CONTENTS

PART TWO ANNUAL FINANCIAL STATEMENTS 229

PREFACE

WHY THIS BOOK?

Financial reporting is changing. Accounting has always been a reactive service, changing and developing to meet the practical needs created by the environment in which it operates. This process of change can be illustrated by both time considerations and place considerations. In particular, in the days when most business operations were largely organized within national boundaries, accounting thought, practices and regulation grew up in significantly different ways in different countries, consistent with national environments and characteristics, a process discussed in more detail in Chapter 2.

Now, however, big business is international, and the process and its implications are moving at a very fast rate. Big business is global in its operations; the demand for finance is global and the supply of finance is global. The provision of information, the oil which lubricates any working market, is global in its reach and instantaneous in its transmission. Financial reporting must of necessity be global too. From slow beginnings, the International Accounting Standards Board (IASB) is now poised to become the generally accepted regulator at this international level. From 2005, every EU/UK/Brexit consideration, Australian and New Zealand company has been required to produce its group financial statements in accordance with International Accounting Standards (IAS) and International Financial Reporting Standards (IFRS). Many countries followed this example and now require IFRS compliance for their listed companies (e.g. Argentina, Brazil, Canada, South Korea). Other countries, as diverse as the USA and China, are seeking closer convergence, as a minimum, with IASB requirements. The USA allows IFRS accounts without reconciliations for US stock exchange listing for foreign registrants.

The effects on accounting and reporting for business entities operating at a national or local level, many of them small and medium-sized enterprises (SMEs), are unclear and are likely to differ in different places. Two points are very clear to us, however. First, national needs, characteristics and ways of thinking will remain significant at the SME level. Second, the application of agreed IAS, a subjective process of necessity, will continue to be influenced by the context and environment in which the application takes place.

This book is written to reflect this situation and its implications. A knowledge of the requirements of IFRS is now essential to anyone studying financial accounting and reporting, whether the aim is the preparer focus implied by a desire to enter the accounting professions or the user focus implied by finance, business or MBA-type programmes aimed at management or the educated public.

But, of course, knowledge is not enough. A critical understanding of issues and alternatives, of the whys and wherefores, is also required. The author team has been carefully constructed to contain significant academic, pedagogic and writing experience and to reflect the diversity of European and international thought and experience. Our approach is to expose the reader to the issues by a carefully developed sequence of exposition, student-centred activity and constructive feedback. This process provides a framework with which the reader can assimilate, understand and appraise the exposition of international requirements that follow. Only with such an overall understanding, enhancing both depth and breadth, will the reader be able to follow, and hopefully participate in, the future development of financial accounting and reporting as the process of international change continues.

It is important to be clear that our emphasis is on the IASB requirements and on a full understanding thereof. How those requirements will actually be applied in detailed practice in the many different countries and cultures involved has to be largely outside our scope. As already indicated, we certainly believe that there will continue to be material differences in the practical interpretation and application of international standards. We give a full justification and explanation of that belief and provide a framework for analyzing its implications. Nevertheless, it has to be up to the individual reader and/or teacher, situated in a 'local' context, to explore what the implications of that local context might be.

The discussion of all standards has been updated for this seventh edition and brought in line with the latest developments in the IFRS standard-setting programme of the IASB. This implies that at the time of writing, attention has been paid to current evolutions and possible changes in the standards taking place in the near future. For this new edition, we have included many more numerical examples and extracts from company reports from a variety of international corporations to provide students with illustrations of standards and real-life insight into financial accounting. In addition, Part One has been changed to better reflect the current theoretical, market, regulatory and societal framework in which IFRS is being developed and used. To this purpose, Chapters 1, 2 and 3 have been rewritten; the chapter on the IASB Conceptual Framework and accounting theory has been partly rewritten and is now Chapter 4. The chapters on accounting models and measurement have been simplified, updated and condensed into two chapters (Chapters 5 and 6), so that Chapter 7 on fair value, value in use and fulfilment value is more easily understandable from a theoretical point of view. Furthermore, there are new chapters on corporate governance (Chapter 9), business ethics, corporate social responsibility, sustainability reporting and responsible investment (Chapter 10) and the ethics of the accounting profession (Chapter 11).

STRUCTURE AND PEDAGOGY

The broad structure of the book is as follows: Part One provides the essential conceptual and contextual background. Parts Two and Three explore the detailed issues and problems of financial reporting both in general and through the specific regulatory requirements of the IASB – for individual company issues in Part Two and for group and multinational issues in Part Three. Part Four provides a summation by an in-depth consideration of financial statement analysis within a dynamic international context.

Each chapter follows a similar pattern in terms of pedagogic structure. Learning objectives set out what the student should be aiming to achieve, with an introduction to put the chapter into context. There are frequent activities throughout the chapter, with immediate feedback so that students can work through practical examples and reflect on the points being made. The chapter closes with a summary and exercises. Answers to some of the exercises can be found on our dedicated CourseMate, the remainder on the Instructor online support resources.

SUPPLEMENTARY MATERIALS

Students have access to the following resources on the book's companion website:

- Answers to students' exercises (at end of chapters).
- An online chapter.
- A glossary of accounting and finance definitions.
- Related links.

Instructors have access to the following additional resources (via specific login details which they can request from the Cengage sales representative after adoption of the book):

- Answers to students' exercises.
- Answers to instructors' exercises.
- PowerPoint slides.
- Online chapter.

The publishers would like to thank Ewan Tracey, University of Northampton, UK, and Collette Kirwan, Waterford Institute of Technology, Ireland, for their contributions to the supplementary materials.

This is not a book for those without prior exposure to accounting. A one-year introductory course in accounting and a basic understanding of the principles of double-entry, or some practical business exposure are assumed. However, we recognize that such earlier work may have taken any variety of different forms, or you may have approached the subject from any one of several different directions; indeed you may well not have studied in the English language. The book will be particularly suitable for the middle and advanced years of undergraduate three- or four-year degree programmes, for post-graduate programmes requiring an internationalization of prior studies of a national system and for MBA-type programmes where a true understanding of the issues and implications of accounting subjectivity and diversity is required.

LIST OF REVIEWERS

The publishers would like to thank the following academics for their insightful feedback and suggestions which helped shape the seventh edition:

Silvia Pazzi, University of Leicester, UK
Ewan Tracey, University of Northampton, UK
Deb Lewis, University of Bath, UK
Ana Isabel Lopes, University Institute of Lisbon, Portugal

OFFICIAL EXAM QUESTIONS

We are grateful to the Association of Chartered Certified Accountants (ACCA) for permission to reproduce past examination questions. The suggested solutions in the exam answer bank have been prepared by us, unless otherwise stated.

We are also grateful to the Chartered Institute of Management Accountants (CIMA) for granting permission to reproduce past examination questions and answers.

IFRS STANDARDS

All IFRS Standards referred to or included in this publication can be accessed via the IFRS website, http://www.ifrs.org/. Copyright © IFRS® Foundation. All rights reserved. Reproduced by Cengage Learning EMEA Ltd with the permission of IFRS Foundation. Reproduction and use rights are strictly limited. No permission granted to third parties to reproduce or distribute. The International Accounting Standards Board, the IFRS Foundation, the authors and the publishers do not accept responsibility for any loss caused by acting or refraining from acting in reliance on the material in this publication, whether such loss is caused by negligence or otherwise.

ACKNOWLEDGEMENTS

We are grateful for constructive help and support from several quarters. We are especially grateful to Karel van Hulle for providing many helpful comments to us regarding earlier editions. For the 7th edition we are grateful to George Georgiou for contributing Chapter 29 to this edition. Five spouses and their offspring have coped with the conflicting demands on our time and thoughts. Now, perhaps, it is your turn to help us, or to help us to help you. Suggestions for further development and improvement would be gratefully received by authors or publisher.

Finally, to come back to where we started, we hope that you, the reader, will be interested and stimulated. The internationalization of accounting is an unstoppable force, which will create new and demanding challenges. We believe that participation in this process will be a fascinating and rewarding experience. We hope that you will agree when you have finished studying this book.

David Alexander, University of Birmingham
Anne Britton, Formerly of Leeds Metropolitan University
Ann Jorissen, University of Antwerp
Martin Hoogendoorn, Erasmus University Rotterdam
Carien van Mourik, Open University

Turn the light on with MindTap

MindTap represents a new approach to online learning. A fully online learning solution, MindTap combines all of your learning tools, readings, multimedia, activities and assessments, into a singular Learning Path that guides you through your course.

Lecturers can easily personalize the experience by customizing the presentation of these learning tools and content to their students so that they have access to course content exactly when they need it.

MindTap can be fully integrated into most Learning Management Systems giving you a seamless experience. You will also have a dedicated team of Digital Course Support professionals to make your use of MindTap a success.

To find out more students can go to **login.cengagebrain.com** and instructors can go to **login.cengage.com** or speak to their local Cengage Learning EMEA representative.

MindTap is available with some of our bestselling titles across multiple disciplines including Accounting, Economics, Management, Psychology, Engineering and Chemistry

CENGAGE
Learning®

Digital
Support
Resources

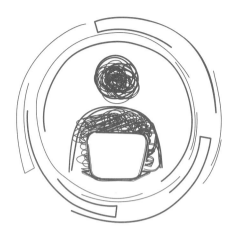

All of our Higher Education textbooks are accompanied by a range of digital support resources. Each title's resources are carefully tailored to the specific needs of the particular book's readers. Examples of the kind of resources provided include:

- A password protected area for instructors with, for example, a testbank, PowerPoint slides and an instructor's manual.

- An open-access area for students including, for example, useful weblinks and glossary terms.

Lecturers: to discover the dedicated lecturer digital support resources accompanying this textbook, please register here for access: login.cengage.com.

Students: to discover the dedicated student digital support resources accompanying this textbook, please search for **International Financial Reporting and Analysis** on: cengagebrain.co.uk.

PART ONE
FRAMEWORK, THEORY AND REGULATION

This first Part is meant to help you structure your thinking about general purpose financial reporting in an international context. We hope that this will help you better grasp the technical aspects of preparing financial statements in Part Two, consolidated financial statements in Part Three and the interpretation of financial statements in Part Four. At the same time, we hope that it will also stimulate you to develop the ability to think critically about the theories, approaches and techniques you will encounter throughout the book.

If you are new to studying accounting, you are likely to find the current level of integration in international financial and capital markets perfectly normal. The International Accounting Standards Board (IASB) and its International Financial Reporting Standards (IFRS) have been around for some 15 years. Chapter 1 will explain what we mean by international financial reporting, what financial reporting standards and IFRS are meant to achieve, who uses general purpose financial reporting information, and the main challenges for IFRS.

Although international trade dates back as long as there have been nation states and international investment was quite common in the late nineteenth century, there was great international diversity of accounting practices and standards. Chapter 2 discusses international accounting differences in the past as well as the present. Before IFRS, multinational companies seeking to raise financing needed to communicate information about their financial performance and financial position to investors in ways that they could understand. Conversely, investors wanting to invest in companies in other countries had to make an effort to understand the information in the financial statements of such companies.

During the 1980s, the globalization of financial, capital and product markets progressed at an unprecedented rate, as did the harmonization of financial reporting practices. Chapter 3 will consider the rise of the IASC and later the IASB and the development of international financial accounting standards going hand in hand with the deregulation of financial and capital markets in most economically advanced countries. As the IASC was a private organization claiming to serve the public interest, it needed to have a conceptual framework that could lend it intellectual credibility and its international accounting standards intellectual legitimacy. Chapter 4 will discuss the history and development of the IASB Conceptual Framework as well as its structure and content. The IASB Conceptual Framework defines the objective of general purpose financial reporting and sets out how to define, recognize, measure, present and disclose the elements of financial statements so as to achieve this objective. Chapter 4 therefore also discusses accounting theory and points to theories that are relevant to the IASB Conceptual Framework and IFRS today.

As the determination of income and equity (financial performance and financial position) are important purposes of financial accounting, it is necessary to understand the main perspectives on income and equity, and how they impact the IASB Conceptual Framework and IFRS today. Chapter 5 discusses the traditional accounting and economic perspectives on income and equity, and Chapters 6 and 7 talk about the theoretical approaches that have developed as compromises between the economic and accounting perspectives. Defining, recognizing and measuring financial statement elements is complemented by the different perspectives on presenting and disclosing the elements on the face of the financial statements or in the notes. Chapter 8 introduces the presentation and disclosure of financial statements in accordance with IAS 1 and the EU Directives.

IFRS applies to companies, predominantly those whose securities are listed on a stock exchange. Financial reporting for companies is one means of alleviating the principle-agent problem and reducing the cost of the information asymmetry between managers and shareholders. Chapter 9 introduces corporate governance as the system by which a company is administrated so as to achieve the objectives of the company in the interests of its shareholders and balance their interests with those of the other stakeholders in the company. Because there are many different stakeholders who are affected by the company's actions, it is not possible to encompass all these conflicting interests and relations in law. Chapter 10 discusses business ethics and corporate social responsibility (CSR) and CSR reporting and how socially responsible investors use CSR reports to inform their investment decisions. It is clear that accounting is very much about conflicting interests, and professionally qualified accountants have a responsibility for the public interest. In Chapter 11 you will learn about the ethics of the accounting profession. On the one hand, professionally qualified accountants are meant to serve the public interest, but on the other, they have to satisfy their customers' needs. This causes a conflict of interest between the customer, the accountant, the accountant's employer and the general public that may never be satisfactorily resolved by a code of ethics and a commitment to public interest. But accountants must try if they are to survive and thrive as a profession.

A BRIEF INTRODUCTION TO INTERNATIONAL FINANCIAL REPORTING

1

OBJECTIVES After studying this chapter you should be able to:

- compare the meanings of international financial reporting before and since IFRS

- compare the roles of financial reporting in different types of business entity

- explain the objectives of financial reporting standards and financial reporting regulation

- explain the objectives of IFRS in the EU and globally

- describe the main functions of general purpose financial reporting

- with reference to these functions, describe the major types of users of published financial information and discuss the implications of their different needs

- discuss two major challenges for the IASB.

INTRODUCTION

This chapter will first compare the meaning of international financial reporting before International Financial Reporting Standards (IFRS) with what it means today. It will then define financial reporting and discuss what financial reporting is meant to achieve in different types of entity and what financial reporting standards are meant to achieve within a jurisdiction as well as globally. Then it will consider the general purpose objective of financial reporting, its users and their various information needs. Finally, this chapter will discuss the main challenges for international general purpose financial reporting and IFRS.

INTERNATIONAL FINANCIAL REPORTING BEFORE AND SINCE IFRS

International financial reporting used to involve two areas of study: first, comparative accounting systems, institutions and practices, and second, the accounting for international transactions and multinational enterprises (Radebaugh and Gray, 2002: 15). The first topic will be discussed in Chapter 2 and the second topic in Part Three of this book and in particular in the chapter on foreign currency translation.

International financial reporting was and still is practised by companies wishing to raise money at capital markets in other countries. There were no international accounting standards until 1973 when the International Accounting Standards Committee (IASC) started to develop its International Accounting Standards (IAS). Even then, companies would adopt IAS on a voluntary basis because they had not been formally adopted in any jurisdiction. Multinational corporations had to follow the accounting standards in the countries of the stock exchanges where they were listed. If they were listed at stock exchanges in five different countries that often meant they had to prepare financial statements in accordance with five different sets of accounting standards. In some cases, they would have to provide a reconciliation of the financial statements in their home country with the standards of the country where they were seeking to be listed.

Companies seeking to raise capital from international investors usually did one of five things in response to the problem of different accounting standards across different countries.

1 Do nothing. For example, a French company might do nothing and hope that international investors would make efforts to understand their financial statements.

2 Provide translations in another language, usually English (convenience translations).

3 Provide translations in the language as well as the currency of the country from which investment was sought (convenience statements). For example, a French company would translate its financial statements from French into English and translate the amounts in to French francs (French currency prior to the adoption of the euro) into US dollars.

4 Provide partial restatements. For example, a French company would reconcile the net income in its income statement with a net income amount using US

accounting standards and do the same for the whole balance sheet or selected items in the balance sheet.

5 Prepare secondary financial statements. In this case, the French company would prepare an additional set of financial statements in accordance with US accounting standards. See Mueller *et al.*, 1994: 56.

As you can imagine, this was an inefficient and costly way of doing things and it also caused much confusion for users of those financial statements.

From the mid-1980s, more and more countries started to deregulate their financial and capital markets. In the UK, the 'Big Bang' was the day the London Stock Exchange rules changed on 27 October 1986. In the US, deregulation happened in stages between 1980 and 1999 when the regulations that were put in place after the stock market crash of 1929 were abolished. Other countries followed suit. Japan's 'Big Bang', modeled on that of the UK, happened between 1996 and 2001. Helped by developments in information technology, financial and capital markets became more globally interconnected. Having a single set of internationally accepted financial accounting standards started to make a lot of sense.

From 2001, the year in which the IASC was reorganized into the International Accounting Standards Board (IASB), international financial reporting increasingly has come to mean financial reporting based on the IASB's IFRS. In effect, the IASB cornered the market for international financial reporting standards to the extent that there is no competition for IFRS as the accepted set of international accounting standards. Hence, in this book, the term 'international financial reporting' will usually indicate financial reporting in accordance with IFRS. Where this is not the case, you will be able to understand this by looking at the context in which the term is used.

FINANCIAL ACCOUNTING AND REPORTING IN DIFFERENT TYPES OF BUSINESS ENTITY

Accounting has been defined in many ways. However, the way the IASB thinks about accounting was informed by an often quoted definition of accounting given in *A Statement of Basic Accounting Theory* by the American Accounting Association (AAA). It reads 'accounting is the process of identifying, measuring, and communicating economic information to permit informed judgements and decisions by users of the information' (AAA, 1966: 1). This definition emphasizes the use of accounting information as a basis for decision making. Alternatively, one could think of the purpose of accounting as providing accountability for the way the accounting entity has achieved or failed to achieve its objectives during the past.

As you will be aware, accounting can be divided into management accounting and financial accounting. Management accounting produces information designed for the management user, i.e. for internal decision making. Senior management, by definition, can obtain whatever information it needs from within the organization. Financial accounting produces information in the form of financial reports designed to be useful to all parties with an interest in the reporting entity. External users have to rely on negotiation or regulation in order to obtain information. As we shall see, there are many different types of external user and they may all require different types of financial accounting information. It could be very costly for business entities to prepare separate financial reports for each type of interested party.

ACTIVITY 1.1

From the above paragraphs, you have learned that from a financial accounting perspective, managers are the internal users of a company's accounting information and that all other interested parties are considered external users of accounting information. Do you agree with this categorization? What about the company's shareholders or its employees?

Activity feedback

It may seem strange that the company's shareholders (its owners) are considered external to the reporting entity. However, the characteristics of listed public limited companies create an arm's length relation between the company and its shareholders. These characteristics include a separate legal personality, limited liability of its shareholders and the fact that the shareholders can sell their shares at will to other prospective shareholders.

Similarly, employees work for the company on an arm's length basis. Although they are responsible for specific tasks or outcomes, they do not have the overall responsibility for the financial performance and financial position of the company and usually will not have access to the same information that the senior managers have. They are dependent on the same general purpose reports as shareholders and other external parties for most of the financial information about the reporting entity.

Financial accounting serves the purpose of determining the financial position (Assets = Liabilities + Equity, as shown by the balance sheet at a certain date) and the financial performance (Profit or loss for the period = Income – Expense, as shown by the income statement) of the business entity. For sole traders and basic partnerships, this enables the owner(s) to file their tax returns, apply for bank loans or other types of loan, and calculate how much of the profit can be withdrawn without jeopardizing the capital base of the business. If the business is managed by a hired professional manager, the financial statements also enable the owner to monitor the performance of the manager, determine the size of the manager's bonus, if any, and determine the extent to which the owner is happy with the financial performance and financial position of the entity. Apart from serving these purposes, there is no legal requirement for sole traders and basic partnerships to produce periodic financial statements.

Financial reporting is the periodic reporting of an entity's financial position, financial performance and other financial information. In this book, we discuss financial reporting in respect of companies. Corporate financial reporting is one of the tools of corporate governance. In short, corporate governance is the system by which companies are directed and controlled. Corporate governance will be discussed in Chapter 9. Within the corporate governance system, financial reporting is the means by which the directors of a company provide accountability to its shareholders for the financial performance and financial position of the company. The regulations that require companies to produce and disclose general purpose financial reporting information are meant to mitigate, to some extent, the information asymmetry which exists between the reporting entity's senior management and the reporting entity's shareholders, investors and other external stakeholders. This book is primarily concerned with general purpose financial reporting.

In this book, we are not concerned with financial accounting and reporting for not-for-profit entities. We are solely concerned with financial accounting and reporting for business entities. Furthermore, this book has been written assuming that you know how to do double-entry bookkeeping and basic financial accounting. In other words, the assumption is that you are able to produce a basic income statement and balance sheet from summary information for business entities such as a sole trader, a basic partnership and a single entity company.

In all jurisdictions, companies are formed under some kind of law (Companies Act, Company Law, Commercial Code, etc.) that requires the company's senior management to produce financial statements periodically for the benefit of its shareholders. Unlimited companies do not offer shareholders the protection of limited liability, which makes the shareholders of unlimited companies similar to the owners of partnerships. The creditors of an unlimited company have a claim on the personal wealth of the unlimited company's shareholders. Unlimited companies are legally obliged to prepare financial statements so their shareholders can monitor the performance of the company's senior management and discharge the managers of their stewardship responsibilities over the past period. Based on this information they can determine the size of the managers' remuneration and determine the dividend to be paid out to the shareholders. Corporation tax payable is calculated using the company's financial performance as a starting point.

Most companies are limited companies. This means that the liability of the shareholders for the business entity's liabilities is limited to the amount that they have invested. A limited company's creditors do not have a claim on the wealth of the company's shareholders. There are private limited companies and public limited companies. Most limited companies are private limited companies. In the UK, private limited companies have the suffix 'Limited' or 'Ltd' as part of their name. The equivalents in certain other European countries are given in Table 1.1. A private limited company can only issue its shares privately. If the shareholders of a private limited company wish to sell their shares, they must do so in a private sale, following the rules set out in the company's constitution. In the UK, such a constitution is called the Articles of Association. In private limited companies, shareholders are often required to obtain permission from the other shareholders to transfer their shares to a new shareholder. Private limited companies do not have to disclose publicly as much information as public limited companies. Financial reporting in private limited companies primarily fulfills the stewardship objectives outlined above, although financial reports are also used to apply for loans and enable the assessment of the entity's credit worthiness.

Public limited companies issue their shares to the general public. In the UK, public limited companies must have the suffix 'public limited company' or the abbreviations 'plc', 'PLC' or 'Plc'. See Table 1.1. for the equivalents in other countries. A minority of public limited companies are listed public limited companies, where have their shares listed on a stock exchange. A stock exchange is a market for trading in the issued shares of public limited companies, but also other types of debt and equity securities. In order to qualify to have its securities listed and traded on a stock exchange, the company has to fulfill strict financial reporting and other requirements issued by the stock exchange. These are usually embedded in the laws of a jurisdiction (or country). Such requirements are intended to protect current shareholders and potential investors. Although financial reporting still fulfills its traditional accountability and stewardship functions, financial reporting is also meant to aid current and potential investors to make decisions about whether to hold, buy or sell the shares or other securities in the company.

Multinational corporations or transnational corporations are not so easy to define. They operate in multiple countries because this offers proximity in terms of markets and natural resources or because of low wages, highly skilled workers, or tax benefits. In terms of financials, they will generate sales, pay expenses, own assets and incur

TABLE 1.1   Examples of the terms for public limited company and private limited company in certain countries

UK	Public limited company (plc)	Private limited company (ltd)
Belgium and the Netherlands	Naamloze Vennootschap (NV)	Besloten Vennootschap (BV)
France	Société Anonyme (SA)	Société à Responsabilité Limitée (SARL)
Germany	Aktiengesellschaft (AG)	Gesellschaft mit beschränkter Haftung (GmbH)
Italy	Società Anónima (SA)	Società per Azioni
Japan	Yugen kaisha	Kabushiki kaisha
Spain	Sociedad Anónima (SA)	Sociedad de Responsabilidad Limitada (SL)

liabilities in multiple countries. Popular at the beginning of the twentieth century, the use of holding companies has again been increasing since 2000. A holding company is a company that is formed for the sole purpose of owning the shares of other companies in order to form a corporate group. This enables a company to register its headquarters in a country where the tax regime is most advantageous for the group. It also enables the owners of the holding company to control a group of companies while minimizing the risk to the companies within the group.

THE OBJECTIVES OF CORPORATE FINANCIAL REPORTING STANDARDS AND REGULATION

Financial reporting standards require the information to be of a reliable quality and presented in a reliable format. This allows investors and other users of financial statement information to compare the financial performance and financial position of a company across time or with other companies in the same industry or across industries. However, accounting standards and accounting systems develop in response to the environment in which they operate. As Mueller *et al.* (1994) observed in the 1990s:

> In a number of countries (such as the United States), financial accounting information is directed primarily towards the needs of investors and creditors, and 'decision-usefulness' is the overriding criterion for judging its quality. However, in other countries, financial reporting has a different focus and performs other roles. For example, in some countries, financial accounting is designed primarily to ensure that the proper amount of income tax is collected by the national government. This is the case in most South American countries. In other countries, financial accounting is designed to help accomplish macroeconomic policies, such as achieving a predetermined rate of growth in the nation's economy.
>
> (Mueller *et al.*, 1994: 1–2)

Since the 1990s, global capital markets have grown in size and reach, the influence of American accounting thought has become stronger, and decision-usefulness is also the criterion adopted by the IASB. Although the differences indicated in the quotation above have become less pronounced, Chapter 2 will show that they can still be observed.

For a long time, investment in stocks, shares and debentures (bonds) was the pre-rogative of wealthy individuals. The general view was that these people knew what they were doing or were able to afford to buy the best advice. Therefore, if these people wanted to speculate with their wealth, there was no need for the government to protect their interests in case things went wrong. However, the 'democratization' of shareholding meant that more and more people who were not rich could invest in the stocks and shares of public limited companies. Shareholder ownership of specific companies became dispersed across many investors rather than concentrated in the hands of a few. The problem was that because of their limited liability, shareholders with well-diversified stock portfolios had little incentive to monitor actively all of the companies included in their portfolios. If they were unhappy with the dividends or returns, they would simply sell their shares and invest in another company. In the US, Berle and Means (1968/2009) observed that corporate managers increasingly ran companies for their own benefit rather than for their shareholders. Financial report-ing and auditing requirements were quite basic, because corporate governance was considered a matter between the company and its owners. The stock market crash of 1929 in the US of 1929 caused an economic depression that spread across the world. In the US, the crash led to the Securities and Exchange Acts of 1933 and 1934, which ultimately resulted in the development of financial reporting standards in the US.

Since then, as more and more countries have embraced capital markets as the way to allocate financial capital to companies, the main functions of financial accounting and reporting standards and financial reporting regulation came to be as follows:

- To establish a minimum standard for the quality, quantity and presentation of useful financial information in order to reduce the information asymmetry between managers (company directors) and investors in equity and debt securities and other users of financial statement information, so as to improve their resource allocation decisions.

- To improve transparency and access to information in order to create a more lev-el playing field for investors. Otherwise, those investors with less access to infor-mation and information processing capabilities may withdraw from the capital market altogether because they tend to lose out to those investors with better access to information and the ability to buy investment advice from analysts with better information processing capabilities. The idea is to prevent capital markets from breaking down due to a lack of the general public's confidence, thereby depriving the national economy of the benefits of allocation of capital through capital markets (Lev, 1988: 7).

For capital markets to function well, they need many different types of investor.

ACTIVITY 1.2

Above we considered the possibility that capital markets will break down due to unequal access to financial informa-tion. What would happen if all investors had equal access to information and equal information processing abilities?

Activity feedback

If all investors had equal access to information and equal information processing capabilities, the market for information might become efficient. However, Grossman and Stiglitz (1980: 404–405) showed that, in theory, informationally efficient capital markets will also break down. In this case the capital markets will break down because investors lack the incentives to spend resources on gaining an information advantage and hence to trade on this advantage and to invest.

THE AIMS OF IFRS IN THE EUROPEAN UNION (EU) AND GLOBALLY

In May 1999, the European Commission agreed on the Financial Services Action Plan. One of the objectives of this Plan was to create a single, large capital market within the EU. To facilitate the creation of a more integrated and efficient European common market, including a common capital market, the European Commission proposed in 2000 that all listed companies should use one set of accounting standards for financial reporting purposes. IASs issued by the IASC were chosen to be that set of accounting standards. In 2002, Regulation (EC) No. 1606/2002 then required the application of IASs/IFRSs as endorsed by the EU for all companies listed on stock exchanges in EU member countries from 2005.

Although the IASB has always stated in its Constitution to be committed to serving the public interest, it was not clear what this meant. In April 2015, the IFRS Foundation issued a Mission Statement. In short, it states that 'Our mission is to develop International Financial Reporting Standards (IFRS) that bring transparency, accountability and efficiency to financial markets around the world. Our work serves the public interest by fostering trust, growth and long-term financial stability in the global economy' (IFRS Foundation, 2015).

ACTIVITY 1.3

From the above paragraphs, we may conclude that IFRS is meant to achieve more integrated and efficient global financial and capital markets. In what ways might IFRS foster trust, growth and long-term financial stability in the global economy? Is this likely to benefit the general public? You may wish to look at the IFRS Foundation's Mission Statement on the internet.

Activity feedback

The Mission Statement (IFRS Foundation, 2015) says that IFRS brings transparency by enhancing the international comparability and quality of financial information. This will then enable international investors and other global market participants to make better informed economic decisions. Furthermore, IFRS strengthens accountability by reducing the information asymmetry between the providers of equity and debt capital and the directors of the companies in which they have invested their money. As a source of globally comparable information, IFRS is also useful to regulators around the world. IFRS contributes to economic efficiency by helping investors to identify opportunities and risks across the world, thus improving global capital allocation. For businesses, the use of a single, trusted accounting language lowers the cost of capital and reduces international reporting costs.

The IASB and IFRS Foundation think that improved global capital allocation, which is in the interests of global investors and global companies, is also in the interests of the international general public. This may be true to the extent that the benefits of a growing global economy are shared internationally and among the general public in different countries. But are they? Maybe in the long term?

THE MAIN FUNCTIONS OF GENERAL PURPOSE FINANCIAL REPORTING

Why does this book focus on general purpose financial reporting? Does this mean that all external users require the same information for the same general purpose? Not really. Specific financial reporting could be aimed at specific user groups, but this would mean that companies would have to prepare several different reports each tailored to the needs of a different user group. This could be quite costly for the company, in particular the costs involved in preparing many reports and, also, the costs associated with the risk of disclosing proprietary information (information that would endanger the competitive position of the company). Sometimes it happens that an external party such as a large lender can demand specific information in order to assess the risk and return of a substantial loan to the company. In the past, the Financial Accounting Standards Board (FASB) and the IASB, like many other national private and public standard setters, decided they should set general purpose financial reporting standards to serve those external parties who do not have this type of negotiating power.

So, what is the general purpose that financial reporting is meant to serve? According to the IASB's 2010 Conceptual Framework:

> The objective of general purpose financial reporting is to provide financial information about the reporting entity that is useful to existing and potential investors, lenders and other creditors in making decisions about providing resources to the entity. Those decisions involve buying, selling or holding equity and debt instruments, and providing or settling loans and other forms of credit.

(IASB, 2010: OB2)

The IASB's view on the general purpose of financial statements is also known as the decision-usefulness objective.

In truth, there are different views on the usefulness of general purpose financial reporting. **Accountability** refers to the action of providing information in order to account for one's actions and decisions to those to whom one is accountable. Accountability also refers to bearing responsibility for those actions and decisions as well as for their intended outcomes and unintended consequences. Historically, corporate financial reporting has been a tool that enables the senior management of a company to provide accountability to the owners of the company for how the managers have performed their stewardship responsibilities.

Traditionally, the **stewardship** function of general purpose financial reporting was twofold. First, the financial statements enabled the senior management of a company (the stewards or agents) to provide accountability for how they have used the company's assets and liabilities during the year to achieve the company's objectives. Second, the financial statements enabled the company's owners (the shareholders) to judge if they were satisfied with the financial performance of the company and the proposed dividends. If they were satisfied, they would approve the financial statements, the dividends and the remuneration for senior management, thereby discharging the managers from their stewardship responsibilities over that period. If the shareholders were not satisfied with the reporting, clarifications from senior management might be needed. If the shareholders were not happy with the entity's financial performance, they could decide to change the company's senior management or their remuneration.

During the 1980s and 1990s, company legislation was changed in some countries (e.g., Japan) so that the shareholders were no longer required to approve the financial statements. They would still approve the dividends and decide on the fate of the company's senior management. However, in an age of portfolio investment and regular rebalancing of their investment portfolio based on an assessment of the market risk of the company's shares or other securities, shareholders increasingly 'voted with their feet' (i.e. sold their shares) rather than at the annual general meeting (AGM). In many internationally listed companies, the monitoring function of the shareholders came to be more abstract and less meaningful. This caused a second interpretation of stewardship to develop. In this interpretation, the stewardship function of financial reporting is subsumed under the decision-usefulness function of financial reporting.

The **decision-usefulness** function of general purpose financial reporting was conceptualised in the 1960s in the US, which had the most advanced capital markets and securities markets at the time. The decision-usefulness function is to provide information to help prospective shareholders and other investors, lenders and creditors in a market setting to make decisions about providing resources to the reporting entity. Ultimately, according to this perspective, the goal is for general purpose financial reporting to contribute to an efficient allocation of financial capital and other resources and stable economic growth. The idea is that financial capital and other scarce resources are allocated to those companies that are using them more productively and efficiently and away from companies that use resources less productively and efficiently.

According to the decision-usefulness perspective, the main function of general purpose financial reporting is to provide information to help investors in debt and equity securities to estimate the entity's future cash flows. This is the thought underlying the IASB's Conceptual Framework, which will be further discussed in Chapter 4. When the stewardship function of financial reporting is subsumed under the decision-usefulness function, it means that it is assumed that the stewardship function and the decision-usefulness function of general purpose financial reporting require the same type of information. The assumption is that both current and future investors need information to make their buy, sell or hold decisions with respect to an entity's securities.

The **efficient contracting** perspective regards the main function of general purpose financial reporting as providing information to enable contracting between entities and lenders or between reporting entities and senior managers. Investors in listed public limited companies will usually have a portfolio of shares and other investments that they can easily adjust based on risk and return criteria. Such shareholders are often not so actively involved in the monitoring of the senior managers (Board of Directors) because it is easier to simply sell their shares in one company and invest in another. In this situation of insufficient monitoring, the senior managers become very powerful. Hence, executive compensation was increasingly designed to align the senior managers' interests with those of the shareholders and other investors by tying the compensation to a mixture of accounting numbers and stock price. The first efficient contracting function of general purpose financial reporting enables the drawing up of contracts for incentivising and monitoring the senior managers. A second efficient contracting function is enabling banks and other lenders to draw up contracts that include covenants related to their lending, such as cash flow ratios, liquidity ratios or compensating balances.

The **social function** of general purpose financial reporting is the reconciliation or at least the balancing of conflicting interests of all parties external to the reporting entity, including but not limited to its shareholders. For example, through the fair and transparent calculation of distributable dividends, financial reporting serves to protect the interests of creditors and lenders. Financial reporting also provides data for negotiations between employers and trade unions, or for other public policy purposes such as the determination of reasonable profit margins in rate-regulated industries. Furthermore, it serves as a basis for the calculation of the reporting entity's taxable income.

USERS OF FINANCIAL REPORTING INFORMATION AND THEIR DIFFERENT INFORMATION NEEDS

When looking at the functions of general purpose financial reporting above, we came across a number of users and their information needs, but there are others. For example, there are also professional advisers, customers or competitors.

ACTIVITY 1.4

There are different ways of grouping the users of general purpose financial reports. For the nine groups suggested below, consider first the sorts of decisions that they are likely to wish to make using accounting information and, second, the implications as to what information they might need.

1 *The equity investor group, including existing and potential shareholders and holders of convertible securities, options or warrants.*

2 *The loan creditor group, including existing and potential holders of debentures and loan stock and providers of short-term secured and unsecured loans and finance.*

3 *The employee group, including existing, potential and past employees.*

4 *The analyst-adviser group, including financial analysts and journalists, economists, statisticians, researchers, trade unions, stockbrokers and other providers of advisory services, such as credit rating agencies.*

5 *Suppliers and trade creditors – past, present and potential.*

6 *Customers – also past, present and potential.*

7 *Competitors and business rivals.*

8 *The government, including tax authorities, departments and agencies concerned with the supervision of commerce and industry, and local authorities.*

9 *The public, including taxpayers, consumers and other community and special interest groups, such as political parties, consumer and environmental protection societies and regional pressure groups.*

Activity feedback

The equity investor group

Essentially, this group consists of existing and potential shareholders. This group is considering whether or not to invest in a business: to buy shares or to buy more shares; or, alternatively, whether or not to disinvest, to sell shares in the business. Equity investors look for one or a combination of two things: income, a money return by way of dividend, or capital gain, a money return by way of selling shares at more than their purchase price. It should be apparent that these two are closely related. Indeed, the only difference is the timescale. However, the simple theory is made immensely more complex in practice by the effects on share prices of other equity investors' expectations.

For example, share prices for a company may rise because higher dividends are expected to be announced by the company. Alternatively, they may rise because other people believe dividends will increase. A buys some shares in expectation of 'good news'. This causes prices to rise. B then buys some shares in the expectation of the price rise continuing. This causes the price to rise again – a self-fulfilling prophecy – which brings in C as a buyer too. The original hope of 'good news' is soon forgotten. If, however, at a later date the news arrives and turns out to be bad, everyone involved – A, B and C – may want to sell and the price will come crashing down.

The motivational and psychological arguments involved here are well beyond the scope of this book. It is the information requirements that concern us. If the investor is taking a short-term view, then current dividends may be a major factor. As the time horizon of our investor lengthens, then future dividends become more important and future dividends are affected crucially by present and future earnings. The focus then is on profits, which both determine future dividends and influence the share price.

One obvious point is that investors, both existing and potential, need information about future profits. The emphasis in published accounting information is almost wholly on past or more or less current profits. These may or may not be a good guide to the future. The need to make the past results useful for estimating (guessing) the future is an important influence on some of the detailed disclosure requirements we shall explore later. The general trend is to make reported accounting statements as suitable as possible for investors to make their own estimations. We should note an alternative possibility, however. This is that the company itself – through management – should make a forecast. After all, management has a much greater insight into possibilities and risks than the external shareholder.

The loan creditor group

This group consists of long-, medium- or short-term lenders of money. The crucial question an existing or potential loan creditor wishes to consider is obvious: Will they get their money back? A short-term loan creditor will primarily be interested, therefore, in the amount of cash a business has or will very soon receive. As a safeguard, they will also be interested in the net realizable value (NRV) of all the assets and the priority of the various claims, other than their own, on the available resources. Longer-term lenders will clearly need a correspondingly longer-term view of the firm's future cash position. Their needs are thus similar to the needs of the equity investor group – they need to estimate the overall strength and position of the business some way into the future.

(Continued)

ACTIVITY 1.4 (Continued)

The employee group

Employees or their representatives need financial information about the business for two main reasons:

- fair and open collective bargaining (i.e. wage negotiations)
- assessment of present and future job security.

They also need to be able to assess the economic stability and vulnerability of the business into the future. The employees, actual or potential, will also have additional requirements, however:

- They will often need detailed information at 'local' level, i.e. about one particular part of the business or one particular factory.
- They will need information in a clear and simple non-technical way.
- They will need other information that is inherently non-financial. They will want to know, for instance, about management attitudes to staff involvement in decision making, about 'conditions of service' generally, promotion prospects and so on.

It can thus be seen that the employee group may require particular statements for its own use and that it may require information not traditionally regarded as 'financial' at all.

The analyst-adviser group

In one sense, this is not a separate group. It is a collection of experts who advise other groups. Stockbrokers and investment analysts will advise shareholders, trade union advisers will advise employees, government statisticians will advise the government and so on. The needs of the analyst-adviser group are obviously essentially the needs of the particular group they are advising. However, being advisers, and presumably experts, they will need more detail and more sophistication in the information presented to them.

Suppliers and trade creditors

Suppliers and trade creditors need similar information to that required by short-term loan creditors. But they will also need to form a longer-term impression of the business's future. Regular suppliers are often dependent on the continuation of the relationship. They may wish to consider increasing capacity specifically for one particular purchaser. They will therefore need to appraise the future of their potential customers both in terms of financial viability and in terms of sales volume and market share.

Customers

Customers will wish to assess the reliability of the business both in the short-term sense (will I get my goods on time and in good condition?) and in the long-term sense (can I be sure of after-sales service and an effective guarantee?).

Where long-term contracts are involved, the customer will need to be particularly on their guard to ensure that the business appears able to complete the contract successfully.

Competitors

Competitors and business rivals will wish to increase their own effectiveness and efficiency by finding out as much as possible about the financial, technical and marketing structure of the business. The business itself will naturally not be keen for this information to become generally available within the industry, and it is generally recognized that businesses have a reasonable right to keep the causes of their own competitive advantage secret. Competitors may also wish to consider a merger, an amalgamation or a straight takeover bid. For this purpose, they need all this information, plus the information required by the equity investor group. They also need information about what they – the bidders – could do with the business. In other words, they need to be able to form an opinion on both:

- what the existing management is likely to achieve
- what new management could achieve with different policies.

The government

Everybody is aware that governments require financial information for the purposes of taxation. This may be the most obviously apparent use by governments, but it is not necessarily the most important. Governments also need information for decision-making purposes. Governments today take many decisions affecting particular firms or particular industries, both in a control sense and in its capacity as purchaser or creditor. Also, governments need information on which to base their economic decisions regarding the economy as a whole. This information is likely to need to be very detailed and to go well beyond the normal historical information included in the usual published accounting reports. Again, there is an obvious need for future-oriented information.

The public

Economic entities, i.e. businesses in the broadest and most general sense, do not exist in isolation. They are part of society at large and they react and interact with society at every level. At the local level, there will be concern for such things as employment, pollution and health and safety. At the wider level, there may be interest in, for example, pollution and 'green' issues, energy usage, effective use of subsidies, dealings with foreign governments and contributions to charities in money or kind. Much of this information is non-financial. Indeed, some of it cannot be effectively measured at all. Whether it is accounting information is an open question. But it is certainly useful information about businesses.

Summary of user needs

Several general points emerge from the preceding discussion:

1 Many, although not all, of the information requirements are essentially forward looking.

2 Different users, with different purposes, may require *different* information about the *same* items.

3 Different users will require (and be able to understand) different degrees of complexity and depth.

4 Not all the information required is likely to be included in financial accounts.

CHALLENGES FOR THE IASB

As we will see in Chapter 2, historically, financial accounting and reporting evolved largely independently across different countries. National differences in financial accounting and reporting arose because the institutional environment (the legal environment, the way the economic activities are organized and financed, the status and organization of the accounting profession and financial reporting regulators) in different countries evolved in response to local needs, corporate governance structures and business practices. As the IASB exists to develop IFRSs and promote their global adoption and implementation, the IASB faces a number of challenges. Here we will discuss two challenges:

1 Promoting the global adoption of IFRS.

2 Consistent application across different institutional environments.

Promoting the global adoption of IFRS

Since 2005 in particular, the number of countries that have adopted IFRS has increased dramatically. All companies listed on a stock exchange within the EU use IFRS (as endorsed by the EU) for their consolidated financial statements for year-ends beginning on or after 1 January 2005. Australia switched to IFRS from the same date. Soon, more and more countries followed suit.

ACTIVITY 1.5

IFRS has been adopted or accepted in many different countries and jurisdictions. Some countries adopted IFRS as issued by the IASB, others have adopted IFRS as their own national standards, or have substantially adopted IFRS but made some changes. Search the IASB website (www.IFRS.org) or the IAS-Plus website (operated by Deloitte) for an overview of the countries where IFRS has been adopted, is accepted or is forbidden. Suggested search term: IFRS jurisdiction profiles.

Activity feedback

Currently, there are more than 100 countries where IFRS are allowed for consolidated financial statements. The countries that require IFRS as issued by the IASB are very diverse. Some have developed capital markets, such as Australia and Canada. Others do not even have a stock exchange, for example Belize, Honduras and Yemen. Countries that have incorporated IFRS into

(Continued)

ACTIVITY 1.5 *(Continued)*

their own standards include Hong Kong. (See Pacter, 2015: www.ifrs.org/Use-around-the-world/Documents/ IFRS-as-global-standards-Pocket-Guide-April-2015.PDF, accessed 1 March 2016).

Some countries, for example China, follow their own standards, which have 'substantially converged with IFRS'. The Chinese Accounting Standards for Business Enterprises (ASBEs) were issued in February 2006

and are similar to IFRS with the exception of a number of items including 'reversal of impairment losses, disclosure of related party relationships and transactions, and accounting for certain government grants' (IFRS Press Release at www.ifrs.org/Alerts/PressRelease/ Documents/2015/2005%20Beijing%20Statement.pdf, accessed on 1 March 2016).

Although many countries have adopted IFRS, a number of important countries have not. Six out of the 20 countries included in the G20 have not adopted IFRS. The 'G20 was initiated in 1999 and consists of Argentina, Australia, Brazil, Canada, China, France, Germany, India, Indonesia, Italy, Japan, Mexico, Republic of Korea, Russia, Saudi Arabia, South Africa, Turkey, the United Kingdom, the United States and the European Union (EU)' (G 20 website: www.g20.org/English/aboutg20/ AboutG20/201511/t20151127_1609.html, accessed 1 March 2016). The six countries are: India, Japan and the US who permit IFRS on a limited voluntary basis for domestic and/or foreign issuers), Saudi Arabia (who requires IFRS for banks and insurance companies only), China (who has substantially converged its national standards to IFRS) and Indonesia (who has adopted national standards that are substantially in line with IFRS but has not announced a plan or timetable for full adoption) (Pacter, 2015) www.ifrs.org/Use-around-the-world/Pages/Analysis-of-the-G20-IFRS-profiles.aspx, accessed on 1 March 2016).

Because of the 2007/2008 financial crisis, the first G20 Leaders' summit was held in 2008. The 2009 G20 (Pittsburg) Leaders' Statement Par. 14 stated:

> We call on our international accounting bodies to redouble their efforts to achieve a single set of high quality, global accounting standards within the context of their independent standard setting process, and complete their convergence project by June 10 2011. The International Accounting Standards Board's (IASB) institutional framework should further enhance the involvement of various stakeholders.
>
> (G20, 2009, www.g20.org/English/Documents/PastPresidency/201512/ P020151225615583055801.pdf, accessed on 1 March 2016)

In 2013, Par. 74 of the G20 Leaders' Declaration stated:

> We underline the importance of continuing work on accounting standards convergence in order to enhance resilience of financial system. We urge the International Accounting Standards Board and the US Financial Accounting Standards Board to complete by the end of 2013 their work on key outstanding projects for achieving a single set of high quality accounting standards.
>
> (G20, 2013, www.g20.org/English/Documents/PastPresidency/201512/ P020151225709417239707.pdf, accessed 1 March 2016)

The full convergence between IFRS and the US FASB's standards is looking increasingly less likely because the balance of power in the IASB is shifting away from the US towards countries that have actually adopted IFRS.

Consistent application of IFRS across different institutional environments

Even if IFRS has been adopted or is accepted in so many different jurisdictions, this does not mean that IFRS is consistently applied and enforced. Often the local business practices make it difficult for people to interpret IFRSs which were written with a different kind of institutional environment in mind. There is also a learning process in the application of IFRS, where accountants keep on doing what they have been doing before, because that is what they know. A further challenge is that auditors may not be able to apply IFRS as it is meant to be applied, because of pressure from their clients. Translations have an impact as well because it is sometimes difficult to translate concepts from English into another language where the customs or the way of thinking is slightly different. IFRS has as a goal to further the globalization of financial and capital markets, but in order to be able to do this, further integration of markets and coordinated regulation may be required.

TERMINOLOGY AND THE ENGLISH LANGUAGE USE

Many readers of this book will be trying not only to master a subject new to them but also doing so in a language that is not their first. One added difficulty is that there are several forms of the English language, particularly for accounting terms. UK terms and US terms are extensively different. Some examples are shown in the first two columns of Table 1.2. At this stage, you are not expected to understand all these terms; they will be introduced later, as they are needed.

The IASB operates and publishes its Standards in English, although there are approved translations in several languages. The IASB uses a mixture of UK and US terms, as shown in the third column of Table 1.2. On the whole, this book uses IASB terms, but UK terms tend to be used in the Fourth EU Directive. Familiarity with both is essential.

TABLE 1.2　Some examples of UK, US and IASB terms

UK	US	IASB
Stock	Inventory	Inventory
Shares	Stock	Shares
Own shares	Treasury stock	Treasury shares
Debtors	Receivables	Receivables (or trade receivables)
Creditors	Payables	Payables (or trade payables)
Finance lease	Capital lease	Finance lease
Turnover	Sales (or revenue)	Sales (or revenue)
Acquisition	Purchase	Acquisition
Merger	Uniting of interests	Uniting of interests
Fixed assets	Non-current assets	Non-current assets
Profit and loss account	Income statement	Statement of financial performance
Balance sheet	Balance sheet/Statement of financial position	Statement of financial position

SUMMARY

This chapter has considered the meaning of international financial reporting prior to and following the introduction of IASB's IFRS. We looked at the different functions of financial accounting and reporting in different types of business entity, and established that this book is about financial accounting and reporting for corporate entities. Financial reporting standards and regulation are to reduce the information asymmetry between corporate directors and shareholders and investors in other securities, and to increase transparency and access to information so as to create a more level playing field for investors with different levels of sophistication. If the general public loses confidence in the markets, they will ultimately break down.

General purpose financial reporting is concerned with the provision of information about business organizations to people outside the management function. We have thought about the various functions of general purpose financial reporting and the users of financial reporting information and their information needs. We have looked at challenges for the IASB in promoting IFRSs as global standards and ensuring consistent application of IFRS across countries with different institutional environments. Chapter 2 will look at the differences in accounting systems across countries and the reasons why they exist.

EXERCISES

Suggested answers to exercises marked ✓ are to be found in the Student online resources, with suggested answers to the remaining questions available in the Instructor online resources.

✓**1** Look up as many definitions of accounting as you can find, noting the source, country, original language and date of publication. Note and try to explain their differences.

✓**2** Consider the relative benefits to users of financial statements of:

- information about the past
- information about the present
- information about the future.

✓**3** Do you think that a single set of financial statements can be prepared that will be reasonably adequate for all major external users and their needs?

4 Which view of the objectives of general purpose financial reporting do you regard as the most important? Why?

5 The IASB assumes that financial information that helps investors and other users of general purpose financial reporting make their investment decisions is useful for all other information users. Do you agree? Discuss.

6   Think of the factors that make it difficult for the IASB's IFRS and the FASB's US GAAP standards to fully converge. Are they mostly political or are they also related to the different views on the objectives of financial reporting? Discuss.

7   In this chapter we read that, on the one hand, financial reporting standards are meant to prevent capital markets from breaking down due to less informed investors withdrawing from the market because they consistently lose out to better informed investors. In other words, financial reporting standards are meant to make capital markets more informationally efficient. On the other, fully informationally efficient capital markets will break down due to a lack of incentives to gain an informational advantage and invest. So, how would a society decide the optimal level of informational efficiency? Is this a technical or a political problem?

INTERNATIONAL ACCOUNTING DIFFERENCES

PAST AND PRESENT

2

OBJECTIVES After studying this chapter you should be able to:

- describe characteristics of accounting systems in terms of accounting standard setting by a public sector body or a private sector body, and in terms of the organization of the accounting profession

- discuss the main characteristics of financial reporting systems in terms of the objectives of financial reporting, the qualitative characteristics of information that achieve these objectives, and the definition, recognition, measurement and disclosure of the elements of financial statements

- describe some of the research on possible classifications of accounting systems between countries

- discuss the meaning of international institutional differences for the IASB and IFRS today.

INTRODUCTION

In the previous chapter, we noted that although IFRS has been adopted or is accepted in more than 100 countries worldwide, this does not mean that IFRS is consistently applied and enforced. In this chapter, we will see that international differences in financial accounting and reporting standards and practices arose because the institutional environments in different countries evolved in response to perceived local user needs, corporate governance structures, and finance and business practices. Because of these differences in institutional environment, there is a local flavour to the ways in which IFRS is interpreted, applied and enforced.

We will first consider international differences in the bodies responsible for accounting standard setting and financial reporting regulation and the organization of the accounting profession. Second, we will look at some characteristics of the accounting practices and or standards that developed in different systems. Third, we will briefly discuss how researchers have used deductive and inductive ways to try to come up with country classifications that captured the systematic nature of international differences in accounting systems. Then we will look at differences that remain and evidence that national differences persist and do affect the application and enforcement of IFRS across countries.

DIFFERENCES IN INSTITUTIONS

Here we will discuss two elements that characterize the institutional elements of accounting systems, namely the organization of financial reporting standard setting and the organization of the accounting profession.

Public or private financial accounting standard setting

In order to understand how some countries have a history of private accounting standard setting and other countries have a history of accounting standard setting by public bodies, it is helpful to draw a parallel between accounting systems and legal systems here. In civil law (or code law) legal systems, the main sources of law are the written Constitution and other Codes. The civil law system originated in Roman law and has developed in continental Europe. It is characterized by a wide set of rules that try to give guidance in all situations. In common law legal systems, there is not always a written constitution, and the main source of law is precedent or jurisprudence in the form of judges' decisions in previous cases.

Anglo-Saxon countries and former English colonies (the Commonwealth countries) are usually classified as common law countries. Historically, in the UK, the US, other Anglo-Saxon countries and countries that are part of the Commonwealth, accounting standards were developed in the private sector, usually the accounting profession. Usually, in a common law situation, accounting rules are not part of law. In common law countries, accounting regulation is in the hands of professional organizations in the private sector. Company law in these countries is kept to a minimum.

Civil law countries comprise most countries in the world, including those countries in continental Europe and many of their former colonies, but also other countries that adopted elements of civil law. Historically, accounting regulation in civil law countries tended to be in the hands of the government, and financial reporting standards require compliance with a set of detailed legal rules. More recently, some countries (for example, Japan) have replaced their public accounting standard setter and delegated developing financial reporting standards to a private standard setting body modelled on the American Financial Accounting Standards Board (FASB).

Walton (1995: 6) argues that the major divide in approaches to accounting standard setting in Europe reflects to some extent the influence of Napoleon's 1807 Commercial Code. Napoleon incorporated Colbert's 1673 Savary Code (or Merchant's Code) into the 1807 Commercial Code. The Napoleonic Empire caused the Code to be applied in Belgium and the Netherlands, but it was later borrowed by Germany and Sweden; Austria, in turn, borrowed from Germany (Walton, 1995: 5). This meant that accounting rules came to be incorporated into law which applied to all types of businesses, not just companies. In many European countries, taxation of corporate income did not occur until the early twentieth century when there was already a substantial body of accounting rules incorporated into law. When corporation tax was introduced, the commercial financial statements formed the basis for determining taxable income as well. In most continental European countries, there was usually a negligible difference between accounting profit and taxable income. After the Second World War, in some continental European countries, accounting standards and regulations came to be used by the government in an attempt to direct the economy back to recovery. For example, in France, the 1947 *plan comptable* (chart of accounts and principles) imposed fixed valuation rules and a standardized terminology (Mikol, 1995: 110). The idea was to allow:

- management to compare costs and financial performance with other companies in the same industry
- shareholders, bankers and suppliers to make judgements based on standardized information
- public authorities to carry out tax audits
- the French state to formulate economic policies and decide on tax incentives based on standardized information (Mikol, 1995: 110).

On the other side of the Channel, in Britain, income tax was introduced in 1799 in order to finance the war with Napoleon, long before Britain had a body of accounting rules incorporated into law. Therefore, in Britain, the determination of taxable income did not rely closely on accounting rules. Joint stock companies had started with the East India Company in 1600, but the South Sea Bubble of 1719–1721 brought the expansion of the corporate sector to a temporary halt. When the Industrial Revolution and the success of the railway companies resulted in the Joint Stock Companies Acts of 1844, amended in 1856 and in 1862, company accounts were seen as a private matter between shareholders and directors (Napier, 1995: 265). The Companies Acts of 1928 and 1929, for the first time specified that public companies had to file the current year's audited balance sheet with the Registrar of Companies at Companies House. A profit and loss account was to be presented to the shareholders, but did not have to be audited or filed (Napier, 1995: 272–273). The 1948 Companies Act stipulated that accounts should give a 'true and fair view' of the state of affairs and of the profit and loss (Napier, 1995: 275). Over time, accounting practices and tax rules diverged and financial statements came to be prepared virtually independently of tax considerations.

Corporate scandals prompted the British accounting profession, in particular Sir Ronald Leach, President of the Institute of Chartered Accountants in England and

Wales (ICAEW), to promote the idea of replacing Accounting Recommendations with Accounting Standards (Napier, 1995: 276). The ICAEW set up the Accounting Standards Steering Committee (ASSC) and began to issue Statements of Standard Accounting Practice (SSAPs). 'Members of the ICAEW who flouted standards would be subject to disciplinary proceedings' (Napier, 1995: 277). Other accounting bodies also started to adhere to the SSAPs. The ASSC was renamed the Accounting Standards Committee (ASC) in 1975 and continued to issue SSAPs until 1990 when the Accounting Standards Board (ASB) took over. The ASB was the standard-setting body of the Financial Reporting Council (FRC). More recent developments will be discussed in Chapter 3. For now, it is important to remember that in the UK, it was the accounting profession that took the initiative for setting accounting standards.

A third type of accounting standard setting is delegated accounting standard setting. In the US, the Securities and Exchange Commission (SEC) is an agency of the United States Federal Government legally responsible for setting accounting standards. The SEC was established by the Securities Act of 1934 in order to enforce the Securities Act of 1933. The SEC has a three-part mission: to protect investors; to maintain fair, orderly and efficient securities markets; and to facilitate capital formation. With a very small majority, the SEC decided to delegate financial accounting standard setting to the accounting profession. The American Institute of Accounting, later to become the American Institute of Certified Public Accountants (AICPA) formed the Committee on Accounting Procedure (CAP) which issued Accounting Research Bulletins (ARB) from 1939. In 1959 AICPA formed the Accounting Principles Board (APB) which issued APB Opinions. ARBs and APB Opinions were not mandatory and hence they allowed much discretion in their application (Baudot, 2014: 222). In 1973, the FASB was established as an independent private sector accounting standard setter committed to serving the American public interest. The FASB's standards are recognized as authoritative by both the SEC and AICPA. Although the accounting profession is represented in the FASB, the organization is independent of AICPA and there are also board members with a background in the financial and corporate sectors. The SEC does appear to have a strong influence on the FASB.

A fourth distinction is between national and international accounting standard setting. The IASB is a private international accounting standard setter. Although modelled on the FASB in terms of organizational independence and structure, the IASB does not have a single jurisdiction to which it is accountable. The IASB is not so much involved in delegated accounting standard setting, but rather setting a body of IFRSs that jurisdictions can choose whether to adopt. The IASB is also committed to serving the public interest, but this is couched in terms of global economic growth and financial stability. As will be discussed in Chapter 4, the adoption of each IFRS involves an endorsement process in the EU.

National or self-regulation of the accounting profession

As you will have guessed from the above, the accounting profession is largely self-regulating in Anglo-Saxon countries. This means that professional accounting bodies set entry requirements, training and examinations for people who want to become qualified accountants. In Britain, there are no fewer than six professional accounting bodies. Traditionally, in most continental European countries, but also in Japan, the state regulated entry to the accounting profession. The accounting profession was larger in the Anglo-Saxon countries than in countries where the profession was regulated by the state.

Table 2.1 shows when professional accountancy bodies were established in selected countries.

TABLE 2.1   Dates of establishment of professional accountancy bodies

Country	Professional body	Founding date (founding date of predecessor)
Belgium	Instituut der Bedrijfsrevisoren/Institut des Reviseurs d'Entreprises	1953
England and Wales	Institute of Chartered Accountants in England and Wales	1880 (1870)
Denmark	Foreningen af Statsautoriserede Revisorer	1912
Finland	KHT-yhdistys	1925 (1911)
France	Ordre des Experts Comptables	1942
Germany	Institut der Wirtschaftsprüfer	1932
Ireland	Institute of Chartered Accountants of Ireland	1888
Italy	Consiglio Nazionale dei Dottori Commercialisti; Collegio dei Ragionieri e Periti Commerciali	1924; 1906
Japan	Japanese Institute of Certified Public Accountants	1948 (1927)
Norway	Den norske Revisorforening	1999 (1930)
Portugal	Sociedade Portuguesa de Contabilidade	1930
Scotland	Institute of Chartered Accountants of Scotland	1951 (1854)
Spain	Institute of Sworn Auditors of Accounts	1943
Sweden	Foreningen Auktoriserade Revisorer (FAR)	1923
	Svenska Revisorsamfundet (SRS)	1899
The Netherlands	Nederlands Instituut voor Registeraccountants	1967 (1895)
New Zealand	New Zealand Society of Accountants	1909 (1894)
United States	American Institute of Certified Public Accountants	1887

Source: Alexander and Nobes (2004), Nobes and Parker (2003) and Ordelheide and KPMG (2001).

ACTIVITY 2.1

Consider Table 2.1, which provides information on when the professional accountancy bodies of selected countries were established. In respect of the discussion on private or public standard setting, can you see a relation between the year that the professional accounting body in a country was established and the likelihood that a country will have a public or private accounting standard setter?

Activity feedback

If we consider Table 2.1, we observe to a certain extent a correlation between the age of the accounting body and a country having a private accounting standard setter. The countries with the oldest accounting bodies, such as Scotland, England and Wales, Ireland and the United States were also the Anglo-Saxon countries where the accounting profession did its utmost to avoid being regulated by a national regulator. These were also the countries where the profession tried to prevent accounting standards from being set by a national standard setter.

DIFFERENCES IN ACCOUNTING STANDARDS AND PRACTICES

Differences in financial reporting characteristics derive from differences in perspectives on the reporting entity and its role in society, the objectives of financial reporting, the qualitative characteristics of information that achieve these objectives, and the definition, recognition, measurement and disclosure of the elements of financial statements. Even within one country where there is only one single institutional environment, people may disagree about how each of these topics should be addressed in the country's accounting standards. You can imagine that across different countries with different institutional environments, there is even more scope for disagreement.

Objective of financial reporting

In any jurisdiction, standard setters define the objective of financial reporting for listed companies in that jurisdiction with the information needs of specific types of users of published financial statements in mind.

The reporting entity and its role in society In some countries, the corporation is predominantly regarded as a vehicle for shareholders to increase their wealth. Proprietary Theory regards shareholders as the owners of the corporation. Proprietary theorists such as Hatfield (1909), Sprague (1913) and Husband (1938, 1954) thought that financial accounting and reporting must be conducted from the perspective of the shareholders. Staubus's (1952, 1959, 1961) Residual Equity Theory extended Proprietary Theory to include investors in equity as well as debt securities.

On the other hand, Entity Theory regards the corporation as an institution in its own right. This institution has a broader role in society by providing goods and/or services, employment opportunities for employees, and a fair return to lenders and investors in equity and debt securities. Early Entity Theorists such as Gilman (1939), Paton and Littleton (1940) and Chow (1942) held that corporations are quasi-public institutions (see Paton and Littleton, 1940: 2). Later Entity Theorists such as Seidman (1956), Raby (1959) and Li (1960a, 1960b, 1961, 1963, 1964) believed that corporations operate for the purpose of their own survival. Entity Theory holds that financial accounting and reporting must be conducted from the perspective of the entity itself. Suojanen's (1954, 1958) Enterprise Theory extended the corporation's role in society to include accountability for the value-added produced and distributed by the company.

Shareholder (or investor) orientation versus stakeholder (or social) orientation Hence, one way to differentiate the objective of financial reporting is between the shareholder (or investor) and the stakeholder (or social) orientations of accounting standards and accounting information. Private accounting standard setters are more likely to adopt a shareholder or an investor orientation, whereas public standards setters are more likely to adopt a stakeholder or social orientation.

For example, the idea behind the 1947 *plan comptable* in France discussed earlier was that the equity investor group is only one among several stakeholders and the state and government are also major users of the information. On the other hand, the IASB and the FASB think that the objective of financial reporting is primarily to serve the interest of investors. In the US and the UK, which have market economies and large and active capital and financial markets and where equity financing is characterized by relatively widespread ownership, financial reporting is mostly aimed at serving the perceived information needs of investors in debt and equity securities. The US has not adopted IFRS but the UK, as an EU member state (at the time of writing), has.

In China, the government is an important user of financial statement information because of significant state ownership in many listed companies. Even though the Chinese Accounting Standards for Business Enterprises (ASBEs) are close to IFRS, the Chinese public standard setter made certain changes to meet the needs of a socialist country. In Germany, financial reporting used to be linked more strongly to taxation and the information needs of banks rather than individual investors. As a result, the emphasis was on unconsolidated financial statements rather than consolidated financial statements and, because of the Maßgeblichkeit principle, there was a negligible difference between the commercial financial statements and the financial statements for taxation purposes, and there would not be any deferred taxation. Furthermore, German companies were not necessarily run solely for the purposes of shareholder value maximization. The interests of employees were also fairly represented in the corporate governance structure.

A further example is Japan before its large scale financial deregulation between 1996 and 2001, which was carried out in an attempt to deal with the collapse of its bubble economy in 1989 and the ensuing free fall of its stock market and economy more generally. Like in Germany, financial reporting was closely linked to taxation. This helped companies make the most of tax exemptions put in place to serve the government's economic policy needs. Another element was that, in practice, income determination served to enable a stable 5 per cent dividend pay-out ratio. In good years, the companies built up (sometimes hidden) reserves, and, in bad years, the companies used these reserves to keep shareholders satisfied. With the globalization of capital and product markets, this kind of management ran into trouble because of intense international competition driving margins down and international investors who were not satisfied with a five per cent dividend yield. Japan after its financial and accounting Big Bang introduced a financial reporting system very similar to that of the US.

Table 2.2 presents some examples of countries in which companies are more shareholder-oriented and countries in which companies are more credit/family/state-oriented. This divide represents the situation in the twentieth century. To a large extent, it is still representative for today's situation, especially for non-listed groups and small and medium-sized enterprises (SMEs).

TABLE 2.2 Shareholder-oriented versus credit-oriented countries

Shareholder-oriented countries	Credit/family/state-oriented countries
United States	Germany
United Kingdom	France
The Netherlands	Belgium
Sweden	Italy
Australia	Spain
Canada	Portugal

Source: Alexander and Nobes (2004), Nobes and Parker (2003) and Ordelheide and KPMG (2001).

ACTIVITY 2.2

Consider what you know about a shareholder orientation and a stakeholder orientation of financial reporting information and the role of the corporation in society. Would you expect the role of corporations to be viewed differently in terms of financial statement information between countries with a shareholder orientation and those with a stakeholder orientation?

Activity feedback

Consider your own country. If you live in the UK, you might think that companies are regarded as vehicles for investors to increase their own wealth and that financial reporting predominantly has a shareholder orientation. However, if you live in Germany, you might think that companies are, on the one hand, vehicles for shareholders to increase their own wealth, but on the other, that they also have responsibilities to their employees and other stakeholders in the company. The corporate financial reporting requirements (and as we will see later, the corporate governance mechanisms) reflect this difference in attitude.

Consolidated accounts In countries where financial reporting has a strong shareholder orientation, the practice of preparing and publishing consolidated financial statements emerged much earlier. Preparing consolidated financial statements was already common practice at the beginning of the twentieth century in the US (in the 1920s). In the UK and the Netherlands, consolidation became common practice in the 1930s. In typical creditor orientation countries, consolidation was introduced by law. This was done in the latter half of the twentieth century (Germany, 1965, *Aktiengesetz* for public companies; France, 1985, a law which obliged listed companies to publish consolidated accounts; Belgium, the Royal Decree of March 1990; in Italy consolidation became compulsory in the early 1990s).

Deferred taxation In countries with no direct link between tax income and accounting income the practice of recording deferred taxes on the balance sheet is well-established and common practice. For countries in which there is a strong link between accounting income and tax income, the practice of recording and calculating deferred taxes is relatively new. Furthermore, in the individual accounts of companies in those countries, the amounts recorded under deferred taxes will be rather small.

Table 2.3 shows the general relationship between accounting and taxation using some examples based on the situation in the 1990s.

TABLE 2.3   General relationship between accounting and taxation

Independence	Dependence
Denmark	Germany
Ireland	France
United Kingdom	Belgium
The Netherlands	Italy
Czech Republic	Sweden
Poland	Norway

Source: Alexander and Nobes (2004), Nobes and Parker (2003) and Ordelheide and KPMG (2001).

Economic substance and legal form In the Anglo-Saxon countries, the aim of financial reporting is to provide a fair representation of the financial situation of the company. In the UK this is called the 'true and fair view' concept. On the other hand, in most continental European countries, financial reporting is focused on compliance with the legal requirements and tax laws. There, the 'legal form' may dominate 'the economic substance'. The most cited example in this respect is the accounting treatment of a lease contract. In countries with strong shareholder orientation and emphasis on fairness, lease contracts are accounted for on the balance sheet although the company is not the legal owner of the assets (e.g. the UK and US). In countries where the legal form prevails, these assets used by the company are often kept off balance sheet as the company is not the legal owner (e.g. until recently, France and Japan.)

Recognition and measurement

Perspectives on the recognition and measurement of assets, liabilities, revenues and expenses can be characterized by conservatism and prudence on the one hand and faithful representation on the other. Accounting in the Anglo-Saxon countries usually aimed at providing a true and fair view, whereas the continental European countries and those influenced by them focused more strongly on conservatism.

Conservatism versus faithful representation In countries in which financial reporting is more creditor-oriented and used for tax purposes, valuation rules will be more conservative or prudent than in countries with a shareholder orientation. Adherence to conservatism will lead to a different choice in valuation rules and accounting practices. For example, with regard to depreciation, the declining balance method will be used more often than the straight line method, if conservatism is an important characteristic in financial reporting. Further, more use will be made of provisions in these countries, especially when they are tax deductible. Conservative accounting is often regarded as a system in which lower profits are reported than under a system driven by accruals accounting. However, with the use of extensive depreciation and creation of provisions, those companies are also able to increase results in periods with weak economic performance.

In countries in which financial reporting is more creditor-oriented and used for tax purposes, valuation rules will be more conservative or prudent than in countries with a shareholder orientation. Conservative recognition rules do not allow the recognition of income if it has not been realised as cash or assets easily convertible into cash through a transaction. Conservative measurement rules do not allow the measurement of assets at current values that are based on subjective expectations. Conservative accounting is often regarded as a system in which lower profits are reported than under a system driven by representational faithfulness. However, the use of provisions and reserves enables the increase of profits in periods with weak economic performance.

Much research has been undertaken with regard to the usefulness of income information. So-called value relevance studies look at the use of accounting data for the prediction of future income or future cash flows. Some studies find that earnings information provided under conservative accounting practices is less value relevant for decision-making purposes (e.g. buying and selling shares) (see Basu, 1997; Pope and Walker, 1999; Penman and Zhang, 2002). Others found that the value-relevance of earnings information decreased over time whereas the relevance of asset and liability information increased (e.g. Francis and Schipper, 1999; Lev and Zarowin, 1999).

Presentation and disclosure of the elements of financial statements

Uniformity, accounting plans and formats In many continental European countries, we observe that the regulator attaches importance to uniformity. Compliance with prescribed accounting plans (France, Spain and Belgium) and detailed formats for the balance sheet and the profit and loss account are a result of this drive for uniformity. When regulation is in the hands of the government, the layout of the balance sheet, profit and loss accounts and notes are much more detailed. The schemes for balance sheet and profit and loss account put forward by the Fourth and Seventh Directives of the EU were more detailed than the layout presented by the IASB. On the other hand, the level of detail in the notes to the balance sheet and profit and loss account is much higher when accounts are prepared in compliance with IFRS.

ACTIVITY 2.3

Consider the above discussion on the characteristics of accounting standards across different countries and Tables 2.2 and 2.3. Can you identify two groups of countries in terms of different types of accounting standards?

Activity feedback

We observe a difference between accounting standards in Anglo-Saxon countries and most continental European countries. In Anglo-Saxon countries, accounting standards focused on the information needs of shareholders and other investors, whereas in continental European countries, accounting standards aimed to meet the needs of a variety of stakeholders, including the government. The needs of investors included consolidated accounts and a focus on financial statements depicting economic substance rather than legal form, which led to separate financial statements for taxation purposes. This was the result of the private sector developing financial reporting rules or standards. In many continental European countries, companies were often financed to a large extent through debt; hence creditor protection was high on the agenda. In these countries, accounting standard setting was in the hands of the government.

COUNTRY CLUSTERS OVER TIME

We have roughly divided accounting systems between the common law-based Anglo-Saxon and the civil law-based continental European inspired systems. However, over time, researchers have tried to use a variety of factors as cluster variables in order to classify different countries into separate, more homogeneous groups according to their characteristics. These classification exercises were very popular in the 1970s and 1980s. Examples include Hatfield (1966); Mueller (1967) (based on economic environment); Seidler (1967) and American Accounting Association (AAA) (1977) (based on colonial spheres of influence); and da Costa *et al.* (1978), Frank (1979) and Nair and Frank (1980), all three based on the same KPMG data set (see Nobes, 2014: figure 3.5). For a long time, an often cited classification pattern of accounting practices in countries was that of Nobes (1983) (see Figure 2.1).

Figure 2.1 Nobes's 1983 suggested classification of 'accounting systems' in some developed countries

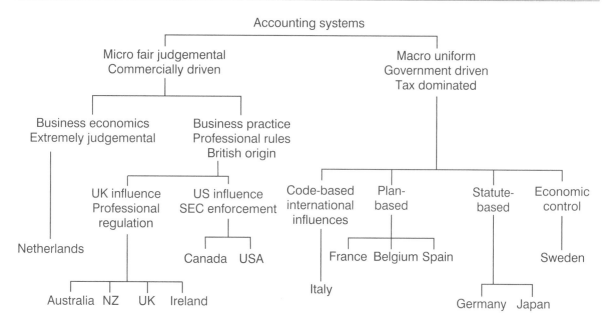

Nobes based his classification research on the financial reporting practices of public companies in the Western world. The classification was made before the enactments in EU countries of the Fourth Directive on company law and before the emergence of IAS. Nobes selected the following nine discriminating variables for the classification of countries into more homogeneous groups:

1 Type of user of the published accounts of listed companies.
2 Degree to which law or standards prescribe in detail and exclude judgement.
3 Importance of tax rules in measurement.
4 Conservatism/prudence.
5 Strictness of application of historical cost.
6 Susceptibility to replacement cost adjustments in main or supplementary accounts.
7 Consolidation practices.
8 Ability to be generous with provisions and to smooth income.
9 Uniformity between companies in application of rules.

However, there was no theory behind this classification. Nobes (1998: 166) suggests that the major reason for international differences in financial reporting practices is 'different purposes for that reporting'. Nobes (1998: 168) proposed that financial accounting systems should be divided into two classes. The defining characteristic is equity financing (Class A) versus debt financing (Class B), and a further characteristic is financing by outsiders (Class A) or insiders (Class B). Class A corresponds to firms in Anglo-Saxon countries and Class B corresponds to firms in continental European countries.

Classification attempts were carried out in the 1990s (e.g. Doupnik and Salter, 1995), but they were becoming less popular. The clustering research of d'Arcy (2001), which is based on data from the second half of the 1990s, shows not only that national differences matter in explaining financial reporting, but also that firm characteristics play an important role in the quality and characteristics of financial reporting (e.g. single versus dual listing status, industry influence, firm dimension, geographical diversification and global player). A number of these variables are still included in current empirical financial accounting research on the accounting quality of published financial information. Today, these national characteristics are still significant variables in explaining differences in accounting quality after the switch to mandatory compliance with IFRS for listed groups.

The clustering exercises illustrated that there are countries in which the accounting systems in place do not result from national characteristics, but are 'exported' to them or 'economically' or 'politically' imposed on them. Western countries have exported their accounting systems to their colonies in the past. For example, the accounting system in place in Singapore and the local Generally Accepted Accounting Principles (GAAP) are very similar to the British system and UK GAAP. In some countries in Africa, which were former French colonies, a uniform chart of accounts (similar to the French *plan comptable*) is in use. A more recent phenomenon is the convergence of accounting standards following the globalization of financial, capital and product markets. In many countries, either IFRS has been adopted for consolidated financial statements as a minimum or their own standards are very similar to IFRS.

A CLOSER LOOK AT SOME CLUSTER VARIABLES

Below we look at four cluster variables used in the literature. The type of legal system was mentioned at the start of the chapter and is fundamental to attitudes towards regulation and self-regulation. The dominant sources of corporate finance, the link between accounting and taxation and cultural differences, are more specific to the perceived main functions of financial accounting standards.

Existing legal system

At the start of the chapter we encountered the so-called common law system and the civil law (or code law) system. Table 2.4 gives some examples of civil law and common law countries. (See also La Porta *et al.*, 1997, 2000.)

Related to the legal system is the degree of enforcement of the legal rules or standards by the judicial authorities or a supervising body. Research evidence reveals that very often in common law countries the degree of enforcement and the mechanisms for investor protection are much stricter than in civil law countries (Bushman and Piotroski, 2006; Jackson and Roe, 2009; Leuz, 2010). Recent research shows that in countries with stricter enforcement, accounting information is of higher quality (see the section on national differences later in this chapter).

Provision of finance

According to Nobes and Parker (2003: 21), 'This difference in providers of finance (creditors) versus (equity) is the key cause of international differences in financial

TABLE 2.4   Common law versus civil law countries

Common law countries	Civil law countries
England and Wales	Scotland
United States	France
Australia	Germany
Canada	Belgium
Ireland	The Netherlands
New Zealand	Portugal
Singapore	Spain
	Japan

Source: Alexander and Nobes (2004), Nobes and Parker (2003) and Ordelheide and KPMG (2001).

reporting'. The Industrial Revolution proceeded in stages from about two centuries ago. Firms had to find extra capital to finance their growth. The countries that were early to industrialize were more likely to actively try to develop capital markets. For example, in the UK and the US, the extra funds tended to be provided by shareholders, often by many shareholders for small amounts. Companies in these countries relied more on equity for the financing of their activities. In these countries, an active stock exchange was and still is present. Countries that were slightly later to industrialize responded differently to this increased need for funds. In countries such as Germany, France, Italy and Belgium, banks became the major supplier of extra funds. Companies in these countries relied more on debt to finance their activities than on equity.

ACTIVITY 2.4

Could you argue why the reliance on debt financing versus reliance on equity financing has an impact especially on financial reporting?

Activity feedback

Insiders or parties that have a power relation towards a company are in a position to ask for internal data about the financial position of the firm towards which they exercise power. The power relation of outsiders is much weaker: they are not in a position to ask for extra informa-tion and have to rely on public information. In countries where widespread shareholder ownership exists, the power of the individual shareholder to obtain financial information is limited. Although the power of the individual shareholder is weak, in those countries where companies rely on the capital market for extra funding, there is a strong incentive towards high-quality external financial reporting. Through financial reports, companies communicate their financial situation to existing and potential shareholders.

So in countries where companies are largely financed through equity, financial statements will have an investor or shareholder orientation. This means that financial statements must provide the kind of information that will enable a potential shareholder to make the best investment decision. Financial information which communicates the underlying economic performance of the firm in a timely manner enables investors to make those investment decisions and is called 'high-quality' accounting information. Earnings are of higher accounting quality if they enable the users of accounting information to assess current performance as well as future performance (Chaney *et al.*, 2011).

Empirical research on the 'quality of accounting earnings' has indicated that in those countries with a strong capital market influence, the quality of accounting earnings is higher than in countries with a creditor orientation (see the discussion of today's role of national differences later in this chapter). In countries where companies rely more on debt financing, the financial statements have a creditor orientation. In these countries, information provided through the annual accounts must be useful to judge whether a company is able to repay its debt. Creditor protection becomes important in this respect and accounting practices will become more conservative.

ACTIVITY 2.5

If you were to compare the financial risk between companies on the basis of the debt/equity ratio calculated from the published annual accounts, in which countries would you come across firms with the highest ratio?

Activity feedback

If we exclude the impact of other influencing factors on the debt/equity ratio (e.g. type of industry, profit distribu- *tion versus reservation) and take into account only these national differences, then you would find, for example, companies with higher debt/equity ratios in Germany and France than in the US or the UK. This difference is then due solely to national differences with regard to the way in which companies are financed.*

These differences in financing are worth bearing in mind when companies from different countries are compared with each other for financial analysis purposes.

Link between accounting and taxation

As discussed under different types of accounting standard setters and regulators, in some countries the fiscal authorities use information provided in the financial statements in order to determine taxable income. In a number of continental European countries, expenses are tax deductible only if they are also recognized in the profit and loss account. As a result, financial reporting becomes tax influenced or even tax biased. In this respect, Germany is well known for its *Maßgeblichkeitsprinzip*, which means that the tax accounts (*Steuerbilanz*) should be identical to the accounts published for external stakeholders (*Handelsbilanz*). This link between financial reporting and taxation is often found in those countries that do not have an explicit investor approach in their financial reporting orientation.

In countries like the US, the UK and the Netherlands, the link between taxable income and accounting income is much weaker. Separate accounts are filed for tax purposes. The measurement and recognition rules and estimates used in the tax accounts can differ from the valuation rules used in the preparation of the financial statements published for all external stakeholders.

This relationship between accounting income and tax income can vary over time. For example, Spain was for a long time in the column of dependence in Table 2.3, which implies that there was a strong link between the accounting income and the tax income; with the reform of 1989, however, the link between taxable income and accounting income became less strong and they are now moving towards independence. The introduction of IFRS will have an impact on the relation between accounting and taxation in those countries characterized by a dependence relationship, especially when SMEs start to use IFRS for private entities in the near future.

Cultural differences

Some people emphasize cultural differences rather than, or in addition to, institutional differences. Cultural differences between nations are identified as an important influencing factor on reporting and disclosure behaviour with regard to financial statements. One of the prominent researchers on cultural differences is Hofstede (1984). Initially, he used four constructs to classify countries according to the cultural differences he observed in his empirical research. The constructs resulted from empirical survey based research in one multinational (IBM; survey population 100 000 employees in 39 countries, 1984). Hofstede labelled his constructs as follows: individualism, power distance, uncertainty avoidance and masculinity. According to Hofstede, these labels describe the following characteristics of a society.

Individualism versus collectivism. Individualism stands for the preference for a loosely knit social framework in society wherein individuals are supposed to take care of themselves and their immediate families only. Collectivism describes the preference for a tightly knit social framework in which individuals expect their relatives, clan or other in-group to look after them in exchange for unquestioning loyalty. The fundamental issue addressed by this dimension is the degree of interdependence a society maintains among individuals. This difference relates to the people's self-concept: 'I' or 'we'.

Large versus small power distance. Power distance is the extent to which the members of a society accept that power in institutions and organizations is distributed unequally. People in larger power distance societies accept a hierarchical order in which everybody has a place that needs no further justification. In small power distance societies, there is less hierarchy and power is distributed more evenly. The fundamental issue addressed by this dimension is how a society handles inequalities among people when they occur.

Strong versus weak uncertainty avoidance. Uncertainty avoidance is the degree to which the members of a society feel uncomfortable with uncertainty and ambiguity. This feeling leads them to beliefs promising certainty and to maintain institutions protecting conformity. Strong uncertainty avoidance societies maintain rigid codes of belief and behaviour and are intolerant of deviant people and ideas. Weak uncertainty avoidance societies maintain a more relaxed atmosphere in which practice counts more than principles, and deviance is more easily tolerated.

Masculinity versus femininity. Masculinity stands for the preference in society for achievement, heroism, assertiveness and material success. Its opposite, femininity, stands for the preference for relationships, modesty, caring for the weak and the quality of life.

More recently Hofstede added a fifth component, namely long-term orientation. Based on Hofstede's classification scheme, Gray (1988) defined 'accounting values' that can be linked to the different cultural values as follows:

- professionalism versus statutory control
- uniformity versus flexibility
- conservatism versus optimism
- secrecy versus transparency.

Professionalism versus statutory control. The accounting value professionalism links to individualism. Professionalism is consistent with a society where the emphasis is on 'I' rather than 'we'. Professionalism also goes together with a society with small power distance. Statutory control is observed in the opposite situation, namely in societies with large power distance. In relation to the accounting profession, professionalism implies self-regulation by the accounting profession itself, as in the US and the UK and much less in continental Europe. Statutory control implies control by the government. Statutory control could also be linked to strong uncertainty avoidance.

Uniformity versus flexibility. First of all, uniformity can be linked to strong uncertainty avoidance. Uniformity leads to detailed regulations embedded in the law and adherence to consistency (e.g. in Belgium, France and Spain uniform accounting plans were imposed on companies by law). Uniformity is therefore also associated with large power distance societies and societies in which the emphasis is on 'we' rather than 'I'. Flexibility, however, can be associated with weak uncertainty avoidance, small power distance and individualism.

Conservatism versus optimism. Conservatism could be linked to uncertainty avoidance. In these societies, one is more conservative with regard to profit recognition and asset measurement. Conservatism is an important value for accountants, especially in continental Europe where financial reporting is more creditor-oriented and where there is a strong link between accounting income and taxable income. Less conservatism in the accounts is applied in the UK, the US and the Netherlands in comparison to France, Switzerland and Germany.

Secrecy versus transparency. Secrecy implies a preference for confidentiality. Secrecy can be linked to uncertainty avoidance, but also to societies with large power distances. Information asymmetry will then reinforce inequalities and power relations between the different parties. Secrecy will have a direct impact on the level of information disclosure by companies. In Japan and continental Europe, lower levels of information disclosure are observed in comparison to disclosure levels in the US and the UK.

The most important economic and cultural elements cited in the literature as causes for differences between national accounting systems have now been discussed. Other factors also listed in the literature as contributors to those differences are, for example, the level of economic development in a country, the degree of industrialization, inflation levels, the adherence to accounting theory (e.g. in the Netherlands, income determination and valuation are inspired by the theory of Limperg (Mey, 1966); financial reporting in Germany was inspired by the theory of Schmalenbach (1927)).

ACTIVITY 2.6

Consider again the cultural values described by Hofstede. How do they link with the accounting value dimensions defined by Gray? Is there a direct link or an indirect link?

Activity feedback

Between some variables there is a direct relationship; between other characteristics and values the relationship is rather indirect. For example, one can distinguish a relation between uncertainty avoidance and conservatism or large power distribution and secrecy versus short power distribution and transparency.

NATIONAL DIFFERENCES AT THE END OF THE TWENTIETH CENTURY

As mentioned earlier in this chapter, classification exercises that attempted to cluster countries in homogeneous groups became less popular in the 1990s. In the 1980s, through the enactment of the Fourth Directive in EU countries, and in the 1990s, under the pressure of the globalization of capital markets, national accounting practices started to move slowly towards each other. This development is still going on and some differences have already become less noticeable or have almost disappeared for certain categories of companies or for certain financial statement items. From the late 1980s onwards, more and more companies sought dual listings. In the early 1990s, many European multinationals went to capital markets abroad, especially to the US. In Germany, for example, Daimler-Benz started to publish two sets of annual accounts – annual accounts presented according to German GAAP and annual accounts presented according to US GAAP. At that time, the differences between equity and earnings presented according to US GAAP and the equity and earnings presented according to German GAAP surprised many. Figure 2.2 became world famous.

Figure 2.2 provides clear evidence of the impact of conservative accounting practices on the reported results. In 1993, the US GAAP result of Daimler-Benz is much lower: conservative accounting leads to a kind of smoothing. Through conservative valuation rules, earnings are decreased in 'good' years, but at times of weak economic performance, results can be increased.

Many Swiss, German and Scandinavian multinationals switched to IAS in the second half of the 1990s. In France, a number of listed companies prepared their consolidated accounts using US GAAP (e.g. Total Fina, Suez) or IAS (e.g. Eutelsat, Rémy Cointreau, Renault). Academics started to study the reaction of the capital market to these voluntary switches of companies from 'conservative or low-quality' accounting standards to a set of 'higher-quality' accounting standards (IAS or US GAAP). Empirical research results showed that capital markets reacted positively to the voluntary switch, since capital markets perceived the switch as a reduction in information asymmetry between firms and investors. As a result, the cost of capital dropped for these companies (e.g. see Leuz and Verrecchia, 2000). The switch of large European

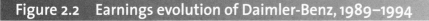

Figure 2.2   Earnings evolution of Daimler-Benz, 1989–1994

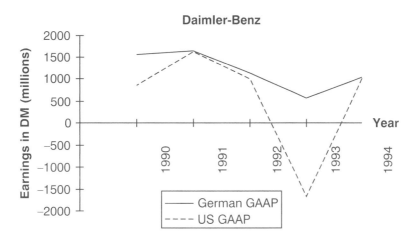

global players from national GAAP to IAS or US GAAP was one of the major triggers for the EU to review its accounting harmonization policy (see Chapter 3).

The switch of the European global players resulted in the emergence of two groups of companies in most countries. This dichotomy still exists today. The first group consists of companies that made an appeal to the international capital market for funds and subsequently started to apply accounting rules that would lead to an increase in comparability of their financial information worldwide. This group started to use 'high-quality' accounting standards such as IFRS, US GAAP and UK GAAP, whereby 'high-quality' standards are defined as follows: 'Financial reporting quality relates to the usefulness of financial statements for contracting, monitoring, valuation and other decision making by investors, creditors, managers and all other parties contracting with the firm' (Ball and Shivakumar, 2002). Nowadays, in more than 100 jurisdictions, listed groups have to comply on a mandatory basis with IFRS. The second group consists of non-listed domestic companies, predominantly small and medium-sized, who so far continue to apply national GAAP.

HOW INTERNATIONAL DIFFERENCES IMPACT ON THE APPLICATION OF IFRS

Even when all companies comply with US GAAP or IFRS, academic research provides evidence that national influences still affect the quality of financial reporting in the different countries. Empirical research provides us with evidence of this influence, and this is another reason why we have paid so much attention to such national variables in this chapter.

The variables pointed out by researchers in the 1970s and 1980s as causes that might explain, and have led to, differences in national accounting systems and national GAAP, are now used in empirical multi-country studies in which different aspects of the financial reporting practices of companies are researched. These studies focus on, among other things, the value relevance of accounting information, earnings management practices and characteristics of the audit market and audit process. A few examples of these empirical studies will be presented here together with their research results. In the first decade of the twenty-first century, most empirical studies analyzed either the quality of the accounting information of firms that adopted IFRS or US GAAP on a voluntary basis, or the quality of accounting information from companies subject to similar types of accounting standards, but different institutional regimes (e.g. risk of litigation, degree of enforcement, degree of investor protection, etc.).

Ali and Hwang (2000) found that the value relevance of accounting information is lower for countries with bank-oriented (as opposed to market-oriented) financial systems. Value relevance was specified in terms of explanatory power of accounting variables (earnings and book value of equity) for security returns. Their results indicate further that value relevance of accounting income is lower for countries where private sector bodies are not involved in the standard-setting process. Ball *et al.* (2000) investigated two properties of accounting income (conservatism and timeliness) and the influence of international institutional factors on accounting income. The property timeliness is defined as the extent to which current period accounting income incorporates current period economic income. Conservatism has been used in this study using the definition of Basu (1997), which regards conservatism as the extent to which current period income asymmetrically incorporates economic losses relative to economic gains. Their central result is that accounting income in common law countries is significantly more timely than in code law countries, due entirely to quicker incorporation of economic losses, which also implies more income conservatism at the same time.

Guenther and Young (2000) investigated how cross-country differences in legal systems, differences in legal protection for external shareholders and differences in the degree of tax conformity, affect the relation between financial accounting earnings and real economic value-relevant events that underlie those earnings. The results provide evidence that the association between financial accounting earnings and real economic activity in a country is related in predictable ways to the legal and economic systems that underlie financial accounting standard setting and the demand for financial accounting standards. The high association for the UK and the US and the low association for France and Germany are consistent with expectations that accounting earnings in common law countries, countries with legal systems that protect external shareholder rights, countries with market-oriented (rather than bank-oriented) capital markets, and countries where financial accounting rules are independent of tax rules, better reflect underlying economic activity. Not only do the traditional elements of differentiation (provision of capital, legal system, link with taxation) seem to be relevant, but also elements such as risk of litigation, investor protection and enforcement of accounting rules are important factors that explain differences in reporting behaviour.

Leuz *et al.* (2003) found that the quality of financial reports increased in countries where investor protection is stronger. Their findings suggest an important link between legal institutions and the quality of financial information provided. The legal rights accorded to outside investors, especially minority investors, and the quality of their enforcement are both associated with the properties of firms' accounting earnings. Their study indicated further that a switch to high-quality standards alone was not a guarantee for high-quality financial information. Other academics had also put forward this issue. For example, Schipper (2000) stated that: 'Reporting quality is not only a function of the set of standards applied. High-quality standards implemented in a defective manner will not result in high-quality financial reports'. Without adequate enforcement, even the best accounting standards will be inconsequential. Hope (2003a, 2003b) constructed an enforcement index which took into account judicial efficiency, rule of law, anti-director rights, audit firm type, audit spending, stock exchange listings and insider trading. Hope found evidence that the enforcement score varied widely among countries. Therefore, accounting quality will still differ among countries even if they apply the same set of accounting standards. Research paying attention to non-listed companies confirms to a large extent the results found in relation to listed companies (Burghstahler *et al.*, 2006).

The research results in the articles cited above are based on financial information published by companies that complied on a voluntary basis with IFRS. The mandatory compliance with IFRS since 2005 for listed companies in many jurisdictions (EU, Australia, New Zealand, South Africa and more recently Argentina, South Korea, Canada, Brazil, Mexico, Turkey and Russia) stimulated a stream of research trying to find out whether accounting quality has improved, and whether comparability of these IFRS accounts has improved after the mandatory country adoptions of IFRS. Many studies find evidence of an increase in accounting quality after the change to IFRS (Beuselinck *et al.*, 2009, 2010; Byard *et al.*, 2011; Horton *et al.*, 2012; Jiao *et al.*, 2012). However a large number of these studies also provide evidence that the beneficial impact of the mandatory compliance with IFRS differs depending upon the characteristics of the institutional environment in which a company operates and a company's reporting incentives (Barth *et al.*, 2008; Daske *et al.*, 2008; Armstrong *et al.*, 2010; Gebhardt and Novotny-Farkas, 2011; Landsman *et al.*, 2011; Christensen *et al.*, 2012; Florou and Pope, 2012; (for an overview see Pope and McLeay, 2011 and Tarca, 2012)). These studies show that the benefits of adopting IFRS with respect to an increase in accounting quality are linked to the extent to which prior national GAAP and IFRS differ and are dependent on the quality of enforcement in the individual countries. Studies focusing on whether or not the mandatory adoption of IFRS increases the comparability of accounting information find similar results. Kvaal and Nobes (2010, 2012) find that pre-IFRS policy choices still influence choices in the IFRS accounts. Lang *et al.* (2010) come to similar conclusions when they analyze earnings co-movement and accounting comparability. Based on the results of these studies, we might state that those national differences which shaped the development of national accounting systems in the twentieth century, are today's drivers of the variation in quality of global comparable accounting information.

SUMMARY

In this chapter we outlined characteristics of national accounting systems and attempts in the literature to cluster countries in order to understand what caused international accounting differences. We identified differences in accounting standards and practices following the two main perspectives on the objectives of financial reporting and had a closer look at some cluster variables used in the literature. Finally, we looked at research investigating how international accounting differences impact on the application of IFRS across countries.

EXERCISES

Suggested answers to exercises marked ✓ are to be found in the Student online resources, with suggested answers to the remaining questions available in the Instructor online resources.

✓**1**   Discuss whether, in essence, accounting is law-based or economics-based.

✓**2**   If accounting is culture-based and national, indeed, local cultures are different, international harmonization will obviously be impossible. Discuss.

3   In this chapter, several causes are discussed which had some influence on existing accounting systems. Which of the causes listed played a significant role in your country? Discuss.

4   If you take Hofstede's (1984) framework for describing cultural differences, how would you describe your own country in relation to these constructs?

5   Do you notice an evolution in the existing accounting system in your country? What would you suggest are the driving forces? Explain.

6   If you consider Gray's (1988) adaptation of Hofstede's (1984) framework in relation to accounting values, could you describe which accounting values are prevalent in your country?

7   Discuss recent research articles which examine the accounting quality or the degree of earnings management after mandatory IFRS adoption.

8   Discuss how the financial reporting infrastructure of a country can have a significant impact on financial statements prepared under IFRS.

FROM HARMONIZATION TO IFRS AS GLOBALLY ACCEPTED STANDARDS

3

OBJECTIVES After studying this chapter you should be able to:

- understand and discuss efforts aimed at the international harmonization of financial accounting standards with reference to the roles of the IASC, the EU and other institutions

- understand and discuss efforts aimed at the international convergence of financial reporting standards with reference to the roles of the IASB, the EU, IOSCO, the SEC and FASB

- outline the IASB's efforts aimed at realizing IFRS as globally accepted financial reporting standards

- discuss the process for the endorsement of IFRS in the EU

- describe the organizational structure and the roles of the IFRS Foundation, the IASB and related institutions

- describe the due process of standard setting of the IASB

- discuss theories of regulation

- discuss some organizational challenges for the IFRS Foundation and the IASB with reference to theories of regulation and what you learned about possible reasons for accounting differences in Chapter 2.

INTRODUCTION

In the previous chapter, we identified international differences in financial accounting systems. We also looked at possible variables for classifying international accounting differences and explored country classifications in the accounting literature. In this chapter, we will look at the process and agents of international financial accounting harmonization and the development towards international financial reporting standards (IFRS). It is useful to keep in mind that these developments took place against the background of deliberate efforts to deregulate and integrate international financial and capital markets. We will also consider theories of regulation, the EU's endorsement process for IFRS, and the organizational structure and due process of the International Accounting Standard Board (IASB).

The first three sections of this chapter will look at three phases in the history of the development of international financial reporting. The period until 1995 was characterized by efforts towards accounting harmonization. We start by looking at harmonization efforts by the International Accounting Standards Committee (IASC), the EU and other organizations. From 1996 to 1999, the idea was to bring about a convergence of accounting standards. Hence, the second section looks at convergence efforts by the IASC, the EU and other organizations. The third section starts in the year 2000 when the IASC was converted into the IASB. The IASB's aim was to develop and promote IFRS as the one and only set of globally accepted standards. We will also discuss how other organizations enabled the IASB to make good progress towards achieving this goal. We continue with a discussion of the IASB's mission to set globally accepted accounting standards and the IASB's organizational structure and due process. We finish by taking a critical look at the contrast between the idea and the reality of IFRS as global standards with reference to the theory of regulation and the global diversity of institutional environments where IFRS has been adopted.

INTERNATIONAL ACCOUNTING HARMONIZATION

As mentioned in Chapter 1, the move towards accounting harmonization was precipitated by the sharp increase in direct investment of American companies in Europe in the 1960s and 1970s and the gradual deregulation of financial and capital markets in many countries around the world in the 1980s and 1990s. In financial accounting:

> [h]armonization (a *process*) is a movement away from total diversity of practice. Harmony (a *state*) is therefore indicated by a 'clustering' of companies around one or a few of the available methods. Standardization (a process) is a movement toward uniformity (a state).
>
> (Tay and Parker, 1990: 72)

Tay and Parker also distinguished between the harmonization and standardization of rules and the harmonization and standardization of actual practices. The efforts towards harmonization of accounting practices and standards lasted until about 1995 when the emphasis shifted to the convergence of standards.

ACTIVITY 3.1

Take a moment to consider the above definitions of har-monization, standardization and the concept of global accounting standardization against the background of what you learned in Chapter 2. To what extent do you think that the idea of 'IFRS as global standards' is feasible? Why?

Activity feedback

'IFRS as global standards' may be possible if we mean de jure standardization because, in principle, all countries could decide to adopt IFRS as their financial reporting standards. Achieving de facto standardiza-tion is already difficult, if not impossible, within one country. It is even less likely across the many different countries in the world, because of differences in busi-ness practices, regulation systems, dominant sourc-es of finance, economic development, etc. However, this is no reason not to try to achieve de jure global standardization.

The creation of the IASC

When the professional accountancy bodies established the IASC in 1973, the IASC's main objective as expressed in its *Agreement and Constitution* was:

[t]o establish and maintain an International Accounting Standards Committee (...) whose function it will be to formulate and publish in the public interest, basic standards to be observed in the presentation of audited accounts and financial statements and to promote their worldwide acceptance and observance.

(IASC Agreement and Constitution, 1973: Par. 1, reproduced in Camfferman and Zeff, 2007: appendix 1).

The emphasis lies on the harmonization of financial reporting and promoting world-wide acceptance of these standards. In order to gain this worldwide acceptance, the IASC allowed many options in the standards it promulgated in the early years.

The IASC was created in 1973 at the initiative of Henry Benson, who was the president of the Institute of Chartered Accountants in England and Wales (ICAEW) in 1966 and 1967 and Douglas Morpeth, who was the president of the ICAEW in 1972 and 1973. The IASC's creation must be regarded against the background of many other developments that were going on at the time. For example, in 1972, the decision was taken for the UK to join the European Economic Community (EEC) as of January 1973. Some say that a primary motive for the professional accounting or-ganizations involved in establishing the IASC was to provide a counter weight for the continental approach to regulation of financial reporting standards and the account-ing profession in the EEC (e.g. Hopwood, 1994: 243). A second motive mentioned by Bocqueraz and Walton (2006: 281) was 'the fear that if the accounting profession did not organise international accounting standards "other agencies" would "take matters into their own hands"'.

A third reason may be that, during the 1960s, an increasing number of interna-tional mergers and acquisitions, particularly the takeover of European companies by American companies took place (Zeff, 2012: 809). There was a practical need to harmonize accounting practices for these companies. Given the political sensitivities at that time, an international accounting standard setter mostly meant an accounting standard setter that was not American. In the US in 1972, the Wheat Committee recommended the creation of the Financial Accounting Standards Board (FASB). In 1973 the FASB took over standard setting in the US from the American Institute of Public Accountants (AICPA)'s Accounting Principles Board. A third person who was important in the establishment of the IASC was Wallace E. 'Wally' Olson (president of the AICPA from 1972 to 1980) who had also been a member of the Wheat Committee.

The IASC's initial members were representatives from the professional accountancy bodies in the UK, the US, Canada, the Netherlands, France, Germany, Australia, Mexico and Japan. According to Bocqueraz and Walton (2006: 282), 'Mexico was "grudgingly" accepted by Benson, at the insistence of the USA, while Japan was added at the later meeting in London in December 1972, again at US insistence'. France, Germany and the Netherlands were included in order that Europe would take the IASC seriously.

> Originally, the IASC was funded and controlled by its founding member bodies. In 1982, this changed to a form of collective ownership by the accounting profession, as appointments to Board positions were from that moment on made by the council of the International Federation of Accountants (IFAC), and IFAC provided a part of the IASC's funding.
>
> (Camfferman and Zeff, 2015: 12)

IFAC had been formed in 1977 to develop and enhance a coordinated worldwide accountancy profession with harmonized International Standards on Auditing (ISAs). According to Mueller *et al.* (1994: 42–43), acceptance of 'IFAC pronouncements received a major boost when the International Organization of Securities Commissions (IOSCO) voted in 1992 to accept IAS for the purposes of multinational registrations and filings with securities commissions'.

National regulatory or standard-setting bodies operate within a national jurisdiction and some form of legal and governmental framework that delineates, defines and provides a level of authority. The IASC, however, operated throughout its existence in the knowledge that, in the last resort, it and its standards had no formal authority. It therefore always had to rely on persuasion and the quality of its analysis and argument. This had two major effects. First, the quality of logic and discussion in its publications was generally high and its conclusions were – if sometimes debatable – feasible and clearly articulated. Second, the conclusions and recommendations of many of the earlier published International Accounting Standards (IAS) documents often had to accommodate two or more alternative acceptable treatments, simply because both or all were already practised in countries that were members of IASC and were too significant to be ignored.

ACTIVITY 3.2

What would be an advantage and a disadvantage of the fact that the IASC often had to accommodate two or more alternative treatments?

Activity feedback

An advantage is that allowing multiple alternative treatments made IASs more acceptable. A disadvantage is that allowing multiple treatments made information less comparable.

Towards the end of the 1980s, the IASC decided it would attempt a more proactive approach, and early in 1989, it published an exposure draft (E32) on the comparability of financial statements. This proposed the elimination of certain treatments permitted by particular IASs and the expression of a clear preference for one particular treatment, even where two alternatives were still to be regarded as acceptable. This 'comparability project' led to a large number of revised standards operative from the mid-1990s, which did indeed considerably narrow the degree of optionality compared with the earlier versions of the standards issued in the 1970s and 1980s. The comparability project, therefore, can be said to have made the set of IASs more meaningful and significant. Of course, it did nothing to increase the formal authority of the IASC.

Harmonization in the EU

The Treaty of Rome led to the establishment of the European Economic Community (EEC) in 1958. The EEC was meant to create a common market of goods, services, capital and workers in the countries that participated in the initiative, i.e. the Benelux countries, France, Italy and West Germany. In order to achieve this, the EEC started to work on a series of Directives intended to harmonize company law and financial reporting in order to enable the free movement of persons, goods, services and capital across EEC member countries (Camfferman and Zeff, 2007: 39). The Fourth Directive was strongly influenced by Germany's tax-oriented approach to accounting (Zeff, 2012: 809) and the concept of the true and fair view in the UK's Companies Act 1948.

For many years, the major method of engendering change across the EU has been by means of Directives. Once agreed, a Directive is a binding agreement by all the Member States of the EU that they will introduce the principles set out in the Directives into national legislation. This means that all Member States are required to implement the Directives. Each Directive must be translated into each of the official EU languages. It is the language version applicable to a particular Member State that is to be enacted into the law of that country. There may not be perfect semantic equivalence between different language versions of the Directives.

Before the Accounting Directive and the Disclosure Directive of 2013, the fundamental EU Directive relating to financial reporting was the Fourth Company Law Directive of 25 July 1978. This related to the annual accounts of limited companies. It was followed by the Seventh Company Law Directive of 13 June 1983, which extended the principles of the Fourth Directive to the preparation of consolidated (group) accounts. The Fourth Directive aimed to provide a minimum of coordination of national provisions for the content and presentation of annual financial accounts and reports, of the valuation methods used within them and of the rules for publication. It applies to 'certain companies with limited liability' – broadly, all those above defined minimum size criteria – and aims to ensure that annual accounts disclose comparable and equivalent information. The Fourth Directive contained many options with regard to recognition and measurement of a substantial number of balance sheet items and profit and loss items. The Seventh Directive, which was developed in the 1980s, contained fewer options than the Fourth Directive. The latter was due to the fact that consolidation practices were less developed in a number of EU Member States, therefore fewer national practices and interests had to be defended during the development of the Seventh Directive.

Crucial to the content of the Fourth Directive was the requirement that published accounts should show a 'true and fair view'. This is a classic example of the cultural divide between the tradition of common law and the tradition of codified law. In the former, definitions of such concepts are typically provided by courts in relation to specific situations rather than by legislative texts intended to apply to many different situations. In the latter, the converse is true: the courts have a role of interpretation and clarification of legislative texts, but not of providing situationally appropriate legal definitions. Thus, the tradition of economic liberalism of the English-speaking countries, the faith in markets and the suspicion of technocracy, go hand in hand with an essentially pragmatic tradition of common law and a belief that the accounting profession can largely lay down its own rules in the form of 'generally accepted accounting principles'. By contrast, many countries in continental Europe have less historical attachment to economic liberalism, more faith in technocracy and a preference for explicit legal texts, which extends to the framing of accounting rules. Harmonization of accounting within the EU has involved bringing these two traditions into some degree of harmony, and it is in this respect that the inclusion of the 'true and fair' requirement in the Fourth Directive was both crucial and controversial.

By the early 1990s, it had become clear, even to the European Commission, that Directives were too cumbersome and slow to achieve further useful harmonization. The Fourth Directive, agreed in 1978, did not cover several topics and it had been too complicated to amend it often. Furthermore, global harmonization had become more relevant than regional harmonization.

Early efforts by other institutions

Two other international institutions, the Organisation for Economic Co-operation and Development (OECD) and United Nations (UN) Commission on Transnational Corporations (UNCTC) also worked on the harmonization of accounting and disclosure standards. Their objective was somewhat different from that of the IASC (and later the IASB) and the EU, in that they focused on producing guidelines for multinational corporations to disclose information that enabled the judgement of social performance as well as financial performance.

Like the EEC, the OECD was also a result of the Treaty of Rome. The OECD was formed in 1960. It has as its founding members 20 of the world's most developed, industrialized countries. Over time, a number of other countries have joined. In 1976, the OECD issued a Code of Conduct for multinational corporations, providing guidelines on voluntarily disclosing financial information. According to the OECD 50th Anniversary Vision statement, the 'OECD will continue to help countries develop policies together to promote economic growth and healthy labour markets, boost investment and trade, support sustainable development, raise living standards, and improve the functioning of markets'.[1]

The UN is an international organization founded in 1945 after the Second World War by 51 countries. Its purposes as currently formulated are: (1) to maintain international peace and security, (2) to promote sustainable development, (3) to protect human rights, (4) to uphold international law, and (5) to deliver humanitarian aid.[2] The UN became involved in accounting standard issues as a result of concerns discussed at the third ministerial session of the United National Conference on Trade and Development (UNCTAD). The UNCTC operated from 1974 until 1993 and answered to the Economic and Social Council (ECOSOC) (Hamdani and Ruffing, 2015: 9–13). Since the end of colonization, transnational corporations proved to be very powerful in negotiating deals that were beneficial for the companies, but less so for the host countries. The UNCTC's purpose was to understand the economic, social and political consequences of the actions of transnational corporations on developing countries, to strengthen the position of these countries vis-à-vis transnational corporations and to try to establish ways of promoting positive contributions for all parties concerned while minimizing the negative effects.

In the 1980s, the IASC attempted to persuade both the OECD and the UN not to set standards as such. The idea was that the IASC would set international accounting standards and the OECD and the UN would address related issues. So the OECD subsequently concentrated on taxation, helping the transition in former USSR countries, and corporate governance. The UN switched to environmental accounting, professional education and SME accounting. See also Camfferman and Zeff (2007: 194–195) and Hamdani and Ruffing (2015: 137–138).

INTERNATIONAL ACCOUNTING CONVERGENCE

By the mid-1990s, it was clear that accounting harmonization was not going to be enough to further the development and integration of international financial and capital markets. The 1990s were a period of unprecedented financial deregulation in many countries. As we shall see below, the IASC received a boost from its 1995 agreement with IOSCO to develop a set of core standards. Although the term convergence suggests that financial accounting standards in different countries would converge to a single set of high-quality financial accounting standards, in reality, convergence was strongly influenced by US Generally Accepted Accounting Principles (GAAP). It also became clear that a number of large European companies voluntary adopted US GAAP as a consequence of being listed on US stock exchanges. However, since the European Commission and other Europeans had no influence over US GAAP, in the second half of the 1990s the European Commission began to support the efforts of the IASC.

Towards acceptance of IAS by IOSCO

In 1995, the IASC entered into an agreement with the IOSCO to complete a 'core set' of IAS by 1999. IOSCO is a confederation of regulatory bodies that had come to be a force on the world stage from the late 1980s. By that time, the US Securities and Exchange Commission (SEC) regarded it as an agent of change to improve the way the world's securities markets were operated and governed (Camfferman and Zeff, 2015: 11).

Completion of a set of comprehensive core standards acceptable to IOSCO's Technical Committee would allow IOSCO to recommend endorsement of those standards in all global securities markets. This meant that one set of financial statements, properly prepared in accordance with IAS, would automatically be acceptable for listing purposes without amendment and without any reconciliation with national (i.e. local) standards on each and all of the world's important stock exchanges. In December 1998 the IASC completed its 'core standards' programme with the approval of IAS 39, *Financial Instruments Recognition and Measurement*.

The US SEC was (and still is) a powerful member of IOSCO. The SEC is also the organization that has entrusted standard setting in the US to the FASB. The SEC and the FASB understood that US GAAP as the de facto set of IAS was not politically feasible in most countries. Nevertheless, the SEC and the FASB considered US GAAP to be the best set of accounting standards and they worked to ensure IFRS convergence with US GAAP.

Apart from IOSCO's endorsement, the SEC also required changes to the future structure, composition and process of the IASC as a standard setter (Camfferman and Zeff, 2015: 15) in order to consider its possible future acceptance of IFRS. Under pressure from IOSCO, the SEC and the G4 + 1 (a group of standard-setting bodies from the US, the UK, Australia, Canada and New Zealand), in late 1999 the Board of IASC approved proposals to make significant changes to IASC's structure. The IASC needed to possess the five characteristics that the SEC and the FASB deemed crucial for a quality international standard setter (Street, 2006: 117). These characteristics were: (1) the independence and technical competence of the IASC Board members, (2) the due process with respect to IASC decision making and actual standard setting, (3) adequate staff, (4) independent fundraising and (5) independent oversight.

The European Commission's 1995 Accounting Strategy and 1999 Financial Services Action Plan

In 1995, the European Commission developed its new 'Accounting Strategy'. Within the frame of that new strategy, the contact committee on Accounting Directives analyzed the degree of conformity between the IASs and the content of the European Accounting Directives. With the results of this analysis, the individual EU Member States could decide whether they would allow national companies to comply with IAS instead of the domestic GAAP for the preparation of consolidated financial statements.

In the wake of the 1997 Asian financial crisis, the G7 finance ministers and the European Commission also wanted to see the IASC restructured. In particular, they wanted the IASC to be detached from the accountancy profession (Camfferman and Zeff, 2015: 15).

In May 1999, the European Commission agreed on the Financial Services Action Plan. The aim of this Plan was to create a single European market for financial services. To facilitate this creation of a large single market for financial services, the European Commission proposed in 2000 that all listed companies should use one set of accounting standards for financial reporting purposes. IAS was chosen to be that set of accounting standards.

The IMF and the World Bank and the adoption of IFRS in some developing countries

Both the IMF and the World Bank have contributed to the adoption of IAS and later IFRS in developing countries, sometimes even those without a stock exchange, demanding the use of IFRS as a condition attaching to their loans to developing countries.

The IMF was conceived at the UN conference in Bretton Woods, New Hampshire, United States, in July 1944. The idea was to build a framework for economic cooperation to address the causes that had contributed to the Great Depression of the 1930s.

> The IMF's primary purpose is to ensure the stability of the international monetary system – the system of exchange rates and international payments that enables countries (and their citizens) to transact with each other. The Fund's mandate was updated in 2012 to include all macroeconomic and financial sector issues that bear on global stability.[3]

The IMF currently has 188 member countries and supports its member countries by providing:

> [p]olicy advice to governments and central banks based on analysis of economic trends and cross-country experiences; research, statistics, forecasts, and analysis based on tracking of global, regional, and individual economies and markets;

loans to help countries overcome economic difficulties; concessional loans to help fight poverty in developing countries; and technical assistance and training to help countries improve the management of their economies.[4]

The World Bank was established in 1944 and consists of two organizations. The International Bank for Reconstruction and Development (IBRD) lends to governments of middle-income and creditworthy low-income countries. The International Development Association (IDA) provides interest-free loans – called credits – and grants to governments of the poorest countries. The World Bank's mission is to reduce poverty.[5]

IFRS

In May 2000, the proposed structural changes were approved by IASC's membership. Also, in May 2000, IOSCO formally accepted the IASC's 'core standards' as a basis for cross-border securities-listing purposes worldwide. For certain countries, notably the US, reconciliations of items such as earnings and stockholders' equity to national GAAP would still be required up until 2007. In June 2000, the European Commission issued a Communication proposing that all listed companies in the EU would be required to prepare their consolidated financial statements using IAS from 2005.

The creation of the IASB

In 2001, the IASC Foundation was established as an independent private standard-setting body in the legal form of a not-for-profit corporation registered in the state of Delaware (Camfferman and Zeff, 2015: 22). In early February 2001, the G4+1 had decided to disband. Formally, the reason was that the G4+1 was no longer necessary. A convenient consequence was that the organizations and people involved in the G4+1 were now free to take up positions in the IASB and the IASC Foundation.

Like the FASB in 1972 and the UK Accounting Standards Board in 1990, which replaced the APB and the ASC respectively, the IASB differed from its predecessor by having a two-tier structure, based on an organ of governance not involved in standard setting (the IASC Foundation's Trustees) and a standard-setting board. This structure was articulated in the IASC Foundation Constitution. The International Accounting Standard Setting Board (IASB) was to be its standard-setting body. The IASC Foundation also established a Standards Advisory Council (SAC) to provide advice on agenda decisions and priorities. The IASC's 1996 Standing Interpretations Committee was reformed into the International Financial Reporting Interpretations Committee (IFRIC) to issue interpretations of individual IFRSs. The IASC Foundation's objective, too, was reformulated. The 2001 *Constitution* of the IASC Foundation included the following objectives:

(a) To develop, in the public interest, a single set of high-quality, understandable and enforceable global standards that require high-quality, transparent and comparable information in financial statements and other financial reporting to help participants in the world's capital markets and other users make economic decisions.

(b) To promote the use and rigorous application of those standards.

(c) In fulfilling the objectives associated with (a) and (b), to take account of, as appropriate, the needs of a range of sizes and types of entities in diverse economic settings.

(d) To promote and facilitate the adoption of International Financial Reporting Standards (IFRSs), being the standards and interpretations issued by the IASB, through the convergence of national accounting standards and IFRSs.

(IASC Foundation, 2001: Par. 2)

The focus is now on developing one single set of high-quality and enforceable standards. The IASB sees itself as performing the role of a global standard setter.

The European Commission's Regulation No. 1606/2002

In June 2000, the European Commission issued a Communication proposing that all listed companies in the EU would be required to prepare their consolidated financial statements using IAS from 2005. In 2002, Regulation (EC) No. 1606/2002 on the application of IFRS was approved by the European Parliament.

Unlike an EU Directive, the Regulation has the force of law and no further action is required by Member States before the Regulation comes into effect. The Regulation applies in all EU Member States plus Iceland, Norway and Lichtenstein. The Regulation requires all listed companies within the EU and the European Economic Area to publish consolidated financial statements for accounting periods beginning on or after 1 January 2005 in accordance with IFRS as endorsed by the EU. The term 'IFRS' in certain contexts is a portmanteau expression including IFRS, IAS, SICs and IFRIC in order to be adopted in the EU. Each new IFRS has to be endorsed by the European Commission.

In June 2001, the European Financial Reporting Advisory Group (EFRAG) was set up as part of the endorsement mechanism. EFRAG is a private sector advisory committee meant to provide input into the development of IFRSs issued by the IASB and to provide the European Commission with technical expertise and advice on accounting matters. Under the IAS Regulation, the Accounting Regulatory Committee (representatives of Member States) were required to endorse individual standards into European law. The Commission puts the standard forward, and the final task in EFRAG's process is to give formal 'endorsement advice' to the Commission, giving its opinion on whether the standard satisfies the criteria established in the IAS Regulation. EFRAG's Technical Expert Group was given the responsibility of providing the actual endorsement advice. In June 2002, EFRAG endorsed the whole body of extant standards (Camfferman and Zeff, 2015: 63). From then on, endorsement was to happen on a standard by standard basis.

IFRS AS GLOBAL STANDARDS?

Like the IASC, the IASB has no power to compel anyone to use its standards. Prior to 2005, a number of mainly European companies used them voluntarily but no national jurisdiction had adopted them directly as mandatory rules. From 2005 onwards, not only EU listed groups were required to comply with IFRS on a mandatory basis. Australian listed groups were now subject to mandatory compliance with IFRS. New Zealand followed this Australian and EU example. Hong Kong and South Africa were also early adopters of IFRS. Since then, worldwide use of IFRS has been increasing. However, although IFRS is accepted for foreign companies listed in the US, IFRS has not been adopted in the US. The argument is that IFRS is not compatible with the institutional characteristics of the US markets and business practices. It is more likely that the US does not want to relinquish its sovereignty when it comes to setting accounting standards.

Although the EU has adopted IFRS, it uses an endorsement mechanism to maintain some level of sovereignty over the accounting standards adopted in the EU. Initially, the endorsement mechanism was meant to be very light touch, but the 2007/2008 financial crisis and the continued economic slowdown caused the EU to reconsider this approach. Although a carve-out to IAS 39 already existed because of French opposition to using fair value by banks, in 2008 the EC forced an amendment to IAS 39 to allow reclassification of financial instruments from available for sale to amortized cost.

Partly as a consequence of the continued economic downturn, in November 2012 the Economics and Finance Ministers of the EU Member States (ECOFIN) Council discussed how the EU could better defend European interests in the accounting standard-setting debate. Philippe Maystadt was commissioned to write a report on how the Accounting Regulatory Committee (ARC) and EFRAG could be reorganized to improve the coordination of the accounting debate in Europe and the consideration of the stakes in the political debate around financial reporting standards (Maystadt, 2013: 5). The Maystadt Report made 12 recommendations. EFRAG was reorganized in June 2014 and its new structure came into effect from December 2014. One important aspect of EFRAG's endorsement process is establishing whether a new IFRS is conducive to the European public good.

ACTIVITY 3.3

On the IAS Plus website and the IASB website you will be able to find the latest list of countries that have adopted, accepted or not adopted IFRS. Have a look and see what countries have chosen which option. Make a note of countries that you find surprising.

Activity feedback

At the time of writing, the IASB claims that IFRS has been accepted in more than 100 countries around the world. However, there are differences between the ways in which countries require or permit IFRS. Even within the EU, some countries require the application of IFRS to both consolidated and unconsolidated financial statements of listed companies, whereas others require local standards for the unconsolidated and IFRS for the consolidated financial statements. Some countries accept IFRS as the IASB pronounces them. Other countries issue their own standards based on IFRS and yet other jurisdictions, such as the EU, endorse each individual standard.

THE IFRS FOUNDATION, THE IASB AND RELATED INSTITUTIONS

As more and more countries adopted IFRS, the IASC Foundation realized that its responsibilities grew correspondingly. One aspect is a transparent due process in order to increase organizational legitimacy. The IASC Foundation's Constitution provided for a regular review of its Constitution and organization. The first review resulted in a *Due Process Handbook* for the IASB in 2006 (Camfferman and Zeff, 2015: 289–290), which was revised in 2008 and 2013. A second aspect is effective communication with the IFRS Foundation's constituency. In 2010 the IASC Foundation, SAC and IFRIC were renamed the IFRS Foundation, the IFRS Advisory Council and the IFRS Interpretations Committee, respectively (Camfferman and Zeff, 2015: 295) to communicate the IFRS brand more strongly and consistently. This brings us to the current structure of the organization.

In the aftermath of the financial crisis, the structure was changed into a three-tier structure in 2009.

ACTIVITY 3.4

Go to the website of the IASB (www.ifrs.org) and look for the organizational structure. What are the three tiers and what organizations comprise this three-tier structure?

Activity feedback

The three tiers are:

1 *The independent standard-setting and related activities of the IASB, the IFRS Foundation and the IFRS Interpretations Committee. The IASB receives advice from the Accounting Standards Advisory Forum, which is made up of representatives of national standard setters.*

2 *The IFRS Foundation's Trustees are responsible for the governance and oversight of the IASB and the IFRS Interpretations Committee's activities.*

3 *The IFRS Foundation's Trustees are accountable to the IFRS Foundation Monitoring Board. The IFRS Foundation Monitoring Board is made up of public capital market authorities. The members of the Monitoring Board include representatives of the Growth and Emerging Markets Committee of the IOSCO, the European Commission (EC), Financial Services Agency of Japan (JFSA), US SEC, Brazilian Securities Commission (CVM), and Financial Services Commission of Korea (FSC). The Basel Committee on Banking Supervision participates in the Monitoring Board as an observer (www.ifrs.org/About-us/Pages/Monitoring-Board. aspx (accessed on 21 January 2016)).*

IFRS Foundation The IFRS Foundation is primarily responsible for the governance of the international accounting standard setter and the organs of this standard setter by appointing the members of these organs in accordance with the provisions of the Constitution. The governance role of the IFRS Foundation includes establishing and maintaining appropriate financing arrangements for the organization. The members of the IFRS Foundation are called the Trustees and they appoint the members of the IASB, IFRIC and the IFRS Advisory Council. The Trustees review broad strategic issues affecting financial reporting standards and they are required to review the Constitution every five years.

The IFRS Foundation comprises 22 Trustees. Trustees are individuals, of whom six are from North America, six from Europe, six from the Asia/Oceania region, one from Africa, one from South America and two from any area, subject to establishing 'overall geographical balance'. Paragraph 7 of the Constitution stipulates that Trustees shall comprise individuals that as a group provide an appropriate balance of professional backgrounds, including auditors, preparers, users, academics and other officials serving the public interest. Two of the Trustees shall normally be senior partners of prominent international accounting firms. To achieve such a balance, Trustees should be selected after consultation with national and international organizations of auditors (including the IFAC), preparers, users and academics. Trustees are appointed for a three-year term, with a possibility for renewal once.

In 2011, a substantial review of the future strategy was undertaken by the Trustees in cooperation with the Monitoring Board. The Due Process Oversight Committee (DPOC) was established. This Committee works on the enhancement of the transparency and oversight of the IASB's standard-setting process.

Of particular importance is the emphasis on the post-implementation reviews when a new standard has been issued or an existing standard has been changed to a large extent.

The IASB The task of standard setting lies with the IASB. The IASB currently consists of 14 members. Up to three members may be part-time members. The expression 'part-time members' means that the members concerned commit most of their time in paid employment to the IASC Foundation. With regard to the composition of the IASB, the main qualifications for membership of the IASB are professional competence and practical experience. The Trustees have to select IASB members so that, as a group, it provides an appropriate mix of recent practical experience among auditors, preparers, users and academics, who represent the best available combination of technical expertise and diversity of international business and market experience in order to contribute to the development of high-quality global accounting standards. The Constitution also ensures the geographical diversity of these members spread over the Asia/Oceania region, Europe, North America, Africa, South America, and two appointed from any area, subject to maintaining overall geographical balance.

ACTIVITY 3.5

Go to the website of the IASB (www.ifrs.org) and look for the IFRS Foundation Constitution. Check for the criteria for IASB members in the Appendix to the Constitution. What are these criteria?

Activity feedback

You will find that eight criteria are found to be of importance to becoming a member of the IASB.

1 demonstrate technical competency and knowledge of financial accounting and reporting

2 ability to analyze

3 communication skills

4 judicious decision making

5 awareness of the financial reporting environment

6 ability to work in a collegial atmosphere

7 integrity, objectivity and discipline

8 commitment to the IASC Foundation's Mission and Public Interest.

Each member has one vote. On both technical and other matters, proxy voting shall not be permitted; neither shall members of the IASB be entitled to appoint alternates to attend meetings. The publication of an exposure draft on final IAS or final interpretation of the Standing Interpretations Committee requires approval by at least 10 of the 16 members of the IASB (by 9 if there are fewer than 16 members). Other decisions of the IASB, including the publication of a discussion paper, shall require a simple majority of the members of the IASB present at a meeting that is attended by at least 60 per cent of the members of the IASB, in person or by telecommunications.

The Monitoring Board The Monitoring Board was established in 2009. The role of the Monitoring Board is to provide a formal link between the Trustees and public authorities. This relationship seeks to replicate, on an international basis, the link between accounting standard setters and those public authorities that have generally overseen accounting standard setters in a national context.

The Monitoring Group consists of public authorities outside the IFRS Foundation's organizational framework. The Monitoring Board comprises the responsible member of the EC, the chair of the IOSCO Emerging Markets Committee, the chair of the IOSCO Technical Committee, the commissioner of the Japan Financial Services Agency, the chairman of the US SEC and, as an observer, the chairman of the Basel Committee on Banking. The Monitoring Group shall participate in the process for appointing the Trustees and approve the appointment of the Trustees. The Trustees report to the Monitoring Group regularly to enable it to address whether and how the Trustees are fulfilling their role as set out in the Constitution.

The IFRS Interpretations Committee Next to the Trustees and the Board, the structure of the international accounting standard setter includes an Interpretations Committee named the International Financial Reporting Standards Interpretations Committee. The Standards Interpretations Committee was established in 1997 and was renamed the IFRIC in 2001. In 2010, the name changed again to the IFRS Interpretations Committee.

People can refer uncertainties about the application of a standard to IFRIC. IFRIC then responds by either (a) saying there is not a problem because the correct reading of the standard has been considered by the Big Four and enforcers, or (b) issuing an Interpretation which is binding but is often later incorporated into the standard, or (c) proposing an amendment to an existing IFRS to clarify the issue.

The Committee consists of 14 members, who are appointed by the Trustees. The Trustees have the task of selecting members of the Committee so that it comprises a group of people representing, within that group, the best available combination of technical expertise and diversity of international business and market experience in the practical application of IFRS and analysis of financial statements prepared in accordance with IFRS. The task of this Committee, according to the Constitution, is to interpret the application of IAS and IFRS and to provide timely guidance on financial reporting issues not specifically addressed in IAS and IFRS, in the context of the IASB framework, and to undertake other tasks at the request of the IASB. In carrying out this work, IFRIC needs to work together with national standard setters to bring about convergence and to reach high-quality solutions.

The IFRS Advisory Council This Council (formerly named the SAC) with 30 or more members, provides a forum for participation by organizations and individuals with an interest in international financial reporting and having diverse geographic and functional backgrounds. The IFRS Advisory Council gives advice to the Board on agenda decisions and priorities and informs the Board of the view of members of the Council on major standard-setting projects. The Council shall be consulted by the IASB in advance of IASB decisions on major projects, and by the Trustees in advance of any proposed changes in the Constitution. The Chairman of the Council is appointed by the Trustees and shall not be a member of the IASB or its staff.

The Accounting Standards Advisory Forum (ASAF) ASAF is an advisory group to the IASB. Its members are national accounting standard setters and regional bodies with an interest in financial reporting. ASAF's principal purpose is to provide technical advice and feedback to the IASB. ASAF was formed in 2013 with the aim of involving national standard setters more directly in developing IFRS.

DUE PROCESS

In order to achieve its objectives, it was necessary for the IASB to develop accounting standards along a transparent process in which the different constituent parties could have their voices heard. The standards promulgated by the IASB are developed through a formal due process in which opportunities for broad international consultation – which involves accountants, financial analysts and other users of financial statements, the business community, stock exchanges, regulatory and legal authorities, academics and other interested individuals – are foreseen.

The IASB's due process of standard setting involves six stages (see the IASB's Due Process Handbook – February 2012) which we will briefly enumerate here.

ACTIVITY 3.6

While you are reading the different stages of the standard-setting process, it is interesting to look at the website of the IASB (www.ifrs.org) and consult its timetable of projects.

Activity feedback

You will find a timetable of the IASB's agenda for the future. This agenda lists the standards, the exposure drafts of standards, the discussion documents and the research projects the IASB is working on in the coming years. A projected timetable of the IASB workplan is posted on the website. A distinction is drawn in their active agenda between new standards, major projects, amendments to standards, the conceptual framework and research projects. Except for the text of a standard which is going to be approved, you will find the texts of all the other documents (exposure drafts, discussion papers, research reports) on the IASB website. Besides the texts of these documents, you are able to consult the comment letters sent by the constituent parties in relation to exposure drafts and discussion documents. Looking at the website helps you better understand the process described below.

Agenda consultation. The IASB will set the agenda for the future by taking into account the users' needs in relation to high-quality accounting standards. The IASB will evaluate the merits of adding a potential item to its agenda mainly by reference to the needs of investors. The IASB discusses potential agenda items with the IFRS Advisory Council, the IFRS Interpretations Committee, ASAF and other interested parties.

Research programme. The IASB is trying to move towards evidence-based standard setting. A topic first goes through an 'assessment stage' where IASB staff consider whether there is a problem that needs to be addressed. It may issue a staff paper, based on which the Board will decide if it is worth pursuing. If so, it stays on the research agenda and moves to the development stage. The research programme consists of research activities and may lead to the development of a discussion paper. When the IASB considers potential agenda items, it may decide that some issues require additional research before it can take a decision on whether to add the item to its active agenda. Such issues may be addressed as research projects on the IASB's research agenda. A research project may be undertaken by the IASB or by another standard setter.

Development and publication of a discussion paper. The IASB publishes a discussion paper as its first publication on any major new topic as a vehicle to explain the issue and solicit early comment from constituents. If the changes are substantial, the Board may re-expose, which it has done with a number of major standards (leases, revenue recognition, insurance). However, a re-exposure can potentially add two years to the process and the IASB avoids it if possible. Typically, a discussion paper includes a comprehensive overview of the issue, possible approaches in addressing the issue, the preliminary views of its authors or the IASB and an invitation to comment. This approach may differ if another accounting standard setter develops the research paper. The IASB normally allows a period of 120 days for comment on a discussion paper, but may allow a longer period on major projects (which are those projects involving pervasive or difficult conceptual or practical issues).

Standards programme. The standards programme consists of the development and publication of an exposure draft, which is a mandatory step in due process before issuing a new standard. Unlike a discussion paper, an exposure draft sets out a specific proposal in the form of a proposed standard (or amendment to an existing standard). The development of an exposure draft begins with the IASB considering issues on the basis of staff research and recommendations, as well as comments received on any discussion paper, and suggestions made by the IFRS Advisory Council, working groups and accounting standard setters and arising from public education sessions.

An exposure draft contains an invitation to comment on a draft standard or amendment to a standard that proposes requirements on recognition, measurement and disclosures. The draft may also include mandatory application guidance and implementation guidance, and will be accompanied by a basis for conclusions on the proposals and the alternative views of dissenting IASB members (if any). The IASB normally allows a period of 120 days for comment on an exposure draft. However, this period can be extended if the standard deals with a major issue, or the period can be shortened to 30 days if there is already broad consensus on the topic.

Development and publication of an IFRS. The development of an IFRS is carried out during IASB meetings, when the IASB considers the comments received on the exposure draft. Changes from the exposure draft are posted on the website. When the IASB is satisfied that it has reached a conclusion on the issues arising from the exposure draft, it instructs the staff to draft the IFRS. Shortly before the IASB ballots the standard, a near-final draft is posted on its limited access website for paying subscribers. Finally, after the due process is completed, all outstanding issues are resolved and the IASB members have been balloted in favour of publication, the IFRS is issued.

Procedures after an IFRS is issued. After an IFRS is issued, the staff and the IASB members hold regular meetings with interested parties, including other standard-setting bodies, to help understand unanticipated issues related to the practical implementation and potential impact of its proposals. For each new IFRS or major amendment to existing IFRSs, a post-implementation review (PIR) is carried out three years after the standard's mandatory application date. The first major post-implementation review that the IASB undertook was the PIR of IFRS 8 'Operating Segments'.

The aim of this elaborate due process of standard setting is that all constituent parties from the different regions of the world participate in this process. Whether or not this goal is achieved is not that easy to observe. Constituent parties often meet with members of the IASB or its staff to discuss items. No tracks are left of this kind of lobbying activity. Lobbying activities which are traceable are the comment letters sent by constituent parties in response to discussion documents and exposure drafts of standards. For a graphical overview of the IASB's due process of standard setting, see their website: www.ifrs.org/how-we-develop-standards/Pages/how-we-develop-standards.aspx.

During the financial crisis, the due process of the IASB was dispensed with on one occasion. Political pressure from governments forced the IASB to bypass its own due process when making amendments to standards in relation to financial instruments. Due to the sharp drop in the stock markets in the late summer and autumn of 2008, a number of financial institutions in Europe, which had large amounts of debt securities classified as 'trading', wanted to avoid having to report huge losses on their holdings in their quarterly figures at the end of September 2008. The financial sector, supported by the French Government, asked the EC to pressure the IASB to approve an amendment of IAS 39 which would allow those financial institutions to reclassify their holdings as 'held to maturity' and back-date the change. If the IASB were to issue this amendment, the financial institutions would not have to report huge losses for their third quarter of 2008. At the beginning of October 2008, the EC threatened the IASB that IFRS would no longer be the accounting standards to comply with by listed companies in EU markets unless the IASB approved the amendment of IAS 39 the Commission had asked for. The IASB asked permission from the IASC Foundation Trustees to override its own due process. By mid-October 2008, the IASB approved an amendment to IAS 39 to enable the reclassification, with the backdating to 1 July 2008.

In order to avoid this breach of the due process in the future, an accelerated due process – to be applied only in exceptional circumstances – is now elaborated. Since receiving input from a diverse range of constituents from diverse professional backgrounds and geographical backgrounds is important for the deliberative process of the IASB, the standard setter now employs many more mechanisms besides the traditional comment letters to be informed on the view of its constituents. On a regular basis, public hearings, field tests and field visits are carried out.

THEORIES OF REGULATION

Some people may believe that (international) financial reporting regulation is not necessary or even desirable. Let us define regulation here as using legal instruments to implement rules and measures that have been specifically designed for the purpose of achieving socio-economic policy objectives. The free market doctrine of classical and neo-classical economics is based on the assumption that the pursuit of self-interest will lead to benefit to society. People opposed to the regulation of financial reporting standards would believe that companies seeking to raise debt or equity capital would provide the information needed by potential investors because it is in their self-interest to do so.

In neo-classical economic theory, regulation is rationalized by the existence of market failure, whereas deregulation is rationalized by government failure. 'Market failure exists when free markets fail to deliver economic efficiency' (Munday, 2000: 29). 'Government failure exists when government intervention in markets leads to economic inefficiency' (Munday, 2000: 82). Economic efficiency comprises productive efficiency (every aspect of production is carried out at the lowest possible resource cost) and allocative efficiency (the right amount of the right products are being produced) (Munday, 2000: 10–13). Reasons for market failure include:

- the existence of externalities (costs or benefits to third parties which are not included in the determination of the private benefits of the parties to a transaction)
- incomplete information, misinformation and asymmetric information between market participants leading to costs associated with adverse selection and moral hazard
- pure public goods (goods that are non-excludable and non-rivalrous) undersupplied by the market because of the free-riding problem
- imperfect competition (monopoly, oligopoly and monopolistic competition) may occur when one or more of the conditions for perfect competition are not met (see also Munday, 2000: 29–46; Stiglitz and Walsh, 2002: 228–238; Groenewegen et al., 2010: 17–24).

Reasons for government failure include:

- Political decision making under imperfect information. Government policies aimed at increasing the public welfare may have unintended side effects such as distorted incentives. For example, financial deregulation together with accounting regulation may incentivize accountants to use their knowledge and creativity to find profitable loopholes, invent new products, or structure transactions so as to circumvent the rules and defeat their purpose.
- Politicians and/or bureaucrats may be acting in their own vested interests or on behalf of the vested interests of a small but well-organized and powerful minority who use lobbying to influence politicians. Vested interests create agency problems in regulators through regulatory capture of the process.

We have already seen that in the US and the UK the accounting profession managed to escape government regulation by exercising self-regulation. This comes in the form of professional codes of conduct and a system of 'social closure' whereby entry into the profession is regulated by the profession itself. In the US, the government initially delegated accounting standard setting to the accounting profession, and, even today, the FASB is still a private standard setter albeit accountable to the SEC. In the UK, the profession was able to pre-empt standard setting by the government. Self-regulation and government regulation are not necessary supplementary activities. They can be complementary modes of regulation as well.

Here we will briefly discuss the main theories of regulation and then focus on setting, implementing and enforcing financial reporting standards within the context of regulating national and international financial and capital markets. Two important groups of theories on regulation are:

- public interest theories
- private interest theories.

Public interest theories of regulation see government regulation as a helping hand meant to protect and benefit society as a whole against the problems caused by market failures. Public interest theories assume that 'governments are benign and capable of correcting these market failures through regulation' (Shleifer, 2005: 440). Critics think that public interest theorists exaggerate the extent of market failures. Others question the assumptions of a benevolent government, or place their faith in well-functioning courts enforcing private property rights.

Private interest theories of regulation include regulatory capture theory and public choice theory. Private interest theories assume that both private and public regulators are self-interested or at least more susceptible to pressure from some constituents than from others. Capture theory predicts that regulatory mechanisms are ultimately controlled by the most powerful regulated parties (Bernstein, 1955; Stigler, 1971). Public choice theory predicts that regulatory processes in democracies tend to be dominated by those groups of constituents who have the strongest incentive or the clearest organizing principle around which to become organized (Olson, 1965, 2000).

Watts and Zimmerman (1978) applied principal/agent theory to the SEC's delegating accounting standard setting to the FASB and concluded that, as long as financial accounting standards have cash flow effects for firms, standard setters will be faced with corporate lobbying. Similarly, Mattli and Büthe (2005) concluded the following:

> Private-sector delegation tends to occur in highly technical and complex issue areas where the creation of specialized public bureaucracies to deal with such

technical issues is either overly costly or simply impractical. Private agents to whom regulatory authority has been delegated, however, are rarely self-reliant bodies. Instead, they almost always are collective actors relying on a prior principal in their owners, funders, or members. In other words, when public regulatory authority is delegated to a private actor, the agent ends up with at least two principals: one public and one private.

(Mattli and Büthe, 2005: 418)

The interesting aspect of IFRS is that the IASB is a private organization that must work very hard to gain and maintain its organizational legitimacy. As the IASB and the IFRS Foundation cannot enforce IFRS, the legitimacy of their organization and the standards they produce must ultimately come from the countries that adopt and enforce them as national standards, the preparers who use IFRS and the users who find the information based on IFRS useful for their purposes.

CHALLENGES FOR IFRS AND THE IASB

The IASB issues standards that have to be applied in a variety of different legal and cultural contexts. IFRS is used by companies that vary considerably in size, ownership structure, capital structure, political jurisdiction and financial reporting sophistication. Financial reports must be comprehensible across countries, across jurisdictions, institutional environments and cultures. This universality of IFRS application was questioned, especially as the direction of US and EU influence pushed IFRS further towards a large enterprise multinational focus.

IFRS for SMEs

The relevance of the focus on multinational companies to SMEs or to developing economies is debatable. After a long due process, starting in 2003, which included all possible steps of the due process (e.g. discussion papers, round tables, extensive field testing), the IASB published in 2009 *The IFRS for SMEs*, which is simplified IFRS, aimed at non-publicly accountable entities that must produce general purpose financial statements. Since the large majority of companies worldwide are private, there is a large potential market for *The IFRS for SMEs*.

At the Trustees' meeting in January 2010, an SME Implementation Group (SMEIG) was set up. The SMEIG has a dual role. First, it needs to consider implementation questions raised by users of IFRS for SMEs. Second, it needs to consider and make recommendations to the IASB on amendments for IFRS for SMEs. The IASB remains the standard-setting body for both groups of standards, namely the 'full' IFRS and IFRS for SMEs. In fact, IFRS for SMEs are simplifications of full IFRS.

The simplification is achieved in many ways:

- By the omission of topics not relevant for SMEs (e.g. segment reporting, interim reporting, earnings per share, insurance, assets held for sale).
- When IFRS have options, only the simpler option is retained and the more complex options are omitted (e.g. financial instruments options including: available for sale, held to maturity, fair value option; proportionate consolidation; revaluation of property, plant and equipment; revaluation of intangibles; free choice on investment property; various options for government grants).

- Recognition and measurement principles are simplified (e.g. goodwill impairment – indicator approach; expense all R&D; cost method for associates and joint ventures; financial instruments: two classifications instead of four; expense all borrowing costs; defined benefit plans: no corridor or deferrals).
- The number of disclosures is reduced. Whereas full IFRS has more than 3000 items in the disclosure checklist, IFRS for SME has about 300 disclosures. Disclosures that are kept in IFRS for SMEs are disclosures about short-term cash flow, liquidity, solvency, measurement uncertainties and accounting policy choices.

In 2011, the IASB formed an Emerging Economies Group to enhance the participation of emerging economies in the development of IFRS and IFRS for SMEs. Members include participants from Argentina, Brazil, China, India, Indonesia, Korea, Malaysia, Mexico, Russia, Saudi Arabia, South Africa and Turkey. The IASB has recently reviewed *The IFRS for SMEs* in order to make it more suitable for smaller companies.

IFRS in developing countries

As Habib (2014: 484) points out:

> [a] sound and reliable financial reporting system relies critically on the successful application of a set of standards suitable to the economic environment of individual countries. However, emerging market countries and NICs rely heavily on accounting standards developed in the Western World, which ignore the unique incentives faced by these countries. Even if the adoption of IFRS can be defended on the grounds that such adoption will increase reporting comparabilities and will affect FDI positively, these countries may lack crucial institutional support, such as a strong regulatory enforcement system and a competent and independent audit profession and, consequently, may fail to achieve the benefits to be expected from IFRS adoption.

This is a big problem with IFRS for SMEs. There is a conflict between the needs of SMEs in developed economies like the EU and the needs of developing countries. The IASB version privileges the former, the UN SMEGA the latter.

IFRS in Islamic countries

In most Muslim countries, the majority of transactions are still conventional rather than Sharia-compliant transactions. Nevertheless, finance and investment in accordance with Islamic Sharia Law are steadily increasing worldwide. Wealthy Muslim individuals in oil rich countries in the Middle East, and the wealthy and middle classes in countries with large Muslim populations such as Indonesia, India, Nigeria, Pakistan and Turkey are seeking Sharia-compliant securities in which to invest.

According to Aissat *et al.* (2014: 492), the IASB and the FASB put the topic of Islamic finance and financial reporting on the agenda in June 2011. On 30 June 2010, the Asian-Oceanian Standard-setters Group (AOSSG)'s Working Group on Financial Reporting Issues Relating to Islamic Finance had issued a paper, which was appended to the IASB Agenda Paper 2D and the FASB Memo 168. It described two contrasting views held in the Islamic world regarding accounting for Sharia-compliant financial transactions. One view holds that IFRS can be applied to Sharia-compliant financial transactions, although extra disclosure may be required. The other view holds that a separate set of Islamic accounting standards is required (AOSSG, 2010: ES2). These contrasting views illustrate the issue that Islamic countries are very diverse in almost every aspect and therefore also in their stance towards the adoption of IFRS.

Aissat *et al.* (2014) identified the status of IFRS adoption in the 57 member countries of the Organization for Islamic Cooperation (OIC) and a few other countries with significant Muslim populations. They also describe the main Islamic accounting regulatory bodies: the Accounting and Auditing Organisation for Islamic Financial Institutions (AAOIFI), which has issued a set of Financial Accounting Standards (AAIOFI FAS), the Islamic Financial Services Board (IFSB) and the Islamic Finance Working Group of the AOSSG.

Aissat *et al.* (2014) also discuss six different reasons why Islamic countries may or may not choose to adopt IFRS (ranging from economic to institutional, historical and political), and provide a brief outline on how conventional and Islamic financial and other transactions might be different in nature and how the IASB Conceptual Framework fits with Islamic principles.

ACTIVITY 3.7

If you accept the capture theory of regulation, where do you think the strongest lobbying for or against specific IFRS will take place?

Activity feedback

It is probably companies rather than investors who will engage in lobbying for or against specific accounting standards. Following the logic of Watts and Zimmerman, this will be because of the most immediate cash flow effects. For investors it is more a matter of adjusting their decisions to new information, so for them possible gains from lobbying are probably not worth the effort.

Furthermore, it is probably companies from more powerful countries that will engage in lobbying the IASB directly or through their government. Companies from smaller countries may not believe that their government has enough political clout.

SUMMARY

This chapter has provided a background of history and understanding behind current international accounting developments with an emphasis on the increasing importance of the IASB. The EU started with the harmonization of financial reporting in the 1980s. The EU changed its accounting strategy in the mid-1990s and started to back the efforts of the IASC and later on the IASB. The new accounting strategy of the EU, the acceptance by IOSCO of IAS for listing purposes and the change in the structure of the international standard setter in 2001 paved the way for the IASB to become a global standard setter. It seems that the final steps towards this status will be taken in the very near future.

EXERCISES

Suggested answers to exercises marked ✓ are to be found in the Student online resources, with suggested answers to the remaining questions available in the Instructor online resources.

✓**1**   The European Commission has handed over accounting regulation in Europe to the IASB. Discuss.

2   Global accounting ignores the needs of developing economies. Discuss.

3   Enumerate which of the steps of the due process of standard setting are necessary in issuing standards.

4   The International Financial Reporting Standards Foundation oversees a number of other international committees, two of which are the IFRS Advisory Council and the IFRS Interpretations Committee. Explain the role of the IFRS Advisory Council and IFRS Interpretations Committee in assisting with developing and implementing International Financial Reporting Standards.

(CIMA P7 – November 2008)

5   Explain the role of the Monitoring Board in the governance structure of the International Accounting Standard Setter.

NOTES

1   www.oecd.org/mcm/48064973.pdf accessed 3 December 2015.

2   www.un.org/en/sections/what-we-do/index.html accessed 3 December 2015.

3   www.imf.org/external/about.htm accessed on 3 December 2015.

4   www.imf.org/external/about/whatwedo.htm accessed on 3 December 2015.

5   www.worldbank.org/en/about/what-we-do accessed 3 December 2015.

THE IASB CONCEPTUAL FRAMEWORK AND ACCOUNTING THEORY

4

OBJECTIVES After studying this chapter you should be able to:

- explain why the IASB needs a conceptual framework

- appraise current developments in the area

- discuss the contents of the 2010 IASB Conceptual Framework

- discuss the contents of the 2015 IASB Conceptual Framework Exposure Draft

- appraise the quality and usefulness of the IASB Framework in the context of its self-declared purposes

- compare the purposes of different types of financial accounting and reporting theory and the purposes of the IASB Conceptual Framework

- describe the main attempts at constructing financial accounting and reporting theory.

INTRODUCTION

In Chapter 3, you learned about the international accounting harmonization, convergence and standardization over the period from the 1970s until today. From 1973, the International Accounting Standards Committee (IASC) pursued harmonization in two ways. The first was to eliminate practices that were generally agreed to be unacceptable. The second was to accept 'all those practices which one or more member bodies were prepared to defend with plausible arguments' (Camffermann and Zeff, 2007: 253). The IASC desperately wanted the Securities and Exchange Commission (SEC) to endorse international accounting standards (IAS) and remove its reconciliation requirements for foreign companies whose securities were listed in the US and who did not use US generally accepted accounting principles (GAAP) for their consolidated financial statements. Pursuing recognition from International Organization of Securities Commissions (IOSCO) and the SEC, the IASC recognized that, in order to be taken seriously, the IASC had to develop standards that contained fewer options and that were founded on an explicit conceptual framework (Camffermann and Zeff, 2015: 11). The Financial Accounting Standards Board (FASB) had developed its Conceptual Framework between 1978 and 1984, and as the SEC's delegated accounting standard-setting body, the FASB Framework emphasized the role of financial statements in providing information for investors in debt and equity securities. Seeking recognition from the SEC and IOSCO, the IASC's 1989 Conceptual Framework also adopted the SEC's emphasis on providing information for investors in debt and equity securities.

When the IASC became the IASB in 2001, the IASB adopted the IASC's Conceptual Framework without making any changes. In 2010, the IASB issued a partially revised Conceptual Framework which was the result of a joint effort by the FASB and the IASB to iron out any differences between their two respective conceptual frameworks. As a result of the IASC Foundation's strategy review in 2011, it became clear that those countries that had actually adopted international financial reporting standards (IFRS) were not happy with the dominant role played by the FASB and the SEC, because the US had not adopted IFRS and did not seem likely to do so in the near future. Hence, the IASB decided to work on completing the revision of the IASB Conceptual Framework on its own. The IASB issued a Discussion Paper in 2013 and an Exposure Draft in 2015 and is expected to issue its revised Conceptual Framework in late 2016. Unfortunately, at the time of writing (early 2016), we do not yet know the exact content of the new IASB Conceptual Framework.

In this chapter, we will first consider the 2010 IASB Conceptual Framework and the 2015 IASB Conceptual Framework Exposure Draft. The IASB has always been careful to emphasize that the IASB Conceptual Framework is not financial accounting theory or financial reporting theory. Nevertheless, if an international financial accounting and reporting conceptual framework is to be coherent and consistent, you would expect it to be based on a set of underlying principles and logic in respect of the goals of financial reporting and how best to achieve them. In other words, a conceptual framework is either based on underlying theory or theories, or is itself an expression of a theory or theories. Finally, we will consider different approaches to developing financial accounting and reporting theory and accounting conceptual frameworks.

ACCOUNTING CONCEPTUAL FRAMEWORKS

A number of attempts have been made since the 1970s to create some form of coherent conceptual framework. In 1978, the FASB issued its Framework. In 1989, the IASC, the predecessor of the IASB, issued the *Framework for the Preparation and Presentation of Financial Statements*. Both belong to the family of conceptual frameworks for financial reporting that have been developed by accounting standard setters in a number of countries where accounting standard setting is carried out by a private sector body. On one level, such conceptual frameworks may be considered attempts to assemble a body of accounting theory (or interrelated concepts) as a guide to standard setting, so that standards are (as far as possible) formulated on a consistent basis and not in an ad hoc manner. On another, but complementary, level, they may be thought of as devices to confer legitimacy and authority on a private sector standard setter that lacks the legal authority of a public body. The IASB as a private sector standard setter shares these reasons for developing a conceptual framework.

In 2001, the EU announced its adoption of IFRS for listed companies from 2005. Soon afterwards, the IASB and the FASB entered into a Memorandum of Understanding for the purpose of convergence and in 2004 started a joint project for convergence between the two conceptual frameworks. It was supposed to happen in different phases. The first phase involved the objectives of general purpose financial statements and the qualitative characteristics of information that are useful for making investment and other economic decisions. In September 2010, the IASB issued its revised Framework, *The Conceptual Framework for Financial Reporting*.

As a result of the completion of the first phase, the objectives and qualitative characteristics have now been converged with the FASB Conceptual Framework. Work on this project had stalled because the 2007/2008 financial crisis required the IASB to work on standards related to financial instruments. In the meantime, the US had still not adopted IFRS. In 2011, the IFRS Foundation's Strategy Review revealed that the public opinion in those countries where IFRS had already been adopted was against the privileged position of the FASB in the determination of the IASB Conceptual Framework and IFRS. However, most respondents had also indicated the great importance attaching to the completion of the Framework. Hence, in late 2012, the IASB announced that it would resume work on its Conceptual Framework. This time, it will not be as part of a convergence project with the FASB. Although the IASB does not appear to see the need to revisit chapters 1 and 3, at least it now recognizes that it is better to work on the Framework as a whole because its elements are interconnected. The IASB expects to issue the completed Conceptual Framework sometime in 2016.

THE 2010 IASB CONCEPTUAL FRAMEWORK FOR FINANCIAL REPORTING

As of September 2010, the IASB Conceptual Framework consists of an introduction (remaining from the 1989 version) and four chapters:

1 Chapter 1 – The objective of general purpose financial statements
2 Chapter 2 – The Reporting Entity (does not yet have any content)
3 Chapter 3 – Qualitative characteristics of useful information
4 Chapter 4 – The Framework (1989): the remaining text

(a) underlying assumptions

(b) the elements of financial statements

(c) recognition of the elements of financial statements

(d) measurement of the elements of financial statements

(e) concepts of capital and capital maintenance.

Introduction to The Conceptual Framework for Financial Reporting (2010)

The Conceptual Framework does not have the status of an IFRS, does not override any specific IFRS and, in case of conflict between the Framework and an IFRS, the latter prevails. The five main purposes of the 2010 IASB Conceptual Framework are as follows:

1 to assist the IASB in the development of individual IFRSs while making sure that IFRS as a body of financial reporting standards is coherent and based on a consistent logic and set of principles

2 to assist the IASB in developing a coherent and consistent approach to the presentation of financial statements and the choice to disclose items on the face of the financial statements or in the notes to the financial statements

3 to assist preparers of financial statements in applying IFRS

4 to assist auditors in forming an opinion on whether financial statements conform with IFRS

5 to assist users of financial statements in interpreting the information contained in financial statements.

In addition, the 2010 IASB Conceptual Framework provides others who are interested in IFRS with information about the underlying thoughts on which IFRS is based. For example, people who want to write comment letters on Exposure Drafts for a specific new standard, teachers who need to explain IFRS to students, accounting bodies aiming to help their members keep up to date and national standard-setting bodies aiming to develop national standards that are aligned with IFRS.

The objective of general purpose financial statements

The 2010 Conceptual Framework states that:

> The objective of general purpose financial reporting forms the foundation of the *Conceptual Framework*. Other aspects of the *Conceptual Framework* – a reporting entity concept, the qualitative characteristics of, and the constraint on, useful financial information, elements of financial statements, recognition, measurement, presentation and disclosure – flow logically from the objective.
>
> (OB1)

> The objective of general purpose financial reporting is to provide information that is useful to existing and potential investors, lenders and other creditors in making decisions about providing resources to the entity. Those decisions involve buying, selling or holding equity and debt instruments, and providing or settling loans and other forms of credit.
>
> (OB2)

ACTIVITY 4.1

What do you think is the logic according to which the rest of the IASB Conceptual Framework flows in terms of general purpose financial reporting? The IASB and the FASB conceptual frameworks share the same objectives of general purpose financial reporting. Hence, if OB1 is correct, should we expect both frameworks to be (more or less) identical?

Activity feedback

Although the idea expressed in OB1 is intuitively appealing, when you start thinking about the logic, it is actually not as straightforward. Unfortunately, the logic and its source have not been explained in the Framework. The objective outlined in OB2 is, in all likelihood, based on Decision-Usefulness Theory (Staubus, 1959, 1961) as Staubus was involved in the development of the 1978 FASB Conceptual Framework. Decision-Usefulness Theory regards assets and liabilities as net cash inflow potential and defines the qualitative characteristics of useful financial reporting information with reference to its relevance to economic decision making. One problem is

that the same information is not necessarily relevant to economic decision making by different types of shareholders (i.e. long-term, speculative, majority or minority shareholders) or holders of debt securities or other types of debt. Short-term investors would find forward-looking information based on managers' expectations regarding future cash flows and the market value of net assets relevant to their decision of whether to buy, hold or sell their securities. Long-term lenders might prefer independently verifiable information based on the actual transactions and recordable events. The 1989 version of the Framework mentioned a trade-off between the qualitative characteristics of relevance and reliability. As you will see below, the focus in the 2010 Conceptual Framework is squarely on relevance at the expense of reliability. As chapters 1 and 3 of the IASB Conceptual Framework are the result of a joint project with the FASB, currently they are indeed identical. However, since then, the boards have decided to each develop the remainder of their conceptual frameworks independently. It is possible that both boards will decide to make some changes to the chapters that they jointly developed.

In accordance with Decision-Usefulness Theory (Staubus, 1959, 1961), OB3 states that 'existing and potential investors, lenders and other creditors need information to help them assess the prospects for future net cash inflows to the entity'. This includes information about 'the resources of the entity, the claims against the entity, and how efficiently and effectively the entity's management and governing board have discharged their responsibilities to use the entity's resources' (OB3).

The 2010 IASB Conceptual Framework then defines the primary users of general purpose financial reports as 'existing and potential investors, lenders and other creditors [who] cannot require reporting entity's to provide information directly to them and must rely on general purpose financial reports for much of the information they need' (OB5).

The balance sheet or statement of financial position provides information about economic resources and claims (OB13 and OB14), and the statement of comprehensive income, or the statement of financial performance, provides information about the changes in economic resources and claims (OB14 and OB16). Financial performance is to be measured as the difference in the entity's resources (i.e. assets) and claims (i.e. liabilities) during a period on an accruals basis because this provides a better basis for assessing past and future performance than information about cash receipts and payments alone (OB17). However, financial performance does not include additional resources directly obtained from investors and creditors (OB18). Furthermore, according to OB19, financial performance includes 'the extent to which events such as changes in market prices or interest rates have increased or decreased the entity's economic resources and claims, thereby affecting the entity's ability to generate net cash inflows'.

OB20 explains that a cash flow statement helps users assess the entity's ability to generate further cash flows in the future and assess the entity's operating, financing and investing activities. Finally, OB21 indicates that it is important to be able to assess the changes in an entity's economic resources and claims that are not the consequence of financial performance. This is then the function of a statement of changes in shareholders' equity.

Qualitative characteristics of useful information

The IASB Conceptual Framework is based on the idea that qualitative characteristics help identify the types of financial information that are likely to be most useful to existing and potential investors, lenders and other creditors for making economic decisions about the reporting entity (QC1). The 2010 Conceptual Framework states: 'If financial information is to be useful, it must be relevant and faithfully represent what it purports to represent. The usefulness of financial information is enhanced if it is comparable, verifiable, timely and understandable' (QC4).

The fundamental qualitative characteristics 'The fundamental qualitative characteristics are *relevance* and *faithful representation*' (QC5). Applying the fundamental characteristics requires:

- identification of an economic phenomenon, information about which is potentially useful to users of the financial reports
- identification of the type of information that would make it relevant and which can be faithfully represented
- determination if that information is available or can be produced (QC18).

Relevance. This is defined as 'capable of making a difference in the decisions made by users' (QC6). 'Financial information is capable of making a difference in decisions if it has predictive value, confirmatory value or both' (QC7). Predictive value consists of the capability of being used as an input in processes or models used to predict future outcomes (QC8). Confirmatory value exists when the information provides feedback about earlier estimations. The information will either confirm or change previous estimations (QC9). 'Information is material if omitting or misstating it could influence decisions that users make on the basis of financial information about a specific reporting entity' (QC10). However, because materiality is an entity-specific aspect of relevance, it is difficult to specify a uniform quantitative threshold.

Faithful representation. To be a perfectly faithful representation of an economic phenomenon, a depiction would be *complete*, *neutral* and *free from error* (QC12). Completeness means that the depiction will include all the information, including descriptions and explanations, necessary for a user to understand the phenomenon (QC13). Neutrality is obtained when a depiction is without bias in the selection or presentation of financial information. In other words, it is not manipulated in order to present a favourable or unfavourable depiction of an economic phenomenon (QC14).

> Faithful representation does not mean accurate in all respects. Free from error means that there are no errors or omissions in the description of the phenomenon, and the process used to produce the reported information has been selected and applied with no errors in the process.

(QC15)

Enhancing qualitative characteristics As mentioned above, these include comparability, verifiability, timeliness and understandability. The enhancing characteristics improve the usefulness of information that is relevant and faithfully represented, and may help decide on the best way to represent an economic phenomenon (QC19). 'Applying the enhancing qualitative characteristics is an iterative process that does not follow a prescribed order' (QC34).

Comparability. This relates to information of an entity that can be compared with other entities as well as with information about the same entity at another time (QC20). Interestingly, QC21 to QC25 discuss what comparability is not, such as consistency or uniformity.

Verifiability. This helps users to have confidence in the faithful representation of the economic phenomenon. Different knowledgeable and independent observers could reach consensus, although not necessarily agreement, about the faithful representation of a depiction (QC26). Direct verification is verification through observation. Indirect verification means checking the inputs to a model, formula or other estimation technique (QC27). When some forward-looking financial information cannot be verified indirectly, at least the underlying assumptions and estimation methods must be disclosed (QC28).

Timeliness. This is defined as financial information being in time to be capable of influencing decisions (QC29).

Understandability. 'Classifying, characterizing and presenting information clearly and concisely makes it understandable' (QC30). Inherently complex phenomena may not be easy to understand, but this information must be included in the financial reports because otherwise they would be misleading (Q31). Users of financial reports are expected to have a reasonable knowledge of business and economic activities, but even well-informed users may occasionally need to seek the aid of a professional adviser (QC32).

The cost constraint on useful financial reporting Cost is a pervasive constraint on the information that can be provided by financial reporting (QC35). The providers of information directly bear the costs of producing the information, and the users of this information directly bear the costs of analyzing and interpreting the information (QC36). The idea is that financial reporting helps users make decisions with more confidence, capital markets become more efficient and costs of capital become lower, which is assumed to benefit the international economy as a whole (QC37). As applying the cost constraint is inherently subjective, the IASB seeks to consider costs and benefits generally, and not in relation to individual reporting entities (QC38–QC39).

The Conceptual Framework for Financial Reporting (2010): chapter 4

As mentioned above, chapter 4 contains the remaining text of the 1989 Framework. It discusses going concern as an underlying assumption, defines the elements of financial statements, discusses recognition and measurement of the elements of the financial statements and concepts of capital and capital maintenance. The IASB is currently working on revising chapter 4.

Underlying assumption: going concern

The financial statements are normally prepared on the assumption that an entity is a going concern and will continue in operation for the foreseeable future. Hence, it is assumed that the entity has neither the intention nor the need to liquidate or curtail materially the scale of its operations; if such an intention or need exists, the financial statement may have to be prepared on a different basis and, if so, the basis used is disclosed.

(para. 4.1)

The elements of financial statements The section of the Framework concerning the elements of financial statements (paras 4.2–4.36) consists essentially of definitions of the elements of financial statements as identified by the Framework. The definitions given in this section, and especially those of assets and liabilities, are the core of the Framework as a prescriptive basis for standard setting. The section on 'Recognition of Elements' (paras 4.37–4.53) acts to reinforce this core. In particular:

1 The Framework defines income and expenses in terms of increases and decreases in economic benefits that are equated with changes in assets and liabilities.

2 The latter are defined in terms of 'resources controlled' and 'present obligations' to exclude some of the types of items that have been recognized as assets or liabilities (accruals and deferrals) in the name of 'matching' expenses and revenues.

In other words, the definitions of assets and liabilities are the starting point for the accounting model. The focus of the accounting model is on the definition, recognition and measurement of balance sheet items first, and the definition, recognition and measurement of income and expense second.

The elements considered to be 'directly related to the measurement of financial position' are assets, liabilities and equity, which are defined as follows (para. 4.4):

1 An asset is a resource:

   (a) controlled by the entity

   (b) as a result of past events; and

   (c) from which future economic benefits are expected to flow to the entity.

Recognition as an asset thus requires that all three components of the definition, (a), (b) and (c), be satisfied.

2 A liability is:

   (a) a present obligation of the entity

   (b) arising out of past events

   (c) the settlement of which is expected to result in an outflow from the entity of resources embodying economic benefits.

Recognition as a liability thus requires that all three components of the definition, (a), (b) and (c), be satisfied.

3 Equity is defined as the residual interest in the assets of the entity after deducting all its liabilities.

Merely satisfying the definition of an element of financial statements does not entail recognition because the recognition criteria must also be satisfied. In the 1989 IASC Framework, the principle of 'economic substance over legal form' had to be respected. For example, this principle requires non-current assets held under finance leases to be recognized by the lessee as non-current assets (with corresponding leasing liabilities), while the lessor recognizes a financial asset. In the 2010 IASB Conceptual Framework, 'substance over form' is assumed to be included in the qualitative characteristic called 'faithful representation' (BC3.26).

Assets. The 'future economic benefit embodied in an asset' is defined as 'the potential to contribute, directly or indirectly, to the flow of cash and cash equivalents to the entity', including 'a capability to reduce cash outflows'. In case that definition should leave unclear the status of cash itself as an asset, it is stated that cash satisfies this definition because it 'renders a service to the entity because of its command over other resources'. Assets embody future economic benefits that may flow to the entity by having one or more of the following capabilities:

- being exchanged for other assets
- being used to settle a liability
- being distributed to the entity's owners.

Cash conspicuously possesses these three capabilities, as well as that of being used singly or in combination with other assets in the production of goods and services to be sold by the entity (paras 4.8–4.10).

Having neither physical form nor being the object of a right of ownership are essential attributes of an asset. Intangible items, such as patents and copyrights, may satisfy the definition of an asset, as may a fixed asset held under a finance lease (by virtue of which it is a resource controlled although not owned by the entity and from which future benefits are expected to flow). Moreover, knowledge obtained from development activity may meet the definition of an asset (capitalized development costs) even though neither physical form nor legal ownership is involved, provided there is de facto control such that, by keeping the knowledge secret, the entity controls the benefits that are expected to flow from it (paras 4.11–4.12).

Assets may result from various types of past transactions and other past events. Normally, these are purchase transactions and the events associated with production, but they may include donation (for example, by way of a government grant) or discovery (as in the case of mineral deposits). Expected future transactions or events do not give rise to assets; for example, a binding contract by an entity to purchase inventory does not cause the inventory in question to meet the definition of an asset of that entity until the purchase transaction that fulfils the contract has occurred. While expenditure is a common way to acquire or generate an asset, expenditure undertaken with a view to generating future economic benefits may fail to result in an asset, for example if the intended economic benefits cannot be expected or are not controlled by the entity (paras 4.13–4.14).

ACTIVITY 4.2

Consider whether each of the following are assets, giving reasons for your answers.

- A heap of rusty metal worth €10 as scrap but costing €20 to transport to the scrap dealer.
- A municipal or trade union social or welfare centre outside the factory that substantially improves the overall working conditions of a firm's employees.
- The benefits derived from next year's sales.

Activity feedback

None of these is an asset because it:
- *has no probable future benefit*
- *is not possessed or controlled by the business*
- *contains no earlier transaction or event.*

Assets are always divided into *non-current (or fixed) assets* and *current assets*. The definition of non-current assets is often misunderstood. A non-current asset is not an asset with a long life. The essential criterion is the *intention* of the owner, the intended use of the asset. A non-current asset is an asset that the firm intends to use within the business, over an extended period, in order to assist its daily operating activities. A current asset, by way of contrast, is usually defined in terms of time. A current asset is an asset likely to change its form, i.e. likely to undergo some transaction, usually within 12 months. Consider two firms, A and B. Firm A is a motor trader. It possesses some motor vehicles that it is attempting to sell, and it also possesses some desks used by the sales staff, management and so on. Firm B is a furniture dealer. It possesses some desks that it is attempting to sell and it also possesses some motor vehicles used by the sales staff and for delivery purposes. In the accounts of A, the motor vehicles are current assets and the desks are non-current assets. In the accounts of B, the motor vehicles are non-current assets and the desks are current assets. Note incidentally that a non-current asset which after several years' use is about to be sold for scrap, remains in the non-current asset part of the accounts even though it is about to change its form.

These two definitions, because they are based on different criteria (one on use and one on time), are not mutually exclusive. It is possible to think of assets that do not conveniently appear to be either fixed or current: investments, for example, or goodwill.

Liabilities. An essential characteristic of (or necessary condition for) a liability is that the entity should have a 'present obligation'. An obligation is 'a duty or responsibility to act or perform in a certain way'. The duty or responsibility may arise from the law, for example the law of contract, or it may arise from normal business practice, which leads to legitimate expectations that the entity will act or perform in a certain way (that is, a constructive obligation). An example of the latter is a constructive obligation to extend the benefits of a warranty for some period beyond the contractual warranty period, because this is an established practice (para. 4.15).

A present obligation (in the relevant sense) is not the same as a future commitment. An entity may have a commitment to purchase an asset in the future at an agreed price; however, this does not entail a net outflow of resources. The commitment does not give rise to a liability: this occurs only after the purchase has actually taken place and title in the asset has passed to the entity, leaving the latter with an obligation to pay for it. In the case of a cash transaction, no liability would arise (para. 4.16).

There are a number of ways in which a liability may be settled or discharged, which include replacement by another obligation, conversion into equity, or the creditor waiving or forfeiting their rights. There are also various types of 'past transactions or past events' from which liabilities may result (paras 4.17–4.18). If a provision involves a present obligation and satisfies the rest of the definition of a liability given in the Framework, it is a liability even if the amount has to be estimated (para. 4.19). Paragraph 4.18 does not emphasize the equally important point that a provision that fails to satisfy the criterion of being an *obligation* arising from a past transaction or past event is not a liability. This point, however, was crucial in arriving at the requirements for recognition of provisions in IAS 22, *Business Combinations* (now IFRS 3), and IAS 37, *Provisions, Contingent Liabilities and Contingent Assets*.

Equity. Paragraphs 4.20–4.23 are concerned with equity. The fact that equity is defined as a residual interest (assets minus liabilities) does not mean that it cannot be meaningfully divided into sub-classifications that are shown separately in the balance sheet. Examples are the differences between the following:

- paid-in capital (capital stock and paid-in surplus)
- reserves representing appropriations of retained earnings
- reserves representing the amounts required to be retained in order to maintain 'real' capital, that is either real financial capital or (real) physical capital (para. 4.20).

There are various legal, tax and valuation considerations that affect equity, such as requirements for legal reserves and whether or not the entity is incorporated. It is emphasized that transfers to legal, statutory and tax reserves are appropriations of retained earnings and not expenses. (Likewise, releases from such reserves are credits to retained earnings and not income, but this is not spelled out.) The rather obvious point is made that the amount at which equity is shown in the balance sheet is not intended to be a measure of the market value of the entity, either as a going concern or in a piecemeal disposal. It is stated that the definition and treatment of equity in the Framework are appropriate for unincorporated entities, even if the legal considerations are different.

Financial performance Paragraphs 4.24–4.36 contain the section of the Framework in which definitions of the financial statement elements relating to financial performance are given. 'Profit is frequently used as a measure of performance or as the basis for other measures, such as return on investment and earnings per share' (para. 4.24). However, this section of the Framework does not discuss the relationship between the elements of performance and the profit measure, except to say that 'the recognition and measurement of income and expenses, and hence profit, depends in part on the concepts of capital and capital maintenance used by the entity in preparing its financial statements'. The determination of profit and related issues are discussed in a later section of the Framework (paras 4.59–4.65). The elements of income and expenses are defined as follows:

1 Income is increases in economic benefits during the accounting period in the form of inflows or enhancements of assets or decreases of liabilities that result in increases in equity, other than those relating to contributions from equity participants.

2 Expenses are decreases in economic benefits during the accounting period in the form of outflows or depletions of assets or incurrences of liabilities that result in decreases in equity, other than those relating to distributions to equity participants (para. 4.25).

These definitions identify the essential features of income and expenses but do not attempt to specify their recognition criteria (para. 4.26). The definition makes it clear that the Framework's approach treats the definitions of assets and liabilities as logically prior to those of income and expenses. This is sometimes characterized as a 'balance sheet approach' to the relationship between financial statements. This term is potentially misleading, however. The Framework's approach should certainly not be understood as implying the subordination of the income statements to the balance sheet from an *informational* perspective.

Income. The Framework's definition of income encompasses both revenue and gains. Revenue is described as arising in the course of the ordinary activities of an entity and includes sales, fees, interest, royalties and rent. Gains may or may not arise in the course of ordinary activities. Gains may arise on the disposal of non-current assets and also include unrealized gains, such as those arising on the revaluation of marketable securities and from increases in the carrying amount of long-term assets. Gains, when recognized in the income statements, are usually displayed separately because their economic significance tends to differ from that of revenue, and they are often reported net of related expenses (paras 4.29–4.31).

The counterpart entry corresponding to a credit for income may be to various asset accounts (not only cash or receivables) or to a liability account such as when a loan is discharged by the provision of goods or services (para. 4.32).

Expenses. The Framework's definition of expenses encompasses losses as well as expenses that arise in the course of the ordinary activities of the entity. Examples given of expenses that arise in the course of ordinary activities are cost of sales, wages and depreciation. They usually take the form (that is, are the accounting counterpart) of an outflow or depletion of assets such as cash and cash equivalents, inventory, property or plant and equipment (para. 4.33).

Losses represent items that may or may not arise in the course of ordinary activities. They include those that result from such disasters as fire or flood, as well as those arising on the disposal of non-current assets and also encompass unrealized losses, such as those arising from the effects of adverse currency exchange rate movements on financial assets or liabilities. Losses, when recognized in the income statement, are usually displayed separately because their economic significance tends to differ from that of other expenses and they are often reported net of related income (paras 4.34–4.35).

Recognition of the elements of financial statements Recognition issues are dealt with in paras 4.37–4.53. Recognition is described as 'the process of incorporating in the balance sheet or [the] income statement an item that meets the definition of an element and satisfies the criteria for recognition set out in paragraph 83'. (The statement of changes in financial position is not mentioned because its elements consist of those that are also elements of financial position or performance.) Failure to recognize *in the main financial statements* items that satisfy the relevant definition and recognition criteria is not rectified by disclosure of the accounting policies used or by use of notes or other explanatory material.

The recognition criteria, set out in para. 4.38, are that an item that meets the definition of an element should be recognized if:

- it is probable that any future economic benefit associated with the item will flow to or from the entity
- the item has a cost or value that can be measured with reliability.

Recognition is subject to materiality. Accounting interrelationships are also signifi-cant, since recognition in the financial statements of an item that meets the definition and recognition criteria for a particular element, for example an asset, entails the recognition of another (counterpart) element, such as income or a liability (para. 4.39). (This refers, strictly speaking, to the initial recognition of an item. However, a similar point could be made about the implications of re-measurement or valuation adjustments.)

Probability of future economic benefit. The concept of *probability* is used in the recognition criteria 'to refer to the degree of uncertainty [as to whether] the future economic benefits associated with the time will flow to or from the entity … in keep-ing with the uncertainty that characterizes the environment in which an entity oper-ates'. Assessments of such uncertainty are made on the basis of the evidence available when the financial statements are prepared. With regard to receivables, for example, for a large population of accounts, some statistical evidence will usually be available regarding collectability (para. 4.40).

Reliability of measurement. Reliability, the second recognition criterion, was discussed earlier in the section on qualitative characteristics of financial statements. If an item does not possess a cost or value that can be measured with reliability (so that the information has that qualitative characteristic), then it is not appropriate to recognize it. However, in many cases, cost or (more particularly) value must be estimated; indeed, the use of reasonable estimates is an essential part of the financial reporting process and need not undermine reliability. In cases where an item satisfied the definition of an element but not the recognition criteria, it will not be recognized in the financial statements themselves, but its relevance is likely to require its disclosure in the notes to the financial statements or in other supplementary disclosures. This applies when the item meets the probability criterion of recognition but not the reliability criterion, but may also apply to an item that meets the definition of an element when neither recognition criterion is met. The key issue here is whether the item is considered to be relevant to the evaluation of financial position, performance or changes in financial position. An item that does not satisfy the recognition criteria for an asset or a liability at one time may do so later, if more information relevant to estimating its probability, cost or value becomes available (paras 4.41–4.43).

It is important to note that 'probable' and 'reliability' are both relative and subjective concepts. The Framework does not pretend otherwise. Professional judgement is required in the context of the particular situation in which the entity concerned operates.

Recognition of assets. An asset is recognized in the balance sheet when it is probable that future economic benefits will flow to the entity (as a result of its control of the asset) and the asset's cost or value can be measured reliably. When expenditure has been incurred but it is not considered probable that economic benefits will flow to the entity beyond the current accounting period, this expenditure will be recognized as an expense, not as an asset. The intention of management in undertaking the expenditure is irrelevant (paras 4.44–4.45).

Recognition of liabilities. A liability is recognized in the balance sheet when it is probable that an outflow of resources embodying economic benefits will result from the settlement of a present obligation and the amount of that settlement can be measured reliably. Obligations under executory contracts – that is, non-cancellable contracts that are equally proportionately unperformed (such as the amount that will be a liability when inventory ordered and awaiting delivery is received) – are not generally recognized as liabilities in the balance sheet, neither are the related assets recognized in the balance sheet. In some cases, however, recognition may be required (para. 4.46).

Recognition of income. Recognition of income occurs simultaneously with the recognition of increases in assets or decreases in liabilities (or a combination of the two). The normal recognition procedures used in practice are applications of the Framework's recognition criteria. An example is the requirement that revenue should be earned (that is, it should be associated with a simultaneous increase in assets or decrease in liabilities). These procedures are concerned with restricting the recognition of income to items that, in effect, meet the Framework's recognition criteria of probability (a sufficient degree of certainty that an economic benefit has flowed or will flow to the entity) and reliability of measurement (paras 4.47–4.48).

Recognition of expenses. Recognition of expenses occurs simultaneously with the recognition of an increase in liabilities or a decrease in assets (or a combination of the two). Expenses are commonly recognized in the income statement on the basis of an association (matching) between the incurrence of costs and the earning of specific items of revenue that result directly and jointly from the same transactions or other events. An example is the matching of the cost of goods sold with the associated sales revenue. However, the Framework does not permit the application of the matching procedure to result in the recognition of items in the balance sheet that do not meet the definition of assets or liabilities (paras 4.49–4.53).

Measurement of the elements of the financial statements Paragraphs 4.54–4.56 deal with measurement issues, in so far as these are covered in the Framework. The treatment here is descriptive and avoids being prescriptive. Measurement is described as 'the process of determining the monetary amounts at which the elements of the financial statements are to be recognized and carried in the balance sheet and income statement'. It involves the selection of a particular basis of measurement.

Four different measurement bases are specifically mentioned and described (without any claim to exhaustiveness): historical cost, current cost (of replacement or settlement), realizable or (for liabilities) settlement value and present value. Historical cost is mentioned as the measurement basis most commonly adopted by entities in preparing their financial statements, usually in combination with other measurement bases. An example of the latter is the carrying of inventories at the lower of historical cost and net realizable value. Marketable securities may be carried at market value and pension liabilities are carried at their present value. Current cost may be used as a means of taking account of the effects of changing prices of non-monetary assets.

Concepts of capital and capital maintenance

Concepts of capital. The Framework identifies two main concepts of capital: the financial concept and the physical concept. The financial concept of capital may take two forms: invested money (nominal financial) capital or invested purchasing power (real financial) capital. In either case, capital is identified with the equity of the entity (in either nominal or real financial terms) and with its net assets measured in those terms. The physical concept of capital is based on the notion of the productive capacity or operating capability of the entity, as embodied in its net assets. Most entities adopt a financial concept of capital, normally (in the absence of severe inflation) nominal financial capital (paras 4.57–4.58).

Capital maintenance and the determination of profit. Choice of a concept of capital is related to the concept of capital maintenance that is most meaningful, given the implications of the choice for profit measurement and the needs of the users of the financial statements in that regard, as follows:

Maintenance of nominal financial capital. Under this concept, a profit is earned only if the money amount of the net assets at the end of the period exceeds the money amount of the net assets at the beginning of the period, after excluding any distributions to, and contributions from, equity owners during the period (para. 4.59 (a)).

Maintenance of real financial capital. Under this concept, a profit is earned only if the money amount of the net assets at the end of the period exceeds the money amount of the net assets at the beginning of the period, restated in units of the same purchasing power, after excluding distributions to, and contributions from, owners. Normally, the units of purchasing power employed are those of the currency at the end of the period into which the net assets at the beginning of the period are restated (para. 4.59 (a)).

Maintenance of physical capital. Under this concept, a profit is earned only if the operating capability embodied in the net assets at the end of the period exceeds the operating capability embodied in the net assets at the beginning of the period, after excluding distributions to, and contributions from, owners. Operating capability embodied in assets may, in principle, be measured by employing the current cost basis of measurement (para. 4.59 (b)).

The main difference among the three concepts of capital maintenance is the treatment of the effects of changes in the carrying amounts of the entity's assets and liabilities. Under nominal financial capital maintenance, increases in the money-carrying amounts of assets held over the period (to the extent that they are recognized as gains) are part of profit.

Under real financial capital maintenance, such increases are part of profit only if they are 'real' increases; that is, increases that remain after money-carrying amounts have been restated in units of the same purchasing power. The total amount of the restatement is known as a 'capital maintenance adjustment' and is transferred to a capital maintenance reserve, which is part of equity (but not of retained profits). Real financial capital maintenance may be used in conjunction with historical cost as a measurement basis, but would more normally be used in conjunction with the current cost basis.

ILLUSTRATION

Let us assume that a company begins with capital stock of €100 and cash of €100. At the beginning of the year, one item of inventory is bought for €100. The item of inventory is sold at the end of the year for €150, its replacement cost at that time is €120 and general inflation throughout the year is 10 per cent. Profit measured using each of the capital maintenance concepts mentioned earlier would be as shown:

	Nominal financial capital maintenance	Real financial capital maintenance	Real physical capital maintenance
Sales	€150	€150	€150
Less cost of sales	(100)	(100)	(120)
Operating profit	50	50	30
Less inflation adjustment	—	(10)	—
Total gain	€50	€40	€30
Capital maintenance adjustment	€0	€10	€20

(Continued)

ILLUSTRATION (*Continued*)

Column 1 shows the gain after ensuring the maintenance of the stockholders' opening capital measured as a sum of money. Column 2 shows the gain after ensuring the maintenance of the stockholders' opening capital measured as a block of purchasing power. Both of these are concerned, under different definitions, with the maintenance of financial capital – in terms either of its money amount or of its general purchasing power. Column 3 shows the gain after ensuring the maintenance of the company's initial operating capacity and is therefore of a completely different nature.

Under real physical capital maintenance, changes in the money prices at current costs of assets and liabilities held over the period are considered not to affect the amount of operating capability embodied in those items and therefore the total amount of those changes is treated as a capital maintenance adjustment and excluded from profit.

Different combinations of measurement bases and capital maintenance concepts provide different accounting models. Management should choose the most appropriate concept for their business, taking into account relevance and reliability. Accounting models will be discussed in Chapters 5, 6 and 7.

THE 2015 IASB CONCEPTUAL FRAMEWORK EXPOSURE DRAFT

In terms of structure, the 2015 IASB Conceptual Framework Exposure Draft (ED) has the following eight chapters.

- Chapter 1 – The objective of general purpose financial statements
- Chapter 2 – Qualitative characteristics of useful information
- Chapter 3 – Financial statement and the reporting entity
- Chapter 4 – The elements of financial statements
- Chapter 5 – Recognition and derecognition
- Chapter 6 – Measurement
- Chapter 7 – Presentation and disclosure
- Chapter 8 – Concepts of capital and capital maintenance.

Here we will briefly consider the main proposed changes to the existing chapters and the main content of the new chapters.

Chapter 1 gives more prominence to the importance of providing information that is useful for assessing management's stewardship of the entity's resources. The IASB does not expect this will lead to any changes in accounting because the IASB believes that the stewardship objective of financial reporting is subsumed under the decision-usefulness objective of financial reporting. In other words, the IASB believes that financial information that helps investors predict the entity's future cash flows is also useful for assessing management's stewardship of the entity's resources.

Chapter 2 proposes to state explicitly that a faithful representation represents the economic substance of an economic phenomenon rather than its legal form.

Chapter 3 states that financial statements must be prepared from the perspective of the entity rather than the perspective of any particular group of its investors, lenders or other creditors. It also discusses the boundary of a reporting entity and proposes that a reporting entity must be an economic entity but does not have to be a legal entity.

Chapter 4 defines assets, liabilities, income and expenses slightly differently from the 2010 IASB Conceptual Framework. Table 4.1 compares the definitions of the elements of the balance sheet in the 2010 IASB Conceptual Framework with the definitions in the 2015 IASB ED.

TABLE 4.1   Comparison of the definitions of the elements of the balance sheet in the 2010 IASB Conceptual Framework with the definitions in the 2015 IASB ED

2015 IASB Conceptual Framework ED (Chapter 4)	2010 IASB Conceptual Framework (Chapter 4)
Asset: An asset is a present economic resource controlled by the entity as a result of past events (para. 4.5). An economic resource is a right that has the potential to produce economic benefits (para. 4.6)	**Assets:** Economic resources controlled by the entity as a result of past transactions or events and from which future benefits are expected to flow to the entity (para. 4.4a)
Liability: A liability is a present obligation of the entity arising to transfer an economic resource as a result of past events (para. 4.24)	**Liabilities:** A present obligation of the entity arising from past events, the settlement of which is expected to result in an outflow from the entity of resources embodying economic benefits (para. 4.4b)
Equity: Equity is the residual interest in the assets of the entity after deducting all its liabilities (para. 4.43)	**Equity:** Equity is the residual interest in the assets of the entity after deducting all its liabilities (para. 4.4c)

Table 4.2 compares the definitions of the elements of the income statement in the 2010 IASB Conceptual Framework with the definitions in the 2015 IASB ED.

Chapter 5 of the 2015 IASB ED defines recognition as 'the process of capturing, for inclusion in the statement of financial position or the statement(s) of financial performance, an item that meets the definition of an element' (para. 5.2). Furthermore, it proposes that an entity recognizes an asset or a liability (and any related income, expenses or changes in equity) if such recognition provides users of financial statements with relevant information about the items concerned, a faithful representation of the items concerned, and the benefits of providing this information exceed its cost (para. 5.9).

TABLE 4.2   Comparison of the definitions of the elements of the income statement in the 2010 IASB Conceptual Framework with the definitions in the 2015 IASB ED

2015 IASB Conceptual Framework ED (Chapter 4)	2010 IASB Conceptual Framework (Chapter 4)
Income: Income is increases in assets or decreases in liabilities, other than those relating to contributions from holders of equity claims (para. 4.48)	**Income:** Increases in economic benefits during an accounting period in the form of inflows or enhancements of assets other than those relating to contributions from equity participants (para. 4.25)
Expenses: Expenses are decreases in assets or increases in liabilities, other than those relating to distributions to holders of equity claims (para. 4.49)	**Expenses:** Decreases in economic benefits during the accounting period in the form of outflow or depletion of assets or incurrences of liabilities that result in decreases in equity, other than those relating to distributions to equity participants (para. 4.25)
Income and expenses include amounts generated by transactions and other events, including changes in the carrying amount of assets and liabilities (para. 4.51)	Income includes revenues and gains

Chapter 5 also states that recognition may not provide relevant information if:

- it is uncertain whether or not an asset or liability actually exists, or if the asset is separable from the business as a whole
- if an asset or liability exists but it is not sufficiently probable that an inflow or outflow of economic benefits will result
- if the level of measurement uncertainty is too high to result in relevant information (para. 5.13).

The 2010 IASB Conceptual Framework did not define derecognition. In the 2015 IASB ED it is defined as 'the removal of all or part of a previously recognised asset or liability from an entity's statement of financial position' (para. 5.25).

Chapter 6 states that measurement:

[i]s the process of quantifying, in monetary terms, information about an entity's assets, liabilities, equity, income and expenses. A measure is the result of measuring an asset, a liability, equity, or an item of income or expense on a specified measurement basis. A measurement basis is an identified feature of an item being measured (for example, historical cost, fair value or fulfilment value).

(para. 6.2)

Chapter 6 categorizes measurement bases as historical cost or current value (para. 6.4). Furthermore, it classifies historical cost and current cost as entry values and regards current value measurement bases as exit values. Current value measurement bases include fair value, value in use for assets and fulfilment value for liabilities (para. 6.20). As you may have suspected by now, the 2015 IASB ED discusses relevance and faithful representation as factors to consider when selecting a measurement basis (paras 6.48–6.58) and states that the enhancing qualitative characteristics of comparability, verifiability and understandability also have implications for the selection of a measurement basis (paras 6.59–6.63).

We will discuss the distinction between entry and exit values, and the reasons for and consequences of using different measurement bases in Chapter 5 of this textbook, and we will discuss fair value, value in use and fulfilment value in Chapter 7.

The 2015 IASB ED's chapter 7 about the presentation and disclosure of information on the face of the financial statements or in the notes to the financial statements or elsewhere (such as the management commentary) is entirely new. The part that is controversial deals with the recognition and presentation of net profit or loss and the items of other comprehensive income in the statement(s) of financial performance. Financial performance can be presented in one statement of profit or loss and other comprehensive income or in a separate statement of profit or loss and a statement of other comprehensive income. In Chapter 8 of this textbook we will investigate what IAS 1 says about how information must be presented in the financial statements.

Although chapter 8 of the 2015 IASB ED presents capital maintenance in a separate chapter, its content has not changed from the 2010 IASB Conceptual Framework.

ACTIVITY 4.3

Do you think that measuring all assets and liabilities at a single measurement basis would produce information in the financial statements that is relevant to investors' decisions and would faithfully represent a reporting entity's financial position and financial performance? Why would you agree? Why might you disagree?

Activity feedback

Some people think that measuring all assets and liabilities at historical costs may provide verifiable and hence reliable information which is not so relevant to investors and does not faithfully represent the entity's financial position and financial performance. Others believe that measuring all assets and liabilities at current values may provide information which is relevant to investors and represents the entity's financial position and financial performance more faithfully than does historical cost.

However, this involves much subjectivity and estimation, which makes information less reliable and ultimately not very useful either. The IASB therefore believes in different measurement bases for different financial statement items. The question then becomes 'What measurement bases should be chosen for which items?'

Increasingly, people have started to think that assets and liabilities that are used by the business to add valuvie, for example non-current assets such as machinery and equipment in a manufacturing company, should be measured at their historical costs. On the other hand, assets and liabilities that are very marketable and used for speculation purposes should be measured at their current values. This line of thought has given rise to the idea that, perhaps, the business model of the company should provide guidance as to what measurement bases to use for its assets and liabilities.

FINANCIAL ACCOUNTING AND REPORTING THEORIES

We will now take a very brief look at theory in financial accounting and financial reporting with a view to gaining some understanding of the extent to which the 2010 IASB Conceptual Framework and the 2015 IASB ED are based on financial accounting theory and financial reporting theory.

What is a theory and what is an argument?

A theory consists of an assertion (also called propositional claim) supported by argument. The argument allows the claim to be evaluated and substantiated. Theories will vary in nature, depending on their objective and scope. Objectives of theories include:

- describing an observed phenomenon
- classifying phenomena into groups based on shared characteristics
- explaining a phenomenon in order to make predictions about future phenomena in the form of testable hypotheses
- explaining a phenomenon with a view to understanding and interpreting an individual action or phenomenon.

In terms of scope, theories may range from the small, specific and sharply delineated, to the generalizing and more broadly defined middle-range, all the way to ambitious grand unifying theories (Van Mourik, 2014a: 36).

An argument is a presentation of one or more reasons (also called premises) offered in support of a claim (also called a conclusion). For a theory to be useful, the supporting argument must be evaluated with respect to the clarity, truth or falsity, and plausibility of the reasons (see, for example, Murray and Kujundzic, 2005) Depending on the purpose of the theory and the type of argument, evidence may be required to support the reasons and substantiate the claim.

A deductive argument is sound, and its conclusion must be true if the argument is valid (its structure is logical) and its premises are true. For example, if we define gross profit as sales less cost of sales, sales of $10 000 less cost of sales of $7000 must equal a gross profit of $3000.

An inductive argument is cogent if the argument is inductively forceful and its premises are true, but the conclusion may still be false because it is a probable conclusion. For example, if the annual profit before interest and taxation of a company over the past five years grew by 8 per cent per year respectively, next year's profit before interest and taxation will also grow by 8 per cent. Given sufficient data, one can calculate the statistical probability that this will happen, but certainty about the outcome will have to wait until the end of the next year.

A practical argument is an argument concerning what to do. Practical arguments are usually neither deductive nor inductive. Practical arguments are often plausible arguments which draw tentative conclusions in conditions of uncertainty, incomplete knowledge and under constraints of time (Fairclough and Fairclough, 2012). For example, the IASB aims to serve the public interest by serving the interest of investors in global financial and capital markets. Investors need information to help them make investment decisions. Hence, the IASB should develop IFRS that help global investors make decisions to buy, hold or sell shares and other securities. The argument is plausible, but we do not really know to what extent IFRS that help global investors make their investment decisions actually do serve the interests of the general public. In practice, most decisions in policy making, standard setting and regulation are made on the basis of norms and/or values, plausibility and compromise.

What is accounting theory?

According to Eldon S. Hendriksen in *Accounting Theory* (1977):

> Theory as it applies to accounting is the coherent set of hypothetical, conceptual and pragmatic principles forming the general frame of reference for a field of inquiry. Thus accounting theory may be defined as logical reasoning in the form of a set of broad principles that:
>
> - provide a general frame of reference by which accounting practices can be evaluated and
>
> - guide the development of new practices and procedures.
>
> Accounting theory may also be used to explain existing practices to obtain a better understanding of them. But the most important goal of accounting theory should be to provide a coherent set of logical principles that form the general frame of reference for the evaluation and development of sound accounting practices.

ACTIVITY 4.4

Compare Hendriksen's definition of accounting theory with the five main purposes of the 2010 IASB Conceptual Framework earlier in this chapter. Do you think that Hendriksen is talking about theories of accounting or a comprehensive theory of accounting? Do you think that the IASB Framework is intended to be a comprehensive theory of accounting?

Activity feedback

Hendriksen appears to be talking about a comprehensive theory of accounting as he mentions that it serves as a general frame of reference. In other words, it has a scope that is broad enough to be comprehensive. He mentions logical reasoning in the form of a set of broad principles, which indicates that the set of principles that constitutes the theory must be coherent and internally consistent. In other words, on the basis of these principles, we would be able to explain and predict which accounting practices and rules are better for a certain specified purpose.

The IASB Conceptual Framework sounds like a comprehensive accounting theory as defined by Hendriksen. But if it is, what is the certain specified purpose for

which accounting practices and rules are developed? How was it determined and who determined it? If there was agreement on the general purpose of financial accounting, would it be the case that this theory would clearly determine how we should provide information to users, and different practices would not prevail? Such agreement may exist on an abstract level. For example, we probably agree that accounting information must be useful. However, at a detailed level, agreement is highly unlikely because accounting is an interested activity and the financial interests of most stakeholders are in conflict with one another. Historically, the FASB Conceptual Framework was called conceptual rather than theoretical because it consisted of generally agreed concepts rather than a coherent set of theoretical principles. The IASC modelled its 1989 Framework on that of the FASB, and the IASB adopted the same in 2001. However, the IASB has a different mandate from that of the IASC and the FASB.

ACTIVITY 4.5

In what ways did the IASB in 2001 (and today) have a different mandate from that of the IASC in 1989 or the FASB (at any time)?

Activity feedback

The FASB's mandate is to set accounting standards in the US in the public interest of the people and businesses in the US. The IASC was not an accounting standard setter.

It was a private organization consisting of representatives of the accounting firms and professional bodies in a number of countries. When the IASC was reorganized into the IASB in 2001, it became a private accounting standard setter committed to act in the international public interest, but the IASB Conceptual Framework then and now is still based on the basic concepts that were agreed upon by the FASB in the American public interest.

In sum, accounting theory as it is described in textbooks consists of many different theories for different purposes. Some are larger in scope whereas others are smaller in scope. A comprehensive theory of accounting is not impossible, but it is not likely any time soon.

APPROACHES TO THE FORMULATION OF ACCOUNTING THEORY

How do we approach the development of theories in accounting? Approaches to the development of theories in accounting are similar to approaches to theory development in other social sciences.

Non-theoretical approaches are concerned with developing accounting techniques and principles that will be useful to users, particularly decision makers. They may lead to the description of generally accepted principles and practices being regarded as a body of theory. These approaches can be developed in a pragmatic or authoritarian way. In essence, in the past the accounting profession adopted a non-theoretical approach to formulating accounting theory. It is fairly apparent that this approach did not lead to the resolution of conflict in accounting practices or principles. An example is the regulatory approach.

Regulatory approach. Some would regard this as the approach we currently have to accounting theory. They hold this view because to them it does not appear that standards, even those of the IASB (in spite of its Conceptual Framework), are based on a coherent set of broad, relevant theories, but are developed as solutions to current conflicts that emerge in our attempts to provide useful information to users. These solutions are sometimes influenced by the politics of standard setting and by political lobbying by interest groups. Indeed, some might argue that new standards are only developed when a particular user complains about misinformation or non-information. But there are ideological questions to consider if we do adopt this approach to the development of accounting theory. In the main, these questions centre on whether we should adopt a free market approach to the regulation, a private sector regulatory approach or a public sector regulatory approach. This regulatory approach is also one that tends to identify solutions to difficulties that have occurred in our reporting, rather than providing us with a theory that anticipates the issues.

Apart from the non-theoretical pragmatic process to the development of an accounting theory from a basic methodological perspective, we can distinguish deductive, inductive or mixed processes.

Deductive approach. This approach involves developing a theory from basic propositions, premises and assumptions that results in accounting principles that are logical conclusions about the subject. A deductive theory ought to be tested to determine whether its results are acceptable in practice. In Chapters 5, 6 and 7 we will discuss the thoughts of some deductive theorists about how to define and measure income and equity. The deductive approach is sometimes considered 'normative' because the propositions, premises and assumptions are a priori truths. That is, you cannot prove the premises or the claim, other than in a circular manner. You may have realized this when we looked at the deductive argument regarding the calculation of gross profit above. In other words, deductive theories are based on beliefs, values and accepted truths and are supported by deductive logic.

Inductive approach. The inductive approach stems from the natural sciences, where theories often take the form of law-like generalizations. It starts with observed phenomena on the basis of which researchers form hypotheses about causal explanations. An inductive theory will usually state one or more hypotheses in respect of regularities between variables. These hypotheses must be tested, i.e. the theory must be supported by sufficient instances/observations that support the validity of the derived conclusions about which variable causes an observed phenomenon and hence might explain and predict it. Generalized conclusions about causality are made on the basis of inference and must be interpreted with reference to the statistical likelihood that the same results will be obtained in the future. Some question whether the inductive approach is suitable for the social sciences, which include economics and accounting. Quite often the deductive and inductive approaches are mixed as researchers use their knowledge of accounting practices, or they may not be aware of the subjectivity with which they interpret their own observations.

Mixed approaches. These attempt to use both conceptual reasoning and empirical observations to formulate and verify a paradigm from which to approach developing and testing an accounting theory. In the social sciences, approaches to doing research and formulating theories can, very roughly, be categorized as those based on positivist, interpretivist and critical methodological assumptions. Positivist assumptions include the belief that social scientists must use the same methods used in the natural sciences, and the belief that researchers can and must base their hypotheses and theories solely on purely objective empirical observations. On this view, the function of theory is to explain presently observed phenomena in terms of causality, which subsequently enables the prediction of behaviour, events and other phenomena in the future. Examples of paradigms based on the methodological assumptions of positivism include:

- informational paradigm
- positive accounting theory
- behavioural paradigm
- new institutional paradigm.

Informational paradigm. This theoretical paradigm is rooted in neo-classical economics. It started with Ball and Brown (1968) and Beaver (1968) and introduced empirical methods based on the assumptions of economic general equilibrium models into accounting research. The aim is to demonstrate how accounting information influences investment decisions. Capital markets-based accounting research is perhaps still the most popular and prolific form of positivist research in accounting.

Positive accounting theory (PAT). This theoretical paradigm was developed in the 1970s. Its best known proponents are Watts and Zimmerman (1978, 1979) and Jensen and Meckling (1976). The approach aims to develop a positive theory of accounting which will explain why accounting is what it is and why accountants do what they do, and predict what effects accounting choices have on people and the allocation and utilization of resources.

The assumption in neo-classical economics (micro-economics, also called positive economics) is that, as long as certain initial conditions are met, individuals freely pursuing their own interests will lead to the greatest economic benefit and happiness for all. PAT is based on the assumptions of positive economics, which includes the proposition that managers, shareholders and regulators are rational and self-interested and that they attempt to maximize their utility. PAT holds that, on aggregate, individual behaviour is predictably rational. Ideally, PAT would not lead to prescriptions of the accounting procedures and policies to be implemented; however, agency theory (Jensen and Meckling, 1976), through the anticipation of predictably rational behaviour, has a big impact on corporate governance and indirectly on accounting as well.

Behavioural paradigm. The behavioural paradigm in economics and finance was developed on the basis of evidence in studies undertaken by psychologists indicating that individuals are not necessarily always predictably rational or self-serving in their decision making. See, for example, Kahneman and Tversky (1972, 1973, 1979), Simon (1979), Statman and Shefrin (1985), Odean (1998), Thaler (1999), Shefrin (2000), Shiller (2000, 2003) and Shleifer (2000). Hence, this approach attempts to take into account human behaviour as it relates to decision making in accounting. In many behaviourist theories in economics, finance and accounting, the assumption is that individuals are predictably irrational.

New institutional paradigm. The new institutional approach in accounting is based on the new institutional approach in economics. The latter was developed by researchers doing comparative economic history because they realized that institutions influence economic growth and development. What is rational in one institutional environment is not necessarily rational in another. Researchers in comparative financial and accounting systems came to the conclusion that legal and financial institutions in particular matter to the development of accounting systems (e.g. La Porta *et al.*, 1997; Nobes, 1998). The gradual progression of the internationalization of capital markets and the increasing number of countries where IFRS has been adopted has focused attention on the importance of differences in institutional environment between countries (e.g. Hail *et al.*, 2010; Leuz, 2010). It is important to understand the difference between the new and the old institutional paradigms in economics in order to appreciate the impact on accounting research. The old institutional paradigm grew out of political economy, which was later split up into political economy and economics. In the old institutional paradigm, importance is attached to the influence of political, economic and military power. If institutions matter so much to economic development and the development of accounting and financial systems, research questions will focus on who has the power to determine what the economic, legal and other institutions are. On the other hand, the new institutional accounting paradigm shares the assumption with neo-classical economic theory that there is no single person, group or country which has the power to shape the development of institutions to their/its own benefit.

Interpretive paradigm. Interpretivist research and theories are based on the belief that it is not always possible for researchers to provide entirely objective interpretations of observed social phenomena (such as accounting practices and rules). In other words, they realize that some a priori truths are actually dependent on context and perspective, and that because of this it is difficult to judge our own ability to be objective about social phenomena. One implication is that these approaches to the formulation of accounting theory do not focus on predicting behaviour and events. They rather focus on explaining and interpreting the meaning of acts and actions from the perspective of the individuals involved. This paradigm is perhaps more popular in managerial than in financial accounting research. On the basis of data collected in case studies and interviews, for example, researchers try to understand motivations behind and the meaning of behaviour and individual acts. They will then form hypotheses, for example, about how workers can be motivated by sharing responsibility for setting performance targets as well as their realization.

Critical paradigm. The critical approach to accounting theory formulation originates in political economy, neo-Marxism and sociology, and focuses on theories about the distributional consequences of financial reporting. Critical researchers try to expose certain accepted truths as false or unfair, and point to how fairness and justice can be improved. In accounting, this approach has led to theories about the social responsibility of managers of large companies, or about the need to report on the social, economic and ecological sustainability or the operations of large companies. The critical paradigm may lead to ethical approaches that centre on social welfare. In other words, accounting principles and techniques are evaluated for acceptance after considering all effects on all groups in society. Writers/researchers in this area include Scott (1940), Yu (1976) and Williams (2002, 2006). Within this approach, we would need to be able to account for a business entity's effect on its social environment.

Finally, there are two more approaches to the formulation of accounting theory that need to be mentioned here:

- economic approach
- eclectic approach.

Economic approach. A macro-economic approach focuses on the economic consequences of accounting policies and standards on general economic welfare. Thus accounting principles and techniques are evaluated for acceptance depending on their impact on the national economy. Sweden, in its national GAAP, uses an economic approach to its development. Theories about macro-economic consequences of accounting policies often relate to taxation and investment fixed capital formation. From a positivist perspective, theories about economic consequences may focus on the effects on businesses or investor behaviour. From a critical perspective, they might focus on the effect of accounting policies on employment and wage levels. Traditionally, accounting standards have been set without considering economic consequences, but lobby pressures from groups who perceive themselves as being affected can be strong. In developing its standards, the IASB does tend to consider an economic approach. For example, the current discussion on accounting for leases focuses on the effect that a standard requiring the capitalization of all leases, whether finance or operating, might have on the economy or business in general.

Eclectic approach. Here we have a combination of all the approaches already identified appearing in our accounting theory. This approach has come about more by accident than as a deliberate attempt due to the interference in the development of accounting theory by professionals, governmental bodies (including the EU) and individuals.

ACTIVITY 4.6

Explain, with reference to the concepts of predictable rationality and bounded rationality, how PAT and behavioural accounting theory might consider disclosing information on the face of the financial statements or in the notes to the financial statements.

Activity feedback

The assumption of rationality under PAT means that it does not matter what form the disclosure of information takes. Users of financial statements will be able to see through any attempt to manipulate their decisions. Behavioural theory probably takes into consideration the fact that most investors do not study the financial statements in great detail. Hence they might miss or discard information that is not presented on the face of the financial statements.

This section has merely listed the main approaches to the development of accounting theories that exist in the literature. For different overviews of this area, please refer to Smith (2011, chapter 1) or Riahi-Belkaoui (2004). Van Mourik (2014a) presents an overview of methodology in financial accounting research and Van Mourik (2014b) outlines different types of issues in financial accounting theory. Other sources for information about accounting research methodology and methods include Ryan *et al.* (2002) and Smith (2011).

Over the past 40 years or so, financial accounting theories have primarily been based on the assumptions of the positive approach and were aimed at explanation and prediction of preparers' and investors' actions and accounting phenomena. Most of the accounting theories developed by financial accounting researchers during this period have been of a relatively small scope.

Some regard the IASB Conceptual Framework as the most promising avenue for the development of a comprehensive theory of financial accounting. A more cynical view held by others is that any conceptual framework is primarily an attempt to legitimize the authority of accounting standard setters and regulators. Yet others regard a conceptual framework as a possible means for private accounting standard setters (such as the IASB) to keep political interference from national regulators at bay. In essence, the IASB's Conceptual Framework is the result of a pragmatic regulatory approach to the determination of accounting principles, which comprises an eclectic mix of deductive, inductive and political elements. As the Framework and IFRS are applied in many different institutional environments, it will be interesting to see what theoretical contributions the old and new institutional paradigms will provide to the field of international accounting theory.

SUMMARY

In this chapter we looked at accounting theory and the IASB Conceptual Framework. We discussed different concepts of accounting theory and approaches to developing accounting theory. The chapter looked at why a conceptual framework is important for the IASB, and discussed the 2010 IASB Conceptual Framework in detail. We also considered the main changes proposed in the 2015 IASB Exposure Draft.

EXERCISES

Suggested answers to exercises marked ✓ are to be found in the Student online resources, with suggested answers to the remaining questions available in the Instructor online resources.

✓**1**   To what extent is financial reporting a suitable subject on which to theorize?

✓**2**   Positive research is a necessary starting point on the road to normative thinking, but it can never be enough by itself. Discuss.

3   Is the 2010 IASB Framework useful in its present form? In what ways might the 2015 IASB Exposure Draft represent an improvement?

4   Accounting standards and regulations should aim to state how all situations should be dealt with. Discuss.

5   If you were to develop an accounting conceptual framework, where would you start and how would you structure it?

ACCOUNTING AND ECONOMIC PERSPECTIVES ON INCOME AND CAPITAL

5

OBJECTIVES After studying this chapter you should be able to:

- understand and explain the allocation problem in financial accounting

- contrast the transactions approach (also called revenue-expense or income statement approach) with the valuation approach (also called assets-liabilities or balance sheet approach) to the determination of profit or loss (income) and equity capital (wealth)

- contrast cash accounting with accrual accounting

- contrast traditional accounting income and capital with ideal economic income and capital

- discuss the difference between return of capital and return on capital with reference to Hicks's income concepts No. 1, No. 2 and No. 3

- contrast the concept of economic income and wealth under the assumptions of certainty with the concepts of ex ante and ex post economic income and wealth under uncertainty

- explain the residual income model perspective on income and wealth

- explain the informational, measurement and efficient contracting perspectives on the objective of general purpose financial reporting.

INTRODUCTION

This chapter is the first of two chapters that explore different approaches to solving the allocation problem in financial accounting. The first section will remind us that the allocation problem in financial accounting presents the challenge of making allocations in accrual accounting in ways that are not arbitrary (purposeful and in accordance with a coherent and consistent set of concepts and principles) and which serve to enable financial reporting to fulfil the objectives we decide it should fulfil.

The second section will contrast the transactions approach and the valuation approach to the determination of accounting profit or loss and equity capital. Both approaches will yield the same profit or loss number and the same equity capital amount, if and only if, the definition, recognition, measurement, presentation and disclosure of the elements of profit or loss articulate with the elements of equity capital in the balance sheet and income statement.

The third section introduces ideal economic income and wealth. Looking ahead, it is useful to keep in mind that the 'traditional accounting perspective' grew out of accountants' pragmatic solutions to practical problems in periodically determining a reporting entity's income and capital in the uncertain and often messy world of business practice. By contrast, the 'economic perspective' grew out of the academic desire to create a theoretically sound approach to personal income and capital determination that would be useful for evaluating different investment opportunities.

The fourth section discusses the distinction between return of capital and return on capital in relation to the determination of financial performance.

The fifth section introduces ex ante and ex post economic income and capital, which is necessary when the assumption of certainty is dropped because actual net cash receipts after the fact are usually different from expected future net cash receipts before the fact.

The sixth section introduces the residual income valuation model, and the seventh section introduces the information, measurement and efficient contracting perspectives on the role of financial reporting information.

THE ALLOCATION PROBLEM IN FINANCIAL ACCOUNTING

In principle, in a financial accounting system based on double-entry bookkeeping, the total recognized income and expenses over a financial reporting entity's entire life must equal the total cash inflows and cash outflows of an entity over its entire life. In other words, over the entity's entire life, cash accounting and accrual accounting produce the same profit or loss. Periodic income under accrual accounting equals net cash receipts for the period (except for capital contributions or withdrawals) plus or minus the appropriate adjustments for accruals.

This is because under double-entry bookkeeping, the flow statements (the statement of profit or loss, the statement of changes in equity and the cash flow statement) articulate with the corresponding accounts in the balance sheet. The balance sheet is a stock statement because it shows the reporting entity's financial position at a point in time. The flow statements show the flows during a period. For example, the cash flow statement for the year ended 31 December 2017 reconciles the amount of cash in the balance sheet of 31 December 2017 with the amount in the balance sheet of 31 December 2016.

The allocation problem in financial accounting (Thomas, 1969, 1974) is a problem of allocating accruals such that they produce information about income and equity capital that satisfies the objective of periodic financial reporting better than cash accounting.

ACTIVITY 5.1

Remind yourself. What accruals do you know?

Activity feedback

There are several types of accruals, only one of which we usually call 'accruals'.

Prepayments: items for which the has been cash paid, but the expense has not yet been incurred (recognized as a current asset in the balance sheet).

Accrued income: items for which the revenue has been earned, but the cash is to be received in arrears in the next accounting period (recognized as an asset in the balance sheet).

Accruals: items for which the expense has been incurred, but the cash has not yet been paid (recognized as a current liability in the balance sheet)

Deferred income: items for which the cash has been received in advance of the revenue having been earned (recognized as a liability in the balance sheet).

However, when we speak of accrual accounting, we mean allocating the cash receipts and payments over the life of the entity in a way that produces information on income and capital that is more useful and relevant to our objective than cash accounting. Thus, this also includes the practice of recording capital expenditure as non-current assets (for which we calculate depreciation), and long-term borrowings as non-current liabilities instead of merely large cash receipts. In an accounting system that adheres to the clear surplus relation, accruals do not include recording provisions and reserves because all recognised changes in assets and liabilities must go through the income statement. In an accounting system that allows dirty surplus, accruals could include provisions and reserves. Note that in this case, 'surplus' means the difference between net assets and shareholders' capital. A clean surplus comprises only retained earnings. A dirty surplus comprises retained earnings and any changes in assets and liabilities that bypass the income statement.

THE TRANSACTIONS APPROACH AND THE VALUATION APPROACH TO THE DETERMINATION OF PROFIT OR LOSS IN ACCOUNTING

The transactions approach and the valuation approach are two procedures to determine the amounts of profit or loss and equity capital. The transactions (also called revenue-expense or income statement) approach determines profit or loss as follows.

Income – Expenses = Net profit or loss

The transactions approach is based on the process of recording the historical transactions and recordable events and focuses on recognizing the realized revenues that were earned through the operations of the business and the matched expenses that were incurred in generating these revenues. The realization concept is fundamental to transactions-based profit or loss. Under the transactions approach, the balance sheet can become a repository for costs that have not yet been realized.

The valuation (also called assets-liabilities or balance sheet) approach determines profit or loss as follows.

Net assets at time $t+1$ – Net assets at time t = Net profit or loss

The valuation approach to income determination starts from the determination of the values of the assets and liabilities in the balance sheet at the start of the period and at the end of the period, and proceeds to conclude that the change in net assets from one period to the next must be the income for the period. In auditing, it tended to be used as an arithmetical check on the income determined using the transactions approach. If the two outcomes were different, it was because a mistake had been made somewhere. Under the valuation approach in combination with adherence to the clean surplus relation, the income statement can include unrealized gains and losses.

Because of the articulation of financial statements, the transactions approach and the valuation approach will yield the same results as long as the definition, recognition and measurement of the elements of the financial statements are the same. That is, under the same set of accounting standards, the results should be the same. We will illustrate this with two Activities. In one, we calculate profit or loss and equity capital on a cash accounting basis and, in the other, we calculate profit or loss and equity capital on an accrual accounting basis. These Activities will also help us better understand the allocation problem in financial accounting.

Profit or loss and equity capital under cash accounting

ACTIVITY 5.2

Consider an investment of €2487 in a single asset firm on 1 January 20X1. The firm has no liabilities. The investment is expected to generate net cash receipts on 31 December each year of €1000 for three years and will have no residual value at the end of the three years.

Required:

(a) *Calculate the profit or loss and equity capital on a cash basis for each of the years 20X1, 20X2 and 20X3.*

(b) *Determine the profit or loss for each year using the valuation approach.*

Activity feedback

(a) *The profit or loss and equity capital on a cash basis are shown in Table 5.1.*

TABLE 5.1   Cash accounting

Income statements	year ended 31/12/20X1	year ended 31/12/20X2	year ended 31/12/20X3	Total
	€	€	€	€
Cash in	1000	1000	1000	3000
Cash out	(2487)	—	—	(2487)
Cash profit (or loss)	(1487)	1000	1000	**513**

Balance sheets	At 1/1/20X1	At 31/12/20X1	At 31/12/20X2	At 31/12/20X3
	€	€	€	€
Opening cash	2487	2487	1000	2000
Net cash added during the period	—	(1487)	1000	1000
Total assets (closing cash)	—	1000	2000	3000
Opening equity capital	2487	2487	1000	2000
Cash profit (or loss)	—	(1487)	1000	1000
Cash based closing equity capital	—	1000	2000	3000

ACTIVITY 5.2 (Continued)

(b) *Profit or loss for each year using the valuation approach*

As you can see, since the measurement basis is historical cost and the recognition basis is the realization concept,

the outcome is the same. In this way, the above calculation provides a mathematical check.

	year ended 31/12/20X1	year ended 31/12/20X2	year ended 31/12/20X3
Valuation approach	€	€	€
Equity capital at 31 December	1000	2000	3000
Equity capital at time 1 January	(2487)	(1000)	(2000)
Cash profit (or loss)	(1487)	1000	1000

In Activity 5.2 we saw how this project reduced equity capital in year 20X1 from €2487 to €1000 because cash accounting shows the financial performance of this one asset firm over year 20X1 as a loss of €1487. Cash accounting shows financial performance over years 20X2 and 20X3 as €1000 per year. However, does this way of showing the financial performance and financial position of a going concern fulfil the objectives of general purpose financial reporting?

For illustrative purposes, in our Activity the life of the investment is only three years, but as discussed in Chapter 1, most firms are going concerns, and there is a need to determine profit or loss periodically on a going concern basis. Because of the large cash investment up front, the cash basis of accounting makes both income (financial performance) and capital (financial position) more volatile than economic reality appears to warrant. But, what is economic reality and how do we faithfully represent it? There is no simple answer to this question because the way we perceive reality is influenced by the way we frame reality, and the way we frame reality is, to a large extent, determined by our main objective.

The revenues realized and recognized for the period less the expenses incurred in generating the revenues is then the periodic profit or loss which increases (or decreases) the residual capital of the business. As a consequence of the focus on realized revenues and matched expenses, the transactions approach regards the statement of profit or loss as the primary statement and the balance sheet becomes a statement of rest posts on their way to becoming revenues and expenses. Hence, this approach is also called the income statement or revenue-expense approach to income determination.

When using the transactions approach to the determination of income, one must attach great importance to the evidence, objectivity, verifiability and reliability of the transactions and recordable events and the historical prices at which they were conducted. In Germany, a similar approach was advocated by Schmalenbach (1959, 1962) who called it the 'dynamic accounting theory' because of the dynamic role played by the income statement. In Finland also, by Saario (1945, 1959) (see Näsi *et al.*, 2014). In the Anglophone world, a similar approach was advocated by Paton and Littleton (1940) who associated it with Entity Theory (See Napier, 2014).

Profit or loss and equity capital under accrual accounting

ACTIVITY 5.3

Consider the same scenario of Activity 5.2 where a firm made an investment of €2487 in a single asset on 1 January 20X1. The firm has no liabilities. The investment is expected to generate net cash receipts on 31 December each year of €1000 for three years and will have no residual value at the end of the three years.

Required:

(a) Calculate the profit or loss and equity capital on an accruals basis for the years 20X1, 20X2 and 20X3.

(b) Determine the profit or loss for each year using the transactions approach and the valuation approach.

(c) Compare the determination of profit or loss and equity capital on a cash basis and on a traditional accruals basis.

(a) *The top part of Table 5.2 shows the calculations on an accruals basis.*

(b) *Profit or loss for each year using the valuation approach is shown in the bottom section of Table 5.2.*

(c) *The accounting profit for each year is €171, which makes a total profit of €513 over the three years. Closing capital at the end of year 3 is €2487 capital + €513 profit = €3000. Comparing the cash and accruals approaches, it is clear that income on a cash basis shows much more volatility than the actual performance warrants. Total profit for both approaches is the same because the accruals basis of accounting does not change the total profit. It merely allocates profit over the years in an attempt to match revenues earned with expenses incurred in the process of earning the revenues. Similarly, because of the higher volatility of profit or loss on a cash basis, equity capital does not represent the financial position as evenly as the economics of the situation seem to warrant.*

Activity feedback

TABLE 5.2   Accrual accounting income and equity capital based on historical cost

	year ended 31/12/20X1	year ended 31/12/20X2	year ended 31/12/20X3	Total
Income statements	€	€	€	€
Income	1 000	1 000	1 000	3 000
Less: Depreciation expense	(829)	(829)	(829)	(2 487)
Accounting profit	171	171	171	513
	At 1/1/20X1	**At 31/12/20X1**	**At 31/12/20X2**	**At 31/12/20X3**
Balance sheets	€	€	€	€
Asset at NBV	2 487	1 658	829	—
Cash	—	1 000	2 000	3 000
Total assets	2 487	2 658	2 829	3 000
Opening equity capital	2 487	2 487	2 658	2 829
Profit or loss	—	171	171	171
Closing equity capital	—	2 658	2 829	3 000

ACTIVITY 5.3 *(Continued)*

Valuation approach	year ended 31/12/20X1 €	year ended 31/12/20X2 €	year ended 31/12/20X3 €
Equity capital at 31 December	2 658	2 829	3 000
Equity capital at time 1 January	(2 487)	2 658	2 829
Cash profit (or loss)	171	171	171

The accounting perspective on the determination of profit or loss and equity capital grew out of accountants' pragmatic solutions to practical problems in the real world of business practice. This is a world characterized by uncertainty about the future and information asymmetry between people who must both compete and collaborate to survive and thrive. This is a world in which people have a limited ability to make rational decisions. Therefore, people often make decisions based on heuristics (simple and pragmatic decision rules) and/or feelings (optimism, pessimism, confidence and fear) and then rationalize these decisions in retrospect. It is a world characterized by problems of agency, moral hazard, information asymmetry, risk, uncertainty, unpredictable markets in terms of supply, demand and market prices, but also in terms of fluctuating levels of market power from and collusion between different market participants and influence from regulators.

IDEAL ECONOMIC INCOME AND WEALTH

The 'economic perspective' on income and wealth arose out of a desire to create a theoretically sound approach to income determination for the purpose of making rational decisions on choosing between alternative actions. The economic income theorists who had the strongest influence on accounting income theorists were Irving Fisher (1867–1947), Friedrich Von Hayek (1899–1992), John Hicks (1904 – 1989), Nicholas Kaldor (1908–1986) and Erik Lindahl (1891–1960).

On the economic perspective, income and wealth (capital) are determined by the present value model. Wealth is the stock of net assets that produces a stream of future net cash receipts. The value of capital is the present value of the future cash flows (benefits) that the capital is expected to generate. Fisher (1912) defined the relation between capital and income to be such that economic income is equivalent to interest, that is, 'economic income can be derived by taking the given interest rate and applying it to the opening capital of each period' (Lee, 1985: 31). The flow of income is distinct from the stock of capital that generated it, but the two are linked through the rate of interest because 'interest is the price of hiring money today in order to obtain a certain amount of money tomorrow' (Lee, 1985: 10).

Economic capital = present value of future net cash inflows:

$$P_0 = V_0 = \sum_{t=1}^{n} \frac{1}{(1+r)^t} C_t$$

Whereby:

P_0 = the market value of the entity's equity capital at time 0

V_0 = the present value of the entity's net assets at the start of the period

r = the interest rate

C_t = the entity's net cash receipts for the period

Fisher's economic income Y = interest rate $r \times$ value of capital at the start of the period V_0:

$$Y = rV_0$$

When you know the interest rate and the future net cash receipts, you can determine the value of the capital by discounting the cash receipts at the rate of interest. When you know the value of capital, you can determine economic income by applying the interest rate to opening capital. For this model to work in a practical sense, one has to know with certainty the future net cash inflows and the interest rate must be both known and constant. That is why this type of economic income is called ideal income.

ACTIVITY 5.4

An investment of €2487 in a single asset firm on 1 January 20X1 is expected to generate cash receipts on 31 December each year of €1000 for three years. The discount rate to reflect the time value of money is 10 per cent.

Required:

(a) Calculate the value of the economic capital as at 1 January for each of the years 20X1, 20X2 and 20X3

(b) Calculate the net present value of the investment in order to decide whether or not this is a good investment.

Net present value is calculated as:

$$NPV_0 = \sum_{t=1}^{n} \frac{1}{(1+r)^t} C_t - I_0 \geq 0$$

Whereby

NPV_0 = the net present value of the investment at time 0

r = the interest rate

C_t = the entity's net cash receipts for the period

I_0 = the amount of the investment at the start of the period

(c) Would you recommend making this investment? Why? Why not?

(d) What is the economic income, according to Fisher, for each of the years 20X1, 20X2 and 20X3?

Activity feedback (see Table 5.3)

(a) The present value of capital at 1 January 20X1 is:

$$\frac{1000}{1.1} + \frac{1000}{(1.1)^2} + \frac{1000}{(1.1)^3} = 909 + 826 + 751 = €2486$$

The present value of capital at 1 January 20X2 is:

$$\frac{1000}{1.1} + \frac{1000}{(1.1)^2}$$
$$= 909 + 826 = €1735$$

ACTIVITY 5.4 (*Continued*)

The present value of capital at 1 January 20X3 is:

$$\frac{1000}{1.1} = €909$$

(b) *The net present value of the investment at 1 January 20X1 is:*

(€909 + €826 + €751 = €2486) – €2487 ≈ –€1

Note that the €2486 and therefore the –€1 are the result of rounding. If you do not round your answer, you will find that the net present value (NPV) is closer to zero.

(c) *The investment has a net present value of –€1. Generally, the rule is:*

If the NPV is greater or equal to zero, the project will add value.

In other words, if the NPV is equal to or greater than 0, it makes sense to pursue the project. One problem, of course, is the assumption that the future cash flows

are €1000 per year for three years. In reality, this is by no means certain. Another problem is the implicit assumption that the rate of discount is the same as the market interest rate and that both are constant. In reality, finding that the rate of discount is influenced by alternative uses of the resource (e.g. interest on money) and by future expectations, which are of necessity subjective, is difficult. Even if a discount rate as of now can be found, the implied assumption used here that the rate remains constant is almost certainly false.

(d) *Fisher's economic income is simply derived by 'taking the given interest rate and applying it to the opening capital of each period' (Lee, 1985: 31). The assumption here is that all of the income is consumed during the year. Hence, the value of the starting capital is not maintained.*

TABLE 5.3   Fisher's economic income and capital

Income statements	year ended 31/12/20X1	year ended 31/12/20X2	year ended 31/12/20X3	Total
	€	€	€	€
Opening capital x 10%	249	174	91	513
Fisher's economic income	249	174	91	513

Balance sheets	At 1/1/20X1	At 31/12/20X1	At 31/12/20X2	At 31/12/20X3	Total
	€	€	€	€	€
Asset at NPV	2 487	1 735	909	—	5 130
Capital	2 487	1 735	909	—	5 130

Unlike Fisher for whom income equalled consumption, for Hicks, income equalled consumption plus savings. The following quote makes it clear what Hicks considers the objective of income determination and how central the concept of capital maintenance is:

> The purpose of income calculations in practical affairs is to give people an indication of the amount which they can consume without impoverishing themselves. Following out this idea, it would seem that we ought to define a man's income as the maximum value which he can consume during a week, and still expect to be as well off at the end of the week as he was at the beginning. Thus, when a person saves, he plans to be better off in the future; when he lives beyond his income, he plans to be worse off. Remembering that the practical purpose of income is to serve as a guide for prudent conduct, I think it is fairly clear that this is what the central meaning must be.
>
> (Hicks, 1946: 172)

Thus applying Hicksian income to a corporate business entity would yield:

$$\text{Income: } Y = P_1 - P_0 = C_1 + (V_1 - V_0)$$

Whereby:

Y = economic income over the period

P_0 = the market value of the entity's equity capital at the start of the period

P_1 = the market value of the entity's equity capital at the end of the period

C_1 = the entity's net cash receipts for the period

V_0 = the present value of the entity's net assets at the start of the period

V_1 = the present value of the entity's net assets at the end of the period

ACTIVITY 5.5

As before, consider an investment of €2487 in a single asset firm on 1 January 20X1 which is expected to generate cash receipts on 31 December each year of €1000 for three years. The discount rate to reflect the time value of money is 10 per cent. According to the Hicksian way of thinking, what is the income for each year?

Activity feedback

Our formula is:

$$Y_e = C + (V_1 - V_0)$$

As you can see in Table 5.4, the economic income calculated for each year according to Fisher's method in Activity 5.4 produces the same outcome when using Hicks's method. This is because the assumptions with regard to the certainty of future net cash inflows and the interest rate are the same. That is why we call the economic income derived under the assumptions of certainty ideal income.

TABLE 5.4   Economic income Y_e = net cash inflow C + (closing capital V_1 – opening capital V_0)

Period	C_1 €	V_1 €	V_0 €	Y_e = economic income €
		2487		
20X1	1000	1735	2487	1000 + (1735 – 2487) = **248**
20X2	1000	909	1735	1000 + (909 – 1735) = **174**
20X3	1000	—	909	1000 – 909 = **91**
	3000	5131	5131	513

Hicks, however, developed three income concepts. Like Fisher, Hicks is obviously adopting a forward-looking approach to valuation and income measurement. Unlike Fisher, Hicks is concerned with capital maintenance in order to secure a constant income stream into the future. Hicks (1946: 173) wrote:

Income No. 1 is thus the maximum amount which can be spent during a period if there is to be an expectation of maintaining intact the capital value of prospective receipts (in money terms). This is probably the definition which most people do implicitly use in their private affairs; but it is far from being in all circumstances a good approximation to the central concept.

What this means, is that Hicksian Income No. 1 must be determined by reinvesting some of the ideal economic profit rather than consuming it all. Otherwise, capital will not be maintained, which makes it impossible to generate a sustainable stream of income into the future.

ACTIVITY 5.6

Following on from Activity 5.5, use the same scenario and extend it by making sure that the €248 economic income of year 20X1 is maintained as an income stream in the later years as well. Like before, the discount rate and interest rate are 10 per cent.

Activity feedback

Income No. 1 is determined as follows. In year 20X1, the cash receipts are €1000, but the income is stated as €248. The difference (€752) needs to be reinvested (saved) in order to facilitate future spending. This reinvestment of €752 on 1 January year 20X2 will by itself earn 10 per cent in the year 20X2, i.e. €75. So, total income in year 20X2 is €174 from the original investment, plus €75 from the reinvestment, i.e. again €248.

In year 20X2 the cash receipts from the original investment are €1000, but the income is stated as €174. The difference (€826) again needs to be reinvested. This investment of €826 will itself earn €83 in year 20X3 giving total cash receipts in that year of €91 from the

original investment + €75 from the first reinvestment + €83 from the second reinvestment = €249 once again. Similarly, in year 20X3, cash receipts will be €1000, but the income is stated as €91. The difference (€909) will be reinvested at 10 per cent, earning itself €91 in each year. Total cash receipts in year 4, all from reinvestments, will therefore be 75 + 83 + 91 = €249 and similarly in year 5 onwards. This of course satisfies our original conditions. The income of year 20X1 is the amount 'that can be spent while still enabling the income of all future periods to be the same amount'. This has been shown to be €249 under the given assumptions. These results are summarized in Table 5.5.

The present value of an annual income stream of €248, to infinity, at a 10 per cent discount rate is €2490. This, allowing for rounding errors, gives us our original 'capital' figure of €2487, which of course is what it should do. So the answer may possibly have come as no surprise. But you should still make sure you understand all the logic involved.

TABLE 5.5 Hicks's economic income model (Income No. 1)

	1	2	3	4	5	6	7	8	9
Year	C_1	V_1	V_0	Y_e	Reinvestment	Cumulative reinvestment	Total reinvestment	Income from reinvestment	Total economic income
20X0	—	2487	—	—	—	—	2487	—	—
20X1	1000	1735	2487	248	752	752	2487	—	≈249
20X2	1000	909	1735	174	826	1578	2487	75	249
20X3	1000	—	909	91	909	2487	2487	158	249
20X4	—	—	—	—	—	2487	2487	249	249

Notes: Col. 4 = 1 + 2 − 3

Col. 5 = 1 − 4

Col. 7 = 2 + 6

Col. 9 = 4 + 8

For Income No. 1, Hicks stressed the expectation of maintaining intact the capital value of prospective receipts (in money terms), which is done by reinvesting the difference between net cash receipts and economic income for each period. However, Income No. 2 and Income No. 3 are the concepts that apply in a world characterized by uncertainty to the extent that interest rates do change and the value of money is not stable. In Hicks's words:

> This leads us to the definition of Income No. 2. We now define income as the maximum amount the individual can spend this week, and still expect to be able to spend the same amount in each ensuing week. So long as the rate of interest is not expected to change, this definition comes to the same thing as the first; but when the rate of interest is expected to change, they cease to be identical. Income No. 2 is then a closer approximation to the central concept than Income No. 1 is.
>
> (Hicks, 1946: 174)

> Income No. 3 must be defined as the maximum amount of money which the individual can spend this week, and still expect to be able to spend the same amount in real terms in each ensuing week. If prices are expected to rise, then an individual who plans to spend €10 in the present and each ensuing week must expect to be less well off at the end of the week than he is at the beginning. At each date he can look forward to the opportunity of spending €10 in each future week; but at the first date one of the €10s will be spent in a week when prices are relatively low. An opportunity of spending on favourable terms is present in the first case, but absent in the second.
>
> (Hicks, 1946: 174–175)

As we are about to leave the world of certainty, it is useful to recap what that world looks like. The assumptions that underpin ideal income are part of the initial assumptions that generally underlie neo-classical economics, such as the economics taught in micro-economics textbooks. The first set of assumptions produces certainty about the economy because all expectations are realized and all future prices of assets and claims are known. The second set of assumptions is regarding the characteristics of markets. Markets are assumed to be perfect and complete.

> The concept of *perfect markets* means that (1) trading of commodities and claims takes place at zero transaction cost, (2) no firm or individual has any special advantage or opportunity to earn abnormal returns on its investments, and (3) prices are invariant to the actions of any individual or firm. The concept of *complete markets* means that markets exist for *all* commodities or claims, and hence the market price for any commodity or claim is publicly observable.
>
> (Beaver, 1998: 38–39)

RETURN OF CAPITAL AND RETURN ON CAPITAL

When discussing Hicksian income and Hicks's three income concepts, we encountered the importance of capital maintenance in order to preserve a constant stream of income into the future. In other words, in order not to impoverish ourselves we must make sure that we achieve a return of capital as well as a constant return on capital. Income concept No. 1 pointed to the importance of reinvesting part of the economic income to achieve this constant stream of income. Income No. 2 showed that when interest rates are not stable, there will be a difference between the expected values of income and capital ex ante and the values ex post. That is, we must adjust our reinvestments based on our updated expectations. Income No. 3 showed that capital maintenance becomes a different type of issue under conditions of inflation. In theory, before we can measure income, we must restate opening capital in order to achieve purchasing power parity. Among other things, Chapter 6 will provide a brief introduction to purchasing power parity accounting.

ACTIVITY 5.7

Obtain a pencil, a measuring rule and an elastic band. Now attempt to measure the length of the pencil: (a) with the rule; and (b) with the elastic band.

Activity feedback

Stupid, isn't it? A centimetre is a precisely defined concept. But the idea of measuring a length with an elastic band is nonsensical because, of course, we do not know how far we have stretched it – it is continually changing by unknown amounts.

But a euro is as elastic a concept as an elastic band! In relative terms, for example in relation to the US dollar, the euro keeps changing, as published exchange rates tell us. Even more importantly, the euro keeps changing in absolute terms – indeed, is undefinable in absolute terms – as published inflation rates confirm. The value of a euro is neither clearly defined nor constant. Yet accountants use it as if it were both.

INCOME EX ANTE AND INCOME EX POST

So far, we have calculated ideal income, which is economic income in a world characterized by ideal conditions under certainty (the firm's future net cash receipts and the interest rate are known with certainty) and perfect and complete markets. We now extend our analysis to include uncertainty about future net cash receipts, but, for now, we stay with the assumption of a fixed interest rate and complete and perfect markets. Ideal conditions under uncertainty imply that future net cash receipts 'are known conditionally on the states of nature' (Scott, 2015: 43). Under these conditions, estimation risk arises because instead of being able to calculate with certainty the present value at time 0, we now have to calculate the expected present value at time 0.

ACTIVITY 5.8

Using the same basic data as in Activities 5.5 and 5.6, let us now suppose that at the end of year 20X2 there is a change in expected net cash receipts for year 20X3 because there are signs that the economy might be picking up pace. The expectation is that in state 1, the firm's net cash receipts will be €1000 but in state 2 the firm's net cash receipts will be €1200. The probability of state 1 occurring is 0.5 and thus the probability of state 2 occurring is also 0.5. Assuming the ideal conditions under uncertainty, calculate the new expected net cash receipt for year 20X3 and the present value of the firm at the start of year 20X3.

Activity feedback

The expected net cash receipt at the end of year 20X3 is:

$$(0.5 * €1000) + (0.5 * €1200) = €1100.$$

The expected present value of the capital is:

$$(0.5 * (€1000/1.1) + (0.5 * (€1200/1.1) = 455 + 545 = €1000$$

This leads to two further concepts: income ex ante and income ex post. Income ex ante means income measured before the event; income ex post means income measured after the event.

Income ex ante

Formally, income ex ante can be expressed as:

$$Y_{ea} = C_1 + (K_c^1 - K_s)$$

Whereby:

C_1 is the expected realized cash flow for the period anticipated at the beginning of the period

K_c^1 is the closing capital as estimated at the beginning of the period

K_s is the capital at the beginning of the period as estimated at the beginning of the period.

ACTIVITY 5.9

Using the same basic data as in Activities 5.5, 5.6 and 5.8, now using an ex ante approach, consider the effects of the change in expectations on the calculations for each of the years.

Activity feedback (see Table 5.6)

Year 20X3 – The opening capital K_s is no longer the same as the closing capital K_e at the end of year 20X2. It will now be:

$$K_s = \frac{1100}{1.1} = €1000$$

TABLE 5.6	Income ex ante					
Period	C	K_e^1	K_s	Y_e	Windfall	Total Y ex ante
	€	€	€	€	€	€
0	—	2487	—	—	—	—
20X1	1000	1735	2487	248	—	248
20X2	1000	909	1735	174	—	174
20X3	1100	—	1000	100	91	191
				522	91	613

Using an ex ante approach, the effects are as follows.

Year 20X1 – No change.

Year 20X2 – Still no change. The calculations for year 20X2 are based on expectations as at the beginning of the year 20X2 and they had not altered at that time.

Comparing this with the corresponding figure of €909 for K_s in year 20X3 under the ideal income calculations, a positive difference of €91 arises. Alternatively: (€1100 – €1000)/1.1 = €91. A positive difference is called a windfall gain and a negative difference is called a windfall loss. Hence, a windfall gain of €91 appears under the ex ante way of thinking in year 20X3. Windfalls are also called 'unexpected' income.

Income ex post

Formally, income ex post can be expressed as:

$$Y_{cp} = C_1 + (K_c^1 - K_s^1)$$

Whereby:

C_1 is the actual realized net cash inflow of the period

K_c^1 is the closing capital estimated at the end of the period

K_s^1 is the opening capital estimated at the end of the period.

ACTIVITY 5.10

Using the same basic data as in Activities 5.5, 5.6, 5.8 and 5.9, now using an ex post approach, consider the effects of the changes in expectations on the calculations for each of the years. In Activity 5.8 we calculated that, at the end of year 20X2, expected net cash receipts in year 20X3 had increased to €1100. Based on these expectations, in Activity 5.9 we calculated income and capital ex ante. At the end of year 20X3, actual net cash receipts in year 20X3 turned out to be €1100. Now using an ex post approach, consider the effects of the change in expectations on the calculations for each of the years.

Activity feedback (see Table 5.7)

TABLE 5.7   Income ex post

Period	C	K_e^1	K_s^1	Y_e	Windfall	Total Y ex post
	€	€	€	€	€	€
20X0		2487				
20X1	1000	1735	2487	248	—	248
20X2	1000	1000	1818	182	83	265
20X3	1100	—	1000	100	—	100
				530	83	613

Again there will be no change in year 20X1.

There will be a change in the calculations for year 20X2, because at the end of year 20X2 our expectations had already altered. Capital at 1 January year 20X2, based on expectations as at the end of year 20X2, is:

$$\frac{1000}{1.1} + \frac{1100}{(1.1)^2}$$
$$K_s = 909 + 909 = €1818$$

This compares favourably with the corresponding figure of €1735 for Ks in year 20X2 under the ideal income calculations, giving rise to a windfall gain of €83 appearing in year 20X2.

Because the changed expectations related to year 20X3 and these expectations turned out to be correct, here is no change in the calculations for year 20X3.

From the above, it is quite clear that the estimation of ideal economic income and capital, ex ante and ex post income and capital do not require any accounting inputs.

THE RESIDUAL INCOME VALUATION MODEL

The residual income model (RIM) is based on the present value model, or more precisely, on the dividend discount model. The RIM expresses the value of an investment in terms of an accounting variable (i.e. the book value of the investment) and the present value of the future unexpected income from the investment (i.e. the present value of the future residual income). Residual income is defined as the all-inclusive or comprehensive income for the period less $(1 + r) \times$ the book value of opening equity, whereby r is the rate of return on equity or the cost of equity capital. Residual income is also called residual earnings, excess profit (Penman, 2003: 142–143) expected abnormal earnings (Beaver, 1998: 77), or goodwill (Feltham and Ohlson, 1995: 961). Thus the value of a 100 per cent investment in a company would be expressed as:

$$P_0 = V_0 = BV_0 + RI$$

Whereby:

P_0 = the market value of the company's equity capital

V_0 = the present value of the company's net assets

BV_0 = the book value of the firm's net assets at time

RI = the expected present value of future abnormal earnings, which is also called goodwill.

RI_1 = Income$_1$ – Future expected normal income$_0$.

Future expected normal income$_0$ = required rate of return (i.e. the cost of equity capital) × the book value of the firm's net assets$_0$

This model works with any accounting measurement basis, although it does not necessarily work with any recognition basis. It is based on two assumptions:

1 The market value of the firm's net assets is equal to the present value of future expected dividends, where the discount rate is the cost of equity capital.

2 Net assets = Equity capital. In other words, the clean surplus condition requires that all changes in equity go through the income statement first.

In their model, Feltham and Ohlson (1995) specified that all realized (recognized) gains and losses go through the income statement. They call this the clean surplus condition which is as follows:

$$NI_1 = BV_1 - BV_0 + d_1$$

Whereby:

NI_1 = net income realized during period 1

BV_1 = book value (or 'owners' equity') at time 1

dt = dividends, net of capital contributions, paid (or received) at time 1.

Net income must therefore be determined on a comprehensive basis, not on a current operating concept of profit basis. In practice, net assets often include items that have bypassed the income statement. For our purposes, this is where we end our discussion about the economic concepts of income and capital and move on to a brief overview of the measurement and information perspectives on decision-usefulness and the main measurement bases that are used in accounting to convey useful information.

INFORMATION, MEASUREMENT AND EFFICIENT CONTRACTING PERSPECTIVES

As discussed in Chapter 4, the International Accounting Standards Board (IASB) has chosen the decision-usefulness perspective as the foundation of its Conceptual Framework and its standards. This means that the IASB gives priority to the information needs of investors in capital markets over the information needs of other financial reporting users. The IASB believes that the main reason why investors use financial reports is to enable them to forecast the future cash flows of the entity they invest in, and ultimately, the cash flows from the entity to the investors (as dividends) or the cash flows from buying, holding or selling the shares of interest to the investor. The IASB believes that information that helps investors estimate the future cash flows of the entity will also be useful for all other financial statement users. We could therefore say that the IASB adheres to an informational perspective on decision-usefulness. This is inspired by the cash flow orientation of the economic valuation models we have discussed above.

Before the 1960 and 1970s, which is before IASB even existed, there were quite a few accounting theorists who adopted a measurement perspective on decision-usefulness. These theorists attempted to come up with an accounting system that approaches the economic income ideal. People believed that the reason that goodwill existed was because accounting measurement underestimated the balance sheet values and consequently did not determine income correctly. Around this time, the Efficient Markets Hypothesis (EMH) was advanced and gained many followers. 'A market in which prices at any time "fully reflect" available information is called "efficient"' (Fama, 1970: 383). The EMH in its semi-strong form is often assumed in capital markets-based research. In a semi-strong efficient securities market, the price of a security traded on that market at all times fully reflects the past stock prices and 'efficiently adjusts to all other information that is obviously publicly available (e.g. announcements of annual earnings, stock splits, etc.)' (Fama, 1970: 383) about this security. Scott (2015: 122) notes four points about this definition.

1 Market prices are efficient with respect to publicly known information, but privately obtained or inside information will exist.

2 Semi-strong market efficiency is a relative concept. Because of the existence of private information, market prices do not necessarily reflect underlying value.

3 Investors cannot expect to gain an excess return in the long term.

4 If market efficiency holds, prices should follow a random walk, that is, they should fluctuate randomly over time.

As we will see in the next chapter, this led a number of theorists advocating the measurement and recognition of assets at current values in order to determine income and capital. Some suggested abandoning the realization concept, whereas others advocated the recognition of unrealized gains and losses directly in equity. However, under uncertainty and in imperfect and incomplete markets, the price of many assets and liabilities does not have the informational characteristics assumed in the measurement models. Neither can we expect the prices of securities themselves to possess the informational characteristics assumed in the EMH.

ACTIVITY 5.11

So far, we have discussed the measurement of financial statement elements based on historical cost and present value. Thinking of the measurement of the assets (for the time being we are not thinking of liabilities) of, say, a chocolate factory, what kind of current values can you think of?

Activity feedback

The current assets, such as inventory, can be measured at their current entry value, which is their replacement cost. They can also be measured at their current exit value, that is, the cost at which they can be sold to customers. In this case, a question is whether or not the costs of selling the inventory must be deducted from the sales price in order to determine the current exit value. In the latter case, we are talking about net realizable value.

The non-current assets, such as plant, property and equipment, can also be measured at their replacement cost. However, here it becomes a little more complicated because you must decide whether you intend to find the replacement cost of the factory with everything in it as a whole, or the replacement cost of each item individually. Similarly, in order to determine the exit value, do you intend to measure the whole factory at its exit value or do you intend to measure the sales value of all the items independently. In other words, what is your unit of account? Is it the whole business, is it the one factory, is it only a group of machines that are used together or is it each item individually?

The efficient contracting perspective on decision-usefulness stresses the role of financial reporting information in drawing up contracts between the firm and lenders (debt contracts), or between the firm and its senior managers and directors (stewardship/governance/executive compensation contracts), and the role of financial reporting in the monitoring associated with both types of contract.

SUMMARY

In this chapter, we first looked at the allocation problem in financial accounting and the transactions approach and the valuation approach to the determination of profit or loss. We compared accounting concepts of income and equity capital under cash accounting and accrual accounting and moved on to the concepts of income and wealth under certainty. Subsequently we progressed to income and capital ex ante and income and capital ex post in ideal conditions under uncertainty. Both in traditional accounting and economic thinking, income and capital are interrelated concepts. Traditional accounting looks to provide information about the past up to the last balance sheet date. Economic thinking starts from forecasting future net cash receipts in order to determine the present value of net assets and capital.

The measurement perspective holds that the determination of true income and capital is possible. The information perspective mostly aims to provide financial reporting information that helps investors and others to forecast future cash flows. The efficient contracting perspective regards financial reporting information as instrumental in drawing up contracts and monitoring the behaviour of the contracting parties.

EXERCISES

Suggested answers to exercises marked ✓ are to be found in the Student online resources, with suggested answers to the remaining questions available in the Instructor online resources.

1   Obtain three sets of published accounts of quoted companies. Look carefully at the consolidated balance sheets and notes thereto and read the 'accounting policies'. Taking each item in the balance sheet separately, describe how the item is evaluated. Are these evaluations consistent, i.e. in mathematical terms, do we have genuine additivity?

✓2   Two retail businesses, *A* and *B,* run a similar trade from similar shops in similar areas. *A* bought its shop in 1950 for €5000 and *B* bought its shop in 1990 for €105 000. Both businesses consistently prepare their accounts on historical cost principles and they have identical operating profits. To what extent do the resulting accounts give a true (and fair) representation of the relative performance of the two businesses?

✓3   It is never possible to define capital or income, only to define capital and income. Do you agree?

4   **(a)** Outline Fisher's thinking on the concept of income.
   (b) Outline Hicks's thinking on this topic.
   (c) Relate and compare the two.

5   Explain the principles of economic income, carefully distinguishing income ex ante and income ex post.

6   'Economic income is an unattainable ideal'. Consider and discuss.

7   Spock purchased a space invader entertainment machine at the beginning of year 1 for €1000. He expects to receive at annual intervals the following receipts: at the end of year 1 €400; end of year 2 €500; end of year 3 €600. At the end of year 3 he expects to sell the machine for €400.

   Spock could receive a return of 10 per cent on the next best investment. The present value of €1 receivable at the end of a period discounted at 10 per cent is as follows:

   End of year 1   0.909
   End of year 2   0.826
   End of year 3   0.751

   Required:
   Calculate the ideal economic income, ignoring taxation, and working to the nearest whole euro. Your answer should show that Spock's capital is maintained throughout the period and that his income is constant.

   (ACCA, adapted)

8   Compare the capitals and incomes of all the Activities in this chapter. Consider how they are the same or different and why this is the case.

CURRENT VALUES, MIXED VALUES MEASUREMENT AND CPPP ACCOUNTING 6

OBJECTIVES After studying this chapter you should be able to:

- discuss the history and objective of current value accounting models

- calculate income and capital on a current entry values (replacement cost) basis

- calculate income and capital on a current exit values basis

- discuss deprival value (or value to the business) as an example of a mixed measurement system

- calculate income and capital on a current purchasing power parity basis.

INTRODUCTION

Having learned about the traditional historical cost (HC) accounting income determination model and the economic income determination model as two different ways of approaching the allocation problem in financial accounting, this chapter will look at current value accounting. Current value accounting is a third approach to producing accounting information that is different from cash accounting in a methodical, theoretically coherent and consistent way that produces financial accounting and reporting information about an entity's financial performance and financial position that better serves the purposes of its users than cash accounting on its own. Broadly speaking, there are two types of current values: entry values and exit values. This chapter first gives a very brief overview of the history of current value accounting models. Second, it looks at current value accounting models using current entry values (or replacement costs (RCs)) and current value accounting models using current exit values (or net realizable values (NRVs)). Third, it discusses deprival value (or value to the business (DV)) as an example of a mixed measurement system. Fourth, it will introduce current purchasing power parity (CPPP) accounting. Finally, this chapter discusses some international practices and traditions.

HISTORY OF CURRENT VALUE ACCOUNTING MODELS

What we called the traditional transactions-based accounting model in Chapter 2 is the model that was dominant from the early twentieth century. Variations of market values or current cost accounting had been used in many countries until then. For example, according to Georgiou and Jack (2011: 314), in the UK:

> [t]he emphasis on a 'full and fair' balance sheet appears with the Joint Stock Companies Acts of 1844 and 1856 that required the 'true and correct view' of the company's state of affairs to be given by the valuation of assets at up-to-date prices, and specifically at selling prices in the ordinary course of business. This was based on the notion that values on the balance sheet should be indicative of the capacity to carry on business and meet outstanding debts.

Similarly, in Germany, exit values had been advocated by Herman Veit Simon (1865–1914) whereas Fritz Schmidt (1881–1950) advocated the valuation of assets at replacement cost (Näsi *et al.*, 2014: 81–85). In the Netherlands, Theodore Limperg (1879–1961) had developed a value theory whereby an asset was valued at the lower of current cost and either the present value of the future benefits associated with the asset, or its current exit value (Camfferman, 1995: 175).

However, it was the economic income ideal that inspired accounting theorists to devise current value accounting systems that were meant to emulate the economic income ideal. Solomons (1961: 376) reconciled accounting income and economic income as follows.

	Accounting income
+	Unrealised changes in the value of tangible assets which took place during the period over and above value changes recognised as depreciation of fixed assets and inventory mark-downs
–	Amounts realised in this period in respect of value changes in tangible assets which took place in previous periods and were not recognised in these periods
+	Changes in the value of intangible assets during the period, hereafter to be referred to as changes in the value of goodwill
=	**Economic income**

According to Solomons (1961: 376), 'Obviously, the main difference between these two concepts lies in the accountant's attachment to realization as the test of the emergence of income'. Over the total life of the enterprise, the total net cash inflows, total net accounting income and total economic income will ultimately have to be the same because unrealized changes in the value of net assets which enter into the determination of economic income are realized over time and expectations with respect to future cash flows, discount rates and values are adjusted as time passes.

Edwards and Bell (1961) advocated an income determination model based on the measurement of assets using entry prices (replacement costs). They believed that the principal function of accounting information is to enable the evaluation of past business decisions (Edwards and Bell, 1961: 3–4). They assumed that managers base their decisions on how to best allocate resources 'largely upon expectations of individual price movements and relationships among these individual prices' (Edwards and Bell, 1961: 17). Furthermore, they claimed that price-level adjustments by themselves are not enough to ensure that a business entity maintains its real capital. 'The latter cannot be determined unless the current values of a firm's assets, not just their historical costs, are recognized' (Edwards and Bell, 1961: 22). They argued that what they call 'realizable profit' based on exit values is the ideal profit concept for short-run purposes and 'business profit' based on entry values has advantages over realizable profit when the decision 'horizon is extended to the long run' (Edwards and Bell, 1961: 26). 'To the extent that securities are purchased on the basis of long-run considerations, the reporting of profit on a current operating basis of profit would appear to be preferable to the reporting on a realizable profit basis' (Edwards and Bell, 1961: 103).

Sterling (1970) and Chambers (1966, 1967) devised an income determination model based on exit prices. Chambers (1967: 733) criticized Edwards and Bell's focus on managerial resource allocation decisions and instead stressed shareholders' need for information that enables them to evaluate the performance of the business more generally, or enable creditors and shareholders to decide whether they are better off allowing the business to continue or forcing it to liquidate its assets. For this purpose, they would need to know the entity's financial position on a current exit values basis (Chambers: 1967: 734). Chambers (1967: 734–736) also criticized Edwards and Bell's distinction between the long run and the short run and instead preferred to see the long-run expectation as equal to the sum of the short-run expectations. Chambers (1967: 736) argued against the restatement of the opening balance sheet in current purchasing power parity terms. He also claimed that income is best measured as the change in the residual equity of the firm using opportunity costs (market resale prices) because this is always the most relevant to every user of financial accounting information.

In this book, we do not go into Edwards and Bell's model and Chambers and Sterling's models in great detail. For those who are interested, the original sources mentioned above are interesting. Also, Lee (1985) provides a detailed comparison and analysis. Here, we are interested in a more general understanding of accounting using replacement cost and net realizable values because this helps us better understand the debates regarding fair value and the presentation of financial performance in the income statement and financial position in the balance sheet.

In the 1980s, the deregulation of financial and capital markets in many economies and developments in IT created opportunities for the development of financial instruments on a large scale. Many companies that had experienced lacklustre performance were able to make up for their operational difficulties through investment in financial instruments. Companies also started to use financial instruments for shifting all kinds of risks on an unprecedented scale. As a consequence, in the early 1990s, calls for the introduction of current value accounting that would abandon the realization concept, particularly when accounting for derivatives and other financial instruments, started to gain momentum (Johnson and Swieringa, 1996). Others advocated the introduction of a financial statement that would show which items had bypassed the income statement because they had been recorded in equity directly (Robinson, 1991).

As we saw in Chapter 4, this is a topic that is controversial. Currently, the IASB must take decisions on how to handle current values, realization and the presentation financial performance and financial position in its Conceptual Framework. Similarly, the FASB will also have to clarify their perspective on the implications of measurement and recognition.

CURRENT ENTRY VALUES

Current entry price is also called replacement cost or reproduction cost.

The valuation of assets and liabilities at current entry prices gives rise to *holding gains* and *losses* as entry prices change during the period of time when they are held or owed by a firm. Holding gains and losses may be divided into two elements: 1. The realized holding gains and losses that correspond to the items sold or the liabilities discharged; and 2. The non-realized holding gains and losses that correspond to the items still held or the liabilities owed at the end of the reporting period.

(Belkaoui, 2004: 489)

ACTIVITY 6.1

Consider the investment of €2487 in a single asset firm on 1 January 20X1 used in the previous chapter. The firm has no liabilities. The investment is expected to generate net cash receipts on 31 December each year of €1000 for three years and will have no residual value at the end of the three years. On 1 January 20X2 the replacement cost of the asset increases to £2550 and on 1 January 20X3 it increases to £2580.

Required:

Calculate the income and capital on a replacement cost basis for the years 20X1, 20X2 and 20X3.

Activity feedback

TABLE 6.1   Replacement cost based accounting income and capital

Income statements	year ended 31/12/X1	year ended 31/12/X2	year ended 31/12/X3	Total
	€	€	€	€
Operating income before depreciation	1 000	1 000	1 000	3 000
Less: Depreciation expense (a)	(829)	(871)	(880)	(2 580)
Profit or (loss)	171	129	120	420

Balance sheets	At 1/1/20X1	At 31/12/20X1	At 31/12/20X2	At 31/12/20X3	
	€	€	€	€	
Asset at cost	2 487	2 487	2 550	2 580	
Less: Accumulated depreciation (c)	—	(829)	(1 700)	(2 580)	
Asset at NBV		1 658	850	—	
Cash	—	1 000	2 000	3 000	
Total assets	2 487	2 658	2 850	3 000	
Opening equity capital	2 487	2 487	2 658	2 850	
Revaluation reserve (b)	—	—	63	30	93
Profit	—	171	129	120	420
Closing equity capital	2 487	2 658	2 850	3 000	513

ACTIVITY 6.1 (Continued)

(a) Depreciation expense for 20X1:
€2487 x ⅓ = €829
Depreciation expense for 20X2:
€2550 x ⅓ = €850 + (€63 x ⅓ = €21) = €871
Depreciation expense for 20X3:
€2850 x ⅓ = €860 + (€30 x ⅔ = €20) = €880

(b) Revaluation in 20X2: Depreciation expense
for 20X1:
€2550 − €2487 = €63
Revaluation in 20X3:
Depreciation expense for 20X2: €2580 − €2550 = €30

(c) Accumulated depreciation for 20X1: €2487 x 1/3 = €829
Accumulated depreciation for 20X2:
€829 + €850 + €21 = €1700
Accumulated depreciation for 20X3:
€1700 + €860 + €20 = €2580

The replacement cost based accounting profit shown in Table 6.1 using the transactions approach gives a profit of €171 in 20X1, a profit of €129 in 20X2 and a profit of €120 in 20X3, which makes a total profit of €420 over the three years.

b) Profit or loss for each year using the valuation approach

Valuation approach	year ended 31/12/20X1	year ended 31/12/20X2	year ended 31/12/20X3	Total
	€	€	€	€
Net assets at 31 December	2 658	2 850	3 000	8 508
Net assets at time 1 January	(2 487)	(2 658)	(2 850)	(7 995)
Profit	171	192	150	513

The replacement cost (current entry values) based accounting profit using the valuation approach for 20X1 is €171, for 20X2 it is a profit of €192 and for 20X3 it is a profit of €150, which makes a total profit of €513 over the three years. On an all-inclusive basis, the revaluation reserve is added back in transactions-based profit or loss, which gives the same result as the valuation approach. Usually, the revaluation reserve is non-distributable as dividends. Hence, the net result is the same.

However, in our example, the revaluation applied to a non-current asset. When revaluation is applied to a current asset, such as inventory, the revaluation amount goes straight to profit or loss irrespective of whether or not the revaluation increase or decrease has been realized, so there will not be a revaluation reserve.

Furthermore, in the example the asset and the business last only three years, in which case it probably does not make much sense to use the replacement cost basis anyway, as you can not assume that the entity is a going concern.

Finally, if you use replacement cost valuation, do you use the cost of replacing the asset by purchasing the same asset brand new? Or do you use the cost of replacing the asset in its used state? What if the asset is unique and cannot be replaced, either new or used?

CURRENT EXIT VALUES

Current exit price:

> [r]epresents the amount of cash for which an asset might be sold or a liability might be refinanced. The current exit price is generally agreed to correspond (1) to the selling price under conditions of orderly rather than forced liquidation, and (2) to the selling price at the time of measurement.
>
> (Belkaoui, 2004: 496)

Current exit price is also called 'net realizable value' if it means the amount of cash for which an asset might be sold less the cost of selling the asset.

ACTIVITY 6.2

Consider the investment of €2487 in a single asset firm on 1 January 20X1 used in the previous activity. The firm has no liabilities. The investment is expected to generate net cash receipts on 31 December each year of €1000 for three years. At the end of Year 20X1 the net realizable value of the asset is estimated at £1600, at the end of Year 20X2 its net realizable value is estimated at £800, and at the end of Year 20X3 the value of the asset is zero.

Required:

Calculate the income and capital on a net realizable values basis for the years 20X1, 20X2 and 20X3.

Activity feedback

TABLE 6.2   Net realizable value based accounting income and capital

Income statements	year ended 31/12/X1	year ended 31/12/X2	year ended 31/12/X3	Total
	€	€	€	€
Operating income before depreciation	1 000	1 000	1 000	3 000
Less: Depreciation (a)	(887)	(800)	(800)	(2 487)
Profit or loss	113	200	200	513

Balance sheets	At 1/1/20X1	At 31/12/20X1	At 31/12/20X2	At 31/12/20X3
	€	€	€	€
Asset at NBV	2 487	1 600	800	—
Cash	—	1 000	2 000	3 000
Total assets	2 487	2 600	2 800	3 000
Opening capital	2 487	2 487	2 600	2 800
Profit or loss	—	113	200	200
Closing capital	2 487	2 600	2 800	3 000

Depreciation expense for 20X1: €2487 – €1600 = €887
Depreciation expense for 20X2: €1600 – €800 = €800
Depreciation expense for 20X3: €800 – 0 = €800
   In Table 6.2, the depreciation expense for each year is simply the difference between the net realizable value of the asset at the start of the year and the net realizable value of the asset at the end of the year. As you can see below, the total profit of €513 over the three years remains the same as under the cash, historical cost, replacement cost (valuations approach) and net realizable value accounting models. Because the entity in our scenario has a life of only three years, it is possible to see this and also see how the measurement methods differ in terms of the profit or loss resulting for each year. However, a going concern presumably has a long life, so the total profits over the life of the entity will not normally be observable.

	year ended 31/12/20X1	year ended 31/12/20X2	year ended 31/12/20X3	Total
	€	€	€	€
Cash profit or loss	(1 487)	1 000	1 000	513
Historical cost based profit	171	171	171	513
Fisher's ideal economic income	249	174	91	513
Replacement cost based profit (t)	171	129	120	*420
Replacement cost based profit (v)	171	192	150	513
Net realizable value based profit	113	200	200	513

Notes: (t) = transactions approach; (v) = valuation approach

* €513 if profit €420 + revaluation reserve €93.

COMPARING CURRENT ENTRY VALUES AND CURRENT EXIT VALUES

By comparing the replacement cost and the net realizable value approaches, it is clear that they each serve a different purpose and are based on a different set of assumptions.

ACTIVITY 6.3

Compare the current entry values accounting model with the current exit values accounting model in terms of purpose, information value, capital maintenance assumptions and the objectivity of measurement.

Activity feedback (see Table 6.3)

TABLE 6.3 Comparison of current entry values model and current exit values model

	Current entry values model	Current exit values model
Purpose	Seeks to evaluate operational business decisions under a going concern assumption	Seeks to answer the question of whether to continue the investment or to invest in an alternative asset/ venture
Information value	Splits total profit into operating profit and gains from revaluation. This enables evaluation of earlier decisions	Follows the opportunity cost principle and reveals the money sacrifice made by keeping an asset. Permits rational decision making on the alternative uses of resources
Capital maintenance	By permitting gains and losses from revaluation to be excluded from reported profit or loss, it aims for the maintenance of the current operating capacity as a going concern	By including holding gains and losses to be included in reported profit or loss, it aims for financial (nominal) capital maintenance
Objectivity of measurement	Replacement cost requires subjective decisions about the unit of measurement (what item or combination of items is to be replaced?) Replace at new value or second-hand value? What are the characteristics of the entry market price observed, identified or estimated?	Net realizable value requires subjective decisions about the unit of measurement (what item or combination of items is to be sold?) What are the characteristics of the exit market price observed, identified or estimated?

MIXED MEASUREMENT MODELS

Mixed measurement models, or mixed attributes models as the IASB calls them, come in different varieties. For example, it is common for companies that broadly follow historical cost accounting principles to use the lower of cost or market value for their inventory, or to revalue some of their fixed assets at intervals. This may well lead to the provision of more useful information as regards particular resources. A current or recent valuation of land or a factory is surely more useful than a 50-year-old cost figure. But, it potentially also increases the inconsistencies within the financial statements as a whole. Here we will discuss deprival value (also called value to the business) as an example of mixed values measurement.

Deprival value or value to the business

The concept of deprival value (DV) (or value to the business) is a systematic approach to the idea of using different valuation bases for different assets – or more accurately, for using different current value measurement bases for assets in different circumstances. Deprival value has a clearly definable concept of capital maintenance. Profit is here being regarded as the excess after maintaining the value to the business of its assets. The value to the business is clearly seen to be related to actual operations (what the business would do). Following on from this, we can say that deprival value seeks to maintain the business's capacity to do things, usually expressed as the *current operating capacity or operating capability*. How does deprival value seek to do this? The following activity will illustrate the thinking behind the concept.

ACTIVITY 6.4

Six people, A to F, are possessors and owners of six assets, U to Z, respectively. The various monetary evaluations (in €) of each asset by its owner are shown in the following table.

Person	Asset	HC	RC	NRV	EV
A	U	1	2	3	4
B	V	5	6	8	7
C	W	9	12	10	11
D	X	16	15	14	13
E	Y	17	19	20	18
F	Z	23	22	21	24

All six people signed a contract with an insurance agent, Miss Prue Dential, under which they shall be reimbursed, in the event of loss of their assets, by 'the amount of money a rationally acting person will actually have lost as a result of losing the asset'. Put yourself in the position of the rationally acting person, decide what action you would take in each circumstance and then calculate the net effect on your monetary position.

Activity feedback

In each situation, the first question to ask is: would the rationally acting entrepreneur replace the asset or not? They will replace it if the proceeds of either selling it (NRV) or using it (economic value (EV)) are higher than the costs of replacing it. If it is going to be replaced, then the loss suffered is clearly the cost of replacement. Thus, in situations where the rationally acting entrepreneur would replace the asset, DV is RC. If they do not replace it, the loss suffered is given by the value of the benefits that would have derived from the asset but which they will now never receive. Being rational, the intention must

have been to act so as to derive the highest possible return, i.e. the higher of NRV and EV. Therefore, in situations where the rationally acting entrepreneur would not replace the asset if deprived of it, deprival value is the higher of NRV and EV. This last element – the higher of NRV and EV – is known as the 'recoverable amount'.

So we can formally state that deprival value is the lower of RC and recoverable amount, where recoverable amount is the higher of NRV and EV (see Figure 6.1). Given three different concepts (RC, NRV and EV), there are in fact only six possible different rankings:

EV	>	NRV	>	RC
NRV	>	EV	>	RC
RC	>	EV	>	NRV
RC	>	NRV	>	EV
NRV	>	RC	>	EV
EV	>	RC	>	NRV

The example contains all six of these alternatives. The DV in each situation is as follows:

Person	DV	Reason
A	2	Cost of replacement
B	6	Cost of replacement
C	11	EV not received
D	14	Realizable value not received
E	19	Cost of replacement
F	22	Cost of replacement

Make sure that you understand the reasons why, in the context of the logic of the DV definition (and notice the irrelevance of the HC figures).

ACTIVITY 6.4 (*Continued*)

Figure 6.1 Relationship between DV, RC, NRV and EV

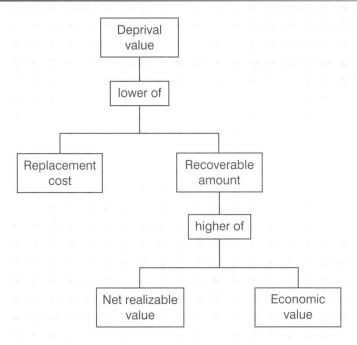

We saw earlier that in four of the six possible rankings, DV equals RC. In the practical business situation, the chances of RC being higher than both NRV and EV will generally be relatively small, so the other two rankings will in practice not occur frequently. This means that, in a practical business context, DV usually comes back to RC (Gee and Peasnell, 1976).

Theoretically, therefore, it can be suggested that DV reduces itself to RC when the economically logical action is to replace and use the more relevant benefit foregone figure in those situations where replacement would logically not occur. DV thinking positively explores the possibilities of refining RC thinking and shows that in most situations the refinements introduce difficulty and subjectivity for very little benefit in terms of extra relevance of information.

ACTIVITY 6.5

Is DV a separate concept, leading to a balance sheet consistently valued in deprival terms? Or is DV merely a formula for choosing which of the three (RC, NRV, EV) valuation bases to use in any particular situation?

Activity feedback

In the UK, many people think the former. Under the latter way of thinking, DV obviously leads to assets and liabilities recognized using a variety of measurement bases in the balance sheet and therefore to a lack of additivity.

The concept of fair value has become popular in recent years. It is certainly a form of current value, but its precise nature and meaning have been a matter of considerable controversy and indeed confusion. It is important enough, with IFRS 13 issued, to warrant a chapter by itself. We therefore defer consideration of fair value to Chapter 7. However, before moving on to fair value, we will first look at current purchasing power parity accounting as a way of dealing with inflation.

CURRENT PURCHASING POWER PARITY ACCOUNTING

Money has no intrinsic value. Its value is related to what we can buy with it, what we can do with it. When most prices are rising, we obtain gradually less and less with any given number of euros. This means that if under any particular valuation basis we have maintained our capital appropriately defined in terms of numbers of euros, we have not necessarily maintained our capital in terms of the purchasing power of those euros. *Current purchasing power* (CPP) accounting attempts to take account of this.

It is vital to understand that current purchasing power is a general purchasing power concept. We are concerned with general inflation, usually expressed as the average rise in the cost of living. If inflation in the last year is 10 per cent, then €100 last year has the same general (i.e. average) purchasing power as €110 this year. This means that in order to know what we are talking about we have to 'date' all our euros. Euros at different dates can no longer be regarded as having the same purchasing power and, strictly speaking, cannot be used as a common measuring unit. In other words, they lack additivity. In order to return to the position of having a common measuring unit, which is essential for proper comparison, we have to convert euros of one date's purchasing power into euros of the other date's purchasing power.

ACTIVITY 6.6

Suppose that on 31 December 20X1 we have €200 in cash and on 31 December 20X2 we have €250 in cash. At face value, this means that we are better off by €50. Now suppose that on 31 December 20X1 the general inflation index stood at 300 and on 31 December the general inflation index stood at 330. How much better off are we in terms of our purchasing power?

Activity feedback

To answer this, we need to make a price-level adjustment to the opening balance of €200 in order to restate it to the equivalent of the value of €200 as at 31 December 20X2.

€200 x 330/300 = €200 x 1.1 = €220

So, we have an increase in 'real' wealth of 250 – €220 = €30.

One way of mitigating the obfuscating effects of inflation in the determination of profit of a reporting entity is to adjust the opening net assets (excluding monetary assets and liabilities) by applying a general price index such as a Retail Price Index (RPI). Note that the idea of CPP adjustments can be superimposed on any valuation basis. Having maintained the reporting entity's financial capital on a nominal basis ($Profit_1 = V_1 - V_0$) does not necessarily mean that the current purchasing power parity of the entity's capital has also been maintained. Similarly, having maintained the current operating capacity of the entity's physical capital ($Profit_1 = V_1 - V_0 - C$) does not necessarily mean that the current purchasing power parity of the entity's capital has also been maintained. In order to maintain the current purchasing power parity of the entity's opening capital, profit must be determined as: $Profit_1 = V_1 - V_0 - ((RPI_1 - RPI_0) / RPI_0) \times V_0$.

When considering CPP accounting, it is important to distinguish between monetary and non-monetary items. Monetary items are items fixed by contract, custom or statute in terms of numbers of euros, regardless of changes in the general price level and the purchasing power of the euros. Examples are cash, debtors and creditors and longer-term loans. Non-monetary items are all items that are not so fixed in terms of number of euros, for example land, buildings, plant, inventory and shares held as investments. With monetary items, when considering two sets of accounts at different dates, no *adjustment* to the euro figure reported is needed, but care must be taken in interpretation. However, when *comparing* two sets of accounts of the same business at different dates it is necessary to adjust all the contents of one balance sheet into the measuring unit (dated euro) of the other.

ACTIVITY 6.7

Mushroom Ltd was established on 1 January 20X4. Its opening balance sheet (on this date) was as follows:

	€
Land	6000
Equipment	4000
Inventory	2000
Equity	12000

During 20X4, the company made the following transactions:

(a) Purchased extra inventory €10000.

(b) Sold inventory for €11000 cash, which had an historical cost value of €9000.

(c) Closing inventory on 31 December 20X4 had an historical cost of €3000 and was bought when the RPI index was 115 (average).

(d) The equipment has an expected life of four years and nil residual value. The straight line method of depreciation is used.

(e) The general price index stood at:

- 100 on 1 January 20X4
- 110 on 30 June 20X4
- 120 on 31 December 20X4.

You should assume that purchases and receipts occur evenly throughout the year. There are no debtors or creditors.

Required:
Calculate the CPP profit for 20X4 and prepare the CPP balance sheet as at 31 December 20X4.

Activity feedback

		$€_{CPP}$	$€_{CPP}$
Sales	11000 × 120/110		12000
Opening inventory	2000 × 120/100	2400	
Add purchases	10000 × 120/110	10909	
		13309	
Less Closing inventory	(3000 × 120/115)	(3130)	
			(10179)
			1821
Less Depreciation			1200
			621
Loss on holding monetary assets (cash)*			(91)
CPP profit			530

*If cash accrues evenly over the year, the loss is
€ (1000 × 120/ 110) − €1000 = €91.

(*Continued*)

ACTIVITY 6.7   (*Continued*)

The historical cost profit (€11 000 – €9000 – €1000 for depreciation = €1000) and the CPP profit can be reconciled as follows:

	€	€$_{CPP}$	€
Sales	11 000	12 000	1 000
Purchases	10 000	10 909	(909)
Net difference			91

	€
Historical cost profit	1 000
Inventory	
Additional charge based on restating the cost of inventory at the beginning and end of the year in euros of current purchasing power, thus taking the inflationary element out of the profit on the sale of inventory. Opening inventory 400 – closing inventory 130 = 270	(270)
Depreciation	
Additional depreciation based on cost, measured in euros of current purchasing power of fixed assets €1200 – €1000	(200)
Monetary items	
Net loss in purchasing power resulting from the effects of inflation on the company's net monetary assets	(91)
Sales, purchases and all other costs*	
These are increased by the change in the index between the average date at which they occurred and the end of the year. This adjustment increases profit as sales exceed the costs included in this heading	91
CPP profit	530

The historical cost profit is based on:

Calculation of balance sheet items, and reconciliation of profit figure with balance sheet:

1 Value of equity, 1 January 20X4   €   12 000
Revalued in terms of €$_{CPP}$ at
31 December
20X4 (€12 000 × 120/100)   €$_{CPP}$ 14 400

2 Mushroom Ltd CPP balance sheet as at 31 December 20X4

		€$_{CPP}$	€$_{CPP}$
Land	6000 × 120/100		7 200
Equipment	4000 × 120/100	4 800	
Less Depreciation	1000 × 120/100	(1 200)	
			3 600
			10 800
Inventory	3000 × 120/115	3 130	
Cash	(11 000 – 10 000)	1 000	
			4 130
NET ASSETS			14 930
Financed by equity and reserves			14 930

CPP closing equity €$_{CPP}$ 14 930 – CPP opening
equity €$_{CPP}$ 14 400 = CPP profit €$_{CPP}$ 530   530

COMBINATION OF METHODS

As already stated, CPP thinking can be applied to any valuation basis, not just historical cost. It is often suggested that CPP adjustments could and indeed should be applied to RC calculations. It is important to remember that:

1 RC accounting deals with specific price rises only

2 CPP accounting deals with general price rises only

3 both types of change are in fact occurring at the same time.

Thus, to take the simplest of examples, if HC = 10 and a year later RC = 13, there is a holding gain of €3. But if the general price index has increased by 10 per cent, then (10 × 110/ 100) = €1 of that holding gain of 3 (closing date) euros is not 'real' because it cannot be translated into increased purchasing power. The 'real' holding gain is arguably only 2 (3 – 1) (closing date) euros. This combined approach is known as *stabilized accounting*.

It is most important when thinking about CPP accounting that you are fully aware of exactly what it is doing and what it is not doing. The crucial point is that it is not producing a current valuation of the term concerned in any sense. In general terms, what it is doing is re-expressing in terms of current euros the figures as originally calculated under the original measurement basis, whatever that was. It does not alter the basis of valuation. It alters the measuring unit which is being applied to the original basis of valuation.

ACTIVITY 6.8

Prepare a list, in point form, of advantages and disadvantages which you think could reasonably be said to apply to current purchasing power accounting.

Activity feedback

Advantages

1 All necessary figures are stated or restated in terms of a common measuring unit (CPP units). This facilitates proper comparison.

2 It distinguishes between gains or losses on monetary liabilities and assets, on the one hand, and 'real' gains or losses through trading activities, on the other.

3 It requires only a simple objective adjustment to HC accounts. Easily auditable.

Disadvantages

1 It is not clear what CPP units are. They are not the same as monetary units.

2 General purchasing power, by definition, has no direct relevance to any particular person or situation.

3 When CPP is applied to HC-based accounts, the resulting figures necessarily contain all the disadvantages of the original HC accounts.

4 It fails to give any sort of meaningful 'value' to balance sheet items although it gives the impression to non-accountants that it has done precisely that.

5 It is extremely difficult to understand and interpret.

SOME INTERNATIONAL PRACTICES AND TRADITIONS

No attempt is made here to replicate a full coverage either of national research traditions or of national practices. Readers wishing to investigate the story as it applies in their own country should look elsewhere. We merely present a brief sketch and overview.

A significant starting point is the publication of a French *ordinance* (law) in 1673 and an authorized (by Royal Decree) commentary on it published in 1675 by Jacques Savary. Savary argued that an annual inventory – which we would now call balance sheet – had two functions. The first function is to give an indication of the position of the business as a performing (and continuing) operation. This function logically requires that assets are measured on a cost basis if not yet sold. The second function is an indication of debt coverage, i.e. to give an indication of the risk of bankruptcy. This function logically requires that assets be measured on a net realizable value basis.

These two functions, and the resulting balance sheets, later became known as dynamic and static respectively. These are the terms used in the German tradition, developed to considerable sophistication by theorists in the early years of the twentieth century. Schmalenbach wrote *Dynamische Bilanz*, in several editions to 1926 (also available in English (1959)), which argues for a reporting system based on historical costs together with a general indexation adjustment. This is in contrast to Schmidt who, in various writings, supported the essentially static view (in the sense already described) that current values should be used, actually current entry (replacement cost) figures under his proposals.

The Dutch academic, Theodor Limperg, broadly followed and developed the Schmidt approach in the years to 1940 (e.g. see Mey, 1966). The essential argument is that replacement cost is the sacrificed value for production resources used. Distributable income is then logically defined as the difference between revenue and the value sacrificed in order to obtain that revenue, i.e. profit is revenue less replacement cost of consumption.

A connection into the English-speaking world was made through the publication by Sweeney of *Stabilized Accounting* (1936). Sweeney had access to the German literature and was strongly influenced by Schmidt. Sweeney went further, however, demonstrating in detail the feasibility of a full-scale combination of RC measurement in combination with general indication, i.e. RC and CPP at the same time. The 'resources sacrificed' approach, essentially an opportunity cost philosophy, can be traced to *The Valuation of Property* by Bonbright, published in the US in 1937. It was this book that provided the foundations for the development of the concept of DV, as already discussed.

Practice since the middle of the twentieth century bears little resemblance to the earlier research developments. The general middle European practical approach has been a strict adherence to historical costs. The same is true in the US, although perhaps more for reasons of objectivity (and fear of the power of lawyers) than for reasons of prudence. The UK and the Netherlands have adopted a more flexible approach, both in law and in practice. The large Dutch company, Philips, used a broadly Limpergian reporting system for several decades.

In the 1970s, the UK experimented with a compulsory supplementary *Current Purchasing Power System* (SSAP 7, 1974). Following the government-sponsored (and influenced) Sandilands Report (1975), an expanded (and excessively complicated) development of DV, known as *Current Cost Accounting* (SSAP 16, 1980) was required (without general indexation). Neither lasted very long. Moves along similar lines were made over this period in a number of other countries, including the US, which briefly introduced additional note disclosures using both specific and general adjustments. But the timing of these events strongly influenced the content and wording of the Fourth European Directive on the accounts of limited companies, published in 1978 and still very much with us today. This Directive allows a very wide variety of different approaches.

In terms of the future, general inflation adjustments are regularly employed in hyperinflationary economies, such as some South American countries and supported by the requirements in IAS 29, discussed in Chapter 22. Specific price change adjustments are not generally in fashion at present. But, as the trend in price rises tends to increase, then the debate is likely to return.

SUMMARY

In this chapter we have explored current entry values, current exit values and mixed values accounting, which were developed as ways of approaching the ideal of economic income. We have discussed current purchasing power parity accounting as a means to increase additivity and identify profit while maintaining the purchasing power parity of the entity's capital in times of inflation. Finally, we attempted to consider the meaning and usefulness of the resulting accounts and statements and to outline some practical developments.

EXERCISES

Suggested answers to exercises marked ✓ are to be found in the Student online resources, with suggested answers to the remaining questions available in the Instructor online resources.

✓**1** What do CPPP adjustments do and how are they calculated?

2 Are general indices more or less useful in financial reporting than specific price changes?

3 To what extent do current purchasing power adjustments to historical cost figures lead to up-to-date valuations in a balance sheet?

4 Current purchasing power adjustments are simple to apply, but hard to explain and interpret. Discuss.

5 From the following historical cost accounts of Page plc, prepare a set of CPPP accounts for the year ended 31 December 20X8.

The movement on the RPI was as follows:

1 January year 20X5	180
1 January year 20X7	200
Average for year 20X7	210
31 October year 20X7	215
31 December year 20X7	220
Average for year 20X8	230
31 October year 20X8	235
31 December year 20X8	240

Balance sheet as at		*31.12.X8*		*31.12.X7*
		€000		*€000*
ASSETS				
Non-current assets				
Cost (purchased 1.1.X5)		500		500
Less: Depreciation		(400)		(300)
		100		200
Current assets				
Inventory (purchased 31.10.X8)	150		100	
Receivables	300		200	
Bank	350		150	
		800		450
Total assets		900		650
EQUITY AND LIABILITIES				
Equity				
Share capital	100		100	
Reserves	400		250	
		500		350
Liabilities				
Current liabilities		400		300
Total equity and liabilities		900		650

Continued

Profit and loss account for the year ended 31 December 20X8:

	€000	€000
Sales		1 850
Cost of goods sold		
Opening inventory	100	
Purchases	1 350	
	1 450	
Less Closing inventory	(150)	
		1 300
Gross profit		550
Expenses	300	
Depreciation	100	
		400
Net profit		150

Assume all sales, purchases and expenses accrue evenly throughout the year.

6 You are the management accountant of a manufacturing company where production is capital intensive, using machinery that is estimated to have a five-year life. The present machinery is now approximately three years old. While raw material inventories have a low turnover due to supply problems, finished goods are turned over rapidly and there is minimal work-in-progress at any one time. The technology incorporated in the means of production is thought to be stable.

In recent years, it has not been possible to increase the price of the company's outputs beyond the rate of general inflation without diminishing market share, due to keen competition in this sector. The company does not consider that it has cash flow problems. The company is all equity financed. Although a bank overdraft is a permanent feature of the balance sheet, this is primarily due to customers being given a 60-day credit period, while most suppliers are paid within 30 days. There is always a positive balance of short-term monetary assets.

In the previous financial year, net profit after taxation on a strict historical cost basis was considered very healthy, and the directors felt that they could prudently distribute a major portion of this by way of dividend. The directors are considering whether, and if so how, to reflect price-level changes in their financial statements. They are concerned that this would affect their profit figure and therefore the amount they could distribute as dividend.

The following price-level changes have been brought to the attention of the directors:

	Retail price index	Index for company's machinery	Raw materials inventory index
3 years previously	100	100	100
2 years previously	104	116	102
1 year previously	107	125	108
Present	112	140	120

You are required to prepare a report for your directors setting out in general terms how to explain to the shareholders the likely impact on the historical cost profit of possible methods of accounting for price-level changes.

(CIMA, adapted)

FAIR VALUES, VALUE IN USE AND FULFILMENT VALUE

7

OBJECTIVES After studying this chapter you should be able to:

- explain and contrast the current exit value concepts of fair value, value in use and fulfilment value

- describe and appraise the requirements of IFRS 13, *Fair Value Measurement*

- discuss the fair value measurement process and disclosure per IFRS 13

- discuss the arguments for and against the usage of fair value, value in use and fulfilment value

- articulate your own views on the various valuation methods considered.

INTRODUCTION

In Chapter 6 you learned about current entry values and current exit values. Here in Chapter 7 we will first look into the development of the concepts of fair value (FV), value in use and fulfilment value. The second section will consider IFRS 13, which is the IASB's Standard on FV measurement. In the third section, we will discuss the process for measuring current exit values such as FV, value in use and fulfilment value. The fourth section will outline disclosure requirements. The final section discusses some overall considerations in respect of valuation and income measurement.

WHAT ARE FV, VALUE IN USE AND FULFILMENT VALUE?

In the 2015 IASB Conceptual Framework ED, the IASB proposed three distinctions in order to classify measurement bases. The first is between historical values and current values. The second is between entry values and exit values. The third is between market values and entity-specific values. It is the latter distinction that indicates the difference between FV (a market value) and value in use and fulfilment value (entity-specific values). Table 7.1 shows these three distinctions.

TABLE 7.1 Three distinctions to classify accounting measurement bases

Historical values	Entry values	Current values	
		Exit values	
Historical cost	Replacement cost	Market values – gross from transaction costs	Entity-specific values
Amortized cost		Fair Value	Value in use (assets)
		1: Market price	Fulfilment value (liabilities)
		2: Mark to market	
		3: Mark to model	

Proponents of value in exchange hold that the current exit price of assets is relevant to investors and decision makers because this enables them to gauge the liquidation values of assets as 'severable means in the possession of an entity' (Chambers, 1966: 92) and evaluate alternative uses of the cash this would generate. Value in exchange also applies to liabilities, as an entity could decide to extinguish a particular liability and refinance in an alternative way on more favourable terms. FV is a value in exchange concept that chimes with the idea that the main purpose of financial reporting is to enable investors to evaluate current alternative investment options, including liquidation.

On the other hand, proponents of value in use maintain that assets that are held rather than sold must be worth more to the owner than their current exit price, otherwise the assets would be sold and the cash invested in an alternative asset or project. Value in use emphasizes the measurement of assets of a business entity as a going concern. Note here that value in use applies to assets. Fulfilment value is the same concept applied to liabilities.

Fair value

The notion of FV has a long and complicated history. It emerged gradually in a number of IASs from the early 1980s. However, without a clear definition, the term could be found rather earlier in the US. As a more clearly defined concept with a coherent theoretical basis, FV has grown up in a rather ad hoc way and it appears to be still crystallizing.

The IASB definition of FV was: 'the amount by which an asset could be exchanged, or a liability settled, between knowledgeable willing parties in an arm's length transaction'.

This definition was used in a number of specific Standards by both IASB and the FASB. The definition had the obvious characteristic of avoiding, or defining away, the problem of exactly what kind of concept and number is represented by FV. An exchange must by definition involve a buyer (to whom a market price or purchase cost represents an entry value) and a seller (to whom a market price or selling price represents an exit value). Because the IASB conceptualizes FV gross of transaction costs, it is necessarily the same number for both buyer and seller. Arguably it represents both an entry and an exit concept at the same time. It is certainly a current value, being updated for each reporting date.

In 2006 the FASB, issued a new Standard, then numbered FAS 157, with a new and different definition, which changed FV to an explicitly exit value concept. Eventually, the IASB accepted this new definition and issued IFRS 13, a completely new Standard relating to the definition of FV as an exit value and its operationalization. Try the following activity to put the general idea of FV into context.

ACTIVITY 7.1

S takes a product to market, incurring transaction costs of €2 and exchanges it with B, in an arm's length (i.e. independent) transaction at an agreed exchange price of €30. B takes the product to his own entity, incurring transaction costs of €3. Calculate each of the following within the limits of the given data:

(a) S's selling price
(b) S's net realizable value (NRV)
(c) B's buying price
(d) B's historical cost
(e) B's current replacement cost
(f) FV to S before the sale
(g) FV to B after the sale.

Activity feedback
Answers would seem to be as follows:

(a)	S's selling price	€30
(b)	S's NRV	€28
(c)	B's buying price	€30
(d)	B's historical cost	€33
(e)	B's current replacement cost	€33
(f)	FV to S before sale	€30
(g)	FV to B after purchase	€30

A number of points emerge: (a) and (c) are necessarily equal, (f) and (g) are necessarily equal at least instantaneously before and after the transaction. Further, (a), (c), (f) and (g) are all necessarily equal. Third, (b) < (c) < (e), i.e. in the general case where disposal and acquisition costs are not nil:

NRV < Fair value < CRG

Value in use and fulfilment value

The 2015 IASB Conceptual Framework ED makes it clear that value in use and fulfilment value are entity-specific values. Value in use is the present value of the cash flows that the entity expects to derive from the continuing use of an asset and from its ultimate disposal. Fulfilment value is the present value of the cash flows that an entity expects to incur as it fulfils a liability (IASB, 2015, para. 6.34). Value in use and fulfilment value are defined inclusive of the present value of transaction costs. Value in use is defined inclusive of the present value of the transaction costs that the entity expects to incur on the ultimate disposal of the asset (IASB, 2015, para. 6.37). Fulfilment value is defined inclusive of the present value of any transaction costs that the entity expects to incur in undertaking transactions that enable the entity to fulfil the liability (IASB, 2015, para. 6.38).

According to the IASB, value in use is useful in predicting the prospects for future cash flows related to the continued use of an asset, and fulfilment value is useful for estimating future cash flows related to the fulfilment of a liability (IASB, 2015, paras 6.40 and 6.41). Furthermore, the updated estimates of value in use and fulfilment value have confirmatory value because they provide feedback about previous estimates (IASB, 2015, para. 6.42).

As with all cash flow based measurement/estimation techniques, the estimation process can be costly and the inputs to the process are likely to be subjective. Both the inputs and the process may be difficult to verify independently (IASB, 2015, para. 6.43). Hence, this may present a challenge to auditors. Furthermore, it may reduce the comparability of financial statements between firms. A further challenge occurs when an asset is used in combination with other assets. For these reasons, value in use may not be practical for periodic re-measurement of assets. However, it may be suitable for occasional re-measurement, such as in the case of impairment testing (IASB, 2015, para. 6.45).

IFRS 13, FAIR VALUE MEASUREMENT

IFRS 13, *Fair Value Measurement*, issued in May 2011 and updated in 2013, does not impose fair value (FV) measurement as a requirement. Instead, it:

(a) defines FV

(b) sets out:
- a framework for measuring FV, including the 'fair value hierarchy'
- requirements for disclosures when FV measurement is used.

In other words, it specifies *how* an entity should measure FV and disclose information about FV measurement, but not *when* FV measurement should be used. When it should or may be used is a matter for individual standards, as discussed extensively in Parts Two and Three of this book.

In IFRS 13, the IASB defines FV as: 'the price that would be received to sell an asset or paid to transfer a liability in an orderly transaction between market participants at the measurement date' (IFRS 13, para. 9). Hence, like the FASB, the IASB regards FV as a market-based exit price established in an orderly transaction.

The objective of FV measurement under IFRS 13 is to estimate an exit price for an asset or a liability from the standpoint of a market participant holding the asset or owing the liability. The estimation assumes an orderly transaction to sell the asset or transfer the liability at the measurement date (IFRS 13, para. 2). Ideally, the price of an asset or liability would be observable in the market. However, if this is not the case, the valuation technique used to estimate FV must, as much as possible, be based on observable inputs and market assumptions (IFRS 13, para. 3). As well as being applied to assets and liabilities, IFRS 13 is to be applied to an entity's own equity instruments (IFRS 13, para. 4).

IFRS 13 applies, in both initial and subsequent measurement, when another IFRS requires or permits FV measurements or requires disclosures about such measurements
or measurements based on FV, with the following exceptions:

1 share-based payment transactions within the scope of IFRS 2, *Share-based
Payments* (see Chapter 21)

2 leasing transactions within the scope of IAS 27, *Leases* (see Chapter 15)

3 measurements that have some similarities to FV but are not FV, such as NRV in
IAS 2, *Inventories* or value in use in IAS 36, *Impairment of Assets* (see Chapters
16 and 14).

Further, the disclosure requirements of IFRS 13 do not apply to:

4 plan assets measured at FV in accordance with IAS 19, *Employee Benefits* (see
Chapter 21)

5 retirement benefit plan investments measured at FV in accordance with IAS 26,
Accounting and Reporting by Retirement Benefit Plans (see Chapter 21)

6 assets for which the recoverable amount is FV less costs of disposal in accordance
with IAS 36 (see Chapter 14).

On the other hand, the measurement requirements (and the disclosure requirements)
apply when FV measurements are disclosed by an entity even if they are not used
in the entity's financial statements, for example being disclosed only in the notes
(IFRS 13, paras 5–8).

FV measurement applies to a particular asset or liability (or a particular interest in
an entity's own equity instruments, e.g. an equity interest issued or transferred in a
business combination). Depending on its unit of account, an asset or liability measured at FV may be either:

• a stand-alone asset or liability such as a financial instrument

• a group of assets or a group of liabilities, which function together

• a group of assets and liabilities which necessarily function together, such as a
business or a cash-generating unit (IFRS 13, para. 13).

The unit of account is determined based on the IFRS in accordance with which the
FV measurement is being applied, except where otherwise stated in IFRS 13.

IFRS 13 can apply to individual assets and liabilities or a group of assets, a group of
liabilities or a group of assets and liabilities (e.g. a cash-generating unit or a business)
(IFRS 13, para. 13). As noted above, an FV measurement assumes that the asset or
liability is exchanged in an orderly transaction between market participants at the
measurement date under current market conditions (IFRS 13, para. 15).

APPLYING IFRS 13

As noted above, an FV measurement assumes that the asset or liability is exchanged
in an orderly transaction between market participants to sell the asset or transfer the
liability at the measurement date under current market conditions (IFRS 13, para.
15). The transaction must take place in the principal market for the asset or liability
or, if there is no principal market, in the most advantageous market for the asset or
liability (IFRS 13, para. 16). The reporting entity must have access to the market in

question, i.e. the practical ability to trade in the market, at the measurement date. The FV measurement represents the price in that market, whether it is directly observable or estimated using another valuation technique.

IFRS 13 states that FV must be estimated using market assumptions regarding the asset or liability, its principal or most advantageous market, and the market participants. Specifically, market participants are assumed to act in their economic best interests (IFRS 13, paras 22–23). FV must be estimated gross of transaction costs because they are not a characteristic of the asset or liability (IFRS 13, para. 25). On the other hand, IFRS 13 states that location can be a characteristic of the asset or liability, in which case the transaction price must be adjusted for the transportation costs (IFRS 13, para. 26).

ACTIVITY 7.2

Does the distinction between transaction costs and transport costs make sense?

Activity feedback

We find it hard to be positive here! The origin of the distinction seems to be the determination to maintain the position that FV is defined in relation to a market and not in relation to an entity. Cows live in fields or barns owned by particular farmers/entities, but are sold in (physical) markets, so their location has to be changed (hence requiring transport costs) before they can be considered as market-related. The commission to the auctioneer is integral to the market, not to the farmer, and presumably is part of transaction costs since it is related to the market and not to the entity itself.

But, we have difficulty with all this. If you wish to sell a cow, or you do sell a cow, there is a selling price. But in order to sell, you have to both transport the cow, and pay the auctioneer. Gross selling (or exchange) price has a clear economic meaning. NRV has a clear economic meaning. FV, as defined and applied here, is in the general case in between. What precisely is its economic meaning or message? To whom and for what is it useful? We find these questions difficult to answer.

Applying IFRS 13 to non-financial assets

Apart from the IFRSs dealing with financial assets and liabilities, several IFRSs require or permit measurement at FV for non-financial assets. These include IAS 16, *Property, Plant and Equipment* (see Chapter 12), IAS 38, *Intangible Assets* (see Chapter 13), IAS 40, *Investment Property* (see Chapter 13) and IAS 41, *Agriculture: Bearer Plants* (see CourseMate) and a number of IFRICs.

IFRS 13, para. 27 stipulates that FV measurement of a non-financial asset take into account a market participant's ability to generate economic benefits by using the asset in its 'highest and best use' (HBU) or by selling it to another market participant that would do so. HBU is a valuation concept used to value many non-financial assets such as real estate. The concept is not relevant to items other than non-financial assets, since they do not have an alternative use without being changed and therefore ceasing to be the same asset or liability.

The HBU of a non-financial asset must be physically possible, financially feasible and legally permissible. Financial feasibility takes into account whether a physically possible and legally permissible use would generate adequate income or cash flows to produce an investment return that market participants would require, and any costs of converting the asset to that use.

The HBU is determined from the perspective of market participants, even if the reporting entity has a different use in mind. Nevertheless, the entity's current use of a non-financial asset is presumed to be its HBU unless market or other considerations suggest otherwise (e.g. in the case of an intangible asset that the entity plans to use defensively so as to prevent others from using it).

The HBU establishes the valuation premise used to measure FV for a non-financial asset which might be used in combination with other assets as a group, or with other assets and liabilities as a business or business unit, as follows:

- If the HBU is the use of the asset in combination with a group of other assets or other assets and liabilities, the FV of the asset is the price that would be received in a current transaction to sell the asset assuming that it would be used with that group of other assets or assets and liabilities (its complementary assets and any associated liabilities) and that these would be available to market participants.

- Associated liabilities for this purpose include those that fund working capital, but not those that fund assets other than those within the group of complementary assets.

- Assumptions about the HBU must be consistent for all the assets included in the group of complementary assets for which HBU is relevant.

- The HBU might provide maximum value to market participants when the asset is used on a stand-alone basis. In that case, the FV of the asset is the price that would be received on the assumption that the buyer would use it on a stand-alone basis.

Applying IFRS 13 to liabilities or an entity's own equity instruments

An FV measurement of a financial or non-financial liability or an entity's own equity instrument (e.g. as issued as consideration in a business combination) assumes that:

- The instrument is transferred to a market participant at the measurement date.

- A liability would remain outstanding and the transferee would be required to fulfil the obligation, which would not be settled with the counterparty or otherwise extinguished on the measurement date.

- An entity's own equity instrument would remain outstanding and the transferee would take on the rights and responsibilities associated with the instrument, which would not be cancelled or otherwise extinguished at the measurement date (IFRS 13, para. 34).

Even when there is no observable market to provide pricing information about such a transfer (for example, because transfer is prevented by contractual or other legal restrictions), if such items are held by other parties as assets this may result in an observable market. In all cases, to meet the objective of FV measurement, which remember is to estimate the price at which an orderly transaction to transfer the item would take place between market participants under current market conditions at the measurement date, an entity maximizes the use of relevant observable inputs and minimizes the use of unobservable inputs.

When a quoted price is not available and an identical item is held by another party as an asset, the FV is measured from the perspective of a market participant that holds the item as an asset at the measurement date (IFRS 13, para. 37).

When a quoted price is not available, and an identical item is not held by another party as an asset, the FV of the item is measured using a valuation technique from the perspective of a market participant that owes the liability or has issued the equity instrument (IFRS 13, para. 40) taking account of the FV hierarchy (see below).

The FV of a liability reflects the effect of the risk that the entity that owes it may not fulfil that obligation, i.e. non-performance risk (IFRS 13, para. 42). Non-performance risk includes, but is not limited to, the entity's own credit risk. Hence, when measuring the FV of a liability, an entity takes into account the effects of its own credit risk as well as other factors that may affect the likelihood that the obligation will be fulfilled. Non-performance risk related to a liability is assumed to be the same before and after the transfer of the liability, for various reasons:

- A market participant taking on the obligation would not enter into a transaction that changed the non-performance risk associated with it without reflecting that change in the price.

- Creditors would not knowingly agree to a transfer to a transferee with a lower credit standing.

- When pricing those assets, those who might hold the liability as an asset would consider the effects of the entity's own credit risk as well as other factors that may affect the likelihood that the obligation will be fulfilled.

THE MEASUREMENT PROCESS

When an asset is acquired or a liability is assumed in an exchange transaction, the transaction price is an *entry* price, whereas FV is defined as an *exit* price. Nevertheless, in many cases, the transaction price will be equal to FV. When this is not the case, the difference (gain or loss) between FV and the transaction price is recognized in profit or loss for the period unless the applicable IFRS specifies otherwise (IFRS 13, para. 60). Reasons why transaction price is not always the same as FV include:

- The transaction is between related parties, although the transaction price may be used as an input where the entity has evidence that the transaction was entered into at market terms.

- The transaction takes place under duress or in a forced sale (e.g. in financial distress of the seller).

- There is a difference in the units of account between the buyer and the seller, for example in a business combination where the transaction includes unstated rights and privileges that are to be measured separately or the transaction price includes transactions costs.

- The market in which the transaction takes place is not the principal or most advantageous market. This might be the case if the entity is a dealer that enters into transactions in the retail market, whereas the principal or most advantageous market is with other dealers in the wholesale market.

The objective of using a valuation technique is to *estimate* the price at which an orderly transaction to sell the asset or transfer the liability takes place between market participants at the measurement date under current market conditions. Valuation techniques that are used should maximize the use of observable inputs and minimize the use of unobservable inputs. They include the market approach (a current transaction price), the cost approach (a historical cost) and the income approach (a present value calculation), all of which have been discussed in previous chapters. If a transaction price is used to measure FV on initial recognition, and a valuation technique that uses unobservable inputs is used to measure FV in subsequent periods, the valuation technique needs to be calibrated so that if applied at initial recognition it would result in the transaction price.

The FV hierarchy was originally included in IFRS 7, but has now been transferred to IFRS 13 (i.e. IFRS 13, paras 72–90). It classifies the inputs to valuation techniques used to measure FV into three levels. The FV hierarchy prioritizes inputs to valuation techniques, not the techniques themselves. Where a combination of inputs from different levels is used, the combined input is classified at the level of the lowest of the inputs. For example, if an observable input requires an adjustment using an unobservable input and the resulting adjustment is of a significant amount, then the resulting measurement is a Level 3 measurement. Hence, the FV hierarchy is also applied to FV measurements based on the lowest level of the inputs used in a particular FV measurement. This then leads to disclosure requirements which are somewhat more onerous for Level 2 measurements than for those at Level 1, and substantially more onerous for Level 3 measurements. The formal definitions are as follows:

(a) Level 1 inputs are unadjusted quoted prices in active markets for identical assets or liabilities that the entity can access at the measurement date. These prices typically provide the most reliable indication of FV and should be used to measure FV whenever available.

(b) Level 2 inputs are all inputs other than quoted prices included in Level 1 that are observable, either directly or indirectly, for the asset or liability, such as quoted prices for similar assets in active markets, or in markets that are not active, or are not quoted prices but are valuation-relevant information such as interest rates and yield curves, credit spreads, etc., or are market-corroborated data derived from or corroborated by observable market data by correlation or other means. Such inputs are substantially less subjective than Level 3 inputs.

Adjustments to Level 2 inputs will vary depending on various factors including the following:

- The condition or location of the asset (for non-financial assets).
- The extent to which inputs relate to items that are comparable to the asset or liability. There may be differences in characteristics such as credit quality or the unit of account.
- The volume or level of activity in the markets within which the inputs are observed.

(c) Level 3 inputs are unobservable inputs to be used to measure FV (or in some cases to adjust Level 2 inputs) to the extent that relevant observable inputs are not available, which reflect the assumptions that market participants would use when pricing the asset or liability, including assumptions about risk. Such inputs might include the entity's own data. Nevertheless, as emphasized earlier, FV is not an entity-specific value, but a market-based value.

Assumptions about risk include the risk inherent in a particular valuation technique used to measure FV, such as a pricing model, and the risk inherent in the inputs to the valuation technique. A measurement that does not include an adjustment for risk would not be an FV measurement if market participants would include such an adjustment when pricing the asset or liability. For example, an adjustment might be called for when there is significant measurement uncertainty. This might be the case when there has been a significant decrease in the volume or level of activity when compared to normal market activity for the asset or liability (or similar assets or liabilities) and the entity has determined that a transaction or quoted price does not, as such, represent FV (for example, there might be transactions that are not orderly, such as forced or distressed sales).

Where a Level 3 input is used to adjust a Level 2 input and the adjustment is significant, the result is a Level 3 measurement.

DISCLOSURE

IFRS 13 requires the disclosure of information that helps users of its financial statements assess the fair values, valuation techniques and inputs used to develop the measurements as well as the impact of FV measurements on profit or loss or other comprehensive income for the period (IFRS 13, para. 91). The disclosures required by IFRS 13 are onerous, especially for FV measurements based on Level 3 inputs. This is intended to mitigate the acknowledged uncertainty and subjectivity of such measurements. Much information is required about the assumptions which underpin the actual measurement process. The detailed disclosure requirements can be found in the standard itself (IFRS 13, paras 91–99).

TOWARDS AN APPRAISAL OF FV, VALUE IN USE AND FULFILMENT VALUE

One of the major issues is the uncertainty of what FV (when marked to market or marked to model), value in use and fulfilment value actually imply in terms of real-life calculation and auditability. Assumptions with respect to inputs to the models such as future cash flows, cost of capital (rate of return, interest rate, or weighted average cost of capital), the models themselves and the process of estimation are all factors that contribute to present value based measurement being regarded as controversial.

Another issue associated with current values accounting in general is what to do with unrealized gains and losses. Do they go to profit and loss and then to retained earnings? Or do unrealized gains and losses bypass the income statement and go straight to equity (in a revaluation reserve)? Or should they not go to profit or loss, but rather go to other comprehensive income and in an accumulated other comprehensive income (revaluation) account in equity? Is this merely a matter of presentation? Or could there be cash flow and other economic consequences?

Both practically and conceptually, FV measurement is problematic insofar as it requires assumptions about 'an orderly transaction between market participants' in situations where there is in fact no active market. Among other things, these assumptions relate to prices, market characteristics, characteristics of market participants, assumed uses and accounting choices. The IASB has insisted that FV measurement is both feasible and meaningful in such circumstances. Its response is the 'Fair Value Hierarchy' of inputs into the FV measurement process. In this three-level hierarchy (passages in quotation marks below are from the text of IFRS 13):

1 The unproblematic Level 1 inputs are 'quoted prices in active markets for identical assets or liabilities that the entity can access at the measurement date'.

2 The Level 2 inputs are those which, while not being quoted prices as in Level 1, are observable, such as quoted prices for similar assets in active markets, or in markets that are not active, or are not quoted prices but are valuation-relevant information such as interest rates and yield curves, etc., or are market-corroborated data derived from or corroborated by observable market data by correlation or other means.

3 The Level 3 inputs are to be used in the absence of Level 1 or Level 2 inputs (or in some cases to adjust Level 2 inputs) and are unobservable inputs which are 'used to measure FV to the extent that relevant observable inputs are not available, ... [but which] reflect the assumptions that market participants would use when pricing the asset or liability, including assumptions about risk. [Such inputs] might include the entity's own data'. Nevertheless, the IASB insists that FV is not an entity-specific value such as net present value or net realizable value, but a market-based value.

It will be clear that it is FV measurement based on Level 3 inputs, which is particularly problematic. IFRS 13 seeks to mitigate this problem by means of disclosure. For both Level 2 and Level 3 inputs, where so-called 'marking to model' is involved, IFRS 13 requires a description of the valuation technique and the inputs used, while for Level 3 inputs assumptions about risk and much more extensive disclosures are required, including the sensitivity of the FV measurement to changes in unobservable inputs.

Particularly with regard to FV, there is political uncertainty regarding the future of, and desirability of, the use of fair values. It follows from the discussions on user needs in Chapter 1, and on international differences in Chapters 2 and 3, that those countries and traditions tending to take a common law economic focus are likely to be more receptive to fair values than those taking a code law legislation focus. It further follows within any given tradition, other things equal, that companies whose shares are actually traded are likely to be relatively favourable towards fair values, whereas companies where the only users in practice are creditors/bankers and taxation authorities are likely to be critical. The implications of these tensions and differences are nowhere near resolution among legal and regulatory authorities.

VALUATION AND INCOME MEASUREMENT: SOME OVERALL CONSIDERATIONS

We have spent a long time and many pages exploring a variety of bases for the evaluation of assets and liabilities and therefore for different measures of performance over time. In Chapter 5 we revised and developed the traditional historical cost model. This is backwards looking and relatively objective. We considered the thinking of important economists in this area, the ideal economic income of Fisher and the work of Hicks with its important capital maintenance implications. These economics-based ideas are properly forward looking and logically relevant to the decision-making process, but they are highly subjective. Current value accounting measurements lie in the middle of this spectrum, both in terms of their time relationship (in between past and future) and in terms of their degrees of objectivity/subjectivity. In this sense, they are clearly worth exploring as a compromise between relevance and verifiability.

There are stronger claims that can be made, however. The usual financial reporting statements essentially claim to report on the position at a (current) date and on the results ending on that date. Current values can properly claim to provide information consistent with this approach. The question follows, of course: 'Which current value should we use?' The discussions in this and previous chapters suggest that each of the suggested bases has particular merits. All provide useful information. All give good and relevant answers to some questions. One obvious suggestion to follow from this is that the preferable method in any situation depends on the particular situation itself – in other words, the abstract question: 'Which is the best method?' has no answer and indeed is simply a silly question. We should be prepared to use different valuation methods and different reporting methods for different purposes.

A second suggestion is an idea for you to take away and think about. The practice and application of double-entry channel us unthinkingly into the assumption that the balance sheet and the income statement are two elements in the same system and that they therefore have to be fully compatible with each other. But, our basic purpose is to produce meaningful reports, and there is no logical reason why they should be in any way constrained by data-recording systems. Perhaps we should consider producing smaller more ad hoc statements, using *combinations* of valuation bases depending on the purpose of each statement, or producing several different versions of a (loosely defined) income statement and a (loosely defined) statement of financial position, so that users can choose between them for their own particular purposes. Would the increased costs of preparation, and the increased complexity of published documents, be justified by the increased usefulness?

Here is an activity, deliberately in two major parts. We suggest you answer them quite independently of each other.

ACTIVITY 7.3

First, suggest, with reasons, which method (or methods) seems likely to produce the most useful measurement of performance (revenues and expenses and therefore income).

Second, suggest, with reasons, which method (or methods) seems likely to produce the most useful measurement of financial position (assets and liabilities and therefore equity).

If the answers are not compatible, consider the implications.

Activity feedback

In a sense, this is the ultimate accounting question. It can be approached in many different ways, and we make no attempt to suggest a definitive answer. It is in the end your own opinions that matter. The qualitative characteristics outlined in Chapter 1 could well point in different directions, depending on which characteristics are given more or less importance. But, we suggest that the best starting point is the users and their needs. One argument which we find persuasive is derived from the Hicks' emphasis on long-run repetitive performance, i.e. on the permanent maintenance of operating capability. This supports the removal of holding gains from the performance (earnings) measure, and therefore current replacement cost. This not only gives an important

indicator for management and for government economic and taxation policy, but also gives current and potential investors a meaningful approximation to long-run cash flows.

But, the resulting balance sheet numbers, for both carrying value of assets and for the reserves section of equity, are more difficult either to explain precisely or to defend in terms of usefulness. If there are no global investors to consider, i.e. the main or only likely users of the financial statements are groups such as banking lenders, tax authorities and lawyers, then some kind of meaningful estimate of asset valuations seems particularly relevant, perhaps either NRV or FV, logically an entity-specific figure being preferable. But, of course, these ideas taken together do indeed mean the usage of multiple bases, which are both relatively costly to prepare and relatively difficult to comprehend. Note also that our discussion takes no account at all of the issue of general inflation, of the decline in value over time of the currency measuring unit in terms of spending power, and the only reason for holding currency is for what it can be exchanged for in terms of further investment or for consumption.

As a general and perhaps evasive conclusion, user needs, and the relevant culture (whether national or international) are likely to significantly affect preferences and desirabilities.

SUMMARY

In this chapter, we have explored the concept of FV, value in use and ful-filment value. We have also discussed the definition, measurement and presentation of FV per IFRS 13. We have considered its characteristics and usefulness, noting that there are uncertainties both conceptually and in terms of practical usage and application. We have also briefly considered the overall 'set' of valuation methods explored so far. It would be good to consider this appraisal again after reading and working through the rest of this book!

EXERCISES

Suggested answers to exercises marked ✓ are to be found in the Student online resources, with suggested answers to the remaining questions available in the Instructor online resources.

✓**1**   What is 'fair value'? Is it a good idea?

2   Investors need an up-to-date forward-looking indication of annual performance, implying a focus on the income statement, and lenders need an up-to-date indication of asset values, implying a focus on the balance sheet. Discuss.

3   In the end, for most practical purposes, historical cost is best. Discuss.

4   Look at the consolidated financial statements of Philips for 2015. The note for financial instruments is on pages 118 and 119 (www.philips.com/corporate/resources/annualresults/2015/PhilipsFullAnnualReport2015_English.pdf, accessed 30 March 2016) and see how Philips has applied the rules of IFRS 13.

PRESENTATION AND DISCLOSURE IN PUBLISHED FINANCIAL STATEMENTS

8

OBJECTIVES After studying this chapter you should be able to:

- understand and explain the difference between presentation and disclosure

- discuss some fundamental conceptual issues concerning the presentation and disclosure of information in the financial statements and the notes

- describe and apply the format and disclosure requirements of IAS 1, *Presentation of Financial Statements*

- understand the requirements of IFRS 1, *First Time Adoption of IFRS* and IAS 8, *Accounting Policies, Changes to Accounting Estimates and Errors*

- describe the requirements of the 2013 Accounting Directive (Directive 2013/34/EU) which specifies simplifications for reporting by SMEs and micro-entities, introduces reporting on payments to governments and country-by-country reporting

- discuss the adequacy of the presentation and disclosure requirements of IAS 1 and the EU Directives and suggest and appraise possible alterations thereto.

INTRODUCTION

So far, we have mainly looked at financial accounting to the extent that it concerns the definition, recognition and measurement of the elements of financial statements. This chapter discusses the presentation and disclosure of financial statement information in accordance with IAS 1, *Presentation of Financial Statements*. It also discusses IAS 8, *Accounting Policies, Changes to Accounting Estimates and Errors* and IFRS 1, *First Time Adoption of IFRS*. In addition, this chapter considers the EU's 2013 Accounting Directive ('EU Directive 2013/34/EU on the annual financial statements, consolidated financial statements and related reports of certain types of undertakings') which consolidates, modernizes and updates the Fourth Company Law Directive (78/660/EEC) and the Seventh Company Law Directive (83/349/EEC).

IAS 1, PRESENTATION OF FINANCIAL STATEMENTS

IAS 1, *Presentation of Financial Statements* was originally issued by the IASC in 1997 and adopted by the IASB in 2001. It was revised in 2003 and has subsequently been amended in 2007, 2011 and 2014. It is the 2014 version that we discuss here. Other Standards have made minor consequential amendments to IAS 1. These include improvements to Standards made between 2009 and 2014. Most of these standards will be considered in detail in Parts Two and Three of this book. Remember that, as a full Standard, IAS 1 automatically takes priority over the IASB Conceptual Framework where there is any overlap or conflict.

IAS 1 prescribes the basis for presentation of general purpose financial statements in order to ensure comparability both with the entity's own financial statements of previous periods and with the financial statements of other entities. To achieve this objective, the Standard discusses the presentation of financial statements, and sets out guidelines for their structure and minimum requirements for the content of financial statements (para. 1). IAS 1 applies to all entities that prepare general purpose financial reports under IFRS, including consolidated financial statements. The other IASs and IFRSs set out the recognition, measurement and disclosure requirements for specific transactions and other recordable events (para. 3).

Broadly speaking, IAS 1 consists of two parts. Part 1 discusses a number of 'overall considerations' consisting of general principles, conventions and requirements. Much of Part 1 is a restatement of aspects of the Framework, as discussed already. Part 2 discusses in some detail the required contents of general purpose financial statements. It is worth noting that most national accounting standards operate, and are designed to operate, within the context of national legislation, especially for corporations. There is, of course, no single international company or corporation statute. To some extent, IAS 1 provides a minimal filling in of this lacuna.

FINANCIAL STATEMENTS UNDER IAS 1

There has been an increasing tendency over recent decades to prescribe not only the contents of published financial statements, but also the precise layout and format in which those contents must be presented. Former country traditions in this respect varied considerably, as Chapter 2 should have made you expect. Traditionally, the degree of precise specification in the UK and US was low, because the idea was that managers know best how to present the information that the users of their particular company's financial statements need. In countries at the other end of the spectrum, for example Japan, the formats of the financial statements, the notes to the financial statements and the supporting schedules to be submitted to the Ministry of Finance and the Tokyo Stock Exchange are standardized. The idea is that standardization makes information easier to find and compare.

Under IAS 1 (para. 10), a complete set of financial statements comprises:

- a statement of financial position as at the end of the period
- a statement of profit or loss and other comprehensive income for the period
- a statement of changes in equity for the period
- a statement of cash flows for the period
- notes, comprising significant accounting policies and other explanatory information
- a statement of financial position as at the beginning of the preceding period when an entity applies an accounting policy retrospectively or makes a retrospective restatement of items in its financial statements.

Below we will discuss the statement of financial position, the statement of profit or loss and other comprehensive income, the statement of changes in equity and the notes. The cash flow statement, the preparation of which is governed by the requirements in IAS 7, *Statement of Cash Flows*, will be discussed in detail in Part Two (see Chapter 23). We will also look at IAS 8, *Accounting Policies, Changes to Accounting Estimates and Errors* and IFRS 1, *First Time Adoption of IFRS*, which require the retroactive restatement of the statement of financial position as at the beginning of the preceding period.

Statement of financial position

It should be noted that IAS 1 does not prescribe any particular balance sheet format. The horizontal and vertical formats are equally acceptable. The descriptions used and the ordering of items may be amended according to the nature of the enterprise and its transactions, to provide information that is necessary for an overall understanding of the enterprise's financial position. For example, a financial institution amends the above descriptions in order to apply the more specific relevant requirements of financial institutions. Other amendments not prescribed by promulgated IFRSs may be necessary in other industrial or commercial situations.

Line items in the balance sheet As a minimum, the face of the statement of financial position (i.e. not the notes to the statement of financial position) should include separate line items that present the following amounts (para. 54):

1 Property, plant and equipment
2 Investment property
3 Intangible assets

  4 Financial assets (excluding amounts shown under 5, 8 and 9)

  5 Investments accounted for using the equity method

  6 Biological assets

  7 Inventories

  8 Trade and other receivables

  9 Cash and cash equivalents

  10 The total of assets classified as held for sale and assets included in disposal groups classified as held for sale in accordance with IFRS 5, *Non-Current Assets Held for Sale and Discontinued Operations*

  11 Trade and other payables

  12 Provisions

  13 Financial liabilities (excluding amounts shown under 11 and 12)

  14 Liabilities and assets for current tax, as defined in IAS 12, *Income Taxes*

  15 Deferred tax liabilities and deferred tax assets, as defined in IAS 12

  16 Liabilities included in disposal groups classified as held for sale in accordance with IFRS 5

  17 Non-controlling interests, presented within equity

  18 Issued capital and reserves attributable to owners of the parent.

Additional line items, headings and subtotals should be presented on the face of the balance sheet when their presentation is relevant to an understanding of the entity's financial position (para. 55). When an entity presents current and non-current assets and current and non-current liabilities as separate classifications on the face of its balance sheet, it must not classify deferred tax assets (liabilities) as current assets (liabilities) (para. 56). Amounts included in line items in relation to IFRS 5 should not also be included elsewhere.

The necessity or otherwise of additional line items is obviously a subjective matter. Judgement on this should be based on assessment of the nature and liquidity of assets; the function of assets within the entity; and the amounts, nature and timing of liabilities.

The current/non-current distinction IAS 1 (para. 60) requires the statement of financial position to present current and non-current assets and current and non-current liabilities as separate classifications. When an entity chooses not to make this analysis, assets and liabilities should still be presented broadly in order of their liquidity, although this alternative is only allowed when it would lead to information that is 'reliable and more relevant'.

Where, as is usually the case, the current/non-current classification is followed, then IAS 1 specifies the distinctions as now described. IAS 1 deals with assets first, by defining a current asset. An asset should be classified as a current asset when (para. 66):

  1 It expects to realize the asset, or intends to sell or consume it, in its normal operating cycle.

  2 It holds the asset primarily for the purpose of trading.

  3 It expects to realize the asset within 12 months after the reporting period.

  4 The asset is cash or a cash equivalent unless the asset is restricted from being exchanged or used to settle a liability for at least 12 months after the reporting period.

All other assets should be classified as non-current assets.

This definition of a current asset requires careful consideration. Only one of the conditions needs to be met for classification as a current asset to be required. Thus, an asset which meets condition 1 in a business with a two-year operating cycle, is a current asset, even if it is not expected to be realized within 12 months.

The classification of liabilities when undertaken by the reporting entity must follow a comparable distinction. A liability should be classified as current when it satisfies any of the following criteria (para. 69):

1 It is expected to be settled in the entity's normal operating cycle.

2 It is held primarily for the purpose of being traded.

3 It is due to be settled within 12 months after the balance sheet date.

4 The entity does not have an unconditional right to defer settlement of the liability for at least 12 months after the balance sheet date.

All other liabilities shall be classified as non-current.

Again, only one of these criteria needs to apply, so a long operating cycle could lead to the classification as current liabilities of items due to be settled in more than 12 months. The 'current' (i.e. due within 12 months) portion of non-current interest-bearing liabilities is to be classified as 'current' in most cases.

It is common for loan agreements to contain clauses such that, in the event of defined undertakings by the borrower not being satisfied (e.g. maintenance of an agreed maximum leverage ratio), the liability becomes payable on demand. If this happens, then the liability would in general immediately become 'current' under IAS 1. The liability would continue to be classified as non-current, however, if the lender has agreed, before the approval of the financial statements, not to demand payment within 12 months of the balance sheet date.

Further subclassifications IAS 1 (para. 59) states that the use of different measurement bases for different classes of assets suggests that their nature or function differs and, therefore, that they should be presented as separate line items. It gives as an example the carrying of certain classes of property, plant and equipment at cost, and other classes at revalued amounts, under IAS 16, *Property, Plant and Equipment* (see Chapter 12).

Further subclassifications of the line items should be presented either on the face of the balance sheet or in the notes, classified in a manner appropriate to the enterprise's operations (para. 77). The detail provided in subclassifications, either on the face of the balance sheet or in the notes, depends on the requirements of specific IFRSs and the size, nature and function of the amounts involved (para. 78). In some cases, other IFRSs provide requirements (subject always to the materiality consideration). Tangible assets, for example, are classified by class as required by IAS 16, *Property, Plant and Equipment* (see Chapter 12), and inventories are subclassified in accordance with IAS 2, *Inventories* (see Chapter 16). Other applications will be more subjective. For example, IAS 1 states that receivables are analyzed between amounts receivable from trade customers, receivables from related parties, prepayments and other amounts, and that provisions are analyzed showing separately provisions for employee benefit costs and any other items.

Equity Paragraph 79 requires extensive detailed disclosure regarding owner's equity. This must be provided on the face of the statement of financial position, or in the statement of changes in equity or in the notes, as follows (para. 79):

1 For each class of share capital:

  (a) the number of shares authorized

  (b) the number of shares issued and fully paid and issued but not fully paid

  (c) par value per share or that the shares have no par value

  (d) a reconciliation of the number of shares outstanding at the beginning and at the end of the period

  (e) the rights, preferences and restrictions attaching to that class, including restrictions on the distribution of dividends and the repayment of the capital

  (f) shares in the entity, held by the entity or by its subsidiaries or associates, and

  (g) shares reserved for issue under options and sales contracts, including the terms and amounts.

2 A description of the nature and purpose of each reserve within equity.

Entities without share capital are required to present equivalent information showing details and movements of each category of equity interest (para. 80).

Table 8.1 provides is an extract of the illustration of the statement of financial position provided by IAS 1. We omit the notes, which of course must be included in practice.

TABLE 8.1 Statement of financial position

XYZ Group – Statement of financial position as at 31 December 20X7

	20X7 €000	20X6 €000
ASSETS		
Non-current assets		
Property, plant and equipment	350 700	360 020
Goodwill	80 800	91 200
Other intangible assets	227 470	227 470
Investments in associates	100 150	110 770
Available-for-sale financial assets	142 500	156 000
	901 620	945 460
Current assets		
Inventories	135 230	132 500
Trade receivables	91 600	110 800
Other current assets	25 650	12 540
Cash and cash equivalents	312 400	322 900
	564 880	578 740
Total assets	1 466 500	1 524 200

TABLE 8.1   *(Continued)*

XYZ Group – Statement of financial position as at 31 December 20X7

EQUITY AND LIABILITIES

Equity attributable to owners of the parent

Share capital	650 000	600 000
Retained earnings	243 500	161 700
Other components of equity	10 200	21 200
	903 700	782 900
Non-controlling interests	70 050	48 600
Total equity	973 750	831 500
Non-current liabilities		
Long-term borrowings		160 000
Deferred tax	28 800	26 040
Long-term provisions	28 850	52 240
Total non-current liabilities	177 650	238 280
Current liabilities		
Trade and other payables	115 100	187 620
Short-term borrowings	150 000	200 000
Current portion of non-current borrowings	10 000	20 000
Current tax payable	35 000	42 000
Short-term provisions	5 000	4 800
Total current liabilities	315 100	454 420
Total liabilities	492 750	692 700
Total equity and liabilities	1 466 500	1 524 200

Source: Slightly adapted from 2016 Blue Book, Guidance on implementing IAS 1.

ACTIVITY 8.1

Having read what IAS 1 says about the statement of financial position and looked at an illustration, it is time to look at a real statement of financial positon. If there is a company whose statement of financial position, you are curious about, please go to the investor relations page on their website and search for the most recent annual financial statements. If you are unable to think of a company, you can look at the financial statements for Nestlé Group.

Does the company comply with IFRS? If so, is the balance sheet similar to the one outlined above? In what ways is it different?

Activity feedback

At the time of writing, the most recent balance sheet I could find for Nestlé Group was for 2014. Nestlé Group prepares its consolidated financial statements in accordance with IFRS and the requirements of Swiss law. Its balance sheet is very similar to the one in Table 8.1. However, there are a few interesting differences.

1 *Nestlé presents assets and liabilities in order of decreasing liquidity, whereas XYZ Group in Table 8.1 presents assets and liabilities in order of increasing liquidity.*

2 *Furthermore, Nestlé presents liabilities before equity whereas XYZ Group presents equity before liabilities.*

These differences reflect traditions in mainland Europe (such as Switzerland) versus traditions in Anglo-Saxon countries (such as the UK).

Statement(s) of financial performance

In Chapter 4, we discussed that the IASB does not distinguish between realized and unrealized changes in assets and liabilities for the recognition of items of income and expenses. Furthermore, we discussed that the IASB aims for the determination of financial performance on an all-inclusive or comprehensive income basis, using the assets-liabilities approach to the determination of income. As a consequence, the requirement to report comprehensive income, mandatory from 1 January 2009, caused major changes in the reporting of performance over the period (and the corresponding comparatives). In 2011, the IAS 1 requirements regarding presentation were amended again to further specify the separate disclosure of reclassification adjustments relating to the components of other comprehensive income.

Although the IASB preferred a single statement of comprehensive income, the comments to the Exposure Draft made it clear that many did not agree. 'They argued that there would be undue focus on the bottom line in the single statement' (BC 52). Hence, IAS 1 (para. 81A) requires that an entity shall present all items of income and expense recognized in a period:

- in a single 'statement of profit or loss and other comprehensive income' or
- in two statements: a separate 'statement of profit or loss' and a separate 'statement of other comprehensive income'.

The IASB does not prescribe the use of an income statement where the line items are classified by nature of expense or an income statement where the line items are classified by function of expense.

Combined statement of profit or loss and other comprehensive income IAS 1 para. 81A states that the statement of profit or loss and other comprehensive income shall present, in addition to the profit or loss and other comprehensive income sections:

- total profit or loss for the period
- total other comprehensive income for the period
- total comprehensive income for the period.

If an entity presents a separate statement of profit or loss, it must not present the profit or loss section in the statement presenting comprehensive income.

If an entity presents the information in one statement of profit or loss and other comprehensive income, the entity shall separately present allocations of profit or loss for the period and other comprehensive income for the period (para. 81B) as follows:

(a) Profit or loss for the period attributable to:
- non-controlling interests and
- owners of the parent.

(b) Comprehensive income for the period attributable to:
- non-controlling interests and
- owners of the parent.

If an entity presents profit or loss in a separate statement, it shall present (a) in that statement (para. 81B).

An entity shall recognize all items of income and expense in a period in profit or loss unless an IFRS requires or permits otherwise (para. 88). Some IFRSs specify circumstances where an entity recognizes particular items outside profit or loss in the current period. For example, IAS 8 specifies the correction of errors and the effect of changes in accounting policies (IAS 1, para. 89).

IAS 1 (para. 82) requires that in addition to items required by other IFRSs, the profit or loss section or the statement of profit or loss shall include line items that present the following amounts for the period:

- revenue
- finance costs
- share of the profit or loss of associates and joint ventures accounted for using the equity method
- tax expense
- a single amount for the total of discontinued operations (see IFRS 5).

An entity is required to present additional line items, headings and subtotals in the statement(s) presenting profit or loss and other comprehensive income, when such presentation is relevant to an understanding of the entity's financial performance (para. 85).

IAS 1 (para. 83) requires that the other comprehensive income section shall present line items for the amounts for the period of:

(a) items of other comprehensive income (excluding amounts in paragraph (b)), classified by nature and grouped into those that, in accordance with other IFRSs:
- will not be reclassified subsequently to profit or loss and
- will be reclassified subsequently to profit or loss when specific conditions are met.

(b) the share of the other comprehensive income of associates and joint ventures accounted for using the equity method, separated into the share of items that, in accordance with other IFRSs:
- will not be reclassified subsequently to profit or loss and
- will be reclassified subsequently to profit or loss when specific conditions are met.

Table 8.2 illustrates the statement of profit or loss and other comprehensive income whereby the line elements are classified by function of expenses.

TABLE 8.2   Income statement (illustrating the presentation of profit or loss and other comprehensive income in one statement and the classification of expenses within profit or loss by function)

XYZ Group – Statement of profit or loss and other comprehensive income for the year ended 31 December 20X7

	20X7 €000	20X6 €000
Revenue	390 000	355 000
Cost of sales	(245 000)	(230 000)
Gross profit	145 000	125 000
Other income	20 667	11 300
Distribution costs	(9 000)	(8 700)
Administrative expenses	(20 000)	(21 000)

(Continued)

TABLE 8.2   (Continued)

XYZ Group – Statement of profit or loss and other comprehensive income for the year ended 31 December 20X7

Other expenses	(2 100)	(1 200)
Finance costs	(8 000)	(7 500)
Share of profit of associates	35 100	30 100
Profit before tax	161 667	128 000
Income tax expense	(40 417)	(32 000)
Profit for the year from continuing operations	121 250	96 000
Loss for the year from discontinued operations	–	(30 500)
PROFIT FOR THE YEAR	121 250	65 500
Other comprehensive income:		
Items that will not be reclassified to profit or loss:		
Gains on property revaluation	933	3 367
Re-measurements of defined benefit pension plans	(667)	1 333
Share of other comprehensive income of associates	400	(700)
Income tax relating to items that will not be reclassified	(166)	(1 000)
	500	3 000
Items that may be reclassified subsequently to profit or loss:		
Exchange differences on translating foreign operations	5 334	10 667
Available-for-sale financial assets	(24 000)	26 667
Cash flow hedges	(667)	(4 000)
Income tax relating to items that may be reclassified	4 833	(8 334)
	(14 500)	25 000
Other comprehensive income for the year, net of tax	(14 000)	28 000
TOTAL COMPREHENSIVE INCOME FOR THE YEAR	107 250	93 500
Profit attributable to:		
Owners of the parent	97 000	52 400
Non-controlling interests	24 250	13 100
	121 250	65 500
Total comprehensive income attributable to:		
Owners of the parent	85 800	74 800
Non-controlling interests	21 450	18 700
	107 250	93 500
Earnings per share (in €'000):		
Basic and diluted	0.46	0.30

Source: Slightly adapted from 2016 Blue Book, Guidance on implementing IAS 1.

Separate statement of profit or loss and separate statement of other comprehensive income Table 8.3 illustrates the use of two separate statements of financial performance. Here you will see clearly the allocation of profit or loss underneath the statement of profit or loss and the allocation of comprehensive income underneath the statement of comprehensive income. This time the statement of profit or loss will classify expenses by nature of the expense.

TABLE 8.3   Income statement (illustrating the presentation of profit or loss and other comprehensive income in two statements and the classification of expenses within profit or loss by nature)

XYZ Group – Statement of profit or loss for the year ended 31 December 20X7

	20X7 €000	20X6 €000
Revenue	390 000	355 000
Other income	20 667	11 300
Changes in inventories of finished goods and work in progress	(115 100)	(107 900)
Work performed by the entity and capitalized	16 000	15 000
Raw material and consumables used	(96 000)	(92 000)
Employee benefits expense	(45 000)	(43 000)
Depreciation and amortization expense	(19 000)	(17 000)
Impairment of property, plant and equipment	(4 000)	–
Other expenses	(6 000)	(5 500)
Finance costs	(15 000)	(18 000)
Share of profit of associates	35 100	30 100
Profit before tax	161 667	128 000
Income tax expense	(40 417)	(32 000)
Profit for the year from continuing operations	121 250	96 000
Loss for the year from discontinued operations	–	(30 500)
PROFIT FOR THE YEAR	121 250	65 500
Profit attributable to:		
Owners of the parent	97 000	52 400
Non-controlling interests	24 250	13 100
	121 250	65 500
Earnings per share (in currency units):		
Basic and diluted	0.46	0.30

Source: Slightly adapted from 2016 Blue Book, Guidance on implementing IAS 1.

XYZ Group – Statement of other comprehensive income for the year ended 31 December 20X7

	20X7 €000	20X6 €000
Profit for the year	121 250	65 500
Other comprehensive income:		
Items that will not be reclassified to profit or loss:		
Gains on property revaluation	933	3 367
Re-measurements of defined benefit pension plans	(667)	1 333
Share of other comprehensive income of associates	400	(700)
Income tax relating to items that will not be reclassified	(166)	(1 000)
	500	3 000

(Continued)

TABLE 8.3 *(Continued)*

XYZ Group – Statement of other comprehensive income for the year ended 31 December 20X7

Items that may be reclassified subsequently to profit or loss:		
Exchange differences on translating foreign operations	5 334	10 667
Available-for-sale financial assets	(24 000)	26 667
Cash flow hedges	(667)	(4 000)
Income tax relating to items that may be reclassified	4 833	(8 334)
	(14 500)	25 000
Other comprehensive income for the year, net of tax	(14 000)	28 000
TOTAL COMPREHENSIVE INCOME FOR THE YEAR	107 250	93 500
Total comprehensive income attributable to:		
Owners of the parent	85 800	74 800
Non-controlling interests	21 450	18 700
	107 250	93 500

Source: Slightly adapted from 2016 Blue Book, Guidance on implementing IAS 1.

Taxation related to components of other comprehensive income An entity shall disclose the amount of income tax relating to each component of other comprehensive income, including reclassification adjustments, either in the statement of profit or loss and other comprehensive income or in the notes (para. 90). An entity may present items of other comprehensive income either:

(a) net of related tax effects or

(b) before related tax effects with one amount showing the aggregate amount of tax relating to these items (para. 91).

In the two illustrations in Tables 8.2 and 8.3 above, XYZ Group had chosen alternative (b) which shows the items of other comprehensive income before tax effects with one amount showing the aggregate amount of tax relating to these items.

Table 8.4 illustrates the statement of other comprehensive income for XYZ Group in the scenario where they had chosen option (a) showing the line items net of tax.

TABLE 8.4 Statement of other comprehensive income illustrating line items shown net of tax

XYZ Group – Statement of other comprehensive income for the year ended 31 December 20X7

	20X7 €000	20X6 €000
PROFIT FOR THE YEAR	121 250	65 500
Other comprehensive income:		
Items that will not be reclassified to profit or loss:		
Gains on property revaluation	600	2 700
Re-measurements of defined benefit pension plans	(500)	1 000
Share of other comprehensive income of associates	400	(700)
	500	3 000

(Continued)

TABLE 8.4   (Continued)

XYZ Group – Statement of other comprehensive income for the year ended 31 December 20X7

Items that may be reclassified subsequently to profit or loss:

Exchange differences on translating foreign operations	4 000	8 000
Available-for-sale financial assets	(18 000)	20 000
Cash flow hedges	(500)	(3 000)
	(14 500)	25 000
Other comprehensive income for the year, net of tax	(14 000)	28 000
TOTAL COMPREHENSIVE INCOME FOR THE YEAR	107 250	93 500
Total comprehensive income attributable to:		
Owners of the parent	85 800	74 800
Non-controlling interests	21 450	18 700
	107 250	93 500

Source: Adapted from 2016 Blue Book, Guidance on implementing IAS 1.

Table 8.5 illustrates the case where an entity discloses the amount of income tax relating to each component of other comprehensive income, including reclassification adjustments, in the notes.

TABLE 8.5   Illustration of disclosure of the amount of income tax relating to each component of other comprehensive income, including reclassification adjustments, in the notes

	(in thousands of currency units) 20X7			(in thousands of currency units) 20X6		
	Before-tax amount	Tax (expense) benefit	Net-of-tax amount	Before-tax amount	Tax (expense) benefit	Net-of-tax amount
	€000	€000	€000	€000	€000	€000
Exchange differences on translating foreign operations	5 334	(1 334)	4 000	10 667	(2 667)	8 000
Available-for-sale financial assets	(24 000)	6 000	(18 000)	26 667	(6 667)	20 000
Cash flow hedges	(667)	167	(500)	(4 000)	1 000	(3 000)
Gains on property revaluation	933	(333)	600	3 367	(667)	2 700
Re-measurements of defined benefit pension plans	(667)	167	(500)	1 333	(333)	1 000
Share of other comprehensive income of associates	400	–	400	(700)	–	(700)
Other comprehensive income	(18 667)	4 667	(14 000)	37 334	(9 334)	28 000

Source: Slightly adapted from 2016 Blue Book, Guidance on implementing IAS 1.

ACTIVITY 8.2

Go back to the financial statements for the company you looked at in Activity 8.1. Alternatively, you can look at the financial statements for Nestlé Group again.

Does the company comply with IFRS? If so, which way of presenting the statement(s) of financial performance does the company use? How does the company deal with the disclosure of the income tax related to the components of other comprehensive income?

Activity feedback

Again, the feedback is in respect of the financial performance statements for 2014 of the Nestlé Group, so we know that Nestlé complies with IFRS and Swiss Law.

Nestlé presents a separate consolidated income statement and a separate consolidated statement of comprehensive income. Interesting about the income statement is the differentiation between trading operating profit and other operating profit. XYZ Group does not make this distinction because the IASB think that this kind of judgement is subjective. Nevertheless, Nestlé thinks it is informative.

In respect of tax related to the components of comprehensive income, Nestlé used option (b) of IAS 1 para. 91. In other words, Nestlé discloses one tax amount for items that are or may be reclassified subsequently to the income statement and one tax amount for items that will never be reclassified to the income statement, and discloses the details in Note 14.2.

Reclassification (recycling) of components of other comprehensive income An entity shall disclose reclassification adjustments relating to components of other comprehensive income (para. 92). These reclassification adjustments may be presented in the statement(s) of profit or loss and other comprehensive income or in the notes. If they are presented in the notes, the items of other comprehensive income must be presented after any related reclassification adjustments (para. 94).

Although the IASB fully embraced comprehensive income in 2009, as the quick revisions in 2011 and 2014 indicate, reclassification is a somewhat controversial concept. The reason is that there are two ways of looking at total comprehensive income. On the one hand, comprehensive income can be regarded as the main performance concept, in which case profit or loss (i.e. realized net income) becomes a secondary measure of performance. Proponents of this approach do not object to abandoning the realization convention and the articulation of financial statements over time. Hence, they regard the reclassification of components of other comprehensive income to profit or loss upon their realization into cash as double counting these components. On the other, realized profit or loss can be regarded as the main performance measure to which the components of other comprehensive income provide additional information.

Proponents of this view, which Cearns *et al.* (1999) called 'the holding tank approach', attach great importance to the realization convention and the articulation of financial statements, because this 'anchors' profit or loss to net cash inflow or outflow via accruals. Therefore, they require components of other comprehensive income to be reclassified into the profit or loss section in the period that they are realized (recycling). The comprehensive income statement under IAS 1 is not fully based on either approach. This is because some IFRSs require recycling (e.g. unrealized gains or losses on available-for-sale financial assets under IAS 39, *Financial Instruments: Recognition and Measurement*) and others explicitly forbid it (e.g. unrealized gains or losses on investments in equity instruments under IFRS 9, *Financial Instruments*). Another example is IAS 16, *Property, Plant and Equipment*, which requires in para. 41 that a transfer from revaluation surplus to retained earnings on realization 'is not made through the profit or loss' (see Chapter 12). Many people have asked the IASB to clarify the theoretical (or conceptual) basis on which some components of other comprehensive income may be recycled and others may not be recycled. However, the IASB would first need to decide which it chooses as the main performance concept.

Other requirements related to the presentation of performance Unlike previously in IAS 1, there is no longer a requirement to present the results of operating activities because IAS 1 does not define 'operating activities'. Presenting operating results is not expressly forbidden. However, an entity shall not present any items of income or expense as extraordinary items in the statement(s) presenting profit or loss and other comprehensive income or in the notes (para. 87). It is important to note that no line item for 'extraordinary items' is allowed. This is the result of an amendment in 2002. The reasons for the amendment are twofold. First, '(t)he Board decided that items treated as extraordinary result from the normal business risks faced by an entity' (BC 63) and second, the Board decided that the distinction between ordinary and extraordinary was too arbitrary (BC 64). IAS 33, *Earnings per Share* requires the disclosure of earnings per share data on the face of the statement of profit or loss (see Chapter 24).

Statement of changes in equity

IAS 1 (para. 106) states that an entity shall present a statement of changes in equity as required by paragraph 10. The statement of changes in equity includes the following information:

1 Total comprehensive income for the period, showing separately the total amounts attributable to owners of the parent and to non-controlling interests.

2 For each component of equity, the effects of retrospective application or retrospective restatement recognized in accordance with IAS 8.

3 For each component of equity, a reconciliation between the carrying amount at the beginning and the end of the period, separately disclosing changes resulting from:

   (a) profit or loss

   (b) other comprehensive income

   (c) transactions with owners in their capacity as owners, showing separately contributions by and distributions to owners and changes in ownership interests in subsidiaries that do not result in a loss of control.

Table 8.6 illustrates the statement of changes in equity for XYZ Group for the year 20X7.

Statement of cash flows

The widespread inclusion of cash flow statements in annual financial reporting packages is a relatively recent phenomenon in some countries. Nevertheless, the rise of the cash flow statement as a necessary part of a comprehensive reporting package has been rapid. Something like it became a standard requirement in the UK in 1975, in IASs in 1977 and eventually in German law, for listed companies, in 1998. There have been a number of developments in the format – and, indeed, in the underlying principles – of such statements and there have been two different versions of an International Accounting Standard in the area, IAS 7. This is dealt with in full in Chapter 23.

TABLE 8.6 Statement of changes in equity

YZ Group – Statement of changes in equity for the year ended 31 December 20X7 (in €'000)

	Share capital	Retained earnings	Translation of foreign operations	Investments in equity instruments	Cash flow hedges	Revaluation surplus	Total	Non-controlling interests	Total equity
Balance at 1/1/20X6	600 000	118 100	(4 000)	1 600	2 000	–	717 700	29 800	747 500
Changes in accounting policy	–	400	–	–	–	–	400	100	500
Restated balance	600 000	118 500	(4 000)	1 600	2 000	–	718 100	29 900	748 000
Changes in equity for 20X6									
Dividends	–	(10 000)	–	–	–	–	(10 000)	–	(10 000)
Total comprehensive income for the year	–	53 200	6 400	16 000	(2 400)	1 600	74 800	18 700	93 500
Balance at 31/12/20X6	600 000	161 700	2 400	17 600	(400)	1 600	782 900	48 600	831 500
Changes in equity for 20X7									
Issue of share capital	50 000	–	–	–	–	–	50 000	–	50 000
Dividends	–	(15 000)	–	–	–	–	(15 000)	–	(15 000)
Total comprehensive income for the year	–	96 600	3 200	(14 400)	(400)	800	85 800	21 450	107 250
Transfer to retained earnings	–	200	–	–	–	(200)	–	–	–
Balance at 31/12/20X7	650 000	243 500	5 600	3 200	(800)	2 200	903 700	70 500	973 750

ACTIVITY 8.3

Go back to the financial statements for the company you looked at in Activities 8.1 and 8.2. Alternatively, you can look at the financial statements for Nestlé Group again.

Does the company comply with IFRS? If so, does the company present the statement of changes in equity in a similar way to the example in Table 8.6?

Activity feedback

Again, the feedback is in respect of the financial per-formance statements for 2014 of the Nestlé Group, so *we know that Nestlé complies with IFRS and Swiss Law.*

Broadly speaking, Nestlé presents the statement of changes in equity in the same way. It is interesting to note that Nestlé holds a significant amount of treasury shares. Furthermore, it is interesting to note that Nestlé discloses retained earnings and other reserves in one amount. It does not separately disclose in the statement of changes in equity the reserves for cash flow hedges and changes in fair values.

Notes to the financial statements under IAS 1

In one sense, the notes to the financial statements are 'where everything else goes'. IAS 1 summarizes the functions of the notes as being to (para. 112):

1 Present information about the basis of preparation of the financial statements and the specific accounting policies selected and applied for significant transactions and events.

2 Disclose the information required by IFRSs that is not presented elsewhere in the financial statements.

3 Provide additional information which is not presented on the face of the financial statements but that is relevant to an understanding of those statements.

Notes to the financial statements should be presented in a systematic manner. Each item on the face of the balance sheet, income statement and cash flow statement should be cross-referenced to any related information in the notes (para. 113).

The Standard suggests that notes 'are normally' presented in the following order (para. 114):

1 A statement of compliance with IFRSs.

2 A summary of significant accounting policies applied.

3 Supporting information for items presented on the face of the balance sheet, income statement, statement of changes in equity and cash flow statement, in the order in which each statement and each line item is presented.

4 Other disclosures, including:

(a) contingent liabilities (see IAS 37, Chapter 19) and unrecognized contractual commitments

(b) non-financial disclosures, such as the entity's financial risk management objectives and policies (see IFRS 7, Chapter 17).

An entity must disclose the following:

In the summary of significant accounting policies – the measurement basis or bases used in preparing the financial statements and the other accounting policies used that are relevant to an understanding of the financial statements (para. 117).

In the summary of significant accounting policies or other notes – the judgements, apart from those involving estimations (see below), management has made in the process of applying the entity's accounting policies that have the most significant effect on the amounts recognized in the financial statements (para. 122).

In the notes – information about the important assumptions concerning the future, and other major sources of estimation uncertainty at the balance sheet date, that have a significant risk of causing a material adjustment to the carrying amounts of assets and liabilities within the next financial year. In respect of those assets and liabilities, the notes shall include details of their nature and their carrying amount as at the balance sheet date (para. 125).

In the notes – the amount of dividends proposed or declared before the financial statements were authorized for issue but not recognized as a distribution to equity holders during the period, and the related amount per share; and the amount of any cumulative preference dividends not recognized (para. 137).

In information published with the financial statements (if not disclosed elsewhere):

- the domicile and legal form of the entity, its country of incorporation and the address of its registered office (or principal place of business, if different from the registered office)
- a description of the nature of the entity's operations and its principal activities
- the name of the parent and the ultimate parent of the group
- if it is a limited life entity, information regarding the length of its life (para. 138).

An entity shall disclose information that enables users of its financial statements to evaluate the entity's objectives, policies and processes for managing capital (para. 134). Para. 135 states that, to comply with para. 134, the entity must disclose the following:

1 Qualitative information about its objectives, policies and processes for managing capital, including (but not limited to):

(a) a description of what it manages as capital

(b) when an entity is subject to externally imposed capital requirements, the nature of those requirements and how those requirements are incorporated into the management of capital

(c) how it is meeting its objectives for managing capital.

2 Summary quantitative data about what it manages as capital. Some entities regard some financial liabilities (e.g. some forms of subordinated debt) as part of capital; other entities regard capital as excluding some components of equity (e.g. components arising from cash flow hedges).

3 Any changes in items 1 and 2 from the previous period.

4 Whether, during the period, it complied with any externally imposed capital requirements to which it is subject.

5 When the entity has not complied with such externally imposed capital requirements, the consequences of such non-compliance.

These disclosures shall be based on the information provided internally to the entity's key management personnel.

ACTIVITY 8.4

Go back to the financial statements for the company you looked at in Activities 8.1, 8.2. and 8.3. Alternatively, you can look at the financial statements for Nestlé Group again. Take a good look at the notes to the financial statements. How are they structured? How many notes are there?

Activity feedback

Again, the feedback is in respect of the financial performance statements for 2014 of the Nestlé Group, so we know that Nestlé complies with IFRS and Swiss Law.

There are 25 notes in Nestlé Group's financial statements for 2014. The notes run from page 65 to page 127. Note 1 Accounting Policies runs from page 65 to page 74. It is very instructive to have a look at the notes. Some notes I found interesting are Note 2 Acquisitions and Disposals of Businesses, which discusses two

major acquisitions in 2014. Note 3 Accounting Segments shows the group's operating segments as well as other segments. Note 6 Inventories explains that a certain amount of inventory has been pledged as securities for financial liabilities. Note 7 Trade and Other Receivables shows that the five major customers represent 11 per cent of total trade and other receivables. Note 8 Property, Plant and Equipment is relevant to what you will learn in Chapter 12. Note 9 Goodwill and Intangibles is relevant to both Parts 2 and 3. Note 10 Employee Benefits discusses pensions and runs from page 92 to page 99. Note 13 Financial Instruments shows in sub-note 13.1b the financial instruments in accordance with the fair value hierarchy discussed in Chapter 7. Note 22 Group Risk Management explains the group's enterprise risk management process.

IAS 8, ACCOUNTING POLICIES, CHANGES TO ACCOUNTING ESTIMATES AND ERRORS

The objective of IAS 8 is to enhance comparability of financial statement data over time within the same firm and between firms. In order to improve comparability, IAS 8 focuses on the criteria for selecting accounting policies, the accounting treatment and disclosure of changes in accounting policies, changes in accounting estimates and errors. The purpose of the Standard is to ensure that entities prepare and present their financial statements on a consistent basis. IAS 8 shall be applied in selecting and applying accounting policies and accounting for changes in accounting policies, changes in accounting estimates and corrections of prior period errors. The tax effects of corrections of prior period errors and retrospective adjustments made to apply changes in accounting policies are accounted for and disclosed in accordance with IAS 12, *Income Taxes*.

The first part of IAS 8, which deals with accounting policies, first determines how to select and apply accounting policies (see paras 7–13). Accounting policies are defined as specific principles, bases, conventions, rules and practices adopted by an entity in preparing and presenting financial statements (para. 5). The selection process for an accounting policy starts with determining whether there is a specific IFRS that deals with the transaction or event that has to be reported.

IAS 8 (para. 7) states that when an IFRS specifically applies to a transaction, other event or condition, the accounting policy or policies applied to that item shall be determined by applying the IFRS and considering the integral guidance to assist entities in applying the IFRS requirements (para. 9).

In the absence of an IFRS that specifically applies to an item in the financial statements, management shall use its judgement in developing and applying an accounting policy that results in information that is (para. 10):

1 Relevant to the decision-making needs of users; and reliable in that the financial statements:

(a) represent faithfully the results and financial position of the entity

(b) reflect the economic substance of transactions and other events, and not merely the legal form

(c) are neutral, i.e. free from bias

(d) are prudent

(e) are complete in all material respects.

In making the judgement described in para. 10, management shall consider the following sources in descending order:

1 The requirements and guidance in Standards and Interpretations of Standards, dealing with similar and related issues.

2 The definitions, recognition criteria and measurement concepts for assets, liabilities, income and expenses set out in the *Conceptual Framework for Financial Reporting* (para. 11).

3 The most recent pronouncements of other standard-setting bodies that use a similar conceptual framework to develop accounting standards, other accounting literature and accepted industry practices, to the extent, but only to the extent, that these are consistent with the first two points of this paragraph (para. 12).

IAS 8 states explicitly that accounting policies should be applied consistently for similar transactions, other events and conditions, unless a Standard or an Interpretation specifically requires or permits categorization of items for which different policies may be appropriate. If an IFRS requires or permits such categorization, an appropriate accounting policy shall be selected and applied consistently to each category (para. 13).

Accounting policy changes Once an accounting policy is chosen, it needs to be applied on a consistent basis over the years. Although consistency is the rule, changes in accounting policies are permitted if the change either:

• is required by an IFRS or

• results in the financial statements providing reliable and more relevant information about the effects of transactions, other events or conditions on the entity's financial position, financial performance or cash flows (para. 14).

ACTIVITY 8.5

Can you think of events or elements which might induce a voluntary change in accounting policies?

Activity feedback

• Company A becomes a subsidiary of company B; subsequently the accounting policies within company A should be harmonized with the accounting policies of company B.

• All changes between benchmark treatments and allowable treatments prescribed in the IAS/IFRS, for example a switch from capitalizing borrowing costs to expensing them, due to changes in the finance policy of a company.

IAS 8 addresses changes of accounting policy arising from three sources:

1 Initial application (including early application) of an IFRS containing specific transitional provisions.

2 Initial application of an IFRS which does not contain specific transitional provisions.

3 Voluntary changes in an accounting policy.

Policy changes under 1 should be accounted for in accordance with the specific transitional provisions of that IFRS.

A change of accounting policy under 2 or 3 should be applied retrospectively, that is applied to transactions, other events and conditions as if it had always been applied (paras 5–19). The Standard goes on to explain that retrospective application requires adjustment of the opening balance of each affected component of equity for the earliest prior period presented and the other comparative amounts disclosed for each prior period presented as if the new accounting policy had always been applied (para. 22). The Standard observes that the amount of the resulting adjustment relating to periods before those presented in the financial statements (which is made to the opening balance of each affected component of equity of the earliest prior period presented) will usually be made to retained earnings. However, it goes on to note that the adjustment may be made to another component of equity (for example, to comply with an IFRS). IAS 8 also makes clear that any other information about prior periods, such as historical summaries of financial data, should also be adjusted (para. 26).

It will frequently be straightforward to apply a change in accounting policy retrospectively. However, the Standard accepts that sometimes it may be impractical to do so. Accordingly, retrospective application of a change in accounting policy is not required to the extent that it is impracticable to determine either the period-specific effects or the cumulative effect of the change (para. 23). The concept 'impracticable' also occurs in relation to the accounting treatment of prior period errors (paras 43–48 and 50–53). As noted above, in the absence of a specifically applicable IFRS, an entity may apply an accounting policy from the most recent pronouncements of another standard-setting body that uses a similar conceptual framework. The Standard makes clear that a change in accounting policy reflecting a change in such a pronouncement is a voluntary change in accounting policy, which should be accounted for and disclosed as such (para. 21).

We have noticed that the IASB introduced the concept of impracticability in relation to the retrospective application of accounting policy changes. Since this concept can be used to circumvent the retrospective application of an accounting policy change, the Standard devotes a considerable amount of guidance to discussing what 'impracticable' means for these purposes, i.e. the limitations on retrospective application (paras 23–27).

The Standard states that applying a requirement is impracticable when an entity cannot apply it after making every reasonable effort to do so. It goes on to note that, for a particular prior period, it is impracticable to apply a change in an accounting policy retrospectively or to make a retrospective restatement to correct an error if:

1 The effects of the retrospective application or retrospective restatement are not determinable.

2 The retrospective application or retrospective restatement requires assumptions about what management's intent would have been in that period.

3 The retrospective application or retrospective restatement requires significant estimates of amounts and it is impossible to distinguish objectively information about those estimates that:

   (a) provides evidence of circumstances that existed on the date(s) as at which those amounts are to be recognized, measured or disclosed

   (b) would have been available when the financial statements for that prior period were authorized for issue, from other information.

IAS 8 observes that it is frequently necessary to make estimates in applying an accounting policy, that estimation is inherently subjective and that estimates may be developed after the balance sheet date. But, developing estimates is potentially more difficult when retrospectively applying an accounting policy or making a retrospective restatement to correct a prior period error because of the longer period of time that might have passed since the affected transaction, other event or condition occurred.

However, the objective of estimates related to prior periods remains the same as for estimates made in the current period, namely, for the estimate to reflect the circumstances that existed when the transaction, other event or condition occurred. Hindsight should not be used when applying a new accounting policy to, or correcting amounts for, a prior period, either in making assumptions about what management's intentions would have been in a prior period or estimating the amounts recognized, measured or disclosed in a prior period. For example, if an entity corrects a prior period error in measuring financial assets previously classified as held-to-maturity investments in accordance with IAS 39, it should not change their basis of measurement for that period if management decided later not to hold them to maturity.

Therefore, retrospectively applying a new accounting policy or correcting a prior period error requires distinguishing information that:

(a) provides evidence of circumstances that existed on the date(s) on which the transaction, other event or condition occurred and

(b) would have been available when the financial statements for that prior period were authorized for issue from other information.

The Standard states that for some types of estimate (e.g. an estimate of fair value not based on an observable price or observable inputs), it is impracticable to distinguish these types of information. When retrospective application or retrospective restatement would require making a significant estimate for which it is impossible to distinguish these two types of information, it is impracticable to apply the new accounting policy or correct the prior period error retrospectively.

The concept of impracticability introduces limitations to the retrospective application of accounting policy changes. The future will tell us if this concept of impracticability will be used to avoid the retrospective application of accounting policy changes.

Although IAS 8 and similar standards of other GAAP systems require all these types of disclosure, we do observe in practice a difference in the quality of disclosure relating to changes in accounting policy or accounting methods. Less quality implies that external parties are hindered in comparing financial data from subsequent years or between firms. If accounting changes are used, for example for earnings management purposes, then there is an incentive to drop the quality level of these disclosures. As disclosure requirements concerning these accounting method changes have become stricter over the years, accounting method changes are now less used for annual accounts' management purposes. The stricter disclosure requirements allow external parties to 'undo' the effect of the change and to detect the 'real' underlying economic performance.

Changes in accounting estimates IAS 8 defines a change in accounting estimates as an adjustment of the carrying amount of an asset or a liability, or the amount of the periodic consumption of an asset, that results from the assessment of the present status of and expected future benefits and obligations associated with assets and liabilities. Changes in accounting estimates result from new information or new developments and, accordingly, are not corrections of errors.

ACTIVITY 8.6

Think of some balance sheet or profit and loss account elements in which estimates are needed for valuation purposes.

Activity feedback

Estimates are required, for example, in the valuation of:

- allowances for bad debts
- inventory obsolescence

- determination of the fair value of assets
- determination of the useful life of an asset.

Indeed, it is difficult to think of elements that do not include estimations.

Valuing balance sheet and profit and loss account items often involves making estimates. The use of reasonable estimates is an essential part of the preparation of financial statements. However, estimates may need to be revised over the years in light of new or changing information. The revision of an estimate does not affect the original classification of the transaction. As changes of accounting estimates imply in most circumstances elements of judgement, the IASB states explicitly in IAS 8 that the change of the estimate should not undermine the reliability of the financial statements.

IAS 8 requires that changes in estimate be accounted for prospectively, defined as recognizing the effect of the change in the accounting estimate in the current and future periods affected by the change (paras 36–38). The Standard goes on to explain that this will mean (as appropriate):

1 Adjusting the carrying amount of an asset, liability or item of equity in the balance sheet in the period of change.

2 Recognizing the change by including it in profit and loss in:

   (a) the period of change, if it affects that period only (e.g. a change in estimate of bad debts) or

   (b) the period of change and future periods, if it affects both (e.g. a change in estimated useful life of a depreciable asset or the expected pattern of consumption of the economic benefits embodied in it).

ACTIVITY 8.7

Think of an example of a change in an accounting estimate which affects only the current period. Then think of an example which might affect the current period as well as subsequent periods.

Activity feedback

For example, a change in the estimate of the amount of bad debts affects only the current period and is therefore recognized in the current period. However, a change in the estimated useful life or the expected pattern of consumption of the future economic benefits embodied in a depreciable asset affects depreciation expense for the remainder of the current period and for each future period during the asset's remaining useful life. In both cases, the effect of the change relating to the current period is recognized as income or expense in the current period. The effect, if any, on future periods is recognized in future periods.

An entity shall disclose the nature and amount of a change in an accounting estimate that has an effect in the current period or is expected to have an effect in future periods, except for the disclosure of the effect on future periods when it is impracticable to estimate that effect (para. 39).

Further, IAS 8 states explicitly that a change in an accounting estimate does not result from a change in the measurement basis or method applied, which is a change in an accounting policy. When it is difficult to distinguish between a change in an accounting policy and a change in an accounting estimate, the change is treated as a change in an accounting estimate, with appropriate disclosure.

Prospective recognition of the effect of a change in an accounting estimate means that the change is applied to transactions, other events and circumstances from the date of the change to estimate. A change in an accounting estimate may affect the current period only or both the current period and future periods.

So a change in an accounting estimate involves less administrative work and is somehow less visible than a change in accounting policy or method. The latter is applied retrospectively, and therefore prior year comparative data need to be restated as well. All these changes will probably catch the eye of the user of the annual accounts sooner or later. Empirical evidence exists (this will be discussed in Chapter 31) that changes in accounting estimates are now more popular for earnings management purposes than accounting policy changes as they are less costly and less visible.

Errors IAS 8 also deals with the treatment of prior period errors. Prior period errors are omissions from, and misstatements in, the entity's financial statements for one or more prior periods arising from a failure to use, or misuse of, reliable information that:

- was available when financial statements for those periods were authorized for issue
- could reasonably be expected to have been obtained and taken into account in the preparation and presentation of those financial statements.

Such errors include the effects of mathematical mistakes; mistakes in applying accounting policies, oversights or misinterpretations of facts, and fraud.

Paragraph 42 stipulates that the correction of the error has to be accounted for in a retrospective way in the first set of financial statements authorized for issue after their discovery, by:

- restating the comparative amounts for the prior period(s) in which the error occurred or
- if the error occurred before the earliest prior period presented, restating the opening balances of assets, liabilities and equity for the earliest prior period presented.

In this way, the financial statements are presented as if the error had never occurred.

Also in the case of prior period errors, comparative information presented for a particular prior period need not be restated if restating the information would be impracticable (paras 43–45).

If the amount of the effect in future periods is not disclosed because estimating it is impracticable, an entity shall disclose that fact (para. 40).

Special disclosure requirements apply in relation to such prior period errors (para. 49):

1 The nature of the prior period error.
2 For each prior period presented, to the extent practicable, the amount of the correction:

(a) for each financial statement line item affected and

(b) if IAS 33 applies to the entity, for basic and diluted earnings per share.

3 The amount of the correction at the beginning of the earliest prior period presented.

4 If retrospective restatement is impracticable for a particular period, the circumstances that led to the existence of that condition and a description of how and from when the error has been corrected.

Financial statements of subsequent periods need not repeat these disclosures.

ACTIVITY 8.8

During 20X2, company A discovered that certain products that had been sold during 20X1 were incorrectly included in inventory at 31 December 20X1 at €3250.

Company A's accounting records for 20X2 show sales of €52 000, cost of goods sold of €43 250 (including €3250 for error in opening inventory), and income taxes of €2625.

In 20X1, company A reported:

	€
Sales	36 750
Cost of goods sold	26 750
Profit from ordinary activities before income taxes	10 000
Income taxes	(3 000)
Net profit	7 000

20X1 opening retained earnings were €10 000 and closing retained earnings were €17 000. Company A's income tax rate was 30 per cent for 20X2 and 20X1.

Show the necessary disclosures in the financial statements for the year 20X2.

Activity feedback

Company A – an extract from the income statement

	20X2	20X1 (restated)
	€	€
Sales	52 000	36 750
Cost of goods sold	40 000	30 000
Profit from ordinary activities before income taxes	12 000	6 750
Income taxes	(3 600)	(2 025)
Net profit	8 400	4 725

Company A
Statement of retained earnings

	20X2	20X1 (restated)
	€	€
Opening retained earnings as previously reported	17 000	10 000
Correction of fundamental error (Net of income taxes of €975) (Note 1)	2 275	—
Opening retained earnings as restated	14 725	10 000
Net profit	8 400	4 725
Closing retained earnings	23 125	14 725

Extract from notes to the financial statements:

1 *Certain products that had been sold in 20X1 were incorrectly included in inventory at 31 December 20X1 at €3250. The financial statement of 20X1 has been restated to correct this error'.*

Once again, we notice that the restatement is made on the judgement of the management of whether or not the restatement is impracticable.

IFRS 1, FIRST TIME ADOPTION OF IFRS

When a company changes from its domestic GAAP to IFRS, this change does not belong to the scope of IAS 8. IFRS 1, *First Time Adoption of IFRS*, provides guidance for all companies which change either compulsorily or voluntarily to IAS/IFRS Standards.

Paragraph 3 states that an entity's first IFRS financial statements are the first annual financial statements in which the entity adopts IFRSs, by an explicit and unreserved statement in those financial statements of compliance with IFRS. Financial statements under IFRS are an entity's first financial statements if, for example, the entity:

1 Presented its most recent previous financial statements:

    (a) under national requirements that are not consistent with IFRS in all respects

    (b) in conformity with IFRS in all respects, except that the financial statements did not contain an explicit and unreserved statement that they complied with IFRS

    (c) containing an explicit statement of compliance with some, but not all, IFRS

    (d) under national requirements inconsistent with IFRS, using some individual IFRS to account for items which national requirements did not exist or

    (e) under national requirements, with a reconciliation of some amounts to the amounts determined under IFRS.

2 Prepared financial statements under IFRS for internal use only, without making them available to the entity's owners or any other external users.

3 Prepared a reporting package under IFRS for consolidation purposes without preparing a complete set of financial statements as defined in IAS 1, *Presentation of Financial Statements*.

4 Did not present financial statements for previous periods.

If a company presents its financial figures for a particular financial year, these figures are usually accompanied by prior year figures. For the sake of comparability, these figures should be prepared using the same GAAP. This implies that the prior year figures in an entity's first IFRS financial statements should also be prepared with the use of IAS/IFRS. If we apply this principle to the compulsory change to IAS/IFRS for listed companies in the EU, we obtain the following situation:

The reporting date for entity A's first IFRS financial statements is 31 December 2005. If entity A decides to present comparative information in those financial statements for one year only, the date of transition to IFRS is the beginning of business on 1 January 2004 (or, equivalently, close of business on 31 December 2003). Entity A will have presented financial statements under its previous GAAP annually to 31 December each year up to and including 31 December 2004. In this case, entity A is required to apply IFRS effective for periods ending on 31 December 2005 in:

- preparing its opening IFRS balance sheet at 1 January 2004 and

- preparing and presenting its balance sheet for 31 December 2005 (including comparative amounts for 2004), income statement, statement of changes in equity and cash flow statement for the year to 31 December 2005 (including comparative amounts for 2004) and disclosures (including comparative information for 2004).

If a new IFRS is not yet mandatory but permits early application, entity A is permitted, but not required, to apply that IFRS in its first IFRS financial statements.

For many preparers who present their first IFRS financial statements, the main question is: 'Which accounting policies need to be applied for the recognition and measurement of the items of the financial statements?' The main rule is that an entity shall use the same accounting policies in its opening IFRS balance sheet and throughout all periods presented in its first IFRS financial statements. Those accounting policies shall comply with each IFRS effective at the reporting date for its first IFRS financial statements. This general rule implies that an entity shall not apply different versions of IFRS that were effective at earlier dates.

In its opening IFRS balance sheet, an entity shall (para. 10):

(a) recognize all assets and liabilities whose recognition is required by IFRSs

(b) not recognize items as assets or liabilities if IFRS does not permit such recognition

(c) reclassify items that it recognized under previous GAAP as one type of asset, liability or component of equity, but are a different type of asset, liability or component of equity under IFRS and

(d) apply IFRS in measuring all recognized assets and liabilities.

The accounting policies that an entity uses in its opening IFRS balance sheet may differ from those that it used for the same date using its previous GAAP. The resulting adjustments arise from events and transactions before the date of transition to IFRS. Therefore, an entity shall recognize those adjustments directly in retained earnings (or, if appropriate, another category of equity) at the date of transition to IFRS (para. 11).

In essence, companies have to use all IFRSs that are effective at the reporting date for all the information included in the annual accounts. However, there are two categories of exception. First, IFRS 1 specifies a number of optional exemptions from retrospective application (paras 13–25). First-time adopters can elect to apply all, some or none of these optional exemptions. Second, IFRS 1 foresees mandatory exceptions from retrospective application.

The switch from a previous GAAP system to IFRS will have an impact on the published figures of a company. IFRS 1 requires that in the notes to the accounts the impact of the transition from the previous GAAP to IAS/IFRS on the financial position, the financial performance and the cash flow should be explained.

Observing reporting practices of companies that have switched to IAS/IFRS, we notice that there is an enormous difference with regard to the level of detail that is presented to users of financial statements in relation to the impact of the switch on a firm's financial position. Some companies provide several pages of explanation with regard to the impact on the company's equity; other companies just disclose a few lines.

A number of companies divided the impact of the IAS/IFRS transition over a number of years. Some companies started complying with IASs which have a favourable impact on equity in the financial years before the 'official' financial transition year. Compliance with IASs that have an unfavourable impact on equity takes place in the 'official' transition year.

EU DIRECTIVE 2013/34/EU (THE 2013 ACCOUNTING DIRECTIVE)

On 26 June 2013, the European Parliament and the European Council issued Directive 2013/34/EU on the annual financial statements, consolidated financial statements and related reports of listed companies, effective from 19 July 2013 and transposed into national company law by 20 July 2015.

Directive 2013/34/EU:

- amends Directive 2006/43/EC of the European Parliament and the Council (on statutory audits of annual accounts and consolidated accounts)
- repeals Council Directive 78/660/EEC (the 'Fourth Company Law Directive' of 25 July 1978 on the annual accounts of certain types of companies)
- repeals Council Directive 83/349/EEC (the 'Seventh Company Law Directive' of 13 June 1983 on consolidated accounts) and
- repeals Council Directive 2012/6/EU (the 'Micros Directive' on the annual accounts of certain types of companies as regards micro-entities).

Directive 2013/34/EU (henceforth the 2013 Accounting Directive) merges and improves the Fourth and the Seventh Company directives and seeks to increase the comparability of financial reports across EU Member States. The idea is to reduce the number of options available to the preparers of financial statements in respect of recognition, measurement, presentation and disclosure.

In addition, the 2013 Accounting Directive protects micro companies and small companies from complexity by simplifying the preparation of financial statements for micro companies and small companies. Small companies are required to prepare a balance sheet, a profit and loss account and notes to satisfy regulatory requirements. Individual EU Member States are allowed to permit small companies to prepare only abridged balance sheets and profit and loss accounts. Any small company is free to provide more information or statements on a voluntary basis. There is no EU requirement for small companies to have an audit. However, individual Member States would nevertheless see the need for assurance and the new Directive will allow for a more proportionate approach.

The 2013 Accounting Directive comprises the following 11 chapters.

- Chapter 1 – Scope, definition and categories of undertakings and groups
- Chapter 2 – General provisions and principles
- Chapter 3 – Balance sheet and profit and loss account
- Chapter 4 – Notes to the financial statements
- Chapter 5 – Management report
- Chapter 6 – Consolidated financial statements and reports
- Chapter 7 – Publication
- Chapter 8 – Auditing
- Chapter 9 – Provisions concerning exemptions and restrictions on exemptions
- Chapter 10 – Report on payments to governments
- Chapter 11 – Final provisions

We will only discuss chapters 1 to 4 here. The full text of Directive 2013/34/EU can be found here: eur-lex.europa.eu/legal-content/EN/ALL/?uri=CELEX:32013L0034 (accessed 14 February 2016).

Chapter 1 – Scope, definitions and categories of undertakings and groups

The 2013 Accounting Directive introduces the obligation for each Member State to distinguish small companies from larger ones, and limits the amount of information that EU Member States are permitted to require small companies to disclose in their annual statutory financial statements. Article 3 of the 2013 Accounting Directive defines the categories of companies and groups whereby on the balance sheet date two out of three criteria are not exceeded, as shown in Table 8.7.

TABLE 8.7	Categories of company sizes		
	Net turnover (€)	Balance sheet total (€)	Average number of employees
Micro	350 000	700 000	10
Small*	4 000 000	8 000 000	50
Medium	20 000 000	40 000 000	250
Large	20 000 000	40 000 000	250

Individual Member States are allowed to define small companies using a maximum turnover of €12 000 000 and a maximum balance sheet total of €6 000 000.

In addition, Article 2 defines public interest entities as entities which are:

(a) governed by the law of a Member State and whose transferable securities are admitted to trading on a regulated market of any Member State

(b) credit institutions as defined in point (1) of Article 4 of Directive 2006/48/EC of the European Parliament and of the Council of 14 June 2006 relating to the taking up and pursuit of the business of credit institutions, other than those referred to in Article 2 of that Directive

(c) insurance undertakings within the meaning of Article 2(1) of Council Directive 91/674/EEC of 19 December 1991 on the annual accounts of insurance undertakings or

(d) designated by Member States as public interest entities, for instance undertakings that are of significant public relevance because of the nature of their business, their size or the number of their employees.

Chapter 2 – General provisions and principles

Article 4 of the 2013 Accounting Directive requires all companies to annually prepare at least a balance sheet, a profit and loss account and notes to the financial statements, which shall give a true and fair view of the undertaking's assets, liabilities, financial position and profit or loss.

Article 6 sets out the principles of going concern, accrual accounting, prudence, consistency, articulation of financial statements, separate valuation of individual assets and liabilities, separate disclosure of individual revenue and expense items, substance over form, historical purchase cost or production cost, and materiality.

Article 7 prescribes that revaluation is allowed, but the amount of the difference between measurement on a purchase price or production cost basis and measurement on a revaluation basis shall be entered in the balance sheet in the revaluation reserve under 'Capital and reserves' and no part of the revaluation reserve may be distributed, either directly or indirectly, unless it represents a gain actually realized.

Article 8 allows EU Member States to require or permit the measurement of financial instruments, including derivative financial instruments, at fair value, and the measurement of specified categories of assets other than financial instruments at amounts determined by reference to fair value. Such permission or requirement may be restricted to consolidated financial statements.

Chapter 3 – Balance sheet and profit and loss account

Article 10 indicates that EU Member States are allowed to prescribe a horizontal or a vertical balance sheet layout. Annex III and Annex IV of the 2013 Accounting Directive show the horizontal layout of the balance sheet and the vertical layout of the balance sheet, respectively.

Article 13 indicates that EU Member States are allowed to prescribe a profit and loss account by nature of expense or a profit or loss account by function of expense. Annex V and Annex VI of the 2013 Accounting Directive show the layout of the profit and loss account by nature of expense and the layout of the profit and loss account by function of expense, respectively.

The balance sheet

In comparison with IAS 1, the 2013 Accounting Directive sets out considerably more detail in its specifications regarding balance sheets. Table 8.8 reproduces a 'horizontal' format with the debits on one side and the credits on the other, following the general continental European tradition.

TABLE 8.8   2013 EU Accounting Directive: Horizontal balance sheet format

Assets

A. Subscribed capital unpaid of which there has been called (unless national law provides that called-up capital is to be shown under 'Capital and reserves' in which case the part of the capital called but not yet paid shall appear as an asset either under A or under D (II) (5)).

B. Formation expenses

as defined by national law, and in so far as national law permits their being shown as an asset. National law may also provide for formation expenses to be shown as the first item under 'Intangible assets'.

C. Fixed assets

I. Intangible assets

1. Costs of development, in so far as national law permits their being shown as assets.

2. Concessions, patents, licences, trade marks and similar rights and assets, if they were:

   (a) acquired for valuable consideration and need not be shown under C (I) (3) or

   (b) created by the undertaking itself, in so far as national law permits their being shown as assets.

3. Goodwill, to the extent that it was acquired for valuable consideration.

4. Payments on account.

(Continued)

TABLE 8.8   (Continued)

II. Tangible assets

1. Land and buildings.

2. Plant and machinery.

3. Other fixtures and fittings, tools and equipment.

4. Payments on account and tangible assets in the course of construction.

III. Financial assets

1. Shares in affiliated undertakings.

2. Loans to affiliated undertakings.

3. Participating interests.

4. Loans to undertakings with which the undertaking is linked by virtue of participating interests.

5. Investments held as fixed assets.

6. Other loans.

D. Current assets

I. Stocks

1. Raw materials and consumables.

2. Work in progress.

3. Finished goods and goods for resale.

4. Payments on account.

II. Debtors

(Amounts becoming due and payable after more than one year shall be shown separately for each item.)

1. Trade debtors.

2. Amounts owed by affiliated undertakings.

3. Amounts owed by undertakings with which the undertaking is linked by virtue of participating interests.

4. Other debtors.

5. Subscribed capital called but not paid (unless national law provides that called-up capital is to be shown as an asset under A).

6. Prepayments and accrued income (unless national law provides that such items are to be shown as assets under E).

III. Investments

1. Shares in affiliated undertakings.

2. Own shares (with an indication of their nominal value or, in the absence of a nominal value, their accounting par value), to the extent that national law permits their being shown in the balance sheet.

3. Other investments.

IV. Cash at bank and in hand

E. Prepayments and accrued income

(Unless national law provides that such items are to be shown as assets under D (II) (6).)

(*Continued*)

TABLE 8.8   (Continued)

Capital, reserves and liabilities

A. Capital and reserves

I. Subscribed capital

(Unless national law provides that called-up capital is to be shown under this item, in which case the amounts of subscribed capital and paid-up capital shall be shown separately.)

II. Share premium account

III. Revaluation reserve

IV. Reserves

1. Legal reserve, in so far as national law requires such a reserve.

2. Reserve for own shares, in so far as national law requires such a reserve, without prejudice to point (b) of Article 24(1) of Directive 2012/30/EU.

3. Reserves provided for by the articles of association.

4. Other reserves, including the fair value reserve.

V. Profit or loss brought forward

VI. Profit or loss for the financial year

B. Provisions

1. Provisions for pensions and similar obligations.

2. Provisions for taxation.

3. Other provisions.

C. Creditors

(Amounts becoming due and payable within one year and amounts becoming due and payable after more than one year shall be shown separately for each item and for the aggregate of those items.)

1. Debenture loans, showing convertible loans separately.

2. Amounts owed to credit institutions.

3. Payments received on account of orders, in so far as they are not shown separately as deductions from stocks.

4. Trade creditors.

5. Bills of exchange payable.

6. Amounts owed to affiliated undertakings.

7. Amounts owed to undertakings with which the undertaking is linked by virtue of participating interests.

8. Other creditors, including tax and social security authorities.

9. Accruals and deferred income (unless national law provides that such items are to be shown under D).

D. Accruals and deferred income

(Unless national law provides that such items are to be shown under C (9) under 'Creditors'.)

Source: Annex III of the 2013 Accounting Directive.

Table 8.9 reproduces a 'vertical' format of the type more traditional in the UK.

TABLE 8.9 2013 EU Accounting Directive: Vertical balance sheet format

A. **Subscribed capital unpaid** of which there has been called (unless national law provides that called-up capital is to be shown under L, in which case the part of the capital called but not yet paid must appear either under A or under D (II) (5).)

B. **Formation expenses** as defined by national law, and in so far as national law permits their being shown as an asset. National law may also provide for formation expenses to be shown as the first item under 'Intangible assets'.

C. **Fixed assets**

I. **Intangible assets**

1. Costs of development, in so far as national law permits their being shown as assets.

2. Concessions, patents, licences, trade marks and similar rights and assets, if they were:

    (a) acquired for valuable consideration and need not be shown under C (I) (3); or

    (b) created by the undertaking itself, in so far as national law permits their being shown as assets.

3. Goodwill, to the extent that it was acquired for valuable consideration.

4. Payments on account.

II. **Tangible assets**

1. Land and buildings.

2. Plant and machinery.

3. Other fixtures and fittings, tools and equipment.

4. Payments on account and tangible assets in the course of construction.

III. **Financial assets**

1. Shares in affiliated undertakings.

2. Loans to affiliated undertakings.

3. Participating interests.

4. Loans to undertakings with which the undertaking is linked by virtue of participating interests.

5. Investments held as fixed assets.

6. Other loans.

D. **Current assets**

I. **Stocks**

1. Raw materials and consumables.

2. Work in progress.

3. Finished goods and goods for resale.

4. Payments on account.

II. **Debtors**

(Amounts becoming due and payable after more than one year must be shown separately for each item.)

1. Trade debtors.

2. Amounts owed by affiliated undertakings.

3. Amounts owed by undertakings with which the company is linked by virtue of participating interests.

4. Other debtors.

(Continued)

TABLE 8.9 *(Continued)*

5. Subscribed capital called but not paid (unless national law provides that called-up capital is to be shown as an asset under A).

6. Prepayments and accrued income (unless national law provides that such items are to be shown as assets under E).

III. Investments

1. Shares in affiliated undertakings.

2. Own shares (with an indication of their nominal value or, in the absence of a nominal value, their accounting par value), to the extent that national law permits their being shown in the balance sheet.

3. Other investments.

IV. Cash at bank and in hand

E. Prepayments and accrued income

(Unless national law provides that such items are to be shown under D (II) (6).)

F. Creditors: amounts becoming due and payable within one year

1. Debenture loans, showing convertible loans separately.

2. Amounts owed to credit institutions.

3. Payments received on account of orders, in so far as they are not shown separately as deductions from stocks.

4. Trade creditors.

5. Bills of exchange payable.

6. Amounts owed to affiliated undertakings.

7. Amounts owed to undertakings with which the company is linked by virtue of participating interests.

8. Other creditors, including tax and social security authorities.

9. Accruals and deferred income (unless national law provides that such items are to be shown under K).

G. Net current assets/liabilities

(Taking into account prepayments and accrued income when shown under E and accruals and deferred income when shown under K.)

H. Total assets less current liabilities

I. Creditors: amounts becoming due and payable after more than one year

1. Debenture loans, showing convertible loans separately.

2. Amounts owed to credit institutions.

3. Payments received on account of orders, in so far as they are not shown separately as deductions from stocks.

4. Trade creditors.

5. Bills of exchange payable.

6. Amounts owed to affiliated undertakings.

(Continued)

TABLE 8.9   (Continued)

7. Amounts owed to undertakings with which the company is linked by virtue of participating interests.

8. Other creditors, including tax and social security authorities.

9. Accruals and deferred income (unless national law provides that such items are to be shown under K).

J. Provisions

1. Provisions for pensions and similar obligations.

2. Provisions for taxation.

3. Other provisions.

K. Accruals and deferred income

(Unless national law provides that such items are to be shown under F (9) or I (9) or both.)

L. Capital and reserves

I. Subscribed capital

(Unless national law provides that called-up capital is to be shown under this item, in which case the amounts of subscribed capital and paid-up capital must be shown separately.)

II. Share premium account

III. Revaluation reserve

IV. Reserves

1. Legal reserve, in so far as national law requires such a reserve.

2. Reserve for own shares, in so far as national law requires such a reserve, without prejudice to point (b) of Article 24(1) of Directive 2012/30/EU.

3. Reserves provided for by the articles of association.

4. Other reserves, including the fair value reserve.

V. Profit or loss brought forward

VI. Profit or loss for the financial year

Source: Annex IV of the 2013 EU Accounting Directive.

The income statement

The implications of the distinction between classification by nature and classification by function are conveniently illustrated by the formats in Tables 8.10 and 8.11. Table 8.10 illustrates the profit and loss account by nature of expense. In this format:

[e]xpenses are aggregated in the income statement according to their nature (for example, depreciation, purchases of materials, transport costs, employee benefits and advertising costs), and are not reallocated among various functions within the entity. This method may be simple to apply because no allocations of expenses to functional classifications are necessary.

(IAS 1, Para. 91 as consolidated by the EU, eur-lex.europa.eu/legal-content/EN/ ALL/?uri=CELEX:32008R1126, accessed on 14 February 2016)

TABLE 8.10   2013 EU Accounting Directive: Profit and loss account by nature of expense

1. Net turnover.

2. Variation in stocks of finished goods and in work in progress.

3. Work performed by the undertaking for its own purposes and capitalised.

4. Other operating income.

5. (a) Raw materials and consumables.

   (b) Other external expenses.

6. Staff costs:

   (a) wages and salaries;

   (b) social security costs, with a separate indication of those relating to pensions.

7. (a) Value adjustments in respect of formation expenses and of tangible and intangible fixed assets.

   (b) Value adjustments in respect of current assets, to the extent that they exceed the amount of value adjustments which are normal in the undertaking concerned.

8. Other operating expenses.

9. Income from participating interests, with a separate indication of that derived from affiliated undertakings.

10. Income from other investments and loans forming part of the fixed assets, with a separate indication of that derived from affiliated undertakings.

11. Other interest receivable and similar income, with a separate indication of that derived from affiliated undertakings.

12. Value adjustments in respect of financial assets and of investments held as current assets.

13. Interest payable and similar expenses, with a separate indication of amounts payable to affiliated undertakings.

14. Tax on profit or loss.

15. Profit or loss after taxation.

16. Other taxes not shown under items 1 to 15.

17. Profit or loss for the financial year.

Source: Annex V of the 2013 EU Accounting Directive.

The second format follows the:

> [f]unction of expense or 'cost of sales' method and classifies expenses according to their function as part of cost of sales or, for example, the costs of distribution or administrative activities. At a minimum, an entity discloses its cost of sales under this method separately from other expenses. This method can provide more relevant information to users than the classification of expenses by nature, but allocating costs to functions may require arbitrary allocations and involve considerable judgement.
>
> (IAS 1, Para. 92 as consolidated by the EU, eur-lex.europa.eu/legal-content/EN/ALL/?uri=CELEX:32008R1126, accessed on 14 February 2016)

Table 8.11 presents the layout of the profit or loss account by function of expense.

TABLE 8.11 2013 EU Accounting Directive: Profit and loss account by function of expense

1. Net turnover.

2. Cost of sales (including value adjustments).

3. Gross profit or loss.

4. Distribution costs (including value adjustments).

5. Administrative expenses (including value adjustments).

6. Other operating income.

7. Income from participating interests, with a separate indication of that derived from affiliated undertakings.

8. Income from other investments and loans forming part of the fixed assets, with a separate indication of that derived from affiliated undertakings.

9. Other interest receivable and similar income, with a separate indication of that derived from affiliated undertakings.

10. Value adjustments in respect of financial assets and of investments held as current assets.

11. Interest payable and similar expenses, with a separate indication of amounts payable to affiliated undertakings.

12. Tax on profit or loss.

13. Profit or loss after taxation.

14. Other taxes not shown under items 1 to 13.

15. Profit or loss for the financial year.

Source: Annex VI of the 2013 EU Accounting Directive.

ACTIVITY 8.9

Consider the relative advantages and usefulness of the two 2013 EU Accounting Directive formats for the income statement.

Activity feedback

As regards the distinction between the classification by nature and by function, both methods have advantages. Showing expenses by nature requires less analysis and less judgement, but is arguably less informative. It shows the amount incurred on production for the period, but does not highlight the total expenses under the accruals convention. It fails to reveal the cost of sales,

and therefore the gross profit and it has the logical disadvantage that it might seem to imply (see Tables 8.10 or 8.11) that changes in inventory are an expense or a revenue in their own right, which they are not. They are logically an adjustment to purchases.

However, because information on the nature of expenses is regarded as useful in predicting future cash flows, IAS 1 and the 2013 Accounting Directive require additional disclosure on the nature of expenses, including depreciation and amortization expenses and staff costs, when the by function classification is used.

Chapter 4 – Notes to the financial statements

Article 15 states that the notes shall be presented in the order in which items are presented in the balance sheet and in the profit and loss account. Article 16 sets out the content of the notes to the financial statements relating to all companies as follows:

1 In the notes to the financial statements all undertakings shall, in addition to the information required under other provisions of this Directive, disclose information in respect of the following:

(a) accounting policies adopted;

(b) where fixed assets are measured at revalued amounts, a table showing:

    (i) movements in the revaluation reserve in the financial year, with an explanation of the tax treatment of items therein, and

    (ii) the carrying amount in the balance sheet that would have been recognised had the fixed assets not been revalued;

(c) where financial instruments and/or assets other than financial instruments are measured at fair value:

    (i) the significant assumptions underlying the valuation models and techniques where fair values have been determined in accordance with point (b) of Article 8(7),

    (ii) for each category of financial instrument or asset other than financial instruments, the fair value, the changes in value included directly in the profit and loss account and changes included in fair value reserves,

    (iii) for each class of derivative financial instrument, information about the extent and the nature of the instruments, including significant terms and conditions that may affect the amount, timing and certainty of future cash flows, and

    (iv) a table showing movements in fair value reserves during the financial year;

(d) the total amount of any financial commitments, guarantees or contingencies that are not included in the balance sheet, and an indication of the nature and form of any valuable security which has been provided; any commitments concerning pensions and affiliated or associated undertakings shall be disclosed separately;

(e) the amount of advances and credits granted to members of the administrative, managerial and supervisory bodies, with indications of the interest rates, main conditions and any amounts repaid or written off or waived, as well as commitments entered into on their behalf by way of guarantees of any kind, with an indication of the total for each category;

(f) the amount and nature of individual items of income or expenditure which are of exceptional size or incidence;

(g) amounts owed by the undertaking becoming due and payable after more than five years, as well as the undertaking's entire debts covered by valuable security furnished by the undertaking, with an indication of the nature and form of the security; and

(h) the average number of employees during the financial year.

(eur-lex.europa.eu/LexUriServ/LexUriServ.do?uri=OJ:L:2013:182:0019:0076:en:PDF, 2013: 17, accessed on 5 August 2016)

Article 16 sets out the additional disclosures required from medium-sized and large companies. Article 17 sets out further disclosures required from large companies and public interest entities.

SUMMARY

This chapter has described and discussed the requirements of IAS 1 and the 2013 EU Accounting Directive in relation to the structure of published financial statements. The major revisions to performance reporting introduced from 1 January 2009 have as their fundamental purpose the prevention of information being 'hidden away' outside the essential statement of performance, now designated the statement of comprehensive income. The word 'comprehensive' is precisely the point. All adjustments and events should be clearly reported in vision. The success of this policy remains to be seen.

This chapter has also considered IAS 8, *Accounting Policies, Changes to Accounting Estimates and Errors* and IFRS 1, *First Time Adoption of IFRS.*

Finally, this chapter also looked at the 2013 EU Accounting Directive's requirements in relation to the structure of published financial statements.

EXERCISES

Suggested answers to exercises marked ✓ are to be found in the Student online resources, with suggested answers to the remaining questions available in the Instructor online resources.

1 Are fixed formats for the key financial statements a good thing? If they are, why are several different ones allowed?

✓2 It is important that revenues as determined under the realization convention are reported in a separate statement from any other gains and asset increases. Discuss.

3 The accountant is entitled to assume that readers of financial statements will read and understand all the notes to the accounts. Discuss.

4 The latest formats of reporting comprehensive income, required by the latest version of IAS 1 and described in this chapter, will now be in regular use. Obtain two sets of consolidated IAS accounts for groups based in different countries. Consider whether these recent requirements:

(a) increase comparability

(b) increase the information content of the reports.

CORPORATE GOVERNANCE 9

OBJECTIVES After studying this chapter you should be able to:

- describe the characteristics of listed public companies

- provide contrasting definitions of corporate governance

- explain the conflicts of interests that corporate governance deals with

- understand and explain the principal-agent problem and information asymmetry

- understand and contrast the following theories in corporate governance: Agency Theory, Stewardship Theory, Stakeholder Theory and their implications for corporate governance mechanisms

- describe the main corporate governance mechanisms and explain how they address specific corporate governance problems

- describe how corporate governance might vary across countries with reference to taxonomies of corporate governance systems

- describe the 2015 G20/OECD Principles of Corporate Governance, corporate governance in the EU and how corporate governance codes might vary between countries

- explain the relationship between corporate governance and financial reporting.

INTRODUCTION

Chapter 1 stated that financial reporting is part of corporate governance and that its purpose is to mitigate information asymmetry between the reporting entity's senior management and the reporting entity's shareholders, investors and other external stakeholders. In this chapter we will take a closer look at corporate governance in order to better understand the different views on the roles that financial reporting plays in addressing problems and mitigating costs caused by information asymmetry.

In order to define corporate governance, this chapter will first look at the causes of information asymmetry between the shareholders, investors and other external stakeholders of the corporation and the senior management of the corporation, and the types of problems and costs associated with it. As financial reporting is only one of the means by which these problems are addressed, we will look at the problems and some of the other corporate governance mechanisms intended to mitigate the associated issues.

This chapter will then consider corporate governance mechanisms and practices in different countries.

DEFINITIONS OF AND PERSPECTIVES ON CORPORATE GOVERNANCE

The term 'governance' indicates the system and structures that govern an organization or society so that its goals are determined, the efforts towards the realization of the goals are organized, adjusted when necessary, and achieved. The term 'corporate' indicates that the subject at issue is the governance of the business corporation. Although corporate governance applies to all business corporations, in this book we focus on the corporate governance of business corporations whose shares are listed on a stock exchange.

Characteristics of large public corporations

Adam Smith (*The Wealth of Nations*, 1776) already understood the challenge arising from the separation of ownership and control. 'The directors of companies being managers of other people's money than their own, it cannot well be expected that they should watch over it with the same anxious vigilance with which the partners in a private copartnery frequently watch over their own'. In 1932, Berle and Means in their *The Modern Corporation and Private Property* observed that the assumption the self-interest of the property owner serves the public interest by guaranteeing economic efficiency, which had underpinned the system of private enterprise, did not hold for large listed corporations (Berle and Means, 1968/2009: 9). The reason that this assumption ceased to hold is that 'a large separation of ownership and control has taken place through the multiplication of owners' (Berle and Means, 1968/2009: 5). Separation of ownership and control means that the ownership of the entity's shares is in the hands of the shareholders, but the control of the entity's assets is in the hands of the company's senior management.

Berle and Means clearly identified that the separation of ownership and control causes what is currently referred to as the agency problem or principal-agent problem. The agency problem arises when a principal entrusts an agent with a responsibility or task and the principal is not able to directly observe the agent when carrying out the task or fulfilling the responsibility. Jensen and Meckling (1976) set out a theory of the corporation and corporate governance commonly referred to as Agency Theory, which is based on the agency problem. Agency Theory will be discussed in the section on corporate governance theories later in the chapter.

The private property rights and obligations of the owner of an item of private property include : 1) the right to possess the property, 2) the right to use the property, 3) the right to manage the property, 4) the right to the income generated from the property, 5) the right to the capital value of the property, 6) the right to security from expropriation, 7) the right to sell or bequeath the property, 8) the absence of term of ownership of the property, 9) the prohibition of harmful use of the property, 10) liability to execution (as repayment for debt), and 11) residuary character (Becker, 1977: 18–19 based on Honoré, 1961: 107–147).

Armour *et al.* (2009: 5) identify five characteristics of the modern corporation. These characteristics include:

1 the legal personality of the company separate from the legal personality of its shareholders
2 limited liability of its shareholders
3 transferable shares (in the case of listed companies: freely tradable shares)
4 centralized delegated management under a board structure
5 absentee investor ownership.

Separate legal personality of a company bestows separate patrimony upon the company's assets. In other words, the company's assets are separate from those of its shareholders. This shields the entity's assets from the personal creditors of the shareholders. Entity shielding also means that the company's creditors have prior claim on the company's assets and the shareholders have the residual claim on the company's assets after any liabilities to its creditors have been paid. Furthermore, as a consequence of its separate legal personality, the company can own assets, its designated managers can enter into contracts on the company's behalf and in the company's name, and the company can sue or be sued.

Limited liability means that the shareholders have limited liability to creditors who have claims on the company's assets. The liability of the shareholders is limited to the amount of their investment in the company. As such, limited liability shields the personal assets of the shareholders from the creditors of the company. As a consequence, limited liability facilitates delegated management and 'shifting downside business risk from shareholders to creditors' (Armour *et al.*, 2009: 11).

Free tradability of shares enables shareholders to buy, hold and sell shares at will. This maximizes liquidity of the shareholdings, which is good for the stock market as well as the investors. From a corporate governance perspective, free tradability of shares potentially reduces shareholders' interest in the company's management and reduces their incentives to perform their monitoring duties.

For this reason, shareholders delegate their monitoring activities to a board of directors. The board of directors comprises a group of people who represent the company's shareholders, who act on behalf of the shareholders and who are accountable to the shareholders. 'Corporate Law typically vests principal authority over corporate affairs in a board of directors or similar committee organ that is periodically elected, exclusively or primarily, by the firm's shareholders' (Armour *et al.*, 2009: 13). Formally, the board is separate from the operational managers of the company. In some countries, there is a two-tier board. The supervisory tier is (at least nominally) separate from the company's hired officers (i.e. its senior managerial employees) and comprises the directors who are elected by the shareholders. The second tier, also called the managing tier, comprises the company's senior managerial employees such as the Chief Operating Officer (COO), the Chief Financial Officer (CFO) and the Chief Information Officer (CIO). The company's top manager, the Chief Executive Officer (CEO), would be part of both tiers. In a single-tier board, hired senior managerial employees may be members of, or even dominate, the board of directors.

> Regardless of the actual allocation of power between the firm's directors and officers, the legal distinction between them formally divides all corporate decisions that do not require shareholder approval into those requiring approval by the board of directors and those that can be made by the firm's hired officers on their own authority.

(Armour *et al.*, 2009: 13)

The board of directors is elected, at least in substantial part, by the company's shareholders. Although entirely or largely chosen by the shareholders, the board of directors is distinct from the shareholders because otherwise decision making would be too costly and inefficient. Finally, the board of directors of a listed company has multiple members so that, at least in principle, authority is not concentrated in the hands of one single person.

The five characteristics of listed companies represent modifications to the private property rights and obligations of an owner of an item of property. On the one hand, these modifications serve society by making it more attractive to engage in relatively risky private investment and contribute to economic growth because they enable risk sharing, fixed capital formation and technological development. On the other, consequences of these modifications include the costs resulting from the conflicting interests between different stakeholders in the company.

ACTIVITY 9.1

Why would the governance of a publicly traded business corporation be different from other types of business organization such as a sole trader, a partnership or a private company?

Activity feedback

In order to answer this question, we need to think about the different characteristics of these business organizations. The owners of sole traders and partnerships bear unlimited liability for all the obligations (including torts) of the business. The governance of these organizations is relatively straightforward because unlimited liability provides a strong incentive for the owners to take an active interest in the business.

In the case of limited companies, the company has a separate legal personality from its owners (the shareholders). The shareholders of limited companies enjoy limited liability for all the obligations (including torts) of the business. In private limited companies the main shareholders are sometimes also directors of the company and can even be involved in the day to day running of the company. In many cases, however, the

company will be run by its senior management on behalf of the shareholders.

This separation of the ownership of the company and the control of its assets creates a situation known as the agency problem (or principal-agent problem). In this situation, the danger exists that the senior managers run the company in their own interests rather than in the interests of the shareholders. Some corporate governance structures and mechanisms are meant to mitigate this problem through monitoring. Financial reporting is an important tool that enables shareholders to monitor the managers' stewardship of the company's assets. Shareholders who are neither directors nor managers of a private limited company have a strong incentive to monitor the performance of the senior managers in discharging their stewardship responsibilities. The shareholders' investment is not very liquid as they cannot simply sell their shares at will. Usually selling one's shares in a private limited company requires approval from the other shareholders.

In the case of public limited companies, and especially publicly traded companies, shareholders can simply sell their shares in the company whenever they see fit. Therefore, shareholders of publicly traded companies have less of an incentive to monitor the senior management. Other corporate governance structures and mechanisms are meant to mitigate the agency problem through the alignment of the senior managers' *interests with those of the shareholders. Unfortunately, sometimes these mechanisms have unintended consequences by aligning the interests of shareholders and managers at the expense of other stakeholders or even the general public.*

Corporate governance definitions

According to Goergen (2012: 6) corporate governance deals with conflicts of interests between:

1 The providers of finance and senior management

2 Different types of shareholders, particularly majority shareholders and minority shareholders

3 The shareholders and the stakeholders.

Many definitions of corporate governance exist. How one defines corporate governance depends on which of the conflicts of interest is the main focus and one's perspective on the purpose of the corporation in society. For example, the principle of shareholder primacy, which focuses on a subset of the first conflict of interest, leads to a definition such as the following:

> Corporate governance is the system by which companies are directed and controlled. Boards of directors are responsible for the governance of their companies. The shareholders' role in governance is to appoint the directors and the auditors and to satisfy that an appropriate governance structure is in place. The responsibilities of the board include setting the company's strategic aims, providing the leadership to put them into effect, supervising the management of the business and reporting to shareholders on their stewardship. The board's actions are subject to laws, regulations and the shareholders in the general meeting.

> (FRC, 2012, para. 2, or, originally, FRC, 1992, para. 2.5)

A focus on the interests of investors would lead Schleifer and Vishny (1997: 737) to say that 'corporate governance deals with the ways in which suppliers of finance assure themselves of getting a return on their investment'.

A broader definition is the one in the G20/OECD Principles of Corporate Governance from the OECD (2015: 9):

> Corporate governance involves a set of relationships between a company's management, its board, its shareholders and other stakeholders. Corporate governance also provides the structure through which the objectives of the company are set, and the means of attaining those objectives and monitoring performance are determined.

ACTIVITY 9.2

Comparing the three definitions of corporate governance above, how do they relate to the three conflicts of interest?

Activity feedback

Both the FRC's and Schleifer and Vishny's definitions focus on the conflict of interests between the providers of finance and senior management. The FRC's definition focuses on shareholder interests and Schleifer and Vishny's definition includes all investors, i.e. providers of finance. The OECD's definition is more all-inclusive because it represents a stakeholder perspective on corporate governance. Like Entity Theory in accounting, the stakeholder perspective regards corporations as institutions in their own right, the managers of which must be responsible to their shareholders as well as the wider stakeholder community. The FRC definition sees the corporate governance structure as a matter between the board of directors and the shareholders. The board of directors monitors whether the managers fulfil their stewardship obligations in the best interests of the shareholders, and the shareholders monitor the board of directors. This FRC definition is more representative of a shareholder perspective on corporate governance. Like Proprietary Theory in accounting, the shareholder perspective regards corporations as the private property of its shareholders. Hence the managers are responsible to the owners of the firm. Schleifer and Vishny's definition is more related to the decision-usefulness theory of general purpose financial reporting.

CORPORATE GOVERNANCE ISSUES

Above we mentioned three types of conflicts of interest, which result in three types of agency problem. Here we will look into the particular agency problems caused by the conflicts of interests between the different groups of stakeholders.

Conflicts of interest between the providers of finance and senior management

Goergen (2012: 9) mentions perks and empire building as the two ways in which senior managers run the company in their own interests rather than in the interests of the shareholders. Perks or fringe benefits are on-the-job consumption of the company's assets by its senior managers. Examples include lavish offices for senior managers, the use of corporate jets or company cars for private purposes, golf memberships and so on which reduce the income available for dividend payments.

Empire building occurs when the senior managers use the company's free cash flows to pursue the firm's growth in cases when this is not necessarily in the interests of the company's shareholders. As mentioned in Chapter 5, companies would normally invest in positive net present value projects in order to maximize the returns to the company's shareholders. A growth strategy can be in the interest of the shareholders in the medium to longer term, but managers can also embark on a growth strategy to increase their own salaries, bonuses, status and power (Goergen, 2012: 11).

When a company is financed by both equity and debt, sometimes managers and or shareholders may collude against the debt holders by seeking to pursue their shared interests at the expense of the debt holders by investing in high risk projects (Goergen, 2012: 11). If the projects fail, it is the debt holders who bear the brunt of the losses. If the projects are successful, payoff to the debt holders is limited and it is the shareholders (as the residual equity holders) who gain the most from the company's investment.

Conflicts of interests between the different types of shareholders

As we will see later in the chapter, in most countries companies' shareholder ownership is not as dispersed as in the US or the UK. In these countries, the agency problem takes the form of the risk of appropriation of the minority shareholders by the majority (controlling) shareholders. According to Goergen (2012: 13), the main forms of appropriation occur via related party transactions either through tunnelling (transferring assets or profits from the company to its largest shareholder) or through transfer pricing. Nepotism is a form of expropriation where shareholders appoint family members into the company's senior management positions.

Conflicts of interest between the shareholders and the other stakeholders

The possibilities are endless. Conflicts of interest occur between shareholders and creditors/lenders, shareholders and employees, shareholders and customers, shareholders and suppliers, shareholders and the government, shareholders and the general public.

THEORIES OF CORPORATE GOVERNANCE

Having looked at the characteristics of large listed companies and the conflicts of interest between different groups that have a stake (financial or otherwise) in the company, we now turn to theories of corporate governance. There are many corporate governance theories, but here we will focus on three existing theories and one area in which theory is needed but not well-developed. Agency Theory and Stewardship Theory (like Proprietary Theory and Residual Equity Theory in accounting) both focus on the company as a vehicle for its owners to increase their wealth. Stakeholder Theory, like Entity Theory in accounting, focuses on the company as an institution in its own right and its responsibility to all its stakeholders in order to best achieve the company's objectives.

Agency Theory

Agency Theory has its roots in the views of economists such as Alchian and Demsetz (1972) and Williamson (1970, 1975), but was developed by Jensen and Meckling (1976) who set out the principal-agent problem in the context of corporations. Agency Theory 'assumes that the company exists for the benefit of its owners, who are assumed to be solely interested in the maximisation of their wealth' (Aras and Crowther, 2012: 193). Both the principals and the agents are assumed to be rational economic persons who are motivated by self-interest.

Agents are assumed to allocate their time at work between productive effort and shirking and allocate the company's resources between productive investments and the consumption of perquisites (Aras and Crowther, 2012: 195). Because the principals cannot directly observe the agents' actions and do not have the same information as the agents, there exists a situation called information asymmetry.

Under information asymmetry (in contracting), adverse selection refers to the situation that an agent has private information about the costs of their private efforts which the principal does not have at the time they enter into an employment contract, hence the contract could be on terms that are disadvantageous to the principal or the principal might hire the wrong agent. Under information asymmetry, moral hazard refers to the situation where the agent may be tempted to shirk and consume perks as much as they think they can get away with, rather than live up to the terms of their contract.

The existence of information asymmetry between principal and agent in companies is one reason why financial reporting plays a role in enabling the company's managers to report on the way that they have discharged their stewardship obligations. Furthermore, the principals will incur monitoring costs, such as the costs of auditing the financial statements, or the costs of employing supervisors (such as the board of directors). The principals may also incur bonding costs, i.e. the costs of aligning the interests of the agents with those of the principals, such as bonuses, managerial ownership of shares, stock options and other incentive systems. After all these efforts, it is likely that there will still be a residual loss borne by the principal (Aras and Crowther, 2012: 196).

Agency Theory predicts that, if the CEO is at the same time the chairperson of the board of directors, it is more likely that the interests of the shareholders are more easily sacrificed because of increased managerial opportunism.

> An implication of agency theory is that where CEO duality is retained, shareholder interests could be protected by aligning the interests of the CEO and the shareholders by a suitable incentive scheme for the CEO, i.e. by a system of long-term compensation additional to basic salary.
>
> (Donaldson and Davis, 1991: 52)

Stewardship Theory

Stewardship Theory, which stems from organizational sociology and organization psychology, posits that agents are more likely to want to do a good job because they are intrinsically motivated by successfully performing challenging tasks, recognition from peers and bosses, responsibility and authority. Unlike according to Agency Theory, in order to achieve the company's objectives, the main challenge is not so much designing the organizational structure to avoid monitoring and bonding costs. Rather, it is to design the organizational structure such that it helps the executive to formulate and implement plans for corporate performance. To this purpose, it must provide clear, consistent role expectations and authorize and empower senior management (Donaldson 1985). Stewardship Theory holds that the dual role of the CEO as CEO and chairperson of the board of directors makes the CEO more effective, which results in higher returns for shareholders.

Stakeholder Theory

As mentioned above, Stakeholder Theory sees the company as an institution in its own right. 'Stakeholder analysts argue that all persons or groups with legitimate interests participating in an enterprise do so to obtain benefits and that there is no prima facie priority of one set of interests and benefits over another' (Donaldson and Preston, 1995: 68). There are three aspects to Stakeholder Theory. The descriptive aspect is that Stakeholder Theory rests on the observation that companies often do identify and manage their stakeholders (e.g. Freeman, 1984; Carroll, 1991). The instrumental aspect predicts that stakeholder management leads to favourable corporate performance and shareholder benefits in the longer term. Finally, the normative aspect of the Theory is that taking into account the interests of all the company's stakeholders is morally the right thing to do (Donaldson and Preston, 1995: 68).

As a consequence, Stakeholder Theory holds that a company's managers have the responsibility to identify and reconcile all the company's stakeholders in order to best achieve the company's objectives.

ACTIVITY 9.3

How would you critique the three theories of corporate governance above?

Activity feedback

Many criticisms exist in the literature. However, intuitively, you may have thought of the fact that Agency Theory assumes people are always acting in their own self-interest. People do act altruistically and are intrinsically motivated by simply doing a good job or by respect or appreciation from their peers.

Conversely, Stewardship Theory assumes that people are mostly intrinsically motivated. It is possible that enabling the CEO to play a dual role does indeed lead to managers behaving opportunistically in some cases.

Stakeholder Theory makes sense to a certain extent. Companies do engage in stakeholder management and this is likely to lead to higher satisfaction of some stakeholders. On the other hand, the Theory says little about the relative importance of each of the stakeholders or what it means to manage the company for the longer term, if the terms of a CEO and other members of the senior officers or the board of directors do not extend into the long term. Finally, what is morally right and morally wrong are issues on which it is often very difficult to obtain general agreement.

Corporate governance in multinational corporations

Some multinational corporations have become richer and more powerful than some small countries. Furthermore, since companies can cherry pick the countries where they wish to be registered and to some extent pay their taxes, it is difficult to see how corporate governance structures are able to ensure that companies and their senior management act in the best interests of all the shareholders or all the stakeholders or the general public whose lives they affect.

TAXONOMIES OF CORPORATE GOVERNANCE SYSTEMS

Parallel to taxonomies of financial accounting systems discussed in Chapter 2, early attempts to categorize the different systems of capitalism included the distinction between market-based economies and bank-based economies made by Hicks and Chandler. Market-based economies are those where companies rely on well-developed capital markets and publicly traded securities to finance their investments (Goergen, 2012: 68). Bank-based economies are those where companies rely on bank loans rather than capital markets for their debt financing and where banks often also have an equity stake in the companies that they lend to.

Franks and Mayer (2001) distinguished between insider systems and outsider systems. Insider systems are characterized by concentrated control and ownership structures, such as often found in Germany, Italy, Korea or Japan. Outsider systems, on the other hand, are characterized by dispersed ownership and control, well-developed stock markets and an active takeover market (Goergen, 2012: 69).

ACTIVITY 9.4

From the following corporate governance mechanisms, can you identify which ones work best in an insider system and which work best in an outsider system?

- monitoring by large banks and creditors
- managerial remuneration
- corporate takeover market
- monitoring by large shareholders
- proxy votes
- dividend policy
- the board of directors
- institutional shareholders
- managerial shareholder ownership.

Activity feedback

Works best in outsider system	Works best in insider system
Dividend policy	*Monitoring by large banks and creditors*
The board of directors	*Monitoring by large shareholders*
Institutional shareholders	*Proxy votes*
Managerial shareholder ownership	
Managerial remuneration	
Corporate takeover market	

As with the financial reporting taxonomies, another way of looking at causes for different systems of corporate governance structures starts with the distinction between civil law and common law legal systems. In corporate governance, this distinction is clearly dependent on the level of legal protection of the property rights of shareholders, investors and creditors. According to La Porta *et al.* (1997, 2000) shareholder and creditor protection is highest in common law countries and lowest in French civil law countries. German and Scandinavian civil law countries are somewhere in between.

Finally, the 'varieties of capitalism' literature distinguishes between liberal market economies (LME) and coordinated market economies (CME) (Hall and Soskice, 2001). The idea is that in LMEs, the coordination mechanism depends to a large extent on arms-length transactions in labour, financial, capital and product markets. On the other hand, in CMEs, the coordination mechanism is based to a somewhat lesser extent on markets which are complemented by complex networks and longer-term relationships.

A BRIEF HISTORY OF CORPORATIONS AND CORPORATE GOVERNANCE MECHANISMS

Early history until 1930

The corporation finds its origin in the Middle Ages. Corporations were often established for a specific social purpose so that churches, universities, etc. could have a life beyond those who operated them. In the sixteenth and seventeenth centuries, at a time when the market economy was only germinating, they were used to raise capital for ventures of a limited period, such as sea voyages to the East. The VOC and East India Companies extended the corporate form again to make these ventures last beyond single voyages. Later, corporations were established for the purpose of building capital-intensive canals and railways, without which the Industrial Revolution would have been difficult, if not impossible. The concept of limited liability was developed to enable projects on an ever increasing scale to be realized. Limited liability makes investing in companies less risky for shareholders and hence more attractive. This was at the time a very controversial concept because it meant doing away with unlimited liability, which is one of the fundamental elements attached to the institution of private property. Public limited corporations listed on stock exchanges made markets more liquid and investment more flexible and thus even more attractive. However, limited liability also limits the incentives for shareholders to perform their monitoring task and, in combination with the ability to sell their shares at will, reduces shareholders' incentives to monitor managers even further, particularly when they invest in portfolios which they regularly adjust. By the third quarter of the nineteenth century, especially in the UK and the US, corporations had lost their social purpose and were primarily regarded as vehicles for individual investors to increase their wealth. With a view to promoting shareholder democratization, ever smaller par value denominations enabled more and more ordinary people to invest in shares. During this period, Proprietary Theory, which holds that accounting for corporations must be done from the viewpoint of the owners, was based on the idea that the company is the private property of the shareholders and that they are, indeed, the effective owners of the company.

1930 to 1960

The stock market crash in the US in 1929 indicated a problem with corporate governance. The consequences of the crash reverberated around the world. Berle and Means (1968/2009) found that the separation of ownership of the company and control of its assets caused a fundamental alteration in the institution of private property rights. They suggested solutions such as voting rights for all shareholders and greater transparency and accountability. The Securities and Exchange Laws (1932 and 1933) included a serious attempt at the regulation of financial reporting disclosure. In other words, this was the start of an increased role for financial reporting in corporate governance. Entity Theory was developed during this period. The Entity perspective on the corporation is based on the idea that it is not effectively owned by the shareholders and that, therefore, the accounting must be done from the perspective of the reporting entity itself. The Second World War may have contributed to the development of the stakeholder perspective on corporate governance, because it forced the introduction of greater equality in many societies in the post-war period.

1960 to 1990

Developed in the 1960s and 1970s, Agency Theory focused solutions to the 'Principal/Agent' (or agency) problem on aligning the incentives of managers with those of the owners. The agency problem concerns potential conflicts of interest arising between the owners (principals) and boards of directors (agents) who have effective control over the company. Bonuses and other incentives became increasingly popular and these are often based, at least partially, on financial reporting information. Later, it became more common to also include market indicators, such as stock price, in the bonus calculations.

The 1970s also saw an emphasis on independent outside directors, audit committees and the establishment of two-tier boards in companies because it became apparent that if the relation between senior management and the board of directors is too close, it would pervert the monitoring function of the board. The EEC, in its fifth draft Directive in 1972, advocated two-tier board governance as seen in Germany and Holland. In the US the same problem caused litigation to increase as shareholders of failed companies sought recompense from directors and so on.

Owing to the gigantic size of some corporations, the 1970s also saw a growth in the idea that public companies, in addition to their duty to shareholders (owners), also had responsibilities to other stakeholders such as employees, customers, suppliers, lenders, community and government.

During the 1980s, action on corporate governance was minimal and more company collapses and questionable practices were seen throughout the world, attributed by many to the power of executive directors who had no checks or balances upon them. In particular, the combination of the CEO and chairperson role was questioned, as was the lack of power of non-executive directors.

1990 to 2008

Until the early 1990s, the assumption was often that ownership of companies was widely dispersed, so that shareholders were often unable to influence management decisions unless they found ways to unite. However, the 1990s saw the growth in power of major institutional investors. In the UK, the issue was brought to the fore by the *Cadbury Report* (Cadbury Committee, 1992) and the establishment of the Cadbury Code that focused on the financial aspects of corporate governance, corporate behaviour and ethics and led to improved boardroom practice. In 1995 the *Greenbury Report* (Greenbury Committee, 1995) added Principles on the Remuneration of Executive Directors in an attempt to curb CEO salaries. These two reports were brought together by the *Hampel Report* of 1998 and formed the first Combined Code. The following year saw the publication of the *Turnbull Report*, which concentrated on risk management and internal controls. All of these reports were as a result of shareholder disquiet over corporate performance and to avoid the threat of government legislation if such codes were not developed voluntarily by the business sector. The *Cadbury Report* had great influence around the world, and several other countries published their own corporate governance reports in the 1990s. All of these reports were concerned with the abuse of corporate power and recommended wider use of audit committees, outside non-executive directors, remuneration committees composed of independent outside directors to advise on director remuneration, and the separation of the chairperson and CEO roles.

Starting in the 1980s, the 1990s also saw the use of (sometimes hostile) takeovers as an effective means to bring managers to heel. From then on, the takeover market was deemed an external corporate governance mechanism to help focus managers on the financial interests of shareholders. Particularly in the Anglophone countries, renewed shareholder power reversed the idea that shareholders were not effectively the owners of the company. During this period, there was a swing back from the Entity perspective on the corporation towards the Proprietary perspective. This can also be observed in the IASB Conceptual Framework and the IFRSs. This trend had started earlier in the US, probably because the influence of Agency Theory, institutional investors and the takeover market had started earlier there. In 1998, the OECD proposed the development of global guidelines for corporate governance and emphasized the difference between the strong external investment culture of the US and UK with the firm corporate governance practices in Japan, France and Germany where employees had more influence and investors seemed to take a longer-term view.

The turn of the century saw the growth in global corporate structures with vast networks of subsidiaries, strategic alliances and related parties. For better or worse, directors of major entities now wield extensive power, and companies have a pervasive influence on communities.

The FRC in the UK took the *Higgs Report* forward together with the *Smith Report* on Audit Committees to publish its *Combined Code of Corporate Governance* in July 2003. This was further revised by the Turnbull Review Group and a revised code issued by the FRC in 2005. About this time, the European Commission also issued its *Corporate Governance and Company Law Action Plan* covering disclosure requirements, exercise of voting rights, cross-border voting, disclosure by institutional investors and responsibilities of board members.

From 2008 onwards

The events of 2008 have shown us that bankers, traders and financial institutions around the world wield extensive power and for all the reports, codes, action plans and publications on corporate governance, it still remains an issue. James Wolfensohn, President of the World Bank, stated in 2008: 'The governance of companies is more important for world economic growth than the government of countries'. However, a potentially socially costly danger is multinational corporations engaging in regulatory arbitrage. This enables them to cherry pick the countries with the most advantageous rules and regulations. Think, for example, of the news in November 2012 that Starbucks, Amazon and Google had not paid corporation tax in the UK for years because ingenious constructions allow them to legally show no profit. Under pressure of public opinion, Starbucks voluntarily decided to pay £10 million. How is it possible that Starbucks can decide how much tax it is going to pay? Recently, in January 2016, Google reached an agreement with Her Majesty's Revenue Service to pay £130 million in back taxes. This amounts to a tax rate of about 3 per cent, despite a UK corporation tax rate of more than 20 per cent (see www.theguardian.com/business/2016/jan/25/mps-launch-corporation-tax-inquiry-criticism-130m-google-hmrc-deal, accessed on 5 February 2016).

Since economic and financial globalization have progressed much faster than political globalization, it may not be so easy for governments to do anything effective about the problems of tax evasion and regulatory arbitrage.

Since 2008, many codes worldwide have been adapted or are in the process of adaptation, implying that new articles are added or that elements are being transferred to the law. The OECD did not reform its 2004 Code straightaway, but issued recommendations in three documents entitled: *Corporate Governance Lessons from the Financial Crisis* (January 2009), *Corporate Governance and the Financial Crisis: Key Findings and Main Messages* (June 2009) and *Conclusions and Emerging Good Practices to Enhance Implementation of the Principles* (February 2010). In September 2015 the G20 and the OECD issued the *G20/OECD Principles of Corporate Governance*. In the UK, the FRC revised its Code in 2010 and issued a new edition in 2012, when it also issued *The UK Stewardship Code* (both of which will be discussed below).

ACTIVITY 9.5

Identify the main corporate governance mechanisms discussed above and indicate what problems they are meant to address. Can you think of any others?

Activity feedback

Corporate governance mechanism	Problem it is meant to address
Governance structure of the company	Specifies the distribution of rights and responsibilities among different participants in the corporation
Incentives for executive directors and other senior managers	Align the interests of the executive directors and senior managers with those of the company's shareholders in order to mitigate the agency problem
Audited annual and interim financial statements	To enable the discharge of managers' stewardship and responsibilities to the shareholders and provide accountability to the other stakeholders
Shareholder participation in the AGM	Monitor and influence the managers' decisions in the interest of long-term shareholders
Corporate takeover market	Discipline the managers to act in the best interests of short-term shareholders

PRINCIPLES AND CODES OF CORPORATE GOVERNANCE

Below we will briefly outline the 2015 G20/OECD Principles of Corporate Governance. Corporate governance in the EU relies on the application of legislation and soft law such as national corporate governance codes of the member countries. We will also discuss the 2014 UK Code of Governance as an example of a national code of corporate governance.

The 2015 G20/OECD Principles of Corporate Governance

The 2015 G20/OECD Principles are intended to help policymakers evaluate and improve the legal, regulatory and institutional framework for corporate governance. The aim of the framework is to support economic efficiency, sustainable growth and financial stability. The idea is that this will be achieved by providing shareholders, board members and executives as well as financial intermediaries and service providers with the right incentives to perform their roles within a framework of checks and balances. Like the 2004 OECD Principles, the 2015 G20/OECD Principles are presented in six different chapters:

Chapter 1: Ensuring the basis for an effective corporate governance framework

This chapter states that the framework for corporate governance must serve the public interest by promoting transparent and fair markets and the efficient allocation of resources. It also recognizes the differences between institutional environments and what works in one country does not necessarily work elsewhere.

Chapter 2: The rights and equitable treatment of shareholders and key ownership functions

This chapter sets out that corporate governance framework should protect and facilitate the exercise of shareholders' rights and ensure the equitable treatment of all shareholders, including minority and foreign shareholders. All shareholders should have the opportunity to obtain effective redress for violation of their rights.

Chapter 3: Institutional investors, stock markets and other intermediaries

The corporate governance framework should provide sound incentives throughout the investment chain and provide for stock markets to function in a way that contributes to good corporate governance.

Chapter 4: The role of stakeholders

The corporate governance framework should recognize the rights of stakeholders established by law or through mutual agreements and encourage active co-operation between corporations and stakeholders in creating wealth, jobs and the sustainability of financially sound enterprises.

Chapter 5: Disclosure and transparency

The corporate governance framework should ensure that timely and accurate disclosure is made on all material matters regarding the corporation, including the financial situation, performance, ownership and governance of the company.

Chapter 6: The responsibilities of the board

The corporate governance framework should ensure the strategic guidance of the company, the effective monitoring of management by the board and the board's accountability to the company and its shareholders. This chapter sets out the responsibilities and functions of the board and discusses ways in which the board could fulfil its responsibilities.

The next step for the OECD working with the G20 and stakeholders is to promote and monitor effective implementation of the revised Principles.

Corporate governance in the EU

In the EU, the distribution of governance-related principles between law and codes in each Member State depends on a number of factors, including legal tradition, ownership structures and the maturity of the corporate governance tradition. In 2006, the European Commission issued Directive 2006/46/EC, introducing the comply-or-explain principle for the first time in European Law. This was strengthened by the Disclosure Directive in 2013 (Directive 2013/34/EU).

> Directive 2013/34/EU of the European Parliament and of the Council of 26 June 2013 on the annual financial statements, consolidated financial statements and related reports of certain types of undertakings requires companies to include a corporate governance statement in their management report if their transferable securities are admitted to trading on a regulated market of any Member State.
>
> (Commission Recommendation 2014/208/EU: Para. 3)

> The corporate governance statement should provide essential information on the corporate governance arrangements of the company, such as information relating to the relevant corporate governance code(s) applied by that company, the internal control and risk management systems, the shareholder meeting and its powers, shareholders' rights, administrative, management and supervisory bodies and their committees.
>
> (Commission Recommendation 2014/208/EU: Para. 4)

> The 'comply-or-explain' principle laid down in Article 20 of Directive 2013/34/EU is a key feature of European corporate governance. According to this principle, companies that depart from the relevant corporate governance code are required

to explain in their corporate governance statement which parts of the Code they depart from and the reasons for doing so.

(Commission Recommendation 2014/208/EU: Para. 6)

The UK Corporate Governance Code 2014

The UK Corporate Governance Code as a whole is meant to identify principles that underpin an effective board of directors. Three of its five main principles, i.e. A. Leadership; B. Effectiveness; and D. Remuneration are entirely dedicated to the functioning of the board. It stresses the collective responsibility of the board for the long-term success of the company and the chairman's responsibility for leadership of the board. Also, C. Accountability and E. Relations with shareholders are presented as functions of the board. The UK Codes are not a rigid set of rules and do recognize that non-compliance may be justified in particular circumstances if good governance can be achieved by other means. The reasons for non-compliance should, however, be explained to shareholders. Thus, the UK Codes rely on a 'comply-or-explain approach'.

You can of course access the *OECD Principles of Corporate Governance* on the website: www.oecd.org and *The UK Corporate Governance Code* and *The UK Stewardship Code* on the FRC website: www.frc.gov.uk.

The Dutch corporate governance code is part of a system based on national and international best practice integrated with Dutch and European legislation and case law on corporate governance, which must be viewed in its entirety. It is also an example of a corporate governance code that lies in between the G20/OECD Principles and the 2014 UK Code discussed above (see www.commissiecorporategovernance.nl/monitoring-committee, accessed 1 May 2013).

ACTIVITY 9.6

Identify the role of financial reporting within corporate governance.

Activity feedback

Financial reporting is about providing useful information to users to enable them to make informed decisions regarding stewardship and the future. Information on whether or not a company complies with the principles of the governance code is of key importance to judge the governance of the firm. In case of non-compliance, a transparent explanation should be provided as to why the company chose not to comply.

ACTIVITY 9.7

What other information might investors and other stakeholders be interested in that is not provided in the published financial statements? You might check the 'investor relations' sections of a few websites of listed companies in order to find out what kind of additional information is provided most frequently.

Activity feedback

You may find many different types of additional report, some of which are meant to give investors more information which helps them to better understand the entity's financial performance, such as a management commentary. Other statements will give more information about the entity's corporate governance structure, such as a corporate governance charter. Yet other statements will give information about the entity's relations with the broader stakeholder community in addition to the relations with its shareholders.

SUMMARY

In this chapter, we have considered the characteristics of large public companies, definitions of corporate governance and issues in corporate governance caused by conflicts of interest between different groups of stakeholders. We discussed three theories of corporate governance: Agency Theory, Stewardship Theory and Stakeholder Theory, and considered taxonomies of corporate governance systems. We looked at a brief history of corporations and corporate governance mechanisms. Finally we considered principles and codes of corporate governance, including the 2015 G20/OECD Principles of Corporate Governance.

EXERCISES

Suggested answers to exercises marked ✓ are to be found in the Student online resources, with suggested answers to the remaining questions available in the Instructor online resources.

1 Consider Agency Theory, Stewardship Theory and Stakeholder Theory. Which theory do you think best describes the problems of corporate governance and why?

✓2 Compare what you have read about taxonomies of financial accounting and reporting systems with taxonomies of corporate governance systems. Identify similarities and differences. Discuss.

3 Appraise the development of corporate governance in meeting the needs of business and its stakeholders in the twenty-first century in your own country.

4 Appraise the relationship between corporate scandals and corporate governance regulation and codes of practice.

✓5 'While La Porta *et al.*'s categorization of legal families ... suggests that there should be little difference between the UK and the USA, the US approach is substantially different' (Goergen, 2012: 137). Look at sources on the internet and try to find out in which ways the US and the UK approaches to corporate governance are different.

6 Appraise the harmonization of corporate governance regulation across the EU.

✓7 Look back at Activity 9.4. Can you think of an underlying reason why some corporate governance mechanisms work better in insider systems and other corporate governance mechanisms work better in outsider systems?

BUSINESS ETHICS, CSR, SUSTAINABILITY REPORTING AND SRI

10

OBJECTIVES After studying this chapter you should be able to:

- define ethics and business ethics

- explain how business ethics relates to corporate governance and financial accounting

- define corporate social responsibility (CSR) and describe different perspectives on CSR

- explain the UN Global Compact's ten principles

- describe:

  - ISO 26000

  - the International Integrated Reporting (IR) Framework

  - the Global Reporting Initiative's (GRI's) *G4 Sustainability Reporting Guidelines*

  - the ISAE 3000 and AA1000 AS assurance standards

- explain the origins of socially responsible investment (SRI)

- describe the two main types of SRI analysis

- describe different SRI fund indices.

INTRODUCTION

In the first section, this chapter looks into definitions of ethics and business ethics. It explores different perspectives on ethics and the need for moral behaviour in business over and above what is required by law. The second section discusses issues in, perspectives on and approaches to practising CSR. We will consider guidance for companies seeking a formal approach to CSR in the United Nation's Global Compact and ISO 26000, and look at the EU's stance on CSR. In the third section, we will look into the practice of CSR reporting and discuss issues in CSR reporting and the verification of CSR reporting. The fourth section discusses CSR indices and considers approaches to SRI.

ETHICS, BUSINESS ETHICS AND THE MORALITY OF THE MARKETS

In this section, we will first define ethics and consider some perspectives on ethics. We will then define business ethics and, finally, we will discuss the need for business ethics with relevance to the morality of free market capitalism.

Ethics

Ethics is a branch of philosophy. It is also called moral philosophy. Other branches of philosophy include theory of knowledge, philosophy of mind, philosophy of science, philosophy of religion and political philosophy. 'Ethics, or moral philosophy asks basic questions about the good life, about what is better and worse, about whether there is any objective right and wrong, and how we know it if there is' (MacKinnon, 2001: 4). We can distinguish three types of enquiry in ethics.

1 Normative ethics provides theories about what is the right thing to do and why this is so.

2 Practical ethics is about what is the right thing to do in a specific situation.

3 Meta-ethics considers the very concepts of 'right' and 'wrong' and where they come from.

In respect of normative ethical theories, we can distinguish between consequentialist (or teleological) moral and non-consequentialist (or deontological) moral theories. The Greek root '*telos*' means goal and the Greek root '*deon*' means duty. Teleological moral theories base moral judgements on the consequences of decisions and actions, whereas deontological moral theories hold that decisions and actions can be wrong irrespective of their positive or negative outcomes (MacKinnon, 2001: 10). The belief that there is an objective right and wrong is called objectivism or non-relativism. On the other hand, the belief that ethical values and beliefs are relative to individuals and societies and that objective moral judgement is not possible, is called ethical relativism. Individual ethical relativism is the idea that moral values and beliefs are the expressions of individuals, but there is no objective standard against which to judge whether these beliefs are right or wrong. Social or cultural ethical relativism 'holds that ethical values vary from society to society and that the basis for moral judgments lies in these social or cultural views' (MacKinnon, 2001: 25). Therefore, an individual must look to the moral values of their society to decide what is right or wrong.

Adopting a stance of moral relativism can lead to tolerance of different people's and different societies' values. However, tolerance may not be a value for all individuals and all societies, hence it could lead to chaos and even violence. Adopting a stance of moral objectivism implies the belief that there is an objective morality that is real because it is independent from cultures or individuals. But how would we know what this objective morality is?

Business ethics is often a matter of practical ethics as it usually requires an assessment of what is the right thing to do in a particular situation. The problem is, of course, how to weight the different factors that need to be taken into consideration. We will look into business ethics as practical ethics below. Meta-ethics is beyond the scope of this book.

Business ethics

In business, economic decisions are made at the individual, organizational and systemic levels (Boatright, 2009: 5–6). Making economic decisions in a business context often involves evaluating the alternative economic actions from strategic, commercial, financial and legal perspectives. Business ethics as an area of practice involves evaluating these alternative economic actions from a moral perspective as well. Business ethics is the study of business decisions, actions and consequences from a moral perspective.

ACTIVITY 10.1

'The law might be said to be a definition of the minimum acceptable standards of behaviour. However, many morally contestable issues, whether in business or elsewhere, are not specifically covered by the law' (Crane & Matten, 2007: 5).

Think of a morally contestable issue in business behaviour that is not specifically covered by law.

Activity feedback

You could have thought of the question of whether or not a tobacco company has the right to exist.

Smoking causes health problems for many people, but tobacco is also a source of tax revenues for the governments of most countries. You may have thought about some employers taking out life insurance on their employees without telling the employees. These are just two examples, but you probably get the gist. In business decisions, the ethical issues are often related to advancing the private interests of an individual, business entity or industry at the expense of the interests of other individuals, communities, animal species or the general public.

The morality of free market capitalism

According to McPhail and Walters (2009: 116), a free market capitalist economic system has four defining characteristics:

- private ownership of the means of production
- competition
- the division of capital and labour
- the profit motive.

Private ownership as opposed to state ownership and communal ownership is the predominant mode of owning the means of production in a capitalist economy. Different levels of state ownership and communal ownership of business organizations will still exist in most countries. The assumption is that competition, through the laws of supply and demand, is the way in which markets allocate scarce resources to their most valued (in financial terms) uses. We observed the division between the suppliers of capital and the suppliers of labour in Chapter 10 on corporate governance in the distinction between the hired officers and the elected directors in the discussion on the board of directors. The profit motive is what incentivizes entrepreneurs to engage in the creative and inventive business activity that has given us the products and services in the market today. Their self-interest works in the public interest through the invisible hand of the market.

The market is not a person. In spite of what you may read in the newspapers or hear on the news, the market does not think, feel or judge. A market merely represents the aggregate of what all of us buy and sell in that particular market. Competition and the profit motive can work in the public interest. However, without an appropriate institutional environment, they can also work in the interests of some who are willing to be opportunistic at the expense of the interests of others.

Free market capitalism works best when there is a high degree of trust in a society. Trust reduces the cost of transactions and the cost of maintaining the institutions that support and complement the system. People need to be able to trust the system to protect their transferable private property rights transparently, reliably and fairly. For the system to work reasonably well, customers need to be able to trust that the people who operate businesses are honest and dependable when they deliver their goods or services. Suppliers need to be able to trust that customers will pay on time to be willing to sell goods or services on credit. Credit is another essential ingredient of free market capitalism today. The legal system and the financial system enable a certain level of trust in the social system and the people in it. Alternatively, in societies with less developed formal institutions, people need to rely on informal institutions. For example, customers value the reputation of a business and will usually buy from the same reliable supplier. This works against arms' length transactions but creates business networks and long-term relationships. A business may choose to hire a family member to fill a crucial position rather than somebody who is better qualified but unknown.

ACTIVITY 10.2

Can you think of some examples where competition and the profit motive have led to unethical business behaviour?

Activity feedback

A recent example is the 2015 case of Volkswagen. It was discovered in the US that the Volkswagen cars were more polluting than Volkswagen claimed. The company had rigged the tests in order to intentionally misrepresent the test results of their diesel cars as much more environmentally friendly than is actually the case. In reality, some cars tested did not even meet the EU's own emission standards. An additional element to this case is that the European Commission has been implicated by allowing outdated testing methods and being aware of the problem before it was made public in the

US. It is possible that Germany's car industry has been able to influence the European Commission and the public opinion in Europe about its diesel cars in this way (www.bbc.co.uk/news/business-34324772, accessed 6 February 2016).

Two examples relate to baby milk powder. In the 1970s, Nestlé promoted bottle feeding babies in order to create a market for its baby formula in African and Asian countries. However, in many of these countries, the water supply was not safe. When mothers switched from breast milk to bottle feeding, mixing the baby formula with water caused many babies to become ill and even die. In 1981, the UN World Health Assembly (the governing body of the World Health Organisation) recommended the adoption of an international code of conduct to govern the promotion and sale of breast milk substitutes

ACTIVITY 10.2 *(Continued)*

(www.theguardian.com/sustainable-business/nestle-baby-milk-scandal-food-industry-standards, *accessed 6 February 2016*).

In 2008, there was a tainted infant formula scandal in China. At least 6 children died and 300 000 children were made ill. Dairy farmers and intermediaries had deliberately added melamine to boost the apparent protein levels of milk so that it would pass nutritional tests (www.theguardian.com/world/2009/nov/24/china-executes-milk-scandal-pair, accessed 6 February 2016).

In the first example above, it is interesting that in Europe many people were led to believe that diesel was more environmentally friendly than petrol. In the US and Japan for many years, scientists had already claimed that diesel was more polluting in some significant ways.

The second example shows that creating a new market, something that is commonplace in business, can have adverse unintended consequences that ought to be taken into account by a company, especially a multinational company. Nestlé at the time defended itself saying that, rather than Nestlé not convincing mothers to bottle feed their babies, the situation should be solved by the local authorities ensuring a safe water supply to their people. The tainted infant formula scandal in China caused Chinese people to distrust Chinese producers and instead parents started to purchase imported baby formula. The Chinese government executed two people involved in the scandal, but the population believed that these were scapegoats and continued to rely on imported product when they could.

WHAT IS CSR?

CSR is also called corporate responsibility, and others refer to it as 'Environmental, Social and Governance responsibility' (ESG). ESG recognizes that it is not only about '(a) the definitions of the responsibilities to society at large, [but it is also about] (b) how these responsibilities are defined and negotiated, and (c) how they are managed and organized' (Blowfield and Murray, 2011: 12).

CSR (or ESG) can be defined in many ways. In *A Renewed EU Strategy EU 2011–14 for Corporate Social Responsibility*, the European Commission defines CSR as 'the responsibility of enterprises for their impacts on society'.

> To fully meet their corporate social responsibility, enterprises should have in place a process to integrate social, environmental, ethical, human rights and consumer concerns into their business operations and core strategy in close collaboration with their stakeholders, with the aim of:
>
> • maximizing the creation of shared value for their owners/shareholders and for their other stakeholders and society at large
>
> • identifying, preventing and mitigating their possible adverse impacts.
>
> (European Commission Communication COM (2011) 681 final, p. 6)

Four types of corporate responsibility

According to Carroll's (1991) pyramid, companies can have four types of responsibility including:

1 The economic responsibility to produce goods and services that society wants in order to be profitable and survive.

2 The legal responsibility to play by the rules and obey the law in the jurisdictions where it operates.

3 The ethical responsibility to do what is right, just and fair and to avoid doing harm.

4 The philanthropic responsibility to contribute to the community and be a good corporate citizen.

An often quoted article by Friedman (1970) entitled 'The social responsibility of business is to increase its profits' argued that in a democratic free market society, extending the social responsibility of corporate managers beyond increasing profits for the company's shareholders amounts to misappropriation of the shareholders' funds. He believed that ultimately pursuing the public interest as a goal in itself would lead to communist or socialist dictatorship. He also believed that managers should follow the rules of the game and not commit fraud, and that it is politicians' responsibility to decide the rules and government's responsibility to enforce them. Friedman's view focusing on Levels 1 and 2 of Carroll's pyramid is consistent with the shareholder perspective on corporate governance and the Proprietary Theory in financial accounting.

A second view which focuses on Levels 1 and 2 is expressed by Freeman (1984) in a book entitled *Strategic Management: A Stakeholder Approach*. According to Blowfield and Murray (2011: 207), 'for Freeman managing stakeholders effectively was essential to the very survival and prosperity of the enterprise'. Identifying a company's main stakeholders and incorporating their needs into the company's strategy becomes a way in which to improve the company's financial performance rather than do what is morally right. Freeman's stakeholder theory of strategic management is compatible with and related to Stakeholder Theory in corporate governance, which adopts the same instrumental approach. The stakeholder approach is also consistent with the Entity Theory in financial accounting.

A third and closely related view stresses the business case for CSR. In *The Market for Virtue*, Vogel (2006: 73) evaluates the business case for CSR and argues that it makes business sense for the few companies where CSR is part of their business strategy and identity (e.g. Patagonia, Ben and Jerry's, M&S and Timberland) and for the few companies who have been targeted by activists (e.g. Shell, Nike and H&M) who use CSR defensively. If there were a general business case for CSR, one might expect that SRI also pays off. Although SRI is on the increase, the verdict is still out. CSR can be very profitable. Think, for example, of fair trade coffee and other products where customers are happy to pay a premium for the fair trade certification.

If one accepts that business managers must evaluate alternative economic actions from strategic, commercial, financial, legal as well as moral perspectives, one is likely to accept that corporations have an ethical (moral) responsibility to all their stakeholders, including society at large. Hence, a fourth group of views extends its focus to Level 3 of the pyramid and is concerned with doing what is right. Their definitions of what is right may be influenced by religion, ideology, ethical and environmental concerns. Socially responsible investors use different screens for different purposes, and investor returns may not be their top priority. This group recognizes the negative externalities caused by companies in their pursuit of profit. Some people focus more on the social consequences of the company's actions for employees, customers or the community. This view is consistent with a focus on social sustainability and the Enterprise Theory in financial accounting. Others focus more on the environmental costs and damage caused by companies' actions and call for ecological sustainability accounting.

Level 4 in Carroll's pyramid is often about 'giving back' to society at large or the community through philanthropic donations (Blowfield and Murray (2011: 24). Companies may sponsor students, charity events or set up foundations. A cynical perspective is to regard philanthropic donations as nothing more than a public relations exercise. This is particularly easy to understand in the case of the so-called 'sin industries', including tobacco, alcohol and fast food.

ACTIVITY 10.3

If you want to find out if there is merit to the cynical perspective, take a look at the IR page of the websites of companies in 'sin industries' such as McDonald's and Heineken. What areas do they focus on in their CSR policies? Do you find the reports credible?

Activity feedback

McDonald's, in its 2012 report, focuses on five areas: nutrition and well-being, sustainable supply chain, environmental responsibility, employee experience and community.

Heineken, in its Sustainability Report 2011, focuses on seven areas: green brewing, green commerce, engaging employees, care about people and environment, promoting responsible alcohol consumption, partnerships to prevent alcohol abuse and enabling sustainability through planning and incentives. For each of these focus areas, Heineken presents an overview of what they said they would do (the measurable targets set in the previous period) and what they have actually done (the extent to which the targets have been reached).

The issue of credibility is a personal one. It is clear that both companies have given sustainability a lot of thought, and the effect is probably more positive than when they did not have these focus areas and policies.

Organized approaches to CSR

Many organizations have issued guidance for companies seeking a formal approach to CSR, including the United Nations Global Compact's ten principles, the ISO 26000 *Guidance Standard on Social Responsibility*, the ILO *Tri-partite Declaration of Principles Concerning Multinational Enterprises and Social Policy*, the OECD *Guidelines for Multinational Enterprises* and the United Nations *Guiding Principles on Business and Human Rights* (European Commission Communication COM (2011) 681 final, p. 6). You will be able to find documents from these organizations on their respective websites. Here we will take a closer look at the United Nations Global Compact's ten principles and the ISO 26000 *Guidance on Social Responsibility.*

The United Nations Global Compact's ten principles

The UN Global Compact is a strategic policy initiative for businesses that are committed to aligning their operations and strategies with ten universally accepted principles in the area of human rights, labour, environment and anti-corruption. By doing so, business as a primary driver of globalization can help ensure that markets, commerce, technology and finance advance in ways that benefit economies and societies everywhere.

(www.unglobalcompact.org/AboutTheGC/index.html)

The ten principles are as follows.

Human rights
Principle 1: Business should support and respect the production of internationally proclaimed human rights and
Principle 2: make sure that they are not complicit in human rights abuses.

Labour
Principle 3: Businesses should uphold the freedom of association and the effective recognition of the right to collective bargaining
Principle 4: the elimination of all forms of forced and compulsory labour
Principle 5: the effective abolition of child labour and
Principle 6: the elimination of discrimination in respect of employment and occupation.

Environment
Principle 7: Businesses should support a precautionary approach to environmental challenges
Principle 8: undertake initiatives to promote greater environmental responsibility and
Principle 9: encourage the development and diffusion of environmentally friendly techniques.

Anti-corruption
Principle 10: Businesses should work against corruption in all its forms, including extortion and bribery

(www.unglobalcompact.org/AboutTheGC/TheTenPrinciples/index.html)

ISO 26000: 2010 Guidance on Social Responsibility

At the end of September 2010, the International Organization for Standardization (ISO) had a membership of 163 national standard setters from countries all over the world. Unlike many other ISO standards, ISO 26000 is not a management system standard and is not for certification or regulatory purposes.

ISO 26000 identifies as the two fundamental practices of CSR: recognition of social responsibility and identifying stakeholders and engaging with them (www.iso.org/iso/sr_schematic-overview.pdf, accessed 9 February 2016). It describes the following core subjects in social responsibility:

- organizational governance
- human rights
- labour practices
- the environment
- fair operating practices (including fair competition, respect for property rights and promoting social responsibility in the value chain, etc.)
- consumer issues (including fair marketing, sustainable consumption and protecting consumers' health and safety, etc.)
- community involvement and development.

In addition, it defines the following principles of social responsibility:

- accountability
- transparency
- ethical behaviour
- respect for stakeholder interests
- respect for the rule of law
- respect for international norms of behaviour
- respect for human rights.

SUSTAINABILITY REPORTING

If you accept the proposition that managers of a large publicly held corporation have wider responsibilities than the financial interests of their shareholders, the need arises to report on more than its financial position and its profit or loss and other comprehensive income or its cash flows. CSR reporting is also called social reporting or sustainability reporting.

Thus far, the IASB has argued that financial reports governed by IFRS are not the place for information on the economic, social and ecological sustainability of the operations of corporations. As a consequence, sustainability reporting by companies and multinational corporations is voluntary unless it is required by regulators within a jurisdiction. In 2011 the European Commission made a commitment to 'present a legislative proposal on the transparency of the social and environmental information provided by companies in all sectors' (Single Market Act, SEC (2011) 467). To this end, there has been a study of *CSR Reporting Practices of EU Companies*. This study finds that the needs of information users are best met when reporting is regulated, CSR reporting is integrated with financial reporting and stakeholders are more involved in reporting.

There are several organizations that are working on establishing guidelines for CSR reporting. We already mentioned ISO 26000 above. Here, we will briefly discuss the International Integrated Reporting Council (IIRC) and the GRI. On 1 February 2013, the GRI and the IIRC signed a Memorandum of Understanding to cement their association. In Article II of this Memorandum of Understanding, the GRI acknowledges that the IIRC's main role is to develop and maintain an International IR Framework, and the IIRC acknowledges that the GRI's primary role is to develop and maintain sustainability reporting guidelines and standards. Below we will first look at the IR Framework that was issued in December of 2013 and then we will briefly discuss the GRI's fourth generation reporting guidelines *G4 Sustainability Reporting Guidelines*, issued in May 2013.

International Integrated Reporting Council (IIRC)

The IIRC is a global coalition of regulators, investors, companies, standard setters, the accounting profession and NGOs aiming to create a global framework for IR. The IIRC's vision is to align capital allocation and corporate behaviour to wider goals of financial stability and sustainable development through the cycle of integrated reporting and thinking (see integratedreporting.org/the-iirc-2/, accessed 9 February 2016).

> The IIRC's long term [sic] vision is a world in which integrated thinking is embedded within mainstream business practice in the public and private sectors, facilitated by Integrated Reporting [(IR)] as the corporate reporting norm. The cycle of integrated thinking and reporting, resulting in efficient and productive capital allocation, will act as a force for financial stability and sustainability.
>
> (The International (IR) Framework, 2013: 2)

IR is a process that results in a periodic integrated report. According to the IIRC's website at www.theiirc.org/, an integrated report shows how an organization's strategy, governance, performance and prospects lead to the creation of value over the short, medium and long term, and should be prepared in accordance with the International Framework.

International (IR) Framework The International (IR) Framework was issued on 8 December of 2013.

Underlying the fundamental concepts is the thinking that investors need to know how an organization creates value over time. The assumption is that value is not created by or within an organization alone. It is influenced by the external environment, created through relationships with stakeholders and is dependent on various resources. Therefore, an integrated report must inform investors about the external environment of the business and its six types of capital, which are categorized as financial, manufactured, intellectual, human, social and relationship, and natural (Para. 2.3).

ACTIVITY 10.4

Providers of financial capital are interested in the value an organization creates for itself. They are also interested in the value an organization creates for others when it affects the ability of the organization to create value for itself, or relates to a stated objective of the organization (e.g. an explicit social purpose) that affects their assessments.

(Para. 2.5 of the 2013 International (IR) Framework)

What does this paragraph tell you about the IIRC's perspective on CSR in respect of Carroll's pyramid? How about the idea of environmental sustainability?

Activity feedback

The IIRC appears to be making the business case for CSR based on strategic stakeholder management. At the same time, the IIRC claims that IR will align capital allocation and corporate behaviour to wider goals of financial stability and sustainable development.

The report must describe the value creation process and its underlying business model. The business model is the business activities through which the company converts its capital into outputs (products, services, by-products and waste) (Para. 2.23).

Para. 3.1 of the International (IR) Framework says that the following Guiding Principles underpin the preparation and presentation of an integrated report, informing the content of the report and how information is presented:

- strategic focus and future orientation
- connectivity of information
- stakeholder relationships
- materiality
- conciseness
- reliability and completeness
- consistency and comparability.

The elements of an integrated report should comprise:

- organizational overview and external environment
- governance
- business model
- risks and opportunities
- strategy and resource allocation
- performance
- outlook
- basis of preparation and presentation
- general reporting guidance.

(integratedreporting.org/wp-content/uploads/2015/03/13-12-08-THE-INTERNATIONAL-IR-FRAMEWORK-2-1.pdf, accessed 9 February 2016)

Global Reporting Initiative (GRI)

GRI is a not-for-profit organization registered in Amsterdam. It has a network-based structure. Its activities involve professionals and organizations from many sectors, constituencies and regions. In May 2013, the GRI issued its fourth generation G4 Sustainability Reporting Guidelines (available from www.globalreporting.org/standards/g4/Pages/default.aspx).

The G4 Sustainability Reporting Guidelines offer reporting principles, standard disclosures and an implementation manual. The Guidelines were developed through a global multi-stakeholder process involving representatives from business, labour, civil society and financial markets, as well as auditors and experts in various fields. Furthermore, their development involved close dialogue with regulators and governmental agencies in several countries. The G4 Sustainability Reporting Guidelines reference internationally recognized reporting related documents (e.g. the UN Global Compact), because the Guidelines were developed in alignment with these documents

As seen above, the UN Global Compact's ten principles are categorized under the four headings of human rights, labour standards, environment and anti-corruption. The GRI categorizes the principles in its G4 Sustainability Reporting Guidelines into the three main categories of environmental, economic and social. Social is further divided into four categories: labour practices and decent work, human rights, society and product responsibility.

The G4 Sustainability Reporting Guidelines operationalize the categories by prescribing reporting on a number of items in each category. For example, the economic category prescribes reporting on economic performance, market presence, procurement practices and indirect economic impacts. As expected, the environmental category prescribes reporting on materials, energy, water, biodiversity, emissions, waste, products and services, compliance with environmental rules and regulations, transport, an environmental assessment of the suppliers of a business, and the existence and procedure for environmental grievance mechanisms. In this way, the G4 Sustainability Reporting Guidelines provide concrete guidelines for businesses to report on the categories of the UN Global Compact while also taking account of the economic sustainability required in a business context.

Application levels To indicate that a report is GRI-based, report makers should self-declare the level to which they have applied the GRI Reporting Framework. There are three levels in the system, entitled A, B and C with A being the highest level. Each level reflects a measure of the extent of application or coverage of the GRI Reporting Framework. A (+) is available at each level (ex. C+, B+, A+) if external assurance was utilized for the report. Reporting organizations can choose to have the level verified by the GRI or by another independent external assessor. GRI will only recognize reports on its website as GRI-based if they contain, at minimum, a GRI Content Index (see www.globalreporting.org/resourcelibrary/G3-Application-Levels.pdf, accessed 9 February 2016).

Metrics and assurance challenges for CSR reporting

We briefly return to Hicks (1946) and his theory of capital maintenance discussed in Chapter 4. Remember the quote: 'The purpose of income calculations in practical affairs is to give people an indication of the amount which they can consume without impoverishing themselves'. This can be applied to the environment, because if we continue to consume the environment, we will impoverish perhaps not ourselves but certainly future generations. Economic activity affects the environment as natural resources are depleted or polluted through, for example, usage, the effects of global warming and acid rain.

However, the indicators of environmental performance and ecological sustainability can be technical. Often there is disagreement between those who take a neo-classical economics perspective and those who take an ecological perspective on the environment, or anything in between. The former is a weak sustainability concept that assumes substitutability of natural resources, whereas the latter is a strong sustainability concept that assumes natural capital is non-substitutable (Neumayer, 2003: 22–24).

The concepts of ecological sustainability, economic and social sustainability are not straightforward. Standards, regulations and policies depend on facts, but also on the interpretation of data and facts, which is often based on personal values, interests, ideology and a sense of urgency. So if deciding on standards and measurement is difficult to agree on (let alone get right), reliable assurance and verification may be hard to realize. Assurers appear more concerned with their own legitimacy and that of their processes than the impact of their assurance on the ecological, social and economic sustainability of the processes and activities of their client business and other organisations (O'Dwyer *et al.*, 2011).

Another problem is who should do the assurance and what assurance standard should they follow? To answer the second question first, two possible standards are ISAE 3000 (2013) and AA1000AS (2008).

ISAE 3000 (2013) The International Standard on Assurance Engagements (ISAE 3000) was issued in 2003 and updated in 2013. It was developed by the International Auditing and Assurance Standards Board (IAASB) of the International Federation of Accountants (IFAC). It is a standard that does not specifically deal with sustainability reporting. It is a generic standard for any assurance engagement other than audits or reviews of historic financial information. According to GRI (2013: 12):

> Its emphasis is on comprehensive procedures for evidence gathering processes and assurer independence. An assurance report 'in accordance with ISAE 3000' can only be issued by professional accountants, as the assurance provider must also comply with the IESBA Code of Ethics for Professional Accountants.

AA1000AS (2008) AccountAbility is a British think tank and consultancy firm which has issued the AA1000 Series, which comprises three standards:

1 AA1000APS (2008) AccountAbility Principles
2 AA1000AS (2008) Assurance Standard
3 AA1000SES (2015) Stakeholder Engagement Standard.

In 2003 AccountAbility issued its AA1000 Assurance Standard, which it revised in 2008. A new revised version is expected in 2016. According to GRI (2013: 12):

> Its emphasis is on whether the organization and its sustainability reporting respond to stakeholder concerns. The standard is used by different types of assurance providers. Organizations seeking to emphasize their commitment to the AA1000APS Principles, including their responsiveness to stakeholder views, often choose assurance based on AA1000AS.

Assurance in accordance with AA1000 (2008) is not limited to professional account-ants and hence they are not necessarily bound by the IESBA Code of Ethics.

AccountAbility's Assurance Standard distinguishes between two types of sustaina-bility assurance engagement. Type 1 is intended to give stakeholders assurance on the way an organization manages sustainability performance, and how it communicates this in its sustainability reporting, without verifying the reliability of the reported in-formation. Type 2 is intended to give stakeholders the Type 1 assurance and provide an evaluation and verification of the specified sustainability performance indicators. Furthermore, the standard distinguishes between providing a high level of assurance and a moderate level of assurance. In para. 4.3, the standard says that the assurance report must provide at a minimum:

- intended users of the assurance statement
- the responsibility of the reporting organization and of the assurance provider
- assurance standard(s) used, including reference to the AA1000AS (2008)
- description of the scope, including the type of assurance provided
- description of disclosures covered
- description of methodology
- any limitations
- reference to criteria used
- statement of level of assurance
- findings and conclusions concerning adherence to the AA1000 AccountAbility Principles of inclusivity, materiality and responsiveness (in all instances)
- findings and conclusions concerning the reliability of specified performance information (for Type 2 assurance only)
- observations and/or recommendations
- notes on competencies and independence of the assurance provider
- name of the assurance provider, and date and place.

With respect to the competence of the assurance provider, the standard requires the individual assurance practitioners and the team to be demonstrably competent in the following areas as a minimum (para. 3.3.1): the AccountAbility Principles, the appli-cation of reporting and assurance practices and standards, the sustainability subject matter (including the specific subject matter of the engagement), and stakeholder engagement.

Assurance providers Broadly speaking, there are three categories of assurance providers. The first is the stakeholders. They can be individuals, experts and oth-ers who comment on the report as a whole or on parts of the report. The second category is corporate responsibility specialists, including certification bodies, techni-cal experts and specialist assurance providers. The third is the Big Four accountancy firms.

What assurance provider to choose depends on the type of assurance the company seeks and why. It also depends on the type of audience the report is aimed at. Simnett *et al.* (2009: 965) provide some evidence that suggests the demand for assurance is higher among companies engaging in more highly visible industrial activity and those with a larger 'social footprint', such as finance, utilities and mining. The findings in Simnett *et al.* (2009: 965) also suggest that companies domiciled in stakeholder-oriented countries are more likely to engage the assurance services of an audit company than companies domiciled in shareholder-oriented countries, which appear more likely to engage the assurance services of specialist assurance providers.

ACTIVITY 10.5

Look online for the most recent sustainability reports of Volkswagen AG, Royal Dutch Shell plc and Nestlé.

- Do they follow the GRI Sustainability Reporting Guidelines? How do you know?
- Do the reports convey an impression of stakeholder management, the business case for sustainability reporting or an attempt to do what is morally right?
- What is your general impression of the structure of the reports?
- What kind of assurance do the reports have?

Activity feedback

The 2014 Sustainability Report for Volkswagen AG is divided into sections on strategy, economy, people, environment, indicators and goals. Very interesting is a section on lobbying on p. 25. 'We at Volkswagen assure politicians of full and open information and reliable and competent advice. We believe in the kind of lobbying that aims to convince people with better arguments and is prepared to expose itself to public criticism'. In the section on the environment (p. 86), it says:

> *By 2018 the Volkswagen Group is aiming to the world's most environmentally compatible automaker. In order to achieve this goal, we have set ourselves some ambitious targets, particularly with regard to environmental protection. In 2014 we continued our pursuit of these goals. Our Environmental Strategy embraces all of our brands and regions, and extends throughout every stage of the value chain.*

On p. 138 it says that the report was prepared taking into account the GRI 4 Guidelines. On p. 116 it says that the sustainability report has been audited by Price Waterhouse Coopers against the GRI G4 requirements taking supplementary account of ISAE 3000.

The 2014 Sustainability Report for Royal Dutch Shell plc is structured into sections on Shell's approach, how Shell operates, Shell's activities and Shell's performance. In the section on how Shell operates we find information about safety, environment, decommissioning, energy and climate change, communities, supply chain, partners and collaborations. The Sustainability Report was prepared in accordance with the GRI G3 Guidelines and has received an A+ rating from GRI. It has received limited assurance from Lloyds Register Quality Assurance Ltd for direct and indirect greenhouse gas emissions for 2014. Shell provides information to the Dow Jones Sustainability Index and the FTSE4Good index.

The 2014 Sustainability Report for Nestlé says that it follows the GRI 4 Guidelines (p. 2). Nestlé introduces its commitment to helping enhance the quality of life of its customers through nutrition, contributing to rural development, water stewardship, environmental sustainability, people, human rights and compliance. The report discusses developments in each of these areas. It is interesting to note that Nestlé (under its water stewardship commitment) is involved in providing access to safe drinking water as well as sustainable management of water usage in its production. It is not clear who provided assurance, if any. The report mentions Nestlé's score of 88 on the Dow Jones Sustainability Index and that Nestlé is included in the FTSE4Good index (which we will discuss in the next section).

SOCIALLY RESPONSIBLE INVESTMENT

SRI is related to business ethics as it is about investment decision making that incorporates other goals than purely financial goals. Those other goals could be related to different types of moral values. Below we will look at the origins of different types of SRI and different SRI fund indices, and the two main types of SRI analysis.

The origins of SRI

SRI practices rooted in religious beliefs started with some investors avoiding companies engaged in industries related to gambling, tobacco, alcohol, weapons and pornography. According to Blowfield and Murray (2011: 232), during the Vietnam War certain investors started to avoid the stocks of companies that supported the war. In the 1980s certain investors avoided the stocks of companies that had operations in South Africa. The 1980s also saw the first investment funds that addressed concerns about the environment. The 1990s saw the establishment of the Domini 400 Social Index (DSI) which applied social screens, and in 1999 the Dow Jones Sustainability Indexes (DJSI) were established. The FTSE4Good was launched in 2001 and from 2004, FTSE4Good introduced a series of regional indices 'including ones for Japan, Australia, the USA, South Africa and emerging economies' (Blowfield and Murray, 2011: 239).

The two main types of SRI analysis

SRI analysis involves screening, which can take the shape of negative screening and positive screening. Negative screening is based on exclusionary screens. Investors and indices applying negative screens would exclude companies:

[w]ith significant involvement in:

- alcohol
- gambling
- firearms
- military weapons
- pornography and
- nuclear power.

(Goergen, 2012: 157)

Other negative screens monitor compliance with internationally accepted norms such as the UN Global Compact or the Millennium Development Goals. Investment funds state their ways of screening in order to create and guard their reputation.

Blowfield and Murray (2011: 237) define positive screening as 'the selection of investments that perform best against corporate governance, social, environmental, or ethical criteria, and which support sustainability'. They also describe 'best-in-class' investment strategies and 'pioneer' screening. In the case of the former, a fund seeks to include only the shares of companies that perform best against different financial, social and environmental criteria. The latter involves the selection of companies who perform best against one specific criterion.

SRI performance

We may expect investors to seek a reasonable financial return as well a social and/or environmental return on their investment. Most investors do not want to lose out financially by investing responsibly. Do SRI indices perform as well as conventional indices? According to Blowfield and Murray (2011: 248–249), the evidence is not convincing either way. In the US, Statman (2006) found that differences in performance of the most important SRI indices for US stocks were not statistically significant in comparison with benchmarks. Schröder (2007) found that the risk-adjusted performance of SRI indices did not differ significantly from that of benchmark portfolios, but SRI indices did exhibit a significantly higher risk. Krosinsky (2008) found that ethical investment funds on average performed worse than conventional funds. On the other hand, investment funds investing in environmental sustainability firms outperformed conventional funds during the period under consideration. Schröder (2014) provides an overview of the empirical literature on any links between SRI,

CSR and the corporate cost of capital and found that most of the studies concerned the US. Schröder (2014: 345) draws the conclusion that 'Greater CSR positively affects stock price performance and the profitability of commercial real estate and it reduces outside capital costs and companies' default risk. However, the question of causality is still a weak point of the studies'.

SUMMARY

In this chapter, we have explored business ethics, CSR, sustainability reporting and the assurance of sustainability reports, types of SRI and SRI performance.

EXERCISES

Suggested answers to exercises marked ✓ are to be found in the Student online resources, with suggested answers to the remaining questions available in the Instructor online resources.

✓**1** Identify and discuss at least four reasons why corporations should take CSR reporting seriously.

✓**2** Freeman's (1984) concept of strategic stakeholder management probably formed the basis for Stakeholder Theory in corporate governance. Explain in what ways Stakeholder Theory in corporate governance may have influenced the International (IR) Framework and the Global Reporting Initiative.

3 Socially responsible investors apply positive and/or negative screening based on values and performance criteria. What kind of criteria would you apply and why?

4 Map the core subjects and the principles of social responsibility of ISO 26000 onto the UN Global Compact's ten principles. In what ways are they similar and in what ways are they different? Can you think of any reasons for the similarities and differences?

5 Some people think that the term 'business ethics' is an oxymoron. What do you think and why?

THE ETHICS OF THE ACCOUNTING PROFESSION

11

OBJECTIVES After studying this chapter you should be able to:

- explain the characteristics of professions in general and the accounting profession in particular

- describe the roles that accountants can fulfil and what makes someone a professional accountant

- compare the functionalist, interactionist and critical perspectives on the formation of the accounting profession

- explain why the accounting profession needs a code of ethics

- discuss ethical challenges for the accounting profession and individual accountants

- describe and explain the fundamental principles outlined in the IESBA Code of Ethics

- describe and explain threats to the fundamental principles outlined in the IESBA Code of Ethics

- describe and explain safeguards against the threats created by the profession, legislation and regulation

- apply the IESBA Code of Ethics to some challenges in the area of financial reporting and auditing.

INTRODUCTION

The first section of this chapter looks at professions in general and at seven characteristics of the accounting profession in particular. It also discusses theoretical perspectives on professions. The second section looks at the way the accounting profession has organized itself internationally, the work accountants do and the difference between accountants in public practice on the one hand and those working in manufacturing, commerce, education or for the government on the other. In the third section we discuss ethical challenges for accountants, consider why the professional accounting bodies usually have a code of conduct and why the international profession has a code of ethics. The fourth section discusses the International Ethics Standards Board for Accountants (IESBA) Code of Ethics, its fundamental principles, threats to these principles and safeguards. It also looks at the IESBA's approach to conflict resolution. The final section is about applying the IESBA Code of Ethics.

PROFESSIONS

In general, we use the words 'profession' and 'professionalism' somewhat loosely. Professionalism denotes performing a task very skilfully. Savage (1994: 131) suggests the following definition: 'A profession is a network of strategic alliances across ownership boundaries among practitioners who share a core competence'. Although a core competence is an important element, a profession has certain characteristics that set it apart from other vocations that require a person to be trained, skilled and competent. Duska *et al.* (2011: 69) present a list of seven characteristics of a profession used by the Commission on Standards of Education and Experience for Certified Public Accountants in the US in the mid-twentieth century when the discipline of accounting was seeking the status of a profession. These characteristics are:

- a specialized body of knowledge
- a recognized formal education process for acquiring the requisite specialized knowledge
- a standard of professional qualifications governing admission to the profession
- a standard of conduct governing the relationship of the practitioner with clients, colleagues and the public
- recognition of status
- an acceptance of social responsibility inherent in an occupation endowed with the public interest
- an organization devoted to the advancement of the social obligations of the group.

Accounting obviously meets the first two characteristics. The third characteristic differs between countries in the sense that in most common law countries and increasingly in many other countries as well, the level for these qualifications is set by the profession as an independent private sector body. At least in the past, in some civil law countries it was the government that set the required exams. Today, in many civil law countries it is more likely that the government has issued a law which sets out the level of skill that the examinations must test, but the actual exams and testing are done by the professional bodies themselves.

A standard of conduct governing the relationship of the practitioner with clients, colleagues and the public is not very specific. Professional accounting bodies have codes of conduct which spell out the ethical obligations accounting professionals must have towards their clients, colleagues and the public. The codes of conduct try to give guidance on what to do in cases where the interests of two or more of these groups conflict. Recognition of status implies that the members of a profession receive public prestige and rewards (McPhail and Walters, 2009: 138), but for the profession itself it means recognition by the state as a profession. For example, in the case where accounting standard setting is left to or delegated to the accounting profession.

In Victorian England, the public interest was taken to mean ensuring that accountants were competent and properly qualified (Lee, 1995). Alternatively, the public interest has also been construed as an obligation to be impartial when producing financial statements so that the information is objective and does not advantage the interests of certain stakeholders over those of others (Sikka *et al.*, 1989). The AICPA (2015: 0.300.030 The Public Interest, para. 02) defines its public and the public interest as follows.

> The accounting profession's public consists of clients, credit grantors, governments, employers, investors, the business and financial community, and others who rely on the objectivity and integrity of *members* to maintain the orderly functioning of commerce. This reliance imposes a public interest responsibility on *members*. The public interest is generally defined as the collective well-being of the community of people and institutions the profession serves.

Finally, a profession has an organization devoted to the advancement of the social obligations of the group. Again, this can mean different things to different people. On the one hand, it means that professional accountants must be loyal to the profession and fellow professionals. Hence they must not do anything that brings the profession into disrepute. Not abiding by the profession's ethical standards may result in a member being expelled from the profession by having their licence revoked. On the other, it means that the organization must set the standards of professional conduct and make sure the members understand and implement them.

ACTIVITY 11.1

Go to the International Federation of Accountants (IFAC) website (www.ifac.org/)and look for a document called 'IFAC's 2015 plan: Delivering on our global advantage'. What are IFAC's strategic objectives? How do they align the public interest with the interests of the accounting profession?

Activity feedback

IFAC's strategic objectives are to serve the public interest in four ways.

1 *Support the development of high-quality standards by independent standard-setting boards, and actively promote the adoption and implementation of these standards in the public interest – thus*

engendering reliable, comparable, consistent, and transparent financial and nonfinancial information.

2 *Develop the accountancy profession – in particular, building strong national and regional PAOs, which in turn support economic growth and stability.*

3 *Promote awareness of how professional accountants facilitate sustainable success and, with member organizations, enhance the competence of professional accountants through sharing and developing knowledge, ideas, and resources.*

(Continued)

4 *Represent and advocate on public interest issues of importance to the profession to
enhance the reputation and credibility of the
profession (see www.ifac.org/system/files/pub-
lications/files/IFAC%27s-2015-Plan-Deliver-
ing-on-Our-Global-Advantage.pdf, accessed 8
February 2016).*

*The first objective states that in providing a high-
quality useful service the accounting profession
fulfils an existing need by contributing towards
making commercial activity orderly and markets
work well. The second objective states that a strong
accountancy profession supports economic growth
and stability, which is in both the interests of the public
as well as the profession. The third objective implies
that by enhancing the competence of professional
accountants the other objectives will be supported.
The fourth objective is to enhance the reputation and
credibility of the profession by advocating on those
public interest issues that are important and relevant
to the profession.*

Theoretical perspectives on why professions exist

Before looking at the accounting profession in more detail, we will first have a
brief look at different theoretical perspectives on why professions exist. Professions
effectively practise a form of social closure whereby they prevent people from entering
a vocation unless they are trained to meet the criteria and are allowed to become
members. On the one hand, this is intended to protect the professional organizations
and their members. On the other, it is intended to protect the public from unwittingly
engaging the services of unqualified people. The same used to apply to guilds in the
Middle Ages.

Theories about the origins of professions include functionalism, interactionism
and critical perspectives (see Wilmott, 1986). Functionalism argues that professions
emerged because they provide an important social function. The audit function is an
essential ingredient of financial reporting as a means of corporate governance. The
role of accountants in insolvency procedures is important to ensure orderly and fair
outcomes.

Interactionism argues that professions emerged as groups competing with each
other for status and economic gains. For example, in the eighteenth and nineteenth
centuries, accountants and lawyers started to compete in the same arena over roles
in insolvency procedures. Finally, critical perspectives often argue that professions
emerged to establish structures in society and helped to bestow power on a particular
group at the expense of other groups. This perspective is often applied to management
accounting where performance measures and targets increasingly came to distinguish
those with knowledge and power in the company (managers) from those who were
being governed (workers).

THE ACCOUNTING PROFESSION

In the UK and a number of other countries, anyone can set themselves up as an
accountant because to be a practising accountant no qualification is required
by law. However, there is a distinction between professional accountants and all
other accountants. Professional accountants are those who are members of certain
professional accountancy bodies by virtue of having obtained the required qualification.
Furthermore, only professionally qualified, registered and inspected accountants are
allowed to work in statutory audit, investment business and insolvency.

In Europe, the European Federation of Accountants/Fédération des Experts Comptables Européens (FEE) is the representative organization for the accountancy profession. FEE's membership consists of 43 professional institutes from 32 countries representing more than 500 000 accountants in Europe. Roughly 45 per cent of these accountants work in public practice. The other 55 per cent work in various capacities in industry, commerce, government and education (see www.charteredaccountants. ie/General/About-Us/Chartered-Accountants-Ireland-Global/FEE---The-European-Federation-of-Accountants/, accessed 7 February 2016).

IFAC is the worldwide organization for the accountancy profession. IFAC was founded in 1977 and is headquartered in New York. The organization has 157 member bodies and associates in 123 countries representing more than 2.5 million accountants employed in public practice, industry and commerce, government and academia. IFAC is responsible for the following standard-setting authorities:

- International Accounting Education Standards Board (IAESB)
- International Auditing and Assurance Standards Board (IAASB)
- International Ethics Standards Board for Accountants (IESBA)
- International Public Sector Accounting Standards Board (IPSASB).

(see www.charteredaccountants.ie/en/General/About-Us/Chartered-Accountants-Ireland-Global/IFAC---International-Federation-of-Accountants/, accessed on 7 February 2016)

Professional accountants in public practice and professional accountants in business

ACTIVITY 11.2

Both the FEE and the IFAC websites mention accountants in public practice. What does this term mean?

Activity feedback

The term 'accountant in public practice' contrasts with 'accountant in business'. According to definitions in the IESBA Code of Conduct in 2005 (IESBA, 2005: 1211):

A professional accountant in public practice is a 'professional accountant, irrespective of functional classification (e.g. audit, tax or consulting) in a firm that provides professional services. This term is also used to refer to a firm of professional accountants in public practice.

A professional accountant in business is a 'professional accountant employed or engaged in an executive or non-executive capacity in such areas as commerce, industry, service, the public sector, education, the not for profit sector, regulatory bodies or professional bodies, or a professional accountant contracted by such entities.

Professionally qualified accountants in public practice work for one of the Big Four multinational accounting firms or smaller international or local accounting firms (including sole practitioners) providing services for a fee in the following areas:

- statutory audit (restricted and more strictly regulated)
- investment business (restricted and more strictly regulated)
- insolvency (restricted and more strictly regulated)
- financial statement preparation
- taxation
- financial management
- forensic accounting
- information and communications technology
- management consulting.

(*Continued*)

ACTIVITY 11.2 *(Continued)*

Professional accountants in business are employed in industry, commerce, government and education. They will use their skills to help the organization that employs them to achieve its objectives. The areas they work in vary from management and financial accounting to finance, compliance, taxation, financial management, operations management and information systems.

In order to be a professional accountant in business, one must qualify by passing the relevant exams and have the practical experience required by the particular accounting body of which one seeks to be a member. Upon qualification, a member must pay a membership fee, obey the rules of the institution and meet the continuing professional development (CPD) requirements in order to remain a professionally qualified accountant. In addition, in order to be a professional accountant in public practice, a member must hold a licence or practising certificate, implement the Code of Ethics of the institution and, at least in the UK, the member must be covered by professional indemnity insurance.

An interesting question is to what extent an accountant who is not professionally qualified can be bound by the same ethical obligations as members of the professional accounting bodies. Someone working as an accountant without having professionally qualified may have the acquired necessary knowledge and expertise through study and experience. It is common sense that they will abide by the standards of professional conduct in order to build up and maintain a reputation and working relationship with their clients. However, it is likely that they will feel they have a responsibility to themselves and their clients rather than to the public or the profession.

ETHICAL CHALLENGES FOR ACCOUNTANTS

Usually, when we talk about the ethics of the accounting profession we think about independent auditors. The audit function is crucial for financial reporting to be able to perform its role in corporate governance. IFAC and the International Accounting Standards Board (IASB) believe that financial reporting and the roles that accounting standard setters, accountants and auditors play in the financial reporting system are fundamental to the investing public's confidence in capital markets, because financial reporting solves the problem of the information asymmetry we discussed in Chapter 9.

Accountants and especially auditors have ethical responsibilities to clients, the public, the profession and (if they are working for an accounting firm) their employer. However, their responsibility to the public overrides their responsibilities to their clients, their employer or the accounting profession. Hence, their self-interest, the interests of their clients, their employer, the profession and the public must all be balanced. Any human being will find this a less than straightforward task. What complicates matters is that although the responsibility to the public of a professional accountant in public practice overrides all other responsibilities in theory, in practice the client pays the fees, the employer pays the salary and superiors have some influence on promotion and career progression.

ACTIVITY 11.3

Based on the introduction above, think of examples of ethical challenges for accountants where:

1 The public interest conflicts with the interests of the client.

2 The accountant's personal interests conflict with the interests of the profession.

3 The accountant's professional interests conflict with the interests of the client.

4 The accountant's professional interests conflict with that of their employer.

Activity feedback

1 *An example of a case where the public interest conflicts with the interests of the client could be that the client asks an accounting firm to devise a legal structure that enables the client to reduce corporate income tax payments to an equivalent of 5 per cent of the average income tax paid over the past five years. The standard corporate income tax rate applicable in the country in question is 20 per cent of income before taxation. The consultancy arm of the accounting firm would not be doing anything illegal and would earn an attractive income from this job, but would the consultancy arm of the accounting firm be doing the right thing by the general public in the country in question?*

2 *An example of a case where an accountant's personal interest conflicts with the interests of the profession could be what is called a 'conflict of interests' situation where the accountant has both professional and personal relations with a client. These relations could be a friendship, a family relationship, a financial relationship or any other type of relationship that makes it more difficult for the accountant to be independent and objective.*

3 *An example of a case where the accountant's professional interest conflicts with the interests of the client could exist when the client proposes to use a level 3 fair value estimate and the accountant cannot assess with sufficient confidence the extent to which the assumptions about future cash inflows and interest rates are reasonable.*

4 *An example of a situation in which an accountant's professional interest conflicts with that of their employer exists when a junior accountant is pressured to perform a certain task within a very short time period. The junior accountant feels that the amount of time is too short for them to perform the task and check the work in order to be confident that no mistakes were made.*

Why do professional accounting bodies have a code of conduct?

It is clear that the public has to trust the accounting profession to be honest, trustworthy and unbiased when preparing and auditing financial statements. Preparing and auditing financial statements often requires the interpretation of rules, judgements about methods and estimations. A code of conduct is meant to provide guidance to the members of professional accounting bodies to make interpretations and judgements in situations where the interests of the client, the employer, the professional accounting body and the public are not clearly aligned or are very much in conflict with one another.

For the public to place their trust in the accounting profession, the public must believe that accountants on average behave ethically and make unbiased (that is, not systematically biased) judgements. Hence, in theory, the accounting profession is best served when accountants serve the public interest first. Without a professional code of conduct, the members of the professional accounting body would not know what rules and guidelines to follow. Similarly, the professional accounting body would not have a way of disciplining its members who do not follow the rules.

Why does the international accounting profession have an international code of ethics?

As capital markets and financial reporting became more globalized, so did the accounting firms. The Big Four have a large share in the global audit market and, in addition, they provide other services as well. In the 1970s, the professional accounting bodies started to see how an international association of national accounting bodies could strengthen the position of the accounting profession worldwide. They established IFAC at the 11th World Congress of Accountants in 1977. IFAC's 12-point programme included: '2. Establish the basic principles which should be included in the code of ethics of any member body of IFAC and to refine or elaborate on such principles as deemed appropriate' (see www.ifac.org/about-ifac/organization-overview/history/12-point-program, accessed 8 February 2016).

Remember the definition of a profession by Savage (1994: 131): 'A profession is a network of strategic alliances across ownership boundaries among practitioners who share a core competence'. If the network of strategic alliances is to extend globally (across both ownership boundaries and national boundaries), and if a code of ethics helps professional accountants to make decisions that inspire the international public confidence, it follows that an international code of ethics could indeed strengthen the position of the accountancy profession worldwide.

THE IESBA CODE OF ETHICS

IFAC 'is the global organization for the accounting profession dedicated to serving the public interest by strengthening the profession and contributing to the development of strong international economies' (IFAC website, accessed 8 February 2016). You can find the IESBA Code of Ethics for Professional Accountants in the Handbook of the Code of Ethics for Professional Accountants on the IFAC website. At the time of writing, the latest edition of the IESBA Code and Handbook is from 2015.

Part A of the IESBA Code of Ethics discusses the five fundamental principles of integrity, objectivity, professional competence and due care, confidentiality and professional behaviour, and the five threats against these principles: self-interest, self-review, advocacy, familiarity and intimidation. Part B applies these principles and threats and safeguards to professional accountants in public practice. Part C applies these principles and threats and safeguards to professional accountants in business practice.

The fundamental principles of the IESBA Code of Ethics

The Code, as much else in accounting, is principles-based not rules-based and therefore does not provide an extensive set of rules to follow. The fundamental principles of the Code (para. 100.5) remain the same as those of the old IFAC Code of Ethics, which are:

- **Integrity** – a professional accountant should be straightforward and honest in performing professional services.
- **Objectivity** – a professional accountant should not allow bias, conflict of interest or undue influence of others to override professional or business judgements.

- **Professional competence and due care** – a professional accountant has a continuing duty to maintain professional knowledge and skill at the level required to ensure that a client or employer receives competent professional service based on current developments. A professional accountant should act diligently and in accordance with applicable technical and professional standards when providing professional services. From the above it is apparent that accountants will need to commit to continuing professional development.

- **Confidentiality** – a professional accountant should respect the confidentiality of information acquired as a result of professional and business relationships and should not disclose any such information to third parties without proper and specific authority unless there is a legal or professional right or duty to disclose. Confidential information acquired as a result of professional and business relationships should not be used for the personal advantage of the professional accountant or third parties.

- **Professional behaviour** – a professional accountant should comply with relevant laws and regulations and should avoid any action that discredits the profession.

The principles of professional competence and due care, confidentiality and professional behaviour are more straightforward to understand and apply than the principles of integrity and objectivity. In 2009 the FEE (FEE, 2009) believed that integrity is the most fundamental of the principles and tried to define it. In 2007 the ICAEW also defined integrity (ICAEW, 2007) and made it more easily operational and less ambiguous. Duska *et al.* (2011: 86) quote the AICPA Professional Code of Conduct, Section 54, Article III.03) as follows:

> Integrity is measured in terms of what is right and just. In the absence of specific rules, standards, or guidance, or in the face of conflicting opinions, a member should test decisions and deeds by asking: Am I doing what a person of integrity would do? Have I retained my integrity? Integrity requires a member to observe both the form and the spirit of technical and ethical standards; circumvention of those standards constitutes subordination of judgement.

Objectivity is also important for inspiring public confidence. If accountants are perceived as producing financial information that is systematically biased towards the interests of one group of stakeholders, the other groups of stakeholders and the general public are unlikely to trust the accounting profession to fulfil its functions of preparing and verifying financial reporting and other information.

Threats to adherence to the IESBA Code of Ethics

As mentioned above, the IESBA Code also considers how relationships or circumstances create threats such as self-interest, self-review, advocacy, familiarity and intimidation, which constitute conditions in which people might be tempted to act contrary to the principles (para. 100.12). The Code recommends the application of safeguards in the form of institutional procedural frameworks and personal responses to minimize or contain threats.

- **Self-interest** – the threat that a financial or other interest will inappropriately influence the professional accountant's judgement or behaviour.

- **Self-review** – the threat that a professional accountant will not appropriately re-evaluate a previous judgement made by the same professional accountant or by another person within the same organization on whose judgement the professional accountant needs to rely.

- **Advocacy** – the threat that a professional accountant promotes a client's or an employer's position or opinion to the point that subsequent objectivity may be compromised.
- **Familiarity** – the threat that due to a long or close relationship with a client or an employer, a professional accountant becomes too sympathetic to their interests or too accepting of their work to remain objective or maintain their integrity.
- **Intimidation** – the threat that occurs when a professional accountant may be deterred from acting objectively by pressures, actual or perceived, including attempts to exercise undue influence over the professional accountant.

ACTIVITY 11.4

The Code states that:

- Self-interest threats can occur as a result of the financial or other interests of an accountant or of an immediate or close family member.
- Intimidation can occur when a professional accountant may be deterred from acting objectively by threats, actual or perceived.

Give examples of self-interest threats and intimidation threats for both accountants in public practice and in business.

Activity feedback

Self-interest threats could be:

- *a financial interest in a client or jointly holding a financial interest with a client*
- *undue dependence on total fees from a client*
- *concern about the possibility of losing a client*
- *having a close business relationship with a client*
- *potential employment with a client*
- *contingent fees relating to an assurance engagement*

- *financial interest, loans or guarantees in the business*
- *incentive compensation arrangements, e.g. bonuses*
- *inappropriate personal use of corporate assets*
- *concern over employment security*
- *commercial pressure from outside the employing organization.*

Intimidation threats could be:

- *threat of dismissal or replacement*
- *threat of litigation*
- *pressure to reduce inappropriately the extent of the work performed to reduce costs*
- *threat of dismissal or replacement of the professional accountant in business or a close or immediate family member over a disagreement about the application of an accounting principle or the way in which financial information is to be reported*
- *a dominant personality attempting to influence the decision-making process, e.g. with regard to the awarding of contracts or the application of an accounting principle.*

Safeguards created by the profession, legislation or regulation

The Code states that safeguards are actions or other measures that may eliminate such threats or reduce them to an acceptable level. Some safeguards are created by the profession, legislation or regulation. Other safeguards must be created and applied in the workplace. Safeguards in the former category include (para. 110.14):

- education, training and experience requirements for entry into the profession
- CPD requirements
- corporate governance regulations for accounting firms

- professional standards (such as those in the Code)
- professional or regulatory monitoring and disciplinary procedures
- external review by a legally empowered third party of the reports, communications and returns produced by the professional accountant.

ACTIVITY 11.5

Identify safeguards to guard against the threats to professional accountants that could be employed in the workplace.

Activity feedback

The safeguard examples given by the Code are:

- the employing organization's systems of corporate oversight or other oversight structures
- the employing organization's ethics and conduct programmes
- recruitment procedures in the employing organization emphasizing the importance of employing high calibre competent staff
- strong internal controls
- appropriate disciplinary processes
- leadership that stresses the importance of ethical behaviour and the expectation that employees will act in an ethical manner
- policies and procedures to implement and monitor the quality of employee performance
- timely communication of the employing organization's policies and procedures, including any changes to them, to all employees and appropri-

ate training and education on such policies and procedures
- policies and procedures to empower and encourage employees to communicate to senior levels within the employing organization any ethical issues that concern them without fear of retribution
- consultation with another appropriate professional accountant (several professional accountancy bodies provide networks to facilitate this).

The Code also includes what might be regarded as the final safeguard:

In circumstances where a professional accountant in business believes that unethical behaviour or actions by others will continue to occur within the employing organization, the professional accountant in business should consider seeking legal advice. In those extreme situations where all available safeguards have been exhausted and it is not possible to reduce the threat to an acceptable level, a professional accountant in business may conclude that it is appropriate to resign from the employing organization.

ACTIVITY 11.6

Identify circumstances that could exist within the workplace that would threaten the ability of the accountant to perform their duties within their given level of expertise. In addition, identify safeguards that the accountant could employ to ensure they maintain this fundamental principle.

Activity feedback

The Code gives the following threats:

- insufficient time for properly performing or completing the relevant duties
- incomplete, restricted or otherwise inadequate information for performing the duties properly
- insufficient experience, training and/or education

- inadequate resources for the proper performance of the duties.

Safeguards that may be considered are:

- obtaining additional advice or training
- ensuring that there is adequate time available for performing the relevant duties
- obtaining assistance from someone with the necessary expertise
- consulting, where appropriate, with superiors, independent experts and a relevant professional body.

The final safeguard is, of course, to refuse to perform the task/duties but remember to communicate to your superiors the reasons for the refusal.

Conflict Resolution

A professional accountant may have to deal with ethical dilemmas. For this purpose, the IESBA Code recommends the following six step systematic approach (para. 100.18):

1 Identify and understand the relevant facts.

2 Identify the relevant parties involved.

3 Identify the ethical issues involved.

4 Identify the fundamental principles that are threatened related to the matter in question.

5 Consider the established internal procedures.

6 Identify the alternative courses of action.

Upon consideration of the relevant factors, the professional accountant shall determine the appropriate course of action, weighing the consequences of each alternative course of action. If the matter remains unresolved, the professional accountant must consult with appropriate persons inside their organization. Only if that does not work can the professional accountant consult with someone outside the organization. As a measure of last resort, the professional accountant should be willing to consider their position in the team or organization. Integrity may require the professional accountant to resign.

APPLYING THE IESBA CODE OF ETHICS

Above, we have briefly discussed the principles of the IESBA Code of Ethics. Now it is time to apply them to a few case studies.

ACTIVITY 11.7

Brief case study

You are a second-year trainee accountant about to go on study leave. Your manager asks you to complete some complicated reconciliation work before your study leave commences as your senior colleague who was due to do the work is on long-term sick leave. You feel the deadline given for the complicated task is unrealistic. You also do not feel sufficiently experienced to complete the work. You have asked your manager for additional supervision to complete the work, but this has been refused. Your manager reiterates that he expects the work to be completed before you can take your study leave.

State which principles of the IESBA Code of Ethics you think the above scenario brings into question, what threats exist and the action you would take to resolve the issue.

Activity feedback

The fundamental principles involved in this scenario are integrity, professional competence and due care, and professional behaviour.

The threat is intimidation.

A suitable course of action would be to explain, politely, to your manager that you do not have sufficient time to complete the work before your study leave; that if you do undertake the work you will need suitable supervision; and that you will of course complete the work when you return from study leave. If this action does not resolve the issue, you must obtain advice from a senior colleague or from your professional body.

(CIPFA ethics code case studies, adapted)

Try another one.

ACTIVITY 11.8

Brief case study

Sunil is a third-year trainee accountant working for an audit firm. Sunil and his superior Janice are auditing a client's financial statements. Sunil finds that the client has spent a material amount on an advertising campaign for the year under consideration. Having negotiated a long payment term, half of the amount is payable in the next year. Instead of recognizing the whole amount as an expense in the year of the advertising campaign, the client has recognized only half of the amount as advertising expense and has not accrued the other half of the expenditure in the current year's financial statements. When asking the client for an explanation, the client provided two reasons.

- Although the advertising campaign took place in the year in which the financial statements are being prepared, the client expects that its effects will last well into the next year.
- The client needs to maintain a consistent net profit margin from year to year in order to be able to enjoy the best interest rate on its overdraft facility.

Sunil knows that this is not the correct way of accounting for advertising expenses. When he discusses the matter with Janice, she says that keeping the client happy is important for the audit firm. Sunil suspects that Janice thinks that losing the client would endanger her prospects for promotion in the short term.

State which principles of the IESBA Code of Ethics you think the above scenario brings into question, what threats exist and the action you would recommend Sunil take to resolve the issue.

Activity feedback

The fundamental principles involved in this scenario are integrity, professional competence and due care, and professional behaviour.

The threat for Sunil is advocacy caused by his loyalty to Janice. The threats for Janice are self-interest (because of her promotion), self-review (relying on the client's information rather than checking for herself) and advocacy (serving the client's interests rather than being objective).

A suitable course of action would be for Sunil to explain, politely, to Janice that this would be compromising her integrity, professional competence and due care and her professional behaviour, because Janice (like Sunil) knows it does not conform with the rules to account for advertising expenditure in this way. If Janice does not agree, Sunil may need to talk to her superior. If this action does not resolve the issue, Sunil must obtain advice from a senior colleague or from his professional body.

SUMMARY

This chapter has considered the ethics of the accounting profession by first understanding the characteristics of professions in general and the accounting profession in particular. We discussed the differences between professional accountants in public practice and professional accountants in business and considered the differences in ethical obligations of these two groups of accountants. We also thought about the moral obligations of accountants who are not members of a professional accountancy body. The chapter looked into ethical challenges for accountants and considered the reasons for them. It discussed why professional accountants need a code of ethics. We considered the IESBA Code of Ethics, its fundamental principles, the threats to these principles and the safeguards for the threats. We also looked at IESBA's framework for conflict resolution and applied it to a few cases.

EXERCISES

Suggested answers to exercises marked ✓ are to be found in the Student online resources, with suggested answers to the remaining questions available in the Instructor online resources.

1 The accounting profession serves the private interests of the profession, the private interests of clients, credit grantors, employers, investors, the business and financial community, governments and others who rely on the objectivity and integrity of the accounting profession to maintain the orderly functioning of commerce. How would accountants weigh their own private interests against the private interests of the other groups they are meant to serve? What does the IESBA Code of Ethics say about this problem?

✓2 According to the IESBA Code of Ethics, integrity is one of the main principles that accountants must apply in order to serve the public interest. For accountancy bodies to teach their prospective members what integrity is and how to apply it is a challenge. What might accountancy bodies do to achieve this goal?

3 Consider the five threats to adherence to the principles of the IESBA Code of Ethics in relation to each of the five principles of the IESBA Code of Ethics. For example, the threat of self-interest can cause an accountant to compromise their integrity, objectivity and professional behaviour by providing an incentive to be dishonest, or to present the facts in a manner that best suits the accountant's private interests.

4 Consider how the threat of self-interest relates to the threat of advocacy, and how the threat of familiarity might lead to the threat of advocacy. What might be solutions to these types of threat?

✓5 Amy is a senior financial accountant for a large manufacturing company listed on the stock exchange. In her professional capacity she has learnt that the company's profit for the year is above the expectations of the company directors and probably also of the financial analysts following the company. She expects that this information, when it will be made public in two weeks' time, will positively impact on the company's stock price. Having had a bit too much to drink with her friends in the pub, Amy recommends they invest in her company's shares before the information is made public, so they are likely to be able to realize a gain when the financial information is released to the public. Think about which principles of the IESBA Code of Ethics you think the above scenario brings into question, what threats exist and the action Amy should take to resolve the issue.

PART TWO

ANNUAL FINANCIAL STATEMENTS

In this Part we look in detail at the international rules that accountants have created for themselves to govern financial reporting. In each case, we explore the underlying issues involved, applying the principles developed in Part One, and consider the International Standards requirements. Do these Standards achieve what they are setting out to do when considered individually? Do they make sense when looked at as a whole? As with Part One, you are invited to form your own opinion on 'the story so far'.

FIXED (NON-CURRENT) TANGIBLE ASSETS

12

OBJECTIVES After studying this chapter you should be able to:

- discuss the measurement of fixed tangible assets at initial recognition

- discuss the major measurement methods of fixed tangible assets after initial recognition

- discuss and apply the principles, concepts and major methods of providing for depreciation

- explain what depreciation does and does not do

- explain the issues involved in determining appropriate treatments for government grants

- describe, apply and appraise the requirements of IAS 20 relating to government grants

- explain the issues involved in determining appropriate treatments for borrowing costs

- describe, apply and appraise the requirements of IAS 23 relating to borrowing costs

- describe, apply and appraise the requirements of IAS 16, *Property, Plant and Equipment*

- discuss alternative treatments for investment properties

- describe, apply and appraise the requirements of IAS 40 related to investment properties

- describe, apply and appraise the requirements of IAS 41 related to biological assets and of IAS 16 to bearer plants.

INTRODUCTION

Assets in general have been defined (in Chapter 4) as follows (Conceptual Framework, para. 4.4):

> An asset is a resource controlled by the entity as a result of past events and from which future economic benefits are expected to flow.

Assets are divided into fixed assets and current assets. The IAS terms are non-current assets and current assets respectively. The distinction is formally defined in IAS 1 (para. 66), discussed in more detail in Chapter 8.

An asset should be classified as a current asset when it is:

- expected to be realized in, or is intended for sale or consumption in, the normal course of the entity's operating cycle

- held primarily for the purpose of being traded

- expected to be realized within 12 months after the balance sheet date reporting period

- cash or cash equivalent (as defined by IAS 7, see Chapter 23), unless it is restricted from being exchanged or used to settle a liability for at least 12 months after the reporting period.

All other assets should be classified as non-current assets.

The definition of non-current assets is often misunderstood. A non-current asset is not an asset with a long life. The essential criterion is the intention of the owner – the intended use of the asset. A non-current asset is an asset that the owner intends to use within the business over an extended period in order to assist their daily operating activities. A current asset, by contrast, is usually defined in terms of time. A current asset is an asset likely to change its form, i.e. likely to undergo some transaction within 12 months.

ACTIVITY 12.1

Consider two firms, A and B. Firm A is a motor trader. It possesses some motor vehicles that it is attempting to sell and it also possesses some desks used by the sales staff, management, and so on. Firm B is a furniture dealer. It possesses some desks that it is attempting to sell and it also possesses some motor vehicles used by the sales staff and for delivery purposes. How are these items treated in each case?

Activity feedback

In the accounts of A, the motor vehicles are current assets and the desks are non-current assets. In the accounts of B, the motor vehicles are non-current assets and the desks are current assets. Note, incidentally, that a fixed asset which, after several years' use, is about to be sold for scrap remains in the fixed asset part of the accounts even though it is about to change its form.

MEASUREMENT OF (NON-CURRENT) TANGIBLE FIXED ASSETS AT INITIAL RECOGNITION

Companies use a wide variety of fixed tangible assets (land, buildings for production purposes, buildings for rental purposes, equipment, installations, machinery, trucks, aeroplanes, vines on which grapes grow, etc.) to run their business. The first question that arises with respect to these fixed tangible assets is do these assets need to be recognized in the books of the company? In order to answer that question, we refer to the definition of an asset under the IASB's Conceptual Framework. According to the Conceptual Framework, an asset is recognized in the statement of financial position when it is probable that the future economic benefits will flow to the entity and the asset has a cost or value that can be measured reliably (art. 4.44). In this definition, we distinguish two elements. First, it must be probable that economic benefits flow to the entity, and second, the asset can be measured reliably. If these two criteria are fulfilled then the asset will be recorded in the books of the entity. But at what value?

Different IASs/IFRSs provide an answer to that second question. Most tangible fixed (non-current) assets fall under the scope of IAS 16, *Property, Plant and Equipment*. When land or buildings are held for rental purposes or for capital appreciation, they fall under the scope of IAS 40, *Investment Property*. If an entity undertakes agricultural activity, then the bearer plants fall under the scope of IAS 16, *Property, Plant and Equipment*, whereas the other biological assets fall under the scope of IAS 41, *Agriculture*. Biological assets are living animals or plants, whereas a bearer plant is a living plant that: (a) is used in the production or supply of agricultural produce; (b) is expected to bear produce for more than one period; and (c) has a remote likelihood of being sold as agricultural produce, except for incidental scrap sales. So the initial measurement of a fixed tangible asset will be determined by one of the following Standards: IAS 16, IAS 40 and IAS 41, depending on the characteristics of the asset. When a tangible fixed asset enters the company under a lease contract, IFRS 16, *Leases* applies.

For example, land and buildings that are used in the production or the supply of goods and services or for administrative purposes are accounted for in compliance with IAS 16, *Property, Plant and Equipment*. When land and buildings are held to sell in the ordinary course of the business of the entity, then these land and buildings are accounted for in compliance with IAS 2, *Inventories*. When land and buildings are held for rental or for capital appreciation, then these land and buildings are called investment property and they are accounted for in compliance with IAS 40, *Investment Property*.

Activity 12.2 introduces you to the scope of these three international accounting standards that deal with the recognition, measurement and disclosure of fixed tangible assets owned by the entity.

ACTIVITY 12.2

Below you will find a list of different assets. Try to figure out which Standard has to be applied for recognition, measurement and disclosure of these assets.

1   A car produced by a car manufacturer.

2   The land used by a farm, dairy cattle is grazing on the land.

3   A car used by the royal mail to deliver packages.

4   A fruit tree in an orchard managed by a large farming company.

5   A building held for capital appreciation.

6   An aeroplane used by an airline company.

7   Land held for rental purposes by a rubber company.

8   A breeding cow on a farm.

(Continued)

ACTIVITY 12.2 (*Continued*)

Activity feedback

1 This car falls under the scope of IAS 2, Inventories.

2 The land falls under the scope of IAS 16, Property, Plant and Equipment.

3 The car falls under the scope of IAS 16, Property, Plant and Equipment.

4 The tree is a bearer plant and falls under the scope of IAS 16, Property, Plant and Equipment.

5 This building has the character of an investment property and falls under the scope of IAS 40, Investment Properties.

6 The aeroplane falls under the scope of IAS 16, Property, Plant and Equipment.

7 This land has the character of an investment property and falls under the scope of IAS 40, Investment Properties. If the land were to be used in the agricultural production of rubber, it would fall under the scope of IAS 16, Property, Plant and Equipment.

8 The cow qualifies as a biological asset and falls under the scope of IAS 41, Agriculture.

In order to understand what value to ascribe to a tangible fixed asset at initial recognition, we need to look in the appropriate Standard (IAS 16, *Property, Plant and Equipment*; IAS 40, *Investment Property*; or IAS 41, *Agriculture*). The recognition, measurement and disclosure of tangible assets used for the exploration and evaluation of mineral resources are accounted for in compliance with IFRS 6, *Exploration For and Evaluation of Mineral Resources*. A discussion of the recognition, measurement and disclosure criteria included in IFRS 6 can be found on the website of this book. In this chapter, we pay attention to all tangible fixed (non-current) assets falling under the scopes of IAS 16, IAS 40 and IAS 41. We will start with a discussion on IAS 16, *Property, Plant and Equipment*.

Initial measurement of property, plant and equipment

IAS 16 defines property, plant and equipment (PPE) as tangible items that are held for use in the production or supply of goods and services, for rental to others or for administrative purposes and are expected to be used during more than one period. A remarkable element in this definition is the fact that tangible items held for rental are included in this definition, whereas IAS 40 specifically deals with tangible assets held for rental purposes. The different development dates of both Standards could be a possible explanation for this observation. IAS 16 was originally developed in 1993, whereas IAS 40 was developed in 2000.

When an asset meets the definition of PPE, it needs to be recognized in the accounts of the entity. IAS 16 relies on the principles set out for assets in the Conceptual Framework for the recognition criteria. So PPE shall be recognized as an asset if, and only if: (a) it is probable that future economic benefits associated with the item will flow to the entity; and (b) the cost of the item can be measured reliably (IAS 16, para. 7).

In determining whether an item satisfies the first criterion for recognition, an entity needs to assess the degree of certainty attaching to the flow of future economic benefits on the basis of the available evidence at the time of initial recognition. Existence of sufficient certainty that the future economic benefits will flow to the entity necessitates an assurance that the entity will receive the rewards attaching to the asset and will undertake the associated risks. The second criterion for recognition usually is readily satisfied because the exchange transaction evidencing the purchase of the asset identifies its cost.

IAS 16 allows for the aggregation of items which may individually be insignificant (para. 9), giving 'moulds, tools and dyes' as an example. The aggregation is then treated as 'an asset', if the recognition criteria are met. Conversely, when it is clear that an asset may initially be acquired as a whole, but significant components of it will have very different useful lives, then the expenditure on the asset should be allocated to the component parts and each part should be accounted for as a separate item. An aircraft and its engines are given as a likely example. This separate treatment allows depreciation figures to reflect properly the different consumption patterns of the various components.

Initial measurement

The measurement at initial recognition of an item of PPE is rather straightforward. It should be measured at cost. IAS 16 specifies three components which need to be included in the cost of the asset at initial measurement (purchase price, directly attributable costs of bringing the asset to working conditions and dismantling costs). The cost of an item of PPE comprises first its purchase price, including import duties and non-refundable purchase taxes. Any trade discounts and rebates are deducted in arriving at the purchase price. Second, the cost of an item of PPE will be augmented with any directly attributable costs of bringing the asset to working condition for its intended use. Examples of directly attributable costs are: cost of site preparation; initial delivery and handling costs; installation costs; and professional fees such as for architects and engineers. The third component of the cost of an item of PPE comprises the initial estimated cost of dismantling and removing the asset and restoring the site, to the extent that it is recognized as a provision under IAS 37, *Provisions, Contingent Liabilities and Contingent Assets* (see Chapter 19). The 'third component', the dismantling costs, arise from the obligation which is incurred at the moment of acquisition of the asset or as a consequence of the use of the asset (IAS 16, para. 16).

In practice, however, a number of complications are likely to arise when determining these items that need to be included in the cost of PPE at initial recognition. The Standard goes into some detail about several aspects (paras 18–28). It notes that in cases where payment is deferred beyond normal credit terms, defined or imputed interest must be removed from the total of the payments, thus reducing the cost to the cash purchase price equivalent. General and administration overheads are not likely to be 'directly attributable costs' as the term was used earlier, but, for example, pension costs of direct labour could be.

The question of what is an essential cost of 'bringing the asset to working condition' is likely to be difficult and subjective. The basic principle is that recognition of costs in the carrying amount of an item of PPE ceases when the item is in the location and condition necessary for it to be capable of operating in the manner intended by management. For example, the following costs are not included in the carrying amount of an item of PPE:

- costs incurred while an item capable of operating in the manner intended by management has yet to be brought into use or is operated at less than full capacity
- initial operating losses, such as those incurred while demand for the item's output builds up
- costs of relocating or reorganizing part or all of an entity's operations
- costs of opening a new facility

- costs of introducing a new product or service (including costs of advertising and promotional activities)
- costs of conducting business in a new location or with a new class of customer (including costs of staff training)
- administration and other general overhead costs.

Subsequent costs

The first and obvious point is that costs of day-to-day servicing of an item of PPE, often described as 'repairs and maintenance', are expenses, not additions to the cost of the PPE. However, major parts of some items of PPE may require replacement at regular intervals. For example, a furnace may require relining after a specified number of hours of use; aircraft interiors such as seats and galleys may require replacement several times during the life of the airframe. Items of PPE may also be acquired to make a less frequently recurring replacement, such as replacing the interior walls of a building or to make a non-recurring replacement. Under the recognition principle in para. 7, an entity recognizes in the carrying amount of an item of PPE the cost of replacing such a part of an item when that cost is incurred if the recognition criteria are met. The carrying amount of those parts that are replaced is derecognized in accordance with the derecognition provisions of the Standard.

Note that in order to facilitate this, the component parts of the original item need to have been accounted for separately in the first place.

A major inspection or refit, even if it does not 'improve' the original item, may logically be treated the same way. Thus, para. 14 notes that a condition of continuing to operate an item of PPE (e.g. an aircraft) may be performing regular major inspections for faults, regardless of whether parts of the item are replaced. When each major inspection is performed, its cost is recognized in the carrying amount of the item of PPE as a replacement if the recognition criteria are satisfied. Any remaining carrying amount of the cost of the previous inspection (as distinct from physical parts) is derecognized. This occurs regardless of whether the cost of the previous inspection was identified in the transaction in which the item was acquired or constructed. If necessary, the estimated cost of a future similar inspection may be used as an indication of what the cost of the existing inspection component was when the item was acquired or constructed.

Measurement subsequent to initial recognition

The IASB has always operated on the basis that a strict adherence to historical cost is not required and, indeed, has recognized the possibility of rejecting historical cost accounting as the normal basis (see Chapter 7). Consistent with this approach, two alternative approaches to the measurement subsequent to initial recognition are allowed under IAS 16 (paras 30 and 31). The first model allowed is the cost model whereby after recognition as an asset, an item of PPE shall be carried at its cost less any accumulated depreciation and any accumulated impairment losses (IAS 16, para. 30).

The second measurement method allowed for PPE is the revaluation model. After recognition as an asset, an item of PPE whose fair value can be measured reliably shall be carried at a revalued amount, being its fair value at the date of revaluation less any subsequent accumulated depreciation and subsequent accumulated impairment losses. Revaluations shall be made with sufficient regularity to ensure that the carrying amount does not differ materially from that which would be determined using fair value at the balance sheet date (IAS 16, para. 31).

The cost model or the revaluation model is applied to a class of assets and not to an individual asset. This requirement is inspired by the fact that if both models could be applied on an individual asset basis, management could choose a valuation model for certain individual assets in order to influence the accounting number in a positive way. A second motive for this requirement is that by choosing the valuation model for a class of assets and not on an individual asset basis, consistency in measurement across assets of the same category is more guaranteed. It is important to note, however, that although the valuation model needs to be chosen for a class of assets, the accounting for the decrease or the increase in the revaluation is done on an individual asset basis. Whether the company uses the cost model or the revaluation model, in both circumstances the assets need to be depreciated if they have a limited life time, and the book value of the asset subsequent to initial recognition is determined as the initial amount (either at cost or fair value) less any accumulated depreciation or any accumulated impairment losses. We will discuss below the concept of depreciation and the concept of impairment is discussed in Chapter 14.

PRINCIPLES OF ACCOUNTING FOR DEPRECIATION

The first major problem with depreciation, perhaps surprisingly, is to agree on what it is and what it is for. The generally agreed view nowadays is that it is in essence a straightforward application of the matching, or accruals, convention. The benefit from a non-current asset is spread over several years. The matching convention requires that the corresponding expense be matched with the benefit in each accounting period. This does not simply mean that the total expense for the asset's life is spread over the total beneficial life. It means, more specifically, that the total expense for the asset's life is spread over the total beneficial life *in proportion to the pattern of benefit*. Thus, to take a simple example, if a non-current asset gives half of its benefit, or usefulness, in year 1, one-third in year 2 and one-sixth in year 3 and the total cost is €1200, then the matching convention requires the charging of €600 in year 1, €400 in year 2 and €200 in year 3, in the annual profit calculation. This charge is known as the *depreciation charge*.

In order to calculate a figure for this charge, it is necessary to answer four basic questions:

1 What is the cost of the asset?

2 What is the estimated useful life of the asset to the business? (This may be equal to, or may be considerably less than, its technical or physical useful life.)

3 What is the estimated residual selling value ('scrap value') of the asset at the end of the useful life as estimated?

4 What is the pattern of benefit or usefulness derived from the asset likely to be (not the amount of the benefit)?

It is perfectly obvious that the second, third and fourth of these involve a good deal of uncertainty and subjectivity. The 'appropriate' figures are all dependent on future plans and future actions. It is important to realize that even if the first figure – the cost of the fixed asset – is known precisely and objectively, the basis of the depreciation calculation as a whole is always uncertain, estimated and subjective.

As usual, the estimates should be reasonable, fair and prudent (whatever precisely that implies!). But the first figure is often not at all precise and objective, for several reasons.

ACTIVITY 12.3

Suggest reasons why the cost of a particular fixed asset may be difficult to determine with precision.

Activity feedback

Possible reasons include the following:

1 Incidental expenses associated with making the asset workable should be included, e.g. installation costs carried out by the business's own staff, probably including some overhead costs.

2 The non-current asset may be constructed within the business by its own workforce, giving rise to all the usual costing problems of overhead definition and overhead allocation.

3 Depending on the accounting policies used by the firm generally, the 'basic' figure for the fixed asset may be revalued periodically. Additionally, if land is not depreciated but the building on the land is, then this requires a split of the total cost (or value) figure for the land and buildings together into two possibly somewhat arbitrary parts.

4 Major alterations/improvements may be made to the asset part way through its life. If these appear to increase the benefit from the asset over the remaining useful life and perhaps also to increase the number of years of the remaining useful life, and are material, then the costs of these improvements should also be capitalized (i.e. treated as part of the non-current asset from then on). However, maintenance costs, including a major overhaul that does not occur frequently, are 'running' expenses and should be charged to the income statement as incurred. In practice, this distinction can be difficult to make.

5 Accounting policies in relation to government grants receivable and to capitalization of borrowing costs may influence the figures. These two issues are the subjects of separate International Standards. They are considered later in the chapter.

The total figure to be depreciated, known as the *depreciable amount*, will consist of the cost of the asset less the residual value. The residual value of an asset is the estimated amount that an entity would currently obtain from disposal of the asset, after deducting the estimated cost of disposal. This depreciable amount needs to be spread over the useful life in proportion to the pattern of benefit. Once the depreciable amount has been found, with revision if necessary to take account of material improvements, several recognized methods exist for spreading, or allocating, this amount to the various years concerned. The more important possibilities are outlined next. It is essential to understand the implicit assumption that each method makes about the pattern of benefit arising, and therefore about the appropriate pattern of expense allocation.

Methods of calculating depreciation

Straight line method. The depreciable amount is allocated on a straight line basis, i.e. an equal amount is allocated to each year of the useful life. When the residual value or the useful life are revised, this change in estimate leads to a different amount in the year of the change and an equal amount after the change. If an asset is revalued or materially improved, then the new depreciable amount will be allocated equally over the remaining, possibly extended, useful life (see Activity 12.3).

ACTIVITY 12.4

Using the straight line method, calculate the annual depreciation charge from the following data:

Cost ('basic' value figure)	€12 000
Useful life	4 years
Scrap value	€ 2000

Activity feedback

$$\text{Annual charge} = \frac{€12\ 000 - €2\ 000}{4}$$

$$= €2\ 500$$

This is by far the most common method. It is the easiest to apply and the easiest to incorporate into the preparation of periodic (e.g. monthly) accounts for internal purposes. This method assumes, within the limits of materiality, that the asset is equally useful, or beneficial, each year. Whether this assumption is as frequently justified as the common usage of the method suggests, is an open question.

Reducing balance method. Under this method, depreciation is calculated each year by applying a constant percentage to the net book value (NBV) brought forward from the previous year. (Note that this percentage is based on the cost less depreciation to date.) Given the cost (or valuation) starting figure and the useful life and 'scrap' value figures, the appropriate percentage needed to make the NBV at the end of the useful life exactly equal to the scrap value can be found from a formula:

$$d = 1 - \sqrt[n]{S / C}$$

where d is the depreciation percentage, n is the life in years, S is the scrap value and C is the cost (or basic value).

This formula is rarely used. In practice, when this method is used a standard 'round' figure is usually taken, shown by experience to be vaguely satisfactory for the particular type of asset under consideration. Notice, incidentally, that the formula fails to work when the scrap value is zero and produces an extreme and possibly distorted allocation of expense when the scrap value is very small.

A particular variant found in practice in some countries is known as the double declining balance method. This involves calculating the appropriate 'straight line' depreciation percentage, then doubling it and applying the resulting percentage on the reducing balance basis.

ACTIVITY 12.5

Using the data from the previous activity and assuming a depreciation percentage of 40 per cent, calculate the depreciation charge for each of the four years using the reducing balance method.

Activity feedback

Year 1	Cost	€12 000
	Depreciation 40%	4 800
Year 2	NBV	7 200
	Depreciation 40%	2 880
Year 3	NBV	4 320
	Depreciation 40%	1 728

Year 4	NBV	2 592
	Depreciation 40%	1 037
	NBV	€1 555

If the estimated scrap value in Activity 12.4 turns out to be correct, then a 'profit' on disposal of €445 would also be recorded in year 4. This is an example of a reducing balance method or of an accelerated depreciation method. The charge is highest in the first year and gradually reduces over the asset's life.

ACTIVITY 12.6

Suggest, and critically appraise, arguments in favour of using the reducing balance method rather than the straight line method.

Activity feedback

1 It better reflects the typical benefit pattern, at least of some assets.

2 It could be argued that, where the pattern of benefit is assumed to be effectively constant, the appropriate 'expense', which needs to be correspondingly evenly matched, is not the pure depreciation element, but the sum of:

   (a) the pure depreciation element, and

   (b) the maintenance and repair costs.

   Because (b) will tend to increase as the asset gets older, it is necessary for (a) to be reduced as the asset gets older in the hope that the total of the two will remain more or less constant. This may be a valid argument in the most general of terms, but of course there is no reason why an arbitrary percentage applied in one direction should even approximately compensate for flexible and 'chancy' repair costs in the other.

3 It better reflects the probable fact that the value (i.e. the market or resale value) of the asset falls more sharply in the earlier years. This argument, often advanced, is questionable in principle. Depreciation is concerned with appropriate allocation of expense, applying the matching convention. It is not concerned with an annual revaluation of the fixed assets, so whether or not a particular method is good or bad from this viewpoint is, or should be, irrelevant. So long as the original estimate of future benefit is still valid, the fact that current market value is small, at an intermediate time, is not of concern.

4 Since it frontloads the depreciation expense charge in the earlier years of the useful life, it is consistent with the prudence principle. It is indeed true that prudence can be said to support the reducing balance method rather than the straight line method. What is not clear is whether this is a valid advantage. This is a particular example of the general debate concerning the relative importance of prudence, on the one hand, and a genuine attempt to apply the matching principle, on the other.

Sum of the digits method. This is another example of a reducing balance method. It is based on a convenient 'rule of thumb' and produces a pattern of depreciation charge somewhat similar to the reducing balance method.

Using the same figures as before, we give the four years weights of 4, 3, 2 and 1, respectively and sum the total weights. In general terms, we give the n years weights of n, $n - 1$, …, 1 respectively, and sum the total weights, the sum being $n(n + 1)/2$. The depreciable amount is then allocated over the years in the proportion that each year's weighting bears to the total.

ACTIVITY 12.7

Use the sum of the digits method to calculate annual depreciation charges for the data in the previous activities.

Activity feedback

1 $4 + 3 + 2 + 1 = 10$ (the 'sum' of the 'digits')

2 Depreciable amount = €12 000 – €2 000

   $$= €10\ 000$$

Depreciation charges are:

Year 1	4/10 × 10 000 = €4 000
Year 2	3/10 × 10 000 = €3 000
Year 3	2/10 × 10 000 = €2 000
Year 4	1/10 × 10 000 = €1 000

This gives NBV figures in the balance sheet of €8000, €5000, €3000 and €2000 for year ends 1–4, respectively.

Unit of production method. This is particularly suitable for assets where the rate of usage or rate of output can be easily measured. For example, a motor vehicle might be regarded as having a life of 100 000 miles, rather than a life of 4 years. The depreciable amount can then be allocated to each year in proportion to the recorded mileage. For example, if 30 000 miles are covered in year 1, then 3/10 of the depreciable amount will be charged in year 1. The life of a machine could be defined in terms of machine hours. The annual charge would then be:

$$\text{Depreciable amount} \times \frac{\text{Machine hours used in the year}}{\text{Total estimated life in machine hours}}$$

Revaluation or arbitrary valuation. This approach is occasionally used with minor items such as loose tools. An estimated or perhaps purely arbitrary figure for the value of the items (in total) is chosen at the end of each year. Depreciation is then the difference between this figure and the figure from the previous year. Strictly, of course, this is not a method of depreciation at all, but a lazy alternative to it.

All these methods can be criticized on the grounds that they ignore the fact that the resources 'tied up' in the fixed asset concerned have an actual cost to the business in terms of interest paid or an implied (opportunity) cost in terms of interest foregone. This could well be regarded as an essential expense that should be matched appropriately against the benefit from the asset. The 'actuarial' methods that attempt to take account of interest expense are complicated to apply and in financial accounting are hardly ever used.

Some misconceptions underlined

The process of depreciation calculation is not designed to produce balance sheet numbers that are either particularly meaningful or particularly useful as measurements of value; in fact, they are measurements of unexpired costs.

It must be remembered that depreciation is a process of matching expenses in proportion to benefits. Given that the depreciable amount has been agreed, the annual charge is based on actual or implied assumptions as to the pattern of benefit being derived and nothing else. In simple bookkeeping terms, all that is happening is that a transfer is being made from the non-current assets section in the balance sheet to the expenses section in the income statement. And it is the expense that is being positively calculated, not the reduction in the asset figure. It follows from this that:

1 The asset figure for an intermediate year has no very obvious or useful meaning. It can only be defined in a roundabout way. For example, under historical cost accounting, it is the amount of the original cost not yet deemed to have been used, or not yet allocated. This intermediate figure is often called the NBV, but it is not a value at all within the proper meaning of the word.

2 Depreciation has nothing to do with ensuring that the business can 'afford' to buy another asset when the first one becomes useless. This is true even if we ignore the likelihood of rising price levels. Depreciation does not increase the amount of any particular asset, cash or otherwise.

3 However, depreciation, like any other expenses figure, does have the effect of retaining *resources* (or total assets) in the business. By reducing profit, we reduce the maximum dividend payable (which would reduce resources) and

therefore increase the 'minimum resources remaining' figure. This is, in fact, a particular illustration of the idea of capital maintenance discussed in Chapter 5.

Before we pay attention to the requirements with respect to depreciation included in IAS 16, we have a final activity on depreciation for you. As a check on your understanding of general principles, try Activity 12.8.

ACTIVITY 12.8

In the year to 31 December 20X3, Hans bought a new fixed asset and made the following payments in relation to it:

	€	€
Cost as per supplier's list	12 000	
Less Agreed discount	1 000	11 000
Delivery charge		100
Erection charge		200
Maintenance charge		300
Additional component to increase capacity		400
Replacement parts		250

Required:

1 State and justify the cost figure which should be used as the basis for depreciation.

2 What does depreciation do and why is it necessary?

3 Briefly explain, without numerical illustration, how the straight line and reducing balance methods of depreciation work. What different assumptions does each method make?

4 Explain the term 'objectivity' as used by accountants. To what extent is depreciation objective?

5 It has been common practice in published accounts of individual entities in Germany to use the reducing balance method for a fixed asset in the early years of its life, and then to change to the straight line method as soon as this would give a higher annual charge. What do you think of this practice? Refer to relevant accounting conventions in your answer.

Activity feedback

1 *This figure should be the total cost of making the fixed asset usable, excluding all costs of actually using it. Therefore:*

11 000 + 100 + 200 + 400 = €11 700

The additional component is the cost of machine as it enhances the revenue earning capacity of the asset, but the replacement parts are a cost of using the machine – hence the difference in treatment between the two. Maintenance is obviously a cost of usage.

2 *Depreciation spreads the cost (or value) of an item over its useful life, in appropriate proportion to the benefit (usefulness). It is necessary in accordance with the matching convention – allocating expense against corresponding benefit, as part of the profit calculation.*

3 *The straight line method charges a constant percentage of the cost (or value) each year. The reducing balance method charges a constant percentage of the NBV (cost less accumulated depreciation brought forward). Thus, the straight line method has a constant charge but the reducing balance method has a charge reducing in each year of the asset's life. The two methods therefore make different assumptions about the usefulness and the trend or pattern of benefit of the fixed asset concerned.*

4 *Objectivity implies lack of bias. It removes the need for and the possibility of subjectivity, of personal opinion. For an accounting figure to be objective, it must be expected that all accountants would arrive at the same figure. Clearly, the figure stated on an invoice has a high degree of objectivity. However, the calculation of depreciation is based on estimates of future life and future usefulness and is therefore highly subjective.*

5 *This practice can claim the advantage of greater prudence, as the expense is always the higher of the two possibilities. However, it seems to lack consistency. Perhaps more importantly, it obviously fails to attempt to follow the matching convention. It makes no attempt to make the trend of expense consistent with the trend of benefit or usefulness.*

DEPRECIATION AND IAS 16

IAS 16 defines depreciation as the systematic allocation of the depreciable amount of an asset over its useful life, whereby the depreciable amount is defined as the cost of an asset, or other amount substituted for cost, less its residual value. We find three other concepts in the definition of depreciation, namely residual value, useful life and cost of an asset. We list below the definitions of these elements in the context of IAS 16.

1 Useful life is:

   (a) the period of time over which an asset is expected to be used by an entity, or

   (b) the number of production or similar units expected to be obtained from the asset by an entity.

2 Cost is the amount of cash or cash equivalents paid or the fair value of the other consideration given to acquire an asset at the time of its acquisition or construction or, where applicable, the amount attributed to that asset when initially recognized in accordance with the specific requirements of other IFRSs, e.g. IFRS 2, *Share-based Payment*.

3 The residual value of an asset is the estimated amount that an entity would currently obtain from disposal of the asset after deducting the estimated costs of disposal, if the asset were already of the age and in the condition expected at the end of its useful life.

4 Entity-specific value is the present value of the cash flows an entity expects to arise from the continuing use of an asset and from its disposal at the end of its useful life, or expects to incur when settling a liability.

5 Recoverable amount is the higher of an asset's fair value less costs to sell and its value in use.

6 Fair value is the price that would be received to sell an asset or paid to transfer a liability in an orderly transaction between market participants at the measurement date.

7 An impairment loss is the amount by which the carrying amount of an asset exceeds its recoverable amount.

8 Carrying amount is the amount at which an asset is recognized after deducting any accumulated depreciation and accumulated impairment losses.

These definitions contain no real surprises and confirm the general earnings calculation focus of the depreciation process. The formal requirement of IAS 16 for the calculation of depreciation should by now have a familiar ring (para. 50). The depreciable amount of an item of PPE should be allocated on a systematic basis over its useful life. The depreciation method used should reflect the pattern in which the asset's economic benefits are consumed by the entity. The depreciation charge for each period should be recognized as an expense unless it is included in the carrying amount of another asset (e.g. as part of the manufacturing cost of inventories).

The Standard goes into detail about a number of aspects. The residual value and the useful life of an asset shall be reviewed at least at each financial year end and, if expectations differ from previous estimates, the change(s) shall be accounted for as a change in an accounting estimate in accordance with IAS 8, *Accounting Policies, Changes in Accounting Estimates and Errors*.

Depreciation is recognized even if the fair value of the asset exceeds its carrying amount, as long as the asset's residual value does not exceed its carrying amount. Repair and maintenance of an asset do not negate the need to depreciate it. The depreciable amount of an asset is determined after deducting its residual value. In practice, the residual value of an asset is often insignificant and therefore immaterial in the calculation of the depreciable amount. The residual value of an asset may increase to an amount equal to or greater than the asset's carrying amount. If it does, the asset's depreciation charge is zero unless and until its residual value subsequently decreases to an amount below the asset's carrying amount. This last point is rather significant. It recognizes and confirms that, while a depreciation charge is *required* for all items of PPE, the correctly calculated charge may well be zero.

Land and buildings are separable assets with different accounting characteristics and should be considered separately, even if acquired as a single purchase.

The Standard mentions three depreciation methods by name: straight line, reducing (or diminishing) balance and the units of production (usage) method (para. 62).

This list is neither exhaustive nor in order of preference. The method used for an asset is selected based on the expected pattern of economic benefits and is consistently applied from period to period unless there is a change in the expected pattern of economic benefits from that asset. This implies that for any particular asset, with its own particular expected pattern of economic benefits, there is one particular appropriate method. Once the method has been chosen, consistency is required. Now look at Activity 12.9.

ACTIVITY 12.9

It is sometimes argued, for example in the case of hotels, that depreciation of the building is not necessary on the grounds that its fair value is being maintained by the incurrence of expensive maintenance costs which are being charged as expenses. To charge depreciation as well could appear to be 'double-counting'. What do you think of this argument?

Activity feedback

Standard setters generally are at pains to counter this argument. It is not valid to argue that maintenance increases residual value at the end of economic life, so in principle the proposition is invalid, although maintenance is certainly a factor in determining the length of the economic life. However, the useful life could, it must be remembered, be significantly shorter than the economic life. It certainly seems theoretically valid for a hotel owner to argue that expected residual value at the end of the expected useful life (to them) is equal to or greater than the initial carrying value. This would suggest that while depreciation needs to be provided, the 'correct' figure would be nil! Auditors may be suspicious of this argument although, as discussed earlier, IAS 16 now recognizes its possible legitimacy.

The depreciation method applied to an asset shall be reviewed at least at each financial year end and, if there has been a significant change in the expected pattern of consumption of the future economic benefits embodied in the asset, the method shall be changed to reflect the changed pattern. Such a change shall be accounted for as a change in an accounting estimate in accordance with IAS 8.

It is necessary to determine whether or not an item of PPE has become impaired. This area is covered by IAS 36, Impairment of Assets (see Chapter 14). Impairments or losses of items of PPE-related claims for or payments of compensation from third parties and any subsequent purchase or construction of replacement assets are separate economic events and are accounted for separately as follows:

- Impairments of items of PPE are recognized in accordance with IAS 36.
- Derecognition of items of PPE retired or disposed of is determined in accordance with IAS 16.
- Compensation from third parties for items of PPE that were impaired, lost or given up is included in determining profit or loss when it becomes receivable.
- The cost of items of PPE restored, purchased or constructed as replacements is determined in accordance with IAS 16.

THE REVALUATION MODEL

If the company chooses to value an item of PPE with the revaluation model, IAS 16 states that companies then have to apply IFRS 13, *Fair Values* to determine the fair value of the asset. IAS 16 states further that the frequency of revaluations depends upon the changes in fair values of the items of PPE being revalued. If the value of the assets changes often, then these items will be more often revalued than in situations where the fair value of assets does not change frequently. A revaluation of an asset can either lead to an increase of the carrying amount of the asset or a decrease of the carrying amount of the asset. Paragraphs 39 and 40 of IAS 16 stipulate the impact of the increase or the decrease on the statement of profit or loss and other comprehensive income. If an asset's carrying amount is increased as a result of a revaluation, their increase shall be recognized in other comprehensive income and accumulated in equity under the heading 'Revaluation surplus'.

ACTIVITY 12.10

Assume Company X owns land. The carrying value of the land before revaluation is £40 000. The fair value of the land has increased and the current market price is £50 000. Company X values its PPE with the use of the revaluation model. What entries need to be made at the end of the period to bring the carrying value of the asset in line with the principles of the revaluation model.

Activity feedback

The journal entry for a revaluation increase is:

Dr Land   10 000
Cr Gain on revaluation of non-current assets (OCI)   10 000

Dr Gain on revaluation of non-current assets (OCI)   10 000
Cr Revaluation surplus   10 000

On the statement of financial position, the land will be shown at its revalued carrying value of £50 000 and under equity (OCI) we observe a revaluation surplus of £10 000.

However if the increase is a reversal of a revaluation decrease of the same asset previously recognized in profit or loss, then the increase shall be recognized in profit or loss to the extent of the amount of the prior reversal decrease.

ACTIVITY 12.11

Assume that another piece of land owned by Company X with an initial value of £20 000 recorded a revaluation decrease last year of £3000. Due to a changing economic climate, the industrial activity in the area in which the land is situated is increasing. The current market price for that land is estimated at £21 000. How much will be credited to the account 'gain on revaluation of non-current assets' (OCI)?

Activity feedback

Only £1000. The carrying value of the land has increased by £4000 from £17 000 to £21 000. However, £3000 of this increase is a reversal of a prior revaluation decrease. Therefore, this prior decrease needs to be reversed by £3000 first. The remaining amount (£1000) will be recorded under other comprehensive income.

We notice that although the choice between the cost model and the revaluation model needs to be made at class level, the accounting is done on an asset by asset basis. We have considered the accounting treatment of an increase in revaluation in the prior activities, but what about a decrease in revaluation? IAS 16 (para. 40) stipulates that when the carrying amount of the asset is decreased as a result of a revaluation in the context of the use of the revaluation model, the decrease shall be recognized in profit or loss. However, the decrease shall be recognized in other comprehensive income to the extent of any credit balance existing in the revaluation surplus in respect of that asset. The decrease recognized in other comprehensive income reduces the amount accumulated in equity under the heading of a revaluation surplus.

ACTIVITY 12.12

Assume Company X owns a piece of land in an area where the economic activity is deteriorating and the market prices of land have fallen. The land has a carrying value prior to revaluation of £30 000. The current market price is £25 000. What are the journal entries that need to be made at the year end?

The revaluation surplus on the statement of financial position will be debited with £5000 to the extent that there is a balance on this reserve and the movement will be shown in OCI. Any outstanding amount will be recognized in profit or loss.

Activity feedback

Dr Loss (revaluation reserve if available,		
otherwise P/L)		5000
Cr Land		5000

ACTIVITY 12.13

Assume that the land in the books of Company X in Activity 12.12, with a carrying value of £30 000, had been revalued two years before from £27 000 to £30 000. What journal entries would then be needed to reduce the carrying value of the land to £25 000?

Activity feedback

Two years ago when the revaluation of the land occurred, Company X would have recorded the following journals in their books:

Dr Land	3000
Cr Gain on revaluation of land (OCI)	3000

Dr Gain on revaluation of land (OCI)	3000
Cr Asset revaluation surplus	3000

Two years later, when Company X needs to record the decrease in the carrying amount of the land to £25 000, they will make the following entries in their books:

Dr Asset revaluation surplus	3000
Cr Land	3000
Dr Loss – downward revaluation of land (P/L)	2000
Cr Land	2000

Such a revaluation surplus reserve is not 'realized', and is therefore not 'earned' and not available for dividend. However, it is likely to become realized over time. Such revaluation surpluses included in equity may be transferred directly to retained earnings when the surplus is realized. The whole surplus may be realized on the retirement or disposal of the asset. However, some of the surplus may be realized as the asset is used by the entity; in such a case, the amount of the surplus realized is the difference between depreciation based on the revalued carrying amount of the asset and depreciation based on the asset's original cost. In all examples given so far, no depreciation was involved. How will accumulated depreciation be treated in the revaluation of PPE accounted for under the revaluation model? IAS 16 foresees two possibilities: a net method and a gross method. The net method is the most straightforward one and foresees that the accumulated depreciation is eliminated against the gross carrying amount of the asset at the date of revaluation.

If a company uses the gross method, then the gross carrying amount is adjusted in a manner that is consistent with the revaluation of the carrying amount of the asset. The gross carrying amount may be restated by reference to observable market data or it may be restated proportionately to the change in the carrying amount. The accumulated depreciation at the date of the revaluation is adjusted to equal the difference between the gross carrying amount and the carrying amount of the asset after taking into account accumulated impairment losses (IAS 16, para. 35(a)).

Both methods will be illustrated with Activities 12.14 and 12.15.

ACTIVITY 12.14

A company has a plant with a carrying amount of €21 000, being an initial cost of €35 000 and accumulated depreciation of €14 000. The fair value of the asset now is €25 000. Show how depreciation will be adjusted under the net method.

Activity feedback

Under this method we first write off the accumulated depreciation of the plant, which reduces the carrying value of the plant to €21 000 (€35 000 – €14 000)

Dr Accumulated depreciation	14 000
Cr Plant	14 000

Subsequently we adjust the carrying amount of €21 000 to the fair value of the asset which is €25 000.

Dr Plant	4 000
Cr Gain on revaluation of plant (OCI)	4 000

ACTIVITY 12.15

Suppose we have an asset to which IAS 16 applies, cost €10 000, a useful life of 5 years, an estimated residual value of nil and it is now 3 years old. The asset is then revalued to a new gross figure of €15 000, that is the new 'cost' is €15 000. Show how the gross method will be used for the depreciation that has accumulated.

Activity feedback
Treatment (a) suggests the following:

Cost	Depreciation	Carrying amount
10 000	6 000	4 000

The asset is now revalued, by index or otherwise, to a new gross figure of €15 000, i.e. the new 'cost' is €15 000. The depreciation is now 'restated proportionately', i.e. it is also increased by 50 per cent. We thus end up with:

Gross revaluation	Depreciation	Carrying amount
15 000	9 000	6 000

This increase in carrying amount of €2000 is then dealt with as discussed later.

Treatment (b) suggests a different sequence. Suppose the asset is again recorded before revaluation:

Cost	Depreciation	Carrying amount
10 000	6 000	4 000

The new carrying value is to be €6000. Other balances will need to be altered or eliminated as shown.

	Asset revaluation account		
Transfer of cost	10 000	6 000	Transfer of depreciation
Surplus (calculated)	2 000	6 000	New carrying value (given)
	12 000	12 000	

Derecognition

The carrying amount of an item of PPE shall be derecognized:

- on disposal or
- when no future economic benefits are expected to arise from its use or disposal.

The gain or loss arising from the derecognition of an item of PPE shall be determined as the difference between the net disposal proceeds, if any, and the carrying amount of the item. The gain or loss is to be included in profit or loss when the item is derecognized (unless IFRS 16 requires otherwise on a sale and leaseback). Gains shall not be classified as revenue.

This confirms that any element of the revaluation reserve relating to the item will not pass through the income statement.

However, an entity that, in the course of its ordinary activities, routinely sells items of PPE that it has held for rental to others shall transfer such assets to inventories at their carrying amount when they cease to be rented and become held for sale. The proceeds from the sale of such assets shall be recognized as revenue in accordance with IFRS 15, *Revenue from Contracts with Customers*. IFRS 5, *Non-current Assets Held for Sale and Discontinued Operations* does not apply when non-current assets that are held for sale in the ordinary course of business are transferred to inventories (para. 68A, inserted in 2008).

The disposal of an item of PPE may occur in a variety of ways (e.g. by sale, by entering into a finance lease or by donations). In determining the date of disposal of an item, an entity applies the criteria in IFRS 15, *Revenue from Contracts with Customers*, for recognizing revenue from the sale of goods. IFRS 16 applies to disposal by a sale and leaseback.

Disclosure

The disclosure requirements under IAS 16 are lengthy and incapable of effective summarization. In general, full details and reconciliations of movements concerning additions, disposals, impairments and revaluations are required.

Accounting for assets held under lease contracts will be explained in Chapter 15 of this book.

DETERMINING THE COST OF A FIXED ASSET: ADDITIONAL ELEMENTS

In the following sections, we look at two particular problem areas regarding cost determination, i.e. government grants and borrowing costs.

GOVERNMENT GRANTS

Entities which receive a material amount of assistance from government or state sources are clearly in a different economic position from otherwise comparable entities which receive no such assistance. In order to allow proper appraisal of the results of the entity activities and to facilitate comparisons, disclosure of this government assistance in as much detail as practicable is necessary.

More specifically, government grants are usually easily quantifiable and the general principle of transparency requires that they are both properly accounted for and clearly disclosed. Government grants typically represent a reduction in net cash outflows and, therefore, at least ultimately, an increase in entity earnings.

Suppose a government grant is paid to an entity because, and under the condition that, the entity purchases a depreciable non-current asset. The figures concerned are as follows:

Purchase price of asset	€12 000
Expected useful life	4 years
Expected residual value	Nil
Government grant	€2 000
Annual profits before depreciation, and grants relating to the asset	€20 000

It is possible to suggest at least four possible different ways of treating the grant:

1 to credit the total amount of the grant immediately to the income statement

2 to credit the amount of the grant to a non-distributable reserve

3 to credit the amount of the grant to revenue over the useful life of the asset by:

(a) reducing the cost of the acquisition of the non-current asset by the amount of the grant or

(b) treating the amount of the grant as a deferred credit, a portion of which is transferred to revenue annually.

ACTIVITY 12.16

Which of these methods do you prefer? Give your reasons.

Activity feedback

The first two methods may be rejected on the grounds that they provide no correlation between the accounting treatment of the grant and the accounting treatment of the expenditure to which the grant relates. The first method would increase the profits in the first year by the entire amount of the grant, failing to associate the grant with the useful life of the asset. It thus ignores both the prudence convention and the matching convention. The second method means that the grant will never affect the profit figure. It therefore also ignores the matching convention and, additionally, leaves the 'non-distributable reserve' in the balance sheet, presumably forever, i.e. it is treated as paid-in surplus.

The third and fourth methods both follow and apply the matching convention. They both have exactly the same effect on reported annual profits, the differences only being concerned with balance sheet presentation.

Illustration of different accounting treatments

Using the data just given, the two 'acceptable' methods give the following results.

Method 3(a)	€	€	€	€
Profit before depreciation, etc.	20 000	20 000	20 000	20 000
Depreciation	(2 500)	(2 500)	(2 500)	(2 500)
Profit	17 500	17 500	17 500	17 500
Balance sheet extract at year end				
Non-current asset at (net) cost	10 000	10 000	10 000	10 000
Depreciation	2 500	5 000	7 500	10 000
Carrying amount	7 500	5 000	2 500	—

Method 3(b)

Profit before depreciation, etc.	20 000	20 000	20 000	20 000
Depreciation	(3 000)	(3 000)	(3 000)	(3 000)
Grant released	500	500	500	500
Profit	17 500	17 500	17 500	17 500
Balance sheet extract at year end				
Non-current asset at (net) cost	12 000	12 000	12 000	12 000
Depreciation	3 000	6 000	9 000	12 000
Carrying amount	9 000	6 000	3 000	—
Deferred credit:				
Government grant	1 500	1 000	500	—

Thus method (a) shows assets of 7500, 5000, 2500 and 0 over the four years and method (b) shows assets of 9000, 6000, 3000 and 0 together with 'liabilities' of 1500, 1000, 500 and 0.

From a pragmatic point of view, method (a) has the obvious advantage of simplicity. No entries and no thought are required in the second and subsequent years. However, method (b) has the advantage that assets acquired at different times and locations are recorded on a uniform basis, regardless of changes in governmental policy. But what is the cost of the asset? Is it 12 000 or is it 10 000? IAS 16, *Property, Plant and Equipment* (see later) states that cost is the amount of cash or cash equivalents paid, net of any trade discounts and rebates. This statement does not seem to resolve the question categorically. The government grant is not a trade discount. It is not a trade rebate, but it is a rebate. This would seem to imply that the cost in the sense of IAS 16 is 10 000. This is surely the net outflow arising because of the purchase. Yet IAS 20, *Accounting for Government Grants and Disclosure of Government Assistance*, as discussed in detail shortly, allows both methods.

A difficult conceptual problem arises with the deferred credit under method (b), for example the 1500 at the end of year 1. We described it earlier as a 'liability'. As discussed in Chapter 8, IASB defines a liability as a present obligation of the entity arising from past events, the settlement of which is expected to result in an outflow of resources embodying economic benefits. On the assumption that the grant cannot be reclaimed by the governmental body concerned (the usual situation), the 1500 is clearly not a liability as no outflow of resources is foreseeable. It is more logically either a reserve (not yet realized) or a contra-asset. It could be suggested that this leads to a different possible treatment, i.e. regular inclusion in the balance sheet as a visible contra-asset, in other words included as a negative balance among the 'assets' instead of as a positive balance among the liabilities. This would raise its own problems – not least the lack of user friendliness involved in the concept of a negative asset. Such conceptual difficulties do not appear to worry either IASB or other national regulators.

The IASB requirements relating to government grants are contained in IAS 20, *Accounting for Government Grants and Disclosure of Government Assistance*, effective since 1984. Its coverage therefore extends beyond the area of fixed assets, but, for completeness, we deal with all aspects of IAS 20 here. Where IAS 41, *Agriculture* applies, government grants are to be treated under IAS 41 (see further in this chapter), not under IAS 20. Key concepts introduced in IAS 20 are as follows.

Government assistance is action by government designed to provide an economic benefit specific to an entity or range of entities qualifying under certain criteria. Government assistance for the purpose of this Standard does not include benefits provided only indirectly through action affecting general trading conditions, such as the provision of infrastructure in development areas or the imposition of trading constraints on competitors.

A specific subset of government assistance is government grants. *Government grants* are assistance by government in the form of transfers of resources to an entity in return for past or future compliance with certain conditions relating to the operating activities of the entity. They exclude those forms of government assistance that cannot reasonably have a value placed on them and transactions with government that cannot be distinguished from the normal trading transactions of the entity.

The notion of government is to be interpreted broadly. *Government* refers to government, government agencies and similar bodies whether local, national or international.

Government grants may be related to revenue/expense items, such as repayment of 10 per cent of the wages bill, or to capital/asset items, such as repayment of 10 per cent of the cost of a machine. These two types are formally distinguished by IAS 20:

1 *Grants related to assets* are government grants whose primary condition is that an entity qualifying for them should purchase, construct or otherwise acquire long-term assets. Subsidiary conditions may also be attached restricting the type or location of the assets or the periods during which they are to be acquired or held.

2 *Grants related to income* are government grants other than those related to assets. The Standard gives two other definitions, including the familiar fair value.

   (a) *Forgivable loans* are loans that the lender undertakes to waive repayment of under certain prescribed conditions.

   (b) *Fair value* is the price that would be received to sell an asset or paid to transfer a liability in an orderly transaction between market participants at the measurement date.

Government assistance

Despite the inclusion of government assistance in the title of IAS 20, the statements about it are brief and rather obscure. The definitions given suggest in effect that government grants are government assistance that is distinguishable and quantifiable. Turning this round, references to government assistance in the Standard are to government activities that cannot be quantified or clearly distinguished. It follows, of course, that government assistance in this sense cannot be included numerically in the financial statements.

Examples of assistance that cannot reasonably have a value placed on them are free technical or marketing advice and the provision of guarantees. An example of assistance that cannot be distinguished from the normal trading transactions of the entity is a government procurement policy that is responsible for a portion of the entity's sales. The existence of the benefit might be unquestioned, but any attempt to segregate the trading activities from government assistance could well be arbitrary.

The significance of the benefit in the examples just presented may be such that disclosure of the nature, extent and duration of the assistance is necessary in order that the financial statements may not be misleading (para. 36). The Standard explicitly stated (para. 37) that while loans at nil or low interest rates are a form of government assistance, the 'benefit is not quantified by the imputation of interest'. This was reversed with effect from 1 January 2009 (see below) by a newly inserted para. 10A.

The disclosure requirement implied in this seems rather weakly stated. Non-quantified government support need not be disclosed at all unless its omission would be so serious as to be 'misleading'.

Treatment of government grants

The major portion of IAS 20 is concerned with the treatment of government grants. The first issue to deal with is the timing of recognition. The IAS requirement (para. 7) is that government grants, including non-monetary grants at fair value, should not be recognized until there is reasonable assurance that the entity will comply with the conditions attaching to them and that the grants will be received. Receipt of a grant does not of itself provide conclusive evidence that the conditions attaching to the grant have been or will be fulfilled.

'Reasonable assurance' is not, of course, definable or defined, but it is clearly less rigorous or demanding than, for example, 'virtual certainty' or 'beyond all reasonable doubt'. The Standard confirms (para. 10) that a forgivable loan (as defined above) is treated as a government grant when there is reasonable assurance that the entity will meet the terms for forgiveness of the loan. Once a government grant is recognized, any related contingency would be treated in accordance with IAS 37, *Provisions, Contingent Liabilities and Contingent Assets* (see Chapter 19).

The benefit of a government loan at a below-market rate of interest is treated as a government grant. The loan shall be recognized and measured in accordance with IAS 39, *Financial Instruments: Recognition and Measurement*. The benefit of the below-market rate of interest shall be measured as the difference between the initial carrying value of the loan determined in accordance with IAS 39 and the proceeds received. The benefit is accounted for in accordance with the Standard. The entity shall consider the conditions and obligations that have been, or must be, met when identifying the costs for which the benefit of the loan is intended to compensate (para. 10A).

The key requirement of the Standard (para. 12) is that government grants should be recognized as income over the periods necessary to match them with the related costs they are intended to compensate, on a systematic basis, i.e. following method 3(a) or (b) as discussed at the beginning of this section. They should not be credited directly to shareholders' interests. SIC 10, *Government Assistance – No Specific Relation to Operating Activities*, effective from 1 August 1998, has confirmed that government assistance to entities is a grant under IAS 20, even if granted generally to all entities within certain regions or industry sectors.

The matching principle will usually be simple to apply, as illustrated earlier in this chapter. Grants related to non-depreciable assets may also require the fulfilment of certain obligations and would then be recognized as income over the periods that bear the cost of meeting the obligations. As an example, a grant of land may be conditional on the erection of a building on the site, and it may be appropriate to recognize it as income over the life of the building. A government grant that becomes receivable as compensation for expenses or losses already incurred or for the purpose of giving immediate financial support to the entity with no future related costs should be recognized as income of the period in which it becomes receivable. Separate disclosure and explanation may be required.

Usually, a careful reading of the contract with the governmental body will determine the appropriate accounting treatment, although an intelligent appraisal of the in-substance thrust of the contract may be required. For example, a grant towards building a factory, stipulating that the factory must remain operating and employ at least 30 people for at least three years, is clearly in essence a grant towards building a factory, not a revenue grant towards reducing net wage costs. However, where a grant clearly relates in material terms to both specific capital and specific revenue items, the Standard is silent on appropriate treatment. Accounting common sense obviously requires an apportionment in such cases.

The Standard is surprisingly vague about non-monetary government grants, such as land donated by a government. IAS 20 merely notes (para. 23) that:

> It is usual to assess the fair value of the non-monetary asset and to account for both grant and asset at that fair value. An alternative course that is sometimes followed is to record both asset and grant at a nominal amount.

This is worded as a description, not as a requirement, although the preference is clear enough. Our view is that merely to record the event at nominal amount lacks transparency to an unacceptable degree. Also, it is not consistent with the substance over form principle and would lead to an inconsistent treatment of assets affecting both inter-entity and intra-entity comparisons.

Presentation of government grants

Regarding the presentation of grants related to assets, IAS 20 allows both methods (a) and (b) as discussed and illustrated earlier. Thus, government grants related to assets, including non-monetary grants at fair value, should (paras 24–28) be presented in the balance sheet either by setting up the grant as deferred income or by deducting the grant in arriving at the carrying amount of the asset. The Standard spells out that separate disclosure of the gross cash flows in the cash flow statement is likely to be necessary, whatever treatment is followed in the balance sheet. IAS 7, *Cash Flow Statements* (see Chapter 23), is more explicit in making this grossing up of cash flows a requirement.

Regarding the presentation of grants related to income, the Standard again accepts either of two alternatives (paras 29–31). It states, with approval, that grants related to income are sometimes presented as a credit in the income statement, either separately or under a general heading such as 'Other income'; alternatively, they are deducted in reporting the related expense.

A proper understanding of the financial statements may require separate disclosure of the grant and its effects on particular items of income or expense.

Repayment of government grants

A grant to which conditions were attached may have been properly recognized under the 'reasonable assurance' criterion discussed earlier. However, it may still become repayable in whole or in part if, in fact, the conditions are not met. IAS 20 requires (para. 32) that such a grant, as soon as the repayment becomes foreseeable (which might be significantly earlier than when the repayment actually occurs), should be accounted for as a revision to an accounting estimate, under IAS 8, *Accounting Policies, Changes in Accounting Estimates and Errors* (see Chapter 8). This essentially requires that the entries be made in the financial statements of the year concerned. Repayment of a grant related to income should be applied first against any unamortized deferred credit set up in respect of the grant. To the extent that the repayment exceeds any such deferred credit, or where no deferred credit exists, the repayment should be recognized immediately as an expense. Repayment of a grant related to an asset should be recorded by increasing the carrying amount of the asset or reducing the deferred balance by the amount repayable. The cumulative additional depreciation that would have been recognized to date as an expense in the absence of the grant should be recognized immediately as an expense. Circumstances giving rise to repayment of a grant related to an asset may require consideration to be given to the possible impairment of the new carrying amount of the asset (see IAS 36, *Impairment of Assets*, discussed in Chapter 14).

Disclosure

Key disclosure requirements are as follows:

- the accounting policy adopted for government grants, including the methods of presentation adopted in the financial statements
- the nature and extent of government grants recognized in the financial statements and an indication of other forms of government assistance from which the entity has directly benefited
- unfulfilled conditions and other contingencies attaching to government assistance that has been recognized.

BORROWING COSTS

The second particular problem area related to the cost of fixed assets is that of interest costs. In general, the interest cost is a straightforward periodic expense; it should be charged against revenues in proportion to the benefit received, i.e. on a time basis.

This is a normal application of the matching principle. The benefit is the existence of the loan and the expense is the interest cost, allocated proportionate to the size of the borrowing.

However, there are circumstances in which accounting theory seems to rationalize an alternative argument. We pointed out in our feedback to Activity 12.3 that 'cost of an asset' includes any item which is necessary to obtain the asset and make it workable. Suppose a loan is necessary in order to obtain the funds without which the asset cannot be obtained. Can it be argued that the cost of the loan (i.e. the interest) is part of the 'cost of the asset'? Clearly, once the asset is workable, i.e. able to function and generate revenues, then there can be no question of this argument justifying the non-expensing of interest. But can interest be capitalized as part of the cost of an asset during the period of its creation or construction (see Activity 12.17)?

ACTIVITY 12.17

From your knowledge of accounting principles, what do you think the answer to the above question should be?

Activity feedback

As far as it goes, the logic of the 'cost' argument seems inescapable. With a typical self-constructed asset, all direct costs, and in some circumstances some allocable indirect costs, are properly regarded as part of the total historical cost. It follows that any borrowing costs that can be directly linked to the financing of the asset concerned are also logically part of the total historical cost, as an application of the matching principle.

However, it is not difficult to find arguments which point in a different direction. It is clearly not very prudent to avoid the immediate expensing of interest payments that undeniably relate to periodic costs of the accounting period in question. Further, is not the economic argument true, i.e. that the cost of necessary finance is part of the cost of production, *whether or not* a separate source of finance related to the particular asset can be distinguished? If it is true, as we would certainly suggest that it is, then an imputed interest charge should be included even if not supported by any payments or external documentation. This arguably departs much too far from the traditional function of accounting as the recording of transactions. A problem of consistency in asset cost calculations thus arises if some interest costs are capitalized (relatable to specific loans) and others are not.

IAS 23, Borrowing Costs

The treatment of borrowing costs is set out in IAS 23, *Borrowing Costs*. The original 1984 version of the Standard permitted a free choice between systematically expensing costs and capitalizing them when certain conditions were met. In its comparability project in the early 1990s, the IASC proposed in ED32 that a 'benchmark' treatment should be for borrowing costs to be expensed, with capitalization as an alternative treatment when certain conditions were met. The responses to ED32 were divided on this issue; however, the IASC then issued ED39, according to which capitalization would be required if certain conditions were met, and expensing would be required otherwise. This position is similar to that in US GAAP (FAS 34). Again, responses to ED39 were mixed. In particular, there is the argument that capital structure would lead to different carrying values of 'qualifying assets'. Hence, IAS 23, *Capitalisation of Borrowing Costs*, issued in 1994, restored the choice between expensing and capitalization subject to certain conditions being met, but expensing became the 'benchmark treatment', and capitalization the 'alternative treatment'.

In March 2007, as part of the programme of convergence between IAS/IFRS and US GAAP, a revised IAS 23, *Borrowing Costs*, was issued which reverted to the position proposed in ED 39. In fact, IAS 23, *Borrowing Costs* now aligns in this respect with US GAAP, with the result that capitalization is required if certain conditions are met, and expensing is required otherwise.

The 'core principle' of the revised IAS 23 is that borrowing costs that are directly attributable to the acquisition, construction or production of a qualifying asset form part of the cost of that asset (i.e. are capitalized). Other borrowing costs are recognized as an expense (IAS 23, para. 1).

IAS 23 is to be applied in accounting for borrowing costs. It does not deal with the actual or imputed cost of equity, including that of preferred capital not classified as a liability. Borrowing costs are not required to be capitalized in the case of qualifying assets that are: (1) measured at fair value (e.g. biological assets), or (2) inventories manufactured or otherwise produced in large quantities on a repetitive basis (IAS 23, paras 2–4). The exclusion of (1) qualifying assets measured at fair value from the scope of IAS 23 is logical in that, as such assets are not measured on the basis of cost, the cost of borrowings is irrelevant to their measurement. The exclusion of (2) inventories manufactured or otherwise produced in large quantities on a repetitive basis is based on pragmatic reasons.

Qualifying assets are assets that necessarily take a substantial period of time to prepare for their intended use or sale, and depending on the circumstances may include certain inventories (e.g. construction work-in-process); manufacturing plants; power generation facilities; intangible assets (e.g. patents); and investment properties.

Qualifying assets do not include financial assets; inventories that are manufactured or otherwise produced over a short period of time; assets that are ready for their intended use or sale when they are acquired. (IAS 23, paras 5–7).

Borrowing costs that are directly attributable to the acquisition, construction or production of a qualifying asset are those borrowing costs that would have been avoided if the expenditure on the qualifying asset had not been made.

When funds are borrowed specifically for the purpose of obtaining a particular qualifying asset, it is clear that these funds are easily identified as directly attributable borrowing costs. If such borrowings are temporarily invested before being expended for the purpose of obtaining the asset, it is likewise clear that any investment income earned is to be deducted from the cost of the borrowings.

In other circumstances, identifying a direct relationship between particular borrowings and a qualifying asset, and determining the borrowings that would otherwise have been avoided, may be difficult, and judgement may have to be exercised. To the extent that funds that have been borrowed for general purposes are used for obtaining a qualifying asset, the amount of borrowing costs that are eligible for capitalization should be determined by applying a capitalization rate to the expenditures on that asset. This capitalization rate is calculated as the weighted average of the borrowing costs applicable to the borrowings that are outstanding during the period, excluding any borrowings made specifically for the purpose of obtaining the particular qualifying asset or any other qualifying asset. The amount of borrowing costs capitalized by an entity during a period must not exceed the total amount of borrowing costs that it incurred during that period.

The commencement date for capitalization is that date on which the entity first meets all of the following three conditions:

- expenditures on the qualifying assets are being incurred
- borrowing costs are being incurred
- activities that are necessary to prepare the asset for its intended use or sale are in progress.

Expenditures on the qualifying asset should include only those that have resulted in payments of cash, transfers of other assets or the assumption of interest-bearing liabilities. They are reduced by any progress payments received (for work-in-process) and grants received in connection with the asset. For the application of the capitalization rate, a reasonable approximation of the balance of expenditures to which it should be applied for a period is given by the average carrying amount of the asset during that period, including all borrowing costs capitalized in prior periods.

Activities necessary to prepare the asset for its intended use or sale include technical and administrative work prior to the start of physical construction. However, the mere holding of the asset in the absence of such work does not count as an activity, and borrowing costs incurred during such a period of inactivity do not qualify for capitalization (IAS 23, paras 17–19).

Moreover, capitalization of borrowing costs is suspended during extended periods in which active development of a qualifying asset is discontinued and no substantial technical or administrative work is carried out, except in the case of a temporary delay that is a necessary part of the process of preparing the asset for its intended use or sale (IAS 23, paras 20–21).

Capitalization of borrowing costs should cease when substantially all of the activities necessary to prepare the qualifying asset for its intended use or sale are complete.

When a qualifying asset is completed in parts, and each part is capable of being sold or used while work continues on the others (e.g. in the case of a business park comprising several buildings), the capitalization of borrowing costs on a substantially completed part should cease.

An asset is normally considered as 'ready for its intended use or sale' when its physical construction is complete, even though: (1) some routine administrative work may still continue, or (2) minor modifications, such as the decoration of the property to the purchaser's or user's specification, may still be outstanding (IAS 23, paras 22–25).

An entity should disclose in the notes to its financial statements:

- the amount of borrowings capitalized during the period
- the capitalization rate used to determine the amount of borrowing costs eligible for capitalization (IAS 23, para. 26).

ACCOUNTING FOR INVESTMENT PROPERTIES

Principles and definitions

The classic perception of a non-current asset is that of a long-term resource that is necessary to support the day-to-day operational activities of a business. It is used in production or administration, but is not itself sold. It generally wears out, as its use value or service potential is consumed, in recognition of which depreciation is charged in the annual profit calculation. These types of assets fall under the scope of IAS 16, *Property, Plant and Equipment*, as discussed in the first part of this chapter. The classic perception of an investment is that of an asset held so that the asset itself will earn positive returns, either through regular inflows such as interest, dividend or rent or through capital appreciation. With an investment, the key issue is impairment or capital appreciation, rather than consumption of use value or service potential.

The specific problem with properties is that they can be held for either purpose or for both purposes at different times. Because of a general tendency over the long term for property prices to rise significantly in nominal terms, the distinction in practice is often particularly significant.

Until at least the 1970s, property held as an investment was generally treated for accounting purposes like any other property, with or without the possibility of revaluation and with or without the possibility of non-depreciation, depending on the jurisdiction. This approach began to be challenged. It was argued that if a property is held as an investment then:

- the matching convention is arguably not relevant as no service potential is being used up
- the current values of such investments and any change therein are of prime importance and relevance.

ACTIVITY 12.18

We have seen that under IAS that a non-current asset is any asset other than a current asset, where a current asset is an asset which (IAS 1, para. 66) is:

- expected to be realized in, or is intended for sale or consumption in, the entity's normal operating cycle
- held primarily for the purpose of being traded
- expected to be realigned within 12 months after the balance sheet date
- cash or cash equivalent (as defined by IAS 7, see Chapter 23, unless it is restricted from being exchanged or used to settle a liability for at least 12 months after the balance sheet date).

If an entity owns a property that it intends to hire out in the short to medium term and then eventually sell, or possibly to sell in the short to medium term, consider:

- whether it is a non-current or current asset
- whether the economic substance of the situation implies a need for annual depreciation.

Activity feedback

The answer seems to depend on the particular situation. If the entity is actually trading in properties as an operating activity, then the property does seem to be a current asset. In this case, the question of depreciation does not arise either logically under the matching principle, or in legal (like for example under EC Directives) or regulatory terms (like for example under IAS/IFRS).

If the entity is intending to hold the property for a number of accounting periods, for rental and/or capital gain, then the current/non-current distinction is less clear, although perhaps non-current better reflects the substance. However, the property is still not being consumed in supporting the operating activities of the entity. Further, the key information of relevance to stakeholders should accord with the expected future outcomes, i.e. some kind of rental income and an eventual profitable disposal, not the wearing out of the asset. Arguably, therefore, depreciation is neither logical nor relevant, although this can raise legal and regulatory issues. This whole area needs separate discussion.

Following on from this criticism, the IASB issued an exposure draft on investment properties in which a mandatory fair value model for investment properties was proposed. However, in the resulting debate, the IASB was forced to backtrack on this proposal and IAS 40, *Investment Properties* now gives a choice between a cost model and a fair value model. An entity applies IAS 40, *Investment Property* rather than IAS 16 to its investment property. With effect from 1 January 2009, IAS 40 applies to property being constructed or developed for future use as an investment property. IAS 40 also applies to existing investment property being redeveloped for future continued use as investment property. Before we discuss the measurement of investment properties further, we zoom in on the definitions included in IAS 40. IAS 40 gives the following key definitions:

Investment property is property (land or a building or part of a building, or both) held (by the owner or by the lessee under a finance lease) to earn rentals or for capital appreciation or both, rather than for:

- use in the production or supply of goods or services or for administrative purposes, or
- sale in the ordinary course of business.

Owner-occupied property is property held (by the owner or by the lessee under a finance lease) for use in the production or supply of goods or services or for administrative purposes.

It follows from the definition of investment property that an investment property will generate cash flows 'largely independently' of other assets held by an entity. It is this which distinguishes investment property from owner-occupied property, as owner-occupied property only generates cash flows in conjunction with other operating assets necessary for the production or supply process.

Recognition criteria of investment property

An investment property within the definition should be recognized as an asset when, and only when:

- it is probable that the future economic benefits that are associated with the investment property will flow to the entity
- the cost of the investment property can be measured reliably.

Figure 12.1 summarizes the various alternatives for treating a property under IAS GAAP (based on a figure in the Appendix to the 2000 version of IAS 40).

Note that in marginal cases, judgement will be needed in distinguishing investment properties from owner-occupied properties. For example, an owner-managed hotel is essentially concerned with the provision of services to guests, so it is not an investment property. However, the owner of a building, which is managed as a hotel by a third party, is in the position of holding an investment, with 'largely independent' cash flows arising, hence creating an investment property. In complex intermediate situations, the substance of the situation and the balance of emphasis should be followed. Disclosure of the criteria used is required when classification is difficult.

ACTIVITY 12.19

Consider each of the assets described in (a) to (i) (below) and indicate whether they are or are not investment properties as defined in IAS 40.

- **(a)** land held for long-term capital appreciation rather than for short-term sale in the ordinary course of business
- **(b)** land held for a currently undetermined future use
- **(c)** property that is being constructed or developed for future use as investment property
- **(d)** a building owned by the entity (or held by the entity under a finance lease) and leased out under one or more operating leases
- **(e)** a building that is vacant but is held to be leased out under one or more operating leases
- **(f)** property intended for sale in the ordinary course of business, e.g. property held for trading by property traders or for development and resale by property developers
- **(g)** property being constructed for third parties
- **(h)** owner-occupied property
- **(i)** property that is leased to another entity under a finance lease.

Activity feedback

(a), (d), and (e) are clearly held for investment purposes and are investment properties. (b) cannot really be regarded as other than a speculative purchase at the time it was acquired and so is an investment property unless and until, presumably, it eventually becomes part of an owner-occupied property. (c), however, does not at present meet the definition; it is property under construction and IAS 16 would apply. None of the final four is an investment property and IAS 40 would not apply to them: (f) would be dealt with as inventory under IAS 2 (see Chapter 16), (g) as a contract with a customer under IFRS 15 (see Chapter 18), (h) and (i) as property PPE under IAS 16.

Figure 12.1   Decision tree for treatment of most property under IAS GAAP

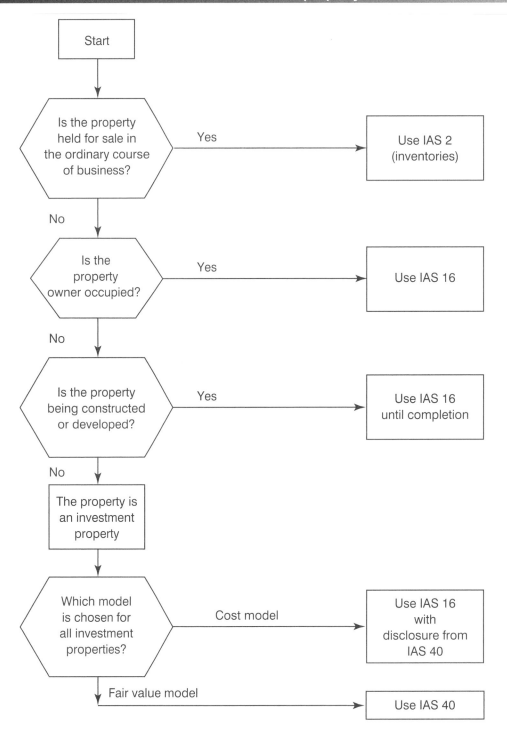

MEASUREMENT OF INVESTMENT PROPERTY

Initial measurement

The initial measurement of a newly acquired investment property under IAS 40 is reasonably simple, but the issue of subsequent measurement is much more complicated. An investment property should be measured initially at its cost, which is the fair value of the consideration given for it. Transaction costs are included in the initial measurement. The cost of a purchased investment property comprises its purchase price and any directly attributable expenditure. Directly attributable expenditure includes, for example, professional fees for legal services and property transfer taxes.

When an investment property has already been recognized, subsequent expenditure on that investment property should be recognized as an expense when it is incurred unless it is probable that this expenditure will enable the asset to generate future economic benefits in excess of its originally assessed standard of performance and the expenditure can be measured and attributed to the asset reliably.

The initial cost of a property investment held under a lease by a lessee and classified as an investment property shall be measured in accordance with IFRS 16, *Leases*.

Measurement subsequent to initial recognition

As suggested, the question of measurement subsequent to the initial measurement is more complicated. Investment property can be treated in either of two ways. Entities can choose between a fair value model and a cost model. The fair value model states that investment property should be measured at fair value and changes in fair value should be recognized in the income statement. The cost model is as defined in IAS 16, *Property, Plant and Equipment*: investment property should be measured at depreciated cost (less any accumulated impairment losses). An entity that chooses the cost model should additionally disclose the fair value of its investment property in the notes to the financial statements.

Although the choice given in IAS 40 between these two models is a free one, and there is no stated 'benchmark' treatment, it is very clear that a preference for a fair value model is expressed. Fair value has to be determined in *all* cases – for measurement in the financial statements if the fair value model is used and for disclosure in the notes if the cost model is used. The Standard notes that IAS 8, *Accounting Policies, Changes in Accounting Estimates and Errors* (see Chapter 8) states that a voluntary change in accounting policy should be made only if the change will result in a more appropriate presentation of events or transactions in the financial statements of the entity. IAS 40 explicitly states that it is highly unlikely that a change from the fair value model to the cost model will result in a more appropriate presentation.

Some insurers and other entities operate an internal property fund that issues notional units, with some units held by investors in linked contracts and others held by the entity. A newly-introduced paragraph (32A) states that an entity may:

(a) choose either the fair value model or the cost model for all investment property backing liabilities that pay a return linked directly to the fair value of, or returns from, specified assets including that investment property and

(b) choose either the fair value model or the cost model for all other investment property, regardless of the choice made in (a).

After initial recognition, an entity that chooses the cost model should measure all its investment property using the cost-based treatment in IAS 16; that is at cost less any accumulated depreciation and any accumulated impairment losses. In other words, if choosing the cost model, an entity proceeds in measurement (but not disclosure) terms to follow IAS 16 as if IAS 40 did not exist.

However, investment properties that meet the criteria to be classified as held for sale (or are included in a disposal group that is classified as held for sale) shall be measured in accordance with IFRS 5, *Non-current Assets Held for Sale and Discontinued Operations* (see Chapter 13).

There is a rebuttable presumption that an entity will be able to determine the fair value of an investment property reliably on a continuing basis. After initial recognition, an entity that chooses the fair value model should measure all its investment property at its fair value, unless this presumption is not valid.

We discussed the concept of fair value in Chapter 7 where we introduced IFRS 13 *Fair Value Measurement*. Fair value is the price that would be received to sell an asset or paid to transfer a liability in an orderly transaction between market participants at the measurement date. By implication, it is automatically assumed in IAS 40 as it stands from 2013 that IFRS 13 is rigorously and properly applied to the relevant investment properties. IAS 40 does note that, as a generality, the various inputs to fair value estimations reflect the assumptions market participants would or do actually make under the market conditions at the relevant time.

A gain or loss arising from a change in the fair value of investment property should be included in net profit or loss for the period in which it arises. The Standard makes it absolutely explicit that changes in fair value are to be taken directly to earnings and not taken to or from reserves.

In the rare situations in which fair value measurement proves impossible for a particular property, the entity should measure that investment property using the cost model treatment in IAS 16. The residual value of the investment property should be assumed to be zero. The entity should continue to apply IAS 16 until the date of disposal of the investment property. In such circumstances, the entity measures all its other investment properties at fair value. IAS 40 requires that once an entity has begun measuring an investment property at fair value, it should continue to do so, even if the measurements subsequently become less reliable.

Transfers and disposals

Under IAS 40, transfers to or from investment property should be made only when there is a clearly evidenced change of use. When the cost model is being used for investment properties, transfers between investment property, owner-occupied property and inventories do not change the carrying amount of the property transferred and they do not change the cost of that property for measurement or disclosure purposes. The Standard does not remind us, but we should note that the fair value of investment properties measured under the cost model has to be disclosed in the notes, a requirement that does not extend to owner-occupied property or to inventory.

A transfer to or from investment properties which are being carried at fair value obviously has potentially very significant effects on the measurement process and the carrying amount of an asset. If an investment property carried at fair value becomes an owner-occupied property or is transferred to inventory, then the property's cost for subsequent accounting purposes is its fair value as at the date of the change in use.

If an owner-occupied property becomes an investment property carried at fair value, then IAS 16 should be applied up to the date of the change of use, i.e. the entity continues to depreciate the property and to recognize any impairment losses. A difference between the carrying amount of the asset under IAS 16 at the date of the change of use and the fair value at that date is dealt with in the same way as a revaluation under IAS 16.

If a property classed as inventory is transferred to become an investment property carried at fair value, then the treatment is consistent with that of a sale of inventory under IAS 2, *Inventories*. A difference between the fair value of the property at that date and its previous carrying amount is therefore part of net profit or loss for the period. Similarly, a self-constructed investment property that will be carried at fair value will give rise, on completion, to an effect on reported net profit or loss for the period equal to the difference between the fair value on the completion date and its previous (cost-based) carrying amount.

ACTIVITY 12.20

Read the immediately preceding paragraph again. Does it meet the requirement in IAS 1 and the underlying concept in the IAS Framework to be prudent?

Activity feedback

There is, certainly in comparison with what many would regard as normal, an apparent lack of prudence, and of strict adherence to the realization principle, inherent in the previous paragraph. However, this is the whole point of the fair value concept. There is, by definition, reliable evidence to determine fair value, which is a market-based concept and it therefore follows logically and consistently with a true sale, that a gain relating to operating processes has been 'made'. Anybody who regards only a completed transaction as providing adequate evidence for fair value should reject the whole notion of fair value accounting.

An investment property should be eliminated from the balance sheet (derecognized) on disposal. The disposal of an investment property may occur by sale or by entering into a finance lease. In determining the date of disposal for investment property, an entity applies the criteria in IFRS 15 for recognizing revenue from the sale of goods (see Chapter 18). IAS 17, Leases applies on a disposal by entering into a finance lease or by a sale and leaseback (see Chapter 15). An investment property must also be derecognized when it is permanently withdrawn from use and no further economic benefits are expected from its disposal. Gains and losses arising on derecognition, i.e. the difference between the net disposal proceeds and the carrying amount are recognized as income or expense in the income statement, unless IAS 17 requires otherwise in the case of a sale and leaseback. This is, of course, consistent with the treatment of annual changes in fair value of a retained investment property, which are likewise taken directly to the income statement.

IAS 40 gives extensive and detailed disclosure requirements. The crucial point to remember is that if the cost model is used, then disclosure of fair values, by way of note, is still required.

ACTIVITY 12.21

An extract from the financial statements of Company Zemla plc for the year to 31 March 20X8 is shown below. Briefly explain how the group measures its properties, and what has happened during the year in relation to them.

At 31 March 20X8, the group book value of properties of £10 469m (20X7: £14 047m) comprises freeholds of £9357m (20X7: £13 118m); virtual freeholds of £303m (20X7: £106m); long leaseholds of £802m (20X7: £820m) and short leaseholds of £7m (20X7: £3m). The historical cost of properties was £7315m (20X7: £8897m).

At 31 March 20X8, the book value of owner-occupied property is £53m (20X7: £50m) after charging £nil (20X7: £nil) depreciation to the income statement for the year.

The property valuation does not include any investment properties held under operating leases (20X7: nil).

Property valued at £7162m (20X7: £9194m) was subject to a security interest and other properties of nonrecourse companies amounted to £2m (20X7: £128m).

Cumulative interest capitalized in investment and development properties amounts to £33m and £84m (20X7: £28m and £46m), respectively.

(Continued)

ACTIVITY 12.21 *(Continued)*

Financial statements of Zembla plc for the year ended 31 March 20X8

	Investment £m	Development £m	Owner-occupied £m	Total £m
Carrying value at 1 April 20X7	12 891	1 106	50	14 047
Additions – property purchases	115			115
Other capital expenditure	253	292		545
Disposals	(2 694)	(24)		(2 718)
Reclassifications	360	(360)		
Revaluations:				
in income statement	(1 569)	(19)		(1 588)
in statement of recognized income and expense		57	3	60
Increase in tenant incentives and guaranteed rent uplift balances	33	10		43
Carrying value at 31 March 20X8	9 389	1 062	53	10 504
Head lease liabilities				(35)
Total group property portfolio valuation 31 March 20X8				10 469

Activity feedback

Most of the group properties are held as investments, with a significant minority under development. They are generally held at fair value. During the year, there has been little acquisition of properties and significant disposals. In addition, a sizeable downward revaluation has been recorded, taken directly to reported earnings. The absolute historical cost of the properties has therefore fallen, as has the excess of valuation over historical cost for those remaining. Note also that most of the properties are pledged as security against group borrowings. The quality of disclosure and transparency seems quite high.

ACCOUNTING FOR AGRICULTURE

Earlier in this chapter, we mentioned the terms 'biological assets' and 'bearer plants'. These terms originate from IAS 41, *Agriculture*. IAS 41 was a completely new Standard issued in 2003, which deals with the accounting treatment of agricultural activity.

Agricultural activity is the management by an entity of the biological transformation and harvest of living animals or plants (biological assets) for sale or for conversion into agricultural produce or into additional biological assets (IAS 41, para. 5). Biological transformation comprises the process of growth, degeneration, production and procreation that cause qualitative or quantitative changes in a biological asset (IAS 41, para. 5). Harvest is the detachment of produce from a biological asset or the cessation of a biological asset's life processes (IAS 41, para. 5). One could say that the biological assets are the PPE of IAS 41, whereas the agricultural produce represents the inventory of IAS 41. The processing of agricultural produce after harvest falls under the scope of IAS 2, *Inventories*. So when the grapes are picked from the vines, they are agricultural produce and accounted for under the scope of IAS 41; when they are processed into wine, they fall under the scope of IAS 2. Another example is when a pig is alive, it is a biological asset and falls under the scope of IAS 41 (measurement of biological assets); when the pig is slaughtered and it is a dead animal, it is still under the scope of IAS 41 but now it qualifies as agricultural produce and is measured accordingly; when in the slaughter house or at the butcher's, the carcass of the pig is processed into meat and bones, then these products fall under the scope of IAS 2.

ACTIVITY 12.22

Let's apply IAS 41 and IAS 2 to the situation of a fish. Assume a fish farm, 'Fresh Fish', specializes in salmon, and when the salmon reaches a mature age it is killed. If Fresh Fish is preparing its annual accounts, how does it account for the living salmon and the dead salmon? Assume at the same time a fishing company, 'Nautilius', sails the seas and the rivers to catch fish. They catch a lot of salmon and, while it is still alive after the catch, it is finally dead when the ship arrives at the harbour. When 'Fresh Fish' and 'Nautilius' prepare their annual accounts, how do they account for the living salmon and the dead salmon?

Activity feedback

Since the fish farm has actively managed the transformation process of the salmon, this company has engaged in agricultural activity and IAS 41 applies. So for the fish farm, as long as the salmon is alive it is a biological asset. When the salmon is killed (= harvested) it changes from being a biological asset to being agricultural produce. Since the salmon is not yet processed further, it still falls under the scope of IAS 41, but as agricultural produce.

The fishing company 'Nautilius' did not manage the transformation process of the salmon at all, so the salmon, dead or still alive, will be accounted for according to IAS 2, Inventories.

Knowing which Standard to apply matters since the measurement of the dead salmon will be different. We will discuss the measurement of agricultural produce further in Chapter 16. We concentrate in this section on the biological assets.

RECOGNITION AND MEASUREMENT OF BIOLOGICAL ASSETS

The traditional recognition criteria of controllability, future benefits and reliable measurement also apply to the recognition of biological assets and agricultural produce. With respect to measurement, IAS 41 (para. 12) stipulates that biological assets shall be measured at initial recognition and at the end of each reporting period at its fair value less costs to sell, except when the fair value cannot be measured reliably. We notice the difference with the other tangible assets where the initial measurement was always at cost. Moreover, for the measurement after the initial measurement, companies always had the choice between the cost model and the revaluation model for tangible assets. In the case of biological assets, the companies do not have a choice. From the moment of initial measurement, the biological assets need to be measured at fair value less costs to sell. Only when the fair value of a biological asset cannot be measured reliably (for example when no quoted market prices are available), should the biological asset be measured at its cost less any accumulated depreciation and any accumulated impairment losses. However, once the fair value of such a biological asset becomes reliably measurable, the company shall measure the asset at its fair value less costs to sell.

Gains and losses arising on initial recognition of a biological asset at fair value less costs to sell and gains and losses from a change in fair value less costs to sell, shall be included in the profit or loss for the period in which it arises. Much agricultural activity involves either the gradual physical expansion and therefore increase in value of a specific item, such as a tree or a cow, or the creation without any market transaction of a new item such as a sapling grown from seed or the birth of a calf. In both situations, the traditional accounting process based on recording the historical cost-of-purchase transaction fails to present fairly the economic reality of the accumulation of agricultural resources. For this reason, IAS 41 focuses on the use of fair values in both the statement of financial position and for the calculation of the profit or loss. However, the immediate result of this valuation model imposed on biological assets is that when market prices of these biological assets are volatile, this volatility is immediately introduced in the profit and loss account of the entity. With respect to the determination of the fair value of biological assets and agricultural produce, the standard setter states that contracts specifying prices at future dates are not necessarily relevant to the determination of fair values to date.

Companies applying IAS 41 encountered many difficulties in determining a fair value for a number of their biological assets, especially for those that qualify as bearer plant (e.g. vines, olive trees, etc.). Therefore, it was decided that biological assets that were bearer plant should be removed from the scope of IAS 41 and, from 2016 onwards, fall under the scope of IAS 16, *Property, Plant and Equipment*. This allows companies to account for bearer plants with the use of the cost model, without having to provide an explanation as to why it is not possible to determine a fair value for the bearer plant.

Disclosure

The purpose of the disclosure is to show to users of financial information the aggregate gain or loss arising during the current period on initial recognition of biological assets and agricultural produce and from the change in fair value less estimated costs to sell of biological assets. The entity also has to provide a description for each group of biological assets. The Standard discusses how this requirement is to be interpreted. The objective that should underlie the interpretation of the word 'group' in this context is to provide information that may be helpful in assessing the timing of future cash flows. The description may be narrative or quantified, but quantified descriptions of each group of biological assets, distinguishing between consumable and bearer biological assets or between mature and immature biological assets are encouraged. For example, livestock intended for the production of meat are consumable biological assets, whereas livestock from which milk is produced are bearer biological assets.

Government grants and agriculture

Companies active in agriculture often receive government grants for their activities. Therefore, IAS 41 pays special attention to how government grants should be accounted for. The fair value based approach of IAS 41 gave the IASB a problem regarding the treatment of government grants. IAS 20, *Accounting for Government Grants and Disclosure of Government Assistance* (discussed earlier in this chapter) requires that government grants should not be recognized until there is reasonable assurance that: (1) the entity will comply with the conditions attaching to them; and (2) the grants will be received. IAS 20 also requires that government grants should be recognized as income over the periods necessary to match them with related costs that they are intended to compensate, on a systematic basis. As regards the presentation of government grants related to assets, IAS 20 permits two methods – setting up a government grant as deferred income or deducting the government grant from the carrying amount of the asset (see earlier in this chapter).

If the latter method is used in the context of a biological asset under IAS 41, then this will reduce the cost of the asset and therefore increase the excess of a fair value over that 'cost' on a dollar-for-dollar basis. Since this excess under IAS 41 is taken directly to income, the effect is that the government grant itself is taken immediately to income, in direct conflict with the IAS 20 requirement to match the grant over the relevant periods. Therefore, government grants received for agricultural activity fall under the scope of IAS 41.

IAS 41 resolves the conflict by requiring a delay in the recognition of such grants when the fair value basis is used. An unconditional government grant related to a biological asset measured at its fair value less estimated point-of-sale costs should be recognized as income, when and only when, the government grant becomes receivable. If a government grant related to a biological asset measured at its fair value less estimated point-of-sale costs is conditional, including where a government grant requires an entity not to engage in a specified agricultural activity, an entity should recognize the government grant as income when, and only when, the conditions attaching to the government grant are met. To illustrate, if a government grant is received in relation to a herd of cattle, which is repayable if the herd is not kept for three years, then none of the grant can be recognized as income until the three years have expired. However, if the amount payable is reduced to 40 per cent of the grant after the end of year two, then 60 per cent of the grant could and should be taken to income at that point. When a biological asset is measured at cost less accumulated depreciation and less accumulated impairment (if no reliable fair value is available), then IAS 20 is applied.

SUMMARY

In this long chapter, we have explored a number of aspects of IAS thinking in relation to the accounting treatment of fixed (non-current) assets. We looked at problems of cost determination, in particular IAS 20 on government grants and IAS 23 on borrowing costs and on the recognition and measurement of PPE (IAS 16), including alternative methods of depreciation calculation. We also exposed alternative views on the treatment of investment properties, and the IAS requirements on this in IAS 40. Finally we discussed the recognition and measurement issues involved with biological assets (IAS 41).

EXERCISES

Suggested answers to exercises marked ✓ are to be found in the Student online resources, with suggested answers to the remaining questions available in the Instructor online resources.

1   What are fixed (non-current) assets?

2   Outline four different depreciation methods and appraise them in the context of the definition and objectives of depreciation.

3   Are government grants related to the purchase of fixed assets by an entity a reduction in cost of acquisition?

4   Can the receipt of a government grant create a liability?

5   In what circumstances, if at all, should borrowing costs be capitalized in your opinion?

✓**6** Should land be allowed or required to be revalued?

✓**7** Should buildings be allowed or required to be revalued?

8 In what circumstances, if any, do you think that regulation should allow the non-depreciation of owned buildings?

9 IAS 40 gives a choice of accounting policies in relation to investment properties. Is a choice acceptable? If not, how should IAS 40 be altered?

✓**10** The following is an extract of Errsea's balances of property, plant and equipment and related government grants at 1 April 2006.

	Cost	Accumulated depreciation	Carrying amount
	$000	$000	$000
Property, plant and equipment	240	180	60
Non-current liabilities			
Government grants			30
Current liabilities			
Government grants			10

Details including purchases and disposals of plant and related government grants during the year are:

(i) Included in the above figures is an item of plant that was disposed of on 1 April 2006 for $12 000 which had cost $90 000 on 1 April 2003. The plant was being depreciated on a straight line basis over four years, assuming a residual value of $10 000. A government grant was received on its purchase and was being recognized in the statement of profit or loss and other comprehensive income in equal amounts over four years. In accordance with the terms of the grant, Errsea repaid $3 000 of the grant on the disposal of the related plant.

(ii) An item of plant was acquired on 1 July 2006 with the following costs:

	$
Base cost	192 000
Modifications specified by Errsea	12 000
Transport and installation	6 000

The plant qualified for a government grant of 25% of the base cost of the plant, but it had not been received by 31 March 2007. The plant is to be depreciated on a straight line basis over three years with a nil estimated residual value.

(iii) All other plant is depreciated by 15% per annum on cost.

(iv) $11 000 of the $30 000 non-current liability for government grants at 1 April 2006 should be reclassified as a current liability as at 31 March 2007.

(v) Depreciation is calculated on a time-apportioned basis.

Required:
Prepare extracts of Errsea's statement of profit or loss and other comprehensive income and statement of financial position in respect of the property, plant and equipment and government grants for the year ended 31 March 2007. Note: disclosure notes are not required.

(ACCA, June 2007, adapted)

✓**11**   Omega is an entity that owns three properties. All three properties were purchased on 1 October 2004. Details of the purchase price and market values of the properties are as follows:

	Property 1 $000	Property 2 $000	Property 3 $000
Purchase price	15 000	10 000	12 000
Market value 30 September 2005	16 000	11 000	13 500
Market value 30 September 2006	17 000	9 000	14 500

Properties 1 and 2 are used by Omega as factories while property 3 is let to a non-related third party at a commercial rent. Omega does not depreciate any of the properties on the basis that they are valued at market values that are generally expected to increase over time.

Required:
(a) Assess whether Omega's policy of non-depreciation of properties 1, 2 and 3 is in accordance with international financial reporting standards.

(b) Show how the movements in the carrying amount of each property will be reflected in the financial statements of Omega for the years ended 30 September 2005 and 2006. You can assume that any relevant depreciation is immaterial.

Where necessary you should justify your treatment with reference to appropriate international financial reporting standards. Where more than one treatment is permitted under international financial reporting standards, you should show the impact of both treatments.

(ACCA, December 2006)

✓**12**   Omega prepares financial statements under International Financial Reporting Standards. In the year ended 31 March 2007 the following transactions occurred:

Transaction 1
On 1 April 2006, Omega began the construction of a new production line. Costs relating to the line are as follows:

Details	Amount $000
Costs of the basic materials (list price $12.5 million less a 20% trade discount)	10 000
Recoverable sales taxes incurred not included in the purchase cost	1 000
Employment costs of the construction staff for the three months to 30 June 2006 (note 1)	1 200
Other overheads directly related to the construction (note 2)	900
Payments to external advisers relating to the construction	500
Expected dismantling and restoration costs (note 3)	2 000

Note 1
The production line took two months to complete and was brought into use on 31 May 2006.

Note 2
The other overheads were incurred in the two months ended 31 May 2006. They included an abnormal cost of $300 000 caused by a major electrical fault.

Note 3
The production line is expected to have a useful economic life of eight years. At the end of that time, Omega is legally required to dismantle the plant in a specified manner and restore its location to an acceptable standard. The figure of $2 million included in the cost estimates is the amount that is expected to be incurred at the end of the useful life of the production plant. The appropriate rate to use in any discounting calculations is 5%. The present value of $1 payable in eight years at a discount rate of 5% is approximately $0.68.

Note 4
Four years after being brought into use, the production line will require a major overhaul to ensure that it generates economic benefits for the second half of its useful life. The estimated cost of the overhaul, at current prices, is $3 million.

Note 5
Omega computes its depreciation charge on a monthly basis.

Note 6
No impairment of the plant had occurred by 31 March 2007.

Transaction 2
On 31 December 2006, the directors decided to dispose of a property that was surplus to requirements. They instructed selling agents to find a suitable purchaser and advertised the property at a commercially realistic price.

The property was being measured under the revaluation model and had been revalued at $15 million on 31 March 2006. The depreciable element of the property was estimated as $8 million at 31 March 2006 and the useful economic life of the depreciable element was estimated as 25 years from that date.

On 31 December 2006 the directors estimated that the market value of the property was $16 million, and that the costs incurred in selling the property would be $500 000. The property was sold on 30 April 2007 for $16.1 million. Omega incurred selling costs of $550 000. The actual selling price and costs to sell were consistent with estimated amounts as at 31 March 2007.

The financial statements for the year ended 31 March 2007 were authorized for issue on 15 May 2007.

Required:
Show the impact of the above transactions on the statement of profit or loss and other comprehensive income of Omega for the year ended 31 March 2007, and on its statement of financial position as at 31 March 2007. You should state where in the statement of profit or loss and other comprehensive income and the statement of financial position relevant balances will be shown.

(ACCA, June 2007, adapted)

13   (i)   Discuss the arguments for and against the capitalization of borrowing costs as part of the cost of an asset.

On 1 April 20X2 Webster commenced the construction of a large development consisting of several separate retail premises. It had a policy of capitalizing borrowing costs under IAS 23. At 31 March 20X3 the amount of expenditure on the development totalled $12 million. These expenditures are deemed to have occurred evenly throughout the year. The development is being financed from funds generally borrowed for the construction of similar development projects. Webster's cost of capital on these funds can be calculated from the following:

- $2 million overdraft at 15 per cent per annum
- $3 million 5 year secured 8 per cent loan note
- $5 million 5 year unsecured 10 per cent loan note.

Construction of the development was halted twice during the accounting period to 31 March 20X3. The first occasion, for a two-week period, was due to the discovery of ancient artefacts unearthed during excavation work. The second, an extended period of two months, was due to an industrial relations dispute.

(ii) Calculate the amount of finance costs that Webster should capitalize for the period to 31 March 20X3.

(ACCA, June 2003, adapted)

14   Kayte operates in the shipping industry and owns vessels for transportation. Kayte's vessels constitute a material part of its total assets. The economic life of the vessels is estimated to be 30 years, but the useful life of some of the vessels is only 10 years because Kayte's policy is to sell these vessels when they are 10 years old. Kayte estimated the residual value of these vessels at sale to be half of acquisition cost, and this value was assumed to be constant during their useful life. Kayte argued that the estimates of residual value used were conservative in view of an immature market with a high degree of uncertainty and presented documentation which indicated some vessels were being sold for a price considerably above carrying value. Broker valuations of the residual value were considerably higher than those used by Kayte. Kayte argued against broker valuations on the grounds that it would result in greater volatility in reporting.

Kayte keeps some of the vessels for the whole 30 years and these vessels are required to undergo an engine overhaul in dry dock every 10 years to restore their service potential, hence the reason why some of the vessels are sold. The residual value of the vessels kept for 30 years is based upon the steel value of the vessel at the end of its economic life.

At the time of purchase, the service potential, which must be restored by the engine overhaul, is measured based on the cost as if it had been performed at the time of the purchase of the vessel. In the current period, one of the vessels had to have its engine totally replaced after only eight years. Normally, engines last for the 30-year economic life if overhauled every 10 years. Additionally, one type of vessel was having its funnels replaced after 15 years, but the funnels had not been depreciated separately.

Required:
Discuss the accounting treatment of the above transaction in the financial statements of Kayte.

(ACCA, Corporate Reporting (International), December 2014, adapted)

15   On 1 January 20X5 Company A commenced the construction of a new office building. The office building was completed on 31 December 20X5. To fund the construction of the building, Company A used both specific borrowings and general borrowings. On 1 January 20X5 Company A obtained a five-year 10% loan of €800 000. This loan was obtained specifically for the purpose of funding the construction of the new office building. During 20X5 interest of €80 000 was incurred on the €800 000 loan. On 1 January 20X5 Company A's general borrowings included a ten-year 8% loan of €1 800 000 and a ten-year 11% loan of €1 500 000. The debt outstanding on the three loans remained unchanged throughout the year. During 20X5 the following payments were made to the building contractor hired to construct the new office building:

Date of payment	Amount €
1 January 20X5	500 000
31 March 20X5	600 000
31 July 20X5	700 000
31 October 20X5	800 000
31 December 20X5	300 000
Total construction costs	2 900 000

Required:

Calculate the amount of borrowings costs that Company A should capitalize for the period to 31 December 20X5.

INTANGIBLE ASSETS

13

OBJECTIVES After studying this chapter you should be able to:

- define and distinguish intangible assets

- discuss the difference between internally generated goodwill and purchased goodwill

- discuss the characteristics of intangible assets under IAS 38

- describe, apply and appraise the requirements of IAS 38 relating to the recognition, measurement and disclosure with respect to intangible assets.

INTRODUCTION

The accounting treatment of goodwill and intangible assets has caused great difficulty and confusion over the years. Part of the trouble was a failure to distinguish clearly between the two. In the 'bad old days', goodwill was often very loosely regarded as a conglomerate figure for all unrecorded net asset values. In other words, if a business was bought for €1 million and the recorded net assets had 'book values' of €600 000, then the difference of €400 000 was considered to be goodwill. This adherence to book values, which are by definition largely meaningless in market terms, is now generally unacceptable. IASB defines goodwill (IFRS 3, Appendix A) as follows:

Future economic benefits arising from assets that are not capable of being individually identified and separately recognized.

In principle, goodwill is in existence all the time. Its value is difficult to define and is constantly changing. Its value can be negative, of course. But goodwill is always there; it is inherent in the business. This is often referred to as *inherent goodwill, non-purchased goodwill* or *internally generated goodwill*. It is contrasted with purchased goodwill. This contrast is not for reasons of principle, but purely for the practical reason that purchased goodwill has a convenient cost figure. There has been a transaction, the cost convention can be applied and we have a figure capable of being audited. If we buy a business for €100 000 and the net separable assets have a fair value of €60 000, then we can certainly say that goodwill is, or at least at that instant was, worth €40 000.

The accounting treatment for purchased goodwill is regarded as an aspect of accounting for business combinations. The IASB covers purchased goodwill in IFRS 3 and therefore we discuss purchased goodwill together with all other aspects of business combinations in Part Three. In this chapter, we consider in detail the problems of accounting for intangibles other than purchased goodwill; this is covered by IAS 38, *Intangible Assets*.

INTANGIBLE ASSETS

In IAS/IFRS, an intangible asset is defined as an '*identifiable* non-monetary asset without physical substance'. This excludes goodwill, which is by definition non-identifiable.

Identifiability in IAS/IFRS does not equal separability, since an asset of an entity is defined as 'a *resource* [that is:] (a) *controlled* by the entity as a result of past events; and (b) from which future economic benefits are expected to flow to the entity'. For an intangible asset to be recognized, the future economic benefits must be 'probable' and it must be possible to measure the cost of the asset reliably. 'Control' encompasses both the right to obtain the benefits and the ability to restrict access to them by others. It is not necessarily considered to imply the ability to sell the item separately from other assets of the entity. These criteria thus permit the recognition as assets, in appropriate circumstances, of non-separable items such as development costs that have not been converted into (separable) patents. They do not permit the recognition of internally generated goodwill.

At the original creation of IAS 38, the IASB was concerned to achieve, as far as possible, uniformity of treatment for all non-current non-financial assets, whether tangible or intangible, and for intangibles whether internally generated or acquired. This concern is manifested in IAS 38 in the following ways:

- Many of the paragraphs of IAS 38 are similar in wording, and in places virtually identical, to paragraphs of IAS 16, *Property, Plant and Equipment*. IAS 38 also foresees initial recognition of intangibles at cost and, following initial measurement, there is the choice between the use of the cost model and the revaluation model. However, more restrictive criteria apply for the use of the revaluation model with respect to intangible assets.

- The recognition as assets of internally generated intangibles is allowed, subject to stringent and cumbersome criteria.

Although the principle is that any intangibles that meet the asset recognition criteria should be recognized, it remains to be seen whether the effect of these criteria acts as a deterrent to a reporting entity from so doing, in the absence of a powerful reason.

In the context of intangible assets, the treatment of R&D costs has always been the subject of particular controversy internationally. While there is general but not universal agreement (e.g. Norwegian law explicitly states the opposite) that research costs do not give rise to intangible values that can be recognized as assets, there is disagreement as to whether development costs may do so, subject to certain criteria. Initially, the IASB (in fact, its predecessor the IASC) was in favour of immediately expensing development costs. Later on, the IASB changed its preferred (benchmark) treatment, namely, the immediate expensing of all development costs, to one of capitalization (i.e. recognition as an asset), provided certain criteria were met. It was thought that this was more consistent with the concept of an asset as set out in the IASB's Framework. IAS 38 now requires capitalization; immediate expensing of development costs is not allowed as an alternative treatment if the recognition criteria are met.

SCOPE OF IAS 38

In the first paragraphs of IAS 38, the scope is defined by stipulating categories of assets that are not included in the scope of IAS 38 (mainly assets that are included in the scope of other IFRSs such as intangible assets held by an entity for sale in the ordinary course of business, IAS 2; assets arising from contracts with customers, IFRS 15; deferred tax assets, IAS 12; goodwill acquired in a business combination, IFRS 3). Thereafter, the subsequent paragraphs provide examples of assets that fall under the scope of IAS 38 and of numerous items of expenditure on what may be termed *intangible resources*, many of which do not meet its asset recognition criteria. A well-known example is computer software. If the software is an integral part of the hardware, then this intangible item is treated as property, plant and equipment and accounted for under IAS 16. When software is not an integral part of the hardware, it is an intangible asset under the scope of IAS 38. So IAS 38 discusses the scope by presenting examples of items which need to be recognized as intangibles and items which should not be recognized as intangibles, but it does not include a straightforward definition of intangible assets.

Recognition under IAS 38

Three criteria need to be satisfied before an item should be recognized as an intangible asset under IAS 38. These are identifiability, control and reliable measurability.

Identifiability (IAS 38, paras 11–12) is necessary in order to distinguish an intangible asset from goodwill. Separability is a sufficient condition for identifiability, but in IAS it is not a necessary one. An asset is separable if the entity could rent, sell, exchange or distribute the specific future economic benefits attributable to the asset without also disposing of other assets or future economic benefits that flow from them. (Future economic benefits include both revenues and cost savings.)

An entity, however, may be able to identify an intangible asset in some other way. If an intangible asset is acquired together with a set of other assets, it may be separately identifiable by virtue of separate legal rights attaching to it. An internally generated intangible asset may also result from an internal project that gives rise to legal rights for the entity. Nevertheless, usually legal rights are transferable so that such assets are separable (an exception is rights resulting from a legal duty on employees to maintain confidentiality). But identifiability in IAS can be achieved even if an asset generates future economic benefits only in combination with other assets; that is, it is not separable, provided the entity can identify the future economic benefits that will flow from the asset. In that case, however, the second criterion, control, is particularly crucial.

Control (IAS 38, paras 13–16) is exercised by an entity over an asset if the entity:

- has the power to obtain the future economic benefits flowing from the underlying resource
- can also restrict the access of others to such benefits.

The resource itself is not recognizable as an asset unless the criterion of control (as well as that of identifiability) is met. Control will generally result from legal rights enforceable in law and such rights provide a sufficient condition for control. IAS 38 does not exclude the possibility that control over the future economic benefits could be exercised in some other way, but give no examples of this.

In the case of such intangible resources as benefits arising from a team of skilled staff and from training, even if the identifiability criterion can be satisfied, the criterion of controllability will most likely not be met in the absence of protection by legal rights. The same is true of customer lists or market shares. Such intangible resources, therefore, do not usually qualify for recognition as intangible assets.

Reliable measurability is also a necessary precondition for the recognition of intangible assets. IAS 38, paras 21 and 24, state that an intangible asset (that has met the other recognition criteria) should be recognized only if its cost can be measured reliably and that it should be measured initially at that cost.

Measurement at initial recognition

For the purposes of determining cost, four different modes of acquisition are considered (paras 25–47): separate acquisition; acquisition as part of a business combination; acquisition by way of a government grant; and acquisition by exchange of assets. Little needs to be said in explanation of this.

In the case of separate acquisition, the rules for determining cost are the same as those for assets generally, as discussed in Chapter 12. The rules for determining cost in the case of acquisition as part of a business combination are given in IFRS 3 (see Part Three). In the case of acquisition by way of a government grant, the rules in IAS 20 are applicable (see Chapter 12).

In general, exchanges of assets are accounted for at fair value, the fair value of the asset given being treated as the cost of the asset acquired subject to any necessary adjustments for any other partial consideration such as cash. In the case of an intangible asset that is exchanged for an equity interest in a similar asset (such as a share in an R&D joint venture), the cost of the new asset is the carrying amount of the asset given up, with no gain or loss being recognized on the transaction, unless the fair value of the asset received is less than the carrying amount of the asset given up.

Internally generated intangible assets

Note that internally generated goodwill cannot be an intangible asset within the terms of IAS 38 and so cannot be capitalized. In order to assess whether an internally generated intangible resource meets the criteria for recognition as an asset, IAS 38 sets out the following methodology (paras 51–64).

The entity first classifies the internal project resulting in the generation of the resource into two phases: a research phase and a development phase. If this distinction cannot be made for the internal project, then the entire project should be considered as a research phase.

Research is defined as original and planned investigation undertaken with the prospect of gaining new scientific or technical knowledge and understanding. Development is the application of research findings or other knowledge to a plan or design for the production of new or substantially improved materials, devices, products, processes, systems or services before the start of commercial production or use (IAS 38, para. 8).

It is worth pausing at this point to remind ourselves about the general principles involved here. It is obvious that the management of an entity will authorize the expenditure of money and resources on either research or development only if there is in some sense or other an expectation of benefit to the entity. It can be argued that an expectation of future benefit from a past event automatically creates the expectation of an asset now. However, the IAS definition of an asset needs to be remembered in full, i.e. an asset is a resource:

- controlled by an entity as a result of past events and
- from which future economic benefits are expected to flow.

ACTIVITY 13.1

From your knowledge of the IASB Framework and general accounting concepts, suggest briefly, with justification, how expenditure in the research and development phases should be treated.

Activity feedback

In essence, the matching convention argues in favour of capitalization now, in order to permit expensing later against the resulting benefit. The asset figure will need to be charged to the P&L account over the period of benefits, in approximate proportion to the benefit pattern. In effect, we would have a fixed asset that would require depreciating. And since there is likely to be a gap, perhaps of several years, between expenditure and eventual benefit in terms of production and sales, it follows that the expense or depreciation may be zero for one or more accounting periods. If the benefit has not begun to appear yet, then under the matching convention we should not yet begin to write off the asset as an expense. It can be suggested that this treatment is inconsistent with the prudence convention. R&D expenditure is by definition speculative and, particularly with more basic investigation, the outcome is highly uncertain. It is perhaps difficult to argue that the existence of future benefit, of greater amount than the expenditure, can be established with 'reasonable certainty'. It is even harder to argue that the relationship to the revenue or benefit in any particular future period can be established with 'reasonable certainty'. It must also be remembered that a successful profitable outcome is crucially dependent on the validity of the going concern convention.

There is clearly a tension regarding R&D expenditure between matching and prudence. Whatever detailed views an individual holds, it is obvious that research is significantly more speculative than development and that development expenditure becomes less speculative and more reasonably predictable in its outcome, as actual production and sale of the product comes nearer. The IASB solution is to forbid the capitalization of all R&D expenditure, except for development phase items which meet specified conditions, in which case they are required (not just permitted) to be capitalized.

Thus, under IAS 38, no intangible asset should be recognized resulting from research or from the research phase of an internal project. Expenditure on research should be recognized as an expense when incurred.

An intangible resource arising from development (or from the development phase of an internal project) should be recognized as an intangible asset if, and only if, an entity can demonstrate all the following:

- The technical feasibility of completing the intangible asset so that it will be available for use or sale.
- Its intention to complete the intangible asset and use or sell it.
- Its ability to use or sell it.
- How the intangible asset will generate probable future economic benefits. Among other things, the following should be demonstrated: the existence of a market for the intangible asset or its output or, if it is to be used internally, its usefulness to the entity.
- The availability of adequate technical, financial and other resources to complete the development and to use or sell the intangible asset, which may be demonstrated by an appropriate business plan.
- The entity's ability to measure reliably the expenditure attributable to the intangible asset during its development, e.g. by means of the entity's costing system.

To demonstrate how an intangible asset will generate probable future economic benefits, the principles set out in IAS 36, *Impairment of Assets*, especially paras 30–57 on value in use, should be applied. If the asset will generate economic benefits only in combination with other assets, the principles for 'cash-generating units' set out in IAS 36 should be followed (IAS 36 is discussed in Chapter 14).

The cost of an internally generated asset is the sum of the expenditure incurred from the date when the intangible asset first meets the recognition criteria set out earlier. Cost includes all expenditure that is either directly attributable to generating the asset or has been allocated on a reasonable and consistent basis to the activity of generating it. Allocations of overheads should follow the principles set out in IAS 2, *Inventories* (see Chapter 16). With regard to the recognition of interest as a cost, IAS 23, *Borrowing Costs* (see Chapter 12) sets out the applicable principles.

Expenditure that is not part of the cost of the intangible asset includes that on selling, administration and training staff to operate the asset. Expenditure on an intangible resource that was initially recognized as an expense in previous financial statements or reports (e.g. expenditure during the 'research phase' of an internal project) should not be recognized as part of the cost of an intangible asset at a later date (IAS 38, para. 71).

Any expenditure that is not part of the cost of an intangible asset properly recognizable as defined and discussed earlier is, naturally, to be recognized as an expense when incurred (unless the expenditure is part of the cost of a business acquisition, when IFRS 3 applies as already stated).

Subsequent expenditure

The view taken in IAS 38 is that only rarely will expenditure incurred after the initial recognition of a purchased intangible asset or after the completion of an internally generated intangible asset result in an addition to the amount of its capitalized cost. This is because it is generally difficult:

- to attribute such expenditure to a particular intangible asset rather than to the business as a whole and

- (even when that difficulty does not arise) to determine whether such expenditure will enhance, rather than merely maintain, the probable economic benefits that will flow from the asset.

Consequently, subsequent expenditure should be recognized as an expense, except in the rare cases where:

- probable enhancement of the economic benefits that will flow from the asset can be demonstrated and
- the expenditure can be measured and attributed to the asset reliably (IAS 38, paras 18–20).

MEASUREMENT SUBSEQUENT TO INITIAL RECOGNITION

Two treatments are available: the cost model and the revaluation model. This measurement approach is similar to the approach of measurement subsequent to initial recognition proposed under IAS 16 (see Chapter 12).

The cost model

According to the cost model, an intangible asset should be carried at cost less any accumulated depreciation and (if any) accumulated impairment losses (IAS 38, para. 74).

Amortization and depreciation

IAS 38 uses the terms *amortization* and *depreciation* interchangeably with reference to intangible assets to refer to the process of systematic allocation of an asset's cost or revalued amount, less any residual value, over its useful life. The residual value should be assumed to be zero, unless either:

- there is a commitment by a third party to purchase the asset at the end of its estimated useful life to the entity (i.e. the period of time over which it is being depreciated) or
- there is an active market for the asset, such that the asset's residual value can be determined by reference to that market and it is probable that the market will exist at the end of the asset's estimated useful life to the entity.

An estimate of an asset's residual value is based on the amount recoverable from disposal using prices prevailing at the date of the estimate for the sale of a similar asset that has reached the end of its useful life and has operated under conditions similar to those in which the asset will be used. The residual value is reviewed at least at each financial year end. A change in the asset's residual value is accounted for as a change in an accounting estimate in accordance with IAS 8, *Accounting Policies, Changes in Accounting Estimates and Errors* (see Chapter 8).

Useful life

IAS 38 requires that an entity shall assess whether the useful life of an intangible asset is finite or indefinite and, if finite, the length of, or number of production or similar units constituting that useful life (paras 88–89). An intangible asset shall be regarded by the entity as having an indefinite useful life when, based on an analysis of all the relevant factors, there is no foreseeable limit to the period over which the asset is expected to generate net cash inflows for the entity.

The accounting for an intangible asset is based on its useful life. An intangible asset with a finite useful life is amortized. If the value of an intangible asset with an indefinite useful life decreases, an impairment needs to be recorded (see Chapter 14).

Factors that need to be considered in estimating an intangible asset's useful life include the following (IAS 38, paras 90 and 94):

- The expected usage of the asset by the entity and whether the asset could be efficiently managed by another management team.
- Typical product life cycles for the asset and public information on estimates of useful lives for similar assets that are used in a similar way.
- Technical, technological, commercial or other types of obsolescence.
- The stability of the industry in which the asset operates and changes in the market demand for the outputs of the asset.
- Expected actions by competitors or potential competitors.
- The level of maintenance expenditure required to obtain the expected future economic benefits from the asset and the entity's intent and ability to spend such amounts.
- The entity's period of control over the asset and legal and similar limits on control or use, such as the expiration dates of related leases. If control over the future economic benefits from the asset is achieved though legal rights that have been granted for a finite period, the useful life of the asset should not exceed the duration of the legal rights unless they are renewable and renewal is virtually certain.
- Whether the asset's useful life is dependent on that of other assets of the entity.

The term 'indefinite' does not mean 'infinite'. The useful life of an intangible asset reflects only that level of future maintenance expenditure required to maintain the asset at its standard of performance assessed at the time of estimating the asset's useful life and the entity's ability and intention to reach such a level. A conclusion that the useful life of an intangible asset is indefinite should not depend on planned future expenditure in excess of that required to maintain the asset at that standard of performance.

INTANGIBLE ASSETS WITH FINITE USEFUL LIVES

The depreciable amount of an intangible asset with a finite useful life shall be allocated on a systematic basis over its useful life. Amortization shall begin when the asset is available for use, i.e. when it is in the location and condition necessary for it to be capable of operating in the manner intended by management. Amortization shall cease at the earliest date that the asset is classified as held for sale (or included in a disposal group that is classified as held for sale) in accordance with IFRS 5, *Non-current Assets Held for Sale and Discontinued Operations* (see Chapter 14), and the date that the asset is derecognized. The amortization method used shall reflect the pattern in which the asset's future economic benefits are expected to be consumed by the entity. If the pattern cannot be reliably determined, the straight line method shall be used. The amortization charge for each period shall be recognized in profit or loss, unless IAS 38 or another Standard permits or requires it to be included in the carrying amount of another asset.

IAS 38 envisages a variety of amortization methods that may be used to allocate systematically the depreciable amount of an intangible asset over the periods making up its useful life. The Standard mentions the straight line, reducing balance and units of production methods. The straight line method should be used unless the time pattern of consumption of the asset's economic benefits can be determined reliably and clearly indicates that one of the other methods is more suitable. There will rarely, if ever, be persuasive evidence to support a method for intangible assets that is less conservative (that is, results in a lower amount of accumulated depreciation) than the straight line method (IAS 38, paras 97–99).

The amortization period and method should be reviewed at least at each financial year end and the amortization period should be changed if the expected useful life of the asset is significantly different from previous estimates (IAS 38, para. 104). If the expected time pattern of economic benefits has changed, the amortization method should be changed accordingly. Such changes should be accounted for as changes in accounting estimates under IAS 8 (see Chapter 8).

In addition to all of the above, the requirements of IAS 36, *Impairment of Assets* (discussed in Chapter 14), will apply.

INTANGIBLE ASSETS WITH INDEFINITE USEFUL LIVES

The essential treatment is very simple. Such assets are not depreciated (i.e. *shall* not be, not *need* not be). IAS 36 is applied and an impairment test is carried out annually and whenever there is an indication that the intangible asset may be impaired. This will lead to reductions in the carrying value to the recoverable amount at the date of the impairment test.

ACTIVITY 13.2

A pharmaceutical company developed over the years a new drug against high blood pressure. Recently they received approval to commercialize the drug from the regulatory authorities. They also obtained patent protection and now have a patent for this new drug for the next ten years. The pharmaceutical company incurred the following costs during the R&D process which led to the marketable drug: labour costs in the research process for molecules €60 000; materials and labour used in the research on possible molecules that could be further developed into drugs €130 000; materials and labour costs in the development of one molecule into a promising drug for blood pressure control €200 000; costs incurred during the testing process on humans €80 000; costs made in the process of the demand for recognition with the regulatory authorities €20 000.

How will this drug and the related costs be accounted for at the initial recognition of the intangible asset? If the pharmaceutical company uses the cost model subsequently to initial valuation, what will be recorded

after initial recognition in the books of the pharmaceutical company?

Activity feedback

Only the costs in the development phase are capitalized. So the value (capitalized costs) of the patent-protected drug for blood pressure at initial recognition will be a total of €300 000 (€200 000 (development of blood pressure drug) + €80 000 (testing on humans) + €20 000 (regulatory expenditure)).

The pharmaceutical company accounts for the drug with the use of the cost model, so no changes in fair value will be recorded. Since the intangible asset has a finite life, the cost of the patent-based drug will be depreciated over a period of ten years with residual value of zero. Over the lifetime of the patent, the pharmaceutical company will record each year:

Dr Depreciation (cost)   30 000

Cr Patents – accumulated depreciation 30 000

THE REVALUATION MODEL

An intangible asset can be valued with the use of the revaluation model after initial recognition. The revaluation model is to carry the intangible asset at a revalued amount. The revalued amount should be the fair value of the asset at the date of revaluation less any subsequent accumulated depreciation and (if any) subsequent accumulated impairment losses (IAS 38, para. 75). Fair value, in the context of this Standard, should be measured by reference to an active market. This revaluation treatment can only be applied after initial recognition, i.e. all the conditions and requirements stated earlier must previously have been fully satisfied.

If an intangible asset is revalued, revaluation of all the other assets in its class should also be carried out (i.e. those of similar nature and use within the entity's operations), except those for which there is no active market, which should be carried at cost less accumulated amortization and impairment losses.

Fair value should be determined by reference to an active market within the requirements of IFRS 13 (see Chapter 7), and revaluations should be made with sufficient regularity so that the carrying amount does not diverge materially from the fair value at the balance sheet date.

It is considered unlikely that such an active market would exist for an intangible asset (IAS 38, para. 78), although there may be exceptions to this generalization; for example, there may be active markets in freely transferable taxi licences, fishing licences, production quotas or airport take-off and landing 'slots'. If an active market is not available, the revaluation model cannot be used.

ACTIVITY 13.3

For which of the following intangibles does an active market exist? Only those intangibles can be measured with the use of the revaluation model.

- the song lyrics of ABBA
- the right to use the character of Mickey Mouse
- a taxi licence in a city with many taxi drivers holding licences
- the publishing rights to Harry Potter
- a patent for a drug
- a franchise right to open a McDonald's restaurant.

Activity feedback

In the list above only the taxi licences can be valued with the revaluation model. All other intangible assets are unique and will therefore be valued using the cost model. Even that is not simple. For the development of a patent, we can capitalize the cost directly attributable to the development of the item which is patent-protected. But how would you value the right to use the character of Mickey Mouse?

The revaluation model cannot apply to the initial recognition of the intangible asset, which should be at cost, or to intangible resources that were not previously recognized as assets. However, if only part of the cost of an intangible resource was recognized as an asset because it did not meet the criteria for recognition until part way through an internal project, the revaluation treatment may be applied to the whole of the asset and not just to that proportion of it that would be represented by the amount recognized as its cost. The revaluation treatment may also be applied to an intangible asset received by way of a government grant and initially recognized at a nominal amount (IAS 38, para. 77).

An active market that has existed for an intangible asset may cease to exist. In that case, if the asset has been accounted for by using the alternative treatment, then its carrying amount should be its revalued amount at the date of the last revaluation by reference to the formerly active market, less any accumulated depreciation and impairment losses. The cessation of the active market may be an indication of possible impairment of the asset's value and this should be tested in accordance with IAS 36, *Impairment of Assets* (see Chapter 14). If, at a subsequent measurement date, an active market is available again so that the fair value of the asset can be determined, the asset should be revalued at its fair value as of that date.

Recognition of revaluation gains and losses

The usual prudence and realization conventions prevail. Increases in an intangible asset's carrying amount (gains) should be credited to other comprehensive income and accumulated in equity under the heading of revaluation surplus, except to the extent that the increase is a reversal of a previous revaluation decrease (loss) recognized as an expense in respect of the same asset, in which case the amount of the reversal is recognized as income.

Revaluation decreases (losses) are recognized as expenses except to the extent that the decrease is a reversal of a revaluation increase (gain) that was previously credited to revaluation surplus (via other comprehensive income) in respect of the same asset, in which case the amount of the reversal should be recognized in other comprehensive income, thus reducing the amount of the revaluation surplus (IAS 38, paras 85–86).

According to IAS 38, para. 87, the cumulative revaluation surplus 'may' be transferred directly to retained earnings when the surplus is realized. Realization of the surplus may occur through retirement or disposal of the asset, or through the process of using up the asset, in so far as the amortization based on the revalued carrying amount exceeds that which would have been calculated on the basis of the asset's historical cost. The transfer from revaluation surplus to retained earnings is not made through the income statement, but directly in the balance sheet, i.e. it does not affect reported earnings in the year the transfer is made.

Retirements and disposals

An intangible asset shall be derecognized:

- on disposal or
- when no future economic benefits are expected from its use or disposal.

The gain or loss arising from the derecognition of an intangible asset shall be determined as the difference between the net disposal proceeds, if any, and the carrying amount of the asset. It shall be recognized in profit or loss when the asset is derecognized (unless IFRS 16, *Leases*, requires otherwise on a sale and leaseback). Gains shall not be classified as revenue. Amortization of an intangible asset with a finite useful life does not cease when the intangible asset is no longer used, unless the asset has been fully depreciated or is classified as held for sale (or included in a disposal group that is classified as held for sale) in accordance with IFRS 5 *Non-current Assets Held for Sale and Discontinued Operations.*

Disclosure

The disclosure requirements are, as usual, long and detailed. Full details of balances, movements over the year and any revaluations or impairment losses are specified. To illustrate the amount of disclosure, we introduce the information disclosed by the adidas Group on intangible assets in the notes to their Statement of Financial Position at 31 December 2014.

Because of the unique nature of R&D and other intangible assets, disclosures in the notes may provide additional useful information that the firm was not able to communicate through accounting numbers. Several academic studies reveal that these additional disclosures convey relevant information to investors and other users of financial information (e.g. Beaver *et al.*, 2012; Merkley, 2014).

REAL LIFE ILLUSTRATION

Intangible assets (except goodwill)

Intangible assets are valued at amortised cost. Amortisation is calculated on a straight-line basis taking into account any potential residual value.

Expenditures during the development phase of internally generated intangible assets are capitalised as incurred if they qualify for recognition under IAS 38 'Intangible Assets'.

Estimated useful lives are as follows:

Estimated useful lives of intangible assets

	Years
Trademarks	indefinite
Software	5–7
Patents, trademarks and concessions	5–15

The adidas Group determined that there was no impairment necessary for any of its trademarks with indefinite useful lives in the years ending December 31, 2014 and 2013. In addition, an increase in the discount rate of up to approximately 1.5 percentage points or a reduction of cash inflows of up to approximately 20% would not result in any impairment requirement.

The recoverable amount is determined on the basis of fair value less costs to sell (costs to sell are calculated with 1% of the fair value). The fair value is determined in discounting notional royalty savings after tax and adding a tax amortisation benefit, resulting from the amortisation of the acquired asset ('relief-from-royalty method'). These calculations use projections of net sales related royalty savings, based on financial planning which covers a period of five years in total. The level of the applied royalty rate for the determination of the royalty savings is based on contractual agreements between the adidas Group and external licensees as well as publicly available royalty rate agreements for similar assets. Notional royalty savings beyond this period are extrapolated using steady growth rates of 1.7% (2013: 1.7%). The growth rates do not exceed the long-term average growth rate of the business to which the trademarks are allocated.

The discount rate is based on a weighted average cost of capital calculation derived using a five-year average market-weighted debt/equity structure and financing costs referencing the Group's major competitors. The discount rate used is an after-tax rate and reflects the specific equity and country risk. The applied discount rate depends on the respective intangible asset being valued and ranges between 6.7% and 8.4% (2013: between 6.8% and 8.8%).

Research and development

Research costs are expensed in full as incurred. Development costs are also expensed as incurred if they do not meet the recognition criteria of IAS 38 'Intangible Assets'.

The Group spent €126 million and €124 million on product research and development (continuing operations) for the years ending December 31, 2014 and 2013, respectively.

REAL LIFE ILLUSTRATION   (*Continued*)

Trademarks and other intangible assets consist of the following:

Trademarks and other intangible assets

(€ in millions)	31/12/2014	31/12/2013
Reebok	1 276	1 123
Rockport	–	158
Reebok-CCM Hockey	107	94
Other	49	44
Trademarks	**1 432**	**1 419**
Software, patents and concessions	772	720
Less: accumulated amortisation and impairment losses	609	556
Other intangible assets	**162**	**164**
Trademarks and other intangible assets	**1 594**	**1 583**

At December 31, 2014, trademarks, mainly related to the acquisition of Reebok International Ltd. (USA) in 2006 and Ashworth, Inc. in 2008, have indefinite useful lives. This is due to the expectation of permanent use of the acquired brand names.

At December 31, 2014, the Rockport trademark was transferred to 'Assets held for sale' due to the concrete plans to sell the Rockport operating segment and is impaired by € 68 million in connection with the fair value measurement of the disposal group /**SEE NOTE 11**.

The reported other trademarks mainly relate to the brand names Ashworth, Adams Golf and Five Ten.

The Group tests at least on an annual basis whether trademarks with indefinite useful lives are impaired. This requires an estimation of the fair value less costs to sell of the trademarks. As part of this estimation, the Group is required to make an estimate of the expected future trademark-specific sales and appropriate arm's length notional royalty rates and also to choose a suitable discount rate in order to calculate the present value of those cash flows. There was no need for impairment for the years ending December 31, 2014 and 2013.

Future changes in expected cash flows and discount rates may lead to impairments of the accounted trademarks in the future.

As part of the goodwill impairment test, the Reebok trademark is allocated on a pro rata basis to the cash-generating units. Thereof, the major shares relate to Retail CIS (€ 276 million), Retail North America (€ 209 million), Wholesale Western Europe (€ 201 million), Wholesale Latin America (€ 119 million) and Wholesale North America (€ 117 million).

Amortisation expenses for intangible assets with definite useful lives were € 58 million and € 52 million for the years ending December 31, 2014 and 2013, respectively/**SEE NOTE 31**.

For details see Attachment I to the consolidated financial statements /**SEE STATE STATEMENT OF MOVEMENTS OF INTANGIBLE AND TANGIBLE ASSETS, P. 246**.

(Continued)

REAL LIFE ILLUSTRATION *(Continued)*

Statement of Movements of Intangible and Tangible Assets
.. / Statement of Movements of intangible and Tangible Assets (€ in millions)

	Goodwill	Trademarks	Software, patents and concessions	Internally generated software	Total Intangible assets
Acquisition cost					
January 1, 2013	**1 569**	**1 484**	**689**	**10**	**3 752**
Currency effect	(35)	(65)	(23)	–	(123)
Additions	–	–	51	1	52
Transfers	–	–	(4)	5	2
Disposals	–	–	(10)	–	(10)
December 31, 2013/January 1, 2014	**1 533**	**1 419**	**704**	**16**	**3 672**
Currency effect	111	193	36	–	340
Additions	–	–	48	2	50
Increase in companies consolidated	–	–	7	–	7
Transfers to assets held for sale	(56)	(180)	(15)	–	(251)
Transfers	–	–	(20)	25	5
Disposals	–	(0)	(31)	(1)	(32)
December 31, 2014	**1 588**	**1 432**	**730**	**41**	**3 792**
Accumulated depreciation, amortisation and impairment					
January 1, 2013	**287**	**0**	**527**	**5**	**819**
Currency effect	(10)	(0)	(19)	–	(29)
Additions	–	0	49	3	52
Impairment losses	52	–	0	–	52
Reversals of impairment losses	–	–	(0)	–	(0)
Transfers	–	–	–	–	–
Disposals	–	–	(9)	–	(9)
December 31, 2013/January 1, 2014	**329**	**0**	**549**	**7**	**885**
Currency effect	38	0	30	–	68
Additions	–	0	47	10	58
Impairment losses	78	–	0	–	78
Reversals of impairment losses	–	–	–	–	–
Transfers to assets held for sale	(26)	–	(12)	–	(38)
Transfers	–	–	0	–	0
Disposals	–	(0)	(21)	(1)	(22)
December 31, 2014	**419**	**0**	**592**	**17**	**1 029**
Net carrying amount					
January 1, 2013	1 281	1 484	162	5	2 933
December 31, 2013	1 204	1 419	155	9	2 787
December 31, 2014	1 169	1 432	138	24	2 763

Rounding differences may arise in percentages and totals.

SUMMARY

Following the exploration of the treatment of tangible non-current assets in Chapter 12, this chapter has looked at the treatment of similar intangible assets. We considered in detail the requirements of IAS 38, dealing with separable intangible assets.

EXERCISES

Suggested answers to exercises marked ✓ are to be found in the Student online resources, with suggested answers to the remaining questions available in the Instructor online resources.

✓ **1**   Is goodwill an asset?

2   Identifiable intangible assets should be treated, for all accounting purposes, identically with tangible assets. Discuss.

3   CD is a manufacturing entity that runs a number of operations including a bottling plant that bottles carbonated soft drinks. CD has been developing a new bottling process that will allow the bottles to be filled and sealed more efficiently.

    The new process took a year to develop. At the start of development, CD estimated that the new process would increase output by 15 per cent with no additional cost (other than the extra bottles and their contents). Development work commenced on 1 May 2005 and was completed on 20 April 2006. Testing at the end of the development phase confirmed CD's original estimates.

    CD incurred expenditure of €180 000 on the above development in 2005/06. CD plans to install the new process in its bottling plant and start operating the new process from 1 May 2006. CD's statement of financial position date is 30 April.

Required:

(i) Explain the requirements of IAS 38, *Intangible Assets* for the treatment of development costs.

(ii) Explain how CD should treat its development costs in its financial statements for the year ended 30 April 2006.

4   Minco often sponsors professional tennis players in an attempt to improve its brand image. At the moment, it has a three-year agreement with a tennis player who is currently ranked in the world's top ten players. The agreement is that the player receives a signing bonus of $20 000 and earns an annual amount of $50 000, paid at the end of each year for three years, provided that the player has competed in all the specified tournaments for each year.

In return, the player is required to wear advertising logos on tennis apparel, play a specified number of tournaments and attend photo/film sessions for advertising purposes. The different payments are not interrelated.

Required:

Discuss how the above items should be dealt with in the financial statements of Minco.

(ACCA, Corporate Reporting (International), June 2014, adapted)

IMPAIRMENT AND DISPOSAL OF ASSETS

14

OBJECTIVES After studying this chapter you should be able to:

- describe, apply and appraise the requirements of IAS 36 relating to impairment of assets

- explain what is meant by non-current assets held for sale

- describe how non-current assets held for sale should be recognized and measured in accordance with IFRS

- explain the purpose of issuing information on discontinuing operations, and how such information should be disclosed.

INTRODUCTION

The previous two chapters have discussed the treatment of various types of non-current assets and their regular expensing. In this chapter we consider first the question of impairment, i.e. of possible additional irregular write-offs, and second, their eventual disposal.

IMPAIRMENT OF ASSETS

The problem

Reference to impairment of assets has been made at a number of points in previous chapters. In very simple terms, the principle of deferring charges to future periods under the matching principle means, of course, that such deferred charges appear in an intermediate balance sheet as assets.

ACTIVITY 14.1

If there is a reasonable expectation of future revenues associated with past expenditure being greater than the deferred expenses, does any other circumstance, such as a low current market value for the asset, lead to a need for immediate writedown to this lower figure?

Activity feedback

Prudence and the informational needs of lenders with a short-term focus might both suggest an argument for such an immediate expense charge and reduction in the balance sheet carrying value of the asset (i.e. the deferred expense). However, matching and the informational needs of investors suggest the opposite. Long-term assets should be appraised in a long-term context, it can be argued. The IASB generally takes this second argument.

Very broadly speaking, purchase transactions are recorded in accounting terms first by including the purchased item as an asset at its cost price, then by expensing the item over one or a number of accounting periods according to its usage or consumption pattern. The going concern convention supports this treatment as it explicitly assumes that there will be future operational accounting periods in which present assets can be transferred to expenses.

Strictly, this means that there is no need, at an intermediate stage in this process, to compare the temporary balance sheet number with any form of value – using the word 'value' in its proper sense of monetary benefit to be derived. This would not be in accordance with the prudence convention, however, and would arguably be dangerously misleading to creditors and lenders. Over the years, accounting has dealt with the inherent tension and conflict here in a variety of ways, all more or less ad hoc, depending on the accounting issue involved (and often depending also on the country involved).

The IASB has quite properly attempted to provide a general Standard, IAS 36, *Impairment of Assets*, to provide consistency and coherence to this whole matter. The principle of the Standard is clear and simple. First, the carrying amount of an asset is determined in accordance with accounting principles and other relevant International Standards. Second, the 'recoverable amount' of the asset is determined as of that date, being the higher of fair value less costs to sell and the asset's value in use (to the existing entity). If the recoverable amount is lower than the carrying value as recorded, then an impairment loss must be recognized immediately; that is, the carrying value is lowered to the recoverable amount. Otherwise, no impairment loss is required. It is important to emphasize that recoverable amount is a very different concept from fair value and, for non-current assets, will often be significantly higher than fair value. IAS 36 does not require assets within its scope to be recorded at the lower of cost and market or fair value.

The question of which assets IAS 36 does apply to is rather complicated, and the following section on scope should be read carefully. Unfortunately, although the principle of IAS 36 is simply stated, the IASB, perhaps influenced by American tradition, found it necessary to specify considerable operational detail in relation to its application. We examine these details later, to the extent that we consider it necessary. However, we are writing a textbook, not a manual for practitioners, and IAS 36 is very much a technical 'how to do it' Standard. It would be unhelpful to attempt to cover all this technical specification here.

Scope and coverage

The essential objective of IAS 36 is to ensure that assets are not carried at a figure greater than their recoverable amount. The Standard itself says nothing about possible or normal methods of arriving at carrying value. The Standard applies whatever the underlying basis of valuation of the asset is.

The Standard begins by saying that it applies to all assets except inventories; contract assets arising from costs to obtain or fulfil a contract that is recognized in accordance with IFRS 15; deferred tax assets; assets arising from employee benefits; financial assets that are included in the scope of IFRS 9; investment property that is measured at fair value; biological assets measured at fair value; deferred acquisition costs and intangible assets arising from insurer's contractual rights under insurance contracts; and non-current assets classified as held for sale. These are generally items that are covered in detail by other International Accounting Standards.

It must be noted that financial assets excluded from IFRS 9 are automatically excluded from the exclusion! Note carefully that the Standard very deliberately describes itself as dealing with impairment of assets, not with impairment of non-current assets. However, it then excludes inventories and contract assets resulting from contracts with customers (IAS 2 and IFRS 15) and accounts receivable and cash (both covered by IFRS 9). In many, if not most, businesses, this will mean that all current assets are excluded from consideration under IAS 36. However, the IAS definition of current assets (discussed in Chapter 8) is more generally expressed, and IAS 36 could be applicable to certain current assets in special cases.

Terminology

IAS 36 gives a number of definitions of key terms. Many of these definitions are interrelated – one term being used in the definition of another (para. 6).

- An *impairment loss* is the amount by which the carrying amount of an asset or a cash-generating unit exceeds its recoverable amount.
- *Carrying amount* is the amount at which an asset is recognized after deducting any accumulated depreciation (amortization) and accumulated impairment losses thereon.
- *Recoverable amount* of an asset or a cash-generating unit is the higher of its fair value less costs of disposal and its value in use.
- *Depreciation* (amortization) is the systematic allocation of the depreciable amount of an asset over its useful life.

- *Depreciable amount* is the cost of an asset or other amount substituted for cost in the financial statements, less its residual value.
- *Useful life* is either:
  - the period of time over which an asset is expected to be used by the entity or
  - the number of production or similar units expected to be obtained from the asset by the entity.
- *Fair value* is the price that would be received to sell an asset or paid to transfer a liability in an orderly transaction between market participants at the measurement date.
- *Costs of disposal* are incremental costs directly attributable to the disposal of an asset or cash-generating unit, excluding finance costs and income tax expense.
- *Value in use* is the present value of the future cash flows expected to be derived from an asset or cash-generating unit.

Most of these terms should be fairly easy to understand, but they can be difficult to calculate. Two further definitions are given, as follows.

- A *cash-generating unit* is the smallest identifiable group of assets that generates cash inflows that are largely independent of the cash inflows from other assets or groups of assets.
- *Corporate assets* are assets other than goodwill that contribute to the future cash flows of both the cash-generating unit under review and other cash-generating units.

When several assets are interrelated in their usage in a way which makes it impossible meaningfully to attribute cash inflows to each individual asset, they are to be considered together as a single cash-generating unit as just defined. In effect, therefore, a cash-generating unit is 'one asset' for the purposes of IAS 36. Corporate assets do not generate their own cash flows, but, as described earlier, are necessary for the generation of cash flows by other units. Special considerations, discussed below, apply to such assets.

Identifying an asset that may be impaired

It is important to be clear that IAS 36 does not require that the recoverable amount of all assets must be determined annually in order to test for impairment. Rather, it postulates a two-stage process. The first stage is to assess, at each balance sheet date, whether there is any indication that an asset may be impaired. If any such indication exists, the entity should estimate the recoverable amount of the asset.

ACTIVITY 14.2

Suggest situations that may indicate that an asset has been impaired.

Activity feedback

IAS 36 suggests that when assessing whether there is any indication that an asset may be impaired, an entity should consider, as a minimum, the following indications (para. 12):

External sources of information

1 During the period, an asset's market value has declined significantly more than would be expected as a result of the passage of time or normal use.

2 Significant changes with an adverse effect on the entity have taken place during the period or will

ACTIVITY 14.2 *(Continued)*

take place in the near future in the technological, market, economic or legal environment in which the entity operates or in the market to which an asset is dedicated.

3 *Market interest rates or other market rates of return on investments have increased during the period and those increases are likely to affect the discount rate used in calculating an asset's value in use and decrease the asset's recoverable amount materially.*

4 *The carrying amount of the net assets of the reporting entity is more than its market capitalization.*

Internal sources of information

1 *Evidence is available of obsolescence of or physical damage to an asset.*

2 *Significant changes with an adverse effect on the entity have taken place during the period or are expected to take place in the near future in the extent to which, or manner in which, an asset is used or is expected to be used. These changes include the asset becoming idle, plans to*

discontinue or restructure the operation to which an asset belongs, plans to dispose of an asset before the previously expected date and reassessing the useful life of an asset as finite rather than indefinite.

3 *Evidence is available from internal reporting that indicates that the economic performance of an asset is, or will be, worse than expected.*

Several of these considerations require some comment. Items 1 and 2 (under 'External sources of information') are fairly obviously indicators of a possible fall in recoverable amount, relating directly to net selling price and value in use, respectively. In neither case, however, does a low or lower recoverable amount necessarily follow, as the recoverable amount is the higher of fair value less costs to sell and value in use. The relevance of item 3 is that value in use, as defined earlier, is the present value of future cash flows. Discounting is thus central to the calculation or recoverable amount and an increase in discount rate may significantly reduce the value in use of an asset, as defined, if the new discount rate is regarded as relevant in the long term. Item 4, again, is a fairly obvious indicator that something is widely perceived as being wrong somewhere, although not, of course, that every, or any one particular, asset is impaired.

There are two different formal requirements. The first relates to all assets (para. 9). This is that an entity should assess at each reporting date whether there is any indication that an asset may be impaired. If such an indication exists, the entity should estimate the recoverable amount of the asset. The second is more stringent, but relates only to certain intangible assets. This is that (para. 10) irrespective of whether there is any indication of impairment, an entity shall also:

(a) test an intangible asset with an indefinite useful life or an intangible asset not yet available for use for impairment annually by comparing its carrying amount with its recoverable amount. This impairment test may be performed at any time during an annual period, provided it is performed at the same time every year. Different intangible assets may be tested for impairment at different times. However, if such an intangible asset were initially recognized during the current annual period, that intangible asset shall be tested for impairment before the end of the current annual period.

(b) test goodwill acquired in a business combination for impairment annually in accordance with paras 80–99. (see part III of this book)

The concept of materiality applies to the general requirement in para. 9, but not to the specific requirement of para. 10, which, in its defined circumstances, is absolute.

Only if an indication of likely impairment exists do we need, in the general case, to move on to the second stage and actually measure the recoverable amount.

Measurement of recoverable amount

IAS 36 devotes no fewer than 39 paragraphs to the measurement of recoverable amount, not including another 42 paragraphs on cash-generating units, and sets out detailed computations. Nevertheless, a number of simplifications may be justified. If either fair value less costs of disposal or value in use exceeds the asset's carrying amount, then the other figure need not be determined at all. If fair value less costs of disposal is unobtainable even by reliable estimate because of the absence of an active market, then the recoverable amount can be taken as equal to value in use. Conversely, the recoverable amount may be taken or given by fair value less costs to sell if the nature of the asset, or the nature of its usage by entity is such that value in use is unlikely to differ materially from fair value less costs to sell, which will usually be the case with active and competitive factor markers (i.e. in developed economies).

Fair value less costs of disposal

This will often be straightforward to determine, being fair value less any incremental costs that would be directly attributable to the disposal of the asset. Fair value will be determined in accordance with IFRS 13 (see Chapter 7). Costs of disposal, other than those that have already been recognized as liabilities, are deducted in determining net selling price. Examples of such costs are legal costs, stamp duty and similar transaction taxes, costs of removing the asset and direct incremental costs to bring an asset into condition for its sale. However, termination benefits (as defined in IAS 19, *Employee Benefits*; see Chapter 21), and costs associated with reducing or reorganizing a business after the disposal of an asset, are not direct incremental costs to dispose of the asset (see IAS 37, *Provisions, Contingent Liabilities and Contingent Assets*; discussed in Chapter 19).

Value in use

Estimating the value in use in a realistic way is often likely to be rather more difficult. It involves the following steps (para. 31):

1 Estimating the future cash inflows and outflows to be derived from continuing use of the asset and from its ultimate disposal.

2 Applying the appropriate discount rate to these future cash flows. Estimates of future cash flows should include:

(a) projections of cash inflows from the continuing use of the asset, net of projections of cash outflows that are necessarily incurred to generate the cash inflows (including cash outflows to prepare the asset for use) and that can be directly attributed, or allocated on a reasonable and consistent basis, to the asset

(b) net cash flows, if any, to be received (or paid) for the disposal of the asset at the end of its useful life.

Future cash flows should be estimated for the asset in its current condition. It follows that estimates of future cash flows should not include estimated future cash inflows or outflows that are expected to arise from:

- a future restructuring to which an entity is not yet committed or
- future (uncommitted) capital expenditure that will improve or enhance the asset in excess of its originally assessed standard of performance.

The issue of when an entity is 'committed to a future restructuring' is discussed in IAS 37, *Provisions, Contingent Liabilities and Contingent Assets* (see Chapter 19). If it is so committed, then obviously the related cash inflows and outflows are to be included.

The estimate of net cash flows to be received (or paid) for the disposal of an asset at the end of its useful life is determined in a similar way to an asset's fair value less costs to sell, except that, in estimating those net cash flows:

1 An entity uses prices prevailing at the date of the estimate for similar assets that have reached the end of their useful life and that have operated under conditions similar to those in which the asset will be used

2 Those prices are adjusted for the effect of both future price increases due to general inflation and specific future price increases (decreases). However, if estimates of future cash flows from the asset's continuing use and the discount rate exclude the effect of general inflation, this effect is also excluded from the estimate of net cash flows on disposal.

Discount rate

The key points can be very briefly stated. The discount rate (or rates) should be a pre-tax rate (or rates) that reflect(s) current market assessments of the time value of money and risks specific to the asset (para. 55). The discount rate(s) should not reflect risks for which future cash flow estimates have been adjusted, as this would involve double counting. The Standard rightly makes no attempt to argue that this process is other than subjective. It does try to suggest a suitable thought process (IAS 36, Appendix A).

As a starting point, the entity may take into account the following rates:

• the entity's weighted average cost of capital determined using techniques such as the capital asset pricing model

• the entity's incremental borrowing rate

• other market borrowing rates.

These rates are adjusted:

• to reflect the way that the market would assess the specific risks associated with the projected cash flows

• to exclude risks that are not relevant to the projected cash flows.

Consideration is given to such risks as country risk, currency risk, price risk and cash flow risk. This makes it clear, for example, that the appropriate discount rate may be different for different types of asset or different circumstances within the same entity. What is crucial, above all else except basic rationality and common sense, is that the chosen method should be applied consistently.

RECOGNITION AND MEASUREMENT OF IMPAIRMENT LOSSES

After all the subjectivity, complexity and detail of earlier sections of IAS 36, it is easy to lose sight of the importance of those paragraphs dealing with recognition and measurement of impairment losses. This is the point and purpose of the entire

Standard. The Standard requires that if, and only if, the recoverable amount of an asset is less than its carrying amount, the carrying amount of the asset should be reduced to its recoverable amount. That reduction is an impairment loss (para. 59).

An impairment loss should be recognized immediately as an expense in the income statement, unless the asset is carried at a revalued amount under another Standard (e.g. under IAS 16, *Property, Plant and Equipment*; see Chapter 12). Any impairment loss of a revalued asset should be treated as a revaluation decrease under the other Standard.

In the general case, if the estimated impairment loss is greater than the carrying value of the relevant asset, the asset is simply reduced to nil, with a corresponding expense. Only if so required by another Standard should a liability be recognized. Common sense indicates, but the Standard feels it necessary to state, that after the impairment loss has been recognized, the depreciation charge for the asset should be adjusted to allocate the revised carrying amount, net of any expected residual value, on a systematic basis over its remaining useful life.

Reversal of an impairment loss

The whole point, in a sense, of impairment losses is that they represent unusual or 'extra' reductions in asset numbers (carrying values) as used in financial statements. If regular depreciation is a downward slope, then an impairment loss is a downward step. The basic cause of this downward step is something unusual and/or extraneous to the asset and its regular accounting treatment. It follows that this cause, this unusual or extraneous factor, may be removed over time. In such a situation, as explained and defined in IAS 36, the original impairment loss must be reversed, *except* for goodwill.

As with impairment losses, we again have a two-stage process. Management will first check to see whether there is any indication that an impairment loss recognized in earlier years may have decreased significantly. IAS 36 spells out a series of likely indicators (para. 111) that mirror those discussed earlier under 'identifying an asset that may be impaired'.

The formal requirement for reversing impairment losses for an asset other than goodwill (para. 114) is that an impairment loss recognized for an asset in prior years must be reversed if, and only if, there has been a change in the estimates used to determine the asset's recoverable amount since the last impairment loss was recognized. If this is the case, the carrying amount of the asset should be increased to its recoverable amount. That increase is a reversal of an impairment loss. It is important to note that an asset's value in use may become greater than the asset's carrying amount, simply because the present value of future cash inflows increases as they become closer. However, the service potential of the asset has not increased. Therefore, such an impairment loss is not reversed, even if the recoverable amount of the asset becomes higher than its carrying amount.

The reversal of an impairment loss should in no circumstances increase the carrying value of an asset above what it would have been at this balance sheet date if no impairment loss had been recognized in prior years. This means, in particular, that the carrying value of assets subject to depreciation cannot be increased above the figure which the pre-impairment depreciation policy, applied to the pre-impairment recoverable amount, would have given at this balance sheet date; that is, the amount of the reversal will be less than the amount of the original impairment. The new carrying value forms the basis for a systematic depreciation policy to allocate the carrying value, less estimated residual value if any, over the remaining useful life.

A reversal of an impairment loss for an asset as above should be recognized as income immediately in the income statement, unless the asset is carried at a revalued amount under another International Accounting Standard (e.g. under the revaluation model in IAS 16, *Property, Plant and Equipment*; see Chapter 12). Any reversal of an impairment loss on a revalued asset should be treated as a revaluation increase under that other Standard.

A reversal of an impairment loss for a cash-generating unit should be allocated to increase the carrying amount of the assets of the unit on a pro rata basis based on the carrying amount of each asset in the unit and then to goodwill allocated to the cash-generating unit.

In allocating a reversal of an impairment loss for a cash-generating unit, the carrying amount of an asset should not be increased above the lower of:

- the recoverable amount (if determinable)
- the carrying amount that would have been determined (net of amortization or depreciation) had no impairment loss been recognized for the asset in prior years.

The amount of the reversal of the impairment loss that would otherwise have been allocated to the asset should be allocated to the other assets of the unit, except for goodwill, on a pro rata basis.

The treatment of a reversal of an impairment loss for goodwill was changed significantly in the revised version of IAS 36 (i.e. with effect from 31 March 2004) as compared with the earlier version. The Standard now completely prohibits the recognition of reversals of impairment losses for goodwill.

Impairment losses have to be recognized whether the asset is valued after initial recognition according to the cost model or according to the revaluation model.

ACTIVITY 14.3

Two companies each own a piece of land adjacent to each other. The surface of both pieces is identical. The two companies, Alpha and Omega bought the land in 20X1 and they each paid €1 million. They both recognized the land at initial measurement at cost in their books for €1 million. Alpha accounts for all its land with the use of the cost model after initial measurement and Omega uses the revaluation model for its land after initial measurement. In 20X2 the market value of the land increased to €1.1 million. A couple of years later in 20X4, due to a decrease in the economic activity of the many steel companies located in that area and the economic crisis hitting the country, the market price of the land dropped to €0.8 million. Three years later, in 20X7, high tech companies settled in the area and replaced the 'old' steel companies. The area again became economically vibrant and the future for these high tech industries looked economically promising. The market price of the land rose in 20X7 to €1.3 million.

How will Alpha and Omega account for their piece of land in their books during this time frame?

Activity feedback

Company Alpha uses the cost model to value land after the initial measurement of the land. The company recorded the land in its books for €1 million when it purchased the land, but did not change the value of the land in the books in 20X2. In 20X4 they recorded an impairment loss of €200 000:

Dr Impairment Loss (expense)	200 000
Cr Land – accumulated impairment losses	200 000

In 20X7, Company Alpha has the possibility of reversing the impairment loss. It is possible to reverse an impairment for all assets other than goodwill. Only in the case of goodwill can impairment losses never be reversed. If company Alpha decided to reverse the impairment, then the carrying amount after the reversal of the impairment can never be higher than the carrying amount before the impairment was recorded. In the case of Company Alpha, that amount is €1 million. In this example, Company Alpha decides to account for the reversal of the impairment loss recorded in 20X4. Therefore, Company Alpha would record the following in its books:

Dr Land – Accumulated impairment losses	200 000
Cr Reversal of previous impairment loss	200 000

Company Omega uses the revaluation model to value its land after initial measurement. So Company Omega records the changes in the fair value of the land in its

(Continued)

ACTIVITY 14.3 (Continued)

books. Therefore, they will record the increase in value of the land in 20X2 and record the following in the books of the company:

Dr Land	*100 000*
Cr Gain on revaluation of land (OCI)	*100 000*
Dr Gain on revaluation of land (OCI)	*100 000*
Cr Asset revaluation surplus	*100 000*

In 20X4 Company Omega first needs to reverse the revaluation surplus of €100 000 and then they need to record the impairment loss of €200 000.

Dr Asset revaluation surplus	*100 000*
Cr Land	*100 000*

Dr Impairment loss (expense)	*200 000*
Cr Land – accumulated impairment losses	*200 000*

In 20X7, Company Omega values the land again at its fair value of €1.3 million. This means that Company Omega has to reverse the impairment loss of €200 000 recorded earlier and record an increase in value of €300 000.

Dr Land – accumulated impairment losses	*200 000*
Cr Reversal of previous impairment losses (income)	*200 000*
Dr Land	*300 000*
Cr Gain on revaluation of land (OCI)	*300 000*
Dr Gain on revaluation of land (OCI)	*300 000*
Cr Asset revaluation surplus	*300 000*

Impairment of a cash-generating unit

This is all very well when 'an asset' means 'an asset'. But when 'an asset' means 'a cash-generating unit', as discussed earlier, the treatment is not so easy in practice – as the Standard's need for over 40 paragraphs on the topic would suggest. If it is not possible to estimate the recoverable amount of an individual asset, an entity should determine the recoverable amount of the cash-generating unit to which the asset belongs (the asset's cash-generating unit) (para. 66). Identification of an asset's cash-generating unit involves judgement. If the recoverable amount cannot be determined for an individual asset, an entity identifies the lowest aggregation of assets that generate largely independent cash inflows from continuing use.

In other words, an asset's cash-generating unit is the smallest group of assets that includes the asset and that generates cash inflows from continuing use that are largely independent of the cash inflows from other assets or groups of assets.

Perhaps inevitably, the Standard resorts to a series of examples in order to try and indicate more precisely how the analysis of any particular situation should proceed. Common sense and economic substance are perhaps the key watchwords. Thus, if an active market exists for the output produced by an asset or a group of assets, this asset or group of assets should be identified as a cash-generating unit, even if some or all of the output is used internally. If this is the case, management's best estimate of future market prices for the output should be used (para. 70):

- in determining the value in use of this cash-generating unit, when estimating the future cash inflows that relate to the internal use of the output
- in determining the value in use of other cash-generating units of the reporting entity, when estimating the future cash outflows that relate to the internal use of the output.

As an indicative illustration, the example given by IAS 36 in relation to this specification is included in Activity 14.4.

ACTIVITY 14.4

A significant raw material used for Plant Y's final production is an intermediate product bought from Plant X of the same entity. X's products are sold to Y at a transfer price that passes all margins to X. Eighty per cent of Y's final production is sold to customers outside the reporting entity. Sixty per cent of X's final production is sold to Y, and the remaining 40 per cent is sold to customers outside the reporting entity.

For each of the following cases, what are the cash-generating units for X and Y?

Case 1: X could sell the products it sells to Y in an active market. Internal transfer prices are higher than market prices.

Case 2: There is no active market for the products X sells to Y.

Activity feedback

Case 1

X could sell its products on an active market and so generate cash inflows that would be largely independent of the cash inflows from Y. Therefore, it is likely that X is a separate cash-generating unit, although part of its production is used by Y.

It is likely that Y is also a separate cash-generating unit. Y sells 80 per cent of its products to customers outside the reporting entity. Therefore, its cash inflows can be considered to be largely independent.

Internal transfer prices do not reflect market prices for X's output. Therefore, in determining value in use of both X and Y, the entity adjusts financial budgets/forecasts to reflect management's best estimate of future arm's length market prices for those of X's products that are used internally (see IAS 36, para. 70).

Case 2

It is likely that the recoverable amount of each plant cannot be assessed independently from the recoverable amount of the other plant because:

- *The majority of X's production is used internally and could not be sold in an active market. So, cash inflows of X depend on demand for Y's products. Therefore X cannot be considered to generate cash inflows that are largely independent from those of Y.*

- *The two plants are managed together.*

As a consequence, it is likely that X and Y together is the smallest group of assets that generates cash inflows from continuing use that are largely independent.

Once the cash-generating unit has been defined, the next step is to determine and compare the recoverable amount and carrying amount of that unit. The Standard reminds us that the carrying amount of a cash-generating unit should be determined consistently with the way in which the recoverable amount of the cash-generating unit is determined.

This means, for example, that the carrying amount of a cash-generating unit includes the carrying amount of only those assets that can be attributed directly or allocated on a reasonable and consistent basis to the cash-generating unit and that will generate the future cash inflows estimated in determining the cash-generating unit's value in use and does not include the carrying amount of any recognized liability, unless the recoverable amount of the cash-generating unit cannot be determined without consideration of this liability. However, the Standard notes that in practice the recoverable amount of a cash-generating unit may be considered either including or excluding assets or liabilities that are not part of the cash-generating unit – for example, a net selling price of a business segment might be determined on the assumption that either the vendor or the purchaser accepts certain obligations. Consistency requires that if the obligation is included in the evaluation of recoverable amount, it is the net carrying value with which this recoverable amount must be compared in determining whether an impairment loss exists.

ACTIVITY 14.5

For cash-generating units, the impairment is obtained at the level of the combined assets. Assume that a health and beauty clinic prepares its accounts in compliance with IFRS. The medical installation to perform nose corrections consists of three separate machines that are responsible for the different steps of a nose correction. A nose correction cannot be executed on a patient unless each of these three machines is used. So the three machines make up a cash-generating unit and each machine has the following carrying value: a special X-ray machine for the measurement of the nose (carrying value €400 000); a laser machine for the cutting (carrying value €200 000) and a special robot for fine stitching (carrying value €800 000). Lately, nose corrections have become less popular and the accountant of the health clinic calculated that the value in use of this cash-generating unit is €1 050 000. The current fair value less costs to sell of the three machines together is €900 000. Will there be an impairment recorded in the books of the health clinic?

Activity feedback

The cash-generating unit has a combined carrying value of €1 400 000. We notice further that the value in use

of the cash-generating unit is higher than the fair value less costs to sell. So the amount of the impairment is equal to the carrying value (€1 400 000) minus the fair value in use (€1 050 000), being €350 000. The carrying value is compared with the value in use, since the value in use (€1 050 000) is higher than the fair value less costs to sell (€900 000). The impairment loss on the cash-generating unit of €350 000 will be apportioned across the three assets using the individual carrying values as the allocation basis. The health clinic will report the impairment loss as follows:

Dr Impairment loss (expense)	350 000
Cr Machine X-Ray – accumulated impairment losses	50 000
Cr Machine Laser – accumulated impairment losses	100 000
Cr Machine Robot – accumulated impairment losses	200 000

There are two problems that need special consideration with respect to impairments, namely goodwill and corporate assets (as already defined). Impairment of goodwill will be discussed in Part Three of the book.

Corporate assets, also by definition, do not generate independent cash flows and, the recoverable amount is determined by reference to the cash-generating unit to which the corporate asset belongs. In testing a cash-generating unit for impairment, an entity shall identify all the corporate assets that relate to the cash-generating unit under review. If a portion of the carrying amount of a corporate asset can be allocated on a reasonable and consistent basis to that unit, the entity shall compare the carrying amount of the unit, including the portion of the carrying amount of the corporate asset allocated to the unit, with its recoverable amount. Any impairment loss shall be recognized in accordance with para. 104, discussed later. If a portion cannot be allocated on a reasonable and consistent basis to that unit, the entity shall:

- compare the carrying amount of the unit, excluding the corporate asset, with its recoverable amount and recognize any impairment loss in accordance with para. 104
- identify the smallest group of cash-generating units that includes the cash-generating unit under review and to which a portion of the carrying amount of the corporate asset can be allocated on a reasonable and consistent basis
- compare the carrying amount of that group of cash-generating units, including the portion of the carrying amount of the corporate asset allocated to that group of units, with the recoverable amount of the group of units. Any impairment loss shall be recognized in accordance with para. 104.

Once the impairment loss for a cash-generating unit has been determined, it has to be deducted from the carrying amounts of specific assets that are part of that unit, in some systematic manner. IAS 36 specifies its requirements with precision (paras 104 and 105).

An impairment loss should be recognized for a cash-generating unit if, and only if, its recoverable amount is less than its carrying amount. The impairment loss should be allocated to reduce the carrying amount of the assets of the unit in the following order:

- first, to goodwill allocated to the cash-generating unit (if any)
- then, to the other assets of the unit on a pro rata basis, based on the carrying amount of each asset in the unit.

In allocating an impairment loss, the carrying amount of an asset should not be reduced below the *highest of*:

- its fair value less costs to sell (if determinable)
- its value in use (if determinable)
- zero.

The amount of the impairment loss that would otherwise have been allocated to the asset should be allocated to the other assets of the unit on a pro rata basis. A liability should be recognized for any remaining amount of an impairment loss for a cash-generating unit, if, and only if, that is required by other International Accounting Standards.

The effect of this is, first, to eliminate goodwill, but then to ensure that the carrying amount of any individual asset is not reduced so far as to produce a figure not economically relevant to that asset.

Disclosure

The disclosure requirements of IAS 36, like much else in the Standard, are extensive. They are also quite straightforward, requiring detailed numerical, explanatory and background information.

NON-CURRENT ASSETS HELD FOR SALE AND DISCONTINUED OPERATIONS

The structure or dimension of most companies changes over the years. On the one hand, companies can grow through acquisitions or/and organic growth. On the other, companies might also discontinue activities and, as a result, may decrease in size. If a relatively large component of the entity is discontinued, then substantial financial disclosure about these discontinued activities is required.

It is intuitively likely that assets associated with discontinued operations, or with operations that are approaching a discontinued status, are likely to suffer impairment, and it seems logical to bring such assets, and the IAS 36 impairment Standard, into proximity. Nevertheless, they are technically separate issues and need to be carefully distinguished when considering the detail.

These requirements are part of IFRS 5, *Non-current Assets Held for Sale and Discontinued Operations*. IFRS 5, which was issued in spring 2004, is one of the first

Standards that is a result of the IASB's convergence project. IFRS 5 is meant to close the gap between, on the one hand, FASB Statement No. 144, *Accounting for the Impairment or Disposal of Long-lived Assets* (SFAS 144), which was issued in 2001, and on the other, the recognition and valuation rules for those assets under IAS/ IFRS. SFAS 144 addressed three areas:

- impairment of long-lived assets to be held and used
- classification, measurement and presentation of assets held for sale
- classification and presentation of discontinued operations.

IFRS 5 only deals with the issues mentioned in the second two. With regard to the impairment of long-lived assets to be held and used, the existing differences between the FASB and the IASB were not resolved. The difference between US GAAP and IAS/IFRS is often called a difference between rules-based versus principles-based accounting standards. If one considers IFRS 5, which is a product of the convergence project, one will notice that the criteria for a non-current asset to be defined as 'held for sale' are rather detailed. It is highly likely that the convergence project might move the IAS/IFRS Standards away from a purely principles-based accounting system and drive them towards a more rules-based system. Although a substantial convergence is reached for these recognition and measurement items (namely non-current assets held for sale and discontinued operations), differences with SFAS 144 still exist. First, we will present the treatment of non-current assets held for sale under IFRS 5 and, second, we will focus on the information to be reported in relation to discontinuing operations.

NON-CURRENT ASSETS HELD FOR SALE

Definition

IFRS 5 presents the definition, the recognition and measurement of non-current assets held for sale. Non-current assets are defined as assets that do not meet the criteria of a current asset. The definition of a current asset is found in IAS 1, para. 66 and is as follows:

An asset shall be classified as current when it satisfies any of the following criteria:

(a) it is expected to be realized in, or is intended for sale or consumption in, the entity's normal operating cycle

(b) it is held primarily for the purpose of being traded

(c) it is expected to be realized within twelve months after the balance sheet date or

(d) it is cash or the cash equivalent (as defined in IAS 7, *Cash Flow Statements*) unless it is restricted from being exchanged or used to settle a liability for at least twelve months after the balance sheet date.

All other assets are classified as non-current assets.

So non-current assets include tangible, intangible and financial assets of a long-term nature. IFRS 5 not only considers individual non-current assets but it also prescribes the definition, recognition and valuation rules for disposal groups. In these circumstances, a common example would be the disposal of a subsidiary. The Standard observes that an entity will dispose of a group of assets, possibly with some directly associated liabilities, together in a single transaction (para. 4). The disposal group might include goodwill acquired in a business combination if the group is a cash-generating unit to which goodwill has been allocated or if it is an operation within a cash-generating unit as defined in Appendix A of IFRS 5. In this respect, a disposal group can be a group of cash-generating units, a single cash-generating unit or part of a cash-generating unit.

IFRS 5 states explicitly that the rules of measurement and recognition stipulated in IFRS 5 do not apply to the following assets since they are covered by other Standards: deferred tax assets; assets arising from employee benefits; financial assets within the scope of IFRS 9; non-current assets that are accounted for in accordance with the fair value model in IAS 40, *Investment Property*; non-current assets that are measured at fair value less costs to sell in accordance with IAS 41, *Agriculture*; and contractual rights under insurance contracts as defined in IFRS 4, *Insurance Contracts*.

Essential to the definition of non-current assets held for sale is that the carrying amount of the assets will be recovered principally through sale rather than continuing use in the business (para. 6). Besides these general definitions on the concept of non-current assets held for sale, IFRS 5 goes further into detail by providing more characteristics that need to be fulfilled before a non-current asset can be classified as held for sale. These characteristics are laid down (in paras 7–14) and have a more rules-based character.

With regard to the interpretation of 'held for sale', we summarize the main items of paras 7–14 here.

For an asset (or disposal group) to be classified as held for sale:

- It must be available for immediate sale in its present condition, subject only to terms that are usual and customary for sales of such assets (or disposal groups).

- Its sale must be highly probable, the appropriate level of management must be committed to a plan to sell the asset (or disposal group), and an active programme to locate a buyer and complete the plan must have been initiated.

- The sale should be expected to qualify for recognition as a completed sale within one year from the date of classification. Exception is permitted if the delay is caused by events or circumstances beyond the entity's control and there is sufficient evidence that the entity remains committed to its plan to sell the asset (or disposal group).

- It must genuinely be sold, not abandoned. The sale transactions, referred to (in paras 7–14) include exchanges of non-current assets for other non-current assets when the exchange has commercial substance in accordance with IAS 16.

MEASUREMENT OF NON-CURRENT ASSETS AND DISPOSAL GROUPS HELD FOR SALE

Measurement on initial classification as held for sale

IFRS 5 requires that immediately before the initial classification of an asset (or disposal group) as held for sale, the carrying amount of the asset (or all the assets and liabilities in the group) should be measured in accordance with applicable IFRSs. In other words, an entity should apply its usual accounting policies up until the criteria for classification as held for sale are met.

Thereafter, a non-current asset (or disposal group) classified as held for sale should be measured at the lower of its carrying amount and fair value less costs to sell. According to IFRS 5, the fair value is defined as 'the price that would be received to sell an asset or paid to transfer a liability in an orderly transaction between market participants at the measurement date'. Costs to sell are defined as 'the incremental costs directly attributable to the disposal of an asset (or disposal group), excluding finance costs and income tax expense'. When the sale is expected to occur beyond one year, the costs to sell should be measured at their present value. Any increase in the present value of the costs to sell that arises from the passage of time should be presented in profit or loss as a financing cost. There is no similar requirement to present that element of an increase in fair value that also relates to just the passage of time as finance income.

For the disposal groups, the Standard adopts a portfolio approach. It requires that if a non-current asset within the scope of its measurement requirements is part of a disposal group, the measurement requirements should apply to the group as a whole, so that the group is measured at the lower of its carrying amount and fair value less costs to sell. It will still be necessary to apportion any write down to the underlying assets of the disposal group, but no element is apportioned to items outside the scope of the Standard's measurement provisions.

If a newly acquired asset (or disposal group) meets the criteria to be classified as held for sale (which are subtly different for assets acquired exclusively with a view to subsequent disposal), applying the above requirements will result in the asset (or disposal group) being measured on initial recognition at the lower of its carrying amount had it not been so classified (e.g. cost) and fair value less costs to sell. This means that if the asset (or disposal group) is acquired as part of a business combination, it will be measured at fair value less costs to sell.

While a non-current asset is classified as held for sale or while it is part of a disposal group classified as held for sale, it should not be depreciated or amortized. Interest and other expenses attributable to the liabilities of a disposal group classified as held for sale should continue to be recognized.

On subsequent re-measurement of a disposal group, the Standard requires that the carrying amounts of any assets and liabilities that are not within the scope of its measurement requirements be re-measured in accordance with applicable IFRSs before the fair value less costs to sell of the disposal group is re-measured.

Recognition of impairment losses and reversals

The requirement to measure a non-current asset (or disposal group) held for sale at the lower of carrying amount less costs to sell may give rise to a write down in value (impairment loss) and possibly its subsequent reversal. As noted earlier, the first step is to account for any items within the scope of the Standard in the normal way. After that, any excess of carrying value over fair value less costs to sell should be recognized as an impairment.

Any subsequent increase in fair value less costs to sell of an asset up to the cumulative impairment loss previously recognized either in accordance with IFRS 5 or in accordance with IAS 36, *Impairment of Assets*, should be recognized as a gain. In the case of a disposal group, any subsequent increase in fair value less costs to sell should be recognized:

> [t]o the extent that it has not been recognized under another Standard in relation to those assets outside the scope of IFRS 5's measurement requirements but not in excess of the cumulative amount of losses previously recognized under IFRS 5 or before that under IAS 36 in respect of the non-current assets in the group that are within the scope of the measurement rule of IFRS 5.

Any impairment loss (or any subsequent gain) recognized for a disposal group should be allocated to the non-current assets in the group that are within the scope of the measurement requirements of IFRS 5. The order allocation should be:

- first, to reduce the carrying amount of any goodwill in the group
- then to the other assets of the group pro rata on the basis of the carrying amount of each asset in the group.

When assets meet the criteria to be classified as held for sale, they have to be presented separately on the balance sheet. In the notes, disclosures have to be made in relation to the facts and circumstances of the sale and the gains or losses recognized after the classification of the non-current assets as 'held for sale'. If assets are no longer used in the operational activities of the firm, they will no longer generate revenues, expenditures and cash. Information on the impact of the disappearance of these items should be presented as information on discontinued operations.

DISCONTINUED OPERATIONS

IFRS 5 also deals with the presentation of information on discontinued operations. This type of information disclosure had been regulated already, namely under the superseded IAS 35. IFRS 5 requires the presentation of a single amount on the face of the income statement relating to discontinued operations, with further analysis either on the face of the income statement or in the notes (see Activity 14.6).

ACTIVITY 14.6

Why do you think financial information about discontinuing operations should be provided to the external user of the financial statements?

Activity feedback

A discontinuing operation is a relatively large component of an entity that is either being disposed of completely or substantially, or is being terminated through abandonment or piecemeal sale. The effects of such discontinuation are likely to be significant both in their own right and in changing the future results of the remaining components of the entity.

Distinguishing between the financial impact of the discontinuing and the continuing operations on the financial situation of an entity will improve the ability of investors, creditors and other users of financial statements to make projections of the entity's cash flows, earnings generating capacity and financial position.

In order to be useful for decision purposes, the results of an entity need to be presented in a manner that will satisfy the two following objectives. First, the activities and results of the year under review must be reported fully and clearly. Second, readers of the financial statements should be able to understand the implications of the current period results for future periods. This relates to the relevance of accounting information. So the objective of IFRS 5 is to establish a basis for segregating information about a major operation that an entity is discontinuing from information about its continuing operations and to specify minimum disclosures about a discontinuing operation.

Definition of a discontinued operation

IFRS 5 defines a discontinued operation as:

a component of an entity that either has been disposed of, or is classified as held for sale, and:

(a) represents a separate major line of business or geographical area of operations

(b) is part of a single coordinated plan to dispose of a separate major line of business or geographical area of operations or

(c) is a subsidiary acquired exclusively with a view to resale.

For the purposes of this definition, a 'component of an entity' is also defined by the Standard as comprising 'operations and cash flows that can be clearly distinguished, operationally and for financial reporting purposes, from the rest of the entity'. In other words, a component of an entity will have been a cash-generating unit or a group of cash-generating units while being held for use.

Business entities frequently close facilities, abandon products or even product lines and change the size of their workforce in response to market forces. Those kinds of termination do not qualify as discontinuing operations, but they can occur in connection with a discontinuing operation. A list of such activities, which do not qualify as discontinuing operations, is presented below:

- gradual or evolutionary phasing out of a product line or class of service
- discontinuing, even if relatively abruptly, several products within an ongoing line of business
- shifting of some production or marketing activities for a particular line of business from one location to another
- closing of a facility to achieve productivity improvements or other cost savings
- selling a subsidiary whose activities are similar to those of the parent or other subsidiaries.

These examples could bring along the recording of impairments or restructuring provisions.

With regard to the presentation of information on those discontinued operations, IFRS 5 stipulates (para. 33) that an entity shall disclose:

(a) A single amount on the face of the income statement comprising the total of:

(i) the post-tax profit or loss of discontinued operations and

(ii) the post-tax gain or loss recognized on the measurement to fair value less costs to sell or on the disposal of the assets or disposal group(s) constituting the discontinued operation.

(b) An analysis of the single amount of (a) into:

(i) the revenue, expense and pre-tax profit or loss of discontinued operations and related income tax expense

(ii) the gain or loss recognized on the measurement to fair value less costs to sell or on the disposal of the assets or disposal group(s) constituting the discontinued operation and related income tax expense.

The analysis may be presented in the notes or on the face of the income statement. If it is presented on the face of the income statement, it shall be presented in a section identified as relating to discontinued operations, i.e. separately from continuing operations. The analysis is not required for disposal groups that are newly acquired subsidiaries that meet the criteria to be classified as held for sale on acquisition.

(c) the net cash flow attributable to the operating, investing and financing activities of discontinued operations.

The Standard also makes clear that any gain or loss on the re-measurement of a non-current asset (or disposal group) classified as held for sale that does not meet the definition of a discontinued operation should not be included within these amounts for discontinued operations, but be included in profit or loss from continuing operations.

Further, IFRS 5 requires that these disclosures be re-presented for prior periods in the financial statements so that the disclosures relate to all operations that have been discontinued by the balance sheet date for the latest period presented. Accordingly, adjustments to the comparative information as originally reported will be necessary for those disposal groups categorized as discontinued operations.

ACTIVITY 14.7

Alpha has three segments: pharmaceuticals, chemicals and soft drinks. In 20X3, after an assessment of the corporate strategy for the future, the company decides to concentrate on chemicals and pharmaceuticals.

On 30 September 20X3 the board of directors voted in favour of a disposal plan which would try either to sell off the soft drinks' segment as a whole, or, if not successful by the end of 20X3, dispose of the assets of the segment in a piecemeal fashion. An announcement of the plan was made the same day. A month later, the company enters into a legally binding sales agreement with one of the major producers of soft drinks in the world. The parties expect the sale to be completed in February 20X4.

The following information for the soft drink segment is available for the financial year 20X3 (figures and transactions are simplified):

	Book value at 30 September	Recoverable amount at 30 September	Book value/ result at 31 December
Assets	450	400	400
Liabilities	200	200	200
Revenue	—	—	300
Operating expenses	—	—	125

An amount of 25 represents non-cash expenses. As you are aware, information relating to a discontinuing operation should be presented separately from continuing operations. You should now prepare the information that needs to be disclosed in the financial statements on 31 December 20X3. Assume a corporate income tax rate of 30 per cent on the accounting profit for the segment.

Also, comment on what other information must be given regarding the discontinuing operation.

Activity feedback

- As a single amount on the income statement, para. 33(a): profit for the period from discontinued operations

(a)	the post-tax result on discontinued operations	122.5
(b)	the post-tax gain or loss on the measurement of the assets held for sale	35.0
	Total	157.5

- An analysis of the single amount, para. 33(b)

	Revenue from discontinued operations	300.0
	Expenses from discontinued operations	125.0
(a)	pre-tax result	175.0
(b)	related income tax expense	52.5
(c)	loss on non-current assets held for sale	50.0
(d)	related income tax result	15.0

On the asset side of the balance sheet, we should present as a single line item:

Non-current assets classified as held for sale	400.0

Among the liabilities, we should disclose as a single line item:

Liabilities directly associated with non-current assets held for sale	200.0
Net cash flow attributable to discontinued operations	200.0

(Continued)

ACTIVITY 14.7   (*Continued*)

Note that comparative figures for 20X2 should be restated as well (para. 34). Disclosure requirements (refer to IFRS 5, para. 41):

- *a description of the segment soft drinks (also comment on the reason for the disposal)*
- *segments in which the discontinuing operation is reported (it is a segment in this case)*

- *the date on which the company announced the plan to discontinue the soft drink segment (also comment on the date when it entered into the binding sales agreement)*
- *the date when the discontinuance is expected to be completed.*

The disclosure on discontinued operations is illustrated with note 3 of the financial statements of the adidas Group for the financial year 2014.

REAL WORLD ILLUSTRATION

Plans to sell the Rockport operating segment became concrete towards the end of 2014 and a divestiture within the next twelve months is considered as highly probable. For this reason, the Rockport operating segment is reported as discontinued operations at December 31, 2014. The focus and the strategic direction of the Group's brand portfolio primarily lies in the field of sports with the result that the Rockport operating segment is no longer regarded as significant in terms of the Group's strategic direction.

The Rockport operating segment was neither classified as assets held for sale nor as discontinued operations at December 31, 2013. The 2013 figures of the consolidated income statement and the consolidated statement of cash flows have been restated to show the discontinued operations separately from continuing operations.

The results of the Rockport operating segment are shown as discontinued operations in the consolidated income statement for all periods:

Discontinued operations

(€ in millions)	31/12/20X4	31/12/20X3
Net sales	283	289
Expenses	264	268
Income from operating activities	**19**	**21**
Income taxes	5	4
Income from operating activities, net of tax	**14**	**17**
Loss recognised on the measurement to fair value less costs to sell	110	–
Income taxes	28	–
Loss recognised on the measurement to fair value less costs to sell, net of tax	**(82)**	–
Losses/gains from discontinued operations, net of tax	**(68)**	**17**
Basic earnings per share from discontinued operations (€)	(0.32)	0.08
Diluted earnings per share from discontinued operations (€)	(0.32)	0.08

Losses from discontinued operations in an amount of € 68 million (2013: gains of € 17 million) are entirely attributable to the shareholders of adidas AG.

SUMMARY

This chapter has completed the coverage, begun in Chapter 12, of the accounting treatment of fixed (non-current) assets. We looked in some detail at the issue of impairment of assets in general and of fixed assets in particular, and at the contents of IAS 36. Finally, we explored the requirements of IFRS 5 relating to non-current assets held for sale, and to the reporting of discontinued operations.

EXERCISES

Suggested answers to exercises marked ✓ are to be found in the Student online resources, with suggested answers to the remaining questions available in the Instructor online resources.

1   If depreciation is calculated properly, impairment adjustments will not arise. Discuss.

2   What is 'recoverable amount' as the phrase is used in IAS 36? How does it relate to the alternative valuation bases?

✓**3**   A cash-generating unit was reviewed for impairment at 31 May 20X3 as required by IAS 36, *Impairment of Assets*. The impairment review revealed that the cash-generating unit has a value in use of $25 million and a net realizable value of $23 million. The carrying values of the net assets of the cash-generating unit immediately prior to the impairment review were as follows:

	$000
Goodwill	5 000
Property, plant and equipment	18 000
Net current assets	4 000
	27 000

The review indicated that an item of plant (included in the above figure of $18 million) with a carrying value of $1 million had been severely damaged and was virtually worthless. There was no other evidence of obvious impairment to specific assets.

Required:
Identify the carrying value of the goodwill relating to the unit immediately after the results of the impairment review have been reflected in accordance with IAS 36.

(CIMA, November 2003, adapted)

4   **(a)** IAS 36, *Impairment of Assets*, was published in June 1998 and subsequently amended in March 2004 and January 2008. Its primary objective is to ensure that an asset is not carried on the statement of financial position at a value that is greater than its recoverable amount.

Required:

(i) Describe the circumstances where an impairment loss is deemed to have occurred and explain when companies should perform an impairment review of tangible and intangible assets.

(ii) Describe the matters to be considered in assessing whether an asset may be impaired.

(b) Avendus is preparing its financial statements to 30 September 20X3. It has identified the following issues:

(i) Avendus owns and operates an item of plant that had a carrying value of $400 000 and an estimated remaining life of five years. It has just been damaged due to incorrect operation by an employee. It is not economic to repair the plant, but it still operates in a limited capacity although it is now no longer expected to last for five years. As the plant is damaged, it could only be sold for $50 000. The cost of replacing the plant is $1 million. The plant does not generate cash flows independently and is part of a group of assets that have a carrying value of $5 million and an estimated recoverable amount of $7 million.

Required:

Explain how the above item of plant should be treated in the financial statements of Avendus for the year to 30 September 20X3. Your answer should consider the situations where the plant continues to be used and where it would be replaced.

(ii) Avendus owns an investment property which has a remaining useful economic life of five years. The property has a carrying value of $200 000 on 30 September 20X3. It is currently let to Marchant at an annual rental of $50 000 per annum. A surveyor has estimated that Avendus could expect net proceeds of $165 000 from the sale of the property. The lease and the rental are due for renegotiation on 1 October 20X3. There is currently a surplus of rental properties and this has affected rental incomes and selling prices considerably. Aware of this, Marchant has offered to rent the property for a further five years, but for an annual rental, payable in advance, of only $40 000. The rental would be payable in full on 1 October each year. The current cost of capital of Avendus is 10 per cent per annum, but current market assessments of a widely expected increase in interest rates means this will soon rise to 12 per cent per annum. Avendus uses the cost method in IAS 40, *Investment Property*. The following information can be taken as correct:

Interest rate	10%	12%
Present value of 4 year annuity	3.2	3.0
Present value of 5 year annuity	3.8	3.6

Required:

Explain how the above investment property should be treated in the financial statements of Avendus for the year to 30 September 20X3. Your answer should be supported with numerical calculations.

(iii) Avendus recently acquired a company called Fishright, a small fishing and fish processing company for $2 million. Avendus allocated the purchase consideration as follows:

	$000
Goodwill	240
Fishing quotas	400
Fishing boats (two of equal value)	1 000
Other fishing equipment	100
Fish processing plant	200
Net current assets	60
	2 000

Shortly after the acquisition, one of the fishing boats sank in a storm and this has halved the fishing capacity. Due to this reduction in capacity, the value in use of the fishing business as a going concern is estimated at only $1.2 million. The fishing quotas now represent a greater volume than one boat can fish and it is not possible to replace the lost boat as it was rather old and no equivalent boats are available. However, the fishing quotas are much in demand and could be sold for $600 000. Avendus has been offered $250 000 for the fish processing plant. The net current assets consist of accounts receivable and payable.

Required:

Calculate the amounts that would appear in the consolidated financial statements of Avendus in respect of Fishright's assets after accounting for the impairment loss.

(ACCA, December 2003, adapted)

5   Outline the requirements of IFRS 5, *Non-current Assets Held for Sale and Discontinued Operations*.

6   **(a)** IAS 36, *Impairment of Assets*, was issued in June 1998 and subsequently amended in March 2004 and January 2008. Its main objective is to prescribe the procedures that should ensure that an entity's assets are included in its statement of financial position at no more than their recoverable amounts. Where an asset is carried at an amount in excess of its recoverable amount, it is said to be impaired and IAS 36 requires an impairment loss to be recognized.

Required:

(i) Define an impairment loss explaining the relevance of fair value less costs to sell and value in use, and state how frequently assets should be tested for impairment. Note: your answer should NOT describe the possible indicators of an impairment.

(ii) Explain how an impairment loss is accounted for after it has been calculated.

(b) The assistant financial controller of the Wilderness group, a public listed company, has identified the matters below which she believes may indicate an impairment to one or more assets:

(i) Wilderness owns and operates an item of plant that cost $640 000 and had accumulated depreciation of $400 000 at 1 October 20X4. It is being depreciated at 12½ per cent on cost. On 1 April 20X5 (exactly halfway through the year), the plant was damaged when a factory vehicle collided with it. Due to the replacement parts being unavailable, it is not possible to repair the plant, but it still operates, albeit at a reduced capacity. Also, it is expected that as a result of the damage, the remaining life of the plant from the date of the damage will be only two years. Based on its reduced capacity, the estimated present value of the plant in use is $150 000. The plant has a current disposal value of $20 000 (which will be nil in two years' time), but Wilderness has been offered a trade-in value of $180 000 against a replacement machine which has a cost of $1 million (there would be no disposal costs for the replaced plant). Wilderness is reluctant to replace the plant as it is worried about the long-term demand for the product produced by the plant. The trade-in value is only available if the plant is replaced.

Required:

Prepare extracts from the statement of financial position and statement of profit or loss and other comprehensive income of Wilderness in respect of the plant for the year ended 30 September 20X5. Your answer should explain how you arrived at your figures.

(ii) On 1 April 20X4 Wilderness acquired 100 per cent of the share capital of Mossel, whose only activity is the extraction and sale of spa water. Mossel had been profitable since its acquisition, but bad publicity resulting from several consumers becoming ill due to a contamination of the spa water supply in April 20X5 has led to unexpected losses in the last six months. The carrying amounts of Mossel's assets at 30 September 20X5 are:

	$000
Brand (Quencher – see below)	7 000
Land containing spa	12 000
Purifying and bottling plant	8 000
Inventories	5 000
	32 000

The source of the contamination was found and it has now ceased. The company originally sold the bottled water under the brand name of 'Quencher', but because of the contamination, it has rebranded its bottled water as 'Phoenix'. After a large advertising campaign, sales are now starting to recover and are approaching previous levels. The value of the brand in the statement of financial position is the depreciated amount of the original brand name of 'Quencher'. The directors have acknowledged that $1.5 million will have to be spent in the first three months of the next accounting period to upgrade the purifying and bottling plant.

Inventories contain some old 'Quencher' bottled water at a cost of $2 million; the remaining inventories are labelled with the new brand 'Phoenix'. Samples of all the bottled water have been tested by the health authority and have been passed as fit to sell. The old bottled water will have to be relabelled at a cost of $250 000, but is then expected to be sold at the normal selling price of (normal) cost plus 50 per cent.

Based on the estimated future cash flows, the directors have estimated that the value in use of Mossel at 30 September 20X5, calculated according to the guidance in IAS 36, is $20 million. There is no reliable estimate of the fair value less cost to sell of Mossel.

Required:

Calculate the amounts at which the assets of Mossel should appear in the consolidated statement of financial position of Wilderness at 30 September 20X5. Your answer should explain how you arrive at your figures.

(ACCA, December 2005, adapted)

7   At 30 November 20X3, Joey carried a property in its statement of financial position at its revalued amount of $14 million in accordance with IAS 16, *Property, Plant and Equipment*. Depreciation is charged at $300 000 per year on the straight line basis. In March 20X4, the management decided to sell the property and it was advertised for sale. By 31 March 20X4, the sale was considered to be highly probable and the criteria for IFRS 5, *Non-current Assets Held for Sale and Discontinued Operations* were met at this date. At that date, the asset's fair value was $15.4 million and its value in use was $15.8 million. Costs to sell the asset were estimated at $300 000. On 30 November 20X4, the property was sold for $15.6 million. The transactions regarding the property are deemed to be material and no entries have been made in the financial statements regarding this property since 30 November 20X3 as the cash receipts from the sale were not received until December 20X4.

Required:
Discuss how the above item should be dealt with in the financial statements of Joey for the year ended 30 November 20X4.

(ACCA, Corporate Reporting (International), December 2014, adapted)

8   **(a)** An assessment of accounting practices for asset impairments is especially important in the context of financial reporting quality in that it requires the exercise of considerable management judgement and reporting discretion. The importance of this issue is heightened during periods of ongoing economic uncertainty as a result of the need for companies to reflect the loss of economic value in a timely fashion through the mechanism of asset write-downs. There are many factors which can affect the quality of impairment accounting and disclosures. These factors include changes in circumstance in the reporting period, the market capitalization of the entity, the allocation of goodwill to cash-generating units, valuation issues and the nature of the disclosures.

Required:
Discuss the importance and significance of the above factors when conducting an impairment test under IAS 36, *Impairment of Assets*.

   (b) **(i)** Estoil is an international company providing parts for the automotive industry. It operates in many different jurisdictions with different currencies. During 20X4, Estoil experienced financial difficulties marked by a decline in revenue, a reorganization and restructuring of the business and it reported a loss for the year. An impairment test of goodwill was performed, but no impairment was recognized. Estoil applied one discount rate for all cash flows for all cash-generating units (CGUs), irrespective of the currency in which the cash flows would be generated. The discount rate used was the weighted average cost of capital (WACC) and Estoil used the 10-year government bond rate for its jurisdiction as the risk-free rate in this calculation. Additionally, Estoil built its model using a forecast denominated in the functional currency of the parent company. Estoil felt that any other approach would require a level of detail which was unrealistic and impracticable. Estoil argued that the different CGUs represented different risk profiles in the short term, but over a longer business cycle, there was no basis for claiming that their risk profiles were different.

   (ii) Fariole specializes in the communications sector with three main CGUs. Goodwill was a significant component of total assets. Fariole performed an impairment test of the CGUs. The cash flow projections were based on the most recent financial budgets approved by management. The realized cash flows for the CGUs were negative in 20X4 and far below budgeted cash flows for that period. The directors had significantly raised cash flow forecasts for 20X5 with little justification. The projected cash flows were calculated by adding back depreciation charges to the budgeted result for the period, with expected changes in working capital and capital expenditure not taken into account.

Required:

Discuss the acceptability of the above accounting practices under IAS 36, *Impairment of Assets*.

(ACCA, Corporate Reporting (International), December 2014)

9   Robby purchased plant, property and equipment (PPE) for $10 million on 1 June 20X9. It has an expected useful life of 20 years and is depreciated using the straight line method. On 31 May 20X1, the PPE was revalued to $11 million. At 31 May 20X2 impairment indicators triggered an impairment review of the PPE. The recoverable amount of the PPE was $7.8 million. The only accounting entry posted for the year to 31 May 20X2 was to account for the depreciation based on the revalued amount as at 31 May 20X1. Robby's accounting policy is to make a transfer of the excess depreciation arising on the revaluation of PPE.

Required:

Discuss how the above item should be dealt with in the financial statements of Robby for the year ended 31 May 20X2.

(ACCA, Corporate Reporting (International), June 2012, adapted)

LEASES

15

OBJECTIVES After studying this chapter you should be able to:

- understand the debate concerning the treatment of leases in financial statements

- explain the issues underlying the accounting treatment of leases

- discuss alternative accounting treatments for leases of various types

- describe, apply and appraise the requirements of IFRS 16 in relation to leased assets for the lessee

- describe, apply and appraise the requirements of IFRS 16 in relation to leased assets for the lessor

- explain in the context of lessor accounting the difference between a finance lease and an operating lease.

INTRODUCTION

A lease is an agreement that conveys to one party (the lessee) the right to use property, but does not convey legal ownership of that property. It follows that if an asset is defined as something which is legally owned (i.e. that has been acquired in an exchange transaction), then leases will not give rise to an asset in the financial statements of the lessee. It also follows that if nothing has been 'acquired', then nothing is unpaid for; that is, the lease agreement will also not give rise to a liability in the financial statements of the lessee.

If, however, the lease agreement allows the lessee to use the property for all or most of its useful life, requires the lessee to pay total amounts close to and possibly greater than the normal buying price of the item, and requires or assumes that the lessee will look after the item as if the item belonged to it (e.g. insurance, repairs and maintenance), then it is clear that in substance the lessee would be in the same position, both economically and in terms of production and operating capacity, *as if* the lessee actually owned the asset. Furthermore, a contractual requirement to make future payments greater than the net cost of a straightforward purchase of the item means that the lessee is in the same position *as if* it had taken out a loan under agreed regular repayment terms and at an agreed rate of interest. Thus, in such circumstances, the economic substance of the situation is that the lessee has an asset and a liability, although the legal form of the agreement makes it quite clear that the legal ownership of the item remains with the other party (the lessor).

ACTIVITY 15.1

A company obtains the use of two identical assets costing €100 000 by obtaining one asset on a credit sale agreement and the other on a lease. Assuming fixed assets are only recorded on a company's balance sheet when it has legal ownership, show the adjustments that would be necessary to the company's accounts and identify the problems, if any, with this method of accounting.

Activity feedback

	€
Fixed assets	100 000
Creditors	100 000

Under this method of accounting only one asset would be shown under fixed assets and only the liability to pay for one asset would be shown. The fact that the company has the use of another fixed asset and that they have the liability outstanding for lease payments is not shown and this could be considered misleading to shareholders and to other potential lenders.

If the two assets are obtained in these different ways by two different companies then the difference will be even more obvious. If the assets are being used equally profitably, then one company will appear to be using significantly fewer resources and significantly less finance than the other one to achieve comparable operating activities. This apparent economic (and managerial) efficiency of the company which leases the asset is not logically justified and, in addition, unavoidable obligations are not being recorded as liabilities.

The general principle of substance over form, discussed in Chapter 8, requires that in such circumstances the lessee *does* record an asset and a liability in its balance sheet and also that the lessor records a sale and a debtor in its financial statements.

ACTIVITY 15.2

A company signs a lease agreement under which it will pay €2000 at the end of each of years 1–6 inclusive. The purchase cost of the asset concerned is €10 000 and the asset is expected to be worthless after six years. Discuss what the accounting entries in year 1 should be.

Activity feedback

In substance, this transaction is clearly a purchase on deferred credit terms. There should be an immediate recording of an asset of €10 000 on day 1, with an equal liability. At the end of year 1, a payment of €2000 is recorded, i.e. a credit. The double entry for this payment will need to be split two ways. There is a total interest cost of €2000 over the six-year period ((2000 × 6) – 10 000), and some of the €2000 payment at the end of year 1 will be payment of the interest relating to year 1, say X^i. This will be an expense of year 1 and the remainder of this payment, i.e. (2000 – X^i), will be a partial settlement

ACTIVITY 15.2 *(Continued)*

of the liability. There will also be a depreciation charge made at the end of year 1 of €1667, if the straight line basis is used. This gives entries as follows:

Leasehold asset		
01/01/X1 cost	10 000	1 667 depreciation 31/12/X1

Lease liability		
	10 000	01/01/X1
	$(2\,000 - X^I)$	31/12/X1

Profit and loss	
31/12/X1 interest	X^I
31/12/X1 depreciation 1 667	

In year 2 the payment, interest and depreciation entries will be repeated, but the interest expense of X^{II} should be less than X^I, because the liability during year 2 was lower than that during year 1. This follows the basic matching principle by allocating the total interest charge of €2000 over the six years pro rata to the benefit, thus the annual interest charge reduces as the amount borrowed reduces.

In this Activity, we did not consider the timing differences of the payments and the implicit interest included in the contract. We do so in Activity 15.4.

In broad terms, the whole issue of accounting for leases can be summarized very simply. If a lease agreement essentially gives the parties rights and obligations similar to those arising from a legal purchase, then the accounting proceeds as if it *were* a legal purchase. This gives rise to a fixed asset and an obligation. If, by way of contrast, a lease agreement is, in the context of the particular characteristics of the object in question, essentially a short-term rental, then the accounting treats it as such, giving rise in the books of the lessee to a simple expense, normally allocated on a time basis.

Unfortunately, this simple division masks a considerable amount of practical difficulty and provides room for creativity for preparers. There are problems involved in creating a clear demarcation line between the two situations, and a number of particular issues and problems have arisen over the years, which IASB and various national Standards have tried to tackle. For years, preparers of financial statements succeeded in keeping a large part of their leasing contracts off their balance sheet. The introduction of the concepts of finance lease and operating lease in the Standard IAS 17, *Leases*, allowed off balance sheet recognition for operating leases in the books of the lessee. According to IAS 17, a *finance lease* was a lease that transfers substantially all the risks and rewards incidental to ownership of an asset. The title may or may not eventually be transferred. The risks of ownership relating to a finance lease are those of breakdown, damage, wear and tear, theft, obsolescence and so on. The rewards of ownership are extracted by using the asset for substantially all its productive usefulness – that is, its economic life – and by receiving its residual value at the time of its disposal. Under IAS 17, an *operating lease* was a lease other than a finance lease. Under IAS 17, finance leases had to be recognized on the balance sheet and operating leases were recognized off balance sheet, which implied that preparers of financial statements only had to report the lease payments as costs and disclose the future lease payments in the notes to the financial statements.

Using the information disclosed in the notes, users of financial statement information could adjust the accounting numbers of the company by adding the information disclosed in IAS 17. This adjustment would allow users to be able to compare more easily the financial statements of companies using finance leases with companies using operating leases. However, according to the IASB, analysis shows that these common-practice adjustments made by investors, credit rating agencies and other providers of capital often over-estimate, but sometimes also under-estimate the value of the leases (IASB fact sheet: IFRS16 – Leases, 13 January 2016).

The accounting for assets under lease contracts just described, is the method according to which lessees will account for these assets in their books up until 2019. From 2019 onwards, this practice will be changed because from then on IFRS 16, *Leases* will become effective (for annual periods beginning on or after 1 January 2019). IFRS 16 abolishes for the lessee the distinction between a finance lease and an operating lease and requires recognition on the balance sheet for all assets held under lease agreements. The accounting treatment for lease contracts in the books of the lessor under IAS 17 will be to a large extent taken over by IFRS 16.

To illustrate the impact the difference in the qualification between a finance lease and an operating lease could have on the accounting numbers of a company, and subsequently on the ratios of the company, we introduce a real life illustration here.

REAL WORLD ILLUSTRATION

The published consolidated financial statements of Euro Disney SCA for the year to 30 September 2000 provided a sharp illustration of how significant the leasing question can be. Broadly speaking, this was a consolidation of the French part of the worldwide Disney organization. It was published in English, but was explicitly stated to follow 'French accounting principles' in the audit report and 'French GAAP' elsewhere. Most of the land and property utilized by Euro Disney is owned, through complicated relationships, by financing companies. Under French GAAP at the time, the leases involved were operating leases and the financing companies are not consolidated. The effect is that major obligations are not revealed. However, a detailed reconciliation is given to US GAAP which, in broad terms, has the same effect as using IAS GAAP as regards the relevant leases.

Four reconciliations are now given.

Reconciliation of net income (loss) (€ in millions)	30 September 2000	1999
Net income, as reported under French GAAP	38.7	23.6
Lease and interest adjustments	(106.0)	(74.5)
Other	1.1	1.0
Net loss under US GAAP	(66.2)	(49.9)

Reconciliation of shareholders' equity (€ in millions)		
Shareholders' equity, as reported under French GAAP	1 247.5	1 140.8
Cumulative lease and interest adjustments	(1 172.9)	(1 067.0)
Effect of revaluing the ORAs and sale/leaseback transactions	178.1	26.7
Other	(14.6)	(15.6)
Shareholders' equity under US GAAP	238.1	84.9

Reconciliation of borrowings (€ in millions)	30 September 2000	1999
Total borrowings, as reported under French GAAP*	873.8	941.4
Unconsolidated Phase 1 SNCs[1] debt	1 245.4	1 249.6
Lease financing arrangements with TWDC[2] (€ in millions)	236.9	236.9
Borrowings including unconsolidated financing companies (€ in millions)	2 356.1	2 427.9
US GAAP adjustments to revalue lease financing arrangements and ORAs[3] Total US GAAP borrowings*	(6.3)	(8.5)

*(excluding accrued interest)

Balance sheet under US GAAP (€ in millions)		
Cash and short-term investments	452.9	347.6
Receivables	203.2	184.6
Fixed assets	2 493.3	2 455.5
Other assets	169.4	161.4
Total assets	3 318.8	3 149.1
Accounts payable and other liabilities	730.9	644.8
Borrowings*	2 349.8	2 419.4
Shareholders' equity	238.1	84.9
Total liabilities and equity	3 318.8	3 149.1

*(excluding accrued interest)

Total assets under French GAAP were 2793.8 for 2000 and 2518.8 for 1999.

Notes: [1] Sociétés en nom collectifs (partnerships); [2] The Walt Disney Company; [3] Obligations remboursables en actions (bonds reimbursable in shares).

ACTIVITY 15.3

Calculate the following ratios, within the limits of the information given in the Euro Disney case study: (a) under French GAAP, and (b) under US GAAP, and comment.

$$\frac{\text{net income}}{\text{shareholders' equity}}$$

$$\frac{\text{borrowings}}{\text{equity + borrowings}}$$

$$\frac{\text{net income}}{\text{total assets}}$$

Activity feedback

(a) French GAAP

	2000	1999
$\dfrac{\text{net income}}{\text{shareholders' equity}}$	$\dfrac{38.7}{1247.5} = 3\%$	$\dfrac{23.6}{1140} = 2\%$
$\dfrac{\text{borrowings}}{\text{equity + borrowings}}$	$\dfrac{873.8}{873.8 + 1247.5} = 41\%$	$\dfrac{941.4}{941.4 + 1140.8} = 45\%$
$\dfrac{\text{net income}}{\text{total assets}}$	$\dfrac{38.7}{2793.8} = 1\%$	$\dfrac{23.6}{2518.8} = 1\%$

(b) US GAAP

$\dfrac{\text{net income}}{\text{shareholders' equity}}$	$\dfrac{(66.2)}{238.1} = -28\%$	$\dfrac{(49.9)}{84.9} = -59\%$
$\dfrac{\text{borrowings}}{\text{equity + borrowings}}$	$\dfrac{2349.8}{2349.8 + 231.8} = 91\%$	$\dfrac{2419.4}{2419.4 + 84.9} = 97\%$
$\dfrac{\text{net income}}{\text{total assets}}$	$\dfrac{(66.2)}{3318.8} = -2\%$	$\dfrac{(49.9)}{3149.1} = -2\%$

To state the obvious, a very different picture is given. When the substance of the situation is recorded and the contracted (legally as well as economically) liabilities related to the operations are involved, the whole entity is shown to be very highly geared (leveraged), as well as unprofitable. Can both sets of figures be validly regarded as equally fairly presenting the position to readers of the financial statements?

As a result of the different accounting treatment between a finance lease and an operating lease hindering the comparability of financial statement information, the IASB promulgated a new Standard, IFRS 16, *Leases*, on 1 January 2016. This new Standard abolished the difference between a finance lease and an operating lease for the lessee and introduced a single accounting model for leases for the lessee (= customer of the leasing contract), whereby all leased assets (with two exceptions) are now recognized on the balance sheet. However, for the lessor, the dual model remains, and IFRS 16 kept the distinction between a finance lease and an operating lease for the accounting model for the lessor (= supplier of the lease contract).

In this chapter, we focus first on the requirements of IFRS 16 for the lessee. IFRS 16 comes into effect on 1 January 2019. Earlier application is permitted if the company also applies IFRS 15, *Revenue from Contracts with Customers*. This requirement is important for the lessors, since the lessees are their customers. In fact, the accounting model for the lessors has not changed a lot from the model prescribed under IAS 17. Since lessees can apply IAS 17 until 2019, we will also pay attention to how the lessee accounted for their lease contract under IAS 17 at the end of this chapter. In the context of leasing, it is important to mention that the measurement and disclosure requirements of IFRS 13, *Fair Value* do not apply to assets that fall under the scope of the 'old' IAS 17, neither to the assets that fall under the scope of IFRS 16.

IFRS 16: LEASE ACCOUNTING BY THE LESSEE

The IASB introduced IFRS 16 to ensure that: (1) a company's assets and liabilities were more faithfully represented, (2) to increase transparency and (3) to improve comparability between companies that lease and companies that borrow to buy assets. By abolishing the difference for lessee accounting between a finance lease (on balance sheet recognition) and an operating lease (off balance sheet recognition), the financial statements of companies that financed their assets mainly through operating lease contracts will be most affected. These industries are the airline industry, the retailers, the travel and leisure industry (see real world illustration of Disneyland Paris earlier in this chapter) and the transport sector in general. Off balance sheet financing for lessees is no longer possible, since a single accounting model now applies for lease accounting in the books of the lessees. All assets that satisfy the recognition criteria of a lease will qualify as lease assets and will be recognized on the balance sheet or in the statement of financial position of the company being the customer of the lease contract. The only permissible exemptions to this balance sheet model are short-term lease contracts of 12 months or less and lease contracts for assets with low value. It will be interesting to follow up whether or not creative preparers of financial statements will use these two exemptions to avoid balance sheet recognition of their lease contracts.

Recognition and initial measurement

IFRS 16 asks a customer of a contract (= lessee) to verify at the inception of the contract whether or not the contract contains a lease. IFRS 16 defines the inception date of the contract as the earlier date of a lease agreement and the date of commitment by the parties to the principal terms and conditions of the lease (IFRS 16, Appendix). In the context of IFRS 16, there is another important date to consider which is the commencement date of the lease. The commencement date of the lease contract is the date on which the lessor makes an underlying asset available for use by a lessee. The commencement date is important for the initial measurement of the lease. But what is a lease contract?

Para. 9 of IFRS 16 defines a lease contract as follows: 'a contract is, or contains, a lease if the contract conveys the right to control the use of an identified asset for a period of time in exchange for consideration'. It is important to note that when a contract contains a lease, the lessee shall account for each lease component in the contract separately as an individual lease. Non-lease components, like services related to the leased asset, do not fall under IFRS 16. When lease contracts contain different lease components and non-lease components (e.g. services), the consideration will be allocated on the basis of the relative stand-alone price of the lease components and the aggregate of the stand-alone prices of the non-lease components.

We distinguish four important items in the definition, which are necessary for the recognition of a lease. It is essential that (1) an entity has the right to control the use of (2) an identified asset (3) for a period of time in exchange for (4) a consideration. This period of time relates to the lease term, which consists of the non-cancellable period of a lease together with both: (a) periods covered by an option to extend the lease if the lessee is reasonably certain to exercise that option and (b) periods covered by an option to terminate the lease if the lessee is reasonably certain not to exercise that option. Since leases with a term of 12 months or less are exempted from IFRS 16, it might be interesting to see whether this lease term will be used as a creative means to escape IFRS 16. However, since the IASB defined the lease term in terms of 12 months or less, a lessor probably does not want to negotiate contracts with a non-cancellable period for 12 months or less with the other periods being optional. Moreover, the lessee would then have to state that it is not reasonably certain they will extend the lease.

When a contract or an element of a contract qualifies as a lease, the lessee has to recognize a right-of-use asset and a lease liability in their books at the commencement date of the lease. The right-of-use asset will be recognized at initial recognition at cost in the books of the lessee. According to para. 24 of IFRS 16, the cost of the right-of-use asset shall comprise:

(a) the amount of the initial measurement of the lease liability (which will be discussed below)

(b) any lease payments made at or before the commencement date, less any lease incentives received

(c) any initial direct costs incurred by the lessee and

(d) an estimate of costs to be incurred by the lessee in dismantling and removing the underlying asset, restoring the site on which it is located or restoring the underlying asset to the condition required by the terms and conditions of the lease, unless those costs are used to produce inventories. The lessee incurs the obligation for those costs either at the commencement date or as a consequence of having used the underlying asset during a particular period.

We notice that the definition of the cost for the right-of-use asset at initial recognition of the lease contract in the books of the lessee is structured in a similar way to the cost at initial recognition of property, plant and equipment. We also distinguish three separate components here: the cost plus directly attributable costs plus dismantling costs (see Chapter 12). At the commencement date of the lease contract, the lessee shall also recognize a lease liability which is equal to the present value of the lease payments that are not paid at that date. The lease payments shall be discounted using the interest rate implicit in the lease contract, if that rate can be readily determined. If that rate cannot be readily determined, the lessee shall use the lessee's incremental borrowing rate.

ACTIVITY 15.4

A lessee leases an asset on a non-cancellable lease contract with a primary term of five years from 1 January 20X1. The rental is €650 per quarter payable in advance. The lessee has the right to continue to lease the asset after the end of the primary period for as long as they wish at a nominal rent. In addition, the lessee is required to pay all maintenance and insurance costs as they arise. The leased asset could have been purchased for cash at the start of the lease for €10 000 and has a useful life of eight years. Calculate the interest rate implicit in the lease.

Activity feedback

From the definition of 'interest rate implicit in the lease' we can state that:

1 €10 000 (fair value) = the present value at implicit interest rate of 20 quarterly rentals payable in advance of €650.

2 The present value of the first rental payable is €650 as it is paid now.

3 Thus €9350 = the present value at implicit interest rate of 19 rentals of €650.

4 Therefore 9350/650 = 14.385 = present value at implicit interest rate of 19 rentals of €1.

5 Using discount tables, we can determine the interest rate as 2.95 per cent per quarter.

Para. 27 stipulates what amounts need to be included in the present value of the lease payments for the determination of the lease liability:

(a) fixed payments, less any lease incentives receivable

(b) variable lease payments that depend on an index or a rate (e.g. payments linked to the consumer price index, a benchmark interest rate, change in market rentals), initially measured using the index or rate as at the commencement date

(c) amounts expected to be payable by the lessee under residual value guarantees (from the viewpoint of the lessee, the *guaranteed residual value* is that part of the residual value which is guaranteed by the lessee or by a party related to the lessee (the amount of the guarantee being the maximum amount that could, in any event, become payable))

(d) the exercise price of a purchase option if the lessee is reasonably certain to exercise that option

(e) payments or penalties for terminating the lease if the lease term reflects the lessee exercising an option to terminate the lease.

ACTIVITY 15.5

Company Trudo acquires the control over an asset through a lease contract with a financial institution which specializes in the leasing of heavy machinery to industry. The lease term is a period of nine years. These nine years represent a non-cancellable lease term. At the commencement date of the lease contract, Company Trudo pays €1 million to the lessor and at the end of each of the nine years of the lease period, Company Trudo also pays €1 million. There is an implicit interest rate embedded in the lease contract of 10 per cent. At what value should Company Trudo recognize the right-of-use asset in its balance sheet at the commencement of the lease contract?

Activity feedback

The net present value of the payments to the lessor consists of the €1 million to be payable at the end of each of the nine years of the lease contract =

$$(1\ 000\ 000)/(1+0.1) + (1\ 000\ 000)/(1+0.1)^2$$
$$+ \dots (1000\ 000)/(1+0.1)^9 = 5\ 759\ 024$$

The amount of 5 759 024 will be the lease liability at the commencement of the contract. However, Company Trudo already paid €1 million on the commencement date of the lease contract. So the cost of the right-of-use asset at initial recognition of the lease contract of the heavy equipment will be €1 000 000 + €5 759 024 = €6 759 024.

Dr Heavy Equipment – right-of-use asset	6 759 024
Cr Cash	1 000 000
Cr Lease liability	5 759 024

Subsequent measurement

After the commencement date of the lease contract, i.e. after initial recognition, the right-of-use asset shall be measured at cost less (a) any accumulated depreciation and any accumulated impairment losses and (b) adjusted for any re-measurement of the lease liability (see also measurement of lease liability discussed below). So we notice that the IASB puts forward the cost model to account for leases in the books of the lessee. There are two exceptions noted in paras 34–35 to the use of the cost model. First, if the leased asset qualifies as an investment property, the leased asset might be valued subsequent to initial recognition using the fair value model embedded in IAS 40, *Investment Property*. Second, when the leased asset relates to a class of property, plant and equipment to which the lessee applies the revaluation model in accordance with IAS 16, *Property, Plant and Equipment*, then the lessee may choose to apply the revaluation model to the right-of-use asset as well. These paragraphs are the result of the IASB's concern for consistent application of standards.

With respect to the subsequent measurement of the lease liability after initial recognition, para. 36 of IFRS 16 states that after the commencement date, a lessee shall measure the lease liability by:

(a) increasing the carrying amount to reflect interest on the lease liability

(b) reducing the carrying amount to reflect the lease payments made

(c) re-measuring the carrying amount to reflect any reassessment or lease modifications specified in paras 39–46, or to reflect revised in-substance fixed lease payments.

After the commencement date, a lessee shall recognize in profit or loss, the interest on the lease liability and the variable lease payments not included in the measurement of the lease liability in the period in which the event or condition that triggers those payments occurs. The depreciation of the right-of-use asset and a possible increase or decrease in revaluation or impairment or reversal of impairment are accounted for in accordance with IAS 16 and IAS 36 and will influence the profit or loss account or the other comprehensive income of the lessee (as discussed in Chapters 12 and 14).

ACTIVITY 15.6

Using the information given in Activity 15.4, and assuming the asset has a nil residual value and that it is leased for a further two years after the primary period, show the accounting entries over the life of the lease required in the lessee's books.

Activity feedback

The lease falls within the definition of a lease therefore the 'rights-of-use asset' will be recognized at a value of €10 000 and the obligation under the lease of €10 000 will be shown as a liability.

The minimum lease payments amount to 20 × €650 = €13 000, the cash price was €10 000, hence the total finance charge will be €3000.

Remembering that this total finance charge should be allocated to accounting periods during the lease so as to produce a constant periodic rate of charge on the remaining balance of the obligation for each accounting period, then an appropriate method of allocation would be the actuarial method as follows:

	€
01.01.XI	
Dr Right-of-use asset	10 000
Cr Creditors (lessor)	10 000

Period	Capital sum at start of period €	Rental paid €	Capital sum during period €	Finance charge (2.95% per quarter)* €	Capital sum at end of period €
1/X1	10 000	650	9 350	276	9 626
2/X1	9 626	650	8 976	265	9 241
3/X1	9 241	650	8 591	254	8 845
4/X1	8 845	650	8 195	242	8 437
				1 037	
1/X2	8 437	650	7 787	230	8 017
2/X2	8 017	650	7 367	217	7 584
3/X2	7 584	650	6 934	205	7 139
4/X2	7 139	650	6 489	191	6 680
				843	
1/X3	6 680	650	6 030	178	6 208
2/X3	6 208	650	5 558	164	5 722
3/X3	5 722	650	5 072	150	5 222
4/X3	5 222	650	4 572	135	4 707
				627	
1/X4	4 707	650	4 057	120	4 177
2/X4	4 177	650	3 527	104	3 631
3/X4	3 631	650	2 981	88	3 069
4/X4	3 069	650	2 419	71	2 490
				383	

(Continued)

ACTIVITY 15.6 (Continued)

	Capital sum at start of period	Rental paid	Capital sum during period	Finance charge (2.95% per quarter)*	Capital sum at end of period
1/X5	2 490	650	1 840	54	1 894
2/X5	1 894	650	1 244	37	1 281
3/X5	1 281	650	631	19	650
4/X5	650	650	—	—	—
				110	
		13 000		3 000	

*As calculated using the actuarial method.

We can now apportion the annual rental of €2600 (i.e. 4 × €650) between a finance charge and a capital repayment as follows:

	Total rental €	Finance charge €	Capital repayments €
X1	2 600	1 037	1 563
X2	2 600	843	1 757
X3	2 600	627	1 973
X4	2 600	383	2 217
X5	2 600	110	2 490
	13 000	3 000	10 000
	(a)	(b)	(a)–(b)

We also need to calculate a depreciation charge. The period for depreciation will be seven years as this is the lesser of economic life (eight years) and lease period (seven years). The annual depreciation charge on a straight line basis is therefore:

$$€10\ 000 \div 7 = €1429$$

	Obligations under leases outstanding at start of year €		Capital repayment €		Obligations under leases outstanding at year end €
31.12.X1	10 000	–	1 563	=	8 437
31.12.X2	8 437	–	1 757	=	6 680
31.12.X3	6 680	–	1 973	=	4 707
31.12.X4	4 707	–	2 217	=	2 490
31.12.X5	2 490	–	2 490	=	—
31.12.X6					—
31.12.X7					—

The accounting entries in the lessee's books will be as follows, assuming the year end is 31 December. Profit and loss account charges:

	Depreciation	Finance charge	Total
X1	1 429	1 037	2 466
X2	1 429	843	2 272
X3	1 429	627	2 056
X4	1 429	383	1 812
X5	1 428	110	1 538
X6	1 428	—	1 428
X7	1 428	—	1 428
	10 000	3 000	13 000

Balance sheet entries
Assets held under leases – right-of-use-assets

	Cost €		Accumulated depreciation €		Net book value of assets held under leases €
31.12.X1	10 000	–	1 429	=	8 571
31.12.X2	10 000	–	2 858	=	7 142
31.12.X3	10 000	–	4 287	=	5 713
31.12.X4	10 000	–	5 716	=	4 284
31.12.X5	10 000	–	7 145	=	2 855
31.12.X6	10 000	–	8 574	=	1 426
31.12.X7	10 000	–	10 000	=	—

Obligations under leases (i.e. the capital element of future rentals payable)

If after the commencement date, the lease liability needs to be re-measured, than that amount shall be recognized as an adjustment to the right-to-use asset. Specific recognition and measurement elements are foreseen when lease contracts are modified (paras 44–46). In the accounts of the lessee, the single model proposed for all lease contracts ensures that the right-to-use asset is recorded among the assets on the balance sheet and that the consideration attached to it is presented under the liabilities on the balance sheet. In the income statement, we observe that the depreciation of the right-to-use asset and the interest expense need to be presented separately. The interest expense is a finance cost of the company. All repayments of the capital amount of the liability are included in the cash outflows from financing activities, and interest payments can also be included in the cash flows from operating activities from financing activities.

IFRS 16: LEASE ACCOUNTING BY LESSORS

IFRS 16 substantially carries forward the lessor accounting requirements of IAS 17. The lessor (supplier of the lease contract) will continue to classify a lease as a finance lease or an operating lease and will account for these two types of leases differently. Since the accounting treatment for lease contracts in the books of the lessor will depend on whether the lease contract is a finance lease or an operating lease, we first pay attention to the different recognition criteria for a finance lease and an operating lease. Thereafter, we discuss the accounting treatment of both leases in the books of the lessor.

Classification of leases into finance lease and operating lease

Para. 62 of IFRS 16 stipulates that a lease is classified as a finance lease if it transfers substantially all the risks and rewards incidental to ownership of an underlying asset. A lease is classified as an operating lease if it does not transfer substantially all the risks and rewards incidental to ownership of an underlying asset.

The Standard makes no attempt to define 'substantially all'. Some national GAAPs take a much more numerical approach to this question, for example requiring the present value of the minimum lease payments to be 90 per cent or more of the fair value of the asset at the inception of the lease (e.g. the US, Germany). Others, such as the UK, suggest that 90 per cent gives a 'presumption' of a finance lease, but make it clear that the determining factor is 'substantially all', not 90 per cent.

What IFRS 16 does do is give a number of examples of situations that 'would normally' (para. 63) or that 'could' (para. 64) point to a lease being properly classified as a finance lease.

Note that the lease classification is to be made at the inception of the lease.

1 The lease transfers ownership of the asset to the lessee by the end of the lease term.

2 The lessee has the option to purchase the asset at a price that is expected to be sufficiently lower than the fair value at the date the option becomes exercisable such that, at the inception of the lease, it is reasonably certain that the option will be exercised (i.e. a bargain purchase option exists).

3 The lease term is for the major part of the economic life of the asset even if title is not transferred.

4 At the inception of the lease, the present value of the minimum lease payments amounts to at least substantially all of the fair value of the leased asset.

5 The leased assets are of a specialized nature such that only the lessee can use them without major modifications being made.

6 If the lessee cancels the lease, the lessor's losses associated with the cancellation are borne by the lessee.

7 Gains or losses from the fluctuation in the fair value of the residual accrue to the lessee (e.g. in the form of a rent rebate equalling most of the residual sales proceeds at the end of the lease).

8 The lessee has the ability to continue the lease for a secondary period at a rent which is substantially lower than market rent (i.e. a bargain rental option).

ACTIVITY 15.7

Explain briefly in your own words why each of these situations (1–8, above) points towards a finance lease.

Activity feedback

Our suggested wording is as follows. Because, under situations 1 and 2 the lessee ends up with legal ownership, the validity of a finance lease classification is obvious. Situation 3 assumes, reasonably enough, that a major part of the economic life (measured in years) must imply transfer of substantially all the risks and rewards of ownership (measured in money). Situation 4 argues that payment of substantially all of the purchase price, after discounting to present value, must again imply that the substance of the transaction is a purchase on credit terms and situation 5 indicates by definition that only the lessee can derive 'rewards' from possession of the particular items. The remaining three situations (6, 7 and 8), while perhaps less definitive, all clearly point to the likelihood of the lessee being in the in-substance ownership position of deriving the benefits and 'paying the price'.

ACTIVITY 15.8

Costa uses three identical pieces of machinery in its factory. These were all acquired for use on the same date by the following means:

1 Machine 1 rented from Brava at a cost of €250 per month payable in advance and terminable at any time by either party.

2 Machine 2 rented from Blanca at a cost of eight half-yearly payments in advance of €1500.

3 Machine 3 rented from Sol at a cost of six half-yearly payments in advance of €1200.

The cash price of this type of machine is €8000 and its estimated life is four years. Are the three machines rented by operating or finance leases?

Activity feedback

Machine 1 is held on an operating lease as there is no transfer of the risks or rewards of ownership. Machine 2 involves a total payment of €12 000. In present value terms this will almost certainly be more than the €8000 fair value of the asset and therefore clearly more than 'substantially all of the fair value of the leased asset' (see our earlier situation 4). Machine 2 is therefore held on a finance lease. Machine 3 involves a total payment of €7200, the present value of which will be significantly less than €8000, so that situation 4 will not apply. The question is whether or not situation 3 applies – that is, whether or not three years is a 'major part of the economic life' of the machine (which is four years). Under US GAAP, which specifies an arbitrary 75 per cent ratio here, this would be a finance lease under situation 3 (in which circumstance the lease agreement would probably have been changed before signing in order to be a week or two shorter). Under UK GAAP, which focuses more exclusively on situation 4, machine 3 would be an operating lease on the information available. Our interpretation of IFRS 16 would be that situation 3 does not apply to machine 3, i.e. that this would be treated as an operating lease under IAS GAAP. This example illustrates well the practical difficulties which may arise in lease classification.

Over the years, a number of detailed requirements relating to leases of land and buildings were added. The essential point is that the land and buildings elements of a lease of land and buildings are considered separately for the purposes of lease classification. If title to both elements is expected to pass to the lessee at the end of the lease term, both elements are classified as a finance lease, whether analyzed as one lease or as two leases, unless it is clear from other features that the lease does not transfer substantially all risks and rewards incidental to ownership of one or both elements. When the land has an indefinite economic life, the land element is normally classified as an operating lease unless title is expected to pass to the lessee at the end of the lease term. The buildings element is classified as a finance or operating lease in accordance with the above specifications.

Separate measurement of the land and buildings' elements is not required when the lessee's interest in both land and buildings is classified as an investment property in accordance with IAS 40 and the fair value model is adopted. Detailed calculations are only required for this assessment if the classification of one or both elements is otherwise uncertain.

ACTIVITY 15.9

Do you think the use of numerical specifications in the finance/operating lease distinction is beneficial?

Activity feedback

The desirability of creating a precise numerical distinction is very much open to question. It has the obvious surface advantage of apparent objectivity and precision. However, the chosen figure is purely arbitrary. More importantly, the creation of a definitive numerical distinction allows, and arguably encourages, business entities to structure lease contracts so that they fall just marginally below the chosen criterion, even though the whole purpose may quite visibly be, in substance, to finance the 'purchase' of major resources by borrowing. The use of a fixed numerical boundary may substantially reduce subjectivity for the accountant and the auditor, but, at the same time, it may substantially increase creative accounting and the likelihood of misleading or unfair financial statements.

The discussion on the criteria of classifying a lease as a finance lease or an operating lease shows that accounting for lease contracts in the books of the lessee is now much more straightforward. However, the difference between finance lease and operating lease remains for the lessor.

ACCOUNTING AND REPORTING BY LESSORS: FINANCE LEASES

If we consider a lease contract from the viewpoint of the lessor, the substance is that the lessor has an amount receivable, much of it usually non-current, due from the lessee. In direct relation to the lease contract, the lessor has no other assets or liabilities. The amounts received from the lessee will embrace two elements – a repayment of 'loan' and an interest revenue.

Lessors should recognize at initial measurement assets held under a finance lease in their balance sheets and present them as a receivable at an amount equal to the net investment in the lease (para. 70). The net investment in the lease is equal to the gross investment in the lease discounted at the interest rate implicit in the lease. The gross investment in the lease is defined as the sum of the lease payments receivable by a lessor under a finance lease and any unguaranteed residual value accruing to the lessor. The determination of the 'net investment in the lease' is similar to the determination of the lease liability under lessee accounting. According to para. 70, at commencement date the lease payments to be included in the measurement of the net investment in the lease comprise the following payments:

- fixed payments, less any lease incentives payable
- variable lease payments that depend on an index or rate, initially measured using the index or rate as at commencement date
- any residual value guarantees provided to the lessor by the lessee, a party related to the lessee or a third party unrelated to the lessor that is financially capable of discharging the obligations under the guarantee

- the exercise of a purchase option if the lessee is reasonably certain to exercise that option

- payments of penalties for terminating the lease, if the lease term reflects the lessee exercising an option to terminate the lease.

Subsequent to the initial measurement, a lessor aims to allocate finance income over the lease term on a systematic and rational basis. This income allocation is based on a pattern reflecting a constant periodic return on the lessor's net investment outstanding in respect of the finance lease. Lease payments relating to the accounting period, excluding costs for services, are applied against the gross investment in the lease to reduce both the principal and the unearned finance income. In fact, the reporting for finance leases in the books of the lessor is almost the opposite of the treatment of a lease in the books of the lessee.

Estimated unguaranteed residual values used in computing the lessor's gross investment in a lease are reviewed regularly. If there has been a reduction in the estimated unguaranteed residual value, the income allocation over the lease term is reviewed and any reduction in respect of amounts already accrued is recognized immediately.

Initial direct costs are often incurred by lessors and include amounts such as commissions, legal fees and internal costs that are incremental and directly attributable to negotiating and arranging a lease. They exclude general overheads such as those incurred by a sales and marketing team. For finance leases other than those involving manufacturer or dealer lessors, initial direct costs are included in the initial measurement of the finance lease receivable and reduce the amount of income recognized over the lease term. The interest rate implicit in the lease is defined in such a way that the initial direct costs are included automatically in the finance lease receivable; there is no need to add them separately. Costs incurred by manufacturer or dealer lessors in connection with negotiating and arranging a lease are excluded from the definition of initial direct costs. As a result, they are excluded from the net investment in the lease and are recognized as an expense when the selling profit is recognized, which for a finance lease is normally at the commencement of the lease term.

An asset under a finance lease that is classified as held for sale (or included in a disposal group that is classified as held for sale) in accordance with IFRS 5, *Non-current Assets Held for Sale and Discontinued Operations*, shall be accounted for in accordance with that IFRS (see Chapter 14).

ACTIVITY 15.10

A lessor leases out an asset on terms which constitute a finance lease. The primary period is five years commencing 1 July 20X0, and the rental payable is €3000 per annum (in arrears). The lessee has the right to continue the lease after the five-year period referred to for an indefinite period at a nominal rent. The cash price of the asset in question at 1 July 20X0 was €11 372, and the rate of interest implicit in the lease is calculated as 10 per cent. Show the entries in the lessor's books.

Activity feedback

The finance charge is simply the difference between the fair value of the asset (in this case being the cash price of the new asset) and the rental payments over the lease period, i.e. of €15 000 less €11 372 or €3628.

Using the actuarial method with an interest rate of 10 per cent, the allocation of the finance charge will be as follows:

ACTIVITY 15.10 (*Continued*)

Year ended 30 June	Balance beginning €		Finance charge (10%) €		Rental €		Balance closing (in year end balance sheet) €
20X1	11 372	+	1 137	–	(3 000)	=	9 509
20X2	9 509	+	951	–	(3 000)	=	7 460
20X3	7 460	+	746	–	(3 000)	=	5 206
20X4	5 206	+	521	–	(3 000)	=	2 727
20X5	2 727	+	273	–	(3 000)	=	—
			€3 628		€15 000		

The relevant extracts from the income statements of the years in question will appear as follows:

	20X1	20X2	20X3	20X4	20X5	Total
Rentals	3 000	3 000	3 000	3 000	3 000	15 000
Less Capital repayments	1 863	2 049	2 254	2 479	2 727	11 372
Finance charges	1 137	951	746	521	273	3 628
Interest payable	(x)	(x)	(x)	(x)	(x)	
Overheads	(x)	(x)	(x)	(x)	(x)	

The relevant extracts from the balance sheets will appear as follows:

	Year ended June 30			
	20X1	20X2	20X3	20X4
Net investment in finance lease:				
Current	2 049	2 254	2 479	2 727
Non-current	7 460	5 206	2 727	—
	9 509	7 460	5 206	2 727

Finance leasing by manufacturers or dealers

The manufacturer or dealer may be the person who actually provides the asset as well as the finance. A finance lease of an asset by a manufacturer or dealer lessor gives rise to two types of income:

- the profit or loss equivalent to the profit or loss resulting from an outright sale of the asset being leased, at normal selling prices, reflecting any applicable volume or trade discounts
- the finance income over the lease term.

The sales revenue recorded at the commencement of a finance lease term by a manufacturer or dealer lessor is the fair value of the asset or, if lower, the present value of the minimum lease payments accruing to the lessor, computed at a commercial rate of interest (para. 71). The cost of sale recognized at the commencement of the lease term is the cost, or carrying amount if different, of the leased property less the present value of the unguaranteed residual value. The difference between the sales revenue and the cost of sale is the selling profit, which is recognized in accordance with the policy followed by the entity for sales, which will be consistent with IFRS 15, *Revenue from Contracts with Customers* (see Chapter 18).

Manufacturer or dealer lessors sometimes quote artificially low rates of interest in order to attract customers. The use of such a rate would result in an excessive portion of the total income from the transaction being recognized at the time of sale. If artificially low rates of interest are quoted, selling profit must be restricted to that which would apply if a commercial rate of interest were charged. Initial direct costs should be charged as expenses at the inception of the lease.

ACCOUNTING AND REPORTING BY LESSORS: OPERATING LEASES

Lessors should present assets subject to operating leases according to the nature of the asset. The asset subject to the operating lease is, in substance as well as in form, a non-current asset of the lessor. Such an asset should be depreciated on a basis consistent with the lessor's policy for similar assets. IAS 16, *Property, Plant and Equipment* or IAS 38, *Intangible Assets* will apply (see Chapters 12 and 13). In addition, IAS 36, *Impairment of Assets* will need to be considered (see Chapter 14).

Costs, including depreciation, incurred in earning the lease income are recognized as an expense. Lease income (excluding receipts for services provided such as insurance and maintenance) is recognized in income on a straight line basis over the lease term even if the receipts are not on such a basis, unless another systematic basis is more representative of the time pattern in which use benefit derived from the leased asset is diminished (para. 81). By definition, no element of selling profit can arise.

Initial direct costs incurred specifically to earn revenues from an operating lease are added to the carrying amount of the leased asset and recognized as an expense over the lease term on the same basis as the lease income.

ACTIVITY 15.11

Assume the asset considered in Activity 15.10 qualified as an operating lease for the lessor. How would the lessor account for this lease in their books?

Activity feedback

At the start of the contract, the lessor would recognize the asset in their books. We assume the lessor bought the asset for cash:

Dr Asset	11 372
Cr Cash	11 372

The lessor will depreciate the asset over the lifetime of the contract. The useful life of the asset is five years, which equals the term of the lease contract and we assume that the residual value at the end of the useful life is zero. The lessor will use a straight line depreciation method, so each year they will record the depreciation as follows:

Dr Depreciation expense 11 372 / 5 =	2 274
Cr Asset – accumulated depreciation	2 274

At the year end the lessor will also record the following in the books:

Dr Cash	3 000
Cr Lease income	3 000

Disclosure

The disclosure requirements are extensive for both lessors and lessees. Leases are a form of financial instrument and disclosure requirements relating to financial instruments generally will apply to leases. IFRS 16 specifies detailed additional requirements. These include details designed to give a clear indication of the timing of future cash movements and future expected expense and revenue outcomes.

SALE AND LEASEBACK TRANSACTIONS

A sale and leaseback transaction involves the sale of an asset by the vendor and the leasing of the same asset back to the vendor. The lease payment and the sale price are usually interdependent as they are negotiated as a package. The principle of substance over form is fundamental in the accounting treatment of a sale and lease back transaction. First of all the buyer-lessor as well as the seller-lessee shall account for the transfer of the contract in compliance with IFRS 16 (para. 98). So the seller-lessee recognizes the now leased asset on its balance sheet and the buyer-lessor will first assess whether the contract qualifies as a finance lease contract or an operating lease contract, and recognize and measure the asset accordingly.

This treatment only applies if the transfer of the asset can be qualified as a sale according to IFRS 15, *Revenue from Contracts with Customers*. A sale and leaseback is a means whereby the lessor provides finance to the lessee, with the asset as security. For this reason, it is not appropriate to regard an excess of sales proceeds over the carrying amount as income because, in substance, there has been no sale. The seller-lessee shall measure the right-of-use asset arising from the leaseback at the proportion of the previous carrying amount of the asset that relates to the right-of-use retained by the seller-lessee. Accordingly, the seller-lessee shall recognize only the amount of any gain or loss that relates to the rights transferred to the buyer-lessor. The buyer-lessor shall account for the purchase of the asset applying applicable standards, and for the lease applying the lessor accounting requirements in this Standard. If the fair value of the consideration for the sale of an asset does not equal the fair value of the asset, or if the payments for the lease are not at market rates, an entity shall make the following adjustments to measure the sale proceeds at fair value: any below-market terms shall be accounted for as a prepayment of lease payments; and any above-market terms shall be accounted for as additional financing provided by the buyer-lessor to the seller-lessee.

If the transfer of the asset cannot be qualified as a sale, the seller-lessee shall continue to recognize the transferred asset and shall recognize a financial liability equal to the transfer proceeds. It shall account for the financial liability applying IFRS 9 (para. 103a).The buyer-lessor shall not recognize the transferred asset and shall recognize a financial asset equal to the transfer proceeds. It shall account for the financial asset applying IFRS 9 (para. 103b).

IAS 17: LEASE ACCOUNTING AND REPORTING BY LESSEES

Because companies can use IAS 17 until 2019, we also discuss the accounting for lease contracts in the books of the lessee in compliance with IAS 17.

Under IAS 17, the lessee also needs to make a distinction between assets held under a finance lease contract and assets held under an operating lease contract. The difference between these two types of leasing contracts under IAS 17 is similar to the difference between these two types of lease contracts under IFRS 16. So for the definitions of a finance lease and an operating lease, we refer to the discussion in the section 'IFRS 16: Lease accounting by the lessor' in this chapter.

IAS 17: Accounting and reporting by lessees – finance leases

In the case of finance leases, the substance and financial reality are that the lessee acquires the economic benefits of the use of the leased asset for the major part of its economic life in return for entering into an obligation to pay for that right an amount approximating to the fair value of the asset and the related finance charge.

Lessees should recognize finance leases as assets and liabilities in their balance sheets at amounts equal at the inception of the lease to the fair value of the leased property or, if lower, at the present value of the minimum lease payments (IAS 17, para. 20). In calculating the present value of the minimum lease payments, the discount factor is the interest rate implicit in the lease, if this is practicable to determine; if not, the lessee's incremental borrowing rate should be used. At the inception of the lease, the asset and the liability for the future lease payments are recognized in the balance sheet at the same amounts.

During the lease term, each lease payment should be allocated between a reduction of the obligation and the finance charge so as to produce a constant periodic rate of interest on the remaining balance of the obligation over the amortization period, in the manner illustrated earlier. The asset initially recorded is depreciated in a manner consistent with that used by the lessee for owned assets.

You will notice that this treatment of finance lease contracts for the lessees under IAS 17 is similar to the accounting for lease contracts by the lessees under IFRS 16. So for an illustration of lease accounting for the lessee of assets held under finance lease contracts we can refer to Activity 15.6, which illustrates lessee accounting under IFRS 16 in this chapter.

IAS 17: Accounting and reporting by lessees – operating leases

Under IAS 17, lease payments under an operating lease can be recognized as an expense in the income statement on a straight line basis over the lease term, unless another systematic basis is more representative of the time pattern of user's benefit (para. 33). Note that the pattern of payment is not relevant. Contingent rent is not included in the original calculations. It therefore follows that the rental expense for any year will consist of:

(a) the minimum rent under the lease divided equally over the number of years plus

(b) any contingent rent relating to that year.

Activity 15.12 will make you familiar with accounting for operating leases in the books of the lessee under IAS 17.

ACTIVITY 15.12

If the lease in Activity 15.6 were to be treated as an operating lease, show the entries in the lessee's books.

Activity feedback

The only entries in the lessee's books would be the following annual entry:

Dr Rental expense (4 × 650)   2 600
Cr Creditors (4 × 650)   2 600

During the negotiation of a new operating lease or the renewal of an existing one, the lessee may receive incentives to sign the agreement from the lessor.

Incentives take many forms, including rent-free periods, reduced rents for a period of time, leasehold improvements on the lessor's account or a cash signing fee. IAS 17 is silent on this matter, but the Standing Interpretations Committee has clarified the position in SIC 15, *Incentives in an Operating Lease*. This requires that the benefit of such incentives be recognized at the inception of the lease and be treated as a reduction of rental expense over the term of the lease. The benefit is recognized on a straight line basis, unless another systematic basis is more representative of the time pattern in which benefit is derived from the leased asset.

SUMMARY

This chapter has explored the accounting measurement and disclosure problems relating to leases in the financial statements of both lessors and lessees. Up until 2019, most lessors and lessees will probably continue to account for assets under a leasing contract according to IAS 17. IFRS 16, which was issued on 13 January 2016, becomes effective from 2019 onwards. The major changes triggered by IFRS 16 are for the lessees of the lease contracts. IFRS 16 abolishes the distinction between a finance lease and an operating lease for lessees. IFRS 16 mandates lessees to recognize all assets under lease contracts on the balance sheet/statement of financial position. For the lessors, IFRS 16 entails far fewer changes. The distinction between a finance lease and an operating lease remains for the lessor under IFRS 16.

EXERCISES

Suggested answers to exercises marked ✓ are to be found in the Student online resources, with suggested answers to the remaining questions available in the Instructor online resources.

✓**1** From the perspective of a lessor, explain the theoretical distinction between finance leases and operating leases.

2 The need to account for lease transactions in a useful way proves that the principle of substance over form is essential. Discuss.

3 All unavoidable obligations relating to all lease contracts should be shown in the statement of financial position of published financial statements. Discuss.

4 The following figures have been extracted from the accounting records of Lavalamp on 30 September 20X3:

	$000	$000
Sales revenue		112 500
Cost of sales (note (i))	78 300	
Operating expenses	11 400	
Lease rentals (note (iii))	2 000	
Loan interest paid	1 000	
Dividends paid	1 200	
Leasehold (20 years) factory at cost (note (ii))	25 000	
Plant and equipment at cost	34 800	

	$000	$000
Depreciation 1 October 20X2 – leasehold		6 250
– plant and equipment		12 400
Accounts receivable	25 550	
Inventory – 30 September 20X3	21 800	
Cash and bank		4 000
Accounts payable		7 300
Ordinary shares of $1 each		20 000
Share premium		10 000
8% Loan note (issued in 20X0)		25 000
Accumulated profits – 1 October 20X2		3 600
	201 050	201 050

(i) Lavalamp has spent $6 million (included in the cost of sales) during the year developing and marketing a new brand of soft drink called Lavaflow. Of this amount, $1 million is for advertising and the remainder is the development costs. A firm of consultants has been reviewing the sales of the new product and based on this, it has valued the brand name of Lavaflow at $10 million and expects the life of the brand to be 10 years. Lavalamp wishes to capitalize the maximum amount of intangible assets permitted under International Financial Reporting Standards.

(ii) Due to a sharp increase in the values of properties, Lavalamp had its leasehold property revalued on 1 October 20X2 with the intention of restating its carrying value. A firm of surveyors contracted to value the property found that it had suffered some damage, which will cost $1.5 million to rectify. They gave a valuation of $24 million for the property on the assumption that the repairs are carried out. Lavalamp has informed Capitalrent, the owner of the property, of the repairs needed. Capitalrent has since sent their own surveyors to inspect the property and have informed Lavalamp that they believe the damage is due to the type of machinery being used in the building and accordingly have requested that Lavalamp pay for the repairs. Lavalamp has taken professional advice on this matter, which concluded that the property was not in good condition when it was originally leased, but the use of the plant is making the damage worse. Lavalamp has offered to share the cost of the repairs with Capitalrent, but it has not yet had a reply.

(iii) Included in the statement of profit and loss charge of $2 million for lease rentals is a payment of $600 000 in respect of a five-year lease of an item of plant (requiring ten payments in total). The payment was made on 1 April 20X3. The fair value of this plant at the date it was leased (1 April 20X3) was $5 million. Information obtained from the finance department confirms that this is a lease with an implicit interest rate of 10 per cent per annum. The company depreciates plant used under leases on a straight line basis (with time apportionment) over the life of the lease. Other plant is depreciated at 20 per cent per annum on cost. The remaining payments were confirmed as being payments in respect of short-term leases and leases of low-value assets.

(iv) A provision for income tax for the year to 30 September 20X3 of $3 470 000 is required.

(v) Lavalamp made and accounted for a rights issue on 1 October 20X2 of 1 new share for every 4 held at a price of $1.60 per share. The issue was fully subscribed.

Required:
Prepare the financial statements for the year to 30 September 20X3 for Lavalamp in accordance with International Financial Reporting Standards as far as the information permits. They should include:

(a) a statement of profit or loss and other comprehensive income

(b) a statement of changes in equity and

(c) a statement of financial position.

(ACCA, December 2003, adapted)

✓**5**   **(i)**   Different accounting practices for leases are an area that, without a robust accounting standard, can be used to manipulate a company's financial statements. IFRS 16, *Leases*, sets out the principles for the recognition, measurement, presentation and disclosure of leases for both parties to a contract, i.e. the customer ('lessee') and the supplier ('lessor').

Required:
(a)   Set out the reasons for issuing IFRS 16, *Leases*.

(b)   Briefly identify the differences between IFRS 16 and IAS 17.

(c)   Summarize the effect on the financial statements of a lessor treating a lease as an operating lease as opposed to a finance lease, and describe the factors that normally indicate a lease is a finance lease.

(ii)   Gemini leased an item of plant on 1 April 20X1 for a five-year period. Annual rentals in advance were $60 000. The cash price (fair value) of the asset on 1 April 20X1 was $260 000. The company's depreciation policy for this type of plant is 25 per cent per annum on the reducing balance basis.

Required:
Assuming the interest rate implicit in the lease is 8 per cent, prepare extracts of the financial statements of Gemini for the year to 31 March 20X3.

(ACCA, December 2003, adapted)

6   Havanna (seller-lessee) has decided to sell its main office building to a third party (buyer-lessor) and lease it back on a ten-year lease. The transfer of the office building qualifies as a sale under IFRS 15. The current fair value of the property is $5 million and the carrying value of the asset is $4.2 million. The market for property is very difficult in the locality and Havanna therefore requires guidance on the consequences of selling the office building at a range of prices. The following prices have been achieved in the market during the last few months for similar office buildings:

(a) $5.0 million

(b) $6.0 million

(c) $4.0 million.

Required:
(a)   Havanna (seller-lessee) would like advice on how to account for the sale and leaseback, with an explanation of the effect which the different selling prices would have on the financial statements, assuming that the fair value of the property is $5 million.

(ACCA, Corporate Reporting (International), December 2013, adapted)

(b)   Explain how the sale and leaseback should be accounted for in the financial statements of the third party (buyer-lessor).

(c)   Briefly outline the accounting treatment in the financial statements of the seller-lessee and buyer-lessor, if the transfer to the buyer-lessor did not qualify as a sale under IFRS 15.

INVENTORIES

16

OBJECTIVES After studying this chapter you should be able to:

- explain the composition of inventories

- describe five inventory cost assumptions, i.e. unit cost; first-in, first-out (FIFO); last-in, first-out (LIFO); weighted average and base inventory

- show the effect on annual profit and profit trends of using different inventory cost assumptions

- discuss IAS 2 requirements relating to inventories

- discuss IAS 41 requirements relating to agricultural produce

- identify the disclosure requirements of IAS 2 and IAS 41.

INTRODUCTION

Inventories, including work in progress, present several problems to the accountant. First, we have to determine the value of the inventories, taking into account that the number of items in inventory changes constantly over time. Second, when inventory items are sold, we need to determine the cost of goods sold and recognize the related revenue. For this purpose, we need to determine the revenue recognition (sale) point. The latter issue was solved in the international accounting standards by IAS 18, *Revenue*. In 2008, a revision of IAS 18 began and in 2015 the new Standard IFRS 15, *Revenue From Contracts with Customers* was published. From 2018 onwards, revenue resulting from contracts with customers will be determined by IFRS 15. The new Standard replaces IAS 18, *Revenue*, but also IAS 11, *Construction Contracts*. More information on the changes IFRS 15 will bring to the definition, measurement and valuation of contracts with customers is included in Chapter 18 of this book.

So the valuation of inventories requires care as it is a key determinant of cost of goods sold and therefore in determining net income. Commercial companies purchase goods with the purpose of reselling them to third party customers. Inventories of commercial companies mainly consist of goods purchased for resale. Industrial companies, on the other hand, produce the products which they sell to their customers. Within industrial companies, inventories consist of raw materials, work in progress and finished goods. Most industrial companies first produce goods and then face the commercial risk of finding a customer for those products. In a number of cases, however, a contract with the customer in which the revenue is determined has already been negotiated and signed before the start of the production of the goods, according to the specifications agreed with the customer. In these cases, companies do not bear a commercial risk after signing the contract with their customers; their main concern is to keep production costs under control. The latter types of contracts were, until 2017, called construction contracts and were treated in a separate Standard, namely IAS 11, *Construction Contracts*. From 2018 onwards, they are included in the scope of IFRS 15, *Revenue from Contracts with Customers*. All other types of inventories are dealt with in IAS 2, except agricultural produce, which at the point of harvest falls under the scope of IAS 41, *Agriculture*.

In this chapter, we consider first all types of inventories for which the firm still bears a commercial risk, so those inventories for which a contract with a customer already exists are excluded. We start with a discussion of all methods available for inventory valuation purposes, and thereafter we focus on those methods which are permitted according to IAS 2. Second, we discuss the valuation of agricultural produce.

INVENTORIES

Inventories include:

- goods or other assets purchased for resale
- consumable stores
- raw materials and components purchased for incorporation into products for sale
- products and services in intermediate stages of completion
- finished goods.

The 'cost' of each item at each of these stages is the key to determining the costs of goods sold and the value of inventory still left in the business – the closing inventory. Commercial companies will include in the valuation of the inventory mainly goods purchased for resale. Industrial companies in determining the cost of their inventory need to consider not only the cost of the raw materials, but also the cost of converting raw materials into products and services for sale. Thus, we need to include in our valuation of inventory the following items: costs of purchase and costs of conversion, including both direct and indirect overhead costs.

A moment's reflection will make it obvious that there are practical problems here. 'Direct' items should present no difficulties as figures can be related 'directly' by definition. But overhead allocation necessarily introduces assumptions and approximations: What is the normal level of activity taking one year with another? Can overheads be clearly classified according to function? Which other (non-production) overheads are 'attributable' to the present position and location of an item of inventory? So for any item of inventory that is not still in its original purchased state, it is a problem to determine the cost of a unit or even of a batch. Methods in common use include job, process, batch and standard costing. All include more or less arbitrary overhead allocations. We will elaborate on this issue when we discuss the IASB's definition of costs of conversion included in IAS 2.

Once we have found a figure for the unit cost per product 'in its present location and position', the next difficulty will arise when we have to select an appropriate method for calculating the related cost where several identical items have been purchased or made at different times and therefore at different unit costs.

Consider the following transactions for company Tradex.

Purchases:	January	10 units at €25 each
	February	15 units at €30 each
	April	20 units at €35 each
Sales:	March	15 units at €50 each
	May	18 units at €60 each

How do we calculate inventory, cost of sales and gross profit? There are several ways of doing this, based on different assumptions as to which unit has been sold or which unit is deemed to have been sold.

Inventory cost assumptions

Five possibilities are now discussed.

Unit cost. Here we assume that we know the actual physical units that have moved in or out. Each unit must be individually distinguishable, for example by serial numbers. In these circumstances, we simply add up the recorded costs of those units sold to give cost of sales and of those units left to give closing inventory. This needs no detailed illustration.

First-in, first-out (FIFO). Here it is assumed that the units moving out are the ones that have been in the longest (i.e. came in first). The units remaining will therefore be regarded as representing the latest units purchased. Work through the following Activity using the FIFO method.

ACTIVITY 16.1

Calculate the cost of sales and gross profit based on FIFO inventory cost assumptions from the data for company Tradex.

Activity feedback

			€	Cost of sales €
January	10 at €25	=	250	
February	15 at €30	=	450	
February total	25		700	
March	−10 at €25 (Jan.)	=	250	
	−5 at €30 (Feb.)	=	150	400
March total	10		300	
April	+20 at €35		700	
April total	30		1 000	
May	−10 at €30 (Feb.)	=	300	
	−8 at €35 (Apr.)	=	280	580
May total	12 at €35		420	
				980

Sales are 750 + 1080 = €1830
Purchases are 250 + 450 + 700
  = €1400

		Cost of sales €
	€	
This gives: Sales		1 830
Purchases	1 400	
Closing inventory	420	
Cost of sales		980
Gross profit		850

Last-in, first-out (LIFO). Here we reverse the assumption. We act as if the units moving out are the ones which came in most recently. The units remaining will therefore be regarded as representing the earliest units purchased. The following Activity demonstrates the use of LIFO, so make sure you complete the Activity carefully.

ACTIVITY 16.2

Calculate the cost of sales and gross profit based on LIFO inventory cost assumptions using the data for company Tradex.

Activity feedback

			€	Cost of sales €
January	10 at €25	=	250	
February	15 at €30 (Feb)	=	450	
February total	25	=	700	
March	−15 at €30 (Feb.)	=	450	450
March total	10 at €25	=	250	
April	+20 at €35	=	700	
April total	30		950	
May	−18 at €35 (Apr.)	=	630	630
May total	12 = 2 @ €35 and 10 @ €25	=	320	
				1 080
This gives:	Sales			1 830
	Purchases	1 400		
	Closing inventory	320		
	Cost of sales			1 080
	Gross profit			750

Weighted average. Here, we apply the average cost, weighted according to the different proportions at the different cost levels, to the items in inventory. Activity 16.3 shows the fully worked out method, involving continuous calculations. In practice, an average cost of purchases figure is often used rather than an average cost of inventory figure. This approximation reduces the need for calculation to a periodic, maybe even annual, requirement. Try the following Activity using the weighted average method.

ACTIVITY 16.3

Calculate the cost of sales and gross profit based on weighted average inventory cost assumptions for company Tradex.

Activity feedback

			Cost of sales	
			€	€
January	10 at €25	=	250	
February	15 at €30	=	450	
February total	25 at €28*	=	700	
March	−15 at €30 (Feb.)		420	450
March total	10 at €28	=	280	
April	+20 at €35	=	700	
April total	30 at €32.67**		980	
May	−18 at €32.67	=	588	588
May total	12 at €32.67		392	
				1 008

This gives:		€	Cost of sales €
	Sales		1 830
	Purchases	1 400	
	Closing inventory	392	
	Cost of sales		1 008
	Gross profit		822

Workings:

This gives:

$$*28 = \frac{(10 \times 25) + (15 \times 30)}{(10 + 15)}$$

$$**32.67 = \frac{(10 \times 28) + (20 \times 35)}{(10 + 20)}$$

Base inventory. This approach is based on the argument that a certain minimum level of inventory is necessary in order to remain in business at all. Thus, it can be argued that some of the inventory viewed in the aggregate is not really available for sale and should therefore be regarded as a fixed asset. This minimum level defined by management remains at its original cost and the remainder of the inventory above this level is treated as inventory by one of the other methods. In our example, the minimum level might be ten units.

ACTIVITY 16.4

Calculate the cost of sales and gross profit based on a minimum inventory level of ten units and using FIFO for company Tradex.

Activity feedback

January purchase of base inventory: 10 at €25 = €250

			€	Cost of sales €
February	15 at €25	=	450	
March	−15 at €30	=	450	450
March total	0		0	
April	+20 at €35	=	700	
April total	20	=	700	
May	−18 at €35	=	630	630
May total	2 at €35	=	70	
				1 080

This gives:		€	Cost of sales €
	Sales		1 830
	Purchases	1 150	
	Closing inventory	70	
	Cost of sales		1 080
	Gross profit		750

In this particular case, the gross profit is the same with this method (base inventory + FIFO) as with LIFO. Can you work out why? This will not generally be the case.

Which approach?

So, which approach or approaches are preferable or acceptable?

In selecting a method, management presumably must exercise judgement to ensure that the methods chosen provide the fairest practicable approximation to cost. If standard costs are used to value inventory, they will need to be reviewed frequently to ensure that they bear a reasonable relationship to actual costs incurred during the period. Methods such as base inventory and LIFO often result in inventories being stated in the statement of financial position at amounts that bear little relationship to recent cost levels. When this happens, not only can the presentation of current assets be misleading, but there also is potential distortion of subsequent results if inventory levels reduce and out of date costs are drawn into the statement of comprehensive income. However, the method of arriving at cost by applying the FIFO method is also not necessarily the same as actual cost and, in times of rising prices, will result in the taking of a profit which has not been realized. To amplify, consider the cost of sales figure for the May sales in the earlier FIFO and LIFO calculations. Is it preferable to match an April cost level against an April revenue (LIFO) or, partially at least, to match a February cost level against an April revenue level (FIFO)? From a statement of financial position viewpoint, the criticism of LIFO perhaps makes sense. The statement of financial position total under both LIFO and base inventory is likely to be badly out of date. Applying the latest purchase price level to all units, sometimes called next-in, first-out (NIFO), could also be rejected in principle for the same reason as LIFO.

Before we consider IAS 2 and how it attempts to answer this puzzle, there is another problem to consider. In the Activities so far, we have virtually been able to match an inventory item with its sale, but this is not generally the case.

INVENTORY SYSTEMS

Periodic systems

Within this system, inventory is determined by a physical count at a specific date. As long as the count is made frequently enough for reporting purposes, it is not necessary to maintain extensive inventory records. The inventory shown in the statement of financial position is determined by the physical count and is priced in accordance with the inventory method used. The net charge between the beginning and ending inventories enters into the computation of costs of goods sold.

Perpetual system

In a perpetual system, inventory records are maintained and updated continuously as items are purchased and sold. The system has the advantage of providing inventory information on a timely basis, but requires the maintenance of a full set of inventory records. Audit practice will certainly require that a physical check of perpetual inventory records be made periodically.

IAS REQUIREMENTS FOR INVENTORY UNDER THE SCOPE OF IAS 2

It is now quite clear that the calculation of the appropriate inventory at 'cost' figure is by no means clear-cut. Assumptions in two respects have to be made. First, the determination of the cost of the unit and, second, the matching of these costs with the items sold. With regard to the first item, IAS 2 states that 'Inventories shall be measured at the lower of cost and net realizable value' (NRV) (para. 9). With regard to the second item, namely the matching issue, IAS 2 allows three of the five methods discussed earlier, namely the unit cost, FIFO and weighted average. In certain circumstances, the retail method is allowed, which we discuss later in this chapter. In the sections below, we concentrate first on the determination of the unit cost of an item in inventory, and then we look at inventory valuation methods allowed by IAS 2. We start the discussion with a review of the scope of IAS 2 and the definitions provided in the Standard for a number of concepts.

Definitions

In para. 6 of IAS 2, inventories are defined as assets:

(a) held for sale in the ordinary course of the business

(b) in the process of production for such sale or

(c) in the form of materials or supplies to be consumed in the production process or in the rendering of services.

Excluded from the scope of IAS 2 are construction contracts, financial instruments and agricultural produce at the point of harvest. With regard to the scope of IAS 2, the text of the Standard (para. 3) mentions further that the Standard does not apply to producers of agricultural and forest products, agricultural produce after harvest, and minerals and mineral products, to the extent that they are measured at NRV in accordance with well-established practices in those industries. Neither does the Standard apply to commodity broker-traders who measure their inventories at fair value less costs to sell. In both cases, changes in fair values are recognized in profit or loss in the period of change.

IAS 2 (para. 6) defines the concepts of NRV and fair value. *Net realizable value* is defined as the estimated selling price in the ordinary course of business less the estimated costs of completion and the estimated costs necessary to make the sale. *Fair value* is defined as the amount for which an asset could be exchanged, or a liability settled, between knowledgeable, willing parties in an arm's-length transaction.

Paragraph 8 of IAS 2 provides a number of examples of items which will be recorded under inventories. For example, merchandise purchased by a retailer and held for resale or land and other property held for resale. They also encompass finished goods produced or work in progress being produced by the entity and include materials and supplies awaiting use in the production process. In the case of a service provider, inventories include the costs of the service for which the entity has not yet recognized the related revenue.

IAS 2 states that inventories must be measured at the lower of cost and NRV. IAS 2 defines (para. 10) the concept of cost of inventories as follows: 'The cost of inventories shall comprise all costs of purchase, costs of conversion and other costs incurred in bringing the inventories to their present location and condition'. The definition of NRV is provided above (see the discussion on the scope of IAS 2). It is obvious that for each separate item of inventory we need to determine both the cost and the NRV.

The separate item point is significant and this is shown in Activity 16.5.

ACTIVITY 16.5

An entity has three products in its inventory with values as follows:

Product	Cost	NRV
A	10	12
B	11	15
C	12	9
Total	33	36

At what value should the inventory be stated in the statement of financial position in accordance with IAS 2?

Activity feedback

If the inventory is not separated into each type, then we would value at the lower of cost of 33 and NRV of 36. The answer is 33. However, IAS 2 requires us to value each type of inventory separately, and therefore the lower in each case is A 10, B 11 and C 9, giving us an inventory valuation of 30.

In the next section, we concentrate on the concept of 'cost of inventory' for industrial companies. In industrial companies, the calculation of the unit cost involves many more decisions in order to arrive at the unit cost which can be used for financial reporting purposes.

COST OF INVENTORY

IAS 2 gives guidance on the costs of the different elements included in the definition of the cost of inventories as follows (see para. 10: 11–18). The cost of inventories should include: all costs of purchase, costs of conversion and other costs incurred in bringing the inventories to their present location and condition. Further amplification of cost is given in para. 11 as follows:

> The costs of purchase of inventories comprise the purchase price, import duties and other taxes (other than those subsequently recoverable by the entity from the taxing authority) and transport, handling and other costs directly attributable to the acquisition of finished goods, materials and services. Trade discounts, rebates and other similar items are deducted in determining the costs of purchase.

It must be noted here that IAS 2 does not permit exchange differences arising directly on the recent acquisition of inventories invoiced in a foreign currency to be included in the costs of purchase of inventories. This change is because the improved IAS 21 has eliminated the allowed alternative treatment of capitalizing certain exchange differences. The cost of purchase applies to the inventories in commercial companies as well as to all materials used in the production process of industrial companies and materials awaiting use in the production process.

The item costs of conversion are explained in paras 12, 13 and 14 of IAS 2, indicating the associated problems. Costs of conversion include direct labour, the systematic allocation of fixed production overheads (e.g. depreciation and maintenance charges), and the allocation of variable production overheads (e.g. indirect materials and labour). (Remember here that fixed overheads are those indirect costs of production that remain relatively constant regardless of the volume of production, whereas variable overheads are those that vary directly or nearly with the volume of production.) IAS 2 prescribes a different allocation procedure for fixed and variable overheads. Variable overheads are allocated to the units produced based on the actual use of production facilities.

The allocation of fixed overheads is based on the normal capacity of production facilities, taking into account the loss of capacity resulting from planned maintenance. However, IAS 2 also proposes two other treatments for the allocation of fixed overhead costs. The actual level of production may be used to allocate the fixed overheads if it approximates to the normal capacity. If the production is lower than the normal production capacity, the amount of unallocated overhead will then be treated as an expense in the period in which it is incurred. When the production is higher than the normal capacity, the costs of the products should still be measured at their normal production cost. Variable production overheads are allocated to each unit of production on the basis of the actual use of the production facilities. Where joint products are concerned, a rational basis for allocation of costs of conversion between them needs to be found.

The Standard suggests the use of relative sale value or gross contribution margin as rational and consistent bases. This can be seen as somewhat arbitrary and subjective but is, nevertheless, at least a consistent, if not entirely logical, method for dealing with a difficult issue.

We now focus on the definition of the third element included in the cost of conversion, namely other costs included in the concept 'cost of inventories'. According to para. 15, other costs are included in inventory only to the extent that they are incurred in bringing the inventories to their present location and condition. Paragraph 16 lists a number of items which are excluded from the cost of inventories and, as a result, they should be recognized as expenses in the period in which they are incurred:

- abnormal amounts of wasted materials, labour and other production costs
- storage costs, unless those costs are necessary in the production process before a further production stage
- administrative overheads that do not contribute to bringing inventories to their present location and condition and
- selling costs.

A good example of storage costs that can be included in the cost of inventory are those involved in the ageing of whisky. As ageing is essential to the production of whisky, whatever storage costs are incurred can be capitalized to the cost of inventory. Work through the following Activities carefully.

ACTIVITY 16.6

Determine the valuation of inventory items A and B from the following data:

	A	B
Direct labour charge per item	2	4

Fixed production overheads total €50 000 and normal capacity of production is 5200 for product A and 10 200 for product B, but this is reduced by 200 for A and 200 for B for planned maintenance. The target of production was 6000 for A and 12 000 for B. Variable production overheads are calculated as €10 000 in total and are to be allocated on a machine hour basis. Each A item takes two hours of machine time and each B item one hour.

Activity feedback

Fixed production overheads will be charged over 5000 A and 10 000 B, as normal capacity is after planned maintenance allowance. The target of production is irrelevant in the calculation unless this high production level is actually achieved, in which case the fixed overheads to each unit will be decreased so as not to measure the item above cost.

	A	B
Direct labour	2.0	4.0
Fixed overheads (allocated in ratio of 1:2 and on number of items)	2.0	4.0
Variable overheads (0.5 per hour)	1.0	0.5
	5.0	8.5

ACTIVITY 16.7

Calculate the cost of inventories in accordance with IAS 2 using the following data relating to Unipoly Company for the year ended 31 May 20X7.

	€
Direct materials cost of can opener per unit	1
Direct labour cost of can opener unit	1
Other direct costs of can opener unit	1
Production overheads per year	600 000
Administration overheads per year	200 000
Selling overheads per year	300 000
Interest payments per year	100 000

There were 250 000 units in finished goods at the year end. You may assume that there were no finished goods at the start of the year and that there was no work in progress. The normal annual level of production is 750 000 can openers, but in the year ended 31 May 20X7 only 450 000 were produced because of a labour dispute.

Activity feedback
The direct costs of the inventory are straightforward to calculate as follows:

	€
250 000 units at €1 direct material cost	250 000
250 000 units at €1 direct labour cost	250 000
250 000 units at direct €1 cost	250 000
	750 000

IAS 2 permits the inclusion of only production overheads in the valuation of inventories and therefore the administration, selling and interest costs (if interest costs meet the requirements identified in IAS 23, Borrowing Costs, see Chapter 13) are not relevant here.

To allocate production overhead, the normal production capacity will be used as an allocation basis (600 000/750 000) = €0.8 per unit. In order to calculate the overhead which will be assigned to the inventory, we multiply the overhead cost per unit by the number of units in inventory (0.8 x 250 000 = 200 000). The abnormal costs associated with the labour dispute will be charged as an expense in the period in which they are incurred. So we arrive at a cost of finished inventory of:

Cost of finished inventory = €950 000

ACTIVITY 16.8

Which of the following costs can be included in the cost of inventory in accordance with IAS 2? Reference to paras 9–20 of IAS 2 will help in completing this Activity.

- discounts on purchase price
- travel expenses of buyers
- import duties
- transport insurance
- commission and brokerage costs
- storage costs after receiving materials that are necessary in the production process
- salaries of sales department
- warranty cost
- research for new products
- audit and tax consultation fees.

Activity feedback

Discounts on purchase price	yes
Travel expenses of buyers	no
Import duties	yes
Transport insurance	yes
Commission and brokerage costs	yes
Storage costs after receiving materials that are necessary in the production process	yes
Salaries of sales department	no
Warranty cost	no
Research for new products	no
Audit and tax consultation fees	no

Techniques for the measurement of the cost of inventories

For companies producing products and services, IAS 2 permits the use of the standard cost method where normal levels of materials, supplies, labour, efficiency and capacity utilization will be used to calculate a standard cost. These standard costs have to be reviewed regularly if this method is used.

IAS 2 also permits the use of the retail method. The retail method is generally used in the retail industry where there are large numbers of rapidly changing items that have similar margins. The cost of the inventory is determined by reducing the sales value of the inventory by the appropriate gross profit margin. Problems occur with this method when a retailer deals in products of widely differing profit margins or discounts slow moving items.

Once the cost of inventories is determined, the following cost formulas are available to determine the value of the costs of goods sold. In the introduction to this chapter, we explained that five methods or cost formulas are available in order to determine the value of the inventory and the costs of goods sold.

Cost formulas for the determination of the value of the inventory and the costs of goods sold

IAS 2 distinguishes between interchangeable goods and non-interchangeable goods. Items that are not ordinarily interchangeable and goods or services produced and segregated for specific projects should be assigned by using specific identification of their individual costs (para. 23). This approach equates to the unit cost method described in the introductory section.

For all other types of inventories, IAS 2 advocates the use of FIFO or the weighted average cost formula. We note that IAS 2 does not permit the use of LIFO.

Remember the use of LIFO in a period of rising costs will reduce profits and value inventory on the statement of financial position at older costs, whereas FIFO shows inventory on the statement of financial position at newer costs and what many would regard as a more relevant cost.

The elimination of LIFO, however, does not rule out specific cost methods that reflect inventory flows that are similar to LIFO. For example, when inventory bins of coal, cement, etc. are replenished by 'topping up', then LIFO may reflect the actual physical flow of inventories.

When inventories are sold, the carrying amount of those inventories shall be recognized as an expense in the period in which the related revenue is recognized. The closing inventory will appear on the statement of financial position at the lower of cost or NRV.

Net realizable value

In order to determine the NRV, the company deducts from the selling price in the ordinary course of the business the estimated costs of completion and the estimated costs necessary to make the sale (= marketing, selling and distribution costs). When the cost of the inventory will not be recoverable due to damage, the cost of the inventory will be written down to NRV. The amount of any write-down of inventories to NRV and all losses of inventories shall be recognized as an expense in the period in which the write-down or loss occurs. The amount of any reversal of any write-down of inventories, arising from an increase in the NRV, shall be recognized in the period in which the reversal occurs.

Disclosure requirements

The disclosure requirements of IAS 2 are similar to the general type of information requirements for other types of assets. The user of the financial statements needs to be informed about the accounting policies adopted in measuring inventories, including the cost formulas used. The carrying amount of inventories has to be disclosed and classified according to how they are measured (cost or fair value less costs to sell). The company also needs to mention the amounts written down on the inventories and the costs of inventories recognized as an expense during the period. If there is a reversal of a write-down, users need to be informed about this as well. Below you will find as illustration Note 12 from the Annual Report of Unilever 2014.

REAL WORLD ILLUSTRATION

INVENTORIES

Inventories are valued at the lower of weighted average cost and net realisable value. Cost comprises direct costs and, where appropriate, a proportion of attributable production overheads. Net realisable value is the estimated selling price less the estimated costs necessary to make the sale.

Inventories with a value of €76 million (2013: €204 million) are carried at net realisable value, this being lower than cost. During 2014, €126 million (2013: €198 million) was charged to the income statement for damaged, obsolete and lost inventories. In 2014, €120 million (2013: €155 million) was utilised or released to the income statement from inventory provisions taken in earlier years.

Inventories	€ million 2014	€ million 2013
Raw materials and consumables	1,364	1,286
Finished goods and goods for resale	2,804	2,651
	4,168	3,937

In the notes to the Financial Statements of the adidas Group, we find the following information on the valuation rules used to measure their inventories.

REAL WORLD ILLUSTRATION

Merchandise and finished products are valued at the lower of cost or net realizable value, which is the estimated selling price in the ordinary course of business less the estimated costs of completion and the estimated costs necessary to make the sale. Costs are determined using a standard valuation method: the 'average cost method'. Costs of finished products include costs of raw materials, direct labour and the components of the manufacturing overheads which can be reasonably attributed. The allocation of overheads is based on the planned average utilization. The net realizable value allowances are computed consistently throughout the Group based on the age and expected future sales of the items on hand.

REQUIREMENTS FOR INVENTORIES UNDER THE SCOPE OF IAS 41

Companies engaged in agricultural activity (see also Chapter 12) manage the biological transformation and harvest of biological assets for sale or conversion into agricultural produce or into additional biological assets. Biological produce can be sold immediately after harvest without any further processing or can be sold after further processing. Biological produce at harvest is recognized and measured according to IAS 41, *Agriculture*. When biological produce is further processed after harvest, it will be recognized and measured according to IAS 2, *Inventories*.

Recognition and measurement

The recognition criteria for biological produce are the traditional criteria employed to recognize assets. They are controllability, future economic benefits and reliable measurement. IAS 41 (para. 13) states that agricultural produce harvested from an entity's biological assets shall be measured at its fair value less costs to sell at the point of harvest. So when agricultural produce right after harvest is present in the company, it shall be presented on the balance sheet at fair value less costs to sell, whereas other inventories are presented at the lower of cost and NRV. When agricultural produce is further processed, the fair value will be augmented with the costs attributable to the further processing of the agricultural produce (e.g. the cost of wine is equal to the fair value of the grapes at harvest augmented with the costs of processing the grapes into wine).

Disclosure

Most disclosure requirements included in IAS 41 relate to biological assets. Only the change in fair value of the biological produce needs to be disclosed.

Most important for agricultural produce is to determine its fair value at the point of harvest. In addition, it is important to know which Standard needs to be applied for the recognition and measurement of the assets. Activity 16.9 sheds further light on the scope of the different Standards.

ACTIVITY 16.9

Choose for the assets below the Standard that will need to be applied in order to determine their recognition and measurement.

- pig carcasses in a meat processing company
- pig carcasses in a pig farm
- salmon (no longer alive) in an ocean fishing company
- salmon (no longer alive) in a fish farm
- olives in an olive plantation
- olives in an oil processing plant
- olive trees in an olive plantation
- trees (harvested) in a company specialized in cleaning forests to create farm land
- trees (harvested) in a furniture company
- trees (harvested) on a plantation forest.

Activity feedback

(1) IAS 2, (2) IAS 41, (3) IAS 2, (4) IAS 41, (5) IAS 41, (6) IAS 2, (7) IAS 16 since the olive tree is a bearer plant, (8) IAS 2 because the company is not involved in agricultural activity as defined in IAS 41, (9) IAS 2, (10) IAS 41.

SUMMARY

This chapter has defined inventories and agricultural produce and identified the accounting requirements for them in accordance with IAS 2. Valuation of inventories using the unit cost, FIFO, LIFO, weighted average and base inventory are all possible, but all lead to a different profit figure and asset figure. Remember, the improved IAS 2 has now eliminated the use of LIFO. We also paid attention to agricultural produce (IAS 41).

It should be clear to you that valuation of inventories is by no means a straightforward task and it requires management to make several judgements.

EXERCISES

Suggested answers to exercises marked ✓ are to be found in the Student online resources, with suggested answers to the remaining questions available in the Instructor online resources.

1 P Forte commences business on 1 January buying and selling pianos. He sells two standard types, upright and grand, and his transactions for the year are given in the table below.

| | Upright | | Grand | |
	Buy	Sell	Buy	Sell
1 January	4 at €400		2 at €600	
31 March		1 at €600		
30 April	1 at €350		1 at €700	
30 June		1 at €600		1 at €1 000
31 July	2 at €300		1 at €800	
30 September		3 at €500		2 at €1 100
30 November	1 at €250		1 at €900	

You observe that the cost to P Forte of the pianos is changed on 1 April, 1 July and 1 October and will not change again until 1 January following.

Required:

(a) Prepare a statement showing gross profit and closing inventory valuation separately for each type of piano, under each of the following assumptions:

(i) FIFO

(ii) weighted average

(b) At a time of rising prices (i.e. using the grand pianos as an example), comment on the usefulness of each of the methods.

2 Using any information you wish from Exercise 1, illustrate and discuss the effects on the statement of profit or loss and other comprehensive income and statement of financial position from using the different cost assumptions available to value closing inventory.

3 Critically appraise the different cost assumptions underlying the valuation of closing inventory.

4 Discuss the solution offered by IAS 2 to the valuation of inventories.

5 The inventory of Base at 30 September 200X was valued at cost €28.5 million. This included €4.5 million of slow moving inventory that Base had been trying to sell to another retailer. The best price Base has been offered for this slow moving inventory is €2 million.

Required:

Identify how Base should record its inventory in its year end accounts at 30 September 200X.

6 Gear Software, a public limited company, develops and sells computer games software. The revenue of Gear Software for the year ended 31 May 20X3 is $5 million, the statement of financial position total is $4 million, and it has 40 employees.

Required:

The directors of Gear Software require advice on the following matter which is relevant to the financial statements for the year ended 31 May 20X3.

Gear Software has two cost centres relating to the development and sale of the computer games. The indirect overhead costs attributable to the two cost centres were allocated in the year to 31 May 20X2 in the ratio 60:40 respectively. Also, in that financial year the direct labour costs and attributable overhead costs incurred on the development of original games software were carried forward as work in progress and included with the statement of financial position total for inventory of computer games. Inventory of computer games includes directly attributable overheads. In the year to 31 May 20X3, Gear Software has allocated indirect overhead costs in the ratio 50:50 to the two cost centres and has written off the direct labour and overhead costs incurred on the development of the games to the statement of profit or loss and other comprehensive income. Gear Software has stated that it cannot quantify the effect of this write-off on the current year's statement of profit or loss and other comprehensive income. Further, it proposes to show the overhead costs relating to the sale of computer games within distribution costs. In prior years, these costs were shown in cost of sales.

(ACCA, June 2003, adapted)

7   At 30 September 20X3, Bowtock had included in its draft statement of financial position inventory of $250 000 valued at cost. Up to 5 November 20X3, Bowtock had sold $100 000 of this inventory for $150 000. On this date, new government legislation (enacted after the year end) came into force, which meant that the unsold inventory could no longer be marketed and was worthless.

Required:
Assuming the amounts are material, state how the information above should be reflected in the financial statements of Bowtock for the year ended 30 September 20X3.

(ACCA, December 2003, adapted)

ACCOUNTING FOR FINANCIAL INSTRUMENTS

17

OBJECTIVES After studying this chapter you should be able to:

- describe financial instruments

- identify the need to account for them

- outline the history of accounting for financial instruments

- define the scope of IFRS regarding financial instruments

- identify and explain the requirements of the IASB for financial instruments

- critically appraise these requirements

- be able to distinguish between financial liabilities and equity

- understand the issues of recognition and derecognition and of measuring different categories of financial assets and liabilities

- identify the need for hedge accounting and understand the basic techniques

- identify and appraise current international accounting requirements for insurance contracts – IFRS 4.

INTRODUCTION

There is a long history on the regulation of accounting for financial instruments. We will discuss that history below, but in this chapter, we will mainly focus on the IFRS that will be applicable from 2018 onwards. That is, we will primarily discuss IFRS 9, but, where relevant, we will also refer to its predecessor, IAS 39. Other financial instruments Standards are IAS 32 and IFRS 7, which have already been effective for a longer time and which are also discussed in this chapter. This chapter also deals with IFRS 4, *Insurance Contracts*.

Financial instruments include such things as swaps (interest rate swaps, credit default swaps, foreign currency swaps), options and forwards, but also more regular items such as bonds, receivables, loans and shares. They have become more complex over the past 20 years. This complexity has led to difficulties in recognizing, measuring, presenting and disclosure of such instruments in the financial statements of an entity. The real stumbling block in the entire debate on financial instruments is around the issue of whether the financial assets and liabilities involved should be valued at fair value.

SHORT HISTORY OF ACCOUNTING FOR FINANCIAL INSTRUMENTS

This section is a background section on the long history of regulating the accounting for financial instruments. You can easily skip this section without having difficulties understanding the rest of the chapter.

The start of the IASC work

The IASC's work on financial instruments began in 1988 following an OECD symposium on the issue. Even at this early stage, the most difficult issue to deal with concerned the valuation of the instruments and whether this should be at fair value or not. The first Draft Statement of Principle (DSOP) was issued in March 1990 and this advocated fair value measurement for financial assets and liabilities held for trading, but not for others. The DSOP was approved by the IASC in November 1990.

ED 40 was issued in June 1991. It advocated a benchmark treatment consisting of fair value for trading items and cost for others, and an allowed alternative of fair value for all items: a compromise solution.

The IASC published a revised Exposure Draft (ED) in 1994 and, after consultation with standard-setting bodies in 20 countries, the IASC decided to split its work on financial instruments into two stages.

IAS 32, IAS 39 and IFRS 7

The first stage was to deal with presentation and disclosure and the second with recognition and measurement. IAS 32 on presentation and disclosure was published in March 1995. IAS 39, *Financial Instruments: Recognition and Measurement*, was issued in 1998 and revised in 2000, and it was seen as an interim solution to accounting for financial instruments. Its publication was driven by the need for the IASB to have a set of core Standards available for approval by IOSCO by early 1999. The Standard was further revised as part of the improvement project and it is this extant version of 2004 that we consider in this chapter, together with its various amendments up to March 2009.

The complexity of the whole area was further demonstrated by the fact that the IASB decided there was a need to issue guidance on IAS 39 in the form of questions and answers. This guidance was included in a publication from the IASB entitled *Accounting for Financial Instruments – Standards, Interpretations and Implementation Guidance*. Several SICs and IFRICs have also been issued on financial instruments. IAS 32, *Financial Instruments: Disclosure and Presentation*, was, as with IAS 39, revised in December 2003, but IAS 32 has now been split into two Standards:

- IAS 32, *Financial Instruments: Presentation*
- IFRS 7, *Financial Instruments: Disclosures.*

Afterwards, several amendments were made, among which the publication in February 2008 of *Puttable Financial Instruments and Obligations Arising on Liquidation* and in December 2011 on *Offsetting Financial Assets and Financial Liabilities.*

In addition to these changes, there was also a very complex situation as regards the adoption of IAS 39 by the EU. In November 2004 the European Commission adopted what became known as a 'carve-out' version of IAS 39. This 'carve-out' version prohibited the use of the fair value option for financial liabilities. The amendment to IAS 39 in June 2005 has dealt with the fair value option, but there still remain some differences between the full IAS 39 and the 'carve-out' version endorsed by the EU.

IFRS 9, Financial Instruments

The IASB had started a project to replace IAS 39 by IFRS 9 in 2009. The objective of this project was to improve the decision usefulness of financial instruments for users by simplifying the classification and measurement requirements for financial instruments and thereby replace IAS 39.

The project consisted of three main phases:

- Phase 1 – Classification and measurement: In November 2009, the IASB published the first part of IFRS 9, *Financial Instruments*, which deals with the classification and measurement of financial assets only. In October 2010 IFRS 9 was expanded to the measurement of financial liabilities and to derecognition of financial assets and liabilities. An ED on Limited Amendments of IFRS 9 on classification and measurement was published in November 2012.

- Phase 2 – Impairment methodology: An ED was issued in respect of this phase in November 2009, *Financial Instruments: Amortized Cost and Impairment.* A supplement was issued in January 2011 and a revised ED in March 2013, *Financial Instruments: Expected Credit Losses.* The final version was published in July 2014 as part of the full version of IFRS 9.

- Phase 3 – Hedge accounting: An ED was issued on *Hedge Accounting* in December 2010 and a final version in November 2013. IFRS 9 only regulates general hedge accounting. There is a separate split-off project on macro-hedge accounting (also called portfolio hedge accounting for interest rate risk).

The final version of IFRS 9 was published in July 2014. IFRS 9 is effective from 1 January 2018 on, with early adoption permitted. At the time of writing, IFRS 9 has not been endorsed by the EU, but endorsement is generally expected.

PROBLEMS IDENTIFIED

Information available

The growth in the variety of financial instruments available over the past 20 years had given rise to a lack of understanding by users of financial statements of the significance of such instruments on an entity's financial performance, position and cash flows. Many of the instruments were traditionally not recognized in the statement of financial position, and the user was unable to assess the effect of these unless there was adequate presentation and disclosure. In addition, an entity can significantly change its financial risk profile by using financial instruments that result in excessive gains or losses depending on whether prices of such instruments move in favour of or against the entity.

Measurement practice

Measuring financial instruments at historical cost does not always provide the most relevant or consistent information for users. Throughout the programme of work on financial instruments, the view grew that using fair values for such assets and liabilities could provide more relevant information.

However, the use of fair values then raises the question of where the unrealized gain or loss should be reported – in profit or loss or in other comprehensive income (as a change in equity). Historically, the principal driver in the recognition of gains was 'realization', but this may have less relevance in a situation where entities are trading underlying risks. Careful consideration would need to be given to information derived by measuring financial instruments at fair value and recognizing that gain or loss in profit or loss as compared with valuation at historical cost.

ILLUSTRATION

Entity A enters into an interest swap with B. The notional amount of the swap is €1m, but this amount is not exchanged. A pays interest to B at three-month intervals at 7 per cent, and B pays interest to A at London Interbank Offered Rate (LIBOR). If LIBOR moves above 7 per cent, then A gains on the deal, otherwise A loses. On a historical cost basis, no asset or liability would be recorded by either party and interest payments would be shown in profit or loss. It could be the case that at a year end, if LIBOR has moved to 10 per cent, the fair value of this interest swap is €50 000. If fair value accounting is used, then the interest rate swap would be recorded at €50 000, and presumably this gain would be shown in profit or loss. In six months' time, the fair value of this swap could have dropped to €10 000 or become negative (when LIBOR is below 7 per cent), and a gain for A is an equivalent loss for B. Which method of accounting for the swap would provide relevant and reliable information to the user? We leave this question for you to debate.

WHAT IS A FINANCIAL INSTRUMENT?

We start by presenting you with the definitions as applied by the IASB, although it is difficult to understand them immediately when reading. IAS 32 defines a financial instrument as 'a contract that gives rise to a financial asset of one entity and a financial liability or equity instrument of another entity'. A financial asset is … any asset that is:

(a) cash

(b) an equity instrument of another entity

(c) a contractual right:

   (i) to receive cash or another financial asset from another entity

   (ii) to exchange financial instruments or financial liabilities with another entity under conditions that are potentially favourable to the entity.

(d) a contract that will or may be settled in the entity's own equity instruments and is:

   (i) a non-derivative for which the entity is or may be obliged to receive a variable number of the entity's own equity instruments or

   (ii) a derivative that will or may be settled other than by the exchange of a fixed amount of cash or another financial asset for a fixed number of the entity's own equity instruments. For this purpose, the entity's own equity instruments do not include instruments that are themselves contracts for the future receipt or delivery of the equity's own equity instruments.

A financial liability is any liability that is:

(a) a contractual obligation:

   (i) to deliver cash or another financial asset to another enterprise entity or

   (ii) to exchange financial instruments assets or financial liabilities with another enterprise entity under conditions that are potentially unfavourable to the entity.

(b) a contract that will or may be settled in the entity's own equity instruments and is:

   (i) a non-derivative for which the entity is or may be obliged to deliver a variable number of the entity's own equity instruments or

   (ii) a derivative that will or may be settled other than by the exchange of a fixed amount of cash or another financial asset for a fixed number of the entity's own equity instruments. For this purpose the entity's own equity instruments do not include puttable financial instruments that are classified as equity instruments or instruments that are themselves contracts for the future receipt or delivery of the entity's own equity instruments.

Some elements of the financial asset and liability definitions are rather clear, others not. This is especially so for (d) in the financial asset definition and (b) in the financial liability definition. We will defer discussion of these elements to the section of equity versus liability below.

From these definitions, we can assert that a financial instrument is the contract, not the asset or liability, and thus we must be clear what is meant by contract, contractual right and obligation. IAS 32 states that 'contract' and 'contractual' refer to an agreement between two or more parties that has clear economic consequences that the parties have little, if any, chance of avoiding, because generally the agreement is enforceable in law. Contracts need not, however, be in writing. Now try the following Activity.

ACTIVITY 17.1

Identify which of the following are financial instruments.

- cash
- gold bullion
- debtors
- creditors
- loans
- bank deposits
- debentures
- a promissory note payable in government bonds
- ordinary shares
- preference shares
- plant and equipment previously bought and paid for by the entity
- pre-payments for goods or services.

Activity feedback

- *Cash: clearly not a financial instrument, but cash is a financial asset.*
- *Gold bullion: this is a commodity or physical asset as there is no contractual right to receive cash or other financial assets.*
- *Debtors: these are financial assets but not financial instruments as they cannot be described as a contract although they quite possibly arose from a contract.*
- *Creditors: they are, likewise, a financial liability.*
- *Loans: these are financial assets of one entity and liabilities of another, but it is debatable whether they are actually a financial instrument as this requires a contract. Presumably there is a con-*

tract behind these assets and liabilities and it should be this that is the financial instrument.
- *Bank deposits: same as for loans.*
- *Debentures: same as for loans.*
- *A promissory note payable in government bonds: this is a financial instrument as the note is the contract that gives the holder the contractual right to receive and the issuer the contractual obligation to deliver government bonds. The bonds themselves are financial assets of one entity and liabilities of another.*
- *Ordinary shares: they can also be regarded as financial instruments if we regard them as a contract that will ultimately result in the entity paying cash to the holder. The Standard defines an equity instrument as any contract that evidences a residual interest in the assets of an entity after deducting all of its liabilities.*
- *Preference shares: same as for ordinary shares.*
- *Plant and equipment previously bought and paid for by the entity: clearly no financial instruments as there is no contract to settle anything in cash or another financial instrument.*
- *Pre-payments for goods or services: again, clearly no financial instruments.*

This Activity is somewhat tortuous given that the Standard uses the terms financial instrument, financial asset and financial liability rather loosely. The Standard tends to confuse the terms financial assets, financial instruments and financial liabilities.

Other examples of financial instruments given in the Standards are derivatives such as financial options, futures and forwards, interest rate swaps and currency swaps. The Standard gives further examples of contracts that do not give rise to financial instruments as they do not involve the transfer of a financial asset. For example, an operating lease for the use of a physical asset can be settled only by the receipt and delivery of services and is therefore not a financial instrument.

However, finance leases are financial instruments as they are contracts which result in a financial asset of one entity and a financial liability of another. (Finance leases are outside the scope of IAS 32 as they are subject to IAS 17, *Leases* to be replaced by IFRS 16).

A derivative is defined in the Standards as a financial instrument:

(a) whose value changes in response to the change in a specified interest rate, security price, commodity price, foreign exchange rate, index of prices or rates, a credit rating or credit index or similar variable (underlying)

(b) that requires no initial net investment or little initial net investment relative to other types of contracts that have a similar response to changes in market conditions and

(c) that is settled at a future date.

Work through the following Activity carefully.

ACTIVITY 17.2

Are the following contracts financial instruments?

1   Entity A enters into both derivatives and an interest rate swap with B that requires A to pay a fixed rate of 7 per cent and receive a variable amount based on three-month LIBOR. The notional amount of the swap is €1 million, but this amount is not exchanged. A pays or receives a net cash amount each quarter based on the difference between 7 per cent and LIBOR.

2   A also enters into a pay fixed, receive variable interest swap with C. The notional amount is for €100m and fixed rate 10 per cent. The variable rate is based on three-month LIBOR. A prepays its fixed interest rate obligation as €100m × 10 per cent × 5 years discounted at market interest rates at inception of the swap.

3   A enters into a contract to pay €10m if X shares increase by 5 per cent or more during a six-month period and to receive €10m if the share price decreases by 5 per cent or more in the same period. No payment is made if the price swing is less than 5 per cent up or down.

Activity feedback

1   *There is no initial net investment; settlement occurs at a future date and its value changes based on changes in LIBOR, the underlying variable. Therefore, this is a financial instrument as it meets the definition of a derivative.*

2   *This is also a derivative and therefore a financial instrument, even though there is an initial net investment. The payment of the fixed interest at inception will be regarded as 'little' compared with other similar contracts such as a variable rate bond where the notional amount of €100m would be paid over.*

3   *There is no initial net investment, settlement occurs at a future date and the underlying variable is the share price. This is a derivative and therefore a financial instrument.*

DISTINCTION BETWEEN FINANCIAL LIABILITY AND EQUITY

At this stage we need to differentiate between a financial liability and equity. Remember the definition of financial liability. An instrument is a financial liability when:

(a) The instrument includes a contractual obligation to deliver cash or another financial asset/liability to another entity or to exchange financial assets or financial liabilities with another entity under conditions that are potentially unfavourable to the issuer.

(b) The instrument will or may be settled in the issuer's own equity instruments, where it is:

(i)   a non-derivative that includes a contractual obligation for the issuer to deliver a variable number of its own equity instruments or

(ii)   a derivative that will be settled other than by the issuer exchanging a fixed amount of cash or another financial asset for a fixed number of its own equity instruments. For this purpose, the issuer's own equity instruments do not include instruments that have all the features of puttable instruments or instruments that are contracts for the future receipt or delivery of the issuer's own equity instruments.

We will now discuss (b) further. The basic idea is that a 'payment' in the form of the entity's own shares (equity instruments) does not result in a liability. However, when the number of shares to be used as payment is variable, this reduces the risk for the holder of the instrument and for that reason the instrument is considered a financial liability.

ILLUSTRATION

A mandatory convertible bond is issued for an amount of €100 000, with a maturity of one year. Ten per cent interest is accrued to the principal (and not paid). The accrued amount at maturity is €110 000. At the time of issue, the fair value of one share is €1000. At the time of conversion, the share price has dropped to €880.

1   At maturity, the bondholder is required to convert the bond into a fixed number of shares. The bond will be converted into 100 shares.

2   At maturity, the bondholder is required to convert the bond into a variable number of shares. The bond will be converted into the number of shares that equals the accrued amount.

In case 1, the bond is classified as equity. In fact, the bondholder, although formally a bondholder, already runs the risk as a shareholder. At maturity, the bond with an accrued amount of €110 000 is converted into 100 shares with a total fair value of €18 000.

In case 2, the bond is classified as a liability. At maturity, the bond is converted into 125 shares (110 000/880): the fair value before and after conversion remain the same.

Note that any variability in the number of shares results in the financial instrument being classified as a liability, even if the variability is small and would result in a significant degree of shareholder risk. To avoid interpretation issues the IASB has chosen a rigid distinction.

The other issue in the definition of a financial liability is that of puttable financial instruments. A puttable instrument is a financial instrument that gives the holder the right to put the instrument back to the issuer for cash or another financial asset, or is automatically put back to the issuer on the occurrence of an uncertain future event or the death or retirement of the instrument holder. An example of a puttable instrument is a redeemable, at the option of the holder, share. Based on the general definition, a puttable financial instrument is a financial liability, as the entity may be required to redeem the financial instrument without having the discretion to avoid payment. However, as an exception to the basic principles, a puttable financial instrument that has all the following features can be classed as equity:

- It entitles the holder to a pro-rata share of the entity's net assets in the event of liquidation.
- It is subordinate to all other classes of instruments, i.e. it has no priority under liquidation before others and it does not need to be converted into another instrument before it is subordinate.
- In the subordinate class, all instruments have identical features.
- It does not include an obligation to deliver cash or another financial asset except for the redemption.
- Its cash flows are based substantially on profit or loss attained.

Compound financial instruments

Some financial instruments can contain both an equity element and a liability element. For example, a bond convertible by the holder into a fixed number of shares of the entity is a compound financial instrument. This is because the instrument comprises a liability to deliver cash or another financial asset on redemption, and a call option granting the holder the right to convert it into a fixed number of shares. IAS 32 requires us to account for the substance of this transaction, both a liability and an equity element, not the legal form. The substance is basically that of issuing a debt instrument with an early settlement provision and warrants to purchase ordinary shares.

IFRS 9 tells us how to measure the component parts and we will deal with this in the measurement section.

Now complete Activity 17.3.

ACTIVITY 17.3

Identify whether the following financial instruments should be classified by the issuer as a liability (debt) or equity in accordance with IFRS.

(a) A has issued a perpetual preference share redeemable only at A's option. A dividend of 8 per cent is paid annually provided there are sufficient distributable profits.

(b) B has issued a perpetual convertible bond. Interest of 10 per cent on the bond is paid if a dividend is paid on the ordinary shares of B.

(c) C issues a perpetual preference share carrying a fixed dividend rate of 5 per cent. If the dividend is deferred, then the dividend is accumulated for future payout together with additional interest at 30 per cent.

(d) D issues specific preference shares to its fund managers. They carry the right to an annual payment based on 25 per cent of realized gains on the fund recorded in the period by D.

Activity feedback

(a) This is a liability as management does not have discretion over payment of a dividend. The critical feature of a liability, remember, is the existence of an obligation to pay cash or to exchange another instrument under conditions that are potentially unfavourable to the issuer.

(b) This should be included in equity as cash is paid over only if a dividend is paid to ordinary shareholders and thus the dividend decision is discretionary.

(c) Given the interest obligation on the non-payment of a dividend, this must be treated as a liability.

(d) Again this is a liability as management has no discretion over the calculation or timing of the amount to be paid.

(Adapted from Accountancy, April 2003, p. 89)

RECOGNITION AND DERECOGNITION OF FINANCIAL INSTRUMENTS

IAS 39 and IFRS 9 are relatively similar on the topics of recognition and derecognition of financial instruments.

Initial recognition

According to both IAS 39 and IFRS 9 (para. 3.1.1), an entity should only recognize a financial asset or liability on its statement of financial position when it becomes a party to the contractual provisions of the instrument. The Standard then deals with something called 'regular way contracts'.

Regular way contracts (IFRS 9, Appendix A) are those for the purchase or sale of financial assets that require delivery of the assets within the timeframe generally established by regulation or convention in the market concerned. For these contracts, recognition is permitted at either trade date or settlement date but the policy chosen must be applied consistently.

However, settlement date accounting, when applied, does require the entity to recognize any change in the fair value of the asset that occurs between the trade and settlement date. This is a somewhat strange requirement given that the financial asset itself is not yet recognized. Regular way contracts actually meet the definition of a derivative as they are forward contracts, but they are not recognized as derivatives because of the short duration of the commitment.

An example of a regular way contract is where a bank makes a loan commitment at a specified rate of interest and then takes a commitment period to enable it to complete its underwriting and to provide time for the borrower to execute the transaction that is the subject of the loan. This commitment period would have to be of a normal duration for such an agreement. The loan, once recognized at either trade date or settlement date, would be carried at amortized cost (see below).

Now complete the Activity below.

ACTIVITY 17.4

On 29 December 20X1 an entity commits to buy a financial asset for €1000, which is its fair value on commitment date (trade date). On 31.12.X1 and 4.1.X2, the settlement date, the fair values of the asset are €1002 and €1003, respectively.

Show the amounts to be recorded for the asset at 29.12.X1, 31.12.X1 and 4.1.X2 using both settlement and trade date accounting and identify where any change in value will be recognized. Assume that the asset is measured at fair value and that all changes in fair value are included in profit or loss. Liabilities are measured at (amortized) cost.

Activity feedback

Table 17.1 explains initial recognition at trade date and Table 17.2 at settlement date.

TABLE 17.1 Trade date accounting

Date of balance	
29.12.X1 (note 1)	
Financial asset	1 000
Liability	(1 000)
31.12.X1 (note 2)	
Financial asset	1 002
Liability	(1 000)
P&L	(2)
4.01.X2 (note 3)	
Financial asset	1 003
Liability	—
P&L	(1)

TABLE 17.2 Settlement date accounting

Date of balance	
29.12.X1	—
31.12.X1 (note 4)	
Financial asset	2
Liability	—
P&L	(2)
4.01.X2	
Financial asset	1 003
Liability	—
P&L	(1)

Notes:

1 At this stage in the recognition we have both a financial asset that we have purchased and the liability outstanding to pay for this asset.

2 The financial asset is measured at fair value and the change is included in profit and loss. We have still not settled this transaction, so the liability still remains and is measured at amortized cost.

3 Settlement date is now reached so the liability is removed, but note that other assets (perhaps cash) would be reduced. There is an additional gain of 1 in profit or loss.

4 We need to recognize the change in fair value that has occurred between trade and settlement date even though the full financial asset is not yet recognized.

Offsetting

A financial asset and a financial liability recognized in the statement of financial position shall be offset, with the net amount presented, when and only when an entity has a legally enforceable right to offset and intends to settle on a net basis or to realize the asset and settle the liability simultaneously (IAS 32, para. 42). When an entity has the right to receive or pay a single net amount and intends to do so, it has, in effect, only one single financial asset or financial liability. Offsetting is different from derecognition (discussed below) and can never give rise to a recognition of a gain or loss.

DERECOGNITION

Derecognition of a financial asset

According to both IAS 39 and IFRS 9, an entity shall derecognize (remove) a financial asset from the statement of financial position when and only when certain criteria are met. Para B3.2.1 of IFRS 9 includes a derecognition flowchart, from which it is clear that it is important to follow the steps in the right order.

First, derecognition is required when the contractual rights to the cash flows from the financial assets have expired. If not, the second criterion would be whether the entity has transferred substantially all the risks and rewards from the asset. If yes, derecognition is required (unless the entity is a pass-through entity). If the entity has retained substantially all risks and rewards, the asset should continue to be recognized. If the entity has neither transferred nor retained substantially all risks and rewards, so if the risks and rewards are shared between parties, derecognition would be required when the entity has lost control of the asset.

In summary, the first criterion in judging whether a transfer of an asset results in derecognition is the transfer of substantially all risks and rewards, and when this criterion does not lead to a clear conclusion, the transfer of control is the second criterion.

This area is again complex given that derecognition of a portion of the asset is permitted and there is the possibility of repurchase options or other derivatives being involved. If you work through the following Activity, you will understand derecognition more clearly.

ACTIVITY 17.5

In each of the following cases, state (with reasons) whether the financial asset should be derecognized in the books of entity A.

1 A transfers a loan it holds to a bank, but stipulates that the bank cannot sell or pledge the loan. (This is to protect the customer to whom the loan was originally made.)

2 A transfers a financial asset to B on terms that stipulate that A can repurchase the asset before the expiry of a specific period at market value at the date of repurchase.

3 A transfers a financial asset to B on terms that stipulate that A must repurchase the asset before the expiry of a specific period and that repurchase is at the value at transfer date plus interest at a fixed rate on that value.

4 A transfers a financial asset to B on terms that stipulate that A can repurchase the asset before the expiry of a specific period and that repurchase is at the value at transfer date plus interest at a fixed rate on that value.

(Continued)

ACTIVITY 17.5   (Continued)

5 A transfers a financial asset to B on terms that stipulate that B has a put option and can oblige A to repurchase the asset before the expiry of a specific period and that repurchase is at the value at transfer date plus interest at a fixed rate on that value.

6 A sells short-term receivables to B and provides a guarantee with that sale to pay for any credit losses that may be incurred on the receivables as a result of the failure of the debtor to pay when due.

Activity feedback

1 Even though the transferee, the bank, cannot sell or pledge the loan, it does receive all other benefits from holding the loan and therefore A would derecognize this financial asset. All significant risks and rewards have been transferred.

2 In this case, the risks and rewards associated with the asset have been transferred to B as it will bear the loss if the market value falls and the gain if it increases. A just has an option to repurchase, not an obligation to do so. The asset will be derecognized by A and recognized when it is repurchased.

3 A does not transfer all significant risks and rewards, as it must repurchase the asset and B just has a lender's return. The significant risks and rewards are retained by A. There is no derecognition.

4 In this case not all significant risks and rewards have been retained, neither have they all been transferred (A still holds the upward risks and rewards, but not the downward risks and rewards). Because A has a repurchase option, A still controls the asset and may therefore not derecognize it.

5 Now B has a put option and as a result A has the downward risks and rewards and not the upward risks and rewards. As B now controls the asset, A would derecognize it, but would provide for the repurchase obligation at fair value.

6 A does not derecognize these receivables. It has retained all significant risks and rewards, as for short-term receivables credit risk is the only major risk.

Derecognition of a financial liability

Derecognition of a financial liability is relatively straightforward. We remove the financial liability from the statement of financial position when the obligation specified in the contract is discharged, cancelled or expires. Occasionally, one financial liability will be exchanged for a similar one with the same lender; if the terms of the new agreement are substantially different from the old, then the old one is derecognized and the new one is recognized. The problem with this requirement from IFRS 9 is that we need to set boundaries for 'substantially'. The terms are considered to be substantially different if the discounted present value of the cash flows, under the new terms, including any fees paid net of any fees received, is at least 10 per cent different from the discounted present value of the remaining cash flows of the original debt instrument.

Derecognition accounting treatment

The accounting treatment on derecognition requires the entity to recognize in the profit or loss for the period the difference between the carrying amount of the asset, or portion, transferred to another party and the sum of the proceeds received or receivable and any prior adjustment to reflect the fair value of that asset that had been reported in other comprehensive income.

Quite often asset derecognition is coupled with the recognition of a new financial asset or liability. When this occurs, IFRS 9 requires recognition of the new financial asset or liability at fair value and the recognition of a gain or loss on the transaction based on the difference between:

- the proceeds and
- the carrying amount of the financial asset sold plus the fair value of any new financial liability assumed, minus the fair value of any new financial asset acquired and plus or minus any adjustment that had been previously reported in equity to reflect the fair value of that asset.

ACTIVITY 17.6

In example 6 in Activity 17.5, A is selling short-term receivables to B and providing a guarantee with that sale to pay for any credit losses that may be incurred on the receivables as a result of the failure of the debtor to pay when due. We have concluded that A does not derecognize these receivables as it has retained all significant risks and rewards. Assume that the amount of receivables transferred from A to B is €40 000. The carrying amount of the receivables in the balance sheet of A, taking into account credit risk, is €39 000. At the moment of transfer, B pays €34 600, taking into account a fee of €400. All receivables will still be paid to A and A transfers the payments to B. The amount of receivables paid is €38 500. Present the journal entries of A at the time of transfer and of the payment of the receivables.

Payment of receivables:

Dr Cash	*38 500*
Dr Bad debt written off	*500*
Cr Receivables	*39 000*
and	
Dr Liability	*35 000*
Cr Cash	*35 000*

The short-term receivables of A would in itself not be recognized by B. B accounts for the cash transfer as a loan receivable that is being redeemed by the cash transfers from A to B. A will of course pay no more than €35 000 to B. The remaining receipts of receivables of €3 500 will be kept by A.

Activity feedback

At the time of transfer:

Dr Cash	*34 600*
Dr Fee expense (given the short-term, immediate expensing)	*400*
Cr Liability	*35 000*

CLASSIFICATION AND MEASUREMENT

IAS 39 and IFRS 9 differ significantly on the classification and measurement of financial assets. For the remaining issues, there are no or limited significant differences. We will therefore discuss IFRS 9 and IAS 39 together, except for the classification and measurement of financial assets.

Initial recognition (IFRS 9 and IAS 39)

At initial recognition, a financial asset or liability should be measured at fair value. Subsequent measurement depends upon the classification of the asset or liability.

Financial assets (IFRS 9)

IFRS 9 applies one classification approach for all types of financial assets. Financial assets are classified in their entirety and not broken down into components.

Measuring all financial assets at fair value is not a feature of IFRS 9, as preparers, auditors and regulators were wary of recognizing changes in fair value in the statement of comprehensive income for financial assets that are not held for trading or not managed on a fair value basis. Problems can occur with fair value measurement when it cannot be determined within a narrow range. This reluctance to move to full fair value measurement is also consistent with the views raised in response to the economic crisis in 2008.

Two criteria are used to determine how financial assets should be classified and measured:

- the entity's business model for managing financial assets and
- the contractual cash flow characteristics of the financial asset.

Financial assets are classified and measured at either amortized cost or fair value, and fair value changes are recognized either in profit or loss or in other comprehensive income.

For debt instruments, amortized cost is required where the asset is held within a business model whose objective is to hold assets in order to collect contractual cash flows, and the contractual terms of the asset give rise on specified dates to cash flows that are solely payments of principal and interest on the principal amount outstanding (so for specific debt instruments). However, it is possible for an entity to designate a financial asset as measured at fair value through profit or loss, if doing so eliminates an accounting mismatch. This mismatch can occur when a financial asset is hedged with a financial liability.

If a financial asset does not meet the conditions above, it is classified and measured at fair value. The fair value would go through other comprehensive income when contractual cash flows are solely principal and interest, and the business model would be that the asset is held for either contractual cash flows or for sale (and the fair value through profit or loss option has not been used). When this is not the case, so when the contractual cash flows are not only held for principal or interest or when the asset is held for sale only, fair value changes should go through profit or loss.

Equity instruments will always be measured at fair value. Equity instruments held for trading should be measured at fair value through profit or loss. For investments in equity instruments that are not held for trading, IFRS 9 permits an entity to make an irrevocable election to present changes in fair value of the investment in the equity instrument in other comprehensive income or through profit or loss. On recognizing fair value changes in other comprehensive income, there would be no recycling to profit or loss upon impairment or sale of the investment. However, dividends from the investment are recognized in profit or loss.

The use of the 'business model' is a fundamental building block of IFRS 9 and aligns the accounting with management's intentions for those financial assets. These intentions are not at the level of individual assets but at the level that reflects how financial assets are managed to achieve a particular business objective. We have seen three business models: generating cash flows by collecting contractual cash flows only (amortized cost measurement), by selling assets only (fair value through profit or loss measurement), or by both (fair value through other comprehensive income measurement). The business model is a matter of fact rather than an assertion. Even within the business model of collecting contractual cash flows only, some sales activity may occur, but they should be infrequent or insignificant. IFRS 9 requires financial assets to be reclassified when, and only when, the entity's business model for managing these assets changes.

The business model is not the only relevant item for classification. For amortized cost measurement and measurement at fair value through other comprehensive income, it is also required that the contractual cash flows of the debt instrument are solely payments of principal and interest. To meet that criterion, the interest can comprise a return not only for the time value of money and credit risk but also for other components such as a return for liquidity risk, amounts to cover expenses and a profit margin. The returns should be consistent with that of a basic lending agreement. Convertible debt instruments do not meet the condition of solely payments of principal and interest, because equity price risk and return is a feature of such an instrument.

Now complete Activity 17.7 below.

ACTIVITY 17.7

State whether the following financial assets would be measured at amortized cost, fair value through comprehensive income, or fair value through profit or loss, in accordance with IFRS 9.

1 An entity holds investments to collect their contractual cash flows of principal and interest, but would sell an investment in isolated circumstances.

2 An entity's business model is to purchase portfolios of loans. If payment on the loan is not made on a timely basis, the entity contacts the debtor by phone, email or post to extract the cash flows.

3 An entity holds bonds in various currencies with stated maturity dates and intends to hold the bonds to maturity. Payments of principal and interest to the entity are linked to the inflation index of the currency in which the loan is issued.

4 An entity holds bonds in various currencies with stated maturity dates and intends to hold the bonds to maturity. Payments of principal and interest to the entity are linked to the bond issuer's net income performance.

5 An entity holds a bond issued by Beta entity with an interest rate of 8 per cent. The bond is redeemable at par or may be converted into Beta equity shares. An equivalent bond without the conversion option would pay an interest rate of 10 per cent.

6 An entity holds a bond portfolio with a variable interest (a 3-month Euribor rate). Some of the bonds will be sold before maturity, others will be held to maturity.

Activity feedback

1 These investments meet the business model definition, even though some sales may occur, as the main objective is to hold the investments for their contractual cash flows. Measure at amortized cost.

2 Again, these purchased loans meet the business model definition and therefore are measured at amortized cost.

3 The business model test is clearly met. Also, the cash flows here are solely payments of principal and interest. Linking the interest rate to the currency inflation rate just reflects the real rate of interest in the instrument and therefore they will be measured at amortized cost.

4 Again, the business model test is clearly met, but the cash flows are not solely payments of principal and interest. The cash flows in this case are not representing the time value of money or credit risk but the debtor's performance, and thus do not meet the business model definition and therefore will be measured at fair value through profit or loss.

5 In any case, the cash flows do not only reflect the time value of money and the credit risk. They are also linked to the value of the equity of the issuer. Measure at fair value through profit or loss.

6 The cash flows are solely payments of principal and interest, and the business model is apparently to held to collect contractual cash flows or to sell the bonds. The bonds should then be measured at fair value through comprehensive income.

Financial assets (IAS 39)

IAS 39 categorizes financial assets into four groups:

- financial assets at fair value through profit or loss
- held-to-maturity investments
- loans and receivables
- available for sale financial assets.

Financial assets at fair value through profit or loss include held for trading assets and assets that have been designated in this category upon initial recognition. The asset is held for trading if, regardless of why it was acquired, it is part of a portfolio for which there is evidence of short-term profit taking or was initially acquired for the purposes of generating a profit through short-term fluctuations in price or dealer's margins. Derivatives are also held for trading assets, unless they are used for hedging. Financial assets may also be designated in this category upon initial recognition, but only when doing so results in more relevant information (by eliminating accounting mismatches or when the performance of the financial asset is evaluated on a fair value basis). This fair value option is open for any financial asset.

Held-to-maturity investments are financial assets with fixed or determinable payments and fixed maturity that an entity has the positive intent and ability to hold to maturity.

Loans and receivables originated by the entity are financial assets created by the entity by providing money, goods or services directly to a debtor.

Available for sale financial assets is the residual category: assets that are not loans and receivables originated by the entity, held-to-maturity or financial assets at fair value through profit or loss.

ACTIVITY 17.8

Applying IAS 39, which categories of financial asset can the following fit into?

1 An investment in a bond acquired with the intent to hold for a long period irrespective of short-term fluctuations in price.

2 A loan issued to a related party with a redeemable on demand option of the entity.

3 Shares held as a temporary investment of cash.

Activity feedback

1 Held for maturity is the most obvious category. Financial asset at fair value through profit or loss and available for sale financial assets are possible alternatives.

2 Loans and receivables is the only possible category.

3 If the shares are to be held for short-term profit making, the category is held for trading. However, if this does not seem to be the case, then the category is available for sale.

What about the measurement of the different categories in IAS 39?

The category 'financial assets at fair value through profit or loss' already indicates the measurement principle: the assets are measured at fair value and re-measurements are recognized in profit or loss.

Available for sale financial assets are also measured at fair value, but re-measurements are recognized outside profit or loss in other comprehensive income. Upon realization or earlier impairment, the cumulative amounts of re-measurements are recycled to profit or loss. Only when the fair value of the asset cannot be reliably measured, is it measured at cost.

Held-to-maturity investments and loans and receivables are measured at amortized cost using the effective interest method.

Financial liabilities (IFRS 9 and IAS 39)

Financial liabilities held for trading should be measured at fair value through profit or loss and entities are permitted to use that measurement for other financial liabilities when particular criteria are met (the fair value option). For most financial liabilities the measurement will be at amortized cost.

In measuring financial liabilities at fair value, an element of discussion was the volatility in profit or loss caused by changes in the entity's own credit risk. When an entity's credit rating declines, the value of the liability will decrease, which would result in a gain in profit or loss (and vice versa). This result is counterintuitive and confusing. For that reason, IFRS 9 requires that the changes in fair value of an entity's own credit risk should be recognized in other comprehensive income rather than in profit or loss (there is no such requirement in IAS 39, so these changes in fair value are also recognized in profit or loss). As an example, assume Company M issues bonds with a face value and fair value of €100 000 at a fixed rate of 6 per cent. Assume that market interest rates do not change. However, M is having a difficult time and two years later its creditworthiness is lower. If M were to issue a fixed rate bond loan at that moment, it would have to pay 8 per cent. The fair value of the loan has now become less than €100 000 (6 per cent interest and repayment cash flows discounted at 8 per cent). Remember, the 2 per cent interest differential is only due to the change in creditworthiness of M, not to market interest rate changes. When M measures the liabilities at fair value through profit or loss, the decrease in the fair value of the liability will normally be a gain. But that is counterintuitive: the worsening of the credit standing would result in a gain. It is for that reason that this fair value change is included in other comprehensive income, outside profit or loss. However, if such accounting were to create or enlarge an accounting mismatch, the credit risk related fair value change would still be recognized in profit or loss.

Amortized cost

As discussed, IFRS 9 and IAS 39 require certain financial debt assets and most financial liabilities to be measured at amortized cost. Amortized cost is the amount at which the financial asset or liability is measured at initial recognition minus principal repayments, plus or minus the cumulative amortization of any difference between the initial amount and the maturity amount, and minus any write-down for impairment or uncollectability.

In profit or loss, the interest is measured in accordance with the effective interest method. The effective interest method is a method of calculating amortization using the effective rate of a financial asset or liability. The effective interest rate is the rate that exactly discounts the expected stream of future cash payments through maturity or the next market-based repricing date to the current net carrying amount of the financial asset or liability. That computation should include all fees and points paid or received between parties to the contract. The effective interest rate is sometimes termed the level yield to maturity or to next repricing date and is the internal rate of return of the financial asset or liability for that period.

Fair value

IFRS 13 defines fair value. The fair value concept is discussed in Chapter 7.

Remember that fair value is the price that would be received to sell an asset or paid to transfer a liability in an orderly transaction between market participants at the measurement date. The fair value of a fixed rate bond or loan is generally estimated as the sum of all future cash payments or receipts discounted using the prevailing market rate of interest for a similar instrument of an issuer with a similar credit rating.

ILLUSTRATION

On 1.1.20X0 an entity acquires €100 000 par value 9 per cent bonds of Paper Co. priced to yield 10 per cent with a maturity date of 31.12.20X4. The value of the bonds on acquisition is:

Present value of interest payments   **€**

9 per cent of €100 000 for five years discounted at 10 per cent = 9000 × 3.79079 (annuity factor at 10 per cent for 5 years):	34 117
Present value of maturity value = 100 000 × 0.62092 (annuity factor at 10 per cent in 5 years):	62 092
Fair value (= market value)	96 209
Discount from par value is therefore:	3 791
Par value	100 000
Thus, the bonds are initially recognized at:	€ 96 209

Remember that financial instruments should be measured at fair value upon initial recognition.

Subsequent recognition of the bonds each year requires amortization using the effective interest rate method. Thus, we need to amortize the discount from par value over the five years recognizing this, together with interest received, as interest income.

Table 17.3 shows the carrying amount (amortized cost) (column E) of the instrument each year and the interest income (column A).

TABLE 17.3   Amortization of bonds

Year	Interest income CA × 10% A	Cash received B	Discount amortized C	Discount remaining D	Carrying amount (CA) E
01.01.X0				3 791	96 209
31.12.X0	9 621	9 000	621	3 170	96 830
31.12.X1	9 683	9 000	683	2 487	97 513
31.12.X2	9 751	9 000	751	1 736	98 264
31.12.X3	9 826	9 000	826	910	99 090
31.12.X4	9 910	9 000	910	—	100 000

COMPOUND FINANCIAL INSTRUMENT MEASUREMENT

We previously identified a redeemable bond with an option to convert to a fixed number of ordinary shares as a compound financial instrument. We now need to deal with the measurement of its separate parts.

IAS 32 tells us to determine the carrying amount of the liability component first by measuring the fair value of a similar liability. The carrying amount of the equity element is then determined by deducting the fair value of the financial liability from the fair value of the compound instrument as a whole. Now complete the following Activity.

ACTIVITY 17.9

On 1 April 20X6 Beta entity issued at par an 8 per cent convertible loan note with a nominal value of £600 000. It is redeemable at par on 31 March 20Y0 or it may be converted into equity shares of Beta on the basis of 100 new shares for each £200 of loan note held. An equivalent loan note without the conversion option would have carried an interest rate of 10 per cent.

Show how the loan note and the interest costs should be presented in the financial statements ended 31 March 20X7 in accordance with IASs.

The present value of £1 receivable at the end of each year, based on discount rates of 8 per cent and 10 per cent, are:

End of year	8%	10%
1	0.9259	0.9091
2	0.8573	0.8264
3	0.7938	0.7513
4	0.7350	0.6830

Activity feedback

IAS 32 (paras 28–32) requires a convertible loan note to be separated into its equity and liability component. The liability component is equal to the fair value of a similar liability that does not have an equity component. In this example we therefore need to determine the present value at a discount rate of 10 per cent (the comparator) of the future cash flows.

End of year	Future cash flows	Discount rate 10%	FV
1	48 000 (interest at 8%)	0.9091	43 637
2	48 000	0.8264	39 667
3	48 000	0.7513	36 062
4	648 000 (capital + interest)	0.6830	442 584
Liability element on 1 April 20x6			561 950
Equity element on 1 April 20x6			38 050
			600 000

Financial statements 31 March 20X7
Statement of financial position

Equity – equity option	38 050
Non-current liabilities – 8% convertible loan note (561 950 + 8195; see below)	570 145

Statement of comprehensive income

Interest costs convertible: 10% × 561 950 = 56 195
Payment: 8% × 600 000 = 48 000
The difference of £8195 is added to the loan note.

Note: the finance costs for the year ending 31 March 20X8 are 10 per cent × 570 145 = 57 014.50. Adding the differences between interest payments and interest costs to the carrying amount of the loan note will result in an amount of £600 000 at the end of year 4.

IMPAIRMENT

Impairment is mainly relevant for those financial debt instruments that are measured at amortized cost. Finding a sound impairment methodology was one of the big challenges of the IASB.

IAS 39

The impairment method within IAS 39 is an incurred loss impairment method, where there should be objective evidence of a credit loss event.

For loans and receivables and held-to-maturity investments carried at amortized cost, the impairment loss is measured as the difference between the asset's carrying amount and the present value of future estimated future cash flows using the original effective interest rate as the discount rate. For available for sale assets exceptionally measured at cost, the carrying amount should be compared to the present value of estimated future cash flows discounted at the current market rate of return for a similar asset. These impairments may not be reversed.

Also for available for sale financial assets measured at fair value, an impairment test should be made at each reporting date. This will not affect the measurement of the asset, which is at fair value and therefore 'automatically' impaired if applicable, but it may affect the amount included in other comprehensive income that should be recycled to profit or loss. There is an impairment in the situation of a significant decline (for example a fair value that is more than 30 per cent below cost) or prolonged decline (for example a fair value that is lower than cost for more than one year).

ACTIVITY 17.10

Determine the amount of the impairment in each of the following cases:

1 An investment in a three-year bond with an amortized cost of €60 000 has a stated and effective interest rate of 7 per cent. After two years, the creditor of the bond faces serious default risk. The reporting entity expects that it will no longer receive the last year's interest on the bond and it expects to receive only 50 per cent of the principal. Current market interest rates are 10 per cent.

2 An investment in listed shares is an available for sale financial asset. Acquisition price was €20 000, current market value €12 000. The fair value reserve is €1000 (ignore taxes).

Activity feedback

1 The expected remaining cash flow at the end of year 3 is €30 000. The present value at the original effective tax rate (7 per cent) is €28 037. This will be the new carrying amount. The amount of the impairment is €31 963.

2 The amount of €1000 would normally be considered a significant decline (a decline of more than 30 per cent). As a result, the full amount (€1000) should be recognized as impairment by transferring it to profit or loss (there will no effect on total comprehensive income as the loss will be compensated by an increase in other comprehensive income).

IFRS 9

The IAS 39 incurred loss model has been heavily criticized, as under this model losses are considered too late to be recognized. IFRS 9 has moved from an incurred loss to an expected loss model. The new model is forward-looking and it eliminates the threshold for the recognition of expected credit losses, so that it is no longer necessary for a trigger event to have occurred before credit losses are recognized. IFRS 9 requires an entity to base its measurement of expected credit losses on reasonable and supportable information that is available without undue cost or effort, and that includes historical, current and forecast information.

There are three stages in impairment recognition:

- Stage 1. As soon as a financial instrument is originated or purchased, 12-month expected credit losses are recognized in profit or loss and a loss allowance is established. 12-month expected credit losses are the portion of lifetime expected credit losses that represent the expected credit losses that result from default events that are possible within 12 months after the reporting date. It is not the expected cash shortfalls over the next 12 months or the loss on actual defaults within 12 months, but the effect of the entire credit loss weighted by the possibility that this loss will occur in the next 12 months. This serves as a proxy for the initial expectations of credit losses. Interest revenue is calculated on the gross carrying amount, so without adjustment for expected credit losses.

- Stage 2. If both the credit risk increases significantly and the resulting credit quality is not considered to be low credit risk, full lifetime expected credit losses are recognized. Credit risk increases significantly when there is a significant increase in the likelihood or risk of a default since initial recognition. Regardless of how an entity assesses a significant increase in credit risk, there is always a rebuttable assumption that credit risk has significantly increased when contractual payments are more than 30 days past due. Lifetime expected credit losses are an expected present value measurement of losses that arise if a borrower defaults on their obligation throughout the life of the financial instrument. A default includes payments that are made later than the contractual dates. Note that lifetime expected credit losses are only recognized when the credit risk has increased significantly from when the entity originated or purchased the financial instrument. When a financial instrument is determined to have low credit risk (a low risk of default), full lifetime expected credit losses will not be recognized, even when the credit risk has increased significantly. The calculation of interest revenue is as in stage 1.

- Stage 3. This stage only involves a change in interest revenue calculation. If the credit risk increases to the point that it is considered credit-impaired, interest revenue is calculated based on the amortized cost, which is the gross carrying amount adjusted for the loss allowance.

Credit losses are the present value of all cash shortfalls. The discount rate used in calculating the impairment of a debt instrument measured at amortized cost is the original effective interest rate, not the market interest rate at the time of the impairment calculation.

ACTIVITY 17.11

1 Bank C originates a five-year single 8 per cent loan for €200 000. At the origination of the loan and at the end of year 1, the entity estimates that the instrument has a probability of default for the next 12 months of 0.5 per cent and it assumes that 25 per cent of the gross carrying amount will be lost if the loan defaults. What will be the measurement of the loan in the statement of financial position at the end of year 1?

(Continued)

ACTIVITY 17.11 (*Continued*)

2 At the end of year 2, the credit risk has increased significantly and the credit risk is not considered to be low. The probability of default for the next 12 months is now estimated to be 3.5 per cent and the entity assumes that 80 per cent of the gross carrying amount will be lost if the loan defaults. The probability of default over the lifetime of the loan is estimated to be 15 per cent, with an expected loss of 90 per cent on default. What will be the measurement of the loan in the statement of financial position at the end of year 2 and the interest revenue in years 2 and 3?

3 At the end of year 3, the probability of default for the next 12 months is now estimated to be 30 per cent and the entity assumes that 100 per cent of the gross carrying amount will be lost if the loan defaults. The probability of default over the lifetime of the loan is estimated to be 45 per cent, with an expected loss of 100 per cent on default. The loan is considered to be credit-impaired. What will be the measurement of the loan in the statement of financial position at the end of year 3 and the interest revenue in year 4?

For the sake of simplicity, you may ignore the effect of discounting.

Activity feedback

1 The loss allowance will be €250 ((0.5 per cent x 25 per cent x €200,000). So the net carrying amount of the loan is €199 750.

2 Because the credit risk has increased significantly and the credit risk is not considered to be low, Bank C will no longer determine its loss allowance on the basis of 12-month but on the basis of lifetime expected credit losses. The loss allowance will therefore be €27 000 ((15 per cent x 90 per cent x €200 000). The net carrying amount of the loan at the end of year 2 is €173 000. The interest revenue in year 2 and 3 is €16 000 (8 per cent x €200 000). In year 2 there is a loss on the loan of €26 750 (€27 000 – €250).

3 The loan is now considered to be credit-impaired. The loss allowance at the end of year 3 will be € 90 000 ((45 per cent x 100 per cent x €200 000). The net carrying amount of the loan at the end of year 2 is €110 000. In year 3 there is a loss on the loan of €63 000 (€90 000 – €27 000). The interest revenue in year 4 will now be based on amortized cost, being €8800 (8 per cent x €110 000).

HEDGE ACCOUNTING

Hedging is about offsetting the loss or potential loss on one item against the gain or potential gain on another. Hedging can be used for managing interest rate risks, foreign currency risks and other price risks. Hedge accounting is a method to show the effects of managing the risks in the financial statements. The loss or gain on the hedging arises from changes in fair values (for instance that of loans) or cash flows (for instance changes in interest cash flows).

IFRS 9 replaces the rules-based design of the regulations in IAS 39 that were criticized as being too complex and arbitrary. Several hedges which are economically sound did not qualify for hedge accounting in the financial statements as they did not meet the detailed rules. IFRS 9 is a move to a principles-based design. The high-level aim is to simplify hedge accounting and to provide a better link with the risk management strategy. An example is the treatment of risk components. IAS 39 did allow components of financial items to be hedged, but not components of non-financial items, like the oil price component of jet fuel. IFRS 9 eliminates this distinction and looks at whether a risk component can be identified and measured and does not distinguish between types of items.

The new model also enables entities to use information produced internally for risk management purposes as a basis for hedge accounting. In IAS 39, there were rules-based anti-abuse criteria to determine whether hedge accounting would be eligible (like the rules-based requirement that to be able to apply hedge accounting, the actual results of the hedged item had to be in the range of 80 per cent to 125 per cent of that of the hedging instrument). IFRS 9 bases the eligibility criteria on an economic assessment of the strength of the hedging relationship, and this can be determined by using risk management data.

IFRS 9 does not yet contain a regulation for macro hedging, a model for fair value hedging of interest rate risk. It is a separate IASB project. As long as macro hedging has not been settled by IFRS 9, the current IAS 39 macro hedging rules may still be applied by entities. There is even a general choice of applying all hedge accounting regulations of IAS 39 instead of IFRS 9, although moving to IFRS 9 for hedge accounting is not considered to be burdensome for entities because of its principles-based approach.

However, although IFRS 9 is more principles-based, the technicalities included in the hedge accounting regulations in IAS 39 remain necessary to prevent abuses and ensure that gains and losses on speculative transactions are recognized immediately in profit or loss, and not hidden away.

One of the difficulties that make hedge accounting complex is that IFRS 9 does not require all financial instruments to be carried at fair value. Remember, many debt investments and most liabilities are carried at amortized cost.

Mostly derivatives will be used as hedging instruments (the items that are used for realizing the hedge); examples include interest rate swaps or foreign currency forward contracts. IFRS 9 also allows non-derivative financial assets or non-derivative financial liabilities that are accounted for at fair value through profit or loss to be designated as hedging instruments. Furthermore, non-derivatives in general are allowed to hedge a foreign currency risk. The hedging relationship only qualifies for using the special treatment of hedge accounting if a formal documentation of the detail of the hedge relationship exists indicating the risk to be hedged, the hedged item (the item that is being hedged), the hedge instrument, and how the entity will assess whether the hedging relationship meets the hedge effectiveness requirements. The hedge effectiveness requirements are:

- there is 'an economic relationship' between the hedged item and the hedging instrument
- the effect of credit risk does not 'dominate the value changes' that result from the economic relationship
- the hedge ratio (the ratio between the amount of the hedged item and the amount of the hedging instrument) may not reflect an imbalance that would create hedge ineffectiveness; in a perfect hedge, the ratio would be 1:1, but less than perfect hedges are allowed.

Hedged relationships are of three types (both in IFRS 9 and IAS 39):

1 *Fair value hedge* where the change in fair value of the asset or liability is hedged.
2 *Cash flow hedge* where the variability to cash flows in the hedged item is hedged.
3 *Foreign currency hedge*, which we consider in Chapter 28.

Fair value hedges

For fair value hedges, the gain or loss from re-measuring the hedging instrument at fair value is recognized immediately in net profit or loss and the gain or loss on the hedged item is also recognized immediately in net profit or loss. Work carefully through the following Activity.

ACTIVITY 17.12

On 1 January 20X0, a fixed 6 per cent interest loan is acquired with a face value and an amortized cost of €100. The loan is measured at amortized cost. Fixed interest loans have a volatile fair value, depending upon the change in market interest rates. To hedge the largest part of the fair value of the loan, the entity acquires an interest rate swap with a nominal amount of €10 where the entity receives 6 per cent interest and pays a variable interest, for instance Euribor + 0.2 per cent. The interest received from the swap is used to pay the interest on the loan. As a result, the entity has swapped a fixed interest loan into a variable interest loan for 80 per cent of the nominal amount.

At 31 December 20X0, due to an increase in the market interest rates, the fair value of the interest rate swap is –€4. The fair value is negative, because the entity pays more interest than it receives.

Show the accounting entries if:

1 hedge accounting is not applied

2 hedge accounting is applied.

Activity feedback

1 *The derivative would be shown at the fair value of –€4. The change in fair value is included in profit or loss. Also the interest paid for the year (Euribor + 0.2 per cent) is included in profit or loss. The carrying amount of the loan remains unchanged (at amortized cost). Although the derivative is* *used for hedging fair value volatility, not applying hedge accounting does result in reported volatility (of both the loan and derivative taken together).*

2 *The derivative would be shown at the fair value of –€4. The change in fair value is again included in profit or loss, as well as the interest paid for the year (Euribor + 0.2 per cent). However, the carrying amount of the loan is now reduced by –€4 (the fair value change of 80 per cent of the loan) and is measured at €96. The reduction is included as a gain in profit or loss. There is no reported volatility, both the loan and derivative taken together remain measured at €100. Only the interest paid is recognized in profit or loss. Note that the loan is not carried at fair value, but at amortized cost plus or minus the fair value changes of the derivative (that only relate to 80 per cent of the loan).*

The accounting seems complicated. Why put all compensating value changes in profit or loss and not have a direct adjustment of the carrying amount of the loan? Or even carrying the derivative at cost (= 0)? One reason for this is that the general principle of measuring all derivatives at fair value and recognizing all fair value re-measurements of derivatives in profit or loss is maintained. The other one is that putting all changes in profit or loss would lead to better accounting of ineffectiveness (not all hedging instruments are perfectly effective hedges).

Cash flow hedges

Cash flow hedge accounting is used when hedging a cash flow risk. This can be both a risk associated with an item recognized in the statement of financial position (such as a loan) and with forecast transactions, like expected future borrowings or expected purchases or sales. A forecast transaction can only be a hedged item when the transaction is highly probable.

Also for cash flow hedges, the derivative should be measured at fair value. However, changes in fair value are not recognized in profit or loss. That portion of the gain or loss on the hedging instrument which is determined to be an effective hedge, should be recognized in other comprehensive income and the ineffective portion shall be recognized in profit or loss.

Now complete Activity 17.13.

ACTIVITY 17.13

Show how the following cash flow hedges should be accounted for.

1 An entity wants to have a two-year fixed rate loan, but the bank only offers a variable rate loan and an interest rate swap. The swap contract requires the entity to pay fixed interest amounts in return for variable interest amounts. The variable interest amounts received will be used to pay the variable interest on the loan. Both the loan and the swap have a nominal amount of €10 000. The fixed rate is 5 per cent, the variable rate is Euribor + 1 per cent. Immediately after the transactions, Euribor increases from 4 per cent to 5 per cent and remains so until the end of year 2.

2 A production entity has a detailed forecast of the raw materials purchases to be made for the next year. To hedge the price risk, it bought two monthly futures (April and June) in November 20X3 at fixed raw material prices. The entity expected to purchase 100 000 units of raw material for these months, and the futures are based on that number of units. At reporting date, the fair value of both futures is –€10 000 each (the raw material price has obviously decreased). At reporting date, the current expectation is that the April purchase will be 80 000 and the June purchase will be 110 000 units.

Activity feedback

1 At the end of year 1, the fair value of the swap, after having swapped the interests for year 1,

is €754 (the difference between interest to be received in year 2 (6 per cent× 80 000) and interest to be paid in year 2 (5 per cent × 80 000), discounted for one year at 6 per cent). The interest rate swap is measured at the fair value of €754 and this amount is included in other comprehensive income and presented in equity as a separate cash flow hedge reserve. In profit or loss the interest costs are €4000 (5 per cent× €10 000). At the end of year 2, the fair value of the swap, after having swapped the interests for year 2, is €0 (a derivative at the end of its lifetime always has a fair value of €0). Interest costs in profit or loss are again €4000, other comprehensive income is –€754. The cash flow hedge reserve is reduced to €0.

2 The April future is partly ineffective. As a result, the fair value should be split into the effective part (–€8000) and the ineffective part (–€2000). The effective part is included in other comprehensive income and presented as a cash flow hedge reserve. The ineffective part is included in profit or loss. The June future is fully effective. There is overhedging (just a part of the purchases are hedged), but overhedging does not result in ineffectiveness of the hedge. Therefore, the full amount of –€10 000 is included in other comprehensive income and presented as a cash flow hedge reserve.

As a real world illustration of hedge accounting, we have included parts of note 16 on Treasury Risk Management from the annual report 2014 of Unilever.

REAL LIFE ILLUSTRATION

16. Treasury risk management

Derivatives and hedge accounting

Derivatives are measured at fair value with any related transaction costs expensed as incurred. The treatment of changes in the value of derivatives depends on their use as explained below.

(I) Fair value hedges[a]

Certain derivatives are held to hedge the risk of changes in value of a specific bond or other loan. In these situations, the Group designates the liability and related derivative to be part of a fair value hedge relationship. The carrying value of the bond is adjusted by the fair value of the risk being hedged, with changes going to the income statement. Gains and losses on the corresponding derivative are also recognised in the income statement. The amounts recognised are offset in the income statement to the extent that the hedge is effective. When the relationship no longer meets the criteria for hedge accounting, the fair value hedge adjustment made to the bond is amortised to the income statement using the effective interest method.

(Continued)

(II) Cash flow hedges[a]

Derivatives are also held to hedge the uncertainty in timing or amount of future forecast cash flows. Such derivatives are classified as being part of cash flow hedge relationships. For an effective hedge, gains and losses from changes in the fair value of derivatives are recognised in equity. Any ineffective elements of the hedge are recognised in the income statement. If the hedged cash flow relates to a non-financial asset, the amount accumulated in equity is subsequently included within the carrying value of that asset. For other cash flow hedges, amounts deferred in equity are taken to the income statement at the same time as the related cash flow.

When a derivative no longer qualifies for hedge accounting, any cumulative gain or loss remains in equity until the related cash flow occurs. When the cash flow takes place, the cumulative gain or loss is taken to the income statement. If the hedged cash flow is no longer expected to occur, the cumulative gain or loss is taken to the income statement immediately.

(III) Net investment hedges[a]

Certain derivatives are designated as hedges of the currency risk on the Group's investment in foreign subsidiaries. The accounting policy for these arrangements is set out in note 1.

(IV) Derivatives for which hedge accounting is not applied

Derivatives not classified as hedges are held in order to hedge certain balance sheet items and commodity exposures. No hedge accounting is applied to these derivatives, which are carried at fair value with changes being recognised in the income statement.

[a]Applying hedge accounting has not led to material ineffectiveness being recognised in the income statement for both 2013 and 2014

The Group is exposed to the following risks that arise from its use of financial instruments, the management of which is described in the following sections:

- liquidity risk (see note 16A);
- market risk (see note 16B); and
- credit risk (see note 17B).

16c. Derivatives and hedging

The Group does not use derivative financial instruments for speculative purposes. The uses of derivatives and the related values of derivatives are summarised in the following table:

	€ million Trade and other receivables	€ million Other current financial assets	€ million Trade payables and other liabilities	€ million Current financial liabilities	€ million Non-current financial liabilities	€ million Total
31 December 2014						
Foreign exchange derivatives						
Fair value hedges	6	–	(1)	–	–	5
Cash flow hedges	9	28	(3)	–	–	34
Hedges of net investments in foreign operations	–	356[a]	–	(23)	–	333
Hedge accounting not applied	106	(225)[a]	(44)	(196)	–	(359)
Cross-currency swaps						
Hedge accounting not applied	–	137	–	(58)	(71)	8
Interest rate swaps						–
Fair value hedges	–	–	–	–	(2)	(2)
Cash flow hedges	–	–	(100)	–	–	(100)
Hedge accounting not applied	–	–	–	–	–	–

REAL LIFE ILLUSTRATION *(Continued)*

	€ million Trade and other receivables	€ million Other current financial assets	€ million Trade payables and other liabilities	€ million Current financial liabilities	€ million Non- current financial liabilities	€ million Total
Commodity contracts						
Cash flow hedges	–	–	(15)	–	–	(15)
Hedge accounting not applied	–	–	(1)	–	–	(1)
	121	296	(164)	(277)	(73)	(97)
	Total assets	417		**Total liabilities**	(514)	(97)
31 December 2013						
Foreign exchange derivatives						
Fair value hedges	2	–	(6)	–	–	(4)
Cash flow hedges	16	–	(15)	–	–	1
Hedges of net investments in foreign operations	–	4	–	(69)	–	(65)
Hedge accounting not applied	48	116	(32)	(98)	–	34
Cross-currency swaps						
Hedge accounting not applied	–	174	–	(32)	(100)	42
Interest rate swaps						
Fair value hedges	–	–	–	–	–	–
Cash flow hedges	–	–	(41)	–	–	(41)
Hedge accounting not applied	–	–	–	–	–	–
Commodity contracts						
Cash flow hedges	16	–	(2)	–	–	14
Hedge accounting not applied	–	–	–	–	–	–
	82	294	(96)	(199)	(100)	(19)
	Total assets	376		**Total liabilities**	(395)	(19)

[a] Swaps that hedge the currency risk on intra-group loans and offset €356 million within 'Hedges of net investments in foreign operations' are included within 'Hedge Accounting not applied'.

DISCLOSURE

According to IFRS 7, para. 7, an entity shall disclose information that enables users of its financial statements to evaluate the significance of financial instruments for its financial position and performance. Specific disclosure requirements include:

- carrying amounts of each category of financial assets and financial liabilities
- details regarding financial assets and financial liabilities at fair value through profit or loss
- reclassifications

- details on offsetting financial assets and financial liabilities
- collateral pledged or held
- allowance accounts for credit losses
- defaults and breaches
- amounts of income, expense, gains or losses
- hedge accounting information
- fair value of financial instruments
- qualitative and quantitative information on risk, including credit risk, liquidity risk and market risk
- details on transfers of financial assets.

IFRS 4, INSURANCE CONTRACTS

Introduction

Before the issue of IFRS 4, *Insurance Contracts* in March 2004, there was no IAS to deal with the diverse practices of insurance contract accounting. The IASC had established a steering committee in 1997 to investigate the issues surrounding insurance contracts, but the IASB did not really discuss the matter until 2001. As with many other controversial issues, the IASB has split the project for insurance contracts into two.

Phase I requirements are:

(a) to make limited improvements to accounting practices for insurance contracts without requiring major changes that may need to be reversed in *Phase II*

(b) to require disclosure that:

    (i) identifies and explains the amounts in an insurer's financial statements arising from insurance contracts and

    (ii) helps users of those financial statements understand the amount, timing and uncertainty of future cash flows from insurance contracts.

Phase I resulted in IFRS 4, which is basically a presentation and disclosure Standard.

Phase II is concerned with the recognition and measurement of an insurance contract. An ED, *Insurance Contracts*, was published in July 2010 and June 2013. If adopted, the ED will replace IFRS 4.

The basic issues with an insurance contract are determining the risks and rewards in the contract, who in substance owns them and how to treat payments received and made within the contract.

Insurance contract

As defined by IFRS 4, this is a contract under which one party (the insurer) accepts significant insurance risk from another party (the policy holder) by agreeing to compensate the policy holder if a specified uncertain future event (the insured event) adversely affects the policyholder.

Several terms used in the above definition are also defined in IFRS 4:

- *Insurance risk*: risk, other than financial risk, transferred from the holder of a contract to the issuer.

- *Insured event:* an uncertain future event that is covered by an insurance contract and creates insurance risk.

Risk is the essence of an insurance contract and as such at least one of the following will be uncertain at the inception of the contract:

1 whether an insured event will occur

2 when it will occur

3 how much the insurer will need to pay if it occurs.

For example, insurance against theft or damage to property is an insurance contract as 1 and 2 above are uncertain and the contract will compensate the policy holder for the loss or damage, albeit generally to a limited amount. Life insurance is also deemed an insurance contract under IFRS 4, as, although death is certain, the timing is uncertain. Now complete the following Activity.

ACTIVITY 17.14

Identify which of the following are insurance contracts.

(a) Compensation in cash or kind to contract holders for losses suffered while travelling.

(b) Financial guarantee contract that requires payment even if the holder has not insured a loss on the failure of the debtor to make payments when due.

(c) A contract that requires specified payments to reimburse the holder for a loss it incurs because a specified debtor fails to make payment when due.

(d) A catastrophe bond in which principal interest payments are reduced significantly if a specified triggering event occurs and the triggering event includes a condition that the issuer of the bond suffered a loss.

(e) Loan contract containing a prepayment fee that is waived if prepayment results from the borrower's death.

Activity feedback

(a), (c) and (d) are insurance contracts.

In (b) there is no specified uncertain future event; the payment is required whatever happens to the debt. Before the contract in (e), the borrower faced no risk corresponding to the prepayment fee, thus no risk has been transferred.

Scope

An entity applies IFRS 4 (para. 2) to:

- Insurance contracts that it issues and reinsurance contracts that it holds. A reinsurance contract is defined as an insurance contract issued by one insurer (the reinsurer) to compensate another insurer (the cedant) for losses on one or more contracts issued by the cedant.
- Financial instruments that it issues with a discretionary participation feature.

Excluded from the requirements of IFRS 4 (para. 4) are:

- Product warranties issued directly by a manufacturer, dealer or retailer.
- Employers' assets and liabilities under employee benefit plans.
- Contractual rights or contractual obligations that are contingent on the future use of, or right to use, a non-financial item (e.g. some licence fees, royalties, contingent lease payments and similar items), as well as a lessee's residual value guarantee embedded in a finance lease.

- Financial guarantees into which an entity enters or retains on transferring financial assets or financial liabilities within the scope of IAS 39 to another party, regardless of whether the financial guarantees are described as financial guarantees, letters of credit or insurance contracts.
- Contingent consideration payable or receivable in a business combination.
- Direct insurance contracts that the entity holds (i.e. direct insurance contracts in which the entity is the policyholder). However, a cedant shall apply this IFRS to reinsurance contracts that it holds.

Now complete the following Activity.

ACTIVITY 17.15

A sells computer hardware and offers an extended warranty to its customers for a fixed period covering servicing, repairs and maintenance for an annual fixed fee. Is this an insurance contract requiring disclosure under IFRS 4?

Activity feedback

A is accepting significant insurance risks under this contract as neither the number of services that A will be required to perform nor their nature is predetermined, so *this does meet the definition of an insurance contract. However, IFRS 4 specifically excludes product warranties issued by a retailer, so this falls outside the scope of IFRS 4. If the extended warranty had been provided by a third party, e.g. a specialist repair firm or even a competing manufacturer or retailer, then the exclusion would not apply and IFRS 4 would need to be applied. The warranty obligation would be accounted for in accordance with IAS 37, Provisions.*

Disclosure

IFRS 4 requires disclosure of information that:

- identifies and explains the amounts in its financial statements arising from insurance contracts
- helps users to understand the amount, timing and uncertainty of future cash flows from insurance contracts.

Under the first one, accounting policies, recognized assets, liabilities, income and expenses will be disclosed as well as processes used to determine assumptions within these amounts and the effects of changes in these assumptions. Under the second one, terms and conditions of the insurance contract that have a material effect on the cash flows of the insurer, and actual claims compared with previous estimates, will be disclosed.

Other main features

Other main features of IFRS 4 are that the Standard:

- exempts an insurer temporarily (until Phase II of the project is complete) from some requirements of other IFRSs
- permits an insurer to change its accounting policies, but only if the resulting financial statements would be more relevant but no less reliable or vice versa
- permits insurers to introduce an accounting policy that would see the insurance liabilities in each period reflected at market interest rates

- does not require the insurer to change its accounting policies even if they are excessively prudent
- requires an insurer to unbundle a deposit component (a financial instrument element of the contract) from the insurance component of an insurance contract when certain conditions are met
- no longer allows catastrophe and equalization provisions
- requires a liability adequacy test at each reporting date.

Financial guarantee contracts

A financial guarantee contract is defined as a contract that requires the issuer to make specified payments to reimburse the holder for a loss it incurs because a specified debtor fails to make payment when due in accordance with the original or modified terms of a debt instrument. These could also be regarded as insurance contracts. However, IFRS 9 states that these financial guarantee contracts are within its scope, but permits an issuer to elect to apply either IFRS 9 or IFRS 4 on those contracts where it has previously asserted explicitly that it regards such contracts as insurance contracts.

IFRS 9 requires that such contracts are initially measured at fair value and subsequently amortized and recorded as income over the period to which the guarantee applies, unless the liability measured in terms of IAS 37 exceeds the carrying amount.

The illustration below should help you understand this.

ILLUSTRATION

Entity Alpha provides a financial guarantee to a third party entity Beta on 1 January 200X. Under the guarantee, if entity Beta defaults on a specific loan of £10 000 that it has with a bank, Alpha will become liable to repay the loan to the bank excluding interest. The guarantee lasts for five years.

On the date of the guarantee being provided, Beta paid Alpha £500, which it considered to be the fair value of granting the guarantee. In 200Y, the credit market has deteriorated to such a degree that it has become probable that Beta will default on its loan to the bank. How should Alpha account for the guarantee in its accounts in accordance with IAS 39?

On initial recognition, the guarantee must be recognized at fair value, that is £500, thus Alpha will show a financial guarantee liability of £500. Subsequently it will

be amortized over its life of five years. Thus, Alpha will credit income with £100 and reduce the liability by £100 for the year ended 31 December 200X.

During 200Y, when the possibility arises that Beta will default on the loan, then Alpha will have to apply IAS 37 to account for the financial guarantee liability. This means Alpha needs to determine the best estimate of the expenditure it would incur if it had to settle the loan. If we assume the best estimate of the liability at 31 December 200Y is £9650 then Alpha will need to charge £9250 as an expense in the statement of comprehensive income and credit the financial guarantee liability account with £9250. The balance on the financial guarantee liability will now be £9650, the amount required to settle the loan.

Insurance contract – Phase II

The IASB has issued two EDs on Insurance Contracts, the first in 2010 and the second, as a replacement, in 2013. The ED proposes a measurement model that provides information about how insurance contracts contribute to the entity's financial position and performance. The balance sheet amount reflects the expected contract profit from the insurance contract and a current estimate of the amount of future cash flows from the contract, adjusted to reflect the timing and uncertainty relating to those cash flows. The statement of comprehensive income reports on operating results which reflects underwriting experience, the change in uncertainty and the profit from services in the period and, through interest and discount rate changes, both a current and a cost-based view of the cost of financing the insurance contract. It is proposed that any changes in estimates relating to the profits to be earned from an insurance contract be recognized over the remaining coverage period.

The new IFRS 4 will not be issued before the second half of 2016. It will probably be effective from 2019 or 2020 on or even later. Check the website of the IASB for the most current information.

SUMMARY

In this chapter, we have summarized the essential parts of what is one of the most complex set of Standards of the IASB: IAS 32, IAS 39, IFRS 7 and IFRS 9 on financial instruments. IFRS 9 will be effective for annual reports from 2018 onwards.

A financial instrument is a contract that gives rise to a financial asset of one entity and a financial liability or equity instrument of another. It is important to distinguish between a financial liability and equity. A financial liability normally includes a contractual obligation to deliver cash; an equity instrument does not. Compound financial instruments should be split. A financial instrument is recognized when an entity becomes party to the contractual provisions of the instrument. Derecognition is required when the contractual rights or obligations expire and when there is a qualified transfer.

In IFRS 9, the classification and measurement of financial instruments depends on the business model for managing financial assets and the contractual cash flow characteristics of the financial asset. When the contractual cash flows of the debt assets are solely principal and interest and the business model is to collect contractual cash flows only, the instruments are measured at amortized cost, unless the choice is made to use the fair value option. For other financial assets, measurement will normally be at fair value either through profit or loss or through other comprehensive income.

The impairment model of IFRS 9 is based on expected losses, as compared to incurred losses in IAS 39, and involves three stages of measurement. When specific conditions are met, entities may apply fair value hedge accounting or cash flow hedge accounting. There are extensive significant disclosure requirements

IFRS 4 fills a gap in IAS but it is a stopgap until Phase II of the project on insurance contracts is complete.

EXERCISES

Suggested answers to exercises marked ✓ are to be found in the Student online resources, with suggested answers to the remaining questions available in the Instructor online resources.

✓**1** Discuss the problems faced by users of financial reports if financial instruments are kept off the statement of financial position.

2 What is a financial instrument?

3 How does the IASB differentiate between financial instruments and other assets and liabilities?

4 What is a derivative?

5 Explain the three classifications of financial assets under IFRS 9.

6 On 1 April 2013, Xtol issued a 5 per cent $50 million convertible loan note at par. Interest is payable annually in arrears on 31 March each year. The loan note is redeemable at par or convertible into equity shares at the option of the loan note holders on 31 March 2016. The interest on an equivalent loan note without the conversion rights would be 8 per cent per annum. The present values of $1 receivable at the end of each year, based on discount rates of 5 per cent and 8 per cent, are:

	5%	8%
End of year 1	0·95	0·93
2	0·91	0·86
3	0·86	0·79

Required:

Identify how the above transaction should be treated in the financial statement of Xtol for the year ended 31 March 2014.

(ACCA, Financial Reporting (International), June 2014, adapted)

7 (i) Coatmin is a government-controlled bank. Coatmin was taken over by the government during the recent financial crisis. At the start of the financial year to 30 November 2013, Coatmin gave a financial guarantee contract on behalf of one of its subsidiaries, a charitable organization, committing it to repay the principal amount of $60 million if the subsidiary defaulted on any payments due under a loan. The loan related to the financing of the construction of new office premises and has a term of three years. It is being repaid by equal annual instalments of principal with the first payment having been paid. Coatmin has not secured any compensation in return for giving the guarantee, but assessed that it had a fair value of $1.2 million. The guarantee is measured at fair value through profit or loss. The guarantee was given on the basis that it was probable that it would not be called upon. At 30 November 2014, Coatmin became aware of the fact that the subsidiary was having financial difficulties with the result that it has not paid the second instalment of principal. It has assessed that it is probable the guarantee will now be called. However, just before the signing of the financial statements for the year ended 30 November 2014, the subsidiary secured a donation which enabled it to make the second repayment before the guarantee was called upon. It is now anticipated that the subsidiary will be able to meet the final payment. Discounting is immaterial and the fair value of the guarantee is higher than the value determined under IAS 37, *Provisions, Contingent Liabilities and Contingent Assets*.

(ii) Coatmin provides loans to customers and funds the loans by selling bonds in the market. The liability is designated at fair value through profit or loss. The bonds have a fair value increase of $50 million in the year to 30 November 2014, of which $5 million relates to the reduction in Coatmin's creditworthiness.

Required:

Discuss, with suitable calculations where necessary, the accounting treatment of the above transactions in the financial statements of Coatmin.

(ACCA, Corporate Reporting (International), December 2014, adapted)

8   Ethan, a public limited company, develops, operates and sells investment properties. Ethan wishes to apply the fair value option rules of IFRS 9, *Financial Instruments* to debt issued to finance its investment properties. Ethan's argument for applying the fair value option is based upon the fact that the recognition of gains and losses on its investment properties and the related debt would otherwise be inconsistent. Ethan argued that there is a specific financial correlation between the factors, such as interest rates, that form the basis for determining the fair value of both Ethan's investment properties and the related debt.

Required:

Discuss how the above transactions should be recorded in the consolidated financial statements of Ethan.

(ACCA, Corporate Reporting (International), June 2012, adapted)

9   The directors of Lizzer, a public limited company, have read various reports on excessive disclosure in the annual report. They have decided to take action and do not wish to disclose any further detail concerning the two instances below.

(i) Lizzer is a debt issuer whose business is the securitization of a portfolio of underlying investments and financing their purchase through the issuing of listed, limited recourse debt. The repayment of the debt is dependent upon the performance of the underlying investments. Debt holders bear the ultimate risks and rewards of ownership of the underlying investments. Given the debt specific nature of the underlying investments, the risk profile of individual debt may differ. Lizzer does not consider its debt holders as being among the primary users of the financial statements and, accordingly, does not wish to provide disclosure of the debt holders' exposure to risks in the financial statements, as distinct from the risks faced by the company's shareholders, in accordance with IFRS 7, *Financial Instruments: Disclosures*.

(ii) At the date of the financial statements, 31 January 2013, Lizzer's liquidity position was quite poor, such that the directors described it as 'unsatisfactory' in the management report. During the first quarter of 2013, the situation worsened with the result that Lizzer was in breach of certain loan covenants at 31 March 2013. The financial statements were authorised for issue at the end of April 2013. The directors' and auditor's reports both emphasized the considerable risk of not being able to continue as a going concern. The notes to the financial statements indicated that there was 'ample' compliance with all loan covenants as at the date of the financial statements. No additional information about the loan covenants was included in the financial statements. Lizzer had been close to breaching the loan covenants in respect of free cash flows and equity ratio requirements at 31 January 2013. The directors of Lizzer felt that, given the existing information in the financial statements, any further disclosure would be excessive and confusing to users.

Required:

Discuss the directors' view that no further information regarding the two instances above should be disclosed in the financial statements because it would be 'excessive'.

(ACCA, Corporate Reporting (International), June 2013, adapted)

REVENUE

18

OBJECTIVES After studying this chapter you should be able to:

- define revenue and what type of transactions it arises from

- understand the basic principles of IFRS 15, including the five major steps in revenue recognition

- apply the concepts of IFRS 15 to real life examples

- identify the specific problems related to construction contracts

- identify the presentation and disclosure requirements in respect of revenue in accordance with IFRS 15.

INTRODUCTION

The income statement or profit or loss statement reports the profit of an entity by matching expenses to revenues, but before we can carry out this matching, we need to define revenues and expenses and identify point at which we should recognize them. Many standards that we have already considered are about the expense side of these issues, but, as yet, we have given very little consideration to the revenue.

Chapter 5 dealt with the general principles in respect of revenue, but this chapter will consider them in more detail. We will discuss the principles included in IFRS 15,

Revenue from Contracts with Customers, published in May 2015. IFRS 15 is effective from 2018 and may be adopted early. IFRS 15 replaces two other primary standards: IAS 18, *Revenue* and IAS 11, *Construction Contracts*. Although IAS 18 and IAS 11 may still be applied for annual reports before 2018, we will limit the discussions in this book to the new IFRS 15. The main difference between IAS 18 and IFRS 15 is the basic concept of revenue recognition. In IAS 18, revenue is recognized when substantially all risks and rewards have been transferred to a third party, while IFRS 15 links revenue recognition to the transfer of control over the asset. For most transactions, IAS 18 and IFRS 15 will have the same impact on financial statements, as the transfer of risks and rewards and that of control over the asset occur at the same time. However, IFRS 15 will result in different accounting in more complex transfers. Furthermore, IFRS 15, although still being principles-based, contains more specific guidance than IAS 18. In this chapter, we will have a special focus on construction contracts. In the majority of cases, accounting for construction contracts will probably not have to be changed when moving from IAS 11 to IFRS 15, although some specifications in the contract might be needed. IFRS 15 contains many illustrative examples. We will use some of these as a basis for the Activities in this chapter.

It is interesting to note that an almost equivalent standard on revenue recognition was published at the same time by the FASB in the US. There had not been a general revenue recognition standard before in the US. Instead, there were many specific and inconsistent revenue recognition rules for specific transactions and industries spread out over many standards. For the US, the move to one general revenue recognition standard is certainly an important change to a more principles-based standard setting.

WHAT IS REVENUE?

Both the *Conceptual Framework for Financial Reporting* and IFRS 15 define income as 'increases in economic benefits during the accounting period in the form of inflows or enhancements of assets or decreases of liabilities that result in increases in equity, other than those relating to contributions from equity participants'. The definition in the 2015 Exposure Draft of the Conceptual Framework is essentially the same. Note that the definition of income is an illustration of the balance sheet approach (or asset-liability approach) of IFRS, as income is defined by reference to (changes in) assets and liabilities.

The Conceptual Framework further states that income encompasses both revenues and gains. Revenues are further described as arising 'in the course of the ordinary activities of an entity'. This is also the definition in IFRS 15. So what is this revenue and how do we distinguish it from other gains?

Revenue is regarded by many as simply the cash that you are paid for selling things and this simple idea also implies exchange – cash for things. We have also carried this idea of exchange through to the balance sheet. Consider the simple exchange of selling an item of inventory for cash – the accounting entries would be to derecognize the item of inventory in the balance sheet and recognize the asset of cash. The asset of cash would qualify as revenue and against this, we would match relevant expenses to determine profit. Traditionally, we have not regarded the item of inventory as revenue until it is sold or at least until we have exchanged it for another asset, perhaps a debtor. This approach seems to equate revenue with economic activity involving exchange with a customer and ignores other items such as gains on assets that are revalued or carried at current value.

There are several important notions in the definition of revenue:

1 Revenue is the *gross inflow*, i.e. before the deduction of any expenses.

2 Revenue results from ordinary activities. This notion distinguishes revenue from other gains. Gains are defined in the Framework as 'other items that meet the definition of income and may, or may not, arise in the ordinary activities of an entity'.

3 Revenue gives rise to an increase in equity.

Now work carefully through Activities 18.1 and 18.2.

ACTIVITY 18.1

An entity receives €100 for the sale of an item of inventory. This amount includes a sales tax at 25 per cent on cost which is payable to the tax authorities. The entity also sells another item of inventory on behalf of an agent for which it only retains a 10 per cent commission charge on sale price. Identify the revenue to the entity in both cases.

Activity feedback

The first item of inventory only results in an increase in equity of €80. The other €20 is paid directly to the tax authorities and is effectively collected by us on their behalf. The second item of inventory has only generated revenue and subsequent increase in equity to the entity of €10. The other €90 is collected on behalf of the agent.

ACTIVITY 18.2

The following transactions occur in an accounting period in separate entities:

1 An entity issued 1m €1 shares at a premium on nominal value of €2.

2 An entity revalued its investment property to fair value, recognizing the fair value change in profit or loss.

3 An entity made a book profit on the sale of its property.

4 An entity dealt in the retail of widgets and made sales of €150 000, 50 per cent of which are on credit.

5 An entity is an audit firm and has provided services by doing audit work.

Identify the revenue for each entity for the period.

Activity feedback

All these transactions give rise to an increase in equity, but only (4) and (5) are always regarded as revenue, (4)
being a transfer of goods and (5) being a transfer of a service. The conclusion for (3) depends on the nature of the entity, which has not been given. If the entity were a property trader, the gross receipt would be revenue, as selling properties is the ordinary course of business. If the entity were, for instance, a production company that irregularly sells some of its properties, property trading is not part of the ordinary business and only the book profit would be recognized in profit or loss (normally part of 'Other income'). This would be called a gain.

The share issue (1) is income received from equity participants, and the revaluation of property (2) is not revenue as it does not arise in the course of an entity's ordinary activities (there is no exchange transactions). The revaluation, however, is income, more specifically a gain. It would also be a gain if it were not recognized in profit or loss, but rather directly in equity (being part of other comprehensive income).

THE BASIC OUTLINE OF IFRS 15

The 'core principle' of the proposals is that an entity should recognize revenue to depict the transfer of promised goods or services to customers in an amount which reflects the consideration to which the entity expects to be entitled in exchange for those goods or services. In order to achieve this principle, an entity should apply all five of the designated steps, which are outlined below:

Step 1. Identify the contract(s) with the customer.

Step 2. Identify the performance obligations in the contract.

Step 3. Determine the transaction price.

Step 4. Allocate the transaction price to the performance obligations in the contract.

Step 5. Recognize revenue when (or as) the entity satisfies a performance obligation.

IFRS 15 also includes a cohesive set of disclosure requirements.

The scope of IFRS 15 is for all contracts with customers, with the exception of lease contracts, insurance contracts and contracts that are financial instruments. So, for example, interest and dividend revenues are out of scope. And there is one more typical scope exemption: IFRS 15 does not apply to non-monetary exchanges between entities in the same line of business to facilitate sales to customers or potential customers. An example would be a contract between two oil companies that agree to an exchange of oil to fulfil a demand from their customers in different specified locations on a timely basis.

STEP 1. IDENTIFY THE CONTRACT(S) WITH A CUSTOMER

A contract is an agreement between two or more parties that creates enforceable rights and obligations. For each separate contract, the requirements in IFRS 15 (steps 2–5) need to be applied. A contract contains identified obligations for all parties (to deliver goods, give services, to pay). For a contract to be under the scope of IFRS 15, it needs to have commercial substance and be probable that payments will be made. In most cases, this last criterion will not be relevant, while an entity will normally not enter into contracts where it is not probable that the customer will pay.

Combining contracts

In some cases, IFRS 15 requires an entity to combine contracts, entered into at or near the same time with the same customer, and account for them as one contract. This will be the case when the contracts are negotiated as a package with a single commercial objective, or when the amount of consideration to be paid in one contract depends on the price or performance of the other contract, or when the contracts are so much related that they together contain just one single performance obligation (see below).

Contract modification

A contract may be modified in a later period. A contract modification is a change in the scope or price or both of a contract (with the approval of all parties to the contract). A contract modification should be accounted for as a separate contract if both of the following conditions exist (para. 20):

(a) the scope of the contract increases because of the addition of promised goods or services that are distinct

(b) the price of the contract increases by an amount of consideration that reflects the entity's stand-alone prices of the additional promised goods or services (which does not prevent a discount being given if it is related to selling costs that would have been made for a new customer).

For changes in a contract that may not be accounted for as a separate contract, it is important to distinguish between two different situations (para. 21):

(a) the remaining goods and services are distinct from the goods and services transferred on or before the date of contract modification: account for the contract modification as if it were a termination of the existing contract and the creation of a new contract

(b) the remaining goods and services are not distinct and therefore form part of a single performance obligation that is partially satisfied at the date of contract modification: account for the contract modification as an adjustment to revenue.

Now try Activity 18.3 on contract modification.

ACTIVITY 18.3

Entity M promises to sell 120 products to a customer for €12 000 (€100 per product). The products are transferred to the customer over a six-month period. After the entry has transferred 60 products, the contract is modified to require the delivery of an additional 30 products (a total of 150 identical products). How would you evaluate this contract modification and what would be the effect on revenue recognition in the following cases:

- Case A. The price of the additional 30 products is €95 per product. The pricing reflects the stand-alone price of the additional products.
- Case B. The price of the additional 30 products was initially agreed to be €80 per product, which is not the stand-alone price. But before modification, the customer had identified minor defects in the 60 units already delivered. Parties agree that for this reason a credit will be given for the amount of €15 per product. The total credit of €900 (60 × €15) results in a price for the 30 additional units of €50 (€80 − (€900/30)).

(Adapted from IFRS 15, Illustrative examples, Example 5)

Activity feedback

In case A, the contract modification is, in effect, a new and separate contract for future products that does not affect the accounting for the existing contract. The entity recognizes €100 per product for the 120 units in the original contract and €95 per product for the 30 additional units.

In case B, the initially agreed price was not on a stand-alone basis. Therefore, the contract modification does not result in a separate contract. Because the remaining products to be delivered are distinct from those already transferred, the entity accounts for the modification as a termination of the original contract and the creation of a new contract. The amount recognized for the remaining products is a blended price of €93.33 (€100 × 60) + (€80 × 30). The €900 credit is accounted for as a reduction of revenue at the time of contract modification.

STEP 2. IDENTIFY THE PERFORMANCE OBLIGATIONS IN THE CONTRACT

A performance obligation is a promise in a contract with a customer to transfer a good or service to that customer. Distinct goods or services are accounted for separately as different performance obligations. Promised goods or services, which are not distinct, are combined until the entity identifies a bundle of goods or services which is distinct, thereby creating a single performance obligation. A series of distinct goods or services that are substantially the same and have the same pattern of transfer to the customer are treated as one performance obligation. In general, a good or service is distinct if the customer can benefit from the good or service either on its own or together with other resources which are readily available to that customer, and the entity's promise to transfer the good or service to the customer is separately identifiable from other promises in the contract (para. 27). The identification of several performance obligations that need to be recognized separately is an important new feature of IFRS 15, compared to IAS 18. This is not to say that in applying IAS 18 multi-element contracts were not separated for recognition purposes, but there were very few specific guidelines on how to do so.

ACTIVITY 18.4

SOFT is a software developer that enters into a contract with a customer to transfer a software licence, perform an installation service and provide unspecified software updates and technical support (online and telephone) for a two-year period. The entity sells the licence, installation service and technical support separately. The installation service includes changing the webscreen for each type of user. It is routinely performed by other entities and does not significantly modify the software. The software remains functional without the updates and the technical support. Identify the performance obligations in the contract.

(Adapted from IFRS 15, Illustrative examples, Example 11)

Activity feedback

Because the customer can benefit from each of the goods and services either on their own or together with *the other goods and services that are readily available, and because the promise to transfer each good and service is separately identifiable, the goods and services are distinct and SOFT identifies four performance obligations: the software licence, an installation service, software updates and technical support. All four are separately accounted for in recognizing revenue.*

If, however, as part of the installation service the software is to be substantially customized to add significant new functionality to enable the software to interface with other customized software applications used by the customer, the installation service and the software licence are not distinct and are to be considered as one performance obligation. Accordingly, the entity would identify three performance obligations in the contract.

Principal and agent

In determining the nature of the performance obligation, it is important to distinguish between a principal and an agent. We saw this issue before in Activity 18.1. If the nature of the promise is a performance obligation to provide the specified good or service itself, the entity is a principal. If the nature of the promise is to arrange for those goods or services to be provided by the other party, the entity is an agent. An entity that is an agent does not control the specified goods or service provided by another party before that good or service is transferred to the customer. An entity determines whether it is a principal or an agent for each specified good or service promised to the customer. When the entity is an agent, the fee or commission is the revenue. Indicators that an entity is a principal are (para. B37):

- The entity is primarily responsible for fulfilling the promise to provide the specified good or service.
- The entity has inventory risk before the specified good or service has been transferred to a customer or after that transfer (for example, on return).
- The entity has discretion in establishing prices for the specified good or service.
- The entity is exposed to credit risk for the amount receivable from the customer.

Warranties

Warranties provided may or may not be a separate performance obligation. IFRS 15 distinguishes between assurance-type warranties and service-type warranties. Assurance-type warranties provide a customer with assurance that the related product will function as the parties intended. This is not a distinct service and therefore not a separate performance obligation. Service-type warranties are separate performance obligations as these warranties can be purchased separately by the customer.

Customer options

Customers might be given options to buy additional goods or services for free or at a discount. If an entity grants such an option in the contract, there is a separate performance obligation only if the option provides a material right to the customer that it would not receive without entering into that contract. An example is a discount that is additional to the discounts that are typically given. Identifying the option as a separate performance obligation implies that part of the cash received for the current delivery of goods or services is not recognized as revenue at the time of delivery, but is deferred until the customer has exercised their option. In measuring the performance obligation, the likelihood that the option will be exercised is included. We will investigate the customer option further later on in this chapter (step 5).

Non-refundable upfront fees

Non-refundable upfront fees, like joining fees in health club membership contracts, will often be advance payments for future goods or services, being the performance obligation(s). Revenues will be recognized when the goods or services are provided.

Licences

A licence establishes a customer's right to the intellectual property of an entity. Licences may relate to software and technology, motion pictures, franchises, patents, etc. If the promise to grant a licence is not distinct from other promised goods or services in the contract, the entity will identify all promises as a single performance obligation. We will return to licences later on in this chapter in discussing revenue recognition (step 5).

STEP 3. DETERMINE THE TRANSACTION PRICE

The transaction price is the amount of consideration to which an entity expects to be entitled in exchange for transferring promised goods or services to a customer, excluding amounts collected on behalf of third parties (such as sales taxes). Note that the amount of revenue is the expected entitlement, not the possibly lower expected receipts (no correction for doubtful debts). The transaction price can be a fixed amount of customer consideration, but it may also include variable consideration or consideration in a form other than cash. Non-cash considerations are to be measured at fair value. The transaction price is also adjusted for the effects of time value of money if the contract includes a significant timing component.

Variable consideration

If the consideration is variable, an entity estimates the amount of consideration to which it will be entitled in exchange for the promised goods or services. The amount of variable consideration may be estimated by determining either the expected value (the sum of probability-weighted amounts in a range of possible consideration amounts), or the most likely amount (the single most likely outcome of the contract), whichever is most suitable. However, the estimated amount of variable consideration will only be included in the transaction price to the extent that it is highly probable that a significant reversal in the amount of cumulative revenue recognized will not occur when the uncertainty associated with the variable consideration is subsequently resolved. At the end of each reporting period, the estimated transaction price shall be updated for the reassessment of the variable consideration.

Right of return

A customer may be entitled to a refund in the case of a sale with a right of return. Because a customer is allowed to return a product, the consideration received from the customer is variable. Revenue may not be recognized for the products expected to be returned. Furthermore, the entity shall recognize a refund liability for the amount of consideration received (or receivable) for which the entity does not expect to be entitled as well as an asset (and corresponding adjustment to the cost of sales) for its right to recover products from customers on settling the refund liability. The refund liability shall be updated at the end of each reporting period.

ACTIVITY 18.5

Buybuy is a retailer company selling consumer electronics by internet. Every customer has the right to return the product within 20 days if they are not satisfied. They will receive a full refund when the product is returned in its original state. One of the products sold is a tablet. The cost of each product is €200; the sales price is €500. Based on its experience, Buybuy expects that 5 per cent of the products sold will be returned. The amount of consideration is estimated by using the expected value method. How should Buybuy account for the sale of a tablet?

Activity feedback

Buybuy recognizes revenue per tablet for an amount of €475 (95% x €500). The journal entry will be:

Dr Cash	500
Cr Revenue (95% x 500)	475
Cr Refund liability (5% x 500)	25
And	
Dr Costs of goods sold (95% x 200)	190
Dr Right on tablet (5% x €200)	10
Cr Tablet	200

The right on tablet signifies that when the tablet is returned and the refund is given, Buybuy again has the asset within its inventory.

Note that in this example, we apply the expected value method on an individual product. In reality, it will be applied on a number of contracts.

Note further that the entity will know whether it is highly probable that a significant reversal in the amount of cumulative revenue recognized will not occur, when the uncertainty associated with the variable consideration is subsequently resolved. Based on experience and the short return period, the entity could do so. But in other more individual or non-routine contracts with a right of return, revenue would probably only be recognized after the return period has expired.

STEP 4. ALLOCATE THE TRANSACTION PRICE TO THE SEPARATE PERFORMANCE OBLIGATIONS IN THE CONTRACT

Having determined the transaction price in step 3 and the performance obligations in step 2, step 4 requires the allocation of the transaction price to the performance obligations in the contract. Of course, if there is only one performance obligation, this allocation is straightforward. If there is more than one performance obligation, the allocation should be done on the basis of the relative stand-alone selling prices of each distinct good or service promised in the contract. If a stand-alone price is not observable, estimations should be made.

A customer may receive a discount for purchasing a bundle of goods or services. The sum of the stand-alone prices then exceeds the promised consideration in a contract. Normally, the entity shall allocate the discount in proportion to all performance obligations in the contract. However, when an entity has observable evidence that the entire discount relates only to one or a subset of all performance obligations, the discount shall be allocated to these and not to all obligations.

Variable consideration may be attributable to a specific part of the contract, like a bonus that is contingent on transferring a specific good or service within a specified period of time.

Changes in the transaction price shall be allocated on the same basis as at contract inception. An entity shall not reallocate the transaction price to reflect changes in stand-alone prices after contract inception. Amounts allocated to a satisfied performance obligation shall be recognized as revenue (or as a reduction of revenue).

ACTIVITY 18.6

An entity enters into a contract with a customer to sell products A, B and C in exchange for €100. The entity will satisfy the performance obligations for each of the products at different points in time. The stand-alone selling prices are €50 (A), €25 (B) and €75 (C), totalling €150. The customer receives a discount of €50 for purchasing the bundle of goods. Determine the transaction price of A, B and C in each of the following cases:

1   The discount could not be allocated to a specific performance obligation

2   The discount would be allocated to B and C, based on objective evidence (for instance the stand-alone price of B and C normally sold together).

(Adapted from IFRS 15, Illustrative examples, Examples 33 and 34)

Activity feedback

1   *The discount of €50 is allocated proportionately, resulting in the following transaction prices: €33 (€50/€150 x € 100) for A, €17 (€25/€150 x €100) for B and €50 (€75/€150 x €100) for C.*

2   *The discount of €50 is allocated to B and C, resulting in the following transaction prices: €50 for A, €12.50 (€25/€100 x €50) for B and €37.50 (€75/€100 x €50) for C.*

STEP 5. RECOGNIZE REVENUE WHEN (OR AS) THE ENTITY SATISFIES A PERFORMANCE OBLIGATION

An entity recognizes revenue when (or as) it satisfies a performance obligation by transferring a promised good or service to a customer. This transfer happens when the customer obtains control of that good or service. The amount of revenue recognized is the amount allocated to the satisfied performance obligation.

Some indicators of the transfer of control are:

(a) The entity has a present right to payment for the asset.

(b) The customer has legal title to the asset.

(c) The entity has transferred physical possession of the asset.

(d) The customer has the significant risks and rewards of ownership of the asset.

(e) The customer has accepted the asset.

An important distinction is between:

(a) Performance obligations that are satisfied at a point in time: typically for promises to transfer goods to a customer. Revenue is recognized at the point in time.

(b) Performance obligations that are satisfied over time: typically for promises to transfer services to a customer. Revenue is recognized over time by selecting an appropriate method for measuring an entity's progress towards complete satisfaction of that performance obligation.

A performance obligation is satisfied over time if one of the following criteria is met:

(a) The customer simultaneously receives and consumes the benefits provided by the entity's performance as the entity performs.

(b) The entity's performance creates or enhances an asset (for example work in progress) that the customer controls as the asset is created or enhanced.

(c) The entity's performance does not create an asset with an alternative use to the entity and the entity has an enforceable right to payment for performance completed to date.

Clear examples of criterion (a) are routine or recurring services, such as cleaning services or payroll processing services. For more difficult services, the criterion is considered to be met if an entity determines that another entity would not need to substantially re-perform the work that the entity has completed to date in order to fulfil the remaining performance obligation.

Criterion (c) implies that the entity is either restricted contractually from readily directing the asset to another use during the creation or enhancement of that asset, or the entity is limited practically from readily directing the asset in its completed state to another use (that might be the case when, in using the asset for another customer, the entity would incur significant costs). The assessment of whether an asset has an alternative use to the entity is made at contract inception. The enforceable right to payment should be at all times throughout the duration of the contract, and the amount must at least compensate the entity for performance completed to date if the contract is terminated by the customer or another party for reasons other than the entity's failure to perform. This criterion is important in accounting for construction contracts, which we will discuss specifically at the end of the chapter.

Note that satisfying a performance obligation at a point in time can be either earlier or later than satisfying it over time. In other words, the point in time can be before or after the time period involved. Think about granting a licence for a defined period (if the criteria are met, the point in time will be when the licence is granted) and a construction contract (the point in time would be at the end of the construction period).

As this is an important step in recognizing revenue, we have included five Activities (18.7–18.11).

ACTIVITY 18.7

The listed entity Hollystone hires the audit firm DEKP, not being the auditor of the financial statements, to write a memo to assist management to account in accordance with IFRS for a major acquisition during the year. DEKP charges on the basis of hours taken. DEKP receives payment even if Hollystone terminates the contract early or management does not agree with the memo, unless the audit firm has performed culpably badly. Analyze whether DEKP satisfies the performance over time, on the basis of hours taken, or at a point in time, upon delivery of the memo. Use the three criteria described above.

Activity feedback

Criterion (a) has not been met. During the writing of the memo ('as the entity performs'), the listed entity does not receive the benefits. Those are received when the listed entity receives the memo. As there is no creation of an asset that Hollystone could control as the asset is created, criterion (b) is not applicable. But criterion (c) has been met: there is not an asset with an alternative use, because the memo is specifically in respect of the acquisition made by Hollystone, and DEKP cannot sell this memo to another entity. Furthermore, DEKP has an enforceable right of payment as it can charge the hours worked on producing the opinion. So the performance obligation is satisfied over time.

ACTIVITY 18.8

An entity enters into 100 separate contracts with customers to provide one year of maintenance services for €1000 per contract. The terms of the contract specify that at the end of the year, each customer has the option to renew the maintenance contract for a second year by paying an additional €1000. The entity charges a significantly higher price (€3000) for customers that do not sign up for the maintenance service in the first year (when the products are new).

This renewal option provides a material right to the customer. A customer's payment of €1000 in the first year is, in effect, a non-refundable prepayment of services to be provided in the second year. Consequently, the entity concludes that the promise to provide the option is a performance obligation. The entity expects that 90 per cent of customers will renew. The expected consideration for each contract is therefore €1900 (€1000 + 90% x €1000). Estimated costs for maintenance are €600 for each contract in year 1 and €750 in year 2. Revenue is recognized on the basis of costs incurred. How much revenue is recognized per contract in year 1 and how much in year 2?

(Adapted from IFRS 15, Illustrative examples, Example 51)

Activity feedback

Total costs per contract are €1275 (€600 + €675 (90% x €750)). Revenue in year 1 will therefore be €894 (€600/€1275 x €1900) and revenue in year 2 will be €1006 (€675/€1275 x €1900).

ACTIVITY 18.9

The supermarket Fresh and Yummer has issued a loyalty card to its customers. The customer receives one or more bonus points when specific products are purchased. The bonus points can be used to buy specific non-food articles at a significant discount. The fair value of one bonus point is considered to be €2.

During the reporting period, the number of bonus points provided is 4000. It is expected that 80 per cent of the bonus points will be used, that is 3200. During the period, 2400 bonus points have already been used, so it is expected that another 800 will be used in later years. The gross revenue during the reporting period is €200 000. What is the amount of revenue to be recognized in the reporting period?

Activity feedback

The loyalty programme results in a separate performance obligation. The total revenue of €200 000 should therefore be allocated to the products already sold and the bonus points provided. As the fair value of the bonus points is €2 per point, and the expectation is that 3200 points will be used, the gross total to use for the allocation is €206 400. The revenue to be recognized initially is €193 798 (€200 000 x (€200 000/€206 400)). This results in deferred revenue of €6202. In IFRS 15 terminology, this deferred revenue is a contract liability.

Because during the reporting period 75 per cent (2400/3200) of the bonus points have been used, 75 per cent of this contract liability is additionally included in revenue, resulting in a total amount of €198 450. The outstanding contract liability at the end of the reporting period is €1550 (25% x €6202).

Note that it would be incorrect to measure the contract liability at the year end at 800 (the number of outstanding bonus points) x €2 (fair value) = €1600.

Licences

We discussed licences in step 2. The performance obligation for a licence might be satisfied over time or at a point in time.

If the promise to grant a licence is distinct, it is a separate performance obligation. When the licence is a right to access the entity's intellectual property that exists throughout the licence period, revenue is recognized over time. When the licence is a right to use the entity's intellectual property as it exists at the point in time at which the licence is granted, revenue is recognized at that point in time.

Revenues for a sales-based or usage-based royalty promised in exchange for a licence shall be recognized at the later of: (a) when the subsequent sale or usage occurs, and (b) the performance obligation concerned has been satisfied.

ACTIVITY 18.10

One of the four performance obligations of the entity SOFT in Activity 18.4 is the software licence, granted over a two-year period. SOFT observes that it does not have any contractual or implied obligations (independent of the updates and technical support) to undertake activities that will change the functionality of the software during the licence period. The software has significant stand–alone functionality and, therefore, the ability of the customer to obtain benefits from the software is not substantially derived from the entity's ongoing activities. Should SOFT recognize revenue at a point in time or over time?

(Adapted from IFRS 15, Illustrative examples, Examples 54 and 55)

Activity feedback

As the contract does not require, and the customer does not reasonably expect, the entity to undertake activities that significantly affect the software (independent of the updates and technical support), the conclusion is that the entity's promise in transferring the licence is to provide a right to use the entity's intellectual property as it exists at a point in time. SOFT therefore recognizes the revenue at a point in time, that is, upon granting the licence for a customer to be able to use it.

If the software updates had been critical to the customer's ability to continue to make use of the licence, as in a rapidly changing technological environment, the promise to the customer would be to provide its most up-to-date intellectual property throughout the contract. The licence and the updates would be a single performance obligation that is satisfied over time.

ACTIVITY 18.11

The entity CHAMPION, a well-known sports team, licenses the use of its name and logo to a customer. The customer has the right to use the name and logo on items including t-shirts, caps, mugs and towels for two years. In exchange for providing the licence, CHAMPION will receive fixed consideration on entering the contract of €2 million and a royalty of 5 per cent of the sales price of any items using the team name or logo. The customer expects that CHAMPION will continue to play games and provide a competitive team. How should CHAMPION recognize its revenue?

(Adapted from IFRS 15, Illustrative examples, Example 61)

Activity feedback

First, CHAMPION needs to identify whether it has one or two performance obligations. As continuing to play games and provide a competitive team do not directly transfer a good or service, this cannot be a separate performance obligation. Therefore, the only performance obligation is the promise to grant the licence.

The next question will be whether the performance obligation is satisfied at a point in time (upon granting the licence) or over time (during two years). Because the customer would reasonable expect that the entity will undertake activities (continue to play games and provide a competitive team) that will significantly affect the intellectual property (the team name and logo), and the ability of the customer to obtain benefit from the name and logo is substantially derived from, or dependent on, the expected activities of the entity, the performance obligation is satisfied over time.

CHAMPION should then determine the measure of progress that will depict the entity's performance for the fixed consideration. For the consideration that is in the form of a sales-based royalty, the entity recognizes revenue as and when the sale of items using the team name or logo occur.

Measuring progress

In measuring satisfaction of a performance obligation over time, a measure of progress should be selected that depicts an entity's performance in transferring control of goods or services to the customer. Appropriate measures include output methods and input methods. Output methods recognize revenue on the basis of direct measurement of the value to the customer of the goods or services transferred to date, relative to the remaining goods or services promised under the contract. Examples of output methods are surveys of performance completed, milestones achieved and units produced or delivered. Use of output methods may be difficult in practice. Therefore, input methods may be necessary. Input methods recognize revenue on the basis of the entity's efforts or inputs to the satisfaction of a performance obligation, such as costs incurred. An entity shall exclude from an input method the effects of any input that do not depict the entity's performance, for instance costs related to inefficiencies and costs incurred that are not proportionate to the progress made in satisfying the performance obligation. For construction contracts, the costs of uninstalled materials is an example of costs to be excluded in determining progress.

As circumstances change over time, an entity shall update its measure of progress to be accounted for as a change in accounting estimate. It is not allowed to recognize revenue for a performance obligation over time when an entity would not be able to reasonably measure its progress towards complete satisfaction as it lacks reliable information. When, for example in the early stages of a contract, an entity is not able to reasonably measure the outcome of a performance obligation, but it expects to recover the costs incurred in satisfying the obligation, the entity shall recognize revenue only to the extent of the costs incurred until such time that it can reasonably measure the outcome of the performance obligation.

ACTIVITY 18.12

Mrs. Jones is a long-term member of the tennis club, Passing Shot. She pays an amount of €1000 a year, to be satisfied by way of prepayment. The membership allows unlimited access to the tennis courts throughout the year. During the autumn and winter seasons, there are indoor facilities. Mrs. Jones will normally only use the tennis courts during spring and summer and has never used the indoor facilities. How should Passing Shot recognize its revenue related to Mrs. Jones: evenly spread over time, or allocated to the spring and summer season when Mrs. Jones uses the tennis facilities?

Activity feedback

The question here is what the performance liability is. Mrs. Jones pays the contribution for making the facilities available during the whole year. She is also entitled to play tennis in the autumn and winter. And she is entitled to use the facilities as many times as she wants. The fact that she has in earlier years decided to use the facilities only in a restricted period of time is not relevant (unless she would be given a discount in exchange for agreeing to use the facilities for only part of the year). So, the performance liability for Passing Shot is to make the facilities available. Evenly spread recognition of revenue over the full year is the best measure of progress.

Repurchase agreements

A repurchase agreement is a contract in which an entity sells an asset and also promises or has the option to repurchase the asset. Generally, there are three forms:

1 A forward: the entity has an obligation to repurchase.

2 A call option: the entity has a right to repurchase.

3 A put option: the entity has an obligation to repurchase at the customer's request.

A forward or call option implies that a customer has not obtained control of the asset. Because there is no transfer of control, the contract shall be accounted for as a lease (when the repurchase amount is less than the original selling price) or a financing arrangement (when the repurchase amount is equal or more than the original selling price). The customer has gained control with a put option, but that does not automatically result in revenue recognition at the time of transfer. IFRS 15 requires that the entity shall consider at contract inception whether the customer has a significant economic incentive to exercise its option right. If so, the contract shall be accounted for as a lease. If not, it shall be accounted for as a sale with a right of return.

ACTIVITY 18.13

An entity enters into a contract with a customer for the sale of a tangible fixed asset on 1 January 2018 for €1 million. How should the contract be accounted for in the following two cases:

(a) The contract includes a call option that gives the entity the right to repurchase the asset for €1.1 million on or before 31 December 2018.

(b) The contract includes a put option that obliges the entity to repurchase the asset at the customer's request for €900 000 on or before 31 December 2018. The market value is expected to be €750 000 on 31 December 2018.

(Adapted from IFRS 15, Illustrative examples, Example 62)

Activity feedback

(a) As the control of the asset was not transferred to the customer, the entity accounts for the transaction as a financing arrangement, because the exercise price is more than the original selling price. The entity also recognizes interest expense for the difference between the exercise price (€1.1 million) and the cash received (€1 million), which increases the liability. When the option expires unexercised, the entity derecognizes the liability and recognizes revenue of €1.1 million on 31 December 2018. The asset is derecognized against cost of sales.

(b) At the inception of the contract, the entity assesses whether the customer has a significant economic incentive to exercise the put option. It concludes that such a significant economic incentive exists, as the repurchase price significantly exceeds the expected market value at the date of the repurchase. Consequently, the entity concludes that control of the asset has not been transferred to the customer and the entity accounts for the transaction as a lease.

Consignment

When an entity delivers a product to another entity, such as a dealer or distributor, for sale to end customers, it might be a consignment arrangement. Under a consignment arrangement, the entity still controls the product until a specified event occurs (sale of the product to the customer). When the delivered product is held on consignment, no revenue is recognized.

Bill-and-hold arrangements

A bill-and-hold arrangement is a contract under which an entity bills a customer for a product, but the entity retains physical possession of the product until it is transferred to the customer at a point in time in the future. For a bill-and-hold arrangement, a customer only has control of a product, and the entity only recognizes revenue when all of the following conditions are met (para. B81):

1 The reason for the bill-and-hold arrangement must be substantive (for example, the customer has requested the arrangement).

2 The product must be identified separately as belonging to the customer.

3 The product currently must be ready for physical transfer to the customer.

4 The entity cannot have the ability to use the product or to direct it to another customer.

CONTRACT COSTS

Contract costs are both costs to obtain a contract and costs to fulfil a contract. IFRS 15 requires an entity to recognize as an asset the incremental costs to obtain a contract if the entity expects to recover those costs. The incremental costs are those costs that an entity would not have incurred if the contract had not been obtained. An example is a sales commission. Non-incremental costs are expensed when incurred.

Costs to fulfil a contract are recognized as an asset when those costs directly relate to the contract and are beneficial, but only as far as they are expected to be recovered. We will discuss cost identification further by including an Activity in the section on construction contracts below (Activity 18.17).

The asset shall be amortized on a systematic basis that is consistent with the transfer to the customer of the goods or services to which the asset relates. A significant change in the timing of the transfer of the goods or services shall be accounted for as a change in accounting estimate. An impairment needs to be recognized to the extent that the carrying amount of the asset exceeds the remaining amount of the consideration to be received less the costs that relate directly to providing the goods or services and that have not been recognized as expenses. If applicable, an impairment shall be reversed.

PRESENTATION AND DISCLOSURE

When either party to a contract has performed, an entity shall present the contract in the statement of financial position as a contract asset or a contract liability, depending upon the relationship between the entity's performance and the customer's payment. An entity is free to use other terminology than 'contract asset' or 'contract liability'. An entity shall present any unconditional rights to consideration separately as a receivable. We will come back to the issue of presentation in the context of a construction contract in Activity 18.18.

The purpose of the disclosure requirements is that an entity will provide users of financial statements with comprehensive information about the nature, amount, timing and uncertainty of revenue and cash flows arising from the entity's contracts with customers. Specifically, IFRS 15 requires an entity to provide information about:

- revenue recognized from contracts with customers, including the disaggregation of revenue into appropriate categories
- contract balances, including the opening and closing balances of receivables, contract assets and contract liabilities

- performance obligations, including when the entity typically satisfies its performance obligations and the transaction price that is allocated to the remaining performance obligations in a contract
- significant judgements, and changes in judgements, made in applying the requirements to those contacts
- assets recognized from the costs to obtain or fulfil a contract with a customer.

ACTIVITY 18.14

On 1 January 2017, Advanced Lithography Machines (ALM), a manufacturer of lithography machines that produce microchips, closes a contract with BCMicroelectronics, a producer of microchips for mobile telephones, to deliver a lithography machine. The machine has already been produced by ALM and is ready for delivery, but, given the production planning of BCMicroelectronics, they want the machine to be delivered on 1 July 2017. ALM requires a prepayment of €2000 on 31 January 2017 and a final payment of €3000 upon delivery on 1 July 2017. Payments are made as required. The contract is cancellable until the delivery date. What journal entries would be required by ALM on 1 January 2017, 31 January 2017 and 1 July 2017?

Activity feedback

No journal entry is made on 1 January 2017. Until the first prepayment is received, the contract is an executory contract (none of the parties had performed). The journal entry on 31 January 2017 is:

Dr Cash	2000	
Cr Contract liability		2000

Because the contract is cancellable, no revenue may be recognized yet.
  The journal entry on 1 July 2017 is:

Dr Cash	3000	
Dr Contract liability	2000	
Cr Revenue		5000

This is the date on which the performance obligation is satisfied.
  If the contract were non-cancellable, the revenue would be recognized on 1 January 2017, as this is a bill-and-hold arrangement (assuming that the conditions as described in the former section have been met). The debit entry would then be a receivable (to be discounted).

CONSTRUCTION CONTRACTS

IFRS 15 replaces IAS 11, a separate standard on construction contracts. Construction contracts are not a separate issue in IFRS 15 (although some of the illustrative examples relate to construction contracts). The accounting for construction contracts is embedded in the general revenue recognition rules. However, taking into account the importance of the construction industry, we believe it is useful and illustrative to pay specific attention to accounting for construction contracts.

One of the criteria in recognizing revenue over time, and not at a specific point in time, is that the entity's performance should not create an asset with an alternative use to the entity, and the entity should have an enforceable right to payment for performance completed to date. Because of this criterion, many construction contracts will remain to be accounted for by the traditional percentage-of-completion (POC) method, as in IAS 11 (outlined below). From a strict 'transfer of control' perspective, one may comment that during the construction phase there will not normally be a transfer of control of the unfinished asset. That would have meant the performance obligation would have been satisfied at a point in time, that is, upon completion of the contract and delivery of the asset. The POC method would then de facto have been replaced by the completed-contract method that had been abolished many years before by the IASB. But, as said, because of criterion (c) (one of the three criteria for satisfying a performance obligation over time, as discussed under step 5), most construction contracts will be accounted for over time, as in IAS 11. This is not to say that IFRS 15 is identical to IAS 11 on construction contracts, but the broad principles are equivalent. However, to be able to retain the POC method, some contractual provisions may need to be adapted or specified, for instance to make sure that there is an enforceable right to payment for performance completed to date.

Nature of construction contracts

Construction contracts were defined in IAS 11 as contracts specifically negotiated for the construction of an asset or a combination of assets that are closely interrelated or interdependent in terms of their design, technology and function of their ultimate purpose or use. IAS 11 distinguished between two types of construction contracts, namely a fixed price contract and a cost plus contract. The essential difference between the two types of contracts is the way in which the revenue of the transaction is determined.

- A *fixed price contract* is a construction contract in which the contractor agrees to a fixed contract price or a fixed rate per unit of output, which in some cases is subject to cost escalation clauses.

- A *cost plus contract* is a construction contract in which the contractor is reimbursed for allowable or otherwise defined costs, plus a percentage of these costs or a fixed fee.

However, in practice, the type of contract is not always so clear-cut and many have characteristics of both types.

Accounting for construction contracts

Construction contracts generally last over a long period of time, certainly longer than one accounting period. Another feature is that the purchase contract for these items is already agreed before production starts. A sales price is determined in the contract. One difficulty is the question of profit allocation over the various accounting periods. If a contract extends over, say, three years, should the contribution to profits be 0 per cent, 0 per cent and 100 per cent, respectively, for the three years? Can we make profits on something before we have finished it? The realization convention might seem to argue against doing so and the old idea of prudence would certainly argue against it too. But would this give a 'fair presentation' of the results for each period? And would it be of any use? All the various users of financial statements want regular information on business progress. Remember the desirability of timeliness of information. Can we not argue that we can be 'reasonably certain' during the contract of at least some profit? This discussion has led to two basic methods of dealing with construction contracts: the completed-contract method and the POC method. This latter requires allocation over accounting periods of the total profit on the contract, while the former delays profit recognition until completion. Try the following Activity.

ACTIVITY 18.15

An entity enters into a contract with a customer to construct a building. The payment schedule in the contract specifies that the customer must make an advance payment of 10 per cent at contract inception, regular payments throughout the construction period amounting to 50 per cent of the contract price and a final payment of 40 per cent after construction is completed. All payments are non-refundable. If the customer terminates the contract, the entity is only entitled to retain any progress payments received. Is the entity allowed to recognize revenue over time in accordance with IFRS 15?

(Adapted from IFRS 15, Illustrative examples, Example 16)

Activity feedback

The answer is no. This is because the entity does not have an enforceable right to payment for performance completed to date. Even though the payments are non-refundable, the cumulative amounts of those payments is not expected, at all times throughout the contract, to at least correspond to the amount that would be necessary to compensate the entity for performance to date. Revenue is recognized when the control of the building has been transferred. This is essentially the completed-contract method. A change of the payment schedules in the contract would be necessary to be able to apply POC accounting.

Remember that we discussed the contract costs that are to be capitalized in fulfilling the contract? We will now apply IFRS 15 to the situation of a construction contract in Activity 18.16 by looking at which costs can and cannot be charged to a specific contract.

ACTIVITY 18.16

Identify four costs that could be charged to a specific contract and four that may not.

Activity feedback

Costs that may be charged are:

- *site labour costs*
- *materials used in construction*
- *depreciation of assets used on construction*
- *costs of moving assets to and from the site*
- *hire charges*
- *design and technical assistance that is directly related*
- *estimated costs of rectification and guarantee work, including warranty costs*

- *claims from third parties*
- *insurance*
- *construction overheads.*

Costs that may not be charged are:

- *general administration costs not specified in the contract*
- *selling costs*
- *research and development costs not specified*
- *depreciation of idle assets not used on a specific contract*
- *costs of wasted materials.*

We will now turn to the mechanics of accounting for construction contracts, using the well-known terminology of the POC method (satisfaction of the performance obligation over time) and the completed-contract method (satisfaction of the performance obligation at a point in time).

ACTIVITY 18.17

Zen entity is contracted to Alpha for $2m to construct a building. The following data are available in relation to the contract:

	20X5	20X6	20X7
Costs incurred during year	500 000	700 000	300 000
Year end estimate costs to complete	1 000 000	300 000	—
Bills raised during year	400 000	700 000	900 000
Cash received during year	200 000	500 000	1 200 000

The contract is completed during 20X7. Show the profit to be included in the accounts under both the POC method and completed-contract method assuming that the measuring of progress is based on costs incurred.

Activity feedback

The contract as a whole has the following outcome:

Sale price (400 + 700 + 900)	2 000 000
Cost of sale (500 + 700 + 300)	1 500 000
Profit	500 000

Under the completed-contract method this profit of $500 000 will not be recognized until 20X7. Under the POC method, the profit has to be allocated to each accounting year on the basis of this formula:

((Total costs to date / total estimated costs to completion) x total profit) – profit previously recognized)

2005: (500 000 / 1 500 000) x 500 000 – 0 = $166 667
2006: (1 200 000 / 1 500 000) x 500 000 –166 667 = $233 333
2007: (1 500 000 / 1 500 000) x 500 000 – 400 000 = $100 000

In presenting the construction contract in the statement of financial position, we might have a receivable, a contract asset and/or a contract liability, as explained in the section on presentation and disclosure. Now, try Activity 18.18.

ACTIVITY 18.18

The following data are available in respect of a contract for P entity carried out by Q entity at the end of the first year of the contract. Show how the contract should be recorded in the financial statements of Q entity.

Contract revenue	400
Contract costs incurred	350
Billings to entity P outstanding	150
Cash received from P	75

Determine the amounts of the receivable, contract asset and/or contract liability.

Activity feedback

The receivable is 150. Furthermore, there is a contract asset of 175, the difference between the revenue recognized because of services transferred (400) and the consideration received and receivable from Q (150 + 75).

Changes in estimates of costs

Estimating the stage of completion of a contract relies on estimates of total costs and these may well change throughout the life of the contract. IFRS 15 requires us to treat the changes as a change in accounting estimate in accordance with IAS 8, *Accounting Policies.* The following illustration demonstrates how this works.

ILLUSTRATION

A construction contract with revenue of £15m is initially estimated to have total costs of £9m and is expected to take four years to complete. In year 2, the costs are re-estimated at £10m, the increased cost being attributed as follows: £0.6m to year 3 and £0.4m to year 4. If we assume the initial costs were attributed as follows, £2m year 1, £2.5m year 2, £3m year 4 and £1.5m year 4, we can calculate the stage of completion of the contract both before and after the re-estimate.

	Year 1 £m	Year 2 £m	Year 3 £m	Year 4 £m
Initial estimate Revenue	15	15.0	15.0	15
Contract costs to date	2	4.5	7.5	9
Contract costs to complete	7	4.5	1.5	—
	9	9.0	9.0	9
Profit estimate	6	6.0	6.0	6
% complete	22.2%	50.0%	83.3%	100%
Profit recognized in year	1.33	1.67	2.0	1.0

Re-estimate

Revenue	15	15.0	15.0	15
Contract costs to date	2	4.5	8.1	10
Contract costs to complete	7	5.5	1.9	—
	9	10.0	10.0	10
Profit estimate	6	5.0	5.0	5
% complete	22.2%	45.0%	81.0%	100%
Profit recognized in year	1.33	0.92	1.8	0.95

Year 2 profit is reduced from £1.67m to £0.92m to take account of the adjustment to the year 1 profit subsequent to the re-estimate. Note that no change is made to the year 1 profit figure in accordance with IAS 8.

Contract outcome unreliable

In applying the POC method, we have dealt with construction contracts where the outcome can be reliably estimated. IFRS states that it is not permitted to recognize revenue for a performance obligation over time if an entity is not able to reasonably measure its progress towards complete satisfaction, as it lacks reliable information. The entity shall then recognize revenue only to the extent of the costs incurred, but only to the extent that the costs are expected to be recovered. Note that this is not the completed-contract method, as that method requires revenues to be recognized at a point in time, that is upon delivering the product.

Now complete the final Activity.

ACTIVITY 18.19

An entity is involved in two construction contracts, the outcome of which cannot be assessed with reliability and for which the following data are available:

Contract A   Contract costs incurred €30 000, all probably recoverable.

Contract B   Contract costs incurred €100 000, similar contracts have shown a loss of 15 per cent on contract sales price due to pending legislation affecting the construction. Contract sale price €1m.

Identify how these two contracts should be treated in the accounts of the entity.

Activity feedback

Contract A	Contract revenue (as contract costs can be recovered)	€30 000
	Contract costs	€30 000
Contract B	Contract revenue (Note 1)	—
	Contract costs recognized as expense	€150 000

Note 1: Estimated contract loss is 15% x 1m = €150 000 and therefore total contract costs are 100 000 + 150 000 = €250 000, which exceeds the contract revenue of €100 000. The excess of total contract costs over total contract revenue, €150 000, is recognized as an expense immediately (provision).

SUMMARY

We have seen throughout this chapter that the recognition of revenue, which is key in the determination of profit of an entity, is dependent on several factors. These factors also require judgements to be made by management, many of which will require subjectivity.

IFRS 15 identifies five major steps in revenue recognition:

1 Identify the contract(s) with a customer. Contracts can be combined and modified.

2 Identify the performance obligations in the contract. One contract can contain several performance obligations with different revenue recognition patterns.

3 Determine the transaction price.

4 Allocate the transaction price to the separate performance obligations in the contract. This might be straightforward, but is more difficult when stand-alone prices of individual obligations do not exist or in the case of discounts.

5 Recognize revenue when (or as) the entity satisfies a performance obligation. This is the major step, where IFRS 15 is based on the principle of revenue recognition on change of control of the asset to the customer. Its predecessor, IAS 18, applied a risks-and-rewards methodology.

We furthermore discussed the identification and recognition of contract costs and the presentation and disclosure requirements of IFRS 15. We specifically discussed the accounting for construction contracts at the end of this chapter.

EXERCISES

Suggested answers to exercises marked ✓ are to be found in the Student online resources, with suggested answers to the remaining questions available in the Instructor online resources.

✓**1** What is revenue? Distinguish it from other gains.

2 Useful information is provided to users by restricting the definition of revenue to that arising from ordinary activities only. Discuss.

3 Previous revenue recognition requirements under IAS 18 were in need of improvement. Discuss.

4 In accordance with IFRS 15, when is revenue recognized in the statement of profit or loss and other comprehensive income. .

5 In accordance with IFRS 15, define the following: (i) a contract with a customer and (ii) a performance obligation.

6 In accordance with IFRS 15, define the transaction price and explain how it should be allocated to the performance obligation(s) in a contract.

7   Under IFRS 15, if the stand-alone selling price is not readily observable, an entity must estimate the stand-alone selling price. Explain the methods in IFRS 15 for estimating the stand-alone selling price.

8   In accordance with IFRS 15, how should an entity determine whether a promise is a distinct performance obligation that should be accounted for separately or a promise that should be bundled with other promises?

9   IFRS 15 provides two methods for recognizing revenue on arrangements involving the transfer of goods and services over time. Explain both methods.

10   Entity A sells medical devices to the healthcare sector. It operates in a number of European countries. On 1 January 20X6, Entity A signed an agreement with Entity B. Entity B is located in America and it manufactures a specific type of medical device. Under the agreement, Entity A has exclusive rights to distribute in Europe the medical device manufactured by Entity B. Entity A sells each device at a fixed price of €1 000 and earns a commission of 10 per cent of sales. During the year ended 31 December 20X6, Entity A sold 8 000 medical devices supplied by Entity B.

Required:
(a) Explain how this transaction should be accounted for in Entity A's financial statements.
(b) Identify and explain the factors that should be considered in determining whether an entity is acting as a principal or an agent.

11   Entity A manufactures and sells electronic goods. One particular product, Product X, is sold with a six-month manufacturer's warranty. Entity A also offers customers the option to purchase an extended warranty on Product X. Under the extended warranty, Entity A will repair products that become defective within 24 months from the date the manufacturer's warranty ends. Product X is sold for €640 per unit. A customer can purchase Product X plus the extended warranty at a combined price of €720. Entity A's financial year ends on 31 December. As at 31 December 20X6, Entity A estimates, based on its past experience and the number of units of Product X sold in 20X6, that costs of €20 000 will be incurred to repair products that become defective within six months of their sale.

Required:
(a) Explain how the sale of Product X plus the related warranties should be accounted for in the financial statements of Entity A.
(b) IFRS 15 identifies two types of warranties: (i) service-type warranties and (ii) assurance-type warranties. Distinguish between the two types of warranties and briefly outline the accounting treatment specified for each warranty type.
(c) Identify and explain the factors that should be considered in assessing whether a warranty provides a customer with a service in addition to the assurance that the product complies with agreed specifications.

12   Entity A sells a range of scooters. When purchasing a scooter, a customer can also purchase an extended warranty. The extended warranty takes effect after the manufacturer's warranty ends. If at the time of purchasing a scooter, a customer does not purchase an extended warranty, the customer can purchase an extended warranty separately at a later stage. The combined sales price for a scooter plus an extended warranty is €7 200. Separately, a scooter can be purchased for €6 900 and the extended warranty can be purchased for €600.

Required:

(a) Explain how this transaction should be accounted for in Entity A's financial statements.

(b) Identify the conditions under which it would be appropriate to allocate the discount to only one performance obligation in the contract rather than to all performance obligations.

13 Discuss the advantages and disadvantages of the 'percentage-of-completion' method for the valuation of construction contracts and appraise whether it results in useful information for users.

14 HS, a contractor, signed a two-year fixed price contract on 31 March 20X8 for $300 000 to build a bridge. Total costs were originally estimated at $240 000. At 31 March 20X9, HS extracted the following figures from its financial records:

	$000
Contract value	300
Costs incurred to date	170
Estimated costs to complete	100
Progress payments received	130
Value of work completed	165

HS calculates the stage of completion of contracts using the value of work completed as a proportion of total contract value.

Required:

Show how this contract should appear in the statement of profit or loss and other comprehensive income and the statement of financial position for the year ended 31 March 20X9.

(CIMA P7, May 2009, adapted)

PROVISIONS, CONTINGENT LIABILITIES AND CONTINGENT ASSETS

19

OBJECTIVES After studying this chapter you should be able to:

- describe the issues IAS 37 attempts to address

- define provisions, contingent liability and contingent asset

- account for provisions and contingencies in accordance with IAS 37

- appraise the recognition and measurement criteria of IAS 37

- describe the presentation requirements in relation to provisions and contingencies

- define an onerous contract.

INTRODUCTION

Financial statements of all entities are prepared at an arbitrary date – the reporting date at the end of the financial period – which is a convenient cut-off point. However, no matter how sophisticated the information systems, judgements still have to be made on the reporting date concerning conditions with uncertain outcomes existing at the end of the reporting period. In essence, IAS 37 deals with situations where obligations to or from an entity are uncertain in either existence of event and/or amount of that event. The accounting, or not, for such conditions can have a marked effect on both the balance sheet/statement of financial position and the statement of profit or loss and other comprehensive income for the period.

PROBLEMS IDENTIFIED

ACTIVITY 19.1

PPR entity, a retailer of washing machines, has a year end of 31 December. During December a washing machine was sold to a customer who carried out the plumbing himself. On 24 December, the washing machine failed to operate correctly, resulting in the customer's house suffering severe damage due to flooding. The customer, together with several relatives, had to spend the festive season in a hotel as his home was uninhabitable. The customer is planning to sue PPR for a considerable amount of damages. Would you, as an accountant for PPR, accrue a loss for the damages pending or not? In other words, would you set up a provision?

Activity feedback

The first question to ask is whether there is a liability. A liability is 'a present obligation of the entity arising from past events, the settlement of which is expected to result in an outflow from the entity of resources embodying economic benefits' (Framework, para. 4.4 (b)). The problem here is that the outcome will presumably only be confirmed when the claim for damages is settled. What view should we take of the outcome of this claim? Will we have to pay out any damages? If so, how much? Should we assume the claim will be found against the entity and estimate how much that claim will be and accrue in the statement of profit or loss and other comprehensive income? The decision as to whether we set up a provision or not is likely to have a profound effect on profits if the claim is substantial.

Reading Activity 19.1, it shows that judgement and estimates play an important role in the set up and measurement of a provision. The area of provisions and contingencies has led to substantial creative accounting within accounts and has given rise to the term 'big bath accounting', which is discussed in more detail in Part Four of this book. The following Activity illustrates this term.

ACTIVITY 19.2

An entity's annual expected future profits are usually in the order of €2.5m. However, in the current year, the expected profits are €4.5m and management decides to recognize a provision (they claim on the grounds of prudence) for reorganization costs for future years of €2m. The reorganization involves a decentralization of all activities relating to purchases and sales to the entity's outlying units from the centre.

ACTIVITY 19.2 (Continued)

In the event of a reorganization, the charges for the reorganization are €0.5m next year (year 2) and €0.5m in year 3, and thereafter no further costs arise. At the end of year 3, the entity notices that it will no longer need the remaining amount of the provision and decides to release the provision to the profit and loss account.

Show the effect of the proposed accounting treatment for the reorganization costs on the profits for the company for the current and future years. Comment on this treatment.

Activity feedback

The entity has charged the provision for the reorganization against the profits in the first year, which were higher than generally expected. In year 2, the entity has released €0.5m from the provision, which neutralized the costs of €0.5m; thus profits in year 2 have not been reduced. In addition, in year 3, as not all of the provision was required, the excess provision has been released back to the income statement in year 3, increasing profits to €3.5m. In effect, the entity has taken a 'big bath' in year 1 when it had substantial profits and has protected future years' profits.

	Year 1	Year 2	Year 3	Year 4
Provision start financial period	0.0	2.0	1.5	0.0
Increase/(decrease) in provision	2.0	(0.5)	(1.5)	0.0
Provision end financial period	2.0	1.5	0.0	0.0
Profits	4.5	2.5	2.5	2.5
Cost of reorganization	—	(0.5)	(0.5)	—
Provision charged/released to income statement	(2.0)	0.5	1.5	0.0
Profit after provision	2.5	2.5	3.5	2.5

Activities 19.1 and 19.2 show the potential for creativity in the area of provisions and therefore the need for a Standard on this issue. Furthermore, if recognition of a provision is based on an intention to incur expenditure rather than an obligation to do so, then this might potentially result in even more creative accounting. We could have the situation arising where a provision is provided for reorganization costs (as per the example just given), and then if this reorganization is not carried out, the whole provision might be released to next year's profits. The recognition of such a provision does not reflect a change in economic position of the entity, since only an external commitment can affect the financial position at the balance sheet date. Without a complete framework for the accounting for and disclosure of provisions, users are not presented with a true and fair view of the state of affairs.

Therefore, IAS 37 effectively bans:

- big bath accounting
- creation of provisions where no obligation to a liability exists and
- the use of provisions to smooth profits.

It also requires disclosure in relation to provisions in order to aid the user's understanding and present a true and fair view. In fact, when IAS 37 was introduced, it significantly reduced the discretion for earnings' management. Before the introduction in 1998, companies could make provisions for future costs that were not present obligations. IAS 37 now defines provisions as liabilities of uncertain timing and amount.

PROVISIONS, CONTINGENT LIABILITIES AND CONTINGENT ASSETS

Scope

IAS 37 is to be applied to all entities when accounting for provisions, contingent liabilities and contingent assets, except for those items resulting from executory contracts (unless the executory contract is onerous) and those items covered by another Standard. Examples of items covered by another Standard are IAS 19, *Retirement Benefits* and IFRS 15, *Contracts with Customers*. The Standard does not apply to financial instruments that are within the scope of IFRS 9, *Financial Instruments*. Executory contracts also need some explanation. These are contracts where neither party has performed any of its obligations, or where both parties have partially performed obligations to an equal amount. Many executory contracts are accounted for under IFRS 15, *Contracts with Customers* unless they become onerous (this will be explained later).

ACTIVITY 19.3

Identify examples of executory contracts within entities.

Activity feedback

Such contracts generally cover delivery of future services, for example:

- *gas, electricity, local taxes*
- *purchase orders*
- *employee contributions in respect of continued employment.*

It is also worth clarifying at this point the provisions that IAS 37 does not cover. These arise because IAS 37 uses the word 'provisions' to mean a liability of uncertain timing or amount, but in the general language of accounting, it is common for the word 'provision' to be applied to:

- provision for depreciation
- provision for doubtful debts
- provision for impairment.

In these cases, the 'provision' is adjusting the carrying amount of the asset; it is not a liability of uncertain timing or amount and therefore should not be recognized as a provision, but as an adjustment of the value of the asset (i.e. depreciation or an impairment).

Many new concepts were introduced in IAS 37: provisions, contingent liabilities, contingent assets and onerous contracts. We will explain these concepts starting with the definition of a liability. A liability is a present obligation of the entity arising from past events, the settlement of which is expected to result in an outflow from the entity of resources embodying economic benefits and can result from a legal obligation or a constructive obligation. One of the key words in the definition of a liability is 'obligation'. So what is an obligation? An obligation can be either legal or constructive. A legal obligation is an obligation that derives from: a contract (through its explicit or implicit terms), or from legislation or from other operation of law (IAS 37, para. 10). A constructive obligation arises from the entity's actions whereby it has indicated to others that it will accept specified responsibilities and, as a result, has created a valid expectation that it will discharge those responsibilities (IAS 37, para 10).

ACTIVITY 19.4

Identify which of the following is a constructive obligation of the entity.

1   A, a leisure entity, causes severe damage to the habitat of wildlife in a country where there is no legal protection for the wildlife. The company has a high profile in the support of wildlife as it makes large contributions to the World Wildlife Fund and campaigns vigorously on its behalf. To rectify the damage to the habitat, a charge of €1m is likely.
2   An entity in the oil industry causes severe pollution when one of its tankers grounds off a

Pacific island. The entity has avoided the costs of cleaning up such contamination in the past and pays little regard to environmental issues.

Activity feedback

1   *This is a constructive obligation as there is a valid expectation that the entity will clean up the habitat.*
2   *This is not a constructive obligation as no valid expectation has been created by the entity that it will repair the damage to the ocean.*

If we consider the definition of a liability then we notice that the outflow of resources is certain and that the amount is known with certainty.

So compared to a liability, we see that in case of a provision an outflow of resources to settle an obligation is more likely than not and the amount is uncertain although a reliable estimate can be made. IAS 37 (para. 10) defines a provision as a 'liability of uncertain timing or amount'.

We have now outlined the difference between a liability and a provision, but what is a contingent liability?

A *contingent liability* is:

(a) a possible obligation that arises from past events and whose existence will be confirmed only by the occurrence or non-occurrence of one or more uncertain future events not wholly within the control of the entity or

(b) a present obligation that arises from past events but is not recognized because:

  (i) it is not probable that an outflow of resources embodying economic benefits will be required to settle the obligation or

  (ii) the amount of the obligation cannot be measured with sufficient reliability.

In essence, a contingent liability is a provision where one or more of the three requirements is not met. IAS 37 provides (in an appendix) a useful decision tree to determine whether a provision or contingent liability exists in a given set of circumstances (included here as Figure 19.1).

Figure 19.1   Decision tree to determine existence of provision or contingent liability

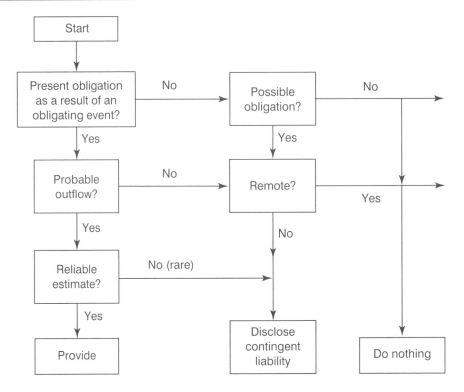

ACTIVITY 19.5

Identify in your own words the key differences between a provision and a contingent liability.

Activity feedback

Provisions require:

- *a present obligation arising from a past event*
- *a probable outflow of economic benefits*
- *an evaluation of timing and amount.*

Contingent liabilities occur when one or more of the conditions for a provision are not met, i.e.:

- *a possible obligation from past event exists*
- *and/or an outflow of economic benefits is not probable*
- *and/or a reliable estimate of outflow cannot be made.*

This can sound rather confusing as a provision is in fact a liability which is contingent as to its timing or amount is uncertain, but it is called a provision not a contingent liability. A contingent liability, as defined by IAS 37, is by its very nature a liability, but it is not recognized as such because it is not charged in the accounts; it is only disclosed. So provisions are included in the statement of financial position, whereas contingent liabilities are only disclosed in the notes.

IAS 37 (para. 10) also defines a contingent asset. A contingent asset is a possible asset that arises from past events and whose existence will be confirmed only by the occurrence or non-occurrence of one or more uncertain future events not wholly within the control of the entity. A contingent asset is only disclosed in the notes.

The last item to define is an onerous contract. An executory contract can become onerous when 'the unavoidable costs of meeting the obligations under the contract exceed the economic benefits expected to be received under it'(IAS 37, para. 10).

ACCOUNTING FOR PROVISIONS, CONTINGENT LIABILITIES AND CONTINGENT ASSETS

If the conditions for a provision are met and a reliable estimate can be made of the amount, then this amount will be recognized in the statement of profit or loss for the year and will be shown as a provision on the balance sheet or statement of financial position. IAS 37 (para. 14) stipulates that a provision shall be recognized when: (a) an entity has a present obligation (legal or constructive) as a result of a past event; (b) it is probable that an outflow of resources embodying economic benefits will be required to settle the obligation; and (c) a reliable estimate can be made of the amount of the obligation. If these conditions are not met, a provision shall not be recognized. A contingent liability is not recognized in the financial statements. However, the notes to the financial statements should disclose: the nature of the contingent liability; an estimate of the possible financial impact on the financial situation of the company; a description of the uncertainties that influence the amount and timing of the outflow; and the possibility of any reimbursement.

A contingent asset is not recognized in the accounts but is disclosed if the inflow of economic benefits is probable (para. 34)

You should have noted by now that how we treat future inflows or outflows of economic benefits in the accounts is dependent on how we/management/experts define the words 'probable', 'not probable', 'possible' and 'remote'. IAS 37, para. 23, states that 'for the purpose of this Standard' an outflow is probable, and requires recognizing if 'the probability that the event will occur is greater than the probability that it will not'. This explicitly indicates that a 51 per cent likelihood is 'probable'. If not 'probable', a contingent liability is disclosed (as 'possible'), unless the likelihood is 'remote', in which case nothing is reported at all. Neither 'possible' nor 'remote' are defined in the Standard. Remote presumably means very unlikely, and possible is everything above remote but lower than probable.

ACTIVITY 19.6

Identify how the following items should be treated in the accounts of the entity at year end 31 December 20X1. All information is at year end 31 December 20X1 unless stated otherwise.

1   An entity has guaranteed a loan taken out by one of its subsidiary entities. In March 20X1, the subsidiary placed itself in liquidation and there would appear to be insufficient funds to repay the loan.

2   An entity catered for a wedding reception in September 20X1. Subsequent to the wedding, several people have died of food poisoning. The entity is disputing liability for the case brought against it by the relatives of the dead and its lawyers advise that it is probable that they will not be found liable.

3   The government of the country in which an entity operates makes substantial changes to the health and safety legislation under which it must operate. The entity will have to retrain a large proportion of its staff to ensure compliance with the new legislation. No retraining has taken place yet.

ACTIVITY 19.6 *(Continued)*

4   An entity at the year end had discounted €600 000 bills of exchange without recourse. At 15 March 20X2, €150 000 are still outstanding and are due to mature in one month's time.

5   No bill has been received for electricity supplied in the last quarter of the year.

Activity feedback

1   *The entity has an obligation to fulfil the guarantee given and it appears that an outflow of funds is probable. A provision should be recognized in the accounts.*

2   *There is no obligation and therefore no provision should be made. It is a contingent liability and a note should be made to the accounts unless the*

lawyers advise that the probability of any transfer of funds is extremely remote.

3   *There is no obligating event as no staff training has taken place yet, and therefore no provision is recognized; neither is there a contingent liability. The entity might need to consider whether there is a possibility it is placing itself in a situation where it will be fined for non-compliance with the new regulations and, if this is the case (that is, the legislation is already in force), then a provision may need to be made for the fines, if any, that could be imposed.*

4   *The bills of exchange are without recourse and therefore no liability falls on the entity.*

5   *This is an accrual as there is very little uncertainty in respect of the timing or the amount due.*

It is a requirement of IAS 37 that provisions be reviewed at each reporting date at the end of the financial period and adjusted where required, and that the expenditure set against a provision is only that in relation to the intent of the provision. Therefore, a provision which is no longer required cannot be used for the offset of other expenditure.

Sometimes an entity can be reimbursed by another party for some of the expenditure in relation to a provision (e.g. insurance contracts, suppliers' warranties). In these cases, the reimbursement must be treated as a separate asset and only accounted for in the statement of profit or loss when the reimbursement is virtually certain.

Measurement of provisions

So far, we have been concerned with the recognition of a provision or a contingent liability, but we must also determine an amount. Remember, a provision can only be recognized in the financial statements if a reliable estimate can be made of the amount. If no reliable estimate can be made of the amount, then a contingent liability is disclosed in the notes.

IAS 37 requires that when determining a reliable estimate this should be 'the best estimate of the expenditure required to settle the present obligation at the reporting date' (para. 36). The best estimate is determined by the judgement of management, supplemented by experience of similar transactions and/or reports from independent experts. The emphasis on present obligation in the measurement rule is deliberate and this means that the effect of future events in this measurement must be carefully evaluated. It is only where such future events are expected to occur with some certainty and objectivity that they will be taken account of.

ACTIVITY 19.7

An entity has a present obligation due to a past event to pay €2m to clean up a waste site. It is currently expected that technological developments that are near completion will decrease this cost to €1.5m. It has also been brought to management's attention that some research is underway (but in its infancy) that might reduce these costs further. At what value would the provision for the clean-up costs be shown in the accounts?

Activity feedback

The technological developments appear to have certainty and objectivity to them, but the other research is much less objective and therefore the provision should be shown at €1.5m.

In practice, the decision may not be as clear-cut as we have just indicated. One future event that is not taken account of in measuring a provision is the gain on the expected disposal of a related asset. The Standard states that these gains must be dealt with in accordance with the Standards dealing with the assets concerned. This is presumably because until there is a binding contract to sell the asset, management can change the decision in respect of the sale. We will deal with this issue again when we look at restructuring and provisions later in this chapter.

The best estimate of a provision can require the use of statistical methods of estimation. This can occur when a provision consists of a large population of items where possible outcomes have various probabilities attached. The method of estimation used in this case is known as 'expected value'.

If the provision relates to a single item or event or a small number of events, then the expected value technique cannot be used. In this case the most 'likely outcome' is used.

ILLUSTRATION

An entity sells goods under warranty. Past experience indicates that 80 per cent of goods sold will have no defects, 15 per cent will have minor defects and 5 per cent major defects. If minor defects occurred in all goods sold, the cost of rectification would be €5m and if all goods had major defects €15m. What is the expected value of the provision to be recorded in the financial statements of the entity at the balance sheet date?

The expected value is:

$$80\% \times 0 + 15\% \times 5 + 5\% \times 15 = 1.5m$$

So, in fact, for a large group of possible obligations, we weight all possible outcomes by their associated probabilities. In the case of a single obligation, the individual most likely outcome is taken as the best estimation, although in practice, some people claim that the expected value of all possible outcomes and their probabilities should be taken into account.

ACTIVITY 19.8

An entity is facing a substantial legal claim for €5m. The lawyers estimate that there is a 40 per cent chance of successfully defending the claim. At what value should this provision be shown in the accounts?

Activity feedback

Care needs to be exercised here as the answer is not 60% x €5m. We have to use the most likely outcome technique here. The most likely outcome, 60 per cent chance, is of an unsuccessful defence against the claim, and therefore the best estimate of the provision required is €5m.

ACTIVITY 19.9

An entity is under warranty to replace a major component in a computer hardware system. The major component costs €0.5m to replace and five of these components are used in the system. Experience shows that there is a 45 per cent chance of only one component failing, a 30 per cent chance of two failing, and a 25 per cent chance of three failures. It has never been known for more than three to fail. What is the value of the provision that should be shown in the accounts of the entity?

Activity feedback

At first glance, the answer to the best estimate would appear to be the costs of one failure, €0.5m, as this is the most likely outcome at 45 per cent occurrence. However, there is a 55 per cent probability that more than one failure would occur, and therefore the best estimate is €1m, that is, of two failures. If the probabilities had been 25 per cent of one failure, 35 per cent of two and 40 per cent of three, then the best estimate would again be €1m (two failures), as there is only a 40 per cent chance of three failures and a 60 per cent chance of fewer than three.

Provisions are measured before the effect of any tax consequences. The tax effect will be shown in accordance with IAS 12, *Income Taxes* (see Chapter 20).

Measurement at present value

'Where the effect of the time value of money is material, the amount of a provision should be the present value of the expenditure expected to be required to settle the obligation' (IAS 37, para. 45). This requirement of the Standard means that we must discount the expenditures required, and the IAS specifies the discount rate as a pre-tax rate that reflects current market assessments of the time value of money and the risks specific to the liability. If future cash flows are adjusted to take account of risk, then the discount rate used must be risk free and vice versa. This is to ensure that the risk involved in future cash flows is not allowed for twice. The best estimate measurement of the provision is becoming somewhat subjective!

ACTIVITY 19.10

The information in an earlier Illustration enabled us to calculate the expected value for the provision for warranties. This provision was not discounted, even though it is expected that the time value of money will have a material effect on the provision. What type of discount rate should be applied: risk free or risk adjusted?

Activity feedback

Risk free, as the specific risk has already been accounted for in the information gathered about the number of warranties taken up.

ACTIVITY 19.11

An entity identifies a provision for €250 000 at the year end 31 December 20X1. The outflow of this amount is expected at year end 20X3. Specific risk associated with this provision has already been taken account of when calculating the best estimate for the provision. A suitable risk free discount rate to use is identified as 5 per cent.

Show the provision charged in the accounts for the year ends 20X1, 20X2 and 20X3, assuming no change takes place in the best estimate and any other related entries required.

Activity feedback

As at 20X1, the provision of €250 000 is due for payment in two years' time and therefore will need to be discounted at 5 per cent for a period of two years:

$$250\,000 \times 0.91 = 227\,500$$

As at 20X2, the provision is now due for payment in one year's time and therefore will be charged at:

$$250\,000 \times 0.95 = 237\,500$$

As at 20X3, the provision should have been paid at €250 000 and therefore will not be required at the year end.

The problem inherent in the discounting of provisions is that the carrying amount of the provision increases as the discount unwinds. Where do we account for this unwinding? The IASB view this unwinding as a charge to interest. There is no doubt that this unwinding is a financial item, but whether it should be regarded as an interest charge is debatable.

In Activity 19.11 in the year ended 20X2, €10 000 would be charged to interest in the statement of profit or loss and at year end 20X3, €12 500.

SPECIFIC APPLICATION OF RECOGNITION AND MEASUREMENT RULES

IAS 37 identifies three specific applications of recognition and measurement of provisions. They are future operating losses, restructuring and onerous contracts.

Future operating losses

These do not meet the definition of a liability as there is no present obligation and thus no liability. The loss will be recognized as it occurs. However, the possibility of future losses should lead management to test assets for impairment.

Restructuring

The issues are presented and discussed in Activity 19.12, which follows.

ACTIVITY 19.12

The management board of Alex take a decision on 24 March to close down one of its divisions. The board also agrees the detailed plan for closure put forward on 24 March. No further action is taken on the closure and the year end for Alex is 31 March. What should Alex provide in the accounts in respect of the closure?

Activity feedback

The first question to ask is whether there is a present obligation (legal or constructive) as a result of a past event (see Figure 19.1).

The answer is no. The board of Alex can change their mind with regard to the closure. A constructive obligation will exist only when the closure is communicated in detail to employees and customers. A problem does exist here, however, as the point of recognition of the constructive obligation is dependent on a subjective judgement – at what point will the company make a sufficiently specific statement as to the closure? No provision will be made in the accounts as at 31 March.

IAS 37, para. 72 tells us that a constructive obligation to restructure arises only when an entity:

(a) *has a detailed formal plan for the restructuring identifying at least:*

  (i) *the business or part of a business concerned*

  (ii) *the principal locations affected*

(iii) *the location, function and approximate number of employees who will be compensated for termination of their services*

(iv) *the expenditures that will be undertaken and*

(v) *when the plan will be implemented and*

(b) *has raised a valid expectation in those affected that it will carry out the restructuring by starting to implement that plan or announcing its main features to those affected by it.*

This still leaves us with a subjective judgement to make.

In addition, we have to be careful about the expenditure included in a restructuring provision as we cannot include those costs associated with ongoing activities of the entity. Thus, we cannot include retraining or relocation costs of continuing staff, marketing or investment in new systems and distribution networks. We can only include the direct expenditures in a restructuring provision. Also, remember that gains from expected disposals of assets should not be taken into account when measuring the provision for restructuring.

Onerous contracts IAS 37 requires us to recognize the present obligation under an onerous contract as a provision. An onerous contract is a contract in which the unavoidable costs of meeting the obligation under the contract exceed the economic benefits to be received under it. These situations can occur when, for example, the economic environment changes and instead of being profit generating, the contract will be loss making. IAS 37 (para. 66) requires that the present obligation under a contract that is onerous shall be recognized and measured as a provision. Many Standards deal with executory contracts (e.g. IFRS 15, *Revenue from Contracts with Customers* and IAS 41, *Agriculture*); however, they remain silent on the recognition and measurement of those contracts when they become onerous. So entities will apply IAS 37 when contracts falling under the scope of other Standards become onerous. The only clarification that is given in the context of onerous contracts is that before a separate provision for an onerous contract is established, an entity recognizes any impairment loss that has occurred on assets dedicated to that contract (IAS 37, para. 69).

Other applications

In Activity 19.13 there are a further two circumstances outlined for the application of the recognition and measurement rules of IAS 37.

ACTIVITY 19.13

1 For many years, an entity has made a provision for repair and maintenance of its assets. Should the entity continue to do so under IAS 37?

2 An entity that operates a chain of retail outlets decides not to insure itself in respect of the risk of minor accidents to its customers, but to self-insure. Based on past experience, it expects to pay €100 000 a year in respect of these accidents. Should a provision be made for the amount expected to arise in a normal year?

Activity feedback

1 The entity has no constructive or legal obligation for repairs and maintenance as a result of a past event. No provision. Charge the amount of repairs and maintenance to the income statement as actually expensed.

2 There is no present obligation as a result of a past event as no event has occurred. No provision. However, as the minor accidents occur, the expenditure associated with them will be charged to the income statement.

ACTIVITY 19.14

Felix, a commercial port operator, is uncertain how to deal with the following issues in its year end accounts:

1 Significant one-off refurbishments of operational port assets that are required in the future.

2 A decision has been taken to alter employee conditions by reducing overtime payments from twice the normal rate to 1½ times at one port. A one-off payment will be made to all employees who accept this change of condition. Employees and unions are aware of the proposed change and have also been informed that if agreement is not given to the proposal, other ways will be found to avoid the overtime.

3 Felix has a contract to purchase items at €1 per unit. The current market price of these items is 50c. The items are used in a part of the business that is profitable. Management believes the contract is onerous.

4 Felix purchased four small ports for €100m during the year; however, the Monopolies and Mergers Commission has directed Felix to sell them. No sale has been made by the year end, but the best estimate of their sale value is €50m.

Activity feedback

1 There is no present obligation, either legal or obligatory, so no provision or contingent liability is shown.

2 The one-off payment is associated with future work, not current, and therefore no provision should be made.

3 The contract is not onerous as no loss is being made by Felix on these items as they form part of a profitable item.

4 A provision of €50m should be made in the accounts as this is a present obligation due to a past event and a reasonable estimate of the loss can be made.

Disclosure

The disclosure requirements are fairly extensive, but are those you would expect in terms of providing relevant information to users.

SUMMARY

You should now realize that the area of provisions, contingent liabilities and contingent assets is controversial and requires a great deal of subjective judgement. Many people would argue that IAS 37 lacks prudence in that it does not require the recognition of, and accounting for, all future expenses. We would not argue this as we view prudence as a state of being free from bias, not being overly pessimistic. The issues involved in this chapter have been quite difficult, and Tables 19.1 and 19.2 summarize the position according to IAS 37.

TABLE 19.1 IAS 37: Summary of provisions and contingent liabilities

Obligation	Accounting result	Disclosure
Present obligation that probably requires outflow	Provision recognized	Amount, nature, uncertainties, assumptions, reimbursements
Possible obligation or present obligation that may require outflow	No provision recognized; contingent liability disclosed	Nature, estimate of financial effect, uncertainties, reimbursement
Possible obligation or present obligation where outflow remote	Nil	Nil

TABLE 19.2 IAS 37: Summary of contingent assets

Economic benefits	Accounting result	Disclosure
Inflow virtually certain	Asset rules apply; no asset recognized	Nature, financial effect
Inflow probable	Contingent asset disclosed	Nature, financial effect
Inflow not probable	Nil	Nil

EXERCISES

Suggested answers to exercises marked ✓ are to be found in the Student online resources, with suggested answers to the remaining questions available in the Instructor online resources.

1   Outline the recommended treatment of provisions, contingent liabilities and contingent assets in accordance with IAS 37, clearly defining and illustrating the meaning of each term.

2   Identify any other methods of accounting for provisions, contingent liabilities and contingent assets, and discuss why IAS 37 rejects these methods in favour of its recommended treatment.

3   Discuss the statement that financial reports prepared under IAS 37 provide a 'true and fair view' to users.

4   Explain the terms: (i) big bath accounting and (ii) profit smoothing. Give an illustration of each.

5   IAS 37 ensures 'consistency between entities in the recognition and measurement of provisions and contingencies and that sufficient information is disclosed about them to users so that they can understand their effect on current and future results'. Discuss.

✓6   The distinction between a provision and a contingent liability is irrelevant. Discuss.

7   Describe the accounting arrangements in accordance with IAS 37 for provisions and contingent liabilities. Comment on whether these arrangements provide useful information to users.

8   Appraise the requirement in IAS 37 to measure a provision at the 'best estimate'.

✓9   Debate the contention that IAS 37 lacks prudence.

10   (i)   In relation to a failed acquisition, a firm of accountants has invoiced Gear Software for the sum of $300 000. Gear Software has paid $20 000 in full settlement of the debt and states that this was a reasonable sum for the advice given and is not prepared to pay any further sum. The accountants are pressing for payment of the full amount, but on the advice of its solicitors, Gear Software is not going to settle the balance outstanding. Additionally, Gear Software is involved in a court case concerning the plagiarism of software. Another games company has accused Gear Software of copying their games software and currently legal opinion seems to indicate that Gear Software will lose the case. Management estimates that the most likely outcome will be a payment of costs and royalties to the third party of $1 million in two years' time (approximately). The best case scenario is deemed to be a payment of $500 000 in one year's time and the worst case scenario that of a payment of $2 million in three years' time. These scenarios are based on the amount of the royalty payment and the potential duration and costs of the court case. Management has estimated that the relative likelihood of the above payments is: best case – 30 per cent chance; most likely outcome – 60 per cent chance; and worst case – 10 per cent chance of occurrence. The directors are unsure as to whether any provision for the above amounts should be made in the financial statements.

   (ii)   In the event of the worst case scenario occurring, the directors of Gear Software are worried about the viability of their business as the likelihood would be that current liabilities would exceed current assets and it is unlikely that in the interim period there will be sufficient funds generated from operational cash flows
        The discount rate for any present value calculations is 5 per cent.

Required:
Write a report to the directors of Gear Software explaining the implications of the above information contained in paragraphs (i) and (ii) for the financial statements.

(ACCA, June 2003)

11   IAS 37, *Provisions, Contingent Liabilities and Contingent Assets* was issued in 1998. The Standard sets out the principles of accounting for these items and clarifies when provisions should and should not be made. Prior to its issue, the inappropriate use of provisions had been an area where companies had been accused of manipulating the financial statements and of creative accounting.

Required:

(a) Describe the nature of provisions and the accounting requirements for them contained in IAS 37.

(b) Explain why there is a need for an accounting standard in this area. Illustrate your answer with three practical examples of how the Standard addresses controversial issues.

(c) Bodyline sells sports goods and clothing through a chain of retail outlets. It offers customers a full refund facility for any goods returned within 28 days of their purchase provided they are unused and in their original packaging. In addition, all goods carry a warranty against manufacturing defects for 12 months from their date of purchase. For most goods, the manufacturer underwrites this warranty such that Bodyline is credited with the cost of the goods that are returned as faulty. Goods purchased from one manufacturer, Header, are sold to Bodyline at a negotiated discount, which is designed to compensate Bodyline for manufacturing defects. No refunds are given by Header, thus Bodyline has to bear the cost of any manufacturing faults of these goods.

Bodyline makes a uniform mark-up on cost of 25 per cent on all goods it sells, except for those supplied from Header on which it makes a mark-up on cost of 40 per cent. Sales of goods manufactured by Header consistently account for 20 per cent of all Bodyline's sales.

Sales in the last 28 days of the trading year to 30 September 2003 were $1 750 000. Past trends reliably indicate that 10 per cent of all goods are returned under the 28-day return facility. These are not faulty goods. Of these, 70 per cent are later resold at the normal selling price and the remaining 30 per cent are sold as 'sale' items at half the normal retail price.

In addition to the above expected returns, an estimated $160 000 (at selling price) of the goods sold during the year will have manufacturing defects and have yet to be returned by customers. Goods returned as faulty have no resale value.

Required:
Describe the nature of the above warranty/return facilities and calculate the provision Bodyline is required to make at 30 September 2003:
(i) for goods subject to the 28-day returns policy and
(ii) for goods that are likely to be faulty.

(d) Rockbuster has recently purchased an item of earth moving plant at a total cost of $24 million. The plant has an estimated useful life of 10 years with no residual value. However, its engine will need replacing after every 5 000 hours of use at an estimated cost of $7.5 million. The directors of Rockbuster intend to depreciate the plant at $2.4 million ($24 million/10 years) p.a. and make a provision of $1 500 ($7.5 million/5 000 hours) per hour of use for the replacement of the engine.

Required:
Explain how the plant should be treated in accordance with International Accounting Standards and comment on the directors' proposed treatment.

(ACCA, December 2003)

12 Nette, a public limited company, manufactures mining equipment and extracts natural gas. The directors are uncertain about the role of the IASB's *Conceptual Framework for Financial Reporting* (i.e. the IFRS Framework) in corporate reporting. Their view is that accounting is based on the transactions carried out by the company and that these transactions are allocated to the company's accounting period by using the matching and prudence concepts. The argument put forward by the directors is that the IFRS Framework does not take into account the business and legal constraints within which companies operate. Further, they have given a situation which has arisen in the current financial statements where they feel that the current accounting practice is inconsistent with the IFRS Framework.

Situation: Nette has recently constructed a natural gas extraction facility and commenced production one year ago (1 June 2003). There is an operating licence given to the company by the government which requires the removal of the facility at the end of its life which is estimated at 20 years. Depreciation is charged on a straight line basis. The cost of the construction of the facility was $200 million and the net present value at 1 June 2003 of the future costs to be incurred in order to return the extraction site to its original condition is estimated at $50 million (using a discount rate of 5 per cent per annum). Of these costs, 80 per cent relate to the removal of the facility and 20 per cent to the rectification of the damage caused through the extraction of the natural gas. The auditors have told the company that a provision for decommissioning has to be set up.

Required:
(a) Explain the importance of the IFRS Framework to the reporting of corporate performance and whether it takes into account the business and legal constraints placed upon companies.
(b) (i) Explain, with reasons and suitable extracts/computations, the accounting treatment of the above situation in the financial statements for the year ended 31 May 2004.
   (ii) Discuss whether the treatment of the items appears consistent with the IFRS Framework.

(ACCA, June 2004, adapted)

13 Blackcutt owns a warehouse. Chemco has leased the warehouse from Blackcutt and is using it as a storage facility for chemicals. The national government has announced its intention to enact environmental legislation requiring property owners to accept liability for environmental pollution. As a result, Blackcutt has introduced a hazardous chemical policy and has begun to apply the policy to its properties. Blackcutt has had a report that chemicals have contaminated the land surrounding the warehouse leased by Chemco. Blackcutt has no recourse against Chemco or its insurance company for the clean-up costs of the pollution. At 30 November 2012, it is virtually certain that draft legislation requiring a clean up of land already contaminated will be enacted shortly after the year end.

Required:
Discuss how the above event should be accounted for in the financial statements of Blackcutt.

(ACCA, Corporate Reporting (International), December 2012, adapted)

14 Verge, a public limited company, operates local and inter-city trains. In February 2012, an inter-city train did what appeared to be superficial damage to a storage facility of a local company. The directors of the company expressed an intention to sue Verge but in the absence of legal proceedings, Verge had not recognized a provision in its financial statements to 31 March 2012. In July 2012, Verge received notification for damages of $1.2m, which was based upon the estimated cost to repair the building. The local company claimed the building was much more than a storage facility as it was a valuable piece of architecture, which had been damaged to a greater extent than was originally thought. The head of legal services advised Verge that the company was clearly negligent, but the view obtained from an expert was that the value of the building was $800 000. Verge had an insurance policy that would cover the first $200 000 of such claims. After the financial statements for the year ended 31 March 2013 were authorized, the case came to court and the judge determined that the storage facility actually was a valuable piece of architecture. The court ruled that Verge was negligent and awarded $300 000 for the damage to the fabric of the facility.

Required:
Advise Verge on how the above accounting issue should be dealt with in its financial statements for the years ending 31 March 2012 (where applicable) and 31 March 2013.

(ACCA, Corporate Reporting (International), June 2013, adapted)

15 Trailer has announced two major restructuring plans. The first plan is to reduce its capacity by the closure of some of its smaller factories, which have already been identified. This will lead to the redundancy of 500 employees, who have all individually been selected and communicated with. The costs of this plan are $9 million in redundancy costs, $4 million in retraining costs and $5 million in lease termination costs. The second plan is to reorganize the finance and information technology department over a one-year period, but it does not commence for two years. The plan results in 20 per cent of finance staff losing their jobs during the restructuring. The costs of this plan are $10 million in redundancy costs, $6 million in retraining costs and $7 million in equipment lease termination costs.

Required:
Advise Trailer on how the above accounting issues should be dealt with in its financial statements for the year ending 31 May 2013.

(ACCA, Corporate Reporting (International), June 2013, adapted)

INCOME TAXES

20

OBJECTIVES After studying this chapter you should be able to:

- explain the concept of deferred taxes

- describe the arguments for and against providing for deferred tax

- identify several possible methods of accounting for deferred tax

- identify the requirements of IAS 12, *Income Taxes*

- critically appraise the IAS approach

- identify possible amendments to IAS 12.

INTRODUCTION

The amount of tax charged against the profit in any period is an important determinant of the amount attributable to the owners of a company (reflected in net profit and earnings per share). It also obviously has an effect on all other ratios which are calculated after tax. However, the tax charge, calculated according to a country's tax legislation, is not necessarily the same as applying the tax rate to the accounting profits. This difference arises because of the different recognition and measurement rules in tax legislation compared to accounting GAAP. The implications arising from these differences have led to a long, complicated and sometimes badly argued debate over the last three decades or more, both in individual countries and internationally.

THE EXPENSE QUESTION

The first question to answer is: 'Is tax a business expense?' At first glance, your answer might be an unequivocal yes, but it needs further consideration. An expense usually takes the form of an outflow or depletion of assets or incurrences of liabilities during a period from delivering or producing goods, services and so on. Expenses are also discretionary in a sense, i.e. the business could avoid them if it wished. Tax is not a charge for the exchange of goods or services and cannot be avoided by the business. Many see tax not as an expense but as a distribution of income, like distributions to shareholders. This view regards the tax authorities as a stakeholder in the business. If this distribution view of tax were adopted, the rest of this chapter would be irrelevant. Tax is internationally treated as an expense, but the argument for doing so is not very well founded.

THE DEFERRED TAX PROBLEM

In many countries, the amount of tax payable by a business for a particular period often bears little relationship to the profit reported by the accountants in the income statement. It is often the case that tax authorities take the accountant's reported profit figure as their starting point, but they make all sorts of adjustments to it in order to determine the amount of taxable income. One of these adjustments can be in respect of depreciation. As we have already seen in Chapter 12, the 'appropriate' charge for depreciation can be a highly uncertain, subjective amount which to many taxation authorities is unacceptable.

Additionally, several national governments have felt that by specifying tax allowances (not equivalent to an accountant's depreciation figure) for capital assets against profits, which they can vary from year to year, they can provide incentives to businesses to invest more or to invest in some particular way. The first thing that such tax authorities do to the accountant's profit figure, as calculated and published in the income statement, is to remove all the depreciation entries put in by the accountant. In other words, the depreciation figure, which will have been deducted in arriving at the accountant's profit figure, is simply added back again. (A profit on disposal that will have been added by the accountant will need to be removed by deduction of course.) From the resulting figure, the tax authority now deducts whatever the tax allowance is for the capital asset, and tax is levied on this taxable profit.

Now consider Activity 20.1, which illustrates the difference between accounting profits and tax authority profits or taxable income.

ACTIVITY 20.1

An asset attracting 25 per cent tax allowances p.a. costs Deftax Ltd €100, and the tax allowances apply to the reducing balance of the asset. The asset has an expected life of five years, at the end of which it is estimated it can be sold for €25. In the books of Deftax, the asset is depreciated each year with an amount of €15.

Taxation is payable at the rate of 30 per cent. Calculate the profit after accounting tax as well as taxable income for each year of the expected life of the asset in the knowledge that the accounting profit before taxes and after a depreciation charge is €100 each year.

ACTIVITY 20.1   (Continued)

Activity feedback

In order to determine both values, we first need to distinguish between the depreciation amounts according to accounting GAAP and the depreciation allowances according to the fiscal rules. The depreciation of the asset according to accounting GAAP is €15 per year (€75/5). The fiscal depreciation is a declining amount calculated each year at 25 per cent of the remaining tax base of the asset, whereby the tax base is the amount attributed to that asset for tax purposes. In order to determine the taxable profit, we start from the accounting profit (after depreciation charge) and add back the depreciation amount according to accounting GAAP. Subsequently, we deduct the tax allowances (depreciation amounts accepted for tax purposes). The outcome is the taxable profit. In the next step, the taxes payable are calculated.

	Year				
	1	2	3	4	5
	€	€	€	€	€
Accounting profit (after depreciation charge)	100	100	100	100	100
Depreciation	15	15	15	15	15
Tax allowance	−25	−19	−14	−10	−8
Taxable profit	90	96	101	105	107
Taxes payable	27	29	30	32	32

Note: the figures have been rounded

	Year				
	1	2	3	4	5
	€	€	€	€	€
Profit before tax	100	100	100	100	100
Taxation 30% of taxable profit	27	29	30	31	32
Profit after tax	73	71	70	69	68
Profit before tax	100	100	100	100	100
Taxation charge if calculated on accounting profit	30	30	30	30	30
Profit after accounting tax	70	70	70	70	70

Activity 20.1 illustrates the difference between profit after accounting tax and taxable profit or taxable income. If the firm uses the taxes payable as tax expense on its income, the profit after tax figures would indicate that in year 2 the performance of the company decreased and continued to do so for the next three years. But, have the firm and management been less successful? Arguably not! Over the five-year period, the company has made the same accounting profit with the same resources each year (excluding the problems of historical cost here). Thus, the profit after accounting tax figures provides a better guide to performance of the company.

If we look carefully at the Activity feedback, we note that the total tax charge is €150 over the five-year period using either method. Thus, the use of tax allowances does not alter the total tax due, only the timing of those tax payments. The difference between the depreciation charge in any year and the tax allowance for that year is referred to as a timing difference or temporary difference.

Timing differences are a potential source of differences between accounting profit and taxable profit. IAS 12 (which will be discussed later in this chapter) defines accounting profit as (para. 5) 'profit or loss for a period before deducting tax expense', profit or loss being the excess of revenues minus expenses for the period. The measurement and recognition of the revenues and expenses for the period is determined by the accounting principles. Taxable profit is defined by IAS 12 as 'the profit or loss for the period, determined in accordance with the rules established by the taxation authorities'. An important point in accounting for income taxes is the identification of these differences between accounting profit or income and taxable income. These differences arise from a different treatment of the same transaction by the accounting principles in comparison to the tax principles. Some of these differences are permanent while others are temporary in nature. A permanent difference between accounting profit and taxable profit arises when the treatment of a transaction by taxation legislation and accounting standards is such that amounts recognized as part of the accounting profit are never recognized as part of the taxable profit or vice versa.

If we return to Activity 20.1, we notice that the tax allowance has the effect of deferring tax payments in year 1 (€3) and 2 (€1), and then collecting these in years 4 (€2) and 5 (€2).

So in future years (4 and 5), we have an eventual payment that relates to years 1 and 2 and arises as a result of the transactions and results of years 1 and 2, and it is therefore arguable that there is a liability created at year 1 (of €3) and increased at year 2 (with €1). We are in effect suggesting that:

1 The tax charge reported on the income statement for years 1 and 2 should really be €33, as this is the amount that must eventually be paid as a result of years 1 and 2 activities.

2 There is a liability of €3 at the end of year 1 in respect of tax related to year 1, but which is payable in later years (4 and 5) and increases to €4 by the end of year 2.

We can easily allow for both these considerations by creating a liability account, known as a deferred tax account. This is shown below. The amount to be transferred to the credit of the deferred tax account can be formally calculated as follows:

$$\text{Amount} = \text{Tax rate} \times (\text{tax allowances given} - \text{depreciation disallowed})$$

Thus, for year 1:

$$30\% \times (25 - 15) = 3$$
$$30\% \times (18 - 15) = 1$$

	Year					
	1	2	3	4	5	Total
	€	€	€	€	€	€
Profit before tax	100	100	100	100	100	500
Taxation: payable for year	27	29	30	32	32	150
Additional charge (credit) to deferred tax account	3	1	0	(2)	(2)	0
Total tax charge	30	30	30	30	30	150
Profit after tax	70	70	70	70	70	350

The tax expense is the aggregate amount included in the determination of the comprehensive income statement for the period in respect of current tax and deferred tax. As an illustration, we present the journal entries which will be made in years 1 and 4 with regard to income taxes.

Year 1:
Dr Tax expense   30
   Cr Taxation payable for the year   27
   Cr Deferred tax liability   3

Year 4:
Dr Tax expense   30
Dr Deferred tax liability   2
   Cr Taxation payable for the year   32

The deferred tax account will be credited in years 1 and 2 and debited in years 4 and 5.

Arguments for deferred tax

From this discussion, we can note:

1 The tax charge by including deferred tax is €30 for years 1–5, which provides a profit after tax figure of €70 that reflects the performance of the company.

2 There is a liability balance remaining at the end of each year in respect of tax related to the current or earlier years, but not yet paid or due for payment. This, we also suggested, was a desirable outcome.

3 The total position viewed over the five years as a whole remains unaltered. This is to be expected as nothing that we or the tax authorities are doing through tax allowances alters the total tax eventually payable as a result of a year's profits.

All this appears totally logical and in accord with accounting principles. So what is the problem?

Arguments against deferred tax

A problem occurs with the previous logic if a company buys assets regularly, which is a realistic assumption. Let us demonstrate the problem.

ACTIVITY 20.2

In addition to the information given in Activity 20.1, Deftax Ltd buys an asset in year 2 for €100, one in year 3 for €120, one in year 4 for €220, and two in year 5 for €250 and €300, respectively. Each of these assets has an expected life of five years but, unlike the first asset in Activity 20.1, these all have an expected scrap value of zero. Complete the table in Activity 20.1 using the new information and show the deferred tax account over the five-year period. Comment on the results.

Activity feedback

To help you with the Activity, we provide the workings for years 2 and 3 for the calculation of depreciation and capital allowances. Years 4 and 5 follow the same pattern.

Workings

Year 2:

Asset 1 depreciation 75/5 =	15
Asset 2 depreciation 100/5 =	20
	35
Asset 1 tax allowance 25% x 75 =	19
Asset 2 tax allowance 25% x 100 =	25
	44

Year 3:

Asset 1 depreciation =	15
Asset 2 depreciation =	20
Asset 3 depreciation 120/5 =	24
	59

(Continued)

ACTIVITY 20.2 (*Continued*)

Asset 1 tax allowance 25% x (75 − 19) = 14
Asset 2 tax allowance 25% x (100 − 25) = 19
Asset 3 tax allowance 25% x 120   = 30
                                           63

	Tax allowance	−25	−43	−63	−102	−214
	Taxable profit	90	92	96	101	99
	Tax charge	27	28	29	30	30
	Deferred tax charge	3	2	1	0	0
	Total tax	30	30	30	30	30
	Profit after tax	70	70	70	70	70

	Year				
	1	2	3	4	5
	€	€	€	€	€
Accounting profit (after deprec. charged)	100	100	100	100	100
Depreciation	15	35	59	103	213

Comparing the tables from Activities 20.1 and 20.2, we see that the total position over the five years is no longer the same. The total tax charge has decreased by €6 (150 − 144). This is not surprising, as it equals the liability provided for at the end of year 5 on the deferred tax account (3 + 2 + 1). The transfer to the deferred tax account can be seen to be the result of an amalgam of positive originating timing differences relating to depreciation. The resultant figure of profit after tax, €70 p.a., reflects the underlying profitability of the company. It does not give an impression of improved profitability because of the effect of tax allowances related to asset acquisitions. Everything appears fine, so what's the problem? The problem is the €6 remaining on the deferred tax account. Does this liability actually exist?

In the long term, we can suggest that:

1 If the entity reaches the state where it has a constant volume of fixed assets, merely replacing its existing assets as they wear out and also the price it has to pay for replacement fixed assets does not rise over time, then the balance of liability on the deferred tax account will remain a more or less constant figure.

2 If the entity finds that it is effectively in the position of paying gradually more and more money for fixed assets each year, then the balance of liability on the deferred tax account will gradually rise, apparently without limit.

3 Only if the monetary amount of reinvestment in fixed assets actually falls will the balance of liability on the deferred tax account start to fall.

How likely is each of these three outcomes? In general, 2 will tend to be the most frequent for three reasons:

1 Entities have a tendency to expand.

2 Entities have a tendency to become more capital intensive.

3 Inflationary pressures tend to cause the amount of money paid for assets to increase over time.

So the most likely outcome, if full provision is to be made for deferred tax in this way, is of a liability figure on the statement of financial position that is apparently ever increasing. But what is a liability? Informally, we can say that it is an amount to be paid out in the future. We have an account representing a liability to the tax authorities. The balance on this account is gradually getting bigger and bigger and, as far as can reasonably be foreseen, this process is going to continue. Therefore, the liability balance never seems to get paid, and it is unlikely to be paid in the foreseeable future. Therefore, it appears that it is not a liability at all within the meaning of the word liability! If the liability account seems all set to keep on growing, is there a probable future sacrifice?

It should be observed that one way of summarizing the two arguments as regards the liability aspect is that we can consider the position for each individual asset or we can consider the position for all assets in aggregate. In the former case, the tax deferred will all have become payable by the end of the asset's life, so a deferred tax provision would seem to be necessary. In the latter case, the aggregate liability is likely to go on increasing, so a deferred tax provision would seem to be unnecessary.

Accountants' response

Formally, three approaches have been distinguished:

1 The *flow through approach*, which accounts only for that tax payable in respect of the period in question, i.e. timing differences are ignored.

2 *Full deferral*, which accounts for the full tax effects of timing differences, i.e. tax is shown in the published accounts based on the full accounting profit and the element not immediately payable is recorded as a liability until reversal.

3 *Partial deferral*, which accounts only for those timing differences where reversal is likely to occur in aggregate terms (because, for example, replacement of assets and expansion is expected to exceed depreciation).

These alternatives are discussed and explained in the following Activities.

ACTIVITY 20.3

Should the flow through approach be identified as the method to be used for accounting for tax? Think of the discussion and illustrations in the Activities above.

Activity feedback

Arguments in favour:

- *Tax is assessed on taxable profits, not accounting profits. The only liability for tax for the period, therefore, is that accordingly assessed.*
- *Future years' tax depends on future events and is therefore not a present liability (see definition of liability, Chapter 19).*

- *Even if current events were to give rise to future tax liabilities, as the tax charge will be based on a complex set of future transactions, it cannot be measured with reliability and therefore should not be recognized.*

Arguments against:

- *As tax charges can be traced to individual transactions and events, any future tax consequences arising from these should be provided for at the outset.*
- *The flow through method can understate an entity's liability to tax.*

ACTIVITY 20.4

Should the full deferral method be adopted as the method to be used for accounting for tax? Think of the discussion and illustrations in the Activities above.

Activity feedback

The view can be taken that the amount of tax saving should not appear as a benefit of the year for which it was granted, but should be carried forward and recredited to *the profit and loss account (by way of reduction of the tax charged therein) in the year or years in which there are reversing time differences.*

In effect, therefore, the full unreversed element is shown as a liability. Applying this to the circumstances of Deftax Ltd, we arrive at the position in Activity 20.2. Thus, we could well be showing a liability that will never crystallize.

ACTIVITY 20.5

Should partial deferral be the method adopted for accounting for tax?

Activity feedback

As we have seen, the one major problem with full deferral is that the balance on the deferred tax account is likely to increase continuously where there is expansion and replacement at increased prices. If, however, timing differences are regarded in aggregate terms rather than as relating to individual assets, then this could be taken as evidence that the differences were not reversing. In short, is a liability that is never likely to become payable a liability at all? In many businesses, timing differences arising from accelerated capital allowances are of a recurring nature and reversing differences are themselves offset, wholly or partially, or are exceeded, by new originating differences thereby giving rise to continuing tax reductions or the indefinite postponement of any liability attributable to the tax benefits received. It is appropriate, therefore, that in the case of accelerated capital allowances, provisions be made for deferred taxation, except insofar as the tax benefit can be expected with reasonable probability to be retained in the future in consequence of recurring timing differences of the same type.

ACTIVITY 20.6

On the assumption that the directors of Deftax Ltd foresee no reversal of timing differences for some considerable time, and using the information from Activity 20.2, show the impact on tax charges and income figures of the firm using the partial deferral method.

Activity feedback

	Year				
	1	2	3	4	5
	€	€	€	€	€
Profit before tax	100	100	100	100	100
Taxation	27	28	29	30	30
Deferred tax charge	0	0	0	0	0
	73	72	71	70	70

The liability for tax will never crystallize, therefore no provision for deferred tax is required.

Deferral versus liability method

The deferred tax amount is dependent on the tax rate used. When calculating the amount we could either use:

- the tax rate applying when the temporary difference originated – deferral method or
- the tax rate (or the best estimate of it) ruling when the tax will become payable – liability method.

A simple example is used to illustrate the difference.

ILLUSTRATION

An entity purchases a non-current asset for €500 000 on 1.1.X0. It is depreciated on a straight line basis over five years. It attracts tax allowances of €300 000 in 20X0 and €200 000 in 20X1. The tax rate in 20X2 is 30 per cent and in 20X1 is 25 per cent.

ILLUSTRATION   *(Continued)*

	20X0	20X1
Depreciation charge	100000	100000
Tax allowance	300000	200000
Temporary difference	200000	100000

Deferred tax provided

	Deferral method		Liability method	
	20X0	20X1	20X0	20X1
	30%	25%	30%	25%
Deferred tax charge	60000	25000	60000	25000
				(10000)
Deferred tax balance	60000	85000	60000	75000

The (10 000) in 20X1 under the liability method adjusts the carry forward of 60 000 to 50 000, which is the temporary difference of 200 000 at 25 per cent tax rate. The 75 000 is now the best estimate of the tax payable if the temporary differences are reversed (300 000 remaining depreciation x 25%), whereas the 85 000 does not represent the best estimate of the likely liability.

Income statement or balance sheet (statement of financial position) view of deferred tax

When the income statement view of deferred tax is taken, there is a focus on the difference between the accounting profit and taxable profit. This was the view of deferred tax taken internationally and in the UK and the US until the 1990s. The balance sheet/statement of financial position (BS) view focuses on the difference between the carrying amount of assets and liabilities and their amount in tax terms, and forms the basis for current IAS and US GAAP.

We identified timing differences as differences in accounting profit and tax profit. This terminology is therefore related to the view. In applying the BS view in IAS 12, the terminology used is that of temporary differences. Temporary differences are defined as differences between the carrying amount of an asset or liability in the statement of financial position and its tax base. Temporary differences may be either taxable or deductible.

In some situations, it makes no difference whether we take an IS or BS view, but in many it does, as the illustration below shows.

ILLUSTRATION

An entity buys an asset for €100, depreciated over five years on a straight line basis. Annual depreciation, according to accounting GAAP, is €20 per year. Tax allowances on capital assets are 50 per cent in the first year and the tax rate is 30 per cent.

Under the income statement view, known as the timing difference, the deferred tax provided at the end of the first year is:

Tax allowance	50
Depreciation	20
Timing differences	30
Deferred tax	9

Under the balance sheet view, the temporary difference, is:

Net book value (NBV) of asset end year 1	80
Tax base (tax written down value)	50
	30
Deferred tax	9

In this example, there is no difference between the two methods.

If the asset had been revalued to €110 at the end of year 1, then only the balance sheet calculation would change:

NBV	110
Tax base	50
Temporary differences	60
Deferred tax	20

IAS 12 AND TAX

Introduction

The current version of IAS 12 has major changes from the one first issued in 1979. This original Standard basically allowed deferred tax to be calculated based on any method available – deferral or liability method, full or partial provision – and was based on an IS approach.

The current IAS 12 is based on a BS approach and the international accounting standard setter has opted for a full provision method for all temporary differences. The IASB plans to revise IAS 12 in the future; however, no specified timeline has been put forward as yet. The IFRS Interpretation Committee and the IASB staff receive many questions on IAS 12, indicating that the Standard is sometimes difficult to apply. Therefore, the IASB had already decided in 2002 to consider undertaking a fundamental review of accounting for income taxes sometime in the future, but, in 2009, the major work was suspended to work on projects with higher priorities. Only limited amendments to IAS 12 were then issued in 2010. Currently, the IASB is doing research of the problems with the current requirements and of how tax information is used when making decisions. It is probable that in the future, IAS 12 will be substantially revised or replaced by a new Standard; however, the timeframe for this project at this time is highly uncertain.

Definitions

The definitions given in IAS 12 (para. 5) are as follows:

- Accounting profit is net profit or loss for a period before deducting tax expense.
- Taxable profit (tax loss) is the profit (loss) for a period, determined in accordance with the rules established by the taxation authorities, upon which income taxes are payable (recoverable).
- Tax expense (tax income) is the aggregate amount included in the determination of net profit or loss for the period in respect of current tax and deferred tax.
- Current tax is the amount of income taxes payable (recoverable) in respect of taxable profit (tax loss) for a period.
- Deferred tax liabilities are the amounts of income taxes payable in future periods in respect of taxable temporary differences.
- Deferred tax assets are the amounts of income taxes recoverable in future periods in respect of:

  (a) deductible temporary differences
  (b) the carry forward of unused tax losses and
  (c) the carry forward of unused tax credits.

- Temporary differences are differences between the carrying amount of an asset or liability in the balance sheet and its tax base. Temporary differences may be either:

  (a) taxable temporary differences, which are temporary differences that will result in taxable amounts in determining taxable profit (tax loss) of future periods when the carrying amount of the asset or liability is recovered or settled or

(b) deductible temporary differences, which are temporary differences that will result in amounts that are deductible in determining taxable profit (tax loss) of future periods when the carrying amount of the asset or liability is recovered or settled. These lead to deferred tax assets.

- The tax base of an asset or liability is the amount attributed to that asset or liability for tax purposes.

Tax base

In many cases, the tax base of an asset or liability is fairly obvious.

ACTIVITY 20.7

An entity buys an asset for €500 000, which it intends to depreciate equally over five years. Under tax legislation, the asset attracts a 50 per cent first year allowance and then an equal allowance each year over the next four to write the asset down to zero.

What is the tax base of the asset (at the end of each year) and its carrying amount in the statement of financial position?

Activity feedback

End year		Tax base	Carrying amount
	1	250 000	400 000
	2	187 500	300 000
	3	125 000	200 000
	4	62 500	100 000
	5	—	—

The tax base of an asset is the amount that will be deductible for tax purposes against any taxable economic benefits that will flow to an entity when it recovers the carrying amount of the asset. If those economic benefits will not be taxable, then the tax base of the asset is equal to its carrying amount.

ACTIVITY 20.8

An entity has interest receivable of €200 and a loan receivable of €300 in its statement of financial position (these amounts are thus the carrying amount of the assets). As far as the tax legislation that the entity is subject to is concerned, the interest will be taxed in full on a cash basis, but the repayment of the loan will have no tax consequences. Identify the tax base for the interest receivable and the loan receivable.

Activity feedback

As the interest is taxed in full when received, there cannot be an interest receivable for tax purposes. Therefore, the tax base is nil.

The tax base of the loan receivable is €300, as the cash flow from the repayment of the loan will be netted with the loan receivable to result in a tax payment of nil. Thus:

	Tax base	Carrying amount	Temp. difference
Interest receivable	—	200	200
Loan receivable	300	300	—

Thus, a deferred tax liability would need to be recognized on the interest receivable but not the loan receivable.

A similar situation occurs in the case of liabilities where the tax base of a liability is its carrying amount, less any amount that will be deductible for tax purposes in respect of that liability in future periods. For example, suppose an entity makes a provision in its accounts for €100 on which tax relief in full will be given when the liability is paid, then:

	Tax base	Carrying amount	Temporary difference
Provision	—	100	100

and a deferred tax asset will be required.

ACTIVITY 20.9

Current liabilities include accrued expenses with a carrying amount of €500. The related expense has already been deducted for tax purposes. Identify the tax base and therefore the temporary difference.

Activity feedback

	Tax base	Carrying amount	Temp. difference
Loan	—	500	500

There are several more examples of tax base calculations in the Standard.

Current tax liabilities and assets

The requirements of IAS 12 here are quite straightforward (paras 12–13). Unpaid current tax in relation to current or earlier periods is shown as a liability and if the amount paid exceeds the amount due, then the excess is recognized as an asset. In addition, where the benefit from a tax loss can be carried back to recover current tax of a previous period, this should also be recognized as an asset.

Recognition of deferred tax liabilities

A deferred tax liability shall be recognized for all taxable temporary differences, except to the extent that the deferred tax liability arises from:

- the initial recognition of goodwill or
- the initial recognition of an asset or liability in a transaction which is not a business combination and at the time of the transaction affects neither accounting profit nor taxable profit.

We will explain the reasoning for these two exceptions to the provision of deferred tax using the information you have acquired so far in this chapter.

First, goodwill is an asset being a residual amount and occurring as a result of a business combination (see Chapter 25). If goodwill is not tax deductible, the tax base is nil. If we assume a goodwill amount of €1000, then a temporary difference of €1000 arises. But if deferred tax is provided on this, then the goodwill, as the residual amount, will change, which will consequently change the deferred tax. This will keep occurring as we try to calculate the deferred tax and thus an exemption is made as the calculation becomes circuitous.

To illustrate the second exemption, suppose a company buys a fixed asset for €1000 with a useful life of five years. Depreciation is not deductible for tax purposes. The tax base is therefore nil. Then, with a tax base of nil and a carrying amount of €1000, a temporary difference of €1000 would arise. This would imply the recognition of a deferred tax liability on the asset of €300 (tax rate 30 per cent). However, the deferred tax liability is not recognized because it results from the initial recognition of the asset. Recognizing a deferred tax asset of €300 would require adjusting the carrying amount of the asset by the same amount. Such adjustments would make the financial statements less transparent.

Temporary differences are differences between the carrying amount of an asset or a liability in the statement of financial position and its tax base. Temporary differences often occur due to timing differences, i.e. when income or expense is recognized in an accounting profit in a different period to when it is included in taxable profit. Remember the example of depreciation here. There are, however, temporary differences that are not timing differences.

Temporary differences that are not timing differences

IAS 12 discusses five circumstances where temporary differences arise that are not timing differences. We have already discussed two of these above – goodwill and initial recognition of an asset or liability – and, as we saw, this temporary difference does not give rise to deferred tax as IAS 12 exempts them.

And we have already illustrated a third one, on revaluations. Where assets are revalued to fair value, there may be a temporary difference. This temporary difference will arise in tax jurisdictions where the tax base of the asset is not adjusted for the revaluation. IAS 12 requires deferred tax to be recognized on this temporary difference. This does seem somewhat illogical. If the tax base of the asset is not adjusted, as there is no tax effect from the revaluation, then how can a liability arise? The IASB justifies the recognition of the liability on the grounds that the asset will generate future taxable income, but this is again debatable as it is difficult to see how future taxable income can equal a past event!

There are two other cases that also give rise to deferred tax.

Business combinations. When a combination occurs under the acquisition method, the acquired assets and liabilities are revalued to fair value. However, the tax base of the asset or liability remains at its original figure within the subsidiary. (NB: a group is not a taxable entity.) A temporary difference therefore arises on which a deferred tax liability is recognized.

Investment in subsidiaries, branches, associates and joint ventures. In the case of an entity with these types of investments, the tax base of the investment is generally cost. The carrying amount of the investment, however, changes over time as undistributed profits are built up in the subsidiary, associate and so on, or due to foreign currency translation or when the investment is reduced to its recoverable amount. These changes will give rise to temporary differences, and IAS 12 requires deferred tax to be recognized except where:

- the parent, investor or venturer is able to control the timing of the reversal of the difference and
- it is probable that the difference will not reverse in the foreseeable future.

One circumstance where a parent can control the difference is the declaration of dividends from the subsidiary, but the parent could not control the difference in relation to foreign currency translation.

Recognition of a deferred tax asset

IAS 12 (para. 5) defines a deferred tax asset as the amount of income taxes recoverable in future periods in respect of: (1) deductible temporary differences, (2) the carry forward of unused tax losses and (3) the carry forward of unused tax credits. There are circumstances when a deferred tax asset should not be recognized and these are when it arises from the initial recognition of an asset or liability in a transaction that:

- is not a business combination
- (at the time of the transaction) affects neither accounting profit nor taxable profit (loss).

These mirror the exemptions under a deferred tax liability. However, there is one clear difference between recognizing deferred tax liabilities and deferred tax assets. Deferred tax liabilities should always be provided for in full, but deferred tax assets may only be recognized to the extent that is probable that taxable profit will be available against which the deductible temporary difference or the unused tax losses and unused tax credits can be utilized (paras 24 and 34). Probable means, as we have seen before, more likely than not, a chance of recovery of more than 50 per cent.

ACTIVITY 20.10

An entity has a tax and accounting loss of €20 000 (pre-tax), creating a right of carry forward of this tax loss for the same amount for three years. After three years, the right expires. The tax rate is 30 per cent. The most probable forecasted tax and accounting profits for the next three years are:

- Year 2: nil
- Year 3: €5000
- Year 4: €8000.

How much of the deferred tax asset should be recognized?

Activity feedback

As only €13 000 profit is expected, a deferred tax asset should be recognized for an amount of €3900 (30% x €13 000). This amount is a benefit in the statement of profit or loss, resulting in a net loss of €16 100. The tax rate in year 1 is 19.5% (€3900/€ 20 000), and not, what would be expected, 30 per cent. When the profits in later years are the same as forecasted, the tax rate will be 30 per cent for these years. For example, year 3: the profit is €5000, the tax expense €1500, the tax payable is nil and the deferred tax asset will be reduced by €1500.

It is important to realize that recognition of deferred tax assets may involve a great deal of estimation. It might be difficult to make forecasts of future profits and management might be inclined to be too optimistic. IAS 12, para. 35, states that the existence of unused tax losses is strong evidence that future taxable profits may not be available. Therefore, when an entity has a history of recent losses, it may only recognize a deferred tax asset to the extent that the entity has sufficient taxable temporary differences (where the reversal of the taxable difference is netted with the deductible difference), or to the extent that there is convincing evidence that profits will be made.

At the end of each reporting period, the entity should reassess the recognized deferred tax asset (is it still probable that future profits will be made?) and the unrecognized part (should this part now be recognized, because financial conditions have improved and it has become probable that future taxable profits will allow the carry forward right to be used?).

Measurement of deferred tax

IAS 12 requires that deferred tax is measured by reference to tax rates and laws, as enacted or substantively enacted by the balance sheet date that are expected to apply in the periods in which the assets and liabilities to which the deferred tax relates are realized or settled. IAS 12 requires an entity to measure deferred tax relating to an asset depending on whether the entity expects to recover the carrying amount of the asset through use or sale. It can be difficult and subjective to assess whether recovery will be through use or through sale when the asset is measured using the fair value model in IAS 40, *Investment Property*. Therefore, IAS 12 provides a practical solution to the problem by introducing a presumption that recovery of the carrying amount will normally be through sale.

Discounting

IAS 12 does not permit the discounting of deferred tax balances, with one exception. IAS 12 allows discounting of deferred tax where it relates to a pre-tax amount that is itself discounted. This exception is obvious, as the application of a tax rate to the discounted item will automatically result in a deferred tax charge that is discounted. Deferred tax is defined as a liability and, as payment is sometime in the future, it is obvious that, under the current regime of IAS 12, the amount shown as a liability does not reflect this deferment to the future. Discounting the deferred tax could be seen as an attempt to reflect the fair value, but could also be seen as a method to reflect the time value of money. The IASB is reflecting on discounting, but for the moment, it does not permit discounting on deferred tax because:

- Reliable calculation is complex and dependent on several factors, not least of which is choice of discount rate, and therefore, if discounting were required, 'reliability' would be questionable.
- If discounting is permitted, some entities would discount and others would not, leading to a lack of comparability.

Activity 20.11 will further test your understanding of the measurement and recognition of deferred taxes.

ACTIVITY 20.11

In each of the following cases, identify the amount of deferred tax that should be recognized and by whom.

1 Entity A, which bought a 35 per cent stake in B, sold goods to B costing £20 000 for £30 000. B still holds these goods at the year end in inventory. A recognizes an adjustment in its consolidated accounts to eliminate its share of the unrealized profit on the goods. A pays tax at 30 per cent and B pays tax at 40 per cent.

2 Entity C recognizes a liability at its year end of £50 000 for accrued warranty costs. For tax purposes, the product warranty costs are not deductible until claimed. The tax rate is 30 per cent.

3 Entity D holds an asset with a carrying amount of £100 and a tax base of £60. A tax rate of 20 per cent would apply if the asset were sold, and a tax rate of 30 per cent would apply to other income.

Activity feedback

1 *There is a temporary timing difference in respect of A's share of the unrealized profit, i.e. 35% × £10 000 = £3500. This timing difference will reverse in the next 12 months if we assume that B sells all the goods, and therefore a deferred tax asset of £3500 × 30% = £1050 is required. Note that A's tax rate is used here, not B's.*

2 *The temporary difference in respect of the warranties is £50 000 on which a deferred tax asset of £15 000 should be recognized.*

3 *If D expects to sell the asset without further use, then a deferred tax liability of 8 (40 × 20%) would be recognized. If it intends to use the asset, a deferred tax liability of 12 (40 × 30%) would be recognized.*

Recognition of movements in deferred tax

The amount recognized in the income statement of a period is the movement in deferred tax from the opening to the closing of the statement of financial position. This difference is recognized in arriving at the net profit or loss for the period, except for tax arising from:

- a transaction or event which is recognized in any accounting period directly in equity, in which case the movement in deferred tax should be accounted for directly in equity or
- a business combination that is accounted for as an acquisition, in which case the movement in deferred tax is included in the resulting goodwill figure.

ACTIVITY 20.12

An entity purchases an asset, cost €50 000, on 1.1.X1. Depreciation is on a straight line basis over its useful life of five years. The taxable allowance for the asset is straight line over four years. On 31.12.X3 the asset is revalued to €45 000, but its useful life and method of depreciation remain unchanged. The revaluation of the asset is irrelevant for tax legislation.

Assume also that yearly income before depreciation and tax is €60 000. Show the charge to the income statement for deferred tax over the life of the asset given a tax rate at 30 per cent for all years, and compare it with the situation where there is no revaluation. Give also the journal entries for tax in the case of the revaluation.

Activity feedback

Revaluation:

Date	Carrying amount	Tax base	Temp. difference
31.12.X1	40000	37500	2500
31.12.X2`	30000	25000	5000
31.12.X3	45000	12500	32500
31.12.X4	22500	—	22500
31.12.X5	—		

When the asset was revalued, €25 000 would have been transferred to revaluation reserve. The charge against this amount (€25 000) for deferred tax is at 30% = €7500. Therefore, the net amount credited to revaluation reserve is €17 500 (€25 000 – €7500).

Deferred tax liability at 30%	Movement in year	IS charge	Equity charge
750	750	750	—
1500	750	750	—
9750	8250	750	7500
6750	(3000)	(3000)	(3750)
—	(6750)	(6750)	(3750)

Transfers from the equity revaluation reserve to retained earnings will be required for the excess depreciation charged over and above the historical cost basis net of deferred tax in each of the final two years as follows:

Historical cost depreciation charge	10 000
Revaluation depreciation charge	22 500
Excess	12 500
Deferred tax 30%	3 750
	8 750

and therefore the €3750 will need to be credited to the revaluation reserve in the last two years.

No revaluation:

Date	Carrying amount	Tax base	Temp. difference	DT liability	Movement in year	Income statement charge
31.12.X1	40 000	37 500	2 500	750	750	750
31.12.X2	30 000	25 000	5 000	1 500	750	750
31.12.X3	20 000	12 500	7 500	2 250	750	750
31.12.X4	10 000	—	10 000	3 000	750	750
31.12.X5	—		—	—	(3 000)	(3 000)

ACTIVITY 20.12   (*Continued*)

Journal entries in the revaluation case (in parentheses means credit; the deferred tax liability is presented on two separate lines for the sake of clarity).

	31.12.X1	31.12.X2	31.12.X3	31.12.X4	31.12.X5
Tax expense	15 000[1]	15 000	15 000	11 250[4]	11 250
Tax payable	(14 250)[2]	(14 250)	(14 250)	(14 250)	(18 000)[6]
Deferred tax liability	(750)	(750)	(750)	(750)	3 000[7]
Deferred tax liability			(7 500)	3 750[5]	3 750
Revaluation reserve / Retained earnings			7 500[3]		

Notes:

1 Income before tax and depreciation 60 000 – depreciation 10 000 (50 000 / 5) = 50 000 x 30%
2 Tax income before tax and depreciation 60 000 – tax depreciation 12 500 (50 000 / 4) = 47 500 x 30%
3 Book value of asset after revaluation 45 000 – book value of asset before revaluation 20 000 (50 000 – 3 x 10 000) = 25 000 x 30%
4 Income before tax and depreciation 60 000 – depreciation 22 500 (45 000 / 2) = 37 500 x 30%
5 Revaluation 7 500 / 2
6 Tax income before tax and depreciation 60 000 – tax depreciation 0 = 60 000 x 30%
7 4 x 750 or taxes payable 18 000 – tax expense without revaluation 15 000.

ACTIVITY 20.13

An entity purchases shares in another entity, leading to a parent/subsidiary relationship. The fair value of the net assets purchased included a deferred tax liability of €50 000, being temporary differences of €125 000 at 40 per cent. In the accounting year after the purchase (year 2) it is announced that the tax rate applicable for the following year is to change to 42 per cent. By the end of the accounting year after the year of the purchase, €40 000 of the temporary difference had reversed. Show the deferred tax liability at the end of the accounting year after the year of purchase and state where any changes would be charged.

Activity feedback

The years are confusing in this Activity and it is therefore easier to see the effects using a table.

Year	Tax rate	Temp. difference	DT liability
1	40%	125 000	50 000
2 without change in tax rate	40%	85 000	34 000
2 with change in tax rate	42%	85 000	35 700

If the tax rate change had not been enacted or substantively enacted, the deferred tax liability account would have been €34 000, but as the change is known about at the year end, the deferred tax under the liability method must be accounted for at €35 700 and thus €1700 will be charged to the income statement for year 2. The charge cannot be debited to any goodwill on acquisition as it results from a post-acquisition event.

Presentation and disclosure requirement

IAS 12 is quite prescriptive in the presentation of tax assets and liabilities in the accounts. IAS 12 (para. 79) states that the major components of the tax expense shall be disclosed separately. These components can include, for example:

• current tax expense (income)
• any adjustments recognized in the period for current tax of prior periods

- the amount of deferred tax expense (income) relating to changes in tax rates or the imposition of new taxes
- the amount of the benefit arising from a previously unrecognized tax loss, tax credit or temporary difference of a prior period that is used to reduce current tax expense
- the amount of the benefit arising from a previously unrecognized tax loss, tax credit or temporary difference of a prior period that is used to reduce deferred tax expense.

The disclosure requirements are extensive and we suggest you read the Standard in detail for these (IAS 12, para. 81). We list a few important disclosures below:

- The following items have to be disclosed separately: (a) the aggregate current and deferred tax relating to items that are charged or credited directly to equity, and (b) the amount of income tax relating to each component of other comprehensive income.
- An explanation of the relationship between tax expense (income) and accounting profit in either or both of the following forms: (a) a numerical reconciliation between tax expense (income) and the product of accounting profit multiplied by the applicable tax rate(s), disclosing also the basis on which the applicable tax rate(s) is (are) computed, or (b) a numerical reconciliation between the average effective tax rate and the applicable tax rate, disclosing also the basis on which the applicable tax rate is computed.
- An explanation of changes in the applicable tax rate(s) compared to the previous accounting period.

In order to illustrate the extensiveness of the disclosure requirements, we introduce a real life illustration of AB Nestlé.

The following disclosure is taken from the 2014 financial statements of Nestlé. Note 14 to the statement of financial position and the statement of comprehensive income provides all necessary information to understand Nestlé's accounting for income tax according to IAS 12.

REAL WORLD ILLUSTRATION

14. Taxes

14.1 Taxes recognised in the income statement

In millions of CHF	2014	2013
Components of taxes		
Current taxes (a)	(3 148)	(2 970)
Deferred taxes	132	(846)
Taxes reclassified to other comprehensive income	(357)	558
Taxes reclassified to equity	6	2
Total taxes	**(3 367)**	**(3 256)**
Reconciliation of taxes		
Expected tax expense at weighted average applicable tax rate	(2 245)	(2 812)
Tax effect of non-deductible or non-taxable items	(527)	(8)

REAL WORLD ILLUSTRATION   *(Continued)*

Prior years' taxes	92	243
Transfers to unrecognised deferred tax assets	(136)	(59)
Transfers from unrecognised deferred tax assets	12	6
Changes in tax rates	9	(15)
Withholding taxes levied on transfers of income	(357)	(381)
Other	(215)	(230)
Total taxes	**(3 367)**	**(3 256)**

(a) Current taxes related to prior years represent a tax income of CHF 133 million (2013: tax income of CHF 172 million).

The expected tax expense at weighted average applicable tax rate is the result from applying the domestic statutory tax rates to profits before taxes of each entity in the country it operates. For the Group, the weighted average applicable tax rate varies from one year to the other depending on the relative weight of the profit of each individual entity in the Group's profit as well as the changes in the statutory tax rates.

14.2 Taxes recognised in other comprehensive income

In millions of CHF	2014	2013
Tax effects relating to		
Currency retranslations	39	317
Fair value adjustments on available-for-sale financial instruments	(48)	64
Fair value adjustments on cash flow hedges	14	(91)
Remeasurement of defined benefit plans	352	(848)
	357	**(558)**

14.3 Reconciliation of deferred taxes by type of temporary differences recognised on the balance sheet

In millions of CHF	Property, plant and equipment	Goodwill and intangible assets	Employee benefits	Inventories, receivables, payables and provisions	Unused tax losses and unused tax credits	Other	Total
At 1 January 2013	(1 508)	(1 549)	2 396	855	450	15	**659**
Currency retranslations	53	31	(68)	(47)	(47)	(79)	**(157)**
Deferred tax (expense)/income	(80)	(94)	(871)	52	38	109	**(846)**
Reclassified as held for sale	—	—	—	—	(10)	(3)	**(13)**
Modification of the scope of consolidation	36	—	(1)	(3)	(1)	(74)	**(43)**
At 31 December 2013	**(1 499)**	**(1 612)**	**1 456**	**857**	**430**	**(32)**	**(400)**
Currency retranslations	(96)	(142)	81	29	(17)	(81)	**(226)**
Deferred tax (expense)/income	(63)	39	257	96	(82)	(115)	**132**
Reclassified as held for sale	12	13	—	—	(4)	(3)	**18**
Modification of the scope of consolidation	(14)	(811)	32	93	58	(15)	**(657)**
At 31 December 2014	**(1 660)**	**(2 513)**	**1 826**	**1 075**	**385**	**(246)**	**(1 133)**

REAL WORLD ILLUSTRATION   *(Continued)*

In millions of CHF	2014	2013
Reflected in the balance sheet as follows:		
Deferred tax assets	2 058	2 243
Deferred tax liabilities	(3 191)	(2 643)
Net assets/(liabilities)	**(1 133)**	**(400)**

14.4 Unrecognised deferred taxes

The deductible temporary differences as well as the unused tax losses and tax credits for which no deferred tax assets are recognised expire as follows:

In millions of CHF	2014	2013
Within one year	35	18
Between one and five years	331	365
More than five years	2 375	1 642
	2 741	**2 025**

At 31 December 2014, the unrecognised deferred tax assets amount to CHF 629 million (2013: CHF 512 million). In addition, the Group has not recognised deferred tax liabilities in respect of unremitted earnings that are considered indefinitely reinvested in foreign subsidiaries. At 31 December 2014, these earning amount to CHF 20.0 billion (2013: CHF 17.1 billion). They could be subject to withholding and other taxes on remittance.

ACTIVITY 20.14

Have a look at the reconciliation of taxes included in note 14.1 of the 2014 Consolidated financial statements of the Nestlé Group as reproduced above. Explain the nature of the reconciling items and why they are positive or negative.

Activity feedback

- *Tax effect of non-deductible or non-taxable items: these items have been included in the profit and loss account, but are not included in determining taxable income. They are permanent differences, not timing or temporary differences. The amount is negative, indicating that there are more non-deductible items than non-taxable items.*
- *Prior years' taxes: taxes that relate to prior period items of profit or loss. The amount is positive, so apparently the tax authorities have accepted more tax-deductible amounts or exempted more taxable amounts than was expected in earlier years.*
- *Transfer to unrecognized deferred tax assets: this is a change in an accounting estimate, where it*

is no longer probable that the deferred tax asset will be realizable. This amount will always be negative.
- *Transfer from unrecognized deferred tax assets: this is the mirror image of the former item and is a change in accounting estimate where it has become probable that the deferred tax asset will be realizable. This amount will always be positive.*
- *Changes in tax rates: changes in tax rates will result in higher or lower deferred tax assets and/or liabilities, depending upon the country where the change is made. The amount in 2014 is positive, indicating either a lower tax rate for a deferred tax liability or a higher tax rate for a deferred tax asset. The situation in 2013 was the reverse.*
- *Withholding taxes levied on transfers of income: deferred tax positions will normally be made under the assumption that income will not be distributed, but upon any distribution (dividend payment), some countries impose an additional withholding tax. This amount will always be negative.*

SUMMARY

Within this chapter, we have considered the principles of the debate on accounting for tax and identified the regulations of IAS 12. We have seen that accounting standard-setting bodies, which all believe that they are issuing Standards within a conceptual framework, can view the principles of deferred tax quite differently. Our debate in this chapter has considered deferred tax from a:

- balance sheet or income statement approach
- flow through, partial or full provision method
- deferral or liability method.

We have also considered the possibility of discounting deferred tax. IAS 12 is based on the balance sheet approach, with full provisioning and applying the liability method. However, deferred tax assets are only recognized to the extent that it is probable that future taxable profits will be available to realize the asset. We leave you with the question: 'Does the required accounting treatment of taxation in published IAS accounts lead to a true and fair view as required by the EU Accounting Directive?'

EXERCISES

Suggested answers to exercises marked P are to be found in the Student online resources, with suggested answers to the remaining questions available in the Instructor online resources.

✓**1** Outline the major arguments in favour of always providing for deferred tax where the amounts are material.

2 Outline the major arguments in favour of only providing for deferred tax when it is probable that a liability will crystallize.

3 Deferred tax should be ignored when preparing financial statements. Discuss.

✓**4** Explain and distinguish between:

- the flow through approach
- full deferral
- partial deferral.

✓**5** Explain and distinguish between:

- the deferral method
- the liability method.

6 Comparability requires that either all entities provide in full for deferred tax or that it is always ignored. Discuss.

✓**7** Explain to a non-accountant the difference between the income statement view and the balance sheet view of deferred tax.

8 Discounting deferred tax balances would provide useful information to users. Discuss.

9 **(i)** IAS 12, *Income Tax* details the requirements relating to the accounting treatment of deferred tax.

Required:
Explain why it is considered necessary to provide for deferred tax and briefly outline the principles of accounting for deferred tax contained in IAS 12, *Income Tax*.

(ii) Bowtock purchased an item of plant for $2 000 000 on 1 October 20X0. It had an estimated life of eight years and an estimated residual value of $400 000. The plant is depreciated on a straight line basis. The tax authorities do not allow depreciation as a deductible expense. Instead, a tax expense of 40 per cent of the cost of this type of asset can be claimed against income tax in the year of purchase and 20 per cent p.a. (on a reducing balance basis) of its tax base thereafter. The rate of income tax can be taken as 25 per cent.

Required:
In respect of the above item of plant, calculate the deferred tax charge/credit in Bowtock's statement of profit or loss and other comprehensive income for the year to 30 September 20X3 and the deferred tax balance in the statement of financial position at that date.

Note: Work to the nearest $000.

(ACCA, December 2003)

10 Nette, a public limited company, manufactures mining equipment and extracts natural gas. The directors are uncertain about the role of the IASB's *Conceptual Framework for Financial Reporting* (the IFRS Framework) in corporate reporting. Their view is that accounting is based on the transactions carried out by the company and these transactions are allocated to the company's accounting period by using the matching and prudence concepts. The argument put forward by the directors is that the IFRS Framework does not take into account the business and legal constraints within which companies operate. Further, they have given a situation which has arisen in the current financial statements where they feel that the current accounting practice is inconsistent with the IFRS Framework.

Situation: Nette purchased a building on 1 June 20X3 for $10 million. The building qualified for a grant of $2 million, which has been treated as a deferred credit in the financial statements. The tax allowances are reduced by the amount of the grant. There are additional temporary differences of $40 million in respect of deferred tax liabilities at the year end. Also, the company has sold extraction equipment which carries a five-year warranty. The directors have made a provision for the warranty of $4 million at 31 May 20X4, which is deductible for tax when costs are incurred under the warranty. In addition to the warranty provision, the company has unused tax losses of $70 million. The directors of the company are unsure as to whether a provision for deferred taxation is required. (Assume that the depreciation of the building is straight line over ten years, and tax allowances of 25 per cent on the reducing balance basis can be claimed on the building. Tax is payable at 30 per cent.)

Required:
(a) Explain the importance of the IFRS Framework to the reporting of corporate performance and whether it takes into account the business and legal constraints placed upon companies.

(b) (i) Explain, with reasons and suitable extracts/computations, the accounting treatment of the above situation in the financial statements for the year ended 31 May 20X4.

(ii) Discuss whether the treatment of the items appears consistent with the IFRS Framework.

(ACCA, June 2004, adapted)

11 The directors of Panel, a public limited company, are reviewing the procedures for the calculation of the deferred tax provision for their company.

The directors wish to know how the provision for deferred taxation would be calculated in the following situations under IAS 12, *Income Taxes*:

(i) On 1 November 20X3, the company had granted 10m share options worth $40m, subject to a two-year vesting period. Local tax law allows a tax deduction at the exercise date of the intrinsic value of the options. The intrinsic value of the 10m share options at 31 October 20X4 was $16m and at 31 October 20X5 was $46m as a result of the increase in the share price in the year to 31 October 20X5. The directors are unsure how to account for deferred taxation on this transaction for the years ended 31 October 20X4 and 31 October 20X5

(ii) Panel is leasing plant over a five-year period. The asset was recorded at $12m at the inception of the lease, which was 1 November 20X4. The asset is depreciated on a straight line basis over the five years and has no residual value. The annual lease payments are $3m payable in arrears on 31 October and the effective interest rate is 8 per cent p.a. The directors have not leased an asset before and are unsure as to its treatment for deferred taxation. The company can claim a tax deduction for the annual rental payment as the lease does not qualify for tax relief.

(iii) Nails, a limited liability company, is a wholly owned subsidiary of Panel, and is a cash-generating unit in its own right. The value of the property, plant and equipment of Nails at 31 October 20X5 was $6m and purchased goodwill was $1m before any impairment loss. The company had no other assets or liabilities. An impairment loss of $1.8m had occurred at 31 October 20X5. The tax base of the property, plant and equipment of Nails was $4m as at 31 October 20X5. The directors wish to know how the impairment loss will affect the deferred tax provision for the year. Impairment losses are not an allowable expense for taxation purposes.

Assume a tax rate of 30 per cent.

Required:
Discuss, with suitable computations, how the situations (i) to (iii) above will impact on the accounting for deferred tax under IAS12, *Income Taxes* in the group financial statements of Panel.

(ACCA 3.5 int., December 2005, adapted)

12 GJ commenced business on 1 October 20X5, and on that date it acquired property, plant and equipment for $220 000. GJ used the straight line method of depreciation. The estimated useful life of the assets was five years and the residual value was estimated at $10 000. GJ's accounting year end is 30 September. All the assets acquired qualified for a first year tax allowance of 50 per cent and then an annual tax allowance of 25 per cent of the reducing balance. On 1 October 20X7, GJ revalued all of its assets; this led to an increase in asset values of $53 000. GJ's applicable tax rate for the year is 25 per cent.

Required:
Calculate the amount of the deferred tax provision that GJ should include in its statement of financial position at 30 September 20X8, in accordance with IAS 12, *Income Taxes*.

(CIMA P7, November 2008)

13 HF purchased an asset on 1 April 20X7 for $220 000. HF claimed a first year tax allowance of 30 per cent and then an annual 20 per cent writing down allowance, using the reducing balance method. HF depreciates the asset over eight years using straight line depreciation, assuming no residual value. On 1 April 20X8, HF revalued the asset and increased the net book value by $50 000. The asset's useful life was not affected. Assume there are no other temporary differences in the period and a tax rate of 25 per cent p.a.

Required:
Calculate the amount of deferred tax movement in the year ended 31 March 20X9 and the deferred tax balance at 31 March 20X9 in accordance with IAS 12, *Income Taxes*.

(CIMA P7, May 2009)

14 On 31 March 20X6, CH had a credit balance brought forward on its deferred tax account of $642 000. There was also a credit balance on its corporate income tax account of $31 000 representing an overestimate of the tax charge for the year ended 31 March 20X5. CH's taxable profit for the year ended 31 March 20X6 was $946 000. CH's directors estimated the deferred tax provision required at 31 March 20X6 to be $759 000 and the applicable income tax rate for the year to 31 March 20X6 as 22 per cent.

Required:
Calculate the income tax expense that CH will charge in its statement of profit or loss and other comprehensive income for the year ended 31 March 20X6, as required by IAS 12, *Income Taxes*.

(CIMA P7, May 2006)

EMPLOYEE BENEFITS AND SHARE-BASED PAYMENT

21

OBJECTIVES After studying this chapter you should be able to:

- explain how short-term employee benefits have to be accounted for

- explain the difference between defined contribution pension plans and defined benefit pension plans

- explain the purpose and function of actuarial cost or funding methods

- list several actuarial assumptions and discuss their impact on the pension cost and pension benefit obligation

- define the concept of total pension cost according to IAS 19

- define the concept of a defined benefit liability according to IAS 19

- describe what is meant by pension plan assets

- describe what is meant by termination benefits

- explain how equity-settled/share-based payment transactions have to be accounted for

- explain how cash-settled/share-based payment transactions have to be accounted for

- explain how equity-settled/share-based payment transactions with cash alternatives have to be accounted for

- explain what is meant by the grant date and vesting date of the benefits

- describe the contents of a pension plan report according to IAS 26.

INTRODUCTION

In every organization, people are a very important resource. Without a competent and loyal staff of personnel, an entity will usually be unsuccessful. To keep the workforce motivated and loyal, most, if not all, employers provide employees with certain benefits in addition to the wages paid. Employee benefits are usually furnished by the employer in full, but some types of benefits are paid for jointly by the employer and the employee. A benefit package may include retirement plans; insurance plans, such as hospital, dental, life and disability insurance; stock options; profit-sharing plans; recreational programmes; vacations and so on.

A number of these employee benefits have a long-term perspective, which implies that elements of uncertainty are involved. As a consequence, accounting for a number of these long-term employee benefits is not that straightforward and of a rather high, technical level.

ACTIVITY 21.1

If you think of employee benefits, which benefits do you consider are short term and which would you regard as long term?

Activity feedback

- *Short-term benefits: salaries, paid holiday, bonuses, medical care.*

- *Long-term benefits: medical care after retirement, pension benefits.*

Equity compensation benefits can be either short term or long term depending on the exercise period.

Most of the employee benefits are dealt with in IAS 19, *Employee Benefits*. One particular type of employee benefit, namely equity compensation or share-based benefits, is dealt with in IFRS 2, *Share-based Payment*. IFRS 2 describes the recognition and valuation rules when an entity undertakes a share-based payment transaction.

As you will notice, the scope of IFRS 2 encompasses all share-based payment transactions made by an entity, not just share-based transactions with employees and top management.

We will first present the definitions, recognition and measurement rules for those employee benefits that fall within the scope of IAS 19. Subsequently, we will discuss the accounting treatment of share-based compensation, which is dealt with in IFRS 2.

IAS 19 defines as short-term benefits: wages, salaries and social security contributions; paid annual leave and paid sick leave; profit-sharing and bonuses (if payable within 12 months of the end of the period); and non-monetary benefits (such as medical care, housing, cars and free or subsidized goods or services) for current employees.

Profit-sharing plans and bonus plans can be long term or short term, according to when they are payable (within 12 months or longer). Examples of long-term benefits are: qualified post-employment benefits such as pensions; other retirement benefits; post-employment life insurance and post-employment medical care. Long-term employee benefits include: long-service leave or sabbatical leave, jubilee or other long-service benefits and long-term disability benefits.

IAS 19 deals with further termination benefits.

If we discuss the issue of how these benefits should be accounted for then it is important to determine when a company is obliged or required to fulfil these employee benefits. The accounting treatment, which IAS 19 prescribes for employee benefits, is applicable if they result from:

- formal plans or other formal agreements between an entity and individual employees, groups of employees or their representatives
- legislative requirements or from industry arrangements, whereby entities are required to contribute to national, state, industry or other multi-employer plans or
- informal practices that give rise to a constructive obligation, for example where the entity has no realistic alternative but to pay employee benefits. An example of a constructive obligation is where a change in the entity's informal practices would cause unacceptable damage to its relationship with its employees.

Accounting for short-term employee benefits is straightforward as these elements do not include many uncertainties. We will look first at these short-term employee benefits. Then we will focus on long-term employee benefits and, more specifically, on pension benefits.

ACCOUNTING FOR SHORT-TERM EMPLOYEE BENEFITS

Short-term benefits are salaries, paid leave and bonus plans to be settled wholly before 12 months after the end of the annual reporting period in which the employees render the related services and other benefits payable. With regard to these benefits, the basic valuation rule is as follows: when an employee has rendered service to an entity during an accounting period, the entity should recognize the undiscounted amount of short-term employee benefits expected to be paid in exchange for that service. The benefit will be reported as an expense, unless another IAS requires or permits the inclusion of the benefits in the cost of an asset (e.g. see IAS 2, *Inventories* and IAS 16, *Property, Plant and Equipment*) and as a liability (accrued expense), after deducting any amount already paid. If the amount already paid exceeds the undiscounted amount of the benefits, an entity should recognize that excess as an asset (prepaid expense) to the extent that the prepayment will lead to, for example, a reduction in future payments or a cash refund.

Compensated absences are short-term employee benefits. IAS 19 pays explicit attention to them. IAS 19 makes a distinction in these short-term compensated absences between accumulating and non-accumulating. The difference between the two will result in a different accounting treatment.

ACTIVITY 21.2

Can you think of some examples of paid absence? Can you distinguish between whether they arise from service rendered in the past (i.e. accumulated absences) or whether they are not related to service rendered at work (i.e. non-accumulated absences)?

Activity feedback

A typical example of an accumulated compensated absence is absence for vacation (holiday). An employee is entitled to a number of days of paid absence according to the number of days worked. Examples of non-accumulated absences are sickness leave, maternity and paternity leave, and military service.

In the case of accumulating compensated absences, the expected cost of the short-term benefit has to be recognized when the employees render the service that increases their entitlement to future compensated absences.

In the case of non-accumulating compensated absence, the benefit should be recognized when the absence occurs, as in the latter case, the absence is not linked to the service rendered by the employees in a period.

ACCOUNTING FOR PROFIT-SHARING AND BONUS PLANS

The compensation package of many executives, but also of higher and middle management these days, often includes profit-sharing plans or bonus plans. When profit-sharing or bonus plans exist, executives and employees receive a variable amount as compensation on top of their salary. These bonuses can be linked to financial indicators, e.g. accounting numbers such as earnings before interest and taxes (EBIT), return on assets (ROA), return on equity (ROE) or non-financial indicators (e.g. customer satisfaction), or a combination of both.

The obligation to pay an amount to the employees under a profit-sharing or bonus plan results from employee service, not from a transaction with the entity's owners. Therefore, an entity has to recognize the cost of profit-sharing and bonus plans as an expense, not a distribution of net profit. The bonus as such qualifies as an obligation. The amount linked to it is dependent on the realized performance in relation to the indicator specified in the profit-sharing or bonus plan.

As a result, the expected cost of profit-sharing and bonus payments should be recognized as an expense and as a liability when, and only when (paras 10 and 17), the entity has a present legal or constructive obligation to make such payments as a result of past events and a reliable estimate of the obligation can be made. A present obligation exists when, and only when, the entity has no realistic alternative but to make the payments.

IAS 19, in itself, unfortunately does not require specific disclosures about short-term benefits; other IASs, however, may require disclosures concerning these short-term benefits. For example, where required by IAS 24, *Related Party Disclosures*, an entity has to disclose information about employee benefits for key management personnel, or IAS 1, *Presentation of Financial Statements*, requires that an entity should disclose staff costs.

IAS 19 does not oblige a company to provide information about the formal terms of a bonus or profit-sharing plan to external stakeholders of the company. This information disclosure is left either to the voluntary disclosure policy of the firm or to corporate governance regulations on disclosure of top management and directors' remuneration in the different jurisdictions. Since empirical research related to earnings management found evidence that these bonus plans and profit-sharing plans can create incentives to manage the reported results of a firm, it would be interesting to know the amounts paid out in respect of these plans, but even more interesting to know the indicator (financial or non-financial) which drives the bonus. The indicator used in the bonus plan would be useful information for financial analysis purposes (for a further discussion of this item, see Chapter 30). Information on the formal terms of the plan (e.g. the indicators to which the bonus is linked) can give the external user of the financial statements an idea concerning the direction in which the results possibly could have been influenced.

ACCOUNTING FOR EQUITY COMPENSATION BENEFITS OR SHARE-BASED PAYMENT

For a long time, bonus plans and profit-sharing plans were the only widely used instruments to increase the compensation of executives and employees. From the beginning of the 1990s, stock-based compensation or share-based payment became very popular. Stock-based compensation can take the form of stock options or gifts of shares for free or at lower than market values. Empirical research on incentives for earnings management also reveals that the existence of stock options might induce management to smooth reported income and to increase income upward in order to boost the share price. These elements are illustrated further in Chapter 30. The instruments that qualify as equity-based compensation are:

- shares, share options and other equity instruments issued to directors, senior executives and other employees and
- cash payments, the amount of which will depend on the future market price of the reporting entity's shares or other equity instruments, again as part of a remuneration plan.

These instruments, without doubt, have an impact on the result, the financial position and the cash flow of an entity. If a company uses existing shares for the equity-based compensation plans, the company has to buy the shares from existing shareholders. This implies a cost to the company. If a company chooses to issue extra shares (in that case employees can subscribe for new shares), there is a dilutive effect when the options are exercised (see Chapter 24).

One of the first issues the Board, in its new composition, wanted to solve is the recognition and valuation of these equity benefit compensation schemes. At the beginning of 2004, IFRS 2, *Share-based Payment* was issued. Equity-based compensation was a hot topic at the turn of the century since many large listed companies in the US accounted for their equity-based compensation off balance sheet. With IFRS 2, the Board has insisted on recognition and measurement of those equity-based remuneration instruments on the balance sheet. A disclosure of these benefits in the notes only and no recognition on the balance sheet was no longer accepted. Studies by Bear Stearns and Credit Suisse First Boston, carried out at the start of the twenty-first century, show that if companies belonging to the Standard & Poor's 500 had accounted for their equity-based remuneration investments on the balance sheet with the use of fair value, the earnings of those companies would have been significantly lower.

The scope of IFRS 2 includes all share-based payment transactions. So IFRS 2 is applicable to more transactions than just equity-based compensation benefits. IFRS 2 defines share-based transactions as those transactions where an entity's equity instruments are transferred by its shareholder to parties that have supplied goods or services to the entity, unless the transfer is clearly for a purpose other than payment for goods or services supplied to the entity. IFRS 2 also applies to transfers of equity instruments of the entity's parent, or equity instruments of another entity in the same group as the entity, to parties that have supplied goods or services to the entity. However, an entity shall not apply this IFRS to transactions in which the entity acquires goods as part of the net assets acquired in a business combination as defined by IFRS 3, *Business Combinations*, in a combination of entities or businesses under common control as defined by IFRS 3, or the contribution of a business in the formation of a joint venture as defined by IAS 31, *Interests in Joint Ventures*. A transaction with an employee (or other party), in their capacity as a holder of equity instruments of the entity, is not considered to be a share-based payment transaction and does not fall under the scope of IFRS 2.

IFRS 2 distinguishes between three different types of share-based transactions with regard to the nature of the share-based payment transactions (para. 2):

- equity-settled share-based payment transactions
- cash-settled share-based payment transactions and

- transactions in which the entity receives or acquires goods or services, and the terms of the arrangement provide either the entity or the supplier of those goods or services with a choice of whether the entity settles the transaction in cash (or other assets) or by issuing equity instruments.

In the absence of specifically identifiable goods or services, other circumstances may indicate that goods or services have been (or will be) received, in which case IFRS applies (e.g. a company which provides shares to a charity in order to improve its image of corporate social responsibility). When IFRS 2 was amended in June 2009, special attention was paid to group share-based payment transactions. A share-based payment transaction may be settled by another group entity (or a shareholder of any group entity) on behalf of the entity receiving or acquiring the goods or services. Paragraph 2 also applies to an entity that:

- receives goods or services when another entity in the same group (or a shareholder of any group entity) has the obligation to settle the share-based payment transaction or
- has an obligation to settle a share-based payment transaction when another entity in the same group receives the goods or services.

Paragraph 2 does not apply in group share-based transactions if the transaction is clearly for a purpose other than payment for goods or services supplied to the entity receiving them.

Although the accounting treatment of these three types of share-based payment transaction will be different, the main objective will be that an entity should reflect in its results, and in its financial position, the effects of share-based payment transactions when the goods are obtained and services are received. We will now present and illustrate the definition, recognition and measurement rules of the three types of share-based payment transactions.

Important elements concerning equity-based compensation are the grant date, the exercise date, the exercise price (strike price), the vesting date and vesting requirements. The difference between the exercise price and the market price is the key value driver of warrants/options. Simple methods (intrinsic value) only use this difference for valuation purposes. More sophisticated methods are using valuation methods (for instance, the Black and Scholes (1973) model) which incorporate additional parameters (e.g. volatility).

Relevant accounting valuation issues concerning these benefits are: how to measure the cost of compensation offered by the company to the employees, when to recognize this cost in the profit and loss account and how to account for the financial impact of stock options (e.g. if existing shares are bought, how will they be financed by the company).

Equity-settled share-based payment transactions

In equity-settled share-based payment transactions, an entity receives goods or services in exchange for equity instruments. For example, an entity acquires equipment from a manufacturer and uses shares as consideration. Another example is a top executive in a company who receives share options or other equity instruments as part of their remuneration schemes.

IFRS 2 (para. 10) states that for these equity-settled share-based payment transactions, the entity shall measure the goods or services received and the corresponding increase in equity directly at the fair value of the goods or services received, unless that fair value cannot be estimated reliably. If the entity cannot estimate reliably the fair value of the goods or services received, the entity shall measure their value and the corresponding increase in equity indirectly by reference to the fair value of the equity instruments granted (see Activity 21.3).

ACTIVITY 21.3

Consider the two examples just given (the acquisition of the equipment and the compensation of the top executive) and determine which amount will be used under IFRS 2 for the valuation of the transaction in the books of the entity.

Activity feedback

In the case of the equipment, the market value of the equipment will be used to measure, on the one hand, the increase in the fixed assets and, on the other, the increase in equity. In the situation where equity instruments are used as remuneration for services rendered by employees, directors or other senior executives, it is usually not possible to measure directly the services received for particular components of the employee's remuneration package. It might also not be possible to measure the fair value of the total remuneration package

independently, without measuring directly the fair value of the equity instruments granted. Furthermore, shares or share options are sometimes granted as part of a bonus arrangement, rather than as a part of the basic remuneration. By granting shares or share options in addition to other remuneration, the entity is paying additional remuneration to obtain additional benefits. Estimating the fair value of those additional benefits is likely to be difficult. Because of the difficulty of measuring directly the fair value of the services received, the entity shall measure the fair value of the employee services received by reference to the fair value of the equity instruments granted. So the share-based remuneration will be recorded in the books of the company in the following manner. The amount of the fair value of the equity instrument will be debited to an expense remuneration account and credited to an equity account.

Determining the fair value of the equity instrument. IFRS 2 distinguishes with regard to the valuation of these equity-settled share-based transactions between two possibilities: first, when the fair value of the goods received and the services rendered can be measured reliably and second, when it is not possible to determine this value in a reliable way. In the first situation, the fair value of the goods received or the services rendered is used for the valuation of the transaction. In the second situation, the fair value of the equity instrument will be used for reporting purposes. For example, if an entity grants shares to a charity organization in order to enhance its image, the transaction shall be accounted for according to IFRS 2, and the value of the transaction is the fair value of the equity instruments.

Grant date. Before focusing further on the recognition and measurement issues of these equity-settled share-based payment transactions, we will explain a number of concepts that play a role in the accounting treatment of these share-based transactions. First, there is the grant date of the share-based payment transaction. This is the date at which the entity and another party (including an employee) agree to a share-based payment arrangement, being when the entity and the other contracting party have a shared understanding of the terms and conditions of the arrangement. At grant date, the entity confers on the other contracting party the right to cash, other assets, or equity instruments of the entity, provided the specified vesting conditions, if any, are met. If that agreement is subject to an approval process (e.g. by shareholders), grant date is the date when that approval is obtained.

Vesting conditions. In the definition of the grant date, we discover the concept of 'vesting conditions'. These are the conditions that must be satisfied for the counterparty to become entitled to receive cash, other assets or equity instruments of the entity, under a share-based payment arrangement. Vesting conditions include service conditions which require the other party to complete a specified period of service, and performance conditions which require specified performance targets to be met (such as a specified increase in the entity's profit over a specified period of time). Only these two conditions, namely service rendered and performance conditions, need to be considered to determine the vesting conditions.

Vesting conditions shall be taken into account by adjusting the number of equity instruments included in the measurement of the transaction amount so that, ultimately, the amount recognized for goods or services received as consideration for the equity instruments granted shall be based on the number of equity instruments that eventually vest. Hence, on a cumulative basis, no amount is recognized for goods or services if the equity instruments granted do not vest because of failure to satisfy a vesting condition (e.g. the counterparty fails to complete a specified service period, or a performance condition is not satisfied, subject to the requirement of para. 21).

ILLUSTRATION

A company, Amax, grants 50 share options to each of its 200 employees. If there is no vesting requirement, the employees are entitled to receive these granted options immediately. The fair value of the share option at the grant date is €30. When the equity instruments granted vest immediately, implying that the counterparty is not required to complete a specific period of service before becoming unconditionally entitled to those equity instruments, the entity shall recognize on grant date the services received in full, with a corresponding increase in equity.

In this situation the expense related to these granted share options is:

$$10\,000 \text{ options} \times €30 = €300\,000$$

This amount will be debited to an expense account and credited to an equity account.

ILLUSTRATION

When company Amax wants to enter its share-based transaction in its books, it needs information on the probability that the employees will remain in service. On the basis of past experience, company Amax estimates that 10 per cent of employees will leave during the three-year period and therefore forfeit their rights to the share options. If we take the example of the share option plan that is only dependent on the vesting condition that the employee remains in service for three years, we will have the following amounts to be entered in the books of company Amax. For this illustration, we assume that after three years the estimates used match exactly with the reality and that the fair value of the option at grant date is €30.

Year	Calculation
1	10 000 options × 90% × €30 × 1/3
2	(10 000 options × 90% × €30 × 2/3) − 90 000
3	(10 000 options × 90% × €30 × 3/3) − 180 000

Over the vesting period, an amount of €270 000 has been reported in the profit and loss account as a remuneration expense, and over the same period that amount has been credited to an equity account.

Amount debited to the expense account	Amount credited to an equity account
€90 000	€90 000
€90 000	€90 000
€90 000	€90 000

If vesting requirements exist, then the grant of the equity instruments is conditional on satisfying specified vesting conditions. For example, a grant of shares or share options to an employee is typically conditional on the employee remaining in the entity's employ for a specified period of time.

Suppose that company Amax still grants 50 share options to each of its 200 employees, but that each grant is conditional on the employee remaining in service over the next three years.

Vesting conditions might also take the form of performance conditions that must be satisfied, such as the entity achieving a specified growth in profit or a specified increase in the entity's share price. Suppose that company Amax grants 50 share options to each of its 200 employees, conditional on the employees remaining in the company for a period of two years. However, the shares will only vest if at the end of year 2 the return on equity of the company has increased by 4 per cent over the vesting period. Company Amax combines a performance condition with a service condition to arrive at the vesting condition.

The entity shall recognize an amount for the goods or services received during the vesting period, based on the best available estimate of the number of equity instruments expected to vest and shall revise that estimate, if necessary, if subsequent information indicates that the number of equity instruments expected to vest differs from previous estimates. On the vesting date, the entity shall revise the estimate to equal the number of equity instruments that ultimately vested. When vesting conditions exist, the amount of the services received, measured by the fair value of the equity instruments, is allocated over the vesting period.

After the vesting period, the entity shall not make any subsequent adjustments to its equity.

Measurement date

The fair value of the equity instruments granted shall be determined at the measurement date. IFRS 2 defines the measurement date as the date at which the fair value of the equity instruments is granted. For transactions with employees and others providing similar services, the measurement date is the grant date. For transactions with parties other than employees (and those providing similar services), the measurement date is the date the entity obtains the goods or the counterparty renders service.

If market prices are available, they should be used as fair value of the equity instruments. If market prices are not available, valuation techniques can be used to estimate the fair value of those equity instruments on the measurement date in an at-arm's-length transaction between knowledgeable willing parties. In relation to share options, the Black-Scholes-Merton formula might be used (see Black-Scholes in Wikipedia). When the fair value of the equity instruments cannot be measured reliably, IFRS 2 stipulates that the intrinsic value of the instrument will be used for valuation purposes. The intrinsic value of the equity instrument is defined in the appendix to IFRS 2 as the difference between the fair value of the shares the counterparty has the right to and the price (if any) the counterparty is required to pay for those shares. In many cases, transactions will have an intrinsic value of nil at the date of the grant. Therefore, IFRS 2 requires that all share-based payments measured at intrinsic value be re-measured through profit or loss at each reporting date until the transaction is settled (e.g. the exercise of options granted).

IFRS 2 describes further the recognition and measurement rules on how to deal with modifications to the terms and conditions on which equity instruments are granted, including cancellations and settlements. Discussing these elements in detail would go beyond the purpose of this book.

Cash-settled share-based payment transactions

For cash-settled share-based payment transactions, the entity shall measure the goods or services acquired and the liability incurred at the fair value of the liability. Until the liability is settled, the entity shall re-measure the fair value of the liability at each reporting date and at the date of settlement, with any changes in fair value recognized in profit or loss for the period.

ILLUSTRATION

Suppose Amax grants 50 share options to each of its 200 employees, on the condition that the employees remain in service for the next three years. The employees may choose to exercise their options at the end of year 3, year 4 or year 5. The payment will, however, be in cash. The amount of cash to be received will be determined by the value of the option at exercise date. During the first year, 8 employees leave the company and the entity estimates that 12 employees will leave the company in the next two years. During year 2, a total of eight employees leave the company and the company estimates that six employees will leave Amax in year 3. In the third year, ten employees leave the company. At the end of year 3, the share options held by the remaining employees vest.

In the third year, 30 employees exercise their options, in the fourth year another 40 employees exercise their options, and in the fifth year the remaining 104 employees exercise their options.

Amax uses the following estimates for the valuation of this cash-settled share-based transaction in its books.

Year	Fair value	Intrinsic value
1	€10	
2	€11	
3	€14	€1 250
4	€17	€1 500
5		€2 000

This cash-settled share-based transaction will lead to the following amounts:

Yr	Calculations	Expense	Liability
1	$(200 - 20) \times 50 \times €10 \times 1/3 = 30\ 000$	30 000	30 000
2	$((200 - 22) \times 50 \times €11 \times 2/3) - 30\ 000 = 35\ 266$	35 266	65 266
3	$[((200 - 26 - 30) \times 50 \times €14) - 65\ 266] + [30 \times 50 \times €12.50] = 35\ 534 + 18\ 750 = 54\ 284$	54 284	100 800
	[calculation of expense of the option plan for year 3] + [30 employees exercise their options at the end of year 3]		
4	$[((144 - 40) \times 50 \times €17) - 100\ 800] + [40 \times 50 \times €15] = -12\ 400 + 30\ 000 = 17\ 600$		
	[value of the outstanding options granted] + [40 employees exercise their options]	17 600	88 400
5	$(104 \times 50 \times €20) - 88\ 400 = 15\ 600$		
	[50 employees exercise their options]	15 600	—

The amount in the column 'Expense' represents the remuneration expense for the period and the amount in the column 'Liability' represents the amount on the liability account. In the example of the cash-settled share-based payment transaction presented above, we need to re-measure the liability at its fair value after the vesting date because not all options have been exercised. If all options are exercised at vesting date, no subsequent re-measurements are necessary.

Share-based payment transactions with cash alternatives

In relation to this third group of share-based payment transactions, a distinction is made between, on the one hand, share-based payment transactions in which the terms of the arrangement provide the counterparty with a choice of settlement and, on the other, share-based payment transactions in which the terms of the arrangement provide the entity with a choice of settlement.

In the first situation, where an entity has granted the counterparty the right to choose whether a share-based payment transaction is settled in cash or by issuing equity instruments, the entity has granted a compound financial instrument which includes a debt component (i.e. the counterparty's right to demand payment in cash) and an equity component (i.e. the counterparty's right to demand settlement in equity instruments rather than in cash). For transactions with parties other than employees, in which the fair value of the goods or services received is measured directly, the entity shall measure the equity component of the compound financial instrument as the difference between the fair value of the goods or services received and the fair value of the debt component, at the date when the goods or services are received.

For other transactions, including transactions with employees, the entity shall measure the fair value of the compound financial instrument at the measurement date, taking into account the terms and conditions on which the rights to cash or equity instruments were granted.

For a share-based payment transaction in which the terms of the arrangement provide an entity with the choice of whether to settle in cash or by issuing equity instruments, the entity shall determine whether it has a present obligation to settle in cash and account for the share-based payment transaction accordingly. The entity has a present obligation to settle in cash, if the choice of settlement in equity instruments has no commercial substance (e.g. because the entity is legally prohibited from issuing shares), or the entity has a past practice or a stated policy of settling in cash, or generally settles in cash whenever the counterparty asks for cash settlement.

If the entity has a present obligation to settle in cash, it shall account for the transaction in accordance with the requirements applying to cash-settled share-based payment transactions.

If no such obligation exists, the entity shall account for the transaction in accordance with the requirements applying to equity-settled share-based payment transactions, in paras 10–29:

(a) If the entity elects to settle in cash, the cash payment shall be accounted for as the repurchase of an equity interest, i.e. as a deduction from equity, except as noted in (c) below.

(b) If the entity elects to settle by issuing equity instruments, no further accounting is required (other than a transfer from one component of equity to another, if necessary), except as noted in (c) below.

(c) If the entity elects the settlement alternative with the higher fair value, as at the date of settlement, the entity shall recognize an additional expense for the excess value given, i.e. the difference between the cash paid and the fair value of the equity instruments that would otherwise have been issued, or the difference between the fair value of the equity instruments issued and the amount of cash that would otherwise have been paid, whichever is applicable.

Group cash-settled share-based payment transactions. In business combinations, employees of subsidiary A might be entitled to share-based compensation whereby they receive shares of the parent entity B. In this situation, subsidiary A accounts for this transaction in its own entity's books according to the principles set out in IFRS 2. For example, in case of an equity-settled share-based payment transaction, the account expenses in relation to employee services of the subsidiary are debited and the equity account of the subsidiary is credited. This credit can be regarded as a capital contribution from the parent, namely entity B in this particular case.

In the parent B's separate financial statements, the parent entity recognizes on the one hand the grant of an equity instrument and, on the other, the capital contribution made to its subsidiary. This event will be recorded in the books of the parent entity by debiting the account investment in subsidiary A and crediting the equity account.

When the consolidated group accounts are prepared, the increase in equity in A's financial statements and the increase in the investment asset in B's separate financial statements are both eliminated upon consolidation.

ACTIVITY 21.4

A parent entity grants 200 employees of its subsidiary the right to receive 200 shares of the parent entity each, conditional upon the completion of two years' service with the subsidiary entity. The fair value of the shares on grant date is €40 per share. The subsidiary estimates that 90 per cent of the employees will complete the two-year vesting period. This estimate remains the same during the whole vesting period. At the end of the vesting period, 92 per cent of the employees had completed the required two years of service.

Account for this transaction in the books of the subsidiary and in the books of the parent entity.

Activity feedback

The subsidiary will recognize this share-based payment transaction by debiting an expense account in relation to employee services and crediting an equity account, representing a capital contribution from the parent. The amounts which will be recorded in year 1 and year 2, are presented below:

Year 1: 200 employees × 200 shares × 90% estimated vesting × 1/2 × €40 = €720 000

Year 2: (200 employees × 200 shares × 92% vesting × 2/2 × €40) – €720 000 = €1 472 000 – €720 000 = €752 000

The parent entity will increase its investment in its subsidiary by debiting this investment account for €720 000 in year 1 and €752 000 in year 2. The equity account will be credited for €720 000 in year 1 and €752 000 in year 2.

Disclosures

Extensive information disclosures about these share-based transactions are required by IFRS 2 (these can be found in the notes to the accounts). In relation to these transactions, an entity shall disclose information that enables users of the financial statement to:

(a) understand the nature and the extent of share-based payment arrangements that existed during the period

(b) understand how the fair value of the goods or services received, or the fair value of the equity instruments granted during the period was determined

(c) understand the effect of share-based payment transactions on the entity's profit or loss for the period and on its financial position.

These information requirements imply that a detailed description of all share-based payment arrangements has to be disclosed (e.g. the different types of share-based arrangements and their nature and conditions; the number and weighted average exercise price of share options for the outstanding options at the beginning of the period; the ones granted, forfeited, exercised and expired during the period, the ones outstanding at the end of the period and the ones exercisable at the end of the period; a description of how the fair value is determined; and details on the expenses recognized and the liabilities recorded).

The disclosure of compensation benefits to the external stakeholders of the company is not only determined by accounting regulation. Codes of corporate governance in many countries include disclosure requirements with regard to top management compensation.

ACTIVITY 21.5

Look at the websites of several companies from different parts of Europe and worldwide and try to find information on stock-based compensation or other elements of compensation. What do you observe?

Activity feedback

Disclosure on equity-based compensation, and about compensation at large, differs among different countries. In the Anglo-Saxon world, information on compensation has for some time found its way into the financial statements. Compensation levels of individuals are disclosed in those financial statements. In continental Europe, the presence of the value 'secrecy' (discussed in Chapter 2) probably has an impact on the amount of and the way in which information is disclosed. Further, a diversity of share-based compensation plans is found in the notes to the financial statements of companies.

The following Real Life Illustration is taken from the 2014 annual report of Unilever.

REAL LIFE ILLUSTRATION

4C. SHARE-BASED COMPENSATION PLANS - Unilever Annual Report 2014

The fair value of awards at grant date is calculated using appropriate pricing models. This value is expensed over their vesting period, with a corresponding credit to equity. The expense is reviewed and adjusted to reflect changes to the level of awards expected to vest, except where this arises from a failure to meet a market condition. Any cancellations are recognised immediately in the income statement.

As at 31 December 2014, the Group had share-based compensation plans in the form of performance shares, share options and other share awards.

The numbers in this note include those for Executive Directors shown in the Directors Remuneration Report on pages 62 to 77 and those for key management personnel shown in note 4A on page 93. Non Executive Directors do not participate in any of the share-based compensation plans.

The charge in each of the last three years is shown below, and relates to equity settled plans:

Income statement charge	€ million 2014	€ million 2013	€ million 2012
Performance share plans	**(186)**	(221)	(147)
Other plans	**(2)**	(7)	(6)
	(188)	(228)	(153)

PERFORMANCE SHARE PLANS

Performance share awards are made under the Management Co-investment Plan (MCIP) and the Global Share Incentive Plan (GSIP). The MCIP allows Unilever's managers to invest up to 60% of their annual bonus in shares in Unilever and to receive a corresponding award of performance related shares. Under GSIP Unilever's managers receive annual awards of NV and PLC shares. The awards of both plans will vest after three years between 0% and 200% of grant level, depending on the satisfaction of performance metrics.

The performance metrics of both MCIP and GSIP are underlying sales growth, operating cash flow and core operating margin improvement. There is an additional target based on relative total shareholder return (TSR) for senior executives.

REAL LIFE ILLUSTRATION   *(Continued)*

A summary of the status of the Performance Share Plans as at 31 December 2014, 2013 and 2012 and changes during the years ended on these dates is presented below:

	2014 *Number of shares*	2013 *Number of shares*	2012 *Number of shares*
Outstanding at 1 January	**18,909,204**	18,031,101	18,642,656
Awarded	**9,724,186**	7,780,730	7,036,147
Vested	**(9,347,225)**	(5,823,102)	(6,277,057)
Forfeited	**(1,817,874)**	(1,079,525)	(1,370,645)
Outstanding at 31 December	**17,468,291**	18,909,204	18,031,101

	2014	*2013*	*2012*
Share award value information Fair value per share award during the year	**€27.80**	€28.91	€25.02

ADDITIONAL INFORMATION

At 31 December 2014, shares and options in NV or PLC totalling 19,428,560 [2013: 23,326,247] were held in respect of share-based compensation plans of NV, PLC and its subsidiaries, including North American plans.

To satisfy the options granted, certain NV group companies hold 18,822,613 (2013: 16,615,696) ordinary shares of NV or PLC, and trusts in Jersey and the United Kingdom hold 1,053,470 [2013: nil] NV or PLC shares. Shares acquired during 2014 represent 0.442% of the Group's called up share capital. The balance of shares held in connection with share plans at 31 December 2014 represented 0.7% (2013: 0.5%) of the Group's called up share capital·.

The book value of €647 million (2013: €507 million) of all shares held in respect of share-based compensation plans for both NV and PLC is eliminated on consolidation by deduction from other reserves. Their market value at 31 December 2014 was €656 million (2013: €489 million).

At 31 December 2014, the exercise price of 167,479 PLC options (NV: nil] were above the market price of the shares. At 31 December 2013, the exercise price of 192,447 PLC options (NV: nil] were above the market price of the shares.

Shares held to satisfy options and related trusts are accounted for in accordance with IAS 32 'Financial Instruments: Presentation' and SIC 12 'Consolidation of Special Purpose Entities'. All differences between the purchase price of the shares held to satisfy options granted and the proceeds received for the shares, whether on exercise or lapse, are charged to reserves. The basis of the charge to operating profit for the economic value of options granted is discussed on page 98.

Between 31 December 2014 and 25 February 2015 (the latest practicable date for inclusion in this report), 4,343,415 shares were granted and 7,840,032 shares were vested or forfeited related to the Performance Share Plans.

ACCOUNTING FOR LONG-TERM EMPLOYEE BENEFITS: PENSION BENEFITS

The most important long-term employee benefits are pension benefits. Other long-term employee benefits, including long-service leave or sabbatical leave, jubilee or other long-service benefits, long-term disability benefits or medical benefits, are accounted for in a similar manner to pension benefits. Therefore, we will only discuss the recognition and valuation issues related to pension benefits extensively. We will start the discussion by defining the concept of a pension benefit and by an analysis of the impact of a company pension plan on the financial situation of the company.

Existence of different pension systems

The purpose of a pension is to grant people some money when they are retired. Worldwide, three different types of 'pension systems' can be distinguished, namely state pensions, pensions received from the employer resulting from an employment contract, and individual pension savings plans. So an individual can be entitled to a state pension, on top of that a retirement benefit resulting from their employment contract (if retirement benefits were included), and finally a payment from an individual pension scheme, if the individual has taken the initiative to contribute to an individual savings account. The importance and presence of each type of pension system in a single country is determined by characteristics of the local or national environment.

In some countries, state pensions are the major source of income for retired people. In other countries, initiatives such as company pension plans and individual pension schemes are stimulated by the government and are common practice because of the lower levels of state pensions.

State pensions do not usually create any accounting problems for entities. The companies are collecting the premium from the employees (a deduction from gross salary) and these amounts, together with employer's contributions (if any), are paid to the government. If the premium due for an accounting period, which will be recorded as an expense, is not equal to the amount transferred to the government, prepaid expenses or accrued expenses can be reported on the balance sheet. According to IAS 19, state pensions should be accounted for as multi-employer plans and these will often have the characteristics of a defined contribution plan (this concept will be defined later in this chapter). The treatment stipulated in IAS 19 concerning state pensions is usually in line with what we have already mentioned.

Individual pension schemes are totally separate from employment contracts, so IAS 19 does not focus on them. IAS 19 deals with company pension plans in particular as they have an impact on the financial situation of a company.

Company pension plans

A company pension plan can be defined as an agreement between an employer and its employees, whereby the former agrees to pay benefits to the latter after their retirement. The terms of the pension plan stipulate the retirement benefit to which an employee is entitled. There are two major categories of pension schemes or pension plans, namely defined benefit plans and defined contribution plans.

Definition of a pension benefit. In a defined contribution plan, the employer agrees to contribute a specific amount to the pension plan with or without a contribution from the employee. The benefits to be received by the employee at retirement are determined by the contributions transferred to the plan, plus the investment return obtained on those contributions. This implies that an employee will only know the amount which they will receive as pension benefit on retirement. The contributions are usually paid into a separate entity (fund or insurance company). Further, the employee bears the risk under this type of pension plan as the amount is, in the end, dependent on the obtained investment return on the amounts contributed and invested.

A defined benefit plan is defined by IAS 19 as all plans other than defined contribution plans. If we want to describe defined benefit plans in somewhat more detail, we would characterize them as those plans where the benefits promised are defined in advance, where the amount of pension benefit to be paid depends on the plan's benefit formula. Plans for which the pension benefit formula is based on compensation levels are called pay-related plans. The three most important types of pay-related plans are:

- the *final pay plan*, in which the benefits are calculated as a percentage of the final salary before retirement
- the *final average pay plan*, where the benefits are calculated as a percentage of the average salary of the last three to five years before retirement
- the *career average pay plan*, in which the benefits are related to the average salary someone has earned during their career.

In some defined benefit plans, the state pensions are included in the benefit formula. This implies, however, that if the level of state pensions drops, the employer faces a higher cost. Plans whereby the benefit formula is not based on compensation levels are called non-pay-related plans or flat benefit plans. For example, a pension plan whereby the pension benefit is defined as a benefit consisting of contributions plus a guarantee of fixed return is categorized as a defined benefit pension plan and shall be accounted for as such.

Organization and financing of a company pension plan. Providing retirement benefits to employees involves many decisions. In addition to the decision about the type of pension benefit promised (defined contribution or defined benefit), decisions regarding the organization and the financing or funding patterns of these benefits also have to be made. The choices made by companies will not only be influenced by company characteristics but also by characteristics of the national environment. When an employer provides its employees with a defined contribution plan, the finance pattern consists of the contributions stipulated in the pension plan made to a pension account. The finance pattern and the responsibility of the employer can be determined in a very straightforward way. The pension account in which the funds are accumulated can be administered by the company or by a bank.

A defined benefit plan can be financed through the so-called pay as you go system or through a funding system. Under the pay as you go system, the pensions are paid directly from the resources of the company as they fall due. The purpose of a funding system, on the contrary, is to make contributions through the whole employment period of the employee in order to accumulate enough funds to guarantee the pension payments. Usually actuarial cost methods (also called actuarial funding methods) are used to determine the amounts to be financed each period in order to have enough funds to pay the pension benefits when the employee retires.

If pension benefits are financed by means of a funding system, two main types of organizational set-ups are possible: internal funding or external funding. In the case of internal funding, resources are allocated in advance for the provision of benefits, but no separation of these amounts from the other assets of the employer is made. Benefit payments, when due, are made directly by the employer. In some countries, employers are allowed to use those funds accumulated within the entity for financing the operational activities of the entity. In other countries, those funds may be kept in the entity but they have to be invested in certain assets. In the Anglo-Saxon world, those plans financed through internal funding are very often called unfunded pension plans. This term might be misleading as it may sound as if no financing arrangements have been made yet, as in the case of the pay as you go system. In fact, internally funded plans is a better way to describe this financing system.

If an employer uses external funding, the resources are accumulated in a separate legal entity (i.e. there is a separate fund). In the Anglo-Saxon world, plans that are funded externally are called funded pension plans. This separate fund may be a unique creation for only one employer or for many employers, or it may be operated by a specialist insurance company running many such schemes. The contract with the insurance company has to stipulate what type of risks and responsibilities are transferred to the insurance company. The terms of this contract are extremely important for accounting purposes as they determine whether insured benefits will be considered a defined contribution type or a defined benefit type. Para. 46 states in this respect:

> An entity may pay insurance premiums to fund a post-employment benefit plan. The entity should treat such a plan as a defined contribution plan unless the entity will have (either directly or indirectly through the plan) a legal or constructive obligation either:
>
> - to pay the employee benefits directly when they fall due or
> - to pay further contributions if the insurer does not pay all future employee benefits relating to employee service in the current and prior periods.

If the entity retains such a legal or constructive obligation, the entity should treat the plan as a defined benefit plan for accounting purposes.

Whether an insured plan qualifies as a defined contribution plan or a defined benefit plan is an extremely important matter, since the way these plans have to be accounted for is totally different. Companies will have a tendency to try to qualify their insured plans as much as possible as defined contribution plans.

Although employers can choose between different types of pension benefit and different ways to organize and finance them, country-specific influences are often encountered. First of all, the importance of the pension benefits granted by the employer versus state pensions differs among countries. In countries like the UK, the US and the Netherlands, the benefits of company pension plans are a major source of income for retired people. In countries in the south of Europe and also in Belgium and Scandinavian countries, state pensions make up an important part of the income of people after retirement. A wide variety of differences in pension systems is also found on a global basis.

Further, companies may choose between internal funding or external funding. Very often the national environment, however, determines the choice. For example, in the Netherlands and the UK, companies usually fund their pension promises externally. A number of German companies use internal funding. This practice is responsible for large provisions on the balance sheets of German companies. Very often, national legal requirements are the drivers for the observed differences. For example, there might be laws which prohibit internal funding. The possibility of withdrawing funds from an external pension fund in times when surpluses are present will also be dependent on the existing laws of a particular country. In fact, IAS 19 has to take into account all these different possibilities existing worldwide. The IASB has to develop accounting regulations concerning these benefits, which can be applied worldwide. IAS 19 is elaborately detailed in order to take into account all of these differences.

Another element which relates to organizational issues is whether an employer joins a multi-employer plan for the organizational and financial aspects in relation to pension benefits, or whether they decide to set up the organization and financing as a single-employer plan. In some countries, such as the Netherlands, employers often join multi-employer plans. In relation to multi-employer plans, IAS 19 stipulates that multi-employer plans are defined contribution plans (other than state plans) or defined benefit plans (other than state plans) that:

- pool the assets contributed by various entities that are not under common control
- use those assets to provide benefits to employees of more than one entity, on the basis that contribution and benefit levels are determined without regard to the identity of the entity that employs the employees concerned.

Whether these multi-employer plans are of a defined benefit or a defined contribution type will depend on the terms of the plan.

ACTIVITY 21.6

How do you think these different types of pension plan affect the financial situation of the sponsoring company, namely the employer?

Activity feedback

- Pensions represent a cash outflow for the company. The timing of the cash flow will be different according to the funding system which is used by the company: pay as you go system, internal or external funding system and the finance pattern determined by the actuarial funding methods.
- The amount of pension benefits represents a cost for the company. This cost can be reduced

through advanced funding if positive investment returns are obtained.
- When an employee renders service, their pension rights accrue. Depending on the terms of the pension plan or the existing company practice, the employer has a legal or constructive obligation.

At the time of retirement, the employer owes the employee a certain amount of money. This amount of money is determined in advance in the case of a defined benefit plan or will be dependent on the realized investment return on the amounts contributed to a plan under a defined contribution plan.

Impact of company pension plans on the sponsoring company. The concept of vested benefits is important as vested employee benefits are those benefits that are not conditional on future employment. The terms of a pension plan stipulate when pension benefits become vested. Usually an employee has to be in service for a minimum period (e.g. five years) before their pension rights become vested. If the benefits are vested, this means that the employee has earned their pension rights independent of whether they stay with the firm in the future.

From the feedback of Activity 21.6, we have learned that pension benefits do have an impact on the result, cash flow and financial position of a company. Further, we know that pensions and other retirement benefits are a major cost for many entities across many jurisdictions.

As a result, these elements have to be accounted for in the financial statements of the employer. The way these benefits are accounted for will depend largely on the type of pension promise which has been made to the employee, namely a defined contribution into a plan or a promise for a defined benefit at the moment of retirement. Defined contribution plans are much simpler to account for. With regard to the recognition and valuation of pension benefits granted under a defined benefit plan, many technical issues have to be agreed on first. For both types of plans, employee contributions to the scheme reduce the employer's expense in the profit and loss account.

Accounting for defined contribution plans

Under a defined contribution plan, the finance pattern and the responsibility of the employer can be determined in a very straightforward way. The amounts to be contributed, according to the terms of the pension plan, should be treated as pension costs for that particular period. If the employer has transferred all the contributions stipulated in the pension plan to a pension scheme, then the employer has fulfilled its pension commitments and no provision has to be shown on the balance sheet.

Paragraphs 51–53 of IAS 19 stipulate reporting and disclosure requirements in relation to a defined contribution plan as follows: when an employee has rendered service to an entity during a period, the entity should recognize the contribution payable to a defined contribution plan in exchange for that service as a liability (accrued expense), after deducting any contribution already paid. If the contribution already paid exceeds the contribution due for service before the balance sheet date, an entity should recognize that excess as an asset (prepaid expense) to the extent that the prepayment will lead to, for example, a reduction in future payments or a cash refund. The contribution payable to a defined contribution plan should also be recorded as an expense, unless another IAS requires or permits the inclusion of the contribution in the cost of an asset (see, for example, IAS 2, *Inventories* and IAS 16, *Property, Plant and Equipment*).

A company should always disclose in the notes the amount recognized as an expense in relation to the defined contribution plans of the company. When a pension plan consists of contributions which guarantee a fixed return, it is considered a defined benefit plan.

Accounting for defined benefit plans

As mentioned earlier, the pension benefit under this type of plan is determined by the pension plan formula and as such is defined in advance. The formula can be a function of the salary of the beneficiary or another variable.

Until recently, most defined benefit plans determined the benefit to be received as a function of the salary of the employee. In the US and in Europe, cash balance plans are becoming more popular. Cash balance plans are pension plans in which the pension benefit is determined by reference to the amounts credited to an employee's account. Those amounts typically comprise in each year a principal amount based on current salary and a specified interest credit. The plan may or may not be funded. If the plan is funded, it may be invested in assets that differ from those which determine the interest credit. On retirement or leaving service (when vesting conditions are met), the employee is entitled to a lump sum equal to the total amount credited to this account.

According to IAS 19, cash balance plans are defined benefit plans. However, they entail specific accounting problems which are not dealt with yet by IAS 19. As a result, the Board will pay attention to these types of plans in the future.

Under a defined benefit scheme, the exact total amount of the benefit is known only at the moment of retirement (in case of a lump sum payment) or when the pensioner dies (in case of annual payments). Only at that moment are all uncertainties gone. The main problem, however, is how to charge this total cost over the subsequent service years of the employee. In many countries, actuarial funding methods are used for this accounting allocation problem, and IAS 19 has also opted for this approach by choosing one particular actuarial funding method for accounting purposes, namely the projected unit credit method. Because of the important role of actuarial funding methods in the recognition of pension costs and pension liabilities for accounting purposes, we will pay attention in this section to the function and the mechanisms of those actuarial funding methods (often called actuarial cost methods by actuaries).

Mechanisms of actuarial funding methods. We will illustrate the purpose and the mechanisms of actuarial funding methods with a numerical example relating to one person, Mr Dupont. This example is highly simplified for pedagogic reasons.

ACTIVITY 21.7

Assume Mr Dupont enters a pension scheme with a pension formula based on his final salary. The pension benefit he is entitled to receive is defined as follows:

$$Br = k(r - y)Sr$$

where:
Br = pension benefit to be received at retirement
k = % of salary
r = retirement age
y = age at which the employee is entitled to receive benefits
Sr = last salary before retirement

The pension benefit for Mr Dupont is a lump sum payment at retirement. We will further assume k = 10% and that Mr Dupont enters the company in year 1. His pension benefits are vested from the first moment of employment. The salary levels over the five years of his employment are:

Year 1: 100 000
Year 2: 110 000
Year 3: 120 000
Year 4: 140 000
Year 5: 160 000

Calculate the amount of earned pension benefit Mr Dupont is entitled to receive at the end of each year of service rendered.

Activity feedback

The pension benefit Mr Dupont is entitled to increases over the years in the following way:

Year 1: B1 = 0.1 × 1 (100 000) = 10 000
Year 2: B2 = 0.1 × 2 (110 000) = 22 000
Year 3: B3 = 0.1 × 3 (120 000) = 36 000
Year 4: B4 = 0.1 × 4 (140 000) = 56 000
Year 5: B5 = 0.1 × 5 (160 000) = 80 000

Several actuarial cost or funding methods exist to determine the financing or funding pattern for the pension benefits. These different methods will all lead to different funding patterns for the same pension benefit to attain in the end; in the case of Mr Dupont, at the end of year 5. The group of actuarial cost or actuarial funding methods which are most commonly used can be divided in two subgroups, namely *accrued valuation methods* and *projected valuation methods*. The first group, the accrued valuation methods, takes into account only the service rendered to date and the current salary level for the calculation of the amounts to be funded. The amount to be funded in a particular year under this method is equal to the present value of the benefit accrual in that particular year. Only the accrued or earned pension rights are financed under this method. Under the accrued valuation method, expected future salary levels can be taken into account as well as in combination with service already rendered. The accrued benefit valuation method, whereby future salary levels are taken into account, is called the projected unit credit method. This method is chosen by IAS 19 for cost recognition and pension liability valuation purposes.

The second group of actuarial cost methods used by actuaries is called the projected benefit cost methods or projected valuation methods. These actuarial funding methods calculate the total pension benefit an employee will receive on retirement by taking into account the expected service to be rendered over the total service period and the expected salary level at retirement. They allocate that final amount over the working life of the employee as a yearly fixed amount or as a fixed percentage of salary.

The main difference in the funding patterns between the two families of actuarial funding methods (accrued valuation methods versus projected valuation methods) is that under the accrued methods, the amounts to be funded at the start of a career of a person are lower than if one were to finance the promised benefit under a projected valuation method, which takes into account the whole expected service period from the start.

Accrued benefit valuation methods use the pension plan formula to determine the accrual of pension rights over the years. The amount of accrued benefits at a particular moment can be defined as follows:

$$AB_x = B_x(_{r-x}P_xT)V_{r-x}\ddot{a}_r$$

where:

AB_x = actuarial value of accrued benefits at age x

B_x = accrued pension benefits at age x

$_{r-x}P_xT$ = the probability that the employee stays with the firm from age x till retirement with

$$P_xT = (1 - q_{mx})(1 - q_{wx})(1 - qd_x)(1 - q_{rx})$$

q_m = probability of mortality

q_w = probability of withdrawal from the plan

q_d = probability of disability

q_r = probability of early retirement

V_{r-x} = discount factor from retirement age to age x

$\ddot{a}_r$ = present value at retirement age of a long life annuity of a single currency unit at the start of each year (needed if the pension benefit will be paid out as an annual payment)

P_xT is often called the plan turnover assumption.

The function of actuarial assumptions. It is clear from the formula just examined that in order to calculate the accrued benefits and the finance patterns related to it, the actuary must make assumptions about a number of variables, such as life expectancy, employee turnover, future salary levels, investment return and so on. These elements are called actuarial assumptions. Some of them are of a demographic nature (e.g. mortality, number of men and women in the plan) and others are of an economic nature (e.g. inflation rate, investment return). When these actuarial funding methods are used to determine the finance pattern of the benefits, a company is free to choose the value of these assumptions. When the outcome of the actuarial funding method is used for accounting purposes, IAS 19 (para. 75) stipulates that the actuarial assumptions used should be unbiased and mutually compatible. By the latter, IAS 19 means that actuarial assumptions are mutually compatible if they reflect the economic relationships between factors such as inflation, rates of salary increase, the return on plan assets and discount rates. For example, all assumptions that depend on a particular inflation level (such as assumptions about interest rates, and salary and benefit increases) in any given future period assume the same inflation level in that period.

Further, IAS states that financial assumptions should be based on market expectations at the balance sheet date for the period over which the obligations are to be settled (para. 75). The choice of the actuarial assumptions is not immaterial. Minor changes in the assumptions might have substantial impacts on the amounts reported; the assumption with the most material effect is the discount rate (also see the example in Activity 21.13). That is the reason why IAS 19 has paid special attention to the choice of the discount rate (para. 83). The rate used to discount post-employment benefit obligations (both funded and unfunded) should be determined by reference to market yields at the balance sheet date on high quality corporate bonds. In countries where there is no deep market in such bonds, the market yields (at the balance sheet date) on government bonds should be used. The currency and term of the corporate bonds or government bonds should be consistent with the currency and estimated term of the post-employment benefit obligations. Moreover, the depth of the market for high quality corporate bonds should be assessed at currency level.

It is important to state here that the discount rate reflects the time value of money and *not* the actuarial or investment risk. In March 2013, IFRIC further stated that the discount rate used to calculate a defined benefit obligation should be a pre-tax discount rate.

ACTIVITY 21.8

Calculate the actuarial value of accrued benefits for Mr Dupont in each of the five years he is in service, based on the service rendered to that date and the current salary level at that time. Assume that the plan turnover assumption is equal to zero and the discount rate is 4 per cent. The pension benefit is paid out as a lump sum at the moment of retirement. The actuarial calculations are made at the end of the year.

Activity feedback

$AB1 = [0.1 \times (1 \times 100\,000)]/(1.04)^4 = 8\,548$
$AB2 = [0.1 \times (2 \times 110\,000)]/(1.04)^3 = 19\,558$
$AB3 = [0.1 \times (3 \times 120\,000)]/(1.04)^2 = 33\,284$
$AB4 = [0.1 \times (4 \times 140\,000)]/(1.04)^1 = 53\,846$
$AB5 = [0.1 \times (5 \times 160\,000)]/(1.04)^0 = 80\,000$

These actuarial calculations can also be made at the start of each year: the interest factor will then be different. The present value of these accrued benefit obligations increases each year due to the year of extra service rendered by the employee and the interest accrual.

We will analyze the impact on the amount of accrued benefits in Activity 21.9 when future salary levels are included in the calculations. IAS 19 requires the use of the projected unit credit method for the determination of the pension liability as well as for the determination of a part of the total pension cost. The projected unit credit method takes into account future salary increases.

During the financial crisis in 2008/09, the yield on government bonds decreased. As a result, there was a lot of critique on the possibility of using the yield on government bonds. The IASB thought of amending this discount rate for measuring employee benefits. The Board considered the responses to the exposure draft issued on this topic in October 2009. The responses indicated that the proposal to use only the corporate bond yield raised more complex issues than expected. The Board therefore decided to adhere to its original plan to address measurement issues only in the context of a fundamental review.

ACTIVITY 21.9

Take into account the expected future salary levels, and calculate the projected benefit obligation (PBO), of Mr Dupont at the end of each year that he is in service. Since we take into account expected future salary levels, we can no longer talk about accrued benefits or amendment earned benefits.

Activity feedback

$PBO1 = [0.1 \times (1 \times 160\,000)]/(1.04)^4 = 13\,677$
$PBO2 = [0.1 \times (2 \times 160\,000)]/(1.04)^3 = 28\,448$
$PBO3 = [0.1 \times (3 \times 160\,000)]/(1.04)^2 = 44\,379$
$PBO4 = [0.1 \times (4 \times 160\,000)]/(1.04)^1 = 61\,538$
$PBO5 = [0.1 \times (5 \times 160\,000)]/(1.04)^0 = 80\,000$

Present value of the defined benefit obligation. The present value of the defined benefit obligation, as calculated in Activity 21.9, plays an important role in the valuation of a possible pension liability under IAS 19. The PBO is the starting point for the recognition of a net defined benefit liability (asset) in the statement of financial position of the employer (see also para. 54).

Paragraph 87 of IAS further stipulates that post-employment benefit obligations should be measured on a basis that reflects:

1 Estimated future salary increases that affect the benefits payable.

2 The benefits set out in the terms of the plan (or resulting from any constructive obligation that goes beyond those terms) at the end of the reporting period.

3 The effect of any limit on the employer's share of the cost of future benefits.

4 Contributions from employees and third parties that reduce the ultimate cost to the entity of those benefits.

5 Estimated future changes in the level of any state benefits that affect the benefits payable under a defined benefit plan, if, and only if, either:

   (a) those changes were enacted before the end of the reporting period or

   (b) historical data, or other reliable evidence, indicate that those state benefits will change in some predictable manner, for example in line with future changes in general price levels or general salary levels.

As a result of point 5 of para. 87, we notice that, in practice, when pension plan formulas are renegotiated or new pension plans are set up, the benefits resulting from state pensions are no longer included as part of the company pension plan benefit formula. Employers clearly want to avoid elements which increase risk and uncertainty.

Now that you are familiar with the workings of actuarial cost methods, we are able to introduce the solution for the determination of the total pension cost and the valuation of pension liabilities and assets which the IASB has opted for. Below is the determination of the defined benefit cost or total pension cost. Thereafter, we pay attention to the impact of the pension benefits on the statement of financial position of the employer. However, first we enumerate a number of decisions the Board has taken in relation to pension accounting:

1 Pension accounting will be based primarily on the plan's terms and benefit formula.

2 For accounting purposes, the projected unit credit method will be used.

3 A net defined benefit obligation will be presented on the balance sheet, rather than a consolidation of pension assets and pension liabilities in the financial statements of the employer or the sponsor.

4 Future salary increases will be incorporated in the measurement of the pension liability.

5 The pension plan assets will be measured at fair value.

Determination of the defined benefit cost in case of a defined benefit plan

The defined benefit cost in a particular year is defined by IAS 19 as the sum of three individual components, namely the service cost, the net interest on the net defined benefit liability (or asset) and the re-measurement of the net defined benefit liability. The former two will be presented in the profit and loss account part of the statement of comprehensive income, whereas the latter will be included in other comprehensive income on the statement of comprehensive income. Two of the three components of the defined benefit cost, namely the service cost and the re-measurement of the net defined benefit liability, each consist of a number of subcomponents. The service cost consists of the current service cost, the past service cost and any gains or losses on settlements. The re-measurements of the net defined benefit liability comprise the actuarial gains and losses, the return on plan assets, excluding amounts included in the net interest on the net defined benefit liability (asset), and any change in the effect of the asset ceiling, excluding amounts included in net interest on the net defined benefit liability (asset).

Below we explain each of the different items which are included in the defined benefit cost in a particular year.

The service cost

Current service cost. The first component of the service cost is the current service cost (CSC). As illustrated in Activity 21.9, the CSC should be calculated with the use of the projected unit credit method. The projected unit credit method attributes the amount to be funded each year on the basis of the plan's benefit formula. The amounts to be funded each year, which result from the projected unit credit method, represent the CSC. However, if an employee's service in later years will lead to a materially higher level of benefit than in earlier years, an entity should attribute the benefit on a straight line basis:

- from the date when service by the employee first leads to benefits under the plan (whether or not the benefits are conditional on further service)
- until the date when further service by the employee will lead to no material amount of further benefits under the plan, other than from further salary increases.

In those cases, the pension plan formula will no longer determine the cost allocation pattern. In fact, IAS 19 allows an allocation pattern in this case which is more similar to the funding patterns used by the projected valuation methods (see earlier in this chapter).

The PBO in Activity 21.9 increases each year due to the service rendered in each year and the interest accrual on the amount of the PBO at the start of the year. Under IAS 19, the increase due to service rendered is called the current service cost.

ACTIVITY 21.10

Calculate the CSC and the interest accrual for Mr Dupont with the use of the projected unit credit method, which takes into account the service rendered to date and the future salary levels. The calculations are made at the end of the year in this example.

Activity feedback

	CSC	Interest accrual	PBO
Year 1	13 677	—	13 677
Year 2	14 224	547	28 448
Year 3	14 793	1 138	44 379
Year 4	15 384	1 775	61 538
Year 5	16 000	2 462	80 000

The CSC is determined each year by the increases in earned pension rights according to the pension benefit formula:

$$CSC1 = [0.1 \times (1 \times 160\,000)]/(1:04)^4 = 13\,677$$
$$CSC2 = [0.1 \times (1 \times 160\,000)]/(1:04)^3 = 14\,224$$
$$CSC3 = [0.1 \times (1 \times 160\,000)]/(1:04)^2 = 14\,791$$
$$CSC4 = [0.1 \times (1 \times 160\,000)]/(1:04)^1 = 15\,384$$
$$CSC5 = [0.1 \times (1 \times 160\,000)]/(1:04)^0 = 16\,000$$

The interest cost (IC) component is determined as follows:

$$IC1 = 0.04\,(0) = 0$$
$$IC2 = 0.04\,(13\,677) = 547$$
$$IC3 = 0.04\,(28\,448) = 1138$$
$$IC4 = 0.04\,(44\,379) = 1775$$
$$IC5 = 0.04\,(61\,538) = 2462$$

Past service cost. The second component of the service cost is the past service cost. The past service costs arise when an employer grants pension rights for the service rendered prior to the establishment of the pension plan, or when an employer grants an increase in pension benefits also for service rendered in past periods. As a result, the PBO will increase. This increase in the amount of the PBO resulting from those past service benefits should, on the one hand, be funded or financed and, on the other, be recognized for accounting purposes. The amounts recognized in relation to those past service benefits in a particular year on the income statement are called *past service costs*. IAS 19 defines past service costs as the change in the present value of the defined benefit obligation for employee service in prior periods, resulting from a plan amendment (the introduction or withdrawal of, or changes to, a defined benefit plan) or a curtailment (a significant reduction by the entity in the number of employees covered by the plan).

ACTIVITY 21.11

Assume that from year 4 onwards Mr Dupont is entitled to a pension benefit of 0.15 per cent of his final salary for each year he has been with the firm instead of 0.10 per cent.

The formula of the pension plan of Mr Dupont then becomes:

$$Br = 0.15 \, (r - y)Sr$$

The employer also grants this increase in pension benefits for the first three years of the career of Mr Dupont. We have to remember that the pension rights of Mr Dupont are vested from the start of his employment.

Calculate the new PBO at the start of year 4, which takes into account this increase in pension benefits granted for past periods.

Activity feedback

PBO start year 4 = 0.15 [3 × (160 000)] = (1:04)^2 = 66 568

Remember that the PBO at the start of year 4 under the old pension benefit formula was 44 379. This is an increase of the PBO of 22 189 = (66 568 – 44 379).

In the example of Mr Dupont where these past service benefits are vested, the amount of 22 189 should be recognized immediately as part of the total pension cost in year 4.

Gains or losses on settlements. The third component of the service cost consists of gains and losses on settlement. A settlement occurs when an entity enters into a transaction that eliminates all further legal or constructive obligation for part or all of the benefits provided under a defined benefit plan, for example, when a lump sum cash payment is made to, or on behalf of, plan participants in exchange for their rights to receive specified post-employment benefits. IAS 19 prescribes that gains and losses on settlements of a defined benefit plan have to be recognized when the settlement occurs. A settlement may arise from an isolated event, such as the closing of a plant, discontinuance of an operation or termination or suspension of a plan. An event is material enough to qualify as a curtailment if the recognition of a settlement gain or loss would have a material effect on the financial statements. Settlements are often linked with a restructuring. Therefore, an entity accounts for a settlement at the same time as for a related restructuring. We notice that it is up to the management to judge whether the effect is material.

Before determining past service cost, or a gain or loss on settlement, the entity shall re-measure the net defined benefit liability using the current fair value of plan assets and current actuarial assumptions (including current market interest rates and other current market prices) reflecting the benefits offered under the plan before the plan amendment, curtailment or settlement (para. 99).

We have now defined the three subcomponents of the service cost. The cost item below is presented together with the service cost on the profit and loss account part of the statement of comprehensive income.

The net interest on the net defined benefit liability (asset)

The second part of the defined benefit cost consists of a single item, namely the net interest on the net defined benefit liability (asset). Based on the data we have available so far, the defined benefit cost for Mr Dupont in subsequent years would be as shown in Table 21.1.

TABLE 21.1   Total defined benefit cost

	CSC	Interest cost component	Total pension cost
Year 1	13 677	—	13 677
Year 2	14 224	547	14 771
Year 3	14 793	1 138	15 931
Year 4	15 384	1 775	17 159
Year 5	16 000	2 462	18 642

In this example, the interest cost component in Activity 21.10 is determined with the use of the discount rate of 4 per cent. IAS 19 calls this interest cost component the net interest on the net defined benefit liability. The interest cost component reflects the time value of money. Para. 123 stipulates that the interest cost component is computed by multiplying the discount rate as determined at the start of the period by the present value of the net defined benefit obligation throughout that period, taking into account any material changes in the obligation. The net interest on the net defined liability (asset) is the change during the period of the net defined liability (asset) that arises from the passage of time. Since the amounts calculated in the Activity are calculated at the end of the year, there is no interest cost in the first year. (As we said earlier, this example is simplified for pedagogic reasons.)

The service cost and the net interest on the net defined benefit liability (asset) are reported on the statement of profit and loss, whereas the next part of the total defined benefit cost, namely the re-measurements of the net defined benefit liability (asset) have to be presented in other comprehensive income.

Re-measurements of the net defined benefit liability (asset)

This third part of the defined benefit cost includes three separate items. Two elements, namely the actuarial gains and losses and the return on plan assets, will be discussed below. The third component, namely the change in the effect of the asset ceiling, will be discussed when the recognition of the net defined benefit liability (asset) is discussed.

Actuarial gains and losses. Actuarial gains and losses arise from two sources. If actuarial assumptions are different from reality, a difference will occur. This difference can be positive or negative. These differences are called experience adjustments in actuarial jargon. If this difference between the actuarial assumption and the reality continues to exist, it could be that the actuarial assumptions used in the actuarial calculations have to be changed. This is a second source of actuarial gains and losses. So, actuarial gains and losses can also result from changes in the actuarial assumptions themselves. A change in the actuarial assumptions used has as a consequence that the future amounts to be funded will be higher or lower. Empirical evidence is available that companies change actuarial assumptions to manage the amount of the net pension (asset) liability (e.g. Baiman and Shaw, 2014). Further, the PBO calculated with the new actuarial assumptions can also be higher or lower than the PBO calculated with the old actuarial assumptions. In the view of an actuary, actuarial gains and losses mean the following: if the PBO (new assumptions) is higher than the PBO (old assumptions) an actuarial loss arises, since the difference is not yet funded and needs to be. In the opposite situation, where PBO (new assumptions) is smaller than the PBO (old assumptions) an actuarial gain arises, since there is now more funded than the present PBO (new assumptions) (see Activity 21.12).

ACTIVITY 21.12

Assume that at the start of year 4 the discount rate used in the calculations in relation to the pension benefit of Mr Dupont will be changed from 4 per cent to 5 per cent. What will be the impact on the PBO at the start of year 4?

Activity feedback

The PBO at the start of year 4 using a discount rate of 5 per cent is equal to:

PBO at the start of year 4 (new assumptions) $= [0.1 \times (3 \times 160\,000)] / (1.05)^2 = 43\,537$.

Remember that the PBO at the start of year 4, using the discount rate of 4 per cent, was PBO4 (old assumptions) 44 379.

In this situation, we have an actuarial gain as the PBO calculated with the new assumptions (in this case a new discount rate) is lower than the PBO calculated with the old assumptions. The actuarial gain is 842 (we talk about a gain because the new PBO (43 537) is lower than the old PBO (44 379)).

A major question subsequently arises. How should we account for this actuarial result? It is obvious that differences between reality and the actuarial assumptions used will occur frequently (e.g. realized salary increases will be higher or lower than estimated salary increases). Since the revision of IAS 19 in 2011, these actuarial gains and losses have to be recognized immediately in other comprehensive income. Before the revision of IAS 19 in 2011, the IASB allowed a so-called corridor approach whereby actuarial gains and losses, which fell within a corridor, need not be recognized. The amount of actuarial gains and losses falling outside the corridor had to be recognized over a certain period of time. This mechanism was meant to reduce the volatility in reported pension costs. Evidence is available that when it became obvious the corridor approach would be abolished, companies shifted pension assets from equity to debt securities (Amir *et al.*, 2010; An *et al.*, 2014).

Return on plan assets. This second component of the re-measurement of the defined benefit liability (asset) consists of the return on plan assets, excluding amounts included in the net interest on the net defined liability. We will illustrate this component with an example. If we take the pension calculations of Mr Dupont in year 3 and year 4, we observe that the CSC is respectively 14 793 and 15 384, and the interest cost component, which results from the change in the net defined liability (discount rate × defined benefit liability at the start of the period) is 1138 and 1775 (see Activity 21.10).

If the return on plan assets were an amount of 1300 in year 3 and an amount of 1500 in year 4, then the following amounts would be represented as return on plan assets under other comprehensive income: in year 3 (1300 – 1138) = 162 and in year 4 (1500 – 1775) = –275.

The following components would then be included in the accounts of the company:

	Year 3	Year 4
Profit and loss account		
Defined benefit cost	14 793	15 384
Service cost	1 138	1 775
Net interest on the net defined liability		
Other comprehensive income	162	(275)
Re-measurement of the defined benefit liability		

All items making up the defined benefit cost have now been discussed except for one item, namely the effect of the limit in relation to the recognition of a net pension asset or asset ceiling, which will be discussed below.

Defined benefit liability

After the analysis of the defined benefit cost, we now focus on the possible impact of company pension plans on the statement of financial position of the employer. According to IAS 19, the net defined benefit liability (asset) shall be reported on the statement of financial position of the employer. The net defined benefit liability (asset) is the deficit or surplus between the present value of the defined benefit obligation less the fair value of the plan assets (if any). The present value of a defined benefit obligation is the present value, without deducting any plan assets, of expected future payments required to settle the obligation resulting from employer service in the current and prior periods. The amounts of the PBOs in the Activities included in the section on defined benefit costs so far are equal to the present value of a defined benefit obligation.

We have a deficit or a net defined benefit liability when the present value of the defined benefit obligation is larger than the fair value of plan assets. There is a surplus or a net defined benefit asset when the present value of the defined benefit obligation is lower than the fair value of the plan assets. In the case of a surplus, the surplus to be reported must never be higher than the so-called asset ceiling. This asset ceiling is the present value of any economic benefits available in the form of refunds from the plan or reductions in future contributions to the plan. The present value of these economic benefits should be determined using a discount rate which is calculated by reference to market yields at balance sheet data on high quality bonds.

We observe that a 'net' amount will appear on the statement of financial position and not the total amount of pension liabilities and pension assets.

After the discussion of the measurement of the pension liability, we now turn our attention to the valuation of the pension plan assets.

Plan assets

Plan assets include (according to the definitions of IAS 19) assets held by a long-term employee benefit fund and qualifying insurance policies. Pension plan assets need to be valued at fair value. On reading the paragraphs on pension plan assets, it becomes clear that the market value is regarded as the value. It is stipulated that when no market price is available, the fair value of plan assets is estimated; for example, by discounting expected future cash flows using a discount rate that reflects both the risk associated with the plan assets and maturity, or expected disposal date of those assets (or, if they have no maturity, the expected period until the settlement of the related obligation). Further, unpaid contributions due from the reporting entity to the fund, as well as any non-transferable financial instruments issued by the entity and held by the fund, may not be included in the pension plan assets. Plan assets should be reduced further by any liabilities of the fund that do not relate to em-ployee benefits. Where plan assets include qualifying insurance policies that exactly match the amount and the timing of some or all of the benefits payable under the plan, the fair value of those insurance policies is deemed to be the present value of the related obligations.

It is tempting for companies to include future reductions in contributions or refunds in the definition of a defined benefit pension asset in order to decrease the amount of the pension liability to be shown on the balance sheet. This resulted in IFRIC 14 being issued. IFRIC 14 addresses the defined benefit pension assets and their minimum funding requirements. If minimum funding requirements exist (depending on the terms of the pension plan and country regulations to improve the security of post-employment benefits), this might limit the ability to reduce future contributions, or these minimum funding requirements might give rise to a liability. IFRIC 14 provides guidance as to when refunds or reductions in future contributions can be regarded as available and as a result be included in the definition of a defined benefit pension asset. Therefore, it stipulates (para. 7) that:

> An entity shall determine the availability of a refund or a reduction in the future con-tributions in accordance with the terms and conditions of the plan and any statutory requirements in the jurisdiction of the plan [e.g. minimum funding requirements]. An economic benefit, in the form of a refund or a reduction in future contributions, is available if the entity can realize it at some point during the life of the plan or when the plan liabilities are settled. In particular, such an economic benefit may be available even if it is not realizable immediately at the end of the reporting period.

IAS 19 states further that an entity should determine the present value of defined benefit obligations and the fair value of any plan assets with sufficient regularity that the amounts recognized in the financial statements do not differ materially from the amounts that would be determined at the balance sheet date. In Activity 21.13, we combine elements from the measurement of the net pension cost and the net pension liability (asset).

ACTIVITY 21.13

Company Alpha has a defined benefit plan for its employees. At 1 January 20X9, the fair value of the pen-sion plan assets was €4 100 000 and the present value of the defined pension liability was €4 250 000. On 31 December 20X9, Company Alpha received the following information from the firm's actuary:

- The service cost for the financial period was esti-mated at €1 050 000.
- During the year, the company paid €250 000 to retired employees covered by the pension plan.
- During the year, the company contributed €950 000 to the plan.

ACTIVITY 21.13   *(Continued)*

- On 31 December 20X9, the fair value of the plan assets was €5 300 000.
- The actuary estimated the discount rate for the year to 31 December 20X9 at 4 per cent.
- The defined pension liability at that date was measured by the actuary and resulted in an amount of €5 500 000.

What amount will be included as net gain or loss in Company Alpha's other comprehensive income (OCI) for the year ended 31 December 20X9? In addition, will Company Alpha record a net defined liability or net defined asset on its statement of financial position at 31 December 20X9 and what will be the amount?

Activity feedback

We will determine the presence of actuarial gains and losses by comparing the movements in the fair value of pension assets and in the present value of the pension liabilities during the financial period 20X9 and compare the outcome with the values determined by the actuary at 31 December 20X9.

	Fair value of pension plan assets	Present value of pension plan liabilities
Opening balance at 1.1.20X9	4 100 000	4 250 000

Service cost		1 050 000
Interest cost (4%)	164 000	170 000
Benefits paid	250 000	250 000
Contributions	950 000	
Total	5 464 000	5 720 000
Values provided by the actuary at 31.12.20X9	5 300 000	5 500 000
Actuarial loss on plan assets	(164 000)	
Actuarial gain on pension liabilities		220 000

The net actuarial gain or loss will be shown in other comprehensive income. In 20X9 Company Alpha had a net gain of €220 000 – €164 000 = €56 000. A net actuarial gain of €56 000 will be recorded in other comprehensive income.

The net defined pension liability of €5 500 000 – €5 300 000 = €200 000 will be shown on the statement of financial position of Company Alpha at 31 December 20X9.

Disclosure in the notes in relation to pension benefits

A liability or an asset will be presented on the face of the statement of financial position of the employer. The underlying elements taken into account to determine this net defined benefit liability or asset have to be disclosed in the notes to the financial statements (para. 135). There are some extensive disclosures.

An entity shall disclose information that:

(a) explains the characteristics of its defined benefit plans and risks associated with them

(b) identifies and explains the amounts in its financial statements arising from its defined benefit plans

(c) describes how its defined benefit plans may affect the amount, timing and uncertainty of the entity's future cash flows.

In order to illustrate the extensiveness of the disclosure on pension benefits in the notes to the accounts, we insert the disclosure made by the adidas Group in 2014 on their pensions and similar obligations.

REAL LIFE ILLUSTRATION

24   Pension and similar obligations

The Group has recognised post-employment benefit obligations arising from defined benefit plans. The benefits are provided pursuant to the legal, fiscal and economic conditions in each respective country and mainly depend on the employees' years of service and remuneration.

Pensions and similar obligations

(€ in millions)	Dec. 31, 2014	Dec. 31, 2013
Liability arising from defined benefit pension plans	271	243
Similar obligations	14	12
Pensions and similar obligations	284	255

Defined contribution pension plans

The total expense for defined contribution plans amounted to € 46 million in 2014 (2013: € 47 million).

Defined benefit pension plans

Given the diverse Group structure, different defined benefit pension plans exist, comprising a variety of post-employment benefit arrangements. The Group's major defined benefit pension plans relate to adidas AG and its subsidiaries in the UK and Japan, The defined benefit pension plans generally provide payments in case of death, disability or retirement to former employees and their survivors. The obligations arising from defined benefit pension plans are partly covered by plan assets.

In Germany, adidas AG grants its employees contribution-based and final salary defined benefit pension schemes, which provide employees with entitlements in the event of retirement, disability and death. In general, German pension plans operate under the legal framework of the German Company Pensions Act ('Betriebsrentengesetz') and under the German Labour Act. A large proportion of the pension plans are closed to new entrants. New employees are entitled to benefits in accordance with the adidas Pension Plan or the adidas Management Pension Plan. The adidas pension plan is a matching contribution plan; the contributions to this pension plan are partly paid by the employee and partly paid by the employer. The contributions are transferred into benefit building blocks. The benefits are paid out in the form of a pension, a lump sum or instalments. The pension plans in Germany are financed using book reserves, a contractual trust arrangement [CTA], a pension fund ('Pensionsfonds') or a provident fund ('Unterstützungskasse'). The benefits granted to some members of the Executive Board are funded via a pension fund ('Pensionsfonds') or a provident fund ('Unterstützungskasse'). An insurance company is responsible for the determination and the implementation of the investment strategy. Further details about the pension entitlements of members of the Executive Board of adidas AG are contained in the Compensation Report /see compensation report, p,28.

The final salary defined benefit pension scheme in the UK is closed to new entrants and to future accrual. The benefits are mainly paid out in the form of pensions. The scheme operates under UK trust law as well as under the jurisdiction of the UK Pensions Regulator and therefore is subject to a minimum funding requirement. The Trustee Board is responsible for setting the scheme's funding objective, agreeing the contributions with the company and determining the investment strategy of the scheme.

In Japan, employees are entitled to benefits from a defined benefit plan that is not funded by plan assets, The benefits in case of retirement are dependent on final salary and service, and are paid out as a lump sum. The pension plan is subject to Japanese labour law. In the first six months of 2015, it is planned to transfer the liabilities from the defined benefit plan to a defined contribution plan.

Breakdown of the present value of the obligation arising from defined benefit pension plans in the major countries

(€ in milllons)	Dec. 31. 2014			Dec. 31, 2013		
	Germany	UK	Japan	Germany	UK	Japan
Active members	178	–	15	123	–	14

(Continued)

REAL LIFE ILLUSTRATION   (Continued)

Former employees with vested rights	49	50	–	31	37	–
Pensioners	78	4	–	70	4	–
Total	**305**	**54**	**15**	**224**	**41**	**14**

The Group's pension plans are subject to risks from changes in actuarial assumptions, such as the discount rate, salary and pension increase rates, and risks from changes in longevity. A lower discount rate results in a higher defined benefit obligation and/or in higher contributions to the pension funds. Lower than expected performance of the plan assets could lead to an increase in required contributions or to a decline of the funded status.

The following tables analyse the defined benefit plans, plan assets, present values of the defined benefit pension plans, expenses recognised in the consolidated income statement, actuarial assumptions and other information.

Amounts for defined benefit pension plans recognised in the consolidated statement of financial position

[€ in millions]	Dec. 31, 2014	Dec. 31, 2013
Present value of funded obligation from defined benefit pension plans	391	95
Fair value of plan assets	[157]	(83)
Funded status	234	12
Present value of unfunded obligation from defined benefit pension plans	37	230
Asset ceiling effect	0	1
Net defined benefit liability	271	243
Thereof: liability	271	243
Thereof: adidas AG	212	199
Thereof: asset	(0)	(0)
Thereof: adidas AG	–	–

The determination of assets and liabilities for defined benefit plans is based upon statistical and actuarial valuations. In particular, the present value of the defined benefit obligation is driven by financial variables (such as the discount rates or future increases in salaries) and demographic variables (such as mortality and employee turnover). The actuarial assumptions may differ significantly from the actual circumstances and could lead to different cash flows.

Weighted average actuarial assumptions

(in %)	Dec. 31, 2014	Dec. 31, 2013
Discount rate	2.4	3.7
Expected rate of salary Increases	3.2	3.2
Expected pension increases	1.7	2.2

The weighted average actuarial assumptions as at the balance sheet date are used to determine the defined benefit liability at that date and the pension expense for the upcoming financial year.

The actuarial assumptions for withdrawal and mortality rates are based on statistical information available in the various countries. In Germany, the Heubeck 2035 G mortality tables are used. In the UK, assumptions are based on the S1NA base table with modified improvement of the life expectancy mortality tables. In Japan, the '21st Life Tables revised in 2010' mortality tables are used. The rate of the expected pension increases in Germany was reduced to 1.5% for the financial year 2014 (2013: 2.0%).

As in the previous year, the calculation of the pension liabilities in Germany is based on a discount rate determined using the 'Mercer Yield Curve (MYC)' approach.

(Continued)

REAL LIFE ILLUSTRATION   *(Continued)*

Remeasurements, such as gains or losses arising from changes in the actuarial assumptions for defined benefit pension plans during the financial year or a return on the plan assets exceeding the interest income, are immediately recognised outside the income statement as a change in other reserves in the consolidated statement of comprehensive income.

Pension expenses for defined benefit pension plans

(€ in millions)	*Year ending Dec. 31, 2014*	*Year ending Dec. 31, 2013*
Current service cost	16	16
Net interest	8	8
Thereof: interest cost	12	11
Thereof: interest income	(4)	(3)
Past service cost	1	0
Expenses for defined benefit pension plans (recognised in the consolidated income statement)	**25**	**24**
Actuarial losses/(gains)	79	(3)
Thereof: due to changes in financial assumptions	79	(7)
Thereof: due to changes in demographic assumptions	0	1
Thereof: due to experience adjustments	0	3
Return on plan assets (not included in net interest income)	(1)	(3)
Asset ceiling effect	(1)	0
Remeasurements for defined benefit pension plans (recognised as decrease/ (increase) in other reserves in the consolidated statement of comprehensive income)	**77**	**(6)**
Total	**102**	**18**

Of the total pension expenses recorded in the consolidated income statement, an amount of € 17 million (2013: € 16 million) relates to employees of adidas AG, € 0.2 million (2013: € 0.2 million) relates to employees in the UK and € 2 million (2013: € 2 million) relates to employees in Japan. The amendment of pension arrangements for members of the Executive Board of adidas AG in 2014 resulted in past service cost of € 1 million. The pension expense is mainly recorded within other operating expenses. The production-related part of the pension expenses is recognised within cost of sales.

Present value of the defined benefit obligation

[€ in millions]	*2014*	*2013*
Present value of the obligation from defined benefit pension plans as at January 1	**325**	**317**
Currency translation differences	7	(6)
Current service cost	16	16
Interest cost	12	11
Contribution by plan participants	0	0
Pensions paid	(13)	(10)
Actuarial losses/(gains)	79	(3)
Thereof: due to changes in financial assumptions	79	(7)

(Continued)

Thereof: due to changes in demographic assumptions	0	1
Thereof: due to experience adjustments	0	3
Past service cost	1	0
Plan settlements	0	0
Present value of the obligation from defined benefit pension plans as at December 31	**427**	**325**

In the following table, the effects of reasonably conceivable changes in the actuarial assumptions on the present value of the obligation from defined benefit pension plans are analysed. In addition, for Germany, UK and Japan the average duration of the obligation is shown.

Sensitivity analysis of the obligation from defined benefit pension plans

(€ in millions)	Dec. 31, 2014			Dec. 31, 2013		
	Germany	UK	Japan	Germany	UK	Japan
Present value of the obligation from defined benefit pension plans	305	54	15	224	41	14
Increase in the discount rate by 0.5%	279	47	14	207	35	13
Reduction in the discount rate by 0.5%	335	63	16	243	47	15
Average duration of the obligations (in years)	18	30	12	16	30	12

Since many pension plans are closed to future accrual or are not dependent on the salary, the salary trend plays a minor role in determining pension obligations. Due to the fact that about half of the benefits of the German pension plans are paid as lump sums or instalment payments, the pension increase rate and the mortality assumption have significantly less impact than the discount rate when calculating the pension obligations. In Germany, the pension increase rate was reduced to 1.5% as at December 31, 2014 (2013: 2%). This resulted in a decrease in the present value of the pension obligations by € 10 million as at December 31, 2014.

Fair value of plan assets

[€ in millions]	2014	2013
Fair value of plan assets at January 1	**83**	**76**
Currency translation differences	4	(2)
Pensions paid	(5)	(2)
Contributions by the employer	68	5
Contributions paid by plan participants	0	0
Interest income from plan assets	4	3
Return on plan assets [not included in net interest income]	1	3
Plan settlements	0	0
Fair value of plan assets at December 31	**157**	**83**

(*Continued*)

Approximately 90% (2013: 83%) of the total plan assets are allocated to plan assets in the UK (2014: 26%, 2013: 44%), Germany (2014: 59%, 2013: 30%) and Switzerland (2014: 4%, 2013: 9%).

The adidas Group has set up a Contractual Trust Arrangement (CTA) in Germany for the purpose of funding the pension obligations of adidas AG and insolvency insurance with regard to part of the pension obligations of adidas AG. The trustee is the registered association 'adidas Pension Trust e.V.', which was established in December 2013. The investment committee of the adidas Pension Trust determines the investment strategy with the goal to match the pension liabilities as far as possible and to generate a sustainable return. In August 2014, an amount of € 65 million in cash was transferred to the trustee. The cash has been invested in equity index funds, hybrid bonds, fixed interest rate bonds and money market funds. adidas AG does not intend to further fund the CTA in the 2015 financial year. Another part of the plan assets in Germany is invested in insurance contracts via pension funds or provident funds.

In the UK, the plan assets are held under trust within the pension fund. The plan assets in Switzerland are held by a pension foundation. The investment strategy is aligned with the structure of the pension obligations in these countries. In the rest of the world, the plan assets consist predominantly of insurance contracts.

The expected payments for the 2015 financial year amount to € 12 million. Thereof, € 7 million relates to benefits directly paid to pensioners by the Group companies and € 4 million to employer contributions paid into the plan assets. In 2014, the actual return on plan assets was € 6 million (2013: € 6 million).

Composition of plan assets

(€ in millions)	*Dec. 31, 2014*	*Dec. 31, 2013*
Cash and cash equivalents	31	14
Equity instruments	51	28
Bonds	41	11
Real estate	1	1
Pension plan reinsurance	27	25
Insurance policies	5	4
Other assets	0	0
Fair value of plan assets	**157**	**83**

All equities and bonds are traded freely and have a quoted market price in an active market. The other assets consist predominantly of foreign insurance products.

At each balance sheet date, the company analyses the over or underfunding and, where appropriate, adjusts the composition of plan assets.

Multi-employer plans

In the introductory discussion on pension benefits, the concept of multi-employer plans was introduced. Paragraphs 32 and 33 of IAS 19 define how a multi-employer plan should be accounted for. The terms of the plan will determine whether a multi-employer plan will be classified as a defined benefit plan or a defined contribution plan. Where a multi-employer plan is a defined benefit plan, the company shall account for its proportionate share of the defined benefit obligation, plan assets and costs with the plan in the same way as for any other defined benefit plans. When insufficient information is available to use defined benefit accounting for a multi-employer plan that is classified as a defined benefit plan, the company might account for the plan as if it were a defined contribution plan. In this situation, the employer has to disclose in the notes to its accounts that the pension plan is in fact a defined benefit plan, together with the reason why there is insufficient information to account for the plan as a defined benefit plan. If there is a surplus or a deficit in the plan that may affect the amount of future contributions, information about the surplus or the deficit (basis for the calculation and the implications) should be provided as well.

Defined benefit plans that share risks between various entities under common control

IAS 19 prescribes the accounting treatment of defined benefit plans that share risks between various entities under common control. How these individual entities under common control have to account for promised pension benefits in their separate annual accounts depends on whether or not a contractual agreement or stated policy exists for charging the net defined benefit cost for the plan as a whole to the individual group entities measured in accordance with IAS 19. If such a contract or policy exists, the total pension cost determined according to IAS 19 for the group as a whole, will be split over the individual accounts of the separate entities under common control. If no such policy or contracts exists, then the total pension cost determined in line with IAS 19 will be recognized in the individual statement of the group entity which is the legally sponsoring employer for the plan. The other group entities account only for their contribution to the plan in their individual accounts. Participation in such a plan is a related party transaction for each individual group entity and the necessary disclosures on related party transactions have to be made.

TERMINATION BENEFITS

Definition

An entity should recognize termination benefits as a liability and an expense when, and only when, the entity is demonstrably committed to either:

- terminate the employment of an employee or group of employees before the normal retirement date or
- provide termination benefits as a result of an offer made in order to encourage voluntary redundancy.

So the definition of termination benefits in IAS 19 also includes employee benefits that are payable as a result of an employee's decision to accept voluntary redundancy in exchange for those benefits, as well as involuntary determination of the employment. Benefits that are payable in exchange for an employee's decision to accept voluntary redundancy are termination benefits only if they are offered for a short period.

Recognition

IAS 19 (165) states that an entity shall recognize a liability and expense for termination benefits at the earlier of the following dates:

(a) when the entity can no longer withdraw the offer of those benefits and

(b) when the entity recognizes costs for restructuring that is within the scope of IAS 37, *Provisions, Contingent Liabilities and Contingent Assets* and involves the payment of termination benefits.

IAS 19 in fact recognizes two situations, namely termination benefits payable as a result of an employee's decision to accept an offer of benefits in exchange for the termination of employment; and termination benefits payable as a result of an entity's decision to terminate an employee's employment. The first are in fact voluntary termination benefits that should be recognized when employees accept the entity's offer of those benefits. In the case of an offer made to encourage voluntary redundancy, the measurement of termination benefits should be based on the number of employees expected to accept the offer (para. 140). The latter are termination benefits that should be recognized when an entity is demonstrably committed to a termination. This occurs when the entity has a detailed formal plan for the termination and there is no realistic possibility of withdrawal. The detailed plan should include, as a minimum:

- the location, function, and approximate number of employees whose services are to be terminated
- the termination benefits for each job classification or function
- the time at which the plan will be implemented. Implementation should begin as soon as possible and the period of time to complete implementation should be such that material changes to the plan are unlikely.

Where termination benefits fall due more than 12 months after the balance sheet date, the entity shall apply the requirements for other long-term employee benefits, and when termination benefits are expected to be settled wholly before 12 months after the end of the annual reporting period in which the termination benefit is recognized, the entity shall apply the requirements for short-term employee benefits.

ACCOUNTING BY THE PENSION FUND

When pension benefits are externally funded, the entity to which the amounts are transferred must also prepare financial statements. When the amounts are transferred to an insurance company, the financial statements of the insurance company will give a picture of the financial position of the insurance company.

Financial reporting by pension funds is regulated by IAS 26, *Accounting and Reporting by Retirement Benefit Plans.* The last revision of IAS 26 dates back to 1994, which is important to stress since IAS 19, which focuses on the financial statements of the employer, has been revised twice since then. The financial situation of a pension fund will not be presented in the 'classical' format of financial statements, namely consisting of a balance sheet and an income statement. IAS 26 defines the contents of a pension fund 'report' which should be prepared. Also, in relation to this report, the type of pension benefit (defined contribution or defined benefit) promised plays a role.

When amounts resulting from a defined contribution plan are transferred to a pension fund, the report (para. 13) contains a statement of net assets available for benefits and a description of the funding policy.

When amounts resulting from a defined benefit plan are transferred to a pension fund, the report of the fund should contain either (para. 17):

(a) a statement that shows:

  (i) the net assets available for benefits

  (ii) the actuarial present value of promised retirement benefits, distinguishing between vested benefits and non-vested benefits—the resulting excess or deficit.

(b) or a statement of net assets available for benefits including either:

(i) a note disclosing the actuarial present value of promised retirement benefits, distinguishing between vested benefits and non-vested benefits or

(ii) a reference to this information in an accompanying actuarial report.

If an actuarial valuation has not been prepared at the date of the report, the most recent valuation should be used as a base and the date of the valuation disclosed.

We notice immediately that the concept of defined benefit obligation is not introduced here; IAS 26 only mentions actuarial present value of promised retirement benefits. In order to improve the information value of the annual reports of pension funds, a revision of IAS 26 in line with the vision of IAS 19 would be welcome. It is not certain, however, whether the business world would also welcome a revision in the near future.

SUMMARY

IAS 19 is considered to be one of the more technical Standards. The same comment applies to IFRS 2, *Share-based Payment*. Pension plans represent assets, liabilities and costs for the sponsoring company. The related amounts are not always easy to determine and the impact on a company may be overlooked. In the acquisition deal of KLM by Air France, the French made a surprising post-acquisition discovery. When the deal was closed and the acquisition price determined, the company management discovered pension surpluses in the pension plan of KLM. This surplus net pension asset could be regarded as an asset of the Air France-KLM group. This meant that Air France had acquired KLM with negative goodwill. The net pension asset was the difference between pension liabilities of €7627 million and pension assets of €8912 million, implying a surplus  of €1285 million. To make sure that they accounted for this surplus, which occurred under IAS (KLM had used Dutch GAAP before the acquisition by Air France), Air France-KLM consulted the IASB on its interpretation of IAS 19. This illustrates that pension valuation and pension accounting is not easy. The level of technicality, however, depends on the type of pension promise made.

Accounting for defined contribution plans is less technical than accounting for defined benefit plans. It has been noticed in recent years that defined contribution plans have become more popular. Could the stricter accounting requirements, which make the uncertainties and the risks involved in a defined benefit plan more visible, have something to do with this?

In response to calls from preparers and users of financial statements, the IASB is currently conducting a project that will result in significant improvements to pension accounting. The IASB intends to complete this project within the next couple of years. Therefore, a fundamental review of all aspects of post-employment benefit accounting is possible in the future.

EXERCISES

Suggested answers to exercises marked ✓ are to be found in the Student online resources, with suggested answers to the remaining questions available in the Instructor online resources.

✓ **1**   Company Rebo has five directors who all participate in the following share-based remuneration plan with cash alternatives. The directors have the right to choose between 600 shares or the value of 500 shares paid in cash at vesting date. If the directors opt for the shares, they may not sell them for three years. The only vesting requirement is that the directors should remain for three years with the company. At the grant date, the entity's share price is €30. At the end of years 1, 2 and 3 the share prices are €33, €36 and €40, respectively. The fair value of the share alternative is €28 per share.

Required:

(i) Calculate the remuneration expense for the equity-based remuneration system of Rebo.

(ii) Indicate which accounts are credited.

In your answer, consider both situations, namely that the directors choose the cash alternative and that the directors choose the equity alternative.

✓**2** Company Crux grants share options to its employees at 1.1.X1. Each employee will receive ten options if they stay with the company for the next three years. At the grant date, the turnover percentage of employees is estimated at 20 per cent. The fair value of the option at the grant date is €20. The company grants these options to the 100 employees in service at the grant date. During the first year, four employees leave and the company revises its estimate on employee turnover from 20 per cent to 15 per cent (= 15 employees leaving). During year 2, another four employees leave, the entity revises the estimate to 12 per cent. At the end of the third year, six employees leave the company. The share options of the remaining employees vest at the end of year 3.

Required:
Calculate the remuneration expense for years 1, 2 and 3 for this share option plan. What is the credit side when this expense is recorded in the books of the company?

✓**3** At the beginning of year 1, an entity grants 1000 share options to 20 senior executives, each based on two conditions. First, the executive has to remain with the entity until the end of year 3. Second, the share options may not be exercised unless the share price has increased from €100 at the beginning of year 1 to above €130 at the end of year 3. If the share price is above €130 at year 3, the share options may be exercised at any time during the next five years.

The entity applies a binomial option-pricing model, which takes into account the possibility that the share price will exceed €130 at the end of year 3 (in this case the share options become exercisable) and the possibility that the share price will not exceed €130 at the end of year 3 (and then the options will be forfeited). It estimates the fair value of the share options with this market condition to be €48 per option.

At the end of year 1, the company estimates the turnover of senior executives at 20 per cent. In the second year, one executive leaves the company but the turnover estimate remains the same. During the third year, two executives leave the company.

Required:
Calculate the remuneration expense for each year in which an expense needs to be recorded. Which account will be credited when the remuneration expense is recorded?

4 An entity grants 100 share appreciation rights to its 200 employees on the condition that they remain with the firm for two years. At the end of these two years, the benefits vest and the employees may exercise the options in the two consecutive years. The benefits will be paid out in cash and the cash amount will be determined by the intrinsic value at the date of exercise. The fair value of the appreciation rights and the intrinsic value of the rights are presented below.

Year	Fair value	Intrinsic value
1	31	
2	36	30
3		40

At the end of the first year, 10 employees leave the company and the company estimates that in the next year 15 more employees will leave. In year 2, 16 employees leave and 74 employees exercise their share appreciation rights immediately when their benefits vest, and the remaining 100 exercise their rights in year 3.

Required:
Calculate the remuneration expenses and the amount of the liability to be recognized as a result of these share-based payment transactions.

5   For the determination and recognition of the current service cost and the defined pension liability, one particular actuarial cost method has been chosen, namely the projected unit credit method. This method takes into account expected future salary increases.

Required:
Comment on this decision. What is your opinion on taking into account these expected salary increases? What arguments could be used in favour of including future salary increases? Are there any arguments against the inclusion of future salary increases?

6   State pension plans are defined in IAS 19 as multi-employer plans. Multi-employer plans can be either of a defined benefit type or of a defined contribution type. Had you been in the position of the standard setter, would you have included the treatment of the state pension plans in the treatment of the multi-employer plans? Present arguments in favour of your answer.

7   Kappa is an entity that operates in a sector where the recruitment and retention of high quality employees is particularly important in order to achieve corporate goals. You are the financial controller of Kappa and you have recently received a memorandum from a member of the board of directors. The memorandum includes the following key issues:

(i)   The board is eager to reward employees appropriately, but is aware that large salary payments have an immediate impact on the liquidity and earnings per share of Kappa.

(ii) A more appropriate method of remuneration is to grant key employees share options that will vest at a future date, if the employees comply with specified conditions (e.g. continued employment) or achieve specific performance targets (e.g. completing an assignment to a specified standard or achieving a specified growth in the share price). This would allow employees to exercise the options at an appropriate time for them and would prevent an immediate impact on the liquidity or earnings per share of Kappa at the grant date.

Required:
Draft a reply that responds to the observations made by the board. Your reply should focus on the impact on the statement of financial position and statement of profit or loss and other comprehensive income of Kappa, rather than the personal tax positions of the employees. Your reply should contain a summary of the appropriate provisions of IFRS 2, *Share-based Payment.*
(ACCA, June 2007, adapted)

8   VB granted share options to its 500 employees on 1 August 20X6. Each employee will receive 1000 share options provided they continue to work for VB for the four years following the grant date. The fair value of the options at the grant date was $1.30 each. In the year ended 31 July 20X7, 20 employees left and another 50 were expected to leave in the following three years. In the year ended 31 July 20X8, 18 employees left and a further 30 were expected to leave during the next two years.

Required:
Prepare the journal entries to record the charge to VB's statement of profit or loss and other comprehensive income for the year ended 31 July 20X8 in respect of the share options, in accordance with IFRS 2 *Share-based Payments*.

(CIMA Financial Management, September 2011)

9   DF granted 1000 share options to each of its 300 employees on 1 January 20X0, with the condition that they continue to work for DF for 4 years from the grant date. The fair value of each option at the grant date was $5. Twenty employees left in the year to 31 December 20X0 and at that date another 65 were expected to leave over the next three years. In the year to 31 December 20X1, 23 employees left and at that date another 44 were expected to leave over the next two years.

Required:
Calculate the charge to DF's statement of profit or loss and other comprehensive income for the year ended 31 December 20X1 in respect of the share options and prepare the journal entries to record this.

(CIMA Financial Management, May 2012)

10   The following information relates to Marchant plc's pension scheme:

	$m
Plan assets at 1 May 20X3	48
Defined benefit obligation at 1 May 20X3	50
Service cost for year ended 30 April 20X4	4
Discount rate at 1 May 20X3	10%
Re-measurement loss in year ended 30 April 20X4	2
Past service cost 1 May 20X3	3

Required:
Calculate the net costs to be recognized in the statement of profit or loss and other comprehensive income for the year ended 30 April 2014 for Marchant plc. Your answer should clearly identify the costs charged to Marchant's profit for the year and the gain/loss to be included in other comprehensive income.

(ACCA, Corporate Reporting (International), June 2014, adapted)

11   MR operates a defined benefit pension plan for its employees. At 1 January 2013, the fair value of the pension plan assets was $3 700 000 and the present value of the pension plan liabilities was $3 900 000. The actuary estimated that the service cost for the year to 31 December 2013 was $1 100 000. The pension plan paid $340 000 to retired members and MR paid $760 000 in contributions to the pension plan in the year to 31 December 2013. The actuary estimated that the relevant discount rate for the year to 31 December 2013 was 5 per cent.

At 31 December 2013, the fair value of the pension plan assets was $4 400 000 and the present value of the pension plan liabilities was $4 700 000.

Required:

In accordance with IAS 19 *Employee Benefits:*

(i)   Calculate the expense that will be charged to MR's profit for the year ended 31 December 2013 in respect of this pension plan.

(ii) Calculate the net actuarial gain or loss on pension plan assets and liabilities that will be included in MR's other comprehensive income for the year ended 31 December 2013. Your answer should clearly state whether it is a net gain or a net loss.

(CIMA, Financial Management, May 2014)

12   MR operates a defined benefit pension plan for its employees. On 1 January 2013, MR made improvements to the benefits offered by the plan and the actuary estimated that the past service costs associated with these improvements totalled $5 million.

Required:

Explain, in accordance with IAS 19 *Employee Benefits*, how:

(i)   the defined benefit pension plan would be accounted for by MR in its financial statements

(ii) the past service costs would be accounted for in the year to 31 December 2013.

(CIMA, Financial Management, February 2014)

13   MLR operates a defined benefit pension plan for all of its employees. On 10 December 2012 improvements were made to the pension plan in respect of the pension rights of members. At that date, the actuary estimated that the present value of these improvements was $5 million. MLR paid $5 million to the pension plan in January 2013. The actuary informed MLR that the present value of the plan liabilities was $15 million as at 31 December 2012 and the fair value of plan assets was $12 million at that date.

Required:

(i)   Explain what MLR will include in its statement of financial position as at 31 December 2012 in respect of its pension plan.

(ii) Explain how MLR should account for the cost of the improvements to the plan in its financial statements for the year ended 31 December 2012.

(CIMA, Financial Management, August 2013)

14   NB operates a defined benefit pension plan for its employees. At 1 April 2013, the fair value of the pension plan assets was $8 200 000 and the present value of the pension plan liabilities was $8 500 000. The actuary estimated that the service cost for the year to 31 March 2014 was $2 100 000. The pension plan paid $500 000 to retired members and NB paid $1 900 000 in contributions to the pension plan in the year to 31 March 2014. The actuary estimated that the relevant discount rate for the year to 31 March 2014 was 6 per cent.

On 31 March 2014, NB announced improvements to the benefits offered by the pension plan to all of its members. The actuary estimated that the past service cost associated with these improvements was $2 million. At 31 March 2014 the fair value of the pension plan assets was $10 200 000 and the present value of the pension plan liabilities (including the past service costs) was $12 500 000.

Required:

In accordance with IAS 19, *Employee Benefits:*

(i)   Calculate the net actuarial gain or loss (stating which) that will be included in NB's other comprehensive income for the year ended 31 March 2014.

(ii) Calculate the net pension asset or liability (stating which) that will be included in NB's statement of financial position as at 31 March 2014.

(CIMA, Financial Management, November 2014)

CHANGING PRICES AND HYPERINFLATIONARY ECONOMIES

22

OBJECTIVES After studying this chapter you should be able to:

- outline regulatory requirements in relation to the issues of accounting for inflation and changing prices discussed in Chapters 6 and 7

- describe, apply and appraise the requirements of IAS 29 concerning hyperinflationary economies

- explain the implications of adjusting, or not adjusting, for changes in general purchasing power in economies with material inflation.

INTRODUCTION

We spent considerable time on the alternative theoretical and practical possibilities regarding measurement alternatives in Part One, Chapters 6 and 7. It is not necessary to repeat this material or to revisit the thinking behind it. This chapter limits itself to coverage of international regulation on the matter.

EU ACCOUNTING DIRECTIVE

The EU Accounting Directive was published on 26 June 2013 and replaced the former Fourth Directive on individual financial statements and the Seventh Directive on consolidated financial statements.

Although the majority of the Directive is couched in historical terms, Articles 7 and 8 provide 'alternative measurements', 'by way of derogation' from the main principle of historical cost.

Article 7 allows Member States to permit or require the measurement of fixed assets at 'revalued amounts'. There is no explanation in the Directive as to what revalued amounts mean. As current replacement cost had been an explicit option in the Fourth Directive that has now been deleted, a reasonable interpretation of law suggests that 'revalued amounts' cannot be current replacement cost. It can also not be 'fair value', as there is a separate article in the EU Directive on that (Article 8, see below). Possible interpretations might be current cost (which is closely related to replacement cost) or revaluation for tax purposes. All changes in the revalued amounts need to be recognized in a revaluation reserve as part of equity.

Article 8 allows Member States to permit or be required to measure financial instruments, including derivatives, at fair value and specified categories of assets to be measured by reference to fair value (for instance at fair value less costs to sell).

Not all financial instruments may be measured at fair value. For liabilities, this is only allowed when they are held as part of a trading portfolio, normally only relevant for banks. Furthermore, fair value is not allowed for non-derivative financial instruments held to maturity, loans and receivables originated by the entity and not held for trading purposes, and investments in subsidiaries, associates and joint ventures.

Examples of the specified categories of assets are investment properties and agricultural inventories.

It is up to the Member States to permit or require whether changes in the fair value are directly included in profit or loss or in a fair value reserve as part of equity.

Note that Article 7 only applies to fixed assets, not to inventory, and that inventory would normally not be a 'specified category of assets' for which the fair value option of Article 8 would apply. So, differently from the Fourth Directive, measuring inventories at current values would normally not be allowed, except for specific categories of inventory, like agricultural items. That comes close to IAS 2.

Based on past experience, it might be expected that countries like the UK, Ireland and the Netherlands will make use of the alternative measurement bases and most other mainland European countries would not.

IAS GAAP

As we pointed out in Part One, inflation and price increases in the 1970s were much higher in the main developed economies than is the case now.

In 1977, the IASC issued IAS 6, *Accounting Responses to Changing Prices*, which required the disclosure of the effect of any procedures applied to reflect the impact of specific or general price changes. Subsequently the IASC replaced IAS 6 with IAS 15, which required the use of restatement on the basis of either the general price level or current costs when the reporting currency was subject to a significant (but unspecified) degree of inflation. In 1989, the IASC followed an approach similar to that of the FASB, by making IAS 15 optional. In the same year, the IASC issued IAS 29, which requires general price-level restatement when the reporting currency is subject to hyperinflation. It is worth noting, however, that IAS GAAP is applied in a number of countries with less developed economies, where significant inflation (but not necessarily hyperinflation) may be prevalent. Yet IAS 15 appears to have been little used in practice. It was completely withdrawn with effect from 1 January 2005.

Currently, there is no general Standard on inflation accounting in IFRS, except for IAS 29 in situations of hyperinflation, discussed below. This does not mean that IFRS is not taking into account changing prices. On the contrary, fair value accounting as discussed in Chapter 7 could be seen as the most important way in which the IASB tackles the issue of the effect of price changes on financial statements.

IAS 29 ON HYPERINFLATIONARY ECONOMIES

IAS 29, *Financial Reporting in Hyperinflationary Economies*, discusses the accounting for changing prices in hyperinflationary economies. As we will discuss further in Chapter 28, an entity uses its functional currency in preparing financial statements. The functional currency is defined as the currency of the primary economic environment in which the group operates. In most cases, this will be the local currency. IAS 29 requires that if the functional currency used by an entity is the currency of a hyperinflationary economy, then the entity's financial statements should be restated in units of the same purchasing power, using the measuring unit current at the balance sheet dates (units of current purchasing power). According to IAS 29, para. 37, this restatement should be made using 'a general price index that reflects changes in general purchasing power' and it is preferable that the same index be used by all entities that report in the currency of the same economy. An entity cannot avoid restatement under IAS 29 by adopting a stable currency as its own functional currency, such as the functional currency of its parent, if that stable functional currency is not the currency of the primary economic environment in which the entity operates.

The restated financial statements should be presented as the primary financial statements and separate presentation of the financial statements that have not been restated is discouraged. The corresponding figures for the previous period required by IAS 1, *Presentation of Financial Statements* (see Chapter 8), and any information in respect of earlier periods should also be restated in terms of units of current purchasing power at the balance sheet date (IAS 29, paras 7–8). The gain or loss on net monetary position (see later) should be separately disclosed as part of net income (IAS 29, para. 9).

Indicators of hyperinflation

IAS 29, para. 3, sets out five characteristics of the economic environment as indicators of hyperinflation, of which the fifth is the most frequently cited:

1 The general population prefers to keep its wealth in non-monetary assets or in a relatively stable foreign currency.

2 The general population regards monetary amounts not in terms of the local currency but in terms of a relatively stable foreign currency.

3 Sales and purchases on credit take place at prices that compensate for the expected loss of purchasing power during the credit period, even when it is short.

4 Interest rates, wages and prices are linked to a price index.

5 The cumulative inflation rate over three years is approaching or exceeds 100 per cent (i.e. the average annual inflation rate over three years is approaching or exceeds $33\frac{1}{3}$ per cent).

Restating assets and liabilities

The general principles of IAS 29, when applicable, are essentially the current purchasing power (CPP) approach discussed in Chapter 6. Monetary items are not restated because they are already expressed in terms of the monetary units current at the balance sheet date (CPP unit). In the case of monetary items that are linked by agreement to changes in prices, such as index-linked bonds and loans, their carrying amounts adjusted in accordance with the agreement are used in the restated balance sheet. Other balance sheet amounts are restated to amounts in CPP units by applying a general price index, unless they are already carried at amounts in CPP units, such as current market value or net realizable value (IAS 29, paras 11–14).

For items carried at cost or cost less depreciation, the restated cost or cost less depreciation is determined by applying to the historical costs and accumulated depreciation (if any) the change in a selected general price index from the date of acquisition to the balance sheet date. For items carried at revalued amounts, the revalued amount and accumulated depreciation (if any) are restated by applying the change in the price index from the date of the latest revaluation to the balance sheet date.

If records of the acquisition of property, plant and equipment do not permit the ascertainment or estimation of the acquisition dates, it may be necessary to use an independent professional valuation of the items concerned as a basis for their restatement when the Standard is first applied. If no general price index is available to cover the period between acquisition and the balance sheet date, an estimate of the changes in general purchasing power of the reporting currency over that period may be made by using the changes in the exchange rate between the reporting currency and a relatively stable foreign currency (IAS 29, paras 11–18).

The restated amount of a non-monetary item is reduced (in accordance with the appropriate IAS) when it exceeds the amount recoverable from the item's future use, sale or disposal (IAS 29, para. 19). It is not appropriate both to restate capital expenditure (fixed assets) financed by borrowing and to capitalize that part of the borrowing costs that compensates for inflation.

At the beginning of the first period of application of IAS 29, the components of owners' equity are restated by applying a general price index from the dates on which the components were contributed or otherwise arose, except for retained earnings and any revaluation surplus. Any revaluation surplus from prior periods is eliminated and restated retained earnings is the residual amount (balancing figure) in the restated balance sheet. Subsequently, all components of owners' equity are restated by applying a general price index from the beginning of the period (or the date of contribution, if later).

The movements for the period in owners' equity should be disclosed in accordance with IAS 1, *Presentation of Financial Statements* (see Chapter 8) (IAS 29, paras 24–25).

Restating the statement of profit or loss

All items in the statement of profit or loss should be expressed in terms of end of year CPP units. Hence, all income statement amounts need to be restated by applying the change in general price index between the dates at which the amounts were recorded and the balance sheet date. In practice, average index values for sub-periods, such as months, would normally be used, as in the case of average exchange rates used for the translation of foreign currency amounts under IAS 21 (see Chapter 28).

According to IAS 29, para. 27, the gain or loss on the entity's net monetary position may be estimated by applying the change in the general price index to the weighted average for the period of the difference between monetary assets and monetary liabilities.

The gain or loss on the net monetary position should be included in net income. Any adjustment to index-linked assets or liabilities (as mentioned earlier) is offset against the gain or loss on net monetary position. It is suggested that the gain or loss on net monetary position should be presented in the income statement together with interest income and expense and foreign exchange differences related to invested or borrowed funds (IAS 29, paras 27–28).

If an investee that has been accounted for under the equity method reports in the currency of a hyperinflationary country, the financial statements of the investee are restated in accordance with IAS 29 in order to calculate the investor's share of its net assets and results of operations (IAS 29, para. 20).

Restating the cash flow statement

All items in the cash flow statement should be restated in terms of CPP units at the balance sheet date (IAS 29, para. 33). Comparative figures from the previous reporting period and other comparative information that is disclosed in respect of prior periods should be restated in terms of CPP units at the balance sheet date (IAS 29, para. 34).

Restating current cost financial statements

These requirements assume an original historical cost set of financial statements. However, IAS 29 also allows for the possibility of 'current cost' financial statements as the basis. Items stated at current cost are already expressed in CPP units and so are not restated. Other items are restated as described for historical cost balance sheets earlier (IAS 29, para. 29).

The current cost income statement reports items in terms of the purchasing power of the monetary unit at the times when the underlying transactions or events occurred. For example, cost of goods sold and depreciation are recorded at their current costs at the time of consumption. Therefore, all amounts need to be restated into CPP units at the balance sheet date (IAS 29, para. 30). Gain or loss on net monetary position should be calculated and accounted for as already described (IAS 29, para. 31).

Other issues

A parent that reports in the currency of a hyperinflationary economy may have subsidiaries that also report in currencies of hyperinflationary economies. The financial statements of such subsidiaries should be restated in accordance with IAS 29, as described earlier, before being included in the process of consolidation. In the case of foreign subsidiaries, financial statements (restated if they are in the currency of a hyperinflationary economy) should be translated into the reporting currency at closing rates as required by IAS 21.

If financial statements with different reporting dates are consolidated, all items, whether monetary or non-monetary, should be restated into CPP units at the date of the consolidated financial statements (IAS 29, paras 35–36).

When an entity discontinues the preparation and presentation of financial statements in accordance with IAS 29 because the economy of its reporting currency is no longer hyperinflationary, the amounts that are expressed in CPP units as at the end of the previous reporting period should be treated as the basis for the carrying amounts in its subsequent financial statements (IAS 29, para. 38). In other words, these increased numbers are retained as the new 'cost' figure, which in a sense they are not.

Disclosures

The following disclosures should be made:

1 The fact that the financial statements and the comparative figures have been restated for changes in the general purchasing power of the reporting currency and are stated in terms of the unit of purchasing power current at the balance sheet date.

2 Whether the underlying financial statements are based on historical costs or current costs.

3 The identity and level of the general price index used at the balance sheet date and the movement in this index during the current and previous reporting periods (IAS 29, para. 39).

REAL WORLD ILLUSTRATION

Entities preparing their consolidated financial statements in accordance with IAS 29 are those in highly inflationary economies. Examples of hyperinflationary countries are Zimbabwe, Malawi and Venezuela. We could not find recent publicly available examples in these countries. However, IAS 29 can also be relevant for companies in countries that are not hyperinflationary by themselves, but have subsidiaries in hyperinflationary countries. The consolidated financial statements for 2014 of Novartis provide an example of this.

> The only hyperinflationary economy applicable to Novartis is Venezuela. The financial statements of the subsidiaries in this country are first adjusted for the effect of inflation with any gain or loss on the net monetary position recorded in the related functional lines in the consolidated income statement and then translated into USD.

SUMMARY

In this chapter, we explored the EU and IAS regulations relating to accounting for inflation. We specifically discussed the accounting in hyperinflationary economies, as described in IAS 29, and related these regulations to the theoretical issues discussed in Part One of this book.

EXERCISES

Suggested answers to exercises marked ✓ are to be found in the Student online resources, with suggested answers to the remaining questions available in the Instructor online resources.

✓**1** Which phenomena is IAS 29 adjusting for when it is applied in the preparation of financial statements?

2 The idea that a regular annual inflation rate of 35 per cent requires CPP adjustments, but a regular annual inflation rate of 25 per cent does not, is quite absurd. Discuss.

3 Rework a numerical exercise from Chapter 7.

STATEMENT OF CASH FLOWS 23

OBJECTIVES After studying this chapter you should be able to:

- identify the need for a statement of cash flows

- describe the requirements of IAS 7, *Statement of Cash Flows*

- prepare a statement of cash flows

- identify any problems in relation to a statement of cash flows

- explain the difference between cash flows from operations, cash flows from investing activities and cash flows from financing activities

- explain how cash flow information is complementary to the information provided in the statement of financial position, the statement of profit or loss and other comprehensive income and the statement of changes in equity.

INTRODUCTION

A statement of cash flows provides additional useful information to users; additional, that is, to the statement of profit or loss and other comprehensive income and to the statement of financial position of an entity. The statement of financial position informs the user on the value of the assets, liabilities and the equity of the firm. The statement of profit or loss and other comprehensive income details the change in net assets of the period, other than those attributable to transactions with equity holders in their capacity as equity holders. The latter changes are presented in the statement of changes in equity.

Despite the usefulness of the information provided in these three statements to support users in their economic-decision making, the user still lacks information on how a company generates resources (incoming cash flows) and uses these resources (outgoing cash flows) and whether the company is able to find a balance between these two. The purpose of the statement of cash flows is to provide users with information that helps them to understand better how companies generate and deploy resources. Moreover, by providing an overview of historic cash flows, the statement of cash flows serves as the starting point for users to estimate a firm's future cash flows. So the statement of cash flows emphasizes cash and liquidity whereas the statement of profit or loss and other comprehensive income focuses on revenue, expenses, profit or loss and elements of other comprehensive income. Therefore, cash flow information is complementary to the information provided in the other statements of a company's financial statements.

The disclosure of cash flow information is dealt with in IAS 7, *Statement of Cash Flows*. In order to illustrate better how cash flow information is complementary to the information included in the other statements, we will pay more attention to the difference between profit (statement of profit or loss) and cash (statement of cash flow).

PROFIT VERSUS CASH

The traditional accounting process is an uncertain and complex process. Not only is profit determination complex but it is also potentially misleading. In any accounting year there will be a mixture of complete and incomplete transactions. Transactions are complete when they have led to a final cash settlement and these cause no profit measurement difficulties. Considerable problems arise, however, in dealing with incomplete transactions, where the profit or loss figure can only be estimated by means of the accruals concept, whereby revenue and costs are matched with one another so far as their relationship can be established or justifiably assumed and dealt with in the profit and loss account of the period to which they relate.

Thus, the profit for the past year is dependent on the validity of many assumptions about the future. For example, the future life of assets is estimated in order to calculate the depreciation charge for the past year.

The greater the volume of incomplete transactions, the greater the degree of estimation and, accordingly, the greater the risk that investors could be misled if actual outcomes deviate from estimates.

To explore the differences between cash flow and profit reporting, consider Activity 23.1 below.

ACTIVITY 23.1

Two short statements about the same business in the same year follow. Summarize what each statement is telling us, and suggest reasons for the differences between them.

Statement A re: the business	€000
Sales	410
Less Cost of sales	329
	81
Less Other expenses	36
	45
Less Depreciation	13
	32
Less Taxation provided	13
	19
Less Dividend provided	8
Retained	11

Statement B re: the business	€000
Sales received	387
Less Payments for goods for sale	333
	54
Less Other expenses paid	32
	22
Less Capital expenditure	20
	2
Less Taxation paid	14
	(12)
Less Dividend paid	7
Increase in borrowing	(19)

Activity feedback

Clearly, statement A is an income statement. It shows the revenues and expenses, calculated on the traditional bases, the taxation charges relating to the year, and the dividends which, it has been decided, should be paid out to shareholders in relation to that year. It shows a profit and implies (although we do not know the size of the business) a successful year.

Statement B is a statement of cash movement in the year – a summary of the cash book, but analyzed into the various reasons the cash has moved. The individual differences between the two statements will be due to changes in accruals, prepayments and the like. Overall, statement B shows a reduction in the cash resources of the business before the payment of the dividend, and obviously shows an even bigger contraction in the cash resources of the business after the dividend payout in the year. Statement B surely implies an unsuccessful year.

CASH FLOW REPORTING

People often talk about 'cash flows' or claim to be in favour of 'cash flow statements' or 'cash flow reporting' without being too precise about what they mean. In fact, different people are likely to mean significantly different things, and it is very important that we are able to separate out the various situations and arguments from one another.

At one level, it can be suggested that cash flow reporting – actual and budgeted – should completely replace both the statement of comprehensive income (on whatever basis) and the statement of financial position. The argument for this (ignoring barter situations) is that only cash represents and demonstrates an increase or decrease in the business resources and suggests that only cash should, and needs to, be reported. This argument is surely untenable. Users need information about changes in the command of a business organization over resources, over goods and services, or the power to obtain goods and services.

At a second level, it could be suggested that some form of statement of cash flows along the lines of statement *B* in Activity 23.1 should be required as an additional statement in the final reporting package, since it obviously gives information which is potentially useful and which is additional to, and different from, the information in the income statement. This is surely logical, because an income statement for the year is not a good indicator of the cash flow position for the year, and a statement of cash flows is not a good indicator of the profit and loss position for the year.

However, one weakness of a statement of cash flows, like that in Activity 23.1, is that it is a historical statement, as is a statement of financial position and a statement of comprehensive income. It gives no indication of future cash flows and whether an entity will be able to meet its debts in the future. A forecast statement of cash flows would be required for this. This historical statement of cash flows then serves as a starting point to estimate a firm's future cash flows.

REQUIREMENTS OF IAS 7

Scope

The IASB viewed cash flow reporting as so important that there are no exemptions for any entities. No matter what an entity's principal revenue-producing activities might be, they need cash to conduct their operation, pay their obligations and provide returns to their investors; their users need this information as they are interested in how the entity uses and generates cash.

Generation of cash flows and definitions

Cash flows within an entity can broadly be generated by three activities:

1 Operating or principal revenue-producing activities, defined by IAS 7 as those activities that are not investing or financing.

2 Investing activities: the acquisition and disposal of long-term assets and investments not included in cash equivalents.

3 Financing activities: activities that result in changes in the size and composition of the equity capital and borrowings of the entity.

Some other definitions from IAS 7, for completeness, are:

- Cash: comprises cash on hand and demand deposits.
- Cash equivalents: short-term, highly liquid investments that are readily convertible to known amounts of cash and which are subject to an insignificant risk of changes in value.

Now complete Activity 23.2.

ACTIVITY 23.2

Provide examples of cash flows, both inflow and outflow, from operating, investing and financing activities.

To help, we provide an example for each category in Table 23.1. Now extend the table.

TABLE 23.1   Examples of cash flows

Operating activities	Investing activities	Financing activities
Cash receipts from sale of goods and rendering of services	Cash payments to acquire fixed assets	Cash proceeds from issue of shares and other equity instruments

ACTIVITY 23.2   *(Continued)*

Activity feedback

You may not have identified all of the following, but the definitive list, as given by IAS 7, is shown in Table 23.2.

TABLE 23.2   Definitive list of cash flows as given by IAS 7

Operating activities	Investing activities	Financing activities
Cash receipts from sale goods and rendering services	Cash payments to acquire fixed assets	Cash proceeds from issue of shares and other equity instruments
Cash receipts from royalties, fees, commissions and other revenue	Cash receipts from sale of fixed assets	Cash payments to owners to acquire or redeem the entity's shares
Cash payments to suppliers for goods and services	Cash payments to acquire equity or debt instruments of other entities and interests in joint ventures	Cash proceeds from issuing debentures, loans, notes, bonds, mortgages and other short- or long-term borrowings
Cash payments to and on behalf of employees	Cash advances and loans made to other parties	Cash repayments of amounts borrowed
Cash payments or refunds of income taxes unless they can be specifically identified with financing or investing activities	Cash receipts from the repayment of advances and loans made to other parties	Cash payments by a lessee for the reduction of the outstanding liability relating to a lease
Cash receipts and payments from contracts held for dealing or trading purposes	Cash payments for futures, forward contracts, options and swaps except when the contracts are held for dealing or trading purposes or the payments are classified as financing activities	Cash receipts and cash payments of an insurance entity for premiums and claims, annuities and other policy benefits

The amount of cash flows from operating activities is highly important for users to assess whether enough cash has been generated from this source for the entity to repay loans, make investments in assets and pay dividends. Cash flows under the heading of operating activities are primarily derived from the principal revenue-producing activities of the entity.

Separating out the cash flows from investing activities is also seen as important as this provides users with information on investments made in resources that will potentially generate future income and cash flows. Users also require information on cash flows within financing activities so that they can predict claims on future cash flows from providers of capital to the entity.

ACTIVITY 23.3

Identify the category in which the following cash flows would be included:

1   An entity purchases a motor vehicle that it intends to sell on to a customer.

2   An entity purchases a motor vehicle that it intends to use as part of its delivery fleet.

3   An entity purchases a motor vehicle using a lease.

4   An entity holds securities for dealing/trading purposes.

5   Interest paid and received and dividends received by an entity.

(Continued)

ACTIVITY 23.3 (Continued)

6 Dividends paid by an entity.

7 An entity purchases a building which it intends to rent to others.

Activity feedback

1 This is a purchase of an inventory item and is therefore shown under operating activities.

2 This is a purchase of a fixed asset for the entity and is therefore part of investing activities.

3 The entity has acquired the use of a fixed asset, but the cash flow of principal payments will be shown under financing activities. There will be no cash flow under investing activities.

4 These are inventory to the dealing house and are therefore part of operating activities as they relate to the principal revenue-producing activities.

5 These are usually classified as operating cash flows for a financial institution, but may also be regarded as operating for other entities as they form part of the net profit calculation (IAS 7, para.

33). This paragraph also allows them to be treated as financing – interest paid, or investing – interest and dividends received. The latter alternative seems more sensible to us.

6 Dividends paid are obviously financing as they are a cost of obtaining finance. However, IAS 7 allows an alternative categorization under operating activities. This is to enable users to judge the ability of the entity to pay dividends out of operating cash flows. We find this lack of consistency in the treatment of interest and dividends received and paid confusing and it will certainly impair comparability of cash flows between entities where different alternatives have been used.

7 This is the purchase of an asset that results in rental income and therefore must be regarded as a cash outflow under operating activities, not investing activities. The rental received will be cash inflow under operating activities.

Cash and cash equivalents

The definitions of these are important as cash flows are defined as inflows and outflows of cash and cash equivalents. It should be apparent to you that an investment, dependent on our view of short-term or highly liquid, could be viewed as a cash and cash equivalent, a cash flow item or an investing activity. Bank borrowings are generally viewed, according to IAS 7, as financing activities, but in certain circumstances bank overdrafts can be viewed as part of cash and cash equivalents. These circumstances are where the overdraft forms an integral part of the entity's cash management. Activity 23.4 demonstrates these definitions, so make sure you complete it.

ACTIVITY 23.4

Determine whether the following items are cash, cash equivalents, investing activities or financing.

1 An account held with a bank where withdrawals require 90 days' notice.

2 An account held with a bank where withdrawals require 95 days' notice.

3 An overdraft with the bank which is seen as short term and part of everyday cash flows of the entity.

4 A loan from the bank for 60 days for a specific purpose.

5 An investment with a bank which has 60 days to maturity, but its final value is subject to significant risk as it is based on the index achievable at that time from a highly fluctuating stock market.

Activity feedback

1 If you view 90 days as short term then this is cash equivalent.

2 If you view 95 days as long term then this would be investing.

ACTIVITY 23.4   *(Continued)*

3 *Cash as part of cash management.*

4 *Financing as a loan for a specific purpose cannot be viewed as everyday cash management.*

5 *This investment has a significant risk attached to it in terms of its final value and therefore must be regarded as investing activities.*

The decision with regard to 1 and 2 in this Activity is clarified by IAS 7 (para. 7) as follows:

An investment normally qualifies as a cash equivalent only when it has a short maturity of, say, three months or less from date of acquisition. It must be readily convertible to a known amount of cash and be subject to an insignificant risk of changes in value.

The decisions required here are quite subjective and it is feasible for one entity to determine an investment as a cash equivalent and for another to determine this as an investing item.

FORMAT OF CASH FLOW STATEMENT

IAS 7 requires entities to report cash flows during a period in a statement identifying cash flows classified by operating, investing and financing activities. This implies a statement as follows:

Statement of cash flows

Cash flows from operating activities	A
Cash flows from investing activities	B
Cash flows from financing activities	C
Net change in cash and cash equivalents	X

However, in order to provide relevant information to users, the Standard requires each of these cash flows to be separated into their constituent parts, i.e. the gross cash receipts and the gross cash payments from operating, financing and investing activities. Note here that if a single transaction has cash flows involving financing, investing and operating activities, then the transaction will need to be split into its constituent parts. An example of such a transaction is a finance lease payment where the principal repayment will be disclosed as a cash flow under financing and the interest payment can be disclosed under operating or financing.

Cash flows under any of the three sections can be reported net where the cash flows reflect the activities of the customer rather than the entity, or where items are large, maturities short and turnover quick. In all other circumstances, gross amounts have to be presented.

In addition, the components of cash and cash equivalents are required, together with a reconciliation of the amounts in the statement of cash flows with the equivalent items reported in the statements of financial position.

Cash flows from operating activities

There are two methods for determining cash flows from operating activities: from cash receipts and payments, known as the *direct method*; or from adjusting net profit for non-cash receipts and payments, known as the *indirect method*.

When entities use the direct method, the major classes of gross cash receipts and gross cash payments are disclosed. The information for the direct method can be obtained in two different ways:

(a) from the accounting records of the entity or

(b) by adjusting sales, cost of sales and other items in the statement of comprehensive income for:

(i) changes during the period in inventories and operating receivables and payables

(ii) other non-cash items and

(iii) other items for which the cash effects are investing or financing cash flows.

For a financial institution, the sales and cost of sales are interest and similar income and interest expense and similar charges (IAS 7, para. 19).

When a company uses the indirect method to determine the cash flow from operating activities, the starting point is the profit or loss of the entity. The profit or loss of the entity is then adjusted for:

(a) changes during the period in inventories and operating receivables and payables

(b) non-cash items such as depreciation, provisions, deferred taxes, unrealized foreign currency gains and losses, and undistributed profits of associates and

(c) all other items for which the cash effects are investing or financing cash flows (IAS 7, para. 20).

Activity 23.5 illustrates both methods (direct and indirect method) to determine an entity's operating cash flow.

ACTIVITY 23.5

From the following information relating to Zen entity, calculate the cash flows from operating activities using both the direct and indirect methods.

Consolidated statement of comprehensive income for the period ended 31 December 20X2

	€000
Sales	30 650
Cost of sales	26 000
Gross profit	4 650
Depreciation	(450)
Administration and selling expenses	(730)
Interest expense	(400)
Investment income	500
Foreign exchange loss	(40)
Net profit before taxation	3 530
Taxes on income	(300)
Net profit	3 230

Consolidated statement of financial position as at 31 December 20X2

	20X2		20X1	
	€000	€000	€000	€000
Assets				
Cash and cash equivalents		410		160
Accounts receivable		1900		1200
Inventory		1000		1950
Portfolio investments		2500		2500
Property, plant and equipment at cost	3730		1910	
Accumulated depreciation	(1450)		(1060)	
		2280		850
Total assets		8090		6660

Liabilities		
Trade payables	250	1890
Interest payable	230	100
Income taxes payable	400	1000
Long-term debt	2300	1040
Total liabilities	3180	4030
Equity		
Share capital	1500	1250
Retained earnings	3410	1380
Total equity	4910	2630
Total liabilities and shareholders' equity	8090	6660

Other information is available as follows:

(a) All the shares of a subsidiary were acquired for €590 000. The fair values of assets acquired and liabilities assumed were as follows:

	€000
Inventories	100
Accounts receivable	100
Cash	40
Property, plant and equipment	650
Trade payables	100
Long-term debt	200

(b) €250 000 was raised from the issue of shares and €250 000 from long-term borrowings.

(c) The interest expense was €400 000, of which €170 000 was paid during the period.

ACTIVITY 23.5 *(Continued)*

€100 000 relating to interest expense of the prior period was also paid during the period.

(d) Dividends paid were €1 200 000.

(e) The liabilities for tax at the beginning and end of the period were €1 000 000 and €400 000, respectively. During the period, a further €200 000 tax was provided for. Withholding tax on dividends received during the period of €200 000 amounted to €100 000.

(f) During the period, the group acquired property, plant and equipment with an aggregate cost of €1 250 000, of which €900 000 was acquired by means of a lease. Cash payments of €350 000 were made to purchase property, plant and equipment.

(g) Plant, with an original cost of €80 000 and accumulated depreciation of €60 000, was sold for €20 000.

(h) Accounts receivable as at end 31 December 20X2 include €100 000 of interest receivable.

(Adapted from example in Appendix A to IAS 7)

Activity feedback

Direct method

Cash flows from operating activities

Cash receipts from customers (working 1)	30 150
Cash paid to suppliers and employees (working 2)	(27 420)
Cash generated from operations	2 730
Interest paid (170 + 100 note c)	(270)
Income taxes paid (1000 + 200 + 100 − 400)	(900)
Net cash from operating activities	1 560

Working 1

Sales – income statement	30 650
Add Opening accounts receivable	1 200
Less Closing accounts receivable (1 900 − 100)	(1 800)
Add Subsidiary accounts receivable	100
	30 150

Working 2

Cost of sales – income statement	26 000
Less Opening stock	(1 950)
Add Closing stock	1 000
Purchases	25 050
Less Closing trade payables	(250)
Add Opening trade payables	1 890
	26 690
Admin and selling expenses	730
	27 420
Subsidiary trade payables (a)	100
Less Subsidiary inventories (a)	(100)
	27 420

(Note: interest and income taxes paid are treated as part of operating activities, dividends paid are not.)

Indirect method

Cash flows from operating activities

Profit before tax	3 530
Add Interest	(100)
Foreign exchange loss	40
Depreciation	450
	3 920
Increase in trade and other receivables (700 − 100 subsidiary − 100 interest receivable)	(500)
Decrease in inventories (950 + 100 subsidiary)	1 050
Decrease in trade payables (1 640 + 100 subsidiary)	(1 740)
Cash generated from operations	2 730
Interest paid	(270)
Income taxes paid	(900)
Net cash from operating activities	1 560

The Standard prefers the direct method as it 'provides information which may be useful in estimating future cash flows which is not available under the indirect method'. Strangely, the UK Accounting Standards Board requires the indirect method as it does not believe that the benefits to the users of the direct method outweigh the costs of preparing it. The IASB prefers the use of the direct method but does not require it in IAS 7 due to the concerns about the cost of preparing a direct method statement of cash flows. Reading IAS 7, para. 19 it emerges that there are two approaches to preparing the direct method of cash flows, however the cost of preparing the information differs.

- The 'bottom-up' or 'cash ledger' approach (referred to as the 'direct-direct method'). Under this approach, cash receipts and payments are determined by aggregating cash flow amounts from cash ledgers. This is a costly approach.
- The 'top-down' or 'financial statement' approach (referred to as the 'indirect-direct method'). Under this approach, cash receipts and payments are determined by adjusting revenues, expenses, and gains and losses for the change in the related accrual over the period. This approach, it is thought, would be cheaper than the direct-direct method.

ACTIVITY 23.6

1 What information would the direct method provide to users that the indirect method would not?

2 Why might the direct method be more costly to prepare than the indirect?

3 How should a non-cash transaction be dealt with in a statement of cash flows?

Activity feedback

1 The direct method would identify cash receipts from customers and cash payments to suppliers and employees, whereas the indirect method would only show net profit with its adjustments for depreciation, profit on disposal, changes in working capital and so on. The actual disclosure of cash receipts and payments enables users to evaluate future cash flows more easily.

2 Entities operate an accounting system that is geared towards accrual accounting. The direct method would require a company to use an accounting system either: (a) to directly record and analyze the cash flow in relation to each transaction, thus operating two accounting systems; or (b) to adjust sales, costs of sales and other items in the income statement for non-cash items, changes in working capital and other items which relate to investing or financing activities – a time-consuming and costly business. If we take the view that information should be provided that is useful to users – the view of the Framework – then we must support the direct method for the disclosure of operating cash flows.

3 Quite obviously, it should not be dealt with as it does not involve a cash flow!

Examples of non-cash transactions given in the Standard are:

- acquisition of assets either by assuming directly related liabilities or by means of a lease
- acquisition of an entity by means of an equity issue
- conversion of debt to equity.

All these involve the exchange of a non-cash asset for a non-cash liability, or conversion from one asset or liability to another. These types of transaction will be reported elsewhere in the financial statements.

Cash flows from investing activities

The second major part of the statement of cash flows relate to the cash flows from investing activities. Cash flows from investing activities are determined by the direct method. This implies that an entity has to report separately the major classes of gross cash receipts and gross cash payments resulting from investing activities.

ACTIVITY 23.7

Now calculate the cash flow from investing activities from the data given in Activity 23.5.

Activity feedback

Investing activities cover cash flows in respect of fixed assets, investments in equity or debt, advances and loans to other parties. The balance sheet changes identify any increases/decreases in portfolio investments and property, plant and equipment, and we were also informed about an acquisition of a subsidiary. Therefore:

Cash flows from investing activities	
Acquisition of subsidiary less cash acquired (590 – 40)	(550)
Purchase of property, plant and equipment (note f and working 1)	(350)
Proceeds from sale of equipment (note g)	20
Dividends received (note c)	200
Interest received (investment income – dividends)	200
Net cash used in investing activities	(480)

Working 1

Opening balance sheet of property, etc. at cost	1 910
Add Subsidiary bought	650
Less Sale	(80)
	2 480
Closing balance sheet at cost	3 730
	1 250
Leased assets so no cash flow	(900)
Therefore, assets bought for cash	350

Cash flow from financing activities

Cash flows resulting from financing activities are the third major part in the statement of cash flows. These are also determined with the use of the direct method. This part of the statement of cash flows therefore shows separately the major classes of gross cash receipts and gross cash payments of financing activities.

ACTIVITY 23.8

Now identify the cash flows from financing activities from the data in Activity 23.5.

Activity feedback

Cash flow from financing activities covers proceeds from the issue of shares, loans, etc. and repayments of amounts borrowed.

Cash flows from financing activities	
Proceeds from issuing shares (note b)	250
Proceeds from long-term borrowings (note b)	250
Lease payments (working 1)	(90)
Dividends paid (note d)	(1 200)
Net cash used in financing activities	(790)

Working 1

Opening balance sheet long-term debt	1 040
Add Lease principal	900
	1 940
Add Subsidiary long-term loan	200
	2 140
New loans	250
	2 390
Closing balance sheet long-term debt	2 300
Therefore, lease principal repaid	90

Statement of cash flows

If you put together the answers of Activities 23.5, 23.7 and 23.8 and add on cash and cash equivalent changes, you have a full statement of cash flows for the data in Activity 23.5 as follows.

Direct method cash flow statement

Cash flows from operating activities

Cash receipts from customers	30 150	
Cash paid to suppliers and employees	(27 420)	
Cash generated from operations	2 730	
Interest paid	(270)	
Income taxes paid	(900)	
Net cash from operating activities		**1 560**
Cash flows from investing activities		
Acquisition of subsidiary less cash acquired	(550)	
Purchase of property, plant and equipment	(350)	
Proceeds from sale of equipment	20	
Dividends received	200	
Interest received (investment income – dividends)	200	
Net cash used in investing activities		**(480)**
Cash flows from financing activities		
Proceeds from issuing shares	250	
Proceeds from long-term borrowings	250	
Payments of lease (working 1)	(90)	
Dividends paid	(1 200)	
Net cash used in financing activities		(790)
Net increase in cash and cash equivalents		**290**
Cash and cash equivalents at beginning of period		120
(160 – 40 (from acquisition of subsidiary))		
Cash and cash equivalents at end of period		410

PREPARATION OF STATEMENT OF CASH FLOWS

The next Activity requires you to prepare a rather more complicated statement of cash flows.

ACTIVITY 23.9

The balance sheet of Axbrit entity for the year ended 31 March 20X2 is as follows:

Assets	20X2	20X1
Cash and cash equivalents	27	21
Accounts receivable	15	18
Inventory	25	20
Property, plant and equipment		
at cost	230	160
Accumulated depreciation	(60)	(44)
Total assets	237	175

Liabilities		
Trade payables	47	39
Income taxes payable	16	12
Long-term debt	32	30
Total liabilities	95	81
Shareholders' equity		
Share capital	33	27
Capital reserves	30	24
Retained earnings	79	43
Total shareholders' equity	142	94
Total liabilities and		
shareholders' equity	237	175

(Continued)

ACTIVITY 23.9   (Continued)

Prepare the statement of cash flows for the year ended 31 March 20X2 given that no property, plant and equipment was sold during the period and that the increase in long-term debt took place on 1 April 20X2 and carried a 10 per cent rate of interest and that dividends paid during the year were €18.

Activity feedback

As we are not given the statement of comprehensive income or any other information to enable us to derive net cash flow from operating activities using the direct method, we have to use the indirect method in this example.
  Indirect method net cash flow from operating activities

Net profit (change in retained earnings + dividends)		54.0
Add Interest on long-term loans	3.2	
Add Taxation charge (assume liability at end is charge for period)	16.0	
		19.2
Net profit before taxation		73.2
Add Depreciation	16.0	
Increase in inventories	(5.0)	
Decrease in accounts receivable	3.0	
Increase in trade payables	8.0	
		22.0
Cash generated from operations		95.2
Interest paid		(3.2)
Income taxes paid		(12.0)
Net cash from operating activities		80.0
Cash flows from investing activities		
Purchase of property, plant and equipment	70.0	
Net cash used in investing activities		(70.0)
Cash flows from financing activities		
Proceeds from issues of shares	12.0	
Proceeds from long-term borrowings	2.0	
Dividends paid	(18.0)	
Net cash used in financing activities		(4.0)
Net increase in cash and cash equivalents		6.0
Cash and cash equivalents at beginning of period		21.0
Cash and cash equivalents at end of period		27.0

The following Activity is a good test of your understanding so far, so complete it before reading the feedback.

ACTIVITY 23.10

From the statement of comprehensive income and statements of financial position of Thomas Manufacturing entity, prepare the statement of cash flows for the year ended 31 December 20X5.

Thomas Manufacturing
Statement of comprehensive income for the year ended 31.12.X5

	€000	€000
Sales		5 000
Change in inventories		500
Own work capitalized		150
Other operating income		50
Raw materials and consumables	(2 000)	
Other external charges	(770)	
		(2 770)

Employee costs	(1 500)
Depreciation and amortization	(400)
Other operating charges	(100)
	930
Income from investments	20
– dividends	
Other interest receivable	5
	955
Interest payable	(160)
Income before income taxes	795
Income taxes	(317)
Income for period	478

(Continued)

ACTIVITY 23.10   (*Continued*)

Thomas Manufacturing
Statement of financial position as at 31.12.X5

	Cost €000	31.12.X5 Deprec €000	Net €000	31.12.X4 Cost €000	Net €000
ASSETS					
Non-current assets					
Intangible	350	200	150	200	100
Property, plant and equipment	2 500	775	1 725	1 500	800
Investments	200	—	200	100	100
	3 050	975	2 075	1 800	1 000
Current assets					
Inventories		1 600		1 000	
Accounts receivable		1 200		1 000	
Investments		—		50	
Cash		30		250	
			2 830		2 300
Total assets			4 905		3 300
EQUITY AND LIABILITIES					
Equity					
Ordinary shares			1 500		1 000
Capital reserves			800		200
Retained earnings			405		177
Total equity			2 705		1 377
Non-current liabilities					
Loans			790		980
Current liabilities					
Accounts payable		750		600	
Loans		257		—	
Taxation		274		243	
			1 281		843
Deferred taxes			129		100
Total liabilities			2 200		1 923
Total equity and liabilities			4 905		3 300

Further information is available as follows:

- Dividends paid for the period were €250 000.
- As at 1 January X5, freehold land was revalued from €500 000 to €1 000 000.
- During the year ended 31 December X5, plant and equipment costing €300 000, written down to €50 000 at 31 December X4, was sold for €75 000. The gain was adjusted in the depreciation charge in the income statement.

- Own work capitalized refers to development work carried forward as an intangible asset.
- Loans with a nominal value of €190 000 were redeemed at par during the year.
- Shares were issued for cash during the year; there were no purchases of the company's own shares.
- The investments shown as current assets at 31 December X4 and not regarded as cash equivalent were sold during the year for €50 000.

ACTIVITY 23.10 (Continued)

Activity feedback

Indirect statement of cash flows for Thomas Manufacturing:

Cash flows from operating activities

	€000	€000
Profit before tax		795
Adjustments for:		
Depreciation (400 + 25 gain adj. on sale into dep.)	425	
Profit on sale of plant and equipment	(25)	
Investment income	(25)	
Interest expense	160	
		535
Operating profit before working capital changes		1 330
Increase in trade and other receivables	(200)	
Increase in inventories	(600)	
Increase in trade payables	150	
		(650)
Cash generated from operations		680
Interest paid		(160)
Income taxes paid (note 1)		(257)
Net cash from operating activities		263

Cash flows from investing activities

Purchase of intangible fixed assets	(150)	
Purchase of property, plant and equipment (note 2)	(800)	
Purchase of investments	(100)	
Proceeds from sale of investments	50	
Proceeds from sale of equipment	75	
Interest received	5	
Dividends received	20	
Net cash used in investing activities		(900)

Cash flows from financing activities

Proceeds from issues of shares	600	
Proceeds from long-term borrowings	257	
Redemption of loans	(190)	
Dividends paid	(250)	
Net cash used in financing activities		417
Net decrease in cash and cash equivalents		(220)
Cash and cash equivalents at beginning of period		250
Cash and cash equivalents at end of period		30

Note 1

Opening balance of taxes (243 + 100)	343
Add income statement charge (325 − 8)	317
	660
Closing balance of taxes (274 + 129)	403
Therefore taxes paid during the year	257

Note 2

Opening balance of assets at cost	1 500
add Revaluation during the year	500
less Sale at cost	(300)
	1 700
Closing balance at cost	2 500
Therefore purchase of assets	800

Disclosure requirements of IAS 7

The disclosure requirements of IAS 7 mainly discuss which classes of cash flows have to be disclosed separately. The most important items are cash flows from interest and dividends received and paid, cash flows from taxes on income and aggregate cash flows resulting from obtaining or losing control of subsidiaries and other businesses. Investing and financing activities that do not involve the use of cash or cash equivalents are not represented on the statement of cash flows. Examples are the acquisition of an asset by means of a lease or the acquisition of an entity by means of a share issue. Since these types of transactions do affect the capital and asset structure of the entity, IAS 7 (para. 43) requires that the impact of these non-cash transactions be disclosed in the notes to the financial statements. An entity also needs to disclose in the notes to the financial statements the components of cash and cash equivalents and whether or not there are restrictions for the group on using any of the cash or cash equivalents.

Recently (early 2016) a new type of disclosure was introduced. IAS 7 now requires an entity to provide a reconciliation of the amounts in the opening and closing statements of financial position for each item for which cash flows have been, or would be, classified as financing activities in the statement of cash flows, excluding equity items. The reconciliation shall include:

(a) opening balances in the statement of financial position

(b) movements in the period, including:

(i) changes from financing cash flows

(ii) changes arising from obtaining or losing control of subsidiaries or other businesses and

(iii) other non-cash changes (for example, the effect of changes in foreign exchange rates and changes in fair values).

(c) closing balances in the statement of financial position.

This amendment resulted from users' requests to the IASB for more information on a company debts. Investors wanted to understand the period-on-period movements in debt. The IASB could have responded to this request by amending IAS 1. However, since they feared that changing IAS 1 would take more time, they decided to respond by introducing an additional disclosure in IAS 7 (see also Disclosure Initiative: Proposed amendment to IAS 7/ ED/2014/6, Basis for conclusion on Exposure Draft, page 15). While the amendment of IAS 7 does not prescribe a net debt reconciliation (the information that was asked for by the users), it ensures that users now have the necessary information to undertake the net debt reconciliation themselves. Fortunately for investors, many companies already provide a net debt reconciliation on a voluntary basis. This amendment illustrates how the IASB sometimes implements practical solutions rather than implementing solutions following the substance of the Conceptual Framework and the Standards.

As an example of disclosure required in respect of statements of cash flows by IAS 7, we present the statements of cash flow from the Adidas Group included in its financial statements of 2014 (page 194). We notice that Adidas includes its interest paid under the cash flows from operating activities. However, Adidas creates additional line items to also show the amount of cash flows from operating activities without interest paid.

REAL WORLD ILLUSTRATION

Consolidated Statement of Cash Flows

.. / adidas AG Consolidated Statement of Cash Flows (IFRS) [€ in millions]

	Note	Year ending Dec. 31, 2014	Year ending Dec. 31, 2013
Operating activities:			
Income before taxes		835	1 113
Adjustments for:			
Depreciation, amortisation and impairment losses	12, 13, 14, 31, 33	405	340
Reversals of impairment losses	30	(1)	(2)
Unrealised foreign exchange losses, net		32	10
Interest income	33	(17)	(25)

REAL WORLD ILLUSTRATION (Continued)

	Note	Year ending Dec. 31, 2014	Year ending Dec. 31, 2013
Interest expense	33	62	73
Losses on sale of property, plant and equipment, net		16	6
Other non-cash income	30, 31	(1)	(1)
Payment for external funding of pension obligations [CTA]		(65)	–
Operating profit before working capital changes		**1 267**	**1 515**
Increase in receivables and other assets		(36)	(1302)
Increase in inventories		(76)	(299)
(Decrease)/increase in accounts payable and other liabilities		(117)	151
Cash generated from operations before interest and taxes		**1 037**	**1 065**
Interest paid		(59)	(68)
Income taxes paid		(284)	(390)
Net cash generated from operating activities - continuing operations		**694**	**608**
Net cash generated from operating activities - discontinued operations		7	26
Net cash generated from operating activities		**701**	**634**
Investing activities:			
Purchase of trademarks and other intangible assets		(49)	(52)
Proceeds from sale of trademarks and other intangible assets		1	1
Purchase of property, plant and equipment		(499)	(422)
Proceeds from sale of property, plant and equipment		4	4
Acquisition of subsidiaries and other business units net of cash acquired	4	(6)	–
Proceeds from sale of short-term financial assets		37	226
Purchase of investments and other long-term assets		(36)	(20)
Interest received		17	25
Net cash used in investing activities - continuing operations		**(531)**	**(237)**
Net cash used in investing activities - discontinued operations		(6)	(6)
Net cash used in investing activities		**(537)**	**(243)**
Financing activities:			
Proceeds from issue of Eurobonds	18	990	–
Repayment of Eurobonds	18.	(500)	–
Repayments of finance lease obligations		(2)	(2)
Dividend paid to shareholders of adidas A3	26	(314)	(282)
Dividend paid to non-controlling interest shareholders		(4)	(1)
Repurchase of treasury shares	26	(300)	–
Proceeds from short-term borrowings		68	67
Repayments of short-term borrowings	18	(56)	(221)
Net cash used in financing activities		**(118)**	**(439)**
Effect of exchange rates on cash		**50**	**(35)**
Increase/(decrease) of cash and cash equivalents		96	(83)
Cash and cash equivalents at beginning of the year	5	1 587	1 670
Cash and cash equivalents at end of period	5	**1 683**	**1 587**

Rounding differences may arise in percentages and totals.
The accompanying notes are an integral part of these consolidated financial statements.

SUMMARY

Within this chapter, we have attempted to show you how to draw up a statement of cash flows using both the direct and indirect methods for cash flows from operating activities. We have highlighted some of the problems associated with the production of the figures and disclosures in the statement of cash flows. These problems are:

- the arbitrary three-month cut-off for cash equivalents
- the choice of category for interest and dividends
- the difficulty of producing direct cash flows
- the lack of user information in indirect operating cash flows
- the historical nature of the statement of cash flows.

On the whole, however, the statement of cash flows under IAS 7 is certainly an improvement on the previous funds flow statement, and the production of cash flow information provides important information to users. We will deal with the analysis of cash flow statements in Chapter 31.

EXERCISES

Suggested answers to exercises marked ✓ are to be found in the Student online resources, with suggested answers to the remaining questions available in the Instructor online resources.

1   Cash is a very difficult figure to fiddle. David Tweedie (former Chairman of the IASB). Discuss.

2   Compare and contrast the direct and indirect methods of preparing a statement of cash flows and identify and comment on the reasons why the IASB prefers the direct method.

✓3   Discuss the proposition that a statement of cash flows is more useful to users than a statement of profit or loss and other comprehensive income.

4   Differentiate, using illustrative examples where necessary, between cash and cash equivalents.

5   Cash flows should be defined as increases or decreases in cash. Discuss.

6   The following information is available in respect of Barn entity.

Statement of profit or loss for the year ended 30 September 20X7

	£m	£m	£m
Gross profit			280
Depreciation		60	
Interest receivable	(10)		
Interest payable	16	6	
Profit on sale of assets		(16)	
Impairment of intangibles		40	90
Net profit before tax			190
Tax			80
Net profit after tax			110
Dividends			80
Retained earnings			30

Statements of financial position as at:	30.9.X6	30.9.X7
	£m	£m
Assets		
Non-current assets		
Intangibles	240	280
Property, plant and equipment	640	778
	880	1 058
Current assets		
Inventory	60	68
Trade receivables	48	44
Cash and bank	128	144
	236	256
Total assets	1 116	1 314
Equity and liabilities		
Equity		
Ordinary share capital	500	600
Share premium	40	60
Retained earnings	192	222
	732	882
Non-current liabilities	200	240
Current liabilities		
Trade payables	64	72
Dividends	30	40
Tax	90	80
	184	192
Total equity and liabilities	1 116	1 314

The sale proceeds from the sale of non-current assets was £72m. All interest due has been received and the interest payable has been paid.

Required:

(a) Prepare the statement of cash flows for Barn entity for the year ended 30 September 20X7 in accordance with IAS 7, *Statement of Cash Flows*. (Notes to the statement of cash flows are not required.)

(b) Identify two limitations of statements of cash flows.

7 The following information is available in respect of Theta entity.

Statement of profit or loss for the year ended 31 December 20X7

	£m	£m	£m
Gross profit			420
Depreciation		90	
Interest receivable	(15)		
Interest payable	24	9	
Profit on sale of assets		(24)	
Impairment of intangibles		60	135
Net profit before tax			285
Tax			120
Net profit after tax			165
Dividends			120
Retained earnings			45

Statements of financial position as at	31.12.X6 £m	31.12.X6 £m	31.12.X7 £m	31.12.X7 £m
Assets				
Non-current assets				
Intangibles	360		420	
Property, plant and equipment	960	1 320	1 167	1 587
Current assets				
Inventory	90		102	
Trade receivables	72		66	
Cash and bank	192	354	216	384
Total assets		1 674		1 971
Equity and liabilities				
Equity				
Ordinary share capital	750		900	
Share premium	60		90	
Retained earnings	288	1 098	333	1 323
Non-current liabilities		300		360
Current liabilities				
Trade payables	96		108	
Dividends	45		60	
Tax	135	276	120	288
Total equity and liabilities		1 674		1 971

The sale proceeds from the sale of non-current assets were £108m. All interest due has been received and the interest payable has been paid.

Required:

(a) Prepare the statement of cash flows for Theta entity for the year ended 31 December 20X7 in accordance with IAS 7, *Statement of Cash Flows*. (Notes to the statement of cash flows are not required.)

(b) Identify information that is provided by a statement of cash flows to users that is not provided by a statement of profit or loss and other comprehensive income and a statement of financial position.

8 The following information has been extracted from the draft financial statements of TEX, a manufacturing entity:

Statement of profit or loss for the year ended 30 September 20X3	$000
Revenue	15 000
Cost of sales	(9 000)
Gross profit	6 000
Other operating expenses	(2 300)
	3 700
Finance cost	(124)
Profit before tax	3 576
Income tax expense	(1 040)
Dividends	(1 100)
Retained earnings	1 436

Statements of financial position at 30 September

	20X3 $000	20X3 $000	20X2 $000	20X2 $000
Assets				
Non-current assets		18 160		14 500
Current assets				
Inventories	1 600		1 100	
Trade receivables	1 500		800	
Bank	150	3 250	1 200	3 100
Total assets		21 410		17 600
Equity and liabilities				
Equity				
Issued capital	10 834		7 815	
Accumulated profits	5 836	16 670	4 400	12 215
Non-current liabilities				
Interest-bearing borrowings	1 700		2 900	
Deferred tax	600	2 300	400	3 300
Current liabilities				
Trade payables	700		800	
Proposed dividend	700		600	
Tax	1 040	2 440	685	2 085
Total equity and liabilities		21 410		17 600

Notes

Non-current assets:

	Property $000	Plant $000	Total $000
At 30 September 20X2			
Cost	8 400	10 800	19 200
Depreciation	1 300	3 400	4 700
Net book value	7 100	7 400	14 500
At 30 September 20X3			
Cost	11 200	13 400	24 600
Depreciation	1 540	4 900	6 440
Net book value	9 660	8 500	18 160

(i) Plant disposed of during the year had an original cost of $2 600 000 and accumulated depreciation of $900 000; cash received on disposal was $730 000.

(ii) All additions to non-current assets were purchased for cash.

(iii) Dividends were declared before the balance sheet dates.

Required:

Prepare TEX's statement of cash flows and associated notes for the year ended 30 September 20X3, in accordance with IAS 7 *Statements of Cash Flows*.

(CIMA, Financial Accounting and Tax Principles, May 2005, adapted)

9 The financial statements of AG are given below:

Statement of financial position as at:	31 March 20X5		31 March 20X4	
Assets	$000	$000	$000	$000
Non-current assets				
Plant, property and equipment	4 500		4 800	
Development expenditure	370	4 870	400	5 200
Current assets				
Inventories	685		575	
Trade receivables	515		420	
Cash and cash equivalents	552	1 752	232	1 227
Total assets		6 622		6 427
Equity and liabilities				
Equity				
Share capital	2 600		1 900	
Share premium account	750		400	
Revaluation reserve	425		300	
Retained earning	1 430	5 205	1 415	4 015
Non-current liabilities				
10% loan notes	—		1 000	
5% loan notes	500		500	
Deferred tax	250	750	200	1 700
Current liabilities				
Trade payables	480		350	
Income tax	80		190	
Accrued expenses	107	667	172	712
Total equity and liabilities		6 622		6 427

Statement of profit or loss for the year ended 31 March 20X5	$000	$000
Revenue		7 500
Cost of sales		4 000
Gross profit		3 500
Distribution costs	900	
Administrative expenses	2 300	3 200
Profit from operations		300
Finance costs		45
Profit before tax		255
Income tax expense		140
Profit for the period		115

Additional information:

(i) On 1 April 20X4, AG issued 1 400 000 $0.50 ordinary shares at a premium of 50 per cent.

(ii) On 1 May 20X4, AG purchased and cancelled all its 10 per cent loan notes at par.

(iii) Non-current tangible assets include properties which were revalued upwards by $125 000 during the year.

(iv) Non-current tangible assets disposed of in the year had a net book value of $75 000; cash received on disposal was $98 000. Any gain or loss on disposal has been included under cost of sales.

(v) Cost of sales includes $80 000 for development expenditure amortized during the year.

(vi) Depreciation charged for the year was $720 000.

(vii) The accrued expenses balance includes interest payable of $87 000 at 31 March 20X4 and $12 000 at 31 March 20X5.

(viii) The income tax expenses for the year to 31 March 20X5 is made up as follows:

	$000
Corporate income tax	90
Deferred tax	50
	140

(ix) Dividends paid during the year were $100 000.

Required:

Prepare a statement of cash flows, using the indirect method, for AG for the year ended 31 March 20X5, in accordance with IAS 7 *Statements of Cash Flows*.

(CIMA, Financial Accounting and Tax Principles, May 2005, adapted)

10 **(a)** Casino is a publicly listed company. Details of its statements of financial position as at 31 March 20X5 and 20X4 are shown below, together with other relevant information:

Statement of financial position as at	31 March 20X5		31 March 20X4	
Assets	$m	$m	$m	$m
Non-current assets (note (i)):				
Property, plant and equipment		880		760
Intangible assets		400		510
		1 280		1 270
Current assets				
Inventory	350		420	
Trade receivables	808		372	
Interest receivable	5		3	
Short-term deposits	32		120	
Bank	15	1 210	75	990
Total assets		2 490		2 260
Equity and liabilities				
Equity				
Ordinary shares of $1 each		300		200
Reserves				
Share premium	60		—	
Revaluation reserve	112		45	
Retained earnings	1 098	1 270	1 165	1 210
		1 570		1 410
Non-current liabilities				
12% loan note	—		150	
8% variable rate loan note	160		—	
Deferred tax	90	250	75	225
Current liabilities				
Trade payables	530		515	
Bank overdraft	125		—	
Taxation	15	670	110	625
Total equity and liabilities		2 490		2 260

The following supporting information is available:

(i) Details relating to the non-current assets are: Property, plant and equipment at:

	31 March 20X5			31 March 20X4		
	Cost/ Valuation $m	Depreciation $m	Carrying value $m	Cost/ Valuation $m	Depreciation $m	Carrying value $m
Land and buildings	600	12	588	500	80	420
Plant	440	148	292	445	105	340
			880			760

Casino revalued upwards the carrying value of its land and buildings by $70 million on 1 April 20X4. On 31 March 20X5, Casino transferred $3 million from the revaluation reserve to retained earnings representing the realization of the revaluation reserve due to the depreciation of buildings. During the year Casino acquired new plant at a cost of $60 million and sold some old plant for $15 million at a loss of $12 million. There were no acquisitions or disposals of intangible assets.

(ii) The following extract is from the draft statement of profit or loss for the year to 31 March 20X5:

	$m	$m
Operating loss		(32)
Interest receivable		12
Finance costs		(24)
Loss before tax		(44)
Income tax repayment claim	14	
Deferred tax charge	(15)	(1)
Loss for the period		(45)
The finance costs are made up of:		
Interest expenses		(16)
Penalty cost for early redemption of fixed rate loan		(6)
Issue costs of variable rate loan		(2)
		(24)

(iii) The short-term deposits meet the definition of cash equivalents.

(iv) Dividends of $25 million were paid during the year.

Required:
As far as the information permits, prepare a statement of cash flows for Casino for the year to 31 March 20X5 in accordance with IAS 7, *Statements of Cash Flows*.

(b) In recent years many analysts have commented on a growing disillusionment with the usefulness and reliability of the information contained in some companies' statements of profit or loss and other comprehensive income.

Required:
Discuss the extent to which a company's statement of cash flows may be more useful and reliable than its statement of profit or loss and other comprehensive income.

(CIMA, Financial Accounting and Tax Principles, June 2005, adapted)

11 Extracts from the consolidated financial statements of the EAG Group for the year ended 30 April 20X8 are as follows:

Consolidated statement of profit or loss for the year ended 30 April 20X8

	$ million
Revenue	30 750.0
Cost of sales	(26 447.5)
Gross profit	4 302.5
Distribution costs	(523.0)
Administrative expenses	(669.4)
Finance cost	(510.9)
Share of profit of associate	1.6
Profit on disposal of associate	3.4
Profit before tax	2 604.2
Income tax	(723.9)
Profit for the period	1 880.3
Attributable to:	
Equity holders of the parent	1 652.3
Non-controlling interests	228.0
	1 880.3

Statement of financial position at 30 April 20X8	20X8 $ million	20X7 $ million
Assets		
Non-current assets		
Property, plant and equipment	22 225.1	19 332.8
Goodwill	1 662.7	1 865.3
Intangible assets	306.5	372.4
Investment in associate	—	13.8
	24 194.3	21 584.3
Current assets		
Inventories	5 217.0	4 881.0
Trade receivables	4 633.6	4 670.0
Cash	62.5	88.3
	9 913.1	9 639.3
Total assets	34 107.4	31 223.6
Equity and liabilities		
Equity		
Share capital	4 300.0	3 600.0
Retained earnings	14 643.7	12 991.4
	18 943.7	16 591.4
Non-controlling interest	2 010.5	1 870.5
Non-current liabilities		
Long-term borrowings	6 133.9	6 013.0
Current liabilities		
Trade payables	5 579.3	5 356.3
Short-term borrowings	662.4	507.7
Income tax	777.6	884.7
	7 019.3	6 748.7
Total equity and liabilities	34 107.4	31 223.6

Notes

1 Depreciation of $2 024 700 was charged in respect of property, plant and equipment in the year ended 30 April 20X8.

2 On 1 January 20X8, EAG disposed of the investment in associate for $18 million. The share of profit in the statement of profit or loss relates to the period from 1 May 20X7 to 31 December 20X7. A dividend was received from the associate on 1 June 20X7. There were no other disposals and no acquisitions of investments in the accounting period.

3 Goodwill in one of the group's subsidiaries suffered an impairment during the year. The amount of the impairment was included in cost of sales.

4 The long-term borrowings are measured at amortized cost. The borrowing was taken out on 1 May 20X6, and proceeds of $6 000 000 less issue costs of $100 000 were received on that date. Interest of 5 per cent of the principal is paid in arrears each year, and the borrowings will be redeemed five years later on 30 April for $6.55 million. All interest obligations have been met on the due dates. The effective interest rate applicable to the borrowings is 7 per cent. The finance cost in the statement of profit or loss includes interest in respect of both the long-term and the short-term borrowing. Short-term borrowing comprises overdrafts repayable on demand.

5 Amortization of 25 per cent of the opening balance of intangibles was charged to cost of sales. A manufacturing patent was acquired for a cash payment on 30 April 20X8.

6 An issue of share capital at par was made for cash during the year.

7 Dividends were paid to non-controlling interests during the year, but no dividend was paid to the equity holders of the parent entity.

Required:

Prepare the consolidated statement of cash flow of the EAG Group for the financial year ended 30 April 20X8. The cash flow statement should be presented in accordance with the requirements of IAS 7, *Statement of Cash Flows*, and using the indirect method. Notes to the financial statements are NOT required, but full workings should be shown.

(CIMA P8, May 2008, adapted)

12 Kingdom is a public listed manufacturing company. Its draft summarized financial statements for the year ended 30 September 2013 (and 2012 comparatives) are:

Statements of profit or loss and other comprehensive income for the year ended 30 September:	2013 $000	2012 $000
Revenue	44 900	44 000
Cost of sales	(31 300)	(29 000)
Gross profit	13 600	15 000
Distribution costs	(2 400)	(2 100)
Administrative expenses	(7 850)	(5 900)
Investment properties – rentals received	350	400
– fair value changes	(700)	500
Finance costs	(600)	(600)
Profit before taxation	2 400	7 300
Income tax	(600)	(1 700)
Profit for the year	1 800	5 600
Other comprehensive income	(1 300)	1 000
Total comprehensive income	500	6 600

Statements of financial position as at 30 September:

	2013		2012	
Assets	*$000*	*$000*	*$000*	*$000*
Non-current assets				
Property, plant and equipment		26 700		25 200
Investment properties		4 100		5 000
		30 800		30 200
Current assets				
Inventory	2 300		3 100	
Trade receivables	3 000		3 400	
Bank	—	5 300	300	6 800
Total assets		36 100		37 000
Equity and liabilities				
Equity				
Equity shares of $1 each		17 200		15 000
Revaluation reserve		1 200		2 500
Retained earnings		7 700		8 700
		26 100		26 200
Non-current liabilities				
12% loan notes		5 000		5 000
Current liabilities				
Trade payables	4 200		3 900	
Accrued finance costs	100		50	
Bank	200		—	
Current tax payable	500	5 000	1 850	5 800
Total equity and liabilities		36 100		37 000

The following information is relevant:

On 1 July 2013, Kingdom acquired a new investment property at a cost of $1.4 million. On this date, it also transferred one of its other investment properties to property, plant and equipment at its fair value of $1.6 million as it became owner-occupied on that date. Kingdom adopts the fair value model for its investment properties.

Kingdom also has a policy of revaluing its other properties (included as property, plant and equipment) to market value at the end of each year. Other comprehensive income and the revaluation reserve both relate to these properties.

Depreciation of property, plant and equipment during the year was $1.5 million. An item of plant with a carrying amount of $2.3 million was sold for $1.8 million during September 2013.

Required:

(a) Prepare the statement of cash flows for Kingdom for the year ended 30 September 2013 in accordance with IAS 7, *Statement of Cash Flows* using the indirect method.

(b) At a board meeting to consider the results shown by the draft financial statements, concern was expressed that, although there had been a slight increase in revenue during the current year, the profit before tax had fallen dramatically. The purchasing director commented that he was concerned about the impact of rising prices. During the year to 30 September 2013, most of Kingdom's manufacturing and operating costs have risen by an estimated 8 per cent per annum.

Required:

(i)   Explain the causes of the fall in Kingdom's profit before tax.

(ii) Describe the main effects which rising prices may have on the interpretation of Kingdom's financial statements. You are not required to quantify these effects.

(ACCA, Financial Reporting (International), December 2013)

13   Monty is a publicly listed company. Its financial statements for the year ended 31 March 2013 including comparatives are shown below:

Statements of profit or loss and other comprehensive income for the year ended 31 March	2013 $000	2012 $000
Revenue	31 000	25 000
Cost of sales	(21 800)	(18 600)
Gross profit	9 200	6 400
Distribution costs	(3 600)	(2 400)
Administrative expenses	(2 200)	(1 600)
Finance costs – loan interest	(150)	(250)
– lease interest	(250)	(100)
Profit before tax	3 000	2 050
Income tax expense	(1 000)	(750)
Profit for the year	2 000	1 300
Other comprehensive income (note (i))	1 350	—
	3 350	1 300

Statements of financial position as at	31 March 2013		31 March 2012	
Assets	$000	$000	$000	$000
Non-current assets				
Property, plant and equipment		14 000		10 700
Deferred development expenditure		1 000		—
		15 000		10 700
Current assets				
Inventory	3 300		3 800	
Trade receivables	2 950		2 200	
Bank	50	6 300	1 300	7 300
Total assets		21 300		18 000
Equity and liabilities				
Equity				
Equity shares of $1 each		8 000		8 000
Revaluation reserve		1 350		—
Retained earnings		3 200		1 750
		12 550		9 750
Non-current liabilities				
8% loan notes	1 400		3 125	
Deferred tax	1 500		800	
Finance lease obligation	1 200	4 100	900	4 825
Current liabilities				
Finance lease obligation	750		600	
Trade payables	2 650		2 100	
Current tax payable	1 250	4 650	725	3 425
Total equity and liabilities		21 300		18 000

Notes:

(i) On 1 July 2012, Monty acquired additional plant under a finance lease that had a fair value of $1.5 million. On this date it also revalued its property upwards by $2 million and transferred $650 000 of the resulting revaluation reserve this created to deferred tax. There were no disposals of non-current assets during the period.

(ii) Depreciation of property, plant and equipment was $900 000 and amortization of the deferred development expenditure was $200 000 for the year ended 31 March 2013.

Required:

Prepare a statement of cash flows for Monty for the year ended 31 March 2013, in accordance with IAS 7 *Statement of Cash Flows*, using the indirect method.

(ACCA, Financial Reporting (International), June 2013, adapted)

14 ER holds investments in a number of subsidiaries and associate entities and made one change to its holdings in 2013, which was the acquisition of LT. The statement of financial position of the ER group as at 31 December 2013 and its comparative are shown below.

Statement of financial position as at 31 December	*2013*	*2012*
Assets	*$000*	*$000*
Non-current assets		
Property, plant and equipment	24 000	20 200
Goodwill	6 300	5 800
Investment in associates	5 200	4 700
	35 500	30 700
Current assets	42 500	31 700
Total assets	78 000	62 400
Equity and liabilities		
Equity attributable to owners of the parent		
Share capital ($1 ordinary shares)	18 000	15 000
Share premium	1 000	—
Revaluation reserve	2 000	—
Retained earnings	12 500	7 600
	33 500	22 600
Non-controlling interests	9 200	8 800
Total equity	42 700	31 400
Non-current liabilities		
Long-term borrowings	16 000	18 000
Current liabilities	19 300	13 000
Total liabilities	35 300	31 000
Total equity and liabilities	78 000	62 400

Additional information:

1 ER acquired 70% of the ordinary shares of LT on 1 July 2013 for a cash consideration of $400 000 plus the issue of 1 million $1 ordinary shares in ER. On 1 July 2013, the fair value of an ER share was $1.50. On 1 July 2013, the fair values of the net assets of LT were as follows:

	$000
Property, plant and equipment	1 000
Inventories	800
Receivables	900
Cash and cash equivalents	150
Payables	(850)
	2 000

ER measured the non-controlling interest in LT at its proportionate share of the fair value of the net assets of LT at the acquisition date.

2   The total comprehensive income attributable to non-controlling interests for the year ended 31 December 2013 was $200 000.

3   There were no disposals of property, plant and equipment in the year. Depreciation charged in the year ended 31 December 2013 was $1 500 000.

4   ER's share of associates' profit after tax for the year ended 31 December 2013 was $900 000.

5   ER paid a dividend in the year of $1 million.

Required:
Prepare the following extracts from the consolidated statement of cash flows for the ER group for the year ended 31 December 2013, in accordance with IAS 7, *Statement of Cash Flows:*

(i)   cash flows from investing activities and

(ii)   cash flows from financing activities.

(CIMA, Financial Management, February 2014)

15   The statement of profit or loss for the FB Group for the year ended 31 December 2013 is shown below:

	$000
Revenue	38 000
Cost of sales	(26 000)
Gross profit	12 000
Distribution costs	(1 800)
Administrative expenses	(2 000)
Finance costs	(1 900)
Share of profit of associate	2 900
Profit before tax	9 200
Income tax expense	(2 500)
Profit for the year	6 700
Profit for the year attributable to:	
Owners of the parent	6 200
Non-controlling interests	500
	6 700

The statement of financial position for the FB Group as at 31 December 2013 and its comparative are shown below:

	2013 $000	2012 $000
Assets		
Non-current assets		
Property, plant and equipment	38 000	32 000
Goodwill	2 000	—
Investment in associate	11 000	9 000
	51 000	41 000
Current assets		
Inventories	28 000	26 000
Receivables	22 000	25 000
Cash and cash equivalents	13 000	1 500
	63 000	52 500
Total assets	114 000	93 500
Equity and liabilities		
Equity attributable to owners of the parent		
Share capital ($1 ordinary shares)	30 000	20 000
Share premium	5 000	—
Retained earnings	18 350	14 300
	53 350	34 300
Non-controlling interests	650	—
Total equity	54 000	34 300
Non-current liabilities		
Long-term borrowings	36 000	42 000
Current liabilities		
Payables	20 000	14 000
Income tax	4 000	3 200
	24 000	17 200
Total liabilities	60 000	59 200
Total equity and liabilities	114 000	93 500

Additional information

1 Depreciation charged in arriving at profit before tax was $4 000 000. There were no disposals of property, plant and equipment in the year to 31 December 2013.

2 FB acquired a controlling interest in SM during the year for $6 350 000. The consideration consisted of $350 000 in cash and the transfer of 4 000 000 of FB's equity shares with a deemed value of $1.50 per share at the acquisition date. The non-controlling interest was measured at its fair value of $450 000 at the acquisition date. FB made no other purchases or sales of investments in the year and had no investments at the start of the year.

3 The fair value of the net assets of SM as at the acquisition date were as follows:

	$000
Property, plant and equipment	2 400
Inventories	3 600
Receivables	2 000
Cash and cash equivalents	200
Payables	(3 800)
	4 400

4   Finance costs relate solely to the long-term borrowing. The effective interest rate of 4.524% was charged on the opening balance of the liability and interest of $1 200 000 was paid in December 2013 together with the capital repayment.

5   An impairment review conducted at 31 December 2013 resulted in goodwill being written down and an amount being charged to profit before tax.

Required:
Prepare the consolidated statement of cash flows for the FB Group for the year ended 31 December 2013 in accordance with IAS 7, *Statement of Cash Flows.*

(CIMA Financial Management, May 2014)

16   A potential investor has approached you for some help in analyzing the financial information on QW, an entity in which he is considering investing. QW has been trading for many years and has recently implemented a new corporate strategy to focus on the core aspects of the business. The statement of cash flows for the QW group for the year ended 31 December 2011 is below:

Cash flows from operating activities	*$ million*	*$ million*
Profit before taxation	950	
Adjustments for:		
Depreciation	450	
Less gain on sale of investments	(80)	
Add back loss on sale of property, plant and equipment	10	
Investment income	(210)	
Interest costs	320	
	1 440	
Decrease in trade receivables	320	
Increase in inventories	(470)	
Increase in payables	210	
Cash generated from operations	1 500	
Interest paid	(140)	
Income taxes paid	(660)	
Net cash from operating activities		700
Cash flows from investing activities		
Disposal of subsidiary (net of cash)	850	
Acquisition of property, plant and equipment	(1 250)	
Proceeds from sale of equipment	40	
Proceeds from sale of investments	390	
Investment income received	120	
Net cash from investing activities		150
Cash flows from financing activities		
Proceeds from share issue	600	
Proceeds from long-term borrowings	280	
Dividend paid to equity holders of the parent	(1 200)	
Net cash used in financing activities		(320)
Net increase in cash and cash equivalents		530
Cash and cash equivalents at the beginning of the period		230
Cash and cash equivalents at the end of the period		760

Required:
Analyse the above statement of cash flows of QW and prepare a brief report that highlights the key features of each category of cash flow that would be of interest to a potential investor.

(CIMA, Financial Management, May 2012)

DISCLOSURE ISSUES

24

OBJECTIVES After studying this chapter, you should be able to:

- explain the purpose of segmental reporting or disclosure of segment information

- describe what is meant by an operating segment

- explain the criteria for the determination of a reportable segment

- describe what is meant by an event after the reporting period

- explain the difference between an adjusting event and a non-adjusting event

- define basic earnings per share

- define diluted earnings per share

- describe the contents and appraise the statement IAS 33 on earnings per share

- describe the main issues of interim financial reporting under IAS 34.

INTRODUCTION

Most of the Standards that we are going to discuss in this chapter have in common that they regulate supplemental information disclosure on top of the data reported in the statement of financial position and the statement of comprehensive income. The aim of the Standards discussed in this chapter is the improvement of the information disclosed in the financial statements for decision usefulness. Stakeholders will make economic decisions based on the reported information. The issues to be discussed are segmental reporting (IFRS 8), communication of information on events after the reporting date (IAS 10), the determination of earnings per share (IAS 33) and interim financial reporting (IAS 34).

DISCLOSURE OF SEGMENT INFORMATION

The first Standard that we will discuss in this chapter is IFRS 8 on the disclosure of segment information.

In the autumn of 2006, the IASB issued a new Standard on segmental reporting, IFRS 8, *Operating Segments*. IFRS 8 replaced the old IAS 14, *Segmental Reporting*. IFRS 8 was part of the convergence programme with the FASB, and its purpose is to achieve convergence in the area of segment reporting with the segmental reporting rules under US GAAP. In practice, this specific convergence project implied that de facto IAS 14 was substituted by SFAS 131, *Disclosures about Segments of an Entity and Related Information*, a financial accounting standard of the FASB. As with any Standards on the agenda of a standard setter, the development of IFRS 8 also generated a lot of discussion and controversy. When the IASB issued IFRS 8, it made three key decisions in that: (1) segments would be identified based on the internal management perspective; (2) information to be disclosed in the segment information would be measured in line with the internal valuation rules that are used for the preparation of the internal management reports; and (3) the line items reported in the segment information would be those items used to communicate to the chief operating decision maker (CODM). In 2012, the IASB undertook a post-implementation review (PIR) of IFRS 8. This was the first major PIR of a Standard undertaken by the IASB. During the PIR of IFRS 8, the IASB posted the views of the preparers, investors and other constituents on its website, as well as the results of academic research on IFRS 8 (www.ifrs.org). In general, preparers think that the Standard works well, while the views of investors are more mixed. Auditors, accounting firms, standard setters and regulators are generally supportive of the Standard (IFRS – Staff paper: Post-implementation review of IFRS 8: Operating Segments). When we discuss the different elements of IFRS 8, we will pay attention to the issues raised by the different stakeholders in the PIR of IFRS 8.

Purpose of the disclosure of segment reporting

Why is disclosure of segment information such a topic of debate?

In order to answer this question, we will first define what segmental reporting means and its purpose. On the statement of financial position and the statement of comprehensive income of a company, aggregated data on sales, expenses, assets and liabilities of a company as a whole are communicated to external parties.

For companies active in a single industry, e.g. Pizza Hut, the risk and volatility of the results disclosed by the company in the statement of comprehensive income are tied to the characteristics of risk and volatility of that specific industry. In this case, external stakeholders are able to make predictions about the future performance of the company based on an assessment of its prior year and current performance and on an assessment of the future evolution of the industry in which the company is active.

Very often, however, companies sell multiple products and compete in different industries and on different regional markets, e.g. companies such as Nike and Adidas are active in both the sports equipment industry and clothing industry, and they sell their products worldwide in markets with different levels of purchasing power. A company such as the Scandinavian SAS Group is active in the airline industry as well as in the hotel business. The corporate risk and the future performance of these companies or groups is influenced, first, by the individual risks and performance patterns of the different product groups and, second, by the individual risks of the different markets in which they are competing. The risks and volatility of the results of these individual products – or services groups or different markets – can be positively or negatively correlated with one another. If there is a positive correlation between the risks and returns of the individual segments, then the company's risk as a whole is increased and the corporate results will then be highly volatile. If the correlation is negative, the corporate risk is reduced. So in order to make predictions about the future performance of multi-business and multinational companies, information on the performance of the individual groups of products or services and the different regional markets is essential.

The provision of financial information about these different product groups and separate markets is called segmental reporting or disclosure of segment information.

ACTIVITY 24.1

Think of some multinationals or other companies you are familiar with and try to determine whether they are single business or multi-business entities and if they are competing in different markets. What kind of information would you like about them?

Activity feedback

Starbucks and McDonald's are typical single businesses. Their performance in the different geographical markets determines the future revenue generating power of the company, together with plans to open new outlets. Unilever and Nestlé are companies active in the area of consumer goods. Information on their different product lines, different brands as well as their performance in the different regions would be welcome information. Car manufacturers produce cars but at the same time develop a financing business to promote the sale of the cars. With respect to car manufacturers, it would be interesting to have the performance of the manufacturing segment and of the financing/leasing segment separately. The old IAS 14 required companies to disclose two types of segment information, namely segment information revealing the different lines of business they were in and segment information revealing the performance of the firm in the different regions of the world.

Segmental reporting or disclosure of segment information is dealt with in IFRS 8, *Operating Segments*. As mentioned in the introductory paragraph, the key objective of this Standard is to assist the user of financial statements in making judgements about the opportunities and risks facing an entity, by the disclosure of more disaggregated information than that provided in the primary financial statements (meaning the statement of financial position and the statement of comprehensive income of the group).

It would be useful to disclose the result obtained in each segment together with the capital employed in each segment. As the segmental information to be disclosed is more disaggregated, it enables the reader of the financial statements to analyze the financial performance of the entity in the various areas or segments in which it operates. In this respect, segmental information increases the value relevance of the accounting information disclosed in the financial statements.

However, companies are not very eager to disclose segmental information as these segmental data are of strategic importance. They could reveal the profitability of individual markets or business lines. Segmental data not only increase the relevance of the accounts for investors but competitors will also make use of those segmental data in their own decision processes. As disclosing segmental data is perceived by companies as communicating proprietary information, firms have often tried in the past to provide segmental information of little relevance. Analysts and investors have consistently criticized the quality and inadequacy of the segment disclosures. Firms often argued that the benefits of informing the capital markets about firm value are smaller than the costs of aiding competitors with the information. The degree of flexibility permitted in segment disclosures was an issue for regulators in the 1980s and the 1990s (Fields *et al.*, 2001). In the mid-1990s, the American FASB issued a new Standard on segment reporting requiring disclosures that are consistent with the firm's internal reporting organization. The IASB took a similar approach with IFRS 8, which does not really differ from the American Standard on segmental reporting.

Before we start with the discussion on the contents of IFRS 8, it is important to stress that IFRS 8 should be applied by those entities whose equity or debt securities are publicly traded and by entities that are in the process of issuing equity or debt securities in public securities markets (IFRS 8, para. 2). Companies that voluntarily issue segmental information in their IAS accounts should also fully comply with IFRS 8 (para. 2). According to IFRS 8, an entity shall disclose information to enable users of its financial statements to evaluate the nature and financial effects of the business activities in which it engages and the economic environments in which it operates.

Definition of segments

In order to provide guidance on the disclosure of segment information, IFRS 8 starts with a discussion on the concept of an operating segment. The first step towards the disclosure of segmental information is the definition of the different operating segments present in the company. The principle underlying the approach in IFRS 8 is that the process of identifying segments for external reporting purposes begins with the information used by the CODM to evaluate past performance and make decisions about future allocations of resources. The term 'chief operating decision maker' identifies a function, not necessarily a manager with a specific title. Whereas in an American context it is clear that the CODM would be an individual like the CEO or the President of the entity, the PIR of IFRS 8 revealed that the identification of the CODM is more complicated in other jurisdictions. Which individual or group of individuals can be identified as the CODM depends on the local corporate governance requirements of the jurisdiction in which the company is located. According to the different national corporate government requirements, the CODM could be either the Board of Directors, the CEO or the Management Committee of the entity.

The former IAS 14 had as underlying principles that similar risks and returns were the basis for defining the business and the geographical segments of a company, which would then be the basis for segmental reporting. Under IFRS 8, however, segments for which financial information has to be disclosed in the notes are identified on the basis of internal reports that are regularly reviewed by the entity's CODM to allocate resources and evaluate the performance of those segments. Through this management approach of segmental reporting, the user of the financial statements will receive segmental information in the same format and according to the same valuation rules as the management of the company. According to this approach, no segments have to be created for external reporting purposes. This certainly facilitates the task for preparers of financial statements. For users of the annual financial statements, however, there is a danger that this 'look through the eyes of management' will create an obstacle to the comparability of segment information between different companies. This approach has already generated many comment letters from users of financial statements at the stage when ED 8 on operating segments was issued.

IFRS 8 (para. 5) provides the following definition for the concept 'operating segment':

An operating segment is a component of an entity:

(a) that engages in business activities from which it may earn revenues and incur expenses (including revenues and expenses relating to transactions with other components of the same entity)

(b) whose operating results are regularly reviewed by the entity's chief operating decision maker to make decisions about resources to be allocated to the segment and assess its performance and

(c) for which discrete financial information is available.

The above definition implies that internal segments which do not earn revenue, such as corporate headquarters, will not qualify as an operating segment. The term 'chief operating decision maker' identifies a function, not necessarily a manager with a specific title.

Generally, an operating segment has a segment manager who is directly accountable to, and maintains regular contact with, the CODM to discuss operating activities, financial results, forecasts or plans for the segment. An operating segment can be a business segment, or a geographical segment or a combination of both. The PIR of IFRS 8 indicates that preparers have no significant remarks concerning the use of this management approach to define segments. Some investors prefer to have information through the 'eyes of management', whereas many other investors mistrust management's intentions and think that segments are reported in such a way as to obscure the entity's true management structure or to mask loss-making activities with individual segments (IFRS Staff paper: Post-implementation review: IFRS 8: Operating Segments, paras 50–53).

As a result of this management perspective to be applied to the disclosure of segment information, a wide variety of different types of segments are reported. Nestlé chooses a combination of geographical and business segments as operating segments (see Appendix I of Chapter 31) and Unilever opts for only business segments as reportable operating segments (see Appendix II of Chapter 31).

Later, we include the segmental reporting of Barry Callebaut, the largest chocolate producer in the world (the value chain of Barry Callebaut is presented in Chapter 30). In the introduction to the segment information of Barry Callebaut, it is explained who the CODM is in their Group.

Reportable segments

A reportable segment is an operating segment for which segment information is required to be disclosed by the Standard. Only segment data for reportable segments have to be disclosed in the notes to the statement of financial position and the statement of comprehensive income.

According to IFRS 8 (para. 11), an entity shall report separately information about each operating segment that has been identified or that results from aggregating two or more of those operating segments (for aggregation criteria, see IFRS 8, para. 12), when an operating segment or the aggregation of operating segments exceeds the quantitative thresholds (for a definition of the thresholds see IFRS 8, para. 13). Therefore, once a company knows which segments qualify under the definition of operating segments, it will focus on the aggregation criteria and work out whether or not operating segments can be combined for reporting purposes into reportable segments. Only information on an operating segment or aggregated operating segments needs to be disclosed if the segment or aggregated segments exceed a number of quantitative thresholds. So, to sum up, operating segments which comply with the aggregation criteria and meet the quantitative thresholds are externally reportable segments.

When operating segments have similar economic characteristics and subsequently similar long-term financial performance, they may be aggregated. The aggregation criteria are defined as follows (para. 12):

Two or more operating segments may be aggregated into a single operating segment if the segments have similar economic characteristics and if they are similar in the following respects:

(a) the nature of the products and services

(b) the nature of the production processes

(c) the type or class of customer for their product and services

(d) the methods used to distribute their products or provide their services

(e) if applicable, the nature of the regulatory environment, for example banking, insurance or public utilities.

Second, only information on operating segments or aggregated operating segments needs to be disclosed if the segment or aggregated segments exceed a number of quantitative thresholds specified in IFRS 8 (para. 13).

An entity shall report separately information about an operating segment that meets any of the following quantitative thresholds:

(a) its reported revenue, including both sales to external customers and intersegment sales or transfers, is 10 per cent or more of the combined revenue, internal and external of all operating segments

(b) the absolute amount of its reported profit or loss is 10 per cent or more of the greater, in absolute amount, of (i) the combined reported profit of all operating segments that did not report a loss and (ii) the combined reported loss of all operating segments that reported a loss

(c) its assets are 10 per cent or more of the combined assets of all operating segments.

Operating segments that do not meet any of the quantitative thresholds may be considered reportable, and separately disclosed, if management believes that information about the segment would be useful to users of the financial statements.

IFRS 8 specifies further (para. 15) that if the total external revenue reported by operating segments constitutes less than 75 per cent of the entity's revenue, additional operating segments shall be identified as reportable segments (even if they do not meet the quantitative thresholds defined in para. 13) until at least 75 per cent of the entity's revenue is included in reportable segments.

Activity 24.2 illustrates the application of the size criteria or quantitative thresholds in order to determine whether or not an individual segment qualifies to be a reportable segment and whether or not sufficient reportable segments have been distinguished for disclosure in the notes to the accounts.

ACTIVITY 24.2

The management of a major multinational has identified the following reportable segments:

	Total segment revenues	Intersegment revenues	Segment result	Identifiable segment assets
Segment A	750		300	800
Segment B	400	40	–50	450
Segment C	950		250	600
Segment D	500	50	200	900
Segment E	350	35	50	500
Segment F	500		150	700
Segment G	550		–150	750
Segment H	650		100	400
Total segments	4 650	125	850	5 100
Intercompany eliminations	125		50	150
Consolidated total	4 525		800	4 950

1 Assume segments A–H are business segments. Determine which of these business segments would classify as reportable segments.

2 Based on your answer to question 1, determine whether the reportable segments represent sufficient operations (75 per cent threshold test).

Activity feedback

1 Reportable segments

	Segment revenue[a] >465 (10% of 4 650)	Segment result >105 (10% of 1 050[b])	Identifiable segment assets >510 (10% of 5 100)	Reportable segment
Segment A	Yes	Yes	Yes	Yes
Segment B	No	No	No	No
Segment C	Yes	Yes	Yes	Yes
Segment D	Yes	Yes	Yes	Yes
Segment E	No	No	No	No
Segment F	Yes	Yes	Yes	Yes
Segment G	Yes	Yes	Yes	Yes
Segment H	Yes	No	No	Yes

Notes:
[a] The majority of the segment revenue is from external sales in all segments.
[b] Combined result of segments in profit 1050; combined result of segments in loss 200; chose the greater in absolute amounts, i.e. 1050.

2 Number of reportable segments

In order to determine the number of reportable segments, the threshold of 75 per cent of the external revenue reported by the segments applies. This implies that if the total external revenue reported by the segments constitutes less than 75 per cent of the entity's revenue, additional segments must be identified as reportable segments until at least 75 per cent of the entity's revenue is included in reportable segments.

So 75% x 4525 = 3394 is the threshold. We will check whether we meet the threshold with individual segments which have passed the size criteria for being an individual reportable segment.

External revenue segment A	=	750
External revenue segment C	=	950
External revenue segment D	=	450
External revenue segment F	=	500
External revenue segment G	=	550
External revenue segment H	=	650
Total	=	3 850

Even without segment D, the threshold of 75 per cent is met.

One of the comments made in the PIR of IFRS 8 is that the criteria for determining the individual reportable segments are not always easy to apply. Moreover, investors argue that too much aggregation of operating segments takes place (Post-implementation review of IFRS 8, Agenda Paper 12C, May 2015, page 40). So more guidance could perhaps be expected on what is meant by similar economic characteristics as a result of the comments made during the PIR of IFRS 8.

Disclosure of segmental data

Once the reportable segments have been determined, information on these segments must be disclosed in the notes in order to enable users of financial statements to evaluate the nature and financial effects of the business activities in which the segments engage and the economic environments in which the segments operate.

First, some general information has to be provided with regard to the reportable segments (para. 22):

- factors used to identify the entity's reportable segments, including the basis of organization (for example, whether management has chosen to organize the entity around differences in products and services, geographical areas, regulatory environments, or a combination of factors and whether operating segments have been aggregated) and
- types of products and services from which each reportable segment derives its revenues.

Second, IFRS 8 states which information needs to be disclosed with regard to each reportable segment. Remember that the internal information communicated and reviewed by the CODM is the basis for segmental disclosure. IFRS 8 (para. 23) states that an entity shall report a measure of profit or loss for each reportable segment even if that information is not included in the communication to the CODM. With regard to segment assets and liabilities, IFRS 8 states that an entity shall report segment assets and liabilities for each reportable segment only if such an amount is regularly provided to the CODM. The following items need to be disclosed for each reportable segment, if they are also reported to the CODM:

- revenues from external customers
- revenues from transactions with other operating segments of the same entity
- interest revenue
- interest expense
- depreciation and amortization
- material items of income and expense disclosed in accordance with para. 86 of IAS 1, *Presentation of Financial Statements*
- the entity's interest in profit or loss of associates and joint ventures accounted for by the equity method
- income tax expense or income and
- material non-cash items other than depreciation and amortization.

With regard to the disclosure of segmental information, investors communicated in the PIR of IFRS 8 that they were very concerned that companies no longer report certain important line items like depreciation. The fact that only information disclosed to the CODM needs to be disclosed in the notes to the statement of financial position provides companies with the discretion not to disclose important line items. Users of financial information would welcome the IASB making the disclosure of a number of line items mandatory. However, the IASB itself is reluctant to do so, since it goes against the adopted principle of 'adherence to the management perspective'.

Measurement

The measurement of the segment data under IFRS 8 is fundamentally different from the measurement under IAS 14. In contrast to segment data reportable under IAS 14, segment data separated under IFRS 8 do not need to comply with IAS regulations. The amount of each segment item reported shall be the measure reported to the CODM for the purposes of making decisions about allocating resources to the segment and assessing its performance. Adjustments and eliminations made in preparing an entity's financial statements and allocations of revenues, expenses, and gains or losses shall be included in determining reported segment profit or loss only if they are included in the measure of the segment's profit or loss that is used by the CODM. Similarly, only those assets that are included in the measure of the segment's assets that is used by the CODM shall be reported for that segment. If amounts are allocated to reported segment profit or loss or assets, those amounts shall be allocated on a reasonable basis. So segmental data can be valued according to rules or principles other than IAS/IFRS. This ability to use internal valuation rules instead of IFRS is another element that might impede comparability of segment data between different companies, as the valuation basis of the segment data could be different. The fact that IFRS 8 introduced the possibility of non-IFRS measurement for segmental data is another major concern for investors and other users of financial statements. This option reduces greatly the comparability of segmental information between entities.

Reconciliations

Since there is no obligation for the disclosed segment data to comply with IAS, the reported totals over all segments might deviate from the figures that appear in the group financial statements, which comply with IAS. In order to link the disclosed segment data with the data published in the statement of financial position and the statement of comprehensive income of the entity, the following reconciliations have to be provided:

- the total of reportable segments' revenues to the entity's revenue
- the total of the reportable segments' measures of profit or loss to the entity's profit or loss before income tax expense or income and discontinued operations; however, if an entity allocates to reportable segments items such as income tax expense or income, the entity may reconcile the total of the segments' measures of profit or loss to the entity's profit or loss after those items
- the total of the reportable segments' assets to the entity's assets
- the total of the reportable segments' amounts for every other material item of information disclosed to the corresponding amount for the entity; for example, an entity may choose to disclose liabilities for its reportable segments, in which case the entity would reconcile the total of reportable segments' liabilities to the entity's liabilities if the segment liabilities are material.

Many investors who expressed their views in the PIR of IFRS 8, would welcome preparers of financial statements enhancing drastically the understandability of the reconciliations they prepare.

Entity-wide disclosures

Besides this requirement to disclose segmental data, IFRS 8 also prescribes the disclosure of entity-wide data. The requirements for entity-wide disclosures also apply to entities that have only one single reportable segment. The IASB is well aware of the fact that some entities' business activities are not organized on the basis of differences in related products and services or differences in geographical areas of operations. In these cases, an entity's reportable segments may report revenues from a broad range of essentially different products and services, or more than one of its reportable segments may provide essentially the same products and services. Similarly, an entity's reportable segments may hold assets in different geographical areas and report revenues from customers in different geographical areas, or more than one of its reportable segments may operate in the same geographical area.

In order to ensure that users of financial statements receive at least some information, which they can use for inter-firm comparison and which is understandable in a straightforward way, IFRS 8 states that entities must disclose the following in addition to their segmental data:

1 Information about products and services (revenues from external customers for each product and service or each group of similar products or services).

2 Information about geographical areas:

(a) revenues from external customers:

   (i) attributed to the entity's country of domicile and

   (ii) attributed to all foreign countries in total from which the entity derives revenues. If revenues from external customers attributed to an individual foreign country are material, those revenues shall be disclosed separately. An entity shall disclose the basis for attributing revenues from external customers to individual countries.

(b) non-current assets other than financial instruments, deferred tax assets, post-employment benefit assets, and rights arising under insurance contracts:

   (i) located in the entity's country of domicile and

   (ii) located in all foreign countries in total in which the entity holds assets. If assets in an individual foreign country are material, those assets shall be disclosed separately.

   The amounts reported in relation to 1 and 2 shall be based on the financial information that is used to produce the entity's financial statements. This implies that this information shall be prepared according to IFRS. If the information is not available in accordance with IFRS and if the cost of producing this information would be excessive, the information can be omitted.

3 Information about major customers. If revenues from transactions with a single external customer amount to 10 per cent or more of an entity's revenues, the entity shall disclose that fact, the total amount of revenues from each such customer, and the identity of the segment or segments reporting the revenues. The entity need not disclose the identity of a major customer or the amount of revenues that each segment reports from that customer. For the purpose of this IFRS, a group

of entities known to a reporting entity to be under common control shall be considered a single customer, and a national government, a local government, or a foreign government shall each be considered a single customer.

These entity-wide disclosures probably compensate for the loss of comparable information on business and geographical segments which was required by IAS 14, but abolished with the introduction of IFRS 8. However, the PIR reveals that entity-wide disclosures are poorly understood and inconsistently applied across entities. During 2015, the IASB's staff proposed a number of amendments to IFRS 8. It is foreseen that by 2017, a number of these amendments will be approved. However, none of the amendments to date changes the principle of 'adherence to the management perspective' included in IFRS 8. The following Real World Illustration is taken from Barry Callebaut's annual report for 2014/15.

REAL WORLD ILLUSTRATION

Consolidated Financial Statements - Barry Callebaut Annual Report 2014-2015

3 Segment information

External segment reporting is based on the internal organizational and management structure, as well as on the internal information reviewed regularly by the Chief Operating Decision Maker. Barry Callebaut's Chief Operating Decision Maker has been identified as the Executive Committee, consisting of the Group Chief Executive Officer, the Chief Financial Officer and the Presidents of the Regions Western Europe, Americas and Global Cocoa as well as the Chief Operations Officer and the Chief Innovation & Quality Officer.

The Executive Committee considers the business from a geographic view. Hence, Presidents were appointed for each region. Since the Group's cocoa activities operate independently of the Regions, the Global Cocoa business is reviewed by the Chief Operating Decision Maker as an own segment in addition to the geographical Regions Western Europe, EEMEA (Eastern Europe, Middle East and Africa), Americas and Asia Pacific. For

the purpose of the Consolidated Financial Statements, the Regions Western Europe and EEMEA were aggregated since the businesses are similar and meet the criteria for aggregation. Furthermore, the Executive Committee also views the Corporate function independently. The function "Corporate" consists mainly of headquarters services (incl. the Group's centralized treasury department) to other segments. Thus, the Group reports Corporate separately.

The segment Global Cocoa is responsible for the procurement of ingredients for chocolate production (mainly cocoa; sugar, dairy and nuts are also common ingredients) and the Group's cocoa-processing business. Most of the revenues of Global Cocoa are generated with the other segments of the Group.

The regional chocolate business consists of chocolate production related to the Product Groups "Food Manufacturers' Products" focusing on industrial customers and "Gourmet & Specialties Products" focusing on products for artisans and professional users of chocolate such as chocolatiers, pastry chefs or bakers as well as products for vending machines.

Financial information by reportable segments

in thousands of CHF	Europe	Americas	Asia Pacific	Global Cocoa	Total Segments	Corporate	Eliminations	Group
Revenues from external customers	2,563,682	1,507,875	269,824	1,900,484	6,241,865	–	–	6,241,865
Revenues from transactions with other operating segments of the Group	4,611	623	–	1,669,368	1,674,602	–	(1,674,602)	–
Net revenue	**2,568,293**	**1,508,498**	**269,824**	**3,569,852**	**7,916,467**	**–**	**(1,674,602)**	**6,241,865**
Operating profit (EBIT)	**289,714**	**130,634**	**26,937**	**47,198**	**494,483**	**(79,662)**	**–**	**414,821**
Depreciation and amortization	**(40,828)**	**(22,978)**	**(6,917)**	**(53,071)**	**(123,794)**	**(2,194)**	**–**	**(125,988)**
Impairment losses	**(569)**	**–**	**–**	**(11,772)**	**(12,341)**	**–**	**–**	**(12,341)**
Total assets	**1,340,869**	**1,080,208**	**162,576**	**2,818,132**	**5,401,785**	**1,371,352**	**(1,343,749)**	**5,429,388**
Additions to property, plant, equipment and intangible assets	(85,877)	(68,558)	(15,406)	(67,586)	(237,427)	(28,726)	–	(266,153)

2014/15

(*Continued*)

REAL WORLD ILLUSTRATION *(Continued)*

in thousands of CHF	Europe	Americas	Asia Pacific	Global Cocoa	Total Segments	Corporate	Eliminations	Group
				2013/14				
Revenues from external customers	2,573,259	1,287,335	249,128	1,756,218	5,865,940	–	–	5,865,940
Revenues from transactions with other operating segments of the Group	66,631	681	–	2,204,104	2,271,416	–	(2,271,416)	–
Net revenue	2,639,890	1,288,016	249,128	3,960,322	8,137,356	–	(2,271,416)	5,865,940
Operating profit (EBIT)	268,097	126,502	27,002	81,951	503,552	(87,307)	–	416,245
Depreciation and amortization	(37,956)	(18,656)	(6,662)	(49,119)	(112,393)	(2,811)	–	(115,204)
Impairment losses	(721)	(3)	(16)	(27)	(767)	(35)	–	(802)
Total assets	1,294,836	897,696	122,754	2,866,872	5,182,158	1,481,385	(1,496,029)	5,167,514
Additions to property, plant, equipment and intangible assets	(71,471)	(76,312)	(14,435)	(58,321)	(220,539)	(32,925)	–	(253,463)

Global Cocoa comprises Group-wide sourcing and Global Cocoa processing functions also for the benefit of all the regions. Therefore some of its operation profits are consequently allocated to the regions.

Segment revenue, segment results (operating profit EBIT) and segment assets are measured based on IFRS principles.

Finance income and costs, the Group's share of result of equity-accounted investees and income taxes are not allocated to the respective segment for internal management purposes.

Additional entity-wide disclosures

Information on geographical regions Barry Callebaut is domiciled in Switzerland; however, its major revenues are generated in other countries. The following table shows revenues and non-current assets excluding investments in equity-accounted investees, deferred tax assets and pension assets allocated to the entity's country of domicile and the major countries where the Group is generating revenues and/or to those countries where the non-current assets as defined above are material.

Information on Product Groups The Group has numerous products that are sold to external customers. Therefore, for internal review by the Chief Operating Decision Maker, information on products is aggregated on a Product Group level. The following table breaks down external revenues into Product Groups:

Segment Information by Product Croup

in thousands of CHF	2014/15	2013/14
Cocoa Products	1,900,484	1,756,218
Food Manufacturers	3,444,664	3,247,374
Gourmet & Specialties	896,717	862,348
Revenues from external customers	**6,241,865**	**5,865,940**

In fiscal year 2014/15, the biggest single customer contributed CHF 912.2 million or 14.6% of total revenues reported across various regions (2013/14: CHF 797.7 million or 13.6%). No other single customer contributed more than 10% of total consolidated revenues.

	Revenues		Non-current assets[1]	
in thousands of CHF	2014/15	2013/14	2014/15	2013/14
United States	1,039,145	905,570	288,580	243,327
Germany	500,936	453,246	90,764	102,231
Belgium	484,030	481,013	338,371	323,598
France	433,135	432,354	73,843	49,139
United Kingdom	421,824	411,419	48,854	78,275
Brazil[2]	335,392	257,243	70,380	81,610
Mexico	306,171	272,754	30,625	32,875
Italy	298,522	308,908	24,879	25,110
Rest of Europe	1,344,030	1,344,533	439,690	461,393
Rest of Americas	329,488	273,614	118,844	129,100
Rest of Asia Pacific	749,192	725,286	555,781	545,719
Total	**6,241,865**	**5,865,940**	**2,080,611**	**2,072,377**

[1] Property, plant and equipment + intangible assets.

[2] Comparatives have been provided to conform to the current period's presentation.

EVENTS AFTER THE REPORTING PERIOD

Financial statements are used mainly for two purposes. First, external stakeholders will use financial statement information in their own decision-making process and, second, financial statements can serve as a basis to assess management's stewardship. The latter means that management and directors could be held accountable for their policy decisions and actions on the basis of information revealed by the financial statements.

With regard to the first aim of providing useful and reliable information, it is important that external stakeholders obtain a clear idea about which transactions and their related financial impact are included in the annual accounts and which transactions or events and their related financial impact have not been taken into account in the financial statements. Time passes between the end of the reporting period and the publication of the financial statements to the public. Accounts, no matter how sophisticated the information technology, are never prepared, audited and approved by directors in a few days. Generally, there is a time lag between the end of the reporting period and the 'signing off' of the accounts by the directors. During this period, numerous events can occur that may or may not have an influence on the information which is provided in the final accounts.

ACTIVITY 24.3

Can you think of activities arising after the reporting period, which might alter the financial picture presented by the financial statements at the end of the reporting period?

Activity feedback

- *The bankruptcy of an important customer*
- *The levy of import tariffs in an important export market of the company*
- *The acquisition of a large part of the shares of a company*
- *A settlement of a court case in which the company is involved.*

The events listed in Activity 24.3 will have an impact on the financial situation of the company, and external stakeholders might well change their decisions in relation to the company if they take into account the financial impact of the information becoming available after the reporting period. IAS 10 deals with the communication of the impact of events occurring after the reporting period on the financial situation of the company.

Definition of events after the reporting period

Paragraph 3 of IAS 10 defines events occurring after the reporting period as those events, both favourable and unfavourable, that occur between the end of the reporting period and the date when the financial statements are authorized for issue. Two types of event can be identified:

- those that provide evidence of conditions that existed at the end of the reporting period (adjusting events after the reporting period)
- those that are indicative of conditions that arose after the end of the reporting period (non-adjusting events after the reporting period).

Date of authorization for issue

In order to judge the relevance of the information provided through the financial statements it is of extreme importance for external stakeholders to know when the financial statements have been authorized for issue, as the financial statements do not reflect events after this date. Therefore, IAS 10 not only requires that the entity disclose the date on which the financial statements were authorized for issue but also who gave that authorization. When an entity's owners or others have the power to amend the financial statements after issue, the entity should disclose this possibility.

ACTIVITY 24.4

Check the financial statements on several websites of listed companies. Is information disclosure clear on this issue (i.e. date of authorization for issue and who gave the authorization)?

Activity feedback

As a user of the annual report and the financial statements you will have found out that it is not easily retrievable and it is not obvious where to find that information, especially with regard to the item 'who gave the authorization'.

An example of such disclosure is found in the 2014 financial statements of the Adidas Group in note 42:

Date of preparation

The Executive Board of Adidas AG prepared and approved the consolidated financial statements for submission to the Supervisory Board on February 13, 2015. It is the Supervisory Board's task to examine the consolidated financial statements and give their approval and authorization for issue.

Herzogenaurach, February 13, 2015
The Executive Board of Adidas AG

The process involved in authorizing the financial statements for issue will vary depending on the management structure, statutory requirements and procedures followed in preparing and finalizing the financial statements (para. 4). In some cases, an entity is required to submit its financial statements to its shareholders for approval after the financial statements have already been issued. In such cases, the financial statements are authorized for issue on the date of original issuance, not on the date when shareholders approve the financial statements (para. 5). In other cases, the management of an entity is required to issue its financial statements to a supervisory board (made up solely of non-executives) for approval. In such cases, the financial statements are authorized for issue when the management authorizes them for issue to the supervisory board. Care may need to be taken in determining the date of 'authorization' for this purpose. The Standard has to allow for a variety of different national systems of corporate governance and management structures.

IAS 10 makes a distinction between adjusting events after the reporting period and non-adjusting events after the reporting period. For both types of event, the financial impact of the events has to be disclosed to the readers of the financial statements, but the disclosure method differs.

Adjusting events

With regard to adjusting events, an entity should adjust the amounts recognized in its financial statements to reflect adjusting events after the reporting period (para. 8).

IAS 10 does not give an explicit definition as guidance for what might be an adjusting event. A list of examples of what the IASB considers to be adjusting events is presented. The following examples should serve as a point of reference for preparers of financial statements (para. 9):

1 The settlement after the reporting period of a court case that confirms an entity had a present obligation at the end of the reporting period.

2 the receipt of information after the reporting period indicating that an asset was impaired at the end of the reporting period or that the amount of a previously recognized impairment loss for that asset needs to be adjusted, for example:

   (a) the bankruptcy of a customer which occurs after the end of the reporting period

   (b) the sale of inventories after the reporting period may give evidence about their net realizable value at the end of the reporting period.

3 The determination after the end of the reporting period of the cost of assets purchased or the proceeds from assets sold before the end of the reporting period.

4 The determination after the reporting period of the amount of profit-sharing or bonus payments, if the entity had a present legal or constructive obligation at the end of the reporting period to make such payments as a result of events before that date (see IAS 19).

5 The discovery of fraud or errors that show that the financial statements were incorrect.

Non-adjusting events

The name reveals that the amounts related to this type of event after the reporting period should not be recognized in the financial statements themselves, but disclosed in the notes to the accounts. If non-adjusting events after the reporting period are material, non-disclosure could influence the economic decisions of users taken on the basis of the financial statements (para. 21). Accordingly, an entity shall disclose the following for each material category of non-adjusting event after the reporting period in the notes to the accounts:

- the nature of the event
- an estimate of its financial effect, or a statement that such an estimate cannot be made.

Again, examples of non-adjusting events are presented as guidance in IAS 10 (para. 22). The following are examples of non-adjusting events after the reporting period that would generally result in disclosure:

- a major business acquisition after the reporting period or disposing of a major subsidiary
- announcing a plan to discontinue an operation
- major purchases of assets, classification of assets as held for sale in accordance with IFRS 5 and other disposals of assets or expropriation of major assets by government
- destruction of a major production plant by a fire after the reporting period
- announcing or commencing the implementation of a major restructuring

- major ordinary share transactions and potential ordinary share transactions after the reporting period
- abnormally large changes after the reporting period in asset prices or foreign exchange rates
- changes in tax rates or tax laws enacted or announced after the reporting period that have a significant effect on current and deferred tax assets and liabilities
- entering into significant commitments or contingent liabilities
- commencing major litigation arising solely out of events that occurred after the reporting period.

Since information on adjusting and non-adjusting events is extremely important for external parties, the disclosure rules on non-adjusting events have become stricter over the years. If an entity receives information after the end of the reporting period about conditions that existed at the end of the reporting date, they are now obliged to adjust disclosures that relate to these conditions, in the light of the new information.

If we study the list of examples of non-adjusting events described in para. 22 of IAS 10, we notice that some events lie within the decision powers of management (e.g. acquisitions, discontinuing operations) and other events are beyond the influence of management (e.g. fire, change in tax laws). It is interesting to observe that many acquisitions or major investments seem to take place between the end of the reporting period and the signing off of the accounts. By signing the contract after the end of the reporting period, the acquisition becomes a non-adjusting event. If, through the acquisition, control was obtained over another entity, full consolidation of the entity in the group accounts could be avoided and the influence of the liabilities of that entity and goodwill paid on acquisition could be postponed for one year on the group's financial statements.

REAL WORLD ILLUSTRATION

To illustrate this observation we include the information on events after the reporting period published by Samsung in its Annual Report 2011, note 35 (page 93).

Annual Report

35. Events after the Reporting Period

A) Merger of Samsung LED

The merger of Samsung LED with SEC was approved by the Board of Directors on December 26, 2011. The approval of the Board of Directors of the Company replaces shareholders' meeting approval of the acquisition, as the acquisition of Samsung LED is a small and simple merger as defined in the commercial law.

The shareholders of Samsung LED will receive 0.0134934 shares of the Company's common stock for each share of Samsung LED common stock owned on the closing date. The Company transferred its treasury stocks to the shareholders of Samsung LED.

B) Acquisition of S-LCD

The Company entered into contracts to acquire the remaining issued shares of S-LCD from Sony on December 26, 2011.

The Company acquired shares of S-LCD with a closing date of January 19, 2011.

(In millions of Korean Won)

Name of the acquired company	S-LCD
Purchase price	₩ 1 067 082
Shares	329 999 999 shares
Percentage of shareholding after acquisition	100 %

C) Spin-off of LCD division

The Company's Board of Directors approved the spin-off of the Company's LCD division on February 20, 2012. The shareholders will approve the spin-off on March 16, 2012, during the shareholders' meeting

Category	Details
Companies subject to stock split	Samsung Display Corporation[1]
Business	LCD

[1]The name of the newly established company is subject to change according to a decision of shareholders' meeting.

150 000 000 shares will be newly issued with par value of W 5000 per share and be assigned to SEC.

In the following disclosure on events after the reporting period, we illustrate different items that can be included. We find different elements disclosed in the notes to the financial statements of Unilever and Nestlé in their accounts of 2014.

Events after the Reporting Period

Note 26. Unilever Annual Report and Accounts – page 128

On 20 January 2015, Unilever announced a quarterly dividend with the 2014 fourth quarter results of €0.2850 per NV ordinary share and £0.2177 per PLC ordinary share. On 3 February 2015, Unilever issued a €750 million 0.50% fixed rate bond which will mature in seven years.

Note 24. Consolidated Statements of the Nestlé Group – page 127

On 15 February 2015, the Swiss National Bank announced that it was removing the ceiling on the exchange rate of 1.20 Swiss francs per euro. This resulted in a significant strengthening of the Swiss franc against all major currencies in which the Group operates. The Group has assessed the impact, particularly on counterparty risk, currency exposures, pensions and intangible assets, including goodwill. The event had no material impact and therefore the Consolidated Financial Statements have not been adjusted for the year ended 31 December 2014.

The Group's approach to management of foreign currency risk is described in Note 13.2c.

At 18 February 2015, the date of approval for issue of the Consolidated Financial Statements by the Board of Directors, the Group has no other subsequent events which either warrant a modification of the value of its assets and liabilities or any additional disclosure.

Dividends

The treatment of dividends was dealt with more explicitly in the latest revision of IAS 10. Paragraph 12 states that if dividends to holders of equity instruments are declared after the reporting period, an entity shall not recognize those dividends as a liability at the end of the reporting period. In many countries, dividends under these circumstances are disclosed as a liability in the national GAAP accounts; the IAS treatment is different.

The issue of going concern

There is one item, however, which applies to the definition of a non-adjusting event, but which entails an adjustment to the financial statements. We refer to para. 14 of IAS 10, which stipulates that if management determines after the reporting period either that it intends to liquidate the entity or to cease trading, or that it has no realistic alternative but to do so, the financial statements should no longer be prepared on a going concern basis.

This implies that the accounts have to be completely redrawn on a non-going concern basis. The latter has a tremendous impact on the data which will subsequently be presented in the financial statements.

EARNINGS PER SHARE

Most people or companies buy shares of other companies for investment purposes. Probably only fans of listed football clubs such as Bayern München or Ajax buy shares for purely emotional reasons. An indicator frequently used in the context of evaluating the investment performance of a company is earnings per share (EPS) (see Part Four of this book). EPS is calculated by dividing profit attributable to ordinary shareholders by the number of ordinary shares in issue. As an absolute, however, it has no meaning or relevance. EPS becomes relevant in the context of the price/earnings (PE) ratio or when the growth rate of the EPS of a company is considered. This will be explained with the following example. If we are told that company A has an EPS of 6c whereas company B has an EPS of 25c, we are unable to compare the performance of the two, because we know nothing about their relative size or, more specifically, about the number or value of shares in issue. For the same reasons, the quoted share price of the two companies provides no basis for comparison of the stock market's perceptions of either.

Thus analysts and investors require a basis of comparison and an indicator of confidence in particular companies. Such an indicator is the PE ratio, which is simply calculated by dividing the share price by the EPS, thereby relating company performance to external perception.

The calculation and use of the PE ratio is illustrated in Activity 24.5, where the PE ratio for company X is calculated to be 7.5 and for company Y, 12.

ACTIVITY 24.5

Which company would you invest in?

Company	X	Y
Price per share (a)	150c	96c
EPS (b)	20c	8c
PE ratio (a)/(b)	7.5	12

Activity feedback

Company X has a higher share price and greater EPS, but company Y is expected to perform better in the future. Why? The normal action of supply and demand has bid up the share price of Y relative to current earnings and the market is therefore saying something about its confidence in Y relative to X. Market participants are willing to pay 12 times the EPS to acquire a share in company Y, whereas investors are only willing to pay 7½ times the EPS to invest in company X. This difference results from an alternative view of the future earnings generating power and prospects of both companies (e.g. markets of company Y represent more growth potential, company Y has more products in the early stage of the life cycle of company X). Clearly, a very high PE would indicate such extravagant expectations that there may be some element of risk, but, generally, a high PE is a good indicator of market support. People are willing to pay more for something they think more highly of.

If the PE ratio is used in this way, being quoted in the financial press and elsewhere, it matters greatly that its derivation is consistent and comparable. There are no problems with the price of the share, but what about the EPS?

In this section, we will discuss the calculation of the EPS and in Part Four of the book we further illustrate the use of EPS in the context of the PE ratio. In order to calculate EPS, the earnings number has to be defined, and the number of shares to be used in the denominator has to be specified. To enhance the comparability of the EPS measure between companies, the IASB has issued IAS 33, *Earnings per Share*, which deals with the determination of EPS. The IASB is well aware of the fact that IAS 33 mainly improves consistency in the determination of the denominator of the EPS ratio. Companies can still influence their results by using different accounting valuation methods and accounting estimates, as we discuss in Chapter 30.

IAS 33 shall be applied by entities whose ordinary shares or potential ordinary shares are publicly traded and by entities that are in the process of issuing ordinary shares or potential ordinary shares in public securities markets (IAS 33, para. 2). An entity that discloses EPS shall calculate and disclose EPS in accordance with IAS 33, if they state that their annual accounts comply with IAS/IFRS. This requirement also applies to companies that disclose voluntary EPS data in their IAS financial statements.

Two types of EPS ratio can be calculated: basic EPS (BEPS) and diluted EPS (DEPS). The main difference between the two EPS figures is the number of shares that are taken into account in the denominator. The outstanding equity share capital during the financial year is taken into consideration in the calculation of BEPS. DEPS also takes this into account, plus adds in the effect of the existence of securities with no current claim on equity earnings, but which will give rise to such a claim in the future. This information gives potential investors an idea about future changes in the EPS.

As the main objective of IAS 33 is achieving consistency in the determination of the denominator of the EPS ratio, the elements to be included in the denominator should be defined first. Paragraphs 5 and 6 of IAS 33 provide the following definitions:

- *An ordinary share* is an equity instrument that is subordinate to all other classes of equity instruments. Ordinary shares participate in net profit for the period only after other types of shares such as preference shares.

- *A potential ordinary* share is a financial instrument or other contract that may entitle its holder to ordinary shares.

- *Warrants, options and their equivalents* are financial instruments that give the holder the right to purchase ordinary shares.

- *Contingently issuable ordinary shares* are ordinary shares issuable for little or no cash or other consideration upon the satisfaction of certain conditions pursuant to a contingent share agreement, whereby a contingent share agreement is an agreement to issue shares that is dependent on the satisfaction of specified conditions.

- *Put options on ordinary shares* are contracts that give the holder the right to sell ordinary shares at a specified price for a given period.

- *Dilution* is a reduction in earnings per share or an increase in loss per share resulting from the assumption that convertible securities were converted, that options or warrants were exercised or that ordinary shares were issued upon the satisfaction of certain conditions. As a result of these events the number of outstanding shares will increase.

- *Anti-dilution* is an increase in earnings per share or a reduction in loss per share resulting from the assumption that convertible instruments are converted, that options and warrants are exercised, or that ordinary shares are issued upon the satisfaction of specified conditions. As a result of these events the number of outstanding shares will decrease.

Listed companies have to disclose BEPS and DEPS. First, we will concentrate on the BEPS figure and all the issues which might arise in the calculation of this.

Basic EPS

The BEPS figure represents the amount attributable to the ordinary shareholders by dividing the earnings figure by the weighted average number of ordinary shares outstanding (the denominator) during the period. The calculation of the earnings figure is determined in para. 12. The earnings are equal to the profit or loss attributable to the parent entity. If there are discontinuing operations in a company, then BEPS should also be calculated on the basis of the profit or loss for the period from the continuing operations attributable to the parent entity. If there are no discontinuing operations, there is just one BEPS figure. Again, this is to improve the relevance of the information communicated.

The calculation of the earnings included in the numerator shall be the profit or loss adjusted for the after-tax amounts of preference dividends, differences arising on the settlement of preference shares and other similar effects of preference shares classified as equity. The reason is that ordinary shares are not entitled to those elements. The weighted average number of ordinary shares outstanding during the period will figure in the denominator.

ACTIVITY 24.6

The summarized income statement for EPS SA for the year ended 20X6 is as follows:

	€	€
Profit before taxation		1 000 000
Taxation (including deferred adjustment)		400 000
		600 000
Preference dividend	50 000	
Ordinary dividend	100 000	
	150 000	
	450 000	

The number of ordinary shares in issue is 200 000. Calculate the basic EPS.

Activity feedback

From the definition of EPS:

$$\text{Basic EPS} = \frac{\text{Profit after tax} - \text{Preference dividend}}{\text{Number of ordinary shares}}$$

$$= \frac{600\,000 - 50\,000}{200\,000}$$

$$= €2.75 \text{ per share}$$

Changes in equity share capital during the year

In Activity 24.6, the number of shares in issue is given and remains constant over the financial period. However, in reality, there can be changes in the equity share capital during the financial year under consideration. For the purpose of calculating BEPS, the number of ordinary shares should be the weighted average number of ordinary shares outstanding during the period. This is the number of ordinary shares outstanding at the beginning of the period, adjusted by the number of ordinary shares bought back or issued during the period multiplied by a time-weighting factor. The time-weighting factor is the number of days that the shares are outstanding as a proportion of the total number of days in the period; a reasonable approximation of the weighted average is adequate in many circumstances.

ACTIVITY 24.7

Fullmar plc had issued share capital on 31 December X5 as follows:

1 500 000 preference shares (value €1 each) to which a preference dividend of 7 per cent is attached.

2 4 000 000 ordinary shares (value €0.25 each).

Profit after tax for the year ended 31 December X5 was €435 000. On 1 October X5 Fullmar issued 1 million ordinary shares at full market price (€0.25 each).

Calculate the basic EPS for Fullmar plc for the year ended 31 December X5.

Activity feedback

The number of ordinary shares in issue on 1 January X5 was 3 million and a further 1 million were issued on 1 October X5.

Thus the time weighted average number of ordinary shares in issue for the year was

$$(3\,000\,000 \times 9/12) + (4\,000\,000 \times 3/12) = 3\,250\,000$$

or

$$(3\,000\,000 \times 12/12) + (1\,000\,000 \times 3/12) = 3\,250\,000$$

The earnings for the year attributable to the ordinary shareholders is €435 000 – €35 000 preference dividend = €400 000. Therefore:

$$\text{EPS} = \frac{400\,000}{3\,250\,000} \text{ per share}$$

$$= €0.1230 \text{ per share}$$

Note that the 1 million ordinary shares are issued at full market price in this example.

In reality, shares can be issued at a price that is different from the market price, or shares can be issued without a corresponding change in the resources of the company. Para. 26 of IAS 33 states that the weighted number of ordinary shares outstanding during the period and for all periods presented shall be adjusted for events, other than the conversion of potential ordinary shares, that have changed the number of ordinary shares outstanding without a corresponding change in resources. Ordinary shares may be issued or the number of ordinary shares outstanding may be reduced, without a corresponding change in resources. Examples include:

- a capitalization or bonus issue (sometimes referred to as a stock dividend)
- a bonus element in any other issue, for example a bonus element in a rights issue to existing shareholders
- a share split
- a reverse share split (consolidation of shares).

In these circumstances, the calculation of the EPS in Activity 24.7 needs to be modified. In all those circumstances where these 1 million ordinary shares have been issued at less than market price or for no consideration, the calculations in Activity 24.7 need to take into account this new element. This is illustrated below. A difference will be made between a change in the number of outstanding shares without a change in the resource of the company (e.g. bonus issue and share split) and a change in the number of outstanding shares with a change in the resources of the company, but by which the shares were not issued at market price. We will first illustrate a change in the number of outstanding shares without a change in the resources of the company.

A bonus issue. In a capitalization or bonus issue or a share split, ordinary shares are issued to existing shareholders for no additional consideration. Therefore, the number of ordinary shares outstanding is increased without an increase in resources. The number of ordinary shares outstanding before the event is adjusted for the proportionate change in the number of ordinary shares outstanding as if the event had occurred at the beginning of the earliest period presented. For example, on a two-for-one bonus issue, the number of ordinary shares that are outstanding before the issue is multiplied by three to obtain the new total number of ordinary shares or by two to obtain the number of additional ordinary shares.

In all of these examples, more shares have been issued at no 'cost'. The earnings of the business during the year can only be regarded as relating to the shares at the end of the year, i.e. to all the shares including the new ones. No distortion arises, as no resources were passed into the business when the new shares were created.

ACTIVITY 24.8

Using the same data as in Activity 24.7, but assuming that the shares issued on October X5 were a capitalization issue, calculate the EPS for the year. This means that we now have a bonus issue for no additional consideration, whereby for each three existing shares a new share is issued.

Activity feedback

We now have a capitalization or bonus issue, not a full market price issue of shares, and therefore we assume 4 million shares are in issue for the whole of the year.

(Note this assumption would be the same no matter what point during the year the capitalization was made.)

Thus, = 3 000 000 + 1 000 000 = 4 000 000.

The number of shares in issue can also be calculated from the following:

$$3\ 000\ 000 \times \frac{9}{12} \times \underset{\text{(bonus factor)}}{\frac{4}{3}} + 4\ 000\ 000 \times \frac{3}{12}$$

$$EPS = \frac{400\ 000}{4\ 000\ 000} = €0.10 \text{ per share}$$

We need to think about the implications of such changes for meaningful comparison with the prior year's figures. Adjusted EPS should be calculated in order to provide meaningful prior year comparative figures. Thus, the EPS figure that relates to year X4 needs to be restated. This figure will consist of the earnings for the year (X4) attributable to ordinary shareholders, divided by the new amount of outstanding shares of the current year, namely 4 000 000.

A consolidation of ordinary shares generally reduces the number of ordinary shares outstanding without a corresponding reduction in resources. However, where a share consolidation is combined with a special dividend and the overall effect is a share repurchase at fair value, the reduction in the number of ordinary shares outstanding is the result of a corresponding reduction in resources. The weighted average number of ordinary shares outstanding for the period in which the combined transaction takes place is adjusted for the reduction in the number of ordinary shares from the date the special dividend is recognized.

We will now discuss the calculation of BEPS when the total number of outstanding shares changes and there is a change in the resources of the company. This can arise when a company has a rights issue at less than full market price.

Rights issue at less than full market price. In a rights issue, the exercise price is often less than the fair value of the shares, for example if Fullmar (see Activity 24.7) had issued the 1 million ordinary shares at a price less than market price. Therefore, such a rights issue includes a bonus element as indicated earlier. The number of ordinary shares to be used in calculating BEPS for all periods before the rights issue is the number of ordinary shares outstanding before the issue, multiplied by the following factor:

$$\frac{\text{Fair value per share immediately before the exercise of rights}}{\text{Theoretical ex-rights value per share}}$$

The theoretical ex-rights value per share is calculated by adding the aggregate fair value of the shares immediately before the exercise of the rights to the proceeds from the exercise of the rights and dividing by the number of shares outstanding after the exercise of the rights or a theoretical ex-rights value per share:

$$\frac{\text{Fair value of all outstanding shares before the exercise of rights} + \text{total amount received from exercise of rights}}{\text{Number of shares outstanding before exercise} + \text{number of shares issued in the exercise}}$$

Where the rights themselves are to be publicly traded separately from the shares before the exercise date, fair value for the purposes of this calculation is established at the close of the last day on which the shares are traded together with the rights.

This is complicated! A rights issue combines the characteristics of a capitalization issue and a full market price issue. New resources are passing into the business, so a higher earnings figure, related to these new resources, should be expected. But at the same time, there is a bonus element in the new shares, which should be treated like a capitalization issue. To the extent that the rights issue provides new resources, i.e. equates to an issue at full market price, we need to calculate the average number of shares weighted on a time basis. To the extent that the rights issue includes a discount or bonus element, we need to increase the number of shares deemed to have been in issue for the whole period. The theoretical ex-rights value per share can be calculated as follows:

Step 1. Calculate the total market value of the equity before the rights issue (actual cumulative rights price × number of shares).

Step 2. Calculate the total proceeds expected from the rights issue (issue price × number of shares).

Step 3. Add these two amounts and divide by the total number of shares involved altogether (i.e. by the total number after the rights issue).

We now introduce Activities 24.9 and 24.10 to illustrate the calculations.

ACTIVITY 24.9

Company TEX wants to raise capital and decides to issue one share for every five outstanding shares. The new shares will be issued at a price of €10. The market value of the shares is €25. The one to five issue takes place on 1 March 20X5 and all shares issued are subscribed. The number of outstanding ordinary shares before the issue was 500. The profit for the year 20X4 is €1600 and the profit for the year 20X5 is €2000. Calculate the EPS for 20X4 and 20X5.

Activity feedback

The increase in resources of company TEX takes place during the year, namely on 1 March 20X5. The shares are issued at less than market price, so this includes a bonus element.

We will first determine the theoretical ex-rights value per share. Using that number, we are able to calculate the factor by which we have to multiply the number of outstanding shares before the issue in order to take into account the bonus element included in this issue.

Theoretical ex-rights value per share:

$$((€25 \times 500 \text{ shares}) + (€10 \times 100 \text{ shares}))/(500 + 100)$$
$$= €22.5 \text{ per share}$$

Second, we calculate the multiplying factor, i.e. the fair value per share immediately before the exercise of the rights/theoretical ex-rights value per share:

$$€25/€22.5 = 1.11$$

We calculate the EPS for 20X5 and take into account when the issue took place:

$$\text{EPS 20X5} = €2000/((500 \times 1.11 \times 2/12)$$
$$+ (600 \times 10/12)) = €3.37$$

We need to recalculate the EPS for 20X4 = €1600/ (500 × 1.11) = €2.88.

ACTIVITY 24.10

Trig plc as at 30 June X5 has 600 000 ordinary shares in issue with a current market value of €2 per share. On 1 July X5 Trig plc makes a four for six rights issue at €1.75 and all rights are taken up. Earnings for the year after tax and preference dividends are €81 579 and the previous year's EPS was declared as 9c. Calculate the EPS figure that should be shown in the financial statements for the year ended 31 December X5.

Activity feedback

First, we calculate the theoretical ex-rights value per share: [(600 000 × €2) + (400 000 × €1.75)]/1000 000. This is equal to 1 900 000/1000 000 = 1.9.

Therefore, the adjustment factor is 2/1.9. The number of ordinary shares to be used in calculating the basic earnings per share for all periods before the rights issue is the number of ordinary shares outstanding before the issue multiplied by the adjustment factor.

Second, we calculate the number of shares outstanding for the whole financial year X5, which is:

$$[600\ 000 \times \tfrac{1}{2} \times 2/1.9] + [1\ 000\ 000 \times \tfrac{1}{2}] = 815\ 789$$

The earnings per share for the year ended 31 December X5 is therefore:

$$81\ 579/\ 815\ 789 = 10c \text{ per share}$$

Third, we need to recalculate the previous year's EPS:

$$9 \times 1.9/2 = 8.55c \text{ per share}$$

A reduction has occurred in the previous year's EPS as we have inserted the bonus element of the rights, and we assume that this element has happened for the earlier period reported.

Diluted EPS

Besides BEPS, a company must also disclose its DEPS. When there are securities existing at the year end that will have a claim on equity earnings from some time in the future, then it is clear that at this future time the claim of each currently existing share will, other things being equal, be reduced (or diluted). It is likely to be useful to current shareholders and others to give them a picture of what the EPS would be if this dilution were to take place. This is done by recalculating the current year's BEPS as if the dilution had already occurred.

For the calculation of the numerator of DEPS, the starting amount will be the earnings amount of the BEPS adjusted for the after-tax effect of:

- any dividends or other items related to dilutive potential ordinary shares deducted in arriving at profit or loss attributable to ordinary equity holders of the parent entity as calculated in accordance with the calculation done for the BEPS
- any interest recognized in the period related to dilutive potential ordinary shares
- any other changes in income or expense that would result from the conversion of the dilutive potential ordinary shares.

In the denominator of the DEPS, the number of ordinary shares shall be the weighted average number of ordinary shares calculated in accordance with paragraphs 19 and 26 (which relate to the denominator of the BEPS), plus the weighted average number of ordinary shares that would be issued on the conversion of all the dilutive potential ordinary shares into ordinary shares. Dilutive potential ordinary shares shall be deemed to have been converted into ordinary shares at the beginning of the period or, if later, the date of issue of the potential ordinary shares.

Further, it is interesting to note that potential ordinary shares shall be treated as dilutive when, and only when, their conversion to ordinary shares would decrease EPS or increase loss per share from continuing operations (para. 41).

This implies that the impact of potential ordinary shares with anti-dilutive effect on EPS is not taken into account when calculating DEPS. Potential ordinary shares are anti-dilutive when their conversion to ordinary shares would increase EPS or decrease loss per share from continuing operations. As a result, an investor will only be informed numerically about the negative impact of potential ordinary shares on the future EPS figure. A positive impact will not be calculated.

We will illustrate the calculation of DEPS in Activity 24.11.

ACTIVITY 24.11

The summarized income statement for EPS plc for the year ended 20X1 is as follows:

	€	€
Profit before taxation		1 000 000
Taxation (including deferred adjustment)		400 000
		600 000
Preference dividend	50 000	
Ordinary dividend	100 000	
		150 000
		450 000

The number of ordinary shares in issue is 2 million.

In addition to the 2 million ordinary shares already in issue, however, there exists convertible loan stock of €500 000 bearing interest at 10 per cent. This may be converted into ordinary shares between 20X3 and 20X6 at a rate of one ordinary share for every €2 of loan stock held. Corporation tax is taken for convenience as 50 per cent. Calculate the fully diluted EPS.

Activity feedback

The fully diluted EPS is found as follows. If the conversion is fully completed, then there will be two effects:

ACTIVITY 24.11 (Continued)

- The share capital will increase by 250 000 shares (1 share for every €2 of the €500 000 loan).
- The profit after tax will increase by the interest on the loan no longer payable less the extra tax on this increase. The interest at 10 per cent on €500 000 is €50 000, but the extra tax on this profit increase would be 50 per cent of €50 000, i.e. €25 000.

So profit after tax, and therefore 'earnings', will increase by 50 000 – 25 000 = €25 000. Fully diluted EPS will be:

$$\frac{600\ 000 + 25\ 000 - 50\ 000}{2\ 000\ 000 + 250\ 000}$$

$$= \frac{575\ 000}{2\ 250\ 000}$$

$$= 25.6c \text{ per share}$$

Remember that the fully diluted EPS is a hypothetical calculation. It assumes total conversion into equity participation. The extent to which this assumption is likely in any particular circumstance is irrelevant.

In determining whether potential ordinary shares are dilutive or anti-dilutive, each issue or series of potential ordinary shares is considered separately rather than in aggregate. The sequence in which potential ordinary shares are considered may affect whether they are dilutive. Therefore, to maximize the dilution of BEPS, each issue or series of potential ordinary shares is considered in sequence from the most dilutive to the least dilutive, i.e. dilutive potential ordinary shares with the lowest 'earning per incremental share' are included in the DEPS calculation before those with a higher earning per incremental share. Options and warrants are generally included first, because they do not affect the numerator of the calculation.

IAS 33 considers a number of financial instruments as potentially dilutive and describes their effect on the DEPS figure in the following order:

- options, warrants and equivalent instruments (paras 45–48)
- convertible instruments (paras 42–51)
- contingently issuable shares (paras 52–61)
- purchase options (para. 62)
- written put options (para. 63).

We will illustrate the impact of options on the DEPS figures in Activity 24.12. The impact of convertible instruments on DEPS figures was illustrated in Activity 24.11.

ACTIVITY 24.12

Company Capsi realized a profit of €600 000 in the financial year 20X6 which is attributable to the ordinary shareholders. In the year 20X6, 300 000 shares are outstanding. The BEPS for company Capsi is €2 (= €600 000/300 000). During the year 20X6, 100 000 share options are outstanding of which the exercise price is €10 per share. The market price of the shares of company Capsi was €15 in 20X6. Calculate the DEPS for 20X6.

Activity feedback

We will assume that from the number of potentially outstanding shares, a part will be issued at market price

(Continued)

ACTIVITY 24.12 *(Continued)*

and a part will be issued without consideration. The number of shares considered to be issued at market price will not influence the calculation of the DEPS. The number of shares considered to be issued with no increase in the resources of the company will be assumed to be present from the earliest period which is reported and will have a dilutive effect. Therefore, the prior year DEPS should also be adjusted.

	Profit for ordinary shareholders	Number of shares	EPS
Profit 20X6	600 000		
Weighted average number of shares outstanding in 20X6 basic EPS		300 000	
Basic EPS			2
Weighted average number of shares under options		100 000	
Weighted average number of shares that would have been issued at average market price (100 000 × €10)/€15		(66 666)	
	600 000	344 444	
Diluted EPS			1.74

The latest version of IAS 33 also looks at retrospective adjustments. IAS 33 (para. 64) states that if the number of ordinary or potential ordinary shares outstanding increases as a result of capitalization, bonus issue or share split, or decreases as a result of a reverse share split, the calculation of basic and diluted EPS for all periods presented shall be adjusted retrospectively. If these changes occur after the balance sheet date but before the financial statements are authorized for issue, the per share calculations for those and any prior period financial statements presented shall be based on the new number of shares. The fact that per share calculations reflect such changes in the number of shares shall be disclosed. In addition, basic and diluted EPS of all periods presented shall be adjusted for the effects of errors and adjustments resulting from changes in accounting policies accounted for retrospectively.

The IASB attaches great importance to the EPS figure, as it requires in IAS 33 that the basic EPS as well as the diluted EPS should be disclosed on the face of the income statement for the current year as well as for all other years for which information is presented. EPS should be presented for each class of ordinary share that has a different right to share in net profit for the period. We know that if there are discontinuing operations, two EPS figures have to be disclosed. An entity that reports a discontinuing operation shall disclose the basic and diluted EPS for this line item either on the face of the income statement or in the notes to the financial statements. Even if the EPS figure is negative, the amounts should still be presented.

EPS is presented as a single figure on the face of the income statement. The user of the financial statements can obtain information in the notes to the accounts on the composition of the numerator and the denominator of the basic EPS and diluted EPS.

REAL WORLD ILLUSTRATION

16. Earnings per share

	2014	2013
Basic earnings per share (in CHF)	4.54	3.14
Net profit (in millions of CHF)	14456	10015
Weighted average number of shares outstanding (in millions of units)	3188	3191
Diluted earnings per share (in CHF)	4.52	3.13
Net profit, net of effects of dilutive potential ordinary shares (in millions of CHF)	14 456	10015
Weighted average number of shares outstanding, net of effects of dilutive potential ordinary shares (in millions of units)	3196	3200
Reconciliation of weighted average number of shares outstanding (in millions of units)		
Weighted average number of shares outstanding used to calculate basic earnings per share	3188	3191
Adjustment for share-based payment schemes, where dilutive	8	9
Weighted average number of shares outstanding used to calculate diluted earnings per share	3196	3200

INTERIM FINANCIAL REPORTING

All of the Standards discussed in this chapter relate to the disclosure of information for the purposes of enhancing the decision usefulness of the data communicated through the financial statements. Investors, creditors, suppliers, the government and the workforce all make use of data taken from the financial statements. The financial statements are prepared on a yearly basis only. The investors' community, however, appreciates the provision of financial information on a more frequent basis.

Many stock exchanges require half-yearly interim reports. The US SEC even asks for quarterly interim reports. In Europe, the normal frequency of reporting is biannual. Relatively few European companies follow the North American practice of reporting every quarter. In Europe, markets' half-yearly financial reports have to be issued and, where the issuer is required to prepare consolidated accounts, the condensed set of financial statements shall be prepared in accordance with the IAS applicable to the interim financial reporting as adopted pursuant to the procedure provided for under Article 6 of Regulation (EC) No. 1606/2002. So this means that half-yearly reports are expected to comply with IAS 34, *Interim Financial Reporting* for firms listed on the stock markets in Europe. A company can publish interim financial reports as a result of a requirement by a stock exchange or another regulatory body. The practice of publishing an interim report can also be voluntary.

ACTIVITY 24.13

Look at websites of listed companies and find out how they present their interim financial reports. Do they present other types of financial short-term information?

Activity feedback

Interim financial reports usually consist of a consolidated statement in a kind of abbreviated format and explan-atory notes accompanied by a management report. Besides interim financial statements, companies also often disclose on their website operating data on a half-year, quarterly or even monthly basis. If you look at the websites of some major airlines, you will even find traffic statistics updated on a monthly basis.

Before we present the contents of IAS 34, we want to underline that IAS does not require companies to publish interim financial reports. For entities reporting under IAS voluntarily or who are required by other authorities to issue interim reports, IAS prescribes the minimum content of an interim financial report and the principles for recognition and measurement for complete or condensed financial statements for an interim period.

According to accounting theory, there are two different theoretical approaches towards interim reporting, namely the 'integral' approach and the 'discrete' approach. The 'integral' approach considers the interim report as part of the yearly financial report. This approach means that in order to prepare the interim reports, preparers will first determine the yearly totals and subsequently allocate these over the different interim periods.

The discrete approach considers an interim report as being independent of the 12-month financial accounts and will recognize assets, liabilities, expenses and revenue in the period in which they occur. For example, the interim report for the first six months should reflect the transactions that arose in the first six months.

In principle, the IASB has opted for the discrete approach; however, for a number of items we notice the influence of the integral approach.

Format of interim reports

IAS 34 gives two options for the format of the interim report, and management may choose which one to use. A company can publish either a complete set of financial statements or a set of condensed financial statements for an interim period. The interim period is defined as a financial reporting period that is shorter than a full financial year. If an entity publishes a complete set of financial statements in its interim financial report, the form and content of those statements should conform to the requirements of IAS 1 for a complete set of financial statements.

If, however, the company opts for a set of condensed financial statements, then the minimum components of the interim financial report are presented in para. 8 of IAS 34, as follows:

- condensed statement of financial position
- condensed statement of comprehensive income
- condensed statement showing either (i) all changes in equity or (ii) changes in equity other than those arising from capital transactions with owners and distributions to owners
- condensed cash flow statement
- selected explanatory notes.

What is meant by 'condensed' is explained further in the Standard: 'Those condensed statements should include, at a minimum, each of the headings and subtotals that were included in its most recent annual financial statements'. Additional line items or notes should be included if their omission would make the condensed interim financial statements misleading. Further basic and diluted EPS should be presented on the face of an income statement, complete or condensed, for an interim period.

It is important to stress that IAS 34 starts from the assumption that anyone who reads an entity's interim report will also have access to its most recent annual report. As a result, virtually none of the notes to the annual financial statements is repeated or updated in the interim report. Instead, the interim notes include primarily an explanation of the events and changes that are significant to an understanding of the changes in financial position and performance of the entity since the last annual reporting date. IAS 34 pays explicit attention to the notes accompanying the interim report.

Notes to the interim reports

Concerning these selected explanatory notes, which are typical for interim reports, paragraph 16 states what information as a minimum should be included if material and not disclosed elsewhere in the interim financial report. The information should normally be reported on a financial year-to-date basis. The requirement to present information on a financial year-to-date basis and to ensure an understanding of the current interim period should be carefully noted. It logically has no effect in the context of half-yearly interim statements, but, if interim statements are issued quarterly, then its implications could be significant. The financial report must satisfy the requirements of providing an understanding of the latest quarter (and its comparatives) and also an understanding of the year-to-date (and its comparatives). For example, a first-quarter report (e.g. 1.1.20X2–31.3.20X2) has to show the data for the three months and comparable figures for the first three months of the previous year (1.1.20X1–31.3.20X1); a third-quarter report has to show the data for the first nine months of the current year (e.g. 1.1.20X2–30.9.20X2) and comparative data for the first nine months of the previous year (1.1.20X1–30.9.20X1) and data of the last three months as well (1.7.20X2–30.9.20X2) and the same period in the previous year (1.7.20X1–30.9.20X1).

The entity should also disclose in the notes to the interim reports any events or transactions that are material to an understanding of the current interim period:

- A statement that the same accounting policies and methods of computation are followed in the interim financial statements as compared with the most recent annual financial statements or, if those policies or methods have been changed, a description of the nature and effect of the change.

- Explanatory comments about the seasonality or cyclicality of interim operations

- The nature and amount of items affecting assets, liabilities, equity, net income or cash flows that are unusual because of their nature, size or incidence

- The nature and amount of changes in estimates of amounts reported in prior interim periods of the current financial year or changes in estimates of amounts reported in prior financial years, if those changes have a material effect in the current interim period

- Issuances, repurchases and repayments of debt and equity securities

- Dividends paid (aggregate or per share) separately for ordinary shares and other shares

- Segment revenue and segment result for business segments or geographical segments

- Material events subsequent to the end of the interim period that have not been reflected in the financial statements for the interim period

- The effect of changes in the composition of the entity during the interim period

- Changes in contingent liabilities or contingent assets since the last annual balance sheet date.

We notice that disclosures required in the interim financial reports mainly include items with respect to commentary about the seasonal or cyclical nature of the operations; issues, repurchases and repayments of debt and or equity; dividends paid and commitments to buy property, plant and equipment if material amounts are involved; and litigation information.

Valuation rules for interim reports

IAS 34 stipulates that an entity should apply the same accounting policies in its interim financial report as are applied in its annual financial statements, except for accounting policy changes made after the date of the most recent annual financial statements that are to be reflected in the next annual financial statements.

In many firms, revenues and costs have a seasonal pattern. Think, for example, of firms in the tourism industry or in the ice-cream industry. But in industries where one would not think about seasonal patterns, they may indeed exist, e.g. the sale of cars.

With regard to revenue and expense recognition, explicit guidance is given on revenues and costs which occur unevenly during the year. Revenues that are received seasonally, cyclically or occasionally within a financial year should not be anticipated or deferred as of an interim date if anticipation or deferral would not be appropriate at the end of the entity's financial year. Costs that are incurred unevenly during an entity's financial year should be anticipated or deferred for interim reporting purposes if, and only if, it is also appropriate to anticipate or defer that type of cost at the end of the financial year.

But, what shall we do with costs and revenues resulting from discretionary decisions by management? The costs can be allocated evenly over the quarters or they can be charged to a specific quarter only if they have occurred in that specific quarter. Consider again the valuation rules of IAS 34 mentioned earlier. They do not give that much guidance. To overcome this issue the IASB has presented in appendix B to IAS 34 a list of examples of how to apply the general recognition and measurement principles in relation to interim reports. The examples relate to maintenance, provisions, pensions, intangible assets, year-end bonuses, tax credits and inventories, among other things.

Explicit attention is paid in IAS 34 to the use of accounting estimates. Paragraph 41 stipulates that the measurement procedures to be followed in an interim financial report should be designed to ensure that the resulting information is reliable and that all material financial information that is relevant to an understanding of the financial position or performance of the entity is appropriately disclosed. While measurements in both annual and interim financial reports are often based on reasonable estimates, the preparation of interim financial reports generally will require a greater use of estimation methods than annual financial reports. Again, an appendix is used to give more guidance. IAS 34, appendix C, presents *Examples of the Use of Estimates* (for example, contingencies, pensions, income taxes, provisions, inventories, etc.). With respect to income tax, IAS 34 mentions that if income tax is calculated by the tax authorities on the results of the full year, the charge in the interim results is calculated using the best estimate of the weighted average annual income tax rate expected for the full year. If the interim results are consolidated results, a tax rate is estimated for each jurisdiction in which the group operates and the average applied to the interim results for that jurisdiction, instead of making one estimate for the group as a whole.

The IASB takes a framework-based approach to interim reporting. As such, it would appear that the IASB sees interim reporting as merely a frequent version of annual reporting, whereas the business community often uses the interim reports as a signalling device towards the total result for the financial year.

SUMMARY

A set of individual Standards (IFRS 8, IAS 10, IAS 33 and IAS 34) has been discussed and illustrated in this chapter. They all have in common one purpose, which is to increase the usefulness of reported information so that external users of the annual accounts can make better decisions. We remember, however, that although the Standards have become stricter over the years, room for judgement still remains and that this might threaten the value and relevance of accounting information. However, we also admit that judgement is always inherent in the process of financial reporting.

EXERCISES

Suggested answers to exercises marked ✓ are to be found in the Student online resources, with suggested answers to the remaining questions available in the Instructor online resources.

✓**1**   Calculate from the following information:

  (a) the basic EPS

  (b) the fully diluted EPS.

The capital of the company is as follows:

  £500 000 in 7 per cent preference shares of £1 each

  £1 000 000 in ordinary shares of 25p each

  £1 250 000 in 8 per cent convertible unsecured loan stock carrying conversion rights into ordinary shares as follows: on 31 December 120 shares for each £100 nominal of loan stock.

The P&L account for the year ended 31 December showed:

  (a) profit after all expenses, but before loan interest and corporation tax £1 100 000.

  (b) corporation tax is to be taken as 35 per cent of the profits shown in the accounts after all expenses and after loan interest.

✓**2**   Norman, a public limited company, has three segments which are currently reported in its financial statements. Norman is an international hotel group which reports to management on the basis of region. It does not currently report segmental information under IFRS 8. The results of the regional segments for the year ended 31 May 2008 are as follows:

Region	Revenue external	Revenue internal	Segment results Profit/(loss)	Segment assets	Segment liabilities
	€m	€m	€m	€m	€m
European	200	3	(10)	300	200
South East Asia	300	2	60	800	300
Other regions	500	5	105	2 000	1 400

There were no significant intercompany balances in the segment assets and liabilities. The hotels are located in capital cities in the various regions, and the company sets individual performance indicators for each hotel based on its city location.

Required:

Discuss the principles in IFRS 8, *Operating Segments*, for the determination of a company's reportable operating segments and how these principles would be applied for Norman plc using the information given above.

(ACCA, June 2008)

✓**3** As the recently qualified accountant of Aveler plc, a food retailer with financial reporting date 31 December 20X1, you notice the following items occurring before the accounts are approved by the directors:

    (a) the sale, during the period from 31 December 20X1 to the date the accounts are approved by the directors, of 1000 tins of baked beans

    (b) the purchase, during the period from 31 December 20X1 to the date the accounts are approved by the directors, of 750 tins of baked beans

    (c) the incurrence of other expenses during the period from 31 December 20X1 to the date the accounts are approved by the directors, amounting to €125

    (d) notification that a customer who owes the company €10 000 as at 31 December 20X1 has gone into liquidation on 17 January 20X2

    (e) a fire on 4 January 20X2 destroys all the stock in one warehouse

    (f) the receipt of a letter from the company's insurers stating that it is unclear whether Aveler was actually insured for loss of stock by fire.

Required:

Which of these items are relevant to the accounts for the period ending 31 December 20X1?

4 Outline the circumstances in which events after the reporting date affect the contents of financial statements. In what different ways are those contents affected? Give examples to illustrate your points.

5 Outline the main difficulties with the disclosure of segmental information and outline possible arguments against the disclosure of segmental information.

6 In preparing the financial statements for the year ended 31 December 20X5, Alpha plc discovers the following, all of which are material in the context of the company's results:

• Development expenditure that met the required criteria of IAS 38 was previously capitalized and amortized. Alpha now believes that writing off all expenditure on development work would give a fairer presentation of the results.

• A debt that was previously considered to be collectable as at 31 December 20X4 now requires writing off.

• The estimate of costs payable in respect of litigation was €250 000 as at 31 December 20X4. This has now materialized at €280 000.

• The directors of Alpha are of the view that depreciating vehicles by the reducing balance method rather than the straight line method as previously used will present a fairer view of the financial performance of the company.

Required:

How would you treat the information above in preparing the financial statements at the end of 31 December 20X5? The treatment should be in line with IAS/IFRS.

7   Discuss the advantages and disadvantages of earnings per share as a measure of corporate performance.

8   The IASB issued IAS 33, *Earnings Per Share*, in 1997 with the objective of determining the principles for the calculation and presentation of earnings per share in order to improve performance comparison. Its main focus is on the denominator of the calculation.

Required:

(a) Explain the usefulness of disclosing:

   (i)   a company's basic earnings per share

   (ii) a company's diluted earnings per share.

(b) Below are extracts from the financial statements of Bovine for the year to 31 March 20X3:

Statement of profit or loss and other comprehensive income:	Continuing operations $000	Discontinuing operations $000	Total $000
Profit (loss) before tax	1 460	(200)	1 260
Tax (charge) relief	(280)	50	(230)
Profit from the ordinary activities	1 180	(150)	1 030

Statement of financial position:	€000
Ordinary shares of 25 cents each	1 800
6% Non-redeemable preference shares	500
10% Convertible preference shares $1 each	1 000
Non-current liabilities – 8% Convertible loan stock	1 500

Notes: All shares and loan stocks were in issue prior to the beginning of the current accounting year. The 10 per cent convertible preference shares are convertible to ordinary shares on the basis of three ordinary shares for every five preference shares on 31 March 20X5 at the option of the preference shareholders. The 8 per cent convertible loan stock is redeemable on 31 March 20X5 or can be converted to ordinary shares on the basis of 120 ordinary shares for each $100 of loan stock at the holder's option.

There are also in issue directors' share options for four million ordinary shares. These were issued on 31 March 20X2 and are exercisable on 31 March 20X5 at a price of $1.40 per share. The market price of Bovine's shares can be taken as $2.00 each.

Preference dividends are paid out of taxed profits. Interest on loan stock is an allowable tax reduction. The rate of income tax is 25 per cent.

Required:

Calculate Bovine's basic and diluted earnings per share for the year ended 31 March 20X3.

(ACCA, June 2003, adapted)

9   **(a)**   IAS 10 deals with the accounting treatment of events occurring after the reporting date.

Required:

In assessing the results of a company for the current year, explain why events occurring after the reporting date may be of importance and describe the circumstances where the financial statements should and should not be adjusted.

    (b)   During a review of Penchant's draft financial statements (for the year ended 30 September 20X3) in October 20X3, the following matters came to light:

- The company's internal auditors discovered a fraud on one of the company's contracts. A senior employee had accepted an inducement of $200 000 for awarding the construction of roadways on one of the company's contracts to a particular subcontractor. Investigations showed that the price of the subcontractor was $1 million higher than another comparable tender offer. At 30 September 20X3, the contract was approximately 50 per cent complete.

- An earthquake occurred on 10 October 20X3. It caused damage to an in-progress contract that it is estimated will cost $500 000 to rectify.

- At 30 September 20X3 the company's head office premises were included in the draft financial statements at a value of $12 million. A building surveyor's report showed that they had fallen in value by $2 million. This was due partly to the discovery of ground subsidence and partly to a general fall of 10 per cent in property prices caused by a sharp unexpected rise in interest rates announced in October 20X3.

- In October 20X3 there was a sharp fall in the value of a foreign currency. Penchant was owed a substantial amount for the final instalment of a completed contract whose price was fixed in that currency. The estimated loss due to the fall in the exchange rate has been translated at $250 000.

Note: you may assume the above figures are material.

Required:

For each of the items above, explain how Penchant should treat them under International Financial Reporting Standards.

(ACCA, December 2003)

10   Classify the events below as adjusting or non-adjusting events according to IAS 10:

    (a) shortly after the financial reporting date a survey of an item of property, plant and equipment revealed significant structural problems with the asset

    (b) a lawsuit alleging damages suffered from an accident that occurred after the financial reporting date

    (c) a bankruptcy of a customer that occurs after the financial reporting date

    (d) at the year end, management has the intention to decide upon implementing a restructuring plan. After the financial reporting date, but prior to the issuance date of the company's financial statements, management approves and announces the plan.

11   AB had 10 million $0.50 ordinary shares in issue at 1 January 20X7. On 1 August 20X7 AB issued 2 million $0.50 ordinary shares at a premium of $0.30. Throughout the year AB had in issue $2 million 7 per cent convertible bonds redeemable in 20X9. The terms of the instrument allow the bondholders to convert every $100 of bonds held to 50 ordinary shares of $0.50.

AB's profit available to ordinary shareholders was $3 million for the year ended 31 December 20X7. AB pays tax at 30 per cent.

Required:

Calculate the basic and diluted earnings per share for AB for the year ended 31 December 20X7.

(CIMA P8, May 2009)

12 GA had 5 million $1 ordinary shares in issue at 1 May 20X8. On 30 September 20X8 GA issued a further 2 million $1 ordinary shares at par. Profit before tax for the year ended 30 April 20X9 was $650 000 and the related income tax charge was $210 000.

Required:

Calculate the basic earnings per share for GA for the period to 30 April 20X9.

(CIMA P8, November 2009)

13 AGZ is a listed entity. You are a member of the team drafting its financial statements for the year ended 31 August 2008. Extracts from the draft statement of profit or loss and other comprehensive income, including comparative figures, are shown below:

	2008 $million	2007 $million
Profit before tax	276.4	262.7
Income tax expense	85.0	80.0
Profit for the period	191.4	182.7

At the beginning of the financial year, on 1 September 2007, AGZ had 750 million ordinary shares of 50¢ in issue. At that date, the market price of one ordinary share was 87.6¢.

On 1 December 2007, AGZ made a bonus issue of one new ordinary 50¢ share for every three held.

In 2006, AGZ issued $75 million convertible bonds. Each unit of $100 of bonds in issue will be convertible at the holder's option into 200 ordinary 50¢ shares on 31 August 2012. The interest expense relating to the liability element of the bonds for the year ended 31 August 2008 was $6.3 million (2007 – $6.2 million). The tax effect related to the interest expense was $2.0 million (2007 – $1.8 million).

There were no other changes affecting or potentially affecting the number of ordinary shares in issue in either the 2008 or 2007 financial years.

Required:

(a) Calculate earnings per share and diluted earnings per share for the year ended 31 August 2008, including the comparative figures.

(b) Explain the reason for the treatment of the bonus shares as required by IAS 33, *Earnings Per Share.*

(CIMA P8, November 2008, adapted)

14 BJS, a listed entity, had a weighted average of 27 million ordinary shares in issue during its financial year ended 31 August 20X6. It was also financed throughout the year by an issue of 12 per cent convertible bonds with a par value of $50 million. The bonds are convertible at the option of the holders at the rate of 12 new ordinary shares for every $100 of bonds at par value. The tax rate applicable to BJS was 30 per cent during the financial year. The profit attributable to ordinary shareholders for the year ended 31 August 20X6 was $100 million.

Required:

Calculate earnings per share and diluted earnings per share for BJS for the year ended 31 August 20X6.

(CIMA, November 2006)

15 A quote from a colleague: 'I never look at the operating segment information in a set of financial statements when I am making investment decisions – it's just lots and lots of numbers I won't understand. It must cost entities a significant amount of money to produce the information, which must outweigh the benefits it provides'.

Required:

(a) Discuss the benefits that could be gained by investors from reviewing the operating segment disclosures when making future decisions on investment.

(b) Discuss the limitations of using operating segment information when making investment decisions.

(c) Discuss how the requirements of IFRS 8 *Operating Segments* assist entities in minimizing the costs of producing these disclosures.

(CIMA Financial Management, March 2012)

16 Which one of the following is not included in the definition of an operating segment in accordance with IFRS 8 *Operating Segments*?

(a) A component of an entity that earns the majority of its revenue from sales to external customers.

(b) A component of an entity that engages in business activities from which it may earn revenues and incur expenses.

(c) A component of an entity whose operating results are regularly reviewed by the entity's chief operating decision maker to make decisions about resource allocations and assess performance.

(d) A component of an entity for which discrete financial information is available.

(CIMA Financial Operations, November 2010)

17 According to IFRS 8, *Operating Segments*, which two of the following apply to reportable segments?

(a) The results of the segment must be prepared using the same accounting policies as are used for the financial statements.

(b) A reportable segment is a component of the entity whose operating results are regularly reviewed by the entity's chief operating decision maker in order to make decisions about resource allocations.

(c) Information for reportable segments is required to be prepared based on products and geographical areas.

(d) A reportable segment is every segment that accounts for 10 per cent or more of the sales revenue.

    1 (a) and (b)

    2 (a) and (c)

    3 (b) and (c)

    4 (b) and (d)

(CIMA Financial Operations, May 2011)

18   Which one of the following would be classified by WDC as a non-adjusting event according to IAS 10, *Events After the Reporting Period?* WDC's year end is 30 September 20X1.

(a) WDC was notified on 5 November 20X1 that one of its customers was insolvent and was unlikely to repay any of its debts. The balance outstanding at 30 September 20X1 was $42 000.

(b) On 30 September, WDC had an outstanding court action against it. WDC had made a provision in its financial statements for the year ended 30 September 20X1 for damages awarded of $22 000. On 29 October 20X1 the court awarded damages of $18 000.

(c) On October 20X1 a serious fire occurred in WDC's main production centre and severely damaged the production faculty.

(d) The year-end inventory balance included $50 000 of goods from a discontinued product line. On 1 November 20X1 these goods were sold for a net total of $20 000.

(CIMA Financial Operations, November 2011)

PART THREE

CONSOLIDATED ACCOUNTS AND THE MULTINATIONAL

In this Part, we look in some detail at the preparation of financial statements for several entities that could be regarded as a group. Such statements are known as consolidated financial statements and the techniques for preparing them are complicated and require detailed regulations. The preparation of consolidated accounts is covered in three chapters. The first, Chapter 25, discusses the accounting for business combinations, where an acquirer obtains control over an acquiree, including accounting for goodwill.

After acquisition, the acquirer becomes a parent and the acquiree a subsidiary. In Chapter 26, the requirements and techniques of consolidated financial statements are discussed, where the parent and its subsidiaries are presented as one economic entity. Chapter 27 deals with other relationships between entities, including associates and joint ventures, and how we should display those relationships within financial statements.

Many groups of entities operate in different countries and, therefore, different currencies, so we need rules and regulations for conversion from one currency to another before we can prepare the consolidated financial statements. We also need to consider the accounting for the relatively simple operation of receiving or making payments in a foreign currency. The accounting for this may not be as easy as it first appears. These foreign currency issues are discussed in Chapter 28.

At the end of this Part, we invite you to form your own opinion as to whether the information provided by consolidated accounts and in respect of foreign entities and different currency transactions is helpful to users.

BUSINESS COMBINATIONS

25

OBJECTIVES After studying this chapter you should be able to:

- understand a business combination and how to account for it

- understand the accounting for goodwill

- be able to determine goodwill in more complex situations, such as non-controlling interests and step-acquisitions

- know how to account for disposals, both with and without loss of control

- know the basic requirements of IFRS 3, *Business Combinations.*

INTRODUCTION

Most people are familiar from their daily newspapers with words such as 'takeover' and 'merger'. In this chapter, we will discuss the issues that arise when a takeover or merger, for which we use the expression 'business combination', takes place.

IFRS 3, *Business Combinations*, defines a business combination as a 'transaction or other event in which an acquirer obtains control of one or more businesses'. Characteristic of a business is that it is an integrated set of activities and assets. The result of nearly all business combinations is that one entity, the acquirer, obtains control of one or more other businesses, the acquiree (IFRS 3, para. 4). This is usually realized by acquiring the shares in the acquiree from the former shareholders.

Control

The concept of 'control' is essential in this respect. An acquirer or investor controls an acquiree or investee when it is exposed, or has rights, to variable returns from its involvement with the investee and has the ability to affect those returns through its power over the investee (IFRS 10, para. 5). The essential features are the existence of power and the use of this power to affect the (variable) returns. We will discuss the concept of control further in the next chapter.

We use the term 'parent' to describe the investor that controls and 'subsidiary' for the investee that is being controlled. In discussing business combinations in this chapter, we will use the terms acquirer and acquiree, as this indicates the process of acquisition; after acquisition, the acquirer becomes the parent and the acquiree the subsidiary. The parent will then prepare consolidated financial statements, bringing the figures of parent and subsidiary together. Preparing consolidated financial statements is the subject of Chapter 26.

ACCOUNTING FOR THE BUSINESS COMBINATION: THE BASICS

IFRS 3 requires an entity to account for each business combination by applying the acquisition method (or purchase method). Applying the acquisition method requires:

- identifying the acquirer
- determining the acquisition date
- recognizing and measuring the identifiable assets acquired and the liabilities assumed
- accounting for goodwill.

Identifying the acquirer

In a business combination, control is obtained for the first time. We need to identify who is the acquirer and who the acquiree. The acquirer is not always easy to identify, but the Standard tells us that we have to identify one and that usually there are indications available to us. For example (IFRS 3, paras B14–15):

- If the combination is effected by primarily transferring cash or other assets or by incurring liabilities, the acquirer is usually the entity that transfers the cash or other assets or incurs liabilities.
- The acquirer is usually the entity whose owners as a group retain or receive the largest portion of the voting rights to the combined entity.
- If the business combination results in the management of one of the combining entities being able to dominate the selection of the management team of the resulting combined entity, the entity whose management is able to dominate is usually the acquirer.
- The acquirer is usually the entity whose owners have the ability to elect or appoint or remove a majority of the members of the governing body of the combined entity.

Note the use of the word 'usually' in the examples.

The Standard also states that a new entity formed to effect a business combination is not necessarily the acquirer. If a new entity is formed to issue equity interests to effect a business combination, one of the combining entities that existed before the business combination shall be identified as the acquirer. The new entity is then considered to be created by, and an extension of, the acquirer.

Determining the acquisition date

The acquisition date is the date on which the acquirer obtains control of the acquiree (IFRS 3, para. 8). This is generally the so-called closing date: the date on which the acquirer legally transfers the consideration, acquires the assets and assumes the liabilities of the acquiree. However, the acquirer might obtain control on a date that is either earlier or later than the closing date.

Recognizing and measuring the identifiable assets acquired and the liabilities assumed

IFRS 3 requires us to allocate the cost of the combination (the acquisition price or purchase price) by recognizing the assets, liabilities and contingent liabilities at their fair values, except for non-current assets (or disposal groups) that are classified as held for sale in accordance with IFRS 5, *Non-current Assets Held for Sales and Discontinued Operations*, which shall be recognized at fair value less costs to sell. The purchase price is the fair value of the consideration without including acquisition costs. The acquirer shall recognize separately the acquiree's identifiable assets, liabilities and contingent liabilities at the acquisition date, but only if they satisfy the following criteria at that date:

- In the case of an asset other than an intangible asset, it is probable that any associated future economic benefits will flow to the acquirer and its fair value can be measured reliably.

- In the case of a liability other than a contingent liability, it is probable that an outflow of resources embodying economic benefits will be required to settle the obligation and its fair value can be measured reliably.

- In the case of an intangible asset or a contingent liability, its fair value can be measured reliably.

It is explicitly recognized that these criteria do 'not preclude' (IFRS 3, para. IE 21) the recognition of brands as separable identifiable assets.

The difference between the purchase price and the fair value of the net assets (assets minus liabilities) is recognized as goodwill. This is commonly known as the purchase price allocation or PPA. Note that it is necessary to determine the fair values of the assets and liabilities and that the acquirer cannot determine the amount of goodwill on the basis of the book values in the financial statements of the acquiree. In identifying the assets and liabilities at fair value, the acquirer might identify intangible assets in accordance with IAS 38 that had not been recognized on the balance sheet of the acquiree. This will be the case for internally generated intangible assets such as brands and customer lists. As we saw in Chapter 13, these may not be recognized in the balance sheet as they are internally generated. However, from the perspective of the acquirer, these intangibles are acquired and therefore need to be recognized at fair value.

Activity 25.1 shows how to account for an acquisition and how to determine goodwill.

ACTIVITY 25.1

H bought 100 per cent of the shares of S at a purchase price of €650 000. The book value of the net assets of S at the acquisition date according to the balance sheet of S was €400 000. The fair value of the net assets of S at the acquisition date was €600 000. Calculate the goodwill on consolidation in accordance with IFRS 3.

Activity feedback

Purchase price	650 000
Net assets at fair value	600 000
Goodwill	50 000

The purchase price or consideration can be in different forms. Activity 25.2 answers this question so you should complete it before reading the answer.

ACTIVITY 25.2

Identify three forms of consideration that could be given in a business combination.

Activity feedback

The consideration given can include:

- *cash*
- *other assets*
- *a business or subsidiary of the acquirer*
- *ordinary or preference equity instruments of the acquirer*
- *options or warrants.*

REAL WORLD ILLUSTRATION

The real world illustrations in this chapter are taken from the integrated annual report 2014 from DSM, a Dutch company in life sciences and materials sciences (pages 120, 121 and 136/137).

Business combinations

Business combinations are accounted for using the acquisition method. The cost of an acquisition is measured as the aggregate of the consideration transferred, including liabilities incurred, measured at acquisition date fair value, and the amount of any non-controlling interest in the acquiree. Acquisition costs incurred are expensed.

As of the acquisition date identifiable, assets acquired, liabilities assumed and any non-controlling interest in the acquiree are recognized separately from goodwill. Identifiable assets acquired and the liabilities assumed are measured at acquisition date fair value. For each business combination, DSM elects whether it measures the non-controlling interest in the acquiree at fair value or at the proportionate share of the acquiree's identifiable net assets.

ACCOUNTING FOR PURCHASED GOODWILL

As stated above, goodwill is the difference between the purchase price and the fair value of the net assets. Goodwill is defined in IFRS 3 (Appendix A) as 'Future economic benefits arising from other assets acquired in a business combination that are not individually identified and separately recognized'.

Why would acquirers pay more than the fair value of the assets and liabilities? In other words, why would the fair value of the shares in the entity acquired be higher than the fair value of the underlying assets and liabilities? The fair value of the shares will normally be determined by reference to the present value of the cash flows from the entity. This present value is normally not fully reflected in assets and liabilities and can be related to 'intangibles' like work force, reputation, innovative capacity, market power, etc.; intangibles that are not specifically identifiable and measurable and are therefore not reflected in the balance sheet. Furthermore, an acquirer might want to pay for goodwill because of synergy possibilities between the entity acquired and the already existing business.

ACTIVITY 25.3

Does goodwill on acquisition meet the IASB's own definition of an asset?

Activity feedback

An asset (Framework, para. 4.4) is a resource controlled by the entity as a result of past events and from which future economic benefits are expected to flow. There is certainly a past event and there must logically be an expectation of future economic benefits in the eyes of the management of the acquirer. But is there a 'resource controlled' by the entity? Remember that, by definition, no 'identifiable asset' is involved. The issue is a complicated, theoretical one and general opinion seems to be that goodwill on acquisition is certainly not a normal asset, but is at least sufficiently asset-like to be treated as if it were one.

We are now in a position to explore the formal requirements of IFRS 3 in relation to goodwill on acquisition. First, look at Activities 25.3 and 25.4.

Goodwill on acquisition might be treated after recognition in a variety of ways. Here are seven possible ways:

1 carry it as an asset and amortize it over its estimated useful life through the profit and loss account

2 carry it as an asset and amortize it over its estimated useful life by writing off against reserves

3 eliminate it against reserves immediately on acquisition

4 retain it in the accounts indefinitely, unless a permanent reduction in its value becomes evident, when an impairment is recognized

5 charge it as an expense against profits in the period when it is acquired

6 show it as a deduction from shareholders' equity (and either amortize it or carry it indefinitely)

7 revalue it annually to incorporate later non-purchased goodwill.

ACTIVITY 25.4

Comment on each of these seven possible treatments in relation to rational justification and usefulness.

Activity feedback

Here are some thoughts, which you may or may not completely agree with:

1 Is a straightforward application of matching the acquisition 'cost' in proportion to the benefit.

2 Seems illogical; amortization represents an expense and therefore should appear in the profit and loss account.

3 This solves the problem as if the item had never existed. It implies that no asset exists, and that equity must face the 'loss' immediately.

4 This is rational if it is accepted that purchased goodwill can be maintained, as a building can. Arguably, however, the reality is that purchased goodwill is gradually being replaced by non-purchased goodwill. It can also be suggested that the costs of maintaining the goodwill are being expensed as they occur and that to charge amortization as well would usually be simple double counting.

5 Seems illogical and excessively prudent.

6 Also seems illogical, and potentially confusing, being essentially a misrepresentation of either 1 or 4.

7 Would be consistent with the trend towards fair value generally, but highly subjective (and inconsistent with legal restrictions in many countries).

Many different methods have been used over the years. The 2013 EU Accounting Directive currently requires method 1, so we find it in all European local GAAPs. Goodwill needs to be amortized over its useful life, with impairment reviews to be made when indications for impairment would exist. In the exceptional situations that a reliable useful life cannot be determined, the useful life will be set at a maximum of ten years. The previous IAS requirement was also method 1. There was a presumption that useful life would not normally exceed 20 years. A longer useful life or an unlimited life with no annual amortization both required annual impairment reviews. In the past, US GAAP allowed a useful life of up to 40 years. IFRS SME still requires method 1.

Method 3 was common for many years in the UK and was found in a number of European national systems. The European Accounting Directive no longer allows this method.

The current IAS requirement is essentially our method 4 (see below).

Goodwill and IFRS 3

The excess of cost over the net fair value of the identifiable assets is the goodwill on acquisition figure. Goodwill is not itself an identifiable asset or liability but a residual amount. Nevertheless, IFRS 3 requires it to be shown as an asset.

IFRS 3 requires that after initial recognition, the business combination goodwill should be measured at cost less any accumulated impairment losses. Thus, this goodwill is not amortized. Instead, the acquirer shall test it for impairment annually, or more frequently if events or changes in circumstances indicate that it might be impaired, in accordance with IAS 36, *Impairment of Assets*. Note that this treatment is exactly consistent with the requirements for identifiable intangible assets with indefinite lives, as discussed in relation to IAS 38 in Chapter 13.

Previously, IFRS did require amortization of business combination goodwill. Whether the new accounting method results in a more robust view of goodwill on the statement of financial position depends on the robustness of the impairment reviews (see below). The rationale for carrying goodwill on the statement of financial position of the combined business at its impaired cost as opposed to amortizing that goodwill through the profit or loss account is outlined in the IASB's Basis for Conclusions to IFRS 3. The Board initially considered three possible treatments for goodwill arising on a business combination:

(a) straight line amortization, but with an impairment test whenever there was an indication that the goodwill might be impaired

(b) non-amortization, but with an impairment test annually or more frequently if events or changes in circumstances indicated that the goodwill was impaired

(c) permitting entities a choice between (a) and (b).

Point (c) was soon discounted in the deliberations because permitting such choices impairs the usefulness to users, as both comparability and reliability are diminished. However, many respondents to the Exposure Draft supported method (a), as the acquired goodwill can be considered to be consumed over time and replaced with internal goodwill. This would be consistent with the general prohibition in IFRS of capitalizing internal goodwill. These respondents felt that straight line amortization over an arbitrary period with impairment tests was a reasonable balance between conceptual soundness and operational issues, given that the pattern of use and the useful life of goodwill are difficult to predict. In other words, (a) was the pragmatic solution. However, the Board was not impressed with pragmatism, being doubtful of the benefits of amortizing acquired goodwill, but not recognizing internal goodwill. They felt that the amortization was unhelpful, as, unlike a tangible fixed asset, goodwill does not have a finite physical utility life. Thus the Board decided that (b) was the way forward; as long as a rigorous and operational impairment test could be devised, then more useful information would be provided to users by the use of (b). Whatever method we use to account for acquired or inherent goodwill in the financial statements has a very large impact on the net assets and profit or loss recorded for the year. If users are not aware of this fact, the decisions they make from using the information given could be flawed.

Negative goodwill

Goodwill is not necessarily a positive amount. The fair value of the net assets might be higher than the purchase price. In this case, the acquirer obtains control of the acquiree company at a discounted price (i.e. as opposed to at a premium). IFRS 3 studiously avoids calling this negative goodwill. The Standard refers to this as a 'bargain purchase'. In practice, this is not so far fetched as it might at first sight appear, in that an acquiring entity may for various reasons (e.g. empire building) be quite willing to purchase an entity with a recent history of trading losses, together with a forecast future of losses. This discount on the purchase price at the date of acquisition may thus be thought of as compensation for anticipated future losses to the acquiring group. One might also reasonably assume that in the medium term future, the group would hope to make this subsidiary profitable.

IFRS 3 states that if the acquirer's interest in the net fair value of the identifiable assets, liabilities and contingent liabilities, recognized in accordance with para. 36, exceeds the cost of the business combination, the acquirer shall:

- reassess the identification and measurement of the acquiree's identifiable assets, liabilities and contingent liabilities and the measurement of the cost of the combination
- recognize immediately in profit or loss any excess remaining after that reassessment.

It follows that negative goodwill, under that or any other label, will not appear in IAS group balance sheets.

Impairment of goodwill

When goodwill is amortized over its useful life (as currently required by the EU Accounting Directive), an impairment review is required whenever there are indications that such an impairment may be required. These were discussed in Chapter 14. In applying the goodwill non-amortization method, an impairment review is required at least once a year and more often when indications for impairment exist (for instance in preparing interim accounts). As we saw in Chapter 14, in an impairment review, the carrying amount of an asset or group of assets (cash-generating units) is compared to its recoverable amount. The recoverable amount of an asset is the higher of its fair value less costs of disposal and its value in use.

Goodwill, by definition, does not generate cash flows independently from other assets or groups of assets and, therefore, the recoverable amount of goodwill as an individual asset cannot be determined. As a consequence, the recoverable amount is determined for the cash-generating unit to which the goodwill belongs. This amount is then compared to the carrying amount of this cash-generating unit and any impairment loss is recognized and attributed first to the goodwill, as discussed later.

It is particularly in relation to the treatment of possible impairment of goodwill that IAS 36 is very detailed and rather complex. The Standard requires goodwill acquired in a business combination to be tested for impairment as part of impairment testing the cash-generating unit(s) to which it relates. It clarifies that:

1 The goodwill should, from the acquisition date, be allocated to each of the acquirer's cash-generating units or groups of cash-generating units that are expected to benefit from the synergies of the business combination, irrespective of whether other assets or liabilities of the acquiree are assigned to those units or groups of units.

2 Each unit or group of units to which the goodwill is allocated should:

   (a) represent the lowest level within the entity at which the goodwill is monitored for internal management purposes

   (b) not be larger than an operating segment as defined by paragraph 5 of IFRS 8, *Operating Segments.*

   (c) If the initial allocation of goodwill acquired in a business combination cannot be completed before the end of the annual period in which the business combination occurs, that initial allocation should be completed before the end of the annual period beginning after the acquisition date.

4 When an entity disposes of an operation within a cash-generating unit (group of units) to which goodwill has been allocated, the goodwill associated with that operation should be:

   (a) included in the carrying amount of the operation when determining the gain or loss on disposal

   (b) measured on the basis of the relative values of the operation disposed of and the portion of the cash-generating unit (group of units) retained, unless the entity can demonstrate that some other method better reflects the goodwill associated with the operation disposed of.

5 When an entity reorganizes its reporting structure in a manner that changes the composition of cash-generating units (groups of units) to which goodwill has been allocated, the goodwill should be reallocated to the units (groups of units) affected. This reallocation should be performed using a relative value approach similar to that used when an entity disposes of an operation within a cash- generating unit (group of units), unless the entity can demonstrate that some other method better reflects the goodwill associated with the reorganized units (groups of units).

By way of example, to illustrate point 4 (above), suppose that an entity sells for €100 an operation that was part of a cash-generating unit to which goodwill has been allocated. The goodwill allocated to the unit cannot be identified or associated with an asset group at a level lower than that unit, except arbitrarily. The recoverable amount of the portion of the cash-generating unit retained is €300. Because the goodwill allocated to the cash-generating unit cannot be non-arbitrarily identified or associated with an asset group at a level lower than that unit, the goodwill associated with the operation disposed of is measured on the basis of the relative values of the operation disposed of and the portion of the unit retained. Therefore 25 per cent of the goodwill allocated to the cash-generating unit is included in the carrying amount of the operation that is sold, and 75 per cent is left in the retained portion.

The Standard permits (not requires) the annual impairment test for a cash-generating unit (group of units) to which the goodwill has been allocated to be performed at any time during an annual reporting period, provided that the test is performed at the same time every year and different cash-generating units (groups of units) are tested for impairment at different times. However, if some of the goodwill allocated to a cash-generating unit (group of units) was acquired in a business combination during the current annual period, the Standard requires that unit (group of units) be tested for impairment before the end of the current period.

The Standard also permits the most recent detailed calculation made in a preceding period of the recoverable amount of a cash-generating unit (group of units) to which goodwill has been allocated to be used in the impairment test for that unit (group of units) in the current period, provided specified criteria are met, as follows:

- The assets and liabilities making up the unit have not changed significantly since the most recent recoverable amount calculation.

- The most recent recoverable amount calculation resulted in an amount that exceeded the carrying amount of the unit by a substantial margin.

- Based on an analysis of events that have occurred and circumstances that have changed since the most recent recoverable amount calculation, the likelihood that a current recoverable amount determination would be less than the current carrying amount of the unit is remote.

REAL WORLD ILLUSTRATION

Intangible assets

Goodwill represents the excess of the cost of an acquisition over DSM's share in the net fair value of the identifiable assets and liabilities of an acquired subsidiary, joint venture or associate. Goodwill paid on acquisition of subsidiaries is included in intangible assets. Goodwill paid on acquisition of joint ventures or associates is included in the carrying amount of these entities. Goodwill recognized as an intangible asset is not amortized but tested for impairment annually and when there are indications that the carrying amount may exceed the recoverable amount. A gain or loss on the disposal of an entity includes the carrying amount of goodwill relating to the entity sold.

We have already calculated goodwill in Activity 25.1. The following Activity contains some further goodwill questions.

ACTIVITY 25.5

1 H acquired 100 per cent of the net assets of S at a fair value of €1 000 000. The net book value of H's net assets was €900 000 and fair value €1 040 000. Identify the value of goodwill.

2 Refer to Activity 25.1. The goodwill was calculated at €50 000 at acquisition date. Assume that the useful life of acquired goodwill is considered to be 10 years. What would be the amount of goodwill after one year?

Activity feedback

1		€
	Purchase price	1 000 000
	Fair value of the net assets acquired	1 040 000
	Negative goodwill on acquisition	40 000

2 *It depends. There is no amortization, so the goodwill is not reduced during its useful life. If there is no impairment, then the goodwill would still be €50 000. If the recoverable amount is lower, this will reduce the amount of goodwill recorded.*

SPECIFIC ISSUES ON ACCOUNTING FOR THE BUSINESS COMBINATION

Non-controlling interests

Until now, we have silently assumed that the acquirer buys 100 per cent of all the shares of the acquiree. This is not necessary in order to obtain control. An acquirer might also buy, for instance, 80 per cent of the shares. An acquirer then still has control over 100 per cent of all the assets and liabilities of the acquiree, but its economic share in equity and results is only 80 per cent. When acquiring only 80 per cent, there is also a so-called 'non-controlling interest' of 20 per cent in the acquiree. The usual expression in the past for a non-controlling interest has been a minority interest, but, as we shall further explain in the next chapter, an entity can have control in another entity without having the majority of the shares. For that reason, the term non-controlling interest is more appropriate.

Why is a discussion of the non-controlling interest of importance in discussing business combinations? After all, if we acquire 80 per cent of the shares, the purchase price is based on 80 per cent of the shares and, from an economical perspective, we only have 80 per cent of the net assets. This is true and is one way of looking at it. Upon consolidation, when the parent consolidates the assets and liabilities for 100 per cent, as we will discuss in the next chapter, a non-controlling interest will be recognized, but this will not affect goodwill. This is how we have accounted for business combinations for some time.

But IFRS 3 allows two views on the measurement of non-controlling interests and related goodwill. Non-controlling interests in the acquiree are required to be measured at either:

1 the non-controlling interest's proportionate share of the acquiree's identifiable net assets at fair value (the view above) or

2 fair value (the new and preferred view).

The second view implies that the purchase price allocation will not be based on the purchase price that the acquirer paid, but on the purchase price that the acquirer would have paid when it acquired 100 per cent of the shares. The goodwill is then also determined on a 100 per cent basis, including the goodwill that is allocated to the non-controlling interest. Thus, depending upon which method is chosen, to value the non-controlling interest will result in different figures in the consolidated financial statements in respect of the non-controlling interest and goodwill.

ACTIVITY 25.6

H bought 80 per cent of the shares of S at a purchase price of €640 000. The fair value of the net assets of S at the acquisition date was €700 000. If H had acquired 100 per cent of the shares of S the purchase price would have been €790 000. The fair value of the non-controlling interest is therefore €150 000 (€790 000 – €640 000). Note that the fair value of the non-controlling interest is not proportional to that of the controlling interest: the price of 80 per cent of the shares is more than four times the price of 20 per cent of the shares. This can be explained by the so-called control premium, the additional value of obtaining control of S. Now calculate the goodwill on consolidation in accordance with IFRS 3, according to both alternatives.

Activity feedback

Alternative 1:

	€
Purchase price	640 000
Net assets at fair value (80%×700 000)	560 000
Goodwill	80 000

Or:

Purchase price	640 000
Non-controlling interests (20% × 700 000)	140 000
	780 000

Net assets at fair value	700 000
Goodwill	80 000

Alternative 2:

Purchase price (on the basis of 100%)	790 000
Net assets at fair value	700 000
Goodwill	90 000

Or:

Purchase price	640 000
Non-controlling interests (at fair value)	150 000
	790 000
Net assets at fair value	700 000
Goodwill	90 000

Activity 25.6 illustrates the accounting for a business combination with a non-controlling interest.

Determining the fair value of the non-controlling interest can be difficult if there is not a ready market in the shares. Furthermore, from the acquirer's perspective, it is somewhat hypothetical to account as if 100 per cent of all the shares have been bought, while the real acquisition was only for 80 per cent.

Business combination achieved in stages

An acquirer sometimes obtains control of an acquiree in which it already holds some of the equity shares. For example, immediately prior to the parent obtaining control of the subsidiary, it may have held a 35 per cent non-controlling interest. If the parent then acquires another 30 per cent, which gives it control, then we have a business combination achieved in stages. IFRS 3 requires us to re-measure the previously held equity interest at its acquisition date fair value, recognizing the resulting gain or loss in profit or loss. The purchase consideration is now the aggregate of the fair value of the non-controlling interest previously held, plus the consideration given for the new purchase to obtain control. The goodwill will be calculated by comparing this total consideration to the fair value of the controlling interest in net assets. Now try Activity 25.7.

ACTIVITY 25.7

H entity holds 30 per cent of the voting shares of S entity which it purchased several years ago at a cost of €250 000. As at 31 December 20X2, H purchased a further 50 per cent of S for a consideration of €600 000. The fair value of S's net assets at 31 December 20X2 is €1 000 000. It is estimated that H paid a control premium of €50 000. Identify the amount to be included in profit and loss, the amount of goodwill and the non-controlling interest to be included in the consolidated financial statements of H as at 31 December 20X2. In calculating goodwill, we will measure the non-controlling interest at the proportionate share of the acquiree's identifiable net assets at fair value (alternative 1 above).

Activity feedback

First, we need to value the original holding at fair value. On the information we have available, we must assume that the fair value of the original holding can be calculated by reference to the consideration paid for the new 50 per cent holding after disregarding the control premium.

	€
Control premium:	50 000
Consideration for 50% without premium	550 000

Fair value of whole of S using consideration (550 000 × 100/50)	1 100 000
Fair value of 30% original holding (30% × 1 100 000)	330 000
Original cost of 30% holding	250 000
Gain on holding (330 000 – 250 000) transferred to profit and loss	80 000
Calculation of goodwill:	
Consideration for 80% in S: 330 000 + 600 000	930 000
Fair value of net assets (80% × 1 000 000)	800 000
Goodwill on consolidation	130 000
Non-controlling interest (20% × 1 000 000)	200 000

The journal entry on the acquisition of the 50 per cent interest in the consolidated accounts would be:

Dr Net assets	1 000 000
Dr Goodwill	130 000
Cr Cash	600 000
Cr Investment in associate	250 000
Cr Gain on investment	80 000
Cr Non-controlling interest	200 000

Subsequent re-measurement of amounts in a business combination

It is not always possible to have a definitive purchase price calculation when drawing up the financial statements. This will especially be the case when acquisitions have been made towards the year end. IFRS 3 allows the inclusion of provisional amounts in the consolidation process. IFRS 3 identifies a measurement period within which adjustments can be made to these provisional amounts to ensure compliance with IFRS 3 requirements. The measurement period cannot exceed one year from the date of acquisition and ends when the acquirer receives the information it was seeking about facts and circumstances that existed as of the acquisition date that would change the provisional figures, or the acquirer learns that more information is not obtainable. Adjustments should be made retrospectively from the acquisition date. When adjusting the provisional figures, the acquirer needs to ensure that only adjustments pertinent to the circumstances at acquisition are included. Now attempt the following Activity.

ACTIVITY 25.8

H entity acquired the whole of the voting shares of S entity on 31 December 20X7. When preparing the consolidated financial statements on 31 December 20X7, H included provisional figures for the fair value of some of S's non-current assets and liabilities. As at 31 March 20X8, the following information was available on these non-current assets and liabilities:

Non-current asset/(liability)	Provisional fair value 31 December 20X7 €	Fair value 31 March 20X8 or sale proceeds €
Building 1	500 000	650 000
Building 2	350 000	400 000
Plant and equipment	90 000	85 500
(Liability to pay damages on accident)	250 000	300 000

Building 1 was sold on 10 January 20X8. Building 2 was sold on 31 March 20X8. The higher sales price of building 2 was caused by an increase during the two months from 1 February 20X8.

Plant and equipment is depreciated on a straight line basis and has an expected remaining life of five years and no residual value.

The damages are finally agreed with the third party involved as at 31 March 20X8.

Identify the assets/liabilities that would require re-measurement in the consolidated financial statements as at the acquisition date.

Activity feedback

Building 1 will be adjusted in the consolidated statements at acquisition date from €500 000 to €650 000 as the sale value on 10 January is likely to reflect the fair value as at 31 December 20X7.

Building 2 will not be adjusted assuming that the increase in value is due to the period between February and the end of March 20X8.

Plant and equipment will not be adjusted as the fall in value reflects the depreciation charged for that three-month period (90 000 / 60 = 1500 depreciation per month, so 4500 for three months).

The damages will be adjusted to €300 000 as the final settlement figure provides evidence of the liability at acquisition date.

The two re-measurements will reduce goodwill on consolidation by €100 000.

Contingent consideration

Acquisition agreements often provide for adjustment to the acquisition price of an acquisition dependent on future events. In terms of IFRS 3, this is a contingent consideration: the consideration (acquisition price) is contingent upon future events. These future events can be:

- the results of the acquiree's operations exceeding or falling short of an agreed level
- changes in the market price of securities issued as part of the purchase consideration.

These contingent considerations are sometimes indicated as 'earn out liabilities'. Changes in the acquisition price resulting from a contingent consideration are not measurement adjustments as discussed above. At the acquisition date, the acquirer should determine the fair value of the contingent consideration. When the contingent consideration is classified as equity (for instance a contingent consideration in the form of shares), there is no re-measurement and the subsequent settlement shall be accounted for within equity. When the contingent consideration is classified as a liability, it will be re-measured to its best estimate at every balance sheet date. Re-measurements will be accounted for in profit and loss.

ACTIVITY 25.9

Should possible subsequent adjustments to the acquisition price of an acquisition be ignored at the date of acquisition or should a reasonable estimate of the probable effect be made?

Activity feedback

Accounting judgements concerned with probability and reliable estimates elsewhere should have led you to the conclusion that we should make a reasonable estimate of the purchase consideration including these future events based on the adjustment being probable and measurement reliable.

ACTIVITY 25.10

Entity A acquired all the issued share capital of entity B when the fair value of B's net assets was €500 000. The cost of the acquisition was €600 000, but included a proviso that an additional payment needed to be made when earnings of B were 10 per cent above the previous year; the consideration would be increased by €100 000 for each percentage point above 10 per cent. A considers that there is a 60 per cent chance that earnings levels will not be above the 10 per cent increase, a 30 per cent chance that the increase will be 11 per cent (additional payment of €100 000) and a 10 per cent chance that the increase will be 12 per cent (additional payment of €200 000), including the time value of money, A calculates the fair value of the earn out liability to be €45 000. In addition, A guaranteed the market price of the securities issued to B's shareholders on the acquisition for six months. The acquisition date was 1 October 20X4 and consolidated financial statements were drawn up as at 31 December 20X4.

In the year ended 31 December 20X5, it was noted that B's earnings were 11 per cent in excess of the previous year and that the market price of the securities had fallen by €25 000.

Identify the goodwill on acquisition and adjustments necessary in the consolidated financial statements as at 31 December 20X5.

Activity feedback

	€
Purchase consideration (fixed)	600 000
Contingent consideration	45 000
Total purchase consideration	645 000
Fair value of net assets	500 000
Goodwill	145 000

Subsequent events create an increase in the earn out liability of €55 000 to €100 000. This increase will be shown in profit and loss and does not affect the purchase consideration and goodwill.

The fall in the market price of the securities will be dealt with by a further issue of securities by A to B. The increase in securities will reduce the premium or increase the discount on the initial issue; it will also not affect the purchase consideration.

It is important to note that the initial estimate of fair value determines the amount of goodwill.

Transactions with the non-controlling shareholder

A parent that already has control can buy shares from the non-controlling shareholder. This is not a business combination as there is no change in control. IFRS 10.23 requires these transactions to be accounted for as equity transactions. It is not allowed to recognize an additional amount of goodwill on the new shares acquired.

A parent can also sell shares to other parties and remain in control. These transactions are also accounted for in equity and do not result in a profit or loss.

ACTIVITY 25.11

The value of a subsidiary's net assets at 31 March 20Y2 is €400 000. At this date the parent, which held a 100 per cent share in the subsidiary, disposes of 40 per cent for €200 000. On the original acquisition of the subsidiary,

goodwill of €80 000 arose. This goodwill has not subsequently been impaired and is in addition to the net assets of €400 000. How should the parent account for this transaction?

ACTIVITY 25.11 *(Continued)*

Activity feedback

	€
Consideration received	200 000
Share of net assets disposed of (including goodwill (40% × (400 000 + 80 000))	192 000
'Profit' on disposal to be recognized in equity	8 000

If, for example, the goodwill had been impaired to €60 000, then the impairment loss would have been recognized in previous profit and loss accounts. The 'profit' on disposal, assuming no change in the proceeds, would then have been calculated as follows:

	€
Consideration received	200 000
Share of net assets disposed of (including goodwill (40% × (400 000 + 60 000))	184 000
'Profit' on disposal to be recognized in equity	16 000

LOSS OF CONTROL

In this section, we discuss the opposite of a business combination: the loss of control. A parent can lose control of a subsidiary by, for example:

- selling part of its ownership such that it is left with less than 50 per cent
- the subsidiary becoming subject to control by a government, court administrator or regulator
- the subsidiary becoming subject to some other contractual agreement that results in another investor gaining control.

In the simplest situation, an entity sells all the shares of the subsidiary. The former parent will then derecognize the assets including any goodwill and liabilities of the subsidiary at their carrying amounts at the date when control is lost. The difference with the fair value of the consideration received is recorded as a gain on sale.

When the former parent still retains an interest in the former subsidiary, IFRS 10, para. 25, requires that the remaining investment is revalued at fair value with the difference being accounted for in profit and loss. This in fact means that the transaction is accounted for as if all the shares held had been sold and a new investment had been acquired at fair value.

ACTIVITY 25.12

We use a slightly different fact pattern than in Activity 25.11.

The value of a subsidiary's net assets at 31 March 20Y3 is €400 000. At this date the parent, which held a 100 per cent share in the subsidiary, disposes of 70 per cent for €420 000. On the original acquisition of the subsidiary, goodwill of €80 000 arose. This goodwill has not subsequently been impaired and is in addition to the net assets of €400 000. The fair value of the remaining 30 per cent is estimated to be €150 000 (this is not proportional to the fair value of the 70 per cent interest as the 70 per cent interest contains a control premium). How should the parent account for this transaction?

Activity feedback

	€
Consideration received	420 000
Share of net assets disposed of (including goodwill (70% × (400 000 + 80 000))	336 000
Profit on shares sold	84 000
Fair value of remaining shares	150 000
Book value of remaining shares (30% × (400 000 + 80 000)	144 000
Profit on shares held	6 000
Total profit (included in profit and loss account)	90 000

DISCLOSURE REQUIREMENTS OF IFRS 3

IFRS 3 requires such disclosures that 'enable users of financial statements to evaluate the nature and financial effect of business combinations' (para. 59). Disclosure is required as follows:

- names and descriptions of combining entities
- acquisition date
- percentage of voting equity instruments acquired
- primary reason for the business combination and a description of how the acquirer obtained control of the acquiree
- cost of the combination and the components of the cost
- details of operations disposed of due to the combination
- details of fair values of assets, liabilities and contingent liabilities acquired
- amount of any negative goodwill in a bargain purchase and a description of reasons why the transaction resulted in a gain
- amount of acquiree's profit or loss since the acquisition date included in the acquirer's profit or loss
- a reconciliation of the carrying amount of goodwill at the beginning and end of the reporting period.

You can read the full disclosure requirements in Appendix B of IFRS 3.

REAL WORLD ILLUSTRATION

DSM Acquisitions 2014

In January 2014 DSM obtained control of Yantai Andre Pectin co., Ltd. a China-based manufacturer of apple and citrus pectin, a key food hydrocolloid providing texture, as well as pectin-related food products. Andre Pectin is the only significant pectin manufacturer in Asia with premier access to the world's fastest growing specialty food ingredients market. DSM already owned 29% of the shares of Andre Pectin together with call options to buy out the other shareholders and obtained control by placing a DSM management team in the company. From January 2014 onwards the financial statements of Andre Pectin have been consolidated by DSM and reported in the Nutrition segment. The acquisition strengthens and complements DSM's position as a pectin manufacturer in Asia with access to the global food ingredients markets. In accordance with IFRS 3 the purchase price of Andre Pectin had to be allocated to identifiable assets and liabilities acquired. Goodwill amounted to € 1 million. The non-controlling interest in Andre Pectin was measured at the proportionate share of the value of net identifiable assets acquired and amounted to €45 million at

the acquisition date. At the acquisition date the fair value of the interest in Andre Pectin was not materially different from the carrying amount. The acquisition of Andre Pectin contributed €36 million to net sales and €7 million to EBITDA in 2014. Andre Pectin-related exceptional items amounted to €3 million before tax (see note 6 Exceptional items).

Up to one year from the acquisition date the initial accounting for business combinations needs to be adjusted to reflect additional information that has been received about facts and circumstances that existed at the acquisition date and would have affected the measurement of amounts recognized as of that date. As a result of such adjustments the values of assets and liabilities recognized may change in the one year period from the acquisition date which resulted in some adjustments to the opening balance sheet of Tortuga. The Purchase Price Allocation (PPA) of Andre Pectin was finalized in the course of the year.

The impact of all acquisitions made in 2014, including adjustments to the initial accounting for Tortuga on DSM's consolidated balance sheet, at the date of acquisition, is summarized in the following table.

2014	Andre Pectin		Tortuga (final PPA)[2]			Total
	Book value	Fair value	Book value	Fair value total	Change in fair value	Fair value
Assets						
Intangible assets	3	29	1	92	(2)	27
Property, plant and equipment	33	36	80	107	—	36

REAL WORLD ILLUSTRATION (*Continued*)

Other non-current assets	9	9	12	7	(5)	4
Inventories	11	12	34	45	—	12
Receivables	12	12	94	96	2	14
Cash and cash equivalents	3	3	3	2	(1)	2
Total assets	**71**	**101**	**224**	**349**	**(6)**	**95**
Non-controlling interests	27	45	—	—	—	45
Liabilities						
Non-current liabilities	—	5	12	26	(1)	4
Current liabilities	33	33	130	131	1	34
Total non-controlling interests and liabilities	**60**	**83**	**142**	**157**	**—**	**83**
Net assets	**11**	**18**	**82**	**192**	**(6)**	**12**
Acquisition price (in cash)		—		350	—	—
Value of associate contributed		19		—	—	19
Consideration		**19**		**350**	**—**	**19**
Goodwill		**1**		**158**	**6**	**7**
Goodwill available for tax purposes (included in the above)		—		152	—	—
Acquisition costs recognized in exceptional items1		2		2	1	3
Contingent liabilities included in fair value		—		—	—	—

¹included in General and administrative: Other costs
² In 2014 the final Purchase Price Allocation (PPA) of tortuga was performed, which has led to the above changes in the fair value, compared to the draft PPA

ALTERNATIVE METHODS IN ACCOUNTING FOR BUSINESS COMBINATIONS

In this chapter, we discussed the accounting for business combinations and identified one method prescribed: acquisition accounting (or purchase accounting). We will now discuss two alternative methods: pooling of interests accounting and carry over accounting.

Pooling of interests accounting

Prior to the issue of IFRS 3, IAS 22, which now no longer exists, identified another method of accounting for a business combination: the pooling of interests method (alternative name: 'merger accounting'). According to this method, the assets and liabilities of the entities would be combined on the basis of their book values. This method was required in a situation of a 'uniting of interests'. IAS 22 defined this as follows:

> A uniting of interests is a business combination in which the shareholders of the combining enterprises combine control over the whole, or effectively the whole, of their assets and operations to achieve a continuing mutual sharing in the risks and benefits attaching to the combined entity such that neither party can be identified as an acquirer.

Many respondents to the IASB on the issue of business combinations believe such uniting of interests (or true mergers) still occur, even if only rarely, and that it will be impossible in such cases to identify an acquirer as required by IFRS 3. IFRS 3 has now eliminated the use of pooling of interests accounting method because:

- it has virtually eliminated the idea that true mergers do occur
- in no circumstances, according to the Board, does the pooling of interests method provide superior information to that provided by the acquisition method.

The Basis for Conclusions to IFRS 3 does conclude that if true mergers exist, which it doubts, then a better accounting method to use for them could be the 'fresh start method'. This method requires both entities in the business combination to value all assets at fair value. However, the IASB also disregarded the fresh start method and has no plans to debate it.

However, pooling of interest accounting is not fully ruled out for entities applying IFRS. Transactions under common control (internal reorganizations within a group) are out of the scope of IFRS 3 and, in practice, pooling of interests accounting (or carry over accounting, see below), is applied in these situations, even if the internal reorganization is not a true merger from the perspective of the entities involved.

Differences between acquisition accounting and pooling of interests accounting

The main differences between the two methods can be examined under the headings of:

- acquisition date
- goodwill
- share premium (paid-in surplus)
- reserves.

Acquisition date Applying pooling of interests accounting does not involve the identification of an acquisition date, as with acquisition accounting. There is no acquisition, and therefore no acquisition date. In fact, there is a new reporting entity and the consolidated financial statements are presented as if the new reporting entity had always existed. Not only are all combined figures presented as from the first date of the statutory year, comparative figures are also presented as if the merger had been effected in that comparative year.

Goodwill With a merger, there is no change in ownership and we merely have a pooling of resources. A consolidated statement of financial position produced for a merger situation will simply combine the existing statements of financial position, and the assets will therefore remain at the book values at which they appear in the original statements of financial position of the separate entities. That is to say, no goodwill is recognized in the new statement of financial position (since none is in fact acquired).

However, with acquisition accounting, the net assets of the entity acquired will be revalued as at the date of acquisition and, of course, the difference between the purchase consideration and this asset revaluation will give rise to goodwill (premium) on acquisition.

Share premium With an acquisition where an entity issues shares to acquire another entity, the cost of the investment is recorded in the acquirer's statement of financial position and, of course, any shares issued in consideration are recorded at fair value, i.e. nominal value plus share premium created. However, with a merger situation, shares issued in the share-for-share exchange involved are recorded at nominal value, i.e. no share premium is created.

Reserves Applying acquisition accounting results in reserves that are equal to those of the acquirer before the acquisition. However, pooling of interests accounting will result in reserves that are the sum of the reserves of the acquirer and the acquiree.

It is obvious when one considers these differences why pooling of interests accounting was popular. Following on from this, it can be seen that with pooling of interests accounting the statement of financial position of the new entity does not carry a goodwill figure that might have to be impaired against income (and have to be amortized during the period that IAS 22 was applicable). Also, the revaluation to fair value of assets would lead to higher depreciation amounts. However, the benefit of presenting higher earnings comes with a lower equity. It is appropriate here to consider an example of the application of pooling of interests accounting and also to contrast it with acquisition accounting (see Activity 25.13).

ACTIVITY 25.13

Two companies, A and M, have the following respective statements of financial position as at 31 December 20X6:

	A	M
	€	€
Ordinary shares (€1)	9 000	6 000
Reserves	2 000	3 000
	11 000	9 000
Net current assets	5 000	2 000
Plant and machinery	6 000	7 000
	11 000	9 000

A acquired the whole of the share capital of M on the basis of a one-for-one share exchange as at the given date, at which point the market values of their respective shares were:

A	€4
M	€4

The fair values of M's tangible assets as at 31 December 20X6 were:

	€
Plant and machinery	8 000
Net current assets	2 500

In accounting for this transaction, what would be the differences between applying the acquisition method, with A being the acquirer, and the pooling of interests method?

Activity feedback

The acquisition method requires us to calculate the acquisition price, the fair value of the net assets and the amount goodwill.

The acquisition price is 6000 (the number of shares A has to issue to acquire all shares of M in a one-for-one share exchange) x €4 (the market value of the shares) = €24 000.

The fair value of the net assets is €10 500 (€8000 + €2500).

Therefore, the goodwill is the difference between the two: €24 000 – €10 500 = €13 500.

The equity of A will be €35 000, consisting of share capital of €15 000 (€9000 + €6000), share premium of €18 000 (6 000 x (€4 – €1)) and reserves of €2000, and represented by net current assets of €7500 (€5000 + €2500), plant and machinery of €14 000 (€6000 + €8000) and goodwill of €13 500.

Applying pooling of interests accounting would result in combining the existing carrying amounts of assets and equity's, without fair value adjustments, goodwill and a share premium. The equity of A will then be € 20 000, consisting of share capital of €15 000 (€9000 + €6000) and reserves of €5000 (€2000 + €3000), and represented by net current assets of €7000 (€5000 + €2000) and plant and machinery of €13 000 (€6000 + €7000).

Carry over accounting

An alternative for applying pooling of interests accounting in mergers and acquisition under common control is carry over accounting. This method is in between acquisition accounting and pooling of interests accounting. Carry over accounting requires identifying an acquisition date, but at this date the business combination is accounted for by combining the entities at their book values, so without revaluation to fair values and without recognizing goodwill. Comparative numbers are not restated, as would be the case in applying pooling of interests accounting.

ACTIVITY 25.14

Refer back to Activity 25.13. Now assume that A and M are both subsidiaries within a group. The financial position on 31 December 20X6 is as given in Activity 25.13. The acquisition date is 31 December 20X6. During 20X6, before the acquisition date, A made a profit of €100 and M made a profit of €90. What would be the comprehensive income for A for 20X6 when applying the following methods:

- acquisition accounting
- pooling of interests accounting
- carry over accounting?

Activity feedback

For both acquisition accounting and carry over accounting, the acquisition date is important. As *the acquisition date was 31 December 20X6, no profit of M would be accounted for by A. So A would report a comprehensive income of €100. Pooling of interests accounting implies that A and M would always have been combined. Therefore, the profits of A and M are added together, and the profit of A, being the sole shareholder of B, would be €190. The comparative figures of A and M would also be combined, both in the statement of financial position and in the statement of comprehensive income.*

After the acquisition, carry over accounting would result in the same statement of financial position as pooling of interests accounting.

SUMMARY

In this chapter, we have dealt with accounting for business combinations. All business combinations are accounted for by applying the acquisition method. The acquirer is the entity that obtains control of the acquiree. The acquisition date is the date that control is obtained. At that date, the purchase price is allocated to assets, liabilities and contingent liabilities (all to be measured at fair value) and the remaining amount is goodwill. Under IFRS, goodwill is not amortized but only tested for impairment. Goodwill might be negative, in which case the amount is recognized in profit and loss.

In the case of acquiring less than 100 per cent of the shares, there will be a non-controlling interest. A business combination can be achieved in stages. The previously held equity interest will then be re-measured at its acquisition date fair value, recognizing the re-measurement in profit and loss. A business combination can also be provisional, in which case the fair values of assets and liabilities might be subsequently re-measured, effecting goodwill if the re-measurement is within a year after the acquisition. Changes in contingent considerations do not affect goodwill, but are accounted for in profit and loss.

All transactions with the non-controlling shareholder, without changing the existence of control, are accounted for in equity. If, however, there is a loss of control, the gains or losses are recognized in profit and loss, including the gain to fair value re-measurement of the remaining investment.

IFRS 3 requires extensive disclosures.

This chapter also discussed two alternative concepts in accounting for a business combination: pooling of interests accounting and carry over accounting. These methods in substance combine carrying amounts of the assets and liabilities of the entities participating in the business combination, with or without restating comparative numbers, and without fair valued adjustments and goodwill.

After the business combination, the acquirer will be the parent company and the acquiree the subsidiary company. The parent will prepare consolidated accounts, which is the topic of the next chapter.

You will find a limited number of exercises at the end of this chapter. There are many more exercises at the end of Chapter 26, many of them integrating the subjects of business combinations and consolidated financial statements.

EXERCISES

Suggested answers to exercises marked ✓ are to be found in the Student online resources, with suggested answers to the remaining questions available in the Instructor online resources.

1   On 30 June 2004, *C* purchased 75 per cent of the equity shares of *D* for $16 million. The statement of financial position of *D* showed net assets of $14 million. This was before taking account of the following items:

- The market value of *D*'s properties at 30 June 2004 (included in the statement of financial position of *D* at a carrying value of $8 million) was $10 million.

- On 30 June 2004, *D* was in the process of negotiating an insurance claim in respect of inventory that was damaged before that date. The claim was for $1 million and although nothing has yet been received, the directors of *D* are confident that the claim will be successful.

Required:
What is the goodwill on consolidation that will appear in the consolidated statement of financial position of C at 30 June 2004?

(CIMA paper, November 2004)

2   Appraise the effects on a group's financial statements of the use of merger accounting as opposed to acquisition accounting in order to account for business combinations.

3   *HA* acquired 100 per cent of *SB*'s equity shares on 1 April 2010 for $185 000. The values of *SB*'s assets at that date were:

	Book value	Fair value
	$000	$000
Property	100	115
Plant and equipment	75	70

On 1 April 2010, all other assets and liabilities had a fair value approximately equal to their book value. *SB*'s equity at 1 April 2010 was:

	$000
$1 equity shares	150
Share premium	15
Retained earnings	(22)

Required:
Calculate the goodwill arising on the acquisition of *SB*.

(CIMA, May 2011)

4   ER acquired 80 per cent of the 1 million $1 equity shares of MW on 1 January 2012 when MW's retained earnings were $1 050 000. The consideration for the acquisition consisted of $400 000 cash paid on the acquisition date and the transfer of 500 000 $1 equity shares in ER with a fair value of $4 each at the acquisition date. The non-controlling interest in MW was measured at its fair value of $560 000 at the date of acquisition.

On 1 January 2012, the carrying value of MW's net assets was considered to be the same as their fair value with the following exceptions:

- Leasehold property with a carrying value of $1 200 000 had a fair value of $1 320 000 and an estimated useful life of 5 years from the date of acquisition. ER depreciates property, plant and equipment on a straight line basis.

- A contingent liability, which had a fair value of $180 000 at the date of acquisition, had a fair value of $60 000 at 31 December 2013. This contingent liability is not reflected in the individual financial statements of MW.

The retained earnings reported in the financial statements of ER and MW as at 31 December 2013 were $7 900 000 and $1 400 000, respectively. An impairment of 10 per cent was recorded in ER's group financial statements as at 31 December 2012. An impairment review performed on 31 December 2013 indicated that goodwill on the acquisition of MW had been further impaired by 20 per cent of its carrying value at that date. ER has no other subsidiaries.

Required:

Calculate the amounts that will be included in the consolidated statement of financial position of the ER group as at 31 December 2013 for:

(a) goodwill

(b) retained earnings

(c) non-controlling interest.

(CIMA, Financial Management, May 2014)

5   Extracts from the financial statements of QA and LM for the year ended 31 March 2014 are presented below.

Summarized statement of profit or loss and statement of other comprehensive income for the year ended 31 March 2014

	QA $m	LM $m
Profit from operations	410	200
Finance costs	(70)	(12)
Profit before tax	340	188
Income tax expense	(100)	(44)
Profit for the year	240	144
Other comprehensive income:		
Items that may be reclassified to profit or loss		
Gains on the investment in LM	10	—
Items that will not be reclassified to profit or loss		
Revaluation of property net of tax	50	20
Other comprehensive income for the year	60	20
Total comprehensive income	300	164

Additional information:

- QA acquired 35 per cent of the equity share capital of LM for $255 million in 2011 when the net assets of LM were $670 million. QA was able to exercise significant influence over LM by virtue of this investment. On 1 January 2014, QA acquired a further 40 per cent of the equity share capital of LM, giving QA control. The consideration paid was $320 million and the net assets of LM had a fair value of $710 million on 1 January 2014. On 1 January 2014, the initial 35 per cent investment in LM had a fair value of $280 million.
- Assume that profits gains and losses accrue evenly throughout the year.

- Non-controlling interest had a fair value of $180 million on 1 January 2014.
- LM has not issued any share capital since 2010.

Required:
Calculate the goodwill arising on the acquisition of LM.

(CIMA, Financial Management, November 2014, adapted)

6   The statements of financial position for ST and UV as at 31 December 2011 are provided below:

	ST	*UV*
ASSETS	$000	$000
Non-current assets		
Property, plant and equipment	2 760	1 000
Investment	1 190	—
	3 950	1 000
Current assets		
Inventories	550	200
Receivables	850	225
Cash and cash equivalents	200	75
	1 600	500
Total assets	5 550	1 500
EQUITY AND LIABILITIES		
Equity		
Share capital ($1 equity shares)	2 500	250
Retained earnings	1 785	1 000
Other reserves	90	—
Total equity	4 375	1 250
Non-current liabilities		
Long term borrowings	675	—
Current liabilities	500	250
Total liabilities	1 175	250
Total equity and liabilities	5 550	1 500

Additional information:
ST acquired 80 per cent of the ordinary shares of UV on 1 May 2008 for $1 100 000. At the date of acquisition UV had retained earnings of $360 000. Goodwill that arose on the acquisition of UV was impaired by 20 per cent in the year to 31 December 2009. On 1 October 2011, ST disposed of 20 000 $1 ordinary shares of UV for $115 000. The proceeds were debited to cash and credited to retained earnings.

Required:
Explain how the disposal of shares in UV should be accounted for in the consolidated financial statements of ST for the year to 31 December 2011.

(CIMA Financial Management, March 2012, adapted)

CONSOLIDATED FINANCIAL STATEMENTS

26

OBJECTIVES After studying this chapter you should be able to:

- outline the need for consolidated financial statements

- prepare consolidated financial statements in accordance with IFRS

- understand and apply the mechanics of preparing consolidated financial statements.

INTRODUCTION

In the last chapter, we discussed accounting for business combinations, where an acquirer acquires an acquiree. After acquisition, the acquirer is a parent and the acquiree is a subsidiary. Both parent and subsidiary need to draw up their financial statements for their legal entity. But this gives just a limited view of what happens in the group, the parent and the subsidiary together. Remember that the parent exercises control over the subsidiary, so it also exercises control over all the assets and liabilities in the subsidiary. A user of financial statements would be interested in financial statements where all assets and liabilities and all revenues and costs that are under the control of the parent are reflected. This is the reason why a parent not only prepares its own legal entity set of financial statements but also consolidated financial statements, financial statements of a parent and all its subsidiaries. In this chapter, we will discuss the issues that arise in preparing consolidated accounts.

CONTROL

We refer back to Chapter 25 where we discussed the concept of control. A parent exercises control over a subsidiary. Control means that a parent is exposed, or has rights, to variable returns from its involvement with the subsidiary and has the ability to affect those returns through its power over the subsidiary (IFRS 10, para. 5). So the three essential elements for an investor (parent) are:

- power over the investee (subsidiary)
- exposure, or rights, to variable returns from its involvement with the investee
- the ability to use its power over the investee to affect the amount of the investor's returns.

An investor has power over the investee when the investor has existing rights that give it the current ability to direct the relevant activities of the investee. Power arises from rights, such as voting rights attaching to shares. Power can also result from one or more contractual arrangements.

An investor is exposed, or has rights to, variable returns from its involvement with the investee when the investor's returns from its involvement have the potential to vary as a result of the investee's performance. The investor's returns can be positive, negative or both positive and negative.

For control to exist, the investor must have the ability to use its power to affect the returns. If an investor is an agent and not a principal, it has delegated decision rights and it acts on behalf and for the benefit of another party. Such an investor would not have control over the investee.

IFRS 10 introduces the concept of de facto control. Even if an investor does not have the majority of the voting rights, the existing voting rights might give the investor the power to direct the relevant activities unilaterally. This will normally be the case when the investor has more voting rights than other investors, and other investors act independently. As an example, given in IFRS 10, para. B43, assume that an investor has 48 per cent of the voting rights, while the remaining voting rights are held by thousands of shareholders, none individually holding more than 1 per cent of the voting rights. Further, assume that none of the shareholders has any arrangement to consult any of the others or make collective decisions. In this situation, the conclusion would be that the 48 per cent investor has (de facto) control.

Another issue in determining control is potential voting rights. For example, take investors A and B, both having an interest in entity C. A has 10 per cent of the voting rights, B has 90 per cent. Based on this scenario alone, B would have control. However, A and B have contracted a substantive call option for A, giving A the current unconditional right to acquire 45 per cent of the shares in C held by B at fair value. As a result, A controls C while it can at any time direct the relevant activities of C (by using the call option and then having 55 per cent of the voting rights).

ACTIVITY 26.1

Identify in each of the following circumstances whether B is a subsidiary of A, i.e. whether A exercises control over B.

1 A owns 40 per cent of the voting rights of B and has an agreement with a shareholder who holds a further 15 per cent of the voting rights that enables A to vote for these shares as well.

2 A owns 42 per cent of the voting rights of B but also has an agreement to govern the financial and operating policies of B.

3 A owns 35 per cent of the voting rights of B and also has the power to appoint or remove five of the nine members of the board of directors.

4 A owns 33 per cent of the voting rights of B and 100 per cent of the voting rights of C which in turn holds 20 per cent of the voting rights of B.

Activity feedback

In cases 1, 2 and 3, A clearly controls the decisions of B and therefore B is a subsidiary of A.

Case 4 is also an example of a subsidiary relationship and Figure 26.1 should show this more clearly. A controls C and therefore also 20 per cent of B, which, together with its own 33 per cent holding, gives it control over 53 per cent of B. This is an example of a mixed group.

Figure 26.1 A subsidiary relationship

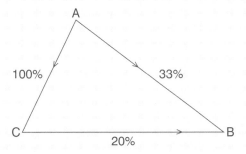

ACTIVITY 26.2

We explore mixed groups a little further in this Activity. In the examples given, identify the parent–subsidiary relationships:

1 H owns 75 per cent of the voting shares of S, which in turn owns 40 per cent of the voting shares of S1. H also owns directly 15 per cent of the voting shares of S1.

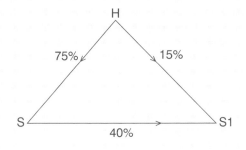

2 H owns 100 per cent of the voting shares of S, which in turn owns 30 per cent of S1. H also owns 75 per cent of S2, which in turn owns 25 per cent of S1.

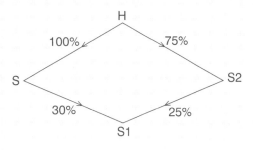

(Continued)

ACTIVITY 26.2 *(Continued)*

3 H owns 60 per cent of the voting shares of S, which in turn owns 20 per cent of the voting shares of S1. H also owns directly 20 per cent of the voting shares of S1.

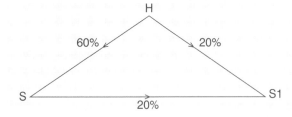

Activity feedback

Example 1

- *S is a subsidiary of H (75 per cent ownership), S1 is not a subsidiary of S (assuming no information in respect of dominant influence).*
- *H directly owns (75% × 40%) of S1 + 15% of S1 = 30% + 15% = 45% which would imply no subsidiary relationship.*

- *However, H controls S and thus controls 40% of S1 plus 15%.*
- *Therefore, S1 is a subsidiary of H and will be consolidated with a non-controlling interest of 55%.*

Example 2

- *S and S2 are subsidiaries of H. S1 requires further analysis.*
- *H directly owns (100% × 30%) + (75% × 25%) of S1 = 30% + 18.75% = 48.75% only.*
- *However, H controls 30% + 25% = 55%.*
- *Thus, S1 is also a subsidiary of H and will be consolidated with a non-controlling interest of 51.25%.*

Example 3

- *S is a subsidiary of H.*
- *H owns 60% × 20% + 20% of S1 = 32% of S1.*
- *H controls 20% + 20% of S1 = 40%.*
- *Thus, S1 is not a subsidiary of H (assuming no indication of dominant influence) and will not be consolidated.*

ACTIVITY 26.3

1 H currently holds 48 per cent of the shares of S. H does not have the power to govern the policies of S, or the power to remove members of the board or the power to cast the majority of votes at meetings. The remaining 52 per cent of S's shares are held by four investors that each have 13 per cent of the shares. Is S a subsidiary of H?

2 Entities A and B currently own 55 per cent and 45 per cent respectively of the ordinary voting right shares of entity C. Entity B also holds debt instruments that are convertible into ordinary shares in entity C at any time. If the debt were converted, entity B would hold 70 per cent of the voting shares and entity A's holding would become 30 per cent. The conversion would require entity B to borrow additional funds to make the conversion payment. Is C a subsidiary of A, B or neither?

Activity feedback

1 *The question is whether H has de facto control in S. In this situation, the four investors can easily*

organize themselves and together outnumber H. So this would not be a case of de facto control. However, if the 52 per cent shares were divided equally among about 30 shareholders, there could be more reason to conclude that H controls S and that S therefore is a subsidiary of H. There is a high degree of judgement involved in determining whether de facto control exists.

2 *The conversion rights owned by B give B the power to set the operating and financial policies of C. Therefore, C is a subsidiary of B not of A. This is an example of potential voting rights. The fact that additional funds have to be borrowed is not relevant. However, if B were unlikely to be able to obtain such funds, the potential voting rights would not have substance and therefore would not be taken into consideration in determining whether a subsidiary exists.*

Non-controlling interest

We discussed the concept of non-controlling interest in Chapter 25. Put simply, non-controlling interest is that part of the subsidiary that the holding (parent) entity does not own. This non-controlling interest is usually less than 50 per cent but, as in example 2 of Activity 26.2, can be more than 50 per cent if ownership does not define the control. This is the reason why the phrase 'non-controlling interest' is better than 'minority interest', as the non-controlling interest does not necessarily reflect a minority of the shares.

THE NEED FOR CONSOLIDATED ACCOUNTS

If we examine the separate accounts of two entities, H and S, where H holds 55 per cent of the ordinary voting shares of S, then we will find the following information available to us. We will refer to H as the 'holding' enterprise, S as the 'subsidiary' and when considering both entities together we will regard them as a 'group'.

In H's statement of financial position the shareholding (interest) in S will traditionally simply appear as an investment recorded at its cost of acquisition, historical cost. IFRS also allows the investment to be measured at fair value, but, as this option is seldom used for investments in subsidiaries, we will not discuss that measurement option any further. With an effective date of 1 January 2016, the IFRS allows a third option for measuring investments in the separate accounts of the parent: the use of equity accounting. The investment is then recorded at its share in equity in the statement of financial position and its share in profits is included in the statement of comprehensive income. This gives more information about the subsidiary's value and profitability. However, we do not know which assets and liabilities contribute to the subsidiary's value and which revenues and costs contribute to its profitability. Equity accounting is discussed further in Chapter 27.

In this chapter, our assumption is that the investment is recorded at historical cost. However, as with other assets in a statement of financial position, the use of historical cost as the basis of valuation would not normally give the shareholders of H any indication of the value of the subsidiary or the underlying assets and liabilities.

In relation to the holding entity's statement of comprehensive income (or statement of profit or loss) the only reference to the subsidiary would be 'dividends received from S' (assuming there were any) and, of course, this would give no indication of the subsidiary's profitability.

As far as the group is concerned, the holding entity's financial statements therefore give no or limited meaningful information about the group's activities, hence it would be useful to find a way to prepare information about the related activities of H and S in a consolidated (combined) format.

This is where the need for group accounts arises: to provide useful information to shareholders and other users of the holding entity's financial statements about the group as a whole.

IFRS 10, para. 19, requires a parent to prepare consolidated financial statements using uniform accounting policies for like transactions and other events in similar circumstances. Consolidated accounts combine assets, liabilities, equity, income, expenses and cash flows of the parent with those of its subsidiaries into a single economic entity.

IFRS 10, para. 4a, however, exempts a parent from presenting consolidated financial statements if it meets all of the following conditions:

- the parent is a wholly owned or partly owned subsidiary of another entity

- the parent's debt or equity instruments are not traded in a public market or the parent is not in the process of issuing any class of instruments in a public market

- the ultimate or any intermediate parent produces consolidated statements available for public use that comply with IFRS.

PREPARATION OF CONSOLIDATED STATEMENTS OF FINANCIAL POSITION

In this section, we will discuss the preparation of consolidated statements of financial position, and, in the next section, the preparation of consolidated statements of comprehensive income. In preparing the consolidated accounts, we will discuss in detail the need for eliminating intercompany relationships. The principles discussed are in line with the requirements of IFRS 10.

Consolidated statement of financial position at the date of acquisition

So far, we have identified a need for group accounts to show useful information to users. But what would be useful information to these users? We can presume that they will need to know the total assets and liabilities of the subsidiary that they control, together with the parent's own assets and liabilities. From this, we can assume that we will add together all the assets and liabilities of the parent and subsidiary. If we do this, we will then need to eliminate the investment from the parent statement of financial position (as we have included the net assets) and add in the goodwill on acquisition. If we have not acquired the whole of the subsidiary, there will also be a non-controlling interest, and we will need to include this in the group statement of financial position or the statement of financial position will not balance. The following example demonstrates the consolidation process where there is no non-controlling interest, i.e. 100 per cent ownership. This example prepares a consolidated statement at the date of acquisition of the subsidiary.

Example 26.1

The statements of financial position of H and S as at 31 December 20X6 are as follows:

	H €	S €
Property, plant and equipment	140 000	45 000
Investment in S	75 000	—
Net current assets	20 000	15 000
	235 000	60 000
Share capital	150 000	50 000
Reserves	85 000	10 000
	235 000	60 000

H acquired the whole of the share capital of S for €75 000 cash on 31 December 20X6. The fair value of S's net assets at this date were €67 000. Prepare the consolidated statement of financial position of H group as at 31 December 20X6.

To do this consolidation there are several steps:

1 calculate the goodwill

2 revalue the net assets of the subsidiary s to fair value

3 consolidate H and S.

1	Purchase price	75 000
	Fair value of net assets acquired	67 000
	Goodwill	8 000
2	S revalued statement of financial position	
	Net assets	67 000
	Share capital	50 000
	Reserves	10 000
	Revaluation reserve	7 000
		67 000
3	Group consolidated statement of financial position	
	Net assets (140 000 + 20 000 + 67 000)	227 000
	Goodwill on acquisition	8 000
		235 000
	Share capital	150 000
	Reserves	85 000
		235 000

Note that the share capital of S and the reserves from S at the date of acquisition, including the revaluation reserve, do not appear in the consolidated statement of financial position. This is because they have been replaced with the net assets acquired and the goodwill value.

The following example shows the preparation of the group consolidated statement of financial position when there is less than 100 per cent ownership. We determine the non-controlling interest on the basis of the proportion in the fair value of the net assets acquired.

Example 26.2

The statements of financial position of A and B as at 31 December 20X2 are as follows:

	A	B
	€	€
Net assets	403 000	87 000
Investment in B	72 000	—
	475 000	87 000
Share capital	350 000	60 000
Reserves	125 000	27 000
	475 000	87 000

A bought 75 per cent of S as at 31 December 20X2 for a purchase price of €72 000 and the value of the net assets bought equalled fair value.

1	Purchase price	72 000
	Fair value of net assets acquired (75% × 87 000)	65 250
	Goodwill	6 750

2   Group consolidated statement of financial position

Net assets (403 000 + 87 000)	490 000
Goodwill	6 750
	496 750
Share capital	350 000
Reserves	125 000
Equity attributable to the shareholders of H	475 000
Non-controlling interest (25% × 87 000)	21 750
Total equity	496 750

Now try Activity 26.4.

ACTIVITY 26.4

On 31 December 20X5, H acquired 1 000 000 shares of S with a nominal value of €0.10 per share, at a fair value of €120 000 for cash (the transaction has not yet been entered). The statements of financial position of H and S at the date of acquisition were as follows:

	H	S
	€000	€000
Land and buildings	650	105
Plant and equipment	110	21
Net current assets	163	11
	923	137
Share capital €1 shares	800	—
Share capital €0.10 shares	—	125
Reserves	123	12
	923	137

The fair value of S's net assets at the date of acquisition was €142 000 (€108 000 land and buildings, €22 000 plant and equipment, €12 000 net current assets).

Prepare the consolidated statement of financial position of H group as at 31 December 20X5 after the acquisition.

Activity feedback

Remember first to amend H's statement of financial position for the purchase of the shares in S. This will require an entry 'investment in S €120 000' and net current assets will be reduced to €43 000 for the cash payment.

H acquired 1 000 000 shares of €0.10 (€100 000) from a total of €125 000 million, i.e. 80 per cent ownership.

Consolidated statement of financial position of H group as at 31 December 201X

1	Purchase price	120 000
	Fair value of net assets acquired	
	(80% × 142 000)	113 600
	Goodwill	6 400
2	Group consolidated statement of financial position	
	Net assets (923 000 – 120 000 + 142 000)	945 000
	Goodwill	6 400
		951 400
	Share capital	800 000
	Reserves	123 000
	Equity attributable to the shareholders of H	923 000
	Non-controlling interest (20% × 142 000)	28 400
	Total equity	951 400

Consolidated statement of financial position later than date of acquisition

We obviously have to prepare consolidated accounts subsequent to the date of acquisition, and as long as we know the fair value of the assets acquired and the cost of that acquisition, this is quite easy. We can only include the parent share of the reserves post-acquisition in the consolidation. The following example shows you how to prepare a consolidated statement of financial position later than the date of acquisition where there is a 100 per cent ownership.

Example 26.3

H entity purchased 100 per cent of the equity share capital of S for cash at 31 December 20Y3 at a price of €2 per share, when the balance on S entity's reserves stood at €4000.

The consolidation is required at 31 December 20Y4, at which point the individual statements of financial position of the two entities are as follows:

	H	S
	€	€
Property, plant and equipment	75 000	13 000
Investment in S (at cost)	20 000	—
Current assets	23 000	4 000
	118 000	17 000
Share capital €1	60 000	10 000
Reserves	58 000	7 000
	118 000	17 000

No further shares have been issued by S during 20Y4.

Purchase price	20 000
Fair value of net assets acquired:	
10 000 (shares) + 4000 (pre-acquisition reserves)	14 000
Goodwill	6 000

Consolidated statement of financial position for H group as at 31 December 20Y4

Property, plant and equipment	88 000
Current assets	27 000
Goodwill	6 000
	121 000
Share capital	60 000
Reserves (58 000 + (7000 – 4000))	61 000
	121 000

Now try Activity 26.5, but note that in this Activity there is also a non-controlling interest.

ACTIVITY 26.5

H entity purchased 80 per cent of the equity share capital of S Ltd for cash at 31 December 20Y7 at a price of €1.50 per share, when the balance on S entity's reserves stood at €2000.

The consolidation is required at 31 December 20Y8, at which point the individual statements of financial position of the two entities are as follows:

	H	S
	€	€
Property, plant and equipment	60 000	5 000
Investment in S entity (at cost)	9 600	—
Current assets	35 000	6 000
	104 600	11 000
Share capital	40 000	8 000
Reserves	64 600	3 000
	104 600	11 000

(Continued)

ACTIVITY 26.5 (Continued)

Activity feedback

The consolidated statement of financial position as at 31 December 20Y8 would then be as follows:

	€
Property, plant and equipment	65 000
Current assets	41 000
Goodwill (note 1)	1 600
	107 600
Share capital	40 000
Reserves (note 2)	65 400
	105 400
Non-controlling interest (note 3)	2 200
	107 600

Notes:	€
1 Cost of investment in S entity	9 600
Acquired ordinary shares at 31 December 20Y7 (80% × 8000)	6 400

		€
	Acquired reserves at 31 December (being 80% of balance of €2000 on reserves of S entity at 31 December 20Y7)	1 600
	Total (80% × 10 000)	8 000
	Goodwill on acquisition	1 600
2	Reserves of H entity at 31 December 20Y8	64 600
	Reserves of S entity accruing to group since date of acquisition to 31 December 20Y8 = (3000 − 2000) × 80%	800
		65 400
3	Share capital as 31 December 20Y8 of S entity accruing to non-controlling interests (20% × 8000)	1 600
	Reserves at 31 December 20Y8 of S entity accruing to non-controlling interests (20% × 3000)	600
	Total (20% × 11 000)	2 200

Intercompany trading and the elimination of unrealized profits

When one member of a group, S, buys goods from an external supplier at a price (say) of €100, and sells those goods to a fellow group entity, S1, at a price of €140, then S can legitimately show a profit of €40 in its own statement of comprehensive income. However, on consolidation of the accounts of S and S1, it should be recognized that this sale from S to S1 could not give rise to a profit as far as the group statement of comprehensive income is concerned, as the sale is in effect an internal group transfer. In order for the group to realize a profit on sale, the sale must be made to a customer outside the group. Now complete the following Activity.

ACTIVITY 26.6

Entity A owns 75 per cent of the shares in entity B, bought when the reserves of B were €200 000. The individual statements of financial position of A and B as at 30 June 20X6 are given below. During the year, B sold goods to A at a profit margin of 25 per cent on cost. €50 000 of these goods lie in A's closing inventory as at 30 June 20X6.

	A €000	B €000
Assets		
Land and plant	1 000	200
Inventory	600	400
Debtors	200	40
Investment in B (at cost)	275	—
Total assets	2 075	640

(Continued)

ACTIVITY 26.6 (Continued)

Equity and liabilities

Equity

Share capital	1 000	100
Reserves	1 045	524
	2 045	624

Liabilities

Creditors	30	16
Total equity and liabilities	2 075	640

Prepare the consolidated statement of financial position as at 30 June 20X6.

Activity feedback

Consolidated statement of financial position as at 30 June 20X6:

	€000
Assets	
Goodwill (note 1)	50.0
Land and plant	1 200.0
Inventory (1000 – 10) (note 2)	990.0
Debtors	240.0
Total assets	2 480.0

Equity and liabilities

Equity

Share capital	1 000.0
Reserves (note 3)	1 280.5
	2 280.5
Non-controlling interest (note 4)	153.5
Liabilities	
Creditors	46.0
Total equity and liabilities	2 480.0

Notes

1	Cost of investment in B		275.0
	Less ordinary shares acquired	75.0	
	Reserves acquired (75% × 200)	150.0	225.0
	Goodwill		50.0
2	Goods in A inventory delivered by B:		50.0
	Profit margin included:		
	(50 – 50/1.25)		10.0
3	Reserves A		1 045.0
	Reserves post-acquisition B 75%		
	× (524 – 10 – 200)		235.5
			1 280.5
4	Non-controlling interest		
	25% ordinary shares		25.0
	25% reserves = 25% × (524 – 10)		128.5
			153.5

Reconciliation of intercompany balances

It is commonplace for entities within a group to shuffle liquidity and inventories between themselves as and when required and indeed this is one of the advantages of a group structure. Obviously, with reference to such transactions, the indebtedness to/from member entities will need to be recorded in the individual entities' books of account as appropriate. Hence, each entity will carry balances within the group. In relation to the group's position as regards the outside world, these balances are internal balances and therefore will not be shown in the group statement of financial position. In fact, they are cancelled on consolidation across the individual statement of financial positions of group members. If, for example, a subsidiary borrows money from its parent, this will be a financial asset in the individual accounts of the parent and a financial liability in the individual accounts of the subsidiary. On consolidation, these balances are eliminated.

Occasionally, however, it is not possible to cancel out such inter-entity balances, and this may often be due to a transfer of goods or cash between group entities straddling the financial year end. A consolidation adjustment is required at the year end to adjust for goods or cash in transit between two entities before we can carry out the consolidation of accounts. The adjustment assumes that we account for the transit item as though it had reached its destination. It is important to note that the adjustments we are making here only affect the consolidated accounts; we make no adjustment for these inter-entity balances to the individual accounts of each entity.

ACTIVITY 26.7

The financial year end of two entities, A and B, within the same group is 31 December. On 29 December, A despatched goods to B to the invoice value of €40 000 and charges B's ledger account accordingly. B does not receive the goods or the invoice until 4 January. Prepare the consolidation adjustment in B's books and note any other adjustment that may be required on consolidation.

Activity feedback

The adjustment will bring the goods into B's books as at 31 December.

Dr Goods in transit	€40 000
Cr A's current account	€40 000

On consolidation, the respective intercompany balances in the current accounts, which are now in agreement, will cancel out.

However, we must remember that this inventory of €40 000 in transit will contain an element of unrealized profit and this will need eliminating on consolidation as well.

Consistency of reporting dates and accounting policies within the group

Generally, the financial statement of a parent and its subsidiaries will be drawn up to the same date to enable easy preparation of consolidated financial statements. However, sometimes it is impracticable to do this and consolidation can take place using the accounts prepared to different dates provided the difference is no greater than a specified number of months, for example three months. Activity 26.8 will test your understanding of the preparation of consolidated statements of financial position for a parent and its subsidiary where there are several adjustments to make before consolidation can take place.

ACTIVITY 26.8

On 1 October 2014, H entity acquired two million of S entity's ordinary shares, paying £4.50 per share. At the date of acquisition, the retained earnings of S were £4 200 000. The draft statements of financial position of the two entities as at 30 September 2016 were as follows:

	H	S
	£000	£000
Assets		
Non-current assets		
Land	11 000	6 000
Plant and equipment	10 225	5 110
Investment in S (at cost)	9 000	—
	30 225	11 110
Current assets		
Inventory	4 925	3 295
Trade receivables	5 710	1 915
Cash	495	—
	11 130	5 210
Total assets	41 355	16 320

Equity and liabilities		
Equity		
Ordinary shares £1	5 000	2 500
Retained earnings	25 920	8 290
	30 920	10 790
Non-current liabilities		
10% loans	6 000	2 000
Current liabilities		
Trade payables	3 200	2 255
Bank overdraft	—	285
Tax	1 235	990
	4 435	3 530
Total equity and liabilities	41 355	16 320

Extracts from the statement of comprehensive income of S entity before inter-group adjustments for the year ended 30 September 2016 are:

	£000
Profit before tax	2 700
Taxation	800
Profit after tax	1 900

(*Continued*)

ACTIVITY 26.8 *(Continued)*

The following information is also relevant:

1 During the year, S sold goods to H for £0.9m. S adds a 20 per cent mark-up on cost to all its sales. Goods with a transfer price of £240 000 were included in H's inventory as at 30 September 2016.

2 The fair values of S's land and plant and equipment at the date of acquisition were £1m and £2m, respectively, in excess of the carrying values. S's statement of financial position has not taken account of these fair values. Group depreciation policy is land not depreciated, and plant and equipment depreciated at 10 per cent per annum on fair value.

3 An impairment review has been carried out on the consolidated goodwill as at 30 September 2016 and it has been found that the goodwill has been impaired by £400 000 during the year.

Prepare the consolidated statement of financial position of H group as at 30 September 2016. Ignore deferred taxes.

Activity feedback

Purchase of 80% (2 million/2.5 million)

	£000
Purchase price (2 million × 4.50)	9 000
Fair value of net assets acquired (80% × (2500 + 4200 + 3000 revaluation))	7 760
Goodwill	1 240

Consolidated statement of financial position for H group as at 30 September 2016

	£000
Assets	
Non-current assets	
Land (11 000 + 6000 + 1000)	18 000
Plant and equipment (10 225 + 5110 + 2000 − 400 (10% × 2 million × 2 years) depreciation)	16 935
Intangible assets (1240 goodwill − 400 impairment)	840
	35 775
Current assets	
Inventory (4925 + 3295 − 40 unrealized profit; 240/120 × 100 = 200 cost for S)	8 180
Trade receivables (5710 + 1915)	7 625
Cash	495
	16 300
Total assets	52 075
Equity and liabilities	
Equity	
Ordinary share capital	5 000
Retained earnings (25 920 + (8290 − 4200 pre-acq. − 400 dep. − 40 unrealized profit) × 80% − 400 impairment)	28 440
	33 440
Non-controlling interest (20% × (10 790 − 400 − 40 + 3000 revaluation))	2 670
Non-current liabilities	
10% loans (6 000 + 2 000)	8 000
Current liabilities	
Trade payables (3200 + 2255)	5 455
Bank overdraft	285
Tax (1235 + 990)	2 225
	7 965
Total equity and liabilities	52 075

Summary so far

We can usefully refresh our memory of group accounts and work through a full example at this point (Activity 26.9), using the rules we have identified so far.

ACTIVITY 26.9

The statements of financial position of Alexander and Britton on 30 June 20X1 were as follows:

	Alexander		Britton	
Non-current assets				
Land and buildings	108 000		64 000	
less Depreciation	20 000	88 000	32 000	32 000
Plant and machinery	65 000		43 000	
Less Depreciation	25 000	40 000	29 000	14 000
		128 000		46 000
Investments				
Shares in Britton (at cost)		35 000		—
Current assets				
Inventory	25 000		27 000	
Trade receivables	48 000		21 000	
Bank	22 000		6 000	
		95 000		54 000
Total assets		258 000		100 000
Equity and liabilities				
Equity				
Share capital		100 000		50 000
Retained earnings		46 000		16 000
		146 000		66 000
Liabilities				
Trade payables		112 000		34 000
Total equity and liabilities		258 000		100 000

1 Alexander acquired 37 500 shares in Britton several years ago when there was a debit balance on the retained earnings of €3000.

2 During the year ended 30 June 20X1, Alexander purchased a machine from Britton for €5000, which had yielded a profit on selling price of 30 per cent to that company. Depreciation on the machine had been charged in the accounts at 20 per cent on cost.

3 Britton purchases goods from Alexander, providing Alexander with a gross profit on invoice price of 33 1/3 per cent. On 30 June 20X1, Britton's inventory included an amount of €8000, being goods purchased from Alexander for €9000 (Britton has reduced the goods to its lower net realizable value by an amount of €1000).

Prepare the consolidated statement of financial position of Alexander and its subsidiary as at 30 June 20X1.

Activity feedback

Purchase of 75%: (37 500/50 000)	€
Purchase price	35 000
Fair value of net assets acquired (75% × (50 – 3)	35 250
Negative goodwill	250

Adjustments:	
Inter-group transfer of machine – unrealized profit (30% × 5000)	1 500
Excess depreciation charged 20% × 1500	300
Britton's accounts unrealized profit	1 200

Inter-group inventory transfer – unrealized profit 33 1/3% × €9000	3 000
Impairment made by Britton	1 000
Net reduction of value	2 000

Consolidated statement of financial position as at 30 June 20X1

Non-current assets		€
Land and buildings (88 000 + 32 000)		120 000
Plant and machinery (40 000 + 14 000 – 1200)		52 800
		172 800
Current assets		
Inventory (25 000 + 27 000 – 2000)	50 000	
Trade receivables (48 000 + 21 000)	69 000	
Bank (22 000 + 6000)	28 000	
		147 000
Total assets		319 800
Equity and liabilities		
Equity		
Share capital		100 000
Retained earnings (note 1)		57 600
		157 600
Non-controlling interest (25% × (66 000 – 1200)		16 200
Liabilities		
Trade payables (112 000 + 34 000)		146 000
Total equity and liabilities		319 800

(*Continued*)

Note 1

Retained earnings of Alexander	46 000
Unrealized profit on inventory	(2 000)
Post-acquisition profits of Britton: 75% × (16 000 (retained earnings 30.6.X1) + 3000 (debit balance at acq. date) – 1200 (unrealized profit on sale of machine))	13 350
Negative goodwill	250
	57 600

Preparation of consolidated accounts involving more than one subsidiary

These are relatively straightforward if you remember the rules already explained. The following example shows how consolidations of more than one subsidiary are made.

Example 26.4

H entity purchased 80 per cent of the equity share capital of S1 for cash at 31 December 20Y6 at a price of €7000 when the balance on S1's reserves stood at €4000. H also purchased 70 per cent of the equity share capital of S2 for cash at 31 December 20Y6 at a price of €12 000 when the balance on S2's reserves stood at €8000. The individual statements of financial position to be consolidated of the three entities at 31 December 20Y7 are as follows:

	H	S1	S2
Current assets	15 000	3 000	10 000
Investment in S1 (at cost)	7 000	—	—
Investment in S2 (at cost)	12 000	—	—
Plant and machinery	30 000	8 000	14 000
	64 000	11 000	24 000
Share capital €1	40 000	4 000	8 000
Reserves	24 000	7 000	16 000
	64 000	11 000	24 000

Net assets of S1 and S2 at acquisition date are assumed to be at fair value.

Purchase S1:	
Purchase price	7 000
Fair value of net assets acquired (80% × (4000 + 4000)	6 400
Goodwill	600
Non-controlling interest (20% × 11 000)	2 200
Post-acquisition reserves accruing to group (80% × (7000 – 4000))	2 400

Purchase S2:	
Purchase price	12 000
Fair value of net assets acquired (70% × (8000 + 8000))	11 200
Goodwill	800
Non-controlling interest (30% × 24 000)	7 200
Post-acquisition reserves accruing to group (70% × (16 000 – 8000))	5 600

Consolidated statement of financial position as at 31 December 20Y7

Current assets	28 000
Plant and machinery	52 000
Goodwill (600 + 800)	1 400
	81 400
Share capital	40 000
Reserves (24 000 + 2400 + 5600)	32 000
Non-controlling interests (2200 + 7200)	9 400
	81 400

We include an Activity here (Activity 26.10) of a consolidation involving several companies to test your understanding and application of the techniques of consolidation.

ACTIVITY 26.10

A plc acquired 5m €1 shares of B Ltd five years ago when the reserves of B stood at £6m. B Ltd acquired 2.25m €1 shares in C Ltd four years ago when the accumulated reserves of C were €0.5m. A plc also acquired 3m €1 shares of D Ltd two years ago when D's reserves were €0.3m. At the date of acquisition, the net book value of all assets equated to fair value. There has been no issue of shares in any of these companies throughout the five-year period. The statements of financial position of the group companies as at 31.12.20Y8 are:

	A	B	C	D
	€m	€m	€m	€m
Fixed assets	45.0	5.0	1.5	2.0
Investment in B	16.0	—	—	—
Investment in C	—	4.5	—	—
Investment in D	4.0	—	—	—
Net current assets	32.0	18.0	2.5	1.0
	97.0	27.5	4.0	3.0
Share capital	18.0	7.5	3.0	4.0
Reserves	79.0	20.0	1.0	(1.0)
	97.0	27.5	4.0	3.0

Prepare the consolidated statement of financial position of A group as at 31.12.20Y8.

Activity feedback

B and D are subsidiaries of A with controlling interests of 66.6 per cent (5m/7.5m) and 75 per cent (3m/4m), respectively. C is a subsidiary of B at an ownership of 75 per cent (2.25m/3m), but as B is a subsidiary of A then C is also a subsidiary of A at a controlling interest of 50 per cent (the economic interest of A in C is 66.6% × 75% = 50%, the remaining 50 per cent being the non-controlling interest). Figure 26.2 aids understanding here.

The goodwill calculations at acquisition are:

	B	C	D	Total
	€m	€m	€m	€m
Purchase price	16.000	4.500	4.000	
Shares bought	5.000	2.250	3.000	
Reserves bought	4.000	0.375	0.225	
	9.000	2.625	3.225	
Goodwill	7.000	1.875	0.775	
Group share (note 1)	7.000	1.250	0.775	9.025
Non-controlling interest calculations:				
Total net assets	23.000	4.000	3.000	
NCI share – %	331/3	50	25	
NCI	7.670	2.000	0.750	10.420

Note 1: Goodwill is 100 per cent for B and D (directly held by A); Goodwill for C is directly held by B (100 per cent); share of A in B is 66.6 per cent (× 1.875 = 1.250).

Consolidated statement of financial position

	€m
Goodwill	9.025
Fixed assets	53.500
Net current assets	53.500
	116.025
Share capital	18.000
Reserves [79 + (20 – 6)2/3 + (1 – 0.5)1/2 + (–1 – 0.3)3/4]	87.605
Non-controlling interest	10.420
	116.025

(Continued)

ACTIVITY 26.10 (Continued)

Figure 26.2   Subsidiaries and controlling interest

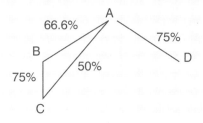

PREPARATION OF CONSOLIDATED STATEMENT OF COMPREHENSIVE INCOME

The principles of preparing a consolidated statement of comprehensive income are the same as those for the statement of financial position. Thus we will add together each individual line from the statement of comprehensive income, deducting inter-entity transactions as we go. At some point, we will need to deduct the profit attributable to the non-controlling interest. A simple example demonstrates the preparation of a consolidated statement of comprehensive income.

Example 26.5

The individual statements of comprehensive income of High and Low as at 31 December 20X6 are as follows:

	High	*Low*
Revenue	100 000	50 000
Cost of sales	75 000	30 000
Gross profit	25 000	20 000
Distribution expenses	4 000	3 000
Administration expenses	7 000	8 000
	14 000	9 000
Investment income: Dividends received	2 250	—
	16 250	9 000
Taxation	7 000	3 000
Net income/Comprehensive income	9 250	6 000

The share capital of Low consists of 100 000 €1 shares of which High bought 75 000 on 1 January 20X6 for €90 000. The fair value of Low's assets at date of acquisition equated to net book values, and the only reserves existing when High bought in were retained profits of €4000. During the year, High sold goods to Low for €12 000, which included a profit of €2000. As at 31.12.X6, 40 per cent of these goods still remain in Low's inventory. The dividends paid and proposed by Low are all paid out of current profits.

First, we need to identify the goodwill on acquisition:

Purchase price		90 000
Bought 75% of Low's shares (100 000)	75 000	
Bought 75% of Low's retained profits (4000)	3 000	
		78 000
Goodwill		12 000

Next, we need to eliminate intercompany trading:

Reduce consolidated Revenue by	12 000
Reduce consolidated Cost of Sales by (10 000 + (60% × 2000))	11 200

Consolidated statement of comprehensive income for the year ended 31.12.X6

Revenue (150 000 – 12 000)		138 000
Cost of sales (105 000 – 11 200)		93 800
		44 200
Distribution expenses	7 000	
Administration expenses	15 000	22 000
		22 200
Taxation		10 000
Consolidated comprehensive income on ordinary activities after tax		12 200
Attributable to non-controlling interest (25% × 6000 (= Low's net income / comprehensive income))		1 500
Attributable to shareholders of High		10 700

Note that all allocation of profits to the non-controlling interest for the year takes place after calculating consolidated earnings after tax and that the intercompany transaction in relation to Low's dividends paid to High is eliminated.

Note also that the total of income and expenditure for the parent and the subsidiary is included in the consolidated statement of comprehensive income. This is in accordance with the inclusion of the total of assets and liabilities in the consolidated statement of financial position. IFRS requires the division between the consolidated comprehensive income attributable to shareholders of the parent and that attributable to the non-controlling interest to be shown separately.

Activity 26.11 requires you to prepare both a consolidated statement of financial position and a consolidated statement of comprehensive income.

ACTIVITY 26.11

The summarized statements for the year ended 30 June 2016 for A, B and C entities are as follows:

Statements of comprehensive income for the year ended 30 June 2016

	A	B	C
	£000	£000	£000
Revenue	15 000	8 000	6 000
Cost of sales	(7 200)	(4 300)	(4 100)
	7 800	3 700	1 900
Expenses	(3 300)	(2 100)	(1 100)
Profit before tax	4 500	1 600	800
Tax	(1 400)	(650)	(260)
Profit for the year	3 100	950	540

Statements of financial position as at 30 June 2016

	A	B	C
ASSETS			
Non-current assets			
Property, plant and equipment	2 652	1 810	1 300
Investment in B (at cost)	1 302	—	—
Investment in C (at cost)	1 256	—	—
	5 210	1 810	1 300
Current assets			
Inventory	630	460	320
Trade receivables	560	370	280
Cash	160	—	90
	1 350	830	690
TOTAL ASSETS	6 560	2 640	1 990
EQUITY AND LIABILITIES			
EQUITY			
Ordinary shares	1 600	850	900
Share premium	100	50	300
Retained earnings	3 850	1 210	360
	5 550	2 110	1 560
NON-CURRENT LIABILITIES			
Loans	450	170	110
CURRENT LIABILITIES			
Trade payables	470	280	300
Bank overdraft	—	70	—
Tax	90	10	20
	560	360	320
TOTAL EQUITY AND LIABILITIES	6 560	2 640	1 990

The following information is also available:

1   A acquired a 70 per cent share in B and an 80 per cent share in C on 1 July 2015. The fair values of B's assets at that date equalled those shown on the statement of financial position. At acquisition date, the fair value of C's property was £500 000 in excess of the statement of financial position value. A, B and C all depreciate their property, plant and equipment on the same basis. Property is depreciated on a straight line basis over 50 years.

2   As at 30 June 2016, the fair value of the consolidated goodwill was reviewed and found to have a value 5 per cent less than its carrying value at the consolidation date. This impairment is to be accounted for in the consolidated accounts.

3   Inter-group sales (A to B) in the period from 1 July 2015 to 30 June 2016 are £3 100 000 on which A made a profit of 15 per cent on selling price. Of these goods, £500 000 (at selling price from A to B) are still in B's closing inventory amount.

Prepare the consolidated statement of comprehensive income for the year ended 30 June 2016 and the consolidated statement of financial position as at that date for the group.

Activity feedback

	£000
Acquisition of B	
Purchase price	1 302.0
Ordinary shares 70% × 850	595.0
Share premium 70% × 50	35.0
Retained earnings at acquisition date (1210 − 950 post-acq. profit) × 70%	182.0
	812.0
Goodwill on acquisition	490.0
Impairment on review 5%	(24.5)
Goodwill at 30 June 2016	465.5
Non-controlling interest	
Ordinary shares 30% × 850	255.0
Share premium 30% × 50	15.0
Attributable to NCI from retained earnings 30% × 1210	363.0
	633.0

(*Continued*)

ACTIVITY 26.11 (Continued)

	£000
Acquisition of C	
Purchase price	1 256.0
Ordinary shares 80% × 900	720.0
Share premium 80% × 300	240.0
Fair value adjustment 80% × 500	400.0
Retained earnings at acquisition date (360 – 540 post-acq. profit) × 80%	(144.0)
	1 216.0
Goodwill on acquisition	40.0
Impairment on review 5%	(2.0)
Goodwill at 30 June 2016	38.0
Non-controlling interest	
Ordinary shares 20% × 900	180.0
Share premium 20% × 300	60.0
Attributable to NCI from retained earnings 20% × 360	72.0
20% fair value adjustment of 500	100.0
Depreciation charge on fair value 20% × 10	(2.0)
	410.0
Total goodwill before impairment (490 + 40)	530.0
Total impairment at 5%	26.5
Total goodwill after impairment (465.5 + 38)	503.5
Total non-controlling interest (633 + 410)	1 043.0
Depreciation required on fair value of property 500/50	10.0

Inter-group sales reduce consolidated revenue by 3100 and consolidated cost of sales by (85% × 3100 + 390) = 3025

Unrealized profit: 3100 − 3025 = 75 [Total profit on sale: 15% × 3100 = 465; realized 15% × 2600 = 390; unrealized 15% × 500 = 75].

Consolidated statement of comprehensive income for the year ended 30 June 2016

	£000	£000
Revenue (15 000 + 8000 + 6000 − 3100)		25 900.0
Cost of sales (7200 + 4300 + 4100 − 3025)		(12 575.0)
		13 325.0
Expenses (3300 + 2100 + 1100 + dep. 10)	(6 510.0)	
Goodwill impairment	(26.5)	
		(6 536.5)
Profit before tax		6 788.5
Taxation (1400 + 650 + 260)		(2 310.0)
Consolidated comprehensive income		4 478.5

Consolidated statement of comprehensive income for the year ended 30 June 2016

(Continued)

	£000	£000
Attributable to NCI (30%× 950 + 20%× (540 + 10)		391.0
Attributable to shareholders of A		4 087.5

Consolidated statement of financial position as at 30 June 2016

	£000
ASSETS	
Non-current assets	
Property, plant and equipment (2652 + 1810 + 1300 + 500 − 10)	6 252.0
Goodwill	503.5
	6 755.5
Current assets	
Inventory (630 + 460 + 320 − 75)	1 335.0
Trade receivables (560 + 370 + 280)	1 210.0
Cash (160 + 90)	250.0
	2 795.0
TOTAL ASSETS	9 550.5
EQUITY AND LIABILITIES	
Equity	
Ordinary shares	1 600.0
Share premium	100.0
Retained earnings (3850 − 3100 + 4087.5)	4 837.5
	6 537.5
Non-controlling interest	1 043.0
Total equity	7 580.5
Non-current liabilities	
Loans (450 + 170 + 110)	730.0
Current liabilities	
Trade payables (470 + 280 + 300)	1 050.0
Bank overdraft	70.0
Taxation (90 + 10 + 20)	120.0
Total liabilities	1 240.0
TOTAL EQUITY AND LIABILITIES	9 550.5

ALTERNATIVE CONCEPTS ON CONSOLIDATION

In this chapter so far, we have discussed the preparation of consolidated financial statements along the lines of IFRS requirements. In the remainder of this chapter, we will discuss alternative concepts that lie behind preparing consolidated financial statements.

Alternative concepts on consolidation are:

- the entity concept
- the parent concept
- proportional consolidation.

These concepts also influence the determination of goodwill on a business combination, within the acquisition accounting method discussed in Chapter 25.

The entity concept

The entity concept (or group entity concept) views the group as a unit and makes no distinction between shareholders. The difference between the entity and parent concept only occurs where there is a less than 100 per cent ownership of the shares of an entity. In preparing consolidated financial statements according to IFRS, the entity concept prevails. This means that non-controlling interests are part of equity, and net comprehensive income includes the net income that is attributable to non-controlling interests. The use of the entity concept has been extensively illustrated in the Examples and Activities in Chapter 25 and this chapter.

IFRS 3 applies the entity concept to account for business combinations, with the exception of accounting for goodwill. For goodwill accounting, there is a choice between the entity concept (the goodwill of the group as a whole) and the parent concept (the goodwill acquired by the parent). We discuss this exception below.

The parent concept

With the parent concept (or parent entity concept or proprietary concept) of accounting, the assumption is made that the consolidated financial statements are being prepared to be primarily of use to the shareholders of the controlling parent entity. The non-controlling interests are credited with their share of the net tangible assets of the subsidiary. This non-controlling shareholding can then be reflected as a quasi-liability: it is not part of equity (as equity is only the amount that belongs to the shareholders of the parent), but it can be labelled as part of group equity. Furthermore, applying the parent concept results in net income being determined excluding the amount that is attributable to the non-controlling interest. In preparing consolidated financial statements, IFRS does not apply the parent concept.

ACTIVITY 26.12

Take a look again at Activity 26.11. What would be the amount of net comprehensive income and equity if applying the parent concept?

Activity feedback

Applying the parent concept would result in a net comprehensive income of £4087.5, being only the net income *that is attributable to the shareholders of A. The amount attributable to the non-controlling interest (£391) would be considered an element of expenses.*

In the consolidated statement of financial position, the equity would be £6537.5. The amount of £7580.5 might be labelled as group equity.

The parent concept also has an impact on accounting for business combinations, especially in the determination of goodwill upon acquisition. In Chapter 25, we discussed the two alternatives that currently exist in IFRS 3 for measuring the non-controlling interest in the acquiree:

- at the proportionate share of the acquiree's identifiable net assets at fair value or
- at fair value.

The goodwill resulting from the first alternative is the goodwill that is paid by the parent in acquiring control and therefore is the goodwill amount that fits within the parent concept. In applying the second alternative, full goodwill would be determined, which fits within the entity concept. As IFRS does not apply the parent concept in preparing consolidated accounts, it seems inconsistent that applying this concept in determining goodwill is acceptable. This inconsistency was not what the IASB had wanted; in an earlier draft, only the full goodwill determination was required. However, this proposal met fierce opposition in Europe, where the parent concept had previously been the dominant concept. For this reason, with the fear of non-endorsement by the European Union, the IASB decided to allow two alternatives. However, the parent concept is not allowed in determining equity and net profit in the consolidated accounts. Also, accounting for transactions with the non-controlling interest within equity does not fit with the parent concept (applying the parent concept would result in an additional amount of goodwill if the parent were to acquire the non-controlling interest).

In all of the Examples and Activities in Chapter 25 and this chapter, we have used the parent concept alternative for goodwill, showing only the goodwill allocated to the parent company. The reason for this is that most European entities apply this method for determining goodwill.

Sometimes a distinction is made within the parent concept in determining the non-controlling interest at acquisition:

- the non-controlling interest is determined on the basis of the fair values of the assets and liabilities at the acquisition date: this is the method discussed above
- the non-controlling interest is determined on the basis of the book values of the assets and liabilities at the acquisition date; in this situation there is no revaluation of assets and liabilities at the time of acquisition.

The latter method is sometimes referred to as *the* parent concept and the first as the parent concept extension method. We use the term parent concept for the first alternative. The second alternative is an easy one from a pragmatic point of view, but is no longer applied or permitted and will therefore not be discussed any further.

Proportional consolidation

The method of consolidation that is in line with IFRS and that has been discussed in the foregoing chapters is that of full consolidation. This means that, even if a parent does not have 100 per cent of the shares, it still consolidates 100 per cent of the net assets as the parent has control of 100 per cent of the net assets. The economic interest is not decisive, it is the fact of having control. This results in a non-controlling interest. When an entity has an economic interest of 80 per cent and has control, it consolidates 100 per cent of the net assets and recognizes a non-controlling interest for 20 per cent of the net assets.

An alternative might be to apply the consolidation on the basis of the economic interest. This is what we call proportional consolidation: consolidation to the proportion of the shares held. In this case, there is no non-controlling interest.

Proportional consolidation is not acceptable by the IASB in a parent–subsidiary relationship. It is, however, a traditional option in accounting for joint ventures. The recent new standard IFRS 11, *Joint Arrangements*, no longer allows proportional consolidation. However, for some specific joint arrangements, the comparable method of proportional accounting will be applicable. This will be discussed further in the next chapter.

Comparison of the three concepts of consolidation

Work through the following Activity carefully.

ACTIVITY 26.13

A buys 80 per cent of B for cash of €2200 when net assets of B have a fair value of €2000 and the net book value is €1500. The fair value of 100 per cent of B is €2700 (this is not proportional to the price for 80 per cent because of the control premium). The fair value of the non-controlling interest is €500 (€2700 – €2200). A's statement of financial position at the date of acquisition was:

	€
Net assets (including investment in B)	5 000
Share capital	4 000
Reserves	1 000
	5 000

Compare and contrast the information provided in the consolidated statement of financial position of A group using the three concepts discussed – entity concept, parent concept and proportional consolidation.

Activity feedback

Table 26.1 gives an overview.

Table 26.1 shows that the consistent figures throughout the three methods are only those of share capital and reserves of the holding company. The net assets change depending on how much of the fair value of the net assets each method considers attributable to the group. The proportional consolidation method excludes all reference to the portion of assets owned by the non-controlling interest, whereas the parent and entity concepts assume that the group might not own all of the subsidiary's assets, but it certainly controls them. The parent concept only incorporates the net book value of the portion of assets owned by the non-controlling interest; it disregards the fair value of this portion. The goodwill under the entity concept includes what could be regarded as the non-controlling interest goodwill. The non-controlling interest is shown at either 25 per cent of the fair value of net assets excluding goodwill (parent concept), or 25 per cent of the net assets at fair value including goodwill (entity concept). The proportional method of course makes no reference to a non-controlling interest.

Applying the parent concept and proportional consolidation, equity is 5000 (excluding the non-controlling interest), whereas the entity concept results in an equity of 5500.

IFRS applies the entity concept, but allows two alternatives, resulting in an equity of 5400 or 5500; the alternative with an equity of 5400 is a mixture between the entity concept (non-controlling interests are part of equity) and the parent concept (the amount of the non-controlling interests).

TABLE 26.1 Information on statements of financial positions (three concepts)

	Entity concept	Parent concept	Proportional consolidation
Net assets (1) (2)	4 800	4 800	4 400
Goodwill (3) (4)	700	600	600
	5 500	5 400	5 000
Share capital	4 000	4 000	4 000
Reserves	1 000	1 000	1 000
Equity	5 000	5 000	5 000
Non-controlling interest (5) (6)	500	400	—
Equity	5 500	5 400	5 000

(1) Net assets (entity concept, parent concept): 5000 – 2200 (investment in B) + 2000 (assets B) = 4800

(2) Net assets (proportional consolidation): 5000 – 2200 + 1600 (80% × 2000) = 4400

(3) Goodwill (parent concept, proportional consolidation): 2200 (purchase price) – 1600 (80% × 2000) = 600

(4) Goodwill (entity concept): 2700 – 2000 = 700

(5) Non-controlling interest (entity concept): 500 (fair value, including allocated goodwill of 100).

(6) Non-controlling interest (parent concept): 20% × 2000 = 400

SUMMARY

In this chapter, we dealt with the preparation of consolidated statements of financial position and consolidated statements of comprehensive income. We first investigated the control concept a little further. The essential elements of control are power of the investor (parent) over the investee (subsidiary), exposure or rights to variable returns from involvement with the investee and the ability to use that power to affect returns. We discussed the need for consolidated accounts and used many Examples and Activities to demonstrate how to prepare them, both at and after the date of acquisition. Specific issues are intercompany trading and the elimination of unrealized profits, the reconciliation of intercompany balances and the consistency of reporting dates and accounting policies within the group. Finally, we discussed alternative concepts of consolidation, being the entity concept, the parent concept and proportional consolidation. This was a rather technical chapter. The many exercises at the end of this current chapter will provide you with plenty of practice in preparing consolidated group financial statements.

EXERCISES

Suggested answers to exercises marked ✓ are to be found in the Student online resources, with suggested answers to the remaining questions available in the Instructor online resources.

1   What is 'control' when used in relation to consolidated financial statements?

2   Construct (using appropriate assumptions) a mixed group structure, bringing together a holding entity, a subsidiary and a sub-subsidiary.

3   The preparation of consolidated financial statements provides useful information to users. Discuss.

4   Appraise the need for consolidated accounts.

5   *D* has owned 80 per cent of the equity shares of *E* since 1 January 1996. *E* has owned 60 per cent of the equity shares of *F* since 1 January 1994. The accumulated profits of *F* at the latest statement of financial position date, 31 December 2003, stood at $30m. The accumulated profits of *F* stood at $12m on 1 January 1994 and $14m on 1 January 1996.

Required:
Ignoring goodwill, what will be included in the consolidated accumulated profits of *D* at 31 December 2003 in respect of *F*?

6   S holds 75 per cent of the shares of U. U sells goods to S. During the year ending 31 March 20X4, U sells goods to S for $100 000. The cost of the goods to U is $80 000. At the year end, S's inventories include $16 000 of goods purchased from U.

Required:
Calculate the adjustment required in respect of unrealized profit, and describe the accounting treatment of the adjustment in the consolidated statement of profit or loss and other comprehensive income and the consolidated statement of financial position.

7   Identify the essence of proportional consolidation and equity accounting and explain when each can be used in the preparation of consolidated financial statements in accordance with International Financial Reporting Standards.

8   On 1 June 2010, Premier acquired 80 per cent of the equity share capital of Sanford. The consideration consisted of two elements: a share exchange of three shares in Premier for every five acquired shares in Sanford and the issue of a £100 6 per cent loan note for every 500 shares acquired in Sanford. The share issue has not yet been recorded by Premier, but the issue of the loan notes has been recorded. At the date of acquisition, shares in Premier had a market value of £5 each. The summarized draft financial statements of both companies are:

Statements of profit or loss for the year ended 30 September 2010	Premier £000	Sanford £000
Revenue	92 500	45 000
Cost of sales	(70 500)	(36 000)
Gross profit	22 000	9 000
Distribution costs	(2 500)	(1 200)
Administrative expenses	(5 500)	(2 400)
Finance costs	(100)	—
Profit before tax	13 900	5 400
Corporation tax	(3 900)	(1 500)
Profit for the year	10 000	3 900

Statements of financial position as at 30 September 2010	Premier £000	Sanford £000
ASSETS		
Non-current assets		
Property, plant and equipment	25 000	13 900
Investments	1 800	—
	26 800	13 900
Current assets	12 500	2 400
Total assets	39 300	16 300
Equity and liabilities		
Equity		
Equity shares of £1 each	12 000	5 000
Land revaluation reserve – 30 September 2009 (note (i))	1 500	—
Other equity reserve – 30 September 2009 (note (iv))	500	—
Profit and loss account	12 300	4 500
	26 300	9 500
Liabilities		
Non-current liabilities: 6% loan notes	3 000	—
Current liabilities	10 000	6 800
	13 000	6 800
Total equity and liabilities	39 300	16 300

The following information is relevant:

(i) At the date of acquisition, the fair values of Sanford's assets were equal to their carrying amounts with the exception of its property. This had a fair value of £1.2m below its carrying amount. This would lead to a reduction of the depreciation charge (in cost of sales) of £50 000 in the post-acquisition period. Sanford has not incorporated this value change into its own financial statements. Premier's group policy is to revalue all properties to current value at each year end. On 30 September 2010, the value of Sanford's property was unchanged from its value at acquisition, but the land element of Premier's property had increased in value by £500 000, although this has not yet been recorded by Premier.

(ii) Sales from Sanford to Premier throughout the year ended 30 September 2010 had consistently been £1m per month. Sanford made a mark-up on cost of 25 per cent on these sales. Premier had £2m of inventory (at cost to Premier) that had been supplied in the post-acquisition period by Sanford as at 30 September 2010.

(iii) Premier had a trade payable balance owing to Sanford of £350 000 as at 30 September 2010. This agreed with the corresponding trade receivable in Sanford's books.

(iv) Premier's investments include investments that have increased in value by £300 000 during the year. The other equity reserve relates to these investments and is based on their value as at 30 September 2009. There were no acquisitions or disposals of any of these investments during the year ended 30 September 2010.

(v) Goodwill has not been impaired as at 30 September 2010.

Required:

(a) Prepare the consolidated profit and loss account for Premier for the year ended 30 September 2010.

(b) Prepare the consolidated statement of financial position for Premier as at 30 September 2010.

(ACCA, December 2010, adapted)

9 The statements of financial position for ER and MR as at 31 December 2012 are provided below.

	ER $000	MR $000
ASSETS		
Non-current assets		
Property, plant and equipment	5 900	2 000
Investment in MR	2 000	—
	7 900	2 000
Current assets	3 200	1 000
Total assets	11 100	3 000
Equity and liabilities		
Share capital ($1 shares)	5 000	500
Retained earnings	3 800	2 000
Total equity	8 800	2 500
Non-current liabilities		
Long-term borrowings	1 300	—
Current liabilities	1 000	500
Total liabilities	2 300	500
Total equity and liabilities	11 100	3 000

Additional information

1   ER acquired 80 per cent of the equity share capital of MR on 1 January 2010 for $2 000 000 when the retained earnings of MR were $1 200 000. There have been no share issues since the date of acquisition of MR.

2   At the date of acquisition, the fair value of the net assets of MR was the same as the book value with the exception of property, plant and equipment. The fair value of property, plant and equipment was $400 000 higher than the book value. Property, plant and equipment had an estimated useful life of ten years from the date of acquisition.

3   Non-controlling interest was valued at its fair value of $450 000 at the date of acquisition.

4   There has been no impairment of goodwill since the date of acquisition.

5   ER purchased goods from MR for $200 000 during the year ended 31 December 2012 and 25 per cent of these items remain in ER's inventories at the year end. MR earns a 20 per cent profit margin on all sales.

Required:

Prepare the consolidated statement of financial position for the ER group as at 31 December 2012.
(CIMA, Financial Management, May 2013)

10   The statements of profit or loss and other comprehensive income and changes in equity for XY and its subsidiary AZ for the year ended 31 December 2012 are shown below:

Statement of profit or loss and other comprehensive income for the year ended 31 December 2012

	XY	AZ
	$000	$000
Revenue	3 200	2 400
Cost of sales	(1 800)	(1 400)
Gross profit	1 400	1 000
Administrative expenses	(350)	(250)
Distribution costs	(300)	(150)
	750	600
Investment income (note 5)	400	—
Finance costs	(140)	(110)
Profit before tax	1 010	490
Income tax expense	(160)	(150)
Profit for the year	850	340

Other comprehensive income that will not be reclassified to profit or loss

Revaluation of property plant and equipment	40	30
Tax effect of other comprehensive income	(12)	(10)
Other comprehensive income for the year, net of tax	28	20
Total comprehensive income for the year	878	360

Notes:

1   XY acquired 80 per cent of the 1 million $1 equity shares in AZ on 1 January 2009 when AZ's retained earnings were $5 000 000. The non-controlling interest was valued at its fair value of $1 350 000 at the acquisition date. The consideration for the acquisition consisted of the following:

- Cash of $1 593 000 paid on 1 January 2009

- Cash of $1 000 000 paid on 1 January 2011 (a discount rate of 8 per cent was applied to value the liability in the financial statements of XY) and

- The transfer of 1 000 000 shares in XY with a nominal value of $1 each and an agreed value on the date of acquisition of $3 each.

2   As at 1 January 2009, the fair value of the net assets acquired was the same as the book value with the exception of property, plant and equipment that had a fair value that was $600 000 higher than its carrying value. The assets were assessed to have a remaining useful life of six years from the date of acquisition. Depreciation is charged to cost of sales.

3   On 31 December 2012, the goodwill arising on the acquisition of AZ has been impaired by 20 per cent. There have been no previous impairments and impairments are charged to administrative expenses.

4   In the year to 31 December 2012, AZ sold goods to XY with a sales value of $300 000. At year end, 20 per cent of the items remain in XY's inventories. AZ earns 25 per cent gross margin on all sales.

5   The investment income recorded in XY's financial statements relates to:

- dividend income from AZ which has been correctly treated in XY's individual financial statements

- income from a trade investment in another entity, LM. XY has a 10 per cent shareholding in LM.

Required:
(a) Prepare the consolidated statement of profit or loss and other comprehensive income and the consolidated statement of changes in equity for the XY Group for the year ended 31 December 2012.

(b) On 1 February 2013, XY acquired a further investment in LM. XY now holds a total of 60 per cent of the equity share capital of LM. Explain how this additional acquisition will impact on the preparation of the consolidated financial statements for the year to 31 December 2013.

(CIMA, Financial Management, November 2013, adapted)

11   Extracts from the financial statements of AZ, B and C are presented below.

Statement of financial position as at 31 December 2012	AZ	B	C
ASSETS	$m	$m	$m
Non-current assets			
Property, plant and equipment	70	44	55
Investment in B	68	—	—
Investment in C	—	38	—
	138	82	55
Current assets	29	24	14
Total assets	167	106	69

EQUITY AND LIABILITIES
Equity attributable to owners of the parent

Share capital ($1 equity shares)	50	40	30
Share premium	20	10	5
Other reserves	3	2	—
Retained earnings	59	30	23
Total equity	132	82	58
Non-current liabilities	15	8	2
Current liabilities	20	16	9
Total liabilities	35	24	11
Total equity and liabilities	167	106	69

Additional information:

1 AZ acquired 80 per cent of the equity share capital of B on 1 January 2009 when the retained earnings of B were $23 million and the balance on B's other reserves was nil. This acquisition resulted in AZ having power over B and AZ used that power to affect its return from the investment. B has not issued any shares since the acquisition date. The non-controlling interest in B was measured at fair value at the date of acquisition. The fair value of one equity share in B was $2.25 on 1 January 2009.

2 B acquired 75 per cent of the equity share capital of C on 1 January 2011 when the retained earnings of C were $8 million and the balance on C's other reserves was nil. This acquisition resulted in B having power over C and B used that power to affect its return from the investment. C has not issued any shares since the acquisition date. The non-controlling interest in C was measured at fair value at the date of acquisition. The fair value of one equity share in C was $1.60 on 1 January 2011.

3 AZ conducted its annual impairment review and concluded that the goodwill on the acquisition of B was impaired by 20 per cent at 31 December 2012. No other impairments of goodwill have arisen.

4 The balance on 'other reserves' for both AZ and B relate to movements in the values of their investments in B and C respectively.

Required:
(a) Explain how the investments in B and C are accounted for in:

  (i) the individual financial statements of AZ and B and

  (ii) the consolidated financial statements of the AZ Group.

(b) Prepare the consolidated statement of financial position for the AZ Group as at 31 December 2012.

(CIMA, Financial Management, August 2013)

12 On 1 January 2014, Plastik acquired 80 per cent of the equity share capital of Subtrak. The consideration was satisfied by a share exchange of two shares in Plastik for every three acquired shares in Subtrak. At the date of acquisition, shares in Plastik and Subtrak had a market value of $3 and $2.50 each, respectively. Plastik will also pay cash consideration of 27.5 cents on 1 January 2015 for each acquired share in Subtrak. Plastik has a cost of capital of 10 per

cent per annum. None of the consideration has been recorded by Plastik. Below are the summarized draft financial statements of both companies.

Statements of profit or loss and other comprehensive income for the year ended 30 September 2014

	Plastik	Subtrak
	$000	$000
Revenue	62 600	30 000
Cost of sales	(45 800)	(24 000)
Gross profit	16 800	6 000
Distribution costs	(2 000)	(1 200)
Administrative expenses	(3 500)	(1 800)
Finance costs	(200)	—
Profit before tax	11 100	3 000
Income tax expense	(3 100)	(1 000)
Profit for the year	8 000	2 000
Other comprehensive income:		
Gain on revaluation of property (note (i))	1 500	—
Total comprehensive income	9 500	2 000

Statements of financial position as at 30 September 2014

	Plastik	Subtrak
Assets	$000	$000
Non-current assets		
Property, plant and equipment	18 700	13 900
Investments: 10% loan note from Subtrak (note (ii))	1 000	—
	19 700	13 900
Current assets		
Inventories (note (iii))	4 300	1 200
Receivables (note (iv))	4 700	2 500
Bank	—	300
	9 000	4 000
Total assets	28 700	17 900
Equity and liabilities		
Equity		
Equity shares of $1 each	10 000	9 000
Revaluation surplus (note (i))	2 000	—
Retained earnings	6 300	3 500
	18 300	12 500
Non-current liabilities		
10% loan notes (note (ii))	2 500	1 000
Current liabilities		
Trade payables (note (iv))	3 400	3 600
Bank	1 700	—
Current tax payable	2 800	800
	7 900	4 400
Total equity and liabilities	28 700	17 900

The following information is relevant:

(i) At the date of acquisition, the fair values of Subtrak's assets and liabilities were equal to their carrying amounts with the exception of Subtrak's property, which had a fair value of $4 million above its carrying amount. For consolidation purposes, this led to an increase in depreciation charges (in cost of sales) of $100 000 in the post-acquisition period to 30 September 2014. Subtrak has not incorporated the fair value property increase into its entity financial statements. The policy of the Plastik group is to revalue all properties to fair value at each year end. On 30 September 2014, the increase in Plastik's property has already been recorded; however, a further increase of $600 000 in the value of Subtrak's property since its value at acquisition and 30 September 2014 has not been recorded.

(ii) On 30 September 2014, Plastik accepted a $1 million 10 per cent loan note from Subtrak.

(iii) Sales from Plastik to Subtrak throughout the year ended 30 September 2014 had consistently been $300 000 per month. Plastik made a mark-up on cost of 25 per cent on all these sales. $600 000 (at cost to Subtrak) of Subtrak's inventory at 30 September 2014 had been supplied by Plastik in the post-acquisition period.

(iv) Plastik had a trade receivable balance owing from Subtrak of $1.2 million as at 30 September 2014. This differed to the equivalent trade payable of Subtrak due to a payment by Subtrak of $400 000 made in September 2014 which did not clear Plastik's bank account until 4 October 2014. Plastik's policy for cash timing differences is to adjust the parent's financial statements.

(v) Plastik's policy is to value the non-controlling interest at fair value at the date of acquisition. For this purpose, Subtrak's share price at that date can be deemed to be representative of the fair value of the shares held by the non-controlling interest.

(vi) Due to recent adverse publicity concerning one of Subtrak's major product lines, the goodwill which arose on the acquisition of Subtrak has been impaired by $500 000 as at 30 September 2014. Goodwill impairment should be treated as an administrative expense.

(vii) Assume, except where indicated otherwise, that all items of income and expenditure accrue evenly throughout the year.

Required:
(a) Prepare the consolidated statement of profit or loss and other comprehensive income for Plastik for the year ended 30 September 2014.

(b) Prepare the consolidated statement of financial position for Plastik as at 30 September 2014.

(ACCA, Financial Reporting, December 2014, adapted)

13 On 1 April 2013 Polestar acquired 75 per cent of the equity share capital of Southstar. Southstar had been experiencing difficult trading conditions and making significant losses. In allowing for Southstar's difficulties, Polestar made an immediate cash payment of only $1.50 per share. In addition, Polestar will pay a further amount in cash on 30 September 2014 if Southstar returns to profitability by that date. The value of this contingent consideration at the date of acquisition was estimated to be $1.8 million, but at 30 September 2013, in the light of continuing losses, its value was estimated at only $1.5 million. The contingent consideration has not been recorded by Polestar. Overall, the directors of Polestar expect the acquisition to be a bargain purchase leading to negative goodwill. At the date of acquisition, shares in Southstar had a listed market price of $1.20 each. Below are the summarized draft financial statements of both companies.

Statements of profit or loss for the year ended 30 September 2013

	Polestar $000	Southstar $000
Revenue	110 000	66 000
Cost of sales	(88 000)	(67 200)
Gross profit	22 000	(1 200)
Distribution costs	(3 000)	(2 000)
Administrative expenses	(5 250)	(2 400)
Finance costs	(250)	—
Profit (loss) before tax	13 500	(5 600)
Income tax (expense)/relief	(3 500)	1 000
Profit (loss) for the year	10 000	(4 600)

Statements of financial position as at 30 September 2013

	Polestar $000	Southstar $000
Assets		
Non-current assets		
Property, plant and equipment	41 000	21 000
Financial asset: equity investments (note (iii))	16 000	—
	57 000	21 000
Current assets	16 500	4 800
Total assets	**73 500**	**25 800**
Equity and liabilities		
Equity		
Equity shares of 50 cents each	30 000	6 000
Retained earnings	28 500	12 000
	58 500	18 000
Current liabilities	15 000	7 800
Total equity and liabilities	**73 500**	**25 800**

The following information is relevant:

(i)   At the date of acquisition, the fair values of Southstar's assets were equal to their carrying amounts with the exception of a leased property. This had a fair value of $2 million above its carrying amount and a remaining lease term of ten years at that date. All depreciation is included in cost of sales.

(ii) Polestar transferred raw materials at their cost of $4 million to Southstar in June 2013. Southstar processed all of these materials incurring additional direct costs of $1.4 million and sold them back to Polestar in August 2013 for $9 million. At 30 September 2013, Polestar had $1.5 million of these goods still in inventory. There were no other intra-group sales.

(iii) Polestar has recorded its investment in Southstar at the cost of the immediate cash payment; other equity investments are carried at fair value through profit or loss as at 1 October 2012. The other equity investments have fallen in value by $200 000 during the year ended 30 September 2013.

(iv) Polestar's policy is to value the non-controlling interest at fair value at the date of acquisition. For this purpose, Southstar's share price at that date can be deemed to be representative of the fair value of the shares held by the non-controlling interest.

(v) All items in the above statements of profit or loss are deemed to accrue evenly over the year unless otherwise indicated.

Required:
(a) Prepare the consolidated statement of profit or loss for Polestar for the year ended 30 September 2013.

(b) Prepare the consolidated statement of financial position for Polestar as at 30 September 2013.

(ACCA, Financial Reporting, December 2013)

14 (a) On 1 October 2012, Paradigm acquired 75 per cent of Strata's equity shares by means of a share exchange of two new shares in Paradigm for every five acquired shares in Strata. In addition, Paradigm issued to the shareholders of Strata a $100 10 per cent loan note for every 1000 shares it acquired in Strata. Paradigm has not recorded any of the purchase consideration, although it does have other 10 per cent loan notes already in issue. The market value of Paradigm's shares at 1 October 2012 was $2 each.

The summarized statements of financial position of the two companies as at 31 March 2013 are:

	Paradigm $000	Strata $000
Assets		
Non-current assets		
Property, plant and equipment	47 400	25 500
Financial asset: equity investments (notes (i) and (iv))	7 500	3 200
	54 900	28 700
Current assets		
Inventory (note (ii))	20 400	8 400
Trade receivables (note (iii))	14 800	9 000
Bank	2 100	—
Total assets	92 200	46 100
Equity and liabilities		
Equity		
Equity shares of $1 each	40 000	20 000
Retained earnings/(losses) – at 1 April 2012	19 200	(4 000)
– for year ended 31 March	7 400	8 000
	66 600	24 000
Non-current liabilities		
10% loan notes	8 000	—
Current liabilities		
Trade payables (note (iii))	17 600	13 000
Bank overdraft	—	9 100
Total equity and liabilities	92 200	46 100

The following information is relevant:

(i) At the date of acquisition, Strata produced a draft statement of profit or loss which showed it had made a net loss after tax of $2 million at that date. Paradigm accepted this figure as the basis for calculating the pre- and post-acquisition split of Strata's profit for the year ended 31 March 2013.

Also at the date of acquisition, Paradigm conducted a fair value exercise on Strata's net assets, which were equal to their carrying amounts (including Strata's financial asset equity investments), with the exception of an item of plant which had a fair value of $3 million below its carrying amount. The plant had a remaining economic life of three years at 1 October 2012.

Paradigm's policy is to value the non-controlling interest at fair value at the date of acquisition. For this purpose, a share price for Strata of $1.20 each is representative of the fair value of the shares held by the non-controlling interest.

(ii) Each month since acquisition, Paradigm's sales to Strata were consistently $4.6 million. Paradigm had marked these up by 15 per cent on cost. Strata had one month's supply ($4.6 million) of these goods in inventory at 31 March 2013. Paradigm's normal mark-up (to third party customers) is 40 per cent.

(iii) Strata's current account balance with Paradigm at 31 March 2013 was $2.8 million, which did not agree with Paradigm's equivalent receivable due to a payment of $900 000 made by Strata on 28 March 2013 that was not received by Paradigm until 3 April 2013.

(iv) The financial asset equity investments of Paradigm and Strata are carried at their fair values as at 1 April 2012. As at 31 March 2013, these had fair values of $7.1 million and $3.9 million, respectively.

(v) There were no impairment losses within the group during the year ended 31 March 2013.

Required:
Prepare the consolidated statement of financial position for Paradigm as at 31 March 2013.

(a) Paradigm has a strategy of buying struggling businesses, reversing their decline and then selling them on at a profit within a short period of time. Paradigm is hoping to do this with Strata.

Required:
As an adviser to a prospective purchaser of Strata, explain any concerns you would raise about basing an investment decision on the information available in Paradigm's consolidated financial statements and Strata's entity financial statements.

(ACCA, Financial Reporting, June 2013)

ACCOUNTING FOR ASSOCIATES, JOINT ARRANGEMENTS AND RELATED PARTY DISCLOSURES

27

OBJECTIVES After studying this chapter you should be able to:

- identify an associate and a joint venture

- identify the need to disclose related party transactions

- consider the mechanics of accounting for an associate and a joint venture

- explain the requirements of IAS 24, *Related Party Disclosures*

- explain the requirements of IAS 28, *Investments in Associates and Joint Ventures*

- explain the requirements of IFRS 11, *Joint Arrangements.*

INTRODUCTION

So far within this Part, we have dealt primarily with the provision of information to users in respect of a holding in a subsidiary entity. However, one entity may have a holding in another that does not give it control but does mean it has significant influence over the net assets of that entity. This chapter considers the appropriate methods to account for holdings/relationships where control is not achieved such that useful information is provided to users.

The dominant accounting method is the equity method. As we referred to in Chapter 26, IFRS also allows this method in accounting for interests in subsidiaries in parent's individual financial statements.

EQUITY ACCOUNTING

In a business combination, one entity obtains control over another entity, resulting in a parent–subsidiary relationship. An entity can also buy shares in another entity without obtaining control, for instance obtaining significant influence or even joint control (control together with another entity). Significant influence normally exists when 20–50 per cent of the shares have been acquired. The entity in which the significant interest exists is named an 'associate'. In this situation, the equity method of accounting might be applicable.

The *equity method* of accounting as a method by which the investment is initially recognized at cost and adjusted thereafter for the post-acquisition change in the investor's share of the net assets of the investee. The profit or loss of the investor includes the investor's share of the profit or loss of the investee.

The equity method in consolidated financial statements provides the user of the statements with much more information than recording the investment at cost and accounting for any distributions from the investee. The user is able to see their share of the results of the investment and calculate more useful ratios.

ILLUSTRATION

On 31 December 2014, A entity acquired 1200 ordinary shares in B entity (4000 ordinary shares) at a cost of €3 per share. B's net assets at 31 December 2014 had a book value (and fair value) of €5600.

The statements of financial position of A and B as at 31 December 2015 are as follows:

	A	B
	€	€
Net current assets	2 000	3 600
Property, plant and equipment	30 000	3 000
Investment in B (at cost)	3 600	—
	35 600	6 600
Ordinary shares €1	16 000	4 000
Reserves	19 600	2 600
	35 600	6 600

A is required to issue consolidated financial statements and decides to apply equity accounting to its investment in B.

First, we need to identify the goodwill in the investment as we did for acquisition accounting.

	€
Cost of investment	3 600
Purchased 30% of B's net assets	
(30% × 5600)	1 680
Goodwill	1 920

Net assets of B at 31 December 2015 are €6600, so the net income of B during 2015 was €1000. A's share of the income of B is 30% × €1000 = €300.

Consolidated statement of financial position of A entity 31 December 2015 using equity accounting for B:

	€
Net current assets	2 000
Property, plant and equipment	30 000
Investment in B 1920	
(goodwill) + (30% × 6600)	3 900
	35 900
Ordinary shares €1	16 000
Reserves (19 600 + 300 share of	
B since purchase)	19 900
	35 900

ACTIVITY 27.1

Using the above illustration, identify the main differences in the preparation of a consolidated statement of financial position using equity accounting as opposed to acquisition accounting.

Activity feedback

The illustration shows us that equity accounting consolidates entity B as a one-line addition and not by *including the fair value of the net assets of B at each individual line of the statement of financial position. This one-line consolidation, however, does show us more than the original cost of the investment in B as it includes the goodwill and A's share of the earnings of B since it made the investment*

IAS 28, INVESTMENTS IN ASSOCIATES AND JOINT VENTURES

IAS 28 requires the use of equity accounting for associates and joint ventures. IAS 28 was originally issued in 1989 and amended several times (the latest major amendment being in 2011). IAS 28's main objective was to reduce alternatives in the application of the equity method, but not to consider the fundamental approach of using the equity method to account for associates.

In this section, we will focus on associates and will discuss joint ventures later in the chapter.

An associate is defined by IAS 28 as an entity over which the investor has significant influence (and that is neither a subsidiary nor an interest in a joint venture) (para. 3).

Significant influence is defined as the power to participate in the financial and operating policy decisions of the investee, but this is not control or joint control over those policies.

Significant influence is amplified in IAS 28 as a situation where the investor holds, directly or indirectly through subsidiaries, 20 per cent or more of the voting power of the investee and, if such a situation exists, that significant influence will be presumed unless it can be clearly evidenced otherwise and vice versa.

Significant influence is usually evidenced by:

- representation on the board of directors or equivalent governing body of the investee
- participation in policy-making processes
- material transactions between the investor and the investee
- interchange of managerial personnel
- provision of essential technical information.

Complete the following Activity.

ACTIVITY 27.2

Identify whether an associate relationship exists in the following examples in accordance with IAS 28.

1 Entity A owns 20 per cent of entity B and appoints one out of the seven directors. The remaining shares are held equally by two entities that both appoint three of the seven directors. A board meeting is quorate if four directors attend. In the event of tied decisions, the chair of the board, who is appointed by one of the other entities, has a casting vote.

2 Entity A owns 15 per cent of B and appoints two of six directors to the board. Each director has one vote

ACTIVITY 27.2 *(Continued)*

at meetings and the chair, who is from entity A, has a casting vote. The other four directors do not represent a shareholding of more than 5 per cent.

3 Entity A manufactures gadgets for retailer B. B designs the gadgets and normally 90 per cent of A's sales are made to B. B owns 12 per cent of the shares of A.

4 Entity A has a 16 per cent holding in B. B retails software packages developed by A, who holds the licence to the software. B retails no other software packages.

Activity feedback

1 Entity A has very little influence in entity B, as at any board meeting they will be outvoted. B is not an associate of A.

2 In this case, although entity A holds less than 20 per cent, A has significant influence given their voting rights on the board, 33.3 per cent, and their chair's casting vote.

3 Although B holds only 12 per cent of the shares, B exerts significant influence as A is reliant on B for the continuation of the business. A is an associate of B.

4 B is dependent on A for technical information and therefore B is an associate of A.

REAL WORLD ILLUSTRATION

Associates

An associate is an entity over which the Group has significant influence and that is neither a subsidiary nor an interest in a joint venture. Significant influence is the power to participate in the financial and operating policy decisions of the investee but do not have control or joint control over those policies.

At the date of acquisition, any excess of the cost of acquisition over the Group's share of the net fair value of the identifiable assets, liabilities and contingent liabilities of the associate is recognised as goodwill. The goodwill is included within the carrying amount of the investment.

The results and assets and liabilities of associates are incorporated in the consolidated financial statements using the equity method of accounting. Under the equity method, investments in associates are carried in the consolidated statement of financial position at cost as adjusted for post-acquisition changes in the Group's share of the net assets of the associate, less any impairment in the value of the investment. The Group's share of post-tax profits or losses are recognised in the consolidated income statement. Losses of an associate in excess of the Group's interest in that associate are recognised only to the extent that the Group has incurred legal or constructive obligations or made payments on behalf of the associate.

Taken from the Vodafone financial statements for the date ended 31 March 2015.

Exemptions from the use of equity method

An investment in an associate shall be accounted for using the equity method, with some exceptions, especially when the investment is held for sale (IFRS 5) or when it is measured at fair value by a venture capitalist or fund.

Goodwill in equity accounting

In accordance with IAS 28, goodwill, if positive, is included in the carrying amount of the investment. (Under a previous version of IAS 28, goodwill was amortized – but remember amortization of goodwill is no longer permitted under IFRS.) Goodwill, unlike that in the case of a subsidiary, is not identified separately or subject to a separate impairment test. The investment in its entirety is tested for impairment. In accordance with IAS 36, the recoverable amount of the investment, which is the higher of value in use and fair value less costs to sell, is compared with its carrying amount whenever there is an indication of impairment. So even though the goodwill included in the measurement of the associate is not amortized, there is no requirement to have an impairment test at least once a year.

If the goodwill on the purchase of the associate is negative, then this is excluded from the carrying amount of the investment and is included as income in the determination of the investor's share of the associate's profit or loss in the period in which the investment is acquired.

Goodwill was discussed in more detail in Chapter 25.

ILLUSTRATION

If the cost of the investment in the illustration at the beginning of this chapter were €1500, then the identified goodwill would be as follows:

	€
Cost of investment	1 500
Purchased (30% of net assets of €5600)	1 680
Negative goodwill	(180)

If the reserves of the parent are €17 500, the statement of financial position would be as follows:

	€	€
Net current assets		2 000
Property, plant and equipment		30 000
Investment in B at cost	1 500	
– share of earnings since purchase		
30% (6600 – 5600)	300	
– exclusion of goodwill	(180)	1 620
		33 620
Capital shares		16 000
Reserves	17 500	
Reserves since purchase	300	
Negative goodwill	(180)	17 620
		33 620

Accounting treatment of losses

Equity accounting requires that the investment in the associate is originally stated at cost and subsequently adjusted for the post-acquisition share of the investor company in the profits or losses of the associate. However, the value of an investment can never be below zero. Continuing losses can affect long-term interests of the investor company in the associate entity. For example, an item for which settlement is neither planned nor likely to occur in the foreseeable future is, in substance, an extension of the entity's investment in that associate. Such items may include preference shares and long-term receivables or loans, but do not include trade receivables, trade payables or any long-term receivables for which adequate collateral exists, such as secured loans. After the interest in the associate is reduced to zero, IAS 28, para. 39, states that additional losses are recognized by a provision (liability) only to the extent that the investor has incurred legal or constructive obligations or made payments on behalf of the associate. If this is not the case, the investor simply keeps a record of its share of losses without recognizing them. If the associate subsequently reports profits, the investor resumes recognizing its share of these profits only after its share of the profits equals the share of losses not recognized (IAS 28, para. 39).

The following Activity illustrates this issue.

ACTIVITY 27.3

Demosthenes plc purchased 30 per cent of Marina Inc. for €3000 on 31.12.X5. During the following three years (20X6, 20X7 and 20X8), Marina Inc. made a loss of €11 000, a profit of €400 and a profit of €700, respectively.

Required:

How would Demosthenes plc account for its investment in Marina Inc. in its accounts for 31.12.X6, 31.12.X7 and 31.12.X8? Assume that Demosthenes' interest in Marina Inc. is the carrying amount of the investment using the equity method.

Activity feedback

	31.12.X6 €	31.12.X7 €	31.12.X8 €
Income statement			
Share of Marina's gains/(losses)	(3 000)	zero	30
Balance sheet			
Investment in Marina	zero	zero	30
Memorandum records			
Marina's profit/(losses)	(11 000)	400	700
Share of profit/(losses)	(3 300)	120	210
Recognized profit/(loss)	(3 000)	zero	30
Unrecognized loss	(300)	(180)	zero

For the year ended 31.12.X6, Demosthenes' share of Marina's loss is €3300 (30% × €11 000), which exceeds its investment of €3000 in Marina by €300. Therefore, Demosthenes will recognize a loss of €3000 (which is equal to its investment) and reduce its investment to zero. At the same time, Demosthenes would keep a record of the unrecognized loss of €300. Note that we assume that Demosthenes did not incur any legal or constructive obligations or make payments on behalf of the associate, so there is no need to make any provisions with respect to Marina's loss.

For 31.12.X7, Demosthenes' share of Marina's profit is €120 (30% × €400). Demosthenes will not recognize this profit as it is lower than the unrecognized loss of €300 and it will continue to keep the investment at zero. However, it will reduce the unrecognized loss to €180 (€300 – €120).

For 31.12.X8, Demosthenes' share of Marina's profit is €210 (30% × €700). However, Demosthenes will recognize only €30 (€210 less unrecognized loss of €180). Its investment in Marina will also be stated at €30.

Disclosure requirements for associates

These are identified in paras 20–23 of IFRS 12 and require the entity to disclose:

(a) the nature, extent and financial effects of its interests in joint arrangements and associates.

This includes requirements to disclose for each associate that is material to the entity: their name and the nature of activities; their principal place of business; proportion of ownership held in them by the entity; summarized financial information, such as: assets, liabilities, revenues, profit and loss from continuing operations and comprehensive income; aggregate financial information for all associates that on their own are immaterial to the entity (IFRS 12, paras 21–22).

(b) the nature of, and changes in, the risks associated with its interests in associates.

This includes a requirement to disclose contingent liabilities (as specified in IAS 37) incurred relating to its interests in associates (including its share of contingent liabilities incurred jointly with other investors' significant influence over the associates) separately from the amount of other contingent liabilities (IFRS 12, para. 23).

The example below is taken from Vodafone's financial statements for the year ended 31 March 2015.

REAL WORLD ILLUSTRATION

Associates

Unless otherwise stated, the Company's principal associates all have share capital consisting solely of ordinary shares and are all indirectly held. The country of incorporation or registration of all associates is also their principal place of operation.

Name of associate	Principal activity	Country of incorporation or registration	Percentage[1] shareholdings
Safaricom Limited[2,3]	Network operator	Kenya	40.0

Notes:

1 Effective ownership percentages of Vodafone Group Plc at 31 March 2015, rounded to the nearest tenth of one percent.

2 The Group also holds two non-voting shares.

3 At 31 March 2015 the fair value of Safaricom Limited was KES 273 billion (£1 989 million) based on the closing quoted share price on the Nairobi Stock Exchange.

On 21 February 2014, the Group disposed of its 45% interest in Cellco Partnership which traded under the name Verizon Wireless. Results from discontinued operations are disclosed in note 7 "Discontinued operations" to the consolidated financial statements. The Group received £4 828 million of dividends in the year to 31 March 2014 (2013: £4 798 million) from Cellco Partnership.

The following table provides aggregated financial information for the Group's associates as it relates to the amounts recognised in the income statement, statement of comprehensive income and consolidated statement of financial position.

	Investment in associates			Profit/(loss) from continuing operations			Other comprehensive (expense)/income			Total comprehensive income/(expense)		
	2015 **£m**	2014 £m	2013 £m	**2015** **£m**	2014 £m	2013 £m	**2015** **£m**	2014 £m	2013 £m	**2015** **£m**	2014 £m	2013 £m
Cellco Partnership	–	–	38 373	–	–	–	–	(1)	–	–	3 190	6 422
Other	328	272	262	88	57	55	–	–	–	88	57	55
Total	**328**	**272**	**38 635**	**88**	**57**	**55**	–	**(1)**	–	**88**	**3 247**	**6 477**

The summarised financial information for each of the Group's material equity accounted associates on a 100% ownership basis is set out below.

	Cellco Partnership		
	2015 **£m**	2014 £m	2013 £m
Income statement and statement of comprehensive income			
Revenue	–	22 122	48 827
Depreciation and amortisation	–	(2 186)	(5 145)
Interest income	–	1	3
Interest expense	–	(38)	(60)
Income tax (expense)/income	–	(111)	29
Post-tax profit from discontinued operations	–	7 092	14 272
Other comprehensive expense	–	(2)	–
Total comprehensive income	–	7 090	14 272
Statement of financial position			
Non-current assets	–	–	
Current assets	–	–	
Non-current liabilities	–	–	
Current liabilities	–	–	
Equity shareholders' funds	–	–	
Cash and cash equivalents within current assets	–	–	
Non-current liabilities excluding trade and other payables and provisions	–	–	
Current liabilities excluding trade and other payables and provisions	–	–	

EQUITY ACCOUNTING IN INDIVIDUAL FINANCIAL STATEMENTS

In Chapter 26, we discussed the accounting for subsidiaries in the individual financial statements of a parent. We identified three alternative measurements:

- at cost
- at fair value
- using the equity method.

The same alternatives exist in accounting for associates (and joint ventures, see below) in those individual financial statements. The following Activity shows how consolidated and individual financial statements interact when subsidiaries are accounted for using the equity method.

ACTIVITY 27.4

Take again a look at Example 26.3 in Chapter 26. Now prepare the individual statement of financial position of H at 31 December 20Y4, measuring the investment in S on the basis of equity accounting. Compare the individual and the consolidated statements of financial position.

(1) 17 000 (100 per cent share in the equity of S at 31 December 20Y4) + 6000 (goodwill, included in the measurement of the investment).

Equity of H in the individual financial statements is now equal to that in H's consolidated financial statements.

Activity feedback

The individual financial statement of position of H at 31 December 20Y4, using the equity method, is as follows:

	H
Property, plant and equipment	75 000
Investment in S (at equity) (1)	23 000
Current assets	23 000
	121 000
Share capital €1	60 000
Reserves	61 000
	121 000

When investments are measured according to the equity method in the individual financial statements, the equity of the parent will normally be equal to consolidated equity. In the case of non-controlling interests, the equity in the parent company's individual statement of financial position will be equal to the part of consolidated equity that is attributable to shareholders of the parent.

If H had had an 80 per cent interest in S in the example in Activity 27.4, and goodwill remained at 6000, the carrying amount of the investment would be 19 600 ((80% × 17 000) + 6000). The equity of H would be 117 600. Consolidated equity would still be 121 000, of which 3400 (20% × 17 000) would be allocated to the non-controlling interest and 117 600 to the shareholders of H.

Applying equity accounting does not always result in equal equity amounts. Differences in equity do arise when subsidiaries have a negative equity and the parent has no legal or constructive obligation to supplement the accrued losses. The measurement of the investment will then be zero and there will be no provision for the negative equity, while the negative equity will be included in the consolidated financial statements.

IFRS 11, JOINT ARRANGEMENTS

Introduction

So far, we have defined investment in another entity as either a subsidiary relationship, an associate relationship or a simple trade investment.

There is one other type of investment we need to consider, and that is a joint arrangement. The IASB issued a standard on such arrangements in 1990, IAS 31, *Interests in Joint Ventures*, and has continued to update it since then. In May 2011, however, it replaced IAS 31 with IFRS 11, *Joint Arrangements*.

Definitions

A joint arrangement is an arrangement in which two or more parties have joint control (IFRS 11, para. 4).

'*Joint control* is the contractually agreed sharing of control of an arrangement, which exists only when decisions about the relevant activities require the unanimous consent of the parties sharing control' (IFRS 11, para. 7). The definition of 'control' is the same as in IFRS 10.

A joint arrangement is dependent on a contractual agreement, usually in writing. This agreement will cover several issues such as duration of the activity, reporting obligations, appointment of the governing body of the entity, capital contributions by the parties involved and the sharing of income, expenses or results. The contract will establish joint control by all ventures involved and will ensure that no one party can control the activity. Quite often though, one party may be appointed as the operator or manager of the joint arrangement but they will still have to act within the financial and operating policies agreed by all parties involved. If this is not the case and one party can act unilaterally, then the arrangement is not a 'joint arrangement' (see Activity 27.5).

ACTIVITY 27.5

Serp Company, a building firm, is involved in the following arrangements with other building entities:

- An interest in a project Castle Residential with Locking entity and Crawford entity. The project involves the renovation of the castle building to provide resident accommodation. The participants have equal shares in the project and are to share profits equally. Invoices are sent to Cork entity, which has contracted with each of the venturers for the work undertaken.
- A 30 per cent interest in Alpha entity to the board of which Serp appoints two directors.
- A 70 per cent interest in Beta entity.
- An equal interest with X entity in Gamma.
- The consent of Serp and X is required for all decisions on financial and operating policies of Gamma essential to activities, economic performance and financial position.
- A 3 per cent interest in Wimp entity.
- A 22 per cent interest in Alpine entity, which is seen as a short-term investment.
- An interest in Delta entity. Serp, Delta and Condo are to share equally in the income, expenses and results

of Delta and they have each contributed the same capital. Condo has the power to vary the financial and operating policies of Delta as it sees fit.

Based on our discussions so far, identify what type of relationship each of these arrangements is as far as Serp is concerned.

Activity feedback

- *Castle Residential is a joint arrangement as the parties have joint control.*
- *Alpha is an associate as we can presume significant influence from two directors.*
- *Beta is a subsidiary if we assume 70 per cent interest implies 70 per cent voting rights.*
- *Gamma is a joint arrangement as it is jointly controlled by Serp and X.*
- *Wimp and Alpine are simple investments as the former investment does not demonstrate any significant influence and the latter is for the short term.*
- *Delta is actually a subsidiary of Condo, not of Serp, and thus Serp will only account for the results of Condo as a trade investment.*

Types of joint arrangement

A joint arrangement can take many different forms both legally and in substance, but IFRS 11 categorizes them into two groups:

- joint operations
- joint ventures.

The classification of joint arrangements into these two categories depends on the rights and obligations of the parties involved.

- *Joint operations* are joint arrangements where the parties that have joint control of the arrangement, known as the *joint operators*, have rights to the assets, and obligations for the liabilities, relating to the arrangement.
- *Joint ventures* are joint arrangements where the parties that have joint control of the arrangement, known as the *joint venturers*, have rights to the net assets of the arrangement.

From the above definitions, it becomes clear that the critical point in assessing whether the arrangement is a joint operation or a joint venture is the determination of the rights and obligations of the parties involved in relation to the joint arrangement. The first step in assessing these rights and obligations is to determine whether the joint arrangement is structured through a separate vehicle, such as the establishment of a corporation or partnership. If this is not the case, then the joint arrangement is a joint operation. For example, two companies may enter into an agreement to operate an asset together and share any resulting output.

If the joint arrangement is structured through the establishment of a separate entity, then the arrangement may be either a joint operation or a joint venture. The determining factor in assessing this is the controlling parties' rights to the assets and obligations for the liabilities, relating to the arrangement that is held in the separate vehicle (para. B20). IFRS 11 specifies that in order to assess these rights and obligations, the following need to be examined:

- the legal form of the separate vehicle (see paras B22–B24)
- the terms of the contractual arrangement (see paras B25–B28) and
- when relevant, other facts and circumstances (see paras B29–B33).

The legal form of the separate vehicle

The scrutiny of the legal form of the separate vehicle is the first step in determining the nature of the arrangement. For example, the legal form may not establish a separation between the parties involved and the separate vehicle. This will be the case if the separate vehicle is a partnership that has unlimited liability. In this case, the parties involved have rights to the assets and obligations for the liabilities of the partnership, which means that the arrangement will be deemed to be a joint operation.

On the other hand, if the separate vehicle is a UK corporation, then this means that from a legal point of view there is a separation between the investors and the assets/liabilities of the vehicle. This, however, is not sufficient to establish whether the arrangement is a joint operation or a joint venture from an accounting point of view. For this purpose, we need to examine the terms of the arrangement and any other facts.

Assessing the terms of the contractual arrangement

Irrespective of the legal form of the separate vehicle, the arrangement may include contractual terms that give the parties involved rights and obligations relating to the assets and the liabilities of the separate vehicle. IFRS 11 provides a number of examples of such terms:

- The parties share all interests (e.g. rights, title or ownership) in the assets relating to the arrangement in a specified proportion.
- The parties share all liabilities, obligations, costs and expenses in a specified proportion.
- The parties are jointly and severally liable for the obligations of the arrangement.
- The parties are liable for claims raised by third parties.

The inclusion of any of these terms will indicate that the arrangement is a joint operation, regardless of the legal form of the separate vehicle. The absence, however, of such terms does not guarantee that the arrangement is a joint venture as other facts may still indicate that the arrangement is a joint operation. This is examined next.

Assessing other facts and circumstances

Besides terms included in the arrangement, certain facts and circumstances may also give the parties involved rights to the assets and obligations for the liabilities of the arrangement that the legal form of the entity does not confer. IFRS 11 specifies two criteria in assessing whether this might be the case: i) whether the joint arrangement primarily aims to provide the parties with an output (i.e. the parties have rights to substantially all of the economic benefits of the assets); and ii) whether the arrangement depends on the parties on a continuous basis for settling its liabilities.

If both of these criteria are met, then the joint arrangement is a joint operation as the rights to the assets and obligation for the liabilities are given to the parties involved.

ACTIVITY 27.6

A, B and C jointly establish a corporation Z over which they have joint control. There are no contractual terms that give A, B and C rights to the assets or obligations for the liabilities of Z. A, B and C agree that they will each purchase a third of all the output produced by Z. The price of the output sold to A, B and C is set by A, B and C, and Z cannot sell output to third parties unless A, B and C approve it. Is Z a joint venture or a joint operation?

Activity feedback

Z is a corporation, which indicates a separation of the three controlling parties and the assets and liabilities of Z. In addition, no contractual terms exist to negate this separation. Both of these factors might indicate that Z is a joint venture. However, they are not sufficient to conclusively establish that Z is a joint venture. Facts and other circumstances also *need to be considered. Z is dependent on the three parties to sell and set the price for its output. Furthermore, in order to sell output to third parties, Z needs the approval of A, B and C. Therefore, from every perspective, Z is dependent on A, B and C, which have all of the economic benefits of Z's assets. The three parties are also effectively responsible for its liabilities given that they buy all of Z's output, which cannot be sold to other parties. These facts indicate that the joint arrangement is a joint operation, not a joint venture.*

Now if Z were allowed to sell to other parties, then this would change the nature of the situation. A, B and C would not have all of the economic benefits and would clearly not assume the liabilities of Z. Therefore, Z would be a joint venture: A, B and C would have rights to the net assets of Z, not rights to assets and obligations to its liabilities.

ACCOUNTING FOR JOINT ARRANGEMENTS

Accounting for joint operations and joint ventures

The determination of whether a joint arrangement is a joint operation or a joint venture is important, as the accounting for these two types of entities is different. This is discussed next.

Joint operations. FRS 11 requires that a joint operator sees through the joint arrangements and accounts for its share of assets, liabilities, revenues and expenses directly. So the interest of the joint operator in a joint operation is not accounted for as an investment in another entity. Instead, each asset and liability (and related income and expense) to which the joint operator has contractual rights are accounted for using applicable IFRSs. For example, assume that parties A and B entered into a joint operation to manufacture a product together. Party A has purchased and provided to the operation the machinery required. Party A will then recognize this machinery as part of its property, plant and equipment under IAS 16 (like any other tangible asset that it owns).

Joint ventures. In contrast to the treatment of a joint operation, a joint venturer recognizes its interest in a joint venture as an investment and accounts for that investment using the equity method in accordance with IAS 28, *Investments in Associates and Joint Ventures* (IFRS 11, para. 24). Therefore, the accounting treatment of joint ventures and associate entities (discussed in an earlier section of this chapter) is the same. It is noteworthy that under the previous standard, IAS 31, a joint venturer had the choice of using either proportional consolidation (as described in Chapter 26) or the equity method.

ACTIVITY 27.7

X entity acquired 600 $1 common shares in Y entity at a price of $1.50 per share on 31 December 20X1, at which point the statement of comprehensive income of Y had a credit balance of $2000. The respective statements of financial position of X and Y as at 31 December 20X2 are summarized here:

	X	Y
	$	$
Net current assets	1 000	1 800
Property plant and equipment	15 000	3 200
Investment in Y – at cost	900	—
	16 900	5 000
Common shares $1	8 000	2 000
Reserves	8 900	3 000
	16 900	5 000

X is required to prepare consolidated financial statements as it has several subsidiaries for the year ended 31 December 20X2. You are required to draft the initial consolidated statement of financial position of the group as at December 20X2 before the inclusion of the subsidiaries but after the inclusion of Y assuming, first, that the investment in Y is a joint venture. How would your answer change if Y were an associate of X?

Activity feedback

Y as a joint venture using the accounting treatment required by IFRS 11:

	€
Net current assets	1 000
Property, plant and equipment	15 000
Investment in Y (see note 1)	1 200
	17 200
Common shares €1	8 000
Reserves (see note 2)	9 200
	17 200

Note 1: Investment in Y	€	Note 2: Reserves calculation	€
Cost of investment	900	X reserves	8 900
Share of Y's post-acquisition profit (30% × 1000)	300	30% of Y post-acquisition profit (1000)	300
	1 200		9 200

If Y were an associate of X, the answer would not change.

Transactions between a venturer and a joint venture

The standard dealing with this issue is IAS 28, which treats transactions between an entity and its associates and transactions between an entity and its joint ventures in the same manner. When a venturer contributes or sells assets to a joint venture (referred to as 'downstream' transactions), recognition of any proportion of a gain or loss from the transaction should reflect the substance of the transaction.

The assets are retained by the joint venture, and provided the venturer has transferred the significant risks and rewards of ownership, the venturer should recognize only that portion of the gain or loss which is attributable to the interests of the other venturers. The same rule applies to 'upstream transactions', transactions in which the joint venture sells or contributes assets to the investor entity, i.e. gains or losses are recognized only to the extent of the unrelated investors' interests in the joint venture (IAS 28, para. 28).

A different rule applies, however, for downstream and upstream transactions when there is evidence of a reduction in the net realizable value of the assets involved or an impairment loss of those assets. In the case of downstream transactions, those losses shall be recognized in full by the investor, while in the case of upstream transactions the investor shall recognize its share in those losses (IAS 28, para. 29).

Now, complete the Activity below.

ACTIVITY 27.8

A joint venture, Gamma entity, is set up between A, B, and C entities. All venturers share equally in the joint venture. After establishment of the joint venture, A sells some items of equipment to Gamma for cash of €1.6m when the carrying value in A's books was €1m.

Show the adjustments to be made in A's consolidated financial statements in respect of the above transaction.

Activity feedback

In A's individual statements (with the investments in the joint venture at cost) the transaction will have been recorded as a sale of equipment thus:

Dr Cash	€1.6m
Cr Equipment	€1.0m
Cr Statement of comprehensive incomes – gain on sale	€0.6m

The gain on sale of €0.6m, in accordance with IAS 28, should only be recognized in the consolidated financial statements as that part which is attributable to the other venturers. Thus only 2/3 × 0.6m = €0.4m should be recognized.

Under the equity method, the following adjustments will be required.

Dr Statement of comprehensive income	€0.2m
Cr Investments in JV	€0.2m

Disclosure in respect of joint ventures

IFRS 11 does not include any disclosure requirements. These are included in IFRS 12 and are almost identical to those for associates (IFRS 12, paras 20–23) that we outlined earlier in this chapter.

The following is an example of disclosure of joint operations and joint ventures from Vodafone's financial statements for the year ended 31 March 2015.

REAL WORLD ILLUSTRATION

Joint operations

The Company's principal joint operation has share capital consisting solely of ordinary shares and is indirectly held, and principally operates in the UK. The financial and operating activities of the operation are jointly controlled by the participating shareholders and are primarily designed for all but an insignificant amount of the output to be consumed by the shareholders.

Name of joint operation	Principal activity	Country of incorporation or registration	Percentage [1] shareholdings
Cornerstone Telecommunications Infrastructure Limited	Network infrastructure	UK	50.0

Note:

1 Effective ownership percentages of Vodafone Group Plc at 31 March 2015, rounded to the nearest tenth of one percent.

Joint ventures

The financial and operating activities of the Group's joint ventures are jointly controlled by the participating shareholders. The participating shareholders have rights to the net assets of the joint ventures through their equity shareholdings. Unless otherwise stated, the Company's principal joint ventures all have share capital consisting solely of ordinary shares and are all indirectly held. The country of incorporation or registration of all joint ventures is also their principal place of operation.

Name of joint venture	Principal activity	Country of incorporation or registration	Percentage [1] shareholdings
Indus Towers Limited[2]	Network infrastructure	India	42.0
Vodafone Hutchison Australia Pty Limited[3]	Network operator	Australia	50.0

Notes:

1 Effective ownership percentages of Vodafone Group Plc at 31 March 2015 rounded to the nearest tenth of one percent.
2 42% of Indus Towers Limited is held by Vodafone India Limited ('VIL').
3 Vodafone Hutchison Australia Pty Limited has a year end of 31 December.

Joint ventures included the results of the Vodafone Omnitel B.V. until 21 February 2014. On 21 February 2014, the Group acquired the remaining 23.1% interest upon which date the results of the wholly-acquired entity were consolidated in the Group's financial statements.

The following table provides aggregated financial information for the Group's joint ventures as it relates to the amounts recognised in the income statement, statement of comprehensive income and statement of financial position.

	Investment in joint ventures			(Loss)/profit from continuing operations			Other comprehensive income			Total comprehensive (expense)/ income		
	2015 £m	2014 £m	2013 £m	**2015** £m	2014 £m	2013 £m	**2015** £m	2014 £m	2013 £m	**2015** £m	2014 £m	2013 £m
Vodafone Omnitel B.V.[1]	–	–	8 441	–	261	731	–	–	(5)	–	261	726
Indus Towers Limited	247	373	(26)	18	21	15	–	–	–	18	21	15
Vodafone Hutchison Australia Pty Limited	(667)	(559)	(609)	(160)	(66)	(223)	1	–	3	(159)	(66)	(220)
Other	89	28	6	(9)	5	(3)	–	–	2	(9)	5	(1)
Total	**(331)**	**(158)**	**7 812**	**(151)**	**221**	**520**	**1**	**–**	**–**	**(150)**	**221**	**520**

Note:

1 Prior to 21 February 2014, the other participating shareholder held substantive veto rights such that the Group did not unilaterally control the financial and operating policies of Vodafone Omnitel B.V.

REAL WORLD ILLUSTRATION (*Continued*)

The summarised financial information for each of the Group's material equity accounted joint ventures on a 100% ownership basis is set out below.

	Vodafone Omnitel B.V.[1]			IndusTower Limited			VodafoneHutchison Australia Pty Limited		
	2015	2014	2013	**2015**	2014	2013	**2015**	2014	2013
	£m	£m	£m	**£m**	£m	£m	**£m**	£m	£m
Income statement and statement of comprehensive income									
Revenue	_	4 931	6 186	1 580	1 547	1 489	1 838	2 032	2 497
Depreciation and amortisation	_	(937)	(999)	(407)	(507)	(256)	(415)	(423)	(454)
Interest income	_	1	2	29	20	8	2	10	6
Interest expense	_	(15)	(6)	(75)	(124)	(103)	(228)	(212)	(191)
Income tax (expense)/income	_	(174)	(430)	(182)	39	(53)	_	1	3
Profit or loss from continuing operations	_	339	951	44	51	34	(320)	(132)	(446)
Other comprehensive (expense)/income	_	_	(6)	_	_	_	2	_	6
Total comprehensive income/(expense)	_	339	945	44	51	34	(318)	(132)	(440)
Statement of financial position									
Non-current assets	_	_		1 482	1 798		2 285	1 916	
Current assets	_	_		278	423		424	590	
Non-current liabilities	_	_		(686)	(801)		(3 473)	(3.150)	
Current liabilities	_	_		(487)	(532)		(743)	(661)	
Equity shareholders' funds	_	_		(587)	(888)		1 507	1 305	
Cash and cash equivalents within current assets	_	_		6	143		90	60	
Non-current liabilities excluding trade and other payables and provisions	_	_		(481)	(701)		(3 325)	(3 060)	
Current liabilities excluding trade and other payables and provisions	_	_		(188)	(258)		(90)	(97)	

Note:

1 Prior to 21 February 2014, the other participating shareholder held substantive veto rights such that the Group did not unilaterally control the financial and operating policies of Vodafone Omnitel B.V.

The Group received a dividend of £166 million in the year to 31 March 2015 (2014: £26 million; 2013: £46 million) from Indus Towers Limited.

OVERVIEW ACTIVITY ON ACCOUNTING FOR ASSOCIATES AND JOINT ARRANGEMENTS

The following Activity illustrates further the accounting treatment for subsidiaries, associates and joint arrangements.

ACTIVITY 27.9

The following information is available with respect to Demos plc and its group of companies for the year ended 31 March 20X8. The income statements are as follows:

	Demos €000	Veta €000	Alpha €000	Sigma €000
Revenue	9 000	6 000	15 000	10 000
Cost of sales	3 900	2 200	8 000	5 000
Gross profit	5 100	3 800	7 000	5 000
Administration and distribution	900	1 200	2 100	1 100
Operating profit	4 200	2 600	4 900	3 900
Dividends received	50	—	—	—
Interest payable	150	170	—	1 100
Profit before tax	4 100	2 430	4 900	2 800
Taxation	1 750	1 100	2 100	1 100
Profit after tax	2 350	1 330	2 800	1 700

The statements of financial position of the group companies as at 31 March 20X8 were as follows:

	Demos €000	Veta €000	Alpha €000	Sigma €000
Assets				
Non-current assets				
Property, plant and equipment	16 500	10 130	30 000	27 500
Investments (at cost):				
Sigma	12 000			
Veta	2 500			
Alpha	5 700			
Brum	5 000			
Total non-current assets	41 700	10 130	30 000	27 500
Current assets	3 200	1 000	4 000	2 500
Total assets	44 900	11 130	34 000	30 000
Equity and liabilities				
Equity				
Share capital	10 000	5 000	4 000	8 000
Retained profits	29 800	1 330	19 800	12 100
Total equity	39 800	6 330	23 800	20 100
Liabilities				
Non-current liabilities	2 200	4 000	7 500	9 000
Current liabilities	2 900	800	2 700	900
Total liabilities	5 100	4 800	10 200	9 900
Total equity and liabilities	44 900	11 130	34 000	30 000

Additional information:

1 Demos plc and SwissCo SA have an equal interest in Veta, which they account for as a joint venture. On 31.3.X7, Veta was stated at €2 500 000 in the consolidated balance sheet of Demos plc.

2 Demos plc purchased 30 per cent of Alpha on 31.3.X4 for €5 700 000. On that date the retained profit of Alpha was €14 000 000. Demos plc treats Alpha as an associate company.

3 Demos plc purchased 70 per cent of the shares of Sigma for €12 000 000 when the net assets of Sigma were €15 000 000.

4 The investment in Brum represents a held for trading investment, the value of which has not changed from the previous year.

Prepare the consolidated financial statements for the Demos group for the year ended 31.3.X8.

Activity feedback

1 Consolidated income statement for the year ended 31.3.X8.

	€000
Revenue (9000 + 10 000)	19 000
Cost of sales (3900 + 5000)	8 900
Gross profit	10 100
Administration and distribution (900 + 1100)	2 000
Operating profit	8 100
Dividends received	50
Interest payable (150 + 1100)	1 250
Share of Alpha's net profit (30% × 2800)	840
Share of Veta's net profit (50% × 1330)	665
Profit before tax	8 405
Taxation (1750 + 1100)	2 850
Profit for the financial year	5 555
Attributable to:	
Equity shareholders	5 045
Non-controlling interests	510

The subsidiary Sigma is fully consolidated, while the equity method of accounting is used to account for the net profit of the associate Alpha and the joint venture Veta. Therefore, Demos reports its shares of the net profit of Alpha (30% × 2800) and Veta (50% × 1330).

2 Consolidated statement of financial position as at 31.3.X8.

	€000
Assets	
Non-current assets	
Property, plant and equipment (16 500 + 27 500)	44 000
Goodwill (Note 1)	1 500
Investments in:	
Veta (Note 2)	3 165
Alpha (Note 3)	7 440
Brum	5 000
	61 105
Current assets (3200 + 2500)	5 700
Total assets	66 805

ACTIVITY 27.9 *(Continued)*

Equity and liabilities	
Equity	
Share capital – Demos' capital	10 000
Retained profits (Note 4)	35 775
Non-controlling interests (Note 5)	6 030
Total equity	51 805
Liabilities	
Non-current liabilities (2200 + 9000)	11 200
Current liabilities (2900 + 900)	3 800
Total liabilities	15 000
Total equity and liabilities	66 805

Note 1: Goodwill relating to Sigma

Cost of investment	12 000
Less 70% of Sigma's net assets (15 000)	10 500
	1 500

See Chapter 26 for alternative method of calculating goodwill and non-controlling interests.

Note 2: Investment in joint venture Veta

Value stated at 31.3.X7 in consolidated SOFP	2 500
Share of profit for the year (50% × 1100)	665
	3 165

Note 3: Investment in Associate Alpha

Cost of investment	5 700
Add Share of post-acquisition profits:	
Retained profits at 31.3.X8	19 800
Less Retained profits at acquisition	14 000
Post-acquisition profits	5 800
Demos' share (30% × 5 800)	1 740
Equity value of investment (5 700 + 1 740)	7 440

Note 4: Retained profits

Demos' retained profits	29 800
Share of Sigma's post-acq. profits (70% × 5100)	3 570
Share of Alpha's retained profit (30% × 5800)	1 740
Share of Veta's profit for the year (50% × 1330)	665
	35 775

Note 5: Non-controlling interests

Share in net assets of Sigma (30% × 20 100)	6 030

RELATED PARTY DISCLOSURES

So far in this chapter and Chapters 25 and 26 we have dealt with accounting for business combinations, subsidiaries, associates and joint ventures. However, what we have not considered is that the parties in these groups often enter into transactions with each other that unrelated parties would not undertake. For example:

- Assets and liabilities may be transferred between parties at values above or below market value.
- One party may make a loan to another at a beneficial interest rate or without taking into account the full risk involved.
- Services carried out by one party for another may be charged at a reduced rate.

When working through the accounting techniques for business consolidation, we learnt that such transactions required elimination in the group consolidated accounts.

However, one of our basic assumptions within accounting is that transactions are carried out at arm's length between independent parties. If they are not, then users of financial statements will be misled if they are not provided with information in respect of these related party transactions. However, if we wish to give such information to users, we need to have uniformity of information provided by enterprises and clearly define when parties are related. This issue is dealt with by the IASB in IAS 24, *Related Party Disclosures*, which was first issued in July 1984 and most recently updated in December 2009.

Related party issues

IAS 24 in its consideration of related party issues maintains that related party relationships could have an effect on the financial position and operating results of the reporting enterprise and that this effect can occur even if no transactions have taken place.

IAS 24 definitions

Related party: a person or entity that is related to the entity that is preparing its financial statements (referred to as the 'reporting entity') (IAS 24.9).

(a) A person or a close member of that person's family is related to a reporting entity if that person:

    (i) has control or joint control over the reporting entity

    (ii) has significant influence over the reporting entity or

    (iii) is a member of the key management personnel of the reporting entity or of a parent of the reporting entity.

(b) An entity is related to a reporting entity if any of the following conditions applies:

    (i) The entity and the reporting entity are members of the same group (which means that each parent, subsidiary and fellow subsidiary is related to the others).

    (ii) One entity is an associate or joint venture of the other entity (or an associate or joint venture of a member of a group of which the other entity is a member).

    (iii) Both entities are joint ventures of the same third party.

    (iv) One entity is a joint venture of a third entity and the other entity is an associate of the third entity.

    (v) The entity is a post-employment defined benefit plan for the benefit of employees of either the reporting entity or an entity related to the reporting entity. If the reporting entity is itself such a plan, the sponsoring employers are also related to the reporting entity.

    (vi) The entity is controlled or jointly controlled by a person identified in (a).

    (vii) A person identified in (a)(i) has significant influence over the entity or is a member of the key management personnel of the entity (or of a parent of the entity).

Close members of the family of a person are those family members who may be expected to influence, or be influenced by, that person in their dealings with the entity and include:

(a) that person's children and spouse or domestic partner

(b) children of that person's spouse or domestic partner and

(c) dependants of that person or that person's spouse or domestic partner.

Compensation includes all employee benefits (as defined in IAS 19, *Employee Benefits*) including employee benefits to which IFRS 2, *Share-based Payment* applies. Employee benefits are all forms of consideration paid, in exchange for services rendered to the entity. It also includes such consideration paid on behalf of a parent of the entity in respect of the entity.

Compensation includes:

(a) short-term employee benefits, such as wages, salaries, and social security contributions, paid annual leave and paid sick leave, profit-sharing and bonuses (if payable within 12 months of the end of the period) and non-monetary benefits (such as medical care, housing, cars and free or subsidized goods or services) for current employees

(b) post-employment benefits such as pensions, other retirement benefits, post-employment life insurance and post-employment medical care

(c) other long-term employee benefits, including long-service leave or sabbatical leave, jubilee or other long-service benefits, long-term disability benefits and, if they are not payable wholly within 12 months after the end of the period, profit-sharing, bonuses and deferred compensation

(d) termination benefits and

(e) share-based payments.

Related party transaction is a transfer of resources, services or obligations between related parties, regardless of whether a price is charged.

Control and *significant influence* are as defined in IFRS 10 and IAS 28.

Disclosure requirements of IAS 24

This breaks down into two areas:

1 Where no transactions have occurred between the parties, but control exists. In this case, the relationship must be disclosed so that the user can form a view on the effect of the relationship on the reporting enterprise.

2 Where transactions have occurred between related parties. In this case, the nature of the relationship, the types of transactions and elements of the transactions necessary for an understanding of the financial statements must be disclosed.

Complete the following Activity.

IAS 24 requires disclosure of four elements:

ACTIVITY 27.10

Identify those elements of a related party transaction that you believe should be disclosed so as to provide an understanding of the financial statements.

Activity feedback

You probably identified:

- *name of related party*

- *volumes and amounts involved in the transactions*
- *amounts and volumes outstanding at the statement of financial position date*
- *amounts written off in respect of debts due from the related party*
- *pricing policies*
- *transfer of a major asset at a reduced price*
- *those where a free service was given.*

1 amount of the transactions

2 amount of outstanding balances

3 provision for doubtful debts

4 expense recognized during the period in respect of bad or doubtful debts together with the name of the entity's parent and key management personnel compensation in total and for each of:

(a) short-term employee benefits

(b) post-employment benefits

(c) other long-term benefits

(d) termination benefits

(e) share-based payment.

The following is an example of disclosure for related party transactions taken from Vodafone's financial statements for the year ended 31 March 2015.

REAL WORLD ILLUSTRATION

Related party transactions

The Group has a number of related parties including joint arrangements and associates, pension schemes and Directors and Executive Committee members (see note 12 "Investments in associates and joint arrangements", note 26 "Post employment benefits" and note 24 "Directors and key management compensation").

Transactions with joint arrangements and associates

Related party transactions with the Group's joint arrangements and associates primarily comprise fees for the use of products and services including network airtime and access charges, fees for the provision of network infrastructure and cash pooling arrangements.

No related party transactions have been entered into during the year which might reasonably affect any decisions made by the users of these consolidated financial statements except as disclosed below.

Dividends received from associates and joint ventures are disclosed in the consolidated statement of cash flows.

Transactions with Directors other than compensation

During the three years ended 31 March 2015, and as of 19 May 2015, neither any Director nor any other executive officer, nor any associate of any Director or any other executive officer, was indebted to the Company.

During the three years ended 31 March 2015, and as of 19 May 2015, the Company has not been a party to any other material transaction, or proposed transactions, in which any member of the key management personnel (including Directors, any other executive officer, senior manager, any spouse or relative of any of the foregoing or any relative of such spouse) had or was to have a direct or indirect material interest.

Dividends received from associates are disclosed in the consolidated statement of cash flows.

	2015 £m	2014 £m	2013 £m
Sales of goods and services to associates	32	231	238
Purchase of goods and services from associates	85	109	97
Sales of goods and services to joint arrangements	6	12	27
Purchase of goods and services from joint arrangements	566	570	568
Net interest income receivable from joint arrangements[1]	79	75	33
Trade balances owed:			
by associates	3	3	21
to associates	4	3	20
by joint arrangements	182	82	260
to joint arrangements	48	170	48
Other balances owed by joint arrangements[1]	61	57	1 065
Other balances owed to joint arrangements[1]	54	63	–

Note:

1 Amounts arise primarily through Vodafone Italy, Vodafone Hutchison Australia, Indus Towers and Cornerstone. Interest is paid in line with market rates.

SUMMARY

Previous chapters explored the financial reporting requirements for subsidiary entities, which are entities over which a holding company has control. This chapter has considered the IFRS requirements for two different types of intercompany investments. First, associate entities, which are entities over which the holding company has significance influence, but not control or joint control. The investments in associates need to be accounted for by way of equity accounting. This method is also one of the alternatives in accounting for investments in subsidiaries in individual financial statements.

Second, joint arrangements where two or more parties have joint control of the arrangement. There are two types of joint arrangements: joint ventures and joint operations. A joint arrangement is a joint operation where the parties have rights to the assets and obligations for the liabilities. If not, the joint arrangement is a joint venture. Joint ventures are also accounted for by way of equity accounting, while for joint operations the assets and liabilities are accounted for according to the applicable IFRSs.

In addition, this chapter considered the disclosures required for related party transactions.

EXERCISES

Suggested answers to exercises marked ✓ are to be found in the Student online resources, with suggested answers to the remaining questions available in the Instructor online resources.

1 Define a subsidiary, associate and related party entity.

2 Identify how a subsidiary, associate and related party will be dealt with in the financial statements of a group.

3 Using any information you can find in respect of 'Enron', discuss the following statement: *If Enron had prepared its financial statements using IFRS/IAS GAAP instead of US GAAP it would have had to account for special purpose entities differently.*

4 Disclosure of related party transactions in financial statements provides no useful information to users. Discuss.

5 Explain what a special purpose entity is and identify how the IASB requires these to be accounted for.

6 Hosterling purchased the following equity investments:

- On 1 October 2005: 80 per cent of the issued share capital of Sunlee. The acquisition was through a share exchange of three shares in Hosterling for every five shares in Sunlee. The market price of Hosterling's shares at 1 October 2005 was $5 per share.

- On 1 July 2006: 6 million shares in Amber paying $3 per share in cash and issuing to Amber's shareholders 6 per cent (actual and effective rate) loan notes on the basis of $100 loan note for every 100 shares acquired.

The summarized statements of profit or loss and other comprehensive income for the three companies for the year ended 30 September 2006 are:

	Hosterling $000	Sunlee $000	Amber $000
Revenue	105 000	62 000	50 000
Cost of sales	(68 000)	(36 500)	(61 000)
Gross profit/(loss)	37 000	25 500	(11 000)
Other income (note (i))	400	—	—
Distribution costs	(4 000)	(2 000)	(4 500)
Administrative expenses	(7 500)	(7 000)	(8 500)
Finance costs	(1 200)	(900)	—
Profit/(loss) before tax	24 700	15 600	(24 000)
Income tax (expense)/credit	(8 700)	(2 600)	4 000
Profit/(loss) for the period	16 000	13 000	(20 000)

The following information is relevant:

(i)   The other income is a dividend received from Sunlee on 31 March 2006.

(ii)   The details of Sunlee's and Amber's share capital and reserves at 1 October 2005 were:

	Sunlee $000	Amber $000
Equity shares of $1 each	20 000	15 000
Retained earnings	18 000	35 000

(iii) A fair value exercise was carried out at the date of acquisition of Sunlee with the following results:

	Carrying amount	Fair value	Remaining life (straight line)
	$000	$000	
Intellectual property	18 000	22 000	Still in development
Land	17 000	20 000	Not applicable
Plant	30 000	35 000	Five years

The fair values have not been reflected in Sunlee's financial statements. Plant depreciation is included in cost of sales. No fair value adjustments were required on the acquisition of Amber.

(iv) In the year ended 30 September 2006, Hosterling sold goods to Sunlee at a selling price of $18m. Hosterling made a profit of cost plus 25 per cent on these sales. $7.5m (at cost to Sunlee) of these goods were still in the inventories of Sunlee at 30 September 2006.

(v) Impairment tests for both Sunlee and Amber were conducted on 30 September 2006. They concluded that the goodwill of Sunlee should be written down by $1.6m and, due to its losses since acquisition, the investment in Amber was worth $21.5m.

(vi) All trading profits and losses are deemed to accrue evenly throughout the year.

Required:

(a) Calculate the goodwill arising on the acquisition of Sunlee at 1 October 2005.

(b) Calculate the carrying amount of the investment in Amber at 30 September 2006 under the equity method prior to the impairment test.

(c) Prepare the consolidated statement of profit or loss and other comprehensive income for the Hosterling Group for the year ended 30 September 2006.

(ACCA, 2.5 int., December 2006, adapted)

7   AC is a listed entity that has made several investments in recent years, including investments in BD and CF. The financial assistant of AC has prepared the accounts of AC for the year ended 31 December 2008. The financial assistant is unsure of how the investments should be accounted for and is not sufficiently experienced to prepare the consolidated financial statements for the AC group. The summarized statements of financial position of *AC, BD* and *CF* are given below.

Summarized statements of financial position	AC	BD	CF
	$000	$000	$000
Assets			
Non-current assets			
Property, plant and equipment	25 700	28 000	15 000
Investments	34 300	—	—
Current assets	17 000	14 000	6 000
TOTAL ASSETS	77 000	42 000	21 000
Equity and liabilities			
Equity			
Share capital ($1 ordinary shares)	30 000	20 000	8 000
Revaluation reserve	3 000	1 000	1 000
Other reserves	1 000	—	—
Retained earnings	22 000	9 000	9 000
	56 000	30 000	18 000
Non-current liabilities	6 000	4 000	—
Current liabilities	15 000	8 000	3 000
TOTAL EQUITY AND LIABILITIES	77 000	42 000	21 000

AC acquired 14m $1 ordinary shares in BD on 1 March 2003 for $18m. At the date of acquisition, BD had retained earnings of $3m and a balance of $1m on revaluation reserve. On 1 July 2008, AC acquired a further 20 per cent stake in BD for $7m. BD made profits of $1.6m in the year to 31 December 2008 and profits are assumed to accrue evenly throughout the year. AC acquired 40 per cent of the $1 ordinary share capital of CF on 1 February 2005 at a cost of $7m. The retained earnings of CF at the date of acquisition totalled $6m. The remaining investment relates to an available for sale investment. The investment has a market value of $2.6m at 31 December 2008. The financial assistant was unsure of how this investment should be treated, so the investment is included at its original cost. CF revalued a property during the year resulting in a revaluation gain of $1m. There were no other revaluations of property, plant and equipment in the year for the other entities in the group. All revaluations to date relate to land, which is not depreciated in accordance with group policy. During the period, AC sold goods to CF with a sales value of $800 000. Half of the goods remain in inventories at the year end. AC made 25 per cent profit margin on all sales to CF. An impairment review was performed in the period and it was estimated that the goodwill arising on the acquisition of CF was impaired by 30 per cent.

Required:

(a) Explain how each of the three investments held by AC should be accounted for in the consolidated financial statements.

(b) Prepare the consolidated statement of financial position of the AC group as at 31 December 2008.

(CIMA, P8, May 2009)

8 On 1 April 2009, Pandar purchased 80 per cent of the equity shares in Salva. The acquisition was through a share exchange of three shares in Pandar for every five shares in Salva. The market prices of Pandar's and Salva's shares at 1 April 2009 were £6 and £3.20 per share respectively. On the same date, Pandar acquired 40 per cent of the equity shares in Ambra paying £2 per share. The summarized profit and loss accounts for the three companies for the year ended 30 September 2009 are:

	Pandar £000	Salva £000	Ambra £000
Turnover	210 000	150 000	50 000
Cost of sales	(126 000)	(100 000)	(40 000)
Gross profit	84 000	50 000	10 000
Distribution costs	(11 200)	(7 000)	(5 000)
Administrative expenses	(18 300)	(9 000)	(11 000)
Investment income (interest and dividends)	9 500	—	—
Finance costs	(1 800)	(3 000)	—
Profit (loss) before tax	62 200	31 000	(6 000)
Corporation tax (expense) relief	(15 000)	(10 000)	1 000
Profit (loss) for the year	47 200	21 000	(5 000)

The following information for the equity of the companies at 30 September 2009 is available:

	Pandar £000	Salva £000	Ambra £000
Equity shares of £1 each	200 000	120 000	40 000
Share premium	300 000	—	—
Profit and loss account at 1 October 2008	40 000	152 000	15 000
Profit (loss) for the year ended 30 September 2009	47 200	21 000	(5 000)
Dividends paid (26 September 2009)	—	8 000	—

The following information is relevant:

(i) The fair values of the net assets of Salva at the date of acquisition were equal to their carrying amounts with the exception of an item of plant which had a carrying amount of £12m and a fair value of £17m. This plant had a remaining life of five years (straight line depreciation) at the date of acquisition of Salva.

In addition, Salva owns the registration of a popular Internet domain name. The registration, which had a negligible cost, has a five-year remaining life (at the date of acquisition); however, it is renewable indefinitely at a nominal cost. At the date of acquisition, the domain name was valued by a specialist company at £20m. The fair values of the plant and the domain name have not been reflected in Salva's financial statements. No fair value adjustments were required on the acquisition of the investment in Ambra.

(ii) Immediately after its acquisition of Salva, Pandar invested £50m in an 8 per cent loan note from Salva. All interest accruing to 30 September 2009 had been accounted for by both companies. Salva also has other loans in issue at 30 September 2009.

(iii) Pandar has credited the whole of the dividend it received from Salva to investment income.

(iv) After the acquisition, Pandar sold goods to Salva for £15m on which Pandar made a gross profit of 20 per cent. Salva had one third of these goods still in its inventory at 30 September 2009. There are no intra-group current account balances at 30 September 2009.

(v) The goodwill of Salva has an indefinite life and no impairment losses on Salva's goodwill have occurred. However, due to its losses, the value of Pandar's investment in Ambra has been impaired by £2.2 million at 30 September 2009.

(vi) All items in the above profit and loss accounts are deemed to accrue evenly over the year unless otherwise indicated.

Required:

(a) (i) Calculate the goodwill arising on the acquisition of Salva at 1 April 2009.

    (ii) Calculate the carrying amount of the investment in Ambra to be included within the consolidated statement of financial position as at 30 September 2009.

(b) Prepare the consolidated profit and loss account for the Pandar Group for the year ended 30 September 2009.

(ACCA, December 2009, adapted)

9 (a) On 1 April 2009, Picant acquired 75 per cent of Sander's equity shares in a share exchange of three shares in Picant for every two shares in Sander. The market prices of Picant's and Sander's shares at the date of acquisition were £3.20 and £4.50 respectively. In addition to this, Picant agreed to pay a further amount on 1 April 2010 that was contingent upon the post-acquisition performance of Sander. At the date of acquisition, Picant assessed the fair value of this contingent consideration at £4.2m, but by 31 March 2010 it was clear that the actual amount to be paid would be only £2.7m (ignore discounting). Picant has recorded the share exchange and provided for the initial estimate of £4.2m for the contingent consideration. On 1 October 2009, Picant also acquired 40 per cent of the equity shares of Adler paying £4 in cash per acquired share and issuing at par one £100 7 per cent loan note for every 50 acquired shares in Adler. This consideration has also been recorded by Picant. Picant has no other investments.

The summarized statements of financial position of the three companies at 31 March 2010 are:

	Picant £000	Sander £000	Adler £000
Assets			
Non-current assets			
Property, plant and equipment	37 500	24 500	21 000
Investments	45 000	—	—
	82 500	24 500	21 000
Current assets			
Inventory	10 000	9 000	5 000
Trade receivables	6 500	1 500	3 000
	16 500	10 500	8 000
Total assets	99 000	35 000	29 000
Equity and liabilities			
Equity			
Equity shares of £1 each	25 000	8 000	5 000
Share premium	19 800	—	—
Profit and loss account			
– at 1 April 2009	16 200	16 500	15 000
– for the year ended 31 March 2010	11 000	1 000	6 000
Total equity	72 000	25 500	26 000

Liabilities			
Non-current liabilities – 7% loan notes	14 500	2 000	—
Current liabilities	4 200	—	—
Other current liabilities	8 300	7 500	3 000
	12 500	7 500	3 000
Total liabilities	27 000	9 500	3 000
Total equity and liabilities	99 000	35 000	29 000

The following information is relevant:

(i) At the date of acquisition, the fair values of Sander's property, plant and equipment were equal to their carrying amounts with the exception of Sander's factory which had a fair value of £2m above its carrying amount. Sander has not adjusted the carrying amount of the factory as a result of the fair value exercise. This requires additional annual depreciation of £100 000 in the consolidated financial statements in the post-acquisition period. Also at the date of acquisition, Sander had an intangible asset of £500 000 for software in its balance sheet. Picant's directors believed the software to have no recoverable value at the date of acquisition and Sander wrote it off shortly after its acquisition.

(ii) At 31 March 2010, Picant's current account with Sander was £3.4m (debit). This did not agree with the equivalent balance in Sander's books due to some goods-in-transit invoiced at £1.8m that were sent by Picant on 28 March 2010, but had not been received by Sander until after the year end. Picant sold these goods at cost plus 50 per cent.

(iii) Impairment tests were carried out on 31 March 2010. It was identified that the value of the investment in Adler was not impaired but, due to poor trading performance, the consolidated goodwill was impaired by £2.7 million.

(iv) Assume all profits accrue evenly through the year.

Required:
Prepare the consolidated statement of financial position for Picant as at 31 March 2010.

(b) Picant has been approached by a potential new customer, Trilby, to supply it with a substantial quantity of goods on three months' credit terms. Picant is concerned at the risk that such a large order represents in the current difficult economic climate, especially as Picant's normal credit terms are only one month's credit. To support its application for credit, Trilby has sent Picant a copy of Tradhat's most recent audited consolidated financial statements. Trilby is a wholly owned subsidiary within the Tradhat group. Tradhat's consolidated financial statements show a strong statement of financial position including healthy liquidity ratios.

Required:
Comment on the importance that Picant should attach to Tradhat's consolidated financial statements when deciding on whether to grant credit terms to Trilby.

(ACCA, June 2010, adapted)

10 Extracts from the financial statements of MAT, X and Y are presented below.

Statements of financial position as at 31 December 2013	*MAT*	*X*	*Y*
ASSETS	*$m*	*$m*	*$m*
Non-current assets	80	70	60
Property, plant and equipment	70	—	—
Investment in X	40	—	—
Investment in Y	190	70	60
Current assets	30	40	20
Total assets	220	110	80

EQUITY AND LIABILITIES
Equity attributable to owners of the parent

Share capital ($1 equity shares)	60	40	30
Share premium	20	5	5
Other reserves	7	—	—
Retained earnings	65	43	25
Total equity	152	88	60
Non-current liabilities	50	—	—
Current liabilities	18	22	20
Total liabilities	68	22	20
Total equity and liabilities	220	110	80

Additional information:

1 MAT acquired 80 per cent of the equity share capital of X on 1 January 2011 when the retained earnings of X were $25 million. This acquisition resulted in MAT having power over X which, when exercised, affects its return from the investment. X has not issued any shares since the acquisition date. The non-controlling interest in X was measured at its fair value of $20 million at the date of acquisition.

2 MAT acquired 50 per cent of the equity share capital of Y on 1 January 2012 when the retained earnings of Y were $11 million. This acquisition was classified as a joint venture in accordance with IFRS 11 *Joint Arrangements*. Y has not issued any shares since the acquisition date.

3 MAT conducted its annual impairment review and concluded that the goodwill on the acquisition of X was impaired by 20 per cent at 31 December 2013. No other impairments of goodwill have arisen.

4 The balance on 'other reserves' relates to movements in the values of investments in X and Y in the books of MAT. $5 million relates to X and the remainder to Y.

5 MAT's non-current liabilities represent a long-term borrowing taken out on 1 January 2013. The borrowing has a coupon rate of 4 per cent per annum and the interest due in respect of 2013 has been paid and charged to profit for the year. The effective interest rate associated with this instrument is 8 per cent per annum.

6 For the first time in November 2013, MAT sold goods to Y with a value of $20 million and a gross margin of 40 per cent. At 31 December 2013, 75 per cent of these items remained in Y's inventories.

Required:

(a) Prepare the consolidated statement of financial position for the MAT group as at 31 December 2013.

(b) MAT acquired a further 4 million of the equity shares of X on 1 January 2014 for $14 million.

   (i) Explain how this additional acquisition will impact on the preparation of the consolidated financial statements of MAT for the year to 31 December 2014.

   (ii) Calculate the adjustment that will be required to be made to the group's statement of financial position in respect of this acquisition.

(CIMA, Financial Management, February 2014)

11 Extracts from the financial statements of AB, CD and EF are presented below.

Statements of profit or loss and other comprehensive income for the year ended 31 December 2011	*AB*	*CD*	*EF*
	$000	*$000*	*$000*
Revenue	1 200	290	150
Cost of sales	(810)	(110)	(80)
Gross profit	390	180	70
Operating expenses	(100)	(40)	(20)
	290	140	50
Investment income	50	—	—
Finance costs	(45)	(10)	(5)
Profit before tax	295	130	45
Income tax expense	(80)	(30)	(15)
Profit for the year	215	100	30
Other comprehensive income:			
Revaluation of property, net of tax	60	20	10
Other comprehensive income for the year, net of tax	60	20	10
Total comprehensive income	275	120	40

Statements of changes in equity for the year ended 31 December 2011	*AB*	*CD*	*EF*
	$000	*$000*	*$000*
Equity at 1 January 2011	1 700	840	500
Total comprehensive income for the year	275	120	40
Dividends	(100)	(50)	—
Equity at 31 December 2011	1 875	910	540

Additional information:

1 AB acquired 80 per cent of the ordinary share capital of CD for $620 000 on 1 January 2008 when the retained reserves of CD were $420 000. CD has 200 000 $1 ordinary shares in issue and there have been no share issues since the acquisition date. The group policy is to measure the non-controlling interest at fair value at the date of acquisition. The fair value of the non-controlling interest at 1 January 2008 was $180 000.

2 On 1 January 2008, the fair value of CD's net assets was the same as their book value with the exception of depreciable property, the fair value of which was $60 000 higher than its book value. The property had a remaining useful life of 15 years at the date of acquisition. Depreciation on property is charged to cost of sales.

3 Goodwill on the acquisition of CD was impaired for the first time by 25 per cent in the year to 31 December 2010. An impairment review conducted at 31 December 2011 indicated a further impairment of 10 per cent of the remaining carrying value of goodwill. Impairment losses on goodwill are charged to group operating expenses.

4 AB acquired 40 per cent of the ordinary share capital of EF on 1 July 2009, when the equity was $435 000.

Required:

(a) Prepare for the AB Group for the year ended 31 December 2011:

(i) a consolidated statement of profit or loss and other comprehensive income

(ii) a consolidated statement of changes in equity.

(b) AB purchased a further 10 per cent of the ordinary share capital of CD on 1 January 2012 for $120 000.

(i) Explain how the acquisition of this additional investment will be accounted for in the consolidated financial statements of the AB Group for the year to 31 December 2012.

(ii) Calculate the debit or credit that will be made to the consolidated retained reserves of the AB Group for the year to 31 December 2012 in respect of this additional 10 per cent share purchase.

(c) AB purchased a further 20 per cent of the ordinary share capital of EF on 1 January 2012.

Explain how the acquisition of the additional investment in EF will be accounted for in the consolidated financial statements of the AB Group for the year to 31 December 2012.

(CIMA, Financial Management, May 2012)

12 On 1 October 2013, Penketh acquired 90 million of Sphere's 150 million $1 equity shares. The acquisition was achieved through a share exchange of one share in Penketh for every three shares in Sphere. At that date the stock market prices of Penketh's and Sphere's shares were $4 and $2.50 per share respectively. Additionally, Penketh will pay $1.54 cash on 30 September 2014 for each share acquired. Penketh's finance cost is 10 per cent per annum. The retained earnings of Sphere brought forward at 1 April 2013 were $120 million. The summarized statements of profit or loss and other comprehensive income for the companies for the year ended 31 March 2014 are:

	Penketh	Sphere
	$000	$000
Revenue	620 000	310 000
Cost of sales	(400 000)	(150 000)
Gross profit	220 000	160 000
Distribution costs	(40 000)	(20 000)
Administrative expenses	(36 000)	(25 000)
Investment income (note (iii))	5 000	1 600
Finance costs	(2 000)	(5 600)
Profit before tax	147 000	111 000
Income tax expense	(45 000)	(31 000)
Profit for the year	102 000	80 000
Other comprehensive income		
Gain/(loss) on revaluation of land (notes (i) and (ii))	(2 200)	3 000
Total comprehensive income	99 800	83 000

The following information is relevant:

(i) A fair value exercise conducted on 1 October 2013 concluded that the carrying amounts of Sphere's net assets were equal to their fair values with the following exceptions:

— the fair value of Sphere's land was $2 million in excess of its carrying amount.

— an item of plant had a fair value of $6 million in excess of its carrying amount. The plant had a remaining life of two years at the date of acquisition. Plant depreciation is charged to cost of sales.

— Penketh placed a value of $5 million on Sphere's good trading relationships with its customers. Penketh expected, on average, a customer relationship to last for a further five years. Amortization of intangible assets is charged to administrative expenses.

(ii) Penketh's group policy is to revalue land to market value at the end of each accounting period. Prior to its acquisition, Sphere's land had been valued at historical cost, but it has adopted the group policy since its acquisition. In addition to the fair value increase in Sphere's land of $2 million (see note (i)), it had increased by a further $1 million since the acquisition.

(iii) On 1 October 2013, Penketh also acquired 30 per cent of Ventor's equity shares. Ventor's profit after tax for the year ended 31 March 2014 was $10 million and during March 2014, Ventor paid a dividend of $6 million. Penketh uses equity accounting in its consolidated financial statements for its investment in Ventor. Sphere did not pay any dividends in the year ended 31 March 2014.

(iv) After the acquisition Penketh sold goods to Sphere for $20 million. Sphere had one fifth of these goods still in inventory at 31 March 2014. In March 2014, Penketh sold goods to Ventor for $15 million, all of which were still in inventory at 31 March 2014. All sales to Sphere and Ventor had a mark-up on cost of 25 per cent.

(v) Penketh's policy is to value the non-controlling interest at the date of acquisition at its fair value. For this purpose, the share price of Sphere at that date (1 October 2013) is representative of the fair value of the shares held by the non-controlling interest.

(vi) All items in the above statements of profit or loss and other comprehensive income are deemed to accrue evenly over the year unless otherwise indicated.

Required:

(a) Calculate the consolidated goodwill as at 1 October 2013.

(b) Prepare the consolidated statement of profit or loss and other comprehensive income of Penketh for the year ended 31 March 2014.

(ACCA, Financial Reporting, June 2014)

13   Joey, a public limited company, operates in the media sector. Joey has investments in two companies. The draft statements of financial position at 30 November 2014 are as follows:

	Joey $m	Margy $m	Hulty $m
Assets			
Non-current assets			
Property, plant and equipment	3 295	2 000	1 200
Investments in subsidiaries and other investments:			
Margy	1 675		
Hulty	700		
	5 670	2 000	1 200
Current assets	985	861	150
Total assets	6 655	2 861	1 350
Equity and liabilities			
Share capital	850	1 020	600
Retained earnings	3 340	980	350
Other components of equity	250	80	40
Total equity	4 440	2 080	990
Non-current liabilities	1 895	675	200
Current liabilities	320	106	160
Total liabilities	2 215	781	360
Total equity and liabilities	6 655	2 861	1 350

The following information is relevant to the preparation of the group financial statements:

1   On 1 December 2011, Joey acquired 30 per cent of the ordinary shares of Margy for a cash consideration of $600 million when the fair value of Margy's identifiable net assets was $1 840 million. Joey treated Margy as an associate and has equity accounted for Margy up to 1 December 2013. Joey's share of Margy's undistributed profit amounted to $90 million and its share of a revaluation gain amounted to $10 million.

   On 1 December 2013, Joey acquired a further 40 per cent of the ordinary shares of Margy for a cash consideration of $975 million and gained control of the company. The cash consideration has been added to the equity accounted balance for Margy at 1 December 2013 to give the carrying amount at 30 November 2014. At 1 December 2013, the fair value of Margy's identifiable net assets was $2 250 million. At 1 December 2013, the fair value of the equity interest in Margy held by Joey before the business combination was $705 million and the fair value of the non-controlling interest of 30 per cent was assessed as $620 million. The retained earnings and other components of equity of Margy at 1 December 2013 were $900 million and $70 million respectively. It is group policy to measure the non-controlling interest at fair value.

2   At the time of the business combination with Margy, Joey has included in the fair value of Margy's identifiable net assets, an unrecognized contingent liability of $6 million in respect of a warranty claim in progress against Margy. In March 2014, there was a revision of the estimate of the liability to $5 million. The amount has met the criteria to be recognized as a provision in current liabilities in the financial statements of Margy and the revision of the estimate is deemed to be a measurement period adjustment.

3   Additionally, buildings with a carrying amount of $200 million had been included in the fair valuation of Margy at 1 December 2013. The buildings have a remaining useful life of 20 years at 1 December 2013. However, Joey had commissioned an independent valuation of the buildings of Margy, which was not complete at 1 December 2013 and therefore not considered in the fair value of the identifiable net assets at the acquisition date. The valuations were received on 1 April 2014 and resulted in a decrease of $40 million in the fair value of property, plant and equipment at the date of acquisition. This decrease does not affect the fair value of the non-controlling interest at acquisition and has not been entered into the financial statements of Margy. Buildings are depreciated on the straight line basis and it is group policy to leave revaluation gains on disposal in equity. The excess of the fair value of the net assets over their carrying value, at 1 December 2013, is due to an increase in the value of non-depreciable land and the contingent liability.

4   On 1 December 2013, Joey acquired 80 per cent of the equity interests of Hulty, a private entity, in exchange for cash of $700 million. Because the former owners of Hulty needed to dispose of the investment quickly, they did not have sufficient time to market the investment to many potential buyers. The fair value of the identifiable net assets was $960 million. Joey determined that the fair value of the 20 per cent non-controlling interest in Hulty at that date was $250 million. Joey reviewed the procedures used to identify and measure the assets acquired and liabilities assumed and to measure the fair value of both the non-controlling interest and the consideration transferred. After that review, Hulty determined that the procedures and resulting measures were appropriate. The retained earnings and other components of equity of Hulty at 1 December 2013 were $300 million and $40 million respectively. The excess in fair value is due to an unrecognized franchise right, which Joey had granted to Hulty on 1 December 2012 for five years. At the time of the acquisition, the franchise right could be sold for its market price. It is group policy to measure the non-controlling interest at fair value. All goodwill arising on acquisitions has been impairment tested with no impairment being required.

5 Joey is looking to expand into publishing and entered into an arrangement with Content Publishing (CP), a public limited company, on 1 December 2013. CP will provide content for a range of books and online publications. CP is entitled to a royalty calculated as 10 per cent of sales and 30 per cent of gross profit of the publications. Joey has sole responsibility for all printing, binding and platform maintenance of the online website. The agreement states that key strategic sales and marketing decisions must be agreed jointly. Joey selects the content to be covered in the publications but CP has the right of veto over this content. However on 1 June 2014, Joey and CP decided to set up a legal entity, JCP, with equal shares and voting rights. CP continues to contribute content into JCP but does not receive royalties. Joey continues the printing, binding and platform maintenance. The sales and cost of sales in the period were $5 million and $2 million respectively. The whole of the sale proceeds and the costs of sales were recorded in Joey's financial statements with no accounting entries being made for JCP or amounts due to CP. Joey currently funds the operations. Assume that the sales and costs accrue evenly throughout the year and that all of the transactions relating to JCP have been in cash.

6 At 30 November 2013, Joey carried a property in its statement of financial position at its revalued amount of $14 million in accordance with IAS 16, *Property, Plant and Equipment*. Depreciation is charged at $300 000 per year on the straight line basis. In March 2014, the management decided to sell the property and it was advertised for sale. By 31 March 2014, the sale was considered to be highly probable and the criteria for IFRS 5, *Non-current Assets Held for Sale and Discontinued Operations* were met at this date. At that date, the asset's fair value was $15.4 million and its value in use was $15·8 million. Costs to sell the asset were estimated at $300 000. On 30 November 2014, the property was sold for $15.6 million. The transactions regarding the property are deemed to be material and no entries have been made in the financial statements regarding this property since 30 November 2013 as the cash receipts from the sale were not received until December 2014.

Required:

Prepare the group consolidated statement of financial position of Joey as at 30 November 2014.

(ACCA, Corporate Reporting (International), December 2014)

14 Coatmin is a government-controlled bank. Coatmin was taken over by the government during the recent financial crisis. Coatmin does not directly trade with other government-controlled banks but has underwritten the development of the nationally owned railway and postal service. The directors of Coatmin are concerned about the volume and cost of disclosing its related party interests because they extend theoretically to all other government-controlled enterprises and banks.

Required:

The directors have requested advice on the nature and importance of the disclosure of related party relationships and specific advice on the disclosure of the above relationships in the financial statements.

(ACCA, Corporate Reporting (International), December 2014, adapted)

FOREIGN CURRENCY TRANSLATION

28

OBJECTIVES After studying this chapter you should be able to:

- explain the necessity for foreign currency conversion and translation

- understand and apply the techniques of currency translation

- understand the concepts of functional currency and presentation currency

- describe the IFRS regulations in respect of foreign currency transactions

- describe the IFRS regulations in respect of translating foreign entities

- explain the basics of hedging foreign currency exposure and the application of hedge accounting

- understand specific issues such as extending the net investment, translating goodwill, accounting for disposals, translating into currencies of hyperinflationary economies

- understand the IFRS disclosure requirements.

INTRODUCTION

Business is increasingly international. Whenever a business has any dealings abroad, it will be involved in 'foreign' currencies. Since an entity generally keeps its accounting records and prepares its accounting reports in its own 'home' currency, figures expressed in foreign money units need to be re-expressed in 'home' units or whatever the reporting currency is. If foreign currency exchange rates remain absolutely constant, i.e. if the value of one currency in terms of the other does not change, then no difficulties arise. But this is rarely the case and, as we all know, exchange rates can and do fluctuate very considerably over relatively short periods of time.

CURRENCY CONVERSION

Currency conversion is required when a foreign currency transaction is completed within an accounting period. A transaction, foreign or otherwise, can be regarded as comprising two events:

- the purchase or sale of an asset or the incurring of an expense or item of income
- the receipt or payment of monies for these assets, expenses or items of income.

These events need to be recorded in an entity's books as they occur (see Activity 28.1).

ACTIVITY 28.1

A UK entity sells goods to a Swiss entity on 1 May 20X2 for SWFr750 000. Payment is received on 1 August 20X2.

> Exchange rate on 1 May 20X2 is £1 = SWFr3.5
>
> and on 1 August 20X2 is £1 = SWFr3.7.

The year end for the entity is 30 September 20X2 and the reporting currency is the British pound. Record this transaction in the entity's books and name the balance on the accounts receivable account.

Activity feedback

Remembering the transaction comprises two events, we need to record the sale of goods immediately, but we must record the event in £s not SWFrs.

Both the sales and the account receivables are recorded for an amount of £214 286 (750 000 / 3.5; exchange rate on 1 May 20X2).

When payment is received on 1 August 20X2, it will be in the form of SWFr750 000, which we must convert to sterling at the exchange rate at the time = 750 000 / 3.7 = £202 703. This event will be recorded as:

Dr Cash	202 703	
Cr Accounts receivable		202 703

Thus, there will be a balance on the accounts receivable account of £11 583, which is obviously a loss on exchange and will need to be reported in profit or loss.

Similarly, if the exchange rate had decreased from May to August, a profit on exchange would have occurred, which again would be reported as profit on ordinary activities.

CURRENCY TRANSLATION

Activity 28.1 involved a transaction that was completed by the year end, but we need to consider how to deal with foreign transactions that are not completed by the year end (see Activity 28.2).

ACTIVITY 28.2

Let us assume in Activity 28.1 that the entity's year end is 30 June 20X2 when the exchange rate is £1 = SWFr3.6. Record this transaction in the entity's books.

Activity feedback

The initial sale will be recorded as before, but at the year end 30 June 20X2 the accounts receivable account will show a balance of £214 286. This balance is not correct, because if the debt was paid at this date we would receive SWFr750 000 = £208 333, which is the value of the debt at 30 June 20X2. Thus, we translate the accounts receivable account at the year end at the exchange rate ruling, which is known as the spot rate, at a given date. The exchange difference of £6253 (£208 033 – £214 286) is the loss on exchange identified as at 30 June 20X2, which will be debited to profit or loss within the statement of comprehensive income:

Dr Exchange loss	6253
Cr Accounts receivable	6253

When the debt is finally paid on 1 August 20X2, a further loss of £5330 is identified for the next year. Notice the total loss of £11 583 is now split over the two years.

The currency translation follows the idea of prudence as we are taking account of the loss as soon as we are aware of it. However, what would we have done if on 30 June 20X2 the exchange rate was £1 = SWFr3.4?

This time at the year end, the debtor would translate as 750 000 / 3.4 = £220 588, giving a profit on exchange of £6302 and on 1 August 20X2 when the debt is finally settled, a loss of £17 885. The gain of £6302 is an unrealized gain and prudence might suggest that we should not recognize this gain. But let us see what IAS 21 says on this issue.

IAS 21 REQUIREMENTS FOR ENTITY'S FOREIGN CURRENCY TRANSACTIONS

The Standard was issued in 1983, revised in 1993 and revised again under the improvement project in 2004. Several small amendments have been made since. According to IAS 21, para. 28, exchange differences on monetary positions following from transactions need to be recognized in profit or loss. These can be either realized in the period (when the monetary position is cleared by payment) or unrealized (when the monetary position is still outstanding at the balance sheet date).

Thus, the IAS is telling us to recognize an unrealized gain in the accounts (in the Activity this was £6302). This treatment can be justified on the grounds that:

- where exchange gains arise on short-term monetary items, their ultimate cash realization can normally be assessed with reasonable certainty and they are therefore realized in accordance with realization conventions
- it provides symmetry with losses.

Now attempt the following Activity.

ACTIVITY 28.3

An entity, Axel, purchases an asset for €12 000 from a foreign entity on 1.3.X2 when the exchange rate between the two currencies involved was 1FC = €2. The currency in which Axel holds its accounts is FCs. At the statement of financial position date of Axel, 30.6.X2, the exchange rate is 1FC = €1.50. Show the entries by Axel to record this transaction initially and those required at the statement of financial position date.

(Continued)

ACTIVITY 28.3 (Continued)

Activity feedback

On 1.3.X2:

Dr Asset	6000
Cr Accounts payable	6000

On 30.6.X2

Dr Exchange loss	2000
Cr Accounts payable	2000

The balance of accounts payable is FC8000 (12.000 / 1.5).

In Activity 28.3, only the monetary item, accounts payable, has been reported using the closing rate at the statement of financial position date. Under the requirements of IAS 21, only foreign currency monetary items should be reported using the closing rate; non-monetary items, which are carried at historical cost denominated in a foreign currency, should be reported using the exchange rate at the date of acquisition or, if the fair value is used, the exchange rate prevalent when the fair value was determined. Therefore, under historical cost accounting, the book value of the asset is not adapted when exchange rates change.

Loans

Transactions can also involve the origination of a loan, which is a monetary item. Thus, a loan will be translated as any other monetary item at the closing rate and the exchange gain or loss credited or charged to income. We might question the rationale for taking the unrealized exchange gain on the loan at the statement of financial position date to profit here, but it at least provides consistent symmetrical treatment with the loss, which is equally unrealized.

Functional currency

In a situation where an entity has many transactions in foreign currencies, the question may arise in which currency the entity should do its accounting. One might think of the local currency in the country where the company is situated, but that is not necessarily the case.

IAS 21 uses the concept of functional currency. The functional currency is the currency of the primary economic environment in which the entity operates. An entity should translate all transactions into its functional currency. All other currencies than the functional currency are foreign currencies. An entity that is situated in the Netherlands, with the euro as its local currency, might have the US dollar as its functional currency, for instance, when the entity is working in the oil and gas industry that is predominantly dollar-based. For this entity, the euro would be a foreign currency. All transactions in euros would need to be translated into US dollars.

When determining its functional currency, an entity has to consider the guidance in accordance with IAS 21, paras 9–14. There is a certain hierarchy in determining the functional currency.

First, the primary economic environment in which an entity operates is normally the one in which it primarily generates and expends cash. An entity considers the following factors in determining its functional currency:

(a) the currency:

(i) that mainly influences sales prices for goods and services and

(ii) of the country whose competitive forces and regulations mainly determine the sales prices of its goods and services.

(b) the currency that mainly influences labour, material and other costs of providing goods or services.

Second, the following factors may also provide evidence of an entity's functional currency:

(a) the currency in which funds from financing activities are generated

(b) the currency in which receipts from operating activities are usually retained.

To summarize, first the currency of sales and costs, and second the currency of assets and liabilities.

Each individual reporting entity, including all foreign entities or foreign operations (a subsidiary, associate, joint arrangement or branch of the reporting entity), should determine its own functional currency. Only individual entities can have a functional currency. A group does not have a functional currency. IAS 21 gives some additional factors to consider in determining the functional currency of a foreign operation. The specific question is whether the foreign operation determines its own functional currency based on sales, costs, assets and liabilities (as indicated above), or whether this foreign operation is so close to the reporting entity that its functional currency should be the same as that of the reporting entity. Factors to take into account are:

- Whether the activities of the foreign operation are carried out as an extension of the reporting entity, rather than being carried out with a significant degree of autonomy. An example of the former is when the foreign operation only sells goods imported from the reporting entity and remits the proceeds to it. An example of the latter is when the operation accumulates cash and other monetary items, incurs expenses, generates income and arranges borrowings, all substantially in its local currency.

- Whether transactions with the reporting entity are a high or low proportion of the foreign operation's activities.

- Whether cash flows from the activities of the foreign operation directly affect the cash flows of the reporting entity and are readily available for remittance to it.

- Whether cash flows from the activities of the foreign operation are sufficient to service existing and normally expected debt obligations without funds being made available by the reporting entity.

When the above indicators are mixed and the functional currency is not obvious, management uses its judgement to determine the functional currency that most faithfully represents the economic effects of the underlying transactions, events and conditions.

We provide below some examples where determination of an entity's functional currency is less than apparent.

Example 28.1

For each of the following, determine the functional currency:

1 An entity operating in France owns several buildings in Paris that are rented to foreign companies, mostly US companies. The lease contracts are determined in US dollars and payment can be made in either US dollars or euros.

   We have a mixed situation here and therefore need to consider the factors outlined in IAS 21:

   (a) The local circumstances in Paris determine the rental yields, thus indicating the euro as functional currency.

   (b) Lease payments denominated and could be paid in US dollars indicates the US dollar as the functional currency.

   (c) Presumably, labour and other expenses are paid in euros indicating the euro as the functional currency.

Overall, it is the euro that would appear to most faithfully represent the economic effects of the entity and therefore should be taken as the functional currency.

2 A US entity has a foreign subsidiary located in Greece. The Greek subsidiary imports a product manufactured by its parent, paying in dollars, which it sells throughout Greece with selling prices denominated in euros and determined primarily by local competition. The subsidiary's long-term financing is primarily in the form of dollar loans from its parent, and distribution of its profits is under parental control. Proceeds of the subsidiary are remitted to the parent on a regular basis.

   Again, we have a mixed situation and need to consider the factors outlined in IAS 21:

   (a) The currency mainly influencing sales prices is the euro.

   (b) The currency mainly influencing labour and other expenses is again presumably the euro except that purchases of inventory are made in US dollars.

   (c) The currency in which funds from financing activities are generated is the dollar and the subsidiary has little autonomy, merely acting as an agent in Greece for the parent.

   Although sales are made in euros, the Greek subsidiary is a foreign entity that seems closely linked to its parent and, on balance, the functional currency is the dollar, being the functional currency of the parent.

An entity entering into a foreign currency transaction records that transaction initially by applying to the foreign currency amount the spot exchange rate between the functional currency and the foreign currency at the date of the transaction. This is what we did in Activity 28.3.

IAS 21 does allow a change in an entity's functional currency. However, this can only happen where there is a change in the underlying transactions, events and conditions. This could occur when there is a change in the currency that mainly influences the sale prices of goods and services.

In accordance with para. 37 of IAS 21, the change in the functional currency is accounted for prospectively. An entity translates all items into the new functional currency using the exchange rate at the date of the change. The resulting translated amounts for non-monetary items are treated as their historical cost.

IAS 21 REQUIREMENTS FOR TRANSLATING FOREIGN OPERATIONS FOR CONSOLIDATION PURPOSES

In a group, each entity has determined its own functional currency. Different foreign operations (subsidiaries, associates, joint arrangements and branches of the reporting entity) should all be translated into one currency for consolidation purposes. This currency is the presentation currency. So the presentation currency is the currency in which the financial statements are presented.

Also, for individual financial statements for each entity, the presentation currency can be different from the functional currency. The reason for this can be due to the currency of the shareholder, for instance a Dutch entity having the euro as its functional currency using the yen as its presentation currency because it is a subsidiary of a Japanese parent.

However, in most cases, translating from functional currencies into a presentation currency will happen when preparing consolidated accounts, and this is what we will focus on.

Translating from functional to presentation currency

According to IAS 21, the translation from functional to presentation currency occurs as follows:

1 Assets and liabilities for each statement of financial position presented shall be translated at the closing rate at the date of that statement of financial position

2 Income and expenses for each statement of comprehensive income shall be translated at exchange rates at the date of the transactions; it is possible to use average rates here

3 All resulting exchange differences shall be recognized in other comprehensive income (therefore outside profit or loss). This is different from translating transactions into the functional currency, as all the resulting exchange differences are then presented as profit or loss. The cumulative exchange differences presented in other comprehensive income are presented as a separate component of equity.

Look at Activity 28.4.

ACTIVITY 28.4

The statement of financial position of Zhou Ltd at 31.12.20X4 is as follows:

	FCs	FCs
Share capital		300
Retained profits		100
		400
Equipment at cost	350	
less Depreciation	50	300
Inventory	80	
Net monetary current assets	60	140
Non-current loans		(40)
		400

The presentation currency for Zhou Ltd is Crowns (CRs) and as at:

	FCs to CRs
1 January 20X4	5
Average for the year to 31 December 20X4	4.5
31 December 20X4	4.2

(Continued)

ACTIVITY 28.4 *(Continued)*

Statement of comprehensive income for the year ended 31.12.X4 is as follows:

	FCs
Revenue	600
less Cost of sales	400
Gross profit	200
less Depreciation	(50)
less Other expenses	(50)
Net profit	100

Translate the financial statements of Zhou Ltd into the presentation currency from the functional currency and show clearly where any exchange difference is recognized.

Activity feedback

Statement of financial position as at 31.12.X4

	Rate	CRs	CRs
Share capital	5		60.0
Retained profits (1)			21.4
Currency translation reserve (2)			13.8
			95.2
Equipment at cost	4.2	83.3	
less Depreciation	4.2	11.9	71.4
Inventory	4.2	19.0	
Net monetary current assets	4.2	14.3	
Long-term loans	4.2	(9.5)	23.8
			95.2

Statement of comprehensive income for the year ended 31.12.X4

Revenue	4.5		133.3
less Cost of sales	4.5		88.9
Gross profit			44.4
Depreciation	4.2	11.9	
Other expenses	4.5	11.1	23.0
Net profit			21.4
Other comprehensive income (2)			13.8
Total comprehensive income			35.2

1 *Retained profits were FC100, being equal to the profit of 20X4 (opening amount was 0). Translated retained profit is the net profit in the statement of comprehensive income.*

2 *The opening amount of the currency translation reserve was zero. The exchange difference for the year is the amount required to balance the statements. This exchange difference is also included as other comprehensive income. The amount of 13.8 can be directly calculated as follows:*

– *Exchange difference on opening balance of assets and liabilities (being 300, the amount of share capital, as the opening balance of retained earnings and currency translation reserve were 0): (300 / 4.2 =) 71.4 – (300 / 5 =) 60 = 11.4, plus the difference between translating net profit at closing rate and net profit as translated: (100 / 4.2 =) 23.8 – 21.4 = 2.4.*

ALTERNATIVE TRANSLATION METHODS FOR FINANCIAL STATEMENTS OF FOREIGN OPERATIONS

We have discussed above the IFRS requirements for the translation of financial statements of foreign entities. Translating assets and liabilities at closing rate is required by IAS 21, but it is just one of the alternative options that have traditionally been identified. In this section, we will explore some of these alternatives.

When translating any particular item, we can take two basic possible views:

1 We can use the exchange rate ruling when the item was created (historical rate).

2 We can use the exchange rate ruling when the item is being reported (current or closing rate).

Since we can apply this choice to each item in the financial statements one at a time, it is clear that many different combinations are possible. Four that have been suggested are now outlined.

Single rate (closing rate)

This is based on the idea that the holding entity has a net investment in the foreign operation and that what is at risk from currency fluctuations is this net financial investment. All assets, liabilities, revenues and expenses will be translated at the closing (statement of financial position date) rate. Exchange differences will arise if the closing rate differs from the previous year's closing rate or from the date when the transaction occurred. This is the method IAS 21 requires.

Mixed rate (current/non-current)

Here, current assets and liabilities would be translated at the closing rate, whereas fixed assets and non-current liabilities would be translated at the rate ruling when the item was established (i.e. current items are translated at current rates and fixed items are translated at fixed rates).

Mixed rate (monetary/non-monetary)

This proposal would translate monetary assets and liabilities at the closing rate and all non-monetary assets and liabilities at the rate ruling when the item was established. There is an analogy here with the arguments for current purchasing power accounting. Monetary items are automatically expressed in current monetary units, so use the current rate for them, and non-monetary items are expressed in out-of-date monetary units, so use the out-of-date rate for them.

Mixed rate (temporal)

This is based on the idea that the foreign operations are simply a part of the group that is the reporting entity. Some of the individual assets and liabilities of the group just 'happen' to be abroad. The valuation basis used to value the assets and liabilities determines the appropriate exchange rate. Those assets recorded on a historical cost basis would be translated at the historical rate – the rate ruling when the item was established. Assets recorded on a current value basis would be translated at the current (closing) rate. Revenues and expenses should theoretically be translated at the rate ruling on the date when the amount shown in the accounts was established, i.e. assuming an even spread of trading at the average rate for the year.

It is important to avoid the assumption that the temporal method means using historical exchange rates. The words temporal and historical are quite wrongly sometimes used interchangeably in this context. 'Temporal' means literally 'at the time', i.e. consistent with the underlying valuation basis. So the temporal method does mean using historical exchange rates when applied to historical cost accounts. But, the temporal method means using current exchange rates when applied to current value accounts. This would broadly reduce the temporal method to the single rate method.

The temporal method is in fact prescribed by IAS 21 for translating transactions and events into the functional currency, before translating the functional currency into the presentation currency at closing rate.

Tables 28.1 and 28.2 provide a useful summary of the IAS 21 requirements using both the temporal method and the closing rate method.

TABLE 28.1   Financial statements of a foreign operation translated into the functional currency (temporal method)

Item	Translation rate
Cost and depreciation of property, plant and equipment and intangible assets	Rate at date of acquisition or fair valuation date
Inventories	Rate when cost incurred
Monetary items	Closing rate
Income and expense items	Rate at date of transaction or average rate for the period if rates do not fluctuate significantly
Exchange differences	Profit and loss

TABLE 28.2   Financial statements of a foreign operation translating from the functional currency into the presentation currency (closing rate method)

Item	Translation rate
All assets and liabilities whether monetary or non-monetary	Closing rate
Income and expense items	Rate at date of transaction or average rates for the period if rates do not fluctuate significantly
Exchange differences	Other comprehensive income

Activity 28.5 shows the differences between the two methods, so complete it carefully.

ACTIVITY 28.5

Home established a 100 per cent ownership of Away on 1 January 20X8 by subscribing to €25 000 of shares in cash when the exchange rate was 12 CU (currency unit) to the €. Away raised a long-term loan of 100 000 CU locally on 1 January 20X8 and immediately purchased equipment costing 350 000 CU, which was expected to last ten years with no residual value. It was to be depreciated on the straight line method. The accounts of Away in CU for 20X8 follow, during which the relevant exchange rates were:

	CU to €
1 January 20X8	12
Average for year	11
Average for period in which closing inventory acquired	10.5
31 December 20X8	10

Statement of comprehensive income for 20X8

	CU
Revenue	450 000
less Cost of sales	(360 000)
Gross profit	90 000
less Depreciation	(35 000)
less Other expenses	(15 000)
Net profit	40 000

(Continued)

ACTIVITY 28.5 (Continued)

Statement of financial position as at 31 December 20X8

	CU
Share capital	300 000
Retained profits (1)	40 000
	340 000
Equipment at cost	350 000
less Depreciation	35 000
	315 000
Inventory	105 000
Net monetary current assets	20 000
less Non-current loans	100 000)
	340 000

(1) Balance of the opening retained earnings was zero, so this amount represents the net profit for the year.

Translate the accounts for the foreign operation using both the closing rate and temporal method and identify what to do with the exchange differences.

Activity feedback

Statement of comprehensive income for 20X8	Rate	Closing	Temporal	Rate
Revenue	11	40 909	40 909	11
less Cost of sales	11	32 727	32 727	11
Gross profit		8 182	8 182	
less Depreciation	10	(3 500)	(2 917)	12
less Other expenses	11	(1 364)	(1 364)	11
Net profit (excluding exchange differences)		3 318	3 901	

Statement of financial position as at 31 December 20x8	Rate	Closing	Temporal	Rate
Share capital	12	25 000	25 000	12
Retained profits (= net profit)		3 318	3 901	
		28 318	28 901	
Equipment at cost	10	35 000	29 167	12
less Depreciation	10	3 500	2 917	12
	10	31 500	26 250	12
Inventory	10	10 500	10 000	10.5
Net monetary current assets	10	2 000	2 000	10
less Non-current loans	10	(10 000)	(10 000)	10
		34 000	28 250	
Exchange difference (balance)		(5 682)	651	
		28 318	28 901	

The share capital figure in the closing rate method (as in the temporal method) is translated at the original rate to highlight the exchange differences.

The exchange difference under the temporal method, (a loss of €651) should be charged to the profit and loss for the current year. Both the net profit and retained earnings, including the exchange difference, are therefore €3250, resulting in equity of €28 250.

Had the exchange difference been a gain, it would have been credited to profit or loss in accordance with IAS 21.

Under the closing rate method, the issue is more complex. Differences have arisen in respect of each type of statement of financial position item because the opening balances (representing the net investment in the overseas subsidiary by the holding company) have been retranslated back into € at the closing rate. The total gain of €5682 can be broken down as in Table 28.3.

(Continued)

ACTIVITY 28.5 (Continued)

TABLE 28.3   Retranslation at closing rate

Item	Opening rate	Closing rate	Difference
Opening fixed assets	350 000/10	350 000/12	CU 5834 credit
Opening net current assets	50 000/10	50 000/12	CU 833 credit
Opening long-term loans	100 000/10	100 000/12	CU 1667 debit
Net profit	40 000/10 = 4000	40 000/average = 3318	CU 682 credit

IAS 21 requires that this gain is taken to other comprehensive income and presented as a separate component of equity (for instance named translation reserve). Total comprehensive income is therefore €9000 (net profit €3318 + other comprehensive income €5682). Total equity is €34 000.
  Summarized:

	Temporal method	Closing rate method
Net profit	3 250	3 318
Total comprehensive income	3 250	9 000
Equity	28 250	34 000

Alternative calculation for other comprehensive income:

- *exchange difference on opening balance of assets and liabilities: 300 000 / 10 – 300 000 / 12 = 5 000 credit, plus*
- *difference between translating net profit at closing rate and net profit as translated: 682 credit (see above).*

We finish this section with two related activities to demonstrate consolidation of a foreign subsidiary.

ACTIVITY 28.6

A UK entity Bei (with the £ as presentation currency) has a wholly owned US subsidiary Jing (with the $ as functional currency), which was acquired for US$1 000 000 on 31 December 20X1. The fair value of the net assets at the date of acquisition was US$800 000 giving rise to goodwill on acquisition of $200 000.
  Exchange rates were as follows:

31 December 20X1	£1 = US$2.0
Average rate during year	£1 = US$1.65
31 December 20X2	£1 = US$1.5

During the year, Jing paid a dividend of $28 000 when the exchange rate was £1 = US$1.75. The summarized financial statements for Jing were as follows:
  Jing statement of profit or loss for the year ended 31 December 20X2

	$000
Operating profit	270
Interest paid	(30)
Profit before tax	240
Tax	(60)
Profit after tax	180

Jing statement of financial position as at 31 December 20X2

	20X2 $000	20X1 $000
Non-current assets at cost	510	450
Depreciation	(196)	(90)
	314	360
Current assets		
Inventory	348	252
Trade receivables	420	290
Cash	480	420
	1 248	962
Total assets	1 562	1 322
Equity and liabilities		
Equity		
Share capital	400	400
Retained profits (1)	552	400
Total equity	952	800

(Continued)

ACTIVITY 28.6 (*Continued*)

Liabilities

Loans	300	260
Current liabilities		
Trade payables	250	226
Tax	60	36
Total liabilities	610	522
Total equity and liabilities	1 562	1 322

(1)   Retained profits 20X2: $400 (pre-acquisition profit) + $180 (profit for the year) minus $28 (dividend).

Translate the financial statements of Jing prior to consolidation with Bei the holding entity. Calculate the exchange differences to be included in other comprehensive income, including the exchange difference on goodwill.

Jing statement of financial position as at 31 December

Activity feedback

Jing's financial statements need to be translated into the presentation currency before consolidation, thus we need to use the closing rate method. Therefore, the statement of comprehensive income items will be translated at the average rate of 1.65 and all assets and liabilities at the closing rate of 1.5 for 20X2 and 2.0 for 20X1.

Jing statement of profit or loss for the year ended 31 December 20X2

	$000		£000
Operating profit	270	1.65	163.7
Interest paid	(30)	1.65	(18.2)
Profit before tax	240		145.5
Tax	(60)	1.65	(36.4)
Profit after tax	180	1.65	109.1

	20X2	1.5	20X1	2.0
	$000	$000	$000	$000
Non-current assets at cost	510	340.0	450	225
Depreciation	(196)	(130.7)	(90)	(45)
	314	209.3	360	180
Current assets				
Inventory	348	232.0	252	126
Trade receivables	420	280.0	290	145
Cash	480	320.0	420	210
	1 248	832.0	962	481
Total assets	1 562	1 041.3	1 322	661
Equity and liabilities				
Equity				
Share capital (1)	400	200.0	400	200
Retained profits	552	434.6	400	200
Total equity	952	634.6	800	400
Liabilities				
Loans	300	200.0	260	130
Current liabilities				
Trade payables	250	166.7	226	113
Tax	60	40.0	36	18
Total liabilities	610	406.7	522	261
Total equity and liabilities	1 562	1 041.3	1 322	661

(1) Share capital remains translated at the original rate (2.0). The retained profit figure of £434 600 includes an exchange difference to be identified separately as follows:
  • exchange difference on opening balance of assets and liabilities: 800 / 1.5 – 800 / 2.0 = £133 300 credit, plus

• difference between translating net profit at closing rate and net profit at average rate: 180 / 1.5 – 180 / 1.65 = £10 900 credit, plus
• difference between translating dividend paid at closing rate and the rate at the date of payment: 28 / 1.5 – 28 / 1.75 = £2700 debit (this is a debit

(*Continued*)

ACTIVITY 28.6 (Continued)

as a dividend payment is a reduction of retained earnings)
- total: £141 500 credit (gain).

From the perspective of Bei, there is another exchange difference: on goodwill. Assuming no impairment, this exchange difference is £33 333 (200 000 / 1.5 – 200 000 / 2) which is a gain.

The total exchange difference of £174 833 is a separate component of equity in the consolidated accounts of Bei (Translation reserve), see Activity 28.7.

ACTIVITY 28.7

This Activity is a follow up to Activity 28.6.

Summarized statement of financial position of Bei 31 December 20X2

	20X2	20X1
Investment in subsidiary (at cost)	500	500
(1m @ 2.0 date of acquisition)		
Cash	416	400
	916	900
Share capital	900	900
Retained profits (dividend received:		
28 @ 1.75 date of translation)	16	—
	916	900

Note that the statement of financial position of Bei uses the temporal method to translate the dividend and investment in subsidiary as we are translating these to the functional currency (£).

Given the feedback of Activity 28.6, complete the consolidation for 20X2.

Activity feedback

Consolidated statement of profit and loss 31 December 20X2

Operating profit of Jing	163.7
Operating profit of Bei	16.0
	179.7
Elimination of inter-entity dividend	(16.0)
	163.7
Interest paid	(18.2)
	145.5
Tax	(36.4)
Consolidated profit for the year	109.1

Consolidated statement of financial position as at 31 December 20X2

Non-current assets	209.3
Goodwill (200/1.5)	133.3
	342.6
Current assets	
Inventory	232.0
Trade receivables	280.0
Cash (416 + 320)	736.0
	1 248.0
Total assets	1 590.6
Equity and liabilities	
Equity	
Share capital	900.0
Retained profits = consolidated profit for the year	109.1
Translation reserve	174.8
	1 183.9
Loan	200.0
Current liabilities	
Trade payables	166.7
Tax	40.0
	206.7
Total liabilities	406.7
Total equity and liabilities	1 590.6

The exchange differences for 20X2 of £174 833 are recognized as other comprehensive income. Total comprehensive income for 20X2 is £283 933 (£109 100 + £174 833).

HEDGE ACCOUNTING

An entity that has transactions or monetary positions in a foreign currency (all currencies other than the functional currency) is exposed to foreign currency risk. We have seen that exchange differences arising from translating the foreign currency monetary positions into the functional currency will affect profit or loss. An entity can protect itself from the exchange risk by, for instance, buying derivatives such as foreign currency swaps, options or forwards. The hedge accounting for these financial instruments was discussed in Chapter 17.

Another form of exchange risk is the result of translating the financial statements of foreign entities from their functional currency into a different presentation currency. These exchange differences do not directly affect profit or loss (although this might happen on disposal, see below), but they have impact on other comprehensive income and equity. Although there are no direct cash flow consequences, unless profit is paid out by way of dividend, an entity might have good reasons to protect itself against these accounting translation differences. One good reason might be to limit the volatility of equity.

One way of hedging the exposure position of the investment (share in equity) in a foreign operation is to raise loans in a foreign country denominated in the functional currency of the foreign operation. From the point of view of the home (investing) entity, it has:

- an asset, exposed to an exchange risk
- a liability also exposed to an exchange risk.

Because the exchange risk of the liability compensates the exchange risk of the asset, this is a form of hedging. Normally, in the consolidated financial statements, the exchange differences on the asset (the net investment = assets minus liabilities of the investee, translated at closing rate) would be recognized in other comprehensive income (outside profit or loss), but the exchange difference on the loan from the foreign currency to the functional currency (being a transaction of the investing entity) would be recorded in profit or loss. As an exception, IAS 21 requires us to classify as other comprehensive income those exchange differences arising on a foreign currency liability, where that liability is used as a 'hedge'.

Interestingly, IAS 21 does not deal with hedge accounting for foreign currency items in much detail and we have to refer to IAS 39 for further guidance. The criteria in IAS 39 used to identify a hedge are as follows:

- At the inception of the hedge, there is a formal document to support classification as a hedge.
- The hedge is expected to be highly effective.
- A forecasted transaction, which is the subject of the hedge, must be highly probable.
- The effectiveness of the hedge can be reliably measured.
- The hedge was assessed on an ongoing basis and determined actually to have been highly effective throughout the financial reporting period.

For a further discussion on hedge accounting, refer to Chapter 17. Now complete the following Activity.

ACTIVITY 28.8

An entity whose year end is 31 March and prepares its accounts in £ sterling, takes out two loans on 1 August, one for €50 000 and one for $30 000, when the exchange rates were £1 = €1.80 and £1 = $1.60. The $ loan is used to make an equity investment of $30 000 at £1 = $1.60. At the same time, another equity investment is made of 100 000 Australian dollars (A$) at £1 = A$1.9. How would this be shown in the entity's books at the year end when £1 = €1.86 = $1.5 = A$1.95, given the reporting currency is £?

Activity feedback

Initially, when the loans and investments are taken up, they will need to be recorded in the books in £s as follows:

- *Loan €: £27 778 (50 000 / 1.8) credit*
- *Loan $: £18 750 (30 000 / 1.6) credit*
- *Investment $: £18 750 (30 000 / 1.6) debit*
- *Investment A$: £52 632 (100 000 / 1.9) debit*

(Continued)

ACTIVITY 28.8 *(Continued)*

In the consolidated financial statements, long-term monetary items, i.e. the € loan and the $ loan, will be translated at year end exchange rates (closing rates), as well as the investments (either the consolidated assets and liabilities of the investments or the investments in associates applying the equity method). Normally, all exchange differences on the loans will be recognized in profit or loss and exchange differences on the investments will be recognized in other comprehensive income. In this case, however, when the investing entity applies hedge accounting documenting that the $ investment is hedged with the $ loan, the exchange difference on the loan avoids profit and loss and is included in other comprehensive income.

At the year end:

- *Loan €: £26 882 (50 000 / 1.86) credit; exchange gain £896 in profit and loss*
- *Loan $: £20 000 (30 000 / 1.5) credit; exchange loss £1250 in other comprehensive income*
- *Investment $: £20 000 (30 000 / 1.5) debit; exchange gain £1250 in other comprehensive income*
- *Investment A$: £51 282 (100 000 / 1.95) debit; exchange loss £1350 in other comprehensive income.*

SOME OTHER ISSUES

In this section, we deal with a few other issues:

- extending the net investment
- goodwill and fair value adjustments
- disposal of a foreign entity
- hyperinflationary economies
- disclosure requirements.

We have concluded in this chapter that exchange differences on accounting for transactions and events in foreign currencies into the functional currency are recognized in profit or loss, while exchange differences that arise on consolidating foreign entities in the presentation currency are recognized in other comprehensive income. As discussed, an exception to this is hedge accounting. There is one more exception: in addition to investing in the equity of the foreign entity, a parent may also give a long-term or permanent loan in the functional currency of the foreign entity. Such a loan would be considered a part of the parent's net investment in the foreign entity: the exchange differences on this loan will also be recognized in other comprehensive income and not in profit or loss. The same holds for the reverse situation, where a foreign entity gives a loan in its functional currency to the parent: this would reduce the net investment, and the exchange differences on this borrowing would also be recognized in other comprehensive income.

Goodwill and fair value adjustments are recognized by the acquirer in a business combination (see Chapter 25). They are not pushed down to the acquiree/subsidiary in their financial statements. However, for translating foreign entities from their functional currency to the presentation currency, all goodwill and fair value adjustments are treated as assets and liabilities of the foreign operation. Thus, they should be expressed in the functional currency of the foreign operation and be translated at closing rate.

Disposal of a foreign entity is dealt with in accordance with para. 48 of IAS 21. On the disposal of a foreign operation, the cumulative amount of the exchange differences deferred in the separate component of equity relating to that foreign operation should be recognized in profit or loss. As a result, both the gain or loss on disposal and all exchange differences recognized in other comprehensive income (both on the investment and on the loans used for hedging) are recognized in profit or loss. This has no effect on total comprehensive income, as these realized exchange differences have already been recognized in other comprehensive income as part of the total comprehensive income. This is what we call 'recycling': the amount included in other comprehensive income in earlier years is now recycled to profit or loss. The exchange gain (or loss) recognized in profit or loss will be fully compensated by the loss (or gain) recognized in other comprehensive income.

IFRS has some specific requirements for those entities reporting in a currency of a hyperinflationary economy. The financial statements of such a foreign entity have to be dealt with in accordance with IAS 29, *Financial Reporting in Hyperinflationary Economies*, before the requirements of IAS 21 are applied. IAS 29 requires that, before translating transactions and events into the functional currency, the effects of general inflation should be taken into account by using a stable current measuring unit. IAS 29 is discussed in Chapter 22.

Paragraphs 51–57 of IAS 21 require certain disclosures, among which:

- the amount of exchange differences recognized in profit or loss
- the amount of exchange differences recognized in other comprehensive income
- the amount of the separate component of equity (translation reserve), and a reconciliation between the beginning and the end of the period
- the functional currency of the parent and the presentation currency of the parent and the group and the reason why they are different, if so.

We include below extracts from the Heineken Annual Report 2014 to illustrate some of these disclosures.

REAL LIFE ILLUSTRATION

(b) Foreign currency

(i) Foreign currency transactions

Transactions in foreign currencies are translated to the respective functional currencies of HEINEKEN entities at the exchange rates at the dates of the transactions. Monetary assets and liabilities denominated in foreign currencies at the reporting date are retranslated to the functional currency at the exchange rate at that date. The foreign currency gain or loss arising on monetary items is the difference between amortised cost in the functional currency at the beginning of the period, adjusted for effective interest and payments during the period, and the amortised cost in foreign currency translated at the exchange rate at the end of the reporting period.

Non-monetary assets and liabilities denominated in foreign currencies that are measured at fair value are retranslated to the functional currency at the exchange rate at the date that the fair value was determined. Non-monetary items in a foreign currency that are measured at cost are translated into the functional currency using the exchange rate at the date of the transaction.

Foreign currency differences arising on retranslation are recognised in profit or loss, except for differences arising on the retranslation of available-for-sale (equity) investments and foreign currency differences arising on the retranslation of a financial liability designated as a hedge of a net investment, which are recognised in other comprehensive income.

(ii) Foreign operations

The assets and liabilities of foreign operations, including goodwill and fair value adjustments arising on acquisition, are translated to Euro at exchange rates at the reporting date. The income and expenses of foreign operations, excluding foreign operations in hyperinflationary economies, are translated to Euro at exchange rates approximating to the

(Continued)

exchange rates ruling at the dates of the transactions. Group entities, with a functional currency being the currency of a hyperinflationary economy, first restate their financial statements in accordance with IAS 29, Financial Reporting in Hyperinflationary Economies (see 'Reporting in hyperinflationary economies' below). The related income, costs and balance sheet amounts are translated at the foreign exchange rate ruling at the balance sheet date.

Foreign currency differences are recognised in other comprehensive income and are presented within equity in the translation reserve. However, if the operation is not a wholly owned subsidiary, the relevant proportionate share of the translation difference is allocated to the non-controlling interests. When a foreign operation is disposed of such that control, significant influence or joint control is lost, the cumulative amount in the translation reserve related to that foreign operation is reclassified to profit or loss as part of the gain or loss on disposal. When HEINEKEN disposes of only part of its interest in a subsidiary that includes a foreign operation while retaining control, the relevant proportion of the cumulative amount is reattributed to non-controlling interests. When HEINEKEN disposes of only part of its investment in an associate or joint venture that includes a foreign operation while retaining significant influence or joint control, the relevant proportion of the cumulative amount is reclassified to profit or loss.

Foreign exchange gains and losses arising from a monetary item receivable from or payable to a foreign operation, the settlement of which is neither planned nor likely in the foreseeable future, are considered to form part of a net investment in a foreign operation and are recognised in other comprehensive income, and are presented within equity in the translation reserve.

The following exchange rates, for the most important countries in which HEINEKEN has operations, were used while preparing these consolidated financial statements:

In EUR	Year-end 2014	Year-end 2013	Average 2014	Average 2013
BRL	0.3105	0.3070	0.3202	0.3486
GBP	1.2839	1.1995	1.2403	1.1775
MXN	0.0560	0.0553	0.0566	0.0590
NGN	0.0049	0.0047	0.0048	0.0049
PLN	0.2340	0.2407	0.2389	0.2382
RUB	0.0138	0.0221	0.0196	0.0236
SGD	0.6227	0.5743	0.5943	0.6017
USD	0.8237	0.7251	0.7527	0.7530
VND in 1,000	0.0387	0.0345	0.0355	0.0358

(iii) Reporting in hyperinflationary economics

When the economy of a country in which we operate is deemed hyperinflationary and the functional currency of a Group entity is the currency of that hyperinflationary economy, the financial statements of such Group entities are adjusted so that they are stated in terms of the measuring unit current at the end of the reporting period. This involves restatement of income and expenses to reflect changes in the general price index from the start of the reporting period and restatement of non-monetary items in the balance sheet, such as P, P & E, to reflect current purchasing power as at the period end using a general price index from the date when they were first recognised. Comparative amounts are not adjusted. Any differences arising were recorded in equity on adoption.

In 2013, hyperinflation accounting was applicable to our operations in Belarus. No hyperinflation accounting was applied in 2014.

(iv) Hedge of net investments in foreign operations

Foreign currency differences arising on the translation of a financial liability designated as a hedge of a net investment in a foreign operation are recognised in other comprehensive income to the extent that the hedge is effective and regardless of whether the net investment is held directly or through an intermediate parent. These differences are presented within equity in the translation reserve. To the extent that the hedge is ineffective, such differences are recognised in profit or loss. When the hedged part of a net investment is disposed of, the relevant amount in the translation reserve is transferred to profit or loss as part of the profit or loss on disposal.

SUMMARY

Foreign currency translation is a fascinating topic, but not an easy one to grasp. It is difficult to get to grips with the logic of applying one set of rules to translation to functional currency and another to presentation currency. Remember:

- Within a group, each individual entity should determine its functional currency. The functional currency is the currency of the primary economic environment in which the entity operates.

- An entity should translate all transactions into its functional currency. For individual entity transactions, non-monetary items are translated at the originating exchange rate, but monetary items are translated at the closing rate if not settled. Thus, unrealized gains and losses due to foreign currency fluctuations will be taken to profit or loss generally as part of ordinary activities. This is the temporal method.

- Foreign entities translating to presentation currency use the closing rate for the statement of financial position and average rate (generally) for the statement of comprehensive income. This usually occurs when there is a need to prepare consolidated financial statements. Exchange differences are taken to other comprehensive income.

- In a few specific cases, exchange differences on transactions are not taken to profit or loss, but are recognized in other comprehensive income: Loans to hedge the net investment and extensions or reductions of the net investment by intercompany borrowings are examples.

- Goodwill and fair value adjustments are treated as assets and liabilities of the foreign operation and need to be translated at closing rates.

- Upon disposal of a foreign entity, the cumulative exchange differences will be included in profit or loss.

- Foreign operations in hyperinflationary economies have to be stated in the measuring unit current at the statement of financial position date before translation.

EXERCISES

Suggested answers to exercises marked ✓ are to be found in the Student online resources, with suggested answers to the remaining questions available in the Instructor online resources.

1   Should exchange differences appear in the statement of profit or loss of an entity or be charged direct to a separate component of equity? State the reasons for your answer.

2   What is the difference between foreign currency conversion and foreign currency translation?

3   On 1 November 2003, DX invested in 100 per cent of the share capital of EY, a new entity incorporated on that date. EY's operations are located in a foreign country where the currency is the Franc. DX has no other subsidiaries. The summary financial statements of the two entities at their 31 October 2008 year end were as follows:

Summary statements of profit or loss for the year ended 31 October 2008	DX $000	EY Franc 000
Revenue	3 600	1 200
Cost of sales, other expenses and income tax	(2 800)	(1 000)
Profit for the period	800	200

Summary statements of changes in equity for the year ended 31 October 2008	DX $000	EY Franc 000
Brought forward at 1 November 2007	5 225	1 500
Profit for the period	800	200
Dividends	(200)	—
Carried forward at 31 October 2008	5 825	1 700

Summary statements of financial position at 31 October 2008	DX $000	EY Franc 000
Property plant and equipment	5 000	1 500
Investment in EY	25	—
Current assets	4 400	2 000
	9 425	3 500
Share capital	1 000	50
Retained earnings	4 825	1 650
Current liabilities	3 600	1 800
	9 425	3 500

Relevant exchange rates were as follows:
1 November 2003 1$ = 2.0 francs
31 October 2007 1$ = 2.3 francs
31 October 2008 1$ = 2.7 francs

Average rate for year ended 31 October 2008 1$ = 2.6 francs

Required:

(a) Explain the meaning of the term 'functional currency' as used by IAS 21, *The Effects of Changes in Foreign Exchange Rates*, and identify THREE factors that an entity should consider in determining its functional currency.

(b) Prepare:

(i) the summary consolidated statement of profit or loss and other comprehensive income for the year ended 31 October 2008

(ii) the summary consolidated statement of financial position at 31 October 2008.

(c) Prepare the summary consolidated statement of changes in equity for the year to 31 October 2008 and a calculation that shows how the exchange gain or loss for the year has arisen. (Work to the nearest $.)

(CIMA P8, November 2008, adapted)

4   AB is planning to acquire 100 per cent of the equity of KM, an entity that operates overseas and which currently prepares its financial statements in euros. The directors of AB intend to require that KM adopts dollars as its functional currency.

Required:
Explain how the functional currency of KM should be determined, in accordance with IAS 21, *The Effects of Changes in Foreign Exchange Rates*.

(CIMA, Financial Management, August 2014)

5   RD operates in Country A and has established the A$ as its functional currency. RD acquired a piece of machinery from an overseas supplier at a cost of B$5 million on 20 November 2013. The invoice remained unpaid at the year ended 31 December 2013.
Relevant exchange rates (where A$/B$ 2.00 means A$1 = B$2.00) are:

20 November 2013   A$/B$2.00
31 December 2013   A$/B$2.15

Required:
In accordance with IAS 21, *The Effects of Changes in Foreign Exchange Rates*:

(i)   explain how RD would have established the A$ as its functional currency

(ii)   calculate the amounts to be included in the financial statements of RD for the year to 31 December 2013 in respect of the above transaction.

(CIMA, Financial Management, February 2014)

6   OVS operates in country G, which has the Grum as its currency. OVS sources all raw materials locally and is subject to local taxes and corporate regulations. The current workforce is recruited locally, although the majority of its sales are to customers from neighbouring countries. OVS has operated autonomously since being acquired by JK and during the year raised a significant amount of finance from the main bank in G to fund its own investment requirements.

Required:
In accordance with IAS 21, *The Effects of Changes in Foreign Exchange Rates:*

(i)   explain the key factors which determine an entity's functional currency and using these factors identify the functional currency of OVS

(ii)   explain how the financial statements of OVS will be translated into dollars prior to preparing the consolidated accounts of JK Group. JK holds 100 per cent of the ordinary shares of OVS

(CIMA, Financial Management, November 2012)

7   Extracts from the financial statements of A and its subsidiary B are presented below.

Summarized statements of profit or loss and other comprehensive income for the year ended 31 December 2012

	A A$000	B B$000
Revenue	8 000	3 000
Cost of sales and operating expenses	(4 500)	(1 800)
Profit before tax	3 500	1 200
Income tax	(1 000)	(400)
Profit for the year	2 500	800

	A A$000	B B$000
Other comprehensive income		
Items that will not be reclassified to profit or loss		
Revaluation gains on property (net of tax)	400	300
Total other comprehensive income	400	300
Total comprehensive income	2 900	1 100

Statements of financial position as at 31 December 2012	**A** **A$000**	**B** **B$000**
ASSETS		
Non-current assets		
Property, plant and equipment	6 700	3 500
Investment in B (held at costs)	1 800	—
	8 500	3 500
Current assets	4 000	3 000
Total assets	12 500	6 500
EQUITY AND LIABILITIES		
Equity		
Share capital (A$1 equity shares/B$1 equity shares)	2 000	1 000
Reserves	8 500	3 500
Total equity	10 500	4 500
Current liabilities	2 000	2 000
Total equity and liabilities	12 500	6 500

Additional information:

1   A acquired 80 per cent of the equity share capital of B on 1 January 2010 for A$1 800 000 when the reserves of B were B$1 900 000. The investment is held at cost in the individual financial statements of A. There have been no issues of share capital since the date of acquisition.

2   The group policy is to value non-controlling interest at fair value at the date of acquisition. The fair value of the non-controlling interest of B was A$410 000 at the date of acquisition.

3   The functional currency of A is the A$. The functional currency of B is the B$. Relevant exchange rates (where A$/B$ 2.00 means A$1 = B$2.00) are:

1 January 2010 A$/B$2.00

31 December 2011 A$/B$2.10

31 December 2012 A$/B$2.30

Average rate for the year ended 31 December 2012 A$/B$2.20

4   An impairment review conducted on 31 December 2011 resulted in the goodwill arising on the acquisition of B being written down by 20 per cent.

Required:

Prepare the following for the A group:

(a) the consolidated statement of profit or loss and other comprehensive income for the year ended 31 December 2012

(b) the consolidated statement of financial position as at 31 December 2012. (Please round all numbers to the nearest $000.)

(CIMA, Financial Management, May 2013, adapted)

8 The statements of profit or loss for HM and OS for the year ended 31 December 2011 are shown below.

	HM A$000	OS Crowns 000
Revenue	5 200	4 500
Cost of sales	(3 200)	(3 000)
Gross profit	2 000	1 500
Distribution costs	(800)	(420)
Administrative expenses	(450)	(450)
Other income	80	—
Profit before tax	830	630
Income tax expense	(250)	(180)
Profit for the year	580	450

Additional information:

1 HM acquired 80 per cent of the ordinary share capital of a foreign entity, OS, on 1 January 2011 for Crowns 13 984 000. At the date of acquisition, the net assets of OS had a fair value of Crowns 15 800 000. The group policy is to value non-controlling interest at fair value at the date of acquisition. The fair value of the non-controlling interest at the date of acquisition was Crowns 3 496 000. The fair value adjustments related to non-depreciable land. At 31 December 2011, the goodwill that arose on the acquisition of OS was impaired by 20 per cent. Impairment is translated at the average rate and is charged to group administrative expenses.

2 The relevant exchange rates were as follows:

1 January 2011 A$/Crowns 1.61 (A$1 = Crowns 1.61)

31 December 2011 A$/Crowns 1.52 (A$1 = Crowns 1.52)

Average rate for 2011 A$/Crowns 1.58 (A$1 = Crowns 1.58)

Required:

(a) Calculate the translation gain or loss for the HM Group for the year ended 31 December 2011.

(b) Prepare the consolidated statement of profit or loss and comprehensive income for the HM Group for the year ended 31 December 2011.

(CIMA, Financial Management, March 2012, adapted)

9 Aspire, a public limited company, operates many of its activities overseas. The directors have asked for advice on the correct accounting treatment of several aspects of Aspire's overseas operations. Aspire's functional currency is the dollar.

(a) Aspire has created a new subsidiary, which is incorporated in the same country as Aspire. The subsidiary has issued 2 million dinars of equity capital to Aspire, which paid for these shares in dinars. The subsidiary has also raised 100 000 dinars of equity capital from external sources and has deposited the whole of the capital with a bank in an overseas country whose currency is the dinar. The capital is to be invested in dinar denominated bonds. The subsidiary has a small number of staff and its operating expenses, which are low, are incurred in dollars. The profits are under the control of Aspire. Any income from the investment is either passed on to Aspire in the form of a dividend or reinvested under instruction from Aspire. The subsidiary does not make any decisions as to where to place the investments. Aspire would like advice on how to determine the functional currency of the subsidiary.

(b) On 1 May 2013, Aspire purchased 70 per cent of a multi-national group whose functional currency was the dinar. The purchase consideration was $200 million. At acquisition, the net assets at cost were 1000 million dinars. The fair values of the net assets were 1100 million dinars and the fair value of the non-controlling interest was 250 million dinars. Aspire uses the full goodwill method. Aspire wishes to know how to deal with goodwill arising on the above acquisition in the group financial statements for the year ended 30 April 2014.

(c) Aspire took out a foreign currency loan of 5 million dinars at a fixed interest rate of 8 per cent on 1 May 2013. The interest is paid at the end of each year. The loan will be repaid after two years on 30 April 2015. The interest rate is the current market rate for similar two-year fixed interest loans. Aspire requires advice on how to account for the loan and interest in the financial statements for the year ended 30 April 2014.

Aspire has a financial statement year end of 30 April 2014 and the average currency exchange rate for the year is not materially different from the actual rate.

Exchange rates	$1 = dinars
1 May 2013	5
30 April 2014	6
Average exchange rate for year ended 30 April 2014	5.6

Required:
Advise the directors of Aspire on their various requests above, showing suitable calculations where necessary.

(ACCA, Corporate Reporting (International), June 2014, adapted)

PART FOUR
FINANCIAL ANALYSIS

In Part One, we focused on what financial reporting is all about – what it is trying to achieve and how the accountant sets about achieving it. Parts Two and Three presented the standards that have been created to govern financial reporting. In those three Parts, a preparer's approach to financial reporting was taken as we described the mechanisms, principles and rules through which financial information is provided to users. In Part Four, a user's approach is followed. In this Part, we analyze how different stakeholders of a company can use the information provided in the annual accounts to gain some insight into the reporting entity's stability, performance, future prospects or whatever else might interest them.

Part Four consists of three chapters. Chapter 29 introduces the basic instruments of financial statement analysis. The presentation of these topics will enable you to understand the discussion in the Chapters 30 and 31 of this book. If you have already mastered the basics of ratio analysis and interpretation of financial statements, you can skip Chapter 29 and continue on to Chapters 30 and 31.

INTRODUCTION TO INTERPRETATION OF FINANCIAL STATEMENTS

29

OBJECTIVES After studying this chapter you should be able to:

- identify the needs of users wishing to make use of accounting information

- explain the technique of ratio analysis and calculate appropriate ratios

- explain what each of the ratios means and discuss their limitations

- identify additional information that users may require to aid their analysis.

INTRODUCTION

In Parts Two and Three of this book we were concerned with the provision of financial information to users which presents a true and fair view of the entity. Users will use this information to gain some insight into the reporting entity's stability, its performance, the future prospects of the entity and/or whatever else might interest them.

In this chapter, we will introduce the basic instruments of financial statement analysis. The presentation of these topics will enable you to understand the discussion on financial statement analysis in the Chapters 30 and 31 of this book. If you have already mastered the basics of ratio analysis and interpretation of financial statements, you can skip this chapter and continue on to the Chapters 30 and 31.

In Chapters 1 and 11 of Part One of this book, we identified the users of accounting information and their differing needs. The following Activity provides a useful piece of revision.

ACTIVITY 29.1

Identify the users of accounting information and their needs/objectives.

Activity feedback

- **Investors/owners**. Is the money invested in the business making a suitable return for them or could it earn more if invested elsewhere? Is the business a safe investment, that is, is it likely to become insolvent/bankrupt? Should the investors invest more money in the business?
- **Suppliers**. Is the business able to pay for the goods bought on credit? Will the business continue to be a recipient of the goods the supplier produces?
- **Customers**. Is the business able to supply the goods the customer requires and when it requires them? Will the business continue in operation so that guarantees on goods purchased will be met?
- **Lenders**. Is there adequate security for the loans made? Does the business make a sufficient profit

and have enough cash available to make the necessary payments to the lenders of interest and capital?
- **Employees**. Does the business make sufficient profit and have enough cash available to make the necessary payments to the employees? Will the business continue in operation at its current level so that employees have secure employment?
- **Government**. For example, to calculate taxation due or to aid decision making in respect of the economy as a whole in a particular country.
- **Public**. The majority of their needs are in respect of employment, pollution, and health and safety, which are not particularly well provided for in financial statements as yet.

A prime source of information for all these economic decision makers is the financial statements published by the company.

ACCOUNTING INFORMATION AND USERS

Financial statements provide valuable information for both the owners of the business and any potential owners/investors, and for other stakeholders of the company. Companies publish general purpose financial statements, which implies that different types of stakeholders will each process different elements of information from the financial statements in order to make the proper economic decisions. Some stakeholders will combine information from the financial statements with other corporate (e.g. sales projections, pro-forma financial information, corporate governance information, integrated reporting information, etc.) or industry information (e.g. industry statistics, market shares, etc.) for their decision-making purposes. A discussion on the use of that other information will be included in the next two chapters.

Whereas Activity 29.1 focused on the different types of users of financial information, Activity 29.2 concentrates on the different types of decisions that stakeholders of financial information face.

Financial statement data serve as an input to the economic decisions of the different stakeholders of the company. The financial statements provide information on the

ACTIVITY 29.2

In its preface to the conceptual framework, the IASB gives a list of examples of different economic decisions which are made by users on the basis of the financial statements of a company. Consider the following list of examples of economic decisions. Try to figure out which group of users will be especially interested in each economic decision:

(a) deciding when to buy, hold or sell an equity investment

(b) assessing the stewardship or accountability of management

(c) assessing the security for amounts lent to the entity

(d) assessing the ability of the entity to pay and provide other benefits to its employees

(e) determining distributable profits and dividends

(f) determining taxation policies

(g) preparing and using national income statistics

(h) regulating the activities of entities.

Activity feedback

The decisions listed in (a) and (b) will be taken by owners of the company and potential owners. Among the owners of the company we can distinguish different groups of owners, such as shareholders with small amounts of shares, or large institutional investors such as pension funds. When shareholders and potential shareholders consider whether to buy, hold or sell their equity investment in a company, they will combine information that informs them about the future prospects of the company (i.e. the company's future revenue and cash generation power) with information that informs them about how successful the company has been in the past (i.e. a profitability analysis). The information on a firm's
past performance allows the owners or the shareholders of the company to evaluate the performance of the management team of the company and to decide on the remuneration of the management team as well as on whether or not the CEO or the management team needs to be replaced.

Decision (c) will concern especially the suppliers of long-term credit to the company, but also suppliers of short-term credit will want to make sure that a company will be able to pay the invoices for the goods and services delivered. Owners of the company will evaluate whether or not the company is able to repay its debt and what level of interest cost is involved with the borrowings. These elements determine the financial risk of the company and will have an impact on the return for the owners.

The decision listed in (d) will be an issue of concern to the owners and also to the creditors of the company and the employees. In a number of countries, including France, Germany and Belgium, the law prescribes that financial information should be provided in specific formats to the workforce. To make sure that the information is reliable, auditors have to certify the economic and financial information provided to the employees by corporate management.

Decision (e) is important for the owners of the company. In order to secure resources for the survival and/or growth of the company, owners might reduce the dividends and make sure that dividend payments never exceed the amount of distributable profit. The dividend policy of a company is useful information for potential investors in a company's equity since it is an element of their return.

Decision (f) is important for owners as well as for the government. Owners try to establish the most favourable tax regime for their operations.

Decisions (g) and (h) refer to governmental decisions or decisions of regulatory authorities. These governmental or regulatory bodies can be national or supranational.

financial position, the changes in the financial position and the performance of the company. These financial data are more appropriate for certain economic decisions than for others. For example, regulatory authorities will probably have to combine financial statement data with other data for their decision-making processes. Regulatory authorities overseeing the competition in certain industries will also need to collect data on market share or pricing policies of the different companies. So financial as well as non-financial data from other sources will be added to financial statement data in order to make decisions.

The analysis of the economic decisions carried out in Activity 29.2 and the discussion on the different types of users in Activity 29.1 indicate that it is possible to identify three general areas of interest in which users' needs and objectives may lie.

Although not all the information needs of users can be met solely by financial statement data, there are needs that are common to all interested parties. The first two items below might interest a wide group of users. The third need relates to owners and potential owners:

1 *Financial status.* Can the business pay its way in the short term as well as in the long-term, so is it in fact *liquid* and *solvent*?

2 *Performance.* How successful is the business? Is it making a reasonable profit? Is it utilizing its assets to the fullest? Is it in fact *profitable* and *efficient*?

3 *Investment.* Is the business a suitable investment for shareholders, or would returns be greater if they invested elsewhere? Is it a good *investment*?

BENCHMARKING

These three general areas of interest require answers to questions which are subjective rather than objective in nature. For instance, how do we judge whether a profit is reasonable? We could do so by comparing current profit or income to profit or income made in previous years or to profit or income made by other businesses. In other words, we use benchmarks against which we compare current performance, financial status and investment potential. However, we need to take great care in carrying out this benchmarking exercise so that we do not invalidate the results. Consider, for example, your opinion of the disco you attended last night. You might think it was the best disco you have ever attended; your friend might think it was the worst night out they had ever had. This is because the experiences/benchmarks you each have are different and you are making a subjective judgement on how the current disco compares with those you attended previously. Thus, in setting benchmarks against which we can compare a company, we must be aware of the limitations of this comparison.

First, we need to identify benchmarks/indicators we can use; then we need to consider their limitations. Four possible benchmarks are:

- past period achievements
- budgeted achievements
- other businesses' achievements
- averages of businesses' achievements in the same area.

ACTIVITY 29.3

Identify for each indicator above its uses and limitations.

Activity feedback

1 *Past periods*

Uses – To identify whether current activity is better or worse than previous periods.

Limitations – External factors may have influenced activity levels, e.g. public awareness of environmental issues may have necessitated a change in manufacturing process leading to increased costs.

2 *Budgets*

Uses – Has current activity matched planned activity?

Limitations – The budget may not be a valid standard of performance, e.g. underlying assumptions may have been unrealistic or set at too high a level.

ACTIVITY 29.3 *(Continued)*

3 *Other businesses*

Uses – Is our business performing as well?

Limitations – Businesses may not be truly comparable with regard to size and type, e.g. grocery sole trader compared to supermarket; manufacturer compared to retailer. External factors may affect one business, e.g. lengthy strike. Accounting policies and bases on which accounting infor-

mation is prepared may be different, e.g. inventory valuations, depreciation, historical cost or revalued amount, treatment of research and development costs, treatment of goodwill.

4 *Industry averages have uses and limitations very similar to those of other businesses. Additionally, an average is simply that – an average which takes account of the best and the worst.*

Each of the four benchmarks identified are commonly used in assessing business status, performance and potential, but interpretation of accounts is highly subjective and requires skilled judgement, bearing in mind the limitations of these benchmarks.

In Chapter 30 of this book, we will discuss further the pitfalls in the interpretation of information included in the annual financial statements of a company. In this chapter, we introduce the techniques of analysis which can be applied to financial statements without elaborating further on the issues of the benchmarks. This will be done in Chapter 31 of this book.

TECHNIQUE OF RATIO ANALYSIS

Financial statements identify for us a multitude of figures, for example profit or income before tax, gross profit, total of non-current assets and net current assets. However, these figures do not mean very much unless we can compare them to something else. For example, looking at a set of financial statements for a high street retailer may tell us that profit before tax is £3 million, but will not tell us if this is a good profit. It will probably be more than the profit of a sole trader in the same industry, but does it mean that the high street retailer is performing better? Now look at Activity 29.4.

ACTIVITY 29.4

You have £1150 to invest and discover that type 1 investment will provide interest of £68 per annum and type 2 investment will provide a single interest payment of £341 after five years. Which investment would you choose, assuming no compound interest and no change in the value of the pound?

Activity feedback

Investment 1 provides a return of 68/1150 = 5.91 per cent per annum. Investment 2 provides a return of

68.2/1150 = 5.93 per cent per annum. Thus, investment 2 provides the highest return. In the above example we compared the return with the amount invested and expressed the figures in the same units – percentage per annum. We were then able to identify which investment provided the better return.

What we did in Activity 29.4 was to calculate a ratio. We will illustrate in the remainder of this chapter how different ratios can be calculated in order to help solve the three information needs mentioned above and facilitate the decision-making process of the different stakeholders of the company.

The next section identifies which figures in a set of financial statements are useful to compare to evaluate the financial status, performance and investment potential of a business. The financial statements used are those of Serendipity plc, which are reproduced below.

Serendipity income statement

	Year ended 31.12.X4		Year ended 31.12.X5	
	£000	£000	£000	£000
Sales		584		972
Opening inventory	31		47	
Purchases	405		700	
	436		747	
Closing inventory	47		62	
Cost of goods sold		389		685
Gross profit		195		287
Wages and salaries	78		101	
Depreciation	16		31	
Debenture interest	—		8	
Other expenses	54	148	62	202
Net profit before tax		47		85
Taxation		16		39
Net profit after tax		31		46
Proposed dividend		16		23
Retained profit for year		15		23

Serendipity Statement of Financial Position

	31.12.X4		31.12.X5	
	£000	£000	£000	£000
Assets				
Non-current assets		280		428
Current assets				
Inventories	47		62	
Debtors	70		156	
Bank	39		16	
Total current assets		156		234
Total assets		436		662
Equity				
Share capital		272		295
Retained earnings		93		116
Total equity		365		411
Non-current liabilities				
10% debentures		—		80
Current liabilities				
Creditors	39		109	
Taxation	16		39	
Proposed dividends	16		23	
Total current liabilities		71		171
Total equity and liabilities		436		662

Note that for simplicity of illustration, the format above is less complex than the layout put forward in IAS 1. The information provided in relation to the company Serendipity relates to the components which determine the profit or loss of the period. We will not include elements of other comprehensive income (which is a part of the income statement under IAS 1) for the period in this example.

Strictly speaking, in IAS jargon, current and non-current refers to the fact of whether or not an asset will be expected to be realized in, or is intended for sale or consumption in, the entity's normal operation cycle (IAS 1, para. 66 (a)) and a liability is expected to be settled in the entity's normal operating cycle or due to be settled within 12 months (IAS 1, para. 69 (a) and (c)). Net current assets are current assets minus current liabilities.

In the format of the previous statement of financial position, total assets and total equity and liabilities are presented separately.

With regard to the income statement, the information on the changes in inventory levels and purchases will be provided in the notes to the accounts. On the face of an IAS income statement itself, you might only find the cost of goods sold which is calculated by combining the changes in inventory levels with purchases.

The ratios which will be introduced to you in the following sections are calculated with information found either on the face of the statement of financial position or on the face of the income statement or in the notes to the accounts.

Before beginning any ratio analysis, it is useful to look at the accounts and identify any changes from one year to the next (see Activity 29.5).

ACTIVITY 29.5

Compare and contrast each item on the statement of financial position and the income statement of Serendipity plc with the figure for the previous year. Note five points of interest from this comparison.

Activity feedback

You should have identified five from the following:

- sales have increased in X5
- cost of sales has increased
- expenses have increased
- profit after tax has increased by 50 per cent
- non-current assets have increased substantially
- net current assets (= current assets – current liabilities) have reduced
- shares and debentures have increased in X5.

Having identified various points of interest in Activity 29.5, we are now ready to carry out the ratio analysis. We will start with those ratios that are helpful in deciding whether or not a business is successful and whether or not it is operated in an efficient way.

Performance

The first ratio to be considered in this respect is 'return on capital employed' (ROCE):

$$\text{ROCE} = \frac{\text{Profit before taxation and long-term loan interest}}{\text{Net assets (Equity + long-term debt)}}$$

This ratio identifies how much profit the business has made from the capital invested in it and answers the question: Would the owners be better off selling the business and placing the proceeds in a bank deposit account?

In fact, this ratio measures the return on investment. However, the question is: What amount do we need to consider as invested capital? In the ROCE ratio above, net assets or equity with long-term debt is used as the denominator. One could also use the total assets instead of net assets as a denominator. In the latter ratio we assume that all assets contribute to the profit of the company. Further, the ratio 'return on assets' (ROA) is not influenced by the financial structure of the company, whereas the ROCE ratio is influenced to a certain extent, namely by the trade-off between short-term and long-term financing. Both ratios are used (ROA and ROCE) in the literature and in practice.

$$ROA = \frac{\text{Profit before taxation} + \text{Interest}}{\text{Total assets}}$$

ACTIVITY 29.6

Calculate the ROCE and ROA for Serendipity plc for X4 and X5.

This ratio has increased from X4 to X5 indicating an increase in profitability of the business.

Activity feedback

	X4	X5
ROCE	47/365 = 12.88%	93/491 = 18.94%
ROA	47/436 = 10.77%	93/662 = 14.04%

But where has this increased profitability come from? Is it because the business has increased sale prices or reduced expenses – that is, increased net profit margins – or is it because the business has increased the volume of trade compared to the capital employed?

We will continue with the ROCE ratio in the following discussion. The sub-analysis of the ROA ratio proceeds in exactly the same way and the interpretations are similar. The only difference is that capital employed is substituted by total assets, and where we need to take into account the interest expense, then the interest expense on short-term liabilities should be added to the interest expense on long-term liabilities.

The change in profitability can be examined using two ratios as follows:

$$\text{Net profit margin} = \frac{\text{Profit before tax and long-term interest}}{\text{Sales}}$$

$$\text{Volume of trade} = \frac{\text{Sales}}{\text{Capital employed}}$$

Calculating these two ratios for Serendipity plc we have:

	X4	X5
Net profit margin	47/584 = 8.0%	93/972 = 9.6%

Net profit margin has increased indicating either greater control over expenses or increased sale prices. An answer to that question will be given later on, with the help of other ratios. If we look at the change in the volume of trade, we see that Serendipity plc is earning more sales per pound of net assets or capital employed in X5 than in X4:

Volume of trade $584/365 = 1.6$ times $972/491 = 1.98$ times

The three ratios we have looked at so far have the following relationship:

$$\text{ROCE} = \text{Margin} \times \text{Volume}$$
$$\frac{\text{Profit}}{\text{Capital employed}} = \frac{\text{Profit}}{\text{Sales}} \times \frac{\text{Sales}}{\text{Capital employed}}$$

This relationship can be shown as a family tree:

```
                        ROCE
                          |
          ┌───────────────┴───────────────┐
(Profit before tax + Long-term interest)/Sales    Sales/Capital employed
```

This family tree can be expanded and will provide a framework for the analysis of the performance and efficiency of the company. For example:

$$\text{Net profit/Sales} = \text{Gross profit/Sales} - \text{Expenses/Sales}$$

whereby:

$$\text{Gross profit} = \text{Sales} - \text{Cost of goods sold}$$

or, in brief:

$$\frac{\text{GP}}{\text{S}} - \frac{\text{E}}{\text{S}}$$

Sales/capital employed can be inverted to capital employed/sales, which is the value of assets held per pound of sales, and then expanded to:

$$\text{Non-current assets (N-CA)/Sales} + \text{Net current assets (NCA)/Sales}$$

or, in brief:

$$\frac{\text{N-CA}}{\text{S}} + \frac{\text{NCA}}{\text{S}}$$

The family tree of ratios, or pyramid, now looks like this:

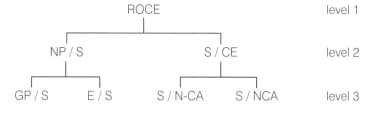

```
                  ROCE                              level 1
            ┌───────┴───────┐
         NP / S            S / CE                   level 2
        ┌───┴───┐        ┌───┴───┐
     GP / S    E / S   S / N-CA  S / NCA            level 3
```

ACTIVITY 29.7

Calculate these four further ratios for Serendipity plc and interpret them.

Activity feedback

	X4	X5
Gross profit margin	195/584 = 33.3%	287/972 = 29.5%

This shows a reduction in gross profit.

This could be due to several reasons. First of all, we observe an increase in the relative cost of goods sold/sales. This percentage has increased from X4 to X5:

	X4	X5
Cost of good sold/sales	389/584 = 66%	685/972 = 70%

This could point to an inflation in the price of purchased goods or less efficient negotiations by the purchasing department.

Another element could be that there has been a decrease in sale prices, which has generated more sales and a resulting increase in cost of goods sold:

	X4	X5
Expenses/sales	148/584 = 25.3%	194/972 = 20%

This has decreased from X4 to X5 indicating greater control over all other expenses:

	X4	X5
N-CA/S	280/584 = 0.48	428/972 = 0.44

If we invert the above, then for X4 we have 2.08 and for X5 2.27; that is, non-current assets have generated 2.08 times their value in sales in X4 and 2.27 times their value in sales in X5.

Non-current assets are earning more sales or are operated in a much more efficient way:

	X4	X5
NCA/S	85/584 = 0.15	63/972 = 0.06

Inverting gives X4 6.87 and X5 15.4.

Net current assets are also earning more sales in X5 than X4.

So, all assets are used more efficiently in X5. Thus, we observe that the overall increase in profitability is positively influenced by the efficient use of the non-current assets and net current assets in X5 and the control of all expenses but not the cost of goods sold. The profitability was negatively influenced by the decrease in the gross profit margin.

The pyramid can be extended to level 4 by comparing individual expenses to sales and breaking down the non-current assets and net current assets into their constituent parts:

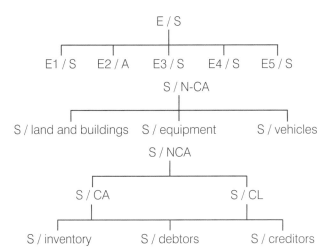

However, as inventory is recorded at cost, not selling price, then a more appropriate ratio than sales/inventory would be cost of goods sold/inventory, and as creditors relates to goods purchased on credit it would be better to look at credit purchases/creditors. Lastly, sales/debtors would be more appropriate as credit sales/debtors.

The following Illustration demonstrates the calculation and interpretation of these level 4 ratios.

ILLUSTRATION

The following information is provided for TAX Ltd as at 31 December 20X4:

	£000
Cost of goods sold	220
Average inventory for the year	50
Trade creditors	86
Credit purchases	216
Trade debtors	96
Credit sales	284

Cost of goods sold/inventory = 220/50 = 4.4; that is, 4.4 times the average inventory level has been used in cost of goods sold for the year. This could be written more simply as: inventory is turned over every 83 days, i.e. 365/4.4 = 83 days.

Creditors' period = 86/216 × 365 = 145 days

The ratio is therefore:

$$\frac{\text{Average inventory}}{\text{Cost of goods sold}} \times 365$$

The lower the ratio, the more efficiently the company is operated. A low ratio means that investment is only tied up in non-income-generating investments for a short period. What is meant by a high ratio or a low ratio is dependent on the industry (see Chapter 31 of this book). These ratios, as with many other ratios, have industry-specific outcomes. Inventory days will be much higher in the steel industry than in industries which sell perishable goods, for example.

The debtors' and creditors' ratios are written as:

$$\frac{\text{Trade debtors}}{\text{Credit sales}} \times 365$$

which will tell us on average how long it takes debtors to pay, and:

$$\frac{\text{Trade creditors}}{\text{Credit purchases}} \times 365$$

which will tell us how long on average it takes the business to pay its creditors.

The information provided above does not give a figure for credit sales or credit purchases, therefore we will have to use total sales and total purchases as an approximation:

Debtors' period = 96/284 × 365 = 123 days
Creditors' period = 86/216 × 365 = 145 days

Whether or not these level 4 ratios should be calculated when carrying out a ratio analysis will depend upon the information produced at previous levels. For example, when considering Serendipity plc, we noted a marked improvement in the efficiency of net current assets; therefore, calculating the fourth level ratios may tell us where this improvement has come from (see Activity 29.8).

ACTIVITY 29.8

Calculate inventory, debtor and creditor turnover periods for Serendipity plc and interpret them.

Activity feedback

	X4	X5
Inventory turnover	((31 + 47)/2)/ 389 × 365	((47 + 62)/2)/ 685 × 365
Number of inventory days	36.6 days	29.0 days

Thus, inventory is being turned over quicker in X5, demonstrating greater efficiency.

	X4	X5
Debtors' turnover period	70/584 × 365	156/972 × 365
Number of debtor days	44 days	58 days

Thus, debtors have been allowed (or have taken) 14 more days on average in X5 than X4 in which to pay their debts to the business. This could possibly indicate that Serendipity plc is losing control of its debtor collection, or that it has purposely allowed debtors more time to pay so as to encourage more sales.

	X4	X5
Creditors' turnover period	39/405 × 365	109/700 × 365
Number of creditor days	35 days	57 days

(Note that cost of goods sold could be used as a substitute for purchases if the financial statements do not provide a figure for purchases.) This indicates that Serendipity plc is taking longer to pay its suppliers – 22 days longer. This may damage relations with suppliers if Serendipity does not take care, but also demonstrates how Serendipity is using creditors to finance its business operations. A balance has to be struck within this dichotomy.

Within the analysis of Serendipity plc at level 3, there was also a benefit gained from control of expenses. Therefore fourth level analysis here would also be beneficial (see Activity 29.9).

ACTIVITY 29.9

Calculate ratios of wages, depreciation and other expenses to sales and interpret them for Serendipity plc.

Activity feedback

	X4	**X5**
Wages/sales	78/584 = 13.3%	101/972 = 10.4%

This indicates that the amount of wages expended to generate £1 of sales has been reduced.

Depreciation/sales	16/584 = 2.7%	31/972 = 3.2%

Depreciation has marginally increased as a proportion of sales. This may be due to an increase in assets.

Other expenses/ sales	54/584 = 9.3%	62/972 = 6.4%

Other expenses have also been controlled as a percentage of sales. As we saw earlier, when we combine these three ratios we see an increase in profit margin – increased profitability. The pyramid also demonstrates that the ratios on the left-hand side show profitability and those on the right-hand side show efficiency in the use of assets. Before moving on to consider financial status within ratio analysis, we need to take another look at the first ratio on the pyramid – ROCE. Capital employed consists of shareholder funds – that is share capital and reserves – and long-term debt, for example debentures. In the example of Serendipity plc, ROCE was:

$$
\begin{array}{ll}
X4 & 12.88\% \\
X5 & 18.94\%
\end{array}
$$

However, the debentures in X5 only required a return to be paid to the holders of 10 per cent, even though the capital invested (£10 000) earned 18.9 per cent. The earnings over and above the 10 per cent will then accrue to the shareholders and their return will be increased beyond the 18.9 per cent that the total capital earned. This phenomenon can be demonstrated by calculating the ratio of return on equity for Serendipity:

$$
\text{ROE} = \frac{\text{Profit before tax, but after interest}}{\text{Shareholders' equity (or owners' equity)}}
$$

$$
\begin{array}{ll}
X4 & X5 \\
47/365 = 12.88\% & 85/411 = 20.68\%
\end{array}
$$

The shareholders have increased their earnings in the business partly due to the benefit gained by borrowing at a lower rate of return than the business is earning. However, the converse can also occur! Note that ROCE and ROE were both the same in X4 as there was no long-term debt.

Whereas ROCE or ROA provides an answer to the question of whether the business is worthwhile to invest in, the ROE ratio takes the perspective of the shareholder and tries to answer the question of whether the investment in the share capital of the company is beneficial for the owners of those shares.

ACTIVITY 29.10

Given the following information, calculate ROCE and ROE for Knight Ltd for X4 and X5.

	X4	X5
	£	£
Profit before tax	80	85
Interest charged	10	10
Capital employed	1 250	1 280
Non-current debt	100	100

Activity feedback

	X4	X5
ROCE	90/1250 = 7.2%	95/1280 = 7.4%
ROE	80/1150 = 7%	85/1180 = 7.2%

The ROCE made in each year is 7.2 per cent and 7.4 per cent, but the return payable to the long-term debt holders is 10 per cent in both years. Therefore the return available to the shareholders reduces to 7 per cent and 7.2 per cent.

This is the opposite of the Serendipity case. Attracting external funds on which interest needs to be paid irrespective of the result of the company might be beneficial to the shareholders if ROA is higher than the interest rate paid by the firm on its debt. It is detrimental to the shareholders if ROA is lower than the interest rate paid by the firm on its debt. We need to compare ROCE with the interest paid on long-term debt.

After the discussion of the ratios which could help in determining whether or not a company is successful and operated in an efficient way, we turn our attention to the information needs in relation to the financial status of the company. The following questions will be asked by interested parties:

1 Can the business pay its way? Is it liquid?
2 Has the company the ability to repay its debt? What is the security for the amounts lent to the company?

FINANCIAL STATUS

It is essential for a business to be able to pay its debts as and when they fall due, otherwise its chances of continuing to operate become remote. Thus, there is a need to analyze the assets available to meet liabilities. This can be done in the short, medium and long-term since some debt will have to be repaid on short notice and other amounts will only fall due in the distant future.

Within the group of ratios which analyze the financial structure of the company, we distinguish on the one hand liquidity ratios, which are used to assess the company's ability to meet its short-term obligations. On the other, we have the group of solvency ratios which concentrate on the question of whether or not a company will repay its debt in the long-term.

Liquidity ratios

Liquidity refers to the capacity of a company to generate liquidity from its current operations to repay its current debt. Therefore, ratios concentrating on the liquidity question will focus on the current assets or short-term assets and the current or short-term liabilities of the firm. The first liquidity ratio is the current ratio:

$$\frac{\text{Current assets}}{\text{Current liabilities}}$$

In most industries, this ratio needs to be higher than one in order to indicate that no liquidity problems will arise. However, within the current assets there are items which might not be realizable in the very short term, for example, inventory items that are damaged. Therefore, there is a second liquidity ratio, the quick ratio or the acid test ratio:

$$\frac{\text{Current assets } - \text{ Inventory}}{\text{Current liabilities}}$$

The acid test is often called the short-term liquidity test and the current ratio the medium-term liquidity test.

Solvency ratios

Solvency ratios try to measure the risk involved in the repayment of debt and the ability of a company to meet its debt in the long run. A key element in this respect is the capital structure of the firm. Companies have two main resources of funds, namely debt and equity. Each has different well-known characteristics (e.g. fixed versus variable rewards, fixed repayment schedules versus repayment when the company liquidates). The financial risk or financial strength of a company is measured by ratios which relate debt to equity. The most commonly used ratio worldwide in this respect is the debt/equity ratio. A high debt/equity ratio implies higher financial risk, since a higher ratio points to higher interest charges and a wider exposure to possible interest changes. Further, debt often needs to be repaid on a fixed date irrespective of whether or not the company has sufficient funds available. There are several alternatives in determining the numerator and the denominator of this ratio, for example:

$$\frac{\text{Debt}}{\text{Equity}} \quad \text{or} \quad \frac{\text{long-term debt}}{\text{Equity}}$$

The ratios mentioned above are often called gearing ratios.

$$\frac{\text{Debt}}{\text{Equity} + \text{Debt}} \quad \text{or} \quad \frac{\text{Equity}}{\text{Equity} + \text{Debt}}$$

The interest cover ratio is a ratio which indicates the safety margin between profits generated and interest charges, and is calculated as follows:

$$\frac{\text{Net profit before interest and taxes}}{\text{Total interest charges}}$$

Whether or not a company is able to repay its debt in the long-term depends on its ability to generate cash flow from operations, from the disposal of assets or from external funding. The future cash flow generating capacity of a company can be estimated on the basis of the current cash flow. Whether or not a company will dispose of its assets depends on its strategy and the role of these assets in implementing the strategy. The possibility of attracting external funding will depend on the appreciation of the company by the capital markets and the suppliers of long-term and short-term credit. These items will be explained further in the following two chapters of this book.

ACTIVITY 29.11

Calculate the two liquidity ratios, the gearing ratio, the interest cover ratio, the debt/equity ratio and the debt/(equity + debt) ratio for Serendipity plc and interpret them.

Activity feedback

	X4	X5
Acid test	$\frac{156-47}{71} = \frac{109}{71}$	$\frac{234-62}{171} = \frac{172}{171}$
expressed as	1.5:1	1:1

The ratio has decreased from X4 to X5 quite considerably, but there are still plenty of liquid assets. The ratio will need careful monitoring to control this downward trend.

Current ratio   156/71 = 2.2:1   234/171 = 1.4:1

Again, this ratio has been substantially reduced but still appears adequate. Monitoring of this downward trend is again required.

Gearing ratio   not relevant   80/411 = 19.5%

This is low and we would consider this company to not be highly geared. If a company is highly geared, then it may have difficulty meeting the required interest payments. However, this needs to be interpreted not only within the specific industry context, but also within the national environment (more on these items in Chapters 30 and 31).

Debt/Equity	71/365 = 19.45%	251/411 = 61.07%
Debt/(Equity + Debt)	71/436 = 16.28%	251/662 = 37.91%

We notice a deterioration in the financial structure.

Interest cover   not relevant   (85 + 8)/8 = 12

In X5 the profit covered the required interest payment 12 times, indicating no immediate problem for Serendipity plc. Notice how consideration of all four ratios helped to build up a picture of the financial status of Serendipity plc.

The last grouping of ratios we will discuss in this chapter relate specifically to the information needs of current and potential shareholders. This group is especially interested in finding out whether or not the investment they make, or intend to make, in a company is a profitable investment compared to other investment possibilities they have (e.g. buying shares in other companies subscribing to debentures or putting their money into a savings account).

Investment potential

Before looking in detail at investment ratios, it is useful to carry out some practical research.

ACTIVITY 29.12

Obtain a fairly recent copy of a financial newspaper (e.g. *The Wall Street Journal* or *The Financial Times*, or the equivalent in your own country). Look up the share information service and make a note of the data provided for each company. Also read the 'company news section' either in a financial newspaper or any other quality newspaper, and note down any ratios or indicators used to evaluate the companies.

Activity feedback

Your list possibly includes the following:

- *book value per share compared with market value per share*
- *net dividend*
- *dividend cover*
- *earnings per share (EPS)*
- *gross dividend yield*
- *price/earnings ratio.*

We will look at each of these ratios in turn.

Book value per share This is the ordinary shareholders' equity/number of shares. This book value is the value each share would have if the company's assets and liabilities were sold at their balance sheet or statement of financial position (book) value. The market value is the price a potential shareholder is willing to pay to acquire a share in the company. Comparing these two values identifies whether the market values the company at more or less than its book value.

Net dividend This is the amount of dividend declared in any one year per share which equals paid and proposed dividends divided by the number of shares. People invest in shares for one of three reasons: to earn dividends, to earn capital growth in the value of the share or both. The level of dividend and its comparison with previous years is generally regarded as an important indicator of future expectations. However, one danger with this comparison is that dividends are not necessarily just paid out of the current year's earnings, but can be paid out of retained earnings. It is, therefore, important to look at dividend cover in any one year.

Dividend cover

$$\frac{\text{Net profit available to ordinary shareholders}}{\text{Total dividend paid}}$$

Earnings per share (EPS) This is another indicator used widely by the investment community. It represents the amount of profit available to ordinary shareholders that the company has earned during the year for each ordinary share. We discussed this ratio in Chapter 24.

For the example of Kit plc (see Activity 29.13), the EPS in X4 is 204 700/1 875 000 = 10.9p and in X5 is 179 100/1 875 000 = 9.6p.

ACTIVITY 29.13

The following information is available in respect of Kit plc:

	X4	X5
	£	£
Ordinary shares issued £1	1 875 000	1 875 000
8% preference shares £1	660 000	660 000
Dividend ordinary shares	225 000	187 500
Net profit after tax	257 500	231 900

Calculate dividend per share in pence for both preference and ordinary shares, and dividend cover.

Activity feedback

	X4	X5
Dividend per preference share	8p	8p

Dividend per	X4	X5
ordinary share	12p	10p
Dividend cover	257 500/277 800	231 900/240 300
	= 0.93	= 0.97

Thus the dividend per share has reduced from X4 to X5, but the dividend cover has improved. However, this dividend cover is less than one which indicates that the company is not earning enough in either year to pay the dividend, and is therefore using past earnings retained to fund the dividend payment. This may be a danger sign for potential investors.

Gross dividend yield This is calculated using the formula:

$$\frac{\text{Gross dividend}}{\text{Market price of ordinary share}}$$

Shareholders may be willing to accept a low gross dividend yield if there is a greater than average capital growth in share value expected, or if the company is a safe investment. Gross dividend is calculated by grossing up the dividend declared in the accounts for basic rate taxation, as dividends are always declared and paid net of basic income tax.

For example, in the case of Kit plc, if the basic rate of tax is 20 per cent, then the gross dividend is:

X4	X5
225 000/80% = 281 250	187 500/80% = 234 375

or per share, 15p (X4), 12.5p (X5)

If the market value per share for Kit was £1.75 in X4 and £1.82 in X5, then the gross dividend yield is:

X4	X5
15/175	12.5/182
8.6%	6.9%

Price/Earnings (PE) ratio The formula for this is:

$$\frac{\text{Market price per share}}{\text{Earnings per share}}$$

For Kit this is:

X4	X5
175/10.9	182/9.6
16.1	19

Like the dividend yield, the PE ratio will change as the market price per share changes. It represents the market's view of the growth potential of the company, its dividend policy and the degree of risk involved in the investment. In general, a high PE indicates that the market has a high/good opinion of these factors, a low PE a low/poor opinion. Another way of looking at the PE is that it represents the number of years' earnings it is necessary to have at the current rate to recover the price paid for the share. For Kit plc this was 19 years at the X5 rate of earnings.

In the discussion on ratios, we have covered the three principal areas in which users need information to make economic decisions (profitability, financial status and investment potential). More ratios and evaluation concepts (like economic value added and total shareholder return) are introduced in Chapter 31 'Techniques of financial analysis'. Although financial statement data represent an important source of information, they have to be interpreted with caution and must be combined with additional information to make sound business decisions. The pitfalls in ratio analysis will be discussed further in the next two chapters of this book, as well as an analysis of the additional information needed. To provide an idea about this additional information, see Activity 29.14.

ADDITIONAL INFORMATION

Ratio analysis is a tool that aids the user in building up an overall picture of the condition/state of a business entity. Other information can help to fill in more of this picture.

Some of the information in Activity 29.14 will be available to users. Companies might release additional information to the capital markets and databases are available with the financial statements of listed companies and large non-listed as well as industry databases with trends and market shares. However, for a number of items, it would be very difficult, probably impossible, for a potential investor to obtain detailed information, for example, in respect of future plans of the business apart from that disclosed in the directors' report in the financial statements.

ACTIVITY 29.14

Identify additional information that you would like when undertaking a ratio analysis of a company.

Activity feedback

- *Inflation effects on the company.*
- *Cash flow throughout the year.*
- *Forecast business plans in the form of budgets and cash flows.*
- *Information in respect of the quality of goods and services and other factors affecting the assessment of goodwill in the business.*
- *Industrial averages of ratios.*
- *Differences in accounting policies between businesses.*

SUMMARY

This chapter has considered the users of financial statements and their needs. We identified a tool that can be used – ratio analysis – to attempt to meet these needs. We have illustrated how individual components of the statement of financial position, the income statement and the notes can be used in ratio analysis in order to provide useful data for economic decision making. In this chapter, the illustrations of performance, liquidity, solvency and investment ratios only allowed us to judge whether or not the position of Serendipity had improved from year X4 to year X5. To make sound business decisions, however, we need to compare the outcomes of the ratios not only over a longer time span than just two years, but we also need to compare them with the outcomes of other companies. This will be elaborated further in the next chapters of Part Four of this book.

EXERCISES

Suggested answers to exercises marked ✓ are to be found in the Student online resources, with suggested answers to the remaining questions available in the Instructor online resources.

✓**1** The following are extracts from an industrial performance analysis for two groups, Alpha Group plc and Omega Group plc.

The two groups operate in different industrial sectors and have accordingly adopted different operating and financial strategies.

Alpha Group plc	20X3 £000	20X2 £000	20X1 £000
Income data			
Turnover	20 915	19 036	16 929
Operating profit	1 386	1 189	943
Depreciation	299	264	214
Income from investments	23	20	14
Interest payable	95	66	60
Statement of financial position data			
Intangible non-current assets	636	660	484
Tangible non-current assets	7 213	5 605	4 654
Investments	234	201	148
Total non-current assets	8 083	6 466	5 286
Inventory	1 405	1 312	1 217
Trade debtors	65	54	57
Cash	97	62	43
Other current assets	1 000	550	700
Total current assets	2 567	1 978	2 017
Total assets	10 650	8 444	7 303

Equity

Ordinary shares	3 000	3 000	3 000
Preference shares, redeemable 20X6	2 000	—	—
Reserves	944	1 606	1 027
Total equity	5 944	4 606	4 027
Liabilities			
Non-current liabilities	904	604	239
Provisions for liabilities and charges	180	159	158
Minority interests	150	132	130
Total non-current liabilities	1 234	895	527
Trade creditors	1 651	1 521	1 381
Overdraft	150	—	160
Short-term loans	300	151	200
Other current liabilities	1 371	1 271	1 008
Total current liabilities	3 472	2 943	2 749
Total liabilities	4 706	3 838	3 276
Total equity and liabilities	10 650	8 444	7 303

Omega Group plc	**20X3**	**20X2**	**20X1**
	£000	£000	£000
Income data			
Turnover	19 540	15 260	16 320
Operating profit	620	340	220
Depreciation	240	220	220
Income from investments	20	20	20
Interest payable	720	660	720
Statement of financial position data			
Tangible non-current assets	1 620	1 360	1 360
Investments	220	280	240
Total non-current assets	1 840	1 640	1 600
Inventory	3 780	2 540	2 040
Trade debtors	3 400	1 920	2 040
Cash	800	480	400
Other current assets	3 260	4 000	3 580
Total current assets	11 240	8 940	8 060
Total assets	13 080	10 580	9 660

Equity and liabilities

Equity

Ordinary shares	600	600	600
Preference shares, redeemable 20X6	200	200	200
Reserves	720	360	60
Total equity	1 520	1 160	860
Liabilities			
Non-current liabilities	5 400	5 100	4 660
Provisions for liabilities and charges	260	300	360
Minority interests	200	180	200
Total non-current liabilities	5 860	5 580	5 220
Current liabilities			
Trade creditors	2 700	1 620	1 020
Overdraft	60	180	—
Short-term loans	1 800	1 200	1 820
Other current liabilities	1 140	840	740
Total current liabilities	5 700	3 840	3 580
Total liabilities	11 560	9 420	8 800
Total equity and liabilities	13 080	10 580	9 660

Required:

(a) A set of five key ratios of use in monitoring the operational performance of the two groups over three years. Show clearly your workings and justify the definitions of the inputs to your ratio calculations.

(b) A set of three key ratios of use in monitoring the financial structure of the two groups over three years. Show clearly your workings and justify the definitions of the inputs to your ratio calculations.

(c) Identify the contrasting operating and financing strategies of the two groups as revealed by your ratio analysis.

(d) For each group suggest an industrial sector for which such a strategy would give a best fit. Give reasons for your suggestions.

(e) List five ways in which financial statements could be improved in order to make them more useful as the basis for input to ratio analysis. Identify the constraints on implementation of these improvements.

(ACCA, adapted)

2   Obtain a set of accounts for a supermarket and a manufacturer. You can do this by accessing the website of the company and searching for the annual report, probably under the information heading 'investor relations'. Compare and contrast the nature of the current assets and liabilities of your two companies.

3 You are given the following information in relation to Olivet Ltd.

Income statement	20X4	20X5
Sales	100 000	100 000
Cost of sales	50 000	60 000
	50 000	40 000
Expenses	30 000	30 000
	20 000	10 000
Dividends	10 000	10 000
	10 000	—
Balance b/d	2 500	12 500
	12 500	12 500

Statement of financial position as at	20X4	20X5
Land	21 500	31 500
Buildings	20 000	39 500
Equipment	3 000	3 000
	44 500	74 000
Investments at cost	25 000	40 000
Inventory	27 500	32 500
Debtors	20 000	25 000
Bank	1 500	—
	118 500	171 500
Ordinary £1 shares	20 000	25 000
Share premium	6 000	7 000
Revaluation reserve	—	10 000
Profit and loss	12 500	12 500
Debentures 10%	50 000	75 000
Creditors	20 000	30 000
Proposed dividend	10 000	10 000
Bank	—	2 000
	118 500	171 500

Required:
You are required to comment on the financial position of Olivet Ltd as at 20X5. Calculate any ratios you feel necessary.

4 You are given the attached information about Fred plc, comprising summarized income statements, summarized statements of financial position and some suggested ratio calculations. You should note that there may be alternative ways of calculating some of these ratios. The holders of a small number of the ordinary shares in the business have come to you for help and advice. There are a number of things they do not properly understand, and a friend of theirs who is an accountancy student has suggested that some of the ratios show a distinctly unsatisfactory position and that holders should sell their shares as quickly as possible.

Required:
Write a report to the shareholders commenting on the apparent position and prospects of Fred plc, as far as the information permits. Your report should include reference to liquidity and profitability aspects and should advise whether, in your view, the shares should indeed be sold as soon as possible.

Fred plc
Some possible ratio calculations (which can be taken as arithmetically correct).

	20X2	20X1
Current ratio	54/147 = 36.7%	56/172 = 32.6%
Acid test ratio	12/147 = 8.2%	15/172 = 8.7%
ROCE	57/249 = 22.9%	41/161 = 25.5%
EPS	31/190 =16.3p	22/190 = 11.6p
Trade debtors' turnover	4/910 × 365 = 2 days	4/775 × 365 = 2 days
Trade creditors' turnover	60/730 × 365 = 30 days	60/633 × 365 = 35 days
Gross profit %	180/910 = 19.8%	142/775 = 18.3%
Operating profit %	57/910 = 6.3p	41/775 = 5.3%
Inventory turnover	42/730 × 365 = 21 days	41/633 × 365 = 24 days
Gearing	61/188 = 32.4%	1/160 = 0.6%

Fred plc
Summarized statements of financial position at year end (£m)

		20X2		20X1
Non-current assets				
Tangible – not yet in use		49		41
– in use		295		237
		344		278
Investments		1		1
Loan redemption fund		1		1
		346		280
Current assets				
Inventory		42		41
Debtors – trade	4		4	
– other	4		4	
		8		8
Bank		2		5
Cash		2		2
		54		56
Total assets		400		336
Equity and liabilities				
Equity				
Ordinary shares of 10p each		19		19
Preference shares of £1 each		46		46
Share premium		1		1
Profit and loss account		122		94
		188		160
Liabilities				
Non-current liabilities		61		1
Provision for liabilities and charges		4		3
Current liabilities				
– trade	60		60	
– other	87		112	
		147		172
Total equity and liabilities		400		336

Fred plc
Summarized income statements for the year (£m)

	20X2		20X1	
Sales		910		775
Raw materials and consumables		730		633
		180		142
Staff costs	77		64	
Depreciation of tangible fixed assets	12		10	
Other operating charges	38		30	
		127		104
		53		38
Other operating income		4		3
		57		41
Net interest payable		5		4
		52		37
Profit sharing – employees		2		1
		50		36
Taxation		17		12
		33		24
Preference dividends		2		2
		31		22
Ordinary dividends		3		2
		28		20
Note:				
Net interest payable:				
interest payable		12		9
interest receivable		(1)		(1)
interest capitalized		(6)		(4)
		5		4

5   You are given summarized results of an electrical engineering business, as follows. All figures are in £000.

Income statement

	Year ended	
	31.12.20X1	31.12.20X0
Turnover	60 000	50 000
Cost of sales	42 000	34 000
Gross profit	18 000	16 000
Operating expenses	15 500	13 000
	2 500	3 000
Interest payable	2 200	1 300
Profit before taxation	300	1 700
Taxation	350	600
(Loss) profit after taxation	(50)	1 100
Dividends	600	600
Transfer (from) to reserves	(650)	500

Statement of financial position

Non-current assets

Intangible	500	—
Tangible	12000	11000
	12500	11000

Current assets

Inventory	14000	13000
Debtors	16000	15000
Bank and cash	500	500
	30500	28500
Total assets	43000	39500

Equity and liabilities

Equity

Share capital	1300	1300
Share premium	3300	3300
Revaluation reserve	2000	2000
Profit and loss	6400	7400
	13000	14000
Non-current liabilities	6000	5500
Current liabilities	24000	20000
Total liabilities	30000	25500
Total equity and liabilities	43000	39500

Required:

(a) Prepar e a table of the following 11 ratios, calculated for both years, clearly showing the figures used in the calculations: current ratio, quick assets ratio, inventory turnover in days, debtors' turnover in days, creditors' turnover in days, gross profit %, net profit % (before taxation), interest cover, dividend cover, ROCE and gearing.

(b) Making full use of the information given in the question, your table of ratios and your common sense, comment on the apparent position of the business and on the actions of the management.

INTERPRETATION OF FINANCIAL STATEMENTS

30

OBJECTIVES After studying this chapter you should be able to:

- explain how industry analysis can be useful in the context of financial analysis

- explain why knowledge of the corporate strategy is important for financial analysis

- describe the different incentives for annual accounts management

- describe the different variables which enlarge the accounting discretion of management

- identify the practices which are used for annual accounts management purposes

- explain the purpose of entity analysis

- describe what is meant by quality of disclosure

- describe what is meant by accounting quality.

INTRODUCTION

Financial statements provide valuable information for different stakeholders. In Chapters 1 and 29, we identified the users of accounting information and their differing needs. In Chapter 29, we also introduced the basics of ratio analysis. In Chapters 30 and 31, we elaborate further on the topic of financial analysis.

Since financial statements serve as a means of communication with the external stakeholders of a firm, they may sometimes be 'managed' to convey a certain message to the outside world. As well as the financial statements, the whole annual report together with interim statements and other releases of financial information and non-financial information, are subject to this phenomenon of 'manipulation' or 'misrepresentation'. Therefore, it is extremely important for users of financial accounting information to be able to 'undo' this manipulation and uncover the underlying economic performance of the firm. Economic decision makers must therefore be aware of the incentives a company's management may have to influence the annual accounts, of the available discretion management enjoys to pursue these incentives and of the means management has available for this purpose.

Knowledge about 'annual accounts management' is as important as a sound knowledge about the techniques of financial analysis in order to understand and judge properly the information provided through the annual accounts. In Chapters 30 and 31, we discuss both elements in depth. The topic of 'annual accounts management' will be discussed in this chapter. The techniques of financial analysis (e.g. trend analysis, common size financial statements, ratio analysis and cash flow analysis) are presented and illustrated in Chapter 31.

Financial statements are a source of information about a company since they present a picture of the economic performance of a firm. This economic performance, however, is determined to a large extent by the adopted business strategy or strategies of a firm and by the economic and industrial environment in which a firm is operating. As a result, accounting numbers are a reflection of the strategy adopted and of the industry environment in which the firm operates. Therefore, it is worthwhile gaining a clear insight into the industry and business characteristics of a company before starting with the analysis of its financial statements. Studying the economic and industrial environment of a company together with its strategy is often called 'industry analysis' in textbooks on financial and corporate reporting and analysis.

INDUSTRY ANALYSIS

In order to determine whether a company is, in fact, able to repay its debt or whether it is making a reasonable profit or is worthwhile to invest in, we need to compare the performance of the company with a benchmark. Besides gaining insight into how a firm's strategy and its business environment have an impact on the data in the annual accounts, industry analysis also provides benchmarking data to financial analysts and all other users of accounting information. For example, boards of directors judge the performance of the top management of the company by comparing the company's performance with the performance of competitors in the same industry. Industry analysis provides benchmarks against which the current performance, the financial status and the investment potential of a particular company can be compared. However, we need to take great care in carrying out this benchmarking so that we do not invalidate the results. In setting benchmarks against which we can compare a company, we must remain aware of the limitations of this comparison. This item will be further elaborated in the next chapter.

ACTIVITY 30.1

Within the scope of industry analysis, data from other businesses in the same industry or industry averages could be used for comparative or benchmarking purposes in order to evaluate the economic and financial situation of a company. What could be their limitations?

Activity feedback

- Other businesses. *Uses – is our business performing as well? Limitations – businesses may not be truly comparable with regard to size and type, e.g. grocery sole trader compared to supermarket; manufacturer compared to retailer. Further external factors may affect one business, e.g. a lengthy strike. Accounting standards and*

accounting policies on which accounting information is prepared may be different, e.g. inventory valuations, depreciation, historical cost or revalued amount, treatment of research and development, treatment of goodwill.

- Industry averages. *Industry averages have uses and limitations very similar to those of other businesses. Additionally, an average is simply a figure which takes account of the best but also the worst.*

Activity 30.2 repeats information from Chapter 29, but it is included here in a slightly different format for pedagogical reasons.

ACTIVITY 30.2

What other benchmarks/indicators could you think of besides benchmarks taken from industry analysis to evaluate the financial and economic situation of the company? Consider also their limitations.

Activity feedback

- Past period achievements. *Uses – to identify whether current activity is better or worse than previous periods. Limitations – external factors*

may have influenced activity levels, e.g. public awareness of environmental issues may have necessitated a change in manufacturing process leading to increased costs.

- Budgets. *Uses – has current activity matched planned activity? Limitations – the budget may not be a valid standard of performance, e.g. underlying assumptions may have been unrealistic or set at too high a level.*

Each of the four benchmarks identified is commonly used in assessing business status, performance and potential, but interpretation of accounts is highly subjective and requires skilled judgement, bearing in mind the limitations of these benchmarks.

In the next two sections, a brief overview will be presented of the elements to be considered in the context of industry analysis.

Analysis of the business environment

As different elements of the business and the economic environment of a company have an impact on the revenue and costs levels of the firm, we may state that the competitive environment determines to a certain extent the profit potential of a company. An important element with regard to industry profitability is the level of competition in an industry. This level of competition is influenced by the type of competition, the barriers to entry, the production capacity available in the industry, the existing relationships, agreements and alliances.

The degree of competition in an industry determines to a large extent on the price which can be charged for the products or services to the customer. The competition can be perfect competition, monopoly or any form in between. Firms in a monopoly position with no substitutes for their products or services can charge higher prices compared to firms in a situation of perfect competition with a high number of substitutes and high price elasticity of demand. The danger of substitute products can be avoided if firms are able to differentiate their products or services. This possibility will be determined by the existing switching costs.

The level of price competition in an industry is also a function of the cost structure, which is related to the technology used and the existence of economies of scale. If the ratio of fixed to variable costs is high, firms have a tendency to engage in price wars in order to fully utilize the production capacity they have invested in. Many economic textbooks mention the airline industry as a typical example of an industry where such a policy is often applied. However, if we analyze more closely the value chain of an airline company, then this observation (= high fixed costs) relates only to the transport activities in the value chain of the airline. Other activities in the value chain (such as reservations and sales, catering, handling) have a higher proportion of variable costs in their total cost structure. Therefore, price wars intended to fill up the empty seats in the airplanes will increase costs in the other activity areas of the value chain of an airline, where costs are much more variable.

Another element which characterizes the competitive environment of a firm is the presence of high or low barriers to entry. In industries with low barriers to entry, the pricing of existing firms within that industry is more constrained and so is the potential for abnormal profits. Barriers to entry could be created through the technology used, the access to channels of distribution, the supplier relationships and the existence of excess capacity.

A further important aspect of industry analysis is the study of the relationship between the input and output market of a firm. As an input market, we distinguish the labour market, the capital market and the suppliers' market. The power relations in these different markets and the scarcity of the resources determine to a large extent the price a company has to pay for those inputs. For example, in times of economic prosperity, the bargaining power of airline pilots with regard to their salaries is much higher than in times of economic downturn, when there is labour-related overcapacity in the airline industry.

The power relations with the buyers in the output market of the firm determine to a large extent the margin which a company can earn. If 80 per cent of the turnover of company X is bought by company Y, then the bargaining position of company X with regard to a price increase on the goods delivered to Y is very weak.

Regulation, or its absence, further characterizes the environment in which a firm operates. Regulation includes, among other things, government regulations, legal requirements and taxation.

The environment of the firm consists mainly of factors that are beyond the control of management. The only way to avoid certain environmental characteristics is often to switch to another industry or another country. Such changes, however, are not always obvious.

Analysis of the business strategy and corporate strategy

Business strategy. The management of a firm will choose what type of business to be in by taking into account environmental and industry characteristics, together with an analysis of strengths and weaknesses of the company. The next step is to decide how the firm is going to compete with other firms within the same industry. This implies choices with regard to the products or services and their characteristics that will be offered, the type of customers to attract and how these products or services will be produced. The firm's business strategy is the strategy that managers choose to achieve a competitive advantage. Several typologies to define strategy exist. The most well known is that of Porter. He defines two generic competitive strategies, namely a low-cost strategy and a differentiation strategy (Porter, 1985). Cost leadership can be achieved through economies of scale and scope, economies of learning, efficient production, simpler product design, lower input costs, cost control and leaner organizational processes. A firm following a low-cost strategy in the automobile industry is Hyundai. In the airline business, Ryanair, easyJet and Southwest airlines are important low-cost airlines. Until now they have been successful in their strategy through a combination of several elements such as lower input costs (lower wage levels), efficient production (higher asset utilization through reduced setup time, so more flights a day can be operated), different organizational processes (ticket sales only through the Internet), the use of secondary airports, negotiations with airport authorities whereby costs (landing fees) which normally had a fixed character (= paid per type of plane landed) were given a variable character (= passenger landed) and simpler product design (only transport is offered and passengers need to pay for the extras, e.g. food and drinks and luggage).

A firm following a differentiation strategy seeks to sell a unique product or service. Uniqueness can be achieved through superior customer service, product design and product features, brand loyalty, distribution network or technology. Mercedes Benz or BMW follow a differentiation strategy in the automobile sector. Whether a firm can develop or sustain cost leadership or differentiation depends on the organization of the value chain. 'The value chain is defined as the sequence of business functions in which utility [usefulness] is added to the products or services of an organization' (Horngren *et al.*, 2002, p. 8). These functions are research and development, design of products, services or processes, production, marketing, distribution and customer service. The activities in the value chain of a low-cost competitor will be organized differently from the activities in the value chain of a differentiator.

Firm profitability will be influenced not only by the chosen strategy but also by structural cost drivers such as scale, scope, experience, technology, complexity, executional cost drivers such as workforce involvement, total quality management, capacity utilization, plant layout efficiency, product configuration, linkages with suppliers or customers (Shank and Govindarajan, 1992) and operational cost drivers, which are cost drivers specific to activities in the value chain. Although these mentioned cost drivers are usually firm specific, certain drivers can be distinguished for an industry as a whole.

Research into the cost drivers in the airline industry (Banker and Johnston, 1993) revealed the existence of two different types of cost driver – those related to actual outputs and those related to output capacity. Actual outputs are the number of passengers carried or tons of cargo handled. The number of passengers is the cost driver for handling and catering. Fuel consumption and labour hours for scheduled flight crews and attendants vary more with aircraft size, seating capacity, distance and other characteristics of flights and aircrafts than with the actual number of passengers carried or tons of cargo handled. The cost of aircraft maintenance varies more with the number of flights, hours flown and characteristics of the aircraft, such as number of engines, than with actual outputs, such as number of passengers carried. Executional cost drivers in the airline business are elements such as density of the network and hub concentration.

So value chain analysis provides insights into how activities in and outside the company are organized and how value is created through these activities for the customer. In the context of value chain analysis, it is important to assess the resources available to a company: physical (i.e. location, equipment), and human and financial resources, together with intangibles (brands, know how). A benchmarking of a company's resources and activities with the resources and activities of a competitor, provides insights into the competitive strength of a company.

Value chain analysis can be taken one step further and be executed on the level of the industry as a whole. In its annual report, SAS presents an overview of the value chain of the aviation industry.

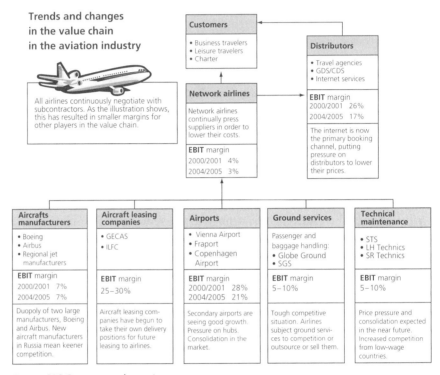

Source: SAS Group annual report 2005, p. 13.

The accounting numbers of a company will be influenced not only by decisions taken with regard to its own competitive position but also by evolutions in the industry value chain in which the company is active. In order to judge the performance or financial position of a firm properly, its value chain should be compared with the value chain of competitors and the industry value chain.

Corporate strategy. Some firms operate in only one industry, but others are competitive in several.

At the corporate level, management can choose to be active only in one business or to operate in multiple businesses. Corporate strategy decisions focus on where corporate resources will be invested. Business strategy decisions are concerned with how to compete in defined product markets. Some companies prosper by competing in one industry whereas others operate successfully in different industries.

For financial analysis purposes, it is important to know whether a company is a multi-business company, in which case the consolidated annual accounts reflect the performance of the group as a whole. In the consolidated profit and loss account, costs of different businesses will be presented in an aggregated way. Only through the segmental data included in the notes to the financial statements can the user of these statements get a glimpse of the profitability of the individual businesses (see Chapter 24 disclosure – segmental reporting). In the case of inter-firm comparison, one must be vigilant to whether or not companies are in the same business or in the same portfolio of businesses. The risks involved in these different business segments may revolve around different patterns.

ACTIVITY 30.3

Think of companies such as Unilever, Walt Disney Corporation, McDonald's and BMW. In how many businesses are they competitive?

Activity feedback

Single industry:	Multiple businesses:
McDonald's (fast food)	Unilever (food, cleansing agents, skincare products)
BMW (car manufacture)	Walt Disney Corporation (movies, TV channel, theme parks, real estate)

The main aim of undertaking industry analysis before one starts with accounting analysis is to get to know the business, because the business context gives meaning to the information presented in the annual accounts. According to the industry's value chain, the company's value chain and strategy chosen, the value of certain ratios will be lower or higher or the volatility of earnings will be different. Quite often, companies present their own value chain or business model in their annual report, or they produce an integrated report in which their business model is key. This type of information allows users to better understand the company, its financial information and their different operating segments. On the next page we include the value chain of Barry Callebaut, the world's largest producer of chocolate and chocolate products in which the company presents its business model.

ACCOUNTING ANALYSIS

We illustrated in the sections above that the economic performance of a firm is influenced to a large extent by the adopted business strategy and by the economic and industrial environment in which the firm is operating. As a result, the business strategy of the firm and the industry characteristics will be reflected in the accounting data. An understanding of that process is useful for an analysis of the accounts in a meaningful way. However, there is more to be taken into account before one can start with financial analysis. As annual accounts are used to communicate the underlying business reality to outside investors, managers may have incentives to manipulate investors' perceptions or the perception of other stakeholders and to present the performance and financial position of the firm more positively than in reality. Managers may choose accounting and disclosure policies that make it more difficult for external users of financial statements to understand the true economic performance of the business.

REAL LIFE ILLUSTRATION

Business at a Glance
Business model

We are the world's leading manufacturer of chocolate and cocoa products, by mastering every step in the value chain from the sourcing of raw materials to the production of the finest chocolates. We are able to provide our customers with added value products and services adapted to specific market needs, ahead of trends and at a competitive price. We serve the entire food industry – from global and local food manufacturers to artisanal and professional users of chocolate, such as chocolatiers, pastry chefs, bakers, hotels restaurants or caterers.

We are a business-to-business company. In order to accommodate price fluctuations in raw materials, most of our business is based on a cost-plus pricing system that passes on raw material costs directly to our customers.

Our input factors are talented people, various raw materials as well as deep chocolate and cocoa know-how. Our output factors are high-quality chocolate and cocoa products as well as value-added services.

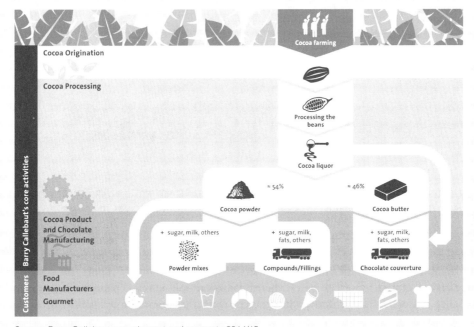

Source: Barry Callebaut annual report and accounts 2014/15.

Besides adopting a business strategy, the management can also adopt what is called an 'accounting reporting strategy'. Management may employ a number of accounting methods, accounting estimates or presentation and disclosure choices as well as real decisions, such that the performance represented through the published accounting numbers deviates from the underlying economic performance. This toolkit of methods, estimates and real decisions used to influence the accounting numbers according to the accounting strategy is used by top management with or without the approval of the board of directors. The purpose of accounting analysis is to try to detect what the incentives, opportunities and mechanisms are to misrepresent the financial situation and the performance of a company, and to provide an indication as to whether there is a possibility that the underlying economic performance might be different from the performance presented through the accounting numbers.

We now proceed with the discussion of the different elements of accounting analysis. First, we analyze the incentives and opportunities management has to influence the accounting numbers. Second, we concentrate on the mechanisms (accounting method choice, accounting estimate choice, presentation and disclosure choices, real transactions) management can use to influence the accounting numbers and which are determined by the amount of accounting flexibility available. This knowledge about the incentives, opportunities and mechanisms available to influence the accounting numbers will enable the external user of the annual accounts to detect more easily the underlying economic performance of the firm, and will allow the user to make a more reliable judgement about the underlying economic performance and financial position of that firm.

Accounting analysis: incentives to manage the annual accounts

The management of a company can have different incentives to manage the accounting numbers which present the performance and the financial position. Academic research into earnings management has shown that earnings management incentives result from the external and internal contracts governing the firm. This stream of research is inspired mainly by the agency paradigm. Among the external contracts governing the firm, we can distinguish between contracts with shareholders, debt holders and the government and other regulatory authorities. The most important internal contract of the firm is that with top management. Academic research provides evidence that incentives to manage accounting numbers are embedded in all contracts. Research into earnings management or financial misrepresentation uses several definitions to describe the phenomenon. We cite two of the most-widely quoted definitions here:

> Earnings management is a purposeful intervention in the external financial reporting process, with the intent of obtaining some private gain (as opposed to, say, merely facilitating the neutral operation of the process).
>
> (Schipper, 1989: 92)

> Earnings management occurs when managers use judgement in financial reporting and in structuring transactions to alter financial reports to either mislead some stakeholders about the underlying economic performance of the company, or to influence contractual outcomes that depend on reported accounting numbers.
>
> (Healy and Wahlen, 1999: 368)

In the sections below, we make a pedagogical presentation of these incentives towards earnings management, taking into account the contract from which they originate.

Incentives driven by the contract with shareholders

In the accounting literature, there is ample evidence of different characteristics of accounting numbers which are viewed favourably by current and potential shareholders. Shareholders will appreciate those accounting numbers and react with higher share prices and a lower cost of capital. High share prices are beneficial for the company, such as when an initial public offering (IPO) is planned, but also for top management, such as when they have stock/share options. These characteristics of accounting numbers and disclosure are small loss avoidance (Burghstahler and Dichev, 1997; Burghstahler and Eames, 2006); recurrent and increasing stream of earnings (Barth *et al.*, 1995; DeAngelo *et al.*, 1996; Bloomfield, 2008); low earnings volatility (Trueman and Titman, 1988; Hand, 1989; Bartov, 1993; Hunt *et al.*, 1995); meeting earnings targets or benchmarks (DeGeorge *et al.*, 1999; Kasznik,

1999; Pope *et al.*, 2007; Koonce and Lipe, 2010; Baginski *et al.*, 2011; Cao and Narayanamoorthy, 2011); and reducing information asymmetry through increased voluntary and mandatory disclosure (Healy and Palepu, 1993; Botosan, 1997; Sengupta, 1998; Healy *et al.*, 1999; Leuz and Verrechia, 2000; Bailey *et al.*, 2006; Rogers and Van Buskirk, 2009).

Small loss avoidance behaviour   It has been noticed that companies tend to avoid small losses and prefer instead to report small profits. Earnings management research has provided evidence for this practice, which the research calls 'small loss avoidance'. DeGeorge *et al.* (1999) and Burgstahler and Dichev (1997) present evidence that managers of US firms use accounting discretion to avoid reporting small losses. Small losses are more likely to lie within the bounds of insiders' reporting discretion and, consequently, can be avoided through earnings management. This implies, further, that if a loss cannot be avoided by accounting decisions, companies have a tendency to go for a one-time big loss, which is known as 'big bath accounting'.

Small losses are probably easy to conceal; hiding larger losses is more difficult and when revealed, it is considered serious accounting fraud. This happened with Olympus Corporation in 2011 when it became clear that it had been hiding losses.

Recurrent and increasing stream of earnings   In periods preceding a capital increase (i.e. pre-IPO period), the management of the company might be tempted to produce a steady stream of increasing earnings over the years. In this situation, earnings are not only smoothed and reported as less volatile but an upward trend of the results is also shown. Some recent studies show that earnings are managed prior to or around IPOs (Friedlan, 1994; Neil *et al.*, 1995) or seasoned equity offerings (Rangan, 1998; Shivakumar, 1998).

Low earnings volatility   Investors and analysts evaluate an investment in a firm as more risky when the reported results are volatile. This volatility has an impact on the market price of the shares. A higher risk perception means a lower share price. Thus, managers may have an incentive to influence the perception of the capital market with regard to the volatility of the business.

Meeting earnings targets and benchmarks   The first earnings target a company must achieve in order to be appreciated by the capital market is to meet the previous year's earnings. In addition, top management usually present targets to the capital markets (e.g. in presentations made to financial analysts) which include an improvement in relation to prior periods. When a company does not meet these targets, the company faces a drop in share price (unless the whole industry is facing the same situation). Therefore, the management of a company will always try to meet the target it has put forward. Further, top management must also make sure that they do not perform below the industry average, since the latter is a benchmark used by current and potential shareholders (An *et al.*, 2014; Isidro and Marques, 2015).

Incentives driven by debt contracts: accounting-based debt covenants

Very often, the terms of a lending agreement involve debt covenants which are specified as accounting ratios and may not be violated. A violation of these debt covenants might entail an increase in the interest rate applied to a loan, or an immediate repayment of that loan or extra collateral. So managers have an incentive to choose those accounting methods and estimates which reduce the violation of the debt covenant (Sweeney, 1994; Easton *et al.*, 2009; Jiang, 2010; Nikolaev, 2010; Christensen *et al.*, 2015). Sweeney found further that firms approaching default respond with income increasing accounting changes. Using actual debt covenant violations, DeFond and Jiambalvo (1994) found support for earnings management by managers of firms with debt covenant violations.

It is not compulsory under most generally accepted accounting principles' (GAAP) systems to disclose information about debt covenants. The following example is taken from the 2014 annual accounts of the adidas Group who discloses this information on a voluntary basis.

REAL LIFE ILLUSTRATION

Borrowings and credit lines

Borrowings are denominated in a variety of currencies in which the Group conducts its business. The largest portions of effective gross borrowings (before liquidity swaps for cash management purposes) as at December 31, 2014 are denominated in euros (2014: 80%; 2013: 76%) and US dollars (2014: 12%; 2013: 14%).

The weighted average interest rate on the Group's gross borrowings decreased to 3.1% in 2014 (2013: 3.8%).

As at December 31, 2014, the Group had cash credit lines and other long-term financing arrangements totalling €3.7 billion (2013: €3.4 billion); thereof unused credit lines accounted for €1.8 billion (2013: €2.0 billion). In addition, at December 31, 2014, the Group had separate lines for the issuance of letters of credit and guarantees in an amount of approximately €0.2 billion (2013: €0.2 billion).

The Group's outstanding financings are unsecured and may include standard financial covenants, which are reviewed on a quarterly basis. These covenants may include limits on the disposal of fixed assets, the maximum amount of debt secured by liens, cross default provisions and change of control, In addition, certain financial arrangements contain equity ratio covenants, minimum equity covenants as well as net loss covenants.

As at December 31, 2014, and December 31, 2013, shareholders' equity was well above the amount of the minimum equity covenant. Likewise, the relevant amount of net income clearly exceeded net loss covenants.

Source: adidas Group annual report and accounts 2014.

Contracts with governments and regulatory authorities In a number of countries, tax authorities use accounting data in order to determine the tax base of a company. Accounting methods might be chosen with a tax effect in mind. In continental Europe in particular (e.g. Germany, Belgium, France), there is a strong link between the reported income in the individual accounts of the company and the tax income.

Regulatory agencies may use accounting data to evaluate regulatory policies (e.g. import tariffs, anti-trust actions). Empirical evidence can be found that earnings management is induced by political or regulatory processes (Guenther *et al.*, 1997; Key, 1997).

Articles in company laws with regard to dividend payments, companies in distress and bankruptcy conditions often refer to ratios in the individual or group accounts of a company which may or may not be exceeded or violated. This results in an incentive to manage these ratios if there is a risk that ratios may be violated. On the following pages you will find an illustration of the remuneration policy of Unilever for its top management (Unilever Annual Report 2014)

REAL LIFE ILLUSTRATION

REMUNERATION PRINCIPLES

SUPPORTING THE DELIVERY OF OUR STRATEGY THROUGH REMUNERATION ARRANGEMENTS

Our business vision is to double the size of Unilever while reducing our environmental footprint and increasing our positive social impact through a focus on our brands, our operations and our people, and the Unilever Sustainable Living Plan (USLP). Remuneration is one of the key tools that we have as a business to help us to motivate our people to achieve our goals.

Our remuneration arrangements are designed to support our business vision and the implementation of our strategy. The key elements of our remuneration package for Executive Directors are summarised below:

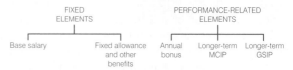

ANNUAL REMUNERATION REPORT

The following sets out how Unilever's Remuneration Policy, which is available on our website, will be implemented in 2015 and how it was implemented in 2014.

☚www.unilever.com/ara2014/downloads

IMPLEMENTATION OF THE REMUNERATION POLICY IN 2015 FOR EXECUTIVE DIRECTORS

ELEMENTS OF REMUNERATION

FIXED ELEMENTS OF REMUNERATION	AT A GLANCE	DESCRIPTION
BASE SALARY	Salary effective from 1 January 2015: • CEO C1,010,000 (unchanged from 2014) • CFO £714 000 (unchanged from 2014)	In its 2011 Report, the Committee signalled its concern that the CEO's salary was positioned at the lower end of market practice compared to similar sized UK and European companies. The Committee expressed its intention to make further increases, as appropriate, to address this over the next few years. Having held their salaries steady for longer than intended and in view of the sustained track record of performance delivery, the Committee recommended, and the Boards approved, salary increases for the CEO and CFO with effect from January 2015. In making these recommendations the Committee considered the strong performance of Unilever and alignment, both to increases in pay for the broader employee population and externally. The CEO and CFO have turned down the salary increases recommended by the Committee for 2015.
FIXED ALLOWANCE	Fixed allowance for 2015: • CEO – £250 000 • CFO – £220 000 The CFO's allowance has been reduced from £260 000 in 2014 to reflect the final stage of the phasing-out of his annual housing allowance.	A fixed allowance not linked to base salary is provided as a simple, competitive alternative to the provision of itemised benefits and pensions.
OTHER BENEFIT ENTITLEMENTS	• Amounts for other benefits are not known until the year end.	In line with Unilever's Remuneration Policy, Executive Directors will be provided with death, disability and medical insurance cover and actual tax return preparation costs in 2015. ☚www.unilever.com/ara2014/downloads In line with the commitments made to the current CEO on recruitment and included in the Remuneration Policy, Unilever also pays the CEO's social security obligations in his country of residence to protect him against the difference between employee social security obligations in his country of residence versus the UK. **Conditional supplemental pension** The CEO also receives a conditional supplemental pension accrual to compensate him for the arrangements forfeited on leaving his previous employer. The CEO will receive a contribution to his

REAL LIFE ILLUSTRATION (*Continued*)

supplemental pension of 12% of the lower of his actual base salary over the year and his 2011 base salary (£920 000) plus 3% per annum. The cap for 2015 has been kept at £976 028 with a maximum contribution of £117 123.

This supplemental pension accrual is conditional on the CEO remaining in employment with Unilever to age 60 and subsequently retiring from active service or his death or total disability prior to retirement.

PERFORMANCE ELEMENTS OF REMUNERATION

The actual targets for the annual bonus and the three business-focused performance measures for the MCIP and GSIP awards to be made in 2015 have not been disclosed up front. The Boards deem this to be commercially sensitive information as targets could reveal information about Unilever's business plan and budgeting process to competitors, which could be damaging to Unilever's business interests and therefore to shareholders. Where appropriate, targets will be disclosed in the Directors' Remuneration Report following the end of the respective performance period.

Performance measures are selected to align with Unilever's clearly stated growth ambition and our long-term business strategy. Unilever's primary business objective is to generate a sustainable improvement in business performance through increasing underlying sales while steadily improving core operating margins and cash flow.

The measures chosen for the annual and long-term incentives support the delivery of this objective. Performance measures focus management on the delivery of a combination of top-line revenue growth and bottom-line profit growth that Unilever believes will build shareholder value over the longer term. The use of a performance measure based on total shareholder return measures Unilever's success relative to peers.

DIRECTORS' REMUNERATION REPORT

Performance Elements of Remuneration	At a Glance	Description
Annual Bonus	• CEO – target 120% of base salary, maximum 200% of base salary • CFO – target 100% of base salary, maximum 150% of base salary	The performance measures for 2015 will be:  In addition, when determining annual bonus awards, the Committee will also consider personal performance and the quality of results in terms of both business results and leadership, including corporate social responsibility and progress against the delivery of USLP goals. The Committee determined that free cash flow would replace underlying volume growth as a performance measure for 2015. This change will assist Unilever in focusing on cost reduction and improving cash generation, as well as top-line growth, in a challenging market environment. Underlying volume growth will remain a factor that is considered by the Committee as part of the quality of results assessment.
MCIP 2015	• Out of their annual bonus awards, Executive Directors are required to invest 25% of their gross bonus and may invest up to 60% of their gross bonus in the MCIP (investment shares which are held in the individual's name) • They are awarded an equal number of MCIP matching shares • Maximum vesting for matching shares is 150% of the initial award	Matching shares awarded under the MCIP in 2015 will be subject to the same measures as GSIP awards made in the year. Further details of the performance measures are disclosed below. The committee considers that using the same performance measures across both the MCIP and GSIP is appropriate, as the performance measures used reflect our key strategic goals and maintain the alignment of our incentive plans to delivering our clearly stated growth ambitions. Given that we use four different performance measures, the Committee believes that the proportion of remuneration linked to each performance measure is not excessive.

REAL LIFE ILLUSTRATION (*Continued*)

	• The maximum award of matching shares for the CEO and CFO (as a percentage of base salary at grant), assuming maximum bonus, maximum deferral under the MCIP, would be 180% of base salary and 135% of base salary respectively
GSIP 2015 Awards	• Target award 200% of base salary for the CEO and 175% of base salary for CFO
	• Maximum vesting of 200% Initial award
	• Maximum vesting of 400% of base salary for the CEO and 350% of base salary for the CFO

Performance targets are assessed over a three year period.

Performance measures for 2015 awards:

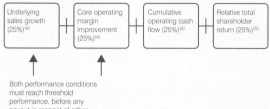

Both performance conditions must reach threshold performance, before any payout in respect of either measure is made.

(a) For the three business-focused measures, 25% of target awards vest for achieving threshold performance. 200% of target awards vest (capped at 150% under the MCIP) for maximum performance.

(b) For the relative TSR measure, Unilever's TSR is measured against a comparator group of other consumer goods companies. TSR measures the return received by a shareholder, capturing both the increase in share price and the value of dividend income (assuming dividends are reinvested). The TSR results are measured on a common currency basis to better reflect the shareholder experience.

The current TSR peer group is as follows:

Avon	Colgate-Palmolive	Henkel	L'Oréal	Reckitt Benckiser
Beiersdorf	Danone	Kao	Nestlé	Shiseido
Campbell Soup	General Mills	Kellogg's	PepsiCo	
Coca-Cola	Estée Lauder	Kimberly-Clark	Procter & Gamble	

The TSR comparator group consists of 18 companies (19 including Unilever). No shares in the portion of the award subject to TSR vest if Unilever is ranked below position 10 in the peer group at the end of the three-year period, 50% vests if Unilever is ranked 10th, 100% vests if Unilever is ranked 7th and 200% (150% under the MCIP) vests if Unilever is ranked 3rd or above. Straight-line vesting occurs between these points. The Committee may change the TSR vesting levels set out above if the number of companies in the TSR comparator group changes.

Source: Unilever annual report and accounts 2014.

Incentives driven by employment contracts

In relation to these contracts with top management, there is the implicit incentive that top managers want to keep their jobs. Research results do indeed indicate that top managers are dismissed when their firms perform below the average industry performance (Pourciau, 1993; Godfrey *et al.*, 2003). Therefore, top management has an incentive to publish a performance which equals the industry average performance.

Alongside such implicit incentives, contracts with top management often also include explicit incentives to manage the accounting numbers.

Management compensation Top management compensation often consists of three individual components: a base salary, a bonus plan linked to a certain indicator and shares or stock/share options. When the bonus plans of top management are linked to reported profits, there is an incentive to choose those accounting methods and accounting estimates which make the company exceed the profit targets stipulated in their compensation contract. This finding not only holds for top management compensation but also for lower-level managers compensated on the basis of accounting numbers. Linking compensation to accounting numbers not only creates incentives for managing those numbers. Jensen and Murphy (1990) claim that paying executives on the basis of accounting profits rather than on changes in shareholder wealth, not only generates incentives to manipulate the accounting system but also generates incentives to ignore projects with large net present values in favour of less valuable projects with larger immediate accounting profits.

In his seminal paper in this area, Healy (1985) found support for earnings management by managers of firms with bonus plans linked to accounting numbers. Healy shows that ceilings (i.e. the upper earnings found in the bonus scheme) in compensation contracts have a predictable effect on accounting accruals. Similar studies revealing a positive association between executives' incentives and the presence of earnings management followed after Healy's seminal paper (Cheng and Warfield, 2005; Erickson *et al.*, 2006; Efendi *et al.*, 2007; Jones and Wu, 2010).

As a result of this possible negative effect of accounting numbers-based compensation, other forms of management compensation emerged. Stock option plans became very popular and 'stock-based performance measures' are often argued to be superior to accounting-based performance measures. However, certain short-term behaviours of management might arise when the exercise period of the options is short.

In order to avoid short-termism, bonuses with a long-term perspective can be introduced and combined with a stock option plan that is in alignment with shareholders' interests, in order to stimulate top management behaviour.

The higher the influence of the bonus and the stock option plan in the total compensation of managers, the stronger the incentive towards earnings management and influencing the accounting numbers of the company in such a way that the capital markets react with an increase in the share price. Despite the expectations that stock option plans would align shareholders' interests with the interests of management, research evidence is now available which shows that stock option plans also induce top management towards earnings management. This information about top management compensation structure can be found in the notes to the annual accounts or in the corporate governance information disclosed by the company.

In 2015, it was revealed that Toshiba had been overstating its earnings by $2 billion from 2009 to 2014. Many press articles pointed at the aggressive profit targets in use in the company as being the main driver for the overstatement of Toshiba's earnings.

Incentives at the time of executive turnover Annual accounts management by top executives may be observed when executive changes take place within companies. Executive changes can be forced or voluntary (e.g. retirement). The outgoing CEO or executive team as well as the incoming CEO or executive team can have incentives to influence the accounts. Research on CEO turnover and annual accounts management distinguishes between CEO turnover in troubled firms and CEO turnover in non-troubled firms. Dechow and Sloan (1991) investigated the hypothesis that CEOs, in their final years of office (before retirement), manage discretionary investment expenditures to improve short-term earnings performance (for example, spending less on R&D). LaSalle *et al.* (1993) reported evidence that is consistent with the hypothesis that new CEOs exploit their accounting discretion to blame their predecessors for poor performance, establish a lower benchmark for subsequent performance evaluation and relieve future earnings of charges that would otherwise have to be made. Murphy and Zimmerman (1993) and Godfrey *et al.* (2003) also found evidence that incoming CEOs of poorly performing firms took 'big baths'.

However, it is important to stress that reduced profits or losses when a new CEO or new management team comes in could also be the result of the 'income borrowing behaviour' of the former CEO. The outgoing CEO might have improved their performance through accounting decisions in the years immediately prior to the increase in reported results, or through income-smoothing behaviour above sustainable levels for several years. So the outgoing CEO in this case would have increased the reported income by using accounting practices which borrow income from the future. In these circumstances, the new CEO would then be faced with less profit or even a loss due to the reversal effects of the practices used by their predecessor (this is discussed later).

The new incoming top management team is often tempted to undertake 'big bath accounting'. In their first year in office, compensation will not be tied greatly to the results of the company. In later years, however, compensation will be tied to the performance of the company. Through this 'big bath', a new CEO is able to front-load costs and secure themselves higher profits in the years to follow.

Big bath accounting, which is observed not only in terms of executive turnover, will be explained below.

Big bath accounting to manage future earnings Setting the objective to maximize the loss is referred to in the literature as big bath accounting. Of course, there are limits to the loss one can present to the stakeholders without influencing their actions. Big bath accounting may occur under any of the following three circumstances:

First, big bath accounting can occur in the case of a (one-time) heavy loss that cannot be avoided by income maximizing accounting interventions (see small loss avoidance). Faced with such a situation, the firm's management may choose to maximize the loss in the current accounting period. This practice is often observed in years of economic downturn.

Second, big bath accounting can occur when the annual accounts are cleaned up before or after an acquisition, a merger or other form of business cooperation. Big bath accounting usually implies the frontloading of costs through large asset write-downs and increases in provisions (restructuring provisions are extremely popular for this purpose) in order to enhance the future performance of the firm. In the financial year where 'a bath is taken', a substantial loss is reported; however, in the following years, performance will rise, partly due to reduced depreciation charges or a decrease in provisions.

Third, big bath accounting may occur at the time of executive handover, especially if the prior CEO was dismissed for poor performance. This practice has received increasing levels of criticism over recent years. The reinforcement of the conditions for creating restructuring provisions under IAS 37, *Provisions, Contingent Liabilities and Contingent Assets* is a result of those practices. The extract below from the speech of Schuetze, Chief Accountant of the SEC, refers to the practice of big bath accounting and the methods used to achieve this accounting strategy:

Cookie jar reserves

One of the accounting 'hot spots' that we are considering this morning is accounting for restructuring charges and restructuring reserves. A better title would be accounting for general reserves, contingency reserves, rainy day reserves or cookie jar reserves.

Accounting for so-called restructurings has become an art form. Some companies like the idea so much that they establish restructuring reserves every year. Why not? Analysts seem to like the idea of recognizing as a liability today, a budget of expenditures planned for the next year or next several years in downsizing, right-sizing or improving operations and portraying that amount as a special, below-the-line charge in the current period's income statement. This year's earnings are happily reported in press releases as 'before charges'. CNBC analysts and commentators talk about earnings 'before charges'. The financial press talks about earnings before 'special charges'. (Funny, no one talks about earnings before credits-only charges.) It's as if special charges are not real. Out of sight, out of mind …

The occasion of a merger also spawns the wholesale establishment of restructuring or merger reserves. The ingredients of the merger reserves and merger charges look like the makings of a sausage. In the Enforcement Division, I have seen all manner and kind of things that ordinarily would be charged to operating earnings instead being charged 'below the line'. Write-offs of the carrying amounts of bad receivables. Write-offs of cost of obsolete inventory. Write-downs of plant and equipment costs, which, miraculously at the date of the merger, become non-recoverable, whereas those same costs were considered recoverable the day before the merger. Write-offs of previously capitalized costs such as goodwill, which all of a sudden are not recoverable because of a merger. Adjustments to bring warranty liabilities up to snuff. Adjustments to bring claim liabilities in line with management's new view of settling or litigating cases. Adjustments to bring environmental liabilities up to snuff or in line with management's new view of the manner in which the company's obligations to comply with EPA will be satisfied. Recognition of liabilities to pay for future services by investment bankers, accountants and lawyers. Recognition of liabilities for officers' special bonuses. Recognition of liabilities for moving people. For training people. For training people not yet hired. For retraining people. Recognition of liabilities for moving costs and refurbishing costs. Recognition of liabilities for new software that may be acquired or written, for ultimate sale to others. Or some liabilities that go by the title 'other'.

It is no wonder that investors and analysts are complaining about the credibility of the numbers.

(Speech by Walter P. Schuetze, Chief Accountant, Enforcement Division, US Securities and Exchange Commission, 22 April 1999. www.sec.gov/news/speech/speecharchive/1999/spch276.htm)

Other incentives to manage accounting numbers

Competitive pressures Data from the annual accounts might be useful for the competition. Especially in a situation where one company is obliged to disclose more proprietary information due to national GAAP requirements, companies have a tendency either to avoid this disclosure or to decrease the quality of disclosure. For example, segmental data will be disclosed on a more aggregated level or high recurring profits might be topped off to avoid entry into the industry by new firms.

Union negotiations Facing forthcoming union negotiations, management might have an incentive to decrease the net result of the company. Strong company profits might incite the unions to ask for a salary increase. These incentives will be more present in companies, industries or countries with strong labour union power.

In research related to earnings management, the notion of implicit contracts is introduced. Contracts can be between the firm and its customers, suppliers, short-term creditors, employees, capital providers and other stakeholders. Bowen *et al.* (1995) and Kasanen *et al.* (1996) find evidence that implicit contracts induce earnings management.

If we consider the incentives listed, we can see that some of them are recurring and others are non-recurring incentives to manage the accounts.

ACTIVITY 30.4

Which of the incentives listed above could be classified as 'recurring' and which could be classified as 'non-recurring'?

Activity feedback

Recurring incentives could be reducing earnings volatility for listed companies and efforts to sustain share prices when stock options are granted. Further, regulatory incentives can be recurring if, for example, a company is located in a country where there is a link between tax income and accounting income. Non-recurring incentives could be present in the situation of an individual public offering, a merger or acquisition or an executive turnover.

In the previous section, we discussed the incentives to manage the accounting numbers embedded in the contracts governing the firm. According to the type of incentive, a different reporting strategy and, as a result, a different type of annual accounts management, will be used. For example, if a firm is involved in union negotiations, the aim will be the decrease of the reported profits in the period before the negotiations. Because each company is subject to a different set of contracts, the incentives for accounting numbers' management and the resulting reporting strategies will also differ between companies. Although general checklists to detect earnings management are available (see Nelson *et al.*, 2003; Penman, 2003), the toolbox used by corporate management will be unique to each company.

ACTIVITY 30.5

Consider some of the different types of incentives presented earlier to manage the annual accounts. What type of accounting strategy would be appropriate for these different types of incentives?

Activity feedback

- **Capital market considerations**.

  (a) **Risk perception**. The accounting strategy of the firm would be to engage in earnings management for the purpose of presenting earnings or results which are less volatile than the underlying economic results that the firm has obtained. In this situation, income smoothing would be pursued and this practice would be a 'recurring activity'. In periods with 'high' economic income, profits would be topped off and in periods with 'lower' income, increasing measures would be used.

  (b) **Preparing for an IPO**. In this case, the accounting strategy could consist of showing a good performance over the years before the IPO and an improvement in the structure of the statement of financial position. Different types of annual accounts' management might be combined into the overall reporting strategy: income smoothing in order to influence the perceived risk of the company, statement of financial position management to improve the structure of the statement of financial position and increasing the results upwards over a period of time before an IPO.

- **Tax incentives**. In countries where there is a link between accounting income and taxable income, the accounting strategy is to decrease the reported profit in order to reduce taxable profit. This type of management will be recurring as long as the company exists.

- **Compensation contracts**. In the case of stock/share options, an increasing share price is desired. The reporting strategy could consist of income-smoothing practices, undertaken to reduce the perceived risk of the company, and further income increasing measures might be used as well. Bonus plans with ceilings might entail one-time earnings management upwards to the ceiling or one-time earnings management below the ceiling.

Discussing the incentives to manage the accounting numbers, it is worthwhile mentioning that, although a distinction is made between earnings management and management of the statement of financial position, the impact of the methods used for those purposes are not isolated to the statement of comprehensive income or the statement of financial position alone. In reality, earnings management also has an indirect impact on certain items in the statement of financial position. For example, an accounting method change with regard to depreciation (change from reducing balance method to straight line method) will influence not only the depreciation expense on the statement of comprehensive income but also the reported book value of the assets on the statement of financial position. The same indirect effect can be observed when a company decides to manage the statement of financial position. If a company wants to improve the debt/equity ratio through switching from owned assets or leased assets to renting assets, not only the liability structure of the statement of financial position will be altered but the character of the costs involved will change as well (from non-cash depreciation costs to cash payments for rentals). A large part of the costs related to the use of the asset will switch from depreciation costs to rental costs. For financial analysis purposes, the former are regarded as non-cash costs whereas the latter are considered as cash costs.

ACCOUNTING ANALYSIS: THE AVAILABLE ACCOUNTING DISCRETION

Accounting analysis tries to detect whether management has not only the incentives to manage the numbers but also the capability to influence the accounting numbers. In order to detect this capability to influence the numbers, it is necessary to gain an insight into the elements which enlarge the accounting discretion of top management. Accounting discretion is first of all influenced by the type of GAAP a company applies. Second, research results indicate that certain company characteristics, board of directors' characteristics, auditors' characteristics and characteristics of the institutional environment, all influence the accounting discretion available to top management. We enumerate below the most important findings of these research streams in order to facilitate a judgement on the available accounting discretion.

Impact of the quality of accounting standards used

Accounting analysis involves an evaluation of the accounting flexibility available to the management of a company. To a large extent, this accounting flexibility is determined by the type of GAAP which is applied. Some GAAP systems allow more valuation choices for one item than others. According to the GAAP applied, the same transactions or operations can be accounted for in a different way, and, depending on the GAAP applied, the flexibility for judgement available to management might be greater.

Preparing financial statements implies complying with the regulation which governs financial reporting (e.g. US GAAP, IAS/ IFRS, UK GAAP, German GAAP, Japanese GAAP). However, since most GAAP are not a rigid set of principles, the management of a company has a certain flexibility with regard to the choice of valuation methods and accounting estimates to use. The level of flexibility will depend on the GAAP being applied. Accounting standards that are characterized by more flexibility allow managers to report income more easily in those financial periods when managers have incentives to present better results. These types of accounting standards are called low-quality accounting standards. High-quality GAAP are recognized as leaving less room for the kind of accounting flexibility which allows management to report the results in the period in which they wish them to appear in the income statement.

The aim of the IASB (Foundation Constitution, part A, para. 2) is:

> [t]o develop in the public interest, a single set of high-quality, understandable and enforceable global accounting standards that require high-quality, transparent and comparable information in financial statements and other financial reporting to help participants in the world's capital markets and other users make economic decisions.

As a result, we have observed over recent years that the flexibility in IAS/IFRS has decreased. In most Standards, the allowable treatment has been removed, leaving only the prior benchmark treatment in place (e.g. with IAS 8, *Accounting Policies, Changes in Accounting Estimates and Errors*, the prospective application of accounting method or policy changes was deleted from the Standard). Since more countries and more regulatory authorities require listed groups to comply with IFRS, it is somewhat easier for users to compare the difference in available accounting flexibility between listed companies. For non-listed companies, and especially SMEs, differences in accounting flexibility to a large extent are influenced by the national GAAP they use.

In their annual report, the corporate management of adidas explained in their own words what the change from a low-quality GAAP to higher-quality GAAP meant for them when they complied with IFRS for the first time.

REAL WORLD ILLUSTRATION

3 Framework for Accounting Policies in accordance with IFRS and Explanation of Major Differences compared with German Accounting Policies

The major differences between the accounting policies and consolidation methods according to IFRS and German law as set out in § 292a section 2 No. 4b of the German Commercial Code (HGB) are outlined below.

a) Framework for Accounting Policies in Accordance with IFRS
The accounting policies of entities in accordance with IFRS are based on the objective of providing investors with decision-relevant information.

Based on the assumption that decision-relevant information should be provided to investors, it follows that accounting policies should be aimed at showing an entity's operating results, rather than determining the amount of distributable profits, whilst bearing in mind the need for protection of creditors.

As a rule, accounting policies in accordance with IFRS have a lower level of prudence than German accounting policies, which leads to the following major differences:

- *Minimization of possibilities for establishing and releasing hidden reserves.*

- *The consistency requirement (recognition, valuation, classification, consolidation) is to be strictly followed; changes in accounting policies are only permitted if it can be proven that the change leads to an improvement in the fair presentation of the financial statements.*

- *Economic substance has precedence over legal form. The principle of substance over form has a stronger influence in accounting policies in accordance with IFRS than in German GAAP.*

Source: adidas annual report and accounts 2004, p. 138.

Empirical research has provided evidence that companies that use the so-called 'low-quality' accounting standards have more flexibility to manage the accounting numbers and as a result more earnings management occurs (Leuz *et al.*, 2003) (see also Chapter 2). These low-quality Standards are found in countries with a code law system and a creditor orientation in financial reporting. However, we also learned in Chapter 2 that 'high-quality' accounting standards on their own are no guarantee of 'high-quality' financial reporting. The institutional environment (shareholder protection, degree of enforcement of accounting standards and risk of litigation) plays a significant role in the quality of financial reporting in a country.

That a Standard's quality is no guarantee of reporting quality implies that it is not sufficient just to check whether or not a company is using high-quality accounting standards to be able to evaluate the accounting flexibility available to management. Since these research results indicate that the application quality might differ between countries, it is also necessary to consider the institutional environment before obtaining a complete picture of the available accounting quality and sources of discretion.

Institutional characteristics

Many authors classify the quality of GAAP to be applied in a jurisdiction as an institutional characteristic. We discussed the quality of GAAP as a separate point above. In this section, we concentrate on those institutional characteristics which do influence accounting quality. In international comparative analysis on accounting quality of published accounting information, the data show that the degree of investor protection (LaPorta *et al.*, 1997, 1998), the risk of litigation (Ball *et al.*, 2000; Leuz and Verrechia, 2000) and the degree of enforcement (Hope, 2003) all create opportunities for earnings management (Bushman and Piotroski, 2006; Djankov *et al.*, 2008; Leuz, 2010; Jennings and Marques, 2011). In countries with low investor protection, low risk of litigation and low degree of enforcement, the accounting quality of published financial information will be low. This implies that the annual accounts could represent less faithfully the underlying economic situation of a company. A switch to a higher-quality GAAP does not automatically imply that the annual accounts represent better accounting quality (see references to Chapter 2).

Next to institutional characteristics, firm specific variables do influence the accounting discretion available to management. Academic research reveals three important variables, namely, the ownership structure, the governance characteristics and the audit quality.

Company characteristics

Research results provide evidence that the degree of ownership concentration affects the nature of contracting and demonstrate that accounting information quality declines as ownership concentration increases (Donnelly and Lynch, 2002; Fan and Wong, 2002; Ajinkya *et al.*, 2005; Fan, 2007; Jaggi *et al.*, 2009). Further, due to improved visibility and more dispersed ownership and listing requirements, the quality of earnings of listed companies is found to be higher than in non-listed companies, especially in those countries where securities regulators have sufficient qualified staff and the legal power to enforce full compliance with the domestic accounting standards or the accounting standards accepted for listing. The amount of accounting flexibility will be less.

Board characteristics

Governance research has focused extensively on the question of whether certain board characteristics are indicators of weaker board monitoring. Research results do indicate that board monitoring becomes weaker when the chairman of the board is also the CEO of the company; when the majority of board members are internal company members or directors with family or economic ties to the company; when there are interlocking directorships; and where no audit committee exists. It is important to note in relation to the research results on company characteristics, audit quality and board characteristics mentioned above that they represent the behaviour of the 'average' firm. They may give an indication in an individual case, but they have no absolute power of prediction in a particular case (Boyd, 1994; Beasley, 1996; Peasnell *et al.*, 2001, 2005; Klein, 2002; Brown and Caylor, 2006; Adams and Ferreira, 2007; Jaggi *et al.*, 2009).

Audit quality

The quality of the auditors has a direct impact on the available accounting discretion of management. Research results so far have provided evidence that the presence of the Big Four auditors seems to constrain earnings management (Johnson *et al.*, 2002; Bedard and Johnstone, 2004; Carcello and Nagy, 2004; Maijoor and Vanstraelen, 2006; Rusmin, 2010). Not only does external auditing of a high quality constrain earnings management, so too do high-quality internal controls (Doyle *et al.*, 2007).

The first steps in accounting analysis consist of investigating whether incentives for annual accounts management are present and whether top management has sufficient accounting discretion to pursue a reporting strategy of influencing the accounting numbers in line with these incentives. The incentives towards financial misrepresentation are driven by the external and internal contracts governing the firm. The available discretion to do so is created by the quality of the GAAP applied and the quality of institutional, ownership, governance and audit characteristics. In the next steps of accounting analysis, we focus our attention on the choices available to management to influence the accounting numbers.

Accounting analysis: methods of accounting numbers management

In most articles and textbooks, the practices, choices or methods used for annual accounts management are usually divided into three broad categories, namely, accounting method choice, accounting estimate choice and real decisions (operating decisions, financing decisions or investment decisions).

Accounting method choice and accounting estimate choice are accounting decisions with no direct first order effect on cash flows (Jiambalvo, 1996). An indirect influence could be present when the amount of taxes payable is affected. This happens in countries where taxable income is based on accounting income. However, when real earnings management is used, there is a direct impact on the cash flow.

Real choices are decisions to structure transactions in certain ways, and real production and investment decisions to achieve a desired accounting outcome. The uses of accounting methods and accounting estimates are called methods of accounting earnings management. In the past, academic research has mainly focused on accounting earnings management (see Armstrong *et al.*, 2010 and Kothari *et al.*, 2010). The presence of earnings management is detected by proxies for earnings management, such as total accruals, working capital accruals, discretionary accruals or performance-matched accruals.

Academic research into real earnings management started later than research into accruals management, but the number of articles on this issue is increasing (Wayne *et al.*, 2004; Roychowdhury, 2006; Gunny, 2010). In practice, a company can pick a single element to manage the accounts, but most often a portfolio of elements is used whereby accounting and real earnings management are combined (Graham *et al.*,

2005; Cohen *et al.*, 2008; Cohen and Zarowin, 2010; Zang, 2012). The management of statement of financial position numbers has received far less research attention.

Besides these three main instruments, other mechanisms can be used to manage the impression of the reader of the financial statements towards one that is more favourable on the performance and financial position of the company. In this respect, Francis (2001) lists the following elements which can be used for accounting numbers management or impression management: timing of adoption of new Standards; choices about display (number of statements, layout of statement); aggregation decisions; classification decisions and disclosure decisions.

We now discuss the three main categories of earnings management.

Accounting method choice An accounting method choice is present when there are several possible valuation methods for the same item under the GAAP that has been applied in the preparation of the annual accounts. Some examples are listed here which could be categorized under the heading of accounting method choice:

- choice of depreciation method (e.g. reducing balance, straight line or accelerated method)
- choice of inventory valuation (LIFO, FIFO or weighted average)
- choice whether or not to capitalize certain expenditures (e.g. R&D, software, advertising)
- choice with regard to the valuation base (historical cost versus fair value).

With regard to accounting method choice, the possibility of influencing the accounts can be limited by the accounting standard setter. A standard setter can always remove options from the available set of accounting valuation methods. Accounting method choice is not the most popular item to be used for annual accounts management purposes as the visibility of those choices is perceived as rather high. If one applies an accounting method change, the impact on the results of the company and the equity should be disclosed in the notes (for further discussion see the section on quality of disclosure). IAS 8, *Accounting Policies, Changes in Accounting Estimates and Errors* presented the accounting treatment of accounting method changes and the necessary information disclosures in relation to such a change. The aim of IAS 8 is to enhance comparability in a situation of an accounting method change.

Different accounting methods available might hinder the comparability of financial information published under different GAAP regimes. But different choices are possible under IFRS as well. The user of the financial statements should take this into account when comparing the figures.

Accounting estimates The preparation of the financial statements and the accounting decisions to be taken relate not only to the choice of valuation methods to be applied but also to the accounting estimates to be used for valuation purposes. The use of accounting estimates for annual accounts management purposes is often preferred by management over accounting method changes, because they are less visible and less costly than changes in accounting methods. A few items contained in financial statements in which accounting estimates play a role are presented below.

- *Bad debt allowances.* Research has revealed that this type of accrual is often used for management purposes (e.g. McNichols and Wilson, 1988). A change in the amount of bad debt allowance is often not visible as it is netted off from the trade receivables. The use of bad debt allowances is one of the oldest methods practised for earnings management purposes. Influencing the amount of the bad debt allowance is a typical example of accounts management.

- *Inventory*: With inventory there is, first, the choice of accounting method (FIFO, LIFO, weighted average). Second, in many GAAP systems, there are requirements to use full costing for inventory valuation purposes for industrial companies. In this case, overhead should be allocated to the costs of production. Many Standards on inventory valuation require the allocation of overhead to be based on the company's normal level of activity. Companies in distress are sometimes tempted to allocate part of the unused capacity to the products instead of charging the amount to profit or loss. As a result, the costs related to the unused capacity would be carried forward through the inventory figure to 'hopefully' more favourable financial years in the future.

- *Provisions*: Provisions are a very popular balance sheet item for managing earnings. Provisions are used for smoothing purposes as well as for one-time increases or decreases of the results. External analysts should always investigate the reasons why provisions are created. Sometimes they have the character of amounts set aside for intentional use later on. This use of provisions to increase the reported profit when 'economic profit' is lower, is also called 'rainy day accounting'. Low-quality GAAP offers more possibilities for creating provisions for earnings management purposes, but possibilities still exist under high-quality GAAP.

- *Choice of the residual value and the useful life*: In order to determine the depreciable amount of property, plant and equipment (PPE), management must estimate its residual value and its useful life. The residual value and the useful life of a PPE will be estimated taking into account the expected usage of the asset, the expected physical wear and tear, and any technical and commercial obsolescence. Higher or lower residual values, and shorter or longer useful lives, will influence the annual depreciable amounts reported in the income statement and the book values recorded on the statement of financial position.

- *Impairment*: The IASB has introduced impairment to move financial reporting from a historical cost basis to a fair value basis (see Chapter 7). An asset is impaired when an entity will not be able to recover that asset's statement of financial position carrying value, through either using it or selling it. Although IAS 36, *Impairment of Assets* made the criteria to determine the carrying value more explicit, there is still room for judgement (see Chapter 7).

Even in the same industry when firms are complying with IFRS, differences in estimates can occur. If we compare, for example, the useful lives and the residual values Lufthansa and easyJet take into account in order to calculate the depreciable amounts, we can see differences.

In the Annual Report 2014 of Lufthansa (p. 164) we read that the commercial aircraft and reserve engines are depreciated over a period of 20 years to a residual value of 5 per cent. Compare this information with the information provided by easyJet on the depreciation policy of their aircraft.

Real transactions Companies are constantly engaged in operating, financing and investment transactions. These real transactions, however, can also be used for annual accounts management purposes. Common examples are the deferral of transactions to future periods, such as purchases or R&D. In some cases, the choice of a particular

REAL LIFE ILLUSTRATION

Property, plant and equipment

Property, plant and equipment is stated at cost less accumulated depreciation. Depreciation is calculated to write off the cost, less estimated residual value of assets, on a straight-line basis over their expected useful lives. Expected useful lives are reviewed annually.

	Expected useful life
Aircraft	23 Years
Aircraft spares	14 Years
Aircraft – prepaid maintenance	7 – 10 Years
Leasehold improvements	5 – 10 Years or the length of lease if shorter
Fixtures, fittings and equipment	3 Years or length of lease of property where equipment is used if shorter
Computer hardware	5 Years

Aircraft held under finance leases are depreciated over the shorter of the lease term and their expected useful lives, as shown above.

Residual values, where applicable, are reviewed annually against prevailing market rates at the balance sheet date for equivalently aged assets and depreciation rates adjusted accordingly on a prospective basis. The carrying value is reviewed for impairment if events or changes in circumstances indicate that the carrying value may not be recoverable.

An element of the cost of a new aircraft is attributed on acquisition to prepaid maintenance and is depreciated over a period ranging from seven to ten years from the date of manufacture. Subsequent costs incurred which lend enhancement to future periods, such as long-term scheduled maintenance and major overhaul of aircraft and engines, are capitalised and depreciated over the length of period benefiting from these enhancements. All other maintenance costs are charged to the income statement as incurred.

Pre-delivery and option payments made in respect of aircraft are recorded in property, plant and equipment at cost. These amounts are not depreciated.

Gains and losses on disposals (other than aircraft sale and leaseback transactions) are determined by comparing the net proceeds with the carrying amount and are recognised in the income statement.

Source: easyJet annual report and accounts 2015.

---

transaction (e.g. financing through a lease contract or a rental contract) is not neutral with regard to the impact on the annual accounts. As a result, the choice of operating, investment and financing decisions might be influenced or even determined by accounting valuation or presentation issues. Sometimes, real transactions are only undertaken for the purpose of annual accounts management. A common example is the sale of assets with a gain on disposal. This has an immediate favourable effect on the result of that year (except for certain sale and leaseback transactions: see Chapter 15). The possibility of creating profit through a sale of assets depends to a large extent on the valuation principles which are applied in the company or are required by the GAAP with which the company complies. In a historical cost environment, the possibilities for these one-time big gains are much larger than in an environment dominated by fair value valuation. The impact of these one-time gains could even be enhanced by combining the real transactions (sale of asset) with a large write-down or impairment the year before the sale. Influencing the earnings through a sale of assets with gains on disposal is easier for companies that are part of a group. In these cases, prices that are not at arm's length can be realized on these transactions. In the consolidated accounts, the impact would be cancelled out by the elimination of intra-group profit or loss, but in the standalone annual accounts the impact of the earnings management would improve the accounts. If the group does not consolidate fully and leaves subsidiaries outside the scope of consolidation, then these intra-group transactions can impact favourably the accounting numbers of the consolidated group accounts.

Under the old IAS 17 leasing Standard, off-balance-sheet leasing could be undertaken in order to improve the solvency ratios of the lessee company. The future payments of the operating lease contracts had to be disclosed in the notes. The user of the annual accounts could adjust the on-balance-sheet debt by the amounts of off-balance sheet debt. However, as already mentioned in Chapter 15, quite often these adjustments either over-estimated or under-estimated the lease debt. However, not all real methods of accounting numbers management are visible. The accounting numbers of consolidated accounts can be influenced to a large extent by not including companies one controls in the scope of consolidation (this happened in the accounting scandals in which Enron, Lernhout and Hauspie, and Ahold were involved). These techniques are more difficult to detect since the user of the annual accounts is not aware of the substance of the relationships between the different companies. In order to illustrate these practices, we now present a section on entity analysis. Sometimes a single accounting method or estimate is used (e.g. the overstatement of its oil reserves by Royal Dutch Shell, the use of supplier payments by Tesco), but quite often different mechanisms are used together in which often third parties or other group companies are involved and whereby consolidation principles are violated such as with Enron in 2001, Lernhout and Hauspie in 2001 and Satyam in 2009 (see also Badertscher, 2011).

ENTITY ANALYSIS

In Part Three of this textbook on consolidated or group accounts, we saw that results of the individual accounts can be influenced through intra-group sales. If there is a relationship of control, these results are eliminated in the group accounts in the consolidation process. This means, however, that it is important to look into the different relationships one company might have with other companies and how this relationship is accounted for. There are different kinds of relationship between an investor company and the company it has invested in. These different kinds of relationship need different accounting treatments. The following treatments are laid down in all GAAP: control (the investee is consolidated), significant influence (equity method) and no influence (valuation at cost).

When there is a control relationship, there is always the possibility of transferring profits from one company to the other by means of transfer prices for goods and services transferred between group members. These intra-group profits are eliminated when all companies over which a holding company has control are fully consolidated.

In the case of a significant influence in a company, but without control, the undertaking is accounted for by the equity method. In situations where there is control, but the undertaking is accounted for by the equity method, the accounts of both parties involved do not present a true picture of the underlying relationship and position of the group.

The 'real' nature of the relationship should be considered and compared with the accounting treatment applied in the annual accounts. Sometimes it might be that the accounting treatment does not comply with the underlying relationship. As an external analyst, it is extremely useful to know why there is this difference and what the impact on the published accounts is. Especially under rules-based GAAP, companies can set up separate entities using the law and legal constructions in such a way that the legal form of the relationship does not comply with the definition of control embedded in the GAAP used by the controlling company. In these circumstances, where new accounting standards are issued over the years, a change in the accounting standards might turn an associated company into a subsidiary for reporting purposes. We will elaborate on this item further at the end of this section.

In the following Activity, we will illustrate the impact on the annual accounts of the investor according to the accounting method applied: full consolidation or equity method. This Activity illustrates further the reporting procedures presented in Part Three.

We notice that if the transactions with associated entities are accounted for in a correct manner, the impact on the net result of the investor company is the same as under full consolidation. The only difference concerning the income statement relates to the lines where the result is eliminated (see Activities 30.6 and 30.7). The operating result under the equity method is always 10 000; in the case of consolidation, the loss or profit made by B on the sale is reflected in the operating result. Although the net result is the same under both the equity method and full consolidation, the amounts representing the operating revenue and the operating result are different. This might have an impact on ratios calculated where sales or operating results are included in the numerator or denominator (see Chapter 31 for more information on ratio analysis). The main difference with regard to full consolidation or equity relates mainly to the statement of financial position. The amount of debt is much higher in the case of full consideration.

ACTIVITY 30.6

Company A owns 45 per cent of the shares of company B; company A bought the shares on 1.1.X. Company A sells goods or services to company B. Company B sells these goods or services to their clients. The beginning statements of financial position of the individual accounts of company A and B follow. Assume that company A sells a product to company B, and at the year end 31.12.X, company B has sold all of its products to third parties. The cost of the products for company A amounts to €40 000. Company A sells the products to company B for €50 000. In the first situation, company B is able to realize a revenue of €56 000 through the sale of these products to its customers. In the second situation, company B realizes revenue of only €42 000. This sale of products is the only activity for company A and B in the year X.

Statement of financial position

	Company A	Company B
	1.1.X	*1.1.X*
Financial assets	45 000	—
Other assets	755 000	400 000
Total assets	800 000	400 000
Equity	300 000	100 000
Liabilities	500 000	300 000
Total equity and liabilities	800 000	400 000

Consider, for both situations, the impact on the statement of comprehensive income for company B. Take the rules on accounting for associated entities into account as well and consider the impact on the statement of comprehensive income of company A, the investor, if the shareholding in B is accounted for under the equity method. When solving this Activity, bear in mind what you learned about

the equity method and accounting for associated companies in earlier chapters of this book.

Activity feedback

Situation 1: Company B is able to sell the products for €56 000.

Statements of financial position

	Individual accounts, company A	Individual accounts, company B	Group accounts, company A
Financial assets	45 000	—	47 700
Other assets	765 000	406 000	765 000
Total assets	810 000	406 000	812 700
Equity	310 000	106 000	312 700
Liabilities	500 000	300 000	500 000
Total equity and liabilities	810 000	406 000	812 700

Income statement

	Individual accounts, company A	Individual accounts, company B	Group accounts, company A
Operating revenue	50 000	56 000	50 000
Operating costs	40 000	50 000	40 000
Operating results	10 000	6 000	10 000
Results from associated undertakings	—	—	2 700
Net result	10 000	6 000	12 700

(Continued)

ACTIVITY 30.6 (Continued)

Situation 2: Company B sells the products for €42 000.

Statement of financial position

	Individual accounts, company A	Individual accounts, company B	Group accounts, company A
Financial assets	45 000	—	41 400
Other assets	765 000	392 000	765 000
Total assets	810 000	392 000	806 400
Equity	310 000	92 000	306 400
Liabilities	500 000	300 000	500 000
Total equity and liabilities	810 000	392 000	806 400

Income statement

Operating revenue	50 000	42 000	50 000
Operating costs	40 000	50 000	40 000
Operating results	10 000	(8 000)	10 000
Results from associated undertakings	—	—	(3 600)
Net result	10 000	(8 000)	6 400

ACTIVITY 30.7

Assume that there are underlying contracts between the management of company A and the shareholders of company B in which agreements are made that company A has the power to control the operating and financing activities of company B. Remember what you learned about consolidation in Part Three. Consider also the definition of control in IFRS 3 and the accounting method prescribed in IAS 27. How should company A now account for company B and what would be the difference with the situation presented under Activity 30.6?

Activity feedback

Company A would now have to consolidate company B. The consolidated accounts of the group AB would present the following picture.

Consolidated statement of financial position

	B sold the products for €56 000	B sold the products for €42 000
Total assets	1 171 000	1 157 000
Equity (capital and reserves)	300 000	300 000
Results for the year	12 700	6 400
Minority interests	58 300	50 600
Liabilities	800 000	800 000
Total equity and liabilities	1 171 000	1 157 000

Consolidated statement of comprehensive income

	B sold the products for €56 000	B sold the products for €42 000
Operating revenue	56 000	42 000
Operating costs	40 000	40 000
Net result	16 000	2 000
Share of minority interests	(3 300)	4 400
Net result for the group	12 700	6 400

A further element with regard to entity analysis is the question of whether all entities with which a company has a link have been included in the consolidated accounts and are properly accounted for (consolidated, equity method or valued at cost according to the relation). In this context, the creation of special purpose entities (SPEs) is important.

In the last decades of the twentieth century, SPVs (special purpose vehicles, also called SPEs) were created, at the start mainly for lease purposes and, later on, for other reasons (e.g. increasing revenue). Feng *et al.* (2009) provided empirical evidence of the use of special purpose vehicles for earnings management purposes during the period 1997–2004.

The entity analysis performed should take into account whether or not all SPEs set up by a company are included or left out from the consolidation process. However, there can be differences according to which GAAP is being applied. It is said that the SPEs which Enron had created and which they could exclude from consolidation under US GAAP would have been consolidated if Enron had applied IAS/IFRS. In the wake of the accounting scandals, the FASB looked into these issues. In January 2003, the FASB issued FASB Interpretation no. 46, *Consolidation of Variable Interest Entities – VIE (FIN 46)*, and amended it in October 2003. Variable interest entities are entities that lack sufficient equity to finance their activities without additional financial support from other parties, or whose equity holders lack adequate decision-making ability based on the criteria set forth in that Interpretation. Economic criteria such as 'lack of sufficient equity to finance the activities' or 'lack of decision-making ability' now dominate the decision of whether an entity should be consolidated in the group accounts.

REAL WORLD ILLUSTRATION

Due to the change in the Standards on variable interest entities, the Walt Disney Company had to include its two theme parks, Euro Disney in France and Hong Kong Disneyland, in its group accounts with the use of the full consolidation method. Up until 2003, both theme parks were included in the group accounts of the Walt Disney Company through the use of the equity method.

The following information is taken from note 2 of the annual accounts of the Walt Disney Company (TWDC) for 2003.

TWDC holds 39 per cent of the capital of Euro Disney SCA, but Euro Disney SCA is managed by Euro Disney SA, which is an indirect 99 per cent owned subsidiary of the Walt Disney Company. Further, in connection with a financial restructuring of Euro Disney in 1994, Euro Disney Associe's SNC, a wholly owned affiliate of the Walt Disney Company, entered into a lease arrangement with a financing company with a non-cancellable term of 12 years related to substantially all of the Disneyland Park assets, and then entered into a 12-year sub-lease agreement with Euro Disney on substantially the same terms. At the conclusion of the sub-lease term, Euro Disney will have the option of assuming Disney SNC's rights and obligations under the lease for a payment of $90m over the ensuing 15 months. If Euro Disney does not exercise its option, Disney SNC may purchase the assets, continue to lease the assets or elect to terminate the lease. In the event the lease is terminated, Disney SNC would be obligated to make a termination payment to the lessor equal to 75 per cent of the lessor's then outstanding debt related to the Disneyland Park assets, which payment would be approximately $1.3 billion. Disney SNC would then have the right to sell or lease the assets on behalf of the lessor to satisfy the remaining debt, with any excess proceeds payable to Disney SNC. Euro Disney's financial difficulties, notwithstanding, the company believes it is unlikely that Disney SNC would be required to pay the 75 per cent lease termination payment as the company currently expects that in order for Euro Disney to continue its business it will either exercise its assumption option in 2006 or that the assumption of the lease by Euro Disney will otherwise be provided for in the resolution to Euro Disney's financial situation.

(Note 2 of the annual accounts of TWDC, 2003)

The subsequent implementation of FIN 46 required the Walt Disney Company to consolidate both Euro Disney and Hong Kong Disneyland for financial reporting purposes from the first quarter of fiscal 2004.

The reversal effect

At the end of the discussion on annual accounts management practices, it is important to highlight that most methods of annual accounts management have what is called a *reversal effect*. Reversal means that income increasing accounting interventions in the current period lead to a decrease in income in future periods, and vice versa. In fact, many of the methods applied involve only inter-temporal shifts in accounting income. In the literature, accounting method choices are often labelled as having a reversal effect (declining depreciation will have lower profits in the beginning than the straight line method, but after a certain moment in the life span of the asset the situation reverses), whereas a real transaction is often labelled as having a one-time effect. However, all three practices (accounting method changes, accounting estimates and real transactions) might entail reversing effects. If one sells, for example, a fuel hedge contract to earn an increase in profits in the year the contract is sold, the company will probably suffer from higher fuel prices in the period thereafter. So the sale of the contract is not limited to a one-time effect.

An element that might differ between the different methods for annual accounts management is the timing of the reversal effect. Now take a look of Activity 30.8.

ACTIVITY 30.8

Think of some methods to be used for annual accounts management purposes with a short reversal time and some with a longer reversal time.

Activity feedback

A change in accounting methods or estimates in the area of the working capital of a firm might have a short reversal period, e.g. a switch from one inventory valuation method to another, a change in the estimates of bad debt allowances.

Working capital accruals reverse in the short term as these elements are short-term assets and liabilities. This implies that if the results fall short the year after, additional earnings influence practices must be used if one does not want the results to fall. The reversal period in relation to non-working capital items is longer. For example, the gain realized on sale and leaseback transactions is spread out over the life span of the leased asset.

Bowen *et al.* (1995) found that management in general chooses accounting interventions with a long-term positive effect on accounting income. However, if the compensation scheme of the management has short-term perspectives, practices with shorter reversal periods are used. Not including a company in the group accounts, although one controls the company, influences the accounting numbers on a permanent basis. We do not see a reversal with regard to these consolidation choices.

So for financial analysis purposes, it is not only important to understand the accounting flexibility which is available but also to know which valuation rules, estimates and other mechanisms are chosen in the presentation of the annual accounts. In order to get an idea about these elements, the quality of disclosure in the financial statements is an important determinant of the visibility of these accounting interventions. Unfortunately, the level of disclosure differs between companies.

Quality of disclosure

When management provides the necessary disclosures in the notes to the statement of financial position, the statement of comprehensive income and the cash flow statement, it facilitates the analysis of the business reality of the company by external parties. Financial statements are meant to inform the stakeholders of the firm about the result, the cash flow and the financial position of the firm. In principle, the published figures should represent the underlying economic situation of the firm. However, due to the flexibility that exists in the accounting standards to be applied and the incentives top executives face towards earnings management, a situation might be created in which the published figures in the financial statements do not translate into the underlying economic condition of the firm. Although companies must provide a minimum level of disclosure as required by the GAAP they are complying with, the management team can always make more voluntary disclosures.

Disclosure quality refers to the compliance of a company with all the disclosures required by the GAAP used and to how informative the voluntary disclosures might be, which are presented in the annual report. So disclosure quality and the level of disclosure can also be extended to the narrative part of the annual report. This will be discussed further in Chapter 31. Empirical and analytical accounting research has paid attention to disclosure practices. Most empirical research studies provide evidence that an increase in disclosure leads to lower costs of capital due to the reduction in information asymmetry (e.g. Leuz and Verrechia, 2000). The analytical research, however, indicates that there is an optimal level of disclosure for a company.

Disclosure quality is an important benchmark when inter-firm comparisons are made and it relates to several aspects. Some examples of disclosure quality will now be illustrated.

Description of accounting methods and accounting estimates So far we have learned that the choice of accounting valuation methods and accounting estimates can influence the reported income and the statement of financial position structure. Adequate disclosure in the notes on the methods and the estimates used might enable external analysts to get an idea of the impact of those choices and to reconcile earnings of different firms when executing a comparative financial analysis of companies. Further, a company can also explain why a particular choice has been made. If we compare the different airlines, we notice that the level of explanation with regard to, for example, how frequent flyer obligations are accounted for, differs. Frequent flyer programmes could create obligations for an airline. However, the obligation is dependent on several terms of the contract between the airline and the customer. On top of that, several ways exist to account for these obligations: the incremental cost approach, whereby the costs are charged to comprehensive income when passengers make use of the bonus miles, or the revenue minus approach, whereby part of the revenue of the ticket sale is deferred to the moment the passenger makes use of the bonus miles (a provision is then created). We illustrate these differences with extracts of the notes of two airlines applying IFRS. The first extract is from the notes to the accounts of the Belgian Airline Sabena that went bankrupt in 2001 (Annual report 2000, page 50, note 5.7).

REAL WORLD ILLUSTRATION

Appropriate provisions are also made for liabilities arising from mileages accrued via the Qualiflyer frequent flyer programme. These provisions are equal to the costs to be incurred as such credits are redeemed.

In the accounts of the International Airline Group (IAG) (the company that arose after the merger of British Airways, Iberia and Vueling), the programmes themselves are described, together with the way they are accounted for.

REAL WORLD ILLUSTRATION

Customer loyalty programmes

The Group operates four loyalty programmes: Executive Club, Iberia Plus, Avios, and Punto. The principal customer loyalty programmes award travellers Avios points to redeem for various rewards primarily redemption travel, including flights, hotels and car hire. In accordance with IFRIC 13 'Customer loyalty programmes', the fair value attributed to the awarded Avios points is deferred as a liability and recognised as revenue on redemption of the points and provision of service to the participants to whom the Avios points are issued.

In addition, Avios points are sold to commercial partners to use in loyalty activity. The fair value of the Avios points sold is deferred and recognised as revenue on redemption of the Avios points by the participants to whom the Avios points are issued. The cost of the redemption of the Avios points is recognised when the Avios points are redeemed.

The Group estimates the fair value of Avios points by reference to the fair value of the awards for which they could be redeemed and is reduced to take into account the proportion of award credits that are not expected to be redeemed based on the results of statistical modelling. The fair value of the Avios point reflects the fair value of the range of available awards.

Explanation of significant changes in accounting methods and accounting estimates

Accounting method changes hinder external users of the financial statements in comparing the income and the statement of financial position structures over the years. Adequate disclosure of the new accounting method applied and the impact on comparability could facilitate the analysis. Changes in accounting methods, estimates and presentation can occur because of a voluntary decision by management or because of a change in accounting regulation. The impact of these changes on the accounting numbers needs to be disclosed, otherwise inter-period and inter-firm comparability of firm information is hindered.

High-quality disclosure is essential for inter-company comparison as well as for inter-period comparability within the same company. Although extensive disclosure requirements are included in many IFRSs, a difference in disclosure quality is found in practice. To enhance disclosure quality, the IASB started a project on disclosure in 2013. In this phase of the Disclosure Project (end 2015), there is still the discussion about whether the IASB could take a highly principled approach (= where preparer's judgement will be important) or a highly prescriptive approach. The choice for one out of these two approaches will determine the next phase of the Disclosure Project. In addition, disclosure is understood in this project as being more specific about the line items to be included in the primary financial statements as well as enhancing disclosures in the notes. At the time of the preparation of this manuscript (January 2016), many options were still open for the IASB with respect to the next steps in the Disclosure Project. It could be interesting to consult the IASB website today when you are reading this part of the book, to see how the Disclosure Project has evolved since early 2016 (see the section on workplan development of standards and projects available at www.ifrs.org).

Non-GAAP or pro-forma accounting measures

Disclosures are not only important to understand IFRS, US GAAP or UK GAAP or simply GAAP accounting numbers properly, but they are even more important when companies present non-GAAP or pro-forma earnings or accounting measures. When companies present non-GAAP measures, they present the financial situation of the company without using any 'officially recognized' GAAP, but rather with the use of their own internally created measures. Often the difference between non-GAAP or pro-forma earnings and IFRS or US GAAP earnings relates to the omission of non-recurring, unusual or infrequently occurring items. However, impairments or depreciations are also often omitted from the earnings figures. Quite often, non-GAAP measures are misleading since the measure does not represent the underlying economic situation and disclosure guiding the user in the interpretation is lacking.

As the use of non-GAAP earnings or pro-forma earnings has increased enormously over the past years, it has caught the attention of regulators. In the US, the Sarbanes-Oxley Act of 2002 contains provisions related to a firm's use of non-GAAP measures. In Europe, ESMA issued the 'Guidelines on Alternative Performance Measures' (APM) on 16 July 2015. The guidelines apply to issuers on EU stock exchanges with securities traded on regulated markets and persons responsible for drawing up a prospectus. The guidelines require a company to provide a reconciliation between the non-GAAP measures or APMs and the GAAP measures. These guidelines became effective in the summer of 2016. A number of companies voluntarily already provided some reconciliation information between their published non-GAAP measures and their GAAP measures.

REAL LIFE ILLUSTRATION

NON-GAAP MEASURES

Certain discussions and analyses set out in this Annual Report and Accounts include measures which are not defined by generally accepted accounting principles (GAAP) such as IFRS. We believe this information, along with comparable GAAP measurements, is useful to investors because it provides a basis for measuring our operating performance, ability to retire debt and invest in new business opportunities. Our management uses these financial measures, along with the most directly comparable GAAP financial measures, in evaluating our operating performance and value creation. Non-GAAP financial measures should not be considered in isolation from, or as a substitute for, financial information presented in compliance with GAAP. Non-GAAP financial measures as reported by us may not be comparable with similarly titled amounts reported by other companies.

In the following sections we set out our definitions of the following non-GAAP measures and provide reconciliations to relevant GAAP measures:

- underlying sales growth;
- underlying volume growth;
- core operating profit and core operating margin;
- core earnings per share [core EPS];
- free cash flow; and
- net debt.

UNDERLYING SALES GROWTH (USG)

Underlying sales growth (USG) refers to the increase in turnover for the period, excluding any change in turnover resulting from acquisitions, disposals and changes in currency. The impact of acquisitions and disposals is excluded from USG for a period of 12 calendar months from the applicable closing date. Turnover from acquired brands that are launched in countries where they were not previously sold is included in USG as such turnover is more attributable to our existing sales and distribution network than the acquisition itself.

The reconciliation of USG to changes in the GAAP measure turnover is as follows:

TOTAL GROUP	2014 vs 2013	2013 vs 2012
Underlying sales growth [%]	2.9	4.3
Effect of acquisitions [%]	0.4	–
Effect of disposals [%]	[1.3]	[1.1]
Effect of exchange rates [%]	[4.6]	[5.9]
Turnover growth [%][a]	[2.7]	[3.0]

REAL LIFE ILLUSTRATION (*Continued*)

PERSONAL CARE	2014 vs 2013	2013 vs 2012
Underlying sales growth [%]	3.5	7.3
Effect of acquisitions [%]	–	–
Effect of disposals [%]	[0.1]	[0.2]
Effect of exchange rates [%]	[5.0]	[6.8]
Turnover growth [%][a]	[1.8]	[0.2]
FOODS	**2014 vs 2013**	**2013 vs 2012**
Underlying sales growth [%]	[0.6]	0.3
Effect of acquisitions [%]	–	–
Effect of disposals [%]	[3.6]	[3.7]
Effect of exchange rates [%]	[3.9]	[3.8]
Turnover growth [%][a]	[7.9]	[7.0]
REFRESHMENT	**2014 vs 2013**	**2013 vs 2012**
Underlying sales growth [%]	3.8	1.1
Effect of acquisitions [%]	0.4	0.1
Effect of disposals [%]	[1.6]	–
Effect of exchange rates [%]	[4.6]	[4.7]
Turnover growth [%][a]	[2.1]	[3.7]
HOME CARE	**2014 vs 2013**	**2013 vs 2012**
Underlying sales growth [%]	5.8	8.0
Effect of acquisitions [%]	1.8	0.1
Effect of disposals [%]	–	–
Effect of exchange rates [%]	[4.8]	[8.6]
Turnover growth [%][a]	2.4	[1.2]

[a] Turnover growth is made up of distinct individual growth components namely underlying sales, currency impact, acquisitions and disposals. Turnover growth is arrived at by multiplying these individual components on a compounded basis as there is a currency impact on each of the other components. Accordingly, turnover growth is more than just the sum of the individual components.

UNDERLYING VOLUME GROWTH (UVG)

Underlying volume growth (UVG) is part of USG and means, for the applicable period, the increase in turnover in such period calculated as the sum of [i] the increase in turnover attributable to the volume of products sold; and [ii] the increase in turnover attributable to the composition of products sold during such period. UVG therefore excludes any impact to USG due to changes in prices.

The relationship between the two measures is set out below:

	2014 vs 2013	2013 vs 2012
Underlying volume growth [%]	1.0	2.5
Effect of price changes [%]	1.9	1.8
Underlying sales growth [%]	2.9	4.3

CORE OPERATING PROFIT AND CORE OPERATING MARGIN

Core operating profit and core operating margin mean operating profit and operating margin, respectively, before the impact of business disposals, acquisition and disposal related costs, impairments and other one-off items, which we collectively term non-core items, due to their nature and frequency of occurrence.

REAL LIFE ILLUSTRATION (*Continued*)

The reconciliation of core operating profit to operating profit is as follows:

	€ million 2014	€ million 2013
Operating profit	7 980	7 517
Acquisition and disposal related cost	97	112
(Gain)/loss on disposal of group companies	(1 392)	(733)
Impairments and other one-off items	335	120
Core operating profit	7 020	7 016
Turnover	48 436	49 797
Operating margin	16.5%	15.1%
Core operating margin	14.5%	14.1%

Further details of non-core items can be found in note 3 on page 92 of the Governance and Financial Report.

CORE EARNINGS PER SHARE

The Group also refers to core earnings per share (core EPS). In calculating core earnings, net profit attributable to shareholders' equity is adjusted to eliminate the post tax impact of non-core items. Refer to note 7 on page 102 of the Governance and Financial Report for reconciliation of core earnings to net profit attributable to shareholders' equity.

FREE CASH FLOW (FCF)

Within the Unilever Group, free cash flow (FCF) is defined as cash flow from operating activities, less income taxes paid, net capital expenditures and net interest payments and preference dividends paid. It does not represent residual cash flows entirely available for discretionary purposes; for example, the repayment of principal amounts borrowed is not deducted from FCF. Free cash flow reflects an additional way of viewing our liquidity that we believe is useful to investors because it represents cash flows that could be used for distribution of dividends, repayment of debt or to fund our strategic initiatives, including acquisitions, if any.

The reconciliation of FCF to net profit is as follows:

	€ million 2014	€ million 2013
Net profit	5 515	5 263
Taxation	2 131	1 851
Share of net profit of joint ventures/associates and other income from non-current investments	(143)	(127)
Net finance costs	477	530
Depreciation, amortisation and impairment	1 432	1 151
Changes in working capital	8	200
Pensions and similar obligations less payments	(364)	(383)
Provisions less payments	32	126
Elimination of (profits)/losses on disposals	(1 460)	(725)
Non-cash charge for share-based compensation	188	228
Other adjustments	38	(15)
Cash flow from operating activities	7 854	8 099
Income tax pad	(2 311)	(1 805)
Net capital expenditure	(2 045)	(2 027)
Net interest and preference dividends paid	(398)	(411)
Free cash flow	3 100	3 856
Net cash flow (used in)/from investing activities	(341)	(1 161)
Net cash flow (used in)/from financing activities	(5 190)	(5 390)

(Continued)

REAL LIFE ILLUSTRATION (*Continued*)

NET DEBT

Net debt is defined as the excess of total financial liabilities, excluding trade and other payables, over cash, cash equivalents and current financial assets, excluding trade

and other receivables. It is a measure that provides valuable additional information on the summary presentation of the Group's net financial liabilities and is a measure in common use elsewhere.

The reconciliation of net debt to the GAAP measure total financial liabilities is as follows;

	€ million 2014	€ million 2013
Total financial liabilities	(12 722)	(11 501)
Current financial liabilities	(5 536)	(4 010)
Non-current financial liabilities	(7 186)	(7 491)
Cash and cash equivalents as per balance sheet	2 151	2 285
Cash and cash equivalents as per cash flow statement	1 910	2 044
Add bank overdrafts deducted there in	241	241
Other current financial assets	671	760
Net debt	(9 900)	(8 456)

Source: Unilever annual report and accounts 2014.

The use of non-GAAP earnings measures attracted a lot of research interests (Barth *et al.*, 2012; Christensen *et al.*, 2014; Curtis *et al.*, 2014; Bentley *et al.* 2015; Isidro and Marques, 2015). These articles study the incentives to use non-GAAP measures and the influence of the institutional environment on the use of these measures. They find incentives to use non-GAAP measures similar to the incentives to manipulate earnings under GAAP. In addition, they also find that the use of non-GAAP measures differs across jurisdictions with different institutional characteristics such as risk of litigation and degree of enforcement. Non-GAAP measures are used much more in jurisdictions with a higher risk of litigation and stricter enforcement.

SUMMARY

The purpose of financial statements is to provide information on the performance and the financial position of a company to external parties. At the same time, however, financial statements are viewed by the management of a company as a means of communication to the outside world. Sometimes, tension may arise to publish a result that is somewhat different from the underlying economic result. In this situation, the company will influence the published accounting numbers. The aim of this chapter was first to illustrate how industrial, economic and company characteristics (i.e. organization of the value chain) have an impact on the accounting numbers. Second, in the part of this chapter on accounting analysis, we discussed how users of annual accounts might be able to determine if the annual accounts have possibly been managed, on the one hand by analyzing the incentives present towards earnings management and the circumstances influencing the available accounting discretion to top management, and on the other, by investigating the choices made by top management in preparing the annual accounts. The purpose of accounting analysis is to gain an understanding of the underlying economic result and financial position, and only this information is useful or relevant for decision-making purposes.

It is important to remember, however, that each toolkit for manipulation (accounting methods, accounting estimates and real decisions) is unique to the needs and environment of each individual company. So each accounting analysis will be unique.

EXERCISES

Suggested answers to exercises marked ✓ are to be found in the Student online resources, with suggested answers to the remaining questions available in the Instructor online resources.

1   Identify as many examples as possible where the choice of accounting policy could significantly affect the analysis and interpretation of published financial statements.

2   Appraise the financial performance and stability of each of these three companies within the limits of the information given. The summarized statements of financial position of three businesses in the same industry are shown below for 200X.

	A £000	B £000	C £000
Intangible non-current assets	100	—	10
Tangible non-current assets	886	582	580
Current assets	920	580	950
Total assets	1 906	1 162	1 540
Equity and liabilities			

Equity			
Share capital	200	40	300
Revaluation reserve	80	—	—
Retained profits	1 056	850	704
Total equity	1 336	890	1 004
Liabilities			
Non-current liabilities	100	20	50
Current liabilities	470	252	486
Total liabilities	570	272	536
Total equity and liabilities	1 906	1 162	1 540

The operating profit and sales for the three companies for the years in question were:

Operating profit	282	194	148
Sales	2 100	1 500	1 750

The companies had different treatments for the intangibles. Company A is amortizing this at £10 000 per annum and company C at £2000 per annum. Company B has written off goodwill of £40 000 to retained profits in the year. Included in the depreciation expense of company A is an extra £4000 over and above the historical cost depreciation caused by an earlier revaluation of its premises.

3   If you consider companies such as McDonald's, Kentucky Fried Chicken, Burger King, etc., what are the value drivers in their industry? What are the critical factors in their industrial environment? Comment on these. Subsequently, contrast your findings with an analysis of the value drivers of companies such as Boeing and Airbus. What do you observe? How will these different industry characteristics and value drivers have an impact on the financial statements of these companies? You might look up their annual reports on their websites for inspiration.

4   Identify as many examples as possible where the choice of accounting methods, accounting estimates or even real transactions could significantly affect the analysis and interpretation of the financial statements. Comment on how these choices affect the financial statements.

5   Consider again the examples you have listed in answering question 3. Relate these findings to the national GAAP of your own country. Does the national GAAP in your country allow accounting flexibility on many of the items listed?

6   Compare the accounting flexibility of the national GAAP in your own country with the flexibility in IAS/IFRS. Which of the two systems allows less flexibility to the preparer of the financial statements?

7   Would the information provided through financial statements improve if you could eliminate accounting flexibility from the standards?

8   You are asked by your financial director to choose suitable companies with which to compare your own company. Explain, in a report to the FD what would influence your choice and how you would adjust for differing accounting policies, if any.

TECHNIQUES OF FINANCIAL ANALYSIS

31

OBJECTIVES After studying this chapter you should be able to:

- identify potential red flags that obstruct comparability of financial accounting data

- perform the following types of analysis and appraise the results:

    - trend analysis

    - common size analysis

    - ratio analysis

    - segmental analysis

    - cash flow analysis.

INTRODUCTION

The purpose of financial analysis is to evaluate the performance and the financial position of a firm given the strategy of the firm, the economic and industrial environment in which the company is competitive, the level of accounting flexibility influenced by the quality of GAAP applied, and the incentives and opportunities that exist towards earnings management. Several techniques of financial analysis exist. The best-known technique is that of ratio analysis, in which items of the statement of financial position and statement of comprehensive income are related to each other. This technique was introduced to you in Chapter 29. In order to review the elements discussed in Chapter 29, we start with the Activities below.

ACTIVITY 31.1

Using the annual accounts of a company, which ratios would you calculate in order to evaluate the performance and financial position of the firm?

Activity feedback

Any reader of this text who has some introduction to this topic will come up with ratios such as:

- *current assets/current liabilities to judge the ability of a company to repay its debt in the short term*
- *debt/equity to evaluate the financial risk of a company in the long term*
- *results/equity to decide whether or not the investments are used in a profitable way.*

ACTIVITY 31.2

Can you judge the financial situation of a company properly, based only on the ratios of one particular year? Why or why not?

Activity feedback

First of all, there is no external benchmark to compare the performance of the firm with, for example, a competitor in the same industry. Second, judging the performance of a firm based on the results of a particular year or even two years is not that meaningful. Information from one or two years is too short a timeframe in which to build an internal benchmark. Moreover, the one year you are considering could be a particular year, for example the first year after a merger, or the year before a mega-merger. It could also be the first year of a new incoming CEO who has joined the company after the dismissal of the prior CEO because of weak economic performance. The new CEO might perhaps apply some big bath accounting.

In order to evaluate the performance of a firm in a meaningful way a comparison is needed with firms in the industry, with the past performance of the firm itself or with an absolute benchmark. In ratio analysis, however, no absolute benchmarks exist, except maybe that profitability should be above the weighted average cost of capital. But even that absolute benchmark in some industries is not always fulfilled.

From the illustrations in the Activities thus far, it becomes clear that the performance of a firm should be judged in a relevant timeframe and against some industry benchmarks. The analysis of the performance or the financial position of the firm over time is called horizontal analysis or trend analysis. The comparison with the performance or financial position of other companies or a whole industry is done by vertical analysis or common size analysis. Before trend analysis and vertical analysis can be undertaken, it is necessary to check that there are no elements present which would disturb the comparison over time and between companies. The elements of industry analysis and accounting analysis (both discussed in Chapter 30) should be kept in mind here.

In the following section, we illustrate the pitfalls related to comparability.

Which elements can you think of that would disturb the comparison of firm performance over time or between companies?

Activity feedback

- *changes in the structure of the company through a merger, acquisition or creation of new subsidiaries*
- *differences in valuation methods or accounting estimates applied*
- *differences in presentation*
- *different time spans.*

ELEMENTS OF NON-COMPARABILITY IN FINANCIAL STATEMENTS

Activity 31.3 listed some red flags that should be checked before analysis of the performance and financial position of a company can be started.

Changes with regard to the time span of the financial year

Companies might decide to change the time span of a particular year for several reasons. We can observe this practice if a company suffers from a huge loss (e.g. trading losses on financial contracts), the company may decide to extend the financial year from 12 months to 15 months by changing the reporting date. As a result, this huge loss is then compensated for by profits of 15 months instead of 12.

Companies can also create very short financial years in which huge losses or restructurings are accounted for. An example can be found in the annual accounts of the 1991 financial year of Sabena. For the purposes of big bath accounting, the financial year 1991 of Sabena, the Belgian flag carrier which went bankrupt in 2001, was split into two financial years. The first financial year covered three months (1.1.1991 – 31.3.1991). The second financial year covered the other nine months (1.4.1991 – 31.12.1991). The bath was located in the first financial report of 1991 and the second financial report of 1991 showed a profit.

Financial year	1.1.1991–31.3.1991 in BEF000	1.4.1991–31.12.1991 in BEF000
Operating (loss)/profit	(2 808 673)	2 161 465
Net (loss)/profit	(30 230 650)	1 132 000

The comparative figures in the annual accounts of 1992 were those of the second report of 1991. A reader of the financial statements who did not pay a lot of attention would then compare the figures of nine months (1991) with the figures of 12 months (1992). This practice was quite popular more than a decade ago. Nowadays, companies have to provide extensive disclosure if they want to change the closing date of the financial period. So this practice occurs less frequently now.

Different statement of financial position dates

Companies use different closing dates for their financial statements. Even within the same industry, differences can be observed. For example, in the airline business the following dates are used as statement of financial position dates by the different airlines:

- 31 March: The Emirates Group
- 30 September: easyJet
- 31 December: Lufthansa and IAG (= International Airline Group: British Airways and Iberia).

If we were to compare the annual accounts of the two low-cost carriers for the financial year with closing dates in 2001, we have to take into account that easyJet closed its financial statements after the 11 September terrorist attacks on the World Trade Center in New York and the Pentagon in Washington, DC by terrorists; British Airways had done so before that event. The same applies to other events affecting the airlines, e.g. SARS and closing airspaces due to events of nature (volcanic eruptions) or events of human origin (terrorist attack).

Changes in company structure

Over the years, companies merge, acquire other companies or parts of other companies or restructure activities into different separate legal business entities. If a company is involved in mergers or acquisitions, observed growth is often not organic growth, but rather growth through acquisition. This should be considered in a different way. Often companies disclose in the notes to the accounts the main drivers of the growth. Growth can be realized through internal growth (some companies correct their internal growth figures for inflation) or through mergers and acquisitions.

These changes in company structures are especially hindering for trend analysis. Some company restructurings can create an impression of decline, although in reality part of the activities have been moved to a separate entity. When operations are discontinued due to a restructuring of activities, shareholders need information on the share of these discontinued activities in the results, the financial position and the cash flow of the group. IFRS 5, *Non-current Assets Held for Sale and Discontinued Operations* stipulates that in case of discontinued activities the impact should be disclosed to the reader of the accounts. The main objective is to ensure comparability for the reader of the annual accounts. This information message is important for financial analysts and investors who estimate a company's future revenue generating power on the basis of revenues from continuing operations and more specifically from the recurring profit from continuing operations.

Companies that merge or are involved in acquisitions have increasing absolute numbers for revenue, earnings before interest and taxes (EBIT) results and total assets. These firms often like to stress this increase in absolute amounts of revenue, EBIT and results, without putting in the spotlight the fact that the increase derives mainly from acquisition. Impression management is often observed in these circumstances; fortunately, we also observe companies that disclose the origin of the increase in these absolute figures in a transparent way. For example, Nestlé used to publish a construct called RIG, which is equal to 'real internal growth'. In this figure, the impact of acquisitions, mergers or spin-offs is eliminated, together with the impact of inflation and price changes.

Accounting method changes and accounting estimate changes

All GAAP have the consistency principle in their Standards: companies are supposed to apply the same accounting policies from one period to the next. The purpose of this consistency principle is enhancing comparability between financial statements over time. However, in practice, changes are observed and the user of the financial statements should take them into account. In the notes to the accounts the impact of the changes has to be discussed (see Chapter 8 for discussion of IAS 8); it will depend, however, on the quality of disclosure whether the user of the accounts is able to judge the impact of the change on the performance and financial position of the company.

A change in GAAP applied

Companies not only change accounting methods or estimates over the years, they sometimes switch from one set of accounting regulations or Standards to another set of Standards. This is a one-time change that might have a serious impact on the results and on the statement of financial position of the company. When new Standards are issued by standard setters and companies have some flexibility to choose the period of first-time adoption of the new Standard, comparability will be threatened. In times where standard setters issue many new Standards, comparability over the years becomes an issue. It is even more important when companies can choose the first period of adoption of the new Standard.

REAL WORLD ILLUSTRATION

01 General

The consolidated financial statements of adidas AG as at December 31, 2014 comprise adidas AG and its subsidiaries and are prepared in compliance with International Financial Reporting Standards (IFRS), as adopted by the European Union (EU) as at December 31, 2014, and the additional requirements pursuant to § 315a section 1 German Commercial Code (Handelsgesetzbuch – HGB).

The following new standards and interpretations and amendments to existing standards and interpretations are applicable for the first time for financial years beginning on January 1, 2014:

/ **IFRS 10 Consolidated Financial Statements** (effective date: January 1, 2014): This new standard had no material impact on the Group's financial statements.

/ **IFRS 11 Joint Arrangements** (effective date: January 1, 2014): This new standard had no impact on the Group's financial statements.

/ **IFRS 12 Disclosure of Interests in Other Entities** (effective date: January 1, 2014): This new standard required additional disclosures in the Group's financial statements.

/ **Consolidated Financial Statements, Joint Arrangements and Disclosure of Interests in Other Entitles: Transition Guidance (Amendments to IFRS 10, IFRS 11 and IFRS 12)** (effective date: January 1, 2014): These amendments had no material impact on the Group's financial statements.

/ **Investment Entities (Amendments to IFRS 10, IFRS 12 and IAS 27)** (effective date: January 1, 2014): These amendments had no impact on the Group's financial statements.

/ **IAS 27 Separate Financial Statements – Revised (2011)** (effective date: January 1, 2014): This amendment had no impact on the Group's financial statements.

/ **IAS 28 Investments in Associates and Joint Ventures – Revised (2011)** (effective date: January 1, 2014): This amendment had no impact on the Group's financial statements.

/ **IAS 32 Amendment – Offsetting Financial Assets and Financial Liabilities** (effective date: January 1, 2014): This amendment had no material impact on the Group's financial statements.

/ **IAS 39 Amendment – Novation of Derivatives and Continuation of Hedge Accounting** (effective date: January 1, 20141: This amendment had no impact on the Group's financial statements.

/ **IFRIC 21 Levies** (effective date: January 1, 2014): This new interpretation had no material impact on the Group's financial statements.

New standards and interpretations as well as amendments to existing standards and interpretations are usually not applied by the Group before the effective

(*Continued*)

REAL WORLD ILLUSTRATION *(Continued)*

date. One exception was the early application of the following standard:

/ IAS 36 Amendment – Recoverable Amount Disclosures for Non-Financial Assets (effective date: January 1, 2014): By having applied this amendment early in the 2013 financial year, the unintentionally introduced requirement to disclose the recoverable amounts of cash-generating units irrespective of whether an impairment has actually occurred is waived.

New standards and interpretations and amendments to existing standards and interpretations that will be effective for financial years beginning after January 1, 2014, and which have not been applied in preparing these consolidated financial statements are:

/ IAS 19 Amendment – Defined Benefit Plans: Employee Contributions (effective date: July 1, 2014): This amendment is not expected to have any material impact on the Group's financial statements.

/ Improvements to IFRSs (2010–2012) (effective date: July 1, 2014): These improvements are expected to require additional disclosures in the Group's financial statements.

/ Improvements to IFRSs (2011–2013) (effective date: July 1, 2014): These improvements are not expected to have any material impact on the Group's financial statements.

The consolidated financial statements have in principle been prepared on the historical cost basis with the exception of certain items in the statement of financial position such as financial instruments valued at fair value through profit or loss, available-for-sale financial assets, derivative financial instruments, plan assets and receivables, which are measured at fair value.

The consolidated financial statements are presented in euros (€) and, unless otherwise stated, all values are presented in millions of euros (€ in millions). Due to rounding principles, numbers presented may not sum up exactly to totals provided.

Source: adidas Group annual report and accounts 2014.

Differences in presentation

We observe two main issues with regard to differences in presentation. First, the contents of 'similar' items used in the annual accounts can be different. Second, different companies use different ways of presentation, classification, aggregation and layout. Standardized formats for the statement of financial position and statement of comprehensive income facilitate comparison. In practice, however, companies use different formats and layouts. Several GAAP require a minimum layout with which companies have to comply (see Chapter 8 for the discussion of the layout of the statement of financial position and the income statement under the Fourth and Seventh EU Directive and IFRS). IAS prescribes only a minimum layout for the statement of financial position and the statement of comprehensive income, which allows substantial room for company-specific choices with regard to the layout.

If we compare the statements of comprehensive income of Nestlé and Unilever (see Appendices I and II to this chapter), we observe a different approach. Although both companies choose a statement of comprehensive income in two parts (first part the profit and loss account and second part the elements charged directly to equity), there are still a lot of differences.

ACTIVITY 31.4

Go to Appendices I and II of this chapter and look at the total assets, total debt and equity of Nestlé and Unilever.

Activity feedback

When you look at both statements of financial position, you will notice that the layout and presentation chosen by both companies is different. With regard to income, *we notice that Nestlé provides more information on the different components of operating costs on the face of the income statement than Unilever does. Unilever provides a breakdown of operating costs, but it does so in the notes to the accounts. It is up to the user to collect this information from the notes to create comparable information.*

Reconciliations, which will lead to more comparable figures, can only be executed if one is analyzing a small number of companies; however, in large-scale analyses (e.g. for large industry analyses or for academic research) these corrections are often not made. So we observe that differences have not vanished with the compulsory introduction of IAS. One might wonder how these differences are taken into account by companies constructing databases like Worldscope, Amadcus, Osiris, Datastream etc. These databases are extensively used for academic research purposes.

TREND ANALYSIS OR HORIZONTAL ANALYSIS

Benchmarks are necessary to make a sound judgement about the performance of a company. With the use of trend analysis, we compare the performance of the firm with its own history. In annual reports, we often find change statistics comparing the figures of two consecutive years. However, some caution is needed when using this published information (see Activity 31.5).

ACTIVITY 31.5

Table 31.1 presents percentages of change between 20X1 and 20X2 in the annual report of a company that went bankrupt one year later. Is a reported increase always positive?

Activity feedback

If negative amounts are involved, care should be taken with the presented statistics. The change in net result and the change in treasury position are not favourable at all, although it is presented as a positive change figure.

TABLE 31.1 Illustration of percentage changes between two financial years

	20X1 (million EUR)	20X2 (million EUR)	% 20X2/20X1
Turnover	2 228	2 436	9.3
Operating result	15	(163)	−1 208.7
Net result	(14)	(325)	2 226.1
Operating cash flow	138	(51)	−137.1
Cash flow net result	124	(108)	−187.1
Changes in treasury position	(80)	(225)	182.1
Total assets	2 471	2 358	−4.6
Equity	223	(97)	−143.3
Ratio long-term debt/equity	5.0	10.9	118.0

With trend analysis or horizontal analysis, we analyze how financial statement items have changed over time. According to the literature, a five-year timeframe is necessary; longer periods, for example ten years, are also possible, although the number of elements which disturb comparison only increases over such a long period. For the purpose of trend analysis, a base year is chosen and all the financial statement items are then expressed as an index relative to the base year. Therefore, the choice of the base year is relatively important, as the performance over the years to follow is bench marked to this base year.

If trend analysis is applied on the items of the statement of comprehensive income, the focus lies on the evolution of revenue and the costs related to it. Whether or not the relation between the evolution of the revenue and the costs should be linear, depends on the industry characteristics. From the section on industry analysis, we know that for the airline industry only catering and handling costs are somewhat variable and are a function of the number of passengers transported. The other costs related to the air transport are a function of the output capacity of the airline, which is measured as available seat kilometre or available tonne kilometre. We illustrate trend analysis on the basis of the evolution of the operating revenue and operating costs of Lufthansa and easyJet in Tables 31.2 and 31.3. The formats of these income statements differ and they reflect the different composition of activities of both companies. Whereas easyJet focuses on passenger transport at low cost and buys most services externally, the Lufthansa group has a large business segment of passenger transport. It also has several other business segments which are active in the value chain of air transportation. So in addition to passenger transport, the Lufthansa group deploys activities in cargo transport (Logistics), in provision of maintenance, repair and overhaul of civilian aircraft (MRO-Lufthansa Technik), in catering and on board services (LSG Skychefs) and in IT-services for selected industries (IT-service). Therefore Lufthansa uses more general line items in their profit and loss account within the statement of comprehensive income, whereas the line items in the profit and loss account of easyJet are more focused on air transport, which is their major single activity.

TABLE 31.2   Horizontal analysis, Lufthansa 2010–2014 (financial reporting date is 31 December)

	Horizontal analysis (%)				
	2010	2011	2012	2013	2014
Operating revenue	100	106	111	110	109
Other revenue	100	95	104	98	99
Total revenue	100	103	109	106	106
Total operating costs	100	105	109	108	108
Material & service	100	108	116	113	112
Staff costs	100	100	105	110	110
Depreciation, amortization	100	102	109	105	90
Other operating costs	100	101	95	92	101
Operating result	100	97	105	69	62

Source: Data taken from the annual reports of Lufthansa.

TABLE 31.3 Horizontal analysis, easyJet 2011–2015 (financial reporting date is 30 September)

	Horizontal analysis (%)				
	2011	2012	2013	2014	2015
Seat revenue	100	138	153	163	168
Other operating revenue	100	9	9	10	10
Operating costs	100	106	118	123	125
Fuel	100	125	128	136	130
Airport	100	103	116	119	121
Crew	100	106	111	117	124
Navigation	100	99	103	107	109
Maintenance costs	100	113	118	118	127
Selling	100	101	100	100	100
Leasing	100	88	94	113	104
Depreciation	100	116	122	127	150
Amortization	100	114	142	171	185
Other costs	100	116	132	143	161
Operating result	100	123	184	115	155

Source: Data taken from the annual reports of easyJet.

Horizontal analysis allows us to see how revenue evolves over a period of time and whether operating costs and the operating result evolve at the same pace. If we compare the horizontal analysis of the revenue, we need to keep in mind that the absolute amount of easyJet is much smaller than the absolute amount of the revenue of Lufthansa. Similar changes in absolute amounts have a larger impact on the trend analysis, when the absolute values are less. When we compare the trends in revenue between both airlines, we notice that the revenue of easyJet grows steadily at a higher pace than the growth of Lufthansa. For easyJet, the growth rate of the operating costs is much slower than the growth rate of the revenue. To a large extent, this is due to the mainly fixed cost structure of the transportation activity. The operational costs of Lufthansa keep pace with the trend in revenue and in a couple of years, the costs grow even faster than revenue. We need to mention that the Lufthansa group is active in a number of business segments with a much more variable cost structure. When cost structures are variable, they tend to follow the revenue trend more closely. EasyJet grew by adding new destinations to the routes it offers and therefore they also needed to invest in aircraft. The increasing depreciation amounts are a result of this growth. If we look at the evolution of the staff costs in the Lufthansa group, we notice that their increase is slightly higher than the increase in revenue. Finally, if we look at the trend in the operating result, we notice a growth scenario for easyJet and a somewhat volatile scenario for Lufthansa.

As an external user of financial statements, one must always keep in mind that competitors also watch evolutions of costs (trend analysis) and the breakdown of those costs (common size analysis). Anecdotal evidence exists that the smoothing of certain levels of cost items is practised in several industries. Consumers also keep an eye on annual accounts. For example, which airline in the world would publish a profit and loss account showing decreasing costs with regard to maintenance if the fleet capacity remains constant or increases?

Horizontal analysis provides us with information on the trend in revenues, costs and profits. If we want to gain more insight into the impact of the different cost components on the results of the company, we perform a vertical analysis.

COMMON SIZE ANALYSIS

The benchmark to compare the performance of a firm within trend analysis is its own past performance. In common size analysis, the benchmarking element is the performance of other firms, usually taken from the same industry. For the purposes of external benchmarking, the size effect needs to be eliminated, and this is done by expressing the items in the statement of comprehensive income as a percentage of revenue and the items in the statement of financial position in terms of a percentage of total assets.

We will use the figures for easyJet and IAG for the vertical analysis of the income statement. IAG was established after the acquisitions of the Spanish airline Iberia, British Airways and Vueling. Both IAG and easyJet's main activities are air transport, and they both buy externally airline-related services like catering and handling. Therefore, they use both much more industry-specific line items in their income statement.

Table 31.4 presents the common size analysis of the operating costs of IAG (financial period ending 31 December 2014) and easyJet (financial period ending 30 September 2015).

TABLE 31.4 Common size analysis of the operational profit of IAG and easyJet

	IAG 100%		easyJet 100%
Transport revenue	100%	Transport revenue	100%
Other revenue	7%	Other revenue	1%
Operating costs	101%	Operating costs	86%
Fuel	31%	Fuel	26%
Staff	24%	Crew	10%
Engineering	6 %	Maintenance	4%
Selling costs	4%	Selling	2%
Handling, catering	10%	Airport charges	24%
Landing costs	8%	Navigation	7%
Leasing	3%	Leasing	2.4%
Depreciation, amortization	6%	Depreciation, amortization	3%
Property, plant, equipment, IT	5%		
Currency	1%	Other operating costs	6%
Operating result	5.4%	Operating result	14%

The first element we notice is that for every £100 of revenue, easyJet realizes £14 profit and IAG £5. Lower costs relative to revenue are one of the main reasons for this difference. These figures confirm that easyJet is a low-cost airline, but low-cost strategy does not imply lower earnings. The vertical analysis shows some interesting differences. First, the fuel costs consume 26 per cent of easyJet's revenue, whereas for

IAG it is 30 per cent. This difference could be driven by a number of factors. For example, one airline uses much more fuel-efficient airplanes, or has substantially shorter distance flights with more take-offs and landings, or is less efficient in hedging future fuel prices. Second, another substantial difference is found with respect to the staff costs. It is possible that easyJet has recorded some staff costs under other line items or that indeed the cost per employee is much lower at easyJet.

Through common size statements of financial position, we are able to compare, on the one hand, the financing structure of different companies and, on the other, where they have invested these resources. So statement of financial position data provide information on the financing and investment policies of a company. The items on the statements of financial position of Lufthansa, IAG, easyJet and The Emirates Group will now be reformulated or regrouped so that the headings include similar items which are comparable (Table 31.5).

ACTIVITY 31.6

Go to the websites of IAG, Lufthansa, easyJet and The Emirates Group and look at all line items presented on the statements of financial position. You will notice that they cannot be used immediately for inter-firm comparability purposes. You need to reconcile the four financial statements into one particular presentation format with line items that allow comparability. How would you start this job?

Activity feedback

In order to choose such a format, it might be helpful to look at IAS 1 and the information to be presented in the statement of financial position (para. 54). One might assume that this has also been the starting point for companies preparing their financial statements in compliance with IFRS. You will notice that Lufthansa uses many more line items in its statement of financial position

than the other airline groups. The line items presented by Lufthansa are often a disaggregation of an item like property, plant and equipment. By aggregating these line items, one arrives at a comparable amount with the other companies. You will also notice that line items are sometimes unique to a particular company. When the amount is small, you can always add it onto another similar amount. When the amount is more material, you could choose to present that amount separately. This is the decision we take for the pension assets presented on the statement of financial position of IAG. You will also notice that some line items are specific to a particular industry. An example for the airline industry is the line item 'unearned flight revenue', which is presented under the current liabilities. The airline has already received the payment for the ticket, but the airline will transport the passenger during the next financial period.

When we compare the structure of the assets of the airline groups, we notice that IAG, Lufthansa and easyJet have around 70 per cent of their assets tied up in non-current assets. The largest of these non-current assets are property, plant and equipment, which comprise the owned aircraft and the aircraft held under financial lease agreements (IAS 17 still applies to that financial period). Planes operated under an operating lease contract are not shown on the statement of financial position, but the annual payments are reported as single line items on the statement of comprehensive income (see vertical analysis of the statement of comprehensive income of IAG and easyJet). The Emirates Group has fewer assets tied up in non-current assets, and we notice that the intangible assets make up half of these non-current assets. Whereas IAG has a pension asset, Lufthansa has a substantial pension provision on its balance sheet. This difference shows the traditional preference for German companies to fund their pension promises internally.

If we consider the current assets, we observe that IAG (+/−20 per cent), easyJet (+/−20 per cent) and The Emirates Group (+/−30 per cent) have a lot of resources tied up in cash or investments. Lufthansa has 10 per cent tied up in these assets.

TABLE 31.5   Common size analysis of group statement of financial position in %

	IAG	Emirates	Lufthansa	easyJet
	31/12/2014	31/3/2015	31/12/2014	30/9/2015
Total non-current assets	68.59	43.73	72.93	73.50
Intangible assets	10.30	22.00	5.20	10.19
Tangible assets	49.82	15.58	55.01	59.79
Financial assets	0.01	4.39	4.00	—
Financial instruments	0.69	—	3.68	1.03
Tax asset	3.25	0.72	4.98	—
Other non-current assets	0.79	1.02	0.03	2.69
Pension assets	3.61	—	—	—
Total current assets	31.40	56.26	27.06	26.49
Inventory	1.79	0.96	2.29	—
Trade receivables	5.29	22.66	13.10	4.26
Financial instruments	0.75	—	1.49	2.65
Investments, securities	14.44	15.66	5.85	5.98
Liquid assets	6.46	16.55	3.12	13.58
Other current assets	2.58	—	0.88	—
Held for sale	0.07	—	0.29	—
Total assets	100.00	100.00	100.00	100.00
Total equity	16.03	50.30	13.22	46.58
Owners' equity	14.73	49.63	13.02	46.58
Minority interests	1.30	0.67	0.20	—
Total non-current liabilities	42.52	12.57	50.76	16.79
Financial liabilities	24.96	3.20	17.60	6.66
Financial instruments	1.51	—	2.35	2.09
Tax liability	1.17	1.20	—	3.73
Other non-current liabilities	0.95	1.66	4.31	0.90
Pension provision	5.59	—	23.72	—
Other provision	8.31	6.50	1.97	3.41
Total current liabilities	41.43	37.11	36.01	36.61
Trade payables	13.87	31.97	15.20	10.25
Unearned flight tickets	16.62	—	9.34	12.82
Financial liabilities	3.01	4.86	1.94	3.76
Financial instruments	5.55	—	2.51	7.62
Taxes	0.24	0.22	0.74	0.89
Provision	2.13	0.05	3.12	1.26
Other	—	—	3.11	—
Total equity and liabilities	100.00	100.00	100.00	100.00

Source: Annual reports of the International Airline Group (IAG = British Airways and Iberia), Lufthansa, easyJet and the Emirates Group.

With respect to the equity/liability side, we find that both easyJet and The Emirates Group are close to 50 per cent financed by equity. IAG and Lufthansa have a smaller equity base and are financed much more by liabilities. Whereas the share of the current liabilities is comparable for the four airlines, the non-current liabilities are an important financial source for IAG (40 per cent) and Lufthansa (50 per cent). However, we need to take into account that in the case of Lufthansa, almost half of the non-current liabilities are related to the pension provision.

ACTIVITY 31.7

Think of the ratios related to solvency discussed in Chapter 29. What does this vertical analysis of the equity/liability side of the statements of financial position of these airlines tell you?

Activity feedback

Lufthansa and IAG are much more leveraged than easyJet and The Emirates Group. As long as the return on their assets is higher than the interest cost, this leverage has a positive influence on the return on equity for the shareholders. However, if the opposite happens, return on equity will be negatively influenced.

Corporate strategic decisions determine the different business lines in which a company is active. The consolidated group accounts represent the overall performance of the different industries or businesses in which a company competes. Segmental information provides an overview of the different businesses and the proportion of each business unit in the total revenue and the results before interest and taxes (EBIT). A discussion on segmental reporting under IAS can be found in Chapter 24. In the next section, we illustrate how the use of segmental data could shed extra light on the analysis of a group's accounts.

SEGMENTAL ANALYSIS

Segmental reporting informs the user of the group accounts about the breakdown of the total revenue over the different business segments. To evaluate the breakdown of the operational costs in the common size analysis (see Tables 31.4 and 31.5) in a more meaningful way, the segmental data included in the accounts also need to be considered.

We learn from the segmental data that the business lines in which the airline companies are active, differ. For example, easyJet is almost exclusively active in the area of passenger transport. As well as passenger transport, other airline companies such as Lufthansa and Air France-KLM are also active in the area of aircraft maintenance, and Lufthansa is also active in catering and IT. The airline group, SAS, also has a large business segment 'hotels'. Therefore, the operating cost items in the income statement of Lufthansa are aggregated figures of different activities.

In the section on ratio analysis below, we compare the performance and financial position of Unilever and Nestlé. Although both companies are active in consumer business, the question of whether they are fully comparable needs to be raised (go to Appendices I and II at the end of this chapter and check their operating segments). If one consults the segmental data in the notes to the accounts of both companies, we notice that the information provided on the reportable segments is not comparable. Unilever opts for a geographical breakdown, whereas Nestlé combines geographical with product-based segments. The entity-wide disclosures on products provide some data which are useful for gaining an insight into the differences between the companies. We notice that a substantial part of Unilever's turnover does not result from food and beverages, but rather from personal care and home care products. Nestlé's turnover results mainly from food and beverages, apart from pharmaceutical products. A comparison of like things would focus on a comparison of the food and beverages activities of Nestlé and Unilever. In the section on ratio analysis, we compare the aggregated information disclosed in the annual accounts of the two groups.

After the IASB issued IFRS 8, *Operating Segments*, the inter-firm comparability of segmental data declined for several reasons. First, because the reportable segments follow the internal reporting documents (see Chapter 24 on IFRS 8), we end up with segments which can only be used with great difficulty for inter-firm comparisons. Second, since IFRS 8, the valuation rules for the presentation of segmental data can be the internal valuation rules instead of IFRSs. Under IAS 14, the predecessor to IFRS 8, segmental data had to be valued according to the IFRSs used in the preparation of the annual accounts. Segmental information disclosed under IAS 14 could therefore be used by external stakeholders for comparative analysis. The loss of this comparable information explains to a large extent why users of financial statements wrote so many comment letters when the exposure draft 'Operating Segments' was issued for comment by the IASB and why this topic generated a lot of attention in the post-implementation review.

Segmental reporting data may also be subject to manipulation. When a company plans for an IPO on a particular segment, there is an incentive to present increasing non-volatile results for that segment. On the other hand, if a company considers segmental data as proprietary data, which it does not want to disclose to the competition, then an incentive for manipulation will arise as well.

RATIO ANALYSIS

Financial statements identify a multitude of figures for us, for example profit before tax, gross profit, total of non-current assets, net current assets. As already mentioned, these figures do not mean very much unless we can compare them with something else. In previous sections of this chapter on techniques of financial analysis, we benchmarked the whole statement of financial position and statement of comprehensive income of a company against its own historical data (trend analysis) or against the data of other companies (common size statements of comprehensive income and common size statements of financial position) in order to be able to evaluate the overall performance. In Chapter 29, we discussed the technique of ratio analysis. This technique enables us to focus on specific questions concerning the financial situation of the company. We repeat the issues analyzed in Chapter 29 here, but in a broader context:

- Can the business meet its financial commitments? Can the business pay its debt? Is it liquid (financial status)?
- How successful is the business? Is it making a reasonable profit? Is it utilizing its assets to the fullest? Is it, in fact, profitable and efficient?

- Is the business a suitable investment for shareholders or would returns be greater if they invested elsewhere? Is it a good investment?

Items in the statement of comprehensive income or the statement of financial position related to these questions will be combined in a ratio to provide useful information to the user of the accounts for their decision making.

With ratios, we relate certain items of the statement of financial position and the statement of comprehensive income to each other in order to evaluate the financial status, performance or investment potential of a business.

Before starting with ratio analysis, one must always check the pitfalls which may hinder comparability of financial statement data. We discussed these pitfalls to a large extent in the first part of this chapter, so we will not repeat them here. As well as data from the airline industry, in this section on ratio analysis we will also use data from the annual accounts of two groups which specialize in consumer goods, namely Nestlé and Unilever. The main objective in including these accounts is to illustrate the different ratios which might be calculated on the basis of these financial statements, rather than compare the financial situation of the two multinationals, which have as similarities that they are recognizable worldwide and are active in consumer goods. Nestlé is active in the following business segments: beverages, milk products, nutrition and ice cream, prepared dishes, cooking aids, pet care, chocolate, confectionery and biscuits, and pharmaceutical products. Unilever is active in the following business segments: savoury and dressings, spread and cooking products, beverages, ice cream and frozen products, foods, and home and personal care products.

In Appendices I and II to this chapter, we include the statement of financial position, the statement of comprehensive income, cash flow statement and statement of changes in equity of both companies. With respect to Unilever, we also provide an extract of the notes in which information on the breakdown of the operating costs is provided. We observe that both companies still use the term 'balance sheet' to describe the presentation of their assets and liabilities and equity at the year end (financial statements 2012). IAS 1 now calls this statement the 'statement of financial position', but companies are still allowed to use the term 'balance sheet'. Both companies use the option of presenting the profit or the loss for the year in one statement for the presentation of the statement of comprehensive income. Then they add a second statement in which all revenues and costs that are charged directly to equity are presented. The amount of total comprehensive income represents the total of all costs and revenues which have been charged to equity in a direct way (through the statement of comprehensive income) or an indirect way (through the income statement). So far, all profitability ratios and EPS figures take only the result into account which is charged to equity through the income statement. When you carry out the activities, please notice the differences in presentation between the two companies.

We start with a discussion of the ratios which are helpful in assessing the following questions:

- How successful is the business?
- Is it making a reasonable profit?
- Is it utilizing its assets to the fullest?
- Is it in fact profitable and efficient?

We will pay attention to the characteristics of IAS accounts.

RATIO ANALYSIS AND THE IAS/IFRS ACCOUNTS

The IASB foresees a minimum content for the statement of financial position and the statement of comprehensive income.

In some countries, domestic GAAP prescribes extensive detailed layouts of the balance sheet and profit and loss account. The IASB did not opt for such an approach. When you look at the profit and loss account of Nestlé and compare it with the layout and the contents of the profit and loss account of Unilever, you will understand the consequence of the IASB's choice. With the approach of the IASB, the preparer of the annual accounts has more freedom with regards to presentation. In these circumstances, classification and presentation decisions may be used to create a certain impression. The user, however, is left with the task of reorganizing the information presented in order to try to achieve some comparability, before even ratio analysis or any other financial technique can be applied.

The issue of comparability relates not only to items on the face of the statement of financial position or the statement of comprehensive income, which are presented under different headings, but also to items which are presented by one company in the notes where the other companies opt for a disclosure on the face of the statement of financial position.

In some countries, national GAAP prescribe the use of a specified layout with a specified number of items which must appear on the statement of financial position and the statement of comprehensive income. If an item is not present or does not apply to the company, the preparer must insert a zero or the words 'not available'. In relation to the IAS/IFRS solution, companies can disclose a certain item under another line item and hide the information from the public by not presenting that specific single line item on the face of the statement of financial position or the statement of comprehensive income. Under IAS/IFRS, a number of items must be recognized in the equity account without influencing the profit or loss reported in the income statement. In relation to other items (e.g. actuarial gains and losses, and past service costs in relation to pension plans), companies have a choice. We need to consider the choices made by companies in order to compare ratios between companies.

IASB mixed valuation model

In the early years, the IASC opted for the historical cost model. In recent years, the fair value approach gained more ground, especially in the later IASs and new IFRS. Adaptations were also made to early IASs in order to allow for revaluations of asset items. As a result, companies often have a choice between the historical cost model and the fair value model. A user of the accounts must be aware of the difference. Ideally, a company would provide the two values (historical cost and fair value) so that users of the accounts could carry out a reconciliation of the asset values in order to improve comparability. The only assets for which both measurements can be found in the financial statements are investment properties.

Performance of the firm

Ratios which try to give a picture of a firm's profitability combine the result with the investments made for the generation of that result. The two most common ratios are return on equity (ROE) and return on assets (ROA).

$$(ROE) = Profit/Equity$$

The profit figure used in this ratio can be before or after tax. In the case of group accounts, one has to make sure that if the minority interests are not added in to the equity of the group, the share in the profit of the company of the minority interests should be excluded from the profit in the numerator as well. Besides ROE, another widely used profitability ratio is ROA:

$$(ROA) = (Profit\ before\ tax + Interest)/Total\ assets$$

Instead of using the total assets in the denumerator, net total assets can be used. The net assets are equal to the equity of the company and the long-term debts. This ratio is also often called return on capital employed (ROCE) or return of net total assets:

$$(ROCE) = (Profit\ before\ tax + Long\text{-}term\ interest)$$
$$/(Equity\ Long\text{-}term\ debt)$$

Applicable to the calculation of all performance ratios, ROA, ROE and ROCE, is the question of with which investment base one should compare the result: investment base at the beginning of the year or an average equity base. In practice, very often the equity base at the end of the year is taken. If data are available for only one year, then there is not much choice.

In order to determine whether the profit obtained is sufficient or excellent, one needs a benchmark. Suitable benchmarks for these ratios, besides the time series data and competitor or industry data, could be the proceeds of an investment in risk-free loans. The latter would answer the question: Would the owners be better off selling the business and placing the proceeds in a bank deposit account?

ACTIVITY 31.8

Calculate the ROA and the ROE of Nestlé and Unilever. Evaluate what the difference between the outcome of the ratios will be according to the different investment bases used [investment base at the beginning of the year (= t – 1) and investment base at the end of the year (= t)]. Compare also the difference of an ROE where minority interests (MI) are included with an ROE where minority interests excluded. We calculate the ROE after tax.

Activity feedback

	Nestlé		Unilever	
ROA_{t-1}	$\dfrac{19\ 043}{120\ 442}$	15.81%	$\dfrac{8\ 146}{45\ 513}$	17.89%
ROA_t	$\dfrac{19\ 043}{133\ 450}$	14.26%	$\dfrac{8\ 146}{48\ 027}$	16.96%
ROE_t	$\dfrac{14\ 904}{64\ 139}$	23.23%	$\dfrac{5\ 515}{14\ 815}$	37.22%
ROE_t with MI	$\dfrac{14\ 904}{71\ 884}$	20.73%	$\dfrac{5\ 515}{14\ 263}$	38.66%
ROE_t without MI	$\dfrac{14\ 456}{70\ 130}$	20.61%	$\dfrac{5\ 171}{13\ 651}$	37.88%

If we compare the profitability ratios of the two companies, we notice that the ROAs are much closer to each other than the ROE. So with respect to the return on total assets, the companies perform in a rather similar way. The difference with regard to ROE is caused by the higher leverage of Unilever (see Activity 31.14) and therefore Unilever is able to realize a larger improvement between ROA and ROE than Nestlé. The leverage of a firm is the result of a financing decision taken by top management on the use of different financial sources by the company (equity versus debt). However, this positive effect of higher ROE results in Unilever scoring higher on the ratios presenting financial risk (see later in this section). When a company is making profit, then ROA and ROE are always lower if the investment base at the end of the year is taken.

The return on total assets can be calculated at corporate level, if the information is available on the level of the operating segments through segmental disclosure; the profitability of the reportable segments can be calculated as well.

The ratios calculated above are the traditional performance ratios calculated on the basis of the profit or loss reported by the company. This type of performance measurement has existed for more than a century. More recently, the concept of other comprehensive income (OCI) was introduced. In addition, in recent years the number of components to be included in OCI increased. Moreover, also the concept of reporting OCI with recycling through the income statement was introduced. So within OCI, we can distinguish items which will be recycled one day through profit or loss and items that will never be recycled through profit or loss. Revaluations of property, plant and equipment and intangibles or actuarial gains and losses on employee benefits are examples of items that will never be recycled through profit or loss. Other items of OCI will be recycled back into income after the occurrence of a specified event or transaction, and then they will influence profit or loss. With respect to whether or not an item is recycled, the choice seems to have been made more ad hoc by the IASB rather than being based on a theory. Stakeholders in the financial reporting process (see EFRAG's report in 2006 'What (if anything) is wrong with the good old income statement?) are still struggling with the concept of OCI and its interpretation. Academic research reveals the problems with it (Rees and Shane, 2012; Brouwer et al., 2014; Mechelli and Cimini, 2014). The critique focuses on the lack of a satisfactory definition of earnings that can differentiate it from OCI. Looking at the differences between earnings and OCI might be that earnings relate more to the core elements of the business and OCI more to elements over which the management of the business has less direct influence (Rees and Shane, 2012). Evidence is available that both sophisticated and unsophisticated users of financial information are better able to extract information about comprehensive income items that are not recycled than about comprehensive income items that get recycled at a later period. According to Tarca et al. (2008), these results show that recycling increases the complexity in the accounting system and hinders users' ability to extract information.

The importance of OCI and its components differs across industries and across companies. In particular, those industries and companies that have a lot of financial instruments, operations in foreign currencies and large pension liabilities might have larger amounts in OCI.

If we take total comprehensive income of Nestlé and Unilever and calculate ROA and ROE using total assets and total equity at the end of the reporting period, we end up with the following figures:

	Nestlé	**Unilever**
ROA	17 576/133 450 = 13.7	4 655/48 027= 9.69
ROE	16 804/71 884 = 23.37	4 155/14 263 = 29.13

For both companies, OCI is negative. The most important items for both companies are the losses on the pension schemes and the foreign currency translations.

To retrieve information on operating decisions and investment decisions, the profitability ratio ROA can be broken down further by relating results to sales and sales to the investment base:

$$ROA = \frac{Profit}{Total\ sales} \times \frac{Total\ sales}{Assets}$$

The first ratio (profit/total sales) is called the profit margin ratio, which expresses the result in a currency generated by each currency unit of sales. This ratio focuses on profitability and is a result of the operating decisions taken by management. The second ratio (total sales/assets) focuses on efficiency and provides information on investment decisions and how efficiently these investments are used.

An analysis of the different cost components in relation to the sales figures could reveal interesting differences between companies. If costs are classified in the statement of comprehensive income according to their function, then the following ratios could be calculated:

- cost of sales/sales
- marketing and sales costs/sales
- distribution cost/sales
- administrative cost/sales.

ACTIVITY 31.9

Recent accounting developments

Which 'profit' is the most meaningful to be combined with sales in the ratio (profit/total sales)? Look at the statements of comprehensive income of Unilever and Nestlé.

Activity feedback

There is the choice between the operating result and the net result of the company. The operating result is related directly to the sales, whereas the net result is also influenced by financing activities. So the most obvious choice is the operating result. If the net result is used, then the combination with the asset turnover (total sales/assets) results in the ROA figure again.

ACTIVITY 31.10

Calculate the profit margin and asset turnover ratios for Nestlé and Unilever.

Activity feedback

	Nestlé		**Unilever**	
Profit margin	$\frac{10\ 905}{91\ 612}$	11.90%	$\frac{7\ 980}{48\ 436}$	16.47%
Asset turnover	$\frac{91\ 612}{133\ 450}$	0.68	$\frac{48\ 436}{48\ 027}$	1.00

Although Nestlé and Unilever arrive at similar ROAs, there are small underlying differences. The product margins of Nestlé are lower than those of Unilever. Nestlé's turnover of total assets is higher than Unilever's.

In the section on industry analysis in Chapter 30, we discussed factors influencing the pricing policy of a company and those influencing the cost levels. Sales price levels and cost levels together determine the profit margin. Asset turnover is often influenced by the type of products in the company's inventory (e.g. perishable goods).

ACTIVITY 31.11

Try to calculate the ratios for cost of sales/sales, marketing and sales cost/sales, distribution cost/sales and administrative cost/sales for the two groups. What do you observe? Nestlé discloses these cost items on the face of the income statement. With regard to Unilever, however, these items are disclosed in the notes. Note 3 informs us that the cost of goods sold is €28 387 million; however €3 079 million of distribution costs are included. Note 3 of the accounts of Unilever further reveals that the selling and administrative costs are €12 069 million. Marketing costs are included in the selling and administrative expenses and are €7 166 million, but R&D is also included in the same line item and those costs amount to €955 million.

Activity feedback

The layouts of the statements of comprehensive income are different and for Unilever the information is not on the

face of this statement, but is found in the notes. The two companies make a different subdivision so that the individual components cannot be compared. For comparative purposes, we use the cost of goods sold for Nestlé of 47 553 and for Unilever of 25 308. We have added up distribution costs, marketing costs and selling and administrative costs, which total 27 868 for Nestlé and 14 193 for Unilever:

	Nestlé	Unilever
Cost of goods sold/ sales	51.90%	52.25%
Marketing, sales, distribution and administrative costs\sales	30.41%	29.30%

The figures confirm what is generally known: these companies spend a lot of money on marketing and sales costs.

The information obtained from these ratios, which relate the different cost components to the sales figure, can also be obtained from a common size analysis of the statement of comprehensive income. See, for example, the common size analysis of the operating cost items of the airlines in Table 31.4.

The next group of ratios to be examined concentrates on the investment decisions and how effectively these assets in which the firm has invested are used. The performance of a firm is influenced not only by the profit margin obtained on its products or services but also by the effectiveness of its operations. The turnover of assets can be regarded as an efficiency ratio, but it is one of a very general nature. Non-current as well as current assets are included in the overall ratio total sales/total assets. With regards to efficiency, the short-term elements are the centre of attention, although in some industries the efficient use of the non-current assets is much more crucial.

The following ratios focus on the turnover of current assets.

Turnover of inventory The turnover of inventory is calculated as the 'cost of goods sold/inventory'. The average inventory level is used as denominator. The turnover of the inventory could also be expressed in days, when the ratio then becomes ((average inventory/cost of goods sold) × 365) (see Activity 31.12.)

Using the same ratio structure, the turnover of trade receivables and trade payables can be calculated, and the average collection or payment period. The following ratios provide that information (and see Activity 31.13):

- sales/trade receivables
- (trade receivables/sales) × 365
- purchases/trade payables
- (trade payables/purchases) × 365.

The outcome of these ratios is not only influenced by efficiency. They could be influenced by industry characteristics. Average collection periods are often determined by industry practice. Also, country influences can play a role.

The ratios concerning the trade payables can only be calculated if information on the purchases is provided in the annual accounts.

ACTIVITY 31.12

Calculate the inventory turnover and the number of inventory days for the Nestlé and Unilever.

Activity feedback

	Nestlé		**Unilever**	
Inventory turnover	$\dfrac{47\ 553}{8\ 777}$	5.41	$\dfrac{25\ 308.0}{4\ 052.5}$	6.24
Number of inventory days		67 days		58 days

These companies are very close to each other. One must be cautious because a higher turnover rate could be due either to more efficient inventory management or to the perishable nature of the products.

ACTIVITY 31.13

Calculate the trade receivables turnover and the collection period for Nestlé and Unilever.

Activity feedback

	Nestlé		**Unilever**	
Trade receivables turnover	$\dfrac{91\ 612}{12\ 832}$	7.13	$\dfrac{25\ 308}{4\ 930}$	5.13
Collection period		51 days		71 days

The usefulness of the ratios presented will differ between industries (e.g. a steel company versus a wholesale company).

Industry-specific ratios The ratio cost of goods sold/sales is more meaningful for companies active in consumer and industrial goods than for companies in a service industry, such as insurance companies and banks. Some industries have their own specific ratios (such as banks, insurance companies, airlines) which characterize the key drivers of performance in that specific industry. For the airline industry, such ratios are, for example, unit revenue or yield, which represent the average amount of traffic revenue per RPK/RPM or RTK/RTM. In this ratio, revenue passenger kilometres/miles (RPK/M) is defined as the number of paying passengers multiplied by the distance they are flown in kilometres/miles. Revenue tonne kilometres/miles (RTK/M) is defined as the number of tonnes of paid traffic (passengers, freight and mail) multiplied by the distance this traffic is flown in kilometres or miles.

These operating statistics or industry-specific key ratios are disclosed by companies on a voluntary basis. Industry practice is usually the driving force for this type of disclosure. This implies that the level of disclosure of these industry-specific ratios differs significantly between companies. The issue of quality of disclosure, which was discussed in Chapter 30, is relevant in this context. Further, it is essential to keep in mind that these operating statistics or ratios are presented in the non-audited part of the annual report. A proper comparison between companies based on these voluntary disclosed industry ratios is therefore not always possible and should be executed with great caution as it concerns non-audited data.

Financial status

In order to judge the financial situation of a firm, the external stakeholders want answers to questions such as: Can the business meet its financial commitments? Can the business pay its debts? Is it liquid? External stakeholders need information on the financial status of a company. It is essential for a business to be able to pay its debts as and when they fall due, otherwise its chances of remaining in operation become remote. For that purpose, there is a need to analyze the assets available to the company to meet its liabilities. This can be done in the short, medium and long term.

Short-term financial status or the liquidity of a firm. If we analyze the assets available in order to meet the short-term liabilities of the firm, we focus on the structure of the working capital of a company, namely the relation between current assets and current liabilities. The acid test ratio or quick ratio and the current ratio can be used for this purpose (see Activity 31.14).

$$\text{Current ratio} = \text{Current assets} / \text{Current liabilities}$$

$$\text{Acid test ratio} = (\text{Current assets} - \text{Inventory}) / \text{Current liabilities}$$

An analysis of the short-term liquidity uncovers a company's ability to pay or satisfy all short-term obligations as they fall due. The acid test ratio is a more conservative indicator of the short-term liquidity risk than the current ratio.

When you calculate current liabilities on the basis of IAS financial statements, you should always check whether long-term borrowings due within 12 months have been mentioned within non-current liabilities. If a company fully complies with IAS 1 and includes this amount of long-term borrowing due within 12 months under non-current debt, then this implies that there is already a refinance agreement for those amounts (IAS 1) and, as such, those amounts are not 'economically speaking' due within 12 months. For the calculation of the above ratios, we have taken the amounts of current liabilities shown on the face of the statement of financial position.

Current assets are supposed to be converted into cash in the current operating cycle of the company. The higher the ratio, the more resources a company has available to repay the short-term debts. In the acid test or quick ratio, inventory is excluded from the current assets as it is the least convertible item of the group. It is often observed that companies in distress keep production levels constant although their sales drop. If these companies use a full cost approach for inventory valuation purposes, then they are able to capitalize part of their overhead in a growing inventory amount. IAS/IFRS only allow the full cost approach for inventory valuation purposes (see Chapter 16). This improves comparability between the data published by firms complying with IAS/IFRS.

ACTIVITY 31.14

Calculate both current and acid test ratios for Nestlé and Unilever.

Activity feedback

	Nestlé		Unilever	
Current ratio	$\dfrac{33\ 961}{32\ 895}$	1.03	$\dfrac{12\ 347}{19\ 642}$	0.62
Acid test ratio	$\dfrac{24\ 789}{32\ 895}$	0.75	$\dfrac{8\ 179}{19\ 642}$	0.41

Unilever has a lower current ratio, which implies that its suppliers are important providers of financial resources.

It is difficult to set absolute benchmarks for short-term liquidity ratios, as the level of the ratio is highly dependent on industry characteristics. So only companies from the same industry can serve as an appropriate benchmark in judging liquidity.

Long-term financial status The long-term financial status of a company refers to the ability of a company to meet its debts in the long run. A key element in this respect is the capital structure of the firm. Companies have two main sources of funds, namely debt and equity. Each has different well-known characteristics (e.g. fixed versus variable rewards, fixed repayment schedules versus repayment when the company liquidates). The financial risk or financial strength of a company is measured by ratios which relate debt to equity. The most commonly used ratio worldwide in this respect is the debt/equity ratio. A high debt/equity ratio implies higher financial risk, since a higher ratio points to higher interest charges and a wider exposure to possible interest changes. Further, debt needs to be repaid often at a fixed date irrespective of whether or not the company has sufficient funds available.

Several alterations can be made to the numerator and the denumerator of this ratio in relation to the focus of the analysis, e.g. debt/(equity + debt), long-term debt/equity.

Further, the debt/equity ratio could be influenced by national or institutional differences (see Chapter 2). In countries with a shareholder orientation, the debt/equity ratio will be lower than in countries with a credit orientation. Information on the financial risk of a company can be provided by the ratios and also by a common size analysis of the statement of financial position structure (see the section on common size analysis in this chapter) or by trend analysis with ratios as input data.

Ratio analysis and common size analysis are complementary techniques of analysis rather than substitutes.

ACTIVITY 31.15

Calculate debt/equity ratios for Nestlé and Unilever.

Activity feedback

	Nestlé		Unilever	
Debt/equity	$\dfrac{61\ 566}{71\ 884}$	0.85	$\dfrac{33\ 764}{14\ 263}$	2.36
Debt/equity + debt	$\dfrac{61\ 566}{133\ 450}$	0.46	$\dfrac{33\ 764}{48\ 027}$	0.70
Long-term debt/equity	$\dfrac{28\ 671}{71\ 884}$	0.39	$\dfrac{14\ 122}{14\ 263}$	0.99
Equity/debt + equity		0.53		0.29

Unilever is more financed through external debt, whereas Nestlé is financed to a large extent by equity. Unilever is able to increase its ROE substantially through this high leverage, as its ROA is above its cost of debt. However, this high leverage also implies that Unilever faces a higher financial risk than Nestlé. In order to know if it is a relatively high risk one needs to compare Unilever's data with all companies in the same industry.

The debt/equity ratio is often used in debt covenants. In Chapter 30, we discussed how a threat of a possible violation of the debt covenants could lead to annual accounts management. One ratio which tries to circumvent the effect of these practices of annual accounts management is the interest cover ratio. This ratio indicates the safety margin between profit and interest charges or the ratio shows how many times operating profit covers net financial expenses:

Interest cover ratio = Profit before interest and taxation / Net interest costs

ACTIVITY 31.16

Calculate the interest cover ratio for Nestlé and Unilever.

Activity feedback

	Nestlé		Unilever	
Interest cover ratio	$\dfrac{19\ 043}{772}$	24.66	$\dfrac{8\ 146}{500}$	16.29

Nestlé has a higher safety margin than Unilever and this is no surprise, since Unilever has a higher leverage. For the calculation of the net interest cost of Unilever, we eliminated the impact of the pension costs recorded under the finance costs in the income statement of Unilever.

The financial risk of a company is directly linked to its capital structure. A company with a high proportion of debt financing is highly leveraged. High financial leverage implies high risk. The debt/equity ratio is often used to gain an understanding of the leverage of the firm. Financial leverage influences the financial risk of a company and, further, it has an impact on the relationship between ROE and ROA. Whether or not ROE is bigger than ROA depends on two elements. First, the leverage of the company and second, the difference between ROA and the interest cost of the firm. The latter is often called the spread. If the obtained ROA is higher than the interest cost, a company can increase the level of ROE compared to ROA by switching from equity financing to debt financing. If, however, ROA is lower than the interest cost of the firm, the relation works in the opposite way. ROE will be lower than ROA and the difference will increase with higher leverage.

Up to now in this section on ratio analysis we have used ratios taken from other companies as benchmarks. Another possibility is to benchmark a ratio against its own historical performance within the same firm. In this type of analysis, trend analysis is combined with ratio analysis. The red flags of comparability should also be taken into account when interpreting the data.

Investment perspective

Potential investors in a company use different sets of information in order to decide whether to buy shares in a particular company. The question on their mind is whether the company is a worthwhile investment. When investors hold shares in a company, they continuously assess their investment. The decision to be taken is a 'hold' or 'sell' decision.

Although for these 'buy' or 'sell' decisions the ratios on the profitability, efficiency and financial status of a company provide useful information, specific ratios are developed with regard to this investment decision. These ratios focus on those elements which are specifically relevant for shareholders, namely the return obtained on their investment. This return can take the form of dividends or capital appreciation.

In Chapter 29, we presented a number of different ratios which could be used by investors to evaluate the profit potential of their investment. These ratios concentrated on the dividend performance of these companies (net dividend and dividend cover ratio), on the earnings potential of the investment (earnings per share) and on the evolution of the share price of those companies (price earnings ratio). The earnings per share ratio and the price earnings ratio have been discussed in Chapter 24.

These investment ratios are usually included and discussed in reports of financial analysts or reports of industry analysts. Investors and potential investors use the information contained in those reports to make buy, hold or sell decisions.

In order to illustrate these investor ratios, we present the EPS and ROE of four airlines based on their financial statements of 2005 and compare these with the price/earnings (PE) ratio taken from Davy European Transport and Leisure Report 2006; see Ryanair website).

	Basic EPS	Diluted EPS	PE	ROE
Air France/KLM	€3.25	€3.25	11.6	11%
British Airways	40.4p	39.8p	10.0	24%
Lufthansa	€0.95	€0.95	23.0	10.4%
Ryanair	€40.00	€39.74	20.0	15.3%

What did these figures mean at that time?

At the time the report was made, the market wanted to pay 20 times the EPS of Ryanair and Lufthansa, whereas investors wanted to pay only 10 times the EPS of Air France-KLM and British Airways. Further, we observe that there is not exactly a link between ROE and PE. This is because in the PE ratio much more information is included than in ROE, which is a historical measure. The appraisal by investors of opportunities for the company and the way in which top management can react to threats and opportunities in the market, all influence the share price and, as a result, the PE ratio. On the other hand, PE ratio of 10 for British Airways and Air France-KLM could also mean that these companies were undervalued at the time of the report.

Companies try to influence the share price not only by providing those accounting numbers to the market which the market appreciates (see Chapter 30) but also by providing information to the market outside the financial statements. Conference calls and financial analysts' presentations have become a 'classic' means of communicating with the investor community, as well as putting information on the website of the company. Very often, the company management stresses more the non-GAAP or pro-forma earnings which suit their message better. In addition to the traditional financial statement data, information on key indicators, which are representative of the strategy and activities of the company, are presented.

Limitations of ratio analysis

The limitations of ratio analysis also apply to analysis of financial statements in general. We have already discussed items such as changes in environment, absence of comparable data and different accounting policies which may limit the usefulness of the information resulting from ratio analysis, horizontal analysis or common size analysis. In this section, we point out a few more limitations.

Non-monetary factors Non-monetary factors are not reflected in financial statements. Thus, factors such as the quality of the product or service are not reflected, neither is whether labour relations are good or bad. In the section on disclosure of non-financial data, we will see how companies are trying to overcome this lack of information. More and more non-financial indicators of performance are being introduced into annual reports.

Historical cost accounting The historical nature of accounts must always be borne in mind, as our interpretation of the business is based on this historical information. But this may not be the best guide to the future performance, financial status and investment potential. However, with recent evolutions in IAS/IFRS and US GAAP, the impact of historical cost accounting might diminish in the coming years.

ACTIVITY 31.17

The following sales figures are available for David plc:

	X0	X1
	£000	£000
	700	800

The price of goods sold was subject to an increase of 10 per cent at the beginning of X1. What is the magnitude of the increase in the volume of trade?

Activity feedback

Sales have increased by £100 000 from X0 to X1, but £70 000 of this is due to the price increase, i.e. inflation in the price of goods sold. Volume of sales has only increased by £30 000, which is 4 per cent not 14 per cent.

Short-term fluctuations Ratio analysis does not identify short-term fluctuations within one year in assets and liabilities, as our appraisal is based on a statement of financial position which provides values of assets and liabilities as at a specific point in time. By using these year-end figures, for example, we may present a better view of liquidity than has been the case throughout the year.

Changes in the value of money We all know how inflation can affect the value of the euro, pound, dollar or yen in our pocket and this is no different for a business. In fact, inflation and price changes could render the whole of our ratio analysis invalid. Short-term fluctuations are better reflected in interim reports.

Multivariate analysis

The ratio analysis we have considered so far is of a univariate type. This is where one ratio is considered at a time and then all ratios, once calculated, are assessed together and the analyst makes a considered judgement on the state of the entity. By way of contrast, multivariate analysis combines some of the ratios together in a specified manner by applying weightings to each of the ratios. The result is an index number that is compared to previous years, other companies and industrial averages. Multivariate analysis has been widely used in predicting corporate failure. In 1968, Altman combined five ratios to produce what he named a Z score:

$Z = 0.012X1 + 0.014X2 + 0.033X3 + 0.006X4 + 0.999X5$
$X1$ = Working capital/Total assets
$X2$ = Retained earnings/Total assets
$X3$ = Earnings before interest and tax/Total assets
$X4$ = Market capitalization/Book value of debt
$X5$ = Sales/Total assets

In his seminal article (Altman, 1968), companies with Z scores above 2.99 had not failed whereas those companies with a Z score below 1.81 had. His research was undertaken in the US manufacturing sector. In the context of this type of multivariate analysis, it is important to remember that results of such analyses in relation to the economic health of a company must be used with extreme caution. The results of these multivariate analyses are only valid for companies located in the same region, active in the same industry and existing more or less in the same time period. The reasons for this limited application are that national environments influence reporting practices (see Chapter 2), the economic climate changes constantly and the value of ratios is influenced by industry characteristics.

Another internationally well-known model is that of Taffler. This group carried out similar work in the UK, but they have not published the details of this as it is used as a working model and they need to retain the commercial interest. What we do know about the model are the ratios included:

$Z = c_0 + c_1 X1 + c_2 X2 + c_3 X3 + c_4 X4$
$X1$ = Profit before tax/Current assets
$X2$ = Current assets/Current liabilities
$X3$ = Current liabilities/Total assets
$X4$ = Length of time which the company can continue to finance its operations using its own assets with no revenue inflow.

The usefulness of these models is, unfortunately, still often limited to the region from which the company data were taken for the estimation procedure. Our view is that the use of several ratios with additional information (such as trend, common size, industry and accounting analysis) and a good deal of common sense should enable you to make a reasonable assessment of a company's financial status, performance, potential and position in the market. The multivariate models used the individual ratios as input without making a proper assessment of the quality and typical characteristics of the data.

DISCLOSURE OF NON-FINANCIAL DATA

A company's short- and long-term performance are influenced by several factors which are called in the literature drivers of performance or drivers of value creation. These drivers relate to elements such as customer satisfaction, internal organization of the business processes, the quality and service of the products or the innovation capability of the firm. In the last two decades of the twentieth century, these drivers of performance started to play a much more prominent role in the management control systems of companies. Internal performance evaluation systems within companies are now built around financial as well as non-financial performance indicators. Many of these indicators are chosen because they are the drivers of future value creation. The most well-known scorecard in which financial indicators are combined with non-financial indicators is the balanced scorecard, a normative concept developed by Kaplan and Norton (1992).

Since elements such as customer satisfaction, innovative capabilities and organizational efficiency are key drivers of performance in the long run, information on these value drivers or performance drivers is also interesting for external users of annual accounts. These indicators might help external users to forecast future performance.

Over recent years, we have observed that companies which have non-financial indicators available in their internal management information systems also include them in their annual reports. The information on non-financial key drivers for success is always included in the narrative or descriptive part of the annual report and is therefore unaudited.

Since these non-financial data became integrated into a number of annual reports, the academic community has started to research the information content of this information. The focus of the research relates to the content of the non-financial data and to the predictive value of this data or what is called the value relevance of the data (e.g. Amir and Lev, 1996; Ittner and Larcker, 2001). Research results so far show that non-financial data are complementary to financial data and the value relevance of financial accounting data continues. Further (using customer satisfaction data), Ittner and Larcker obtained evidence that non-financial data have predictive value, but the relationship is non-linear.

The communication of information additional to the statement of financial position, the statement of comprehensive income, the changes in equity and the notes to the accounts was discussed in Chapter 11. Most popular these days are additional statements on corporate social responsibility, sustainability and the environmental policy of the company, product information and market growth. Very often, this information is bundled in a sustainability report. These additional reports contain interesting information to relate to the annual report. However, one must keep in mind that this information is unaudited. In order to provide some guidance on this extra information, the IASB has looked at the disclosure of management information in annual accounts with its ED on Management Commentary, which will lead to a guidance on this issue in the near future.

Listed companies provide a lot of information on their websites. Interesting data can be found in the presentations made to financial analysts, which companies usually post on their website among other information for investors. However, one has to bear in mind that the information provided is unaudited and that companies often use pro-forma financial data in those presentations. In these pro-forma financial data, companies undo the impact of some accounting Standards and use their own valuation rules.

CASH FLOW STATEMENT

The cash flow statement, its preparation and its contents were discussed in Chapter 23. Cash flow information helps the external user to gain an understanding of whether a company is able to generate net positive cash flows. To be able to sort out the different origins of cash, the cash flows are divided into three groups in the cash flow statement, namely cash flow from operating activities, cash flow from investment activities and cash flow from financing activities.

Studying cash flow data, users of this statement want to know, in the first instance, if a company can generate cash from its operations. In the second instance, the analyst will try to find out whether this internally generated cash is sufficient to finance the investments of the company or whether the firm needs to rely on external borrowing or an equity increase. The relations between the three components of cash flow will differ according to the financial status of the company. The cash flow patterns in a fast-growing company will differ from those of a company in distress. In companies in distress, the cash flow generated from operating activities is often negative. This negative cash flow can be compensated for by a disposal of assets and borrowing extra funds from creditors or from an increase in capital. Fast-growing companies might generate a positive operational cash flow or even a negative cash flow. In most cases, the operational cash flow is not enough to finance growth. Therefore, these fast growers have to rely on additional external financing either from creditors or from an increase in capital from shareholders. These parties will provide the necessary funds since the prospects of a fast grower look much more promising than the prospect of a company in distress.

Although you might have the impression that comparability issues are less important with cash flow data, you still need to be alert to differences. For example, dividends, taxation and interest can be presented differently by companies. Further, you have to be sure that the bottom line represents an increase or decrease in cash and cash equivalents available in the company. Sometimes the bottom line is working capital movements.

Based on cash flow information, a number of ratios providing insights into a company's liquidity position can be calculated. They are complementary to the current ratio, the acid test ratio and the solvency ratios. First, we can substitute the current assets in the numerator of the current ratio with the figure 'cash flow from operations'. Through this substitution, we avoid the convertibility-to-cash problem of current assets. The current ratio then becomes:

Cash flow to short-term debt: Cash flow from operations / current liabilities

Similar to the cash flow to short-term debt ratio, we can calculate the cash flow to debt ratio. This ratio calculates the coverage of the repayment of the debt (interest expenses or other costs are not taken into account in this calculation) by the current cash flow of the company.

Cash flow to debt: Cash flow from operations / total debt

The interest cover ratio uses EBIT in the numerator. This amount is influenced by accruals items. As an alternative, we can calculate this interest cover ratio by substituting EBIT with cash flow from operations.

Interest cover ratio (cash) = cash flow from operations / net finance expense

A ratio which shows the proportion of investments a company is able to fund through its own operations is shown below:

Capital expenditure ratio = cash flow from operations / investments

This ratio provides an idea of a firm's long-term risk.

ACTIVITY 31.18

Calculate these ratios based on the cash flow information included in the statements of cash flow of Nestlé and Unilever.

Activity feedback

	Nestlé In million €	Unilever In million €
Cash flow to short-term debt	14 700 / 32 895 = 0.44	5 543 / 19 642 = 0.28
Cash flow to debt	14 700 / 61 566 = 0.23	5 543 / 33 764 = 0.16
Interest cover ratio (cash)	14 700 / 772 = 19.04	5 543 / 500 = 11.08
Capital expenditure ratio	14 700 / 3 072 = 4.78	5 543 / 341 = 16.25

From Chapter 30 we know that information provided through the statement of financial position and the statement of comprehensive income might be biased or distorted through annual accounts management (accounting method choices, changes in accounting estimates or real transactions). It is believed that in situations where large accruals are recorded, cash flow information gives a more reliable picture of the performance of the firm than the result reported in the statement of comprehensive income. However, the usefulness of cash flow information in general and in relation to undoing the effect of accrual accounting varies from firm to firm (empirical evidence can be found in Dechow, 1994). Cash flow figures can be influenced by real decisions. Further, clarification and presentation decisions can be made in order to give the impression of a healthy operating cash flow. So in order to make a proper assessment about the economic situation and performance of a company, data from the statement of financial position, the statement of comprehensive income, the notes and the cash flow statement should always be combined. This is often called the cash flow check. The most important techniques of financial analysis have now been discussed with the discussion on the analysis of the cash flow statement.

The financial statements of Nestlé 2014

Consolidated income statement for the year ended 31 December 2014

In millions of CHF	Notes	2014	2013
Sales	3	**91 612**	**92 158**
Other revenue		253	215
Cost of goods sold		(47 553)	(48 111)
Distribution expenses		(8 217)	(8 156)
Marketing and administration expenses		(19 651)	(19 711)
Research and development costs		(1 628)	(1 503)
Other trading income	4	110	120
Other trading expenses	4	(907)	(965)
Trading operating profit	3	**14 019**	**14 047**
Other operating income	4	154	616
Oilier operating expenses	4	(3 268)	(1 595)
Operating profit		**10 905**	**13 068**
Financial income	5	135	219
Financial expense	5	(772)	(850)
Profit before taxes, associates and joint ventures		**10 268**	**12 437**
Taxes	14	(3 367)	(3 256)
Income from associates and joint ventures	15	8 003	1 264
Profit for the year		**14 904**	**10 445**
of which attributable to non-controlling interests		448	430
of which attributable to shareholders of the parent (Net profit)		14 456	10 015
As percentages of sales			
Trading operating profit		15.3%	15.2%
Profit for the year attributable to shareholders of the parent (Net profit)		15.8%	10.9%
Earnings per share (in CHF)			
Basic earnings per share	16	4.54	3.14
Diluted earnings per share	16	4.52	3.13

Consolidated statement of comprehensive income for the year ended 31 December 2014

In millions of CHF	Notes	2014	2013
Profit for the year recognised in the income statement		**14 904**	**10 445**
Currency retranslations			
– Recognised in translation reserve		2 660	(3 160)
– Reclassified from translation reserve to income statement		1 003	214
Fair value adjustments on available-for-sale financial instruments			
– Recognised in fair value reserve		191	9
– Reclassified from fair value reserve to Income statement		(4)	(532)
Fair value adjustments on cash flow hedges			
– Recognised in hedging reserve		31	161
– Reclassified from hedging reserve		(87)	85
Taxes	14	5	290
Share of other comprehensive income of associates and joint ventures	15		
– Recognised in the reserves		83	40
– Reclassified from the reserves		(436)	–
Items that are or may be reclassified subsequently to the income statement		3 446	(2 893)
Remeasurement of defined benefit, plans	10	(1 745)	1 632
Taxes	14	352	(848)
Share of other comprehensive income of associates and joint ventures	15	(153)	47
Items that will never be reclassified to the income statement		(1 546)	831
Other comprehensive income for the year	18	**1 900**	**(2 062)**
Total comprehensive income for the year		**16 804**	**8 383**
of which attributable to non-controlling Interests		556	371
of which attributable to shareholders of the parent		16 248	8 012

Consolidated balance sheet as at 31 December 2014 before appropriations

In millions of CHF	Notes	2014	2013
Assets			
Current assets			
Cash and cash equivalents	13/17	7 448	6 415
Short-term investments	13	1 433	638
Inventories	6	9 172	8 382
Trade and other receivables	7/13	13 459	12 206
Prepayments and accrued income		565	762
Derivative assets	13	400	230
Current income tax assets		908	1 151
Assets held for sale	2	576	282
Total current assets		**33 961**	**30 066**
Non-current assets			
Property, plant and equipment	8	28 421	26 895
Goodwill	9	34 557	31 039
Intangible assets	9	19 800	12 673
Investments in associates and joint ventures	15	8 649	12 315
Financial assets	13	5 493	4 550
Employee benefits assets	10	383	537
Current income tax assets		128	124
Deferred tax assets	14	2 058	2 243
Total non-current assets		**99 489**	**90 376**
Total assets		**133 450**	**120 442**
Liabilities and equity			
Current liabilities			
Financial debt	13	8 810	11 380
Trade and other payables	13	17 437	16 072
Accruals and deferred income		3 759	3 185
Provisions	12	695	523
Derivative liabilities	13	757	381
Current income tax liabilities		1 264	1 276
Liabilities directly associated with assets held for sale	2	173	100
Total current liabilities		**32 895**	**32 917**
Non-current liabilities			
Financial debt	13	12 396	10 363
Employee benefits liabilities	10	8 081	6 279
Provisions	12	3 161	2 714
Deferred tax liabilities	14	3 191	2 643
Other payables	13	1 842	1 387
Total non-current liabilities		**28 671**	**23 386**
Total liabilities		**61 566**	**56 303**
Equity	18		
Share capital		322	322
Treasury shares		(3 918)	(2 196)
Translation reserve		(17 255)	(20 811)
Retained earnings and other reserves		90 981	85 260
Total equity attributable to shareholders of the parent		**70 130**	**62 575**
Non-controlling interests		1 754	1 564
Total equity		**71 884**	**64 139**
Total liabilities and equity		**133 450**	**120 442**

Consolidated cash flow statement for the year ended 31 December 2014

In millions of CHF	Notes	2014	2013
Operating activities			
Operating profit	17	10 905	13 068
Non-cash items of income and expense	17	6 323	4 352
Cash flow before changes in operating assets and liabilities		**17 228**	**17 420**
Decrease/(increase) in working capital	17	(114)	1 360
Variation of other operating assets and liabilities	17	85	(574)
Cash generated from operations		**17 199**	**18 206**
Net cash flows from treasury activities	17	(356)	(351)
Taxes paid		(2 859)	(3 520)
Dividends and interest from associates and joint ventures	15	716	657
Operating cash flow		**14 700**	**14 992**
investing activities			
Capital expenditure	8	(3 914)	(4 928)
Expenditure on intangible assets	9	(509)	(402)
Acquisition of businesses	2	(1 986)	(321)
Disposal of businesses	2	321	421
Investments (net of divestments) in associates and joint ventures [a]	15	3 958	(28)
Outflows from non-current treasury investments		(137)	(244)
Inflows from non-current treasury investments		255	2 644
Inflows/(outflows) from short-term treasury investments		(962)	400
Inflows from other investing activities [b]		294	1 273
Outflows from other investing activities		(392)	(421)
Cash flow from investing activities		**(3 072)**	**(1 606)**
Financing activities			
Dividend paid to shareholders of the parent	18	(6 863)	(6 552)
Dividends paid to non-controlling interests		(356)	(328)
Acquisition (net of disposal) of non-controlling interests		(49)	(337)
Purchase of treasury shares		(1 721)	(481)
Sale of treasury shares		104	60
Inflows from bonds and other non-current financial debt		2 202	3 814
Outflows from bonds and other non-current financial debt		(1 968)	(2 271)
Inflows/(outflows) from current financial debt		(1 985)	(6 063)
Cash flow from financing activities		**(10 637)**	**(12 158)**
Currency retranslations		42	(526)
Increase/(decrease) in cash and cash equivalents		**1 033**	**702**
Cash and cash equivalents at beginning of year		6 415	5 713
Cash and cash equivalents at end of year		**7 448**	**6 415**

(a) Mainly relates to the partial disposal of L'Oréal shares. The Group sold part of its shares to L'Oréal for a price of CHF 7342 million (see Note 15) in exchange for the remaining 50% stake in Galdorma for an equity value of CHF 3201 million (see Note 2) and cash of CHF 4141 million.
(b) In 2013 mainly relates to the disposal to Givaudan shares.

CONSOLIDATED STATEMENT OF CHANGES IN EQUITY
FOR THE YEAR ENDED 31 DECEMBER 2014

In millions of CHF

	Share capital	Treasury shares	Translation reserve	Retained earnings and other reserves	Total equity attributable to shareholders of the parent	Non-controlling interests	Total equity
Equity as at 31 December 2012	322	(2 078)	(17 924)	80 687	61 007	1 657	62 664
Profit for the year	—	—	—	10 015	10 015	430	10 445
Other comprehensive income for the year	—	—	(2 887)	884	(2 003)	(59)	(2 062)
Total comprehensive income for the year	—	—	(2 887)	10 899	8 012	371	8 383
Dividend paid to shareholders of the parent	—	—	—	(6 552)	(6 552)	—	(6 552)
Dividends paid to non-controlling interests	—	—	—	—	—	(328)	(328)
Movement of treasury shares	—	(612)	—	190	(422)		(422)
Equity compensation plans	—	214	—	(39)	175	—	175
Other transactions settled with treasury shares[a]	—	280	—	—	280	—	280
Changes in non-controlling interests	—	—	—	(297)	(297)	(136)	(433)
Total transactions with owners	—	(118)	—	(6 698)	(6 816)	(464)	(7 280)
Other movements[b]	—	—	—	372	372	—	372
Equity as at 31 December 2013	322	(2 196)	(20 811)	85 260	62 575	1 564	64 139
Profit for the year	—	—	—	14 456	14 456	448	14 904
Other comprehensive income for the year	—	—	3 556	(1 764)	1 792	108	1 900
Total comprehensive income for the year	—	—	3 556	12 692	16 248	556	16 804
Dividend paid to shareholders of the parent	—	—	—	(6 863)	(6 863)	—	(6 863)
Dividends paid to non-controlling interests	—	—	—	—	—	(356)	(356)
Movement of treasury shares	—	(1 943)	—	204	(1 739)	—	(1 739)
Equity compensation plans	—	221	—	(48)	173	—	173
Changes in non-controlling interests	—	—	—	(297)	(297)	(10)	(307)
Total transactions with owners	—	(1 722)	—	(7 004)	(8 726)	(366)	(9 092)
Other movements	—	—	—	33	33	—	33
Equity as at 31 December 2014	322	(3 918)	(17 255)	90 981	70 130	1 754	71 884

(a) The other transactions relate to the acquisition of a business (see Note 2).
(b) Relates mainly to the adjustment for hyperinflation in Venezuela, considered as a hyperinflationary economy.

3. Analyses by segment

3.1 OPERATING SEGMENTS REVENUE AND RESULTS

In millions of CHF — 2014

	Sales[a]	Trading operating profit	Net other trading income/(expenses)[b]	of which impairment[c]	of which restructuring costs	Impairment of good will
Zone Europe	15 175	2 327	(105)	(27)	(81)	—
Zone Americas	27 277	5 117	(316)	(59)	(59)	(1 835)
Zone Asia, Oceania and Africa	18 272	3 408	(110)	(11)	(31)	(52)
Nestlé Waters	7 390	714	(34)	(7)	(28)	(1)
Nestlé Nutrition	9 614	1 997	(105)	(45)	(13)	(4)
Other businesses[d]	13 884	2 654	(35)	(6)	(4)	(16)
Unallocated items[e]	—	(2 198)	(92)	(4)	(41)	—
Total	**91 612**	**14 019**	**(797)**	**(159)**	**(257)**	**(1 908)**

In millions of CHF — 2013[f]

	Sales[a]	Trading operating profit	Net other trading income/(expenses)[b]	of which impairment[c]	of which restructuring cost	Impairment of good will
Zone Europe	15 567	2 331	(115)	(33)	(54)	(2)
Zone Americas	28 358	5 162	(415)	(31)	(91)	—
Zone Asia, Oceania and Africa	18 851	3 562	(37)	(7)	(13)	—
Nestlé Waters	7 257	665	(24)	(11)	3	(5)
Nestlé Nutrition	9 826	1 961	(78)	(11)	(34)	(84)
Other businesses[d]	12 299	2 175	(67)	(43)	(18)	(23)
Unallocated items[e]	—	(1 809)	(109)	(7)	(67)	—
Total	**92 158**	**14 047**	**(846)**	**(143)**	**(274)**	**(114)**

(a) Inter-segment sales are not significant.

(b) Included in Trading operating profit.

(c) Impairment of properly, plant and equipment and intangible assets.

(d) Mainly Nespresso, Nestlé Professional, Nestlé Health Science and Nestlé Skin Health (renamed following the integration of Galdorma as from July 2014).

(e) Refer to the Segment reporting section of Note 1 – Accounting policies for the definition of unallocated items.

(f) 2013 comparatives have been restated following the transfer of responsibility for Nestea RTD businesses in geographic Zones to Nestlé Waters effective as from 1 January 2014.

Refer to Note 3.3 for the reconciliation from trading operating profit to profit before taxes, associates and joint ventures.

ASSETS AND OTHER INFORMATION

In millions of CHF 2014

	Segment assets	Of which goodwill and intangible assets	Capital additions	Of which capital expenditure	Depreciation and amortisation of segment assets
Zone Europe	11 308	2 050	749	747	(473)
Zone Americas	20 915	7 952	1 226	1 039	(681)
Zone Asia, Oceania and Africa	15 095	4 580	803	697	(510)
Nestlé Waters	6 202	1 569	327	308	(403)
Nestlé Nutrition	24 448	15 352	501	363	(330)
Other businesses[a]	21 345	13 295	10 399	573	(525)
Unallocated items[b]	11 892	9 559	258	187	(136)
Inter-segment eliminations	(1 928)	—	—	—	—
Total segments	**109 277**	**54 357**	**14 263**	**3 914**	**(3 058)**
Non-segment assets	24 173				
Total	**133 450**				

In millions of CHF 2013[c]

	Segment assets	of which goodwill and intangible assets	Capital additions	of which capital expenditure	Depreciation and amortisation of segment assets
Zone Europe	11 779	2 229	980	964	(517)
Zone Americas	21 243	9 058	1 134	1 019	(769)
Zone Asia, Oceania and Africa	14 165	4 284	1 279	1 280	(520)
Nestlé Waters	6 046	1 575	405	377	(442)
Nestlé Nutrition	22 517	14 089	562	430	(337)
Other businesses[a]	9 564	3 709	1 091	642	(437)
Unallocated Items[b]	11 060	8 768	293	216	(143)
Inter-segment eliminations	(2 021)	—	—	—	—
Total segments	**94 353**	**43 712**	**5 744**	**4 928**	**(3 165)**
Non-segment assets	26 089				
Total	**120 442**				

(a) Mainly Nespresso, Nestlé Professional, Nestlé Health Science and Nestlé Skin Health (renamed following the integration of Galdorma as from July 2014).
(b) Refer to the Segment reporting section of Note 1 – Accounting policies for the definition of unallocated items.
(c) 2013 comparatives have been restated following the transfer of responsibility for Nestea RTD businesses in geographic Zones to Nestlé Waters effective as from 1 January 2014.

3.2 PRODUCTS

REVENUE AND RESULTS

In millions of CHF   2014

	Sales	Trading operating profit	Net other trading Income/(expense)[c]	of which impairment[b]	of which Restructuring costs	Impairment of goodwill
Powdered and Liquid Beverages	20 302	4 685	(51)	(23)	(28)	(16)
Water	6 875	710	(34)	(7)	(27)	(1)
Milk products and Ice cream	16 743	2 701	(162)	(19)	(62)	(1 028)
Nutrition and Health Science[c]	13 046	2 723	(121)	(45)	(16)	(4)
Prepared dishes and cooking aids	13 538	1 808	(148)	(39)	(29)	(807)
Confectionery	9 769	1 344	(129)	(4)	(42)	(52)
PetCare	11 339	2 246	(60)	(18)	(12)	—
Unallocated Items[d]	—	(2 198)	(92)	(4)	(41)	—
Total	**91 612**	**14 019**	**(797)**	**(159)**	**(257)**	**(1 908)**

In millions of CHF   2013

	Sales	Trading operating profit	Net other trading Income/(expense)[a]	of which impairment[b]	of which Restructuring costs	Impairment of goodwill
Powdered and Liquid Beverages	20 495	4 649	(95)	(21)	(27)	—
Water	6 773	678	(21)	(9)	3	(5)
Milk products and Ice cream	17 357	2 632	(177)	(14)	(44)	—
Nutrition and Health Science[c]	11 840	2 228	(120)	(44)	(38)	(107)
Prepared dishes and cooking aids	14 171	1 876	(120)	(28)	(61)	—
Confectionery	10 283	1 630	(86)	(19)	(23)	—
PetCare	11 239	2 163	(117)	(1)	(17)	—
Unallocated items[d]	—	(1 809)	(109)	(7)	(67)	(2)
Total	**92 158**	**14 047**	**(845)**	**(143)**	**(274)**	**(114)**

(a) Included in Trading operating profit.

(b) Impairment of property, plant and equipment and intangible assets.

(c) Renamed following the integration of Galderma as from July 2014).

(d) Refer to the Segment reporting section of Note 1 – Accounting policies for the definition of unallocated items.

Refer to Note 3.3 for the reconciliation from trading operating profit to profit before taxes, associates and joint ventures.

ASSETS AND LIABILITIES

In millions of CHF	Assets	of which goodwill and intangible assets	Liabilities
			2014
Powdered and Liquid Beverages	11 599	648	4 790
Water	5 928	1 532	1 764
Milk products and Ice cream	14 387	4 874	3 818
Nutrition and Health Science [a]	32 245	21 578	4 325
Prepared dishes and cooking aids	13 220	6 099	2 934
Confectionery	7 860	1 964	2 561
PetCare	14 344	9 182	2 004
Unallocated items [b] and intra-group eliminations	1 179	2 176	(2 668)
Total	**100 762**	**48 053**	**19 528**

In millions of CHF	Assets	Of which goodwill and intangible assets	Liabilities
			2013
Powdered and Liquid Beverages	11 044	477	4 607
Water	6 209	1 621	1 747
Milk products and Ice cream	14 805	5 220	3 773
Nutrition and Health Science [a]	28 699	18 648	3 838
Prepared dishes and cooking aids	13 289	6 373	2 761
Confectionery	8 190	2 071	2 611
PetCare	14 064	9 185	1 819
Unallocated items [b] and intra-group eliminations	1 081	2 146	(2 821)
Total	**97 381**	**45 741**	**18 335**

(a) Renamed following the integration of Galderma as from July 2014).

(b) Refer to the Segment reporting section of Note 1 – Accounting policies for the definition of unallocated items.

3.3 Reconciliation from trading operating profit to profit before taxes, associates and joint ventures

In millions of CHF	2014	2013
Trading operating profit	14 019	14 047
Impairment of goodwill	(1 908)	(114)
Net other operating income/expenses) excluding impairment of goodwill	(1 206)	(865)
Operating profit	**10 905**	**13 068**
Net financial income/expense)	(637)	(631)
Profit before taxes, associates and joint ventures	**10 268**	**12 437**

3.4 Customers

There is no single customer amounting to 10% or more of Group's revenues.

3.5 Geography (top ten countries and Switzerland)

In millions of CHF	2014		2013	
	Sales	Non-current assets[a]	Sales	Non-current assets[b]
USA	23 489	15 028	23 334	15 161
Greater China Region	6 638	6 020	6 618	5 414
France	5 507	1 708	5 578	1 683
Brazil	5 117	1 186	5 116	1 057
Germany	3 340	1 556	3 321	1 598
United Kingdom	2 987	1 232	2 824	1 111
Mexico	2 960	796	3 179	697
Philippines	2 489	958	2 410	877
Italy	2 108	823	2 098	849
Canada	1 962	578	2 064	552
Switzerland[b]	1 566	4 616	1 512	2 846
Rest of the world and unallocated items	33 449	48 277	34 104	38 762
Total	**91 612**	**82 778**	**92 158**	**70 607**

(a) Relate to property, plant and equipment, intangible assets and goodwill.

(b) Country of domicile of Nestlé S.A.

The analysis of sales by geographic area is stated by customer location.

APPENDIX II

The financial statements of the Unilever Group 2014

CONSOLIDATED INCOME STATEMENT

for the year ended 31 December 2014

	Notes	€ million 2014	€ million 2013	€ million 2012
Turnover	2	**48 436**	49 797	51 324
Operating profit	2	**7 980**	7 517	6 977
After (charging)/crediting non-core items	3	**960**	501	(73)
Net finance costs	5	**(477)**	(530)	(535)
Finance income		**117**	103	136
Finance costs		**(500)**	(500)	(526)
Pensions and similar obligations		**(94)**	(133)	(145)
Share of net profit/(loss) of joint ventures and associates	11	**98**	113	105
Other income/(loss] from non-current investments		**45**	14	(14)
Profit before taxation	6A	**7 646**	7 114	6 533
Taxation		**(2 131)**	(1 851)	(1 697)
Net profit		**5 515**	5 263	4 836
Attributable to:				
Non-controlling interests		**344**	421	468
Shareholders' equity		**5 171**	4 842	4 368
Combined earnings per share	7			
Basic earnings per share (€)		**1.82**	1.71	1.54
Diluled earnings per share (€)		**1.79**	1.66	1.50

CONSOLIDATED STATEMENT OF COMPREHENSIVE INCOME

for the year ended 31 December 2014

	Notes	€ million 2014	€ million 2013	€ million 2012
Net profit		**5 515**	5 263	4 836
Other comprehensive income	6C			
Items that will not be reclassified to profit or loss:				
Remeasurement of defined benefit pension plans net of tax	15B	**(1 250)**	697	(497)
Items that may be reclassified subsequently to profit or loss:				
Currency retranslation gains/(losses) net of tax[a]	15B	**(25)**	(999)	(316)
Fair value gains/losses) on financial instruments net of tax	15B	**(85)**	106	(125)
Total comprehensive income		**4 155**	5 067	3 898
Attributable to:				
Non-controlling interests		**404**	339	444
Shareholders' equity		**3 751**	4 728	3 454

[a]Includes fair value gains/(losses) on net investment hedges and exchange differences in net investments in foreign operations of €412 million (2013: €(275) million; 2012: €(160) million.

FINANCIAL STATEMENTS UNILEVER GROUP (CONTINUED)

CONSOLIDATED BALANCE SHEET

As at 30 December 2014

	Notes	€ million 2014	€ million 2013
Assets			
Non-current assets			
Goodwill	9	**14642**	13917
Intangible assets	9	**7532**	6987
Property, plant and equipment	10	**10472**	9344
Pension asset for funded schemes in surplus	4B	**376**	991
Deferred tax assets	6B	**1286**	1084
Financial assets	17A	**715**	505
Other non-current assets	11	**657**	563
		35680	33391
Current assets			
Inventories	12	**4168**	3937
Trade and other current receivables	13	**5029**	4831
Current tax assets		**281**	217
Cash and cash equivalents	17A	**2151**	2285
Other financial assets	17A	**671**	760
Non-current assets held for sale	22	**47**	92
		12347	12122
Total assets		**48027**	45513
Liabilities			
Current liabilities			
Financial liabilities	15C	**5536**	4010
Trade payables and other current liabilities	14	**12606**	11735
Current tax liabilities		**1081**	1254
Provisions	19	**418**	379
Liabilities associated with assets held for sale	22	**1**	4
		19642	17382
Non-current liabilities	15C	**7186**	7491
Financial liabilities		**161**	145
Pensions and post-retirement healthcare liabilities:			
Funded schemes in deficit	4B	**2222**	1405
Unfunded schemes	48	**1725**	1563
Provisions	19	**916**	892
Deferred tax liabilities	6B	**1534**	1524
Other non-current liabilities	14	**378**	296
		14122	13316
Total liabilities		**33764**	30698
Equity			
Shareholders' equity			
Called up share capital	15A	**484**	484
Share premium account		**145**	138
Other reserves	15B	**(7538)**	(6746)
Retained profit		**20560**	20468
Shareholders' equity		**13651**	14344
Non-controlling interests		**612**	471
Total equity		**14263**	14815
Total liabilities and equity		**48027**	45513

CONSOLIDATED CASH FLOW STATEMENT

for the year ended 31 December 2014

	Notes	€ million 2014	€ million 2013	€ million 2012
Net profit		5515	5263	4836
Taxation		2131	1851	1697
Share of net profit of joint ventures/associates and other income/(loss) from non-current investments		(143)	(127)	(91)
Net finance costs	5	477	530	535
Operating profit		7980	7517	6977
Depreciation, amortisation and impairment		1432	1151	1199
Changes in working capital:		8	200	822
Inventories		(47)	168	(9)
Trade and other receivables		82	(917)	1
Trade payables and other liabilities		(27)	949	830
Pensions and similar obligations less payments		(364)	(383)	(369)
Provisions less payments		32	126	(43)
Elimination of (profits)/losses on disposals		(1460)	(725)	(236)
Non-cash charge for share-based compensation		188	228	153
Other adjustments		38	(15)	13
Cash flow from operating activities		7854	8099	8516
Income tax paid		(2311)	(1805)	(1680)
Net cash flow from operating activities		5543	6294	6836
Interest received		123	100	146
Purchase of intangible assets		(359)	(377)	(405)
Purchase of property, plant and equipment		(1893)	(1791)	(1975)
Disposal of property, plant and equipment		207	141	237
Acquisition of group companies, joint ventures and associates .		(313)	(142)	(133)
Disposal of group companies, joint ventures and associates		1741	1053	246
Acquisition of other non-current investments		(82)	(273)	(91)
Disposal of other non-current investments		69	302	88
Dividends from joint ventures, associates and other non-current investments		162	136	128
(Purchase)/sale of financial assets		4	(310)	1004
Net cash flow (used in)/from investing activities		(341)	(1161)	(755)
Dividends paid on ordinary share capital		(3189)	(2993)	(2699)
Interest and preference dividends paid		(521)	(511)	(506)
Acquisition of non-controlling interests		—	(2901)	—
Purchase of Estate shares	24	(880)	—	—
Net change in short-term borrowings		338	350	(870)
Additional financial liabilities		5174	4219	1441
Repayment of financial liabilities		(5305)	(3294)	(3565)
Capital element of finance lease rental payments		(16)	(11)	(15)
Other movements on treasury stock		(467)	24	48
Other financing activities		(324)	(273)	(456)
Net cash flow (used in)/from financing activities		(5190)	(5390)	(6622)
Net increase/decrease) In cash and cash equivalents		12	(257)	(541)
Cash and cash equivalents at the beginning of the year		2044	2217	2978
Effect of foreign exchange rate changes		(146)	84	(220)
Cash and cash equivalents at the end of the year	I7A	1910	2044	2217

NOTES TO THE CONSOLIDATED FINANCIAL STATEMENTS
UNILEVER GROUP (CONTINUED)

2. SEGMENT INFORMATION

SEGMENTAL REPORTING

Personal Care – including sales of skin care and hair care products, deodorants and oral care products.

Foods – including sales of soups, bouillons, sauces, snacks, mayonnaise, salad dressings, margarines and spreads.

Refreshment – including sales of ice cream, tea-based beverages and weight-management products.

Home Care – including sales of home care products, such as powders, liquids and capsules, soap bars and a wide range of cleaning products.

CORE OPERATING PROFIT

Core operating profit represents our measure of segment profit or loss as it is the primary measure used for the purpose of making decisions about allocating resources and assessing performance of segments. Core operating margin is calculated as core operating profit divided by turnover.

	Notes	€ million Personal Care	€ million Foods	€ million Refreshment	€ million Home Care	€ million Total
2014						
Turnover		17 739	12 361	9 172	9 164	48 436
Operating profit	3	3 259	3 607	538	576	7 980
Non-core items		66	(1 302)	273	3	(960)
Core operating profit		3 325	2 305	811	579	7 020
Share of net profit/(loss) of join! ventures and associates		(1)	3	96	—	98
Depreciation and amortization		307	257	371	192	1 127
Impairment and other non-cash charges[a][b]		198	122	393	100	813
2013 Turnover		18 056	13 426	9 369	8 946	49 797
Operating profit	3	3 078	3 064	851	524	7 517
Non-core items		128	(687)	5	53	(501)
Core operating profit		3 206	2 377	856	577	7 016
Share of net profit/(loss) of joint ventures and associates		5	9	96	3	113
Depreciation and amortisation		327	293	330	201	1 151
Impairment and other non-cash charges[b]		267	139	97	179	682
2012 Turnover		18 097	14 444	9 726	9 057	51 324
Operating profit	3	2 925	2 601	908	543	6 977
Non-core items		160	(73)	—	(14)	73
Core operating profit		3 085	2 528	908	529	7 050
Share of net profit/(loss) of joint ventures and associates		1	5	99	—	105
Depreciation and amortisation		336	311	340	212	1 199
Impairment and other non-cash charges[b]		189	141	106	128	564

[a]See note 3 for further information.
[b]other non-cash charges include charges to the income statement during the year in respect of the share-based compensation and provisions.

2. SEGMENT INFORMATION (CONTINUED)

Transactions between the Unilever Group's reportable segments are immaterial and are carried out on an arm's length basis. The Unilever Group is not reliant on revenues from transactions with any single external customer and does not receive 10% or more of its revenues from transactions with any single external customer.

Segment assets and liabilities are not provided because they are not received or reviewed by our chief operating decision-maker, which is the Unilever Leadership Executive (ULE) as explained in the Corporate Governance section.

2014	€ million Netherlands/ United Kingdom	€ million United States	€ million Others	€ million Total
Turnover	3851	6684	37901	48436
Non-current assets[c]	3921	7668	21714	33303
2013				
Turnover	3872	7084	38841	49797
Non-current assets[c]	3390	7626	19794	30810
2012				
Turnover	3980	7834	39510	51324
Non-current assets[c]	3353	8670	19676	31699

[c]Non-current assets excluding financial assets, deferred tax assets and pension assets for funded schemes in surplus.

No other country had turnover or non-current assets (as shown above) greater than 10% of the Group total.

ADDITIONAL INFORMATION BY GEOGRAPHIES

	€ million Asia/AMET/ RUB[d]	€ million The Americas	€ million Europe	€ million Total
2014	**19703**	**15514**	**13219**	**48436**
Turnover				
Operating profit	**2626**	**3233**	**2121**	**7980**
Non-core items	**(15)**	**(959)**	**14**	**(960)**
Core operating profit	**2611**	**2274**	**2135**	**7020**
Share of net profit/(loss) of Joint ventures and associates	**—**	**68**	**30**	**98**
2013	20085	16206	13506	49797
Turnover				
Operating profit	2765	2859	1893	7517
Non-core items	(85)	(542)	126	(501)
Core operating profit	2680	2317	2019	7016
Share of net profit/(loss) of joint ventures and associates	(1)	63	51	113
2012	20357	17088	13879	51324
Turnover				
Operating profit	2637	2432	1908	6977
Non-core items	30	(13)	56	73
Core operating profit	2667	2419	1964	7050
Share of net profit/(loss) of joint ventures and associates	(2)	68	39	105

[d]Refers to Asia, Africa, Middle East, Turkey, Russia, Ukraine and Belarus.

NOTES TO THE CONSOLIDATED FINANCIAL STATEMENTS
UNILEVER GROUP (CONTINUED)

3. GROSS PROFIT AND OPERATING COSTS

	€ million 2014	€ million 2013	€ million 2012
Turnover	**48 436**	49 797	51 324
Cost of sales[n]	**(28 387)**	(29 065)	(30 530)
of which: Distribution costs	**(3 079)**	(3 139)	(3 264)
Gross profit[a]	**20 049**	20 732	20 794
Selling and administrative expenses[d]	**(12 069)**	(13 215)	(13 817)
of which: Brand and Marketing Investment[a]	**(7 166)**	(7 383)	(7 311)
Research and Development	**(955)**	(1 040)	(1 003)
Operating profit	**7 980**	7 517	6 977

SUMMARY

External parties use financial statement data to obtain information on several aspects of a company, e.g. is the company liquid, can the company repay its debts, is the company performing well? Several techniques exist to extract information from the financial statements in order to answer those questions. One purpose of this chapter was to explain and illustrate these techniques (trend analysis, common size analysis, ratio analysis, segmental analysis and cash flow analysis). A common characteristic of all these techniques is that benchmarks (internal and external) with which to compare the company data are needed in order to have information valuable for decision-making purposes. A necessary condition for benchmarking is the comparability of data. As a result, the second purpose of this chapter was to point out and illustrate several pitfalls which might hinder the comparability of financial accounting data. If accounting analysis is combined with several techniques of financial analysis, external parties should be able to judge the performance and financial position of a company in a proper perspective.

EXERCISES

Suggested answers to exercises marked ✓ are to be found in the Student online resources, with suggested answers to the remaining questions available in the Instructor online resources.

1   You are the management accountant of Expand, a company incorporated in Dollarland. The company is seeking to grow by acquisition and has identified two potential investment opportunities. One of these, Hone, is also a company incorporated in Dollarland. The other, Over, is a company incorporated in Francland.

You have been presented with financial information relating to both companies. The financial information is extracted from their published financial statements. In both cases, the financial statements conform to domestic accounting Standards. The financial statements of Hone were drawn up in dollars while those of Over were drawn up in francs. The information relating to Over has been expressed in dollars by taking the figures in francs and dividing by 1.55 – the $/franc exchange rate at 31 December 20X1. The financial information is given below.

Income statements

Year ended	Hone		Over	
	31/3/20X2	31/3/20X1	31/12/20X1	31/12/20X0
	$ million	$ million	$ million	$ million
Revenue	600	550	620	560
Cost of sales	(300)	(250)	(320)	(260)
Gross profit	300	300	300	300
Other operating expenses	(120)	(105)	(90)	(85)
Profit from operations	180	195	210	215

Income statements

	31/3/20X2	31/3/20X1	31/12/20X1	31/12/20X0
Finance cost	(20)	(18)	(22)	(20)
Profit before tax	160	177	188	195
Income tax expense	(50)	(55)	(78)	(90)
Net profit for the period	110	122	110	105

Statements of changes in equity

Year ended	Hone		Over	
	31/3/20X2	31/3/20X1	31/12/20X1	31/12/20X0
	$ million	$ million	$ million	$ million
Balance brought forward	470	418	265	240
Net profit for the period	110	122	110	105
Dividends	(70)	(70)	(80)	(80)
Balance carried forward	510	470	295	265

Statements of financial position

	Hone		Over	
	31/3/20X2	31/3/20X1	31/12/ 20X1	31/12/20X0
	$ million	$ million	$ million	$ million
Non-current assets	600	570	455	440
Inventories	60	50	55	50
Trade receivables	80	75	90	80
Cash	10	20	15	15
	750	715	615	585
Issued share capital	150	150	110	110
Reserves	360	320	185	155
	510	470	295	265
Interest-bearing borrowings	150	150	240	240
Current liabilities	90	95	80	80
	750	715	615	585

Expand is more concerned with the profitability of potential investment opportunities than with liquidity. You have been asked to review the financial statements of Hone and Over with this concern in mind.

Required:

(a) Prepare a short report to the directors of Expand that, based on the financial information provided, assesses the relative profitability of Hone and Over.

(b) Discuss the validity of using this financial information as a basis to compare the profitability of the two companies.

(CIMA, May 2001)

✓**2** It has been suggested that cash is king and that readers of a company's accounts should pay more attention to information concerning its cash flows and balances than to its profits and other assets. It is argued that cash is more difficult to manipulate than profit and that cash flows are more important.

Required:

(a) Explain whether you agree with the suggestion that cash flows and balances are more difficult to manipulate than profit and non-cash assets.

(b) Explain why it might be dangerous to concentrate on cash to the exclusion of profit when analyzing a set of financial statements.

(CIMA, adapted)

3 Look up the financial statements of two companies competing in the same industry in your country. Calculate their return on equity (ROE). First, try to explain the difference observed with the use of ratio analysis. Subsequently, add trend analysis, common size analysis, segmental analysis and cash flow analysis to it. What extra information do these supplemental analyses give you? If you were to carry out an industry analysis, would this provide you with any extra information?

4 Look up the PE ratios of several airlines; what do you observe? How does the market value the prospects of each of these companies? Do the underlying financial statements confirm the market appreciation? Or do you observe conflicts?

5 Question 4 can be repeated for listed companies in several industries. Do you observe industry differences?

6 In which industries would you expect inventory turnover to be lower and in which industries would you expect it to be higher? Comment on this. Repeat this exercise for asset turnover.

7 In which industries would you expect profit margins to be lower and in which industries would you expect it to be higher?

8 Heavy Goods plc carries on business as a manufacturer of tractors. In 20X4, the company was looking for acquisitions and carrying out investigations into a number of possible targets. One of these was a competitor, Modern Tractors plc. The company's acquisition strategy was to acquire companies that were vulnerable to a takeover and in which there was an opportunity to improve asset management and profitability.

The chief accountant of Heavy Goods plc has instructed his assistant to calculate ratios from the financial statements of Modern Tractors plc for the past three years and to prepare a report based on these ratios and the industry average ratios that have been provided by the trade association. The ratios prepared by the assistant accountant and the industry averages for 20X4 are set out as follows.

Required:
You are required to write a full appraisal and report.

	20X2	20X3	20X4	Industry average (%) 20X4
Sales growth	30.00	40.00	9.52	8.25
Sales/total assets	1.83	2.05	1.60	2.43
Sales/net non-current assets	2.94	3.59	2.74	16.85
Sales/working capital	−21.43	−140.00	38.33	10.81
Sales/debtors	37.50	70.00	92.00	16.00
Gross profit/sales	18.67	22.62	19.57	23.92
Profit before tax/sales	8.00	17.62	11.74	4.06
Profit before interest/interest	6.45	26.57	14.50	4.95
Profit after tax/total assets	9.76	27.80	13.24	8.97
Profit after tax/equity	57.14	75.00	39.58	28.90
Net non-current assets/total assets	62.20	57.07	58.54	19.12
Net non-current assets/equity	3.64	1.54	1.75	0.58
Equity/total assets	18.29	37.07	33.45	32.96
Total liabilities/total assets	81.71	62.93	66.55	69.00
Total liabilities/equity	4.47	1.70	1.99	2.40
Long-term debt/total assets	36.59	18.54	29.27	19.00
Current liabilities/total assets	45.12	44.39	37.28	50.00
Current assets/current liabilities	0.84	0.97	1.11	1.63
(Current assets − inventory)/current liabilities	0.43	0.54	0.72	0.58
Inventory/total assets	17.07	18.54	14.63	41.90
Cost of sales/inventory	8.71	8.55	8.81	4.29
Cost of sales/creditors	6.10	6.25	6.17	12.87
Debtors/total assets	4.88	2.93	1.70	18.40
Cash/total assets	15.85	21.46	25.08	9.60

Note: Total assets = non-current assets at net book value + current assets
Net non-current assets = non-current assets at net book value.

(ACCA, adapted)

9 Seville plc is a rapidly expanding trading and manufacturing company. It is currently seeking to extend its product range into new markets. To achieve this growth, it needs to raise
   €800 000. The directors are considering two sources of funds:
   (i) A rights issue at €2.00 per share. The shares are trading at €2.50 (20X0 €2.20) per share.
   (ii) A bank loan at an interest rate of 15 per cent and repayable by instalments after two
       years. The bank would want to secure the loan with a charge over the company's
       property.

   The following are extracts from the draft financial statements.

Seville plc Draft financial statements
Extracts for the year ended 31.12.X1

Draft income statements	20X0	20X1
	€000	€000
Revenue	1 967	1 991
Operating profit	636	698
Interest payable	(45)	(55)
Profit before taxation	591	643
Taxation	(150)	(140)
Profit after taxation	441	503
Extraordinary item	(90)	—
Profit for the year	361	453

Draft statement of financial position

	20X0	20X1
Non-current assets		
Tangible	1 132	1 504
Intangible	247	298
	1 379	1 802
Current assets		
Inventory	684	679
Debtors	471	511
Cash in hand and at bank	80	117
	1 235	1 307
Total assets	2 614	3 109
Equity		
Ordinary share capital €1 shares	800	800
Revaluation reserve	144	144
Profit and loss	664	1 037
	1 608	1 981
Non-current liabilities		
10% debentures, repayable 2004	450	450
Finance lease	—	100
	450	550
Current liabilities		
Trade	336	308
Taxation	140	190
Dividends	80	80
	556	578
Total liabilities	1 006	1 128
Total equity and liabilities	2 614	3 109

Operating profit
Operating profit has been arrived at after charging or crediting the following:

	20X0	20X1
	€000	€000
Depreciation	110	150
Gain on disposal of property (as part of a sale and leaseback transaction)	—	95

Notes:
Extraordinary item: The extraordinary loss consists of reorganization costs in a branch where a reduction in activity involved various measures including redundancies. Attributable tax credit is €38 000.

Deferred taxation: Deferred taxation has not been provided because it is not considered probable that a liability will crystallize. If deferred taxation had been provided in full then a liability for the year of €7000 would have arisen (20X0 €8000).

Contingent liability: There is a contingent liability of €85 000 (20X0 €80 000) in respect of bills of exchange discounted with bankers.

Further investigation has revealed that inventory includes items subject to reservation of title of €40 000 and obsolete or slow moving items of €28 000 (20X0 €28 000).

An age analysis of debtors has revealed that debts overdue by more than one year amount to €40 000 (2000 €40 000).

The auditors are yet to report and there is some discussion as to the classification of the gain on disposal and the reorganization costs.

The directors forecast that the new funds will generate an operating profit of €300 000, and that the 20X1 operating profit will be repeated. If new shares are issued, the dividend will increase to €150 000.

Required:

Prepare a full report on progress, strengths and weaknesses, supported by ratio analysis.

(ACCA, adapted)

10   Recycle plc is a listed company which recycles toxic chemical waste products. The waste products are sent to Recycle plc from all around the world. You are an accountant (not employed by Recycle plc) who is accustomed to providing advice concerning the performance of companies, on the basis of data which are available from their published financial statements. Extracts from the financial statements of Recycle plc for the two years ended 30 September 20X7 are as follows:

Statements of comprehensive income – year ended 30 September

	20X7	20X6
	€m	€m
Revenue	3 000	2 800
Cost of sales	(1 600)	(1 300)
Gross profit	1 400	1 500
Other operating expenses	(800)	(600)
Operating profit	600	900
Interest payable	(200)	(100)
Profit before taxation	400	800
Taxation	(150)	(250)
Profit after taxation	250	550
Proposed dividend	(200)	(200)
Retained profit	50	350
Retained profit b/fwd	900	550
Retained profit c/fwd	950	900

Statements of financial position at 30 September

	20X7 €m	20X6 €m
Tangible non-current assets	4 100	3 800
Current assets		
Inventory	500	350
Debtors	1 000	800
Cash in hand	50	50
	1 550	1 200
Total assets	5 650	5 000
Equity and liabilities		
Equity		
Called-up share capital (€1 shares)	2 000	2 000
Profit and loss account	950	900
	2 950	2 900
Liabilities		
Non-current liabilities		
Non-current loans (repayable 20X9)	1 000	1 000
Current liabilities		
Trade creditors	600	600
Taxation payable	150	250
Proposed dividend	200	200
Bank overdraft	750	50
	1 700	1 100
Total liabilities	2 700	2 100
Total equity and liabilities	5 650	5 000

You ascertain that depreciation of tangible non-current assets for the year ended 30 September 20X7 was €1200m. Disposals of non-current assets during the year ended 30 September 20X7 were negligible. You are approached by A, who is a private investigator considering purchasing shares in Recycle plc. A considers that Recycle plc has performed well in 20X7 compared with 20X6 because turnover has risen and the dividend to shareholders has been maintained.

Required:
Write a full report, addressed to A, supported by appropriate ratios.

(CIMA, adapted)

11   H plc manufactures vehicle parts. The company sells its products to a number of independent distributors who resell the goods to garages and other retail outlets in their areas. H plc has a policy of having only one distributor in any given geographical area. Distributors are selected mainly on the basis of financial viability. H plc is keen to avoid the disruption of sales and loss of credibility associated with the collapse of a distributor. The company is currently trying to choose between two companies which have applied to be its sole distributor in Geetown, a new sales area.

The applicants have supplied the following information:

	Applicant X			Applicant Y		
	20X3	20X4	20X5	20X3	20X4	20X5
Sales (£000)	1 280	1 600	2 000	1 805	1 900	2 000
Gross profit %	22	20	18	23	22	24
Return on capital employed %	8	12	16	14	15	16
Current ratio	1.7:1	1.9:1	2.1:1	1.7:1	1.65:1	1.7:1
Quick ratio	1.4:1	1.1:1	0.9:1	0.9:1	0.9:1	0.9:1
Gearing %	15	21	28	29	30	27

Required:

(a) Explain why trends in accounting ratios could provide a more useful insight than the latest figures taken on their own.

(b) Using the information provided above, explain which of the companies appears to be the safer choice for the role of distributor.

(CIMA, adapted)

12 Arizona plc has carried on business for a number of years as a retailer of a wide variety of do-it-yourself goods. The company operates from a number of stores around the United Kingdom. In recent years, the company has found it necessary to provide credit facilities to its customers in order to achieve growth in turnover. As a result of this decision, the liability to the company's bankers has increased substantially.

The statutory accounts of the company for the year ended 31 March 20X8 have recently been published, and extracts are provided below, together with comparative figures for the previous two years.

Statements of comprehensive income for the years ended 31 March

	20X6 £m	20X7 £m	20X8 £m
Turnover	1 850	2 200	2 500
Cost of sales	(1 250)	(1 500)	(1 750)
Gross profit	600	700	750
Other operating costs	(550)	(640)	(700)
Operating profit	50	60	50
Interest from credit sales	45	60	90
Interest payable	(25)	(60)	(110)
Profit before taxation	70	60	30
Taxation	(23)	(20)	(10)
Profit after taxation	47	40	20
Dividends	(30)	(30)	(20)
Retained profit	17	10	—

Statements of financial position at 31 March

	20X6	20X7	20X8
	£m	£m	£m
Tangible non-current assets	278	290	322
Inventory	400	540	620
Debtors	492	550	633
Cash	12	12	15
Trade creditors	(270)	(270)	(280)
Taxation	(20)	(20)	(8)
Proposed dividends	(30)	(30)	(20)
Bank overdraft	(320)	(520)	(610)
Debentures	(200)	(200)	(320)
	342	352	352
Share capital	90	90	90
Reserves	252	262	262
	342	352	352

Other information:

- Depreciation charged for the three years was as follows:

Year ended 31 March	20X6	20X7	20X8
	£m	£m	£m
	55	60	70

- The debentures are secured by a floating charge over the assets of Arizona plc. Their repayment is due on 31 March 20X8.
- The bank overdraft is unsecured. The bank has set a limit of £630m on the overdraft.
- Over the past three years, the level of credit sales has been:

Year ended 31 March	20X6	20X7	20X8
	£m	£m	£m
Credit sales	213	263	375

Given the steady increase in the bank overdraft which has taken place in recent years, the company has recently written to its bankers to request an increase in the limit. The request was received by the bank on 15 May 20X8, two weeks after the 20X8 statutory accounts were published.

You are an accountant employed by the bankers of Arizona plc. The bank is concerned at the steep escalation in the level of the company's overdraft and your regional manager has asked for a report on the financial performance of Arizona plc for the last three years.

Required:

Write a report to your regional manager which analyzes the financial performance of Arizona plc for the period covered by the financial statements.

Your report may take any form you wish, but should specifically address the particular concern of the bank regarding the rapidly increasing overdraft. Therefore, your report should identify aspects of poor performance which could have contributed to the increase in the overdraft.

(CIMA)

13 You are an investment analyst. A client of yours, Mr A, owns 3.5 per cent of the share capital of Price. Price is a listed company and prepares financial statements in accordance with International Accounting Standards. The company supplies machinery to agricultural businesses. The year end of Price is 31 July and the financial statements for the year ended 31 July 20X1 were approved by the directors on 30 September 20X1. Following approval, copies of the financial statements were sent to all shareholders in readiness for the annual general meeting, which is due to be held on 30 November 20X1. Extracts from these financial statements are given below:

Statement of comprehensive income – year ended 31 July

	20X1	20X0
	$000	$000
Revenue	54 000	51 000
Cost of sales	(42 000)	(40 000)
Gross profit	12 000	11 000
Other operating expenses	(6 300)	(6 000)
Profit from operations	5 700	5 000
Finance cost	(1 600)	(1 000)
Profit before tax	4 100	4 000
Income tax expense	(1 200)	(1 200)
Net profit for the period	2 900	2 800

Statement of financial position as at 31 July

	20X1		20X0	
	$000	$000	$000	$000
Non-current assets				
Property plant and equipment		44 200		32 000
Current assets				
Inventories	8 700		7 500	
Receivables	13 000		12 000	
Cash and cash equivalents	200	21 900	1 500	21 000
		66 100		53 000
Capital and reserves				
Issued share capital		20 000		20 000
Reserves		20 300		14 000
		40 300		34 000
Non-current liabilities		15 400		10 000
Current liabilities				
Trade payables	8 000		7 800	
Tax	1 200		1 200	
Bank overdraft	1 200	10 400	—	9 000
		66 100		53 000

Statement of changes in equity

	$000
Balance at 31 July 20X0	34 000
Surplus on revaluation of properties	5 000
Net profit for the period	2 900
Dividends	(1 600)
Balance at 31 July 20X1	40 300

Extracts from notes to the financial statements finance cost – year ended 31 July

	20X1 $000	20X0 $000
On 10% interest-bearing borrowings	1 000	1 000
On zero-rate bonds	400	—
On bank overdraft	200	—
	1 600	1 000
Non-current liabilities at 31 July		
10% borrowings repayable 31 July 20X6	10 000	10 000
Zero-rate bonds	5 400	—
	15 400	10 000

The zero-rate bonds were issued for proceeds of $5m on 1 August 20X0. The lenders are not entitled to interest during their period of issue. The bonds are repayable on 31 July 20X4 for a total of $6 802 450. The bonds are quoted on a recognized stock exchange. However, the company intends to hold the bonds until they mature and then repay them.

Revaluation of properties: This is the first time the company has revalued any of its properties.

Depreciation of non-current assets: Depreciation of non-current assets for the year to-talled $4m (2000 – $3m).

Your client always attends the annual general meeting of the company and likes to put questions to the directors regarding the financial statements. However, he is not a financial specialist and does not wish to look foolish by asking inappropriate questions. Mr A intends to ask the following three questions and seeks your advice based on the information provided. The points he wishes to make are as follows:

Point 1: Why, when the company has made almost the same profit as last year and has borrowed more money through a bond issue, has the company got a bank overdraft of $1.2m at the end of the year when there was a positive balance of $1.5m in the bank at the end of the previous year? This looks wrong to me.

Point 2: The company has a revaluation surplus of $5m included in the statement of changes in equity. I have never understood this statement. Surely surpluses are shown in the income statement. Perhaps our accountants are unaware of the correct accounting treatment?

Point 3: I don't understand the treatment of the zero-rate bonds. The notes tell me that these were issued for $5m and no interest was paid to the investors. The accounts show a finance cost of $400 000 and a balance owing of $5.4m. Is this an error? On the other hand, perhaps the $5.4m is the fair value of the bonds? I feel sure an International Accounting Standard has been issued that requires companies to value their borrowings at fair value.

Required:

Prepare a reply to Mr A that evaluates the issues he has raised in the three points and provides appropriate advice. You should support your advice with references to International Accounting Standards.

(CIMA, November 2001)

14 You are the Management Accountant of Drax. The entity prepares financial statements to 31 March each year. Earnings per share is regarded as a key performance indicator and the executive directors receive a bonus if the earnings per share exceeds a given target figure. Good corporate governance is ensured by the appointment of a number of non-executive directors, who rigorously scrutinize the financial statements each year to ensure that the earnings per share figure has been correctly computed.

Drax has recently appointed a new non-executive director who seeks your advice regarding the financial statements for the year ended 31 March 20X3. Extracts from these financial statements (excluding the comparative figures) are given below. The financial statements comply with relevant Accounting Standards in all material respects.

STATEMENTS OF FINANCIAL PERFORMANCE Income statement – year ended 31 March 20X3

	Continuing operations $ million	Discontinuing operations $ million	Total $ million
Revenue	1 000	100	1 100
Cost of sales	(520)	(70)	(590)
Gross profit	480	30	510
Other operating expenses	(200)	(40)	(240)
Profit from operations	280	(10)	270
Loss on disposal of discontinuing operations (note 1)	—	(30)	(30)
Profit before finance costs	280	(40)	240
Finance costs			(55)
Profit before tax			185
Income tax expense			(55)
Profit after tax			130
Minority interests			(45)
Group profit for the period			85
Earnings per equity share			**59.13 cents**

Statement of changes in equity – year ended 31 March 20X3

	$ million	$ million
Balance at 1 April 20X2		270
Profit for the financial year		85
Unrealized surplus on the revaluation of properties		22
Currency translation differences on foreign currency net investments	12	
Less exchange losses on related foreign currency loans	(9)	3
Dividends (all equity)		(50)
Issue of share capital (note 2)		60
Balance at 31 March 20X3		390

NOTES TO THE FINANCIAL STATEMENTS:

Note 1

During the year, Drax disposed of a subsidiary. The loss on disposal shown in the income statement consists of two elements: Disposal proceeds less related net assets less related goodwill $45 million loss; Gain on curtailment of retirement benefits relating to disposal $15 million profit.

Note 2

At the start of the period, Drax had 120m $1 equity shares in issue. Drax had no non-equity shares. On 1 July 20X2, Drax made a rights issue to existing shareholders of one share for every four held at $2 per share. The market value of each share immediately before the rights issue was $2.50.

Note 3

Defined benefit pension plan

	At 31 March 20X3 $ million	At 31 March 20X2 $ million
Present value of funded obligations	500	4 500
Fair value of plan assets	(2 600)	(2 700)
Unrecognized actuarial losses	(380)	(350)
Net liability in statement of financial position	2 020	1 450

The new non-executive director has sent you a list of questions to which he requires answers:

(a) Please show how the earnings per share figure has been computed.

(b) I am a non-executive director for another entity operating in the same industry as Drax with roughly the same revenue and with very similar unit costs of raw materials. The nominal value of the shares of this other entity is $1 yet its earnings per share is quite different from that of Drax. How can this be?

(c) I am very suspicious about some of the figures in the statement of changes in equity and in the pension plan liability. It would seem to me that exchange losses on loans and actuarial losses relating to the pension plan should be in the income statement. Are the executive directors trying to maximize the earnings per share for their own ends?

(d) I don't understand how the 'gain on curtailment of retirement benefits' is a gain that goes to the income statement. Shouldn't it be treated in the same way as the actuarial losses that seem to be included in the balance sheet figure for the pension plan liability?

Required:

Prepare a reply to the questions the non-executive director has raised. You should refer to the provisions of relevant Accounting Standards where appropriate. Assume that the non-executive director has a reasonable general knowledge of business but that he is not familiar with the detail of Accounting Standards.

(CIMA, May 2003)

15   You are the accountant of Acquirer. Your entity has the strategy of growth by acquisition and your directors have identified an entity, Target, which they wish to investigate with a view to launching a takeover bid. Your directors consider that the directors of Target will contest any bid and will not be very cooperative in providing background information on the entity. Therefore, relevant financial information is likely to be restricted to the publicly available financial statements.

Your directors have asked you to compute key financial ratios from the latest financial statements of Target for the year ended 30 November 20X2 and to compare the ratios with those of other entities in a similar sector. Accordingly, you have selected ten broadly similar entities and have presented the directors with the following calculations:

Ratio	Basis of calculation	Ratio for Target	Spread of ratios Highest	For comparative Average	entities Lowest
Gross profit margin	$\dfrac{\text{Gross profit}}{\text{Revenue}}$	42%	44%	38%	33%
Operating profit margin	$\dfrac{\text{Profit from operations}}{\text{Revenue}}$	29%	37%	30%	26%
Return on total capital	$\dfrac{\text{Profit from operations}}{\text{Total capital}}$	73%	92.5%	69%	52%
Interest cover	$\dfrac{\text{Profit from operations}}{\text{Finance cost}}$	1.8 times	2.5 times	1.6 times	1.6 times
Gearing	$\dfrac{\text{Debt capital}}{\text{Total capital}}$	52%	56%	40%	28%
Dividend cover	$\dfrac{\text{Profit after tax}}{\text{Dividend}}$	5.2 times	5 times	4 times	3 times
Turn of inventory	$\dfrac{\text{Cost of sales}}{\text{Closing inventory}}$	4.4 times	4 times	4 times	3.2 times
Receivables days	$\dfrac{\text{Trade receivables}}{\text{1 day's sales revenue}}$	51 days	81 days	62 days	49 days

Required:

(a) Using the ratios provided, write a report that compares the financial performance and position of Target to the other entities in the survey. Where an issue arises that reflects particularly favourably or unfavourably on Target, you should assess its relevance to a potential acquirer.

(b) Identify any reservations you have regarding the extent to which the ratios provided can contribute to an acquisition decision by the directors of Acquirer. You should highlight the extent to which the financial statements themselves might help you to overcome the reservations you have identified.

(CIMA, November 2003)

16 BHG is a successful listed entity that designs and markets specialist business software. BHG's directors have decided to adopt a policy of expansion into overseas territories through the acquisition of similar software businesses possessing established shares of their domestic markets. BHG's aim is to obtain control, or at the minimum, significant influence (represented by at least 40 per cent of issued share capital) of investee entities. Target investee entities are likely to be listed entities in their own countries, but the acquisition of unlisted entities is not ruled out.

You are a senior accountant in BHG, and you have been asked by the Chief Financial Officer (CFO) to establish a set of key accounting ratios for use in:

(i) the initial appraisal of potential acquisitions

(ii) ongoing appraisal following acquisitions.

The ratios will be used as part of a suite of quantitative and non-quantitative measurements to compare businesses with each other. The CFO has suggested that it would be appropriate to identify no more than five to seven key financial ratios.

One of your assistants has suggested a list of five key accounting ratios as suitable for both initial and ongoing appraisal and comparison. She has provided reasons to support the case for their inclusion as key ratios.

1 Earnings per share: 'one of the most important investor ratios, widely used by all classes of investor to assess business performance'.
2 Dividend yield: 'this ratio provides a very useful measurement that allows comparison with yields from other equity and non-equity investments'.
3 Gearing: 'this is of critical importance in determining the level of risk of an equity investment'.
4 Gross profit margin: 'allows investors to assess business performance, and is of particular use over several accounting periods within the same organization. It is also very useful for comparing performances between businesses'.
5 Asset turnover ratios: 'allow the investor to compare the intensity of asset usage between businesses and over time'.

Required:

(a) Discuss the extent to which each of the five suggested accounting ratios is likely to be useful to BHG for both initial and ongoing appraisal and comparison, and the extent to which your assistant's assessments of the value of the ratios are justified.

(b) Explain the problems and limitations of accounting ratio analysis in making inter-firm and international comparisons.

(CIMA, May 2008)

17   ST, UV and WX are listed entities operating in the same business sector. At 31 October 20X6, their PE ratios were reported as follows:

ST 16.2
UV 12.7
WX 8.4

Which ONE of the following statements about these PE ratios is correct?

The PE ratios suggest that:

(a) ST is regarded by the market as the riskiest of the three entities.

(b) ST has the highest earnings per share of the three entities.

(c) UV represents the safest investment because its PE lies approximately mid-way between the other two.

(d) WX's share price may be relatively lower than that of ST and UV because of an adverse effect such as a profit warning.

(CIMA, May 2006)

REFERENCES

Chapter 1

AAA (1966) *A Statement of Basic Accounting Theory*. New York, American Accounting Association.

Berle, A.A. and Means, G.C. (1968/2009) *The Modern Corporation and Private Property Rights*, New Brunswick, NJ, Transaction Publishers. Originally published in 1932 by Harcourt, Brace and World, Inc.

G20 (2009) 'Leaders' Statement', The Pittsburgh Summit, 24–25 September 2009. www.g20.org/English/Documents/PastPresidency/201512/P020151225615583055801.pdf (accessed 1 March 2016).

G20 (2013) 'G20 Leaders' Declaration', Saint Petersburg Summit, 5–6 September 2013. www.g20.org/English/Documents/PastPresidency/201512/P020151225709417239707.pdf (accessed 1 March 2016).

Grossman, S.J. and Stiglitz, J.E. (1980) 'On the impossibility of informationally efficient markets', *American Economic Review* 70(3):393–408.

IASB (2010) *Conceptual Framework for Financial Reporting*. London, International Accounting Standards Board.

IFRS Foundation (2015) Mission Statement. www.ifrs.org/About-us/Pages/IFRS-Foundation-and-IASB.aspx (accessed 1 March 2016).

Lev, B. (1988) 'Toward a theory of equitable and efficient accounting policy', *The Accounting Review* 63(1):1–22.

Mueller, G.G., Guernon, H. and Meek, G.K. (1994) *Accounting: An International Perspective*, 3rd edn, New York, Richard D. Irwin, Inc.

Pacter, P. (2015) *IFRS as Global Standards: A Pocket Guide*, London: IFRS Foundation.

Radebaugh, L.H. and Gray, S.J. (2002) *International Accounting and Multinational Enterprises*, New York, Wiley.

Chapter 2

Alexander, D. and Nobes, C. (2004) *Financial Accounting: An International Introduction*, 2nd edn, Harlow, UK, Pearson Education.

Ali, A. and Hwang, L.-S. (2000) 'Country-specific factors related to financial reporting and the value relevance of accounting data', *Journal of Accounting Research* 38(1):1–21.

American Accounting Association (1977) *Accounting Review* 52(4 supp.).

Armstrong, C., Barth, M., Jagolinzer, A. and Riedl, E. (2010) 'Market reaction to the adoption of IFRS in Europe', *Accounting Review* 85(1):31–61.

Ball, R. and Shivakumar, L. (2002) 'Earning quality in UK private firms', Working paper, London Business School.

Ball, R., Kothari, S.P. and Robin, A. (2000) 'The effect of international institutional factors on properties of accounting earnings', *Journal of Accounting and Economics* 29(1):1–51.

Barth, M., Landsman, W. and Lang, M. (2008) 'International accounting standards and accounting quality', *Journal of Accounting Research* 46(3):467–98.

Basu, S. (1997) 'The conservatism principle and the asymmetric timeliness of earnings', *Journal of Accounting and Economics* 24(1):3–37.

Baudot, L. (2014) Perspectives on the role of and need for accounting regulation, in Van Mourik, C and Walton, P. (eds) *The Routledge Companion to Accounting, Reporting and Regulation*, Abingdon, UK, Routledge, pp. 207–227.

Beuselinck, C. Joos, P., Khurana, L. and Van der Meulen, S. (2009) 'Mandatory IFRS reporting and stock price informativeness' SSRN-eLibrary.

Beuselinck, C., Joos, P., Khurana, L. and Van der Meulen, S. (2010) 'Mandatory adoption of IFRS and analysts' forecasts information properties', SSRN-eLibrary

Burghstahler, D.C., Hail, L. and Leuz, C. (2006) 'The importance of reporting incentives: Earnings management in European private and public firms', *Accounting Review* 81(5):983–1016.

Bushman, R. and Piotroski, J. (2006) 'Financial reporting incentives for conservative accounting: The influence of legal and political institutions', *Journal of Accounting and Economics* 42:107–48.

Byard, D., Li, Y. and Yu, Y. (2011) 'The effect of mandatory EFRS adoption on financial analysts' information environment', *Journal of Accounting Research* 49(1):69–96.

Chaney, P., Faccio, M. and Parsley, D. (2011) 'The quality of accounting information in politically connected firms', *Journal of Accounting and Economics* 51:58–76.

Christensen, H., Hail, L. and Leuz, C. (2012) 'Mandatory IFRS reporting and changes in enforcement', SSRNeLibrary.

Da Costa, R.C., Bourgeois, J.C. and Lawson, W.M. (1978) 'A classification of international financial accounting practices', *International Journal of Accounting (Education and Research)* 8(7):73–85.

Daimler-Benz (1989–94) Annual Reports.

D'Arcy, A. (2001) 'Accounting classification and the international harmonization debate – an empirical investigation', *Accounting, Organizations and Society* 26:327–49.

Daske, H., Hail, L., Leuz, C. and Verdi, R. (2008) 'Mandatory IFRS reporting around the world: Early evidence on the economic consequences', *Journal of Accounting Research* 46(5):1085–142.

Doupnik, T.S. and Salter, S.S. (1995) 'External environment, culture and accounting practice: A preliminary test of a general model of international accounting development', *International Journal of Accounting* 30: 189–207.

Florou, A. and Pope, P. (2012) 'Mandatory IFRS adoption and investor asset allocation decisions', *The Accounting Review* 87(6):1993–2025.

Francis, J. and Schipper, K. (1999) Have financial statements lost their relevance?. *Journal of accounting Research* 37(2): 319–52.

Frank, W.G. (1979) 'An empirical analysis of international accounting principles', *Journal of Accounting Research* 17(2):593–605.

Gebhardt, G. and Novotny-Farkas, Z. (2011) 'Mandatory IFRS adoption and accounting quality of European banks', *Journal of Business Finance and Accounting* 38(3–4):289–333.

Gilman, S. (1939) *Accounting Concepts of Profit* (New York: Ronald Press).

Gray, S. (1988) 'Towards a theory of cultural influence on the development of accounting systems internationally', *Abacus* 24(1):1–15.

Guenther, D. and Young, D. (2000) 'The association between financial accounting measures and real economic activity: A multinational study', *Journal of Accounting and Economics* 29(1):53–72.

Hatfield, H. R. (1909) *Modern Accounting: Its Principles and Some of its Problems*, New York: D. Appleton.

Hatfield, H.R (1966) 'Some variations in accounting practices in England, France, Germany, and the United States', *Journal of Accounting Research* 4(2):169–82.

Hofstede, G. (1984) *Culture's Consequences: International Differences in Work-related Values*, Beverly Hills, CA, Sage.

Hope, O.K. (2003a) 'Disclosure practices, enforcement of accounting standards, and analysts' forecast accuracy: An international study', *Journal of Accounting Research* 41(2):235–72.

Hope, O.K. (2003b) 'Firm-level disclosures and the relative roles of culture and legal origin', *Journal of International Financial Management and Accounting* 14(3):218–48.

Horton, J., Serafeim, G. and Serafeim, I. (2012) 'Does mandatory IFRS adoption improve the information environment', *Contemporary Accounting Research* 30(1):388–423.

Husband, G.R. (1938) 'The corporate-entity fiction and accounting theory', *The Accounting Review* 13(3): 241–253.

Husband, G.R. (1954) 'The entity concept in accounting', *The Accounting Review*, 29(4): 552–63.

Jackson, H. and Roe, M. (2009) 'Public and private enforcement of securities laws: Resource-based evidence', *Journal of Financial Economics* 93:207–38.

Jiao, T., Koning, M., Mertens, G. and Rosenboom, P. (2012) 'Mandatory IFRS adoption and its impact on analysts' forecasts', *International Review of Financial Analysis* 2(1):343–71.

Kvaal, E. and Nobes, C. (2010) International differences in IFRS policy choice: A research note.

Kvaal, E. and Nobes, C. (2012) 'IFRS policy changes and the continuation of National Patterns of IFRS Practice', *European Accounting Review* 21(2):343–71.

Landsman, W., Maydew, E. and Thornock, J. (2011) 'The information content of annual earnings announcements and mandatory adoption of IFRS', *Journal of Accounting and Economics* 53(1–2):34–54.

Lang, M., Maffet, M. and Owens, E. (2010) 'Earnings comovement and accounting comparability: The effects of mandatory IFRS adoption', Simon School Working Paper No. FR 11–03. Available at ssrn.com/abstract=1676937 or dx.doi.org/10.2139/ssrn.1676937

La Porta, R., Lopez-de-Silanes, F., Shleifer, A. and Vishny, R.W. (1997) 'Legal determinants of external finance', *Journal of Finance* 52(3):1131–50.

La Porta, R., Lopez-De-Silanes, F., Shleifer, A., and Vishny, R.W. (2000) 'Investor protection and corporate governance', *Journal of Financial Economics* 58(1–2): 3–27.

Leuz, C. (2010) 'Different approaches to corporate reporting regulation: How jurisdictions differ and why?', *Accounting and Business Research* 40(3):229–56.

Leuz, C. and Verrecchia, R.E. (2000) 'The economic consequences of increased disclosure', *Journal of Accounting Research* 38(3 supp.):91–124.

Leuz, C., Nanda, D. and Wysocki, P. (2003) 'Earnings management and investor protection: An international comparison', *Journal of Financial Economics* 69(3):505–27.

Lev, B. and Zarowin, P., (1999) 'The boundaries of financial reporting and how to extend them (Digest Summary)', *Journal of Accounting Research* 37(2):353–85.

Li, D.H. (1960a) 'The nature of corporate residual equity under the entity concept', *The Accounting Review* 35(2):258–63.

Li, D.H. (1960b) 'The nature and treatment of dividends under the entity concept', *The Accounting Review* 35(4):674–79.

Li, D.H. (1961) 'Income taxes and income tax allocation under the entity concept', *The Accounting Review* 36(2):265–68.

Li, D.H. (1963) 'Alternative accounting procedures and the entity concept', *The Accounting Review* 38(1):52–5.

Li, D.H. (1964) 'The objectives of the corporation under the entity concept', *The Accounting Review* 39(3):946–50.

Mey, A. (1966) 'Theodore Limperg and his theory of values and costs', *Abacus* 2(1):3–23.

Mikol, A. (1995) 'The history of financial reporting in France', in Walton, P. (ed.) *European Financial Reporting: A History*, London: Academic Press Limited, pp. 91–122.

Mueller, G.G. (1967) *International Accounting*, New York, Macmillan.

Nair, R.D. and Frank, W.G. (1980) 'The impact of disclosure and measurement on international accounting classifications', *Accounting Review* 55(3):426–50.

Napier, C. (1995) 'The history of financial reporting in the UK', in Walton, P. (ed.) *European Financial Reporting: A History*, London: Academic Press Limited, pp. 259–283.

Nobes, C.W. (1983) 'A judgemental classification of financial reporting practices', *Journal of Business Finance and Accounting* 10(1):1–19.

Nobes, C.W. (1998) 'Towards a general model for the reasons for international differences in financial reporting', *Abacus* 34(2):168–187.

Nobes, C.W. (2014) *International Classification of Financial Reporting*, 3rd edn, Abingdon, UK, Routledge.

Nobes, C.W. and Parker, R. (2003) *Comparative International Accounting*, 7th edn, London, Prentice Hall.

Ordelheide, D. and KPMG (eds) (2001) *Transnational Accounting*, 2nd edn, London, Palgrave.

Paton, W. A. and Littleton, A.C. (1940) *An Introduction to Corporate Accounting Standards*, Monograph No. 3, New York: American Accounting Association.

Penman, S.H. and Zhang, X.-J. (2002) 'Accounting conservatism, the quality of earnings, and stock returns', *Accounting Review* 77(2):237–64.

Pope, P. and McLeay, S. (2011) 'The European IFRS experiment: Objectives, research challenges and some early evidence', *Accounting and Business Research* 41(3):233–66.

Pope, P. and Walker, M. (1999) 'International differences in the timeliness, conservatism, and classification of earnings', *Journal of Accounting Research* 37(3 supp.):53–87.

Raby, W.L. (1959) 'The two faces of accounting', *The Accounting Review* 34(3):452–61.

Schipper, K. (2000) 'Accounting research and the potential use of international accounting standards for crossborder securities listings', *British Accounting Review* 32(3):243–56.

Schmalenbach, E. (1927) 'Der Kontenrahmen', *Zeitschrift fur betriebswirtschaftliche Forschung* 21:385–402.

Seidler, L.J. (1967) 'International accounting – the ultimate theory course', *Accounting Review* 42(4):775–81.

Seidman, N.B. (1956) 'The determination of stockholder income', *The Accounting Review* 31(1):64–70.

Sprague, C.E. (1913) *The Philosophy of Accounts*, New York: Ronald Press.

Staubus, G.J. (1952) 'Payments for the use of capital and the matching process', *The Accounting Review* 27(1):104–113.

Staubus, G.J. (1959) 'The residual equity point of view in accounting', *The Accounting Review* 34(1):3–13.

Staubus, G.J. (1961) *A Theory of Accounting to Investors*, Berkeley and Los Angeles, CA: University of California Press.

Suojanen, W.W. (1954) 'Accounting theory and the large corporation', *The Accounting Review* 29(3):391–98.

Suojanen, W.W. (1958) 'Enterprise theory and corporate balance sheets', *The Accounting Review* 33(1):56–65.

Tarca, A. (2012) 'Report to the Trustees of the IFRS Foundation: Appendix – The case for Global Accounting Standards: Arguments and evidence', Staff paper prepared by the IFRS Foundation Staff – 22 October 2012, pp. 68–84. ssrn.com/abstract=2204889 or dx.doi.org/10.2139/ssrn.2204889

Walton, P. (1995) 'International accounting and history', in Walton, P. (ed.) *European Financial Reporting: A History*, London: Academic Press Limited, pp. 1–10.

Chapter 3

AOSSG (2010) 'Financial reporting issues relating to Islamic finance', Asian-Oceanian Standard Setters Group, Working Group on Financial Reporting Issues Related to Islamic Finance, Research Paper, 15 September 2010.

Aissat, S., Boulkeroua, L., Lucas, M. and van Mourik, C. (2014) 'Accounting regulation and IFRS in Islamic countries', in Van Mourik, C. and Walton, P. (eds) *The Routledge Companion to Accounting Regulation, Reporting and Regulation*, Abingdon, UK, Routledge.

Bernstein, M.H. (1955) *Regulating Business by Independent Commission*, Princeton, NJ, Princeton University Press.

Bocqueraz, C. and Walton, P. (2006) 'Creating a supranational institution: The role of the individual and the mood of the time', *Accounting History* 11(3):271–88.

Camfferman, K. and Zeff, S.A. (2007) *Financial Reporting and Global Capital Markets: A History of the International Accounting Standards Committee*, Oxford, UK, Oxford University Press.

Camfferman, K. and Zeff, S.A. (2015) *Aiming for Global Accounting Standards: The International Accounting Standards Board 2001–2011*, Oxford, UK, Oxford University Press.

Groenewegen, J. Spithoven, A. and van den Berg, A. (2010) *Institutional Economics: An Introduction*, London, Palgrave Macmillan.

Habib, A. (2014) 'Accounting regulation in emerging markets and newly industrializing countries', in Van Mourik, C. and Walton, P. (eds) *The Routledge Companion to Accounting Regulation, Reporting and Regulation*, Abingdon, UK, Routledge.

Hamdani, K. and Ruffing, L. (2015) *United Nations Centre on Transnational Corporations: Corporate Conduct and the Public Interest*. Routledge.

Hopwood, A.G. (1994) 'Some reflections on "The harmonization of accounting within the EU"', *European Accounting Review* 3(2):241–54.

IASC Foundation (2001) *Constitution*. London: International Accounting Standards Committee Foundation.

Mattli, W. and Büthe, T. (2005) 'Accountability in accounting? The politics of private rule making in the public interest', *Governance: An International Journal of Policy, Administration and Institutions* 18(3):399–429.

Maystadt, P. (2013) Should IFRS standards be more 'European'?: Mission to reinforce the EU's contribution to the development of international accounting standards. ec.europa.eu/internal_market/accounting/docs/governance/reform/131112_report_en.pdf (accessed on 18 December 2015).

Mueller, G.G., Gernon, H. and Meek, G.K. (2004) *Accounting: An International Perspective*, 3rd edn, Homewood, IL, Richard D. Irwin, Inc.

Munday, S. (2000) *Markets and Market Failure*, Oxford, UK, Heinemann Educational Publishers.

Olson, M. (1965/1971) *The Logic of Collective Action: Public Goods and the Theory of Groups*, Cambridge, MA, Harvard University Press.

Olson, M. (2000) *Power and Prosperity: Outgrowing Communist and Capitalist Dictatorships*, New York: Basic Books.

Shleifer, A. (2005) 'Understanding regulation', *European Financial Management* 11(4):439–51.

Street, D.L. (2006) 'The G4's role in the evolution of the international standard setting process and partnership with the IASB', *Journal of International Accounting, Auditing and Taxation* 15:109–26.

Stigler, G.J. (1971) 'The theory of economic regulation', *The Bell Journal of Economics and Management Science* 3(3):3–21.

Stiglitz, J. and Walsh, C.E. (2002) *Principles of Microeconomics*, 3rd edn, New York, W.W. Norton & Company, Inc.

Tay, J.S.W. and Parker, R.H. (1990) 'Measuring international harmonization and standardization', *Abacus* 26(1):71–88.

Watts, R.L. and Zimmerman, J.L. (1978) ,Towards a positive theory of the determination of accounting standards', *The Accounting Review* 53(1):112–134.

Zeff, S. A. (2012) 'The evolution of the IASC into the IASB, and the challenges it faces', *The Accounting Review* 87(3):807–37.

Chapter 4

Ball, R. and Brown, P. (1968) 'An empirical evaluation of accounting income numbers', *Journal of Accounting Research* (Autumn):159–78.

Beaver, W. (1968) 'The information content of annual earnings announcements', *Journal of Accounting Research* (Supplement) 6:67–92.

Camfferman, K. and Zeff, S.A. (2007) *Financial Reporting and Global Capital Markets: A History of the International Accounting Standards Committee*, Oxford, UK, Oxford University Press.

Camfferman, K. and Zeff, S.A. (2015) *Aiming for Global Accounting Standards: The International Accounting Standards Board 2001–2011*, Oxford, UK: Oxford University Press.

Fairclough, I. and Fairclough, N. (2012) *Political Discourse Analysis: A method for Advanced Students*, Oxford, UK, Routledge.

Hail, L., Leuz, C. and Wysocki, P. (2010) 'Global convergence and the potential adoption of IFRS by the US (Part I): Conceptual underpinnings and economic analysis', *Accounting Horizons* 24(3):355–94.

Hendriksen, E.S. (1977) *Accounting Theory*, 3rd edn, Homewood, IL: R.D. Irwin.

IASB (2001) *Framework for the Preparation and Presentation of Financial Statements*, London: International Accounting Standards Board.

IASB (2010) *Conceptual Framework for Financial Reporting*, London: International Accounting Standards Board.

Jensen, M.C. and Meckling, W.H. (1976) 'The theory of the firm: Managerial behavior, agency costs and ownership structure', *Journal of Financial Economics* 3:305–60.

Kahneman, D. and Tversky, A. (1972) 'Subjective probability: A judgment of representativeness', *Cognitive Psychology* 3:430–54.

Kahneman, D. and Tversky, A. (1973) 'On the psychology of prediction', *Psychological Review* 80:237–51.

Kahneman, D. and Tversky, A. (1979) 'Prospect theory: An analysis of decisions under risk', *Econometrica* 47:313–27.

La Porta, R., Lopez-de-Silanes, F., Shleifer, A. and Vishny, R.W. (1997) 'Legal determinants of external finance', *Journal of Finance* 52(3):1131–50.

Leuz, C. (2010) 'Different approaches to corporate reporting regulation: How jurisdictions differ and why', *Accounting and Business Research* 40(3):229–56.

Murray, M. and Kujundzic, N. (2005) *Critical Reflection: A Textbook for Critical Thinking*, Montreal, Canada: McGill-Queens University Press.

Nobes, C. (1998) 'Towards a general model of the reasons for international differences in financial reporting', *Abacus* 34(2):162–87.

Odean, T. (1998) 'Are investors reluctant to realize their losses?', *Journal of Finance* 53(5):1775–98.

Riahi-Belkaoui, A. (2004) *Accounting Theory*, 5th edn, Boston, MA, South-Western, Cengage Learning.

Ryan, B., Scapens, R.W. and Theobald, M. (2002) *Research Method and Methodology in Finance and Accounting*, 2nd edn, London, Thomson.

Scott, D.R. (1940) 'The accounting exchange: Selling accounting short', *The Accounting Review* 15(4):507–9.

Shefrin, H. (2000) *Beyond Greed and Fear: Understanding Behavioral Finance and the Psychology of Investing*, Boston, MA, Harvard Business School Press.

Shiller, R.J. (2000) *Irrational Exuberance*, Princeton, NJ, Princeton University Press.

Shiller, R.J. (2003) 'From efficient markets theory to behavioral finance', *Journal of Economic Perspectives* 17(1):83–104.

Shleifer, A. (2000) *Inefficient Markets*, Oxford, UK, Oxford University Press.

Simon, H.A. (1979) 'Rational decision making in business organizations', *American Economic Review* 69(4):493–513.

Smith, M. (2011) *Research Methods in Accounting*, 2nd edn, London, Sage.

Statman, M. and Shefrin, H. (1985) 'The disposition to sell winners too early and ride losers too long: Theory and evidence', *Journal of Finance* 40(3):777–90.

Staubus, G.J. (1959) 'The residual equity point of view in accounting', *The Accounting Review* 34(1):3–13.

Staubus, G.J. (1961) *A Theory of Accounting to Investors*, Berkeley, CA, University of California Press.

Thaler, R.H. (1999) 'Mental accounting matters', *Journal of Behavioural Decision Making* 12:183–206.

Van Mourik, C. (2014a) 'Methodology in financial accounting theory', in Van Mourik, C. and Walton P. (eds) *The Routledge Companion to Accounting, Reporting and Regulation*, Abingdon, UK, Routledge.

Van Mourik, C. (2014b) 'Fundamental issues in financial accounting and reporting theory', in Van Mourik, C. and Walton P. (eds) *The Routledge Companion to Accounting, Reporting and Regulation*, Abingdon, UK, Routledge.

Watts, R.L. and Zimmerman, J.L. (1978) 'Towards a positive theory of the determination of accounting standards', *The Accounting Review* 53(1):112–34.

Watts, R.L. and Zimmerman, J.L. (1979) 'The demand for and supply of accounting theories: The market for excuses', *The Accounting Review* 54(2):273–305.

Williams, P.F. (2002) 'Accounting and the moral order: Justice, accounting and legitimate moral authority', *Accounting in the Public Interest*, 2:1–21.

Williams, P.F. (2006) 'Accounting for economic reality: Whose reality? Which justice?', *Accounting in the Public Interest* 6:37–44.

Yu, S.C. (1976) *The Structure of Accounting Theory*, Gainesville, FL: University Presses of Florida.

Feltham, G.A. and Ohlson, J.A. (1995) 'Valuation and clean surplus accounting for operating and financial activities', *Contemporary Accounting Research* 11(2):689–731.

Fisher, I. (1912) *The Nature of Capital and Income*, New York, Macmillan.

Hicks, J. (1946) *Value and Capital: An Inquiry into Some Fundamental Principles of Economic Theory*, 2nd edn, Oxford, UK, Clarendon Press.

Kieso and Weygandt (2004) *Intermediate Accounting*, 12th edn, New York, Wiley.

Lee, T.A. (1985) *Income and Value Measurement: Theory and Practice*, 3rd edn, London, Chapman & Hall.

Napier, C. (2014) 'English-language theories of financial reporting', in Van Mourik, C and Walton, P. (eds) *The Routledge Companion to Accounting, Reporting and Regulation*, Abingdon, UK, Routledge.

Näsi S., Saccon , C., Wüstemann, S. and Walton, P. (2014) 'European accounting theory: Evolution and evaluation', in Van Mourik, C and Walton, P. (eds) *The Routledge Companion to Accounting, Reporting and Regulation*, Abingdon, UK, Routledge.

Paton, W.A. and Littleton, A.C. (1940) *An Introduction to Corporate Accounting Standards*, American Accounting Association.

Penman, S.H. (2013) *Financial Statement Analysis and Security Valuation*, 5th edn, New York, McGraw-Hill, International Edition.

Saario, M. (1945) 'Realisointiperiaate ja käyttöomaisuuden poistot tuloslaskennassa' [Summary: Realization Principle and Depreciation], Doctoral thesis, Liiketaloustieteellisen tutkimuslaitoksen julkaisuja 6, Helsinki.

Saario, M. (1959) 'Kirjanpidon meno-tulo-teoria' [The Expenditure–Revenue Theory of Bookkeeping], Liiketaloustieteellisen tutkimuslaitoksen julkaisuja 28, Keuruu, Finland.

Schmalenbach, E. (1959) *Dynamic Accounting*, trans. G.W. Murphy and K.S. Most, London, Gee and Co.

Schmalenbach, E. (1962) *Dynamische Bilanz* [Dynamic accounting theory], 13th edn, revised by R. Bauer, Cologne and Opladen, Germany: Westdeutscher Verlag.

Scott, W.R. (2015) *Financial Accounting Theory*, 6th edn, New York, Pearson.

Thomas, A.L. (1969) *The Allocation Problem in Financial Accounting Theory*, Studies in Accounting Research No. 3, Sarasota, FL: American Accounting Association.

Thomas, A.L. (1974) *The Allocation Problem: Part Two*, Studies in Accounting Research No. 9, Sarasota, FL: American Accounting Association.

Chapter 5

Beaver, W.H. (1998) *Financial Reporting: An Accounting Revolution*, 3rd edn, Englewood Cliffs, NJ, Prentice Hall.

Fama, E.F. (1970) Efficient capital markets: A review of theory an empirical work, *The Journal of Finance* 25(2):383–417.

Chapter 6

Belkaoui, A.R. (2004) *Accounting Theory*, 5th edn, New York, South-Western, Cengage Learning.

Camfferman, K. (1995) 'The history of financial reporting in the Netherlands,' in P. Walton (ed.) *European*

Financial Reporting: A History, London, Academic Press, pp. 169–87.

Chambers, R.J. (1966) *Accounting: Evaluation and Economic Behavior*, Upper Saddle, NJ, Prentice-Hall.

Chambers, R.J. (1967) 'Continuously contemporary accounting – Additivity and action', *The Accounting Review* 4(4):751–7.

Edwards, E.O. and Bell, P.W. (1966) *The Theory and Measurement of Business Income*, Berkeley, CA, University of California Press.

Gee, K.P. and Peasnell, K.V. (1976) 'A pragmatic defence of replacement cost', *Accounting and Business Research* 6(24):242–9.

Georgiou, O. and Jack, L. (2011) 'In pursuit of legitimacy: A history behind fair value accounting', *The British Accounting Review* 43(4):311–23.

Johnson, L.T. and Swieringa, R.J. (1996) 'Derivatives, hedging and comprehensive income', *Accounting Horizons* 10(4):109–22.

Lee, T.A. (1985) *Income and Value Measurement: Theory and Practice*, 3rd edn, London, Chapman & Hall.

Mey, A. (1966) 'Theodore Limperg and his theory of values and costs', *Abacus* 2(1):3–23.

Näsi, S., Saccon, C., Wüstemann, S. and Walton, P. (2014) 'European accounting theory: evolution and evaluation', in Van Mourik, C. and Walton, P. (eds) *The Routledge Companion to Accounting, Reporting and Regulation*, Abingdon, UK, Routledge, pp. 54–71.

Robinson, L.E. (1991) The time has come to report comprehensive income', *Accounting Horizons* 5(2):107–12.

Solomons, D. (1961) 'Economic and accounting concepts of income', *The Accounting Review* 36(3):374–83.

Sterling, R.J. (1970) *Theory of the Measurement of Enterprise Income*, Lawrence, KS, The University Press of Kansas.

Sweeney, H.W. (1936) *Stabilized Accounting*, New York: Harper & Brothers.

Chapter 7

Chambers, R.J. (1966) *Accounting, Evaluation and Economic Behavior*, Englewood Cliffs, NJ: Prentice Hall.

IASB (2015) Exposure Draft, Conceptual Framework for Financial Reporting. London: International Accounting Standards Board.

IFRS 13, *Fair Value Measurement*. Issued in 2012, revised 2103. London, The International Accounting Standards Board.

Chapter 8

2013 EU Accounting Directive eur-lex.europa.eu/legal-content/EN/ALL/?uri=CELEX:32013L0034 (accessed 14 February 2016).

International Accounting Standard 1 (IAS 1) *Presentation of Financial Statements*. London, The International Accounting Standards Board.

International Accounting Standard 8 (IAS 8) *Accounting Policies, Changes in Accounting Estimates and Errors*. London, The International Accounting Standards Board.

International Financial Reporting Standard 1 (IFRS 13) *Fair Value Measurement*. London, The International Accounting Standards Board.

Chapter 9

Alchian, A.A. and Demsetz, H. (1972) 'Production, information costs and economic organization', *The American Economic Review* 62(5):777–95.

Aras, G. and Crowther, D. (2012) *Governance and Social Responsibility: International Perspectives*, Basingstoke, UK, Palgrave Macmillan.

Armour, J., Hansmann, H. and Kraakman, R. (2009) 'Chapter 1: What is corporate law?', in Kraakman, R., Armour, J., Davies, P., Enriques, L., Hansmann, H., Hertig, G., Hopt, K., Kanda, H. and Rock, E. (2009) *The Anatomy of Corporate Law: A Comparative and Functional Approach*, Oxford, UK and New York, Oxford University Press.

Becker, L.C. (1977) *Property Rights: Philosophic Foundations*. London, Routledge & Kegan Paul Ltd.

Berle, A.A. and Means, G.C. (1968/2009) *The Modern Corporation and Private Property Rights*, New Brunswick, NJ, Transaction Publishers. Originally published in 1932 by Harcourt, Brace and World, Inc.

Carroll, A.B. (1991) 'The pyramid of corporate social responsibility: Toward the moral management of organizational stakeholders', *Business Horizons* 34(4):39–48.

Commission Recommendation 2014/208/EU eur-lex.europa.eu/legal-content/EN/TXT/?uri=CELEX%3A32014H0208 (accessed 16 June 2016).

Committee on Corporate Governance (1998) *Final Report (Hampel Report)* of January 1998, London: Gee (a division of Professional Publishing Ltd).

The Committee on the Financial Aspects of Corporate Governance and Gee and Co. Ltd. (Cadbury Committee) (1992) *Report of the Committee on the Financial Aspects of Corporate Governance*. London: Gee (a division of Professional Publishing Ltd).

Donaldson, L. (1985) *In Defence of Organization Theory: A Reply to the Critics*, Cambridge, UK, Cambridge University Press.

Donaldson, L. and Davis, J.H. (1991) 'Stewardship theory or agency theory: CEO governance and shareholder returns', *Australian Journal of Management* 16(1):49–64.

Donaldson, L. and Preston, L.E. (1995) 'The stakeholder theory of the corporation: Concepts, evidence and implications', *The Academy of Management Review* 20(1):65–91.

Directive 2013/34/EU of the European Parliament and of the Council of 26 June 2013 on the annual financial statements, consolidated financial statements and related reports of certain types of undertakings eur-lex. europa.eu/legal-content/EN/TXT/?uri=CELEX% 3A32013L0034 (accessed 16 June 2016).

European Commission Directive 2006/46/EC eur-lex.europa.eu/legal-content/EN/ALL/ ?uri=celex%3A32006L0046 (accessed 16 June 2016).

Franks, J. and Mayer, C. (2001) 'Ownership and control of German corporations', *Review of Financial Studies* 14(4):943–77.

FRC (2012) *UK Corporate Governance Code*, UK Financial Reporting Council. www.slc.co.uk/media/5268/ uk-corporate-governance-code-september-2012.pdf (accessed 28 March 2016).

Freeman, R.E. (1984) *Strategic Management: A Stakeholder Approach*, London, Pitman Publishing.

Goergen, M. (2012) *International Corporate Governance*, Harlow, UK, Pearson Education Limited.

Hall, P.A. and Soskice, D. (eds) (2001) *Varieties of Capitalism: The Institutional Foundations of Comparative Advantage*, Oxford, UK, Oxford University Press.

Honoré, A.M. (1961) 'Ownership', *Oxford Essays in Jurisprudence*, Guest, A.G. (ed.) Oxford, UK, Clarendon Press (in Becker, 1977).

Jensen, M.C. and Meckling, W.H. (1976) 'Theory of the firm: Managerial behavior, agency costs and ownership structure', *Journal of Financial Economics* 3(4):305–60.

La Porta, R., Lopez-de-Silanes, F., Shleifer, A. and Vishny, R. (1997) 'Legal determinants of external finance', *Journal of Finance* 52:1131–50.

La Porta, R., Lopez-de-Silanes, F., Shleifer, A. and Vishny, R. (2000) 'Investor protection and corporate governance', *Journal of Financial Economics* 58:3–27.

OECD (2015) *G20/OECD Principles of Corporate Governance*. www.oecd.org/daf/ca/Corporate-Governance-Principles-ENG.pdf (accessed 29 March 2016).

Schleifer, A. and Vishny, R.W. (1997) 'A Survey of corporate governance', *The Journal of Finance* 52(2):737–83.

The Study Group on Directors' Remuneration (Greenbury Committee) (1995) *Directors' Remuneration: Report of a Study Group Chaired by Sir Richard Greenbury*, London: Gee (a division of Professional Publishing Ltd).

Williamson, O.E. (1970) *Corporate Control and Business Behavior: An Inquiry into the Effects of Organization Form on Enterprise Behavior*, Englewood Cliffs, NJ, Prentice Hall.

Williamson, O.E. (1975) *Markets and Hierarchies: Analysis and Antitrust Implications*, New York: Free Press.

Chapter 10

Blowfield, M. and Murray, A. (2011) *Corporate Responsibility*, 2nd edn, Oxford, UK, Oxford University Press.

Boatright, J.R. (2009) *Ethics and the Conduct of Business*, 6th edn, Upper Saddle River, NJ: Pearson Education, Inc.

Carroll, A.B. (1991) 'The pyramid of corporate social responsibility: Toward the moral management of organizational stakeholders', *Business Horizons* 34(4):39–48.

Crane, A. and Matten, D. (2007) *Business Ethics: Managing Corporate Citizenship and Sustainability in the Age of Globalization*, 2nd edn, Oxford, UK, Oxford University Press.

European Commission Communication COM (2011) 681 final, p. 6. eur-lex.europa.eu/legal-content/EN/ TXT/?uri=celex%3A52012AE1301 (accessed 16 June 2016).

Freeman, R.E. (1984) *Strategic Management: A Stakeholder Approach*, London, Pitman Publishing.

Friedman, M. (1970) 'The social responsibility of business is to increase its profits', *The New York Times Magazine*, 13 September 1970. umich.edu/~thecore/doc/ Friedman.pdf (accessed 28 March 2016).

Goergen, M. (2012) *International Corporate Governance*, Harlow, UK, Pearson Education Limited.

GRI (2013) *The External Assurance of Sustainability Performance.* www.globalreporting.org/ resourcelibrary/GRI-Assurance.pdf (accessed 12 February 2016.

Hicks, J. (1946) *Value and Capital: An Inquiry into Some Fundamental Principles of Economic Theory*, 2nd edn, Oxford, UK, Clarendon Press.

Krosinski, C. (2008) 'Sustainable equity investing: The market –beating strategy', in *Sustainable Investing: The Art of Long-Term Performance*, Krosinski, C. and Robins, N. (eds) London: Earthscan, pp. 19–30.

MacKinnon, B. (2001) *Ethics: Theory and Contemporary Issues*, 3rd edn, Belmont, CA: Wadsworth/Thomson Learning.

McPhail, K. and Walters, D. (2009) *Accounting and Business Ethics: An Introduction*, Abingdon, UK, Routledge.

Neumayer, E. (2003) *Weak versus Strong Sustainability*, Cheltenham, UK and Northampton, MA: Edward Elgar Publishing Limited.

O'Dwyer, B., Owen, D. and Unerman, J. (2011) 'Seeking legitimacy for new assurance forms: The case of assurance on sustainability reporting', *Accounting, Organizations and Society* 36(1):31–52.

Schröder, M. (2007) 'Is there a difference? The performance characteristics of SRI equity indexes', *Journal of Business Finance and Accounting* 34(1–2):331–48.

Schröder, M. (2014) 'Financial effects of corporate social responsibility: A literature review', *Journal of Sustainable Finance & Investment* 4(4):337–50.

Simnett, R., Vanstraelen, A. and Chua, W.F. (2009) 'Assurance on sustainability reports, an international comparison', *The Accounting Review* 84(3):937–67.

Statman, M. (2006) 'Socially responsible indexes: Composition, performance and tracking errors', *Journal of Portfolio Management* 32(3):100–9.

Vogel, D. (2006) *The Market for Virtue*, Washington, DC, The Brookings Institution.

Chapter 11

AICPA (2015) AICPA Code of Professional Conduct. New York: American Institute of Certified Public Accountants. pub.aicpa.org/codeofconduct/Ethics.aspx (accessed 27 March 2016).

Duska, R., Duska, B.S. and Ragatz, J. (2011) *Accounting Ethics*, 2nd edn, New York, John Wiley and Sons.

FEE (2009) Integrity in Professional Ethics: A Discussion Paper. European Federation of Accountants/Fédération des Experts Comptables Européens. www.icaew.com/~/media/corporate/files/technical/ethics/integrity%20in%20professional%20ethics%20fee%20discussion%20paper.ashx (accessed 27 March 2016).

ICAEW (2007) *Reporting with Integrity*, London: The Institute of Chartered Accountants in England and Wales. ISBN 978–1–84152–455–9. www.icaew.com/~/media/corporate/files/technical/ethics/reporting%20with%20integrity%20report.ashx. (accessed 27 March 2016).

IESBA (2005) www.ethicsboard.org/iesba-code (accessed 19 June 2016).

IFAC International-Federation-of-Accountants www.ifac.org/ (accessed 19 June 2016).

Lee, T. (1995) 'The professionalization of accountancy: A history of protecting the public interest in a self-interested way', *Accounting, Auditing and Accountability Journal* 8(4):48–69.

McPhail, K. and Walters, D. (2009) *Accounting and Business Ethics: An Introduction*, Abingdon, UK, Routledge.

Savage, D.A. (1994) 'The professions in theory and history: A case of pharmacy', *Business and Economic History* 23(2):129–60.

Sikka, P., Wilmott, H. and Lowe, T. (1989) 'Guardians of knowledge and public interest: Evidence and issues of accountability in the UK Accountancy Profession', *Accounting, Auditing and Accountability Journal* 2(2):47–71.

Wilmott, H. (1986) 'Organising the profession: A theoretical and historical examination of the development of the major accountancy bodies in the UK', *Accounting, Organizations and Society* 11(6):555–80.

Chapter 13

Beaver, W., Correia, M. and Mc Nichols, M. (2012) 'Do differences in financial reporting attributes impair the predictive ability of financial ratios for bankruptcy?', *Review of Accounting Studies* 17:996–1010.

Merkley, K. (2014) 'Narrative disclosure and earnings performance: Evidence from R&D disclosures', *The Accounting Review* 89(2):725–57.

Chapter 21

Amir, E., Guan, Y. and Oswald, D. (2010) 'The effect of pension accounting on corporate pension asset allocation', *Review of Accounting Studies* 15:345–66.

An, H., Lee, Y. and Zhang, T. (2014) 'Do corporations manage earnings to meet/exceed analyst forecasts? Evidence from pension plan assumption changes', *Review of Accounting Studies* 19:698–735.

Bauman, M. and Shaw, K. (2014) 'An analysis of critical accounting estimate disclosures of pension assumptions', *Accounting Horizons* 28(4):819–45.

Black, F. and Scholes, M. (1973) 'The pricing of options and corporate liabilities', *Journal of Political Economy* 81(3):637–54.

Chapter 24

Fields, T., Lys, T. and Vincent, L. (2001) 'Empirical research on accounting choice', *Journal of Accounting and Economics* 31(1–3):255–307.

Chapter 30

Adams, R. and Ferreira, D. (2007) 'A theory of friendly boards', *Journal of Finance* 62(1):217–50.

Ajinka, B., Bhojraj, S. and Sengupta, P. (2005) 'The association between outside directors, institutional investors and the properties of management earnings forecasts', *Journal of Accounting Research* 43(3):343–76.

An, H., Lee, Y. and Zhang, T. (2014) 'Do corporations manage earnings to meet/exceed analyst forecasts? Evidence from pension plan assumption changes', *Review of Accounting Studies* 19:698–735.

Armstrong, C., Barth, M., Jagolinzer, A. and Riedl, E. (2010) 'Market reaction to events surrounding the adoption of IFRS in Europe', *The Accounting Review* 85(1):31–61.

Badertscher, B. (2011) 'Overvaluation and the choice of alternative earnings management mechanisms', *The Accounting Review* 86(5):1491–1518.

Baginski, S., Hassell, J. and Wieland, M. (2011) 'An examination of the effects of management earnings forecast form and explanations on financial analyst forecast revisions', *Advances in Accounting* 27(1):17–25.

Bailey, W., Karolyi, G. and Salva, D. (2006) 'The economic consequences of increased disclosure: Evidence from international cross-listings', *Journal of Financial Economics* 81(1):175–213.

Ball, R., Kothari, S.P. and Robin, A. (2000) 'The effect of international institutional factors on properties of accounting earnings', *Journal of Accounting and Economics* 29(1):1–51.

Banker, R. and Johnston, H. (1993) 'An empirical study of cost drivers in the US airline industry', *Accounting Review* 68(3):576–601.

Barth, M., Elliot, J. and Finn, M. (1995) 'Market rewards associated with increasing earnings patterns', Working paper, Cornell University.

Barth, M., Gow, I. and Taylor, D. (2012) 'Why do pro forma and street earnings not reflect changes in GAAP, Evidence from SFAS 123R', *Review of Accounting Studies* 17:526–62.

Bartov, E. (1993) 'The timing of asset sales and earnings manipulation', *Accounting Review* 68:840–55.

Beasley, M.S. (1996) 'An empirical analysis of the relation between the board of director composition and financial statement fraud', *Accounting Review* 71(4):443–65.

Bedard, J. and Johnstone, K. (2004) 'Earnings management risk, corporate governance risk, and auditors planning and pricing decisions', *The Accounting Review* 79(2):277–304.

Bentley, J., Christensen, T., Gee, K. and Whipple, B. (2015) Disentangling Managers' and Analysts' Non-Gaap reporting incentives. Working Paper.

Bloomfield, R. (2008) 'Discussion of annual report readability, current earnings, and earnings persistence', *Journal of Accounting and Economics* 45(2–3):248–52.

Botosan, C.A. (1997) 'Disclosure level and the cost of equity capital', *Accounting Review* 72(3):323–49.

Bowen, RM., DuCharme, L. and Shores, D. (1995) 'Stakeholders' implicit claims and accounting method choice', *Journal of Accounting and Economics* 20(3):255–95.

Boyd, B.K. (1994) 'Board control and CEO compensation', *Strategic Management Journal* 15(5):335–44.

Brown, L. and Caylor, M. (2006) 'Corporate governance and firm valuation', *Journal of Accounting and Public Policy* 25(4):409–34.

Burgstahler, D. and Dichev, I. (1997) 'Earnings management to avoid earnings decreases and losses', *Journal of Accounting and Economics* 24(1):99–126.

Burgstahler, D. and Eames, M. (2006) 'Management of earnings and analysts' forecasts to achieve zero and small positive earnings surprises', *Journal of Business Finance and Accounting* 35(5):633–52.

Bushman, R. and Piotroski, J. (2006) 'Financial reporting incentives for conservative accounting: The influence of legal and political institutions', *Journal of Accounting and Economics* 42:107–148.

Cao, Z. and Narayanamoorthy, G. (2011) 'The effect of litigation risk on management earnings forecasts', *Contemporary Accounting Research* 28(1):125–73.

Carcello, J. and Nagy, A. (2004) 'Audit firm tenure and fraudulent financial reporting', *Auditing: A Journal of Practice and Theory* 23(2):55–69.

Cheng, J. and Warfield, T. (2005) 'Equity incentives and earnings management', *The Accounting Review* 80(2):441–76.

Christensen, T., Drake, M. and Thornock, J. (2014) 'Optimistic reporting and pessimistic investing: Do pro forma earnings disclosures attract short sellers?', *Contemporary Accounting Research* 31(1):67–102.

Christensen, T., Pei, H., Pierce, S. and Tan, L. (2015) Non-Gaap Reporting following debt covenant violations. Working Paper.

Cohen, D. and Zarowin, P. (2010) 'Accrual-based and real earnings management activities around seasoned equity offerings', *Journal of Accounting and Economics* 50(1):2–19.

Cohen, D., Dey, A. and Lys, T. (2008) 'Real and accrual based earnings management in the pre and post Sarbanes Oxley periods', *The Accounting Review* 83(3):757–87.

Curtis, A., Mc Vay, S. and Whipple, B. (2014) 'The disclosure of Non-Gaap Earnings information in the presence of transitory gains', *The Accounting Review* 89(3):933–58.

DeAngelo, H., DeAngelo, L. and Skinner, D. (1996) 'Reversal of fortune: Dividend signaling and the disappearance of sustained earnings growth', *Journal of Financial Economics* 40(3):341–71

Dechow, P.M. and Sloan, R.G. (1991) 'Executive incentives and the horizon problem: An empirical investigation', *Journal of Accounting and Economics* 14(1):51–89.

DeFond, M.L. and Jiambalvo, J. (1994) 'Debt covenant violation and manipulation of accruals', *Journal of Accounting and Economics* 17(1–2):145–76.

DeGeorge, F., Patel, J. and Zeckhauser, R. (1999) 'Earnings management to exceed thresholds', *Journal of Business* 72(1):1–33.

Djankov, S., La Porta, R., Lopez-de-Silanes, F. and Shleifer, A. (2008) 'The law and economics of self-dealing', *Journal of Financial Economics* 88:430–65.

Donnelly, R and Lynch, C. (2002) 'The ownership structure of UK firms and the informativeness of accounting earnings', *Accounting and Business Research* 32(4):245–57.

Doyle, J., Ge, W. and McVay, S. (2007) 'Accruals quality and internal control over financial reporting', *The Accounting Review* 82(5):1141–70.

Easton, P.D., Monahan, S.J. and Vasvari, F.P. (2009) 'Initial evidence on the role of accounting earnings in the bond market', *Journal of Accounting Research* 47(3):721–66.

Efendi, J., Srivastava, A. and Swanson, E. (2007) 'Why do corporate managers misstate financial statements? The role of option compensation and other factors', *Journal of Financial Economics* 85(3):667–708.

Erickson, M., Hanlon, M. and Maydew, E. (2006) 'Is there a link between executive equity incentives and accounting fraud?', *Journal of Accounting Research* 44(1):113–43.

Fan, Q. (2007) 'Earnings management and ownership retention for initial public offering firms: theory and evidence', *The Accounting Review* 82(1):1–27.

Fan, J.P.H. and Wong, T.J. (2002) 'Corporate ownership structure and the informativeness of accounting earnings in East Asia', *Journal of Accounting and Economics* 33(3):401–25.

Feng, M., Gramlich, J. and Gupta, S. (2009) 'Special purpose vehicles: empirical evidence on determinants and earnings management', *Accounting Review* 84(6):1833–76.

Francis, J. (2001) 'Discussion of empirical research on accounting choice', *Journal of Accounting and Economics* 31(1–3):309–19.

Friedlan, J.M. (1994) 'Accounting choices of issuers of initial public offerings', *Contemporary Accounting Research* 11(1):1–31.

Godfrey, J., Mather, P. and Ramsey, A. (2003) 'Earnings and impression management in financial reports: The case of CEO changes', *Abacus* 39(1):95–123.

Graham, J., Harvey, C. and Rajgopal, S. (2005) 'The economic implications of corporate financial reporting', *Journal of Accounting and Economics* 40(1–3):3–75.

Guenther, D., Maydew, E. and Nutter, S. (1997) 'Financial reporting, tax costs and book-tax conformity', *Journal of Accounting and Economics* 2(3):225–48.

Gunny, K. (2010) 'The relationship between earnings management using real activities manipulation and future performance: Evidence from meeting earnings benchmarks', *Contemporary Accounting Research* 27(3):855–88.

Hand, J.R.M. (1989) 'Did firms undertake debt-equity swaps for an accounting paper profit or true financial gain?', *Accounting Review* 64(4):587–623.

Healy, P.M. (1985) 'The effect of bonus schemes on accounting decisions', *Journal of Accounting and Economics* 7(1–3):85–107.

Healy, P.M. and Palepu, K.G. (1993) 'The effect of firms' financial disclosure strategies on stock prices', *Accounting Horizons* 7(1):1–11.

Healy, P.M. and Wahlen, J.M. (1999) 'A review of the earnings management literature and its implications for standard setting', *Accounting Horizons* 13(4):365–83.

Healy, P.M., Hutton, A. and Palepu, K.G. (1999) 'Stock performance and intermediation changes surrounding sustained increases in disclosure', *Contemporary Accounting Research* 16(3):485–520.

Hope, O.K. (2003) 'Disclosure practices, enforcement of accounting standards and analysts' forecast accuracy: An international study', *Journal of Accounting Research* 41(2):235–72.

Horngren, C.T., Bhimani, A., Datar, S.M. and Foster, G. (2002) *Management and Cost Accounting*, 2nd edn, London, Financial Times-Prentice Hall.

Hunt, A., Moyer, S.E. and Shevlin, T. (1995) 'Earnings volatility, earnings management, and equity value', Working paper, University of Washington.

Isidro, H. and Marques, A. (2015) 'The role of institutional and economic factors in the strategic use of Non-Gaap disclosures to beat earnings benchmarks', *European Accounting Review* 24(1):95–128.

Jaggi, B., Leung, S. and Gul, F. (2009) 'Family control, board independence and earnings management: Evidence based on Hong Kong firms', *Journal of Accounting and Economic Policy* 28(4):281–300.

Jennings, R. and Marques, A. (2011) 'The joint effects of corporate governance and regulation on the disclosure of manager-adjusted Non-Gaap earnings in the US', *Journal of Business Finance and Accounting* 38(4):364–94.

Jensen, M.C. and Murphy, K.J. (1990) 'Performance pay and top-management incentives', *Journal of Political Economy* 98(2):225–64.

Jiambalvo, J. (1996) 'Discussion of: "Causes and consequences of earnings manipulation: An analysis of firms subject to enforcement actions by the SEC"', *Contemporary Accounting Research* 13(1):37–47.

Jiang, J. (2010) 'Beating earnings benchmarks and the cost of debt', *The Accounting Review* 83(2):377–416.

Johnson, V., Khurana, I. and Reynolds, J. (2002) 'Auditfirm tenure and the quality of financial reports', *Contemporary Accounting Research* 19(3):637–60.

Jones, R. and Wu, Y. (2010) 'Executive compensation, earnings management and shareholder litigation', *Review of Quantitative Finance and Accounting* 35(1):1–20.

Kasanen, E., Kinnunen, J. and Niskanen, J. (1996) 'Dividend-based earnings management: Empirical evidence from Finland', *Journal of Accounting and Economics* 22(1–3):283–312.

Kasznik, R. (1999) 'On the association between voluntary disclosure and earnings management', *Journal of Accounting Research* 37(1):57–81.

Key, K.G. (1997) 'Political cost incentives for earning management in the cable television industry', *Journal of Accounting and Economics* 23(3):309–37.

Klein, A. (2002) 'Audit committee, board of director characteristics and earnings management', *Journal of Accounting and Economics* 33(3):375–400.

Koonce, L. and Lipe, M. (2010) 'Earnings trend and performance relative to benchmarks: How consistency influences their joint use', *Journal of Accounting Research* 48(4):859–84.

Kothari, S, Ramana, K. and Skinner, D. (2010) 'Implications for GAAP from an analysis of positive accounting research in accounting', *Journal of Accounting and Economics* 50:246–86.

LaPorta, R., Lopez-de-Silanes, F., Shleifer, A. and Vishny, R (1997) 'Legal determinants of external finance', *Journal of Finance* 52(3):1131–50.

LaPorta, R., Lopez-de-Silanes, F., Shleifer, A. and Vishny, R (1998) 'Law and finance', *Journal of Political Economy* 106(6):1113–55.

LaSalle, R.E., Jones, S.K. and Jain, R. (1993) 'The association between executive succession and discretionary accounting changes: Earning management or different perspectives?', *Journal of Business Finance and Accounting* 20(5):653–71.

Leuz, C. (2010) 'Different approaches to corporate reporting regulation: How jurisdictions differ and why?', *Accounting and Business Research* 40(3):229–56.

Leuz, C. and Verrechia, RE. (2000) 'The economic consequences of increased disclosure', *Journal of Accounting Research* 38 (supp.):91–124.

Leuz, C., Nanda, D. and Wysocki, P.D. (2003) 'Earning's management and inventor protection: An international comparison', *Journal of Financial Economics* 69(3):505–27.

Maijoor, S. and Vanstraelen, A. (2006) 'Earnings management within Europe: The effects of member state audit environment, audit firm quality and international capital markets', *Accounting and Business Research* 36(1):33–52.

McNichols, M. and Wilson, G.P. (1988) 'Evidence of earnings management from the provision for bad debts', *Journal of Accounting Research* 26(3 supp.):1–31.

Murphy, K.J. and Zimmerman, J.L. (1993) 'Financial performance surrounding CEO turnover', Journal of Accounting and Economics 16(1–3):273–315.

Neil, J.D., Pourciau, S.G. and Schaefer, T.F. (1995) 'Accounting method choice and IPO valuation', *Accounting Horizons* 9(3):68–80.

Nelson, M.W., Elliott, J.A. and Tarpley, R.L. (2003) 'How are earnings managed? Examples from auditors', *Accounting Horizons* 17(supp.):17–35.

Nikolaev, V.V. (2010) 'Debt covenants and accounting conservatism', *Journal of Accounting Research* 48(1):51–89.

Peasnell, K.V., Pope, P.F. and Young, S. (2001) 'The characteristics of firms subject to adverse rulings by the Financial Reporting Review Panel', *Accounting and Business Research* 31(4):291–311.

Peasnell, K.V., Pope, P.F. and Young, S. (2005) 'Board monitoring and earnings management: Do outside directors influence abnormal accruals?', *Journal of Business Finance and Accounting* 32(7/8):1246–311.

Penman, S.H. (2003) *Financial Statement Analysis and Security Valuation*, 2nd edn, Boston, MA, McGraw-Hill.

Pope, P., Gore, P. and Singh, A. (2007) 'Earnings management and the distribution of earnings relative to

targets: UK evidence', *Accounting and Business Research* 37(2):151–66.

Porter, M.E. (1985) *Competitive Advantage: Creating and Sustaining Superior Performance*, New York, Free Press.

Pourciau, S. (1993) 'Earnings management and non-routine executive changes', *Journal of Accounting and Economics* 16(1–3):317–36.

Rangan, S. (1998) 'Earnings management and the performance of seasoned equity offerings', *Journal of Financial Economics* 50(1):101–22.

Rogers, J. and Van Buskirk, A. (2009) 'Shareholder litigation and changes in disclosure behavior', *Journal of Accounting and Economics* 47(1–2):136–56.

Roychowdhury, S. (2006) 'Earnings management through real activities manipulation', *Journal of Accounting and Economics* 42(3):335–70.

Rusmin, R. (2010) 'Auditor quality and earnings management: Singaporean evidence', *Managerial Auditing Journal* 25(7):618–38.

Schipper, K. (1989) 'Commentary earnings management', *Accounting Horizons* 3(4):91–102.

Sengupta, P. (1998) 'Corporate disclosure quality and the cost of debt', *Accounting Review* 73(4):459–74.

Shank, J.K. and Govindarajan, V. (1992) 'Strategic cost management and the value chain', *Journal of Cost Management* Winter:5–21.

Shivakumar, L. (1998) 'Market reaction to seasoned equity offering announcements and earnings management', Working paper, London Business School.

Sweeney, A.P. (1994) 'Debt-covenant violations and managers' accounting responses', *Journal of Accounting and Economics* 17(3):281–308.

Trueman, B. and Titman, S. (1988) 'An explanation for accounting income smoothing', *Journal of Accounting Research* 26(3):127–39.

Wayne, T.B., Herrmann, D.R. and Inoue, T. (2004) 'Earnings management through affiliated transactions', *Journal of International Accounting Research* 3(2):1–25.

Zang, A. (2012) 'Evidence on the tradeoff between real manipulation and accruals manipulation', *The Accounting Review* 87(2):675–703.

Chapter 31

Altman, E.I. (1968) 'Financial ratios, discriminant analysis and the prediction of corporate bankruptcy', *Journal of Finance* 23(4):589–609.

Amir, E. and Lev, B. (1996) 'Value-relevance of nonfinancial information: The wireless communications industry', *Journal of Accounting and Economics* 22 (1–3):3–30.

Brouwer, A., Farmazi, A. and Hoogendoorn, M. (2014) 'Does the new conceptual framework provide adequate concepts for reporting relevant information about performance?', *Accounting in Europe* 11(2):235–57.

Dechow, P.M. (1994) 'Accounting earnings and cash flows as measures of firm performance: the role of accounting accruals', *Journal of Accounting and Economics* 18(1):3–42.

Ittner, C.D. and Larcker, D.F. (2001) 'Assessing empirical research in managerial accounting: A value-based management perspective', *Journal of Accounting and Economics* 32(1–3):349–411.

Kaplan, R. and Norton, D. (1992) 'The balanced scorecard: Measures that drive performance', *Harvard Business Review* (Jan–Feb):71–9.

Mechelli, A. and Cimini, R. (2014) 'Is comprehensive income value relevant and does location matter? A European Study', *Accounting in Europe* 11(1):59–87.

Rappaport, A. (1998) *Creating Shareholder Value: A Guide for Managers and Investors*, New York, Free Press.

Rees, L. and Shane, P. (2012) 'Academic research and standard-setting: The case of other comprehensive income', *Accounting Horizons* 26(4):789–815.

Tarca, A., Hancock, P., Woodliff, D., Brown, P., Bradbury, M. Van Zijl, T. (2008) 'Identifying decision useful information with the matrix format income statement', *Journal of International Financial Management and Accounting* 19(2):184–217.

IFRS Standards

INDEX